THE BLACKWELL ENCYCLOPEDIA OF MANAGEMENT

BUSINESS ETHICS

THE BLACKWELL ENCYCLOPEDIA OF MANAGEMENT

SECOND EDITION

Encyclopedia Editor: Cary L. Cooper
Advisory Editors: Chris Argyris and William H. Starbuck

THE BLACKWELL
ENCYCLOPEDIA
OF MANAGEMENT

SECOND EDITION

BUSINESS ETHICS

Edited by
Patricia H. Werhane and
R. Edward Freeman
Darden Graduate School of
Business Administration,
University of Virginia

Blackwell
Publishing

BLACKWELL PUBLISHING
350 Main Street, Malden, MA 02148-5020, USA
9600 Garsington Road, Oxford OX4 2DQ, UK
550 Swanston Street, Carlton, Victoria 3053, Australia

First published 1997 by Blackwell Publishers Ltd
Published in paperback in 1999 by Blackwell Publishers Ltd
Second edition published 2005 by Blackwell Publishing Ltd

Library of Congress Cataloging-in-Publication Data
The Blackwell encyclopedia of management. Business Ethics / edited by
Patricia H. Werhane and R. Edward Freeman.
p. cm.— (The Blackwell encyclopedia of management; v. 8)
Rev. ed. of: The Blackwell encyclopedic dictionary of business ethics / edited by
Patricia H. Werhane and R. Edward Freeman.
Includes bibliographical references and index.
ISBN-13: 978-1-4051-0013-7 (hardcover : alk. paper)
1. Business Ethics—Dictionaries. 2. Management—Dictionaries.
I. Werhane, Patricia Hogue. II. Freeman, R. Edward, 1951–. III. Blackwell Publishing Ltd. IV. Blackwell
encyclopedic dictionary of business ethics. V. Title: Business ethics. VI. Series.
HD30.15. B455 2005 vol. 2
[HF5387]
658'.003 s—dc22
[174'.4'03]
2004007693

ISBN-13: 978-1-4051-0013-7

A catalogue record for this title is available from the British Library.

The publisher's policy is to use permanent paper from mills that operate a sustainable forestry policy, and
which has been manufactured from pulp processed using acid-free and elementary chlorine-free practices.
Furthermore, the publisher ensures that the text paper and cover board used have met acceptable
environmental accreditation standards.

For further information on
Blackwell Publishing, visit our website:
www.blackwellpublishing.com

Contents

Preface

The second edition of the *Blackwell Encyclopedia of Management: Business Ethics* is again a labor of love undertaken by over 220 contributors. When we began the first edition we did not realize that it would entail asking so many of our friends, colleagues, acquaintances, and strangers freely and willingly to write entries. The result is amazing. Each entry to this volume was written without complaint by philosophers, theologians, social scientists, professors of management, and practitioners. A few contributors even volunteered to write second, third, even fourth pieces, should we need them. Such enthusiasm was again demonstrated in putting together the second edition. This volume is dedicated to its contributors.

The idea of an eleven volume *Encyclopedia of Management* that would include a dictionary of business ethics was the brainstorm of the two senior editors, Cary L. Cooper and Chris Argyris. For us, it was a positive indication that business ethics had become part of mainstream management, management teaching and research, and management practice. This is reinforced with the publication of this new edition. *The Blackwell Encyclopedia of Management: Business Ethics* will again be listed in Blackwell's philosophy catalogue, indicating that perhaps applied ethics will now become part of mainstream philosophy as well. This inclusion reflects on the foresight of Blackwell editors, and is a compliment to our contributors, many of whom are academic philosophers or professors of religious studies.

There are a number of other people who deserve special mention for making this book possible. The premier encyclopedia in the field is Larry and Charlotte Becker's monumental work, the *Encyclopedia of Ethics*, now in its second edition. In that work, the Beckers set out exemplary criteria for all encyclopedias of its kind. In addition, because their work is on *ethics* we learned a great deal from their topic headings, and indeed, we asked some of the same authors to write on the same or similar topics. Surprisingly, in the interests of advancing *applied* ethics, most of these authors changed their Becker entry to be more appropriate for *business* ethics. Our deepest, heartfelt gratitude to Charlotte and Larry Becker.

The first edition of this volume could not have been possible without the fine editorial work of Henry W. Tulloch, a retired executive and Senior Fellow at the Olsson Center for Applied Ethics at the Darden School, Tara Radin, Maura Mahoney, Susan Crandell, and our tireless editorial assistant on this project, Kirsti Severance. Entries for the second edition were read and edited by Jenny Mead, the associate editor, with the assistance of Henry Tulloch. Without their tireless efforts, there would be no dictionary. Karen Musselman, the administrator of the Olsson Center at Darden, has assisted all of us in a myriad of ways throughout this project. To all of these people, each of whom has made invaluable contributions – and there are others we have neglected to mention – we give our deepest thanks. The Darden School of the University of Virginia has been most supportive of our work on this project in every way. A number of faculty contributed entries, and the administration provided encouragement, space, equipment, and release time as well as financial resources. Additional financial assistance for the volume was provided by the Olsson Center for Applied Ethics, the Ruffin Foundation, and the Batten Institute.

The shortcomings of the book are, unfortunately, the sole responsibility of its editors.

Patricia H. Werhane and R. Edward Freeman

EDITORIAL STAFF

Jenny Mead, *Associate Editor*

Henry W. Tulloch, *Assistant Editor*

The editors gratefully acknowledge Lawrence C. Becker and Charlotte B. Becker (eds.), *Encyclopedia of Ethics*, New York: Garland Publishing, 1992, and Lawrence C. Becker and Charlotte B. Becker (eds.), *Encyclopedia of Ethics*, 2nd edition, New York: Routledge, 2001, for permission to reprint substantial portions of "Justice, circumstances of" (published here as JUSTICE) and RIGHTS. The reader is also directed to the following entries in the *Encyclopedia of Ethics:* Acts and Omissions; Altruism, Authenticity; Autonomy of Ethics; Business Ethics; Coercion; Computers; Envy; Guilt and Shame, Harm and Offense; Interests; Kantian Ethics; Liberalism; Liberty, economic; Moral Dilemmas; Needs; Partiality; Practical Reason(ing); Promises; Reciprocity; Responsibility; Self-deception; Technology; Universalizability; Utilitarianism.

About the Editors

Editor in Chief
Cary Cooper is based at Lancaster University as Professor of Organizational Psychology. He is the author of over 80 books, past editor of the *Journal of Organizational Behavior*, and Founding President of the British Academy of Management.

Advisory Editors
Chris Argyris is James Bryant Conant Professor of Education and Organizational Behavior at Harvard Business School.
William Haynes Starbuck is Professor of Management and Organizational Behavior at the Stern School of Business, New York University.

Volume Editors
Patricia H. Werhane, Ruffin Professor of Business Ethics and Senior Fellow of the Olsson Center for Applied Ethics, holds a joint appointment at Darden and at DePaul University, where she is Wicklander Chair in Business Ethics and Director of the Institute for Business and Professional Ethics. Werhane teaches Ethics Courses in the Darden MBA program, heads the school's Doctoral Program Operating Committee, and is Academic Advisor for the Business Roundtable Institute for Corporate Ethics. She is a prolific author, an acclaimed authority on employee rights in the workplace, one of the leading scholars on Adam Smith, and founder and former editor-in-chief of *Business Ethics Quarterly*, the leading journal of business ethics. She was a founding member and past president of the Society for Business Ethics.

R. Edward Freeman, Elis and Signe Olsson Professor of Business Administration, heads Darden's Olsson Center for Applied Ethics, one of the world's leading academic centers for the study of ethics, and is also Academic Director of the Business Roundtable Institute for Corporate Ethics. Freeman has written or edited ten books on business ethics, environmental management, and strategic management. His latest book, *Environmentalism and the New Logic of Business: How Firms Can be Profitable and Leave Our Children a Living Planet*, helps executives meet the challenge of being profitable while being environmentally responsible. He has also authored more than 40 Darden case studies and 50 scholarly articles. Freeman serves on the advisory board of the University of Virginia Institute for Practical Ethics.

Contributors

Julia J. Aaron
Philosophy Department, Clarion University of Pennsylvania

Raj Aggarwal
Graduate School of Management, Kent State University

Kenneth D. Alpern
Department of Philosophy, Hiram College

Sita C. Amba-Rao
School of Business, Indiana University Kokomo

Lyn Suzanne Amine
School of Business and Administration, St. Louis University

Mary Beth Armstrong
Orfalea College of Business, California Polytechnic State University

Denis G. Arnold
Department of Philosophy, University of Tennessee

Kaushik Basu
Department of Economics, Cornell University

Alan R. Beckenstein
Darden Graduate School of Business Administration, University of Virginia

Daniel A. Bell
City University of Hong Kong

Rosalyn W. Berne
School of Engineering and Applied Sciences, University of Virginia

Frederick Bird
Department of Religion, Concordia University

Lawrence Blum
Department of Philosophy, University of Massachusetts

John R. Boatright
School of Business Administration, Loyola University Chicago

Norman E. Bowie
Carlson School of Management, University of Minnesota

F. Neil Brady
Romney Institute of Public Management, Brigham Young University

George G. Brenkert
McDonough School of Business, Georgetown University

Richard N. Bronaugh
Department of Philosophy, University of Western Ontario

Allen Buchanan
Department of Philosophy, Duke University

Rogene A. Buchholz, emeritus
College of Business Administration, Loyola University New Orleans

Martin Calkins
Leavey School of Business, Santa Clara University

Joan C. Callahan
Department of Philosophy, University of Kentucky

Archie B. Carroll
Terry College of Business, University of Georgia

Thomas Carson
Department of Philosophy, Loyola University Chicago

Barry Castro
Seidman School of Business, Grand Valley State University

Gerald F. Cavanagh
College of Business Administration, University of Detroit Mercy

Susan Chaplinsky
Darden Graduate School of Business Administration, University of Virginia

Joanne B. Ciulla
Jepson School of Leadership Studies, University of Richmond

Max B. E. Clarkson (deceased)
Clarkson Centre for Business Ethics & Board Effectiveness; Rotman School of Management, University of Toronto

James G. Clawson
Darden Graduate School of Business Administration, University of Virginia

Peggy A. Cloninger
Victoria School of Business, University of Houston

Dana R. Clyman (deceased)
Darden Graduate School of Business Administration, University of Virginia

Phillip L. Cochran
Kelley School of Business, Indiana University

Jane Collier
Judge Institute of Management, University of Cambridge

Robert M. Conroy
Darden Graduate School of Business Administration, University of Virginia

J. Angelo Corlett
Department of Philosophy, San Diego State University

Maria Cecilia Coutinho De Arruda
Fundação Getulio Vargas Business School, Brazil

Kendall D'Andrade

John M. Darley
Department of Psychology, Princeton University

Martin N. Davidson
Darden Graduate School of Business Administration, University of Virginia

Sharon L. Davie
Women's Center, University of Virginia

Michael Davis
Center for the Study of Ethics in the Professions, Illinois Institute of Technology

Michael Deck
PricewaterhouseCoopers LLP

J. Gregory Dees
Fuqua School of Business, Duke University

Richard T. De George
Department of Philosophy, University of Kansas

Robbin Derry
Kellogg Graduate School of Management, Northwestern University

Joseph R. DesJardins
Department of Philosophy, College of St. Benedict and St. John's University

Paul de Vries
New York Evangelical Seminary Fund

John N. Dienhart
Albers School of Business and Economics, Seattle University

John Dobson
College of Business, California Polytechnic State University

Thomas J. Donaldson
Wharton School, University of Pennsylvania

Thomas W. Dunfee
Wharton School, University of Pennsylvania

Craig P. Dunn
Department of Management, San Diego State University

Ronald F. Duska
American College

Deni Elliott
Department of Journalism and Media Studies, University of South Florida – St. Petersburg

Dawn R. Elm
Department of Management, University of St. Thomas

Robin J. Ely
Harvard Business School, Harvard University

Georges Enderle
Mendoza College of Business, University of Notre Dame

Amitai Etzioni
George Washington University

Paul W. Farris
Darden Graduate School of Business Administration, University of Virginia

Paul Fiorelli
Center for Business Ethics and Social Responsibility, Xavier University

Richard E. Flathman
Department of Political Science, Johns Hopkins University

Timothy L. Fort
School of Business Administration, University of Michigan

Leslie P. Francis
Department of Philosophy, University of Utah

Robert H. Frank
Johnson Graduate School of Management, Cornell University

Robert E. Frederick
Center for Business Ethics, Bentley College

William C. Frederick, emeritus
Katz Graduate School of Business, University of Pittsburgh

James R. Freeland
Darden Graduate School of Business Administration, University of Virginia

R. Edward Freeman
Darden Graduate School of Business Administration, University of Virginia

Peter A. French
Lincoln Center for Applied Ethics, Arizona State University

James C. Gaa
School of Business, University of Alberta

Christopher Gale, emeritus
Darden Graduate School of Business Administration, University of Virginia

Alan Gewirth, emeritus
Department of Philosophy, University of Chicago

Christine Gichure
Department of Philosophy, Kenyatta University

Daniel R. Gilbert, Jr.
Department of Management, Gettysburg College

A. R. Gini
Department of Philosophy, Loyola University Chicago

James R. Glenn, Jr.
College of Business, San Francisco State University

Alan H. Goldman
Department of Philosophy, College of William and Mary

Kenneth E. Goodpaster
Graduate School of Business, University of St. Thomas

Carol C. Gould
Department of Philosophy, George Mason University

Joseph Grcic
Department of Philosophy, Indiana State University

Mitchell S. Green
Department of Philosophy, University of Virginia

Barbara A. Gutek
Department of Management and Policy, University of Arizona

Richard M. Hare (deceased)
Department of Philosophy, Corpus Christi College, Oxford

Robert S. Harris
Darden Graduate School of Business Administration, University of Virginia

David Kirkwood Hart, emeritus
Marriott School of Management, Brigham Young University

Edwin M. Hartman
Department of Management, Rutgers University

Brian Harvey
Manchester Business School, Manchester University

Mark E. Haskins
Darden Graduate School of Business Administration, University of Virginia

John Hasnas
School of Law, George Mason University

W. Michael Hoffman
Center for Business Ethics, Bentley College

Rachelle D. Hollander
National Science Foundation

LaRue Tone Hosmer, emeritus
School of Business Administration, University of Michigan

Lynn A. Isabella
Darden Graduate School of Business Administration, University of Virginia

Dove Izraeli (deceased)
Leon Recanati Graduate School of Business Administration, Tel-Aviv University

Robert Jackall
Department of Anthropology and Sociology, Williams College

Kevin T. Jackson
Graduate School of Business Administration, Fordham University

Deborah G. Johnson
School of Engineering and Applied Sciences, University of Virginia

Robin D. Johnson
Management and Human Resources Department, California Polytechnic University

Thomas M. Jones
Business School, University of Washington

Albert R. Jonsen, emeritus
School of Medicine, University of Washington

Kenneth Kipnis
Department of Philosophy, University of Hawaii-Manoa

George Klosko
Department of Government and Foreign Affairs, University of Virginia

Daryl Koehn
Cameron School of Business, University of St. Thomas

James M. Kouzes
The Leadership Challenge R

Nancy B. Kurland
School of Business, University of Southern California; novelist

Gene R. Laczniak
College of Business Administration, Marquette University

C. Jay Lambe
Pamplin College of Business, Virginia Tech

William L. Langenfus
Department of Philosophy, John Carroll University

Andrea Larson
Darden Graduate School of Business Administration, University of Virginia

William S. Laufer
Wharton School, University of Pennsylvania

D. Jeffrey Lenn
School of Business and Public Management, George Washington University

Jeanne M. Liedtka
Darden Graduate School of Business Administration, University of Virginia

Henk van Luijk, emeritus
Nijenrode University, Netherlands School of Business

David Lyons
Department of Philosophy and School of Law, Boston University

John J. McCall
Department of Philosophy, St. Joseph University

Deirdre N. McCloskey
Department of English, Department of Economics, Liberals Arts & Sciences, University of Illinois at Chicago

Michael Maccoby
Maccoby Group

Tibor R. Machan
School of Business & Economics, Chapman University

Eric Mack
Murphy Institute of Political Economy and Department of Philosophy, Tulane University

Christopher McMahon
Department of Philosophy, University of California – Santa Barbara

Rev. Thomas F. McMahon, CSV, emeritus
School of Business Administration, Loyola University Chicago

John McVea
Undergraduate Division of Business, University of St. Thomas

Wesley A. Magat (deceased)
Duke University

John Marshall, emeritus
Department of Philosophy, University of Virginia

Deryl W. Martin
College of Business Administration, Tennessee Technological University

Marilynn Cash Mathews
International Consulting and Executive Development

Larry M. May
Department of Philosophy, Washington University

Jenny Mead
Darden Graduate School of Business Administration, University of Virginia

David M. Messick
Kellogg Graduate School of Management, Northwestern University

Alex C. Michalos
Institute for Social Research and Evaluation, University of Northern British Columbia

Ann E. Mills
Center for Biomedical Ethics, University of Virginia

Barry Mitnick
Katz Graduate School of Business, University of Pittsburgh

Christopher W. Morris
Department of Philosophy, University of Maryland

Kevin W. Mossholder
E. J. Ourso College of Business Administration, Louisiana State University

Patrick E. Murphy
School of Business Administration, Notre Dame University

Jan Narveson
Department of Philosophy, University of Waterloo

Samuel M. Natale
School of Business, Adelphi University

Lisa Newton
Department of Philosophy, Fairfield University

James W. Nickel
College of Law, Arizona State University

Kai Nielsen
Department of Philosophy, Concordia University

Richard P. Nielsen
Wallace E. Carroll School of Management, Boston College

William G. O'Neill
Department of Philosophy, Iona College

Daniel R. Ortiz
School of Law, University of Virginia

Daniel T. Ostas
Michael F. Price College of Business, University of Oklahoma

David T. Ozar
Center for Ethics and Social Justice, Loyola University Chicago

Lynn Sharp Paine
Graduate School of Business Administration, Harvard University

Moses Pava
Sy Sims School of Business, Yeshiva University

Tom Peters
Tompeterscompany!

Jeffrey H. Peterson
School of Business, St. Bonaventure University

Michael J. Phillips
Kelley School of Business, Indiana University

Robert A. Phillips
School of Business Administration, University of San Diego

Deborah C. Poff
College of Arts, Social and Health Sciences, University of Northern British Columbia

Lawrence A. Ponemon
Ponemon Institute

Barry Z. Posner
Leavey School of Business, Santa Clara University

Frederick R. Post
College of Business Administration, University of Toledo

Patrick Primeaux
Department of Theology and Religious Studies, St. John's University

Michael H. Prosser
Department of English, Beijing Language and Culture University

Tara J. Radin
Frank G. Zarb School of Business, Hofstra University

Robert J. Rafalko
Department of Philosophy, University of New Haven

David J. Reibstein
Wharton School, University of Pennsylvania

Alan J. Robb
Department of Accounting, Finance and Information Systems, University of Canterbury, Christchurch

Donald P. Robin
Calloway School of Business & Accountancy, Wake Forest University

Joanne Rockness
Cameron School of Business, University of North Carolina at Wilmington

Julie A. Roin
University of Chicago Law School

Sandra B. Rosenthal, retired
Department of Philosophy, Loyola University – New Orleans

Gedeon J. Rossouw
Department of Philosophy, Rand Afrikaans University

Mark Rowe
Center for Business Ethics, Bentley College

Brother Leo V. Ryan, CSV
College of Commerce, DePaul University

Abdulaziz A. Sachedina
Department of Religious Studies, University of Virginia

Robert J. Sack, emeritus
Darden Graduate School of Business Administration, University of Virginia

Mark Sagoff
Institute for Philosophy and Public Policy, University of Maryland

Steven R. Salbu
McCombs School of Business, University of Texas at Austin

Howard S. Schwartz
Elliott School of Business Administration, Oakland University

Maureen A. Scully
Center for Gender in Organizations, Simmons School of Management

S. Prakash Sethi
Zicklin School of Business, Baruch College, City University of New York

William H. Shaw
Department of Philosophy, San Jose State University

Jon M. Shepard, emeritus
Pamplin College of Business, Virginia Polytechnic Institute and State University

Kristin Shrader-Frechette
Department of Philosophy and Department of Biological Sciences, University of Notre Dame

William W. Sihler
Darden Graduate School of Business Administration, University of Virginia

A. John Simmons
Department of Philosophy, University of Virginia

Alan E. Singer
Department of Management, University of Canterbury, Christchurch

Ming S. Singer
Department of Psychology, University of Canterbury, Christchurch

Walter Sinnott-Armstrong
Department of Philosophy, Dartmouth College

Michael W. Small
Curtin Business School, Curtin University of Technology

Patricia G. Smith
Department of Philosophy, Baruch College & the Graduate Center, City University of New York

Scott Sonenshein
School of Business Administration, University of Michigan

Sebastian A. Sora
School of Business, Adelphi University

Robert E. Spekman
Darden Graduate School of Business Administration, University of Virginia

Roger D. Staton
Attorney, Lebanon, Ohio

Paul Steidlmeier
School of Management, Binghamton University (State University of New York)

Carroll U. Stephens, emerita
Pamplin College of Business, Virginia Polytechnic Institute and State University

John A. Stieber
Cox School of Business, Southern Methodist University

Iwao Taka
Business Ethics and Compliance Research Center, Reitaku University

Jesse Taylor
Department of Philosophy, Appalachian State University

Barbara Ley Toffler
Columbia Business School, Columbia University

Rosemarie Tong
Department of Philosophy, University of North Carolina – Charlotte

Linda Klebe Treviño
Smeal College of Business Administration, Pennsylvania State University

Thomas M. Tripp
School of Business, Washington State University – Vancouver

Manuel Velasquez
Leavey School of Business, Santa Clara University

Sankaran Venkataraman
Darden Graduate School of Business Administration, University of Virginia

Sandra Waddock
Carroll School of Management, Boston College

Clarence C. Walton (deceased)
Charles Lamont Post Chair in Ethics and the Professions, American College

Douglas N. Walton
Department of Philosophy, University of Winnipeg

Gary R. Weaver
Alfred Lerner College of Business & Economics, University of Delaware

Jack Weber
Darden Graduate School of Business Administration, University of Virginia

Vivian Weil
Center for Study of Ethics in the Professions, Illinois Institute of Technology

Carl P. Wellman
Department of Philosophy, Washington University

Patricia H. Werhane
Darden Graduate School of Business Administration, University of Virginia and Institute for

Business and Professional Ethics, DePaul University

Alan Wertheimer
Department of Political Science, University of Vermont

Laura Westra
Department of Philosophy, University of Windsor

Andrew C. Wicks
Darden Graduate School of Business Administration, University of Virginia

James B. Wilbur (deceased)
State University of New York – Buffalo

Paul G. Wilhelm
School of Business, University of Texas of the Permian Basin

Rev. Oliver F. Williams, CSC
Graduate School of Business, University of Cape Town

Donna J. Wood
College of Business Administration, University of Northern Iowa

Thomas Wren
Department of Philosophy, Loyola University Chicago

Shaker A. Zahra
F. W. Olin Graduate School of Business, Babson College

A

accounting ethics

James C. Gaa

Accounting is difficult to define precisely, but it is generally agreed that its focus is on the production of financial information, and its use for various purposes. The ethical issues and problems of accounting may be divided into two types. One type relates to the production and use of accounting information as an economic good. The second type relates to the practice of accounting (i.e., accountancy) as a professional occupation, including the role of accounting information in organizations.

Two characteristics of accounting information are central to the ethical issues of accounting. One is that, depending on whether and how it is disclosed to interested parties, accounting information may have the characteristics of a private good or of a public good. Welfare issues relating to the amount of information produced, the extent to which market forces may be relied on to produce the "optimal" amount of information, who is to benefit from its production and use, and how it is distributed follow immediately from this.

The other characteristic is that accounting information is normally asymmetrically distributed among individuals and groups who have a stake in the organization, and therefore a stake in the production and use of accounting information. Information asymmetry exists when one party possesses information that another party lacks. The imbalance has an ethical dimension because the asymmetry confers an advantage on the party who possesses the information. Because information asymmetry concerns the distribution of information, it is clear that it presents a wide range of ethical issues, in which the question is whether a given asymmetry ought to be maintained or reduced. In some cases, for example the protection of intellectual property and privacy, judgments are in favor of maintaining an asymmetry, so that protection of privacy is tantamount to protecting the asymmetry (*see* INTELLECTUAL PROPERTY; PRIVACY). On the other hand, many securities market regulations (such as Regulation Fair Disclosure of the Securities and Exchange Commission in the US) are intended to ensure that asymmetries are minimized. The focus of many of the ethical issues relating to accounting information is on information asymmetry. For example, corporate insiders may engage in insider trading in the capital market to their own advantage (*see* INSIDER TRADING). The existence of information asymmetry is consistent with the adage "knowledge is power." Insofar as they are about accounting, the recent financial scandals, mainly in the US in the last few years, have centered around information asymmetry.

These scandals also demonstrate the importance of addressing the ethical issues of accounting as a social practice. For example, the financial frauds relating to Enron and WorldCom, and the collapse of Andersen (a major multinational public accounting firm) concern the practice of accounting (and auditing) as social institutions with major social dimensions.

The accounting profession contains three main branches: managerial accounting, external financial accounting and reporting, and public accounting. Although accountants perform a great variety of managerial tasks, the activities that define accountancy focus on recording, analyzing, and reporting of financial information about the affairs of individuals and organizations. Accountants may be members of any of a number of professional associations, which control admission into the professional ranks and define the norms of competence and conduct governing their actions. With few exceptions, public accountants who perform audits of financial statements must be licensed by an agency of the jurisdiction in which they practice.

ETHICAL ISSUES IN ACCOUNTING

Although a small amount of work (e.g., Carey, 1946; Mautz and Sharaf, 1961) dates from an earlier period, the ethics of the accounting profession has emerged as a scholarly field only in the last few years. Theories of the ethics of the accounting profession and even an adequate understanding of the issues are at an early stage of development. A primary reason for this is that, although the accounting profession is closely linked with the administration of organizations and the conduct of business activity, few attempts have been made to link it explicitly to the older and better-established field of business ethics. For example, many of the ethical issues that arise in public accounting are not professional problems *per se*; rather, they result from the way public accounting firms are organized and managed, and are thus instances of generic business ethics issues. Nor has much of the conceptual framework of business ethics entered the accounting literature to date. (For an examination of the limited use of stakeholder literature in accounting, see Roberts and Mahoney, 2004.)

The issue of whose interests should be served by accountants pervades all parts of the profession (*see* ROLES AND ROLE MORALITY). The scope of services issue (discussed below) is essentially the question of whether public accountants are able successfully to act in the interest of the readers of audited financial statements when they are also acting in the interest of their client in other areas. Financial accountants regularly face the problem of being expected to act in the interest of their employers by controlling the content of financial statements (and thereby perpetuating an information asymmetry), and also to provide information to the readers of these statements. In managerial accounting, the content and flow of information (e.g., budgets and expected levels of performance) from superiors to subordinates can be used to manipulate the latter's behavior. In addition, accountants place a high value on the confidentiality of information about their employer or client, but often possess information about misdeeds that might, on ethical grounds, merit unauthorized disclosure (*see* WHISTLE BLOWING).

ETHICAL ISSUES IN MANAGERIAL ACCOUNTING

Managerial accountants, that is, corporate financial officers, produce a large variety of financial and non-financial information for use within organizations of all kinds, including accumulating information about the cost of producing goods and services, budgets, forecasts, non-routine cost analyses, transfer prices, and the measurement of economic performance. In addition to working with the accounting information system, management accountants may perform many of the general management functions in such organizations.

Managerial accounting developed around the end of the nineteenth century with the ascendancy of the scientific management movement, which magnified the need for detailed financial information and sophisticated analyses of cost of production.

Most of the basic techniques of managerial accounting were developed by about 1925 (with some recent developments such as activity-based costing, economic value added, and the balanced score card). Recent developments in the managerial accounting profession, including the above but also major changes in information technology, have caused the professional associations of managerial accountants to promote the idea that the primary role of managerial accountants is management, rather than accounting *per se*.

The ethics of managerial accounting has almost completely escaped serious attention by either scholars or practicing accountants. This may be an implicit recognition that most of the ethical issues of managerial accounting are essentially business ethics issues, where the role of managerial accountants is to design information systems and provide information to aid the management of organizations. The key ethical factor for managerial accounting is that many uses of accounting information involve the manipulation of people to perform in ways the organization prefers, but which are not necessarily in the interest of the individual being manipulated (*see* BLUFFING AND DECEPTION).

Managerial accountants are subject to the codes of professional conduct of the professional organizations of which they are members. As the codes apply to managerial accountants, their provisions are generally non-restrictive and they do not provide for significant enforcement powers. The provisions applying to managerial accountants focus on avoiding conflict of interest and maintaining confidentiality. They are silent on many issues, including (surprisingly, in view of accountants' close involvement with confidential information) whistleblowing. More generally, the codes do not deal with the common problem of conflict between the requirement to follow the instructions of superiors and professional values or standards which may conflict with those instructions.

ETHICAL ISSUES IN FINANCIAL ACCOUNTING AND REPORTING

Many accountants employed by organizations also engage in financial accounting and reporting, which focuses on the preparation of general-purpose financial statements (e.g., the financial statements found in the annual reports of corporations and in filings with securities market regulators), primarily for use by parties who are external to the organization (*see* FINANCIAL REPORTING).

A basic ethical principle governing financial accounting is that readers of financial statements should be provided with "full and fair disclosure" of all the important and relevant aspects of the organization's activities and financial position. However, as agency theory suggests, managers have powerful economic incentives to disclose only that information to outsiders which gives the organization and/or its management a strategic advantage (*see* AGENCY THEORY).

The ethical dimension of this situation does not seem to have received serious attention. For example, a number of people believe that earnings management is the most important ethical issue facing the accounting profession. A widely accepted definition of the concept is the following: "Earnings management occurs when managers use judgment in financial reporting and in structuring transactions to alter financial reports to either mislead some stakeholders about the underlying economic performance of the company or to influence contractual outcomes that depend on reported accounting numbers" (Healy and Wahlen, 1999). Thus, financial accountants frequently engage in "income smoothing," i.e., manipulation of the calculation of an organization's income for strategic reasons. Many practicing accountants believe that some techniques for smoothing income are more ethically acceptable than others (Merchant and Rockness, 1994), even though the result may be equally deceptive. Financial accountants are rarely punished by their professional associations for misrepresentation of corporate financial statements.

Although there is a burgeoning literature on earnings management, it has almost entirely focused on the economic aspects of the phenomenon. A distinction is often made between "good" earnings management (i.e., that which benefits its stakeholders, such as shareholders of a corporation) and "bad" earnings management and fraud (i.e., that which benefits some stakeholders, such as management, at the expense of others). However, the normative issues have not been addressed in a serious way. For example, it is apparently implicitly assumed that "good" earnings management is ethically acceptable, while "bad" earnings management is ethically unacceptable. However, the situation is more complex than that. For example, some instances of earnings management may benefit current shareholders at the expense of future shareholders, creditors, or the general public. An example of the focus on shareholder interests is found in Arya, Glover, and Sunder (2003).

ETHICAL ISSUES IN PUBLIC ACCOUNTING

Public accounting firms are usually identified with the audit, or independent examination of, external financial statements of their clients. However, more than half of the revenues (and even more of the profits) of most public accounting firms come from income tax planning and preparation, and a wide range of other management advisory services for their clients. This situation has been a major focus of attention in recent years, culminating in the financial scandals in the US. Although ethical issues exist in managerial accounting and non-audit aspects of public accounting, the bulk of work on accounting ethics has focused on the role of public accountants in the relationship between management and owners of business enterprises.

Auditing. Auditing, or more generally, assurance, is regarded by many as the essence of public accounting for a number of reasons, including the fact that it is the only activity for which accountants are exclusively granted licenses to practice by government agencies. In addition, from society's point of view, there is a clear public interest in auditing, in view of its role in capital markets and the fact that the right to perform audits is a legally recognized monopoly. In this regard, a quid pro quo exists between members of the profession and the rest of society.

The role of auditors is quite different from that of other professionals. According to virtually all statements of professional ethics, professionals are supposed to have an overriding responsibility to act in the public interest, in exchange for the benefits they obtain through the right to organize (Gaa, 1991). For most professions (such as law, medicine, and engineering, as well as the non-audit services provided by public accountants), the public interest is supposed to be served by acting (within limits) in the interest of the client, i.e., the party paying for the services. While this is also the case for non-audit services provided by public accountants, for auditing it may mean acting against the client's interest.

It is generally agreed that auditors owe a FIDUCIARY DUTY to the non-management owners and other external stakeholders of the organizations they audit. The exact nature of that duty has, however, been a source of continual controversy (accompanied by lawsuits alleging professional negligence) since the 1880s. This is the so-called "expectations gap" between the profession's and the public's opinion about the ethical (and legal) duties of auditors, specifically the extent to which auditors are responsible for detecting fraud and other illegal and unethical acts by their clients. Generally, auditors have taken a narrow view, limiting the scope of both their examinations and their legal liability, while the general public, courts, and government agencies have regularly taken a broader view.

Closely related to the expectations gap, the nature of the auditor–client relationship has been problematic. Since the interests of their clients and of the external stakeholders are generally in conflict, auditors must make judgments that leave one of these groups better off and others worse off. Furthermore, auditors themselves have their own economic interest, which may conflict with one or more of these stakeholder groups. According to the concept of auditor independence, auditors are supposed to be able to provide objective and unbiased opinions of their clients' financial statements, and are not supposed to subordinate their judgment to their clients' interests. The difficulty is that auditors and their clients inevitably develop a close economic and personal relationship that threatens this independence. The essence of this problem is CONFLICT OF INTEREST, in which there is some likelihood that the auditor will act in the client's interest at the expense of the external stakeholders to whom their auditor's report is addressed (Gaa, 1994).

The chance that auditors may fail to act in accordance with their duty to external stakeholders has increased in recent years because of increased competition in the market for public accounting services. Although one of the primary rationales for organizing as a profession is to restrict competition and thus enable its members to earn economic rents, it is also true that competitive forces may pressure professionals either to cut costs and do substandard work or to violate the independence principle. Increasingly, auditors must provide fixed-price bids for audits, and may engage in "low-balling" (i.e., bidding below the cost of providing the service, in the hope of recovering the lost profit through subsequent audits or the provision of non-audit services).

Non-audit services. Both income tax consulting and management advisory services are essentially conventional business consulting. As such, the public accountant *qua* business consultant faces the same kinds of ethical problems as other business consultants (*see* CONSULTING, ETHICS OF). However, some commentators believe that providing such services is incompatible with the independence required for the audit function. The question is: what is the appropriate scope of services which a public accounting firm may provide for a client, while still remaining independent while performing audits (Mautz and Sharaf, 1961; Briloff, 1990)? In addition, fee arrangements common in business consulting may be incompatible with auditor independence. The Sarbanes-Oxley Act of 2002 has drastically reduced (but not eliminated) this conflict by restricting the type and amount of consulting work that may be performed for audit clients.

REGULATION OF FINANCIAL ACCOUNTING AND AUDITING

Financial accounting and auditing are highly regulated, both by professional associations and by public and private sector regulatory agencies. In addition to a code of ethics, financial accountants and auditors must act in accordance with a number of auditing standards, accounting principles, and a whole host of disclosure regulations (see PROFESSIONAL CODES). These standards of behavior are promulgated by a large variety of professional associations, and private sector and public sector agencies. The professed primary purpose of these agencies and regulations is to protect external stakeholders from the self-interested behavior of management. Extensive regulation (by both government and the profession) in North America dates back to the CORPORATE GOVERNANCE debates in the early 1930s in the US, with passage of the Securities Acts of 1933 and 1934.

Scholars and practitioners have devoted significant attention to the process of setting financial accounting and reporting standards. The primary issue is how a standard-setting agency (such as the Financial Accounting Standards Board in the US) should fulfill its responsibilities to stakeholders. Discussions of stakeholders have been generally limited to individuals and groups that have a direct connection to business activities, such as actual and potential investors and creditors, suppliers, customers, employees, regulators, and the business press. Two problems have been addressed. The standard

problem of stakeholder theory (i.e., how to rank the claims of the various stakeholders) has received only minor attention. Focusing on the conflicting interests of management and groups of financial statement users, Gaa (1988) provided theoretical foundations for the "user primacy" principle based on INTEGRATED SOCIAL CONTRACTS THEORY. Although it is clear that other stakeholder groups are affected by accounting and auditing standards, the role of their interests has not been explored. The other ethical problem is the identification of principles underlying standard setters' choices among alternative regulations. Various approaches have been offered, including rights theory (Gaa, 1988), duty theory (Ruland, 1984), justice theory (Williams, 1987), and a version of utilitarianism (Zeff, 1978).

CRITICAL APPROACHES TO ACCOUNTING

Although much of the literature on accounting focuses on the role of accounting in representing reality, in some sense, a significant literature exists which focuses on the ways in which our conceptions of "reality" are shaped by the institution of accounting. In the last twenty years or so, a literature has appeared which seeks to explain accounting as a social institution. Two primary streams have developed. One employs various continental and postmodern theories (e.g., Arrington and Francis, 1989; Cooper and Taylor, 2000; Shearer, 2002). The other stream is based on political theory.

Both focus on several basic ideas, including a collective, rather than individual, approach to ethical issues; and the concepts that accounting is part of a power structure, and plays an active role in the success of corporations; that accountants are therefore not passive or neutral, but are partisans in a struggle for economic power; and that the accounting profession is regulated for the benefit of its members. In addition, many advocates of this point of view believe that more conventional approaches to accounting ethics serve to perpetuate the traditional understanding of accounting as a purely technical and neutral activity by providing rationalizations for the status quo. Examples of this literature include Burchell et al., 1980; Cooper and Sherer, 1984;

6 accounting ethics

Tinker, 1984; Miller and O'Leary, 1987; Hines, 1988; and Power, 2003. For a review of a wide range of alternative research in management accounting, see Baxter and Chua, 2003.

See also *information, right to*

Bibliography

Arrington, E. and Francis, J. R. (1989). Letting the chat out of the bag: Deconstruction, privilege and accounting research. *Accounting, Organizations, and Society*, 15, 1–28.

Arya, A., Glover, J. C., and Sunder, S. (2003). Are unmanaged earnings always better for shareholders? *Accounting Horizons* 17 (supplem.): 111–16.

Baxter, J. and Chua, W. F. (2003). Alternative management accounting research: Whence and whither. *Accounting, Organizations, and Society*, 28, 97–126.

Briloff, A. (1990). Accountancy and society: A covenant desecrated. *Critical Perspectives on Accounting*, 1, 5–30.

Burchell, S., Clubb, C., Hopwood, A., Hughes, J., and Nahapiet, J. (1980). The roles of accounting in organizations and society. *Accounting, Organizations, and Society*, 5, 5–27.

Carey, J. L. (1946). *Professional Ethics of Certified Public Accountants*. New York: American Institute of Accountants.

Commission on Auditors' Responsibilities (1978). *Report, Conclusions, and Recommendations*. New York: Commission on Auditors' Responsibilities (American Institute of Certified Public Accountants).

Cooper, C. and Taylor, P. (2000). From Taylorism to Ms. Taylor: The transformation of the accounting craft. *Accounting, Organizations, and Society*, 25, 555–78.

Cooper, D. and Sherer, M. J. (1984). The value of corporate accounting reports: Arguments for a political economy of accounting. *Accounting, Organizations, and Society*, 9, 207–32.

Financial Accounting Standards Board (1978). Statement of financial accounting concepts no. 1: Objectives of financial reporting by business enterprises. Stamford, CT: Financial Accounting Standards Board.

Gaa, J. C. (1988). Methodological foundations of standard setting for corporate financial reporting. *Studies in Accounting Research*, 28, Orlando, FL: American Accounting Association.

Gaa, J. C. (1990). A game-theoretic analysis of professional rights and responsibilities. *Journal of Business Ethics*, 9, 37–47.

Gaa, J. C. (1991). The expectations game: Regulation of auditors by government and the profession. *Critical Perspectives on Accounting*, 2, 83–107.

Gaa, J. C. (1993). The auditor's role: The philosophy and psychology of independence and objectivity. In R. Srivastave (ed.), *Proceedings of the 1992 Deloitte and Touche/University of Kansas Symposium on Auditing Problems*. Lawrence: University of Kansas Press, 7–43.

Gaa, J. C. (1994). *The Ethical Foundations of Public Accounting*. Research Study No. 22. Vancouver, BC: CGA-Canada Research Foundation.

Healy, P. M. and Wahlen, J. M. (1999). A review of the earnings management literature and its implications for standard setting. *Accounting Horizons*, 13 (4): 365–83.

Hines, R. (1988). Financial accounting: In communicating reality, we construct reality. *Accounting, Organizations, and Society*, 13 (3), 251–61.

Lowe, H. J. (1987). Ethics in our 100-year history. *Journal of Accountancy*, 163, 78–87.

Macdonald, W. A., chairman (1988). Report of the Commission to Study the Public's Expectations of Audits. Toronto: Canadian Institute of Chartered Accountants.

Mautz, R. K. and Sharaf, H. A. (1961). *The Philosophy of Auditing*. Sarasota, FL: American Accounting Association.

Norman, B. Macintosh, Shearer, T., Thornton, D. B., and Welker, M. (2000). Accounting as simulacrum and hyperreality: Perspectives on income and capital. *Accounting, Organizations, and Society*, 25, 13–50.

Merchant, K. A. and Rockness, J. (1994). The ethics of managing earnings: An empirical investigation. *Journal of Accounting and Public Policy*, 13: 79–94.

Miller, P. and O'Leary, T. (1987). Accounting and the construction of the governable person. *Accounting, Organizations, and Society*, 12 (3), 235–65.

Noreen, E. (1988). The economics of ethics: A new perspective on agency theory. *Accounting, Organizations, and Society*, 13, 359–69.

Petitioner vs. Arthur Young and Company et al. No 82-687. March 21, 1984. US Supreme Court Opinions, October Term, 1983. Reprinted in *The United States Law Week*, 52 (36) March 20, 1984.

Power, M. (2003). Auditing and the production of legitimacy. *Accounting, Organizations, and Society*, 28, 379–94.

Roberts, R. W. and Mahoney, L. 2004. Stakeholder conceptions of the corporation: Their meaning and influence in accounting research. *Business Ethics Quarterly*, forthcoming.

Ruland, R. G. (1984). Duty, obligation, and responsibility in accounting policy making. *Journal of Accounting and Public Policy*, 3, 223–37.

Shearer, T. (2002). Ethics and accountability: From the for-itself to the for-the-other. *Accounting, Organizations, and Society*, 27, 541–73.

Tinker, T. (1984). Theories of the state and the state of accounting: Economic reductionism and political voluntarism in accounting regulation theory. *Journal of Accounting and Public Policy*, 3, 55–74.

Treadway Commission (National Commission on Fraudulent Financial Reporting) (1987). Fraud commission issues final report. *Journal of Accountancy*, **164** (5), 39–48.

Williams, P. F. (1987). The legitimate concern with fairness. *Accounting, Organizations, and Society*, **12**, 169–89.

Zeff, S. (1978). The rise of economic consequences. *Journal of Accountancy*, **158** (6) 56–63.

accounting, liability in

Joanne W. Rockness

Sole practitioners to large public accounting firms continue to face potentially devastating legal liabilities. Since the mid-1980s there has been a dramatic increase in lawsuits against public accounting firms resulting in billions of dollars in legal settlements. The savings and loan cases began the litigation flurry leading to the downfall of Laventhol and Horwath. Substantial firm settlements in the late 1990s followed, involving companies such as Cendant and Waste Management. Now the profession faces a new magnitude of litigation that is only beginning to surface as a result of Enron, WorldCom, HealthSouth, Rite Aid, Xerox, etc. What the future holds is certain major litigation and enormous settlements for accounting professionals.

The legal basis of accountants' liability primarily lies in the US Securities Acts of 1933 and 1934 and the common-law theories of fraud, breach of contract, and negligence. The 1933 Securities Act imposes liability for actions related to initial public offerings of securities. It imposes civil and criminal liability for false statements or omissions in registration statements or if securities are sold without an accurate prospectus. The 1934 Securities Act regulates purchases and sales of securities. It imposes civil and criminal liability for false or misleading statements filed with the Securities and Exchange Commission, or if an accountant intentionally deceives others through oral or written misstatements or omissions in connection with a sale or purchase of securities. Prior to 1994, the 1934 Act imposed liability for aiding and abetting; however, in April 1994, the US Supreme Court eliminated aider and abettor liability in the *Cen-tral Bank of Denver vs. First Interstate Bank of Denver* case.

Common-law theories impose contract liability, criminal liability, and tort liability on the accounting profession. When accountants or public accounting firms enter into contracts with clients, they agree to act as reasonable, prudent professionals and to perform all terms of the contract. If they fail to do so, they can be sued for either breach of contract or negligence. Breach of contract suits fall under contract liability and are usually brought by the client against the accountant. Accountants are subject to criminal liability for willfully certifying false documents, altering or tampering with records, forgery, and so forth.

Fraud involves the intentional misstatement of material information. Most accountants do not purposely misstate facts on behalf of clients. The most devastating legal liability for accountants is the tort theory of negligence. Negligence involves the failure to act as a reasonably prudent professional under the circumstances. Lawsuits for negligence may be instigated by clients or non-clients. The litigation by non-clients is based on the extent to which accountants should be held liable to third-party financial statement users. This responsibility to third parties varies by state, with three major approaches being utilized: Credit Alliance, Restatement of Torts, and Reasonable Foreseeable User. Some states do not follow a specific, prescribed approach.

Under the Credit Alliance approach the accountant is not liable for negligence to third parties unless the accountant is aware that the third party intended to rely on the auditor's opinion and the financial statements. The third party must be specifically identified to the accountant. This is the most conservative approach and the most favorable for the accounting profession. This approach is based on the rulings in the *Credit Alliance vs. Arthur Andersen and Co.* case and the landmark case of *Ultramares vs. Touche*, and is followed in nine states.

Restatement of Torts subjects accountants to more liability by permitting recovery by foreseen third parties even if they are not specifically identified. The accountant must only be aware that the audited financial statements will be used by a third party. This approach is followed in nineteen states.

The Reasonable Foreseeable User approach subjects accountants to the highest degree of liability exposure. It permits recovery by all parties that are reasonably foreseeable recipients of financial statements. There is no privity requirement, and in effect the accounting profession is viewed as the public watchdog. This approach is currently only followed in three states.

The concept of joint and several liability applies in all of the above three theories. A successful plaintiff is permitted to collect an entire judgment against any defendant regardless of the degree of fault attributable to the individual defendant. Joint and several liability remains a primary concern of the accounting profession. The Litigation Reform Act of 1995 attempted to limit joint and several liability but contains a provision limiting it to one and one-half times the liability determined by the court. Thus, the relief the profession sought was not achieved.

The organizational structure of public accounting firms also affects the extent of the individual accountant's liability exposure. Historically, accounting firms have been organized as proprietorships or partnerships, resulting in unlimited personal liability for the partners. In 1992 the AICPA changed its bylaws to permit CPAs to practice in any organizational form allowed by state law. Limited Liability Partnerships (LLPs) and Limited Liability Corporations (LLCs) are emerging as states change their restrictions. LLCs and LLPs remove much of the partners' personal liability for other employees' negligent or wrongful acts. Most large accounting firms have converted to LLP status since state laws usually permit LLPs to practice in non-LLP states, and the conversion to a LLP from a general partnership is much less complicated.

Recent developments, including the Sarbanes-Oxley legislation, resulting SEC rules, and SAS 99, further define the accountant's legal responsibilities with regard to services provided and determination of fraud. The profession is now reacting and implementing the new rules and only the future will tell the extent of additional liability.

One certainty is that accounting liability will remain at the forefront of the accounting profession. It is not clear whether the profession as we know it today can withstand another Enron.

Bibliography

Arthur Andersen, Coopers and Lybrand, Deloitte and Touche, Ernst and Young, KPMG Peat Marwick, Price Waterhouse (1992). *The Liability Crisis in the United States: Impact on the Accounting Profession*. Position Paper.

Epstein, M. and Spalding, A. (1993). *The Accountants Guide to Legal Liability and Ethics*. New York: Richard D. Irwin.

Hanson, R. and Rockness, J. (1994). Gaining a new balance in the courts: some of the liability burden has disappeared – but a heavy weight remains. *Journal of Accountancy* (Aug.), 178 (2), 40–4.

Hanson, R., Rockness, J., and Woodard, R. (1995). Litigation support liability – the Mattco decision. *CPA Journal* (March), 65 (3), 28.

Simonetti, G. and Andrews, A. (1994). A profession at risk/a system in jeopardy. *Journal of Accountancy* (April), 177 (4), 50; (3), 46–54.

advertising, ethics of

Gene R. Laczniak

The systematic study of how moral standards are applied to advertising decisions, behaviors, and institutions. It is a subset of business and marketing ethics (*see* MARKETING, ETHICS OF). It should be noted that many of the practices that critics of advertising consider to be "unethical" may also be violations of the law. Thus, the discussion which follows mentions some advertising practices that are outright transgressions of the law (e.g., deceptive advertising), but also discussed are actions that are legal but are nevertheless called into question because they arguably lack the degree of moral propriety that society would like to see advertising uphold. For instance, advertising practices which are perfectly legal but still raise ethical questions include ads for target pistols in teen magazines, featuring bevies of bikini-clad women in beer commercials, and health claims for products that are not especially healthy.

THE NATURE AND SCOPE OF ADVERTISING

Given the economic importance of advertising as well as its social visibility, it is not surprising that it comes under great public scrutiny. Critics have often complained about the lack of ethical evaluations of certain business practices (e.g., security trading by insiders), but there has been no shortage of attention devoted to advertising ethics and the social questions that it raises. One survey of the literature, using the ABI/Inform database, found 127 articles published on the topic of advertising ethics between 1987 and 1993 (Hyman, Tansey, and Clark, 1994). No doubt, part of the attention garnered by advertising is due to the fact that it is such a significant economic force in society. Over $148 billion was spent on advertising in the US in 1994. The cost of running a single 30-second commercial on US TV for the 1995 Super Bowl was over $1 million. Recognizing that advertising is *by definition* a one-sided, persuasive communication using the mass media and intending to advocate a sponsor's product or service, it should not be startling that much advertising fails to tell a fully informative story about the products that it endorses. In other words, a big part of the ethical concern about advertising stems from the fact that by its nature it is propaganda about the products and services that are available for sale. Some of this intentionally persuasive information may be valuable to potential buyers, while other parts may be misleading.

MACRO- AND MICRO-CRITICISMS OF ADVERTISING

The ethical criticisms of advertising can be categorized as *macro* or *micro*. Macro-criticisms of advertising generally deal with the negative impact of advertising upon society. For example, could the $148 billion allocated to advertising be more usefully spent attempting to achieve other economic goals? Does advertising help foster a culture of materialism? Micro-ethical criticisms of advertising focus on the propriety of specific advertising practices. For example, should cartoon characters be allowed to pitch products on programs targeted for children? Should ads for contraceptives be shown on network TV? Should subliminal messages be permitted?

Historically, the macro-debate about advertising ethics has a long tradition. For instance, in 1907, one critic of advertising wrote, "On the moral side, it [advertising] is thoroughly false and harmful. It breeds vulgarity, hypnotizes the imagination and the will, fosters covetousness, envy, hatred, and underhand competition" (Logan, 1907).

Some of the macro-ethical problems of the advertising industry might be summarized along the following lines. First, there is the contention that such persuasion violates people's inherent rights. The issue here is that so much advertising is persuasively one-sided that it violates the principle of fairness by depriving consumers of unbiased input with which to make an informed buying decision. Second, there is the charge that advertising encourages certain human addictions. The focus here would be upon the societal appropriateness of *any* advertising campaigns for controversial products such as cigarettes, tobacco, pornography, and firearms. Third, there is the fact that the motivation behind advertising involves trying to make money, not to foster the truth. The question here is the extent to which a certain proportion of advertising will always be inherently misleading because it nurtures false implications or associates product usage with a lifestyle or social image that may have little to do with the product. For example, can drinkers of Old Milwaukee beer really expect to find themselves in a situation where "it doesn't get any better than this"? Fourth, there is the belief that advertising frequently degenerates into vulgarization. For example, the exploitation of women in advertising as well as the use of fear appeals (e.g., you will be socially ostracized without fresh breath gum) would be representative of this criticism. The use of ads which parody great books and famous quotations, as well as notable art, architecture, or people, is a further illustration of this critique.

The most common response to many macro-criticisms of the advertising industry is that advertising is little more than a mirror of the current character of society (Pollay, 1986). The argument goes as follows: as a "looking glass" that reflects the attitudes of society, one should expect that sometimes advertising is deceptive just as other forms of communication might be deceptive or misleading. And sometimes advertising will be in "bad taste" just as some art or movies or political speeches might prove to be in poor taste. These defenders of advertising would further contend that the vast majority of advertising provides useful information which allows consumers to glean important facts and thereby enhances the efficiency of product choice (Levitt, 1970). Therefore, despite the use of inherently persuasive techniques, having corporation-sponsored information about the products and services available in a complex, consumption-driven economy provides more benefits than dysfunctions. Such pragmatic and utilitarian analysis is commonly employed by defenders of advertising (see UTILITARIAN-ISM.

Consider the following as a "case in point" concerning the utilitarian trade-off inherent in advertising. Recent analysis of six decades of research dealing with consumer perceptions of advertising concludes that the typical consumer finds most advertising definitely informative and the best means of learning what is available on the market (Calfee and Ringold, 1994). However, the study also suggests that, consistent over time, approximately 70 percent of consumers believe that advertising is often untruthful and may persuade people to buy things they do not want. But, on balance, the valuable information provided by advertising is worth the deficiencies caused by its inherent persuasiveness (Calfee and Ringold, 1994).

With regard to the micro-objections to advertising, the list of criticisms is long. A recent survey of advertising practitioners shows that the current area of advertising practice generating the highest level of ethical concern is the continued use of deceptive advertising. Other concerns in the "top five" involve exploitative advertising to children, ads for tobacco and alcoholic beverages, the increased use of negative political ads, and stereotyping in advertising (Hyman, Tansey, and Clark, 1994). While granting the problematic nature of many of these specific practices, defenders of advertising are quite adamant in their view that most advertising is not only ethical but also helpful. Though beyond the scope of this entry, philosophers such as Arrington (1982) have provided

tightly argued analyses suggesting that the vast majority of advertising is neither manipulative nor deceptive because it generally does not violate the various criteria which constitute consumer autonomy.

REGULATION OF ADVERTISING PRACTICES

In theory at least, the consumer is protected from many questionable advertising practices via government regulation as well as the self-regulation provided by the advertising industry. In the USA, industry regulation is provided by the National Advertising Division (NAD) of the Better Business Bureau. This group, established in 1971, investigates almost 200 cases of alleged unfairness in advertising annually. Many of the questionable ads brought to the NAD are identified by fellow competitors, which would seem to indicate that advertisers are guardians of their own honesty. Most of the disputes brought at this level (approximately 98 percent) are resolved, but for those cases still at question, the National Advertising Review Board (NARB) becomes a court of appeal. The NARB is staffed by members of the advertising profession as well as informed persons from the general public. Given that this control process is an industry-wide effort to maintain the integrity of advertising, endorsed and adjudicated by the industry itself, there is great pressure upon advertisers to abide by the findings of the NAD/NARB. Still, there might be advertising practices that would require a stronger form of intervention which can only be provided by the force of government regulation.

The linchpin of government oversight of advertising in the US is provided by the Federal Trade Commission (FTC). The commission was established in 1914. It has jurisdiction to police all forms of false and deceptive trade practices, including advertising. The FTC has gone through relative periods of activity and inactivity, depending upon the political climate of the country. In part, the level of regulatory fervor is due to the zeal of the commissioners who control the FTC and who are political appointees. Nonetheless, at all times the FTC protects the public from the most egregious forms of deceptive advertising. The FTC is assisted by various other government agencies, such as the Food and Drug Administration (FDA) which, as its name implies, has jurisdiction over the advertising of food and drug products. For example, the recent regulatory changes requiring improved nutritional labeling and disclosure were the result of cooperation between the FDA and the FTC. Still another government agency important in the oversight of advertising is the Bureau of Alcohol, Tobacco, and Firearms (BATF), a division of the US Department of Treasury. It regulates all aspects of the sale of products for which the division is named.

THE CREDIBILITY OF ADVERTISING

While many feel the combination of industry self-regulation and the Federal Trade Commission provides an appropriate safety net against deceptive advertising, regulatory efforts are not without their critics, some of whom believe that much unethical advertising remains. For example, Preston (1994), in a comprehensive analysis, contends that advertisers, by providing only partial truth (i.e., one-sided argumentation) about their products and services, contribute to the "diminishment of the truth." Why? Partial truth is a form of falsity that harms many consumers who cannot be expected to gather sufficient buying information without reliance upon advertising claims. Preston proposes a reinvention of advertising regulation via the "reliance rule" which would require that the only product claims allowed would be those that advertisers advocate as being important enough for consumers to make buying decisions on. In other words, advertisers would be limited to making claims about product attributes which embody distinct reasons for purchasing a particular product. Thus, claims such as "Pontiac is excitement" would have no standing because it is an unprovable "puff." Whereas a claim such as "This model Pontiac will provide 30 miles per gallon" would be permitted – assuming the mpg figure can be substantiated.

THE ETHICS OF THE ADVERTISING INDUSTRY

Another set of issues to be addressed has to do with the set of actors that orchestrate modern advertising. Major players in the advertising industry are *sponsors* of advertising (e.g., corporations), *advertising agencies* (the makers of ad campaigns), and the *media* which carry advertising messages. The complexity of relationships among these three groups often creates ethical conflicts. For example, the media are dependent for much of their operating revenues upon the advertising dollars that underwrite their programming. Thus, the ethical question is often raised about the extent to which advertising is able to shape media programming – especially its influence over news media content that is critical of an advertising sponsor. Similarly, advertising agencies are often financially rewarded based on the amount of media time that they buy rather than the quality of the advertising they produce. Thus, there can be inherent pressures on ad agencies to push for more advertising rather than searching for the optimal ad campaign that best serves the sponsoring company.

To understand how ethical issues are addressed by advertisers, some questions must be asked about the values inherent in the advertising community. What do advertising people consider to be unethical? What is the prevailing professional ethic of advertising? Some of the substance of this ethic can be ascertained by looking at the codes of ethics which have been promulgated by the American Association of Advertising Agencies (4As) and the American Advertising Federation (AAF) (*see* PROFESSIONAL CODES). Both codes contain the following provisions:

- There are prohibitions against false and misleading statements.
- Testimonials that do not reflect the real opinion of individuals involved are forbidden.
- Price claims that are misleading are not allowed.
- Statements or pictures offensive to the public decency are to be avoided.
- Unsubstantiated performance claims are never to be used.

Such admonitions serve as absolutes in guiding advertising practice. In effect, they become the lowest common denominator in shaping the professional ethic of advertising practitioners. One major disadvantage of the approach used by the 4As and the AAF in their codes is that their prohibitions are formulated in terms of "negative" absolutes – in other words, practices that formulators of advertising should *not* engage in.

These negative absolutes have value because they suggest (for example) that to be ethical, advertisers should not lie to customers, should not steal competitor ideas for their own campaigns, should not cheat the media, etc. However, some observers of the advertising industry have suggested that "positive" absolutes, which stress the meritorious duties advertisers ought to engage in, provide a more inspirational avenue for shaping advertising practice. An example of a positive meritorious duty would be the "principle of fairness." Applied to advertising, it might be stated as follows: "Advertisers must take fairness into consideration in their dealings with consumers, clients, suppliers, vendors, the media, employees, and agency management." And taking this meritorious duty a step further and linking it with elements of Kant's well-known categorical imperative, one could further add: "advertising should never treat its audience or spokespersons as mere means." An illustration of a TV ad campaign to which the above principle might be applied is the controversial Swedish bikini team commercial which was used by Heilemann Brewing Company to promote one of its brands of beer. In this situation, one could apply the principle and contend that while the use of such blatant sex appeals constituted a memorable television commercial, the salacious portrayal of women featured in the ad was an inappropriate means for seeking economic success.

The difficulty of all moral imperatives such as the fairness principle is that they are often difficult to apply to specific situations. For example, the vast majority of advertising practitioners would agree with the guideline that testimonial ads should not use celebrity spokespeople to endorse products which the spokespeople have never used. Suppose, however, a company hires a well-known actor who has never previously used a particular product but upon signing his endorsement contract, honestly concludes that the product is a superior one. Is this a misleading use of testimonials? The case is debatable.

CONCLUSION

In the end, many advertising practitioners fall back to a pragmatic defense of the current system of advertising. They argue from a conse-quentialist point of view that "if you don't like the advertising, consumers won't buy the product and the ad sponsors will be punished at the cash register."

In summary, advertising contributes much informational value to consumers. The most obvious forms of deception and unfairness in US advertising are mitigated by industry self-regulation, governmental controls, and the inherent professional ethic of the ad industry. But because advertising is undertaken for the primary purpose of selling specific products and services, it undoubtedly will continue to generate much ethical controversy because it is fundamentally an exercise in commercial persuasion.

Bibliography

Arrington, R. L. (1982). Advertising and behavior control. *Journal of Business Ethics*, 1, 3–12.

Calfee, J. E. and Ringold, D. J. (1994). The 70 % majority: Enduring consumer beliefs about advertising. *Journal of Public Policy and Marketing*, 13, 228–38.

Hyman, M. R., Tansey, R., and Clark, J. W. (1994). Research on advertising ethics: Past, present, and future. *Journal of Advertising*, 23, 5–15.

Laczniak, G. R. and Caywood, C. L. (1987). The case for and against televised political advertising: Implications for research and public policy. *Journal of Public Policy and Marketing*, 6, 16–32.

Levitt, T. (1970). The morality (?) of advertising. *Harvard Business Review*, 48, 84–92.

Logan, J. D. (1907). Social evolution and advertising. *Canadian Magazine*, 28, 333.

Pollay, R. W. (1986). The distorted mirror: Reflections on the unintended consequences of advertising. *Journal of Marketing*, 50, 18–36.

Preston, I. L. (1994). *The Tangled Web They Weave: Truth, Falsity, and Advertisers*. Madison: University of Wisconsin Press.

Rotzoll, K. and Haefner, J. (1990). *Advertising in Contemporary Society*. Cincinnati, OH: South-Western.

advertising to children, ethics of

Christopher Gale

It has been estimated that children between the ages of 4 and 12 spent over $6 billion in the United States in 1989, and that expenditures in major media directed explicitly to children might be as high as $750 million (McNeal,

1992). In addition, many other channels are used to reach children, including in-store merchandising, in-class TV shows and school hall billboards (*Consumer Reports*, 1995), 30- to 60-minute TV cartoon shows based on commercially available toy personalities, product placements in the movies, product packaging ads ostensibly directed to parents, and "kids clubs," all of which mean that the actual expenditures are much higher.

The historical criticisms of advertising – even when the claims are factually correct – have included a putative ability to manipulate persons to buy products "they don't need," a tendency to materialism in society, and a development of "false values" (Drumwright, 1993). False and grossly misleading advertising is universally condemned, and while "puffery" – partial truths and/or exaggerated suggestions and tone – is accepted, it is said to develop cynicism toward the practice and worth of advertising in particular and to market economies in general. The ethical issues surrounding advertising are magnified when children become the target. In a survey of 124 *Journal of Advertising* reviewers and a random sample of American Academy of Advertising members, respondents ranked "advertising to children" (after "use of deception in ads") as the second most important topic for the study of advertising ethics (Hyman, Tansey, and Clark, 1994).

Most societies hold children in special regard: the mistreatment of children is seen as more odious than that of adults, and their protection is given high priority. The major concerns with respect to children's advertising center on a child's relative inexperience with money and shopping, and therefore with his/her poorly developed sense of critical judgment. Children have, fundamentally, an undeveloped sense of "self" – and so critics view advertising as engendering a false sense of needs, a short-term horizon for satisfaction, and a taste for banal or even harmful products. In this view, the child is seen as an easier prey, a dupe to the lure of slickly packaged advertising claims, and is exhorted to put pressure on mom or dad to "make me happy." Studies have shown that children "lack the conceptual wherewithal to research and deliberate about the relative merits of alternative expenditures in light of their economic resources" (Paine, 1993). In the extreme, there is the concern that children are "trained" to be materialistic and will become cynical about society through what critics feel will be inevitably unfulfilled product expectation.

The increasing use of television advertising to children led to consumer pressure for more US government regulation starting in the late 1960s. After continued pressure from parents, the Children's Television Act of 1990 was passed, which limits advertising to 10.5 minutes per hour of weekend shows and to 12 minutes per weekday hour, and which requires television stations to document how they have served the "education needs" of children as part of their license renewal review (Drumwright, 1993).

Bibliography

Consumer Reports (1995). Selling to school kids. *Consumer Reports*, May, 327–9.

Drumwright, M. E. (1993). Ethical issues in advertising and sales promotion. In N. Craig Smith and J. A. Quelch (eds.), *Ethics in Marketing*. Homewood: Irwin.

Hyman, M. R., Tansey, R., and Clark, J. W. (1994). Research on advertising ethics: Past, present, and future. *Journal of Advertising (Special Issue on Ethics in Advertising)*, **23** (3), 5–15.

McNeal, J. U. (1991). *A Bibliography of Research and Writings on Marketing and Advertising to Children*. New York: Lexington Books.

McNeal, J. U. (1992). *Kids as Customers: A Handbook of Marketing to Children*. New York: Lexington Books.

Paine, L. S. (1993). Children as consumers: The ethics of children's television advertising. In N. Craig Smith and J. A. Quelch (eds.), *Ethics in Marketing*. Homewood: Irwin.

affirmative action programs

Lisa H. Newton

are efforts to increase the representation, in certain positions of organizations, of groups that have not traditionally been part of such organizations or have not held such positions. These efforts are especially to be found in cases where the groups in question have traditionally been discriminated against for such positions, or actively discouraged from applying for them. Affirmative action includes attempts to recruit men as nurses and women as engineers; attempts to recruit African-American students at Amherst College and white students at Howard University. Affirmative action can occur on a national level: since women, Hispanics, and African Americans have traditionally not attained positions of high rank in business or in government, all efforts to place persons of that description in such positions count as affirmative action. More familiarly, it occurs on a local level: for historical reasons, Jews and African Americans may be in short supply at some universities, and Hispanics and Asians lacking in some occupations, in which cases it would be an effort of "affirmative action" to find members of just those groups to become part of just those institutions.

Affirmative action is justified primarily by an appeal to justice, and derives from a national commitment to equality of opportunity to participate in all occupations and all educational programs. On its usual rationale, it is argued that all groups of people are fundamentally equal in distribution of talents; therefore, if we find one group participating in some occupation or profession in percentages well below that found in the population (especially the local population) it's probably because the members of that group have been discriminated against in the past. Because of that history, it is no longer sufficient just to open the doors and say that from now on one will honor the principles of equal opportunity, for the members of the disfavored group have given up looking to enter by those doors. Therefore, it is argued that one must seek out and find qualified members and actively work to incorporate them in professions and enterprises. This effort is demanded by the duty of compensatory justice to make up for past wrongs.

Affirmative action can also be justified by utilitarian considerations, since a richer social environment is better than a poorer one, and persons of many groups and backgrounds make for a more interesting organization (*see* UTILITARIANISM). It is also good for students and managers to get used to having African Americans and women in the roles of authority from which they had been excluded, since it will be more difficult for them to work productively with supervisors whose legitimacy they doubt on grounds of group membership. Multinational corporations often seek a diversified workforce to represent the diverse nations in which they carry on their operations.

If the duty to engage in affirmative action spills over into "reverse discrimination" (i.e., a requirement that *only* a person of the previously disfavored group may be accepted or hired), then a serious injustice occurs unless all advertising for that position makes the exclusion clear. It cannot be fair to advertise a job as open to all on the basis of equal opportunity, while privately intending to examine the credentials of only certain groups.

Bibliography

Cahn, S. M. (1995). *The Affirmative Action Debate*. New York: Routledge.

Gold, S. J. (1993). *Moral Controversies: Race, Class and Gender in Applied Ethics*. Belmont, CA: Wadsworth.

Gross, B. R. (1977). *Reverse Discrimination*. Buffalo, NY: Prometheus Books.

Africa, business ethics in

Christine Gichure

Business ethics is a relatively new subject in most countries of the world. In Africa one could say that it is an absolutely new field. The first signs of academic life in business ethics on the African continent can be traced back to the 1980s, mostly in South Africa, Nigeria, and Kenya (Rossouw, 2000). As a new discipline, business ethics has been received with varying appreciation, some viewing it with skepticism, others receiving it with great excitement as one of the major highways toward the much-awaited African renaissance.

Those who receive it enthusiastically have been hard at work to popularize it. A survey conducted in 1999 (Barkhuysen, 1999: 39) showed that people's perception of business ethics as an academic field was polarized between those who believe its role should be to study and understand the central ethical dimension of business, and those who think that the focus should be more on the improvement of the behavior of those who are involved in business (Barkhuysen and Rossouw, 2000: 223).

An analysis of publications on business ethics in Africa seems to indicate there is very little reflection on the field of business ethics as such or on its development. What one finds from time to time are publications written in response to the needs and problems of Africa regarding ethics in business. This indicates a dire need for contributions toward business ethics as an academic discipline. This will be achieved once those who are involved in the field get together to reflect on what they are doing and what they are perhaps neglecting.

The survey reported in Barkhuysen (1999), for example, revealed that although prior to this period no record existed of the number of business ethics courses being taught in the continent, there in fact existed no less than 77 courses at 40 departments in universities, technikons, and colleges in six African countries. It also recorded that most of these courses were hosted in a variety of disciplines, ranging from Business Management and Human Resource Management to Philosophy and Law, with Business Schools topping the list. No less than seven centers were dealing with business ethics in Africa, even though none of them were exclusively focused on business ethics as such. These centers were located in Kenya, Nigeria, South Africa, and Uganda.

All these efforts to promote business ethics tended to occur in isolation from one another, as academics were often unaware of the existence of colleagues interested in business ethics, or did not know what those colleagues were doing. The reason for isolation was simple: Africa is a vast continent with over 45 different sovereign states and hampered by difficulties of communication and transport (Rossouw, 2000: 225).

The isolation of those working in the field of business ethics has increasingly been reduced through the availability and use of the Internet. The most significant impact of this system of communication for African business ethics has been the creation of a Business Ethics Network of Africa (BEN-Africa) in 1999 at the Uganda Martyrs University at Nkozi, Uganda. This forum was established to bring together Africans who share an interest in business ethics and who are willing to expand it on the African continent. It was formed in the belief that through interaction both theoretical knowledge and practical skill in managing ethics would be enhanced in Africa. The projects of the network include a Case Study Project, which is working toward the compilation of case studies of ethical dilemmas that occur in African organizations; an Ethics Codes Project, the objective of which is to collect ethical codes on the African continent in order to build a database of such codes; and a Whistle-blowing Project, which aims to provide descriptions of cases of whistleblowing. To date the network has membership in 25 African countries. Several of its members, including its president, are also members of the International Society of Business, Ethics and Economics (ISBEE).

FIGHTING CORRUPTION

Even before the formation of BEN-Africa, concern about escalating ethical scandals in Africa prompted the convening of various conferences and conventions in business ethics. Top on the agenda of these gatherings has nearly always been how to fight corruption in its various forms and eradicate poverty in Africa. Dialogue with international bodies such as Transparency International has to some extent helped the enthusiasts of business ethics to focus on specific areas of corruption, and to popularize business ethics in the continent, enabling people in the private and public sectors and academia to reflect on the crucial role of business ethics in curbing corruption.

Research carried out in selected areas has sometimes revealed the need to embark on a wider inquiry to probe the roots of some of the problems of corruption. A good example is a study carried out by KPMG in South Africa and published in 1996, which prompted business ethicists there to employ greater expertise on the ethical dimensions of fraud to the economic underdevelopment of African states. A survey was subsequently carried out in 17 African countries by the Forensic Division of Deloitte and Touche (South Africa) to find out the extent, causes, and major types of fraud experienced in Africa, their major perpetrators, and the amounts of assets lost per year (Rossouw, 2000: 227; Gichure, 2000: 236–47). The study gave encouragement to people of different academic and professional backgrounds to get involved in the expansion and dissemination of business ethics.

Corruption and business ethics are two terms people tend to place together, one being conceived as the negation of the other. In independent Africa, corruption has become perhaps the greatest challenge to leaders and citizens, threatening to undermine economic development and the stability of young democracies. Palmer-Buckle (1999) of Ghana defines it as acts by which the market and business sector (which has the economic strength) makes an alliance with the money-hungry political sector in exchange for protection and cover for the unethical and even criminal deals.

Scholars continue to debate the reasons why corruption has become so deeply entrenched in contemporary Africa, whereas it seems not to have been so significant before independence. There are those who attribute it to Africa's colonial history and its aftermath. Others believe that its roots are to be found in the conflict between African culture and Western ethical values, while some others link it to political growing pains and natural human greed. Corruption, as a human moral weakness, is not confined to Africa, as recent world events such as Enron have shown. African scholars tend to agree that what makes it more significant in Africa is that its effects are more devastating. They are devastating because the continent is still passing through a transitional period in which it has to cope with the effort and pain of globalization in order not to be isolated. Consequently, loopholes in political and economic management are made use of by the corrupt, to the detriment of the whole economic fiber.

At the political and economic level the fact that Africa is still finding its feet in democratic governance and a culture to sustain it often leaves sufficient space for clever but corrupt people to operate. For example, there remains the problem of finding the right mechanisms to control a modern cash economy, still a new concept in the African set up, in matters such as banking systems and international economic and financial cooperation and transactions, etc. The educational system has often failed to foster political economic maturity by neglecting comprehensive civic education. Some theorists have blamed the educational system itself, claiming it has been turning out educated persons who nevertheless remain utterly ignorant of their right to demand integrity, accountability, and transparency in the delivery of services. Over-arching all these things, African ethicists also contend that the underpinning of corruption in Africa stems from the disintegration of African ethical and moral values, the presence of foreign ideologies of what is right and wrong, as well as the absence of national values and true patriotism.

THE WAY FORWARD

Theorists attribute most of Africa's economic development problems to the lack of an African business ethics. Thus, the "history of economic activities in Africa is that they have been pursued without ethics. Some of the Western economic values, such as the pursuit of individual self-interest, were simply incompatible with the African worldview and the individual ontology. For a long time business values that originated from the Western culture have been unintelligible to the mind of the African people" (Murove, 2003).

Consequently, it is suggested that "an intelligible African business ethics should arise from the African anthropological presuppositions and the implicated core ethical values." Such an African-focused business ethics, it is claimed, should be based on an African worldview and African humanism which, given current world economic trends, can have an immense contribution to make to world business ethics (Lotriet, 2003).

GOOD CORPORATE AND BUSINESS ETHICS IN AFRICA

Political philosophers and scientists in their turn are increasingly linking good governance with the economic development of a country. They point out, however, that crucial to good governance are two concepts that are mutually reinforcing: transparency and accountability. Hence, good governance as a means of protecting the vulnerable members of society is a moral question (Aseka, 2003: 2). But morality is not just a means to good leadership: it is also a means to civility and good citizenship. For that reason it is observed that responsibility for the misfortunes of others lies with those who rise to positions of leadership. This has been one major problem in Africa which, "faced with various crises of legitimacy, regulatory and territorial crises as evidenced in its instabilities, fluctuations, uncertainties and social ruptures ... needs good leadership. A good leadership is morally obligated to its citizens and its moral obligation determines its moral integrity" (Aseka, 2003). Without moral obligation and moral integrity, there can be no moral authority, and without moral authority, there arises a crisis of legitimacy. One major task of business ethics in Africa today is to foster good governance.

CORPORATE SOCIAL RESPONSIBILITY: A CHALLENGE

According to the International Leaders Forum Report of 2001, it is only lately that companies in most parts of the world have begun to embrace economic, social, and environmental accountability (Yambayamba, 2003). The report also acknowledges that gaps still remain even where corporate social responsibility has been embraced. Africa is no exception. Business ethics programs in the continent need to urgently address this question because corporations within most African countries, whether indigenous or multinational, have hardly adopted CSR measures and where they have done so it is still at the level of unstructured and unprofessional philanthropy. For many corporations, CSR is not expected to form any part of the corporation's obligations. Any actions of the corporations carried out for the benefit of society are still perceived as being simply "something nice for" rather than something the corporation has the mandate "to do" for society. This perception could be due to the fact that the business sector is still struggling to understand what CSR is all about, what to do and how to ensure the best impact. To date there does not exist any clearly defined national agenda for this practice, which may be what has hampered it. African scholars – particularly political scientists and ethicists – are working towards a change of attitudes in this realm. African governments are also now moving toward reinforcing those efforts through the formation of such bodies as NEPAD (New Partnership for Africa's Development), currently being addressed by African states, in which member states have pledged to work together toward the eradication of the continent's poverty before the end of the twenty-first century. The task of business ethics in Africa as regards CSR is to get the business sector to realize that it can do good to people while enhancing its own shareholder value. Consequently, some business ethics projects in Africa involve the compilation of "Best Practices," which can later serve as a model to stimulate greater awareness of social responsibility (Yambayamba, 2003).

GLOBALIZATION AND BUSINESS ETHICS IN AFRICA

Globalization and the ideology of neoliberalism imply increasingly outward-oriented economies. This provides real challenges for the regulation of economic interactions between vastly differing players, who perceive their own interests differently. Africa is aware that the global order in the making is organized mostly around dominant world economic cultures. Thus, it is only logical for Africa to wonder whether the results may not be adverse to her own interests (Lotriet, 2003).

In an effort to be part of the globalization agenda, many African countries have striven to attract foreign investment in their economies through commercialization and privatization policies. Since globalization of the rich economies is driven by the desire of the rich to make money, there are certain concerns for the poor countries that must be addressed in terms of the health of the global environment and the long-term security of the ecology of those countries (Emiri, 2003). Globalization, much as it is desirable, raises various questions for African business ethics. One such question is how to expand and diversify its production base, reduce its commodity dependence, reinvest its technological capacities, and cope with the debt burden and its adverse effect on the continent.

Another crucial question that arises has to do with the understanding of ethics in the Western model applied to African values. Faced with what the developed countries consider unethical, poor continents like Africa, which host a myriad of multinational companies, still find it difficult to believe that certain practices are really unethical. This in turn makes it difficult for those multinational investors whose headquarters, main facilities, and charter are located in their home countries, to understand certain aspects of the behavior of local management and employees. Examples of such behavior include nepotism, the contentious issue of child labor, and bribery. Nepotism – often cited as a source of disagreement between home and host countries – may be wrong, yet local managers might not hesitate to place family, clan, and tribal loyalties over meritocracy when jobs are scarce. Similarly, the boundary between a bribe and a gift in a continent where social graces require certain exchanges of gifts prior to tackling the essential issues is seen to be more a matter of culture than of ethics.

Bibliography

Aseka, E. M. (2003). Culturing the principles and practices of transparency and accountability in African leadership. Paper presented at the 14th Biennial Congress of the Association of African Political Science (AAPS) on the theme of New Visions for Development in Africa, Durban, 26–28 June.

Barkhuysen, B. and Rossouw, G. J. (2000). Business ethics as academic field in Africa: Its current status. *Business Ethics: A European Review*, 9 (4), 229–35.

Emiri, O. F. (2003). Ethics and economic globalization. Paper presented at the 3rd Business Ethics Network of Africa Conference at Victoria Falls, 20–22 July.

Gichure, C. W. (2000). Fraud and the African renaissance. *Business Ethics: A European Review*, 9 (4), 236–47.

Lotriet, R. A., (2003). Globalization and Transcending Boundaries. Paper presented at the 3rd Business Ethics Network of Africa Conference at Victoria Falls, 20–22 July.

Murove, F. (2003). The voice from the periphery: Towards an African business ethics beyond the Western model. Paper presented at the 3rd Business Ethics Network of Africa Conference at Victoria Falls, 20–22 July.

Palmer-Buckle, C. (1999). The church's role in the fight against fraud. *Fraud and the African Renaissance: Proceedings of the Pan-African Conference held at Uganda Martyrs University, Nkozi,* 8–10 April, 99–107.

Rossouw, G. J. (2000). Out of Africa: An introduction. *Business Ethics: A European Review*, 9 (4), 225–8.

Walligo, J. M. (1999). The historical roots of unethical economic practices in Africa. *Fraud and the African Renaissance: Proceedings of the Pan-African Conference held at Uganda Martyrs University, Nkozi,* 8–10 April, 43–53.

Yambayamba, K. E. S. (2003). Corporate social responsibility: Challenge for Africa. Paper presented at the 3rd Business Ethics Network of Africa Conference at Victoria Falls, 20–22 July.

agency theory

Barry M. Mitnick

The theory of agency, an approach that has seen many applications across the social sciences and the disciplines of management, seeks to understand the problems created when one party is acting for another. Agents typically face a variety of problems when acting for their principals, and principals face many problems in ensuring that the actions of their agents realize the principal's preferences. Thus agency, and the agency theory constructed to provide understanding of agency behaviors, shows two faces: the activities and problems of identifying and providing services of "acting for" (the agent side), and the activities and problems of guiding and correcting agent actions (the principal side).

One of the key observations in agency theory is that all action has real or perceived costs, so that the corrections necessary to improve the quality of agent and principal actions in their relationship all have costs. As a result, it may not pay the agent, the principal, or third parties to invest in correction of this behavior where the gains from correction do not exceed the costs of performing the correction. A similar reasoning applies to the identification and specification of actions to be taken by the agent; it may not pay to find out exactly what the principal wants, nor to tell the agent that. In addition, a host of factors can produce specification and correction attempts that occur imperfectly; they may even fail to occur at all. Such factors include errors in perception, inadequacies in detection and/or in performance skills, failures in communication, conflicts of interest and/or risk preference, variations in information possession, emergent processes from system or network behavior, and problematic institutional structures. Deviant behaviors may even be institutionalized and socially protected. Kenneth Arrow terms the critical problems of agency "hidden information" (adverse selection) and "hidden action" (moral hazard) problems (Arrow, in Pratt and Zeckhauser, 1985); these terms may not, however, capture the full range of factors at work. Indeed, the careful identification of the sources of problems in agency is still a current area of research.

The logic of agency therefore predicts that deviant behaviors can persist, and be tolerated. Indeed, "perfect agency" rarely occurs, and agency theory itself becomes a study in the production, the persistence, and the amelioration of failures in service and in control.

Because agency typically occurs not only in dyads but also in organizational and higher-level systems, the complexity of agency problems, as well as of their remediation, can multiply. Agency theory seeks to build theoretical explanations of behavior within such dyadic relationships, as well as within the complex networks in which they are embedded. To date, relatively little agency theory has examined organizational systems, networks, and extended emergent structures composed of agency relations; there is indeed work in this area, but most study has been directed at more accessible problems within dyads, simple multiple agent/multiple principal conditions, and relatively simple supervisory or hierarchical structures. Agency relations can be viewed as building blocks of more complex settings, however, and so future work may tackle such contexts.

Though it is most closely associated with the modeling of firm behavior by financial economists and accountants, agency theory in fact is not, nor has it ever been, limited to theoretical contexts constrained by particular assumptions embedded in economic theory, nor to the modeling of the corporation alone. Its potential lies in its status as a general social theory of relationships of "acting for" or control in complex systems. The trend in work in agency is to introduce ever more descriptive analysis, with better grounding in the descriptive details of organizational life.

Despite this, references in the literature to "agency theory" often assume that agency theory is a narrow approach rooted in economics. As such it is assumed to make relatively simple or incomplete assumptions about human motivation (either self-interest or utility maximization) and to model organizations in terms of decision structures, assignments, and processes, thereby greatly simplifying institutional features. A great deal of criticism has been directed at the agency approach as a result, but at least some of that criticism really applies only to a particular modeling subset of work in agency.

In fact, work in agency theory extends considerably beyond the economics paradigm and includes attention to a variety of normative, institutional, cognitive, social, and systemic factors. In addition, agency theory should not be viewed as a theory of the firm alone, which is merely one application of it. Agency is a general approach to the study of a common social relation, that of "acting for."

The intellectual ancestors of agency theory go back at least to the 1930s, with Ronald Coase's work on the firm and Chester Barnard's classic work on the functions of the executive. There are forebears as well in sociology in some of the classic works of Mead and Simmel.

In economics, the stream passes through the series of studies in the divergence of owner and manager interests and behavior (from scholars such as Berle and Means, through Papandreou, Penrose, Marris, and Baumol, to Williamson's theory of managerial discretion; see also work on agency and the firm by Harvey Leibenstein). Marshak and Radner's work on the theory of teams and Spence and Zeckhauser's work on risk and insurance highlighted the effects of differing information states and risk preferences. Oliver Williamson's transaction-costs approach applied a costs model to the study of exchange and its internalization in organization that has a cousin in agency's use of costs of correction in its modeling of control. Alchian and Demsetz explained the emergence of organization based on the need to monitor individual contributions in situations of joint production; it is often seen as one of the foundational works in an agency theory of the firm. In several works, Arrow observed the importance of considering non-economic factors in relations in which one party acts for another. Several other early papers used agency concepts in an economics context, though they did not appear to see or propose agency as a coherent and general theoretical approach; these included works by Victor Goldberg and Barry Weingast.

In political science, Herbert Simon's work on administrative behavior and on the employment relation (see also the later related work on this in economics by Williamson, Wachter, and Harris), March and Simon's inducements-contributions model, and Clark and Wilson's incentive systems theory constructed a stream out of Barnard that flows directly into modern institutional agency theory. Those who view agency as a creature of economics often miss these critical theoretical ties. In addition, work in sociology on exchange theory by such scholars as George Homans, Peter Blau, Richard Emerson, Bo Anderson, Karen Cook, and Peter Marsden should be seen as theoretical development cognate to that in agency and in the transaction-costs literature in economics.

The first explicit proposals that a systematic theory of agency would be valuable and ought to be constructed, and the first works explicitly beginning such construction, apparently came from Stephen Ross (1973) and Barry Mitnick (1973, 1975), independently. Ross's work was anchored in financial economics; Mitnick's was more generally based in social science, including political science and sociology. Each reflected the tools then currrent in their disciplines. Ross was the first to clearly identify and worry about the resolution of "agency problems" and to try to derive formal conclusions about the nature of successful incentive contracts in agency; Mitnick's work was the first to lay out a broad framework structuring agency theory and to actually develop a series of small theoretical applications of agency, such as the consequences of agents bargaining with each other. Ross's work may be seen as the explicit start of the "economic" theory of agency; Mitnick's, of what may be termed the "institutional" theory of agency.

The work that has probably had the biggest impact on agency studies is the classic piece by Jensen and Meckling (1976), which provided an explicit agency theory of the firm as a "nexus of contracts" (see CONTRACTS AND CONTRACT-ING). Subsequent work by Eugene Fama and Jensen identified the decision process in firms as central, and argued that study of the assignment of rights to "decision management" and "decision control" could explain many features of firm behavior. The contexts of this work usually concern the economic theory of the firm, not necessarily a general theory of agency relations in social behavior.

At present there is no unified, coherent "theory of agency." Depending on the research tradition in which the particular work in agency has been developed, different explicit logics, based in different social science literatures, such as economics or sociology, and sometimes displaying divergent approaches even within disciplines, are used to construct explanations. This produces the appearance of streams of work, each stream tending to operate within its own assumptional world. This is true even within the economics area, where agency work divides into formal mathematical modeling and modeling based in a more descriptive theory of the firm. The accounting literature also features behavioral/descriptive theoretic works in such areas as auditing relationships, ethical issues (see Noreen, 1988), and contract design (including such public sector application areas as contracting out and municipal bond decisions). The formal work in economics, finance, and accounting features proofs of theorems based in assumptions about such characteristics of the agency situation as the preferences (including risk) of the agent and principal, the contract between them and its incentive structure, the sequencing of action in the relation, and conditions of information held by the parties about each other and the state of the environment.

In contrast, some of the work in management, sociology, and political science has explored agency using variables and perspectives that are of more traditional interest within those fields. For example, there is work in agency now examining the role of trust and of sociological norms (e.g., Mitnick, 1973, 1975, on norms in agency; Shapiro, 1987, on trust; there is work by Mitnick and by the sociologist Arthur Stinchcombe on what they call the "fiduciary norm") (see FIDU-CIARY DUTY). The study of control has been linked to older traditions in those fields, as well as to newer networks approaches, by such scholars as Robert Eccles, Kathleen Eisenhardt (1989), and Harrison White. Agency analysis has been applied to such older topics for study as political corruption and bureaucratic behavior by such scholars as Edward Banfield, Gary Miller, Barry Mitnick, Terry Moe (1984), and

Susan Rose-Ackerman. In addition, agency has been used to study corporate political activity (e.g., Mitnick, 1993). There are quite a number of applications of agency to government regulation, for example, by Mitnick, Barry Weingast, Pablo Spiller, and Jeffrey Cohen. In management, scholars have used (or modified) agency approaches to explore such topics as behavior in boards of directors (e.g., work by Barry Baysinger, Gerald Davis, and Edward Zajac), organizational control (e.g., work by Donaldson and Davis, Kathleen Eisenhardt, Huseyin Leblebici, Benjamin Oviatt, and James Walsh), bargaining (e.g., work by Lax and Sebenius), and compensation practices (e.g., work by Luis Gomez-Mejia, Henry Tosi, and Conlon and Parks) (*see* CORPORATE GOVERNANCE). Agency has also seen some attention in the marketing literature. The appearance of each body of work more nearly resembles the kinds of theory construction and hypothesis testing practiced in these disciplines.

In an important stream of work, Lex Donaldson and James Davis (e.g., Donaldson and Davis, 1994) demonstrate via their "theory of stewardship" how theory development on the firm can escape or modify the constraints of the economics model. Indeed, given our view of the duality of agency, the economic theory of agency seems biased toward the analysis of corrections; it is a theory of control (or of who gets control, such as decision rights). But agency has two sides: control and service. There is no reason why a viable theory of the firm cannot be constructed taking the service side as primary (e.g., other things being equal, managers seek performance; correction is then taken as a secondary, marginal activity). Of course, the most descriptive theory of the firm may take a contingent approach that simply uses the conceptual tools of both service and control to understand the production of behavior in and around the firm.

It is probably true that the scholars using agency theory have tended to rely on the sources for that theory with which they are most familiar. Because most scholars have assumed that agency originated in economics they have tended to use the major works there, such as Jensen and Meckling (1976), and adapted its features to the study at hand. This tends to lead to more limited kinds of analysis as assumptions more appropriate to the economics paradigm are imported into settings for which social science has additional tools available.

It is important to be aware of the differences between agency theory and the law of agency. In the law of agency it is presumed that the agent is acting under the orders of the principal; the law itself acts, of course, as a normative guide to behavior and to the resolution of disputes regarding appropriate action in agency roles (see the *Restatement of the Law, 2d, Agency*). Agency theory is just that, a group of descriptive theoretical approaches that seek to provide understanding of a broad class of social behaviors; agents need not be presumed to be under explicit direction and hence possessing particular obligations. The law of agency does, however, provide rich materials for exploration via agency theory, and contributes central insights that can expand the quality and domain of agency theory (the first such use of the law of agency was by Mitnick, 1973, but there has been a scattering of work by such scholars as Robert Clark, Frank Easterbrook, and Daniel Fischel, and in a number of law reviews). The same may be said of the related bodies of law and legal analysis in contracts and trusts; of particular interest is work on "relational contracting" by Ian Macneil.

Applications of concepts relevant to agency are found in numerous places in the business ethics literature, but, with the exception of the volume edited by Bowie and Freeman (1992) and some scattered work elsewhere (e.g., Noreen, 1988, and work in accounting by Wanda Wallace), most applications in business ethics use materials based in the law of agency (e.g., the concept of fiduciary duty) and in moral philosophy (e.g., the obligations of the moral agent) (*see* CORPORATE MORAL AGENCY). Agency as a descriptive theory of service and control ought to be capable of providing increased understanding of the dilemmas produced in the pervasive agency relations of business.

Bibliography

American Law Institute (1958). *Restatement of the Law, 2d, Agency.* St. Paul, MN: Thomson-West.

Bowie, N. E. and Freeman, R. E. (1992). *Ethics and Agency Theory: An Introduction*. New York: Oxford University Press.

Donaldson, L. and Davis, J. (1994). Boards and company performance: Research challenges the conventional wisdom. *Corporate Governance: An International Review*, **2**, 151–60.

Eisenhardt, K. M. (1989). Agency theory: An assessment and review. *Academy of Management Review*, **14**, 57–74.

Jensen, M. C. and Meckling, W. H. (1976). Theory of the firm: Managerial behavior, agency costs and ownership structure. *Journal of Financial Economics*, **3**, 305–60.

Mitnick, B. M. (1973). Fiduciary responsibility and public policy: The theory of agency and some consequences. *Proceedings of the 1973 Annual Meeting of the American Political Science Association, New Orleans, La.*, **69**, Ann Arbor, MI: UMI.

Mitnick, B. M. (1975). The theory of agency: The policing "paradox" and regulatory behavior. *Public Choice*, **24** (winter), 27–42.

Mitnick, B. M. (1992). The theory of agency and organizational analysis. In N. Bowie and R. E. Freeman (eds.), *Ethics and Agency Theory*. New York: Oxford University Press, 75–96.

Mitnick, B. M. (1993). *Corporate Political Agency: The Construction of Competition in Public Affairs*. Newbury Park, CA: Sage.

Moe, T. M. (1984). The new economics of organization. *American Journal of Political Science*, **28**, 739–77.

Noreen, E. (1988). The economics of ethics: A new perspective on agency theory. *Accounting, Organizations and Society*, **13**, 359–69.

Pratt, J. W. and Zeckhauser, R. (eds.) (1985). *Principals and Agents: The Structure of Business*. Boston, MA: Harvard Business School Press.

Ross, S. A. (1973). The economic theory of agency: The principal's problem. *American Economic Review*, **62**, 134–9.

Shapiro, S. P. (1987). The social control of impersonal trust. *American Journal of Sociology*, **93**, 623–58.

AIDS

Craig P. Dunn

AIDS is an acronym for Acquired Immunodeficiency Syndrome. AIDS is generally, although not universally, thought to be associated with the presence of HIV, the Human Immunodeficiency Virus. All persons with HIV cannot appropriately be said to have AIDS. The United States Center for Disease Control's (CDC's) technical descriptor of AIDS has to do with either the presence of an opportunistic infection associated with HIV, and/or a diminution of the body's CD4 (T-lymphocyte or T-cell) count to below 200 per cubic millimeter of blood. Evidence suggests that HIV is spread through transmission of bodily fluids typically associated with intimate sexual contact and/or intravenous drug use, though cases of *in utero* mother-to-child transmission are on the rise. HIV is fragile once outside the body, and is therefore not transmittable through casual contact. AIDS is treatable but not curable. With proper treatment, it is not unusual for individuals to live ten years or even longer from time of initial diagnosis with HIV to eventual death.

The CDC currently estimates that globally more than 16 million people have died of AIDS and more than 16,000 people become newly infected each day. Geographic impacts have been disparate. Developing countries are currently being hardest hit, particularly those in Sub-Saharan Africa where over 23 million adults and children are living with HIV/AIDS and more than 13 million have died, accounting for more than 80 percent of the world's deaths due to AIDS. In the United States there are now 800,000 to 900,000 people living with HIV, with approximately 40,000 new HIV infections occurring every year. In the US, HIV-related illness and death historically have had a tremendous impact on men who have sex with men (MSM); even though the epidemic has increased during the last decade among injection drug users and heterosexuals, MSM continue to account for the largest number of people reported with AIDS each year. Though they represent only 13 percent of the US population, more than half of new HIV infections occur among blacks (http://www.cdc.org).

HIV/AIDS should be a core business issue for every company – particularly those with interests in heavily affected countries – according to the Global Business Coalition on HIV/AIDS (http://www.businessfightsaids.org/). Estimates by the World Bank suggest that the macroeconomic impact of HIV/AIDS may reduce the growth of national income by up to a third in countries where the prevalence among adults is 10 percent. Additionally, rates of HIV infection worldwide are highest for the young and for women, who are major contributors to the workforce (http://www.bsr.org/BSR Resources/IssueBriefDetail.cfm?DocumentID = 49032). In some countries – most notably South Africa – the tendency of a significant proportion of employers has been to discriminate against employees and job applicants living with HIV/AIDS through use of HIV testing to exclude those that are HIV-positive. In the case of *Hoffmann vs. South African Airways*, the Constitutional Court ruled against this practice (Ngwena, n.d.). In response to such expansions of workplace protections to those infected with HIV/AIDS, several global companies have policies in place underpinned by principles of inclusion, non-disclosure, confidentiality, tolerance, and non-discrimination. BP asserts their "global approach prohibits unfair discrimination against people living with HIV/AIDS ... it promotes an environment in which people who are HIV-positive are able to be open about their status, without fear of stigma or rejection" (http://www.bp.com/environ_social/bus_ethics/hum_rights/hiv.asp).

HIV/AIDS has become such a critical business issue that academic programs focusing specific attention on this dimension of the pandemic are now emerging. In response to their belief that unevenness, inadequate training, and distrust between managers and workers characterize the management of HIV/AIDS in workplaces and cause negative effects on the quality of life and work, the African Centre for HIV/AIDS Management in the World of Work at Stellenbosch University and the National School of Public Health at Medunsa have partnered in offering a Postgraduate Diploma in the Management of HIV/AIDS in the World of Work (http://www.aidscentre.sun.ac.za/diploma.html). Case materials focusing on a variety of ways to manage people with AIDS at work and a broad range of perspectives informing managers' decisions about this painful and complex issue have been developed (http://www.caseplace.org/newsletter-url3128/ newsletter-url_show.htm?doc_id = 180238).

Underlying the pragmatic impacts of HIV/AIDS reside deep ethical concerns. Links between HIV infection and such social "baggage" as homosexuality and drug abuse make this a volatile issue for those formulating corporate policy. From the view of KANTIAN ETHICS, or deontology, there is a potential clash of rights (*see* RIGHTS) between the HIV+ worker and the HIV− co-workers. The concern on the part of some individuals is that the ease of transmitability of HIV has been grossly understated. One study of corporate and public service employees found that "thirty percent of the respondents expressed skepticism about the accuracy of public information" related to AIDS, with nearly one in four stating they would be "afraid of getting AIDS from working near PWAs [Persons with AIDS]" (Barr, Waring, and Warshaw, 1992: 226). Such individuals typically advocate for disclosure of co-workers' HIV status. Conversely, those infected with HIV are concerned with the variety of discriminatory practices, including erosion of the right to PRIVACY, revocation of health benefits or escalation of the cost of such benefits (*see* HEALTHCARE ETHICS AND BUSINESS ETHICS), shunning by co-workers, and even termination of employment, which often accompany making a positive diagnosis with HIV a matter of public record. Additionally, the right of the AIDS sufferer to his or her WORK must be considered against the backdrop of the right of the employer to exercise the doctrine of EMPLOYMENT AT WILL. This particular conflict is compounded by the Americans with Disabilities Act (ADA), which in part treats workers with AIDS as a disabled class subject to the protections contained in this legislation.

The issue of resolving rights conflicts with respect to persons with AIDS in the workplace is necessarily complicated by consideration of RISK tolerance. Few, if any, rights are absolute; therefore, the challenge for the deontologist is to decide which among a competing set of rights is most foundational. This determination is in some sense dependent upon the probability, or risk, of alternative realizable policies. Neither the view that the rights of the AIDS sufferer must be protected at all cost, nor the view that the rights of co-workers are inviolate, seems correct. However, the suggestion that determination of a "rights hierarchy" – and thereby of one policy versus another – is dependent upon risk assessment necessarily moves the argument toward consideration of the utilitarian consequences of alternative policies.

UTILITARIANISM requires that we consider the consequences of including or excluding AIDS sufferers from the workplace, with an eye toward bringing about the "greatest good for the greatest number." Those familiar with the debate over whether HIV+ medical providers should be compelled to disclose their HIV status to patients have seen this particular issue evolve from one in which rights were of central importance, to concern over the impact of mandatory disclosure policies on the healthcare profession in general and ultimately the welfare of society at large. The presupposition of utilitarian argumentation is that relevant benefits and costs can be both identified and quantified. While utilitarians are well versed in dealing with such complexities, when it comes to workplace AIDS transmitability, the issue is so emotive as to make consensual policy formulation a virtual impossibility. What is known is that the well-being of the AIDS sufferer is to a great extent a function of AIDS policy. Research into the longevity of HIV+ individuals indicates that a supportive community (*see* COMMUNITARIANISM) leads to life extension. One of the drawbacks of traditional utilitarianism, however, is its compatibility with injustices: in seeking to promote the greatest good for the greatest number, the interests of the non-majority are rather easily overridden. For the HIV+ minority, the consequences of restrictive workplace AIDS policy might well be the foreshortening of their very lives.

At least one writer suggests Kantian and utilitarian ethics can be meaningfully combined. Brady suggests we should make "exceptions to rules when so doing recognizes or promotes the affiliation and connectedness of persons" (1990: 144–5). With this understanding, should HIV+ individuals be offered organizational membership in spite of a general rule affording all employees a safe working environment? Consistent with designation of HIV infection as a disability under the ADA, Brady's principle implies that the objective of affiliation should override more general workplace safeguards. In effect this principle injects classical utilitarianism with JUSTICE considerations. The objective is to have the manager approach the crafting of workplace AIDS policy with specific reference to the idiosyncrasies of each specific work environment.

Consideration of the personal – and relational – implications of AIDS policy formulation and implementation suggests we consider the ethics of care. The topic of AIDS in the workplace needs to be a matter of conversations about how we as human beings live, and more particularly how we live in caring relationship with one another. Such caring conversation is hindered by language which creates unnecessary – or even inflammatory – distinctions. As Sedgwick (1990: 1) has noted, "many of the major nodes of thought and knowledge in twentieth-century Western culture as a whole is structured – indeed, fractured – by a chronic, now endemic crisis of homo-heterosexual definition, indicatively male, dating from the end of the nineteenth century." This is nowhere more true than in conversations about the appropriate policy response to persons in the workplace who happen to have been infected by HIV. Jonsen (1991: 660) offers perhaps the best closing to this discussion of policy alternatives relating to AIDS in the workplace: "In all epidemics, fear stimulates isolation and responsibility requires inclusion – this might even be called the moral law of epidemics."

Bibliography

Barr, J. K., Waring, J. M., and Warshaw, L. J. (1992). Knowledge and attitudes about AIDS among corporate and public service employees. *American Journal of Public Health*, 82 (2): 225–8.

Brady, F. N. (1990). *Ethical Managing: Rules and Results*. New York: Macmillan.

Cohen, E. D. and Davis, M. (eds.) (1994). *AIDS: Crisis in Professional Ethics*. Philadelphia, PA: Temple University Press.

Deka, D. (1994). "AIDS in the workplace." Graduate thesis: College of Business Administration, San Diego State University.

Feldblum, C. R. (1991). The Americans with Disabilities Act: Definition of disability. *The Labor Lawyer*, 11: 11–26.

Gilbert, D. R. and Freeman, R. E. (1994). AIDS in the workplace: A critique from lesbian/gay theory. Presentation within Social Issues in Management Division, Academy of Management Annual Meeting.

Gini, A. and Davis, M. (1994). AIDS in the workplace: Options and responsibility. In E. D. Cohen and

M. Davis (eds.), *AIDS Crisis in Professional Ethics*. Philadelphia, PA: Temple University Press.

Heacock, M. V. and Orvis, G. P. (1990). AIDS in the workplace: Public and corporate policy. *Harvard Journal of Law and Public Policy*, 13 (2): 689–713.

Jonsen, A. R. (1991). Is individual responsibility a sufficient basis for public confidence? *Arch Intern Med*, 151: 660–2.

Ngwena, C. (n.d.). Constitutional values and HIV/AIDS in the workplace: Reflections on *Hoffmann vs. South African Airways*. *Law and Bioethics* (http://www.blackwell-synergy.com/links/doi/10.1111/1471–8847.00007/abs/).

Paul, R. J. and Townsend, J. B. (1997). AIDS in the workplace: Balancing employer and employee rights. *Review of Business*, 18 (2), 9–14.

Sedgwick, E. K. (1990). *Epistemology of the Closet*. Berkeley: University of California Press.

Stone, R. A. (1994). AIDS in the workplace: An executive update. *Academy of Management Executive*, 8 (3): 52–61.

Alliances

Lynn A. Isabella

"Forming alliances" is a phrase often used in today's business environment. While the concept seems simple – unite with other individuals within a company or with another organization – to collaborate rather than compete, not all alliances are really alliances. The word is fashionable to use, and used liberally within companies, but the philosophy behind a *true* alliance is anything but business as usual.

Defining an Alliance

An alliance is a close, collaborative relationship between two (or more) firms with the intent of accomplishing mutually compatible goals that would be difficult for each to accomplish alone (Spekman and Isabella, 2000). This definition is carefully worded. An alliance implies that the relationship between the parties is not competitive, it is strategic, each needs the other to accomplish a business objective, and goals are complementary (though not necessarily identical). At its core, alliances are about shared control and decision-making. In a business world frequented by competition and transactions, alliances require a different mindset for action and interaction.

What can be confusing is that, given this definition, alliances can take a number of different forms and still be alliances. The most "organized" alliance is a joint venture (JV) between two firms in which a third and separate firm is created. Such an alliance, governed by a board of directors represented by both partner companies, is often formed to bring specific strategic capabilities of each partner to a new or existing market. At the other end of the alliance continuum might be co-marketing arrangements, through which two companies market each other's products. In between, other alliance forms can include channel partnerships or manufacturing alliances.

Common Characteristics

Despite their appearance each of these types of alliance share certain characteristics. An alliance is not a transaction. Transaction implies an exchange, such as money for services or products. True alliances are not simply an item-for-item exchange but include:

- *Goal complementarity*: Both parties in an alliance give and get something from the partnership. While they may be different things, the goals for which each member of the partnership is striving are compatible.
- *Recognized interdependence and coordination*: Within an alliance each partner must recognize that their actions may have implications for their partner, making each partner interdependent with the other. As a result, coordination between alliance partners must be high in order to ensure true collaboration and cooperation.
- *Trust and commitment:* By definition, alliances require relational trust and commitment. Both partners must work hard to ensure that trust is nurtured and commitment ensured. Without trust and commitment, there can be no alliance.
- *Symmetry:* Alliances are about equity over time, not necessarily at any one moment in time. Partners want an equitable share of the decision-making, share of the rewards and share of the success. Without symmetry or with a banker's mentality (meaning

everything balances at the end of the day), there is not an alliance.

- *Open and two-way flows of information:* Alliances are about sharing and breaking the traditional thinking that information is power. In alliances, shared information is power. This does not mean that each partner is obliged to reveal its proprietary secrets or technology; it does mean that relevant alliance information is not held by one partner when needed by the other partner.
- *Joint decision-making:* No alliance can be an alliance unless there is mutual joint decision-making. If one partner makes the decision for another, an alliance does not exist. Both partners make decisions for the alliance.
- *Long-term focus:* True alliances act as if they are going to be an alliance over the long term. While realizing that the competitive environment may change, or reasons unseen now might make the reason for alliance moot later on, alliance partners act as if the alliance were headed forward in perpetuity. To think this way means that each partner takes a long-term interest in the future of the alliance.
- *Cultural humility:* Whether speaking of national culture or corporate culture, an alliance may bring together two partners with different cultures. Who's to say, for example, that it is better to have lunch at your desk or to take a 2-hour break for a leisurely lunch with wine? Who's to say that how Partner A does project management is not as good as Partner B? Alliances require a sense of humility that one's own culture is not necessarily the only one for the alliance.

More than just Business

Alliances are about business and relationships. Consider the DNA model of a double helix with strands of DNA intimately intertwined. So it is with the business and relationship side of an alliance. The business side of an alliance is the task of the alliance – what the alliance is charged with doing; the relationship side encompasses the relationship between the partners. An alliance cannot exist without both. On average if the percent of time spent on one dimension (either business or relationship) exceeds 70 percent, the alliance is most likely in trouble. Business and relationship activities need to be balanced. Managers find it easy to conduct the business of an alliance; relationship activities are harder to identify and to remember to do.

Alliance Spirit

While business and relationship activities are visible, there is a more important aspect of an alliance: the alliance spirit. Alliance spirit represents the answer to the question: What does it mean to partner? Ideally, alliance spirit is about solidarity (we are in this together), mutuality (for both our benefits), flexibility (maintaining a sense of adaptability and change), and harmony (yet realizing we will need to reach agreement when we disagree). The alliance spirit is created through the actions of each and every member of the alliance. Collectively, alliance spirit is about trust and sharing, not power and control. Having a similar and strong alliance spirit can help an alliance through its difficult times.

Conclusion

Alliances are valid and valued business forms. Most certainly they will increase across our organizations in the future. Alliances open up companies to markets beyond their immediate reach, to technology they don't have or could not develop quickly, to partners that might share development risks or costs or to any number of other capabilities and skills. What most companies don't realize, however, is that using the word "alliances" connotes a set of expectations and behaviors around sharing and collaboration. Calling something an alliance when it is really a transaction sends mixed messages and increases the probability of failure. Companies can be alliance-like in their interactions, but that doesn't mean that everything between two partners is an alliance.

Bibliography

Spekman, R. and Isabella, L. A. (2000). *Alliance Competence: Maximizing the Value of Your Partnerships.* New York: John Wiley.

altruism and benevolence

Lawrence A. Blum

A concern for the well-being of persons other than oneself. (Both contrast with "beneficence," which refers to actions that promote the welfare of others, independent of the motive behind them.) This concern cannot, however, be in service of one's own interest, as when we help out another with the expectation that our doing so will result in greater benefit to ourselves. The concern must be directed toward the other *for her own sake*, otherwise it is not altruism or benevolence. Altruism concerns not merely the results of action, but also the agent's *motivation* to engage in such action.

Concern for others for their own sake does not necessitate actual self-sacrifice, or, more moderately, a loss of personal well-being. The view that it does may stem from the false belief that every situation presents us with a choice between fostering our own good and fostering the good of others. Bishop Joseph Butler (1692–1752) gave the classic arguments showing that action on behalf of others need involve no loss to the self.

Beyond this, to say that someone is "altruistic" does seem to carry the implication that the person neglects her own well-being in favor of others'. (The same implication is not carried by "benevolence," however.) Yet we need to retain a term for a concern for the good of others *without* the further implication of self-sacrifice or self-neglect.

However, when altruism *does* involve great personal risk or sacrifice it is generally thought to be more admirable than altruism with minimal risk. Thus, rescuers of Jews during the Nazi era – a group extensively studied as exemplars of heroic altruism – exhibited the highest moral virtue. Nevertheless, self-sacrifice is not a virtue in its own right. It must be in the service of a great good, or at least a good greater than the loss to the agent (as in the rescuers' case), otherwise it might just be foolish. And even self-denying altruism is not always admirable or advisable. Some persons may give too much of themselves, even to promote a great good for others. Feminists have claimed that women have been victims of just such a debilitating self-denying ideology.

Still, by and large, appropriate self-sacrificing altruism is good and admirable.

Altruism and self-interest need not be opposed; they may be mutually enhancing. Often those with the most secure sense of self and self-worth are also very altruistic persons. Their self-confidence allows them to respond to the plight of others without a debilitating self-absorption. They are happy people who derive satisfaction from their altruistic activities, though these may involve a sacrifice of comfort, convenience, and missed pleasures. Some take this truth a step further and argue that the *most* fulfilled and flourishing individuals are those whose lives involve a substantial degree of altruism. They claim that persons who are non-altruistic, whose lives are devoted to the pursuit of self-oriented satisfaction are, paradoxically, less likely to achieve such self-satisfaction.

Yet if altruism is satisfying to the self, is it still really altruism? More generally, many question whether altruism actually exists. Psychological egoism is the view that behind all beneficent action lies a pursuit of self-benefit, whether conscious or unconscious. It is true that the most apparently altruistic actions may be egoistically driven. If my beneficent pursuits are in the service of an image of myself as an altruistic person, because I think that will make me happy, then I am not altruistic (*see* EGOISM, PSYCHOLOGICAL EGOISM, AND ETHICAL EGOISM).

However, being *aware* of the satisfaction one derives from altruistic pursuits is not the same as being *motivated* by that satisfaction. In fact it is impossible to gain altruistic satisfaction by deliberately aiming at it; for then it will not involve a true regard for the other for her own sake. The satisfaction derived will not be altruistic but egoistic.

Since altruism is a matter of motivation, it cannot guarantee that the results of altruistic action will actually be beneficial, even if that is the agent's intent. An altruistic person may be mistaken as to the interests of the party she wishes to help; her action may thus fail to benefit. Yet since an altruistic person does wish for the good of the other, she should also be concerned about understanding what that good is, and open to revising her view of that good in light of new information. Thus, an ideally altruistic person will be concerned not only for the other's good, but also to figure out what that good is. Nevertheless, it would be misleading to deprive the term "altruism" of application when the agent seeks the good of the other for its own sake but is non-culpably mistaken about the nature of that good.

Motivations are sometimes difficult to discern. And so some say, "Why should we care what the agent's motive is, as long as she gets results, that is, as long as others are benefited? We should arrange our political and social institutions so that self-interested motives will produce beneficent results and we will not need to rely on people acting altruistically." It can be doubted whether such a social order is possible; political, social, and even economic life depends in all sorts of ways on people not pursuing their own self-interest to the utmost, but rather taking some account of the interests of others (see Mansbridge, 1990). Beyond this, we do in fact take a moral interest in people's motivations and character. We admire the benevolent and altruistic person but not the selfish, opportunistic person, even if we are relieved when the latter's actions happen to produce beneficial results.

See also *feminist ethics*

Bibliography

Baron, L., Blum, L., Krebs, D., Oliner, P., Oliner, S., and Smolenska, M. Z. (1992). *Embracing the Other: Philosophical, Psychological, and Historical Perspectives on Altruism.* New York: New York University Press.
Blum, L. (1980). *Friendship, Altruism, and Morality.* London: Routledge and Kegan Paul.
Butler, J. (1983) [1726]. *Five Sermons Preached at the Rolls Chapel.* Indianapolis, IN: Hackett.
Mansbridge, J. (1990). *Beyond Self-Interest.* Chicago: University of Chicago Press.
Social Philosophy and Policy (1993). **10** (1), winter.
Thomas, L. (1989). *Living Morally: A Psychology of Moral Character.* Philadelphia, PA: Temple University Press.

anti-competitive practices in marketing

C. Jay Lambe and Robert E. Spekman

Marketing practices that reduce or discourage competition, typically thought of in terms of antitrust violations. Antitrust: of, relating to, or being legislation against or opposition to trusts or combinations; consisting of laws to protect trade and commerce from unlawful restraints and monopolies or unfair business practices (*Webster's College Dictionary*, 1993).

Under certain conditions, examples of anti-competitive practices in marketing, which are considered violations of US antitrust law, include the following: conspiring to monopolize a market by using a size advantage to underprice competitors and drive them from the market (predatory pricing), offering larger business customers lower prices than smaller business customers with whom they compete (discriminatory pricing), and conspiring to monopolize a market through mergers or collusion with competitors.

Perhaps the best way to understand the rationale behind antitrust legislation, and why it has evolved as it has, is to place these events in a historical perspective. Essentially, the industrial revolution, and its expanding scope in the late 1800s, led to the initiation of antitrust legislation in the US. As technology expanded and developed, the size and power of certain companies grew tremendously, which led to heightened social and political concern about large business enterprises. The general consensus was that the market power of these large industries (e.g., steel, oil, railroads) discouraged competition. As a result, the period of 1861 to 1901, often called the age of "Robber Barons," was accompanied by populist movements that contended that big business was endangering the livelihoods of small, independent businessmen and farmers. These movements led to the first major federal regulatory antitrust enactment, the Sherman Anti-trust Act of 1890.

The Act regulated the form and size of organizations and expressly prohibited monopolies. In a monopoly a firm has sole, or nearly sole, control of a certain market. Section 1 of the Act forbids entering into a contract, combination, or conspiracy in restraint of trade. Section 2 of the Sherman Act prohibits monopolizing or attempting to monopolize trade, including acts such as predatory pricing. Perhaps the most famous example of alleged predatory pricing involved Standard Oil Company of New Jersey. In evidence presented before the Supreme Court, the government demonstrated that Standard Oil would sharply reduce prices in local markets where competition existed, while holding prices at a much higher level in other markets, with the objective of persuading competitors to merge.

Although the Sherman Act discouraged monopolistic practices, it was only effective against a few obvious monopoly consolidations. In order to more specifically attack the methods by which firms developed monopoly power, the federal government passed the Clayton Act and the Federal Trade Commission Act in 1914. The Clayton Act provisions are an effort to deny firms the ability to develop monopolies through mergers or collusion with other firms. Specifically, Section 7 of the Act prohibits stock acquisitions by any corporation "where the effect of such an acquisition may be to substantially lessen competition . . . or to restrain such commerce in any section or community, or tend to create a monopoly of any line of commerce." Section 3 prohibits entering into exclusive dealing and tying contracts in order to develop monopoly power. The Federal Trade Commission Act created the Federal Trade Commission (FTC) to police anti-competitive conduct.

Two later Acts amended the Clayton Act, addressing what some considered to be loopholes in the existing legislation. In 1936 the federal government initiated the Robinson-Patman Act to address the issue of discriminatory pricing by amending Section 2 of the Clayton Act. Provisionally, discriminatory pricing is selling or purchasing different units of the same product at price differentials not directly attributable to differences in the cost of supply. Pressure for this enhancement to the Clayton Act came from relatively small wholesalers and retailers who competed against A&P and other emerging retail chain organizations. These businesses complained that the favorable pricing received by larger competitors created an advantage that was competition-threatening. The argument was that these larger companies could establish prices that were profitable for them, but unprofitable for the smaller firms that must pay more for inputs, and thus could eliminate competition. In agreement with this logic, the Robinson-Patman provision prohibits price discrimination among business purchasers to an extent that cannot be justified by a difference in cost or as a good-faith attempt to meet the price of a competitor. Addressing another omission, the 1950 Celler-Kefauver Act amended Section 7 of the Clayton Act. This amendment made asset acquisitions of competitors that substantially lessen competition illegal. Proponents of this amendment successfully pointed to anti-competitive acquisitions, such as those made by Standard Oil when it bought competing oil refineries, not by buying the stock of the target firm, but by purchasing its assets.

Given the past development of antitrust laws and the legacy that remains, what does the future hold for antitrust? As it has in the past, antitrust legislation will continue to evolve as it is presented with new challenges. A major difference, though, is that some existing legislation may be rolled back, or at least softened, particularly in the area of mergers and interfirm collusion. Several phenomena seem to be responsible for this retreat. Based on a trend that started with the emergence of strong Japanese competition and the Reagan presidency, it appears that the American public and the government view a lessening of these antitrust provisions, and regulation as a whole, as vital to the international competitiveness of the US. Recent consortia of high-technology firms engaged in research to improve US global competitiveness attest to a shift in the interpretation of antitrust behavior. In addition, the increasingly dynamic nature of technology often ensures that no one firm will have long-lived market dominance. Thus, given the increasingly tenuous position of market leaders, there is naturally less concern about monopolistic practices. And some have questioned the efficacy of the Robinson-Patman Act. The argument here is that a too-literal interpretation of the Act protects inefficient firms and, therefore, does not promote free-market competition. As always, though, future legislation will be dependent upon the prevailing political climate.

See also *advertising, ethics of; marketing, ethics of*

Bibliography

Caves, R. (1982). *American Industry: Structure, Conduct, Performance.* Englewood Cliffs, NJ: Prentice-Hall.

Stern, L. W. and Eovaldi, T. L. (1984). *Legal Aspects of Marketing Strategy: Antitrust and Consumer Protection Issues.* Englewood Cliffs, NJ: Prentice-Hall.

Stern, L. W. and Grabner, J. R., Jr. (1970). *Competition in the Marketplace.* Atlanta, GA: Scott, Foresman.

Wall Street Journal (1995). Land of the giants. May 5, A12.

Werner, R. O. (1989). *Legal and Economic Regulation in Marketing.* New York: Quorum Books.

applied ethics

Joan C. Callahan

Although applied (or "practical") ethics borrows insights from theories of moral axiology (i.e., theories of the morally good and evil), theories of moral obligation (i.e., theories regarding what is morally permissible, morally required, and morally impermissible), and from metaethics (i.e., theories regarding the meaning of moral terms, the nature of moral discourse, and the justification of moral claims), the task in engaging in practical ethics is not simply to work out applications of existing ethical theories. It is, rather, to attempt to find acceptable resolutions of moral problems of present and practical urgency. This involves much more than merely doing some sort of philosophical technology where high-level theory is simply brought over to practice. When done well, questions addressed within practical ethics continually raise important theoretical and methodological questions for general theories of moral good and moral right, and for metaethics. For example, attempting to answer questions pertaining to

choosing and changing jobs raises a number of significant questions about what it means for any choice to be rational and genuinely voluntary. Similarly, questions in professional ethics regarding the distribution of certain goods and services raise deep questions regarding basic human goods and the possibility of maximizing the potential of characteristically human lives. In raising and addressing these questions, theorists working in practical ethics are inseparable from theorists working in more familiar areas of ethics. What is true, however, is that engaging in practical ethics is in some important ways quite different from attempting to construct a full and general moral theory. Specifically, there are differences in the content of the questions asked, and differences in focus, goals, and method.

GOALS

The differences in content and focus in moral theory and practical ethics provide some clues as to how goals in engaging in these projects might differ. A legitimate goal in studying and engaging in moral theory construction might consist in acquainting oneself with one branch of the history of philosophy or one branch of systematic philosophy as a matter of purely intellectual interest, much as an academic approach to religious studies might focus on understanding certain religious traditions as a way of deepening one's appreciation of a culture's heritage. That is, a study of moral theory need not concern itself with resolving any real-life moral dilemmas, any more than studying a religious tradition need concern itself with resolving any theological dilemmas. Genuine engagement in practical ethics, on the other hand, disallows neutrality on the goal of attempting to resolve some morally dilemmic issues, since practical ethics takes the resolution of such issues as its proximate concern. This concern issues in several projects to be pursued in engaging in practical ethics.

1 Recognizing moral issues. A first step in practical ethics is developing skill in recognizing moral issues. Issues that have a moral content are those that involve the rights and/or welfare of persons (and/or other sentient beings), the character of the acting agent, the flourishing of relationships and communities, and/or special obligations that attach to special roles. Being able to recognize such issues where they often go unnoticed is crucial. In business ethics, seeing that some rather standard behaviors are unjustifiably manipulative or even coercive is to be aware of morally crucial dimensions of conventional, unreflective action or practice. An important first project in engaging in practical ethics, then, is a kind of consciousness raising that enlivens one to the moral complexity of the world in a number of domains.

2 *Developing the moral imagination.* Closely connected to the task of developing skill in recognizing moral issues is the task of developing the moral imagination. As elementary as it may seem, we are often unaware that our attitudes toward (or indifference to) what is morally acceptable issue in actions or failures to act that can have serious effects on the rights and well-being of other individuals as well as the various communities to which we belong. Thus, for example, people who are not enlivened to the fact that certain public policies or institutional policies are oppressive to women or members of certain minorities or persons generally, may support those policies or miss opportunities to oppose those policies. Such enlivening often requires nurturing the capacity to imagine what it feels like to be a person directly affected by a certain practice or policy. To genuinely understand, say, the vulnerability of workers in sweatshops, one must be able imaginatively to assume the place of the worker, who may be desperate for work, bored, confused by complex machinery and terminology, feeling displaced, and affected by any number of the other daunting features of work. Similarly, being able to imagine what it is like to be an elderly person on a fixed income might lead one to see how problematic it is that pharmaceutical companies spend more money on marketing than on research and development, and that those marketing costs get carried over to one of the most vulnerable segments of the community – the elderly who are ill. Developing moral imagination is closely related to the skill of recognizing moral problems, since in using a well-developed moral imagination, we often see moral issues where we had not noticed them before.

3 *Sharpening analytical/critical skills.* At least two more tasks of practical ethics are connected to issues of moral relativism (*see* RELATIVISM, CULTURAL AND MORAL). Many of us are extremely reluctant to call *any* action (or practice) morally wrong. To be sure, calling another person's action morally wrong does amount to a strong and important claim. And establishing exact criteria for moral rightness and wrongness has eluded philosophers for centuries. Aware of the hazards of moral evaluation, we often do not want to "pass judgment" – we want to be careful about condemning the actions of other persons, the practices of other societies, and practices in earlier stages of our own society. We want to be tolerant of differences, and this is a good thing. But when "tolerance" becomes so extreme that we are left morally resourceless, the virtue of tolerance swells into its excess and everything becomes permissible.

One of the goals of thoughtful engagement in applied ethics is to help reveal that even though moral questions are difficult, we can go a long way before we need to say, "Well, we just disagree on our fundamental moral commitments." By honing analytical skills, we can come to see that we share a large common moral ground that can be defended on the basis of reasonable moral principles, and that ground can provide us with reasons for ruling out certain kinds of actions and practices as morally unacceptable. This is not to suggest, of course, that all morally aware, imaginative, and reasonable persons will always agree on how morally dilemmic cases and issues are to be decided. But it is to suggest that careful reflection on what might initially seem to be an utterly unresolvable case or issue will often at least reveal that some potential resolutions are not consistent with moral principles to which disputants are committed, or that what was initially thought to be a case or issue requiring some substantive resolution might be given a procedural resolution. For example, in some cases careful reflection might reveal that the question to be resolved is not what should be done, but rather who should decide what should be done. Thus, sharpening analytical skills can help to rule out certain potential resolutions that might initially seem acceptable, and can help with the engendering and consideration of potential resolutions that were not initially apparent.

4 Sorting out disagreements. Hard moral questions are hard because they tend to leave residues of disagreement among even the most sensitive and astute moral agents. No matter how refined one's analytical skills become, such residues will tend to remain. It is here that tolerance in ethics has its proper place. Among the chief tasks in practical ethics is the twofold task of learning not only to put *oneself* in the position of others, but learning to put oneself in the position of *others*. That is, part of the task is to realize that there are legitimately differing ways of ordering values and that some differences in value judgment are inevitable and acceptable. In many cases, decisions to be made will need to be made collectively; and an important part of careful reflection in practical ethics is to encourage others to express their moral misgivings about proposed resolutions to morally dilemmic cases and issues, to sort out disagreements that are morally reasonable from those that are not, and to work toward acceptable moral closure despite some residual disagreement. Indeed, often decisions will need to be made despite serious and morally responsible disagreements.

5 Affecting decisions and behavior. If applied ethics is worth doing and worth doing well, it is precisely because doing applied ethics holds out the promise of affecting individual behavior, public policy, corporate practices, and so on, in a morally positive way. Indeed, the main difference between studying ethical theory and engaging in practical ethics lies in the practical ethics goal of contributing directly and immediately to behavior and policy creation that is reflective, well-reasoned, intellectually responsible, and morally sensitive.

IMPLEMENTATION: CLOSURE AND PROCESS

If we accept the goals sketched above as proper to applied ethics, what kinds of problems might be expected in pursuing them, and what might be some strategies for avoiding these problems?

One problem has already been mentioned – the problem of hasty relativism. Given the pluralism of our society, the desire to be tolerant, and the very real problems that intrapersonal and intrasocietal disagreements about morality raise, temptation to retreat into a relativism or subjectivism where everything is permitted, or a simple pragmatism – that is, a view that morality is one thing, getting through life is another – is pervasive. But such retreats make moral reflection irrelevant, since they are really failures to attempt to come to satisfactory moral closure in the face of moral pluralism and moral complications. A theory of retreat from morality cannot possibly serve as an adequate moral theory. But tolerance and taking pluralism seriously are certainly consistent with responsible moral reflection which works toward moral closure. "Closure" is the resolution of a moral dilemma or debate, a resolution that is supported by the best reasons available and recognized by the disputants as a morally responsible solution that takes seriously the positions of those who may still disagree. That is, when there is serious moral disagreement, the task is to search for a decision that everyone involved can "live with," even though not everyone might agree that the solution is ideal. When coming to closure is difficult, the reasons for failure to come to closure can be explored. Is the remaining disagreement one that can be well defended? If not, why not? If so, can anyone offer a solution that avoids the problem(s) giving rise to the disagreement? If not, given that a decision must be made, what can be done or decided to ensure that the least morally problematic decision is made? Pressing for closure by asking such questions can help disputants to discover the moral ground that they share and can lead to considerable confidence in decisions made after responding to such questions.

In the moral realm, we often labor under conditions of uncertainty. This is the case whether we are trying to make a hard moral decision alone or with others. Because of the intrinsic uncertainty that moral dilemmas involve, often the best that can be done is following a decision procedure that is careful to take into account the morally relevant considerations that support deciding a case or issue in various ways. Although we may never enjoy complete certainty about the content of our decisions in morally hard cases, we can enjoy confidence in the procedures we use to make such decisions. One helpful procedure involves the following steps.

1 Set out the various possible resolutions of the case. Be sure to tax your imagination. The case may admit of more alternatives than are initially obvious.

2 Set out the facts relevant to supporting each resolution you have identified. Generate as complete a set of lists as possible of the facts (known, possible, probable) that might be used to support each of the options you have identified on how the case might be resolved. Relevant facts might include: someone will be or is likely to be harmed (physically, emotionally, financially, in reputation, etc.) if a certain resolution is chosen; limited resources expended in one way could be expended in another way, meeting some (other) pressing need; some decision will interfere with the liberty of an individual; a proposed resolution involves coercion, deception, manipulation, breach of trust, keeping a promise, breaking a promise, exploitation, unequal treatment, and so on.

3 Set out the moral principles that underpin the selection of the facts on your lists. That is, each fact that you identify as supportive of a possible resolution will be relevant because of some underlying moral principle. Articulate these principles clearly. Relevant principles might include: Prevent harm; Do good; Be fair; Be loyal; Keep your promises; Do not inflict harm on other persons/sentient beings; Maintain integrity; Be candid; Live up to the requirements of your office or role; It is permissible to protect one's own interests; Respect the liberty/autonomy of persons; Contribute to the flourishing of relationships within this community or that one; and so on. Combining these principles with the relevant facts you have selected provides moral arguments for the possible resolutions you have identified.

So, for example, an argument from your lists for some option (call it "Option A") might look like this:

Premise 1, Principle: Keep promises.
Premise 2, Fact: Doing X, which will be done if Option A is selected, involves keeping a promise.
Conclusion: Choose Option A.

4 Reflect on the options you have identified on your lists. Ask yourself (again) if you have included all potentially acceptable options; and if your lists of facts, and the principles that lead you to select those facts as supportive of the options you've identified, include all the plausible arguments for each of the alternatives you have identified. Are the lists of facts and principles supporting the view you are inclined to take, longer than your other lists? If so, be sure that you have been as thorough as possible in laying out the facts and principles supportive of the resolutions that differ from the one you are inclined to favor.

5 Make and articulate your decision. After careful consideration of the options you have identified and the arguments supporting each of those options that you have identified, select the option you think is the one that should be chosen.

6 Justify your decision. Set out your positive reasons for the decision you have made. This will take you back to your lists. Make explicit which considerations on your lists of facts and principles you found the most compelling.

7 Anticipate and respond to the most serious potential objection to your decision. Go back to the lists supporting the option(s) other than the one you have chosen. Use these lists to help you clarify what you take to be the strongest potential objection to your position or to your positive argument for your decision. What is your reply to that objection? Given your reply, is it reasonable to believe that a proponent of that objection could be brought to see the preferability of the resolution you support?

8 Clarify the costs or downside of your decision. Go back to your lists a final time and use them to help you articulate what you take to be the most morally significant cost(s) of your decision. (This may be related to what you take to be the strongest potential objection to your decision.)

A procedure incorporating such steps goes a long way toward fulfilling the goals that are suggested here as proper to engagement in practical ethics, which is direct engagement with the hard moral questions that inevitably challenge us all in the lived world of moral responsibility.

Bibliography

This article has been adapted from Callahan (1990), with permission.

Bayles, M. (1989). *Professional Ethics*, 2nd edn. Belmont, CA: Wadsworth.

Callahan, D. (1980). Goals in the teaching of ethics. In D. Callahan and S. Bok (eds.), *Ethics Teaching in Higher Education*. New York: Plenum, 61–80.

Callahan, J. (ed.) (1988). *Ethical Issues in Professional Life*. New York: Oxford University Press.

Callahan, J. (1990). From the "applied" to the practical: Teaching ethics for use. *American Philosophical Association Newsletter on Teaching Philosophy*, **90** (1), 29–34.

Caplan, A. (1980). Ethical engineers need not apply: The state of applied ethics today. *Science, Technology, and Human Values*, **6** (33), 24–32.

Gorovitz, S. (1985). *Doctors' Dilemmas: Moral Conflict and Medical Care*. New York: Oxford University Press.

Klinefelter, D. S. (1990). How is applied philosophy to be applied? *Journal of Social Philosophy*, **21** (1), 16–26.

Midgley, M. (1990). Homunculus trouble, or, What is applied philosophy? *Journal of Social Philosophy*, **20** (1), 5–15.

Singer, P. (1986). *Applied Ethics*. New York: Oxford University Press.

auditing, ethical issues in

Mark E. Haskins

At its most fundamental level, the objective of an external financial-statement audit is to render an independent, professional opinion regarding the fairness (or lack thereof) of a set of financial statements in depicting a company's financial condition, results of operations, and cash flows. Such an opinion is based on an auditor's accumulated evidence pertinent to the company's financial assertions and the auditor's informed evaluation of that evidence. In the United States, and in most other industrialized countries, the company audited is the buyer of the audit. That is to say, the company (technically, in the US it is now the audit committee of a company's board of directors) hires, pays the fees of, expects value from, and evaluates the auditor. The audit of a publicly traded company is usually mandated by securities regulators or stock exchanges for the benefit of the investing public, not the company being audited. Thus, a fundamental tension exists as to this three-part relationship: the au-

ditor has both a fiduciary responsibility to the investing public that desires full and fair company disclosures, and a cost-efficient responsibility to the engagement client that desires value-added audits. Given the headline-making audit fiascos occurring at the dawn of the twenty-first century involving Enron, World-Com (now MCI), Tyco, Xerox, HealthSouth, and others, the US federal government has responded in an assertive manner to help restore public confidence in audits. With the 2002 passage of the Sarbanes-Oxley Act and the 2003 creation of the Public Companies Accounting Oversight Board (PCAOB), it is clear that: (1) the pendulum of auditor orientation will swing back toward the investing public's needs and, (2) depending on the audit guidelines issued by the PCAOB, the actual conduct of audits is likely to change.

Embedded in this fundamental tension are two additional phenomena, each generating additional ethical issues. First, at the engagement-client level, auditors have historically attempted to redirect a client's value-added expectations (i.e., the desire for advice and ideas that extend beyond an auditor's mere rendering of an audit opinion) to the audit firm's consulting divisions (this is often referred to as the cross-selling of services – a practice legislatively restricted of late but not eliminated). As a byproduct of the audit, auditors frequently do offer company management a number of recommendations for how the auditee might improve various aspects of their financial reporting and control systems. There is an ongoing debate as to whether auditors are truly independent if they or their firms are also providing client management with recommendations for, and assistance in, implementing any number and type of improved business processes. Indeed, an auditor's opinion regarding the fairness of a client's financial statements is valuable, in large measure, because the auditor is perceived to be an independent, objective party qualified to render such an opinion. It is the perception of independence, as well as independence in fact, that is critical to the viability of the audit.

The second phenomenon occurs at the audit profession level. It is important to note that while a set of financial statements involves the adherence to many accounting guidelines, some of which are very prescriptive, they are also replete with many financial figures that are the result of management estimations and judgments. The performance of an audit and the evaluation of audit evidence entails a similar dual phenomenon for the auditors – i.e., adherence to professional guidelines *and* the constant exercising of professional judgment. In this context two pervasive ethical issues exist.

One of these has to do with what is known as "opinion shopping" by clients. There are times when a company's management judges as acceptable and preferable a certain accounting treatment for a significant transaction in a way different from their auditor's judgment. Such differences of opinion may not be reconcilable, and client management may dismiss the current auditor and embark on a search for a new auditor who will agree with management's judgment. (A minimal control mechanism in this regard applicable to publicly held companies is that companies must file an 8–K statement with the Securities and Exchange Commission (SEC), spelling out the reasons for an auditor's dismissal. Many of these 8–Ks, however, are not very detailed or informative.) Clearly, at one level, if the original auditor was exercising extreme care and competency in his/her concern for fairness of the financial statements, all other similarly professional auditors should come to the same conclusion. For any number of reasons (e.g., propensity for risk-taking or competitive pressures), however, the reality is that company management may find an auditor who accepts their judgment, with or without any modification. Thus, both the current auditor and any prospective auditor are faced with a possible moral dilemma of doing what is right (i.e., insisting on a certain accounting treatment) and losing an audit client versus justifying what is perhaps not totally right or preferable and keeping/gaining a client.

The second ethical issue at the level of the audit profession's tension between judgment and guidelines has to do with auditor liability. Corporate managements and astute observers of business agree that reports on financial condition and performance are by nature relative and imprecise, not absolute and exact. Thus, an auditor must exercise judgment in rendering an audit opinion. Audit opinions are not the mechanical result of a series of precisely specified formulae and tasks. It is a fact, however, that auditors are increasingly being sued, for huge sums of money, on matters related to their exercising of professional judgment. As auditors face an increasing number of lawsuits, from a public seeking audit assurances that look more and more like guarantees of a company's reported financial results rather than opinions as to their fairness, auditors are quite naturally interested in the safe harbors of more authoritative guidance on audit procedures and accounting rules for a myriad of business transactions. The conundrum is that more authoritative guidance generally means less need for the exercising of professional judgment, which many view as at the heart of the value of a professional audit. Auditors do not audit merely to serve the public need – they audit with the need to do so at a profitable level. Lawsuit costs are a substantial cost of the audit business. There may be a not-too-distant future in which professional, well-intentioned auditors cannot profitably conduct judgment-laden audits that satisfy an increasing public demand for assurances.

An auditor faces several ethical tensions at several levels. At the economy level, there is the issue of who is the real versus *de facto* client (i.e., the company being audited or the investing public). At the engagement level, there is the issue of auditor independence when the audit firm provides an audit and also advises auditee company management on ways to improve various business processes. At the audit profession level, there are the judgment-related issues of (1) auditee opinion shopping and (2) legal liability costs.

Bibliography

American Institute of CPAs (1993). *The Expectation Gap Standards.* New York: American Institute of CPAs.

Campbell, D. R. and Parker, L. M. (1992). SEC communications to the independent auditors: An analysis of enforcement actions. *Journal of Accounting and Public Policy,* winter, 297–330.

Elliott, R. K. (1994). Confronting the future: Choices for the attest function. *Accounting Horizons,* September, 106–24.

Hanson, R. K. and Rockness, J. W. (1994). Gaining a new balance in the courts. *Journal of Accountancy,* August, 40–4.

PricewaterhouseCoopers (2003). *The Sarbanes-Oxley Act of 2002 and Current Proposals by NYSE, Amex, and NASDAQ.* New York: PricewaterhouseCoopers.

Schultze, W. P. (1994). A mountain or a molehill? *Accounting Horizons*, March, 69–75.

Wallace, W. A. (1980). *The Economic Role of the Audit in Free and Regulated Markets.* New York: Touche Ross.

auditor–client relationships

Mary Beth Armstrong

Auditors play a significant role in a free-market economy. They lend credibility to published financial information, thereby enabling investors to more efficiently make investing choices and enhance society's ability to optimize its allocation of scarce financial resources. Most models of professional–client relationships include two actors, the professional and the client (see Faber, 2003). In contrast, the model of auditors' role in society includes three actors: the auditor, the auditee (business entity), and the investing public. Who is the client in such a model?

Historically, auditors have understood they had a responsibility to the investing public to perform their services with independence, integrity, and objectivity. Nevertheless, the business entity's management hired them, paid them, and negotiated their fees. Auditors understood that the client was the corporation's management. Hence the model contained an inherent conflict of interest. The accounting profession has traditionally attempted to manage the conflict by emphasizing the requirements of their code of professional conduct to act with integrity and objectivity while maintaining independence in fact and in appearance. Independence can be conceptualized as the "golden mean" between the extremes of a mutuality of interests with the client and a conflict of interests between auditor and client.

In 1994 an Advisory Panel to the profession's Public Oversight Board issued a report suggesting that the boards of directors of public companies should be considered the client, not management. "Boards," they said, "particularly independent directors, and auditors are, or should be, natural allies in protecting shareholder interests." After all, boards are elected by the shareholders and serve as their representatives. During the remainder of the 1990s the Securities and Exchange Commission and others proposed various measures to strengthen boards of directors and audit committees of boards.

It took a watershed event, the financial fraud scandals of the turn of the century (Enron, WorldCom, Adelphia, and others) and the resultant legislation (Sarbanes-Oxley Act of 2002), to actually bring about a shift in power and responsibilities to boards of directors. Today, if you ask an auditor who the client is, she will not hesitate to point to the audit committee of the board. Now the audit committee hires, fires, and sets the compensation of the auditor.

However, a shift in mentality concerning who is the client has not eliminated all conflicts of interest. Management often hires the auditing firm to perform tax or consulting engagements for the company. In those cases, management is the client. The Sarbanes-Oxley Act requires that boards of directors approve instances where auditors perform consulting for the auditee company, but the fact remains that in some situations the audit firm has two clients: management (for consulting and tax work) and the board of directors (for the actual audit). If the interests of management and the board are in conflict, the auditing firm is caught in that conflict.

Bibliography

Advisory Panel on Auditor Independence (1994). *Strengthening the Professionalism of the Independent Auditor.* Report by the Oversight Board of the SEC Practice Section, American Institute of Certified Public Accountants, September 13 ("Kirk Panel Report"). Stamford, CT.

Faber, P. (2003). Client and professional. In J. R. Rowan and S. Zinaich, Jr. (eds.), *Ethics for the Professions.* Belmont, CA: Wadsworth, 125–34.

Australia, business ethics in

Michael W. Small

ETHICS IN BUSINESS – SOME EXAMPLES

"Business Ethics as an academic discipline is relatively new in Australia." So began the article about Australia in the first edition of this book (1997). Since that time, the print media and TV stations have been publishing reports, in a seemingly never-ending stream, about people in the business world who have gained notoriety by their excesses in business. The article for this second edition is a narrative, which identifies some of the cases and individuals in the business world who have been so publicized. The amount of information, therefore, which is now available for inclusion and subsequent analysis into business ethics courses is considerable. Yet it seems that business schools, with perhaps one or two exceptions, have not taken up the challenge to develop programs to help counteract the ongoing breakdown of morally correct behavior in business. This is despite the expressions of concern that business schools should take a lead and develop core (i.e., compulsory) programs in this area.

Business ethics is taught in most universities, but as stated in the first edition, it is still not a mainstream subject in the majority of business schools. However, in a news report (August 2003), one business school, Mt. Eliza, announced that ethics would be a core component of its MBA program. With the publicity generated by unethical and criminal activities of business identities it might have been expected that more business schools would have responded and developed appropriate course material to counter some of these excesses. The Australian and Securities Investments Commission's (ASIC) Annual Report for 2001–2, entitled *Tackling Ethics and Governance*, summarized some of its activities. To illustrate, nineteen criminals were jailed for terms totalling seventy-four years; eleven dishonest company officers and eight others who cheated investors were jailed for periods varying from ten years to sixteen months.

Business schools at the present time are not receiving good press coverage. Reports about poor financial performance have appeared, which identify three leading business schools which failed to put "theory into practice." Losses of $A8.4 million, $A2.3 million, and $A1.1 million have been reported. In another media report, one business school was stated to have relocated the portrait of one of their benefactors from a prominent position to a less obvi-

ous spot. The benefactor, who at one time had described himself as the "beer and jam king of Australia," was banned for four years, commencing on July 28, 2003, from managing a corporation, had to pay compensation of $A1.428 million, had to pay pecuniary penalties of $A15,000, and pay ASIC's taxed costs.

In academia, articles are appearing in quality journals and texts are being produced by Australian academics. Conferences in Australia now include tracks for "business ethics and social responsibility." For example, the International Society of Business, Economics and Ethics (ISBEE), in association with ARC Special Research Centre for Applied Philosophy and Public Ethics (CAPPE), and the University of Melbourne, planned a World Congress in Melbourne for July 2004. Areas to be addressed included "freedoms and responsibilities; ethics, leadership and corporate governance in a global economy." Business periodicals and business newspapers give the impression that an ethical approach in business is becoming more common, but so far this is unwarranted. For example, in an advertisement (which appeared regularly) in one financial newspaper it was stated that the staff of a financial investment firm acted with "integrity, competence, dignity and in an ethical manner." The advertisement included the comment that the firm's investment professionals worldwide had been tested extensively on ethics, and that every year they reaffirmed their continuing commitment to their code of ethics. "Ethics come first" was the headline (May 2003) in another report on the appointment of the new chairman of the Australian Competition and Consumer Commission (ACCC). The newly appointed chairman stated that the role of the ACCC was to enforce the Trade Practices Act and he would continue the work of the retiring chairman. In another item, directors were told to "get personal over ethics." This item advised large investors in public companies to get to know the directors personally, so they could assess their honesty and integrity.

There are, however, encouraging signs of change. For example, there is the active pursuit of corporate criminals by ASIC, ISBEE's decision to hold a world congress in Melbourne, and a project being developed by Macquarie

Graduate School of Management (MGSM) and Reputation Measurement (Reputex) – all point to promoting a change in business culture. The project is described as "ground-breaking and a response to meet the growing demand for major corporations to operate in a more socially responsible manner." "Ethical and unethical practices of Australia's top one hundred companies are being investigated, and will be revealed in a new community-based company rating system." One hundred companies will be rated according to their behavior in four areas: environmental impact, governance (including payments to executives), social impact, and workplace practices. Research in the four areas will be carried out with the assistance of special interest groups. For example, in respect to environmental impact, the expertise of the Environmental Protection Authority (EPA) Victoria, the Wilderness Society, and Greenpeace will be utilized. In respect to corporate governance, the expertise of the University of Melbourne's CAPPE, the Institute of Chartered Accountants, and the Securities Institute of Australia will be utilized. In respect to social impact, the expertise of the Australian Council of Social Services, the Consumers' Federation of Australia, and the Australia Business Arts Foundation will be utilized. Finally, in respect to workplace practices, the expertise of the Australian Institute of Management (AIM), the Australian Council of Trade Unions (ACTU), and Employers First will be utilized. MGSM will analyse the results and trends. The purpose of the exercise is to expose companies which are identified as socially irresponsible.

To illustrate the changes in the business ethics culture that are now occurring, be they ever so minimal, Australian Ethical Investments and banks such as Bankers Trust, Rothschilds, and Westpac (which offers funds with a socially responsible ethos, but they can invest in gaming stocks) have set up ethical funds management divisions. The amount invested in ethical funds in Australia is growing, and was estimated in June 2003 to be $A14 billion. Reports suggest, however, that poor performance and stock selection have led to a decrease in socially responsible investment. Screening eliminates companies involved in gambling, animal testing, weapons manufacturing, nuclear power, and alcohol. By comparison, the amount invested in ethical funds in the United States is estimated to be $US2 trillion.

It might be assumed, therefore, that an ethical approach to business and administration is now the norm, and is having a positive effect on contemporary business practice. However, the reality is that there is still an absence of an ethical culture in many business organizations. This is illustrated by regular reports in the media of criminal business practices and the annual reports of agencies such as ASIC. The outgoing chairman of the ACCC in a farewell speech had some harsh words to say about business. Under the banner headline "farewell blitz on business" the chairman focused on big business, retailers, brick companies, hoteliers, and surgeons. The retiring chairman, soon to take up an academic post, called for tougher laws to make it easier for the ACCC to prosecute big business. Examples included money laundering (complete with diagrams showing where the millions went), manipulating the market on three consecutive days, and an HIH Insurance director being charged with making false statements. A similar charge against a Sydney-based stockbroker was brought on by ASIC. This case involved manipulating the market in respect to mining shares.

Other examples such as bribery, forgery, conspiracy, and obtaining benefits by deception have been reported. Accounts of "unethical and socially irresponsible business practices" which contributed in part to the collapse of companies such as HIH Insurance (and Pacific Eagle Equities), One.Tel, Harris Scarfe, and Ansett (airline) were also in the news. In respect to Harris Scarfe, the former chief financial officer was jailed for six years for falsifying company accounts. HIH was an insurance company which collapsed in 2001 with debts of about $A5.3 billion. Two directors were banned from holding office, fined, and made liable for compensation. By the time these inquiries will have been completed, the Commonwealth will have spent a total of $A82 million in the most expensive court case of this type undertaken by the government. The repercussions (social, personal, and political) of this collapse will be felt for many years. In respect to the investigations into the collapse of HIH Insurance, an area of concern which was raised at the Royal Commission into HIH was the subject of directors' duties. These were reported to have included a wide range of conduct that covered the majority of the suspected criminality that was under investigation. Some of Counsel Assisting's comments were relevant. For example, comments in reference to the founder and CEO of HIH Insurance were: "conduct might have been grossly improper, involved in undesirable corporate governance and might not have met professional standards." Comments referring to the second major partner in this collapse were: "might have acted dishonestly on numerous occasions and might have failed to discharge his duties." The third major figure's conduct was described as: "might have been grossly dishonest over a long period."

As a direct consequence of the HIH Royal Commission, two former senior executives of FAI Insurance were charged with providing false and misleading information, and with using their positions to the detriment of the company. These charges could result in two-year jail sentences. In respect to the case of the failed telecom One.Tel, the former directors face the possibility of paying their own substantial defense costs in a civil claim brought about by ASIC. One director was banned from being a director, or otherwise being involved in the management of any corporation for ten years, was liable to pay compensation of $A92 million to One.Tel and agreed to pay ASIC's costs of $A750,000. The director agreed to this settlement without necessitating further costly proceedings, a decision which the court viewed favorably.

In respect to insider trading, a prominent news report stated: "top judge delivers business a lashing." The judge commented in August 2003: "big sections of the business community were thumbing their noses at the law, and showing the sort of cavalier attitude that led to financial crises. This approach to doing business was to blame for financial scandals that erupted every ten years and it was very tough to catch those responsible." The comments were made at the trial of a businessman who was convicted of six counts of insider trading. He was sentenced to a suspended 18-month prison sentence and a fine of $A20,000. The judge is reported to have stated: "large sections of the business community seem to regard the Corporations Law as a bundle of inconvenient pieces of paper which should not be allowed to get in the way of whatever they want to do."

One case (June 2003) involved Australia's most experienced stockbroker and trader, who contravened the insider provisions of the Corporations Act. The judge stated, *inter alia*: "insider trading was hard to detect and had the capacity to undermine to a serious degree the integrity of the market. There is a need to sound, in effect, a clarion call to discourage illegal and unethical behavior among company directors, company officers, brokers, traders, advisors, and those who have close connection through merchant banking, to the stock market." The penalty for this particular instance of trading with inside information in Qantas Airways shares was nine months' imprisonment, to be served by way of periodic weekend detention, and a fine of $A30,000. ASIC commented: "insider trading is a serious offense that undermines the fairness and integrity of our stock market. The fact that he made a relatively small profit from the transaction does not alter its criminal nature."

In respect to unethical behavior in the workforce, reports occur at regular intervals about abusive and intimidatory behavior by employers and those in superordinate positions who are "control freaks or bullies." One report suggested this type of behavior contributed to corporate collapses and affected the health of those subjected to it, leading to increased risk of heart disease and stroke. In such situations it was to be expected that temporary and less experienced staff would be less likely to report flagrant breaches of conduct involving ethical issues because they would see themselves as vulnerable and liable to lose their jobs. Reports about bullying and abusive behavior by those in superordinate positions were not confined to blue-collar and semi-skilled workers. They also occurred in organizations which one would assume to be the least likely places for this type of behavior to occur. The executive director of AIM stated that a bad boss was someone who was "unnecessarily autocratic, non-inclusive, and condescending."

Whistleblowing has also received publicity. The ACCC announced it would become more involved in breaking up market-rigging conspiracies by big business. Immunity from prosecution would be given to the first member of any cartel who blew the whistle and who cooperated with the ACCC. Whistleblowing was a subject for discussion in respect to Royal Commissions into the activities of the different state police services. In one Royal Commission – "into whether there has been any corrupt or criminal conduct by police officers" – police officers were encouraged to roll over and give evidence against former colleagues. One state police service, in an attempt to address alleged corruption and lack of integrity in its service, now includes sections on "integrity," "corruption," and "strategies to counter unethical practices" in its officer development courses. The same service intends to produce a plan promoting "corruption prevention strategies." These can be summarized as follows: (1) universal interventions targeted at an entire police service and which are intended to produce a positive police culture; (2) selective interventions described as activities targeted at high-risk groups; (3) indicated interventions described as activities highly targeted and which frequently involve corruption identification at individual and workplace level.

In another case, known locally as "Western Australia, Inc.," which involved some well-known business figures, one of the major players was apprehended in June 2003 in Poland, where he had been living for seven years in an attempt to avoid extradition. Now described as a "business consultant," he was returned to Australia to face fifteen fraud charges in relation to the $A12 million collapse of another major business. This story revolves around an individual who had built up a huge business empire and had established himself as a major figure in the world of international business and finance. Some of his activities – such as winning the America's Cup in 1986 – made him a local folk hero. He had undertaken land deals, acquired a brewery, and operated an airship advertising his business. He developed a taste for valuable French and early Australian paintings. He acquired property in London and a complete English village. The activity which caused authorities in Australia most frustration was his skill in hiding billions in family trusts and bank accounts around the world, with most of it hidden in Switzerland. In

an amazing turn of events, he was described as "richer, smarter and more determined than most corporate criminals." He tricked the legal system by stalling the judicial processes through questionable medical-related conditions, thumbing his nose at the Australian Federal Police and the investigators who were trying to uncover his money trail. This was a ploy to avoid paying what he owed to his creditors. At one stage he agreed to repay at the rate of .000415293 cents in the dollar, or 4 cents for every $A10,000 owed. It was a case, *par excellence*, of the meltdown of any pretense of ethical and moral behavior in business. In addition to this effrontery, an army of business and financial consultants, medical and legal practitioners, art fanciers, assorted wheelers, dealers and hangers on, all offered advice and support. These people displayed a lack of ethical and moral behavior in their business practices. The extraordinary feature of this episode was that there were so many professional people (lawyers, doctors, etc.) who were prepared to become involved in questionable practices. The repercussions from this period, and the breakdown of any sense of moral responsibility by the participants, will be felt for a long time. For a brief account of "Western Australia, Inc." see "Business Ethics in Australia" in the first edition of this book.

It might be assumed that the events described above would have prompted business schools and others with a vested interest in business education to take some preemptive steps in an attempt to forestall such actions. However, business ethics as a subject in business schools' curricula is still sidelined, and not yet a mainstream subject in business management programs. The idea has been proffered that business schools should raise the profile of courses in business ethics and social responsibility by making them a part of mainstream curricula. The subject should also be taught more effectively. In the meantime, professional bodies are stepping in where the business schools have defaulted. For example, one major accounting body offered a symposium on corporate governance "designed to meet the challenges of today's competitive business environment." The course addressed topics such as the significance of ethics, making ethics work, and principles of good corporate governance. Police services, referred to earlier, now include short courses in applied ethics in their in-service programs.

A news report in August 2003 stated: "top companies sidestep governance guidelines." This referred to a survey by Chartered Secretaries Australia, which found that 55 percent of respondents would not comply with some of the Australian Stock Exchange's corporate governance guidelines. The recommendation causing most trouble was the one concerning the number of independent directors on the board. The occurrence of such items implying some sort of unethical approach to business is ongoing and constant. The onus therefore is on business schools across Australia to review and reconsider their course offerings in the light of those business people and business organizations which gain publicity for all the wrong reasons. The best that can be said is that a small number of university business schools are making a stand against unethical and criminal corporate behavior by promoting business ethics courses within their degree programs. Two – MGSM and Mt. Eliza Business School – now include ethics in their core programs. Incorporating a sense of business ethics and corporate social responsibility is a challenge which is only now being addressed.

B

bankruptcy, ethical issues in

Paul E. Fiorelli

The philosophy behind bankruptcy laws was to preserve assets for creditors, and allow debtors to have a "fresh start." This philosophy has changed recently to include a new reason for filing bankruptcy – use it as a business strategy to improve your bargaining position in restructuring debt. Three of the largest examples of bankruptcy filings with this newest philosophy occurred in the 1980s: (1) Manville Corporation, trying to deal with class-action asbestos claims; (2) A. H. Robbins, trying to deal with class-action Dalkon Shield claims; (3) Texaco, trying to deal with a $10 billion judgment for Pennzoil.

One could argue that bankruptcy laws are inherently improper because they do not promote one's moral obligation to satisfy one's debts. By their very nature, these laws seem to allow individuals to avoid personal responsibility. Irrespective of these challenges, a discharge of debts in bankruptcy should allow a person to escape oppressive debt and gain a second chance. The "fresh start" theory makes sense because there is little to be gained from debtors who are so burdened with bills that they have no hope of repayment. Since we no longer have debtors' prisons or sell people into slavery for failing to pay their bills, insolvents should be allowed to develop a payment plan which gives creditors the maximum amount available, and discharge the remainder. This way, debtors can use their efforts to start new (more successful) ventures, or develop better spending and saving habits.

BANKRUPTCY AS A PLANNING TOOL

The newest debate focuses on the use/abuse of the bankruptcy laws to gain a strategic advantage in business negotiations. This is not to suggest that companies enter into the bankruptcy decision lightly, nor that they do not pay a price. Stockholders may suffer, management may lose their jobs, and the company will incur substantial legal fees. Even with these negatives, it may still be the best business decision to enter into bankruptcy. The question becomes whether the best business decision is the best ethical decision.

Bankruptcy filing used to carry the stigma of financial ruin and failure. With its increased usage and acceptance, bankruptcy is no longer shameful. Since a company or individual does not need to be insolvent to file bankruptcy, a strategic filing (or the threat of one) may be considered a savvy business decision. While the Manville, A. H. Robbins, and Texaco filings satisfied the letter of bankruptcy laws, one may question whether they met its spirit. These companies gained substantial profits respectively from (1) selling asbestos, (2) selling Dalkon Shields, and (3) acquiring Getty, after it (Getty) had agreed in principle to be acquired by Pennzoil. In order to avoid or renegotiate their burdensome liabilities, each company declared bankruptcy. This strategy gives the debtor more time to deal with creditors. Strategic filings may also give the debtor an unfair advantage by allowing it to bargain with creditors within the bankruptcy system, a system that typically favors compromise.

OTHER ETHICAL ISSUES

Two additional bankruptcy situations violating both law and ethics are fraudulent conveyances and preferential transfers. In a fraudulent conveyance, debtors attempt to cheat their creditors by selling assets – before filing for bankruptcy – to family members at deeply discounted prices. An example would be a president of a closely held corporation selling a company car valued at $15,000 to her daughter for $1,000, then filing for bankruptcy. Due to this scheme, the bankrupt estate has $14,000 less to pay its creditors. To complete the cycle, after the bankrupt's remaining debts are discharged in bankruptcy, the daughter who purchased the car would transfer use back to the discharged debtor.

Preferential transfers occur when a debtor wants to treat some unsecured creditors better than others. This desire is a clear violation of bankruptcy laws, but insolvents may have hopes of using their skills in similar businesses after the bankruptcy proceedings. They may need the goodwill of certain suppliers. These suppliers may extort "preferential" treatment from the debtor before they file for bankruptcy, by threatening never to do business with them in the future if *their* bills are not paid. These preferred creditors do not care whether the other unsecured creditors will receive less on their claims. The law and ethics concur on how to treat both fraudulent conveyances and preferential transfers. Bankruptcy laws allow the Trustee in Bankruptcy to invalidate both transactions and collect full value into the bankrupt's estate for a ratable distribution to all unsecured creditors.

CONCLUSION

Even if the Manville, A. H. Robbins, and Texaco bankruptcy filings were both legal and ethical, will the bankruptcy filings of the future be the same? Will companies make short-term profits by cutting environmental costs, polluting the environment, then declaring bankruptcy, leaving someone else to pay their bills? Will unscrupulous business people enter into contracts they know they cannot afford, with the expectation that they can always declare bankruptcy and receive more favorable terms? The original intent was to allow bankruptcy laws to be used as a "defensive shield" against oppressive debt. The ethical question becomes whether its current application as an "offensive sword" frustrates this intent.

Bibliography

Ayer, J. D. (1986). How to think about bankruptcy ethics. *American Bankruptcy Law Journal*, fall, 355–98.

Henwood, D. (1992). Behind the bankruptcy boom: Failures in the system. *The Nation*, October 5, 345.

Hiltzik, M. A. (1987). Bankruptcy: Beyond failure; big business sees Chapter 11 shield as a potent tool. *Los Angeles Times*, July 26, business section, 1.

Moskowitz, D. and Ivey, M. (1987). You don't have to be broke to need Chapter 11. *Business Week*, April 27, 108.

Newborn, M. J. (1994). The new Rawlsian theory of bankruptcy ethics. *Cardozo Law Review*, 16, 111–46.

Schlangentstein, M. (1987). Pennzoil chairman denounces Texaco's bankruptcy filing. *United Press International*, April 30.

Thompson, T., Tell, L. J., Vogel, T., Davis, J. E., Norman, J. R., and Mason, T. (1987). Bankruptcy court for Texaco: The lesser evil – barely. *Business Week*, April 27, 102.

biodiversity

Andrea Larson

Biodiversity – a shorthand way of saying biological diversity – is defined as the full variety of life, from genes to species to ecosystems. It is the cumulative total of plants and animals on the planet. Scientists estimate anywhere between 5 and 30 million species with only about 1.5 million currently described (newly discovered life on the ocean floor may raise the upper end of this range). As a species we have dramatically expanded our influence and reach worldwide. Within a very short period of time – the last decades of the twentieth century and the early years of the twenty-first – humans have extended their control over life forms on the planet. While public sector policies have their role to play, the ascension of corporations to historically new heights of influence over economic growth has focused greater attention on their strategies and behavior with respect to biodiversity. This reality, combined with our increasing knowledge of how biodiversity works, what actions disrupt and degrade its functions, and our self-conscious capacities to change our behavior, require elevated responsibility for current and future actions.

Accumulated knowledge of species diversity, habitat destruction, earth systems functions, extinctions, and economic globalization's interactions with biological diversity is focusing unprecedented multidisciplinary attention on the value of the vast mosaic of plants and animals encompassed by the term biodiversity. Biodiversity comprises the plant and animal species visible to the human eye and the microscopic protist and invertebrate species on land and water. The concept also includes the processes of co-evolution and interdependence of living organisms within their ecological system contexts of food supply and nutrient cycling processes. Biodiversity definitions are inextricably linked to ecosystem services defined as flows of resources, energy, and information from the biosphere that supports human activity. From this perspective, counting distinct species as a way to measure biodiversity loss seems a very conceptually constrained exercise. Biodiversity in fact provides regulation of atmosphere and climate, purification and retention of fresh water, creation and cyclical enrichment of soil, nutrient recycling, detoxification of waste, and crop pollination. These system services support human life *and* provide the commonly considered natural services of a biodiverse planet, such as timber, fuels, medicines, food, clothing, oils, dyes, spices, etc. The more far-reaching systemic and process understanding of biodiversity needs to be maintained in the face of typically narrower treatment of the concept in economic discussions.

There is general agreement among natural science experts that biodiversity decline and species extinction is accelerating. These changes are a function of extreme reduction and fragmentation of physical areas into biogeograph islands. Species numbers decline and genetic variation is reduced as land is appropriated for human needs. Precise rates of and implications of biodiversity reduction are difficult to calculate due to lack of knowledge of species magnitude and the still poorly understood effects of repeatedly removing pieces of an interdependent co-evolving system of life support units and processes.

Yet humans must respond to the signals of biodiversity at risk. The biophysical demands of historically dramatic and unprecedented population growth requiring relatively staggering volumes (compared with 50 years ago) of fuel, raw materials for manufacturing, and food, are increasing. World population has grown from insignificant levels relative to the resource base that supported it 100 years ago to estimates of 8–10 billion people in the next few generations. The evidence grows that appropriation of land and biodiversity resources to meet the economic growth demands of a world society rapidly adopting a Western growth model fundamentally challenges the system's capacities.

The approach of the industrialized countries' economic development model is to place a value on biological diversity and then to determine the choices and trade-offs required between economic growth and biodiversity. Through this lens, species are assigned value and certain species are seen as having more value than others as commodities, amenities, or as moral value. Commodity value is determined by price in the marketplace or indirect value as in biologically produced chemicals that are copied in synthetic production methods, for example, for medical uses. Amenity value provides pleasure and translates into economic market value as recreation and eco-travel. Moral value enters when people are willing to pay to protect biodiversity for its own sake because it has value in and of itself, independent of human use, or if it serves as a stimulus of inspiration for human value system development (e.g., the existence of a species which is catalytic for reflection on human larger purposes and the search for meaning). Economists, through cost-benefit calculations, seek quantitative answers to such value questions. More recently, option value calculations try to determine the present benefit of holding open the opportunity or possibility for a species to serve human needs in the future. If a species or insufficiently understood biodiversity process may be discovered to have value, how much is society willing to pay to retain the option of having that resource continue to be available through current lifetimes or into future generations?

The utilitarian value, or economic income flow now or in the future, of biodiversity and species effectively triggers certain levels of value recognition. For example, the commodity value of biodiversity resources in terms of medicines accounts for approximately 40 percent of prescriptions at pharmacies in the United States: 25 percent of prescriptions come from plants, 13 percent from micro-organisms, and 3 percent from animals. In 1998 the US over-the-counter value of drugs from plants was estimated at $20 billion, worldwide at $84 billion. This argument is used to support tropical ecosystem preservation. In 1997 a team of economists and environmental scientists estimated world ecosystem services value at $33 trillion, or double the global GNP. The biodiversity that enables those services to function properly in support of human objectives is increasingly viewed as having clear market value.

Regardless of motivations, preserving biodiversity in service of short-term and long-term human prosperity and health seems a worthwhile goal. And while commodification of biodiversity may sound distasteful, failure to assess and assign currency value to increasingly scarce or pivotally critical biodiversity resources creates significant problems in a global society increasingly, not less, focused on economic returns. The current practice of little or no acknowledgment of biodiversity value places insufficient or even zero economic value on biodiversity resources, leaving them open to unfettered degradation. Accounting for this destruction may come later at a high cost.

The problems with placing economic value on biodiversity resources in the same way that human-made products and services are valued are several. First, the process encourages decisions that cannot be reversed. Calculations today may be found inaccurate in ten years' time, yet species cannot be brought back. Furthermore, partial knowledge of biodiversity value forces decisions with risky uncertainties. For example, new knowledge of keystone species – the notion that some species carry disproportional weight in the maintenance of life process webs – and rapidly evolving understanding of co-evolution (each species depending on a complex of interrelated other species and intricate processes) – complicate efforts to apply simple economic trade-off calculations.

The limits to human understanding and what appears appropriate humility in the face of such limits suggest the questions being asked may not be the right ones. Questions such as what is the value of biodiversity, and how do we place an economic value on an endangered species, lead us only to more conflicts. This path of traditional economic reasoning could well lead us to destroy biodiversity as perceived cheaper substitutes are found. This economic logic brings biodiversity resources conceptually within the economy as a subset of human activity, a questionable intellectual leap given human dependency on the life support functions provided by biodiversity resources. The question is how to simultaneously hold in human minds the dominant industrial development economic model *and* the reality of biodiversity destruction. Can it be done, and if it cannot, what alternative vision of the future will reconcile the collision between business and biodiversity?

In the end we come back to questions not of economic valuation but of how we view ourselves within the biosphere and what options we might forge in the face of our rapidly evolving understanding of human impacts on natural systems. How can prosperity be shaped to reinforce rather than degrade the integrity of biodiversity elements, systems, and processes? Ultimately, the decision on how to proceed is a moral one that flows from what we value, which in turn reflects the image we want of ourselves in our own lives and for our descendants. Ways around the conundrums raised by biodiversity and economic growth can be fashioned only by understanding the mental models and moral reasoning that placed humans in this position in the first place. From there, a different future can be forged.

Bibliography

Daily, G. C. (ed.) (1997). *Nature's Services.* Washington, DC: Island Press.

Daly, H. E. and Townsend, K. N. (eds.) (1993). *Valuing the Earth.* Cambridge, MA: MIT Press.

Larson, A. (1998). Consuming oneself: The dynamics of consumption. In L. Westra and P. H. Werhane (eds.), *The Business of Consumption.* Lanham, MD: Rowman and Littlefield.

Novacek, Michael J. (ed.) (2001). *The Biodiversity Crisis.* New York: New Press.

Wilson, E. O. (ed.) (1988). *Biodiversity.* Washington, DC: National Academy Press.

biotechnology

John McVea

WHAT ARE BIOTECHNOLOGY ETHICS?

The ethics of biotechnology (biotech) is an emergent field of applied ethics which has a number of overlaps with the fields of biomedical ethics, professional medical ethics, and business ethics. While biotech ethics addresses distinctive and important questions, the subject has probably gained most attention in recent years because of the extraordinary rate of scientific progress of the underlying science itself, and because of the related ability to "hit the headlines" with claims of our newly acquired ability to control and manipulate nature. Important issues addressed by the field at the time of writing involve genetics, including the privacy of genetic information and gene therapy as well as genetically modified plants and animals; research involving human participants; cloning; stem-cell research; and the storage, manipulation, and ownership of genetic data.

THE EMERGENT FIELD OF BIOTECHNOLOGY ETHICS

The ethics surrounding biotechnology have emerged at the intersection of the fields of biomedical ethics, professional medical ethics, and business ethics. Therefore, it is worthwhile to briefly outline the dominant approaches within these spheres. These fields have traditionally drawn on different texts and foundations to address the distinctive ethical challenges within each discipline. The most influential approach to biomedical ethics has been the "principlism" developed by Beauchamp and Childress (2001); however, this approach has been subjected to vigorous criticism over the last decade or so. Professional medical ethics has traditionally leaned heavily on the ethics of the professions, emphasizing conflicts of interest and professional–client relationships (Davis and Stark, 2001; Emmanuel and Steiner, 1995; Korn, 2000). Finally, business ethics has failed to cohere around a single dominant approach. This has resulted in a number of competing strands based on deontological approaches (Bowie, 1999; Donaldson and Dunfee, 1999), consequentialist approaches (Singer, 1993), and virtue approaches (Solomon, 1993; Hartman, 1996)

Because of the range of competing approaches, and because of the high public profile raised by ethical biotechnology issues, there is considerable debate over how to address these new and difficult questions and over the appropriateness of existing ethical frameworks.

THE HISTORY OF THE BIOTECHNOLOGY INDUSTRY

While much of the impetus for the interest in biotechnology ethics comes from recent technological innovations, biotechnology has been harnessed for our benefit for thousands of years. The US government has defined biotechnology as "any technique that uses living organisms (or parts of living organisms) to make or modify products, to improve plants and animals, or to develop micro-organisms for specific uses." Thus, biotechnology is a broad family of technologies and sciences, including some that have been around for millennia, and some for hundreds of years (for example, selective breeding of plants and animals; wine, beer, cheese, and bread manufacture; septic waste treatment; vaccination). Nevertheless, despite the long history of biotechnological innovation in food/ agriculture production, medicine, and environmental science, it is the technological innovations that have occurred since the 1970s that have created most of the concerns that have stimulated the recent interest in biotechnology ethics. These breakthroughs include the manipulation of recombinant DNA; the ability to transfer genes from one organism to another; the ability to fuse cells to create monoclonal antibodies; genetic engineering of cells to "manufacture" scarce materials; the decoding and manipulation of genetic structures; and the automation and computerization of genetic analysis. Thus, the challenges and opportunities faced by the biotechnology industry today were barely imaginable only twenty years ago.

CURRENT AREAS OF CONTROVERSY

Gene therapy. Research in this area has focused on severe and life-threatening diseases. This work has raised a number of difficult ethical issues, such as procedures for the selection of human subjects for protocols; access to unproven treatments by patients with advanced symptoms; the appropriate balance of caution and urgency in regulatory approval of protocols; sharing of experimental safety data versus patient confidentiality; protection of commercial secrecy.

Privacy and genetic discrimination.   Genetic medical information greatly complicates the traditional issue of medical privacy because the creation of personal genetic information can have distinct implications for others, and because some such information might have powerful scientific or societal value. Individual genetic testing may inevitably constitute testing by proxy for others who share the same bloodline and who may have not given their consent. Furthermore, tests are commonly available for genetic disorders before treatments for the underlying disorder have been developed. Thus, the individual "right to know" can come into conflict with the professional duty of care. Additionally, concerns have been raised with regard to the possibility of genetic discrimination; whether in the workplace – where employers might attempt to screen for certain characteristics – or in insurance markets – where insurers might refuse coverage to individuals with particular genetic profiles.

Stem cells.   This controversy demonstrates one of the characteristic difficulties of the ethics of biotechnology. The debate around the use of stem cells is fraught with change even at the time of writing. Scientific knowledge and techniques change within a matter of months, with definitions, capabilities, and scientific facts and beliefs in permanent transition. Stem cells are undifferentiated cells which have the ability to transform themselves into any cell in the human body, and they can also reproduce themselves. Researchers believe that these cells hold the key to breakthrough treatments for diseases from cancer to aging. However, the research currently involves both embryonic stem cells, which are separated from the blastocysts that will eventually form an embryo, and other types of stem cells that may be derived from non-embryonic cells, such as fat cells. Some groups have raised concerns about the ethics of the experimentation, harvesting, and manipulating of "pre-embryonic cells." In August 2001 the US government amended its policy on human embryonic stem cells. This decision resulted in a partial lifting of the federal funding restrictions on embryonic stem-cell research. However, under this policy research programs were restricted to using only embryonic stem-cell lines that had been created before the date of announcement. Thus, the creation of new lines of stem cells would not be supported. Privately funded research was unaffected.

Cloning.   Much of the debate around cloning revolves around the fear of the development of human reproductive cloning. The National Bioethics Advisory Commission (USA) has stated it has "grave moral, ethical, and safety concerns" over such practices. There is currently a voluntary moratorium on human reproductive cloning in the USA. However, ethical concerns still arise over the possibility of such research being carried out outside of government regulation. Furthermore, there are numerous alternative techniques – sometimes referred to as "non-reproductive cloning" – through which many researchers hope to pursue medical breakthroughs. There is currently much debate about which of these techniques should be referred to as cloning, and over which ethical guidelines should apply to which techniques. (See the 2002 report of the US President's Council on Bioethics on cloning for research, the successor to NBAC.)

Food and agriculture.   Some of the greatest advances in biotechnology have been in the genetic modification of the plants and animals that constitute the food production business. There has been a distinctive difference in ethical response to these breakthroughs between the USA and Europe, with much of the rest of the world currently under pressure to take sides. On the one hand, the modified plants and animals offer the potential to greatly increase both agricultural yields and quality in a world where malnutrition affects millions, and where others are demanding more healthy foods. On the other hand, many people worry about the scientists' ability to foresee the consequences and to control the genetic changes once they have been made.

CHARACTERISTICS

The examples listed above illustrate some of the distinctive characteristics and challenges of biotechnology ethics.

Creativity.   Biotechnology is one of the most dynamic and creative areas of scientific progress. The creative and novel aspects of the process are ultimately responsible for both the economic value of the work, and for the ethical intensity of the situations. These types of products have never before been created. These types of decisions have never before been taken. Under these circumstances scientific progress can generate what has been referred to as "an ethical time lag" (Marshall, 1999). According to this view, during periods of rapid technological progress there is an inherent gap between the technological advances and the development of ethical guidelines that govern their use. Social and ethical consensus can take a great deal longer to achieve than scientific consensus. Thus, technology has a tendency to run ahead of the ethical limits we wish to place on it. As a result, scientists and entrepreneurs must rely a great deal on their own judgment and analysis when making decisions that occur at the edges of scientific capability – a problem greatly compounded by the level of knowledge required to understand the issues at stake.

Science/business.   Biotechnology research occurs at the intersection of the worlds of academic science and business. Much of the original breakthrough research has been carried out within private and public research institutions and universities. However, most of these ideas have made their way to market through entrepreneurial firms that have raised a great deal of private capital to finance the development of the technology. These public/private, academic/commercial characteristics influence a number of ethical dimensions within biotechnology. For example, the relationship between the scientific norms of open publication and corporate secrecy; the appropriate rewards and incentives for scientific researchers; conflicts of interest; ownership of intellectual property; the relationship between the scientific ethic and the entrepreneurial ethic.

Uncertainty/newness.   The ever-progressing nature of science within biotechnology, the uncertainty over unforeseen consequences, and the fundamental nature of the implications of some of these breakthroughs have led some to raise the issue of the ethics of scientific progress itself. "In areas of great uncertainty, how should we proceed forward? Boldly? There are surely some buccaneers in the world who would say let's go

ahead and seize it. That's part of human adventure. We can, on the other hand proceed nervously" (Callahan, 1996). The question of placing ethical limits on scientific progress is one on which public debate has barely begun. Some have proposed that, where the stakes are high, scientific progress should adopt a *precautionary ethic* (Gollier, Jullien, and Treich, 2000). This would challenge the traditional approach to scientific decision-making of assembling a reliable and complete set of facts before drawing conclusions. A precautionary approach would, in highly uncertain and potentially catastrophic circumstances, encourage the drawing of conclusions and the taking of action in advance of what is normally considered complete scientific knowledge. However, others see the precautionary principle as a barrier to progress.

Emotions/politics.   A fourth distinctive aspect of biotechnology ethics is due to the way the issues tend to impact us as individuals. Many of the issues in biotechnology touch on some of our more fundamental beliefs, for example reproductive issues, the definition of life, even the meaning of humanness. As such these topics often invoke a strong emotional response. This has led some to observe that our positions on the issues of biotechnology are based on our emotional experiences as much as on our personal principles.

Many traditional ethical frameworks take little account of emotional responses. Indeed, the primacy of rationality over emotions is central to many mainstream approaches to ethics. However, there are a number of important critical responses and alternatives to the neglect of the emotions within ethics, notably Aristotelian virtue ethics (Aristotle, 1985; Nussbaum, 1986, 1990; MacIntyre, 1988) and the ethics of care. More recently, others have proposed that an ethical approach based on the ethical pragmatism of John Dewey could contribute to the field of biomedicine by taking fuller account of the roles of imagination and community (McGee, 1999; Hester, 2001).

SUMMARY

The ethics of biotechnology is an emergent field. While there are a number of influential approaches that have been successfully used in adjacent fields, there has yet to emerge a dominant paradigm or framework. Successful approaches will have to deal with the challenges of a field where the scientific "facts" are in constant change, where the public will always lag the field in expertise and knowledge, where the potential for progress that enriches our lives is immense, but where the risks of harm are equally large, where there are tensions between the traditional worlds of business and academia, and where public debate is likely to remain protracted and, at times, emotional.

Bibliography

Aristotle (1985). *Nicomachean Ethics*, trans. Terence Irwin. Indianapolis, IN: Hackett.

Beauchamp, T. L. and Childress J. F. (2001). *Principles of Biomedical Ethics*, 5th edn. Oxford: Oxford University Press.

Bowie, N. E. (1999). *Business Ethics: A Kantian Perspective*. Malden, MA: Blackwell.

Callahan, D. (1996). Biotechnology and ethics: A blueprint for the future. Center for Biotechnology, Northwestern University, www.biotech.nwu.edu/nsf/callahan.html.

Davis, M. and Stark A. (2001). *Conflicts of Interest in the Professions*. Oxford: Oxford University Press.

Donaldson, T. and Dunfee, T. W. (1999). *Ties That Bind: A Social Contracts Approach to Business Ethics*. Cambridge, MA: Harvard Business School Press.

Engelhardt, H. T. (1996). *Foundations of Bioethics*, 2nd edn. Oxford: Oxford University Press.

Emmanuel, E. J and Steiner, D. (1995) Institutional conflicts of interest. *New England Journal of Medicine*, 332 (4), 262–7.

Gert, B., Culver, C., and Clouser, K. D. (1997). *Bioethics: A Return to Fundamentals*. Oxford: Oxford University Press.

Gollier, C., Jullien, B., and Treich, N. (2000). Scientific progress and irreversibility: An economic interpretation of the Precautionary Principle. *Journal of Public Economics*, 75.

Hartman, E. M. (1996). *Organizational Ethics and the Good Life*. Oxford: Oxford University Press.

Hester, M. (2001). *Community as Healing*. Oxford: Rowman and Little.

Korn, D. (2000). Conflicts of interest in biomedical research. *Journal of the American Medical Association*, 284 (17), 2234–7.

McGee, G. (ed.) (1999). *Pragmatic Bioethics*. Nashville, TN: Vanderbilt University Press.

MacIntyre, A. C. (1988). *Whose Justice? Which Rationality?* Notre Dame, IN: University of Notre Dame Press.

Marshall, K. P. (1999). Has technology introduced new ethical problems? *Journal of Business Ethics*, March, 1999.

Nussbaum, M. (1986). *The Fragility of Goodness*. Cambridge: Cambridge University Press.

Nussbaum, M. (1990). *Love's Knowledge*. Oxford: Oxford University Press.

Singer, Peter (1993). *Practical Ethics*, 2nd edn. New York: Cambridge University Press.

Solomon, Robert C. (1993). *Ethics and Excellence*. Oxford: Oxford University Press.

Treich, N. (1997). Economics of uncertainty: Analysis of precaution. PhD thesis (in French). Toulouse: University of Toulouse.

Veatch, R. M. (2000). *The Basics of Bioethics*. Englewood Cliffs, NJ: Prentice-Hall.

Wildes, K. W., SJ (2000). *Moral Acquaintances: Methodology in Bioethics*. Notre Dame, IN: University of Notre Dame Press.

bluffing and deception

Thomas L. Carson

Deception can be defined as causing someone to have false beliefs (or intentionally causing someone to have false beliefs). To bluff in a negotiation is to attempt to deceive the other party about one's intentions or negotiating position. Another kind of deception that is common in both negotiations and sales is deception about the features of the good or service being sold.

BLUFFING

It is generally contrary to one's own self-interest to reveal one's intentions while negotiating. A seller who is negotiating with a potential customer usually has a minimum price below which she is unwilling to sell. Generally, it would be contrary to her own self-interest for her to reveal her minimum price, for, if she does, the buyer will be unwilling to offer anything more than that minimum. It can be to one's advantage to make false claims about one's negotiating position (e.g., a seller stating a minimum acceptable price that is higher than her actual minimum or a buyer misstating the maximum price she is willing to pay). Such claims can enable one to reach a more favorable settlement than one would have otherwise obtained. However, if (as in most cases) the parties to the negotiation don't know the negotiating position of the other party, misstating one's intentions in this way risks losing an opportunity to reach a mutually acceptable agreement. (One might state a position unacceptable to the other party when, in fact, one's actual position is acceptable to him.)

Is it morally wrong for negotiators to make deliberate false claims about their intentions or negotiating positions? For example, would it be wrong for me to tell you that $90,000 is absolutely the lowest price that I will accept for my house, when I know that I would be willing to accept as little as $80,000? Such statements count as lies according to most dictionary definitions of lying; they are intentional false statements that are intended to deceive others. However, Carr (1968) argues such statements are not lies since people do not expect to be told the truth about such matters in negotiations. On Carr's account, nothing said by a notoriously dishonest person could constitute a lie, because others do not expect her to speak truthfully. (See Carson 1993 for a detailed discussion of the question of whether bluffing constitutes lying.)

According to Carr, it is morally permissible for people to misstate their intentions in negotiations, because "it is normal business practice" and is "within the accepted rules of the business game." Carr claims that actions which conform to normal and generally accepted business practices are *ipso facto* morally permissible. This principle seems highly implausible in light of reflection on such things as slavery and child labor, which were once normal and "generally accepted" business practices. Carson, Wokutch, and Murrmann (1982) argue that the morality of misstating one's negotiating position depends on the actions of the other parties to the negotiation: there is a strong presumption against misstating one's negotiating position if the other party is not misstating her position, but little presumption against doing this if the other person is misstating her position. Carson (1993) develops a "generalized principle of self-defense." This principle implies that the moral presumption against lying and deception does not hold when one is dealing with people who are, themselves, engaged in lying and deception and thereby harming one.

DECEPTION ABOUT THE NATURE OF THE PRODUCTS BEING SOLD

In negotiations sellers often provide prospective buyers information about the goods or services being sold. What are the obligations of sellers in such cases? This question is central to ethics of sales. We need to distinguish between deception, lying, withholding information, and concealing information. Roughly, deception is causing someone to have false beliefs. Lying arguably requires the intent to deceive others, but lies that don't succeed in causing others to have false beliefs are not instances of deception. A further difference between lying and deception is that, while all lies are false statements, deceiving someone needn't involve making false statements; true statements can be deceptive and some forms of deception don't involve making any statements. Withholding information does not constitute deception. It is not a case of *causing* someone to have false beliefs; it is merely a case of failing to correct false beliefs or incomplete information. On the other hand, actively concealing information usually constitutes deception. Both negotiators and sales people make factual representations about goods and services they are selling. Deceptive statements about what is being sold (whether or not they are lies) raise serious ethical questions. There is, on the face of it, a strong moral presumption against such statements due to the harm they are likely to cause potential buyers.

Discussions of the ethics of sales often focus on the ethics of withholding information. The legal doctrine of *caveat emptor* ("buyer beware") says that sellers are not obligated to inform prospective buyers about the properties of the goods they sell. Buyers, themselves, are responsible for determining the quality of the goods they purchase. *Caveat emptor* permits sellers to withhold information about the things they sell, but it doesn't permit lying or (active) deception about such matters. Many take this legal principle to be an acceptable moral principle and hold that sellers have no moral duty to provide buyers with information about the goods they are selling. David Holley argues *caveat emptor* is no longer an acceptable standard. Given the complexity of many modern goods, it is impossible for most people to judge their quality with any accuracy. Holley claims that sales people are obligated to reveal all information they would want to know if they were considering buying the product. This seems too strong; it implies that a sales clerk in a store is obligated to inform customers if he knows that the product they are looking at can be purchased at a lower price elsewhere.

See also *advertising, ethics of; marketing, ethics of; truthtelling*

Bibliography

Carr, A. (1968). Is business bluffing ethical? *Harvard Business Review*, **46**, 143–53.

Carson, T. (1993). Second thoughts about bluffing. *Business Ethics Quarterly*, 3, 317–41.

Carson, T., Wokutch, R., and Murrmann, K. (1982). Bluffing in labor negotiations: Legal and ethical issues. *Journal of Business Ethics*, 1, 13–22.

Dees, J. and Crampton, P. (1991). Shrewd bargaining on the moral frontier: Towards a theory of morality in practice. *Business Ethics Quarterly*, 1, 135–67.

Ebejer, J. and Morden, M. (1988). Paternalism in the marketplace: Should a salesman be his buyer's keeper? *Journal of Business Ethics*, 7, 337–9. (This paper criticizes both *caveat emptor* and Holley's views.)

Holley, D. (1986). A moral evaluation of sales practices. *Business and Professional Ethics Journal*, 5, 3–22.

Kavka, G. (1983). When two "wrongs" make a right: An essay in business ethics. *Journal of Business Ethics*, 2, 61–6.

bourgeois virtue

Deirdre N. McCloskey

The moral excellence of business people, such as responsibility, honesty, prudence, and enterprise. The bourgeois virtues are contrasted with aristocratic virtues such as courage and magnanimity, or with peasant virtues such as faith and solidarity. Since the middle of the nineteenth century most philosophers and novelists have rejected bourgeois virtue, seeing it as a contradiction in terms, a disguise for the vice of greed. The "ethics of the virtues," an approach as old as Aristotle but revived since the 1970s, suggests another view: that any practice develops a set of virtues, and that a practice as widespread as business is unlikely to thrive without them. Bourgeois virtue reinvents an eighteenth-century project, especially in Scotland, of developing a vocabulary of virtue for a commercial society.

The bourgeois virtues apparent in business practice might include enterprise, adaptability, imagination, optimism, integrity, prudence, thrift, trustworthiness, humor, affection, self-possession, consideration, responsibility, solicitude, decorum, patience, toleration, affability, peaceability, civility, neighborliness, obligingness, reputability, dependability, and impartiality. The point of calling such virtues "bourgeois" is to contrast them with non-business virtues, such as (physical) courage or (spiritual) love. Bourgeois virtues are the townsperson's virtues, as distinct from those of a military camp for the aristocracy or a commons for the peasantry. Sometimes the distinction between bourgeois and other virtues is mere verbal shading. An aristocrat has wit, a peasant or worker jocularity. A business person must have humor. But the contrast can be more than shading. Physical courage, shown by aristocrats in war and sport, resembles bourgeois enterprise. But to make the two into one virtue is to encourage warfare in business, which has led sometimes to shooting wars bad for business. Trustworthiness is a business virtue, paralleled in some ideals of a peasant or working-class community by a loving solidarity. But solidarity has socialist outcomes, also bad for business.

The usual vocabulary of the virtues, persisting to the present, tells only of a world of heroes or laborers. Our moral talk overlooks the growing world of management, negotiation, leadership, persuasion, and other business. The eighteenth century began to construct an ethical vocabulary for merchants, especially in Scotland, and most especially in the writings and teaching of Adam Smith. As Michael Novak (1990) put it, "Smith saw his own life's work as moral teaching for the 'new class' of his era." In a dedication to the memory of Mr. William Crauford, a merchant of Glasgow, Smith praised his "exact frugality...downright probity and plainness of manners so suitable to his profession...unalterable cheerfulness of temper...the most manly and the most vigorous activity in a vast variety of business" (Smith, 1980: 262). Smith's *The Theory of Moral Sentiments* (1759, 2nd edn. 1790) is often neglected in favor of *The Wealth of Nations*, but both of the books published in Smith's lifetime exposit a bourgeois virtue. Many eighteenth-century people admired commerce, as distinct from the violence of aristocrats and the piety of peasants. As Doctor Johnson put it, "There are few ways in which a man can be more innocently employed than in getting money." The eighteenth-century admiration for commerce was overwhelmed in the middle of the next century by anti-business sentiments on the left and right, what George Bernard Shaw called "the great conversion" and what others have called "the treason of the clerks."

The oldest argument in favor of bourgeois virtue is that it is good for business. A roofer in a small town who installs a bad roof will not be in business long. The pressures of entry and exit force the bourgeoisie to exhibit virtue. The trouble with such an argument is that pressure is the absence of ethics. A business person induced by prospective profits or forced by potential loss to speak honestly to her customers is not behaving out of ethical motives. The reply would be that it does not matter why she is virtuous: anyway, she is. And the rejoinder would be that as soon as the balance of advantage turns to lying, she will.

A deeper argument is that bourgeois life is good for ethics. This is what European novelists and philosophers have denied since the middle of the nineteenth century. In Flaubert's *Madame Bovary* (1857) or Sinclair Lewis's *Babbit* (1922) the only way to be a good bourgeois is to stop being one. It has become conventional wisdom that the market eats away at virtue, and at society and the environment as well. As someone put it recently, "the expansion of the exchange system by the conversion of what is outside it into its terms . . . is a kind of steam shovel chewing away at the natural and social world."

The new research in bourgeois virtue mistrusts such conventional views, and wishes to return to the eighteenth-century project of recognizing our bourgeois character. The economist Albert Hirschman (who himself speaks of "bourgeois virtues") has recounted the career from Montesquieu to Marx of the phrase *doux*

commerce, quoting for instance the Scottish historian William Robertson in 1769: sweet commerce "tends to wear off those prejudices which maintain distinctions and animosity between nations. It softens and polishes the manners of men."

See also *virtue ethics*

Bibliography

Hirschman, A. (1977). *The Passions and the Interests: Political Arguments for Capitalism Before its Triumph.* Princeton, NJ: Princeton University Press.

McCloskey, D. N. (1994). Bourgeois virtue. *American Scholar*, **63** (2), 177–91.

Novak, M. (1990). *This Hemisphere of Liberty.* Washington, DC: American Enterprise Institute.

Smith, A. (1980) [1790]. *Essays on Philosophical Subjects*, Glasgow edn. of *The Works and Correspondence of Adam Smith*, ed. W. P. D. Wrightman and J. C. Bric. Oxford: Oxford University Press; Indianapolis, IN: Liberty Classics.

bribery

Kendall D'Andrade

I hand you some money, you deliver a good or service; have I bribed you? Have you extorted money from me, or is this a simple exchange, and thus presumably legal as well as morally acceptable? If we insist that this simple description "captures the essence of the act" then bribery becomes just another way of doing business, with extortion merely the report of the payer's unhappiness over the cost. To retain our moral intuitions that bribery and extortion are morally objectionable, we will need to accept some limits on freedom of exchange.

Two examples (treating blackmail as one species of extortion): the person who pays the blackmail prefers to pay rather than risk the threatened exposure. That that person would prefer a third alternative, neither paying nor being exposed, is not enough to show that blackmailing is wrong; compared to either having my electricity turned off or paying the current rates, I would much prefer to have my electric service for a penny a day, but that alone does not show that the utility has acted improperly in setting its rates. Bribes are even more willingly given and received, with both parties feeling they have benefited; I may be happy to slip you $10,000 if you will commit your company to a $10 million purchase from mine. And we both claim to benefit from the transaction. Just as with extortion, one obvious objection condemns too much; while my competitors disapprove of my action, they might object to any act which resulted in the sale not going to them.

If there were only two parties to the bribe, the one who gives it and the one who takes it, then it's hard to find anything to object to. So let's bring in a third party, the person or entity that the bribe-taker has a prior obligation to. For the purchasing agent, that's the company in whose name he's making the purchase. To see that this role of representing another, acting for that other, is essential, try imagining how you could bribe someone to spend her own money buying from you. An offer of cash is simply an offer of a lower price, which is perfectly reasonable market behavior. The "bribe" doesn't buy you anything just because all the costs and all the benefits go to the same person; quite the opposite of the purchasing agent's situation where the costs and some benefits go to the company while some other benefits, the bribe especially, go to the person authorizing the purchase. Here is a definition that exposes what is wrong with the practice: bribery is persuading the bribe-taker to act as the bribe-giver's agent while pretending to continue acting as another's agent. That third being can be a person, a corporation, another more or less organized body, even an ideal. What is vital is that the bribe-taker has accepted an obligation to act in the interests of that third being, which is part of the reason the bribe-taker was given the power to act for the other, committing its resources and generally acting in the name of that other.

From this definition, it follows that bribes can only be given for services, in fact for the specific service of acting as my agent, not the agent of the person to whom you have a prior and continuing obligation. But that doesn't help much, since acting as my agent may mean delivering another's good to me, as when I bribe you to let me into the vault you are supposed to be guarding. The legality or illegality of what one is paid to do is irrelevant to deciding whether the payment is a bribe. Murder for hire requires a payment, but the murderer is not acting as if he were another's agent while covertly acting as mine when committing the murder. And the purchasing agent may have the authority to conclude a perfectly proper purchase, even believe that in this case the order he is bribed to place also happens to be in the company's best interest, yet still be taking a bribe because he is surrendering his independence of judgment, or at least action, by agreeing to act as the bribe-giver wishes.

The real interest in bribery as a topic in business ethics comes from claims that certain payments should not be counted as bribes, or that, even though they are bribes, they are still acceptable, generally as the lesser of two evils.

"Grease" and "tips" are two ways to characterize small payments which are an expected, though not quite legally required, part of the implicit contract for a service. Insofar as they are both small, as measured by the receiver, and part of the normal course of doing business, this type of payment does not change the receiver's loyalties; only their absence does, and then to the non-giver's cost. So if there is anything wrong with these payments, it is that they are extorted. But that claim fails when the payments are seen by all to be part of an implicit contract, one based on common industry practice. However, even industry practice changes. Where those with influence over large purchases could once expect expensive gifts at Christmas and other "tokens" throughout the year, many companies now place a ceiling on the value of what their employees can accept, usually around $50. Such a policy recognizes that even the hope for continuing gifts may have some influence on the receiver's decisions, and thus compromise her independence from the suppliers. Then they would be non-specific bribes, bribes to create "good will," which it was hoped would result in favorable actions at some point, although no specific action would be mentioned, or implied.

Some have extended this model to very large payments ($1–10 million), often to very high officials in other countries, a type of payment specifically outlawed by the Foreign Corrupt Practices Act of 1977. This extension only works if amounts do not matter, a highly questionable claim, and if the practice of receiving these payments is acceptable in at least the receiver's own country. But the second claim is clearly false; every public exposure of acceptance brought disgrace, virtually always with at least the loss of office.

Initially more promising was the view that these bribes were necessary for consideration of a proposal. If in fact the purchasing agent evaluated only those proposals accompanied by bribes but evaluated them without regard to the amount of the bribe or any expectation of future bribes, then such payments are extorted. We may wonder whether anyone can ignore even the hope for a continuing supply of side payments in evaluating competing proposals; thus such an official might award an occasional contract just to keep that supplier competing in his market, and paying the "fees for consideration." If the payments have some effect on the recipient, even one he is unaware of, then they function to affect his actions and his reasons for choosing, and so are bribes. Then the company, and its representative, are offering bribes. But even if they could show that making the payments was simply bowing to extortion, they are not off the hook. Since both bribery and extortion are wrong, what is the extortion payer doing to resist the extortion? What is she doing to combat the practice? If the answer is nothing, then she seems satisfied with the current arrangement, in which case the payments look a lot like bribes *and* extortions.

Since bribery is undermining the agreement to act in another's interest, in situations where it is appropriate for the agent not to act in the principal's interest, there bribery will at least seem less offensive. What if you bribed me to give evidence about my company's dumping hazardous wastes in the river? Ideally, I should simply act in the public interest; but if I need a little extra persuading, your offer is at least a lot more defensible than the standard examples of bribery. Many things besides money will influence a person's choices: love, friendship, another's support of a cause or program one values highly. So unless a person is prepared to commit himself solely to the corporation, or other principal, there will always be some limits to his faithful service. The most that the principal can expect is that both parties understand in advance approximately what those limits are.

Bibliography

Alpern, K. (1985). Moral dimensions of the Foreign Corrupt Practices Act. In Werhane and D'Andrade (1985).

Calero, T. (1985). Business and the Foreign Corrupt Practices Act. In Werhane and D'Andrade (1985).

D'Andrade, K. (1985). Bribery. *Journal of Business Ethics*, 4, 239–48.

Danley, J. R. (1983). Toward a theory of bribery. *Business and Professional Ethics Journal*, 2 (3), 19–39.

Pastin, M. and Hooker, M. (1985). Ethics and the Foreign Corrupt Practices Act. In Werhane and D'Andrade (1985).

Philips, M. (1984). Bribery. *Ethics*, 94, 621–36.

Werhane, P. and D'Andrade, K. (eds.) (1985). *Profit and Responsibility: Issues in Business and Professional Ethics*. Lewiston, NY: Edwin Mellen Press.

business and society

William C. Frederick

Business and Society has two meanings. (1) It refers to the relationships that business firms have with society's institutions and nature's ecosystems. (2) The term also refers to the field of management study that describes, analyzes, and evaluates these complex societal and ecological linkages.

BUSINESS AND SOCIETY RELATIONSHIPS

Business, while recognized as an economic activity, is strongly affected by the surrounding social and ecological environment. A society's legal system, its politics and government regulations, community attitudes and public opinion, concepts of morality and ethics, and the forces of social change including science, technology, and rivalry among nations, can exert both negative and positive influences upon a business firm's costs, prices, and profits. Global business firms particularly must learn to deal effectively with demographic diversity, religious and ethnic movements, and public concerns about ecological impacts of business operations.

Business exerts a reciprocal influence upon society through its economic decisions and policies, such as providing jobs, creating income, producing goods and services, and investing capital in plant, equipment, and new product development. These beneficial economic impacts are frequently accompanied by negative social impacts, such as environmental pollution, hazardous working conditions, unsafe or unreliable consumer products, various forms of discriminatory practices, illegal and unethical actions, and excessive political influence on a society's political and governmental systems. A positive social influence may be felt when business firms provide social services not otherwise available, such as healthcare and retirement plans for employees; when they design and build attractive and environmentally sensitive plants and offices, or lend executives to local governments or non-profit institutions, or support local community initiatives through philanthropic contributions to educational, cultural, and charitable organizations.

Quite clearly, in these and other ways, business and society influence one another, sometimes negatively and sometimes with positive results for both (Paul, 1987; Sethi and Falbe, 1987).

Business and Society as a Field of Management Study

In the United States, the two central questions that led to the formation of a new field of management study, variously called "Business and Society," "Business and Its Environment," and "Social Issues in Management," were rooted in the reciprocal ties that bind business and society to one another. The questions were: (1) Should a business firm deliberately and voluntarily try to promote social goals and purposes other than those involved in the pursuit of profits? (2) If so, what criteria should determine the content, scope, and limits of business's social responsibilities?

Two schools of thought developed. One asserted that corporations should voluntarily act in socially responsible ways, even if doing so lowered profits. Howard Bowen's 1953 book, *Social Responsibilities of the Businessman*, was the first comprehensive statement of this doctrine. Earlier in the century, however, a few corporate leaders had acknowledged the need for business firms to look beyond profit goals by accepting a measure of social responsibility for their actions (Heald, 1970). The Committee for Economic Development (1971) affirmed this position by proposing a social contract between business and society that broadened business's social responsibilities.

Others (Friedman, 1970) opposed these views, saying that business makes its main contribution to society by producing goods and services at a profit under competitive market conditions. Nothing should be allowed to interfere with this economic function, as long as business operations are conducted legally and ethically. Voluntarily seeking social goals would be economically diversionary, would penalize socially responsible firms by imposing extra costs not experienced by their less responsible competitors, would substitute private corporate judgments for public policy, and would reintroduce a corporate paternalism hostile to free choice. A related view (Chamberlain, 1973) expressed doubt that even the most well-intentioned social initiatives undertaken by corporations could have a significant impact due to their interference with deeply ingrained profit motives, economic growth, and the public's preference for high levels of consumer goods and services.

This basic philosophical argument was gradually replaced by three further theoretical developments, each of which became a conceptual pillar of this new field of study. Some scholars (Preston and Post, 1975; Buchholz, 1992) argue that corporate social performance is best monitored through the instruments of public policy and government regulatory agencies such as the Environmental Protection Agency, the Consumer Product Safety Commission, the Equal Employment Opportunity Commission, the Occupational Safety and Health Commission, etc. Companies could take their cues for publicly desired social actions by adhering to the nation's laws, public policies, and government regulations, rather than relying on the social conscience of the firm's executive managers.

Other scholars (Freeman, 1984) believe that corporations can best attain their overall strategic objectives, both economic and social, by responding positively to stakeholder demands, thus substituting corporate social performance for the more philosophical principle of social responsibility (Ackerman, 1975; Frederick, 1994; Miles, 1987). A closely related view is that specific social issues affecting a given company can be identified, tracked, and managed to the firm's advantage (Wartick and Cochran, 1985). Theories incorporating the public policy/stakeholder responsiveness/issues management approaches had become the field's dominant conceptual paradigm by the early 1990s.

During the 1980s, business ethics also became a significant component of Business and Society studies. Introduced into the field by business ethics philosophers, it represents an effort to apply moral principles to ethical issues that arise in the workplace (Beauchamp and Bowie, 1988; Donaldson, 1989).

To summarize, the Business and Society field of management study attempts to clarify business's multiform relations with society and thereby to improve the ability of firms to plan and manage their interactions with this broad social and ecological environment. Because economic, social, political, ecological, and ethical interests are affected by these linkages, many of the questions studied are controversial and ultimately philosophical in nature, while nevertheless bearing on the effective management of the firm (Preston, 1986; Wood, 1991).

In the United States, four professional academic organizations promote Business and Society teaching and research: the Social Issues in Management division of the Academy of Management, founded in 1971; the Society for Business Ethics, founded in 1978; the Society for the Advancement of Socioeconomics, founded in 1989; and the International Association for Business and Society, founded in 1989–90.

See also *economics and ethics; socioeconomics; stakeholder theory*

Bibliography

Ackerman, R. W. (1975). *The Social Challenge to Business.* Cambridge, MA: Harvard University Press.

Beauchamp, T. and Bowie, N. E. (1988). *Ethical Theory and Business*, 3rd edn. Englewood Cliffs, NJ: Prentice-Hall.

Bowen, H. R. (1953). *Social Responsibilities of the Businessman.* New York: Harper.

Buchholz, R. A. (1992). *Business Environment and Public Policy: Implications for Management and Strategy*, 4th edn. Englewood Cliffs, NJ: Prentice-Hall.

Chamberlain, N. W. (1973). *The Limits of Corporate Responsibility.* New York: Free Press.

Committee for Economic Development (1971). *Social Responsibilities of Business Corporations.* New York: Committee for Economic Development.

Donaldson, T. (1989). *The Ethics of International Business.* New York: Oxford University Press.

Frederick, W. C. (1994). From CSR_1 to CSR_2: The maturing of Business and Society thought. *Business and Society*, 33, 150–64.

Freeman, R. E. (1984). *Strategic Management: A Stakeholder Approach.* Boston, MA: Pitman.

Friedman, M. (1970). The social responsibility of business is to increase its profits. *New York Times Magazine*, September 13, 122–6.

Heald, M. (1970). *The Social Responsibilities of Business: Company and Community, 1900–1960.* Cleveland, OH: Case-Western Reserve Press.

Miles, R. H. (1987). *Managing the Corporate Social Environment: A Grounded Theory.* Englewood Cliffs, NJ: Prentice-Hall.

Paul, K. (1987). *Business Environment and Business Ethics: The Social, Moral, and Political Dimensions of Management.* Cambridge, MA: Ballinger.

Preston, L. E. (1986). Social issues in management: An evolutionary perspective. In D. A. Wren and J. A. Pearce (eds.), *Papers Dedicated to the Development of Modern Management.* Ada, OH: Academy of Management.

Preston, L. E. and Post, J. E. (1975). *Private Management and Public Policy: The Principle of Public Responsibility.* Englewood Cliffs, NJ: Prentice-Hall.

Sethi, S. P. and Falbe, C. M. (eds.) (1987). *Business and Society: Dimensions of Conflict and Cooperation.* Lexington, MA: Lexington Books.

Wartick, S. L. and Cochran, P. (1985). The evolution of the corporate social performance model. *Academy of Management Review*, 10, 758–69.

Wood, D. J. (1991). Corporate social responsiveness revisited. *Academy of Management Review*, 16, 691–718.

business ethics

Kenneth E. Goodpaster

The study of ethics is the study of human action and its moral adequacy. Business ethics, then, is the study of business action – individual or corporate – with special attention to its moral adequacy. Business persons confront ethical issues, whatever their position in the corporate structure and whatever the size and complexity of the organization. Sometimes responsible judgment and action are clear, but not always. Consider the problems surrounding whistleblowing and loy-alty, sexual harassment in the workplace, intellectual property, the limits of product safety, and ethical differences across cultural borders. What managers often need is an orderly way to think through the moral implications of a policy decision – a perspective and a language for appraising the alternatives available from an ethical point of view. For many, this is the most operational definition of business ethics.

The field of business ethics is at least as old as commerce itself, but in the modern period we can date it from the industrial revolution. Individuals, corporate forms of organization, and even capitalism as a socioeconomic system have come under moral scrutiny from proponents and critics alike. In the second half of the twentieth century there was a renaissance of interest in the subject, spurred by events and by disciplinary realignments. The events included political and social movements for civil rights, women's equality, and environmental awareness. Also deserving of mention in relation to ethical reflection in the US are Watergate, the Wall Street Insider Trading scandal, the Savings and Loan crisis, and the collapse of the Soviet Union. In terms of disciplinary focus, business education has expanded beyond psychology and the social sciences in search of a more humanistic outlook, so that recent efforts in the field are philosophical, theological, and literary.

The modern corporation is a microcosm of the community in which it operates and also a macrocosm of the individual citizen living and working in that wider community. Insofar as the corporation resembles the wider community, issues arise that are similar to those in classical political philosophy: the legitimacy of authority; the rights and responsibilities associated with entry, exit, membership, promotion, and succession; civil liberties; moral climate. Insofar as the corporation resembles an individual person in the community, issues arise that are similar to those in classical moral philosophy: responsibility, integrity, conscience, virtue; duties to avoid harm and injustice; respect for the law; provision for the needs of the least advantaged. There are differences in each realm, of course, since the respective analogies are imperfect, but the similarities are strong enough to help organize the normative issues that present themselves to

business management (*see* MORAL STATUS OF CORPORATIONS).

MODES OF ETHICAL INQUIRY

It has often been observed that ethical inquiry can take three forms: descriptive, normative, and analytical. Descriptive ethics is not, strictly speaking, philosophical. It is better classified among the social sciences, since it is aimed at empirically neutral descriptions of the values of individuals and groups. To say, for example, that a business executive or an organization disapproves of workplace discrimination or approves of bribery is to make a descriptive ethical observation, one that can presumably be supported or refuted by pointing to factual evidence.

Normative ethics, by contrast, is not aimed at neutral factual claims, but at judgments of right and wrong, good and bad, virtue and vice. To say that a business executive or an organization disapproves of workplace discrimination or approves of bribery and is right or wrong in doing so is to add a normative ethical claim to a descriptive one. If it is to be supported or refuted, of course, some criteria of "rightness" or "wrongness" must be provided.

Analytical ethics (sometimes called metaethics) is neither a matter of describing moral values nor advancing criteria for right and wrong. Instead, it steps back from both of these activities in order to pose questions about the meaning and objectivity of ethical judgments. At this remove, the aim is to explore differences among scientific, religious, and ethical outlooks; the relation of law to morality; the implications of cultural differences for ethical judgment, and so forth.

THE DYNAMICS OF NORMATIVE ETHICS

Within normative ethics, there are two interacting levels of reasoning that need to be distinguished. First, and most familiar, is reasoning from moral common sense. In our personal lives and in our professional lives, most of us operate with a more or less well-defined set of ethical convictions, principles, or rules of thumb that guide decision-making. Seldom are such values or rules spelled out explicitly in a list, but if they were, the list would probably include such items as:

- Avoid harming others
- Respect others' rights (Be fair, just)
- Do not lie or cheat (Be honest)
- Keep promises and contracts (Be faithful)
- Obey the law

Such a repertoire of commonsense moral judgments is often sufficient. It functions as an informal checklist that we are prepared to live by both for the sake of others and for our own inner well-being. In the context of business behavior, the toleration of toxic workplace conditions, racial discrimination, and false advertising are as clearly contrary to moral common sense as honoring agreements with suppliers and obeying tax laws are in accord with it.

Unfortunately, problems arise with common sense both hypothetically and in practice. And when they do, we seem forced into another kind of normative thinking. The problems come from two main sources: (1) internal conflicts or unclarities about items on personal or corporate checklists, and (2) external conflicts in which others' lists (persons or corporations) differ (e.g., are longer, shorter, or display alternative priorities). How can we keep this promise to that supplier while avoiding risk to those customers? What does it mean to be fair to employees? When, if ever, does "affirmative action" become "reverse discrimination"? If competitors don't value honesty, why should we? Such questions drive us beyond moral common sense to what is called critical thinking. Here the search is for principles or criteria that will justify the inclusion or exclusion of commonsense norms, clarify them, and help resolve conflicts among them. It is the dynamic interaction between moral common sense and our attempts at critical thinking that lead to what some call "reflective equilibrium" (Rawls, 1971: 20ff.).

Aspects of the Moral Point of View

The history of ethics reveals a widely shared conviction that ethics can and should be rooted in what has been termed the moral point of view. For many, the moral point of view is understood in religious terms, a perspective that reflects God's will for humanity. For others, it is understood in secular terms and is not dependent for its authority on religious faith. But setting aside differences about its ultimate source, there is significant consensus regarding its general character. The moral point of view is a mental and emotional standpoint from which all persons are seen as having a special dignity or worth, from which the Golden Rule gets its force, from which words like "ought," "duty," and "virtue" derive their meaning. It is our principal guide for action. Two basic features of action deserve special notice. Any action or decision has:

1 *An aretaic aspect*, highlighting the expressive nature of our choices. When a person acts she or he is revealing and reinforcing certain traits or "habits of the heart" which are called virtues (and vices). The same may be true of groups of persons in organizations. Sometimes we refer in the latter cases to the culture or mindset or value system of the organization. The key to the aretaic aspect of action is its attention to actions as manifestations of an inner outlook, character, set of values or priorities. Four classical virtues that have often been the focus of ethical analysis and reflection in the past are: prudence, justice, temperance, and courage. Others include honesty, compassion, fidelity (to promises), and dedication to community (the common good). Vices of individuals or groups include greed, cruelty, indifference, and cowardice.

2 *A deontic aspect*, highlighting the effective nature of our choices – the way in which our actions influence our relationships with others and change the world around us. Actions have stakeholders and consequences when viewed from this perspective; they are transactions that affect the freedom and well-being of others (*see* STAKEHOLDER THEORY). The deontic aspect of actions relates to their effects on the world, in particular, their effects on living creatures whose interests or rights might be at stake. Management and the board are bound legally and ethically to a fiduciary role in relation to the shareholders of the enterprise, but they must also be attentive to other stakeholders. This kind of extended moral awareness, despite the ambitions of some of the great thinkers of the past, is no more reducible to a mechanical decision procedure than is balanced judgment in education, art, politics, or

even sports. Ethics need not be unscientific, but it is not a science. It may be more akin to staying healthy. Acknowledging our limitations regarding knowledge and certainty in ethics is not the same as embracing the motto "There's no disputing tastes." Sometimes stakeholder interests and rights, as well as the needs of the wider community, are in tension with one another, making ethical judgment very difficult for individuals and for managers of organizations.

This "bifocal" perspective on action (expressive and effective) signals a duality in what we referred to as the moral point of view. Through one set of lenses, moral judgment concentrates on the expressive meaning of actions and policies – what they reveal about those who initiate them. Through another set of lenses, the focus shifts to the effective or transactional significance of what we do. If our inquiry concentrates on an individual's or an organization's habits or culture (content, genesis, need for maintenance or change, etc.) it is aretaic. If the focus is on the interests and rights of stakeholders of personal or corporate decisions, it is deontic.

While a comprehensive review of the many ways in which philosophers, past and present, have organized critical thinking is not possible here, we can sketch several of the more important normative views that have been proposed. These views provide avenues for ethical analysis in the sense that discussions of cases or pending decisions often can be illuminated (and even resolved) by one or more of them. Three of these avenues fall under the heading of "stakeholder-based" thinking (figure 1), while the fourth maps onto "virtue-based" thinking (see figure 2.)

STAKEHOLDER-BASED THINKING

Stakeholder thinking is the most highly developed approach to ethical analysis, and displays three distinctive "logics" or avenues: interest-based, rights-based, and duty-based.

Interest-based avenues. One of the more influential avenues of ethical analysis, at least in the modern period, is what we can call interest-based. The fundamental idea behind interest-based analysis is that the moral assessment of actions and policies depends solely on consequences, and that the only consequences that really matter are the interests of the parties affected (usually human beings). On this view, ethics is all about harms and benefits to identifiable parties. Moral common sense is thus disciplined by a single dominant objective: maximizing net expectable utility (happiness, satisfaction, well-being, pleasure). Critical thinking, on this view, amounts to testing our ethical instincts and rules of thumb against the yardstick of social costs and benefits.

There is variation among interest-based analysts, depending on the relevant beneficiary class. For some (called egoists), the class is the actor alone – the short- and long-term interests of the self. For others, it is some favored group – Greeks or Englishmen or Americans – where others are either ignored or discounted in the

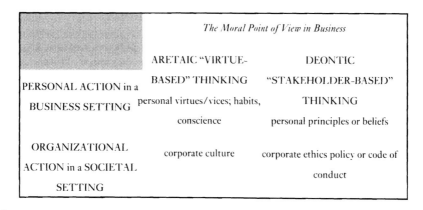

	ARETAIC "VIRTUE-BASED" THINKING	DEONTIC "STAKEHOLDER-BASED" THINKING
The Moral Point of View in Business		
PERSONAL ACTION in a BUSINESS SETTING	personal virtues/vices; habits, conscience	personal principles or beliefs
ORGANIZATIONAL ACTION in a SOCIETAL SETTING	corporate culture	corporate ethics policy or code of conduct

Figure 1

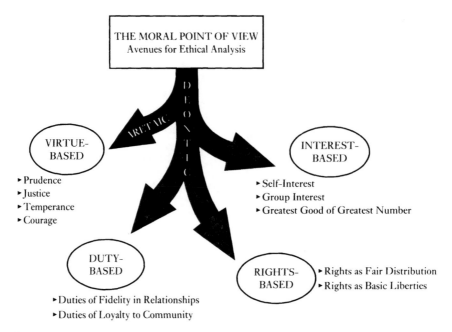

Figure 2

ethical calculation of interests (*see* EGOISM, PSYCHOLOGICAL EGOISM, AND ETHICAL EGOISM). The most common variation (called utilitarianism) enlarges the universe of moral consideration to include all human beings, if not all sentient (feeling) beings. In business management, interest-based reasoning often manifests itself as a commitment to the social value of market forces, competitive decision-making, and (sometimes) regulation in the public interest. Problems and questions regarding interest-based avenues of ethical analysis are several: How does one measure utility or interest satisfaction? For whom does one measure it (self, group, humankind, beyond)? What about the tyranny of the majority in the calculation?

Rights-based avenues. A second influential avenue is rights-based analysis. Its central idea is that moral common sense is to be governed not by interest satisfaction, but by rights protection. And the relevant rights are of two broad kinds: rights to fair distribution of opportunities and wealth (contractarianism), and rights to basic freedoms or liberties (libertarianism) (*see* COMMUNITARIANISM). Fair distribution is often

explained as a condition that obtains when all individuals are accorded equal respect and equal voice in social arrangements. Basic liberties are often explained in terms of individuals' opportunities for self-development, property, work's rewards, and freedoms including religion and speech.

In management practice, rights-based reasoning is evident in concerns about stakeholder rights (consumers, employees, suppliers) as well as stockholder (property) rights. Questions regarding this avenue include: Is there not a trade-off between equality and liberty when it comes to rights? Does rights-based thinking lead to tyrannies of minorities that are as bad as tyrannies of majorities? Is this avenue too focused on individuals and their entitlements with insufficient attention to larger communities and the responsibilities of individuals to such larger wholes?

Duty-based avenues. The third avenue of ethical analysis is duty-based. While this avenue is perhaps the least unified and well-defined, its governing ethical idea is duty or responsibility not so much to other individuals as to communities of individuals. In the duty-based outlook, critical thinking turns ultimately on individuals conforming to the legitimate norms of a healthy community. According to the duty-based thinker, ethics is not finally about interests and rights, since those are too individualistic. Ethics is about playing one's role in a larger enterprise – a set of relationships (like the family) or a community (communitarianism). The best summary of this line of thinking was echoed in John F. Kennedy's inaugural speech: "Ask not what America can do for you, ask what you can do for America."

In practice, duty-based thinking underlies appeals to principles of fiduciary obligation, public trust, and corporate community involvement (see FIDUCIARY DUTY). Problems and questions regarding this avenue include the fear that individualism might get swallowed up in a kind of collectivism (under the communitarian banner) and that priorities among conflicting duties are hard to set.

VIRTUE-BASED THINKING

Virtue-based thinking lies on the expressive side of the distinction made earlier between deontic and aretaic outlooks on human action. The focus of virtue-based thinking is on developing habits of the heart, character traits, and acting on them. Actions and policies are subjected to ethical scrutiny not on the basis of their effects or their consequences (for individuals or for communities), but on the basis of their genesis – the degree to which they flow from or reinforce a virtue or positive trait of character. *Newsweek* magazine devoted its June 13, 1994 issue to the theme of virtue-based ethics in American culture. In an article entitled "What is Virtue?," Kenneth L. Woodward observed: "The cultivation of virtue makes individuals happy, wise, courageous, competent. The result is a good person, a responsible citizen and parent, a trusted leader, possibly even a saint. Without virtuous people, according to this tradition, society cannot function well. And without a virtuous society, individuals cannot realize either their own or the common good."

There is an emphasis in virtue-based analysis on cultivating the traits and habits that give rise to actions and policies, on the belief that too often "the right thing to do" cannot be identified or described in advance using one of the other avenues. The most traditional short list of basic (or "cardinal") virtues includes prudence, temperance, courage, and justice. Some of the most popular management books in recent years have suggested virtue-based thinking in their titles: *The Art of Japanese Management* (Pascale and Athos, 1981), *In Search of Excellence* (Peters and Waterman, 1982), *The Seven Habits of Highly Effective People* (Covey, 1989). In the wider philosophical and cultural literature, *After Virtue* (MacIntyre, 1981) and *A Book of Virtues* (Bennett, 1993) have extended the rediscovery of virtue-based thinking.

In management contexts the language of virtue is frequently encountered in executive hiring situations as well as in management development training. Another management context that may prove to be more amenable to virtue-based thinking than to stakeholder-based thinking is environmental awareness. Often, debates over the impacts of business behavior on the environment have focused on the economic inclusion of "special" stakeholders (like future generations or animals or living creatures generally). While this approach is, logically speaking, an option, it may be less practically compelling than an approach which interprets management ethics in this arena, alongside community involvement, as a virtue akin to temperance.

Questions associated with virtue-based thinking include: How are we to understand the central virtues and their relative priorities in a secular world that does not appear to agree on such matters? Are there timeless character traits that are not so culture-bound that we can recommend them to anyone, particularly those in leadership roles? And can virtue(s) be taught?

Each of the four avenues (figure 2) represents a concentration of critical thinking in ethical matters from which specific ethical challenges might be addressed, if not resolved. All have in common a sustained effort to give practical voice to the moral point of view in business life.

Bibliography

Beauchamp, T. and Bowie, N. (eds.) (1993). *Ethical Theory and Business*, 4th edn. Englewood Cliffs, NJ: Prentice-Hall.

De George, R. T. (1993). *Competing with Integrity in International Business*. New York: Oxford University Press.

Donaldson, T. and Werhane, P. H. (1993). *Ethical Issues in Business: A Philosophical Approach*, 4th edn. Englewood Cliffs, NJ: Prentice-Hall.

Freeman, R. E. and Gilbert, D. R. (1988). *Corporate Strategy and the Search for Ethics*. Englewood Cliffs, NJ: Prentice-Hall.

Matthews, J., Goodpaster, K., and Nash, L. (eds.) (1991). *Policies and Persons: A Casebook in Business Ethics*, 2nd edn. New York: McGraw-Hill.

Novak, M. (1993). *The Catholic Ethic and the Spirit of Capitalism*. New York: Free Press.

Rawls, J. (1971). *A Theory of Justice*. Cambridge, MA: Harvard University Press.

Regan, T. (1984). *Just Business: New Introductory Essays in Business Ethics*. New York: Random House.

Stone, C. (1975). *Where the Law Ends: The Social Control of Corporate Behavior*. New York: Harper and Row.

Velasquez, M. (1992). *Business Ethics: Concepts and Cases*, 3rd edn. Englewood Cliffs, NJ: Prentice-Hall.

Walton, C. (1988). *The Moral Manager*. Cambridge, MA: Ballinger.

Werhane, P. (1991). *Adam Smith and His Legacy for Modern Capitalism*. New York: Oxford University Press.

C

Canada, business ethics in

Deborah C. Poff

Some might argue it is unnecessary to specify a particular nation-state when speaking about business ethics. Since all human action has moral consequences and ethical theories about assessing the morality of human action, surely business ethics can be discussed in universal rather than country-specific terms?

While it is true that the particular activities of any business in any country can be discussed by appeal to general mainstream ethical theories (e.g., utilitarianism or deontology), individual characteristics are important. The specific ethical issues of relevance to a given country have a great deal to do with its political and legal history, its religious history, its economic status, its natural resources, its industrial base, and its relationship to other nation-states.

For Canada, two key relationships have conditioned the development of law and the evolution and context in which business and ethics converge. First, Canada was a British colony and is, consequently, a member of the Commonwealth of nations. Consequently, the Canadian government is a parliamentary government and Canada has had closer ties with other Commonwealth countries than geography alone would make evident. Secondly, Canada shares a boundary with the United States, its largest trading partner, a neighbor with ten times its population.

Canada's historic relationship with Great Britain is partly evidenced by its recent constitutional autonomy. Canada's Charter of Rights and Freedoms was "repatriated" or came into constitutional legal existence in 1982. With the exception of the Quebec provincial judicial system, Canada's legal history is grounded in British common law. Canada has not had the litigious history of its American neighbor and Canadian victims of ethical wrongdoing by corporations have not sought class-action suits to rectify the wrong even when evidence of the wrongdoing has been significant and well documented (e.g., compare the series of lawsuits against US asbestos companies with the virtual lack of suits by Canadian victims of the asbestos industry).

It is perhaps not surprising that cultural and economic autonomy are common themes in Canadian business ethics. Canadians have one state-subsidized radio and television network (the Canadian Broadcasting Corporation) and a partially subsidized film industry, the National Film Board. Over the past decade, these cultural industries have received significant budget cuts and cultural nationalists debate the seriousness of this. Most Canadians watch American television, read American magazines, and go to American films for entertainment. The extent to which Canada as a nation-state has a different cultural and national identity distinct from the United States and whether, in fact, state-subsidized initiatives should bolster such differences is an ongoing and familiar debate within the country.

As a sparsely populated, traditionally resource-based economy, Canada has had a high quality of life with state-subsidized education (including post-secondary education) and universal healthcare. Recently, the value of state-subsidized education and healthcare has become an issue in free trade discussions, particularly between the United States and Canada.

While the national debt and economic health of Canada has improved significantly since the first edition of this encyclopedia, the pressures of globalization, trade liberalization, and deregulation are still common themes in articles and books on business ethics in Canada. The critics of the North American Free Trade Agreement (NAFTA) in Canada focused primarily on two issues. First, would NAFTA increase unemployment in Canada by shipping low-paying jobs to a poorer nation-state (i.e., Mexico), where lower wages and less stringent worker and environmental protection laws are the norm? Secondly, even if the quality of Canadian life were advanced through NAFTA, would it be ethical to benefit by shipping the worst jobs to a third world country? The debates have shifted from NAFTA for the most part in Canada to discussions of the role of the IMF and the World Trade Organization and the ethics of transnational corporations. Critics of the IMF and WTO in Canada have questioned whether Canada as a democratic national state is playing a strong enough role in voicing concerns about global justice and global sustainability.

Canada's economic autonomy as a nation of the Americas is significantly tied to the American market. The boycott on Canadian beef, following one diagnosed case of mad cow disease, has cost millions of dollars in lost revenue and many bankruptcies in the agricultural industries in Canada, where the majority of beef is exported to the United States. The impact of this disaster has raised the issue of economic autonomy in agri-business in Canada and the role of the state in subventions and financial relief during disaster. Such issues are clearly related to free trade talks. The soft-wood lumber talks between the United States and Canada and the position of the US in this dispute has cost thousands of jobs in Canada and resulted in unemployment rates in some forestry-based communities of 20 percent. Much of the Canadian tourist industry is dependent upon American tourists and the recent SARS-related illness in Canada seriously compromised the economic viability of many tourist-based community economies.

The environment and sustainability of natural resources within Canada remain critical in a country that built its economic base, to a large extent, on resource extraction. The successive Canadian governments over the past decade have stressed the need for the diversification of the Canadian economy from primary resource extraction and emphasized the importance of increasing global competitiveness through value-added industries.

Canadian business ethics is not, however, solely idiosyncratic and concerned only with issues circumscribed by Canadian boundaries. *The Corporate Ethics Monitor*, the bi-monthly newsletter of EthicScan Canada Ltd. (a private company), regularly features Canadian companies' ratings on a series of ethical indicators, including: code of ethics; community relations; employment of women (at all levels of the co - poration); charitable donations; extended maternity leave; corporate-sponsored daycare; environmental performance; international relations; labor relations; health and safety; military and nuclear involvement.

Canadian concern with the impact of globalization of the economy on national and international ethics and law, as noted above, is shared internationally with other industrialized and developing nations. Employment equity (Canada's term for affirmative action); First Nations' land claims over privately owned land and crown land; criminal wrongdoing; taxation of businesses; corporate donations to political parties; the online civilization and regulation – all are ethical business issues Canadians share with the world. The recent Enron scandal, as well as similar infamous violations of law and morality with respect to accountability, honesty, and integrity, has resulted in more scrutiny of business in Canada as it has in the United States. Canada has not been immune to similar scandals, the most notable being Livent, Inc., a Canadian-based entertainment corporation operating in Canada and the United States.

Recently, Canadian business ethics has joined the world of cybernet with the growth of a number of Internet think-tanks on business ethics. The Canadian Business and Professional Ethics Network (CBPENET) links the majority of academics working on business ethics in Canada. SUSNET links ethicists concerned with sustainability, justice, and global economic development, while members of ESAC-L (the network of the Environmental Studies Association of Canada) discuss environmental issues and problems. These networks also connect Canadian ethicists with a number of US and international Internet lists.

While Canadian history makes the discussion of business ethics somewhat culture-specific, the Canadian future may include the erosion of such specificities through free-trade agreements, information highways, and a globalized economy that diminishes the importance of national boundaries and the strength of autonomous nation-states. If this does prove to be the case, business ethics and international standards and the monitoring of those standards will supersede and transform current political boundaries and political realities.

Bibliography

Bienefeld, J. P. (1992). Financial deregulation: Disarming the nation-state. *Studies in Political Economy*, 37, 31–58.

Brooks, L. (ed.) (n.d.) *The Corporate Ethics Monitor*. Published six times per year by EthicScan Canada Ltd., Box 54034, Toronto, Ontario, M6A 3B7.

Cragg, W. (1992). *Contemporary Moral Issues*. Toronto: McGraw-Hill Ryerson.

Michalos, A. (1995). *A Pragmatic Approach to Business Ethics*. Thousand Oaks, CA: Sage.

Poff, D. (1994). Reconciling the irreconcilable: The global economy and the environment. In T. Schrecker and J. Dalgleish (eds.), *Growth, Trade and Environmental Values*. London, Ont.: Westminster Institute for Ethics and Human Values.

Poff, D. and Waluchow, W. (eds.) (1991). *Business Ethics in Canada*. Scarborough, Ont.: Prentice-Hall.

Schrecker, T. and Dalgleish, J. (eds.) (1994). *Growth, Trade and Environmental Values*. London, Ont.: Westminster Institute for Ethics and Human Values.

Snider, L. (1993). *Bad Business: Corporate Crime in Canada*. Toronto: Nelson.

Swift, J. and Tomlinson, B. (eds.) (1991). *Conflicts of Interest: Canada and the Third World*. Toronto: Between the Lines.

care, ethics of

Robbin Derry

Moral reasoning that derives from a concern for others and a desire to maintain thoughtful mutual relationships with those affected by one's actions. The concern of this approach is the responsibility of the individual to respond to another in the other's terms, acting out of care for the other person (Gilligan, 1982). This is distinct from conceptions of morality as justice in that it does not attempt to follow impartial rules or ensure equitable treatment. It focuses on responsiveness to another's needs. It also includes caring for oneself in a nurturing rather than a self-maximizing way. Because the voices expressing an ethic of care are most frequently women's voices, this orientation has become the focal point of extensive research and debate about whether men and women differ in their moral reasoning.

DISTINCT MORAL ORIENTATION

A moral orientation toward caring was initially observed by Carol Gilligan in her interviews of women facing abortion decisions (Gilligan, 1977, 1982). Gilligan's articulation of morality as care emerged in contrast to Kohlberg's stage theory of moral development, which Gilligan argued relied on a conception of morality as justice.

In 1977 Carol Gilligan challenged the field of moral development to consider the sex bias inherent in Kohlberg's model. The longitudinal sample which had given Kohlberg his critical model-building data was composed of 84 males. Women, when measured on Kohlberg's scale, rarely reached the higher stages, and most often seemed to demonstrate stage three reasoning, that of helping and pleasing others.

In conducting interviews for a project with Kohlberg, Gilligan had found what she subsequently called "a different voice," the perspective, voiced more frequently by women, that morality was not defined by justice, fairness, or universal rights, as Kohlberg argued. Instead, this perspective described a morality based on care, on responsibility to others, on the continuity of interdependent relationships. Gilligan described this perspective as a morality of care and argued it was a distinct moral orientation, not merely one of Kohlberg's stages of moral development. She believed this orientation resulted in clearly different reasoning and unique ways of resolving moral conflict situations.

Kohlberg's response to Gilligan was to acknowledge the importance of recognizing the concept of morality which focuses on special relationships and obligations, but to deny that it was a distinct moral orientation. He saw it as a supplement rather than an alternative to justice solutions (Kohlberg, Levine, and Hewer, 1983: 21).

THE RELATIONAL CONTEXT OF CARE

Nell Noddings (1984) elaborated an ethic of care characterized by a fundamental grounding in relation. According to Noddings, the act of caring requires moving away from oneself and becoming engrossed in the reality of another's life. This ethic of care involves the "one-caring" and the "cared-for," in acts of giving and receiving, understanding and sharing, which establish their relatedness. Accepting this relationship as necessary to our existence and well-being is a premise for the ethic of care. Noddings suggests that we are not fundamentally alone in this world, driven by the anguish of isolation and motivated by self-interested individualism. Rather, we are most basically in relation to each other, and a deep and profound joy is the basic human affect. The ethical ideal is the nurturing of the understanding of our mutual interdependence. How ethically good any of us can be as the "one-caring" depends on the reception and response of each of us as the "cared-for." Education in ethics, therefore, should focus on both aspects of the caring relationship.

Similarly, the successful development and practice of an ethic of care demands a consistent integration of the awareness of our relatedness. That which creates difficulty and suffering for the cared-for is also suffered as a difficulty for the one-caring. The reality of the joys and pains of the cared-for is shared by the one-caring as she realizes the possibility of such reality. Ethical action is driven by the feeling of "I must" act in a way to alleviate the pain of another. This aroused sense of concern for another is our natural ethical self. We may learn to listen to that self or to silence it.

The emphasis on feeling rather than thinking as the key route to an ethical life distinguishes the ethics of care from other formal systems of ethics which rely on rational thought and the ability to abstract the general from the specific. Noddings and Gilligan both argue for the critical relevance of an emotional basis for ethical decisions. Rather than trying to create rules for ethical action that would hold in all similar situations, or to calculate the good or evil to the general population, the ethics of care encourage learning to respond to the uniqueness and context of each situation.

The ethics of care have frequently been considered to be an approach more natural for women, and as such, have contributed to substantial debate over the existence of measurable differences in the moral reasoning of women and men. Both Gilligan and Noddings identify women's experience as that which gives rise to the articulation of the ethics of care. Gilligan offers an extended argument for the inclusion of the morality of care in the social repertoire of ethical behavior, citing the systematic exclusion of and bias against women's logic, priorities, and concerns within the development of moral philosophy (Gilligan, 1982: 30).

RELATED RESEARCH

Numerous important contributions to ethical theory have emerged from the distinction of the ethics of care. Although these do not all support the entire conception of care reasoning presented by Gilligan or Noddings, each has derived significant impetus from the initial thesis. As a result, the ethics of care can be seen as an array of ideas, broadly encompassing such topics as what care consists of, who engages in it and why, what an understanding of care teaches us about our society, how care is experienced, and how care is researched.

Seyla Benhabib develops a critical view of traditional moral philosophy by elaborating the relational self found in the ethics of care. She suggests that contractarian theories from Hobbes to Rawls rely on a "generalized other." Universalistic moral theories hypothesize disembodied and disembedded rational beings in an attempt to establish a system in which all will be treated fairly and equally. In contrast, Benhabib argues for an understanding of "every rational being as an individual with a concrete history, identity and affective-emotional constitution" (Benhabib, 1987: 87). Only with this perspective of "the concrete other" are we able to make ethical decisions which are good for individuals as well as humanity. The relational self described by both Noddings and Gilligan is deeply embedded in personal feelings, values, and experiences. An individual's own "concreteness" as well as that of the people she cares about are critical components of her moral reasoning.

The importance of drawing on women's experience in the construction of theoretical models is one of the hallmarks of feminist research. Accordingly, Gilligan is recognized for listening to the voices of women in a field where the uniqueness of women's experience was unnoticed. In her discussion of feminist morality, Virginia Held (1993) acknowledges Gilligan's contribution of examining actual relationships in the lives of women. This methodology is critical for Held, as she develops a "mothering person" model to replace the more abstract "rational economic man" paradigm. The mothering person, an ostensibly gender-neutral concept, looks to the maternal experience of women as a reliable guide for moral behavior. Held's model specifically values the integration of emotion to the process of moral reasoning.

The use of emotion and familial experience to develop moral theory stands in stark contrast to the insistence on impartiality and detachment found in theories articulated by most male philosophers and derived from men's experience and values.

Further drawing on the methodology of Gilligan, Jonathan Adler (1987) argues that the value placed on autonomous, universalizable moral reasoning by Kant and Kohlberg neglects the personal point of view. In doing so, it overlooks the importance of contextual variables in individual decisions and establishes a standard of consistency that undermines effective ethical action. Gilligan's articulation of care embraces the inconsistency in practical moral evaluations, thereby relinquishing the necessity of generalizing action to all similar situations. Adler suggests that abstraction from situational realities results in a "widening of the gap between theory and our actual moral practices" (1987: 206). By contrast, the ethics of care look deeply into contextual specifics to formulate a moral solution.

The use of context in moral reasoning is also addressed by Marilyn Friedman in her criticism of Kohlberg's theory of moral development. Friedman (1987) suggests that the essential aspect of contextual thinking is not the use of real as opposed to hypothetical moral dilemmas,

as Gilligan proposes, but rather the presence of rich detail in the situational variables. Friedman challenges Kohlberg's emphasis on the primacy of justice and suggests that sometimes considerations of care and community, of special relationships, override considerations of justice and rights. Whereas justice reasoning envisions abstract persons crafting a mutually respected social contract, care reasoning envisions the unique bonds of an individual relationship. Therefore, care reasoning is most able to be articulated within a rich contextual framework. Friedman's insight suggests that research instruments for the assessment of care reasoning should enable reference to details and contextual variables.

CARE AND BUSINESS ETHICS

There is a paucity of theoretical and empirical research applying the ethics of care to business ethics. Surveying ethics education for accountants, Sara Reiter signaled the need for full narratives, similar to those used in Gilligan's research, portraying real individuals in concrete situations. She argued: "The lack of research on the ethical problems of practicing accountants presents a barrier to development of appropriate narratives and cases" (Reiter, 1996: 27). Creating such models for business ethics education would encourage both professors and students to weigh contextual components in addition to the rights and duties found within cognitive moral development theory.

Thomas White (1992) noted the potential contribution of Gilligan's ethic of care to a better understanding of how women manage organizations. John Dobson and Judith White further suggested that a "feminine-oriented relationship-based value system complements the essential nature of the firm as a nexus of relationships between stakeholders" (Dobson and White, 1995: 19). Each of these scholars urged extensive incorporation of the ethics of care into business ethics research.

The moral reasoning of a sample of men and women managers of a Fortune 100 company was investigated by Robbin Derry (1989) using interviews and real-life dilemmas. Finding little evidence of care reasoning among any of the participant managers, she suggested that the organizational culture and the promotional system in the conservative, high-tech organization may have fostered moral reasoning focused on rights and rules: strong components of justice reasoning. Those participants who used care reasoning in other areas of their lives seemed to believe it was inappropriate at work. In addition, Derry argued that the lack of a reliable and valid research instrument to measure care reasoning, as readily as the Kohlberg or Rest instruments measure justice in moral development, has hampered further investigation of the ethics of care.

The potential for the application of the ethics of care to business ethics is significant. As indicated above, such potential is evident in several distinctive features. First, the ethics of care emphasize the maintenance of relationships and their myriad commitments. In the corporate environment, there is an increasing demand for business to be attentive to its many stakeholders, particularly customers and employees, in caring ways. As organizations attempt to build such relationships, they must define the responsibilities of initiating and maintaining care. The ethics of care may be able to facilitate an understanding of these responsibilities. Second, the use of real-life dilemmas, or rich hypotheticals, would enable a broader definition of ethical issues, inclusive of the specifics of the market and work environments. This offers an alternative to the abstraction utilized in traditional philosophical models. Third, the ethics of care draw on women's lives and perspectives as informative and instructive. The much-heralded change in demographics over the next few decades, with an increasing number of women and minorities taking on significant roles in management, creates a greater need to build models and paradigms on the experience of these people. While the ethics of care may not be fully representative, understanding this perspective opens the way for inclusion of other "different" voices.

Bibliography

Adler, J. (1987). Moral development and the personal point of view. In E. F. Kittay and D. T. Meyers (eds.), *Women and Moral Theory*. Totowa, NJ: Rowman and Littlefield, 205–34.

Belenky, M. F., Clinchy, B. M., Goldberger, N. R., and Tarule, J. M. (1986). *Women's Ways of Knowing*. New York: Basic Books.

Benhabib, S. (1987). The generalized and the concrete other: The Kohlberg–Gilligan controversy and feminist theory. In S. Benhabib and D. Cornell (eds.), *Feminism as Critique*. Minneapolis: University of Minnesota Press, 77–95.

Derry, R. (1989). An empirical study of moral reasoning among managers. *Journal of Business Ethics*, 8, 855–62.

Dobson, J. and White, J. (1995). Toward the feminine firm. *Business Ethics Quarterly*, 5 (3), 463–78.

Friedman, M. (1987). Care and context in moral reasoning. In E. F. Kittay and D. T. Meyers (eds.), *Women and Moral Theory*. Totowa, NJ: Rowman and Littlefield, 190–204.

Gilligan, C. (1977). In a diffferent voice: Women's conception of the self and of morality. *Harvard Educational Review*, 47, 481–517.

Gilligan, C. (1982). *In a Different Voice*. Cambridge, MA: Harvard University Press.

Held, V. (1993). *Feminist Morality: Transforming Culture, Society, and Politics*. Chicago: University of Chicago Press.

Kohlberg, L., Levine, C., and Hewer, A. (1983). *Moral Stages: A Current Formulation and a Response to Critics*. New York: Karger.

Noddings, N. (1984). *Caring: A Feminine Approach to Ethics and Moral Education*. Berkeley: University of California Press.

Reiter, S. A. (1996).The Kohlberg-Gilligan controversy: Lessons for accounting ethics education. *Critical Perspectives on Accounting*, 7.

Tong, R. (1993). *Feminine and Feminist Ethics*. Belmont, CA: Wadsworth.

White, T. (1992). Business, ethics, and Carol Gilligan's "two voices." *Business Ethics Quarterly*, 2, (1), 51–61.

caring organizations

Jeanne M. Liedtka

A caring organization is one whose values and practices are consistent with, and supportive of, an ethic of care. An ethic of care focuses on the self as connected to others, with an emphasis on the care-giver's responsibility to the "other" to maintain that connection (Gilligan, 1982). It is often compared with the stereotypically masculine ethic of justice, with its focus on defining the self as separate and its use of rights to protect boundaries between the self and other. Gilligan's metaphor of the web to represent feminine thinking has been juxtaposed against the use of hierarchy to represent masculine thinking (White, 1992).

A decade of writing in feminist morality has focused on the concept of an ethic of care. In examining the relevance of an ethic of care for business practice, the question has been raised, can organizations care? In other words, is it possible to take this essentially individual-level theory and extend it to the level of an organization, without subverting it in the process?

Central to the question of whether organizations can care is Noddings's (1984) distinction between "caring for" and "caring about." Ethical caring, she argues, only applies to those *persons* that we care *for*. She uses the term "aesthetical caring" for objects and things that we care *about*. She is concerned about the extent to which our caring for things subverts our caring for people, by encouraging us to use them instrumentally to achieve other ends. Similarly, if it is people that we care *about*, versus *for*, she views this as representing only a "verbal commitment to the possibility of care." We cannot, she argues, care "for" those who are beyond our reach. Caring represents a personal investment that must always remain at the level of "I"; caring at the more abstract level of "We" is an illusion. This quality of particularity is essential. Without particularity the caring connection is lost and we must relabel the new process: no longer "caring," it becomes "problem-solving," in Noddings's terminology.

But what does it mean, within the literature on feminist moral theory, to "care for" this particular other? Noddings remains vague on this point, alluding to an "inclination" toward them. Along with other scholars (Held, 1993; Ruddick, 1989), Noddings has used the relationship between a mother and her child to illustrate, at its deepest level, her notion of what it means to care. Thus, the essence of caring becomes a focus on acceptance of the other, both in his or her current state, *and* as one capable of growth. Nurturing the development of the one cared-for becomes the critical activity in caring relationships. To say that I care about my customers, then, would be to place them and the potential that they represent at the center of my attention, and to work with them to realize that potential. In addition, caring always involves

"feeling with" – receiving the other, rather than projecting one's own view onto the other. Thus, the development process evolves out of the aspirations and capabilities of the cared-for, rather than being driven by the needs and goals of the care-giver.

Thus, Noddings would maintain that, in order for an organization to "care," such caring would need to be:

1 focused entirely on *persons*, not "quality" or "profits," for example;
2 an *end* in and of itself, and not merely a means toward achieving quality, profits, etc.;
3 developmentally focused at a personal level, in that it involves particular individuals engrossed, at a subjective level, in nurturing the development of other particular individuals.

Does, then, an assembly of appropriately caring individuals constitute a "caring" organization? Considerable precedent exists, of course, for such anthropomorphizing – we speak of organizations that have values, that learn, that reward. Yet it would certainly be possible for a subgroup of caring individuals to exist within an organization that worked to subvert their efforts. Thus, we would argue that a caring organization, in addition to being comprised of individuals who met the conditions, would need to actively support their efforts.

In fact, some authors have argued that individual caring is only sustainable, in the long term, within caring systems (Kahn, 1993): "To be cared for is essential for the capacity to be caring" (Gaylin, 1976). Caring, though a particular relationship between individuals, is situated within the context of a community and derives its focus from the needs of that community. We care, not because we are inherently "good," Noddings asserts, but because it is self-serving for the group, as a whole, to care for each other; care is self-reinforcing within that context. Thus, both because it derives its meaning within the context of community, and because of the personal investment required to care, organizations that support individual caring, that create self-reinforcing systems of caring, are not only possible – they are essential if caring is to persist at all.

At this point, however, given Noddings's concerns about instrumentality, we must raise the question, can *business* organizations care? The question of instrumentality and the profit motive is a thorny one. At one level, we might read Noddings as asserting that positive outcomes for anyone other than the cared-for could never be allowed to provide the incentive to care, but must be viewed as mere byproducts. Yet she acknowledges that, at the community level, an ethic of care is clearly self-serving. We might deduce, then, that caring which both honors the growth and development of the particular individual *and* perpetuates the health of a vibrant caring community (which, in turn, fosters more growth of particular individuals) is not instrumental. Thus, the instrumentality caveat would be breached only by the subordination of the particular other cared-for to the interests of the abstract cared-about.

Other concerns raised in the literature relate to questions about the utility of using the mother/child dyad, so prevalent in feminist moral writings, as a model for non-familial relationships and issues around freedom and fairness that a more rights-focused perspective offers. The "mothering" image of caring that is so powerful also raises significant concerns. One of these relates to the issue of power. Is the power differential between parent and child one that we want to embrace as a model for relationships at work? What are the risks of replacing patriarchy with matriarchy? Few, asserts Held (1993), in proposing her "post-patriarchal" model. Disparity in power is a given in our society and cannot be avoided. Yet traditional notions of power are useless in the mothering context. Mothers, she argues, do not "wield" power. Instead, "the power of a mothering person is to empower others – to foster transformational growth" through *influence*.

Ferguson (1984) believes otherwise, asserting that both the presence of inequality and the "natural love" inherent in mothering make it unsuitable for generalization outside the bounds of the family. Instead, she offers the model of citizenship, and uses the town meeting with its decentralization, public decision-making, and openness to conflicting views as a guide for care-based organizations. Her view is strikingly similar to that contained in Charles Handy's call for "federated structures," which contain local and separate activities served by a common center. Such structures, he believes, led by the center and managed by the parts, "combine the benefits of scale and autonomy, while retaining a sense of meaning that connects people to purpose" (1994: 110).

But how are concerns related to fairness and equality addressed within a care-based ethic? Again, Held (1993) argues that our definitions need reframing. Equality no longer corresponds with equal rights or equal treatment; rather, it requires that we view each member as worthy of equal respect and consideration, and respond to the unique needs they bring with them. In a similar vein, Ferguson asserts freedom is essential. But rather than viewing freedom as "an arena of privacy surrounding each individual, [where] community is a secondary arrangement among already autonomous beings; freedom must be located in relations among others… caring for others by caring for their freedom" (1984: 31).

Thus, the issues of freedom, fairness, and power can be reconciled within the framework of a care-based organization. Gilligan, in fact, believes that rights are an essential, though not dominant, component of caring. Without rights, "the injunction to care is paralyzing, rights allow us to appropriately value self-interest… to act responsively towards self *and* others and thus to sustain connection" (1982: 149).

Bibliography

Belensky, M., Clinchy, G., Goldberger, N., and Tarule, J. (1986). *Women's Ways of Knowing*. New York: Basic Books.

Ferguson, K. (1984). *The Feminist Case Against Bureaucracy*. Philadelphia, PA: Temple University Press.

Gaylin, W. (1976). *Caring*. New York: Knopf.

Gilligan, C. (1982). *In a Different Voice*. Cambridge, MA: Harvard University Press.

Handy, C. (1994). *The Age of Paradox*. Boston, MA: Harvard Business School Press.

Held, V. (1993). *Feminist Morality*. Chicago: University of Chicago Press.

Kahn, W. (1990). Psychological conditions of personal engagement and disengagement at work. *Academy of Management Journal*, 33 (4), 692–724.

Kahn, W. (1993). Caring for the caregivers: Patterns of organizational caregiving. *Administrative Science Quarterly*, 38, 539–63.

Lyons, N. (1983). Two perspectives: On self, relationships, and morality. *Harvard Educational Review*, 53 (2), 125–45.

Noddings, N. (1984). *Caring: A Feminine Approach to Ethics and Moral Education*. Berkeley: University of California Press.

Ruddick, S. (1989). *Maternal Thinking*. Boston, MA: Beacon Press.

White, T. (1992). Business, ethics, and Carol Gilligan's "two voices." *Business Ethics Quarterly*, 2 (1), 51–9.

case method

James G. Clawson

The use of descriptions of situations, called "cases," as a basis for discussion in teaching. Cases, which may be oral or written, actual or invented, provide students with a common set of data that they can read, analyze, and discuss. The Harvard Business School borrowed the technique from the medical and legal educational processes to become, in 1919, the first champion of the use of written, actual cases in business education. Two other schools, the Darden Graduate School of Business at the University of Virginia and the University of Western Ontario in Canada, later also became primarily case-oriented schools. Many other schools use cases to varying degrees and in various ways. Written cases vary in length from one to almost 100 pages; the usual length is between 15 and 25 pages.

Case method is used to refer to a wide range of case-based instructional methodology, most clearly seen in the proportion of teacher to student talk. The "classical" Harvard method was intended to provide intelligent, experienced students with actual, current descriptions of difficult business problems and let the students, at their own pace and level of insight, debate the different aspects of the problems with their peers. This was a "student-centered" approach in that the discussion relied heavily on the experience, analysis, contributions, and insight of the students. Some Harvard professors occasionally said nothing during a class. This approach relied on a four-step learning process: careful pre-class individual preparation, continued analysis in small study groups, large, full-class debate, and post-class personal distillation of general principles.

At the other end of the scale, cases are often used by instructors elsewhere as illustrations of lectured, theoretical points. This "instructor-based" use of cases proceeds at the pace and level of insight comfortable to the professor such that students might never speak. Here, what is to be learned is determined by the instructor rather than the student.

Case advocates argue that the classical case method is more effective because it begins where students are, proceeds at their pace on pragmatic rather than theoretical problems, and infuses energy into the learning process, hence accelerating the development of business judgment. Dissidents argue that cases are single examples missing the generalizable lessons of larger sample pools, that the classical case approach ignores the input of more experienced instructors, and that case classes are easily manipulated by case instructors in case selection and presentation.

Current decision-based cases and skilled instructors are the lifeblood of the case method. Finding, researching, and writing good cases is a mixture of science and art that is time consuming and expensive, often requiring a month or more of a researcher's time. Good cases present rich data surrounding an important decision to be made in such a way that many avenues could be argued reasonably. Case courses are built by the selection of cases that present a sequential series of decisions that follow the design intentions of the instructor.

Bibliography

Christensen, C. R. (1987). *Teaching and the Case Method*. Boston, MA: Harvard Division of Research.

Clawson, J. G. and Frey, S. C., Jr. (1986). Mapping case pedagogy. *Organizational Behavior Teaching Review*, now titled *Journal of Management Education*, 11 (1), 1.

Dooley, A. R. and Skinner, W. (1977). Casing case method methods. *Academy of Management Review*, 2 (2).

Gragg, C. I. (1940). Because wisdom can't be told. *Harvard Alumni Bulletin*, Harvard University.

casuistry

Albert R. Jonsen

A word coined, and almost always used, with a pejorative intent: it refers to the ability of clever and devious persons to argue, under the cover of specious moral reasons, for the rightness of their own case. Historically, this negative meaning arose out of theological disputes of the seventeenth century. At that time, Roman Catholic theologians commonly presented "cases of conscience," short analyses of a wide variety of moral dilemmas, to educate believers about their moral duties and to help confessors judge the seriousness of sins and faults revealed to them in confession. Although this study had been common since the late Middle Ages, it aroused vigorous opposition from the Protestant Reformers and, in particular, from rigorist French Catholics, called Jansenists, in the mid-1660s. One of those, the brilliant mathematician Blaise Pascal, attacked the professors of cases of conscience, accusing them of a lax and self-serving interpretation of the laws of God and the church. His attack, *The Provincial Letters*, was a literary success and tarnished the reputation of "cases of conscience." The word "casuistry" itself was coined in a similarly sarcastic vein by the English poet Alexander Pope in 1702. Since that time it is applied almost exclusively to a moral argument that is seen as overly complex, devious, and self-justifying. A patently obvious example: the general said that Vietnam villages had to be destroyed in order to save them.

This pejorative meaning, however, hides an important feature of moral reasoning and a respectable method for analyzing it. The important feature of moral reasoning arises from the fact that moral dilemmas are posed in particular cases. The conflict of moral principles appears in a set of unique circumstances. The circumstances and their relationship to the principles must be understood as precisely as possible in order to reach a judgment. An appreciation of this fact gave rise to the method of "cases of conscience." That method, in essence, called for a careful examination of the proposed case and a comparison of the case to other cases in which similar problems appeared. Such comparison would often show why a change of circumstances rendered one case a more or less

serious matter than the other. Careful methods were developed to analyze the relevant features of cases and to draw appropriate comparisons. The authors of these cases of conscience carried on incessant critique of each other's work, attempting to show inconsistencies in argument or offering stronger reasons to support conclusions. This constant dialogue about cases kept the classical casuists honest, although there were exaggerated practitioners of the art. The value of the method was that it made persons sensitive to the special features of cases and refined their moral judgment about them.

This method contrasts with the broad, abstract study of morality that appears in the standard academic disciplines that deal with morality, moral philosophy, and theological ethics. These disciplines usually devise comprehensive theories of morality. In recent times the moral disciplines have neglected case analysis. However, the interest in the ethics of medicine and healthcare that emerged in the 1970s under the title "bioethics" drew attention to the need for close case analysis: cases are the stuff of medicine. Thus, casuistry, as a method for ethical analysis, was rediscovered.

Other areas of ethical concern, such as business, journalism, politics, and media, find the case approach congenial. It allows practitioners in the field to work with materials familiar to them and brings the moral issues close to the practical realities of their activities. It is interesting to note that in one of the earliest case discussions in an ethical treatise, the Roman philosopher Cicero offers two cases about business ethics, one in which a seller of property wonders how truthful he must be about the condition of the house, the other in which a merchant wonders how to set a fair price for grain in a famine (*On Duties* III, 13–15). In both cases, the considerations offered by the ancient philosopher are relevant to modern business.

The case method is familiar to all students of business and finance, since it was introduced at the Harvard Business School as a basic teaching technique in the 1920s. The Business School adopted the method from the Harvard Law and Medical Schools, which had initiated this technique in the late 1890s. When used as a teaching technique, it can stimulate vivid discussion and creative solutions to problems. However, in business, law, and medicine, the ethical dimensions are seldom factored into the cases. The contemporary interest in ethics in these fields may encourage a more sophisticated attempt to create a casuistry. This requires not only the presentation of the facts of the case in a realistic way, but also the invention of a method of interpreting ethical values in the setting of those facts.

This method must include statements of the goals and essential elements of the enterprise, in addition to its place within the wider society. These features are associated with the range of moral values and principles that naturally come to mind when the enterprise is considered. Thus, in medicine the doctor's duty to benefit the patient and the autonomy of the patient's choice; in diplomacy, the responsibility of furthering the interest of the nation and fidelity to agreements; in business, the legitimacy of profit and the value of honesty. Even in the abstract, these values and principles are somewhat in opposition and, in the concreteness of the case, may come into conflict. Thus a casuistry for each enterprise will work at the intersection of the general features and values of the enterprise and the particular circumstances of the case. The results of this analysis will sometimes show that there is no conflict, but more often suggest ways of minimizing or eliminating conflict. In some cases, it will reveal the stark choice, unavoidable by the responsible person, between good and evil, right and wrong.

Bibliography

Cicero, Marcus Tullius (1975). *On Duties.* Loeb Classical Library. Cambridge, MA: Harvard University Press.

Jonsen, A. and Toulmin, S. (1987). *The Abuse of Casuistry: A History of Moral Reasoning.* Berkeley: University of California Press.

McNair, M. (ed.) (1954). *The Case Method at Harvard Business School.* New York: McGraw-Hill.

Pascal, Blaise (1967). *The Provincial Letters*, trans. A. Krailsheimer. London: Penguin Books.

Catholic social teaching

Oliver F. Williams

The view that capitalism considered in isolation from a context of a humane community seems inevitably to shape people into greedy and insensitive human beings.

While there has always been some reflection on the social and political implications of biblical teaching, within the last one hundred years there has developed a body of official Catholic Church teaching on social ethics known as Catholic Social Teaching. The insight of church teaching accepts the market economy but with a key qualification that the state intervene where essential to promote and protect human dignity. Most official church teachings are promulgated as pastoral letters of a national conference of bishops or as encyclicals, pastoral letters issued by the pope as the chief shepherd of the church. An encyclical's title is taken from the first two words in the Latin edition.

At their best, church statements that reflect on and offer guidance to capitalist economies are attempts to be a moral force, ensuring that an acquisitive economy does not degenerate into an acquisitive society. For example, Pope Leo XIII in *Rerun Novarum* (1891) put the church squarely on the side of the workers in the struggle for recognition of labor unions. Monsignor John A. Ryan was most influential in Catholic circles, writing *A Living Wage* (1906) and *Distributive Justice* (1916). Ryan drafted a crucial document of the National Catholic Welfare Conference (the predecessor of the United States Catholic Conference), issued in 1919 by the US bishops and often cited as the forerunner of some of Franklin Roosevelt's New Deal policies. Titled *Social Reconstruction: A General Review of the Problems and Survey of Remedies*, Ryan's document offered a moral perspective on the economy and made suggestions for such reforms as minimum-wage laws, child-labor laws, the right of labor to organize, and unemployment and health insurance. For the most part, Ryan's suggestions have become public policy in the United States.

In 1931 Pope Pius XI issued *Quadragesimo Anno*. While its proposed alternative model of society is of dubious value today, the role of the church as an agent of change in the sociopolitical order was clearly established. Three principles enunciated in the document have been dominant in all subsequent Catholic social theory: the need to protect the dignity of the person; the concern that organizations be no larger than necessary – subsidiarity; and the focus on the necessity for mediating structures (family, professional associations, church, etc.) between the person and the state.

Quadragesimo Anno outlined a vision of society and its relationship to the state which has continued to develop in Catholic social thought. Society is composed of all the various groupings that people find necessary or helpful – families, churches, unions, professional associations, business corporations, social clubs, neighborhood associations, and so on. The role of the state is to be *in the service* of society, that is, its role is primarily to facilitate the cooperation and well-being of all these groupings or "mediating structures" as they are often called today. The encyclical uses the verbs *direct, watch, urge,* and *restrain* "as occasion requires and necessity demands" when describing the role of the state (para. 80). The 1961 encyclical of Pope John XXIII, *Mater et Magistra*, employs similar terms: the role of the state is to "encourage, stimulate, regulate, supplement, and complement" (para. 53).

Catholic social thought is ever vigilant against collectivist tendencies which tend to obliterate legitimate mediating structures. This defense of personal rights is clearly evident in the 1981 encyclical *Laborem Exercens*, in which Pope John Paul II vigorously defends the solidarity of workers and their right to come together in organizations to defend common interests. Eschewing the model of interest-group pluralism which tends to view the world exclusively through the prism of one set of interests, Catholic social thought repeatedly returns to the notion of the common good as the appropriate context in which to consider one's own interests. John Paul II emphasizes this point in *Laborem Exercens*.

Assuming that human nature is flawed, one of the roles of the state, according to this religious perspective, is to facilitate the growth of desirable character traits and mute those that are less noble. Yet there is a confidence in the goodness, the cooperative dimension of the person, so that the social constraints of the state are designed to enhance human freedom and curtail selfishness for the common good.

This confidence in the fundamental goodness of the person underlies the church's basic strategy of appealing to the consciences of those who control wealth and power, to bring about basic changes in society that are designed to alleviate the plight of the poor. Pope Paul VI in *Populorum Progressio* (Development of Peoples) argues for a new international economic order, but he appeals for strategies of negotiation and consensus rather than any violent means.

The 1991 encyclical *Centesimus Annus* of Pope John Paul II is perhaps the most forthright defense of the wealth-creating capacity of a market economy, but it too stresses a modest role for government intervention to ensure a humane community. A major theme of the criticism of capitalism by the church is summed up well by John Paul II, in speaking of alienation. He notes that the Marxist analysis of alienation is false, but there is a type of alienation in our life today. The point is that it is quite possible for people in a market economy to lose touch with any real meaning or value in life (para. 4). One of the ways this happens is called "consumerism," an easily misunderstood term. Consumerism, as a pejorative term, is certainly not referring to the consumption of material goods, which is, after all, required for a market economy to function and for people to have employment. Consumerism refers to that aberration where people are led to believe that happiness and self-fulfillment are found solely in acquiring material goods. The values of friendship, music, and beauty, for example, come to pale in importance and, because basic, non-materialistic needs are not met, there is alienation. Consumer advocates in the United States have long been critical of certain kinds of advertising because of their adverse cultural and social effects similar to those described above. Seeking ways to strengthen the influence of the family, the schools, and the church is the challenge put forward. Some disciples of Adam Smith believed in God's providence working to ensure the common good, a self-regulating economy. Catholic social teaching says, in effect, that we must make God's work our own.

Bibliography

Byers, D. M. (1985). *Justice in the Marketplace: Collected Statements of the Vatican and the US Catholic Bishops on Economic Policy, 1891–1984.* Washington, DC: United

States Catholic Conference, Inc. (The periodical *Origins* prints all encyclicals and pastoral letters.)

Curran, C. E. (1985). *Directions in Catholic Social Ethics*. Notre Dame, IN: University of Notre Dame Press.

Houck, J. W. and Williams, O. F. (eds.) (1983). *Co-Creation and Capitalism: John Paul II's Laborem Exercens*. Washington, DC: University Press of America.

Houck, J. W. and Williams, O. F. (eds.) (1984). *Catholic Social Teaching and the US Economy: Working Papers for a Bishops' Pastoral*. Washington, DC: University Press of America.

Ryan, J. A. (1942). *Distributive Justice*. New York: Macmillan.

Williams, O. (1993). Catholic social teaching: A communitarian democratic capitalism for the new world order. *Journal of Business Ethics*, 12, 919–32.

Williams, O. F. and Houck, J. W. (eds.) (1991). *The Making of an Economic Vision*. Washington, DC: University Press of America.

Williams, O. F. and Houck, J. W. (eds.) (1993). *Catholic Social Thought and the New World Order*. Notre Dame, IN: University of Notre Dame Press.

character

Edwin M. Hartman

Character is revealed in a person's typical behavior in important matters, including moral ones. Your character may be good or bad according to whether you are virtuous or vicious, and strong or weak according to whether you can be relied on to act on your values even under pressure. Ethicists and psychologists, particularly personality theorists, study character and the causal and conceptual links among traits.

To identify your self with your character is misleading in this sense: a significant character change would not by itself mean that you have ceased to exist and have been replaced by someone else. Yet an extreme change in character may justify saying, meaningfully but with some exaggeration, that Jones is a different man, or not the man I married. Strong character does have to do with consistency of thought, value, and action over time. One who is consistent in this way, especially one who acts according to the values one espouses, is a person of integrity.

Aristotle famously claims that ethics is primarily about the virtues of character rather than about principles, though he grants principles a role in ethics. His view is no longer quaint: in recent years the notions of virtue and character have gained respectability among business ethicists.

This is not to say that character and virtue have obviated principles. We cannot assume that any single sort of ethical theory will address all issues equally well, but principle-based theories seem particularly ill-suited to certain practical moral issues with which managers and others must often deal. Faced with a moral problem that requires action, a manager will likely find that (for example) Kantian ethics and utilitarianism yield no determinate results, but instead create subsidiary arguments about the right sort of preference, or the precise maxim of the act in question. If those arguments could be settled, there would be a further one about which of the general approaches is right. If that problem could be solved, moreover, there would still be the practical issue of whether people will actually do the right thing, as those of good character do. Depending in part on the nature, size, and environment of an organization, a manager may be able to bring about morally good behavior most effectively by populating the organization with employees of good and strong character rather than by enforcing moral rules.

If the virtues of character were simply dispositions to act according to certain principles, then virtue and character ethics would not differ from principle-based ethics; but virtue and character ethicists deny that there are algorithms linking virtues to action-guiding principles. On the contrary, a person of good character does not merely act according to principles, but in cases in which principles give little guidance is also sensitive to all significant aspects of the situation, including possible indirect and long-term consequences. This practical wisdom resembles the ability of a consistently successful business person to assess opportunities and act effectively; it is not a matter of simply knowing textbook rules, important as these may be.

A person of good and strong character is one whose interests are such that being moral makes him or her happy and fulfilled. For such a person the question "Why is it in my best interests to be moral?" can hardly arise. A life anchored by a set of clear and coherent values will likely be preferable to one in which happiness is based on ephemera. But couldn't a bad person of strong character be equally well off? Probably not: such people arouse opposition and lose the benefits of cooperation.

A person of bad character is capable of good acts where these serve that person's interests or fit enforced norms comfortably, much as a person who lacks knowledge may make true statements. But just as education is a matter of imparting actual knowledge, so training in morality should build good character. Acting morally need not be painful – for the person of good character it is not – but it cannot be based on self-interest alone.

To understand how your virtues are related and why you have them requires understanding your character, of which virtues are its iceberg's tip. Teachers, parents, and managers who would affect character must consider psychological relations, which are not relations merely among virtues. Here is another reason why a character is not simply a disposition to act in a certain way: a character trait has no less ontological status than does a psychological state, which is not a mere disposition. A description of a character trait may explain a whole set of virtues. In fact, a particular trait (firmness, for example) may be the psychological basis of both a virtue (courage) and a vice (obstinacy), especially in one who is not perfectly rational.

A pervasive organizational culture can make people of weak character act against their values, though it may occasionally support good character. There is no obligation for managers to improve their employees' character, but they should maintain an organization in which good character does not put one at a disadvantage.

Can character be taught, by business ethics professors or anyone else? If, as Aristotle claims, habituation creates character, there is a problem: how can character be related to the rationality definitive of humans, whereby the agent controls ephemeral desires in aid of an appropriate long-term conception of happiness? If building character is just a matter of forming habits, then moral education should proceed not by appeals to the intellect but by positive and negative reinforcement, and business ethics courses taught in the usual way are a waste of time, and too late.

Yet a business ethics course may indeed help build character. The case study method, or case method, can assist students in developing prac-

tical wisdom, including the sensitivity to details, consequences, and nuances that we attribute to a person of character. Insofar as it deals with issues of character, moreover, a course in business ethics can show the moral importance of corporate culture and of a human resources policy that takes character into account.

Bibliography

Aristotle (1985). *Nicomachean Ethics*, trans. T. Irwin. Indianapolis, IN: Hackett. (Includes a glossary of key terms.)

French, P., Uehling, T., and Wettstein, H. (eds.) (1988). *Ethical Theory: Character and Virtue*, Midwest Studies in Philosophy 13. Minneapolis: University of Minnesota Press. (Includes several essays on character.)

Hartman, E. M. (1996). *Organizational Ethics and the Good Life*. New York, Oxford University Press.

Kupperman, J. (1991). *Character*. New York: Oxford University Press.

Schoeman, F. (1987). *Responsibility, Character, and the Emotions*. New York: Cambridge University Press. (Includes several essays on character.)

Solomon, R. C. (1992). *Ethics and Excellence: Cooperation and Integrity in Business*. New York: Oxford University Press. (An important analysis of business ethics from an Aristotelian point of view.)

China, business ethics in

Georges Enderle

Business ethics faces a vast array of daunting challenges in China. Many observers of China's development, particularly from outside the country, see an urgent need to address these ethical challenges, while others believe that the time for business ethics has not yet come. Because of the size of the country, with its 1.3 billion people, and the pace of change, developing business ethics in China is a highly complex task. Thus, the approach must be comprehensive as well as differentiated (see Enderle, 2003). To focus solely on what individuals and organizations can and should do (which is a tendency of business ethics in the USA) does not suffice; and to deal only with questions of the economic system or economic order (as many Europeans tend to understand business ethics) is not sufficient either. Instead, business ethics in China has to come to grips with all three levels: the individual, organizational and systemic. It is best expressed in Chinese by the now commonly used term *jingji lúnli*, that is, ethics in the economic sphere of life, including and going beyond "business ethics" as "corporate ethics" or "management ethics."

Although it appears premature to assess the emergence of business ethics in China in the last ten or more years, four important features already have become unmistakably clear.

1   Contrary to a belief widely held in Western countries, there is no "ethical vacuum" in China. Confucian ethics, with its 2,500-year history, socialist ethics promulgated since 1949, and many Western and other influences have combined to create a kind of ethical awareness that sharply contrasts with a "value-free" view of business. This does not mean that China has a unified and consistent ethical understanding. Indeed, one can observe not only moral pluralism but also much moral confusion (which, by the way, also characterizes other countries in varying degrees). To put it simply, the question is less whether or not ethics matters and more what kind of ethics should be applied.

2   Given the extremely complex and dynamic transformation process being experienced by China, there is an urgent need to build up formal institutions that are effective, stable, and fair. Of course, institution building is a difficult and lengthy process and cannot succeed without numerous trials and errors. Yet such a buildup is essential from the ethical perspective because institutions and the lack thereof shape, for better or worse, the behavior of individuals and organizations. Those who conceive ethics in only personal terms have difficulty recognizing the crucial importance of institutional ethics. Well understood, it does not diminish in any way the indispensability of personal ethics.

3   With national economic reform the world of enterprises in China has changed dramatically. Not only have business organizations multiplied and taken on a wide variety of forms; more importantly, they have gradually gained more autonomy and greater freedom. Accordingly, the presuppositions for corporate ethics have been established.

There is no doubt that, for the development of business ethics in China, the roles and responsibilities of business organizations, be they Chinese, joint ventures, or foreign companies, are becoming increasingly important. If, as stated above, a kind of ethical awareness exists in China today, it will be interesting to observe how this impacts the shape of business organizations.

4   Talking about business ethics in China evokes many questions in the West as to whether or not the cultural differences between the two prevent a genuine mutual understanding. Such questioning is part of a necessary and healthy process to neutralize naive assumptions about Chinese attitudes and behavior and to identify real cultural differences. At the same time, to take all cultural differences as insurmountable seems equally naive and unacceptable. Continuous and open communication can certainly reduce the "cultural obstacles" significantly, and cultural diversity does not necessarily mean ethical relativism. The development of business ethics in China needs to address cultural differences and to find a common ethical ground supported by a majority of Chinese and in accord with international standards.

These four essential features form the backdrop against which the following challenges gain a clearer profile.

SUSTAINABLE HUMAN DEVELOPMENT

The overall challenge for China (as for other "developing" and "developed" countries) is striving for "sustainable human development." This means, in a nutshell, "a process of enlarging people's choices," as proposed by the United Nations Development Program in its *Human Development Reports* since 1990 (see, particularly, the report on China, UNDP 1999). It involves the long-term perspective of "sustainability," defined by the World Commission on Development and Environment in 1987 as follows: "to meet the needs of the present without compromising the ability of future generations to meet their own needs." China faces enormous environmental challenges, to a considerable extent because of rampant economic growth and despite fairly advanced environmental laws and regulations. Among the most important problems is the widespread reliance on polluting coal energy, the effects of acid rain, the pollution of Chinese cities, and the waste of energy sources in the building and transportation sectors.

Moreover, the concept of human development has been enriched by Amartya Sen with five types of "real freedoms that people enjoy," namely "political freedoms, economic facilities, social opportunities, transparency guarantees, and protective security" (Sen, 1999). Benchmarked against these freedoms, China has a mixed record. In terms of economic facilities and social opportunities (providing basic healthcare and education to all citizens), China has been widely successful. With regard to political freedoms and transparency guarantees, the record indicates that the country has much catching up to do. This matters not only because these freedoms are important in themselves, but also because they are instrumental in achieving other types of freedom. Protective security also presents a big challenge for China, as the country steadily moves from a centrally planned economy (guaranteeing an "iron bowl" to everybody) to a market economy that needs to be complemented with a social security system. Regarding economic facilities in the future, China has to pursue a policy of sustainable economic growth with equity. It would be myopic to concentrate all economic efforts on production and efficiency while disregarding the distributional side of this process. The reduction of poverty, the containment of income inequality, and the creation of employment on a large scale are imperatives for the survival of the nation. Suffice it to mention that China needs to create approximately 40 million new jobs per year in 2000–20 in order to employ the surplus labor from the agricultural sector (a staggering number compared to the 5–9 million jobs created annually by the modern sector in recent years, with the economy growing at an annual rate of not less than 7 percent; see Pastor, Videla, and He, forthcoming).

A MODERN SYSTEM OF RELATIVELY AUTONOMOUS SOCIAL INSTITUTIONS

In China, personal relations (*guanxi*) have traditionally played a pivotal role in business and other spheres of life. However, with the introduction of the rule of law and a modern market economy that heavily rely on anonymous rules and transactions, the importance of personal relations has been reduced considerably, and respecting institutional requirements without undue influence of personal relations has been a continuous struggle. Moreover, the transition from a centrally planned economy to a market economy involves multiple trends of "separation" or disentanglement: the political sphere and the economic sphere become more distinct entities. A civil sphere with a certain independence from the political and economic sphere is emerging. Within the economic sphere, many different forms of companies have developed. State-owned enterprises and state agencies have changed into "legal persons" and independent enterprises. And ownership rights and management rights are split up. This process of disentanglement, characteristic of "modernization," allows for more autonomy of different social institutions, a better focus on their specific roles, agents, and objectives, and more efficiency and effectiveness in pursuing these multiple purposes. But it also threatens the existing power structure and administrative monopoly, and calls for a common ethical ground and a strong legal framework in order to hold Chinese society together in this process of disentanglement.

It goes without saying that such a transition creates considerable uncertainties and conflicts. What is the proper role of personal relations in modern business? How far can and should the process of institutional disentanglement go? As a matter of fact, as long as personal relations are the decisive factor of decision-making in government and business, the public suffers from a bewildering lack of transparency and understandably becomes more suspicious and distrustful. And as long as social institutions keep being closely entangled (particularly through the "government approval system"), the already rampant problem of corruption expands even further.

WHAT KIND OF COMMON ETHICAL GROUND?

For these (and other) reasons, the quest for a common ethical ground is imperative for the survival and flourishing of business and society in China. As mentioned earlier, China can tap powerful ethical resources (such as Confucianism, socialist ethics, and many Western and other ethical traditions), which should be considered assets rather than liabilities. Moreover, despite the frenzy of searching for a quick profit and worshiping money, there is still a widespread desire for a long-term and balanced perspective, and the five types of "real freedoms that people enjoy" (Sen) can enlighten this quest substantially.

Confucianism, an ethics of virtue (see Cua, 2001), guided by the ethical ideal of a good human life as a whole (*dao*), stresses character formation or personal cultivation of virtues (*de*); first the basic, interdependent virtues of *ren* (love and care for one's fellows), *li* (a set of rules of proper conduct), and *yi* (reasoned judgment concerning the right thing to do); then the dependent virtues of filiality, respectfulness, trustworthiness, and others. It emphasizes the Golden Rule ("What I don't want others to do to me, I do not want to do to others": Confucius, *Analects* 5:12). Like other traditional Chinese approaches to ethics, Confucian ethics is of a communitarian nature. It aims for a well-ordered society based on good government that is responsive to the needs of the people, to issues of wise management of natural resources, and to just distribution of burdens and benefits. Contemporary challenges are: how to come to grips with gender equality, how to apply this virtue ethics to economic and political institutions, and how to fully recognize the importance of the law.

Characteristic of socialist ethics is a strong concern for the interests of society, including "social stability," urged by the Chinese government over the last twenty years. Compared to Confucianism, an important socialist objective has been the advancement of the role of women and gender equality. In order to clarify and promote socialist ethics, the Central Committee of the Communist Party of China issued various key documents on the reform of the economic system (October 1984, November 1993, October 2003) and on ethical and spiritual civilization (October 1996, November 2001). As a case in point, the resolutions of October 1996 vigorously and directly emphasize the crucial role of ethical and cultural progress. They do not speak

of "individual rights," but rather of "the personal legitimate interests of the citizens" which should be fully respected. Since then, it is noteworthy that the discussion about individual rights has intensified in academic and business circles, and there are Chinese companies (though not many) that are committed to respecting and promoting the human rights of their employees.

The third set of ethical resources available to the Chinese are derived from other cultures, and an overview, limited to Western resources, will be even sketchier than the previous discussion of China's internal resources, since it cannot account for the ethical thoughts offered by Japan, India, and other countries. A major contribution of the West is certainly the notion of basic individual freedoms and rights, which embody an essential part of human dignity and should be incorporated in and respected by any social institution. Another important value is transparency based on a modern system of relatively autonomous social institutions. It is an indispensable condition for building and maintaining the confidence needed for the functioning of any complex society. In addition, there is a basic assumption, though often ignored, that ethical responsibility presupposes freedom, and the bigger the space of freedom of the moral actor, the greater is his or her ethical responsibility. If the market economy is not just a "mechanism," but a place in which human freedom is at stake, ethics, epitomized in responsibility, must play a central role in the market economy. Similar to other resources, caveats are in order. The emphasis on individual rights does not necessarily imply an individualistic philosophy, but can be supported by a communitarian view as well. And the "value-free" view of business and economics, widely advocated in the West, avoids addressing tough questions about a common ethical ground and appears unable to take up this crucial challenge for business ethics in China.

MORE SPECIFIC CHALLENGES

As China is becoming the manufacturing powerhouse of the world, not only the quality of the goods but also the quality of the working conditions is increasingly coming under scrutiny (see Santoro, 2000) and the treatment of employees – including recruitment, training, promotion, and layoffs – needs serious ethical examination. The reform of the banking and financial sector is a top priority. It can learn from recent developments in the USA and should promote, as an important objective, professional ethics in accountancy and financial services. As they gain more autonomy and freedom, companies in China (including state-owned enterprises) must bear more moral responsibility. Increasingly exposed to public criticism, they have to establish and live up to high standards of corporate governance and improve their cultures in ethical terms as well. Multiple experiences with business leaders, ranging from the scandalous to the exemplary, have made the question of ethical leadership a hotly debated issue. On top of these and other challenges, China faces globalization. It has to speed up and strengthen its reform to adjust itself to international technical, legal, and ethical standards. At the same time, as a major economic power, it is expected to play a constructive and responsible part in shaping globalization. (For an early report on business ethics in China, see Lu 1997; for a recent discussion on major issues, see Lu and Enderle, 2004.)

Bibliography

Cua, A. S. (2001). Confucian ethics. In L. C. Becker and C. B. Becker (eds.), *Encyclopedia of Ethics*, 2nd edn. New York: Routledge, 287–95.

Enderle, G. (2003). Business ethics. In N. Bunnin and E. P. Tsui-James (eds.), *The Blackwell Companion to Philosophy*, 2nd edn. Oxford: Blackwell, 531–51.

Lu Xiaohe (1997). Business ethics in China. *Journal of Business Ethics*, October, 1509–18.

Lu Xiaohe and Enderle, G. (2004). *Developing Business Ethics in China*. Notre Dame, IN: University of Notre Dame Press. (In Chinese: Shanghai Academy of Social Sciences Press, Shanghai, 2003.)

Pastor, A., Videla, P., and He, W. (forthcoming). *China and the WTO: How Much Truth Is There in the Threat Theory?*

Santoro, M. (2000). *Profits and Principles: Global Capitalism and Human Rights in China*. Ithaca, NY: Cornell University Press.

Sen, A. (1999). *Development as Freedom*. New York: Knopf.

UNDP (1999). *The China Human Development Report*. United Nations Development Program, China. New York: Oxford University Press.

codes of ethics

Leo V. Ryan

(Also called codes of conduct or professional codes): statements of behavioral expectations and ideals common to various groups which may be general or specific; aspirational, educational or regulatory; prescriptive or proscriptive; usually developed to affirm organizational goals and ideals stressing adherence to legal, moral, cultural, and ethical standards and relating them to constituencies served. Codes usually combine both philosophical and the practical elements.

Codes also relate to value statements and credos. Value statements expand mission statements and describe how these ideals influence organizational performance (e.g., the Golden Rule). A credo describes ethical responsibilities to shareholders (e.g., the Johnson and Johnson Credo).

Codes present detailed information on organizational moral values and ethical policies, frequently designed to influence personal behavior and to promote positive interpersonal relationships. Codes are acknowledged as the primary means of institutionalizing ethics into the culture, religion, professions, learned societies, and in domestic and international corporations.

Historically, the Code of Hammurabi contained almost 300 paragraphs of rules governing business, moral, and social life reaching back into the third millennium BC, to the earlier Codes of UrNammu (ca. 2060–2043 BC), the Code of Lipit-Ishtar (ca. 1983–1733 BC), and the Code of Eshnunnia (ca. 1950 BC). These codes were compilations of customs, laws, and rules of ancient Mesopotamia, going back to Sumerian times.

The 1993 Centennial Parliament of the World's Religions adopted a *Declaration Toward a Global Ethic* signed by fourteen world religions. The Declaration promotes a universal Code of Ethics to augment, neither to diminish nor replace, the ethical codes defined by the Torah (Jewish), the New Testament (Christian), the Qur'an (Muslim), the Bhagavad-Gita (Hindu), and the Discourses of Buddha (Confucian). Also in 1993, a "Code of Ethics in International Business" was developed by Christian, Muslim, and Jewish business, government, and religious leaders meeting in Amman, Jordan.

Universal codes of conduct have been developed and promoted by the United Nations, by various UN agencies, and by governmental and intergovernmental bodies. Codes of conduct are essential elements of the historically recognized professions (medicine, law, and clergy). Most learned societies, corporations, and trade associations have adopted codes, and increasingly non-governmental organizations (NGOs), grassroots organizations (GROs), and grassroots support organizations (GRSOs) have also developed codes of conduct.

William Frederick identified six "landmark multilateral international codes developed from 1948–1998." They were:

1 UN Declaration of Human Rights (1948)
2 European Convention on Human Rights (1950)
3 Helsinki Final Act (1975)
4 Organization for Economic Cooperation and Development (OEDC) Guidelines for Multinational Enterprises (1977)
5 International Labor Office (ILO) Tripartite Declaration (1977)
6 UN Code of Conduct on Transnational Corporations (1972–1990)

(Williams, 2000: 173)

The UN initiative promoting codes began in 1977 with the establishment of the UN Commission on Transnational Corporations (UNCTC), with an initial mandate to give "highest priority" to drafting a "Code of Conduct for Transnational Corporations." In 1976 the UN Secretariat presented a report on *Transnational Corporations: Issues Involved in the Formulation of a Code of Conduct.* The final draft, introduced in 1991, took 14 years to develop, which illustrates the complexity of achieving code consensus among corporations and NGOs. The draft had yet to be adopted by the UN in 2003 (www.unglobalcompact.org).

Even before the UN initiative, the American Management Association (AMA) analyzed and promoted corporate "creeds" and "credos" (1958). The Conference Board (1987) found 76 percent of the 300 major corporations surveyed, developed or had codes before 1984. The Business Road Table (1988) published "Corporate Ethics: A Prime Business Asset." A 1992 study showed 93 percent of the 800 Company *Forbes 500* firms had codes of ethics, while 43 percent had credos and 65 percent had value statements.

Corporate ethical crises increase the demand for codes. The 1958–61 Justice Department investigation of the electrical industry antitrust practices prompted Secretary of Commerce Luther H. Hodges to establish the Business Ethics Advisory Council (1961). The 1973–6 SEC investigations of defense contractors for domestic and foreign bribery led to the Foreign Corrupt Practices Act (FCPA) in 1977. Events around Michael Milken and Ivan Boesky in the 1980s activated interest in codes governing security regulations. The Enron, Arthur Andersen, WorldCom, and Martha Stewart scandals of 2002–3 prompted the Sarbanes-Oxley Corporate Responsibility Act (2002), which focuses on corporate conduct and governance. Such events heightened interest in ethical codes and hastened their adoption or revision by domestic and international corporations.

The Caux Roundtable (CRT) was founded in 1986 by senior business executives from Japan, Europe, and North America. Initially, they organized a meeting in Caux, Switzerland, to explore ways to lessen trade tensions but, by 1992, CRT realized that moral and ethical principles were essential for efficient global business. Earlier Minneapolis-St. Paul business leaders established the Minnesota Center for Corporate Responsibility (MCCR) (1976) and by 1991 had adopted "Minnesota Principles: Toward an Ethical Basis for Global Business." The CRT discovered that MCCR had already designed a code; after two CRT–MCCR meetings, CRT adopted the Minnesota Code, incorporating their Preamble verbatim. "The Caux Principles for Business Behavior for a Better World" was launched in July 1994. The Caux Principles are widely accepted by business because knowledgeable business executives participated in writing the code (www.cauxroundtable.org).

The Interfaith Center for Corporate Responsibility (ICCR) developed between 1995 and 1998 "Global Corporate Responsibility: Benchmarks for Measuring Business Performance." The ICCR Principles incorporated eleven additional codes as appendices.

The Reverend Leon Sullivan, concerned about developments in South Africa, enlisted a small group of business executives to help develop the document "Principles of US Firms with Affiliates in the Republic of South Africa." The draft document (December 1976) enunciated six principles governing business relations with South Africa. By March 1987 the Sullivan Principles were launched with twelve corporate signatories. "The Global Sullivan Principles" are among the most widely known codes addressing external business practices in a particular country. The McBride Principles for Ireland are another. Another, "The International Code of Ethics for Canadian Business," was developed jointly by the Ministries of Foreign Affairs and International Trade (September 1977).

The International Chamber of Commerce (ICC) in 1991 published "The Business Charter for Sustainable Development." "The Code of Best Practice," popularly called the Cadbury Code after the chairman, was produced by the Committee on Financial Aspects of Corporate Governance (UK) (1992). The Coalition for Environmentally Responsible Economics, representing investors and four environmentally concerned NGOs, reacting to the Alaska Exxon oil spill at Valdez, in 1992 devised the Ceres Principles, initially called Valdez Principles. General Motors adopted the Ceres Principles (1994), as did various British companies. Both the Sullivan and Ceres Principles were initially rejected as radical and unrealistic, but subsequent revisions, executive involvement, and sponsor education prompted their eventual acceptance and adoption.

Multiple governments and NGOs have devised codes with minimal success, due to difficulties in monitoring and meaningful enforcement mechanisms. Individual corporate codes have been more successful because of more immediate control over enforcement. Effective codes require precise drafting, specific focus, a monitoring system, and a process for effective enforcement. Equally essential are a critical mass of persons committed to systemic change, who have the capacity to effect change.

Enforcement of codes presumes promulgation, implementation, and incorporation into the system to ensure compliance. Advocates and critics agree that code enforcement often fails because of inadequate communication, inconsistent implementation, and weak systems of enforcement. Complying with the "spirit of the code" is often too general and sporadic; complying with the "letter of the law" too legalistic and stultifying. Because codes mix ideals, rules, protocols, laws, and etiquette, enforcement often allows various interpretations, suffers the risk of unequal application, and potentially results in discrimination and injustice. Internal code compliance involves supervision, ethics training, ethics officers or ombudsmen, and review panels. External compliance involves audits, government regulation and enforcement, and the courts.

Only cooperatively developed, carefully articulated, clearly understood, widely promulgated, and sympathetically enforced codes preserve the individual conscience, promote the ethical environment, and permit the code to be efficacious – whether in the corporate or public sector.

Future codes will continue to address company authority, employee rights and obligations, and introduce more specific stakeholder references, with increasing emphasis on accountability, consumer sovereignty, corporate citizenship, corporate social responsibility, transparency, globalization, environmental protection, and emerging public-interest areas. Codes are recognized as only one aspect of a larger system of institutional efforts directed to developing and promoting an ethical environment.

Bibliography

Donaldson, T. (1989). *The Ethics of International Business.* New York: Oxford University Press.

Interfaith Declaration (1993). "A Code of Ethics on International Business for Christians, Muslims and Jews." Amman, Jordan.

Küng, H. and Kuschel, K.-J. (eds.) (1993). *A Global Ethic: Declaration of the Parliament of the World's Regions.* New York: Continuum.

Manley, W. W., II (1992). *Good Business Practice: Corporate Codes of Conduct.* London: Routledge.

Messick, D. M. and Tenbrunsel, A. (eds.) (1996). *Codes of Conduct: Behavioral Research into Business Ethics.* New York: Russell Sage Foundation.

Murphy, P. E. (1998). *Eighty Exemplary Ethics Statements.* Notre Dame, IN: University of Notre Dame Press.

Thompson, S. (1958). *Management Creeds and Philosophies,* Research Study 32. New York: American Management Association.

United Nations Economic and Social Council (1976). *Transnational Corporations: Issues Involved in the Formation of a Code of Conduct.* New York: United Nations, E/C, 10/17.

Walton, C. C. and Cleveland, F. W., Jr. (1964). *Corporations on Trial: The Electric Cases.* Belmont, CA: Wadsworth.

Welby, S. (1997). *Codes of Ethics and International Business.* London: Institute of Business Ethics.

Williams, O. F. (ed.) (2000). *Global Codes of Conduct: An Idea Whose Time Has Come.* Notre Dame, IN: University of Notre Dame Press.

coercion

Alan Wertheimer

is one of a family of concepts such as duress and force. It refers to one method by which one person can motivate another to do something. We typically say that A coerces B to do X when A gets B to do something by threatening to harm B or by making B worse off in case B should not do X. We also often say that coercion interferes with one's freedom or autonomy, that if B is coerced into doing X (or does X under duress), then B's action is involuntary.

Roughly speaking, there are two philosophical questions about coercion: (1) what *counts* as coercion? (2) when are individuals or the state *justified* in using coercion? The second question is, of course, a central problem of political philosophy (*see* LIBERTY). This entry focuses on (1).

Understanding what counts as coercion is important for several reasons. First, we do not hold individuals responsible for actions that are the products of coercion. A coerced promise or contract is neither morally nor legally binding; a defendant is not guilty if he was coerced into performing a crime. Second, various social practices such as surrogate motherhood, sales of bodily parts, and the volunteer army, have been criticized on the grounds that poverty effectively coerces people into such an arrangement. Third, capitalist theory assumes that market transactions are free, even if they are made against a background of economic necessity. What sort of coercion invalidates an agreement or excuses wrongdoing or interferes with one's liberty? To answer these questions, we must know what counts as coercion.

Consider three examples: (1) Gunman says to Victim: "Your money or your life." Victim turns over his wallet. (2) Prosecutor says to Defendant: "Plead guilty to manslaughter or I will convict you on a murder charge." Defendant pleads guilty. (3) Doctor says to Patient: "Consent to amputation or you will die of gangrene." Patient consents (*see* CONSENT). We think that Victim is coerced but that Defendant and Patient are not. Are we right? Why?

One view maintains that coercion is essentially *empirical*. On this view, A coerces B because A's threat puts B under great psychic pressure or leaves B with no other rational choice. But this view has trouble explaining why Victim is coerced but Defendant and Patient are not. A second view maintains that coercion is essentially moralized. On this view, one is coerced only when one's rights are violated, even if one has "no choice" but to agree. This view is compatible with our intuitions about the cases, but how do rights violations relate to coercion?

On the standard view, threats coerce and offers do not. A makes a *threat* when B will be *worse off* than in some relevant baseline position if B does not accept A's proposal. A makes an *offer* when B will be *better off* than in some relevant baseline position if B accepts A's proposal. The key to coercion is to establish B's baseline. In *Coercion* (1987) I argue that a moral tenet for B's baseline can explain why Gunman threatens Victim, but Prosecutor and Doctor both make offers. Only Gunman proposes to violate a right if the proposal is not accepted.

Interestingly, some coercive proposals do not actually coerce. If Gunman says to Victim, "Kill C or I will break your arm," Victim cannot claim to have been coerced into killing C. An adequate account of coercion will explain why this is so. It will also consider these questions: Are there coercive *offers*? Can one be coerced by background conditions? Are coerced actions involuntary?

Questions as to what constitutes coercion can arise within several different business contexts. Within the workplace, we may want to know when sexual harassment is coercive. If a supervisor offers an employee a promotion she would not otherwise receive if she has sexual relations with him, has she been coerced? (Note that sexual harassment can be seriously wrong even when it is not coercive.) With respect to market transactions, some people have argued that one is coerced into purchasing a drug if one would die without it, or that one can be coerced into employment if one's only alternative is a life of desperation.

Bibliography

Frankfurt, H. (1973). Coercion and moral responsibility. In T. Honderich (ed.), *Essays on Freedom of Action*. London: Routledge and Kegan Paul, 65–8.

Nozick, R. (1969). Coercion. In S. Morgenbesser, P. Suppes, and M. White (eds.), *Philosophy, Science and Method*. New York: St. Martins Press, 440–72.

Pennock, J. R. and Chapman, J. (eds.) (1972). *Nomos XIV: Coercion*. New York: Aldine-Atherton.

Wertheimer, A. (1987). *Coercion*. Princeton, NJ: Princeton University Press.

Wertheimer, A. (1992). Coercion. In L. C. Becker and C. B. Becker (eds.), *Encyclopedia of Ethics*. New York: Garland, 172–5.

Zimmerman, D. (1981). Coercive wage offers. *Philosophy and Public Affairs*, 10, 121–45.

collective bargaining

Frederick R. Post

Legally mandated group bargaining between an employer, or employers, and organized employees seeking to reach an agreement on wages, hours, and other working conditions. Unlike other bargaining which allows either party to freely terminate the negotiation, the process of collective bargaining is legally regulated both substantively as to work-related issues discussed and procedurally as to both timetable and process of bargaining, the purpose of which is to pressure the parties to reach a collective bargaining agreement.

The US National Labor Relations Act of 1935, usually called the Wagner Act, ensures the right of employees to form unions and to negotiate as a group with employers. Absent such legal compulsion, there would be no collective bargaining. The employer would be free to establish and change conditions of employment unilaterally at will, based solely on its conceptions of fairness, attitudes toward maximizing of profit and social responsibility, and knowledge of current labor-market condi-

tions (Taylor and Whitney, 1987). With the advent of an organized workforce, usually represented by an outside labor union, such unilateral employer action ceases and is replaced by a joint determination of employment conditions.

This unique regulated group bargaining replaces the legal right of individual freedom of contract in the workplace when employees conclude it is a worthless right due to the inordinate imbalance of power between an individual employee and an employer. The process seeks to resolve a series of ethical issues relating to fairness, power sharing, and profit sharing previously left to the employer's sole discretion. While collective bargaining provides a mechanism for resolving such issues, the process generates additional ethical issues as the parties seek victory through the assertion of power while complying with the several "good faith" bargaining duties required by law.

As an adversarial process, the efforts of the parties are directed solely toward concluding an agreement most favorable to their self-interest based exclusively on their relative bargaining power. Since the remedies for illegal bargaining are minimal, the parties are encouraged to manipulate and exploit each other based upon self-interest (Post, 1990). Typical unethical behaviors practiced during collective bargaining include deception, bluffing, and lying. Such practices usually produce sub-optimal agreements characterized by an undermining of the moral value of truth and honesty. This promotes distrust throughout the organization, the development of confused, divided loyalties, the ignoring of broader stakeholder interests, the frustration of efforts to encourage team and quality commitments. An over-emphasis on bargaining over extrinsic (wages, fringes, seniority) job conditions is often at the expense of higher level intrinsic (job responsibility, job content, recognition) job conditions (Post, 1990). Such behaviors are cited as part of the reason for the alleged shortcomings of American business to compete effectively in the global marketplace (Dertouzos et al., 1989; Kochan, Katz, and McKersie, 1986).

Carson, Wokutch, and Murrmann (1982) argue that to the extent there are unethical behaviors practiced in collective bargaining, they are the result of preexisting dispositions of the bargainers. Post (1990) disagrees and asserts that the legal environment of collective bargaining dictates that the parties act unethically to win. Bowie (1985) proposes a "family model" to effectuate attitude change when bargaining. Post (1990) proposes the "collaborative collective bargaining" process as a moral approach to labor negotiations and later reports on its implementation via an in-depth case study (Post, 1994).

Bibliography

Bowie, N. (1985). Should collective bargaining and labor relations be less adversarial? *Journal of Business Ethics*, **4**, 283–91.

Carson, T., Wokutch, R., and Murrmann, K. (1982). Bluffing in labor negotiations: Legal and ethical issues. *Journal of Business Ethics*, **1**, 13–22.

Dertouzos, M., Lester, R., Solow, R., and the MIT Commission on Industrial Productivity (1989). *Regaining the Competitive Advantage*. Boston, MA: Houghton Mifflin.

Kochan, T., Katz, H., and McKersie, R. (1986). *The Transformation of American Industrial Relations*. New York: Basic Books.

Post, F. (1990). Collaborative collective bargaining: Toward an ethically defensible approach to labor negotiations. *Journal of Business Ethics*, **9**, 495–508.

Post, F. (1994). Use of the collaborative collective bargaining process in labor negotiations. *International Journal of Conflict Management*, **5**, 34–61.

Taylor, B. and Whitney, F. (1987). *Labor Relations Law*. Englewood Cliffs, NJ: Prentice-Hall.

collective responsibility

J. Angelo Corlett

A collective is any collection of persons and/or non-persons which constitutes a diversified whole. Collectives vary in structure, from highly organized conglomerates such as large corporations, universities, and the like, to random collectives such as mobs having minimal or no organizational structure. The problem of collective responsibility concerns the possibility of such collectives being responsible agents.

"Responsibility" is an ambiguous term, with several senses. There are duty, blame, praise, causal, and liability senses of "responsibility," each of which might be construed either legally

or morally (Corlett, 1992). There are also different ways in which a collective might be responsible: retrospectively, for the future, or *tout court* (Feinberg, 1988–9). In the context of moral philosophy, however, discussion has focused on the extent to which collectives of certain kinds (Corlett, 1992; French, 1984; Held, 1970; May, 1987) are (French, 1984; May, 1987) or could be (Corlett, 1992) properly deemed retrospectively and morally liable for an untoward action, event, or state of affairs. Such collective liability is discussed in contexts of racism (McGary, 1986), corporate crimes or torts (Corlett, 1988a, 1988b; French, 1984, 1992; May, 1987; Wilkins, 1992), military groups (French, 1972; Wilkins, 1992), random collectives (Held, 1970; May, 1987), the law in general (Feinberg, 1970), and even in more general terms (Corlett, 1992; French, 1991, 1992; May, 1992; Mellema, 1988). Focus in the present article is on collective, retrospective, moral liability responsibility for wrongdoings.

There are at least two opposing views on collective moral responsibility, each founded on certain metaphysical presuppositions. *Methodological individualism* states that to attribute moral properties to collectives is to mistake what are fundamentally and irreducibly properties of individuals for collective ones. That is, language about collective moral properties is reducible to the language of individual relations. More precisely, "Social processes and events should be explained by being deduced from (a) principles governing the behavior of participating individuals, and (b) descriptions of their situations" (Watkins, 1973). This position is dubbed "strong analytic individualism," and its content is described in the following way: "everyday collectivity concepts are analyzable without remainder in terms of concepts other than collectivity concepts, in particular, in terms of the concept of an individual person, his goals, beliefs, and so on" (Gilbert, 1989). As a species of this sort of position, *moral responsibility individualism* holds that it is unjustified to ascribe moral responsibility to collectives because statements about collective moral responsibility are reducible to those of morally responsible individual agents within the collective (Lewis, 1948). From this, it is argued, talk of collective moral responsibility is meaningless. There are pure ontological versions of individualism, but I am here concerned with its reductionist counterpart.

Just what does the moral responsibility individualist mean when she argues that collective moral responsibility statements are reducible to those of individual moral responsibility? "Reducible" seems to mean something like "linguistically reducible" or "redescribable in terms of." In other words, the moral responsibility individualist argues that all statements of collective moral responsibility are linguistically redescribable in terms of those individuals (being members of the collective) who are morally responsible for something. But what does this mean? "Linguistic reducibility" means that collective moral responsibility statements are redescribable, without loss of cognitive meaning, in terms of individual moral responsibility statements.

Notice, however, for what the reductionist (individualist) seems to argue. She is claiming that all statements of collective moral responsibility are linguistically redescribable, without loss of cognitive meaning, to statements of individual moral responsibility. Yet for individualism to succeed it must be shown that collective moral responsibility ascriptions are *unreasonable* or *unjustified*. But from the supposition that collective moral responsibility statements are completely redescribable in terms of individual moral responsibility, it does *not* logically follow that collective moral responsibility ascriptions are unreasonable or unjustified.

The reason for this is because the successful redescription of collective moral responsibility statements provides one with an *identity* relation between the collectivist statements on the one hand, and the individualist ones on the other hand. This means that the set of collective moral responsibility statements being redescribed or "reduced" is logically equivalent to the set of individual statements which redescribe it. Given Gottlob Frege's law of the substitutivity of co-referential terms or expressions in propositional attitude contexts ("If a declarative sentence S has the very same cognitive information content as a declarative sentence S′ then S is informative ('contains an extension of our knowledge') if and only if S′ is (does)" (Frege, 1984; Salmon, 1986)), equivalent expressions retain truth and are substitutable for one another

in *any* propositional attitude context. Thus the belief (or proposition attitude) that "The Exxon Corporation is morally responsible (liable) for the oil spill in Prince William Sound and ought to be severely punished with impunity" is indeed reducible to and redescribable in terms of the moral responsibility and punishability of certain individuals of Exxon at the time of the disaster (perhaps in terms of Exxon's president at the time of the disaster, as well as certain members of the board of directors and higher-level managers who served Exxon at the time of the decisions made which "caused" the incident, etc.). But this hardly shows that *collective* responsibility ascriptions are unreasonable or unjustified. The point here is that the linguistic reducibility of collectivist statements does not affect the *elimination* of the sense or meaningfulness of such language. For if the moral responsibility individualist's reduction preserves truth (and sense), then both the collectivist *and* the individualist statements about moral responsibility share the same truth-value. It would appear, moreover, that the moral responsibility individualist is in fact committed to the very meaning of the statements she seeks to eliminate or render senseless! On what basis, then, would collective moral responsibility claims (at least some of them) be unreasonable or unjustified?

A view which affirms the meaningfulness of collective moral responsibility talk is *moral responsibility collectivism*. This position, in its various forms, is well represented (Bates, 1971; Cooper, 1968; Corlett, 1992; French, 1984; Held, 1970; May, 1987, 1992). But the failure of the moral responsibility individualist's reductionism to render senseless collective moral responsibility statements is insufficient reason to infer that the information content of collective moral responsibility language is meaningful. Substance must be provided for such claims. One way to attempt this is by providing conditions which, if satisfied, would make a collective morally liable for a wrongful act, event, or state of affairs.

One condition of collective moral responsibility in the context, for instance, of corporate-collective wrongdoing and harm to others, is that those officially working "for" the corporation *act intentionally* in regard to the wrongdoing. For an agent to act intentionally, she must act according to her beliefs, wants, and desires (Goldman, 1970). To be sure, there are degrees to which agents within a collective might be said to act intentionally and liably concerning a wrongdoing. One might do so in a strong sense, such as when a higher-level manager or the board of directors acts or omits to act in such a way so as to become a contributory cause of the untoward event, act, or state of affairs. There is also a weak sense of intentionality, whereby those in lower-level managerial positions act or omit to act as contributory causes of the wrongdoing. Here a hierarchical notion of the power to effect corporate change is assumed.

The case for collective intentionality has been set forth, defended (French, 1984; May, 1987), and criticized (Corlett, 1988a, 1988b) in various ways. But the way the typical corporation in the United States is organized, few individuals act intentionally. Yet a collective's acting intentionally is crucial for its being legitimately ascribed moral liability.

It would seem, then, that collective moral liability ascriptions are justified to the extent that each and every individual member of the collective has significant power to act intentionally in relation to the specific wrongdoing in question. This might well require the restructuring of the typical US corporation, which is currently structured along the lines of a hierarchical model of organization (Hersey and Blanshard, 1977; Katz and Kahn, 1966). It might very well imply that to legitimately hold collectives liable for wrongdoings (and hence make US capitalism a morally viable economic system which can and does take corrective justice seriously), such entities must resemble something akin to a democratically organized structure. For within such a structure, collectives will be more likely to provide each and every individual with sufficient power to intentionally effect change within the organization to make collective liability ascriptions less problematic. Under such conditions, it would make much better sense to say of Exxon that it (e.g., the individuals of Exxon) is (are) liable for the oil spill which destroyed Prince William Sound.

There are at least two different ways in which a corporate structure might be democratized: representatively or directly. When a corporation is democratized in a representative manner, a corporation's top managers are elected by its employees to represent the employees on matters of institutional obligations, rights, etc. However, representative corporate democracy provides the employees with insufficient opportunities to significantly determine corporate policy, which in turn affects employees' activities (McMahon, 1989). Thus, directly democratic corporate structures are preferred over less direct ones insofar as the empowerment of all members of the corporation is concerned. This might mean that "some form of co-determination" of corporate policy, "in which boards of directors contain in equal numbers representatives of employees of non-employee investors," is preferable to representative corporate democracy (McMahon, 1989).

However, there is more to collective intentional agency (action or omission) than the empowerment of employees. What is also required is a *publicity condition* which would clearly state to each and every individual that he or she will be held accountable (either personally and/or as a corporate agent) for corporate wrongs to the extent that he or she was an intentional agent concerning them. Currently, no such communication is made to corporate employees in a consistent and unambiguous manner. So it is far from obvious that (in their assuming a position in a corporation) employees willingly or intentionally assume liability for some other individual's action or omission. It is important, then, that the publicity condition is satisfied for collective liability ascriptions to be plausible.

If both a restructuring of US corporations and the empowering of each and every individual within such collectives are effected, then it is less morally problematic to say of an organized, decision-making corporation that *it* can legitimately be held liable for "its" wrongs.

However, collective intentionality is not the only condition requisite for legitimate attributions of collective responsibility. For it is possible that a corporation is democratically structured for intentional action (or inaction, as the case may be), yet lacks a crucial capacity for *voluntariness* which would render it nonresponsible for an untoward event.

To say that a corporation is a voluntary agent means, at the very least, that the corporation "acts freely." This means it is sufficient that a corporation has the capacity to have a higher-order volition concerning an action, event, or state of affairs. In turn, this means that it would be able to "really want" to do what it does, even if it lacks the ability to do otherwise. But acting freely, if it is a condition at all, is but a sufficient condition of voluntariness and moral responsibility (Frankfurt, 1988). And some would argue that the ability to do otherwise is a necessary condition of freedom. There are higher-order compatibilists who argue that the ability to do otherwise is a necessary condition of freedom (Lehrer, 1991), and there are incompatibilists who arrive at the same conclusion (van Inwagen, 1983). In any case, it is clear that in general voluntariness is necessary for an agent's being legitimately held morally liable for wrongdoing. And collective moral responsibility requires voluntariness, which in turn requires at least either the corporate capacity to act freely or the corporate ability to do otherwise.

Not only are collective intentionality and voluntariness required for collective moral responsibility, so too is collective epistemic action. What this means is that a collective, in order to qualify as a morally liable agent concerning a certain untoward action, event, or state of affairs, must have acted knowingly. *Acting knowingly* involves more than an agent's merely believing that such and such is the case in regards to a certain policy and its possible outcomes. It involves, among other things, that agent's being justified in believing certain things about a policy enacted by the agent. Moreover, it involves that agent's duty to reflect on and consider various alternative actions or policies. In short, it involves critical reflection on the part of the agent.

The answer to the question of whether or not collectives are the kinds of agents which qualify as epistemic agents which act knowingly is contingent, at least in part, on the extent to which the collective is directly democratic and solidary, and the extent to which collectives qualify as epistemic agents at all (Corlett, 1991, 1996; Fuller, 1988; Goldman, 1992; Schmitt, 1994). What is clear is that the capacity to act knowingly is requisite for a collective's being legitimately ascribed moral liability.

But even if a collective acts intentionally, voluntarily, and knowingly, there are cases in which these conditions do not jointly suffice for our ascribing to it moral liability. Consider the Schmexxon Corporation, an oil conglomerate with the same strength of assets as Exxon, except that Schmexxon is directly and democratically structured, acts with intent, voluntariness, and knowledge to transport oil by way of Prince William Sound. And, just as with Exxon, a Schmexxon tanker loses thousands of gallons of crude oil into the Sound. Even though Schmexxon (unlike Exxon) takes precautions well beyond what is required by law, and above and beyond what any competing corporation has even considered taking, there was a spill. But it is discovered that the spill was caused by natural disaster of some sort (say, an earthquake sending the tanker crashing into a reef), not the result of human error. So even though Schmexxon acted intentionally, voluntarily, and knowingly in shipping the oil through the Sound, it is not morally liable for the oil spill, though it might be held "strictly liable" by the law for a variety of reasons.

The example of Schmexxon is intended to demonstrate that additional requirements must be satisfied by morally liable agents, namely, guilt and fault. A guilty agent must be "at fault" in doing X for that agent to be morally liable for X. So it is for corporations. Since Schmexxon cannot reasonably be held at fault for the oil spill in question (because it was caused by a natural disaster), it cannot be held morally liable for it. Again, this does not imply that Schmexxon cannot be held *legally* liable for the oil spill. For considerations of social utility might suggest that there is good reason to hold corporations in the oil transport industry strictly (legally) liable for oil spills. In any case, collective *fault* must obtain in order for the corporation to be legitimately construed as being morally liable for the disaster.

Bibliography

Bates, S. (1971). The responsibility of "random collections." *Ethics*, 81, 343–9.

Cooper, D. E. (1968). Collective responsibility. *Philosophy*, 43, 258–68.

Corlett, J. A. (1988a). Corporate responsibility and punishment. *Public Affairs Quarterly*, 2, 1–16.

Corlett, J. A. (1988b). Schefflerian ethics and corporate social responsibility. *Journal of Business Ethics*, 7, 631–8.

Corlett, J. A. (1991). Social epistemology and social cognition. *Social Epistemology*, 5, 135–49.

Corlett, J. A. (1992). *Moral compatibilism: Rights, responsibility, punishment and compensation*. PhD dissertation, University of Arizona.

Corlett, J. A. (1996). *Analyzing Social Knowledge*. Lanham, MD: Rowman and Littlefield.

Feinberg, J. (1970). *Doing and Deserving*. Princeton, NJ: Princeton University Press.

Feinberg, J. (1988–9). "Responsibility for the future" and "responsibility *tout court*." *Philosophy Research Archives*, 14, 73–113.

Frankfurt, H. G. (1988). *The Importance of What We Care About*. Cambridge: Cambridge University Press.

Frege, G. (1984). *Collective Papers on Mathematics, Logic, and Philosophy*, ed. B. McGinnis; trans. M. Black, V. H. Dudman, P. Geatch, H. Kaal, E.-H. W. Kluge, B. McGinnis. Oxford: Blackwell.

French, P. (ed.) (1972). *Individual and Collective Responsibility*. Cambridge: Schenkman.

French, P. (1984). *Collective and Corporate Responsibility*. New York: Columbia University Press.

French, P. (ed.) (1991). *The Spectrum of Responsibility*. New York: St. Martin's Press.

French, P. (1992). *Responsibility Matters*. Lawrence: Kansas University Press.

Fuller, S. (1988). *Social Epistemology*. Bloomington: Indiana University Press.

Gilbert, M. (1989). *On Social Facts*. Princeton, NJ: Princeton University Press.

Goldman, A. (1970). *A Theory of Human Action*. Princeton, NJ: Princeton University Press.

Goldman, A. (1992). *Liaisons*. Cambridge, MA: MIT Press.

Held, V. (1970). Can a random collection of individuals be morally responsible? *Journal of Philosophy*, 67, 471–80.

Hersey, P. and Blanshard, K. H. (1977). *Management of Organizational Behavior: Utilizing Human Resources*. Englewood Cliffs, NJ: Prentice-Hall.

Katz, D. and Kahn, R. L. (1966). *The Social Psychology of Organizations*. New York: John Wiley and Sons.

Lehrer, K. (1991). *Metamind*. Oxford: Oxford University Press.

Lewis, H. D. (1948). Collective responsibility. *Philosophy*, 23, 3–18.

McGary, H. (1986). Morality and collective liability. *Journal of Value Inquiry*, 20, 157–65.

McMahon, C. (1989). Managerial authority. *Ethics*, 100, 33–53.

May, L. (1987). *The Morality of Groups*. Notre Dame: Notre Dame University Press.

May, L. (1992). *Sharing Responsibility*. Chicago: University of Chicago Press.

Mellema, G. (1988). *Individuals, Groups, and Shared Moral Responsibility*. New York: Peter Lang.

Salmon, N. (1986). *Frege's Puzzle*. Cambridge, MA: MIT Press.

Schmitt, F. (ed.) (1994). *Socialising Epistemology*. Lanham, MD: Rowman and Littlefield.

Synthese (1987). Issue devoted to social epistemology, guest editor F. Schmitt.

van Inwagen, P. (1983). *An Essay on Free Will*. Oxford: Oxford University Press.

Watkins, J. W. N. (1973). Ideal types and historical explanation. In A. Ryan (ed.), *The Philosophy of Social Explanation*. Oxford: Oxford University Press.

Wilkins, B. (1992). *Terrorism and Collective Responsibility*. London: Routledge.

communitarianism

Daniel A. Bell

A theory that contends that the individual develops and can flourish morally and politically only within the context of a community. Modern-day communitarianism began in the upper reaches of Anglo-American academia in the form of a critical reaction to John Rawls's landmark book of 1971, *A Theory of Justice*. Drawing primarily upon the insights of Aristotle and Hegel, political theorists such as Alasdair MacIntyre (1984), Michael Sandel (1981), and Charles Taylor (1985) disputed Rawls's assumption that the principal task of government is to secure the liberties and economic resources individuals need to lead freely chosen lives.

These critics of Rawlsian liberalism identified two main problems with this approach. First, Sandel among others argued that Rawlsian liberalism rests on an overly individualistic conception of the self. Whereas Rawls argues that we have a supreme interest in shaping, pursuing, and revising our own life plans, he neglects the fact that our selves are often defined or constituted by various communal attachments (e.g., ties to the family or to a religious tradition) so close to us that they can only be set aside at great cost, if at all. Hence, politics should not be concerned solely with securing the conditions for individuals to exercise their powers of choice, as there may also be a need to sustain and promote the social attachments crucial to our sense of well-being and respect.

Second, communitarians have sought to deflate the universal pretensions of liberalism.

Whereas Rawls seemed to present his theory of justice as universally true, critics argued that moral judgment will depend on the language of reasons and the interpretive framework within which agents view their world, that it makes no sense to begin the political enterprise by abstracting from the interpretive dimension of human beliefs, practices, and institutions. And whatever the philosophical appeal of liberal universalism, Michael Walzer (1983) has developed at length the additional argument that *effective* social criticism must derive from and resonate with the habits and traditions of actual people living in specific times and places.

Liberals have of course responded to these criticisms (Rawls, 1993, in particular has cleaned up his theory of individualist and universalist presuppositions), but a growing number are settling on the conclusion that communitarian critics of liberalism may have been motivated not so much by philosophical concerns as by certain pressing *political* concerns, namely, the negative social and psychological effects related to the atomistic tendencies of modern liberal societies. Whatever the soundness of liberal principles, in other words, the fact remains that many communitarians seem worried by a perception that traditional liberal institutions and practices have contributed to, or at least do not seem up to the task of dealing with, such modern phenomena as alienation from the political process, unbridled greed, loneliness, urban crime, and high divorce rates. And given the seriousness of these problems in the United States, it was perhaps inevitable that a "second wave" of 1990s communitarians such as Amitai Etzioni and William Galston would turn to the more practical political terrain of emphasizing social responsibility and promoting policies meant to stem the erosion of communal life in an increasingly fragmented world.

Such "political" communitarians blame both the left and the right for our current malaise. The political left is chastised not just for supporting welfare rights economically unsustainable in an era of slow growth and aging populations, but also for shifting power away from local communities and democratic institutions and toward centralized bureaucratic structures better equipped to administer the fair and equal distribution of benefits, thus leading to a growing sense of powerlessness and alienation from the political process. Moreover, the modern welfare state with its universalizing logic of rights and entitlements has undermined family and social ties in civil society by rendering superfluous obligations to communities, by actively discouraging private efforts to help others (e.g., union rules and strict regulations in Sweden prevent parents from participating voluntarily in the governance of the daycare centers to which they send their children), and even by providing incentives that discourage the formation of families (e.g., welfare payments are cut off in most American states if a recipient marries a working person) and encourage the break-up of families (e.g., no-fault divorce in the US is often financially rewarding for the non-custodial parent, usually the father).

Libertarian solutions favored by the political right have contributed even more directly to the erosion of social responsibilities and valued forms of communal life, particularly in Britain and the US. Far from producing beneficial communal consequences, the "invisible hand" of unregulated free-market capitalism undermines the family (e.g., few corporations provide enough leave to parents of newborn children), disrupts local communities (e.g., following plant closings or the shifting of corporate headquarters), and corrupts the political process (e.g., since the mid-1970s, special economic interests in the US have gained more power by drawing on political action committees to fund political representatives, with the consequence that representatives dependent on PAC money for their political survival no longer represent the community at large). Moreover, the valorization of greed in the Thatcher/Reagan era justified the extension of instrumental considerations governing relationships in the marketplace into spheres previously informed by a sense of uncalculated reciprocity and civic obligation.

More specifically in the American context, communitarians such as Mary Ann Glendon (1991) indict a new version of rights discourse that has achieved dominance of late. Whereas the assertion of rights was once confined to matters of essential human interest, a strident rights rhetoric has colonized contemporary political discourse, thus leaving little room for reasoned discussion and compromise, justifying the neglect of social responsibilities without which a society could not function, and ultimately weakening all appeals to rights by devaluing the really important ones.

To remedy this imbalance between rights and responsibilities, "political" communitarians propose a moratorium on the manufacture of new rights and changes to our "habits of the heart" away from exclusive focus on personal fulfillment and toward concern with bolstering families, schools, neighborhoods, and national political life, changes to be supported and reinforced by certain public policies.

While communitarians generally emphasize that changes ought to be made in the context of basic civil and political liberties (e.g., see Etzioni, 1993, part II), critics may nonetheless worry that communitarians are embarking on a slippery slope to authoritarianism. Others may worry that marginalized groups demanding new rights (e.g., homosexual couples seeking the right to legally sanctioned marriage) will be paying the price for the excesses of others if the communitarian proposal to declare a moratorium on the minting of new rights is put into effect. Most serious from the standpoint of those generally sympathetic to communitarian aspirations, however, is the worry that some communitarian ideals may conflict if translated into practice. Etzioni, for example, argues for a whole host of pro-family measures: mothers and fathers should devote more time and energy to parenting (in view of the fact that most childcare centers do a poor job of caring for children), labor unions and employers ought to make it easier for parents to work at home, and the government should force corporations to provide six months of paid leave and another year and a half of unpaid leave. The combined effect of these "changes of heart" and public policies in all likelihood would be to make "citizens" into largely private, family-centered persons.

Yet Etzioni also argues that the American political system is corrupt to the core, concluding that only extensive involvement in public affairs by virtuous citizens can remedy the situation: "once citizens are informed, they must make it their civic duty to *organize others* locally,

regionally, and nationally to act on their understanding of what it takes to clean up public life in America" (1993: 244). But few can afford sufficient time and energy to devote themselves fully to family life and public affairs, and favoring one ideal is most likely to erode the other. Just as liberals sometimes have to choose between ideals (e.g., freedom and equality) that come into conflict with one another if a serious effort is made to realize any one of them fully, so communitarians may have to make some hard choices between valued forms of communal life.

Bibliography

Bell, D. A. (1993). *Communitarianism and Its Critics.* Oxford: Clarendon Press.

Etzioni, A. (1993). *The Spirit of Community: Rights, Responsibilities, and the Communitarian Agenda.* New York: Crown. (Written primarily for the general public.)

Galston, W. A. (1991). *Liberal Purposes: Goods, Virtues, and Diversity in the Liberal State.* Cambridge: Cambridge University Press.

Glendon, M. A. (1991). *Rights Talk: The Impoverishment of Political Discourse.* New York: Free Press.

MacIntyre. A. (1984). *After Virtue*, 2nd edn. Notre Dame, IN: University of Notre Dame Press.

Rawls, J. (1971). *A Theory of Justice.* Cambridge, MA: Harvard University Press.

Rawls, J. (1993). *Political Liberalism.* New York: Columbia University Press.

Sandel, M. (1981). *Liberalism and the Limits of Justice.* Cambridge: Cambridge University Press.

Taylor, C. (1985). *Philosophy and the Human Sciences: Philosophical Papers, 2.* Cambridge: Cambridge University Press.

Walzer, M. (1983). *Spheres of Justice: A Defence of Pluralism and Equality.* Oxford: Blackwell.

comparable worth

John R. Boatright

is a strategy for raising wages in traditionally female job categories by making the pay of women in such jobs equal to the earnings of men in comparable male-dominated lines of work.

The implementation of comparable worth begins with a *comparable-worth study*, in which a *job evaluation* is conducted to determine the skill, effort, responsibility, and working conditions of each job category in a place of employment. These factors are assigned point values, and the resulting sums are used to rank the value of all jobs to an employer. The study then identifies wage disparities among job categories with the same or a similar number of points, and a *comparable-worth policy* is adopted that adjusts the pay of job categories so as to reduce or eliminate the wage disparities.

Comparable worth assumes that disparities in income between men and women are due to sex-segregated job categories and that women's jobs have been systematically undervalued by the market. Other remedies for sex discrimination, such as the US Equal Pay Act of 1963 and Title VII of the 1964 US Civil Rights Act, do not address the wage disparities that result from the undervaluing of work done by women. In particular, removing barriers to the entry of women into traditionally male job categories so as to reduce job segregation – a strategy known as *alignment* – does not increase the wages of women in female-dominated areas.

Supporters of comparable worth generally accept the standard economic view that the value of a job is the price of a worker's productivity in a competitive labor market. Insofar as productivity is a function of skill, effort, responsibility, and working conditions, jobs that are comparable in these respects would be paid the same in a market free of discrimination. Alternatively, the lower pay of women in comparable female-dominated job categories can be assumed to result from discrimination and not lower productivity. Thus, comparable worth is offered not as an alternative to the market but as a means of identifying and correcting the distorting effects of discrimination on an otherwise free-market economy.

Comparable worth has been adopted in the United States by some municipalities, counties, and states for public-sector employees, but it has been largely rejected on the federal level. Elsewhere in the world, Australia and Canada have adopted comparable-worth policies that apply to both the public and private sectors. US courts have ruled that the failure to pay the same wages for comparable work is not a violation of law, except in cases where the intent to discriminate can be proved. Virtually no US business firms have adopted comparable-worth policies, although the widespread use of job evaluation to set wages and the efforts of corporations to comply with discrimination law have resulted in some reduction of wage disparities between male- and female-dominated job categories.

The prevalence of sex-segregated job categories and the lower wages of women in traditionally female jobs are well-documented features of the workplace, but whether these are due to discrimination is widely disputed. Many economists argue that the wage disparities between men and women can be explained by two models of occupational choice: (1) the human capital model, which holds that women choose not to acquire the knowledge and skills and to make the sacrifices that would increase their value to employers; and (2) the model of compensating differentials, according to which women, in choosing jobs, express preferences for clean, safe working conditions and other desirable features over higher pay. Critics counter that women invest less in their own human capital and prefer certain kinds of work because of discriminatory forces in the socialization process. Women may also rationally choose to invest less in themselves if their human capital is worth less in a labor market that discriminates against them. The available evidence suggests that after controlling for the variables of human capital and compensating differentials, some wage disparities still exist as a result of discrimination.

One objection to comparable worth is that job evaluation is inherently subjective and arbitrary. Studies have revealed considerable variation in evaluators' judgments of the relevant features of jobs and the number of points assigned to them. The judgments of evaluators tend, in particular, to reflect the prevailing status and pay of jobs, thereby ratifying existing patterns of discrimination. Scientifically designed, statistically reliable methods for job evaluation are available, however. Experts in the field recommend that decisions be made by consensus among groups of people who are familiar with the jobs being evaluated. Job evaluation methods can also be validated by applying them to male-dominated job categories and comparing the predicted wages with those actually earned.

Opponents of comparable worth also argue that ignoring market forces in setting wages would produce an inefficient allocation of labor with a resultant lowering of productivity. Comparable-worth policies are apt to include complex administrative structures that would further reduce productivity by increasing the involvement of government in business. This argument is criticized, however, for ignoring the extent to which the personnel practices in both government and business do not conform to the market ideal. Employers in the public sector have long used comparable-worth studies in order to match the wages of private-sector employees. And private-sector employers already use job evaluation extensively as a rational means for setting wages for the multitude of jobs in large organizations where individual productivity is difficult to measure. Comparable worth, according to its supporters, would not be a substantial departure from the existing labor market.

Comparable worth addresses a serious problem: women are paid less than men for performing comparable work. Whether comparable worth ought to be adopted, however, depends on complex empirical and normative analyses of the causes of the wage disparities and the effectiveness and desirability of the possible solutions.

Bibliography

Aaron, H. and Lougy, C. (1986). *The Comparable Worth Controversy*. Washington, DC: Brookings Institution.

Acker, J. (1989). *Doing Comparable Worth*. Philadelphia, PA: Temple University Press.

England, P. (1992). *Comparable Worth: Theories and Evidence*. New York: Aldine de Gruyter.

Gold, M. E. (1983). *A Dialogue on Comparable Worth*. Ithaca, NY: ILR Press.

Hartmann, H. I. (1985). *Comparable Worth: New Directions for Research*. Washington, DC: National Academy Press.

Remick, H. (1984). *Comparable Worth and Wage Discrimination*. Philadelphia, PA: Temple University Press.

Sorensen, E. (1994). *Comparable Worth: Is It a Worthy Policy?* Princeton, NJ: Princeton University Press.

Treiman, D. J. and Hartmann, H. I. (eds.) (1981). *Women, Work, and Wages: Equal Pay for Jobs of Equal Value*. Washington, DC: National Academy Press.

compensation, ethics of

Denis G. Arnold

In contemporary capitalist societies, ethical issues regarding compensation in the private sector may be divided into three main categories: desert, wage limits, and wage equity. In determining ethical, or just, wages, it is necessary to put aside considerations such as the hereditary rank and relative power of individuals. Nor can efficiency, while a relevant ethical consideration, be regarded as the only ethically relevant consideration for determining compensation. Other ethically relevant considerations include respect for persons, merit, loyalty, and justice.

At its core, compensation for work provided is justified on the grounds that the relevant parties to the transaction must be regarded as ends in themselves. If workers are to be regarded as ends in themselves, then, at a minimum, wages that individual employees deserve should be determined by assessing their effort, productivity, education, the difficulty and danger of the work involved, and the relative value of their work to others. It is the invocation of such factors that justifies significant differences in the wages of individuals even when they work in the same field. For example, a physician who has completed a medical degree and four to nine years of additional specialized training, and who regularly takes 24-hour calls, has a morally legitimate claim to greater remuneration than a registered nurse with two years of medical training, and who works a regular shift. Additional considerations such as the loyalty of the employee, or the extent to which the employee adheres to employer defined, professional, or statutory regulations, may also be ethically relevant factors for determining what compensation a worker deserves.

In circumstances where there is a large surplus of workers who are able and willing to perform a job, the employer is in a distinct bargaining advantage. In such cases, it is typical for compensation to remain low. In cases where lawful wages are below the threshold of what is required for a "living wage," that is, to live with dignity in a particular society, there is disagreement over whether employers have an ethical obligation to provide a living wage to employees.

Some authors argue such an obligation is grounded in the inherent dignity of employees *qua* persons (Arnold and Bowie, 2003; Ryan, 1912). Others argue that paying such workers a living wage would reduce the overall welfare of society (Maitland, 1997).

At the other end of the continuum, the wages of executives have increasingly come under ethical scrutiny. In recent years there have been significant increases in executive compensation, increases that are typically not linked to increased revenues or profits. Defenders of record executive compensation packages point to a purported scarcity of qualified executives as a justification for these increases. Critics typically deny there is a scarcity, and point to greed as the primary cause of the increase. Surprisingly little philosophical attention has been devoted to justifying or criticizing limits on executive compensation. On one version of a Rawlsian analysis of executive compensation, increases in executive pay packages would be justified only in cases where the increases resulted in benefits to the least well off employees in the firm (Rawls, 1999).

A final issue in assessing ethical compensation is that of wage equity. This issue developed historically around gaps in the earnings of women and men (Evans and Nelson, 1989). Women who are paid less than men for the same work should be entitled to equitable compensation on grounds of fairness. The question of paying women the same wages as men for comparable work hinges largely on questions regarding the comparability of different occupations. If different occupations are found to be comparable, then equitable compensation is a requirement of fairness. Differences in pay to women and men with comparable occupations are sometimes defended by appealing to assumptions regarding who is, or who should be, the primary wage earner for a family. Such claims are illegitimate on two grounds. First, they are illegitimate if they are based on sexist assumptions about family life. Second, they are illegitimate insofar as they introduce contingent factors regarding an employee's personal life that have no obvious connection to ethically legitimate concerns such as the employee's effort, productivity, training, education, or dignity as a person.

Bibliography

Arnold, D. G. and Bowie, N. E. (2003). Sweatshops and respect for persons. *Business Ethics Quarterly*, **13** (2), 221–42.

Evans, S. M. and Nelson, B. J. (1989). *Wage Justice: Comparable Worth and the Paradox of Technocractic Reform.* Chicago: University of Chicago Press.

Maitland, I. (1997). The great non-debate over international sweatshops. *British Academy of Management Conference Proceedings.*

Rawls, J. (1999). *A Theory of Justice*, revd. edn. Cambridge, MA: Harvard University Press.

Ryan, J. A. (1912). *A Living Wage: Its Ethical and Economic Aspects.* New York: Macmillan.

Sher, G. (1987). *Desert.* Princeton, NJ: Princeton University Press.

Walzer, M. (1983). *Spheres of Justice.* New York: Basic Books.

compensatory justice

Manuel Velasquez

The fairness that obtains when an agent adequately compensates a party whom he or she has injured for the losses that party suffered. Compensatory justice is sometimes wrongly confused with retributive justice, which is the fairness that obtains when a person is adequately punished for wrongdoing. Just compensation is limited to the losses suffered by the injured party, may imply no wrongdoing, and is focused on making the injured party whole, but just retribution may be more or less severe than the injuries inflicted on victims, always implies wrongdoing, and is focused on punishing the wrongdoer. That the two notions are distinct is recognized in contemporary torts law, which allows both "punitive damages" and "compensatory damages."

The earliest treatment of compensatory justice is Aristotle's discussion of "corrective justice" in "involuntary exchanges" such as theft, assault, or murder in *Nicomachean Ethics*, book 5. Unfortunately, Aristotle's overly mathematical analysis of corrective justice conflates retributive justice and compensatory justice. Aquinas, in his thirteenth-century *Summa Theologiae* (II–II, 61, 4), more carefully distinguishes the two notions. Later moralists discussed compensatory justice under the rubric of "just restitution."

In business ethics compensatory justice is of central importance in discussions of product liability, employer liability for employee injuries, and the justification of affirmative action. In these areas the main controversies over compensatory justice have revolved over questions of (1) how much compensation injured parties are due, (2) under what conditions compensation is due, and (3) to whom and from whom compensation is due. First: some claim that compensatory justice requires that compensation should equal the actual losses suffered by the injured party. But this claim assumes it is possible to quantify all losses, which may be incorrect. What, for example, constitutes just compensation for the loss of reputation, life, or sight, or for the infliction of pain and suffering? Second: traditional moralists have held that an agent owes compensation to an injured party when (a) the agent voluntarily performed the action that inflicted the injury, (b) the injury was caused by that action and not by the injured party's own actions, and (c) the agent's action was wrongful or negligent. But twentieth-century product liability law has stretched the notion of negligence to include also an agent's failure to exercise "due care" even when an injury is due to the injured party's own actions, and strict liability theories have imposed liability even on agents who have done all they could to protect parties from harm, and so whose actions were neither wrongful nor negligent. Third: some arguments supporting affirmative action programs claim that such programs constitute the just compensation that whites as a group owe to minorities as a group for past injuries. But this raises the question whether present-day minorities should be compensated, and whether present-day whites should pay compensation, for injuries that past generations of whites inflicted on past generations of minorities. Can mere membership in a group make a person deserving of, or liable for, compensation?

Bibliography

Chapman, J. W. (1991). *Compensatory Justice*. New York: New York University Press.

computers and computer technology, ethical issues in

Deborah G. Johnson

Many ethical issues have arisen as a result of the increasing use of computers and computer technologies. Most of the issues can be classified and analyzed using traditional ethical concepts such as property, responsibility, rights, and authority, and most involve relationships that exist independent of computers – employer/employee, citizen/government, producer/vendor/consumer, professional/client, professional/society. Nevertheless, when a situation involves computers it takes on special features that may transform its moral character or create uncertainty about norms, rights, and responsibilities. The special features of the situation necessitate a rethinking of traditional norms and values, a new understanding of how traditional values and norms apply. Hence, it seems fitting to call the issues new *species* of generic moral issues.

The new and old in computer ethical issues can be illustrated using the threat to personal privacy that computer technology seems to create. Information about individuals was being gathered and kept in increasing quantities by government and business for centuries before computers were invented. Still, the development of computer technology facilitated a radically increased *scale* of record keeping. It has facilitated an increased level of exchange of information about individuals (increased speed of exchange, quantity of information being exchanged, and number of organizations exchanging); an increased endurance of such information (rather than being discarded, records remain because they take up little space); and the creation of new kinds of information (especially transactional information produced when, for example, individuals use credit cards or automated teller machines). The new scale of activities needs to be evaluated morally, but when we do this we are *not* entering a wholly new domain; we are evaluating new versions of behaviors, relationships, and institutions that existed before computers.

Similarly, workplace monitoring made possible by computer technology illustrates the new and old in computer ethical issues. As a result of developments in computer technology, it is now possible for an employer to purchase software that will allow supervisors within the company to keep a complete record of everything that employees do while working on computers. The software allows supervisors to keep track of keystrokes so as to measure the speed or accuracy of work being done or simply to view work as it appears on a worker's computer screen. So, the software creates a new possibility for employers, but the ethical issue posed by this new possibility can be classified as a new version of the tension between employer and employee rights – a tension that has been in play for many centuries and has been addressed in law and in practice with regard to such matters as wages and safety conditions, political speech, and drug testing. Computer monitoring is a new species of an old issue.

Computer technology is now a fundamental part of doing business and its incorporation into the business world has created a wide variety of issues which can be understood to be new species of issues in business ethics. Indeed, one major change brought about by computer technology has been the creation of a whole new industry (or set of industries), producing computer hardware and software and other computer peripherals. As these new industries have developed, it has been necessary to work out laws, policies, and rules to ensure that the industry (and computer usage in general) is organized in ways that lead to beneficial consequences for society. One such area of concern has been defining property rights in the domain of computing – what should individuals and companies be allowed to own and what should be *un*ownable; that is, what should be proprietary and what not?

PROPERTY

Computer software is what makes computers the enormously powerful tools that they are. The stakes involved in successfully creating and bringing new and better software to the marketplace are now extremely high. This has meant that companies and individuals want to lay claim to ownership of as much as they possibly can. In the domain of the "technological arts," the primary way to do this is by using the legal protection offered by patents, copyrights, and trade

secrecy. These legal mechanisms, however, were developed long before computers, and extending them to computer technology has been awkward and uncertain. Their applicability is being worked out primarily through legal suits, and the outcomes of these legal suits will define the "rules of the game" in computer and computer-related industries.

The patent and copyright systems aim at encouraging development in the technological arts and sciences so that society benefits. The presumption is that individuals are more likely o create and invent *and* bring their inventions o the marketplace when they can profit from doing so. Inventors will not be able to profit from their useful inventions unless they have proprietary rights in them. Hence, the patent and copyright systems are designed to give such rights to inventors. However, both systems recognize that the benefits to society will be undermined if too much is owned. In particular, if the building blocks of science and technology were owned, then the owners could restrict invention, making it difficult or expensive for others to use fundamental knowledge to make yet newer inventions. For this reason, each system of legal protection restricts what can be claimed. The patent system does not allow ownership of abstract ideas, laws of nature, and mathematical formulas. One can only obtain a patent on an application or implementation of such. Similarly, the copyright system disallows ownership of ideas and grants copyright only in the expression of ideas.

Both the distinction made in patent law between an idea and the application of an idea, and the distinction in copyright law between idea and expression, have been problematic when used to protect computer software. In the case of patents, initially the problem was fear that granting ownership in software might, in effect, grant ownership of numerical sequences or mental steps – since all the steps in a computer program can, in principle, be done by an individual performing the steps mentally. More recently there has been uncertainty as to whether computer algorithms for solving abstractly defined problems can be patented; will this mean ownership of mathematical algorithms or of the building blocks of computing? The distinction between idea and expression used in copyright has also proved problematic for computer software. There is presently a good deal of uncertainty about the copyrightability of such things as the "structure, sequence, and organization" of a computer program, and the "look and feel" of a user interface. It is unclear whether such things constitute an idea or an expression. The copyright system also leaves a good deal of uncertainty about what is "fair use" when it comes to computer programming. One is allowed, in the copyright system, to use the ideas one learns from reading something. One is even allowed to use what another has created as long as one makes a significant improvement upon it and gives credit. These conditions do not, however, clarify whether one can use lines of computer code written by another. It does not make clear when one has stepped over the line between "fair use" and violation of copyright.

Legal problems aside, because of the nature of computer software, it is easy for individuals and companies to makes copies of what is proprietary. Rampant illegal copying has meant millions of dollars in lost revenues for the computer software industry. While software developers have developed a variety of techniques to protect their software from copying or at least to discourage it, illegal copying persists. Some compare software copying to drinking alcohol during Prohibition, claiming it is a form of behavior that cannot be stopped; hence we ought to give up and develop some other system for protecting the valuable aspect of software.

In any case, the copying of proprietary software raises ethical questions for businesses as well as for individuals. For individuals, the question seems straightforward: is it wrong for me to make a copy of proprietary software? For companies, the issue is more complicated. Of course, the company should not intentionally break the law (for example, by buying one copy of a useful piece of software, making multiple copies, and distributing them throughout the company). But what responsibility does a company have for preventing illegal copying within the company? Does it have a responsibility to make internal policies that discourage employees from illegal copying? If so, how far should it go to enforce these policies? Should it periodically check what is stored on every computer and require employees to show proof of purchase for any software found on a corporate computer?

PRIVACY

The increase in the scale of information gathering facilitated by computer technology was mentioned earlier. Information about individuals is now big business. Databases containing financial information, addresses and telephone numbers, magazine subscription information, as well as information from government agencies (e.g., driver's license information) are now routinely bought and sold. The ethical issues surrounding this activity are generally placed in a framework of understanding that the need of organizations and institutions for information is in tension with the desires of many individuals for privacy. Organizations want and need the information in order to make better and more efficient decisions. They argue that individuals are the beneficiaries because the increased efficiency made possible by more and better information leads to better services and lower prices for individuals. At the same time, many individuals are uncomfortable with their personal information being circulated without their knowledge or consent, and without their ability to check its accuracy.

Framing the issue as a tension between the need of organizations for information about individuals and the desires of individuals for privacy seems to tip the scales in favor of information gathering. At least in the US, where there is no explicit constitutional protection for personal privacy and no comprehensive legislative protection, the value of information gathering to companies and government agencies generally seems to outweigh the desires of individuals for privacy. The ethical issue here may be better understood by framing it as a matter of differential power. Organizations make powerful decisions about individuals, deciding whether they receive benefits, go to jail, get insurance, and so on, and they make these decisions on the basis of personal information. Individuals do not have control over that information and, hence, do not know whether these agencies are basing decisions on accurate or appropriate information. Hence, individuals have very little power in relation to these organizations.

The differential in power raises a variety of ethical issues in business. First, and perhaps foremost, it raises questions about how we might better organize an information industry so as to benefit society and respect the desire for personal privacy. This is complex insofar as we want both efficient private and public institutions and a high degree of individual autonomy. Another set of privacy issues in business has to do with how businesses handle information about individuals. Shouldn't they have policies informing employees about the confidential nature of information and restricting how they use it? Shouldn't companies inform their customers as to how they will treat information the customers provide? Does the company gather more information than it needs? Does the company's use of personal information lead (directly or indirectly) to racial or gender discrimination?

RESPONSIBILITY

Computer technology often changes or diffuses understanding of who is responsible for what. The legal liability of those who produce and sell software (mass-market software, custom systems, and hybrid systems) for errors and malfunctions in the software is still being worked out in the courts. Law aside, there are special issues of responsibility in software because of its power and complexity. Software that automates an activity such as an industrial process is based on a model of that activity. A computer system is then built on the basis of the model and may consist of millions and millions of lines of computer code. Those who design and program computer systems admit that they can never be sure that the software is perfect: the model may be incomplete and the code may have errors in it. While there may be ways to test a system, often it cannot be tested under every condition so as to eliminate the possibility of error. This, of course, must be figured into our understanding and use of computer systems, but its implications for responsibility are problematic. It seems to mean, for example, that errors and consequent accidents or harms will occur for which no one is responsible. What can be done to minimize accidents? What sort of system of liability or insurance can be worked out to compensate those who are harmed?

More and more decision-making is now being done by computer or based on complex computer analysis. Computers now manage indus-

trial processes, monitor patients in hospitals, route airplanes, approve and assign credit limits, and so on. Even when computers do not make decisions, human decision-makers now routinely base their decisions on computer analysis – computer analysis that the decision-maker may not fully understand because he or she does not understand the inputs and algorithms used in the program. In such a situation the human decision-maker may feel compelled to act on the computer output because it justifies a decision. Imagine, for example, a person who manages funds for a pension plan. She believes this is not a good time to invest more money in bonds, but the computer system that her company uses regularly is recommending bonds. If she does not follow the system recommendations, she may be accused of mismanaging funds and the computer output can be used as evidence of her "incompetence." She does not understand how the system works but her years of experience tell her it is wrong this time. If she follows the advice of the computer system, is she abdicating responsibility or acting in a responsible way?

THE INTERNET

In the last decade, use of the Internet (by individuals and companies) has increased at unprecedented speed, and with its development has come a good deal of speculation as to what it will mean and do to individual lives, global politics, and the global economy. The Internet has changed the environment of business and this has meant, among other things, that many of the standard issues in business ethics arise in new ways and with a global and international twist. The Internet links individuals and companies, making it possible to do business instantaneously, and to intensively manage companies, on a global scale. Individuals, industries, and governments send and receive digitalized information in literary, audio, and video form. Property rights, privacy, and responsibility issues arise between nations with a greater intensity than ever before. With companies so dependent on the Internet, its security has become a major issue. The Internet and the relationships and activities it facilitates are likely to continue to evolve and change the way business is done, and consequently the ethical issues in business.

Bibliography

Bennett, C. J. and R. Grant (eds.) (1999). *Visions of Privacy: Policy Choices for the Digital Age.* Toronto: University of Toronto Press.

Bynum, T. W. and S. Rogerson (eds.) (2004). *Computer Ethics and Professional Responsibility: Introductory Text and Readings.* Oxford: Blackwell.

De George, R. T. (2003). *Ethics of Information Technology and Business.* Oxford: Blackwell.

Ermann, M. D. and Shauf, M. S. (2002). *Computers, Ethics, and Society.* Oxford: Oxford University Press.

Hester, D. M. and Ford, P. J. (eds.) (2001). *Computers and Ethics in the Cyberage.* Upper Saddle River, NJ: Prentice-Hall.

Johnson, D. G. (2001). *Computer Ethics*, 3rd edn. Upper Saddle River, NJ: Prentice-Hall.

Johnson, D. G. and Nissenbaum, H. (eds.) (1995). *Computers, Ethics and Social Values.* Englewood Cliffs, NJ: Prentice-Hall.

Spinello, R. (2003). *Case Studies in Information Technology Ethics*, 2nd edn. Upper Saddle River, NJ: Prentice-Hall.

Spinello, R. and Travani, H. T. (eds.) (2001). *Readings in CyberEthics.* Sudbury, MA: Jones and Bartlett Publishers.

Tavani, H. T. (2004). *Ethics and Technology: Ethical Issues in Information and Communication Technology.* New York: John Wiley and Sons.

conflict of interest

Michael Davis

occurs if and only if a person *P* is in a relationship with one or more others requiring *P* to exercise judgment in their behalf, and *P* has a (special) interest tending to interfere with the proper exercise of judgment in that relationship. The crucial terms in this definition are "relationship," "judgment," "interest," and "proper exercise of [that] judgment."

Relationship. This term is quite general, including any connection between *P* and another person justifying that other's reliance on *P* for a certain purpose. So, for example, employers typically have such a connection with their employees.

Judgment. Judgment (as used here) is the ability to make certain decisions correctly more often than would a simple clerk with a book of rules and all – and only – the same information. Some jobs, such as assembly-line worker, require little or no judgment; most, especially at the professional level, require a good deal.

Interest. An interest is any loyalty, concern, emotion, or other feature of a situation tending to make *P*'s judgment (in that situation) less reliable than it would normally be (without rendering *P* incompetent). Financial influences and family connections are the most common interests discussed in this context, but love, prejudice, gratitude, and the like can also be interests.

Proper exercise. What constitutes proper exercise of judgment is generally a question of social fact, including what people ordinarily expect, what *P* or the group *P* belongs to invite others to expect, and what various laws, professional codes, or the like require. What is proper exercise of judgment in one job may well not be in another. For example, a lawyer who resolves every reasonable doubt in favor of an employer when presenting the employer's case in court exercises professional judgment properly; an industrial chemist who does the same thing when presenting research at a conference does not.

What's wrong with conflict of interest? To have a conflict of interest is to be less reliable than one normally is (that is, to be less deserving of reliance). In this respect, the interest in question is *special*: to exercise one's judgment when one has a conflict of interest is to take an unusual risk of error. A conflict of interest is not simply a conflict within one's interests, commitments, or values. Rather, it is a conflict between some special interest and the proper exercise of competent judgment. So, for example, I do not have a conflict of interest just because I promised to work here and also promised to work somewhere else during the same period. That conflict of commitment does not threaten my judgment. I would, however, have a conflict of interest if, as director of purchasing, I had to choose among suppliers when one was my daughter. I would find it harder than a stranger to judge accurately the relative quality of her product or service. Would I be harder on her than a stranger would, easier, or just the same? Who knows?

Accountants often describe this inability to judge as someone less involved would as a loss of "objectivity"; other professions have other terms.

But the underlying idea is the same: the judgment in question depends on something it does not ordinarily depend on, something it should not depend on. A conflict of interest is therefore objectionable for at least one of three reasons:

1   Insofar as *P* is unaware of the conflict, she is incompetent. We generally suppose people in positions of responsibility to know their limits, especially when these are obvious.
2   If those justifiably relying on *P* for a certain judgment do not know of *P*'s conflict of interest and *P* knows (or should know) that they do not, *P* is allowing them to believe that she is what she is not; she is, in effect, deceiving them (since their reliance on her is justified until she reveals what she knows).
3   Even if *P* informs those justifiably depending on her judgment that she has a conflict of interest, her judgment will still be less reliable than it ordinarily is. *P* therefore risks appearing less competent than usual (and perhaps less competent than someone in her position should be). Conflict of interest can be a technical problem even when no longer a moral problem (and, even as a technical problem, can harm the reputation of the profession, occupation, or individual in question).

What can be done about a conflict of interest? One can *avoid* some conflicts of interest (for example, by putting one's stocks in a blind trust or by refusing a gift); *escape* others (for example, by divesting oneself of the conflicting interest or by withdrawing from, or redefining, the relationship of dependence); or, in some cases, *disclose* the conflict to those relying on one's judgment (thereby preventing deception and allowing those relying on one to adjust their reliance accordingly). In general, disclosure does not end the conflict of interest but merely renders it less likely to be harmful.

P has a *potential* conflict of interest if and only if *P* has a conflict of interest with respect to a certain judgment, but is not yet in a situation where he must make that judgment. Potential conflicts of interest, like time bombs, may or may not go off.

P has an *actual* conflict of interest if and only if *P* has a conflict of interest with respect to a certain judgment and is in a situation where he must make that judgment.

P has a (mere) *apparent* conflict of interest if and only if *P* does not have a conflict of interest (actual or potential), but someone other than *P* would nonetheless be justified in concluding (however tentatively) that *P* does have a conflict. An apparent conflict is objectionable for the same reason that any apparent wrongdoing is objectionable. It may mislead people about their security, inviting waste of resources on unnecessary precautions. An apparent conflict is resolved by making available enough information to show that there is no actual or potential conflict.

Bibliography

Davis, M. (1992). Conflict of interest. *Business and Professional Ethics Journal*, 1, 17–28.
Davis, M. (1993). Conflict of interest revisited. *Business and Professional Ethics Journal*, 12, 21–41.
McMunigal, K. (1992). Rethinking attorney conflict of interest doctrine. *Georgetown Journal of Legal Ethics*, 5, 823–77.

consent

A. John Simmons

An act by which one freely changes the existing structure of rights and obligations, typically by undertaking new obligations and authorizing others to act in ways that would otherwise have been impermissible for them.

Consent is a concept of central importance in moral, political, legal, and economic contexts. In typical cases, a person's consent to another's acts removes moral or legal objections to, or liability for, the performance of those acts. In medical practice, for instance, the "informed consent" of a patient to a procedure can justify the physician's actions. In law and business, the maxim *volenti non fit injuria* (the willing person is not wronged) governs a wide range of acts and transactions. And in politics, it is often supposed that it is "the consent of the governed" that justifies the use of official coercion to compel obedience to law.

Consenting is closely associated with acts like promising, contracting, entrusting, etc. Justification by appeal to consent is especially central within liberal thought. Liberalism conceives of persons as self-conscious sources of value who have rights to govern themselves (within the bounds set by the rights of others). Consent is seen as the means by which this individual moral liberty may be limited in a fashion consistent with respect for liberty.

Consent may be either express or tacit. Express consent is consent given by an explicit verbal or written undertaking or by other direct but non-verbal consensual acts (such as raising one's hand). Tacit consent is given by actions or omissions (such as inactivity or silence) that do not involve an explicit undertaking, but that nonetheless constitute the making of a morally significant choice in the context of a clear, non-coercive choice situation. Some attempted justifications by consent appeal not to actual (express or tacit) consent, but to hypothetical consent. Hypothetical consent can be ideal (what fully rational persons would consent to) or dispositional (what real persons would have consented to, had they been able). Only appeals to the latter (by which we justify, for example, imposing medical treatment on an unconscious injured person) seem to be genuine justifications by consent. Appeals to the former are really disguised attempts to justify by showing that an arrangement is best or acceptable, independent of people's consent.

Consent of whatever form can only justify acts or arrangements given the satisfaction of a complex set of conditions for binding consent. First, there are knowledge conditions (consent must be "informed"). Second, binding consent must be intentional. Third, consent can only be given by the competent (which may exclude in various contexts apparent consent given by the insane, severely retarded, emotionally disturbed, immature, intoxicated, etc.). Fourth, binding consent must be voluntary (limiting it to cases not involving the extraction of consent by coercion, undue influence, exploitation, unfair bargaining advantage, etc.). Finally, consent only binds given acceptability of content. In most legal systems, for instance, agreements you make to commit crimes, become a slave, or allow yourself to be killed are not enforceable.

See also *contracts and contracting; liberalism; obedience, to authority and to the law*

Bibliography

Beran, H. (1987). *The Consent Theory of Political Obligation*. London, Croom Helm.
Feinberg, J. (1986). *Harm to Self*. New York: Oxford University Press.
Kleinig, J. (1982). The ethics of consent. *Canadian Journal of Philosophy*, supp. vol. 8, 91–118.
Rawls, J. (1971). *A Theory of Justice*. Cambridge, MA: Harvard University Press.
Simmons, A. J. (1993). *On the Edge of Anarchy: Locke, Consent, and the Limits of Society*. Princeton, NJ: Princeton University Press.

consequentialism

William L. Langenfus

is the claim that the moral evaluation of acts, dispositions, or any other possible object of moral assessment, is exclusively related to their contribution to an impartially good overall state of affairs. The continued appeal that such a conception of morality has for many of its adherents – even in the face of strenuous objections by critics – rests upon this fundamental idea. Somehow, it is thought, morality *must* have something essentially to do with how our acts, dispositions, etc., affect the world and make it either a better or worse place. A consequentialist perspective inherently captures this idea and makes it the ultimate basis of morality.

This very general characterization covers a multitude of complexities, however, which call for some discussion. First of all, consequentialist theories can be differentiated, in part, by their reliance upon different conceptions of the good. The actual application of any consequentialist conception of ethics will necessarily presuppose some specified general conception of the good where this is defined independently of moral evaluation. Obviously, if the *moral* evaluation of our acts, dispositions, etc., depends on how these contribute to an impartially good state of affairs, to actually make such an evaluation, we must first have some conception of what is "good" or "valuable" that is independent of the moral evaluation itself. Otherwise, the consequentialist moral assessment could not get started – it would have nothing to work on. Because of this, consequentialist ethical theories must rely upon conceptions of value that are independent from *moral* evaluation.

There are a number of well-known candidates for this. For instance, the classical utilitarianism of Jeremy Bentham (along with that of Henry Sidgwick) was fundamentally a combination of a consequentialist conception of moral evaluation with a hedonistic conception of the good that defines the good ultimately in terms of pleasure. John Stuart Mill's form of this theory incorporates a more complicated idea of the good that cannot be reduced easily to the pure form of hedonism of the type Bentham held. Recent versions of utilitarianism have employed a conception of the good that is defined in terms of individual "preference" or "desire" satisfaction (see Griffin, 1986: chs. 1 and 2). And there are other (non-utilitarian) consequentialist theories that employ fundamentally different conceptions of the good besides these (see Nagel, 1979: ch. 9; Griffin, 1986: chs. 3 and 4). Hence, although all consequentialist theories are alike in maintaining that moral evaluation is strictly a matter of contribution to an impartially "good" state of affairs, they can be differentiated, in part, by the various conceptions of the good that might be incorporated within them.

A second major element underlying a consequentialist approach to moral evaluation is its conception of rationality. Consequentialist theories are regarded as embodying a certain form of practical rationality. This is where they gain their normative force – moral requirement being essentially a dictate of practical reason in its impartial or impersonal form. It is often thought that such practical rationality involves a "maximization" of the good. For this reason, consequentialist ethical theories are most often defined in terms of requiring a *maximizing* relation between the objects of moral assessment (acts, dispositions, etc.) and the production of an impartially good outcome.

However, this is not the only possible way to view this relation. It has been claimed by some that it is rational to be satisfied with a resulting state of affairs that is judged to be good enough even though it may be less than the best possible one, given the various open alternatives. It is therefore possible to develop a consequentialist ethical theory incorporating this (less demanding) "satisficing" conception of practical rationality (see Slote, 1985: ch. 3). The result would be a form of consequentialism requiring a promotion of the good that is "satisfactory." Hence, consequentialist theories can also be differentiated by whether they embody either a maximizing or satisficing conception of rationality.

Because a consequentialist approach to ethics places its exclusive emphasis on (good) outcomes, *any* factor associated with moral agents that has an influence on states of affairs can be assessed in consequentialist terms. Such factors have what might be called "consequentialist relevance." The most obvious such factor is an agent's *acts*. What actions are performed in the various circumstances in which one finds oneself can have a significant effect on states of affairs. Indeed, consequentialism has most often been defined exclusively in terms of the moral assessment of particular acts – that is, as providing a criterion of morally right action. However, there are other factors that have a clear influence on the acts that agents perform, and thus, at least, have an important *indirect* consequentialist relevance. Prominent in this regard is the whole host of dispositions that provide the motivational background against which agents perform many (if not all) of their acts. Many of these dispositions have to do with how agents are deeply motivated to act or, more broadly, how to live their lives. And many of the acts that agents perform in the course of their lives depend, ultimately, on such motivational elements. A concern, therefore, for the development and maintenance of those dispositions (including deep traits of personal character) that will tend to bring about a good overall state of affairs can be regarded as a crucial part of any complete consequentialist approach to ethics.

The version of the theory that is most often discussed is a maximizing one, whose exclusive focus is the consequentialist assessment of particular acts – so-called "act-consequential-ism." This is essentially defined by its criterion of right action that holds that an act is morally right if and only if that act will promote as much good – impartially considered – as any other feasible act open to the agent. In other words, the only acts of an agent that are morally permissible on this view are those that produce a maximally good outcome from an impartial or impersonal point of view, relative to the available alternatives. This conception of ethical requirement is a very demanding one. This is because of its inherently "impersonal" standpoint (that is, that the good produced must be regarded as such from the perspective of the interests of no particular agent), and its maximizing conception of practical rationality (requiring that such good be maximally produced). As a result of its impersonal character, the moral requirements that would typically be generated by this criterion of right acts are likely to be very demanding on the personal projects and interests of most human agents. In addition to this, because one can always be doing *something* (whatever it happens to be) to produce such maximally good outcomes, the theory is *pervasively* demanding. Agents are literally *always* subject to such possibly sacrificial moral requirements on this view.

The most prominent objections to act-consequentialism stem, in various ways, from this extremely demanding character. First of all, it is simply un-intuitive from the perspective of ordinary commonsense morality to be pervasively under such demanding moral requirements. Ordinary moral intuitions usually allow for a rather large area of life where one is free from moral requirement, and thus able to pursue, without moral compunction, one's own personal projects and interests. Since this area of optional moral freedom is ruled out by the pervasiveness of the act-consequentialist perspective, so the argument goes, so much the worse for that approach. While this objection might seem question-begging (in favor of the commonsense, non-consequentialist, perspective), the sway of ordinary moral intuitions in this matter has tended to exert a strong influence in discussions of the viability of this theory.

A second, perhaps more influential, way in which the demanding nature of the act-consequentialist conception has been regarded

as problematic has been to argue that it cannot adequately account for, or reflect, the "personal" perspective of ordinary human agents. According to this objection, ordinary human moral agents, as a matter of their very nature, are deeply motivated to act and, indeed, live their lives, from a *personal* perspective. Their own interests and projects have a significance that is disproportionate to that given to them by the impersonal perspective of the consequentialist conception. The act-consequentialist conception can be regarded as problematic in this regard in essentially two different ways. First, it can be alleged that it is *motivationally futile* to require such agents to abide by the pervasive, impersonally generated, consequentialist demands. Such requirements, it can be argued, simply cannot have a secure motivational backing given the deep personal bias of ordinary moral agents. Hence, it is claimed, act-consequentialism is ill-suited to the actual motivational capacities of ordinary moral agents and is, thus, to be rejected as a reasonable theory grounding such requirements. Second, it can be argued that even the *attempt* to live one's life according to such a moral conception can be positively destructive of this valuable element of human nature. It has been argued, for instance (notably, by Williams, 1973: esp. 108–18), that the integrity of an agent's personal projects and commitments can be fragmented by the attempt to abide by this sort of impersonal morality. One must, it seems, be willing to "step aside" from any personal commitment (e.g., career, friends, family, etc.) any time the consequentialist morality requires it. But this seems incompatible with the sort of attitude one must necessarily take to such deeply personal, significant, pursuits. If this is so, the attempt to live the pervasive consequentialist life would likely end up destroying the ability to maintain this sort of integrity and authenticity of one's own personal projects and commitments. If, as Williams and others claim, this is regarded as a loss of something inherently valuable, then this would certainly be a troubling aspect associated with the act-consequentialist approach.

A number of different responses to these objections to the alleged overly demanding nature of act-consequentialism have been offered. Four of these will be discussed here. The first involves defining the act-consequentialist criterion of right acts itself in terms of the "satisficing" conception of rationality discussed above. This, at least, would appear to generate moral requirements that may be far less sacrificial from an agent's personal perspective than the usual maximizing version. One would not be required to act in a way that leads to the *best* overall outcome, but rather, in such a way that the outcome is judged to be good enough. One problem with this is that if the criterion is not going to end up involving a basic indeterminacy regarding actual moral requirement, a determinate standard of satisfactoriness must be established. But it is not at all clear how one would go about doing this without relying, ultimately, upon an agent's own discretion. But, if this is so, the objective nature of the consequentialist theory might be jeopardized.

A second alternative has been to modify the act-consequentialist conception by reflecting, directly, the personal point of view. Samuel Scheffler (1982) has argued along such lines for the inclusion of what he calls an "agent-centered prerogative" which would make it *permissible* for agents to devote energy and attention to their own projects (including, perhaps, a personal commitment to promote the overall good) out of proportion to the strictly impersonal or impartial weighting involved in the pure consequentialist conception. The theory would still allow, however, for the incorporation of an act-consequentialist moral commitment *as part of* an agent's own framework of personal motivation. In this way, it is claimed, the theory would not place an excessive strain on the personal integrity of agents, and yet, could still incorporate much of the act-consequentialist conception of moral requirement. However, a major problem encountered here is, again, the apparent difficulty in determining when the (strict consequentialist) requirements should override the agent's own prerogative. If this cannot be answered in some non-arbitrary fashion, this "hybrid" theory is in danger of collapsing into a view which would place no real, clearly determinable, *requirements* on agents at all.

A third response to the demandingness objection to the act-consequentialist conception concedes that the criterion (in its usual maximizing form) is extremely demanding, but holds, nonetheless, that it is still a true account of moral requirement. Those who take this route usually attempt to show that the consequentialist conception maintains a basic coherence and rationality that has not been able to be equalled by rival, non-consequentialist moral perspectives (see, most notably, Kagan, 1989). Further, it is often argued that human nature is much more malleable – capable of being motivated to much more highly demanding moral requirements – than critics of the consequentialist view tend to think. This being so, such agents can, indeed, be motivated to act in accordance with the strict consequentialist conception (without unduly fragmenting their own personal integrity). Hence, this conception can continue to be regarded as plausible, and true, even in light of its extremely demanding nature. The issue here is whether this portrays a true picture of the motivational capacities of ordinary human moral agents, and whether certain non-consequentialist conceptions can better respond to it.

A final response on the part of some consequentialists attempts to redefine the whole theory in a way that simply excludes the act-consequentialist criterion of right action (at least as part of the motivational framework of agents generally). Moral assessment, on such views, is *primarily* directed at the inculcation and maintenance of general dispositions (including, perhaps, certain moral beliefs) and character traits which will best tend to promote the good. Morally right action, accordingly, is that which would be motivated by the best overall framework of such general dispositions. Because, on such views, there is no direct appeal to (or inclusion of) an act-consequentialist criterion of right action, and the moral assessment is directed exclusively at certain value-generating dispositional factors, there is far less likelihood of this moral conception generating demands that will tend to fragment an agent's personal integrity. Whether such indirect forms of consequentialism can be maintained in a coherent manner (excluding, as they do, an act-consequentialist assessment of acts) is a matter of some controversy.

Consequentialism in its (growing) variety of forms continues to be a major alternative in general ethical theory. Much of its plausibility depends upon a widely shared (although, not universal) intuition that, somehow, consequences count in our moral assessments, and that those assessments should be grounded in an impartial practical rationality. However, the complete establishment of such a theory depends upon whether a stable and coherent form can be developed which will adequately reflect a plausible and complete view of human motivation.

Bibliography

Brink, D. (1986). Utilitarian morality and the personal point of view. *Journal of Philosophy*, 83, 417–38.
Griffin, J. (1986). *Well-Being*. Oxford: Clarendon Press.
Kagan, S. (1984). Does consequentialism demand too much? *Philosophy and Public Affairs*, 13, 239–54.
Kagan, S. (1989). *The Limits of Morality*. Oxford: Clarendon Press.
Nagel, T. (1979). *Mortal Questions*. Cambridge: Cambridge University Press.
Railton, P. (1984). Alienation, consequentialism, and the demands of morality. *Philosophy and Public Affairs*, 13, 134–71.
Scheffler, S. (1982). *The Rejection of Consequentialism*. Oxford: Clarendon Press.
Scheffler, S. (ed.) (1988). *Consequentialism and Its Critics*. Oxford: Oxford University Press.
Slote, M. (1985). *Common Sense Morality and Consequentialism*. London: Routledge and Kegan Paul.
Williams, B. (1973). A critique of utilitarianism. In J. J. C. Smart and B. Williams, *Utilitarianism: For and Against*. Cambridge: Cambridge University Press, 75–150.
Williams, B. (1985). *Ethics and the Limits of Philosophy*, London, Fontana Press.

consulting, ethics of

Barbara Ley Toffler

deals with the responsibilities of individuals who serve as consultants to institutions and their members. Consulting can be defined as an intervention into an organization with the goal of helping that organization (1) understand its beliefs and practices and how they affect organizational outcomes, (2) design appropriate structures, systems, and processes to manage or change those beliefs and practices to result in more effective outcomes, and (3) implement the mechanisms designed.

The institutions served by consultants are in the private, public, and non-profit sectors of our society. They can be business corporations or partnerships; they can be hospitals and other healthcare facilities; they can be governments and government agencies; they can be foundations, charities, and other non-profit organizations. Any organized setting in which individuals and groups work for a broad common purpose is a potential client for consultation.

Consulting in any field and under any circumstances requires a carefully honed sense of ethics, since by its very nature, any consultation involves intervening in the lives of individuals, having an impact on a system simply by being present, and dealing with values in a way that could result in the inappropriate imposition of the consultant's values on the client institution.

In some ways, the consultant is similar to the health professional. The client institution, like a patient, is seeking remedy to a "condition" (or conditions) its members believe is preventing the institution's achieving "good health." Like the medical practitioner, the consultant is asked to "make things better." Therefore, to continue the medical analogy, the moral minimum of consulting must be: *Do No Harm*. This principle may be easier said than done. Unlike the medical profession in which there are licensing and accrediting bodies for members and the institutions in which they serve, the occupation of consulting, *per se*, is not monitored, reviewed, nor guided by any organization which sets standards or tests practitioners. In addition, there is no prescribed course of study; there are no standard "treatments" which clients may anticipate. (These descriptive statements provide the reasons one must call consulting an occupation and not a profession.) For the client, there can be only trust that the consultant is knowledgeable and well trained, and is a responsible, ethical person. Given these realities, the principle "Do No Harm" requires the consultant to be critically cognizant of his or her own limitations.

To emphasize the importance of the "Do No Harm" rule, and the potential pitfalls to enacting it, consider the consulting field relevant to this volume: business ethics consulting.

BUSINESS ETHICS CONSULTING

Business ethics consulting formally came into being in the early 1980s, so, by the 1990s, it could truly be called "teenaged." Further, it was an adolescent in that it had some early successes and showed promise of having an impact on the world, but it is still unpredictable, often self-centered, sometimes undisciplined, and very frequently hard to understand.

PRACTITIONERS

One of the effects of occupational adolescence is that the characteristics of the practitioner have not been specified. The business ethics consult-ant body is composed of individuals trained in a number of different academic disciplines with varied amounts of knowledge about and experi-ence in the professions, industries, businesses, and organizations to which they consult. Many ethics consultants are trained in philosophy, the-ology, and related fields; others come from the social sciences: psychology, sociology, anthro-pology, and the like; some were trained in the professional area to which they consult: medi-cine, law, and engineering, among others. In addition, there are individuals marketing them-selves as business ethics consultants who have taken one- or two-day programs offered by vari-ous organizations. Because there is no accredit-ing body for business ethics consultants (as is the case with many fields of consultancy), anyone choosing to act as a business ethics consultant may do so. Consequently, the mandate to "Do No Harm" at present must be paired with a client message of "*caveat emptor* – buyer beware."

WHY DO ORGANIZATIONS INITIATE AN ETHICS CONSULTATION?

Just as there are a variety of reasons a patient will seek medical assistance or guidance, there are several reasons an organization will choose to bring in a business ethics consultant:

1   The organization and/or its members or others in its industry have been found to have done something legally or ethically "wrong" and it wants to prevent future mis-conduct as well as generate positive public relations.
2   The organization or its industry is undergo-ing major regulatory or structural changes in which the new "rules" are unclear or signifi-cantly different than in the past and it wants

to anticipate and, thus, prevent uninten-tional wrongdoing.
3   The organization engages in professional ac-tivities with acknowledged health and safety impact on the public (e.g., medicine, engin-eering) and it wants to manage the dilemmas of professional delivery of services.
4   There is a legal mandate, such as the 1991 US Corporate Sentencing Guidelines.
5   A soon-to-retire CEO or senior official wishes to leave a legacy of "Ethics."

These reasons that institutions seek ethics consultation further confirm the importance of the injunction to do no harm. In a majority of cases, client organizations consider themselves to be in reasonably good shape, seeking preven-tion or enhancement as much or more than remedy. While prevention or betterment may be impossible to promise, a commitment to not making things worse is imperative! If clients cannot feel assured that, at the very least, they will end up no worse than they started, then consultants cannot claim they are acting respon-sibly.

ETHICAL OBLIGATIONS BEYOND "DO NO HARM"

Beyond the avoidance of harm, ethical consult-ing demands other considerations. A critical eth-ical obligation of the consultant is *respect* for the client institution and its members. Respect means holding in regard the work that the members of the institution do and their know-ledge related to that work. While consultants are brought in as outside "experts," they should never forget that the organization to which they are providing guidance is the expert in its busi-ness: almost no consultant can know as much about an organization as its members.

Similarly, consultants are obligated to *not impose their values* on the institutions to which they consult. This injunction can become com-plicated, in that most guidance and advice is not value-free. Consequently, consultants must walk the line between *suggesting* and *imposing* ways of thinking and acting. A responsible consultant needs never to say to a client "You must see things my way."

However, respect for the client's values does not mean the consultant must always "follow orders." The ethical consultant must *recognize his or her personal bottom line*, and be willing to turn down or step aside from work with a client whose beliefs and actions fall below that line.

Respectful, responsible consultation must include listening to and hearing the concerns of the client institution's members, learning whatever is necessary to understand the business of the client organization, designing and implementing interventions that meet the client organization's needs, and valuing the skills, capabilities, and knowledge of the organization's membership. There is an old joke that goes: "A consultant is someone who borrows your watch to tell you what time it is." A wise consultant knows that comment contains more than a grain of truth – as well as an ethical mandate. As a consultant, one is being entrusted with the real and the emotional "property" of one's client: proprietary information, the hopes, fears, and beliefs of its membership, and, perhaps above all, the institution's reputation and its image in the world. The responsible consultant employs that "property" (along with other tools) to reflect back to the client institution what it has not been able to see, and to help the institution use its resources to build its capabilities as a responsible and successful organization.

consumer prices and advertising

Paul W. Farris and David J. Reibstein

TWO MODELS

Economists use two principal models to describe the effects of advertising on the prices consumers pay. In the Advertising = Market Power model, advertising is thought to change consumer tastes, establish brand loyalty, and ultimately raise profits and consumer prices while decreasing price sensitivity and competition. In the Advertising = Information model, advertising is seen as providing information to consumers, resulting in increased price sensitivity, lower prices, and reduced monopoly power.

Of course, price sensitivity, as well as brand loyalty, are created and supported by other factors, such as product quality, better packaging, favorable user experience, market pos-

ition, warranty, and/or service. Also, the observation that companies with relatively higher advertising budgets also usually charge the higher prices can be confusing. Some see the higher prices of advertised products as clear-cut evidence that advertising causes consumers to pay more. The relationship between advertising and price is anything but clear-cut. When other factors, such as high quality, give marketers "something to say" in advertising, they are more apt to say it with more advertising support. Similarly, if quality helps increase prices and margins, then the evidence is confounded by the fact that when the profit on an individual item is higher, there is more incentive to advertise, as the return on investment will be proportionately greater. Unfortunately, it is easy for this "evidence" to be misinterpreted. Some critics of advertising have even gone so far as to imply that all advertising is wasteful and that consumer prices would be reduced by the percentage that advertising constitutes of sales (about 2–3 percent for a wide variety of products, but as much as 30–40 percent for some).

ADVERTISING AND PRODUCT QUALITY

The argument that advertising "explains" and communicates product quality to consumers is considered specious by some. They argue that advertising too often creates the impression of higher quality when no real differences exist. Advertising is often thought to raise costs, instill artificial preferences (i.e., create excessive product differentiation), and increase consumer prices. Indeed, there is little doubt that in many cases marketers attempt to justify price premiums and escape the intensity of price competition by using advertising to communicate marginal product benefits to consumers. Even without clear product differences advertising may enable some marketers to charge higher prices relative to competition. In the alcoholic beverage market, for example, without advertising, certain brands, such as "Absolut" vodka, could not charge their current prices.

Can we reconcile the idea that highly advertised brands charge higher prices than competitors with the notion that advertising is essential to competition? The answer is yes, as will be shown. Our arguments rely on the distinction between manufacturer price and retail price on the one hand, and relative price and absolute price on the other.

MANUFACTURER PRICES, RETAIL PRICES, RELATIVE PRICES, ABSOLUTE PRICES

For our purposes, manufacturer price is the manufacturer's selling price, and, except in situations where there are intervening parties such as distributors, this price is usually the retailer's purchase price. The retailer's selling price refers to the retail price, and as used here is synonymous with consumer purchase price. Relative price is a ratio or difference between the price of one brand versus the price of another, measured either in retail or manufacturer prices. Absolute price is an average of all prices of products in a category. In the main, we believe that it is the effect of advertising on the long-term level of absolute consumer prices that is the primary concern. On the other hand, it is the sums spent by manufacturers for advertising that are argued to increase prices. Retail advertising almost always features prices and has, to our knowledge, never been argued to increase prices.

In studies conducted to examine the effect of manufacturer advertising on prices, as one might imagine, support exists for both the "power" and the "information" models. It is relevant that, with a single exception, the studies examining manufacturer price reported that advertising decreases price sensitivity, while studies examining retail price concluded the opposite, that manufacturer advertising increases price sensitivity.

These studies are not necessarily in conflict. The reason is that advertised brands are often the subject of intense inter-store price competition. The manufacturer's price may initially be low to encourage retailers to carry a product and, when advertising creates product demand, the manufacturer may charge a higher price to the retailer. The retailer could pass on this increase to the consumer, but this does not often happen because of the retailer's desire to remain competitive with other retailers (inter-store competition). If a retailer wants to be known as the low-priced store it will be especially competitive on advertised products that are stocked by other retailers. Such low-priced, highly advertised brands are often used as traffic builders. Indeed,

manufacturers sometimes fear that the extreme popularity of some advertised brands causes retailers to become unhappy with the intense retail price competition. When retailers are unhappy with the retail margins they earn on the manufacturer's product they may try to switch consumers to one that "is just as good," but on which the retailer earns a higher margin. The overall level of prices is a mix of the advertised products and the unadvertised products.

The real issue is not what one brand in a particular category costs consumers in relation to another, but what the absolute price level of the entire category would be without advertising. This is relevant because, although we often observe that advertised brands charge more, in reality it is the unadvertised brands that cost less. In other words, advertised brands set the price ceiling for unadvertised brands. These unadvertised brands may be able to "ride free" on the reputation created by the advertisers. "Just as good as ..." is often the argument (sometimes valid, sometimes not) for buying the unadvertised brand.

Advertising may create brand differentiation, but this brand differentiation is relative to the products of other manufacturers. For retailers, advertised products are more of a commodity (less differentiated) as concerns retail price competition. Advertising can create additional value to the retailer for products that can create an image, act as traffic builders, and experience quick inventory turnover. For the retailer, a "quick nickel is as good as a slow dime." Indeed, advertising can "force" distribution, and it often results in far lower retail profits. In some extreme cases, the manufacturer's price of one product could be higher than for another, but because of the difference in retail profit margins the retail price is higher for the product with the lower manufacturer price.

Such effects depend on the manufacturer's distribution policy. With exclusive or selective distribution, intense inter-store competition is mitigated. The best competition involves comparison between brands and between retailers, that is, both intra-store and inter-store competition. Private labels and retail discounts counterweight the power of advertising to enable marketers to charge a higher retail price. Private-label products are not subject to inter-store comparison; however, they are usually priced below the highly advertised brands, and provide a price control through intra-store competition.

It is almost impossible to believe that consumers would be willing to pay more for a product whose sole distinction is that it is unadvertised, even if these products were of the same quality. This remains so in spite of the fact that the higher sales volume of advertised products often imparts substantial economies in product, distribution, or overhead costs, so that unadvertised products have higher costs. Why should you pay the manufacturer not to advertise the product?

Advertising can certainly help establish barriers to entry into a market in which it has differentiated brands, and created brand loyalty that new entrants must overcome. But whether such potential barriers cause consumers to pay more in the long term is highly questionable. The reasons are that manufacturer brand loyalty can cause retailers to compete more fiercely and that prices for advertised brands can set ceilings for unadvertised brands. In some sense, advertised brands can take credit for the low prices they forced competitors and retailers to charge. Unadvertised brands are responsible for keeping the prices of advertised brands from rising too high. Together, they help balance retail and manufacturer power, give the consumer more choices, and enhance price and quality competition at all levels of the distribution system.

Whether consumers, in general, are wise to pay the premiums that advertised brands charge is quite another question.

Bibliography

Albion, M. S. and Farris, P. W. (1980). The impact of advertising on the price of consumer products. *Journal of Marketing*, **44** (3), 17–35.

Farris, P. W. and Reibstein, D. J. (1979). How price, ad expenditures, and profits are linked. *Harvard Business Review*, **57** (6), 173–84.

Steiner, R. (1991). Manufacturer's promotional allowances, free riders, and vertical restraints. *Antitrust Bulletin*, **36** (2), 383–411.

contingent work

Julia J. Aaron

Since this classification encompasses a wide variety of part-time, temporary, and contract workers, employees who are considered contingent workers are engaged in a wide variety of occupations, including migrant farming and college teaching. Contingent work may also be either voluntary, when the employee does not desire a permanent position, or involuntary, when the employee desires a permanent position but is unable to find one. Because of this diversity of the contingent workforce, it is difficult to make broad generalizations about contingent workers. Perhaps the best way to define contingent workers is as "those who have a loose affiliation with their employers" (Parker, 1994: 145).

Although statistics vary, in part due to the types of employees that are included in the category of contingent workers, an estimated one-fifth to one-third of all workers in the United States are contingent. Contingent jobs in the US have been produced at a much higher rate than other types of jobs, and most of these positions are within the service industry (Hearing, 1990; Parker, 1994). This increase in the number of contingent workers has also occurred within other industrialized nations (Uzzi and Barsness, 1998). With this increase in contingent hiring, one can also expect that it will be more difficult for employees to leave a contingent position for a permanent one. Businesses provide a few reasons for this international trend in hiring. The first is to increase profit margins. Profit margins are increased because contingent workers often do not earn the same wages as other employees and are not eligible for many benefits. However, there is disagreement concerning the long-term profitability of hiring a contingent workforce (Hearing, 1990). Another reason is to produce more flexibility in a volatile business environment with varying demands for products and services. The use of contingent workers is claimed to allow businesses to easily adjust their workforce to the changing market. Additionally, the contingent workforce offers employers the advantage of being able to screen potential permanent employees (Segal and Sullivan, 1997: 128).

The practice of hiring employees in contingent positions involves several ethical issues. A primary concern regarding contingent work is the disproportionate representation of minorities and women (Smith, 1997: 326). Because these populations often are over-represented in the contingent workforce, the increase in contingent workers may perpetuate discriminatory practices in hiring (*see* DISCRIMINATION IN EMPLOYMENT). Another concern is that contingent workers are often hired for short periods of time. Thus, contingent work increases instability for many employees and may require them to regularly rely on social resources during their periods of unemployment. Additionally, those contingent workers who remain with a company for an extended period of time are usually not entitled to the same pay increases that permanent employees would receive. This decrease in earnings over time will impact all aspects of that employee's life as well as the lives of their dependents. Since income level is an important factor in determining where a person lives, lower paid contingent workers are less likely to live in neighborhoods that provide a healthy environment with a quality education for their children.

The reduced benefits for contingent workers also have ethical implications. In the United States, contingent workers are much less likely to have health insurance coverage. This is even true of white-collar workers who find jobs using the temporary services industry (Segal and Sullivan, 1997: 126). This lack of medical benefits makes it difficult to acquire quality, or preventative, medical care, and a major illness could result in financial ruin. In any nation in which medical benefits typically provided by the employer are denied to contingent workers, medical treatment for these employees is affected. Healthcare for these workers and their family members may be provided through government agencies. If this is the case, an increase in contingent workers is likely to increase the social costs of medical care. Other benefits are also not available to contingent workers. Contingent workers who do not have retirement benefits in any society that offers little support to workers once they are elderly will have difficulty providing for themselves when they are no longer working. All of these factors negatively impact the lives of the contingent workers and produce social costs that will increase as the percentage of contingent workers increases.

Bibliography

Bartkowiak, J. J. (1993). Trends toward part-time employment: Ethical issues. *Journal of Business Ethics*, 12, 811–15.

Callaghan, P. and Harman, H. (1991). *Contingent Work*. Washington, DC: Economic Policy Institute.

Hearing Before the Committee on Labor and Human Resources (1990). *Meeting the Challenges of a New Work Force*. United States Senate, One Hundred First Congress, Second Session, July 19.

Parker, R. E. (1994). Race, sex, class: The contingent workforce in the United States. *Race, Sex and Class*, 2 (1), 145–59.

Segal, L. M. and Sullivan, D. G. (1997). The growth of temporary services work. *Journal of Economic Perspectives*, 11 (2), 117–36.

Smith, V. (1997). New forms of work organization. *Annual Review of Sociology*, 23, 315–39.

Uzzi, B. and Barsness, Z. (1998). Contingent employment in British establishments: Organizational determinants of the use of fixed-term hires and part-time workers. *Social Forces*, 76 (3), 967–1005.

contracts and contracting

Richard N. Bronaugh

The civil wrong identified by contract law is the existence of a broken promise. However, to show that a legal obligation was transgressed, a broken promise is not enough. Indeed, so much of contract doctrine is about when a promise breaker is *not* bound, it may look as if the law has been designed for those who elude responsibilities rather than for those who keep their word. Nonetheless, contract law is rooted in an aspect of morality; *promise* by its nature is a moral concept and failing to keep one's promise is a moral wrong.

When does a promise become a legally binding contract? In common-law jurisdictions a single written promise with a red seal affixed is a contract. However, as a thing anachronistic or too often morally abused, the seal has lost legal support in over half of US states and is limited in effect elsewhere. A contract can exist even though it is not in writing, though some (e.g., for land) must be in writing to be enforced. When one puts all issues about writing to the side, what is required in essence for a contract to exist? Broadly, there are three kinds of requisite.

First of all, putative contracts are subject to various *invalidating conditions*; for example, the contractors were legal infants, a party was insane at the time of contracting, has promised a crime or sexual immorality, sought to oust the jurisdiction of the courts, or the agreement was secured by force or fraud. "On Sunday" was once on the invalidity list, as was "wife acting without her husband's permission." In the absence of such conditions, the contract is valid so far. Next, there is the basic requisite, known as *consideration*.

There is a promise to give a gift. The common law was clear that, even when there was substantial reliance by the promisee in expectation, the promisor could not be held to the promise of a gift (unless under seal) because there had been no consideration. Each who receives a promise must *during the life of the offer and in return* give something back, either as an act or a promise of one's own, for the promise received. "Consideration must extend from the promisee," as it is put, to make the other's promise legally enforceable. If promises of future action are exchanged (in what is known as a bilateral contract, as distinguished from a unilateral contract) then each party is a promisee as well as a promisor. The promise of a gift lacks this element of exchange. (To suggest that substantial reliance can serve as "consideration" makes no sense, because reliance must come, if it does, after the formation of the contract.)

In two similar situations, one person invites another to "take 48 hours to think it over – I'll wait"; or says "OK, pay me half you owe and I'll be satisfied." These were not contractual promises at common law and could not be enforced. Many North American jurisdictions now have enacted statutes to protect those who were once told that their reliance on a "bare" promise was misplaced. While not everything, reliance is important to the law. Indeed, when no obvious reliance had been placed upon a promise, some courts have demanded that the promisee (seeking enforcement) must show that at least some opportunity was forgone as a result of having made the agreement.

It would be natural to think when courts *enforce* a contract that they compel the promised act. But that remedy is rare. Typically, the relief for a breach of contract is "damages" not "specific performance." (Too often the act is no longer available, as it were, to be done.) What these damages provide is the money equivalent of the performance (its expectation) – as if the contract had been fulfilled and then reduced to cash.

The final requisite involves what might be called *overarching* concerns. Must parties *be* in agreement to have an agreement? The logic of "offer and acceptance" (as a way of characterizing the exchange needed for contract formation) requires a subjective meeting of minds, that is, being "in agreement." Nonetheless, because confusion (and misrecollection) within communications is so common, the law tends to be objective in this area. The court may discover – as a matter of what is reasonable – "an agreement" that neither party quite imagined it had made. "Reward cases" raise another issue about the logic of offer and acceptance. Someone finds a lost child but knew nothing of the reward offered. Logic would deny her any reward unless she knew of the offer in order to accept it. If things come out otherwise in court, some overarching concern about the fair and reasonable would have been in play.

Contract is often characterized as a bastion of individualism, where, having created one's own "law" through the contract, one stands by its terms whatever (barring frustration or impossibility). Common-law courts always said they would not make people's bargains for them, outside the area of unreasonable miscommunication. Yet courts today will consider a gross imbalance of bargaining power between the parties at the time of contract formation. Mr. Big may not have made a valid contract with Mr. Little when the terms were, or the particular bargaining context was, "unconscionable" for Mr. Big to have enjoyed. Here, individualism is tempered by a standard of fair play aimed against undue influence.

A final related overarching concern involves promising away one's contractual remedies in an exemption clause written by the other side. You rent a car and declare (without a shred of truth) that you have read and understood the conditions and exclusions of the contract of bailment. The circumstantial pressure at the counter is neither undue nor fraudulent. So you jeopardize your rights, hoping that not too many devils can dance on the head of a pen. Exemption clauses as such are a fact of life, yet one may condemn some of them as morally unjust, as "unfair contract terms."

See also *freedom of contract; justice*

Bibliography

Atiyah, P. (1979). *The Rise and Fall of Freedom of Contract.* Oxford: Clarendon Press. (Historical study.)

Cheshire, G. C. and Fifoot, C. H. S. (1945). *The Law of Contract*, 1st edn. London: Butterworths. (Classic English text with many updated editions.)

Collins, H. (1986). *The Law of Contract.* London: Weidenfeld and Nicolson. (A restatement of contract to reflect interventions designed to correct free-market injustices.)

Corbin on Contracts (1952). St. Paul: West Publishing. (US classic, with updates.)

Fried, C. (1981). *Contract as Promise.* Cambridge, MA: Harvard University Press. (Philosophical analysis.)

Waddams, S. M. (1977). *The Law of Contract*, 1st edn. Toronto: Canada Law Book. (Canadian textbook.)

copyright

Roger D. Staton

1   Pursuant to authority provided under Article I, Section 8 of the United States Constitution, Congress enacted Title 17 United States Code, known as the Copyright Act. The purpose of the Copyright Act is to protect authors and artists from the unauthorized exploitation of their creations, and to provide financial incentives to the copyright holders. A 1980 amendment to Title 17, Section 106, provides protection for computer programs.

2   Under the present copyright law, protection begins immediately upon creation of the work. Individuals are given statutory protection for the life of the creator plus 50 years, and a corporation is given protection for 100 years from the date of creation or 75 years from the date of publication.

3   Copyright protection is not absolute, and the law permits some limited unauthorized use through the Fair Use Doctrine. This doctrine has been codified under Section 107 United States Code. A number of factors are recognized as providing an exemption for Fair Use under copyright law. These factors include purpose and character of use, nature of copyrighted work, amount and substitutability of the portion used, and the effect on potential market for copyrighted works. In order to be protected under the Fair Use Doctrine, the copied portions of the work can be used for criticism, comment, news reporting, teaching (including multiple copies for classroom use), scholarship, or research. If these copied works are used for these purposes and meet tests of brevity and spontaneity, and the cumulative-effect test, the copier and user of copyrighted works without the permission of the owner will not be considered an illegal infringer.

Most legal experts would not argue against the existence of the Fair Use Doctrine. Although the Copyright Act has as its primary intent to protect authors from the unauthorized exploitation of the economic benefit of their works, there is also the important need to encourage widespread dissemination and use of the works for teaching and scholarship. The Fair Use Doctrine is an attempt to permit certain users to ethically and legally assist the dissemination of copyrighted works while generally protecting the financial incentive of the creator.

Bibliography

Basic Books, Inc. et al. vs. Kinko's Graphics Corporation in Nimmer, Copyright (1989). Mathew Bender, 758 F. Supp. 1522 (SDNY 1991).

corporate citizenship

Sandra Waddock

The degree of responsibility evidenced in a company's or other organization's practices (i.e., policies, procedures, and processes) with respect to its relationships with and impacts on stakeholders and the natural environment; also associated with the rights and responsibilities granted to a company or organization by governments in the locales within which the enterprise operates (Waddock, 2002). Corporate citizenship as defined broadens the understanding of a company's stakeholder and environmental responsibilities from earlier conceptions of corporate social responsibility (CSR), which focused more narrowly on discretionary responsibilities of the firm with respect to social issues (Carroll, 1979, 1998), i.e., actions and functions specifically intended to enhance society and the natural environment. Corporate functions relating to CSR include public affairs/business–government relations, corporate community relations, and issues management.

In its evolving usage, the term "corporate citizenship" carries much the same meaning as the increasingly popular term "corporate responsibility," which is integrally related to business strategies and operating practices, behaviors, actions, and decisions and their impacts. With this definition, some degree of positive or negative corporate citizenship can be said to exist with respect to corporate actions and decisions that have impacts and influences on stakeholders, including primary stakeholders that constitute the firm (employees, shareholders, customers, and suppliers), secondary stakeholders in the broader society (e.g., governments and local communities), and the natural environment on which human civilization depends.

Unlike earlier conceptions of CSR, which focused on voluntary activities explicitly aimed at improving society, corporate citizenship and the analogous term corporate responsibility imply an integrated approach to a firm's responsibilities and impacts as they relate to day-to-day business operations and strategies. In a 1997 report, Logan, Roy, and Regelbrugge emphasized: "Today, the phrase leading companies are using to define their relationship with the wider society is 'corporate citizenship.' It implies a responsibility to provide useful goods and services while operating legally, acting ethically, and having concern for the public good. Corporate citizenship is a multi-faceted concept that brings together the self-interest of business

and its stakeholders with the interests of society more generally" (1997: iii).

Similarly, Marsden and Andriof argued: "Corporate citizenship needs to be perceived not as a bolt-on activity but as something which pervades the whole of a company's operations. It should also be seen not always as a business cost, a trade-off against additional profits, but more often as a significant contributor to long-term business success and entirely coincident with the goal of profit maximization" (1998: 330)

Use of the politically charged word "citizenship" implies that companies are, like individual citizens, granted rights and responsibilities in society by relevant governments. Indeed, social contract theorists argue that companies, in being incorporated, are granted charters by societies and thus have obligations to benefit those societies in return. Because companies are not human beings and granting these rights and responsibilities reifies the firm, this usage is sometimes viewed as problematic, in particular because companies control significantly more resources and wield significantly more power than do most individual citizens (Matten, Crane, and Chapple, 2003). Companies are legal fictions, not individual human beings; they are also tools for achieving economic productivity and efficiency rather than other ends, hence they are subject to laws and regulations of the societies where they operate (Laufer, 1996; Frederick, 1995), even though they are sometimes bigger in economic terms than some of those societies. Critical observers question whether the linking of citizenship rights and responsibilities and corporate power might not represent efforts to mask or disguise less beneficial impacts that companies have on stakeholders and nature in the guise of rights granted to citizens.

The term "corporate citizenship" became popular during the mid-1990s. Its roots, however, can be traced at least as far back as the work of Dow Votaw. Votaw, a legal scholar, argued in the early 1960s that the corporation needed to be understood as a political actor and corporate citizen because its size, influence, and power enabled it to significantly affect society. In language that still echoes in more recent writing about corporate citizenship, Votaw stated: "If the corporation can properly be examined as a political institution [corporate citizen], then the important issues become those which are important to other political institutions: power, legitimacy, accountability, influence, and sanctions, to name a few" (1961: 111). In focusing on the impacts of the company on societies, or as might be said today, stakeholders and the natural environment, Votaw implicitly argued for the holistic conception of corporate citizenship given above, which defines a company's responsibilities as inherent in the fundamental practices that have the biggest impacts on stakeholders and the natural environment. In assessing the size and clout of corporations, Votaw worried, as many people still do, about how a corporation's legitimacy as a corporate citizen can be retained when there are few formal ways of restricting its power, noting that public opinion, capital markets, competition, and laws and regulations seemed then – and still seem – to have limited effect holding companies accountable for their impacts.

Other interpretations of the term corporate citizenship focus more narrowly on the discretionary or voluntary activities of the firm to improve society and on the company's responsibility to live up to its citizenship obligations by complying with existing laws and regulations. The interpretation of corporate citizenship as discretionary activities equates corporate citizenship with corporate *social* responsibility and generally is more narrowly construed than the definition above to mean only the company's charitable giving and philanthropic activities, community relations (sometimes referred to as "feel good" programs), and volunteering and service by employees. Interpreting corporate citizenship largely as community or social involvement represents an effort to delimit the breadth of corporate responsibilities and sometimes leads to charges that corporate citizenship is nothing more than window dressing or a marketing ploy.

A more legalistic interpretation of corporate citizenship equates *compliance* with law and regulation with corporate *integrity* and good citizenship. In this view, having a code of conduct or ethics and a compliance program can be conceived as sufficient evidence of corporate citizenship as long as the company is in legal compliance. As Laufer (1996) points out, however, such a narrowly legalistic interpretation is problematic where few corporate crimes are actually investigated or punished. Demands by human and labor rights, anti-corruption, anti-corporate, anti-globalization, and environmental activists during the late 1990s and early 2000s, along with the exposure of significant corruption and abusive practices within many large corporations, have led to increasing recognition that a legalistic perspective alone will not ensure adequate levels of corporate integrity or good citizenship, or address the concerns about legitimacy raised early on by Votaw (1961).

Reasons for anti-corporate activism and consequent demands for greater corporate citizenship in the broadest sense include the increasing global clout, power, and resource control, not to mention the impact of branding, on different societies in the world. In 2000 the Institute for Policy Studies (Anderson and Cavanagh, 2000) reported that of the largest 100 economies in the world, 51 are companies, not countries, a finding that provides a rationale for why the attention to corporate citizenship grew rapidly during the 1990s and early 2000s. According to the United Nations, by 2003 there were more than 65,000 transnational companies with some 850,000 foreign affiliates. Additionally, there are millions of small and medium-sized corporations, each with the full range of primary stakeholders that actually constitute the firm (employees, owners, customers, and suppliers) – and hence with the need to develop relationships with each of these groups. These statistics suggest that the largest corporations have global reach and great economic power.

There are now many pressures on companies for better corporate citizenship, including some new legal mandates, such as those in Great Britain requiring pension fund managers to report how – or if – they evaluate corporate responsibility and sustainability measures, the US Sarbanes-Oxley Act, and similar measures in other nations. But pressures go well beyond mandate. Fueled by the connectivity of the worldwide web, activists and other concerned stakeholders are now able to demand greater corporate accountability, transparency, and responsibility and attempt to ensure that companies fulfill their legitimate responsibilities in society, which are notably the same issues raised nearly a half century earlier by Votaw (1961). Anti-corporate and anti-globalization activism, combined with efforts by stakeholders like employees, labor and trade unions, consumer groups, and social/ethical investors, have pushed progressive companies toward explicit corporate citizenship initiatives. Companies that have brand names to protect are particularly vulnerable to charges of poor citizenship, since their corporate *reputation* is a valuable resource that can potentially be damaged by direct activism against them.

Company executives who want their companies to have corporate reputations as good citizens typically adopt specific corporate citizenship practices. Such practices can include issuing environmental and social reports that account for the companies' social and ecological impacts and practices; some progressive companies now issue *triple bottom line reports* (Elkington, 1998), which integrate three bottom lines: economic, social, and ecological. There is as yet no globally accepted reporting standard for these currently voluntary reports; however, many companies are following the common reporting guidelines promulgated by the Global Reporting Initiative (GRI) (www.globalreporting.org) in an effort to provide some degree of standardization in their external reporting. Some companies' executives have signed the United Nations Global Compact (GC) (www.unglobalcompact.org), founded in 1999 by UN Secretary General Kofi Annan to create a "compact" between businesses and societies in which businesses agree to uphold nine fundamental principles related to human rights, labor rights, and environmental sustainability. Companies that sign the GC sometimes also follow GRI guidelines in their reporting, because the two initiatives are linked. Many companies have developed (and publicize) internal codes of conduct/ethics or have signed onto other globally recognized codes, such as the Caux Principles, the Global Sullivan Principles, the OECD Guidelines for Multinational Corporations, and a multitude of other codes of conduct that emerged since the beginning of the 1990s.

Numerous lists and rankings emerged in the last part of the twentieth century, which publicize various aspects of corporate citizenship in specific companies (e.g., diversity management, best companies to work for, sustainability and other social indices, most admired companies), not to mention explicit corporate citizenship rankings. Social researchers and investment houses now provide investors concerned about issues of corporate citizenship and ethics with information on corporate practices, as well as developing investment vehicles that track performance on multiple dimensions beyond financial performance. New stock market indices that highlight corporate citizenship (e.g., the Dow Jones Sustainability Index, the Domini Social Index, and the FTSE4 Good Index) emerged during the 1990s and early 2000s.

Some companies with recognizable brand names, particularly those with long supply chains where labor, human rights, and environmental problems draw significant negative publicity, have adopted internal responsibility management systems to improve conditions throughout their supply chains as part of their corporate citizenship efforts. To ensure that their own internal standards and codes of conduct are being met, some of these companies contract with monitoring, certification, and verification agencies to audit their labor, human rights, and environmental practices and feed that information into the companies' external reports. Still others actively engage in what is called *multi-stakeholder dialogue or engagement*, with government officials, non-governmental organizations (NGOs), activists, and concerned community members, among others, both to forestall problems and to produce joint solutions to problems that do arise. Many companies use charitable giving, volunteering, and community relations programs to provide direct and explicit support to communities in which they operate. The most progressive companies do many of these things simultaneously to provide evidence of their intentions as good corporate citizens.

Much activity related to corporate citizenship is voluntary and clearly intended to enhance companies' legitimacy, provide a degree of accountability and transparency, and convey companies' responsibility publicly and through engagement with important stakeholders. Concerns remain as to whether all companies will voluntarily develop the types of good corporate citizenship practices described above, particularly companies that are out of the public limelight because their names are not well recognized or because they are small enough to escape the radar screen of activists. Progressive companies are likely to continue to develop their corporate citizenship practices because public demands for better citizenship, broadly defined, are increasing with the growing sophistication of both internal and external stakeholders.

Bibliography

Anderson, C. and Cavanagh, J. (2000). The rise of corporate global power. Institute for Policy Studies, released 2000. Posted at: http://www.ips-dc.org/downloads/Top_200.pdf, 8/11/03).

Carroll, A. B. (1979). A three-dimensional conceptual model of corporate social performance. *Academy of Management Review*, 4: 497–505.

Carroll, A. B. (1998). The four faces of corporate citizenship. *Business and Society Review: Journal of the Center for Business Ethics at Bentley College*, 100–1, 1–7.

Elkington, J. (1998). *Cannibals with Forks: The Triple Bottom Line of Sustainability*. Gabriola Island: New Society Publishers.

Frederick, W. C. (1995). *Values, Nature, and Culture in the American Corporation*. New York: Oxford University Press.

Laufer, W. S. (1996). Integrity, diligence, and the limits of good corporate citizenship. *American Business Law Review*, 35 (2), 157–81.

Logan, D., Roy, D., and Regelbrugge, L. (1997). *Global Corporate Citizenship – Rationale and Strategies*. Washington, DC: Hitachi Foundation.

Marsden, C. and Andriof, J. (1998). Towards an understanding of corporate citizenship and how to influence it. *Citizenship Studies*, 2 (2), 329–52.

Matten, D., Crane, A., and Chapple, W. (2003). Behind the mask: Revealing the true face of corporate citizenship. *Journal of Business Ethics*, part 2, 45 (1/2), 109–21.

Votaw, D. (1961). The politics of a changing corporate society. *California Management Review*, 3 (3), 105–18.

Waddock, S. (2002). *Leading Corporate Citizens: Vision, Values, Value Added*. New York: McGraw-Hill.

corporate crime

Marilynn Cash Mathews

Any act that is committed by a corporation that is punished by the state, regardless of whether it is punished under administrative, civil, or criminal law (Clinard and Yeager, 1980: 16).

While some authors have used the terms white-collar crime and corporate crime to mean the same thing, the distinction between the two types is important to note. Corporate crime is illegal activity that is undertaken on behalf of the company in order to benefit the organization (such as the manufacture and sale of unsafe products). In contrast, white-collar crime (such as embezzlement) is crime that is undertaken against the company and solely benefits an individual or individuals. Because government regulatory agencies (e.g., Environmental Protection Agency, Food and Drug Administration, Securities and Exchange Commission, etc.) are the bodies that generally deal with corporate lawbreakers, regulatory reform has been the primary means of controlling corporate wrongdoing.

While many companies and their executives are law abiding and socially responsible, the public perception has been that most large corporations and their executives are lawbreakers with little or no concern for the well-being of the public. The attempt to achieve a balance among business, society, and government has produced the concept of stakeholders – all those individuals and groups who are directly affected by the actions of the corporation (*see* STAKEHOLDER THEORY). While many notable researchers have engaged in the study of corporate crime in recent years, Edwin Sutherland's systematic approach to the study of corporate crime in the late 1930s and the 1940s laid much of the substantial groundwork for researchers. Sociologist and criminologist Donald Cressey (1976) followed up on Sutherland's work, concluding that corporate criminal behavior was learned by executives just as street crime is learned by juvenile delinquents. Clinard and Yeager's (1980) oft-cited study of corporate crime provoked much of the interest from both the academic world and the popular press. Mathews's (1988) study of corporations and their codes of conduct/ethics demonstrated that codes alone did not lower or prevent incidents of corporate illegalities (*see* CODES OF ETHICS). Because executives and managers are in essence role models, they set the tone for the organization – law-abiding or lawbreaking.

Corporate illegalities have had a peculiar position within both the legal and social worlds. The early English common-law view was that a corporation could not commit a crime because it had no mind and thus could not form intent. Further, because the corporation had no body, it could not be imprisoned. From these concepts it was concluded that a corporation could not be guilty of a crime. Therefore, tort law was often used to handle the illegal behavior of corporations and their employees, especially in areas where consumers' interests conflicted with manufacturers' interests, such as in the area of products liability. As Friedman (1973: 454) suggests, "In nineteenth-century law, where there was a corporate will, there was generally a corporate way, at least eventually."

In earlier eras, because of a corporation's status as a fictional entity, corporate executives who engaged in illegal activities on behalf of a corporation generally were able to avoid prosecution. Further, the criminal justice system historically focused on lower-class or street crime. Penal sanctions were almost exclusively reserved for those in the lower income brackets – the corporate "criminal" has been regarded as highly unusual. Holding corporate officials/actors liable for illegal acts of the corporation is an idea that is gaining acceptance in the legal world, yet is steeped in controversy. In some instances, managers and directors can be held responsible for illegal acts taken by others on behalf of the corporation – even if the managers and/or directors had no knowledge of the illegal acts (see CORPORATE PUNISHMENT).

The progression from caveat emptor to the notion of social responsibility of corporations and their executives has been the result of social change over the past century (Nader and Shugert, 1980). The evolution in tort law is particularly a reflection of the change from a laissez-faire economic model to one in which the government is considered a major force in effecting social change and promoting the general welfare of the public.

There have been three distinct periods in the last 100 years in the United States when the public's distrust of big business reached extremely high levels. The first period extended from the late 1800s up to World War I, when the American public became increasingly irate over abuses by the business world. As a result, the Interstate Commerce Commission was estab-

lished in 1887 and the Sherman Antitrust Act was passed in 1890. In the first part of the new century, Upton Sinclair's (1906) treatise helped to create federal regulation of food and drugs, and other reforms followed, including the establishment of the Federal Reserve system, the passage of the Clayton Antitrust Act (1914), and the creation of the Federal Trade Commission (1914) to police business. Public displeasure subsided until the Great Depression of the 1930s, when once again distrust of big business was rampant. In this, the second era, the end result was New Deal legislation, including the establishment of the new regulatory agencies such as the Federal Deposit Insurance Corporation (1933), the Securities and Exchange Commission (1934), and the National Labor Relations Board (1935).

Discontent with the business world did not emerge again until the 1960s, the years of the Vietnam War and the period when Ralph Nader became a nationally known consumer activist. Nader popularized the issue of corporate crime by making the issue accessible to the public. (Vilified by corporate heads and beloved by corporate critics, Nader's name is synonymous with corporate crime investigation.) This incipient stage was followed in the early 1970s by the overseas payments scandals and the Watergate fiasco (see FOREIGN CORRUPT PRACTICES ACT). Respect for the business world plummeted. The third era, like the earlier ones, brought about the establishment of a host of new federal regulatory agencies (e.g., the Consumer Product Safety Commission (1972), Environmental Protection Agency (1970), National Highway Traffic Safety Administration (1970)) and new legislation regulating corporations. The following years of 1973 to 1980 ushered in the era of social responsibility. It was during this time that corporations and their executives began to be seriously concerned with consumer calls for social responsibility. In the hope of staving off further external regulation, many corporate leaders attempted to demonstrate effective internal regulation, through gestures of social responsibility and social responsiveness such as written codes of ethics, community involvement, philanthropic endeavors, and the like.

The 1980s were generally considered a time of corporate excess and avarice. By the latter part of the decade the public perception of corporate greed resulted in greater scrutiny of corporations and their executives. By the mid-1990s, discontent with the corporate world was once again on the upswing.

Bibliography

Braithwaite, J. (1984). *Corporate Crime in the Pharmaceutical Industry*. London: Routledge and Kegan Paul.

Clinard, M. B. (1983). *Corporate Ethics and Crime: The Role of Middle Management*. Beverly Hills, CA: Sage.

Clinard, M. B. and Yeager, P. C. (1980). *Corporate Crime*. New York: Free Press.

Coleman, J. W. (1988). *The Criminal Elite: The Sociology of White Collar Crime*, 2nd edn. New York: St. Martin's Press.

Cressey, D. R. (1976). Restraint of trade, recidivism, and delinquent neighborhoods. In J. F. Short, Jr. (ed.), *Delinquency, Crime and Society*. Chicago: University of Chicago Press.

Cullen, F. T., Maakestad, W. J., and Cavender, G. (1987). *Corporate Crime Under Attack: The Ford Pinto Case and Beyond*. Cincinnati, OH: Anderson.

Friedman, L. (1973). *A History of American Law*. New York: Simon and Schuster.

Keenan, J. (1996). Whistle-blowing and the first level manager: Determinants of feeling obliged to blow the whistle. *Journal of Social Behavior and Personality*.

Mathews, M. C. (1988). *Strategic Intervention in Organizations: Resolving Ethical Dilemmas*. Newbury Park, CA: Sage.

Nader, L. and Shugert, C. (1980). *No Access to Law*. New York: Academic Press.

Nader, R. (1972). *Unsafe at Any Speed*. New York: Grossman.

Shapiro, S. (1984). *Wayward Capitalists: Target of the Securities and Exchange Commission*. New Haven, CT: Yale University Press.

Sinclair, U. (1980) [1906]. *The Jungle*. New York: New American Library.

Sutherland, E. H. (1949). *White Collar Crime*. New York: Holt, Rinehart, and Winston.

Westin, A. (1981). *Whistle-Blowing: Loyalty and Dissent in the Corporation*. New York: McGraw-Hill.

corporate finance, ethical issues in

William W. Sihler

For many, the conjunction of corporate finance and ethics is oxymoronic. This reaction is justified by the financial scandals of recent years, when financial activities were reported with an intensity not seen since the Depression. In fact, for centuries financial activities of necessity have had to be conducted according to higher than existing normal standards of trust and responsibility. Of all human endeavors, financial transactions are most dependent on the exchange of intangible items (clay tablets, pieces of paper) and on the exchange of promises to perform at some time, often distant, in the future. This does not mean, of course, that finance has not attracted its share of charlatans – often the development of new financial tools has been accompanied by those eager to cash in on the desperation of the distressed and the naiveté of the ignorant. Many depositors lost money in the period of Wildcat Banking, and the early days of the insurance industry were characterized by widespread fraud.

Although particular institutions and structures are characteristic of each historical period, there is evidence that the basic functions have been in operation for over 5,000 years. The Code of Hammurabi, which dates to about 2,100 BC, contains provisions that indicate active business and financial sectors were already well developed. The ethical responsibilities of the parties have probably not changed since then, although they were undoubtedly much less complex in a less complex and interdependent society.

THE FINANCIAL FUNCTION

The financial function, in its broadest sense, assists in the efficient allocation of scarce resources between those who hold surplus resources and those who can use the resources productively. The holders of surplus resources (who can be individuals, corporate bodies, or financial institutions such as pension funds) are often not in a position efficiently to allocate the surplus to those that can use it. Second, the principle of diversification (which virtually guarantees some small level of loss in order to avoid the overwhelming loss that can come from a concentration of investment) suggests that the surplus units may benefit from a mechanism that allows the surplus to be invested in many smaller positions. The costs of direct investment make accomplishing diversification prohibitively expensive on a small scale.

These requirements create a need for financial intermediaries to bring savers and investors together efficiently. The intermediaries can take virtually any form of legal structure. They can perform the task without any commitment of their own resources (although there is often some out-of-pocket expense at risk), or they can invest some of their own capital in the process. Banks are in the latter category, as are insurance companies. This type of intermediary accepts savers' funds, adds some of its own capital, and provides the mix to those whose earnings on the funds is expected to be greater than the cost (including an allowance for loss). If problems develop with the borrower, this type of intermediary is expected to bear the losses first out of the capital it contributed.

At the other extreme, investment banks traditionally have acted as agents, for a fee, and at most have their capital invested for a few days while an issue is being placed. The saver and the user are then placed in a direct relationship, with the saver bearing the entire risk of ultimate loss. The agent's potential loss is confined to that associated with the placement process.

COMPLEXITIES OF MODERN SOCIETY

The nature of financial ethical violations and dilemmas has naturally changed over time as the economy has become more sophisticated and increasingly relies on intangibles as ways in which wealth is held and traded. The US government did not issue paper money until the Civil War; its transactions were largely in specie. Even after the first US Legal Tender Notes were issued, they were not valid for payment of interest on the US government debt, nor for payments to the US government for excises and taxes. As late as the start of the twentieth century, the US economy was still primarily agrarian. The commercial ethical issues were largely physical: short measure, clipped coins, non-delivery. Even the management of inheritances was largely left to family, friends, or local attorneys, and the assets in the estates were primarily real assets.

With the growth of intangible assets (often merely impulses in a computer) and of financial intermediaries, ethical problems in finance have taken on correspondingly less physical and more characteristically financial dimensions: account-

ing fraud, misappropriation of funds, misleading information, and conflicts of interest in the handling of financial transactions and obligations.

The general ethical obligation in financial transactions, however, has remained honesty – although there is a buyer-beware clause. If the buyer asks the right question, the ethical mandate is for the question to be answered honestly. There has been little obligation until recently, however, to disclose what is not asked about.

Because of the perceived differences in modern society between the power of the individual investor and of the large intermediary or large user of savings, the legal system in the United States now requires that the user of savings disclose all material facts of its situation and interpret them for the small investor. This requirement, however, does not apply to transactions between large and presumably knowledgeable parties and institutions.

FINANCIAL INTERMEDIARIES

The most interesting questions in contemporary corporate financial ethics indeed relate to these large financial intermediaries. Following the end of World War II, pension and retirement plans became significant holders of funds for their beneficiaries. Between 1950 and 1991 the assets of pension funds grew six times as fast as the Gross National Product. In recent years, as individuals have been allowed to direct the investment of their share of these funds (rather than leaving these decisions to the plan trustees), equity and balanced mutual funds began to grow rapidly. Because of the regulatory structure of the banking system, money-market mutual funds were also established and eventually accounted for 15 percent of the deposits in commercial banks. In sum, institutional investors are now thought to hold some 70 percent of the value of the stocks listed on the New York Stock Exchange and probably a larger proportion of taxable corporate bonds.

At the simplest intermediary level, the securities broker or customer's representative is acting as an intermediary, often recommending investments to a client and then holding the assets in the broker's name until the client decides to sell them. What, for example, should the broker's (or the firm's) trading practices be with respect to the trades recommended for the broker's customers? Can the broker ever sell a stock that is being recommended for customer purchase (or vice versa)? Can the broker buy (or sell) in advance of recommendations to the firm's customers? Which customers get called first or have their transactions placed first? How hard does the broker work to get the best price for the customer?

Although the Securities and Exchange Commission and the securities exchanges themselves have many regulations (particularly with respect to use of inside information) attempting to prevent brokers from profiting at the expense of the investment community (and, to a lesser extent, from profiting at the benefit of the users of funds), these are minimal expectations. Some brokerage firms have established regulations that are considerably more demanding. For example, some firms allow their employees to invest only in mutual funds managed by another firm. Some go as far as to restrict employees' investments to US government securities.

Similar regulations with similar intentions have been established in the United States for the users of funds, the issuers of securities, so they will provide investors with complete and accurate material information. Issuers of securities, particularly those corporations issuing securities to the public for the first time, are increasingly being subject to legal attack from disgruntled investors if the price of the security subsequently declines. Issuing the security at such a low price that a decline is improbable, however, penalizes the existing equity owners – another ethical problem.

The question of favoring existing owners over future owners is more easily settled than the issue of which customers a broker or other financial intermediary should favor. The general rule is to favor the existing owners subject to full disclosure but buyer-beware on the part of the new owners. As one corporate treasurer responded when asked if the company would issue shares if the treasurer believed them to be overvalued: "Yes, I'd issue the shares. The investors are entitled to their opinions, and mine may be wrong."

A much more complex set of ethical problems arises among the relationships of the investor, the intermediary, and the user of the funds when the investor is not making the ultimate buy-and-sell decisions. For example, what are the ethical responsibilities of a pension fund when the sponsoring employer encounters financial difficulties? Should the fund invest in the employer's securities, trying to help stabilize the situation and protect the company's current employees – the later beneficiaries of the fund? Or is the responsibility of the fund to protect the fund's assets by putting them in safe investments so they will be more certain to be there to meet the eventual claims on the fund? The question is further complicated because some former employees may have already retired. What risks should be taken to protect the current employees? These were the difficult questions faced by a number of labor unions and their pension funds during the financial problems of New York City in the late 1970s.

ETHICAL ASPECTS OF THE SOCIALIZATION OF RISK

Another emerging trend places on the economic sector and indirectly on the financial sector responsibility for activities that have been for several generations considered governmental responsibilities. This has been termed the "socialization of risk" (see RISK). Less genteelly phrased, it might be expressed as "Somebody else has to pay!"

Starting with the economic problems of the 1930s, society accepted the government's obligation to step in to assist society in resolving major social problems and distributing the associated costs. It was considered fair to spread the costs over the whole society, usually through individual income tax, rather than to assess it against the segment of the society that had the problem.

The tax "revolt of the middle class" that appeared during the late 1980s, however, created serious problems with this consensus. The middle class, which pays the majority of the income taxes (and indirect taxes) by virtue of its large size in the United States, appears to have decided that it was paying too much and getting too little in return. On the other hand, the electorate did not wish to have services curtailed, particularly those services that involved transfer payments to the poor, the elderly, and the environment. The legislative response was to try to pass those costs on to the corporate sector.

The socialization of risk has been most evident in the retrospective establishment of liability for activities that were legal and not known to be harmful at the time they were undertaken. Judgments and settlements in these circumstances are then charged to insurance companies, whose rates had not been set with this knowledge and which were therefore much too low. The insurance company's owners are thus damaged (perhaps pension and retirement funds), its existing customers are damaged if the firm fails, and its future customers are damaged because their premiums are raised to allow the company to rebuild its equity. This latter may be difficult to accomplish in the face of competition from new companies and those that did not happen to write insurance in the problem area.

Risk socialization has also been evident in the effort to mandate actions for certain financial sectors, apparently on the presumption that the sectors are natural monopolies that can easily spread these additional costs over their existing customer base. One instance has been the demand that insurance companies provide health insurance for individuals who are sick at the time they request the insurance. This is akin to mandating that payment be made to a person whose car has been stolen even though the individual had not taken out insurance. The costs must be passed on to those who have taken out the insurance or who will be taking it out in the future. Another instance is the demand that financial institutions provide free services to designated economic sectors or allocate credit to sectors deemed not to have adequate access to credit.

In the case of true natural monopolies, such as electric power companies, such mandates may provide a substitute for direct governmental support. Mandates placed on institutions that do not have natural monopolistic power usually undermine those institutions because their customers find more efficient ways to obtain the desired services. The public is far less ignorant than legislators tend to assume when they put mandates into effect.

The effort to avoid having to balance in an ethical manner the demands of various segments of society is creating these serious new ethical financial issues for the corporate sector and financial intermediaries. Colleges, for example, must offer health insurance coverage for pregnancy as part of the insurance provided to their students. Students who do not think they will require this coverage may find it less expensive to get insurance elsewhere that more nearly suits their needs. The smaller base then makes the cost of the college-sponsored insurance much more expensive. Those who really need the coverage may not be able to afford any. The effort to mandate that all college students should buy into the college-sponsored pool foundered for fear of the protest of parents whose children were already being covered by the parent's employer's plan.

Thus, although the core ethical precept in finance remains honest disclosure and dealing, the operational definition of these terms changes to reflect society's overall sense of who should be responsible to whom for what and in what priority. As of the late twentieth century, these norms are undergoing substantial changes. Whether the economy can provide the resources to support these new demands is not clear.

corporate governance

Philip L. Cochran

In the *broad sense* "corporate governance" is concerned with those decisions made by the senior executives of a firm and the impacts of their decisions on various stakeholder groups. Normally these executives are the officers in charge of specific functional areas (finance, marketing, etc.) and, depending on the corporate structure, could also include officers in charge of geographic areas or major product lines. In the *narrow sense* "corporate governance" refers only to the activities of the actual board of directors. In this sense the term refers to the relationship between the board and the firm.

The ethical issues in corporate governance are more subtle than in many of the other areas of firm/stakeholder relations. The reason for this is that, following a strict interpretation of neo-classical economics, it is possible to make an argument that would *favor* the "exploitation" of various stakeholder groups such as customers or employees if the shareholders would thus benefit. Many products entail a certain degree of risk to the consumer. For example, it is all but impossible to manufacture an automobile that is 100 percent safe. From a neoclassical perspective, the firm should increase the safety of a product until the marginal costs of more safety equals the marginal benefits of more safety. Thus, from the neoclassical perspective, the level of safety built into a product should be a function of the costs (such as bad public relations, lost sales, costs of lawsuits and regulations, and so on) and benefits (generally higher profits) to shareholders.

According to a strict reading of neoclassical economics the one and only responsibility of senior management is to the firm's shareholders. In the case of corporate governance the principal stakeholders are the shareholders. The senior management team and the board are in both theory and law the agents of the shareholders. Their goal, according to the theory, should be to maximize the utility of the shareholders.

Even from a neoconservative perspective, no argument can be made that senior management should "exploit" the firm's shareholders. Miles Mace has noted that a major finding of his path-breaking work "was that directors of large- and medium-sized companies did not do much to represent their principal constituency, the stockholders" (1986: vii). Whom then do they represent? In general they appear to represent the interests of senior management. Excessive executive pay, lavish perquisites, and insider trading are all cases where senior management can and often does exploit the shareholders. Thus, even if it is possible to weave an argument that would defend exploitation of customers, workers, and other stakeholders, it is not possible to make such an argument with respect to shareholders.

The structure of boards of directors is a key area of study in corporate governance. In the United States, Canada, and Great Britain most corporations have boards of directors that are composed of a mix of "inside" and "outside" directors. Inside directors are corporate employees (such as the CEO, executive vice-presidents of functional areas, and general counsel who also

sit on the board). Outside directors (also known as "non-executive" or "independent" directors) are individuals who are not employees of the company (such as university presidents, politicians, union leaders, representatives of institutional investors, or executives from other firms).

Historically, boards were dominated by outside directors. However, earlier in this century, as professional managers began to replace founder-owners, the composition of boards began to shift in the direction of more insiders. Some have argued that this could be a serious problem. An inside director is "in a very precarious position at a board meeting. Unwilling to say anything in disagreement with his boss, he usually sits quietly and waits until he is called upon to speak" (Nader, Green, and Seligman, 1976: 98). As a result, some reformers such as Harold Williams (US Securities and Exchange Commission chair 1977–81) suggested that boards should have only one inside director – the CEO. Others, such as retired ITT chair Harold Geneen, have suggested that boards should have no inside directors (Braiotta and Sommers, 1987: 10). In part as a result of this pressure there has been a trend over the last several decades away from insider-dominated boards and back toward outsider-dominated boards.

Pay differentials and executive compensation are other major issues in corporate governance. One company that is often regarded as one of the more socially responsible firms in the world, Ben and Jerry's Homemade, Inc., until recently capped the CEO's salary at seven times that of the entry-level employees. However, in the United States today the average CEO of a major firm earns more than 150 times the salary of an average employee (Monks and Minow, 1995: 157). This is considerably higher than the differentials in any other major industrialized country.

Ethical issues in corporate governance are a particularly interesting subset of issues encountered in the field of business ethics because of the distinctive roles of the board and senior management in the modern corporation. Theoretically, no argument can be made that would justify the "exploitation" of the firm or its stockholders by the senior management team. Nonetheless, in the "real world" there are innumerable examples of such behavior.

Bibliography

Braiotta, L., Jr. and Sommers, A. A., Jr. (1987). *The Essential Guide to Effective Corporate Board Committees.* Englewood Cliffs, NJ: Prentice-Hall.

Crystal, G. (1991). *In Search of Excess.* New York: W. W. Norton.

Cochran, P. L. and Wartick, S. L. (1988). *Corporate Governance: A Review of the Literature.* Morristown, NJ: Financial Executives Research Foundation.

Conference Directorship Practices (1967). Joint report from National Industrial Conference Board and American Society of Corporate Secretaries (Studies in Business Policy no. 125), New York.

Demb, A. and Neubauer, F.-F. (1992). *The Corporate Board: Confronting the Paradoxes.* New York: Oxford University Press.

Lorsch, J. W., with MacIver, E. (1989). *Pawns or Potentates: The Reality of America's Corporate Boards.* Boston, MA: Harvard Business School Press.

Mace, M. L. (1986). *Directors: Myth and Reality.* Boston, MA: Harvard University Press.

Monks, R. A. G. and Minow, N. (1995). *Corporate Governance.* Oxford: Blackwell.

Mueller, R. K. (1982). *Board Score: How to Judge Board-worthiness.* Lexington, MA: Lexington Books.

Nader, R., Green, M., and Seligman, J. (1976). *Taming the Giant Corporation.* New York: W. W. Norton.

corporate moral agency

Peter A. French

(or the theory of the corporation as a moral person): the theory that corporations and corporate-like entities, in and of themselves, can and do satisfy the conditions of being intentional actors and so should qualify as full-fledged subjects of moral principles and rules. It argues that corporations can be held morally responsible for what they do or fail to do. It offers an alternative to atomistic or methodological individualism's interpretation of the corporation.

According to agency theory, a currently popular transposed version of individualism, a corporation is understood to be nothing more than a contractual nexus, a collection of self-interested humans acting either as principals or agents with respect to each other. Principals hire agents to represent their interests in various dealings. In the corporate setting, stockholders hire directors

and managers to try to maximize the return on their investments in the corporation. The agents, agency theory assumes, only work for their principals because of what those agents expect personally to gain from the relationship. A corporation is but the financial and contractual "playing field" for a number of individual dealings, and it has no existence independent of those dealings. The "agency problem": how to create an incentive system that can align the self-interests of the agents with those of their principals – how to get managers to act in the best interests of the stockholders – dominates that conception of a corporation.

Corporate moral agency theory opposes the individualist tradition and agency theory. It argues that though corporations are artificial entities, they exist in much more than the "contemplation of law" (*Trustees of Dartmouth College vs. Woodward* 17 US (4 Wheat.) 518 (1819)). Corporate moral agency reflects the findings of many sociologists, who, like James Coleman (1982, 1990), regard corporate entities as the dominant "players" on our social scene. It is squarely in the tradition of German law known as the Reality Theory and identified with Gierke (1868), which understands corporations to be sociological persons independent of being conferred legal status. But it is one thing to treat corporations as sociological/legal persons and quite another to maintain, as does corporate moral agency, that they also have the status of moral persons.

In order to qualify as a moral person, to be a moral agent, at least minimally, philosophers, as far back as Aristotle, are likely to agree that an entity must be capable of genuine rational intentional (or voluntary) actions. To say that something is an intentional rational agent is to say that it motivates itself because it has reasons for doing so, and those reasons typically reflect its desires, wants, interests, goals, etc. It is rational in that it seeks to maximize its satisfaction of its interests at minimal cost. Corporate moral agency theory has the burden of providing a convincing argument that some of the things a corporation does are intended by the corporation itself. It must counter the claim that its actions, as the methodological individualist maintains, always are reducible to or a shorthand way of talking about the intentions and actions of humans who happen to comprise, say, its management or its board of directors.

Peter A. French (1979, 1984, 1995) has argued that all corporations have corporate internal decision structures (CID structures) that provide the grounds for attributing moral agency to them. He identifies two elements in CID structures: (1) an organizational flow chart that delineates stations and levels within the corporation; and (2) rules that reveal how to recognize decisions that are corporate ones and not simply personal decisions of the humans who occupy the positions identified on the flow chart. These rules are typically embedded, whether explicitly or implicitly, in statements of corporate policy. Its CID structure is an organization of personnel (agents) for the exercise of the corporation's power with respect to its ventures and interests. As such, its primary function is to draw various levels and positions within the corporation into rational decision-making, ratification, and action processes, forming a functioning intentional entity.

To get a sense of how this works, think of the CID structure of a corporation as containing two sorts of rules: organizational rules and policy/procedure rules. These rules make descriptions of events possible that would not be possible if those rules did not exist. These rules play a role similar to the role that rules play in our descriptions of sporting events. A person may toss a round ball into a hoop on a gymnasium wall, but without the rules of basketball the activity is not describable as sinking a jump shot and scoring two points. In basketball there are also two types of rules: those that define positions, the dimensions of the court, the number of players per side, etc., and those that allow certain activities of the players and forbid others – rules that permit attempting to shoot the ball into the basket in some ways and not others, that forbid certain ways of stopping an opponent from scoring, etc.

The organizational chart of a corporation distinguishes players and clarifies their rank and the interwoven lines of accountability within the corporation. It maps the interdependent and dependent relationships, line and staff, that produce corporate decisions and actions. The organizational chart provides what might be called the grammar of corporate decision-making. The policy/procedure rules provide its logic.

Policy/procedure rules are, in effect, recognition rules (following H. L. A. Hart) because they yield conclusive and affirmative grounds for describing a decision or an act as having been made or performed for corporate reasons in the structured way. Some of the procedural rules are already embedded in the organizational chart. For example, by looking at the chart, we should be able to see that certain kinds of decisions are to be reached collectively at certain levels, but that they must be ratified at higher levels.

A corporate decision, and subsequently a corporate action, is recognized, however, not only by the method of its making, but by the policy that it reflects. Every corporation creates a general set of relatively transparent policies (as well as an image) that must inform its decisions if they are properly described as decisions of that corporation. Such policies must be clearly knowable by both its agents and those with whom it interacts. These policies are necessary for the attribution of intentionality to corporations and so for the identification of the actions of corporate agents as corporate. When an action performed by someone in the employ of a corporation is an implementation of its corporate policy, then it is proper to describe the act as done for corporate reasons or for corporate purposes and so as an action of the corporation.

Corporate moral agents appear in their full form at the level of description that CID structures make available to us. Corporate moral agency depends on the possibility of truthfully describing an event as (1) the intentional action(s) of a human or humans, *and* also as (2) the intentional action(s) of a corporation for whom that/those human(s) works. French, following Donald Davidson, maintains that there may be a number of different layers of description of a single event at which intentional agents appear on the moral scene or, simply, intentionality and morality are not limited to only one level of description: the one where we describe events as the intentional actions of individual humans. For example, the same event might be truthfully described as the president of a company signing a document, but also as the company raising the wholesale price on one of its products. The corporate moral agency theory uses the CID structure idea as a way of justifying redescriptions of events from the individual human to the corporate intentional type.

Consider again the two descriptions of the same event: "The corporation's president signed a document" and "The corporation raised its wholesale prices." The human act and the corporate act certainly have different properties. They also have different causal ancestries, even though they are causally inseparable. The president's signing the document is not the cause of the corporation's raising its wholesale prices, nor vice versa. But if the corporation's raising wholesale prices has a certain causal effect, for example, losing its contract with a small distributor, then the president's signing the document has the same effect.

The way a corporation typically has of trying to achieve its goals, realize its interests, is through the actions of its human personnel. However, corporate goals, interests, etc. may be radically different from those of the humans who occupy positions in the corporation, even very senior positions. Corporations now may even act through computers while humans in the company are left unaware of what is actually happening.

Corporate moral agency theory maintains that corporations themselves have rational reasons for doing things because they have interests in realizing their established corporate goals regardless of the transient self-interests of directors, managers, etc. Corporations, on this account, are intentional actors, capable of being motivated to respond to ethical considerations. They should therefore be treated in ethics as full-fledged moral persons and not as fictions that disappear completely when questions of moral responsibility are raised with respect to corporate activities. Corporate moral agency does not entail that if a corporation is held morally responsible for some state of affairs, individual humans may not also be held responsible as well. Instead, it argues for a broadening of the spectrum of subjects of morality by identifying non-moral reasons why corporations should join humans within the boundaries of the moral community.

Bibliography

Coleman, J. (1982). *The Asymmetric Society*. Syracuse, NY: Syracuse University Press.

Coleman, J. (1990). *Foundations of Social Theory*. Cambridge, MA: Harvard University Press.

Curtler, H. (ed.) (1986). *Shame, Responsibility, and the Corporation*. New York: Haven.

Donaldson, T. (1982). *Corporations and Morality*. Englewood Cliffs, NJ: Prentice-Hall.

Drucker, P. (1946). *The Concept of the Corporation*. New York: John Day.

French, P. (1979). The corporation as a moral person. *American Philosophical Quarterly*, 16, 207ff.

French, P. A. (1984). *Collective and Corporate Responsibility*. New York: Columbia University Press.

French, P. A. (1995). *Corporate Ethics*. Fort Worth, TX: Harcourt Brace.

French, P. A., Nesteruk, J., and Risser, D. (1992). *Corporations in the Moral Community*. Fort Worth, TX: Harcourt Brace.

Gierke, O. (1868). *Das deutsche Genossenschaftrecht*. Berlin: Weidmann.

Ladd, J. (1970). Morality and the idea of rationality in formal organizations. *Monist*, 54, 488–516.

May, L. (1987). *The Morality of Groups*. South Bend, IN: Notre Dame University Press.

Schrader, D. E. (1993). *The Corporation as Anomaly*. Cambridge: Cambridge University Press.

corporate punishment

Robert J. Rafalko

The question of whether some form of punishment is appropriate and warranted for corporations that break the law centers around two chief issues. The first issue is the metaphysical status of the corporation: is "corporate punishment" a *meaningful* pairing of terms? In other words, is the corporation the sort of entity that can be punished? The second issue concerns the justice and effectiveness of punishment, assuming we answer the previous questions in the affirmative.

Another way of phrasing the first issue is to ask whether the corporation is a moral agent. Only moral agents are punishable. For example, a person who is judged criminally insane will not be punished: rather, his activities will be curtailed or monitored, or he will be separated from society at large or confined and treated. This may be done to protect the person so judged, or to protect the public from that person.

One school of thought regarding the metaphysical status of the corporation is what Thomas Donaldson (1982) refers to as the Structural Restraint View. This point of view holds that the corporation is tightly bound to its charter and as such lacks the basic moral prerequisite of freedom to act morally or immorally. If this view is correct, then the concept of punishment is irrelevant, and we must treat the offending corporation in much the same way that we treat the criminally insane: by way of regulations and restrictions.

Another school of thought holds that corporations are best thought of as "artificial and invisible" persons. According to this view, advanced first by the philosopher Peter French, corporations are sufficiently like persons to be held morally accountable for their actions. Like persons, corporations display intentional behavior because they have in place central decision-making units such as boards of directors, which "direct" the conduct of the corporation. Thus, the problem of assigning moral responsibility to corporations vanishes because corporations are *collective* persons and all persons are morally accountable for their actions.

These considerations about the metaphysical status of the corporation are important for the application of the kinds of theories of punishment that are found in the study of ethics. Such theories conceive of justifiable punishment along grounds of retribution, rectification, rehabilitation, deterrence, and others. Aristotle defines retribution as "suffering in return for one's action." He defines rectification as "taking away the gain, restoring the equilibrium" for wrongs done by one and inflicted on another. Rehabilitation is the theory which holds that just punishment should show the offender the error of his ways, allowing him one day to return to society as a respectable citizen. Punishment as deterrence holds that justice is served if the nature of the punishment is so fearful that it discourages the offender or others from committing crimes.

Notice that justice as retribution seems to have little application to the punishment of corporations unless the corporation is sufficiently like a person that it can be "made to suffer" – an intentional notion that seems to have little relevance to the nature of corporations. However, the other notions of punishment – rectification, rehabilitation, and deterrence – do seem to have meaningful applications where corporate lawbreaking takes place, so we do not need to be driven to the other extreme, the Structural Restraint View. Corporations may be moral agents in the way that nation-states are conceived of as moral agents – and nations can be and are punished by way of reparations, and such punishments can set an example to that nation and others as deterrents for similar conduct in the future.

Thus, it is clear that in order to decide whether a corporation is the sort of entity that can be punished, we must decide the appropriateness of referring to this institution within a framework of a close family of moral terms: responsibility, liability, moral blame and censure, moral freedom, and agency. The fact that corporations are best defined as "liability-limiting mechanisms" makes the ascription of moral responsibility (and the assignment of punishment) especially problematic.

The second issue concerns the balance between justice and effectiveness of punishment of corporations which have broken the law. Corporations, unlike persons, cannot be incarcerated, so we are left to the recourse of imposing fines on them. Unfortunately, the levying of fines by judges on lawbreaking corporations can have unintended and unwanted effects. If the fines are truly weighty, they can easily harm innocent people. For example, a large fine imposed on a chemical corporation for illegal disposal of toxic wastes can have the unintended and undesirable effect of causing layoffs in the company, thus harming employees who had no part in the decision to dump wastes illegally and no part in the activity of illegal dumping. Such fines can also result in a company's decision to close down a less profitable plant in a small community, possibly depriving that community of its largest tax base and source of employment. Ponderous fines can also cause higher prices for the company's product, thus making the product less competitive and narrowing the range of consumer choice. If the fine is very large, it may even have the effect of putting the company out of business altogether.

Because of these considerations, judges have been understandably reluctant to impose large fines on lawbreaking corporations. The US Sentencing Commission learned that between 1984 and 1987, the average federal fine imposed on corporations for violations of the law was $48,000, and 67 percent of those fines amounted to $10,000 or less. Thus, it is understandable that many corporate executives began to reason that it was often cheaper to break the law and pay the fine than it was to treat hazardous chemicals or eliminate smokestack emissions – the fines became part of the "cost of doing business."

In November 1991 the US Sentencing Commission, after years of deliberation, issued a new set of guidelines for federal judges sentencing individuals and especially organizations convicted of breaking the law. In part, these sentencing guidelines were inspired by the success of the Defense Industry Initiatives (DII) – a voluntary agreement signed by 46 defense contractors in 1986 designed to prevent fraud and overcharging on government contracts. The DII mandated the creation of codes of conduct, designated officers of the corporation whose responsibility it was to oversee ethics of compliance, required internal reporting systems made up of telephone "hotlines" and ethics "ombudsmen" to allow reporting of legal and ethical violations without fear of retribution, and provided for compulsory ethics training for each of the company's employees and agents.

The 1991 US Sentencing Guidelines likewise mandated the creation of such an ethics compliance program, but broadened the requirement to include *all* organizations, defense or otherwise, profit or non-profit. Under the new guidelines, fines are to be assessed against lawbreaking organizations on a multiple of three to four times the cost of harm or damage done by the violating corporation. However, these fines could be reduced to less than 1 percent of that total provided that the offending organization fully and sincerely took part in the investigation of the wrongdoing (which can lead to mandatory jail sentences for individuals responsible for the crime), and provided that the company or organization had already in place a seven-step ethics

and legal-compliance program similar to the one developed for the DII.

How extensive the ethics training and compliance program must be in order to be granted leniency under these guidelines depends on three factors: the size of the organization, the ethically sensitive nature of its business, and the organization's prior history of enforcement actions taken against it.

Bibliography

Donaldson, T. (1982). *Corporations and Morality.* Englewood Cliffs, NJ: Prentice-Hall.

Ewing, A. C. (1970). *The Morality of Punishment.* Montclair, NJ: Patterson Smith.

French, P. (1979). The corporation as a moral person. *American Philosophical Quarterly,* 16, 207ff.

Rafalko, R. (1989). Corporate punishment: A proposal. *Journal of Business Ethics,* 8, 917–28.

Rafalko, R. (1994). Remaking the corporation: The 1991 US Sentencing Guidelines. *Journal of Business Ethics,* 13, 625–36.

Werhane, P. (1985). *Persons, Rights and Corporations.* Englewood Cliffs, NJ: Prentice-Hall.

corporate social performance

Donna J. Wood

Corporate social performance (CSP) is defined as a business organization's configuration of principles of social responsibility, processes of social responsiveness, and observable outcomes as they relate to the firm's societal relationships (Wood, 1991: 693). CSP scholars envision societies as complex webs of interconnected stakeholders, multiple cause and effect, and they see business as a social institution with both power and responsibility. CSP, then, has to do with the full range of antecedents, processes, and outcomes of business organization operations, and does not focus narrowly on maximizing shareholder wealth.

CSP forms an intellectual framework for grasping the structure of business and society relationships. It is a theory of how corporations are held accountable to stakeholders and the societies in which they operate. In the CSP model, three principles of corporate social responsibility – institutional legitimacy, public responsibility, and managerial discretion – define structural relationships among society, the business institution, business organizations, and people.

The principle of institutional legitimacy states that society grants legitimacy and power to business, and that the business institution must use its power in a way that society considers responsible. General institutional expectations are made of any business organization, and organizational legitimacy is achieved and maintained by complying with these institutional expectations. Furthermore, individuals working in and on behalf of business organizations are obliged to abide by these general norms applying to the institution of business.

The principle of public responsibility states that business organizations are responsible for outcomes related to their primary (mission- or operations-derived) and secondary (related to, but not derived from, mission or operations) areas of societal involvement (Preston and Post, 1975). Each business organization has unique responsibilities because of the type of business it is – its size, industry, markets, product/service mix, workforce, location, etc. For example, some businesses pollute the air and water more than others do; some are uniquely situated to take advantage of or aid poor populations; some routinely face ethical issues of honest disclosure and others more often face product safety issues.

The principle of managerial discretion states that managers are moral actors and are obligated to exercise all available discretion toward socially responsible outcomes. Responsibilities of business organizations include (a) economic duties such as providing jobs, creating wealth, and paying taxes; (b) legal and regulatory compliance; (c) responsiveness to ethical norms and principles; and (d) discretionary social welfare or cultural contributions (Carroll, 1979). The principle of *individual* responsibility emphasizes that within these various domains of business, managers are responsible for balancing their moral decision-making autonomy and their agency relationship to the firm and its stakeholders. Even more, it emphasizes that the support of moral choice is the fundamental responsibility of a business organization (Kang and Wood, 1995).

Processes of corporate social responsiveness, the second dimension of CSP, represent characteristic boundary-spanning behaviors of businesses. These processes, linking social responsibility principles and behavioral outcomes, include (a) environmental assessment: gathering and assessing information about the external environment; (b) stakeholder management: managing the organization's relationships with those persons, groups, and organizations that can affect or are affected by the company's operations (Freeman, 1984); and (c) issues management: tracking and developing responses to social issues that may affect the company. Responsive processes can be implemented without reference to principles of social responsibility, but the result is purely self-interested rather than society-oriented organizational behavior, thus leaving the firm subject to external control processes such as regulation (Wartick and Cochran, 1985).

Outcomes, finally, show the answers to the question of "to whom does organizational behavior make a difference, and what difference does it make?" In the neoclassical economic model, business outcomes are thought of as narrow financial measures such as profit, share value, and market share, making a difference primarily to owners. In the stakeholder view of organizations, outcomes are defined as consequences to stakeholders, including persons, organizations, and societies; for example, product safety, human rights, natural resource use, pollution, and effects on local communities as well as profitability, and to the firm itself as policies and practices are adapted to achieve better CSP.

Current research focuses on linking CSP to theories of stakeholders, ethics, and organizations; systematizing the assumptions and theoretical implications of the CSP model; empirically testing ideas about how people perceive, interpret, and enact CSP; using a CSP framework to broaden causal investigations of financial performance (Margolis and Walsh, 2001); extending the fundamental ideas of CSP in cross-cultural and multinational settings; efforts to integrate CSP with underlying moral values; and critiques of existing CSP theory. Current issues relevant to CSP include corporate governance, ethics in practice, accountability, and transparency via social reporting. The globalization of corporate social responsibility and performance, in the absence of supranational regulatory capacity, is of particular current concern (Logsdon and Wood, 2002).

See also *ethics*

Bibliography

Carroll, A. B. (1979). A three-dimensional model of corporate performance. *Academy of Management Review*, 4 (4): 497–505.

Freeman, R. E. (1984). *Strategic Management: A Stakeholder Approach*. Boston, MA: Pitman.

Kang, Young-Chul, and Wood, D. J. (1995). Before-profit social responsibility: Turning the economic paradigm upside down. *Proceedings of the International Association for Business and Society*, Vienna, Austria, June.

Logsdon, J. M. and Wood, D. J. (2002). Business citizenship: From domestic to global level of analysis. *Business Ethics Quarterly*, 12 (2), 155–87.

Margolis, J. D. and Walsh, J. P. (2001). *People and Profits? The Search for a Link Between a Company's Social and Financial Performance*. Hillsdale, NJ: Lawrence Erlbaum Associates.

Preston, L. E. and Post, J. E. (1975). *Private Management and Public Policy: The Principle of Public Responsibility*. Englewood Cliffs, NJ: Prentice-Hall.

Wartick, S. L., and Cochran, P. L. (1985). The evolution of the corporate social performance model. *Academy of Management Review*, 10 (4), 758–69.

Wood, D. J. (1991). Corporate social performance revisited. *Academy of Management Review*, 16 (4), 691–718.

corporations and the law

Michael J. Phillips

This broad subject involves at least four inter-related topics.

CORPORATION LAW AND ECONOMIC GROWTH

The law defines a corporation as an artificial legal person created by the state. This artificial corporate person has long been able to hold and transfer property, make contracts, sue, and exercise other legal powers for conducting business. Traditionally, however, the law limited those powers. Early in the nineteenth century, so-called special charters restricted the use of the corporate form and the powers corporations could exercise; most corporations only pursued quasi-public purposes such as banking, insurance, and the operation of turnpikes, canals, and bridges; and the doctrine of *ultra vires* ensured that the charter's statement of corporate powers was strictly construed. By 1900, however, general incorporation statutes allowed widespread use of the corporate form, corporations increasingly could pursue any lawful purpose, and *ultra vires* had lost most of its teeth. These changes helped make corporations the devices through which entrepreneurial energies found expression, provided entrepreneurs the freedom and flexibility to pursue new opportunities, and thus facilitated economic growth.

American corporation law also promoted economic growth by establishing shareholder ownership of corporations. By creating the possibility of dividends and share appreciation, and by granting investors some control over the firm's operation, shareholder ownership gave owners of capital an incentive to invest in corporations. This incentive was increased by another important feature of corporation law: shareholders' limited liability for the corporate entity's obligations. In these ways, shareholder ownership of corporations has enabled businesses to amass the capital required for industrialization and economic growth.

LEGAL CONTROLS OVER CORPORATIONS

Due partly to the legal doctrines just noted, business corporations have grown tremendously in size and power. Despite that power, they are not as accountable to the public as are the formal organs of government. In addition, corporations mainly pursue profits, and may compromise other important values in that pursuit. For such reasons, checks on corporate activities are necessary. The law provides many such checks, most of which reside outside the law of corporations.

Perhaps the most important legal check on corporate misbehavior is government regulation in all its forms, including the imposition of criminal liability on corporations and their officers and employees. But actual and potential civil liability also restrains business misconduct. In addition to these familiar controls, there have been many proposals for changing the internal governance of corporations, relatively few of which have been adopted in any aggressive form. These include giving increased power to shareholders (e.g., the ability to pass binding resolutions), requiring that certain constituencies be represented on the board of directors (e.g., environmentalists), requiring that the board have fewer inside directors or that it contain some public-interest directors, and changing the corporation's internal management structure so that it can better correct the harms its activities generate.

PROBLEMS WITH LEGAL CONTROLS

Despite its immense importance in checking business misbehavior, the law is an imperfect corporate control device. For example, legal controls (1) consume money and resources; (2) provide at best an after-the-fact remedy when the relevant risks were unknown to lawmakers at the time they arose; (3) often bear the marks of business influence in both their content and their enforcement; and (4) may be consciously disobeyed if penalties are too light or their imposition too improbable. Also, the law sometimes fails to deter corporate misconduct because deterrence requires rationality from the party to be deterred, and some intra-organizational phenomena make corporations behave irrationally on occasion. Examples include "groupthink" and the tendency for bad news not to get to the top. Besides suffering from all these problems, criminal sanctions pose some special difficulties of their own. Because firms often can pass on the costs fines impose, they may fall on innocent consumers, shareholders, or employees rather than the responsible managers. As for criminal sanctions targeting those managers, the diffused nature of corporate decision-making sometimes makes their identification difficult, and such people often get light penalties even when they are identified and convicted.

The proposals comprising the corporate governance agenda also have their difficulties. Due to the pecuniary orientation of most shareholders, why should greater shareholder power generate more responsible corporate behavior? The various proposals for changing the board's composition suffer from some practical problems – for example, which constituencies and how much representation for each? By allowing competing social interests representation on the board, moreover, some of these proposals may impair corporate decision-making. On the other hand, constituency directors also may be coopted by management, especially if they lack business experience. Finally, changes in internal management structure have not been adopted to any great extent, and business's political influence may prevent their future adoption.

THE PROBLEM OF CORPORATE MORAL PERSONHOOD

The law's inadequacy as a corporate control device is one (but only one) reason for the growing interest in business ethics and corporate social responsibility. Partly underlying that interest is the perception that if corporations can be made to recognize certain ethical obligations, the law's inadequacies may prove less troubling and the need for legal controls may even decline. Any such program, however, must confront at least two basic questions. First, are corporations capable of having moral obligations and being blameworthy for failing to meet those obligations? Second, even if corporations can be morally culpable, does such responsibility "buy" society more control over corporate misconduct than the purely individual moral responsibility of corporate managers and employees? The first question, which has been extensively discussed in the business ethics literature, seems to depend critically on what corporations are. Specifically, it seems to depend on whether a corporation is a real entity distinct from the people who form it, and on whether this entity can have moral obligations. The standard answer to the second question is that purely corporate moral responsibility assumes importance in situations where the corporate entity is morally responsible but its human constituents are not. Identifying such situations, however, is a difficult matter.

See also *corporate social performance; corporate moral agency; corporate crime; corporate governance; moral status of corporations; economic efficiency; corporate punishment*

Bibliography

Friedman, L. (1985). *A History of American Law*, 2nd edn. New York: Simon and Schuster.

Herman, E. (1981). *Corporate Control, Corporate Power*. Cambridge: Cambridge University Press.

Kempin, F. (1990). *Historical Introduction to Anglo-American Law*, 3rd edn. St. Paul, MN: West Publishing.

Phillips, M. (1992). Corporate moral personhood and three conceptions of the corporation. *Business Ethics Quarterly*, 2, 435–59.

Stone, C. (1975). *Where the Law Ends: The Social Control of Corporate Behavior*. New York: Harper and Row.

Werhane, P. (1985). *Persons, Rights, and Corporations*. Englewood Cliffs, NJ: Prentice-Hall.

cross-cultural consumer marketing

Lyn Suzanne Amine

Marketing goods and services to consumers who have a culture different from one's own and live outside one's own country. Cross-cultural consumer marketing often involves marketing simultaneously in many different cultures and environments.

Ethical problems arise when managers apply different ethical standards in their home and overseas markets. A key danger is the exploitation of vulnerable consumers abroad. "Vulnerable" describes consumers who, for various reasons, find themselves at a disadvantage relative to a business entity, not being fully able to understand, express, claim, or defend their rights as consumers. Since passage of the Consumer Bill of Rights in the US in the early 1960s, at least four basic rights have been identified: the right to safety; the right to be informed; the right to choose; and the right to be heard (i.e., to have one's interests fully and fairly considered in the formulation and administration of government policy). Children, the elderly, the poor, and the illiterate may not have the necessary cognitive ability with which to defend their rights to information, choice, and due consideration. The burden of responsibility for consumer safety would appear to fall on the sellers of goods and services and national governments and their agencies.

The US Consumer Bill of Rights is not always honored in cross-cultural marketing. Examples from the 1970s and 1980s of exploitation of vulnerable consumers in developing countries included over-the-counter sales of high-dosage contraceptives banned in developed markets; weaning food promoted using high-pressure sales tactics; continued sale of pesticides and high-tar cigarettes after their forced withdrawal from Western markets; inadequate health and safety precautions during production of asbestos; and the explosion of a chemical plant due to lax safety standards. Numerous cases of cross-cultural marketing were seen in Malaysia during the early 1980s (Newman, 1980). Problems included adulterated products, use of known carcinogens, deceptive and misleading labeling, inadequate product information and warnings, phony discounts, short weights, and unlicensed practitioners. Perpetrators included both domestic and foreign companies. When queried about these practices, some foreign company managers claimed they were doing their best in a largely under-regulated market; others said it was not their responsibility to act for the government, which they claimed was conniving in the exploitation of its citizens.

One might reasonably wonder why well-educated, professionally trained managers in companies with international reputations might take decisions that risk provoking public censure and harming unsuspecting consumers. Shue (1981: 599) tried to explain this behavior as follows: "It has a great deal to do with the discounting of the welfare of people across national boundaries, especially when the boundaries also mark cultural, ethnic, or racial differences. Harm to foreigners is simply not taken as seriously."

One may argue that discounting others' welfare results from the unequal interplay of *deontological* (process) and *teleological* (outcome) evaluations during decision-making (see Hunt and Vitell, 1986). It seems more likely that it comes either from a failure to recognize the existence of an ethical choice or from a misplaced sense of loyalty to the company or one's superiors. Failure to identify a moral choice may be the result of a low level of *cognitive moral development*, or a lack of ethical sensitivity, or a lack of moral character (see Kohlberg, 1969; Hunt and Vitell, 1993; Williams and Murphy, 1990).

Managers may attempt to justify questionable ethical behavior overseas by invoking the following specious arguments:

1 *Moral projection*: Organizations cannot be expected to have the same moral attributes as individuals.
2 *Level of economic development in overseas markets*: Any national government is at fault if it does not adequately protect its people. It is not a foreign company's role to stand "in loco parentis."
3 *Why us?*: The argument here boils down to the naive question of "Why should we change when everyone else is doing it?"
4 *Conflict of duties*: Company resources belong to the shareholders, not the managers. Shareholders should decide on any act of social responsibility that will increase the company's cost of doing business in other national markets.
5 *Competence and legitimacy*: Managers may not feel sure about what ethical decisions are within their purview or how to go about actively "doing good."

Smith (1990: 56–60) summarized these arguments as four types of managerial attitude toward corporate social responsibility:

1 *Profit maximization and social irresponsibility*: Companies may do good as a result of serving their own self-interest but may also cause harm to consumers and would not act to prevent such harm.
2 *Profit maximization tempered by the "moral minimum" operating through self-regulation*: This means avoiding causing harm. Most firms and managers appear to operate at this level.
3 *Profit as a necessary but not sufficient goal, with affirmative action extending beyond self-regulation*: This is where actively doing good starts to be an important element in company missions and managers' decisions. Companies may elect to play the role of "moral champions" (Amine, 1996).
4 *Profit as a necessary but not sufficient goal, with social responsibility extending beyond self-regulation and affirmative action to include the championing of political and moral causes unrelated to the corporation's activities*: An example would be Bata Shoe Company's sponsorship of the Boy Scouts in Kenya.

In order to protect vulnerable consumers from potentially harmful effects of unethical cross-cultural marketing, companies should adopt a proactive policy of information disclosure. All stakeholders should be provided with sufficient relevant information to allow them to make informed choices about buying and using products and services (*see* STAKEHOLDER THEORY). This avoids casting potentially vulnerable consumers in the role of victim. As Shue (1981: 599) has asked: "Why is informed consent not more appealing when it does in fact relieve a firm of the responsibility of having inflicted harm upon unsuspecting people?"

In the age of satellite news and computerized communications, managers cannot pursue unethical behavior undetected for long. Fear of discovery, if nothing else, should discourage managers from pursuing questionable actions in their cross-cultural markets. One would hope that moral championship would be considered a far preferable mode of conduct in all cross-cultural markets.

See also *multiculturalism; regulation*

Bibliography

Amine, L. S. (1996). The need for moral champions in global marketing. *European Journal of Marketing*, **30** (2).
Hunt, S. D. and Vitell, S. J. (1986). A general theory of marketing ethics. *Journal of Macromarketing*, **6** (1), 5–16.
Hunt, S. D. and Vitell, S. J. (1993). The general theory of marketing ethics: A retrospective and revision. In N. C. Smith and J. A. Quelch (eds.), *Ethics in Marketing*. Homewood, IL: Irwin, 775–801.
Kohlberg, L. (1969). Stage and sequence: The cognitive developmental approach to socialization. In D. A. Goslin (ed.), *Handbook of Socialization Theory and Research*. Chicago: Rand-McNally, 347–480.

Newman, B. (1980). Consumer protection is underdeveloped in the Third World. *Wall Street Journal*, April 8, 1/23.

Shue, H. (1981). Exporting hazards. *Ethics*, **91** (July), 579–606.

Smith, N. C. (1990). *Morality and the Market: Consumer Pressure for Corporate Accountability*. New York: Routledge.

Williams, O. F. and Murphy, P. E. (1990). The ethics of virtue: A moral theory for marketing. *Journal of Macromarketing*, **10** (spring), 19–29.

D

decision analysis

Dana R. Clyman

It is often believed that quantitative methods are insufficient to explore fully the qualitative elements of important decisions, particularly when one is concerned with such ethical considerations as individual rights, interests of multiple stakeholders, and non-financial societal concerns. Indeed, in their famous book *Decisions with Multiple Objectives: Preferences and Value Tradeoffs*, Keeney and Raiffa write,

> It is almost a categorical truism that decision problems in the public domain are very complex. They almost universally involve multiple conflicting objectives, nebulous types of non-repeatable uncertainties, costs and benefits accruing to various individuals, businesses, groups, and other organizations – some of these being non-identifiable at the time of the decision – and effects that linger over time and reverberate throughout the whole societal superstructure. (Keeney and Raiffa, 1976: 12)

The fundamental objections to formal quantitative methods are (1) all models, whether qualitative or quantitative, necessarily abstract away some of the richness of particular situations, and (2) complex problems require subjective evaluations, and it is exactly these subjective evaluations that are often missed by the analysis. While it is tautologically true that "bad" models leave much to be desired, the trouble with formal analysis is not that subjective evaluations cannot be incorporated, but that too often, too few decision-makers are willing to formalize their personal preferences and subjective assessments.

Many decision-makers are concerned that formal analysis tries to quantify the "unquantifiable." But it is at least as wrong, if not quite a bit more so, not to quantify that which can be quantifiable. While an artist may be hard pressed to provide a formula that captures her sense of the quality of her work, she is certainly able to compare any two and say which she prefers. This, of course, leads to rank orderings, and where there are rank orderings, numbers cannot be far behind. Indeed, most artists, when pressed, are able to attach a price tag to each work, thereby quantifying at least one aspect of the subjective evaluation.

This sort of quantification is not done by formula, but through the much more complex process of subjective introspection. Thus, the question becomes: Is it legitimate to work with numbers that are determined not objectively, but rather are arrived at subjectively? The answer is a resounding yes, and decision analysis provides the framework for accomplishing this task.

So what is decision analysis? It is a formal and coherent, theoretical methodology for modeling complex decisions in an uncertain world that integrates objective inputs with subjective judgments and personal preferences. It takes the point of view of an individual decision-maker contemplating alternative actions (decisions) in an uncertain environment. The approach combines systematic analysis, with various analytical techniques, to help clarify the optimum choice for that particular decision-maker given her values, preferences, and risk tolerance.

> In this sense, the approach is not *descriptive*, because most people do not attempt to think systematically about hard choices under uncertainty. It is also not *normative*, since it is not an idealized theory designed for the super-rational being with an all-powering intellect. It is, instead, a *prescriptive* approach designed for normally intelligent people who want to think hard and systematically

about some important real problems. (Keeney and Raiffa, 1976: vii)

The paradigm consists of five basic steps, usually conducted sequentially and iteratively. The first step is one of *identification*. In this step, the decision-maker and other stakeholders are identified, their objectives and values are examined, and a preliminary collection of action alternatives is established (*see* STAKE-HOLDER THEORY). Indeed, whole books have been written about this step, most notably, *Value-Focused Thinking* by Ralph Keeney (1992), which explores in detail how to create and integrate the objective hierarchies of multiple stakeholders.

The second step is one of *structural analysis*. Here, the qualitative anatomy of the problem is explored. What information is available and what will become available without further intervention? What data can be collected, and what are the experiments that can be conducted to augment our understanding? Similarly, which of the decisions that must be addressed must be made immediately, and which can be deferred? Questions like these are explored in this phase of the process, and the information is arranged in an orderly and systematic fashion, often utilizing decision trees or influence diagrams to organize it.

The third step is *uncertainty analysis*. Here, both objective and subjective assessments are incorporated to capture the best understanding possible of the chances of various events occurring. The techniques used to accomplish this task include analysis of prior empirical data, examination of assumptions, results of stochastic models, expert testimony (calibrated to account for any personal biases or idiosyncrasies that might affect the expert's judgment), and the subjective assessments of the decision-maker.

The fourth step is *utility and value analysis*. Here, the decision-maker formally assigns to every possible consequence, or outcome, a series of attribute values that completely describes the implications of that outcome. It is in the collection of attributes used to measure outcomes that the rights and interests of the various stakeholders are incorporated. The decision-maker then encodes her preferences for these consequences with cardinal utility numbers that not only

enable ordinal rankings of consequences, but also encode the decision-maker's tolerance for risk. When the accomplishment of these tasks conforms to the desiderata of the theory, the result is a complete description of the problem such that expected utility becomes the appropriate criterion for determining the decision-maker's optimal action.

The final step is one of *optimization*. After the decision-maker identifies the objectives and values, structures the problem, and assigns probabilities and utilities, it is possible to calculate the optimal strategy – that is, the strategy that maximizes that decision-maker's expected utility. This strategy indicates what to do at the start of the decision tree and what choices to make at every other decision node that can be reached along the way. Nevertheless, the analysis is not complete, because, as already noted, all models must abstract away from the full richness of the situation. Therefore, as part of the optimization analysis, one conducts what has become known as sensitivity analysis to assess the sensitivity of the model to the various assumptions underlying it. This is accomplished by testing how the model's results change with changes in those assumptions and with the inclusion of excluded factors.

So does it work in practice? Can the rights and interests of multiple stakeholders be incorporated? Can soft qualitative factors and subjective judgments be included? Can the full complexity of real-world problems be analyzed? The answer is yes, and the case is substantiated by the many successful decision-analysis applications that have been conducted over the past several decades. These applications have ranged from common business issues to large-scale public policy debates. And while no list could begin to be complete, by way of example, the applications have included issues of public policy and disease control, medical diagnostics and treatment, technology choice, power generation and the disposal of nuclear waste, air pollution, validity of legal evidence, and a host of business and financial applications like research and development, product introduction, capital budgeting, and so on and so forth. In *Value-Focused Thinking*, well over 100 examples and applications are presented and discussed, ranging broadly from such personal decisions as identifying the best job opportunity and deciding whether to have a child, to such large public policy questions as deciding on the appropriate leadership role for NASA in space exploration and deciding what to do about the possibility of global climate change.

Bibliography

Clemen, R. T. (1991). *Making Hard Decisions: An Introduction to Decision Analysis*. Belmont, CA: Duxbury.

Keeney, R. L. (1992). *Value-Focused Thinking: A Path to Creative Decision-Making*. Cambridge, MA: Harvard University Press.

Keeney, R. L. and Raiffa, H., with a contribution by R. F. Meyer (1976). *Decisions with Multiple Objectives: Preferences and Value Tradeoffs*. New York: John Wiley and Sons.

Raiffa, H. (1968). *Decision Analysis: Introductory Lectures on Choices under Uncertainty*. Reading, MA: Addison-Wesley.

defense industry, ethical issues in the

Nancy B. Kurland

Common charges levied against the defense industry include procurement and overbilling charges and violations of the Foreign Corrupt Practices Act. Some factors potentially encouraging these practices include the complex legal and regulatory environment surrounding the defense industry, conflict of interest and "revolving doors" between government officials and defense industry leaders (Wrubel, 1989), a one-customer market, and the pressures to meet the contracted budget and schedule.

In light of the numerous scandals in the defense industry, the federal government responded in several ways: passing the amended False Claims Act of 1986, proposing mandatory ethics programs, and creating a blue-ribbon commission to investigate the scandals. The amended False Claims Act of 1986, through its "qui tam" provisions, grants monetary incentives to defense contractor employees who whistleblow (*see* WHISTLE BLOWING). Critics argue that this Act promotes bounty hunting (Singer, 1992). The Defense Acquisition Regulatory Council has called for mandatory ethics programs to become part of the Department of

Defense's procurement rules. However, it still remains in the proposal stage.

In 1986 President Ronald Reagan created a blue-ribbon commission headed by Dave Packard to investigate defense procurement fraud. The commission's major recommendation was for defense contractors to adopt ethics programs, and it thereby created the Defense Industry Initiative (DII). The DII was drafted by 18 defense contractors, is voluntary, and wholly self-regulating.

On becoming a signatory company, a company must adhere to the following six principles of business ethics and conduct (President's Blue Ribbon Commission, 1986: 251):

1   Each company will have and adhere to a written code of business ethics and conduct.
2   The company's code establishes the high values expected of its employees and the standard by which they must judge their own conduct and that of their organization; each company will train its employees concerning their personal responsibilities under the code.
3   Each company will create a free and open atmosphere that allows and encourages employees to report violations of its code to the company without fear of retribution for such reporting.
4   Each company has the obligation to self-govern by monitoring compliance with federal procurement laws, and adopting procedures for voluntary disclosure of violations of federal procurement laws and corrective actions taken.
5   Each company has a responsibility to each of the other companies in the industry to live by standards of conduct that preserve the integrity of the defense industry.
6   Each company must have public accountability for its commitment to these principles.

These six principles are intended to promote sound management practices, ensure that companies are in compliance with other complex regulations, and restore public confidence (*1990 Annual Report*: 3).

The DII remains one of the most ambitious attempts by an industry to implement ethics.

However, its success in engendering ethical behavior remains undetermined (cf. Kurland, 1993, for a critique of the initiative).

See also *codes of ethics*

Bibliography

1990 Annual Report to the Public and the Defense Industry (1990). Defense Industry Initiative on Business Ethics and Conduct. Available on request from Alan Yuspeh, DII Coordinator, c/o Howrey and Simon, 1299 Pennsylvania Avenue NW, Washington, DC 20004.

Kurland, N. B. (1993). The Defense Industry Initiative: Ethics, self-regulation, and accountability. *Journal of Business Ethics*, **12**, 137–45.

President's Blue Ribbon Commission on Defense Management (1986). *A Quest for Excellence: Final Report to the President*. Washington, DC.

Singer, A. W. (1992). The whistle-blower: Patriot or bounty hunter? *Across the Board*, **29** (11), 16ff.

Wrubel, R. (1989). Addicted to fraud?: Why the Defense Industry just can't seem to clean up its act. Even when it tries. *Financial World*, June 22, 58–61.

disclosure

Robert J. Sack

In our complex society few people would argue for complete *laissez-faire*, but in this era of individualism few will argue for complete centralized control over any significant aspect of the community's life. In the United States the notion of full disclosure has become an accepted compromise between those two extremes. Calling on a current example, we have evidently agreed (through our elected representatives) that something needed to be done to reduce the social costs of cigarette smoking, and that it was not enough for the Surgeon General to take to the bully-pulpit. We have also evidently agreed that regulated prohibition of smoking was inappropriate because it would conflict with individual freedoms. We have, however, agreed that we would insist on warning labels on cigarette packs and advertisements – providing full disclosure of the risks of smoking – as the best compromise. Interestingly, that disclosure of the risks of smoking was imposed on the tobacco companies by federal regulation, but it is now

being used by the companies as a defense against product damage litigation.

In their classic text on securities regulation, Loss and Seligman quote Louis D. Brandeis as arguing for publicity as the remedy for social and industrial diseases. In *Other People's Money*, published in 1942, Brandeis said, "Sunlight is said to be the best of disinfectants; electric light the most efficient policeman" (Loss and Seligman, 1989: 173). Although that full-disclosure philosophy is central to most of the regulatory schemes in the US, different times and different areas have relied more or less on central control. Loss and Seligman also cite Justice William O. Douglas, who criticized the proposal for a disclosure-based securities law (which became the Securities Act of 1933), arguing that the law would not protect the people who needed it because "They either lack the training or intelligence to assimilate [the disclosures] and find them useful, or are so concerned with a speculative profit as to consider them irrelevant" (Loss and Seligman, 1989: 174).

We continue to have examples of that conflict between control and disclosure. In prior years, the US Food and Drug Administration was criticized because it insisted on strict control over drug distribution, and rejected proposals to allow distribution of new drugs even if accompanied by full disclosure of the attendant risks and uncertainties. The spirit of deregulation in the 1980s – and the magnitude of the AIDS crisis – forced the FDA to adopt more flexible policies, allowing speedier clearance of drugs directed to life-threatening diseases. But a change in the time required to approve the drug does not change the approach to regulation – the regulation remains centralized and controlling. Salbu (1994) describes that approach to regulation as paternalistic and suggests that the FDA should instead adopt a contractual approach to regulating new drugs. In that way, a patient suffering from a threatening disease would be able to obtain an unproven drug by signing a "waiver of informed consent," accepting responsibility for the risks which might accompany the use of the drug.

In many commercial transactions the terms of the contract between the buyer and seller are implied, rather than "informed," and it is the ambiguity in those implied terms which causes subsequent disputes. Enhancing the disclosure reduces the ambiguity of the terms of a transaction, and helps to establish responsibility between the parties.

In the corporate world the announcement of large salary payments to executives created calls for controls. Villasana (1995) reported that in the early 1980s the average pay of the CEO was $624,996, which was 42 times the pay of the average factory worker. By 1990 the average executive's pay had increased to $1,214,090, which was 85 times that of the average factory worker. In response to that development, Congress amended the tax law in 1993 to deny the payor company a tax deduction for any compensation (other than from a performance-based plan) which was in excess of $1 million. As with all categorical rules, that tax provision can be circumvented in a number of ways. In 1992 the SEC adopted new proxy rules which required every publicly traded company to disclose (among other things) (1) a summary of all forms of compensation paid to their top executives; (2) a performance graph that compares the 5-year cumulative total return of the company's stock to a broad market index and a peer-group index; and (3) a report from the compensation committee of the board which sets out the rationale for the compensation program followed by the company. Regarding the new SEC requirements, Robert Lear (1993) commented that the disclosures would provide a wonderful opportunity for every company to reappraise its compensation systems. He concluded, "After all, it is about time executive compensation came out of the closet. It is through compensation that a company says its executives have done a (superb, excellent, good, fair, poor) job of managing in the light of current conditions and competition. This is too important a measurement to be left to a small committee of senior directors and the CEO. It must be viewed in the open and judged fairly in the marketplace."

The world of accounting demonstrates an interesting ambivalence about controls and disclosures, perhaps reflecting Justice Douglas's concerns. Academic studies have demonstrated that the securities market – as a whole – processes information efficiently, regardless of the vehicle used for the dissemination of the information. That theory suggests that the market will respond exactly the same whether a company discloses the terms of a lease by which it acquired a new piece of equipment, or whether the company buys the equipment and records the purchase and the related debt. Based on that research, it can be argued that accounting rules should be flexible and allow for a wide variety of choice in the dissemination of information, or at least accountants ought not to impose significant costs on society in pursuit of specific accounting rules. Regardless of that evidence, a significant superstructure has been established to formulate accounting rules for specific transactions, going far beyond simple disclosure. Confronting that policy question, Imhoff, Lipe, and Wright (1993) found that the securities market in general was able to use disclosure in lieu of explicit transaction accounting, but also found that (1) the level of disclosure is important, and (2) not all users of financial information were similarly influenced by disclosure – some were only influenced by the explicit accounting. As a consequence, they suggested that regulators were faced with the task of identifying "the point on the continuum between no disclosure and full recognition [full transaction accounting] that best serves the target user group, while minimizing the cost to other constituents" (1993: 363).

Bibliography

Imhoff, E. A., Jr., Lipe, R., and Wright, D. W. (1993). The effects of recognition versus disclosure. *Journal of Accounting, Auditing and Finance*, 8 (4), 333–63.

Kotner, K. B. (1993). Final SEC proxy disclosure rules. *Benefits Quarterly*, second quarter, 22–30.

Lear, R. W. (1993). Read my proxy. *Chief Executive*, 87, 10.

Loss, L. and Seligman, J. (1989). *Securities Regulation*. Boston, MA: Little Brown.

Salbu, S. R. (1994). Regulation of drug treatments for HIV and AIDS: A contractarian model of access. *Yale Journal on Regulation*, 11 (2), 402–53.

Villasana, G. A. (1995). Executive compensation and RRA '93. *CPA Journal*, February, 3640.

discrimination in employment

Daniel R. Ortiz

is treating some employees or job applicants less favorably than others on the basis of characteristics that have little or no relationship to a person's abilities to perform a particular job. Most such behavior is unregulated. Under the traditional EMPLOYMENT AT WILL doctrine, unless bound by contract or law, an employer may make whatever employment decisions it wishes for any reason whatsoever or, indeed, for no reason at all.

The United States Constitution and various federal and state statutes abrogate the traditional "at will" rule in several respects. The Fourteenth Amendment's equal protection clause, for example, prevents public employers from intentionally discriminating on the basis of some characteristics, including race, sex, national origin, religion, illegitimacy, and, in some cases, citizenship, absent a persuasive justification. Section 1981, a Civil War era statutory provision, prohibits racial discrimination in the making, enforcing, and performance of employment contracts by private employers.

Four modern federal statutes fill out the picture. The Age Discrimination in Employment Act prohibits both private and public employers of 20 or more employees from discriminating against workers 40 years old or older. The Rehabilitation Act and the Americans with Disabilities Act prohibit public and private employers with at least 15 employees from discriminating against the disabled. Title VII of the Civil Rights Act of 1964 prohibits public and private employers with 15 employees or more from discriminating on the basis of race, color, religion, sex, national origin, and citizenship. Of these statutes, Title VII is the most important. It provides the widest coverage and, in many respects, served as the model for the others.

Title VII covers discrimination in all aspects of employment. It makes it unlawful for an employer

> to fail or refuse to hire or to discharge any individual, or otherwise to discriminate against any individual with respect to his compensation, terms, conditions, or privileges of employment ... [or] to limit, segregate, or classify his employees or applicants for employment in any way which would deprive or tend to deprive any individual of employment opportunities or otherwise adversely affect his status as an employee, because of such individual's race, color, religion, sex, or national origin. (Title VII, § 2000e–2(a) (1)–(2))

It also prohibits labor unions and employment agencies from engaging in similar activities.

There are two primary restrictions on Title VII's reach. It covers discrimination on the basis of only a few specified characteristics and it requires that the challenged practice concern the employment relationship. Thus, Title VII does not prohibit employment discrimination on the basis of sexual orientation, although some state statutes and local ordinances do, and it does not prohibit an employer from discriminating against minority-owned vendors, although other federal and state civil rights provisions may.

Title VII regulates both practices whose aim is to discriminate and practices pursued for other, perhaps legitimate, reasons that have a discriminatory effect. The first type of practice is called disparate treatment. To prove such intentional discrimination, the employee or applicant must show that a prohibited characteristic, such as race or sex, was a motivating factor in an employment decision adverse to her. She can prove this in many different ways. In a hiring discrimination suit, for example, she can show that she is a member of a protected class and possesses the minimal qualifications for the job, that she applied for it and was rejected, and that the employer continued to seek applications from people with the same qualifications that she has. If she shows all this, then the employer must provide a legitimate business reason for its refusal to hire her, which the applicant can then try to rebut.

The second type of practice may be challenged under a theory of disparate impact. If an employee or applicant can show that an otherwise valid practice has an adverse, disproportionate impact on individuals in a protected group, the burden of proof switches to the employer to show that the challenged practice is "job related ... and consistent with business necessity" (Title VII, §2000e–2(k) (1) (A) (i)). If an employer fails to carry this burden, the practice is declared unlawful and liability follows. Although disparate treatment actions can challenge employment practices affecting individuals or whole groups, disparate impact actions can challenge only practices affecting groups of employees or applicants. By its nature, a disparate impact action requires statistical evidence of how a disputed employment practice affects various groups differently.

In addition, Title VII requires employers to make reasonable accommodations for employees whose religious beliefs make it difficult, if not impossible, for them to fulfill standard employment requirements. An employer must, for example, ask other employees whether they would be willing to substitute for an employee whose religion forbids her from working on a day the employer requires her services. Whether an accommodation is reasonable depends on the burden it would place on the employer and other employees. Similarly, the Americans with Disabilities Act requires covered employers to make reasonable accommodations for employees' and applicants' disabilities if they are otherwise qualified for a particular job. Thus, for example, an employer would have to make training materials available in large print or otherwise accessible to a sight-impaired employee who would otherwise be able to fulfill a particular job's requirement.

Strictly speaking, accommodation requirements embody a different theory of anti-discrimination than do ordinary anti-discrimination provisions. Whereas ordinary provisions prohibit an employer from taking some characteristic into account on the ground that the characteristic should make no difference, accommodation requirements place an affirmative duty on the employer to recognize and alleviate certain differences. Accommodation provisions, in other words, require the employer to take into account characteristics that ordinary anti-discrimination provisions would insist that it be blind to.

See also *affirmative action programs; racism; sexual harassment*

Bibliography

Brest, P. (1976). Foreword: In defense of the anti-discrimination principle. *Harvard Law Review*, 90, 1–54.
Epstein, R. (1992). *Forbidden Grounds: The Case Against Employment Discrimination Laws.* Cambridge, MA: Harvard University Press.
Rutherglen, G. (1987). Disparate impact under Title VII: An objective theory of discrimination. *Virginia Law Review*, 73, 1297–345.

distributive justice

Kevin T. Jackson

Fairness in the allocation of societal benefits and burdens by the state and other institutions. Taxation, minimum wage laws, welfare payments, housing subsidies, healthcare, and retirement benefits are common methods by which the state distributes wealth in a society.

THE CONCEPT OF DISTRIBUTIVE JUSTICE

A liberal concept of distributive justice is provided by John Rawls. He expounds two principles of justice that people would rationally choose in an imaginary "original position" where they are unaware of their own status in society. One of these principles – dubbed the "difference principle" – gives criteria for distributive justice. It states that social and economic inequalities should be allowed only insofar as such differences will lead to the greatest advantage of all (including the least advantaged), and attach to opportunities open to everybody (*see* JUSTICE).

In contrast, a libertarian conception of distributive justice stresses the individual's liberty to acquire, own, and transfer holdings without the state intervention that a liberal understanding of distributive justice contemplates (*see* LIBERTARIANISM).

CORPORATIONS AND DISTRIBUTIVE JUSTICE

The changeover from public to private ownership of business and the transition to free-enterprise market economies occurring in many parts of the world raise issues of distributive justice for corporations. The legal and ethical question arises whether a corporation purchasing a factory previously owned by a communist-style government owes workers benefits (such as pensions and retirement payments) formerly expected by the workers from the state.

With the dismantling of apartheid in South Africa, a debate erupted concerning large conglomerates built up during the former regime. It is uncertain whether distributive justice permits such conglomerates to remain intact or requires them to "unbundle" into smaller businesses that might be more amenable to egalitarian ownership and control of the sort denied under apartheid laws.

INTERNATIONAL DISTRIBUTIVE JUSTICE

Philosophers dispute whether, and to what extent, principles of distributive justice apply internationally. One view contends that the international arena lacks the requisite background institutions and cooperative arrangements to permit redistribution of wealth from developed countries to poor countries. Opponents contend that proper respect for distributive justice dictates that concerted efforts be made to further develop global institutional mechanisms (such as the United Nations) to this end. Even if such institutions are dissimilar to nation-states, they might lend greater warrant to the redistributive mandates of global justice.

International distributive justice may be seen as requiring fair risk distribution by multinational corporations. The idea is that by transferring hazardous technology to less-developed countries, multinational businesses should not impose significantly higher risks by operations in host countries than would be permitted in a home country. In addition, international distributive justice encompasses the controversial question of whether corporations ought to render assistance to people deprived of basic human rights in less-developed countries with which they do business.

EXECUTIVE SALARIES

Executive salaries are sometimes criticized as inimical to the requirements of distributive justice. This is especially so in cases where a company's profits decline while the executive's salary increases, and those in which there is an unconscionably high ratio between the salaries of the lowest-paid employees and executives. Even if an executive's salary is lowered, his or her overall compensation may appear excessive due to bonuses and stock options. However, to the extent that such latter forms of compensation are tied to successful corporate performance from the executive's leadership, arguments that such compensation is undeserved tend to carry less weight (*see* EXECUTIVE COMPENSATION).

Bibliography

Arthur, J. and Shaw, W. (eds.) (1978). *Justice and Economic Distribution*. Englewood Cliffs, NJ: Prentice-Hall.

De George, R. T. (1993). *Competing with Integrity in International Business*. New York: Oxford University Press.

Donaldson, T. (1989). *The Ethics of International Business*. New York: Oxford University Press.

Jackson, K. (1994). *Charting Global Responsibilities: Legal Philosophy and Human Rights*. Lanham, MD: University Press of America.

Nozick, R. (1974). *Anarchy, State and Utopia*. New York: Basic Books.

Rawls, J. (1971). *A Theory of Justice*. Cambridge, MA: Harvard University Press.

diversity

Sharon L. Davie

refers to (1) an array of characteristics of human beings which significantly mark their own and/or others' perceptions of their individual and group identities, especially characteristics of race, gender, ethnicity, age, national origin, sexual orientation, religion, physical ability, and class; and (2) the heterogeneity of a group or organization based on the inclusion of individuals of different backgrounds or experiences, especially in the areas listed above. As a positive goal for organizations, achieving diversity usually refers not only to numerical inclusion, but also to the creation of an organizational climate in which diverse individuals are able to perform optimally as individuals, in teams, and as a community member.

THE CONCEPT OF DIVERSITY

Diversity as a concept involves complexity and ambiguity along several dimensions. First, the differences between individuals which are seen to constitute "diversity" vary according to the observer. Characteristics other than those listed above which are sometimes perceived to indicate the "diversity" of human beings include veteran's status, educational status, and marital/parental status; geographic origin; learning styles; "functional" differences (the function played by an individual within the organization, e.g., engineering, human resource management); status within an organization (managerial or non-managerial, for instance, or exempt or non-exempt); and corporate personnel identification, in the case of acquisitions and mergers.

The differences between individuals are myriad; usually only those we invest with cultural importance are seen as aspects of "diversity." "Cultural" here refers to that which carries with it a pattern of beliefs, perceptions, or experiences adhering to a group. Thus the opening definition indirectly suggests that the characteristics of race, gender, ethnicity, age, national origin, sexual orientation, religion, physical ability, and class may be invested with cultural importance – patterns of experiences, beliefs, self-perceptions, or perceptions by others – for members of that group.

A second complication immediately emerges: all of us occupy a number of these "categories of identity" at once. For instance, a wealthy heterosexual African-American woman and a white lesbian living close to the poverty line share the category of gender. But economic class, race, and sexual orientation will mark their experiences as well as gender; and the very meaning of gender – the particular way in which it is constructed for and by them – will be shaped by the particular ways in which our culture constructs and invests with meaning other categories that they occupy. Companies assessing and responding to diversity issues for "women" find that diversity *among* women must be responded to as well. Xerox Corporation's attempt in the 1970s to create a monolithic "women's caucus" was unsuccessful; today, female employees at Xerox may be in one or more of numerous caucuses, whether focused primarily or partially on gender (the Women's Alliance, the Black Women's Leadership Council) or other aspects of their identity (the Hispanic Association for Professional Development, Pride at Work – Gay and Lesbian Employees, the National Black Employee Association, Asians Coming Together) (Sessa, 1992: 49; Xerox, 2003) (*see* FEMINIST ETHICS).

A third abiding tension in the diversity movement stems from the organization's – and employee/manager's – need to recognize a particular individual's complexity, even as the significance of her or his group identities and needs is recognized. If this tension is not maintained, recognizing "difference" based on group categories can come perilously close to the stereotyping that diversity programs aim to eliminate. Clearly, the unique complexity of a particular individual exceeds the shaping of her

or his identity by race or gender or any other category or combination of categories of experience. Cultural studies scholar Eve Kosofsky Sedgwick suggests that the cultural categories we use to define diversity are a "tiny number of inconceivably coarse axes of categorization," but argues also that they are "indispensable." However, she goes on, identity categories are inevitably limited:

> But the sister or brother, the best friend, the classmate, the parent, the child, the love, the ex-: our families, loves, and enemies alike, not to mention the strange relations of our work, play, and activism, prove that even people who share all or most of our own positions along these crude axes may still be different enough from us, and from each other, to seem like all but different species. (Sedgwick, 1990: 22)

Legal scholar Peter Schuck puts the point succinctly: "Even within a particular, well-defined group, differences among its members may be greater than those between its members and outsiders" (2003: 21).

Fourth, it is useful to notice the relational nature of diversity: we see a characteristic in ourselves or others as constituting "difference" when that characteristic varies from the culturally prescribed norm. Thus, in many fields of work, women add "diversity" – because men are seen as the norm in that field. In a field traditionally dominated by women, like nursing, men add "diversity" and represent "difference." As Martha Minow points out, "If difference is no longer presumed to be inherent in the 'different' person but is instead a feature of a comparison drawn between people, the relationships behind the comparisons become salient and crucial... The [individual]... in a wheelchair becomes less 'different' when the building, designed without him in mind, is altered to permit his access" (1990: 12).

A final aspect of complexity in the concept of diversity can also be understood with this example. Equality in a diverse workplace may sometimes be achieved through providing different treatment for the "different" group, and sometimes through ensuring the same treatment for the different group as for those in the majority group. To ensure equal access to the workplace for the individual in a wheelchair, different accommodations for that individual are necessary. Perhaps an even clearer example is the case of schoolchildren in the 1960s in San Francisco public schools who spoke primarily Chinese, who were falling behind in classes taught only in English. After their concerned parents were met by the school system with the argument that the children simply were being given equal treatment, the same provided by the schools for all children, their parents took the matter to court. Finally, in 1974, the Supreme Court ruled that in order to ensure "equality" – equal access to education – for these children, "difference" in treatment was necessary: some affirmative plan was necessary "to rectify the language deficiency" (Minow, 1990: 19–20).

Perhaps more than any other aspect of diversity, this concept – that organizational equality may mean "difference" rather than "sameness" of treatment – has been a source of friction. A tension between majority rights – often couched as "individual rights" – and minority rights – often couched as "group rights" – often exists within efforts to diversify organizations (see *Regents of the Univ. of California vs. Bakke*, which popularized the concept of "reverse discrimination": 347 US 483, 74 S. Ct. 686, 98 L.Ed. 873 [1954]). This tension particularly resides around legal mandates for affirmative action. Embedded in many arguments against affirmative action is the assumption that the status quo situation is neutral and "natural," and that thus a neutral stance toward the individual who is judged "different" from the norm is indicated. Proponents of affirmative action reply that a neutral stance will simply perpetuate an inequity – not "natural" but historical – that is part of the status quo.

ROOTS OF THE DIVERSITY MOVEMENT

The current movement in the US aimed at addressing diversity issues in organizations was immediately preceded and made possible by the civil rights movement of the 1950s and 1960s, and the women's movement of the 1960s and 1970s. Since those two seminal social-change movements, various other group movements have emerged – for the rights of immigrants, lesbians and gays, those with disabilities, Latinos, Native Americans, Asian Americans,

and others – that have also been interwoven into the fabric of what we understand to be diversity.

Legal decisions, executive orders, and regulations have paved the way for an increased attention to diversity issues in organizations. Probably the most powerful of these was *Brown vs. Board of Education* (438 US 265, 98 S. Ct. 2733, 57 L.Ed.2d 750 (1978)), which ruled as illegal the practice of creating so-called "separate but equal" systems of racially segregated public schools.

Rulings during the 1960s which have had particular impact in the area of current diversity initiatives include Title VII, the 1964 Civil Rights Act (as amended in 1972), which prohibits employment discrimination on the basis of race, religion, gender, or national origin; Executive Order 11246 (1965), which requires employers holding federal contracts to create affirmative action plans for minorities, women, persons with disabilities, and veterans; the 1965 Amendments to the Immigration and Nationality Act; and the Age Discrimination in Employment Act (1967). Title IX of the Educational Amendments of 1972, which stated that no one could be excluded from participation or benefits, by reason of sex discrimination, in educational programs which receive federal assistance, was important as well. Educational opportunities for women were widened, with the result of opening fields of employment to women: "In 1994, women received 38 percent of medical degrees, compared with 9 percent in 1972; in 1994, women received 43 percent of law degrees, compared with 7 percent in 1972; in 1994, 44 percent of all doctoral degrees to US citizens went to women, up from 25 percent in 1972" (University of Iowa Gender Equity in Sports Project). Clearly, there are other reasons for this upsurge of women's participation, but Title IX was an important contributor to this changed career landscape.

More recently came the Immigration Reform and Control Act of 1986, prohibiting discrimination by employers on the basis of national origin; the Americans with Disabilities Act of 1990; and the Civil Rights Act of 1991, which granted to individuals charging discrimination on the basis of race, color, gender, age, disability, and/or national origin the right to a jury trial, and the possibility of compensatory and punitive damages. The Civil Rights Act of 1991 also specifically provides that victims of sexual harassment, who previously could receive settlements only of back wages, can win punitive and legal damages.

Rulings in 2003 by the Supreme Court pertaining to affirmative action in admissions at the University of Michigan hold significance for affirmative action and diversity programs within the workplace. The Court ruled in *Grutter vs. Bollinger* that the University of Michigan's consideration of race as one factor in their Law School admissions process was constitutional: "The Law School's narrowly tailored use of race in admissions decisions to further a compelling interest in obtaining the educational benefits that flow from a diverse student body is not prohibited by the Equal Protection Clause" (Supreme Court website). In a parallel case concerning Michigan's undergraduate admissions policy and its inclusion of race in considering which applicants to admit to the university (*Gratz vs. Bollinger*), the ruling was the opposite: the court found that the policy was too broad, not "narrowly tailored" enough to be acceptable. The implications for workplace diversity and affirmative action programs are many, but perhaps most important are two. First, the highest court in the land found that diversity is in the state's interest, saying: "American businesses have made clear that the skills needed in today's increasingly global marketplace can only be developed through exposure to widely diverse people, cultures, ideas, and viewpoints." On the other hand, the Supreme Court made it clear that race or ethnicity can only be considered in a "narrowly tailored" way, as part of a much more inclusive comparison of candidates.

Civil rights legislation and court decisions have been joined by the forces of demographic and social change in shaping the diversity movement within business. Though Friedman and DiTomaso (1994) argued convincingly that the projections of workforce diversity in the Hudson Institute's *Workforce 2000* (Johnson and Packer, 1987) had been misunderstood and thus exaggerated, they pointed out some demographic forces shaping the workforce which have in fact been powerful: (1) white women have been entering the workforce in unprecedented numbers; and (2) while the percentage of African-American men and women in the workforce is fairly stable, immigration has supported increased percentages of other minorities in the workplace (see US Department of Labor, 2003). As population studies authority Douglas S. Massey points out, from 1970 to the present, there has been a marked upsurge of immigration of Asians and Latinos. The yearly flow of immigrants was on average 675,000 between 1971 and 1993, and the total of over 15.5 million immigrants was "overwhelmingly non-European: about half came from Latin America and a third originated in Asia; only 13 percent were from Europe" (Massey, 2002: 84).

Massey provides a succinct summary of the differences inherent in this wave of immigration compared to the European immigration of the early twentieth century, including "high income inequality and growing labor market segregation" and "highly concentrated ... distinctive linguistic and cultural communities" (Massey, 2002: 92). This has led to a fear of immigration on the part of some non-Hispanic whites, and in particular a fear that what is familiar in their country's culture – including their cultural dominance, and their language – may be displaced. On a very different front, it is important to note that, as Farrell Bloch notes, "Despite almost thirty years of anti-discrimination and affirmative action regulation in the United States, the unemployment rate of blacks has remained twice that of whites" (Bloch, 1994: 1). Bloch argues convincingly that recruitment practices are a major stumbling block.

Social change, though inseparable from both legal and demographic change, has manifestations that affect business which are beyond either of these. Xerox Corporation, for instance, began a powerful commitment to affirmative action and diversity after race riots occurred in 1964 in Rochester, New York, where corporate headquarters are located; confirming that commitment were legal actions (the Civil Rights Act of 1964, Executive Order 11246, a class-action suit), a second race riot in Rochester in 1967, and the initiation of black caucus groups within Xerox (Sessa, 1992: 41). Another kind of revolution among women in terms of self-perception has led to vastly increased numbers of white women in the workplace (African-American women already having been involved in the workplace in relatively high percentages), and more recently to increased emphasis on the quality of life in that workplace for all women, regardless of race. As Fernandez points out, by the early 1990s, "Nearly 90 percent of Fortune 500 companies... [had] received complaints of sexual harassment, and more than one third have been sued at least once" (1993: 203). Legal remedies to sexual harassment continue to inspire intensely conflicting opinions in legal scholars; see Catharine MacKinnon's classic *Sexual Harassment of Working Women* (1979), as well as the conflicting assumptions of Mane Hajdin's *The Law of Sexual Harassment* (2002).

CURRENT AND DEVELOPING TRENDS

Based on several decades of involvement with affirmative action programs and with the diversity movement, many business organizations are recognizing the continued need for both. Building the critical mass necessary to escape tokenism and combat stereotyping is a first step that is still necessary in many organizations (see Bowens et al., 1993: 40). What is increasingly evident is the need to diversify business organizations across strata. Least successful have been attempts to infiltrate the top levels of American management, which remain peopled almost solely with white males. Inevitably, this is an increasing focus as middle management becomes more diverse by gender, race, and ethnicity, and ready to take on top leadership positions.

Five trends seem to be developing in the area of diversity in business organizations. First, diversity is seen increasingly as part of a "business strategy" – that is, something that is integrated into the strategic plan for the business, and inseparable from the goals of the organization as a whole. Effective communication between diverse employees; the ability of management to make decisions that are not distorted by stereotypes; service to customers who are increasingly diverse; responsiveness to (and good public relations with) the surrounding community; and not just competent but visionary leadership for change within both domestic and international workplace and market arenas – these are joining the traditional goals of legal mandates to foster diversity in business organizations.

Second, it has become clear that recruiting increasing numbers of employees who are "different" from the white male norm is not sufficient to create a stable and optimally functioning diverse workforce. Assimilation, a mistaken goal of some affirmative action programs, has been replaced by the goal of reshaping the organization so that it is flexible enough to meet different needs. The "norm" once aimed at through assimilation is itself shifting.

Demographics may not be destiny, as the Hudson Institute's *Workforce 2000* would have had it; but demographics may provide a map which if followed will lead to a new destination. For instance, the participation of women in the workforce is steadily increasing (see Johnson and Packer, 1987: 85; US Department of Labor, 2003). More than two of every three children under the age of six have mothers who are part of this labor force (Morrison, 1993: 57). Other studies show that three-quarters of working women are in their childbearing years (Morrison, 1993: 58). Some business organizations have begun to respond to this reality with maternity and family leave policies, childcare support, flex time, job sharing, part-time and work-at-home options, and other "family friendly" policies. Many more will do so in the future. Again, economic reasons will drive this: in the 1990s, for instance, staff turnover at Corning dropped 50 percent after family friendly policies were introduced (Fernandez and Barr, 1993: 209).

Reshaping the organization may be the solution in other ways in the future as well. Demographic studies show a projected shortage of new entry workers who are educated or trained sufficiently to fill positions which are increasingly technical or communication-oriented in nature. The California Franchise Tax Board, faced with such a situation in the context of mandated hiring of ethnically diverse and under-educated welfare recipients, chose to build into the company itself onsite responses to the issues facing their employees. The result was a visionary sweep of onsite programs aimed at upgrading skills at every level of the organization: FTB felt that "making the program inclusive reinforced the participative element of the organization's culture... training programs ranged from basic skills for operators to a Master's degree in taxation for auditors"

(Barzelay and Moukheibir, 1993: 2). Even more impressive in their innovation were support programs for employee needs like childcare and transportation to work. The latter was a particularly egregious problem for many low-level workers; FTB worked with the Sacramento public transit system to extend the light-rail service to FTB's front door.

The California Franchise Tax Board worked closely with the local school system as well, going so far as to collaboratively design courses which would ensure students had the skills to fulfill positions at FTB upon graduation. At the managerial level, many major corporations have introduced successful "grow-your-own" programs to support minority college and graduate students who then fill management positions in the companies upon graduation. This is a technique increasingly used successfully by companies which want to shape the demographic picture rather than be shaped by it.

A third trend in responding to diversity in the workplace is the recognition that issues of climate demand attention, if diverse individuals are to flourish. "Climate" is a term that refers to the comfort level of a particular workplace environment for diverse individuals. The norms of language and behavior of a particular workplace can lead either to the perception of a respectful, nurturing workplace environment, or on the other hand, to the perception of an uncomfortable, or even harassing, environment or "climate." Approaches aimed at creating a positive workplace climate vary widely, from sensitivity training to skills training; increasingly, it appears that a combination of the two may be most effective. A survey of 55 major corporations in the 1990s showed that more than half were conducting diversity training of some kind (Laabs, 1993). Some of the impetus here is avoidance of litigation: between 1985 and 1992, for instance, more than 7,500 sexual harassment complaints were filed with the Equal Employment Opportunity Commission (EEOC) (Fernandez and Barr, 1993: 203).

A fourth trend is related to this: there is much less trepidation about support for initiatives that focus on difference than when, for instance, the first black caucus groups formed at Xerox Corporation in 1965. But part of this trend is an increasing recognition of the complexity of difference – the diversity of diversity. At Xerox, for instance, where Hispanic, Asian, Black women's, Gay and lesbian, and Pan-racial women's caucuses now exist in addition to the Black employee caucus group, this diversity among caucus groups has affected the very categories that Xerox uses to monitor its Balanced Work Force goals; from the previous groupings of majority and minority male and female, the categories shifted to reflect gender categories of specific minority groups (African American, Asian American, Hispanic, and Native American).

Inevitably, there has been and will be a backlash against diversity movements within business organizations. The very attention to the complexity of difference can be threatening to those who perceive that ethnic or racial or gender identity can fracture community wholeness and harmony. Partly for this reason, a fifth trend is to approach diversity within an organization as a reality and an opportunity for the whole. "Difference" is recognized not as residing only within the ethnicity or gender or sexual orientation or other quality of those who do not fit the putative "norm," but as part of every individual within the organization. At its worst this can be a watering down of the meaning of "diversity" until it has no meaning (see Fraiman, 1997). At its best this trend becomes not a pulling back from hard issues of race or gender or other "minoritized" categories, but a deepening of an organization's commitment to genuine change.

Again, different approaches are taken here, ranging from the emphasis on skill improvement for all sectors and strata at California Franchise Tax Board, to the small group dialogues promoted in earlier years at Digital through their "Valuing Differences" program. What seems strongest about this trend toward exploring the diversity of the whole is related to the insights of the "learning organization" movement, as espoused by Peter Senge (1990) and others: through suspending and testing assumptions in dialogue with others, relationship may be fostered; through risking the surfacing of mental models, learning will be experienced.

That fostering of relationship and learning, on both the organizational and interpersonal levels, is the ultimate goal of managing diversity in business organizations. In more applied terms, Xerox, in describing the benefits of inclusive diversity programs, asserts the company will "leverage differences as a competitive advantage; develop leadership that values unique perspectives; embrace a framework within which diverse work groups can consistently perform and improve their work" (Xerox, 2003: 3).

Whether celebrating differences among employees or responding to bias and potential abuse of power in the workplace, diversity initiatives are increasingly integrated into business policy and practice.

See also *affirmative action programs; equal opportunity; multinational marketing; multiculturalism; racism; sexual harassment; women in leadership; work and family*

Bibliography

Barzelay, M. and Moukheibir, C. (1993). *The California Franchise Tax Board: Strategies for a Changing Workforce*, Case Program, Kennedy School of Government. Cambridge, MA: Harvard University Press.

Bloch, F. (1994). *Antidiscrimination Law and Minority Employment: Recruitment Practices and Regulatory Constraints*. Chicago: University of Chicago Press.

Bowens, H. et al. (1993). Managing cultural diversity toward true multiculturalism: Some knowledge from the black perspective. In R. R. Sims and R. F. Dennehy (eds.), *Diversity and Differences in Organizations: An Agenda for Answers and Questions*. Westport, CT: Quorum Books, 33–46.

Denton, N. A. and Tolney, S. E. (eds.) (2002). *American Diversity: A Demographic Challenge for the Twenty-first Century*. Albany. NY: State University of New York Press.

Fernandez, J. P. and Barr, M. (1993). *The Diversity Advantage: How American Business Can Out-Perform Japanese and European Companies in the Global Marketplace*. New York: Lexington Books of Macmillan.

Fraiman, S. (1997). Diversity in adversity: The retreat from affirmative action. *NWSA Journal*, spring, 34–43.

Friedman, J. and DiTomaso, N. (1994). What managers need to know about demographic projections. Unpublished paper, presented at the AACSB/GMAC Conference on New Models of Management Education, Philadelphia, 23–24 September.

Gregory, R. F. (2001). *Age Discrimination in the Workplace: Old at a Young Age*. New Brunswick, NJ: Rutgers University Press.

Hajdin, M. (2002). *The Law of Sexual Harassment: A Critique*. London: Associated University Presses.

Jackson L. (2003). Supreme Court ruling shows national importance of diversity goals but sets limits on methods. *Jackson Lewis Preventive Strategies: A Bulletin of Workplace Law for Employers*, fall, http://www.jacksonlewis.com/publications/newsletters/PS/2003, 1–3.

Johnson, W. B. and Packer, A. H. (1987). *Workforce 2000: Work and Workers for the 21st Century*. Indianapolis, IN: Hudson Institute.

Laabs, J. (1993). Interest in diversity training continues to grow. *Personnel Journal*, October, 18–20.

MacKinnon, C. A. (1979). *Sexual Harassment of Working Women*. New Haven, CT: Yale University Press.

Maschke, K. J. (1989). *Litigation, Courts, and Women Workers*. New York: Praeger.

Massey, D. S. (2002). The new immigration and ethnicity in the United States. In N. A. Denton and S. E. Tolney (eds.), *American Diversity: A Demographic Challenge for the Twenty-First Century*. Albany, NY: State University of New York Press.

Minow, M. (1990). *Making All the Difference: Inclusion, Exclusion, and American Law*. Ithaca, NY: Cornell University Press.

Morrison, P. A. (1993). Congress and the year 2000: Peering into the demographic future. *Business Horizons*, November/December, 55–63.

Schuck, P. H. (2003). *Diversity in America: Keeping Government at a Safe Distance*. Cambridge, MA: Belknap Press of Harvard University Press.

Sedgwick, E. K. (1990). *Epistemology of the Closet*. Berkeley: University of California Press.

Senge, P. M. (1990). *The Fifth Discipline: The Art and Practice of the Learning Organization*. New York: Doubleday.

Sessa, V. I. (1992). Managing diversity at the Xerox Corporation: Balanced workforce goals and caucus groups. In S. E. Jackson and Associates, *Diversity in the Workplace: Human Resource Initiatives*. New York: Guilford Press, 37–64.

Supreme Court website (2003). http://www.supremecourtus.gov/opinions/02pdf/02–516.pdf (*Grutter vs. Bollinger*).

University of Iowa Gender Equity in Sports Project (2003). What Title IX is and what it strives to accomplish. http://bailiwick.lib.uiowa.edu/ge/TitleIX.html.

US Department of Labor, Bureau of Labor Statistics (2003). *Labor Force Statistics from the Current Population Survey*. http://data.bls.gov.servlet/SurveyOutletServlet, 1–12.

Xerox (2003). *Different Ideas, Diverse People, Dramatic Results.* Xerox Corporation brochure, 1–4.

due process

Patricia H. Werhane and Tara J. Radin

A means by which one can appeal a decision in order to get an explanation of that action and/or a disinterested, objective, or fair judgment of its rightness or wrongness. In the law, due process guarantees people protection from governmental action. According to the Fifth and Fourteenth Amendments of the US Constitution, every accused person has a right to a fair hearing and an impartial evaluation of his or her guilt or innocence.

There are two components of due process: procedural and substantive. Procedural due process demands that people have access to channels through which they can challenge decisions; substantive due process entails inquiry into the types of reasons that undergird decisions.

In the context of the workplace, due process is, or should be, a formal procedural right: the right of employees and employers to grievance, arbitration, or some other appeals procedure to evaluate an employer's decision in firing, promotion, or demotion, or to judge questionable activities of employees. At a minimum, it would give a person a right not to be transferred, demoted, or fired without a hearing or some other grievance procedure. Procedural due process would give employees rights to some form of grievance procedure; substantive due process would require that there be good reasons for employment decisions. Substantive due process does not preclude demotion or firing, but it questions the arbitrariness of employment decisions.

Traditionally, courts have recognized the rights of corporations in the private sector of the economy to procedural due process without requiring due process for employees within those companies. The justification put forward is that since corporations act in the public interest, they, like persons in the public areas, should be afforded the right to due process. Persons in private employment, on the other hand, are not subject to or protected by the principles that govern the public domain.

The rationale for not requiring due process in the workplace is grounded in the distinction between the public and the private. This distinction falls out of a tradition in Western thinking that distinguishes between the public and private spheres of life. The public sphere contains that part of a person's life that lies within the bounds of government regulation; the private sphere contains that part that lies outside those bounds. This is essentially an appeal to the right to privacy: at home a person may do as she wishes, but in public these activities are restricted by the rights of others. By analogy, what goes on in a privately owned business or corporation lies outside the public domain of jurisdiction (Wallace, 1986).

Recently, however, there has been an increasing overlap between private enterprise and public interests such that at least one legal scholar argues "developments in the twentieth century have significantly undermined the 'privateness' of the modern business corporations, with the result that the traditional bases for distinguishing them from public corporations have largely disappeared" (Frug, 1980: 1129). Yet, despite this trend, the failure to recognize employee rights, including the right to due process, has not been affected.

Interestingly, due process *is* guaranteed for permanent full-time workers in the public sector of the economy, that is, for workers in local, state, and national government positions. The reasoning for this is as follows. The Constitution restricts governmental actions, even when the government is acting as an employer. The constitutional provisions that protect liberty and property rights guarantee that any alleged violation or deprivation of those rights may be challenged by some form of due process, and employment falls within the relevant category of liberty and property rights. According to recent US Supreme Court decisions, when a state worker is a permanent employee he or she has a property interest in his or her employment. Because his or her productivity contributed to the place of employment, a public worker is entitled to his or her job unless there is good reason to question that (e.g., poor work habits, habitual absences, and other abuses). Moreover, if a discharge would prevent him or her from obtaining other employment, that employee has a right to due process before being terminated.

This justification for extending due process protections to public employees is grounded in a public employee's proprietary interest in her job. If that argument makes sense, it is curious that this justification does not apply to rights of employees in the private sector as well, since the distinction between public and private employment rests on the nature of the employer, not on the proprietary interests or lack thereof in one's job.

The expansion of employee protections in the private sector to what might be considered just claims to due process gives to the state and the courts more opportunity to interfere with the private economy, and thus might further skew a precarious but delicate balance between the private economic sector and public policy. But, if the distinction between public and private institutions is no longer clear cut, and the tradition of the public versus private spheres is no longer in place, it is increasingly difficult to distinguish rights of public employees from those of employees in the private sector. It is inconsistent not to recognize and extend constitutional guarantees so as to protect all citizens equally. Moreover, if due process is crucial to political relationships between the individual and the state in all areas, even in employment, why is it not central in relationships between employees and corporations, since at least some of the companies in question are as large and powerful as small nations? It is, in fact, not in keeping with our democratic tradition *not* to mandate such rights.

Bibliography

Ewing, D. (1977). *Freedom Inside the Organization*. New York: McGraw-Hill.

Frug, G. E. (1980). The city as a legal concept. *Harvard Law Review*, **93**, 1059–154.

Wallace, R. (1986). Union waiver of public employees' due process rights. *Industrial Relations Law Journal*, 8, 583–600.

Werhane, P. (1985). *Persons, Rights, and Corporations*. Englewood Cliffs, NJ: Prentice-Hall.

Werhane, P. and Radin, T. (1995). Employment at will and due process. In T. Donaldson and P. Werhane (eds.), *Ethical Issues in Business*, 4th edn. Englewood Cliffs, NJ: Prentice-Hall.

E

e-business

Timothy L. Fort

During the e-commerce fervor of the late 1990s, it often seemed that the Internet might be ushering in an entirely new set of ethical issues for business. With the passage of time, it is more accurate to say that there were many old issues that were dressed in a new form and that there were some technologically driven issues that, if not entirely new, were strangely enough presented to have the effect of dealing with new ethical issues for business.

Many electronic business issues are simply new versions of old themes. Fraud is an issue reaching back to ancient sacred literature and in oral traditions before that. But experiencing instantaneous fraud perpetrated by someone never seen before, but with whom a person is contracting – such as in an E-Bay auction – does seem different. Even in contrast with earlier electronic contracting through telegrams, the instantaneous nature of a transaction and the physical disembodiment from a face-to-face transaction makes it much harder to make a wrongdoer accountable.

Similarly, businesses have accumulated marketing information on consumers for years and also have listened in on employees' telephone conversations. Yet the ease with which a business can do this through the monitoring of computer movements represents new twists on old issues. Defaming another person is a long-standing problem, but the ability to duplicate infinitely the libelous remark exacerbates the possibility of harm to the defamed person and increases the possibility of liability for the person making the remark as well as the repeater of the information.

Thus, the novelty of electronic business provides the impression of something dramatically new. What frequently seemed new, however, was a new guise for conventionally unethical and illegal behavior. There are, however, some issues that if not totally new, are so different that applying ethical and legal principles is significantly challenged.

First, while globalization has made it difficult to know what political sovereign's rules apply, the Internet does truly introduce a level of borderless transactions and communications that make cultural relativism almost seem quaint. Examples of this have occurred domestically within the United States, where operators of adult websites in California were convicted of violating Tennessee obscenity laws because the offending websites were accessible by paying Tennessee customers. This conviction, undoubtedly surprising to the couple operating the website, has been replicated in other instances where because an Internet site can be accessed wherever one has a computer and a modem, a business can find itself liable for civil and even criminal wrongs in places it never anticipated reaching. The examples become even more interesting internationally where insulting a country's police force could make one criminally liable in that country even without setting foot in it. The jurisdictional questions surrounding the Internet raise profound legal issues, but they also lay bare the differing cultural values that are no longer separated by oceans, land, or air. This has prompted efforts to develop a single body of rules applicable anywhere. In the United States, that effort has resulted in the Uniform Computer Information Transaction Act (UCITA), which recommends a standard set of contractual rules for software.

Internationally, the United Nation's UNIC-TRAL initiative serves a similar function for trying to systematize international rules.

Second, as mentioned previously, there is a long history of companies intruding on consumer and employee privacy (sometimes within legal constraints and sometimes not), but today's technology does present challenges of a different nature. The ability of companies to install "keystroke" monitoring gives employers the ability to not only track what messages and statements an employee may make, but also to track the thoughts of the employee who may type a sentence and change her mind, but whose original construction of a message has been captured by a centralized recording system. Such monitoring goes beyond tracking messages – it tracks thought itself.

Third, the desirability of transacting business on the Internet gives rise to issues such as what constitutes an authorizing signature. To be valid and enforceable, many kinds of contracts must be in writing and must contain the signature of a person to verify the authenticity of the proposed offer and acceptance. Does an "electronic signature" meet legal standards, and do they, in fact, adequately protect against fraud? Users of fax machines faced these issues in the 1980s, but even with that technology, a person or court could observe whether or not the purported signature did match an original, executed validation. Signatures, however, are much different in Internet transmissions. Anyone can type "Tim Fort" so that the words "Tim Fort" authenticate nothing in an e-mail offer. As a result, various kinds of encryption and biometric technologies exist in order to try to replicate the security offered by a handwritten signature.

Thus, many issues in electronic business are ethical and legal issues as old as business itself. But new technologies tend to roil perceptions as to whether old rules remain relevant. In most instances they do, as demonstrated in a slightly different context with respect to accounting rules and the valuation of e-businesses. In other cases, however, the issues are new enough or are entirely novel so as to require significant rethinking of what is necessary to deal with ethical and legal ambiguities.

economic efficiency

Patrick Primeaux and John A. Stieber

The ethical implications of economic efficiency arise within a behavioral definition of profit maximization and focus on long-term opportunity cost decisions about the allocation of scarce resources.

From a technical perspective, profit maximization is defined as the set of conditions where marginal revenue is equal to marginal cost (MR = MC), and the marginal-cost curve intersects the marginal-revenue curve from below. It is at that point, and only at that point, that a firm operates at a level of output that guarantees the community the maximum amount of goods and services produced from a given set of scarce resources.

From a behavioral perspective, MR = MC can be translated into producing the right kind and the right amount of goods and services consumers want at the lowest possible cost. The right kind and amount of goods and services are determined by the market, that is, supply and demand. Producing at the lowest possible cost is probably the most recognizable tenet of business behavior. Assuming consumer sovereignty (consumer wants) and low-cost market advantage (lowest possible cost), the behavior of profit maximization also recognizes that all resources used in production are scarce. Accordingly, inefficient use of any scarce resource is unethical because it yields fewer goods and services to the community of individual consumers. Efficient use of scarce resources is ethical because it yields more goods and services to the community of consumers.

Within profit maximization, economic efficiencies are tied to cost allocation decisions. These costs are usually defined as fixed, variable, and opportunity costs. In accounting, these cost allocation decisions are defined in terms of fixed and variable costs. From this perspective, efficiency is focused on the allocation of fixed and variable costs. In economics, these cost allocation decisions are defined in terms of fixed, variable, and opportunity costs. This difference in determining profits is crucial.

Opportunity costs are forgone goods and services that could have been produced from a given set of resources that were used to produce other goods and services. Once resources are allocated to establishing a used-car lot in an Amish community, or to producing chairs rather than automobiles, these resources are forgone. They can never be used to provide other goods and services for the community.

Rather than centering allocation decisions simply on fixed and variable costs, economic efficiency and profit maximization would situate the allocation of these costs within the wider context of opportunity costs. Internally, the focus would be on efficient use of the factors of production: capital, labor-time, land, creativity–entrepreneurship.

The costs associated with the factors of production are described as payments: the payment to capital is interest; to labor-time, wages; to land, rent; to creativity–entrepreneurship, profits. When each of the factors of production is regarded as a scarce resource, it is a matter of economic efficiency and of good ethics to pay each according to market standards, that is, the value of its marginal product. To pay either more or less is economically inefficient and unethical. It would also result in opportunity costs for the company. Paid less than the value of his/her marginal product, the employee, a scarce human resource, would leave the company. Paid more, the company's opportunity costs would result in fewer resources from which to produce the goods and services the community wants.

Externally, a firm's opportunity costs are tied to every consideration arising from the greater community in which the firm exists, from the immediacy of geographical location to philosophical, religious, legal, sociological, and cultural implications of the greater world. To choose to establish a used-car lot within an Amish community would be inefficient and unethical because the religious practices of a certain people within a certain place were not considered. Likewise, to ignore gift exchanging in Japan would be inefficient and unethical.

From an ethical perspective, profit maximization and the efficiencies of profit maximization become the primary standard of judgment. Other implications, for example, legal, religious, philosophical, enter into judgment as opportunity cost considerations. These considerations can and do change. The changing medical and political sentiment against smoking cigarettes would be an opportunity cost consideration for the tobacco industry. Similarly, social and legal prohibitions against certain drugs can and do change. Profit maximization and economic efficiency, valuing the sovereignty of the individual consumer and of the individual producer, reserves judgment, in the final analysis, to the market. However, it brings all of these market interests into the equation through long-term opportunity cost considerations.

Opportunity cost decision-making does not ignore conflict of interest between individual ethics and corporate ethics. Rather, it assumes a distinction between an individual's ethics and a company's ethics. As the individual's ethics could be religiously or philosophically determined, the firm's ethics should be economically determined. It is, therefore, of tremendous importance that the individual defines his/her own ethics and that the company does the same. The individual is, then, in a position to judge whether to enter into, and contribute to, a certain industry or company. The ethical mandate of the company is to profit maximize through economic efficiencies. Ethical concerns about the company's product (the right kind of goods and services) are determined primarily by the market and individual producers and consumers.

This paradigm for business ethics focuses on economic efficiency as explained in the behavior of profit maximization and measured by opportunity costs. It is grounded in business theory and practice, uses the language of business, and relates directly to the ordinary behavior of men and women in business.

See also *profit, profits, and profit motive*

Bibliography

Primeaux, P. and Stieber, J. (1994). Profit maximization: The ethical mandate of business. *Journal of Business Ethics*, 13, 287–94.

Primeaux, P. and Stieber, J. (1995). *Profit Maximization: The Ethical Mandate of Business*. San Francisco: Austin and Winfield.

Stieber, J. and Primeaux, P. (1991). Economic efficiency: A paradigm for business ethics. *Journal of Business Ethics*, 10, 335–9.

economic justice

William H. Shaw

The core problem of economic justice is straightforward: On what basis should economic goods and services be distributed? This question has long interested philosophers and other thinkers, but it gains urgency in light of the vast disparities in income and wealth we see all around us. How, for example, can it be just or fair that some eat food scrounged from garbage cans while others dine at expensive restaurants, that the top 1 percent of US households own more than the entire bottom 90 percent, or that since 1980 the compensation of the average CEO has jumped from 42 to 157 times that of a production worker?

Various principles of economic justice have been advanced. Some believe that justice requires an equal distribution of goods and resources. Others recommend that distribution correspond to individual need, effort, merit, or social contribution. Each of these principles seems plausible in some circumstances – for example, merit seems the appropriate basis for promotion, need the basis for distributing food stamps. Yet each of these common principles has its problems, and none seems to work in enough circumstances to be successfully defended as *the* principle of economic justice.

Some philosophers are content with saying that there are various principles of economic justice and that one must simply choose the one that best applies to the situation. If several principles apply, one must weigh them as best one can. Other philosophers, however, have offered more comprehensive theories of economic justice as a basis for assessing rival economic systems. Among the most influential of these theories have been utilitarianism, libertarianism, and the social contract approach of John Rawls.

Utilitarianism

Utilitarians assess actions, policies, and institutions in terms of the happiness or unhappiness they produce. Economic justice, too, is a function of what maximizes happiness. Thus, John Stuart Mill (1806–73) argued that whether more talented workers should receive greater remuneration cannot be determined by abstract principles but only by social utility. Utilitarianism ties questions of economic justice to the promotion of social well-being or happiness, and utilitarians thus favor whatever economic system will produce the most social good. But which system is that? The answer depends on the utilitarian's understanding of the relevant social, economic, and political facts and possibilities. Utilitarians in the early nineteenth century typically advocated *laissez-faire* capitalism, believing that unregulated markets and free competition would best promote the total social good. Today, there is no consensus among utilitarians on economic matters, but they are likely to favor social welfare and a more equal distribution of income. The reason for this rests on "the declining marginal utility of money" – the idea that successive additions to one's income produce, on average, less happiness or welfare than did earlier additions. This suggests that increasing the income of those who now earn less would do the most to boost total welfare.

Libertarianism

Libertarians reject utilitarianism's concern for total social well-being and contend that justice consists in permitting each to live as he or she pleases, free from the interference of others. Libertarians place individual liberty at center stage and believe that we possess certain natural rights, including the right to property and the right not to be coerced by others, independently of any social or political institutions.

The influential libertarian Robert Nozick has argued that a state that uses taxes to redistribute income violates individual liberty by forcing people to support projects or people they have not freely chosen to support. Nozick's *entitlement theory* states that one is entitled to one's holdings (that is, goods, money, and property) as long as one has acquired them fairly, that is, without injuring others, defrauding them, or otherwise violating their rights. If you have acquired your holdings justly, you are entitled to do with them as you wish. No one else has a legitimate claim on them. Even though other people may be going hungry, justice imposes no obligation on you to help. Nozick rejects theories that require distribution to fit some pattern. His theory is historical: what matters is how people come to have what they have. If people are entitled to their possessions, then the distribution of economic holdings is just, regardless of what it happens to look like. Rival theories inevitably involve violations of liberty by forbidding "capitalist acts between consenting adults."

RAWLS'S THEORY

Although Rawls represents his hypothetical contract theory as an alternative to utilitarianism, he conceives of society as a cooperative venture for mutual advantage, and does not base his theory, as Nozick does, on the postulate that individuals possess certain natural rights. Rawls's strategy is to ask what principles people would choose to govern society if, hypothetically, they were to meet for this purpose in what he calls the "original position." Although in the original position people choose on the basis of self-interest, they are imagined to be behind a "veil of ignorance," not knowing their race, sex, personal talents and characteristics, or whether they are rich or poor. Rawls argues that people in the original position would not insist on absolute equality. Rather, they would embrace the *difference principle*, which permits social and economic inequalities but only if they are to the greatest expected benefit of the least advantaged. Inequalities are not justified if they maximize total happiness; rather, they must make the least-well-off segment of society better off than it would otherwise have been. Rawls suggests that either a democratic socialist system or a liberal form of capitalism with sufficient welfare provisions might satisfy his principle.

Whether a theory like Rawls's can be extended internationally and whether one can talk meaningfully of global economic justice have been debated issues. Even more controversial has been communitarianism's critique of liberalism (seen as embracing utilitarianism, libertarianism, and Rawls) and its skepticism toward abstract theories of economic justice. Communitarians insist instead on the complexity of justice and stress its intimate connection to particular practices and historically evolved conceptions of the good that characterize different communities. The debate over communitarianism and among the theories of economic justice described above lies at the heart of contemporary political and moral philosophy.

Bibliography

Arthur, A. and Shaw, W. H. (eds.) (1991). *Justice and Economic Distribution*, 2nd edn. Englewood Cliffs, NJ: Prentice-Hall.

Brandt, R. B. (1992). Utilitarianism and welfare legislation. In *Morality, Utilitarianism, and Rights*. Cambridge: Cambridge University Press, 370–87.

Kymlicka, W. (1990). *Contemporary Political Philosophy*. Oxford: Oxford University Press.

Mill, J. S. (1979) [1861]. *Utilitarianism*. Indianapolis, IN: Hackett.

Nozick, R. (1974). *Anarchy, State, and Utopia*. New York: Basic Books.

Pogge, T. W. (1989). *Realizing Rawls*. Ithaca, NY: Cornell University Press.

Rawls, J. (1971). *A Theory of Justice*. Cambridge, MA: Harvard University Press.

economic liberty

Eric Mack

consists in the freedom of agents to dispose, for economic purposes, of the objects or powers to which they are entitled in any way they choose as long as this disposition does not prevent other agents from enjoying a comparable discretionary control over the objects and powers to which they are entitled. Thus, economic liberty is a major subcategory of liberty understood as the freedom to dispose of one's own as one chooses. As the definition of economic liberty makes clear, determining whether an agent enjoys or suffers a loss of economic liberty requires prior judgments about what entitlements that agent has.

Since there are many competing views about what entitlements people have, there are many particular conceptions of economic liberty. An advocate of everyone's joint entitlement to all economically useful objects and powers will have to hold that economic liberty is fully realized only when collective decisions determine the economic use of everything. Any individual's private economic deployment of anything will count as an infringement upon economic liberty. At the other end of the ideological spectrum, the advocate of the justice of private rights in economically useful objects and powers will hold that economic liberty is fully realized only when each individual rightholder has full discretionary control over her own property (subject to the limitations to which she has freely agreed).

This familiar capitalistic conception of economic liberty envisions an economic regime of extensive and robust private property in which single agents or voluntary associations coordinate the exercise of their rights through market and contractual relationships. In search of economic gains and guided by the price signals generated by competitive markets and by their special knowledge of their own skills and circumstances, agents will deploy, recombine, transform, or exchange their holdings so as maximally to meet others' demands for goods and services. Capitalist economic liberty (CEL) is compromised whenever any agent, including any governmental agent, constrains private owners in their separate or mutually agreed-to utilizations of their legitimate holdings.

Among the justifications offered by advocates of CEL are:

1 Respect for CEL is respect for people's underlying rights over themselves and their holdings.
2 CEL tends to move existing skills and resources to their most highly valued uses and to motivate the discovery of talents and resources and their development by those generally best situated to deploy them.
3 CEL's requirement that people interact on the basis of voluntary exchange, and not on the basis of force or fraud, guarantees that all interacting parties benefit from their interactions.
4 As long as individuals are not subject to force or fraud, any negative externalities they may suffer from others' transactions are likely to be counterbalanced by positive externalities.
5 The introduction of regulatory and redistributive mechanisms which contravene CEL tends increasingly to divert effort, talent, and resources from productive economic activity to the unproductive pursuit of political clout.
6 Even if large-scale economic coordination of an efficiency comparable to that achieved through CEL could be achieved through central planning or regulation, imposed coordination would require a vast and dangerous expansion of the state's coercive powers.

Thoroughgoing critics of CEL reject most or all of these contentions. They reject the model of individual rights to human and extra-human resources and may even challenge the presumption that individuals are the loci of moral claims. Such critics will reject the idea that complex and mutually beneficial economic coordination is more likely to emerge endogenously out of market and contractual processes than out of conscious political design and organization. Thoroughgoing critics will often reject the conception of voluntariness presupposed within the capitalist model of economic liberty, arguing instead that many capitalist relationships are coerced or exploitative. This charge of exploitation will often be linked to the claim that the distribution of holdings which sets the stage for capitalist transactions is itself unjust, while other critics will charge that the distributive outcome of CEL is unjust. (These last two charges suggest a program of melding CEL with some system of resource redistribution.)

Other critics of CEL raise more technical objections about the tendency of CEL to give rise to harmful economic monopolies, for example, or to fail to promote unprofitable public goods. Many additional criticisms of CEL are essentially cultural. The central and honored place advocates of CEL propose for economic self-interest, bargaining, commerce, and profit-making is said to create a world which is mean-spirited, dehumanizing, alienating, and/or corrupting. Cultural critics from both ends of the conventional political spectrum argue that the rise of capitalist interactions and the dispositions and values they foster undermine our affective ties and capacities and thereby damage both ourselves and those who otherwise would be beneficiaries of our affections. These critics maintain that, in a social order which gives considerable scope to CEL, the perception of certain objects or activities (e.g., bodily organs, blood, sexual encounters, the bearing of babies) as commodities to be delivered if the price is right leads to the displacement or degeneration of valuable, non-market forms of life and interaction – spontaneous donations of organs and blood, loving sex, meaningful maternity. Cultural critics of CEL believe that the seductive allure of the rewards and practices of commercial society generates distorted or inauthentic preferences. Individuals can only be protected from succumbing to these damaging preferences by legal restrictions upon those rewards and practices or on people's pursuit of them – legal restrictions formulated by those with undistorted insight about people's authentic preferences.

Bibliography

Buchanan, A. (1985). *Ethics, Efficiency, and the Market.* Totowa, NJ: Rowman and Allanheld. (Especially for moral arguments against economic liberty.)

Cowen, T. (1988). *The Theory of Market Failure.* Fairfax, VA: George Mason University Press.

Hayek F. A. (1960). *The Constitution of Liberty.* Chicago: University of Chicago Press.

Machan, T. R. (1990). *Capitalism and Individualism.* New York: St. Martin's Press.

Mack, E. (1992). Economic liberty. In L. C. Becker and C. B. Becker (eds.), *Encyclopedia of Ethics.* New York: Garland. (Especially describes cultural criticisms.)

Murphy, J. (1981). Consent, coercion, and hard choices. *Virginia Law Review,* **67,** 79–95.

Radin, M. (1987). Market-inalienability. *Harvard Law Review,* **100,** 1865–1937. (A version of cultural criticism.)

Siegan, B. H. (1980). *Economic Liberties and the Constitution.* Chicago: University of Chicago Press.

economics and ethics

Allen Buchanan

Economics

Economics is frequently defined as the science of choice, where choice is understood to be the selection of one course of action (or policy) from among a set of options, on the basis of weighing costs and benefits. Essential to the economic conception of choice is the recognition that every choice involves costs – at the very least, the cost of the most valued forgone alternative that could have been chosen. Economics attempts to explain particular choices of individuals by applying a model of rationality. Large-scale social phenomena, such as the behavior of markets, are then explained by showing how they emerge from the interactions of large numbers of individual choices.

The model of rationality that mainstream economics employs is that of *individual utility maximization*. The rational individual is understood to be an agent who attempts to maximize his expected utility. In contemporary economics, utility is identified with the satisfaction of preferences.

As a *positive* (that is, explanatory and predictive) theory, economics purports to be able to account for human behavior so far as individuals act rationally (in the defined sense). However, to the extent that human beings care about being rational, to describe an action as rational is to commend it, while to characterize an action as irrational is usually taken to be a criticism. For this reason, the model of rationality with which economics operates is viewed as *normative* as well as positive. In other words, economics purports not only to explain and predict behavior (so far as it is rational), but also to guide behavior by determining how agents, including policymakers, should act if they wish to act rationally.

Ethics

Ethics is sometimes understood to refer to a code of conduct, but in the literature of contemporary ethics generally and of business ethics in particular it is more often understood to be a *practical activity* – a reflective and self-critical process of making decisions about which acts (or policies) are right, wrong, or permissible. As a practical activity, ethics is also understood to include the process of making judgments about the praiseworthiness or blameworthiness of particular agents. Furthermore, ethics is a *rational* practical activity at least in the sense that both in ethical theorizing and in everyday ethical discourse, *reasons* are given to support or to criticize the moral judgments individuals make.

It is therefore appropriate to request that one who advances a moral judgment be prepared to support it, and to support it with relevant considerations. Generally speaking, only certain sorts of considerations are widely recognized to be relevant in moral discourse – only certain types of reasons count as reasons to support or criticize moral judgments. Among the most important are appeals to basic and widely shared values – fairness, human welfare, and individual autonomy being among the most common. One distinctive feature of moral reasons is their *im-*

personal character. If *A* declares that abortion is wrong, it is appropriate for *B* to ask "And why is it wrong?" Moreover, if *A* were to answer "Because it makes me ill" he would not have given the right sort of reason to support his judgment, because a statement of personal distaste does not qualify as the sort of consideration that can support a moral judgment.

Many ethical theorists have also observed that moral judgments themselves have an equally important characteristic: they are made from a point of view which purports to be impartial. Thus if a person sincerely makes a moral judgment (for example, about the rightness of a certain act) then he is understood to be committed to universalizing the judgment – that is, to judging that the same type of act, in the same circumstances, would be right if another person performed it.

THE APPARENT CONFLICT BETWEEN ECONOMICS AND ETHICS

Economics appears to recognize only one reason for acting – namely, that doing this rather than that will maximize one's expected utility. Ethics, in contrast, not only offers a variety of considerations (human welfare, individual autonomy, fairness, etc.), but also requires that individuals sometimes act contrary to their own interests. On the surface at least, then, ethics and economics advance opposing conceptions of how one ought to choose. Moreover, if the model of economic rationality is accepted as a positive theory, an account of how human beings do in fact invariably behave, it seems to rule out the possibility of ethical conduct. If all people actually do – and all they can do because of the laws of human psychology – is to seek to maximize their expected utility, then it is futile to exhort them to act ethically. To the extent that economic thinking dominates the methodology of the sorts of courses that are taught in business schools and pervades the characteristic patterns of decision-making of business people, the very idea of business ethics becomes problematic.

THE THEORY OF THE MARKET AS THE RECONCILIATION OF ETHICS AND ECONOMICS

Some of the most eloquent advocates of the extensive market systems of social interaction that emerged in Western Europe in the seventeenth and eighteenth centuries proposed a way of reconciling economics and ethics. DeMandeville (1714) argued that in a market system "private vices" make "public virtues": purely self-interested conduct that fits the traditional description of moral vices, if it occurs within the context of market institutions, produces public benefits. Similarly, Adam Smith (1776) extolled the market as a system that harnesses self-interested action for the common good. DeMandeville and Smith presaged the First Fundamental Theory of Welfare Economics: in a perfectly competitive market, free exchanges among individual utility maximizers will result in an equilibrium that is efficient in the Paretian sense of efficiency – there will be no redistribution of goods that will make anyone better off without making someone worse off.

According to this simple conception of the relation between ethics and economics, the realm of market exchanges is an area of human life in which ethics is not needed for the production of morally admirable results. Human welfare emerges, in the aggregate, as a fortunate byproduct of amoral or even immoral behavior.

This simple view of the relationship between economics and ethics is itself subject to ethical criticism, however. One obvious difficulty, of course, is that markets in the real world are not perfectly competitive and lack other features, such as perfect information, which the ideal market of the First Fundamental Theorem possesses. Thus the justification for reliance upon market systems, and for tolerating unethical behavior within them, cannot be that market systems are necessarily efficient.

More importantly, however, a number of ethical theories, as well as much commonsense moral thinking, challenge the assumption that efficiency is a sufficient standard for evaluation. The main difficulty is that outcomes can be efficient (in the technical economic sense explained above) and yet grossly unfair. For example, a system in which a minority of masters owned everything and a majority of slaves owned nothing would be efficient in the Paretian sense if it were not possible to improve the lot of the slaves without worsening that of the masters.

The basic point can be put in a different way, without recourse to such an extreme example.

Economic theory only tells us that in perfect markets efficient outcomes will emerge from free exchanges for gain, but market processes cannot be expected to correct for inequities in the initial distribution of assets which individuals bring to the market. Some individuals, through no fault of their own, simply have fewer assets to bargain with. Ethical reasoning is needed to determine whether, or under what conditions, undeserved differences in initial endowments are unjust; and if so, what means of correcting or preventing them are permissible.

A second major area in which economic thinking by itself is inadequate and in which reliance upon ethical reasoning is unavoidable is the problem of *externalities*. In all real-world markets there are externalities or "spill-over" effects, costs or benefits that arise from exchanges but that accrue to others than (or in addition to) the exchangers themselves. A familiar example is pollution. When a manufacturer and a supplier of raw materials make an exchange which allows the manufacture of a chemical, they each calculate the costs and the benefits of the exchange to themselves. However, if, as a result of the exchange, toxic fumes are discharged into the air, costs will be imposed on others and these costs will not be fully taken into account in the exchange. In some cases economics can offer suggestions as to how to "internalize external costs" (for example, by a policy in which the government issues exchangeable permits to spill certain amounts of pollution into the air), but economics cannot by itself tell us whether such a policy is fair or even whether the harm which the externality represents is important enough to require such remedies.

Two more examples will illustrate the dependence upon ethics of economics, as a discipline which purports to provide guidance for policy. First, consider the pervasive policy question of which sorts of goods or services ought to be offered for sale in markets. Should not only cars and legal services but also recreational drugs, sex, or babies for adoption be marketable? Positive economics can tell us under what conditions marketing an item will contribute to efficient outcomes, but it cannot tell us whether it ought to be marketed if it is admitted that there are other considerations that are relevant besides efficiency. To assume that efficiency is the only

thing that matters is to endorse a particular moral theory – namely utilitarianism – not to avoid moral theory, and economics by itself cannot tell us which moral theory to endorse.

Second, consider a basic tool of economic analysis for government bureaucracies and businesses as well: cost-benefit analysis. Although cost-benefit analysis is often presented as if it were a value-neutral, scientific procedure for making decisions about the use of scarce resources, in fact a number of difficult ethical questions must be answered before it can be employed. The first of these, of course, is "Whose costs and benefits are to count?" The second is "Whose judgments about costs and benefits are to be used?" (For example, in deciding whether to commit public funds for abortion, do we count costs to fetuses?) A third question is a variant of a complaint noted above concerning the use of efficiency as the sole or overriding standard for evaluation: "Why should we be concerned only with maximizing the ratio of benefits to costs rather than with how costs and benefits are distributed among people who will be affected?" (For example, if we think that one element of a just healthcare system is the fair distribution of the costs of providing access to care for all, then we are denying that distribution of costs and benefits is irrelevant.) In addition, the standard ways of measuring costs and benefits are themselves subject to serious moral criticisms. For example, when cost-benefit analysts assign a value to lives they typically either equate the value of a life with total expected life-time earnings or with how much the individual would be willing to pay to avoid some specified probability of death. The former measure systematically disadvantages women and minorities who have lower expected life-time earnings, due to historical patterns of educational and employment discrimination. The latter, if taken literally, automatically assigns higher value to the lives of the wealthy, since how much an individual is willing to pay is a function of how much resources he or she has access to.

None of this is to deny, of course, that ethics does not also depend upon economics. Any ethical theory in which a consideration of the consequences of actions and policies for human welfare or freedom is understood to be relevant will require some way of estimating costs and benefits. Similarly, any acceptable view of the ethically responsible use of resources will have to be concerned with efficiency to some extent.

THE NEW ECONOMICS: MAKING ROOM FOR ETHICS

One of the most striking and fruitful developments in economics in recent years has been a growing awareness that people's ethical commitments do in fact influence their behavior in all areas of human life, even the life of "economic man" in the market. As a consequence, economists are rethinking the very foundations of their discipline, as well as their conception of its subject matter. Instead of assuming that all behavior is self-interested and in consequence proposing far-fetched egoistic explanations of what certainly seems to be non-self-interested behavior, more and more economists are attempting to see how the standard tools of economic analysis can be adapted to model moral behavior. Thus far, four main areas of research have been especially prominent: (1) the role of moral commitments in solving or avoiding problems in the supply of public goods; (2) the function of moral commitments in fostering successful cooperation within organizations; (3) the necessity of moral commitments for the well-functioning of markets; and (4) the contribution which moral commitments make to the welfare of the individuals who have them.

1 Morality and public goods. Standard economic analyses which assume that most agents act in purely self-interested ways in all circumstances predict that public goods will not be supplied or will be undersupplied if contribution to them is left voluntary. The prediction is that if he can expect to enjoy the good if it is produced through the contributions of others, each self-interested individual will refrain from contributing because he will regard his own contribution as an available cost. Unfortunately for the analysis, there are many cases in which public goods are supplied at higher levels than the analysis predicts, even without resorting to coercion to ensure contributions. Substantial voter turn-out is one example among many: if voters behaved as standard economic theory predicts no one would vote in elections in which the

chance that his vote would determine the outcome are negligible, yet many people do vote in these circumstances. Once we allow the possibility that significant numbers of people may vote because they believe it is their *duty* to do so and that their sense of duty overrides or suspends a purely self-interested calculation of the expected costs and benefits of contributing to the public good of substantial voter turn-out, we have the beginnings of a more satisfactory analysis of voting behavior.

2 The contribution of morality to successful cooperation in organizations. A number of empirical studies (e.g. Guth, Schmittberger, and Schwarze, 1982) have revealed the role that moral values play in fostering successful and sustained cooperation in organizations, including business firms. In particular, there is considerable evidence that commitment to moral norms concerning fairness is often crucial in avoiding or resolving conflicts between labor and management and that recognition of workers' rights to participate in decision-making can increase productivity.

3 The moral underpinnings of markets. Unless most participants in market exchanges have a modicum of trust and honesty, for example, transaction costs and enforcement costs for commercial contracts would be prohibitively high. Moreover, since the efficiency of markets depends upon competitiveness, moral inhibitions against engaging in anti-competitive practices (including sabotaging one's rivals) play an important role even if they are viewed only as supplementing the fear of prosecution for violations of antitrust law. For these reasons what may be called the morality of the market is sometimes described as a public good for all who seek to benefit from markets: it is in everyone's interest that there be sufficient moral commitments among others so that markets can function well, even though from a purely self-interested point of view, being moral is a cost to the individual and he has reason to attempt to take a free ride on the moral restraint of others.

4 The contribution of an individual's moral commitments to his own self-interest. The final area of economic research on ethics challenges the preceding assumption that individual self-interest only speaks in favor of encouraging moral commitments in *others*, as opposed to oneself. To take only one example that has been studied in some detail (Frank, 1988), the fact that an individual who is a potential cooperator is known to be honest can make it possible to overcome "commitment problems" that otherwise might block mutually advantageous cooperation. Commitment problems are ubiquitous in business and wherever there are principal–agent relationships with significant agency risks. An agency risk exists whenever there is a divergence between the interests of an agent to whom a principal entrusts some activity and the interests of the principal which he engaged the agent to further. Often, close monitoring of the agent's activity is not feasible or would be too costly to the principal. Under such circumstances the ability of the agent to make a credible commitment to serve the principal's interest even when not doing so would further his own interests is a valuable economic asset for the agent. Moreover, for a number of reasons, the least costly way for an agent to be able to convince others that he has certain moral qualities (such as honesty) may be to actually cultivate those qualities, not merely to try to feign them.

In all of these areas of research, economists are expanding what has traditionally been regarded as the proper subject matter of economics to include moral behavior, not just self-interested behavior. In doing so, they are recognizing a more complex and mutually enriching relationship between economics and ethics.

Bibliography

Bowie, N. (1991). Challenging the egoistic paradigm. *Business Ethics Quarterly*, 1, 1–21.

Buchanan, A. (1985). *Ethics, Efficiency and the Market.* Totowa, NJ: Rowman and Allanheld.

Collard, D. (1978). *Altruism and Economy: A Study in Non-Selfish Economics.* New York: Oxford University Press.

DeMandeville, B. (1989) [1714]. *The Fable of the Bees*, ed. P. Harth. Harmondsworth: Penguin Books.

Etzioni, A. (1988). *The Moral Dimension: Toward a New Economics.* New York: Macmillan.

Fox, A. (1974). *Beyond Contract: Work, Power and Trust Relations.* London: Faber.

Frank, R. (1988). *Passions within Reason: The Strategic Role of the Emotions.* New York: W. W. Norton.

Guth, W., Schmittberger, R., and Schwarze, B. (1982). An experimental analysis of ultimate bargaining. *Journal of Economic Behavior and Organization*, 3, 367–88.

Hausman, D. and McPherson, M. (1993). Taking ethics seriously: Economics and contemporary moral philosophy. *Journal of Economic Literature*, 31, 671–731.

Isaac, R. M., Mathieu, D., and Zajac, E. E. (1991). Institutional framing and perceptions of fairness. *Constitutional Political Economy*, 2, 329–70.

Smith, A. (1976) [1776]. *An Enquiry into the Nature and Causes of the Wealth of Nations*, ed. R. H. Campbell and A. S. Skinner. Oxford: Clarendon Press.

efficient markets

D. Jeffrey Lenn

The operation of the market system that uses and allocates resources by means of the price mechanism so as to minimize cost while satisfying demand.

In a capitalist economy, markets for labor, capital, and goods will reach an equilibrium at the point where demand equals supply. The free movement of prices is the coordinating mechanism for the large and varied decisions made by buyers and sellers. This invisible hand allows individuals in the market to fulfill their needs efficiently without the costly intervention of a central authority. A subset of this concept, the "efficient market theory," focuses on efficiency in capital markets, building on the assumption that the current price of an asset reflects all of the information available to buyers and sellers.

Vilfredo Pareto (1848–1923) refined and specified the criteria by which to evaluate the operation of the market under the direction of the invisible hand. He focused on the outcomes of the market in relationship to the well-being of the individuals within the total economy. Pareto optimality (or Pareto efficiency) means that efficiency is achieved only if a change in the market leads to some people being better off without making anyone else worse off. Individuals will exchange with each other so that the ratios of the marginal utilities of goods are equal to the ratios of their prices. Pareto argued that the optimum point of exchange does not require any comparison between the total utility of each person involved.

Three conditions are necessary to achieve Pareto optimality (Pareto efficiency): exchange, production, and product-mix efficiency (Stigler, 1993). Exchange efficiency means that goods are distributed among individual buyers to satisfy their preferences. The price system encourages continued exchanges up to the point where no further trade can take place. Production efficiency is achieved when it is no longer possible to produce more of some goods without producing less of others. The price system signals the scarcity of the resources needed by producers. This leads them to make more efficient use of resources and drives down costs. When the mix of products offered for sale in the economy fully reflects the preferences of consumers, product-mix efficiency is achieved. Increased demand for one product translates into higher prices, which leads producers to shift their production in order to gain greater profit.

Pareto's work laid the foundation for the development of the field of welfare economics, which is concerned with defining the necessary conditions for efficiency because of market imperfection. The unequal distribution of income within an economy, which was not important to Pareto for assessing market efficiency, is a major point of contention in determining these conditions. Some contend that income inequity is an inevitable consequence of the operation of efficient markets. Any attempt to modify the market process will create inefficiencies. Others argue that significant differences in income have severe consequences for individuals and society. Therefore, it is necessary to alter the market operation to narrow this gap. The debate is often framed as a trade-off between efficiency and equality.

Bibliography

Okun, A. M. (1975). *Equality and Efficiency: The Big Tradeoff.* Washington, DC: Brookings Institution.
Pareto, V. (1971) [1927]. *Manual of Political Economy.* London: Macmillan.
Reiter, S. (1987). Efficient allocation. In J. Eatwell, M. Milgate, and P. Newman (eds.), *The New Pelgrave: A Dictionary of Economics,* vol. 2. London: Macmillan, 107–20.
Sen, A. (1987). *On Ethics and Economics.* Oxford: Blackwell.
Stigler, J. E. (1993). *Economics.* New York: W. W. Norton.

egoism, psychological egoism, and ethical egoism

Tibor R. Machan

The term "egoism" is ordinarily used to mean "exclusive concern with satisfying one's own desires, getting what one wants." Dictionaries tend to support this. They call "egoism," for instance, "1. selfishness; self-interest. 2. conceit" (*Webster's New World Dictionary*). The term "egotist" is often a substitute, although it's defined differently, for example, as "excessive reference to oneself." The ego is the self. But we should distinguish first between "selfishness," "self-interest," and "interest of the self." They usually mean, respectively, "concern exclusively and for indulging one's desires," "consideration based first on what is good for oneself without the exclusion of others," and "that which motivates an autonomous person." These will help us appreciate what follows (*see* RATIONAL CHOICE THEORY).

"Egoism" is also used in ethical considerations of how human beings do or ought to live. It is thus often qualified by such terms as "ethical" and "psychological." So what determines the most sensible meaning of the term? It is crucial, first of all, what the *ego* is. If it is the unique identity of the individual human being or self, what exactly is this?

Some argue that everyone is, to use Karl Marx's term, a collective or *specie*-being. Others, in turn, hold that the human being is first and foremost related to a supernatural God and has a body (which is of this earth) and a soul (of the spiritual realm) combined in one person. Some others say a human being is an integral and unique whole, comprised of many diverse facets. Egoisms differ depending on which of these is taken to be true.

PSYCHOLOGICAL EGOISM

Some hold we are all automatically selfish. So just as it is a constitutive part of us that we have certain physical organs and functions – a heart, brain, liver, blood circulation, motor behavior – so it is that we *will* act to advance our own well-being, that we will attempt to benefit ourselves at all times. We are supposed to be instinctively moved to act selfishly. Here is one way of giving expression to what seems to be the gist of this idea: "Every individual serves his own private interest...The great Saints of history have served their 'private interest' just as the most money grubbing miser has served his interest. The *private interest* is whatever it is that drives an individual" (Friedman, 1976).

Egoism concerns itself with *benefiting oneself*. To do this is to provide oneself with what one requires for flourishing, excelling, developing in positive ways. Different explanations of what that comes to can be given. For example, some hold that to benefit oneself is to become satisfied. Benefiting oneself would be to obtain whatever one would like to have, or to enable one to do what one wants to do. Here is how Thomas Hobbes put the point: "But whatsoever is the object of any man's Appetite or Desire, that is it which he for his part calleth Good: and the object of his Hate and Aversion, Evill...For these words of Good and Evill...are ever used with relation to the person that useth them: there being nothing simply and absolutely so; nor any Common Rule of Good and Evill" (Hobbes, 1968: 120).

Yet the above paradoxically implies that if someone were to want to do or have something obviously self-destructive, the person would be benefited. Being benefited, then, may be different from having one's desires satisfied or one's wants fulfilled. If so, then psychological egoism would mean that everyone does what one benefits from in terms of some objective standard of well-being, not based just on what one desires or likes.

We might make this more sensible by adding that what we desire or want is always something *we take to be* of benefit to ourselves. When we take a job, go on a vacation, seek out a relationship, or, indeed, embark on an entire way of life, we may be doing what *seems to us best*. Is this what is meant by the view that we are necessarily selfish?

Yet what is meant by "what seems to be best"? If one says, "This *seems* to me to be a vase," we know what is meant because we know

what it *is* to be a vase. So could one tell what *seems to be of benefit* to oneself, *seems to contribute to one's well-being*, without any standard independent of what one desires or wants determining what *is to one's benefit, contributes to one's well-being*? No.

Some argue that despite its troubles, we can make good use of psychological egoism as a technical device, for example, in the analysis of market behavior – of how people act when they embark on commercial or business tasks. By assuming that's how people act in markets, we can anticipate trends in economic affairs. In fact, however, when these estimates are made, usually certain assumptions are invoked about what *in fact is of benefit to us*. So even as an analytic device the psychological egoist position by itself seems to be difficult to uphold as a cogent doctrine.

ETHICAL EGOISM

Ethical egoism states that one *ought to* benefit oneself, first and foremost. Yet this by no means tells it all, as we have already seen in connection with psychological egoism. The precise meaning of ethical egoism also depends upon what the ego is and what it is to be benefited.

Subjective egoism. The most commonly discussed version of ethical egoism differs only in one basic respect from psychological egoism. According to this *subjective* egoism, the human self or ego consists of a bundle of desires (or drives or wishes or preferences) and to benefit oneself amounts to satisfying these desires in their order of priority, which is itself something entirely dependent upon the individual or, as it is often put, a subjective matter. Why this is still a type of *ethical* egoism is that everyone is supposed to *choose* to satisfy the desires he or she has – that is, one *ought to* attempt to satisfy oneself.

Criticisms. This view is said to have serious problems, too. First, if John desires, first and foremost, to be wealthy; next, to be famous; then, to find a beautiful mate; then, to please some of his friends; then, to give support to his country; then, to conserve resources; and finally to assist some people who are in need, John ought to strive to achieve these goals in this order of priority. But how John ought to rank these goals cannot be raised. (Here is where the position is similar to the first version of psychological egoism: the desires are decisive in determining what benefits John.) Yet that is crucial in ethics.

Next, a *bona fide* ethical theory must be *universalizable* (i.e., needs to apply to all choosing and acting persons), *unambiguous* (provides clear guidance as to what one ought to do), *consistent* (does not propose actions which contradict one another), and is *comprehensive* (addresses all those problems that are reasonably expected to arise for a person). And this subjective egoist position fails to satisfy these conditions. For one, even for an individual, desires often oppose another. Any ethical theory has to avoid the problems cited above. Subjective egoism is, thus, often used as an example of a failed ethical theory (Machan, 1983: 185–202).

CLASSICAL EGOISM

A more promising ethical egoism states that each person should live so as to achieve his or her *rational self-interest*. (I have called this "classical" egoism to indicate its pedigree in Aristotelianism. It is also captured by the term "eudaimonist ethics.") Accordingly, as living beings we need a guide to conduct, principles to be used when we cannot assess the merits of each action from the start. As living beings we share with other animals the value of life. But life occurs in individual (living) things. And human living, unlike that of other animals, cannot be pursued automatically. We must learn to do it. And the particular life we can pursue and about which we can exercise choices is our own. By understanding *who and what we are*, we can identify the standards by which our own life can most likely be advanced properly, made successful, become a happy life.

In short, this ethical egoist holds that one's human life, the basis of all values, is to be lived with the aid of a moral outlook. Since (the value of) one's own life is the only one a person can advance in a morally relevant way (by choice), each person should live it successfully within that person's own context (as the individual one is, within one's circumstances). Even more briefly put, people should pursue their own individual happiness, and the principles that make this possible are the moral principles and virtues suited for leading a human life. The benefit one ought to seek and obtain is, then, not subjective

but objective: it is one's own successful, flourishing human life.

The prime virtue in egoistic ethics is rationality, the uniquely human way of being (conceptually!) aware of and navigating the world. Success in life or happiness for any human being must be achieved in a way suited to human life. Accordingly, being *morally virtuous* consists of choosing to be as fully human as possible in one's circumstances, *to excel at being the human being one is*. Each person is a human being because of the distinctive capacity to choose to think, to attend to the world rationally (by way of careful and sustained principled thought); therefore, to succeed as a person, everyone should make that choice. All the specialized virtues in egoism must be rationally established (or at least capable of such establishment).

Egoism, unlike other ethical positions, considers the proper attitude in life to be informed selfishness – not, however, pathological self-centeredness (egotism). Pride, ambition, integrity, honesty, and other traits that are by nature of value to any human life are considered virtues. It is with regards to the sort of self that is proper to a human being that one ought to be selfish, not just any sort of self. (Indeed, whether selfishness is to be thought of as good or bad depends on what the *self* is.) The worst, most reprehensible way of conducting oneself is to fail to think and exercise rational judgment, to evade reality and leave oneself to blind impulse, others' influence, the guidance of thoughtless clichés, and the like. Since knowledge is indispensable for successful realization of goals, including the central goal of happiness, failure to exert the effort to obtain it – thus fostering error, misunderstanding, and confusion – is most disastrous to oneself and, hence, immoral.

Finally, in classical egoism the goal, one's happiness, is something that should be sharply distinguished from pleasure, fun, or thrills. This type of egoism sets as our primary goal to be happy, which is a sustained positive reflective disposition, resulting from doing well in one's life *qua* the individual human being one is (Rand, 1964; Norton, 1976).

BUSINESS ETHICS AND EGOISM

Egoism is of concern in the examination of business ethics, both when we use the latter to refer to how people in commercial and business endeavors ought to act, and what kinds of public policy should govern business and industry – to whit, capitalism, which arises from a legal system that respects and protects private property rights, and is an economic system that is closely linked to versions of egoism. Adam Smith, the founder of modern economic science, advanced something like a psychological egoist position about human motivation (although arguably Smith was not thoroughgoing in this – for example in his *Theory of Moral Sentiments* he advances a different position). Many neoclassical economists incline toward psychological egoism when they discuss why people behave as they do, although since they refer to "utility maximization" rather than "the pursuit of self-interest," it is not always simple to classify their position.

If there is something morally right about commerce and the profession of business, something along the lines of an egoistic principle must be included in the set of virtues human beings ought to practice. Thus, some argue that *prudence* ultimately gives moral support to commerce and business (Den Uyl, 1991; Machan, 1988).

Unless room is made for egoistic conduct as morally praiseworthy, commerce and business could be seen as having nothing morally significant about them. In which case "business ethics" would be an oxymoron. (Many seem to believe just that, going on to require that corporate managers, executives, or owners do their morally good deeds apart from business – unlike the case with physicians, artists, or educators.) Indeed, in terms of classical egoism, commerce is a morally worthwhile undertaking and business an honorable profession. They are to be guided by both the general moral principles of human living and their specific professional ethics. The last posits the creation of wealth as its primary objective, to be pursued without violating principles of morality and through the effective achievement of prosperity with the appropriate enterprises selected accordingly. A banker ought to earn a good income from safeguarding and investing the deposits and savings of customers, honestly, industriously, and with attention to the need to balance these undertakings with others that mor-

ality requires. So should an automobile executive, the CEO of a multinational corporation, or the owner of a restaurant. And this requires the institution of the right to private property and freedom of enterprise, lest the moral component – self-direction – be missing from how those doing business comport themselves.

Bibliography

Den Uyl, D. J. (1991). *The Virtue of Prudence*. New York: Peter Lang.
Friedman, M. (1976). The line we dare not cross. *Encounter*, **47**, (5), 11.
Hobbes, T. (1968). *Leviathan*, with an intro. by C. B. Macpherson. Baltimore, MD: Penguin Books.
Machan, T. R. (1983). Recent work in ethical egoism. In K. G. Lucey and T. R. Machan (eds.), *Recent Work in Philosophy*. Totowa, NJ: Rowman and Allanheld. (For a discussion of this and other forms of ethical egoism.)
Machan, T. R. (1988). Ethics and its uses. In T. R. Machan, *Commerce and Morality*. Lanham, MD: Rowman and Littlefield.
Norton, D. L. (1976). *Personal Destinies: A Philosophy of Ethical Individualism*. Princeton, NJ: Princeton University Press.
Rand, A. (1964). *The Virtue of Selfishness*. New York: New American Library.

employee stock ownership plans

Susan Chaplinsky

Employee Stock Ownership Plans (ESOPs) are defined contribution pension plans that have two distinctive features: (1) they can be leveraged (though they need not be), and (2) they are designed to primarily hold the sponsoring firm's equity securities. In contrast, other pension plans typically are restricted from borrowing to acquire the securities for the plan and by law must be diversified with respect to their investment holdings. The stock held in an ESOP, usually common or convertible preferred stock, can be repurchased from the firm's outstanding shares or be newly issued treasury shares. In either case, the shares are considered outstanding and therefore have cash flow and voting rights.

Because of the ability of an ESOP to be leveraged, a firm can quickly place a large block of shares in the plan. This ability has raised questions about whether ESOPs can be used as anti-takeover devices in control contests by management to help fend off unwanted bids. However, as pension plans, there is a high degree of oversight and a number of regulations that affect how the plans can be used. At the initiation of a leveraged ESOP, most shares are placed in a suspense account; these shares are called *unallocated shares*. As the ESOP loan is repaid, shares are allocated to individual employee accounts, and the employees receive the associated voting rights. Non-voting securities used to fund the plans, such as convertible preferred stock, must convert to voting securities when allocated to employees. Since the allocation of shares to individual employees is usually based on salary, management typically receives more shares than other employees. However, for the ESOP to receive preferential tax treatment under the Internal Revenue Code (IRC), the allocation rule must not discriminate in favor of high-income employees. These provisions make it difficult for top management to own a significant portion of the firm's stock through an ESOP.

Under the Employee Retirement Income Security Act (ERISA), the ESOP trustee is directed to vote and tender unallocated shares in the best interests of plan participants and beneficiaries. Although management may attempt to influence a trustee, court rulings suggest that a trustee's decision with respect to voting or tendering shares is more likely to be upheld when the trustee can demonstrate his/her independence from management. For public companies with an ESOP, the plan must allow for *pass-through voting* of the shares. This requires the trustee to vote and tender unallocated shares in a control contest in the same manner that employees vote and tender allocated shares. Thus, non-managerial employees typically control the voting of ESOP shares. As a result, an ESOP's effectiveness as an anti-takeover device usually relies on non-managerial employees siding with management, perhaps out of fear of a bidder's action with respect to compensation or jobs, rather than with management's overt control of the shares.

employment at will

Patricia H. Werhane and Tara J. Radin

The principle of Employment at Will (EAW) is a common-law doctrine stating that, in the absence of law or contract, employers have the right to hire, promote, demote, and fire whomever and whenever they please. The principle was stated explicitly in 1887 by H. G. Wood, who wrote, "a general or indefinite hiring is prima facie a hiring at will."

In the United States, EAW has been interpreted as the rule that when employees are not specifically covered by union agreement, legal statute, public policy, or contract, an employer "may dismiss their employees at will . . . for good cause, for no cause, *or even for causes morally wrong*, without being thereby guilty of legal wrong" (Blades, 1967: 1405). Today, at least 60 percent of all employees in the private sector of the economy, from part-time or temporary workers to corporate presidents, are "at will" employees.

EAW has been widely interpreted as allowing employees to be demoted, transferred, or dismissed without having a hearing and without requirement of good reasons or "cause" for the employment decision. This is not to say that employers do not have reasons, usually good reasons, for their decisions. But there is no legal obligation to state or defend their decisions. Thus EAW sidesteps the requirement of due process or grievance procedures in the workplace, although it does not preclude the institution of such procedures.

As a recognized common-law principle, traditionally EAW has been upheld in the US state and federal courts. However, in the last 15 years legal statutes have increased the number of employees who are protected from EAW, including those protected by equal opportunity and age discrimination legislation. Moreover, what is meant by "public policy" has been expanded. For example, cases in which an employee has been asked to break a law or to violate a stated public policy, cases where employees are not allowed to exercise certain constitutional rights such as the right to vote, serve on a jury, or collect worker compensation are all considered wrongful discharges. Employees won 67 percent of their suits on wrongful discharge during a recent three-year period. These suits were won, not on the basis of a rejection of the principle of EAW, but rather because of breach of contract, lack of just cause for dismissal when a company grievance policy was in place, or violations of public policy (Geyelin, 1989).

EAW is often justified for one or more of the following reasons:

1   The proprietary rights of employers guarantee that they may employ or dismiss whomever and whenever they wish.
2   EAW defends employee, managerial, and employer rights equally, in particular the right to freedom of contract, because an employee voluntarily contracts to be hired and can quit at any time.
3   In choosing to take a job, an employee voluntarily commits herself to certain responsibilities and company loyalty, including the knowledge that she is an "at will" employee.
4   Extending due-process rights and other employee protections in the workplace often interferes with the efficiency and productivity of the business organization.
5   Legislation and/or regulation of employment relationships further undermine an already over-regulated economy.

On the other side, there are a number of criticisms of EAW. Perhaps the most serious is that while EAW is defended as preserving employer and employee rights equally, it is sometimes interpreted as justifying arbitrary treatment of employees. This is analogous to considering an employee as a piece of property at the disposal of the employer or corporation. When I "fire" a robot, I do not have to give reasons, because a robot is not a rational being; it has no use for reasons. On the other hand, if I fire a person arbitrarily I am making the assumption that she does not need reasons for the decision, a questionable logic. If I have hired persons, then I should treat them as such, with respect throughout the employment process. This does not preclude firing, but it does ask employers to give reasons for their actions, for reasons are appropriate when one is dealing with persons.

There are other grounds for not abusing EAW as part of recognizing equal obligations implied by freedom of contract. Arbitrariness, although not prohibited by EAW, violates the managerial model of rationality and consistency. This ideal is implied by a consistent application of this common-law principle, that EAW protects employees, managers, and employers equally and fairly. We expect managers, in their roles as employers, to act reasonably and consistently in their decision-making. Not giving reasons for employment decisions belies that expectation. Thus, even if EAW itself is justifiable, the practice of EAW, when interpreted as condoning arbitrary employment decisions, is not.

Looking ahead, the signs are clear that the doctrine of EAW will continue to be refined and challenged. Within the corporation new approaches to work and organizational activity are bringing new modes of employee participation that encourage greater employee expression. The challenge for management and employees is to find creative ways to minimize burdensome litigation while at the same time balancing employer and employee rights.

Bibliography

Arvanites, D. and Ward, B. T. (1990). Employment at will: A social concept in decline. In J. J. Desjardins and J. J. McCall (eds.), *Contemporary Issues in Business Ethics*, 2nd edn. Belmont, CA: Wadsworth Publishing, 147–54.

Blades, L. E. (1967). Employment at will versus individual freedom: On limiting the abusive exercise of employer power. *Columbia Law Review*, 67, 1404–35.

Ewing, D. (1983). *Do It My Way or You're Fired!* New York: John Wiley.

Feinman, J. M. (1991). The development of the employment at will rule revisited. *Arizona State Law Journal*, 23, 733–40.

Geyelin, M. (1989). Fired managers winning more lawsuits. *Wall Street Journal*, September 7, B1.

Hutton vs. Watters (1915). 132 Tenn. 527, S.W. 134.

Payne vs. Western. (1884). 81 Tenn. 507.

Summers, C. B. (1980). Protecting *all* employees against unjust dismissal. *Harvard Business Review*, January/ February, 132–9.

Werhane, P. H. (1985). *Persons, Rights, and Corporations.* Englewood Cliffs, NJ: Prentice-Hall.

Wood, H. G. (1887). *A Treatise on the Law of Master and Servant.* Albany, NY.

empowerment

Barry Z. Posner and James M. Kouzes

may be defined in many specific ways, but in common is the idea of providing people the "power" necessary to fulfill their job responsibilities without having to secure approval from others (i.e., supervisors). With empowerment, control over the means of getting the job done is left with the person doing the job, creating greater control over the results produced. This responsibility for producing results leads to greater ownership on the individual's part for both the input and output of production.

Some argue that empowerment is nothing new but, for example, just today's equivalent for previous management concepts such as participative decision-making, team building, job enrichment, and the like. Others argue that empowerment is "oversold," really nothing more than a buzzword or slogan; or that it is an overrated concept that ignores or minimizes, among other things, political realities and workload increases. Furthermore, failures in implementation have led to feelings ranging from disappointment to disillusionment and anger about empowerment.

Research has found that empowered employees, teams, and organizations outperform their less democratic and more bureaucratic counterparts. Some common misconceptions about empowerment are: (1) managers and leaders lose power by empowering others; (2) empowered people do not need leaders; and, (3) empowerment and delegation are synonymous.

"The problem with empowerment is that it suggests that this is something leaders magically give or do for others. But people already have tremendous power. It is not a matter of giving it to them, but of freeing them to use the power and skills they already have. It is a matter of expanding their opportunities to use themselves in service of a common and meaningful purpose. What is often called empowerment is really just taking off the chains and letting people loose" (Kouzes and Posner, 1993: 157). In essence, organizations can only create environments where people feel powerful and choose to create and use their power.

Research into the times when people feel powerful and powerless reveals that feeling powerful comes from a deep sense of being in control of one's life. When people feel able to determine their own destiny, when they believe they are able to mobilize the resources and support necessary to complete a task, then they will persist in their efforts. When people report feeling controlled by others, and when they feel that resources and support are lacking, they may comply but they experience little motivation or commitment to excel.

The initial challenge is to articulate a clear vision of what empowerment entails, including both boundaries and opportunities. Empowerment is akin to "guided autonomy" in which people feel that they not only can, but should, make a difference, and that consensus and strong feelings (values) exist about the right way to do things in the organization. The psychological process of empowerment involves enhancing an individual's sense of self-efficacy. This is accomplished through role models, persuasion, and facilitating personal mastery.

The organizational process of empowerment is multi-faceted and cannot flourish without institutional support and nourishment. Here are some essential management practices:

Developing capacity. Organizations that invest more than the average amount of money in training and development activities enjoy higher levels of employee involvement and commitment, along with higher levels of customer service and productivity. Unless people know how, there is no "can do" possible. Educational activities are often needed to ensure that people have the capacity to handle additional responsibility and autonomy.

Facilitating discretion. Given the latitude and opportunity to exercise choices and make decisions, people feel a sense of ownership – ownership as a state of mind resulting from having the knowledge and skills (education) necessary to make a decision, and then the motivation and will to act. Able to exercise discretion, people feel in control of their own lives: broad job descriptions, multiple customers and suppliers, and tasks requiring a range of skills all facilitate discretion.

Opening communications.   Being able to influence and see the results of their efforts, people will take great interest in what is happening. With detailed feedback, including such factors as quality, timeliness, and customer delight, people can become self-corrective. Information ensues from being involved and included in important planning and problem-solving efforts. Being "in the know" and understanding the premises on which decisions are based increases one's influence.

Building confidence.   Confident people feel powerful, and persist in the face of challenge and adversity. In a simulated series of management situations, managers led to believe that decision-making was an innate capability (rather than an acquired capability) lost their confidence in themselves when they encountered difficulties. Their problem-solving deteriorated, they lowered their aspirations, and organizational performance suffered – and they also tended to place blame for the situation on others. The most effective means of raising people's self-confidence is through the experience of performing successfully.

Fostering innovation.   In any new endeavor there is a learning curve, meaning that performance generally goes down before it goes up. A willingness to take risks and experiment with innovative ideas characterizes an empowered organization, as does making it safe for people to make mistakes, since this is the means for development. Discretion, as the ability to take non-routinized actions and exercise independent judgment, is the first cousin of innovation and the opportunity to be flexible, creative, and adaptive. Doing one's job the way it has always been done is the antithesis of empowerment.

Providing recognition and visibility.   Power does not flow to unknown sources. Being noticed is a key precursor to developing key strategic alliances with others. Recognition for one's efforts and achievements, important in its own right, creates interest in being connected and having one included in relationships, as well as access to higher-level sponsors and to the increased resources which generally flow to successful people.

"It is common to think of empowerment," say organizational scholars, "as a principal quality of leaders" (Coffey, Cook, and Hunsaker, 1994: 153). However, it is ironic that so much of what leaders accomplish is through enabling their constituents to become leaders (empowered) themselves.

See also *leadership; participatory management; trust*

Bibliography

Blanchard, K., Carlos, J. P., and Randolph, W. A. (1995). *Empowerment Takes More than a Minute.* San Francisco: Berrett-Kohler.

Coffey, R. E., Cook, C. W., and Hunsaker, P. L. (1994). *Management and Organizational Behavior.* Homewood, IL: Austen Press.

Kanter, R. M. (1983). *The Change Masters: Innovation for Productivity in the American Corporation.* New York: Simon and Schuster.

Kouzes, J. M. and Posner, B. Z. (1993). *Credibility: How Leaders Gain and Lose It, Why People Demand It.* San Francisco: Jossey-Bass.

Kouzes, J. M. and Posner, B. Z. (1995). *The Leadership Challenge: How to Keep Getting Extraordinary Things Done in Organizations.* San Francisco: Jossey-Bass.

Wood, R. E. and Bandura, A. (1989). Impact of conceptions of ability on self-regulatory mechanisms and complex decision-making. *Journal of Personality and Social Psychology,* **56,** 407–15.

engineers and business ethics

Vivian Weil

Engineers depend on their technical knowledge and skills to carry out their responsibilities for research, design, development, testing, and maintenance of technological products and systems. Their responsibilities can include quality control, safety management, implementation of government regulations, and sales. A great majority of engineers practice in business organizations; they are so integral to so many areas of business that any comprehensive account of business ethics has to consider engineers' roles and responsibilities.

The surge in growth of the engineering profession from the last third of the nineteenth century onward coincided with the rise of modern large-scale business organizations.

These organizations needed engineers to remove some of the guesswork from operations on a large scale, and they could afford the skills of large numbers of trained engineers. The process by which new industries arose in close association with the growth of fields of engineering continues to the present (Layton, 1986).

Engineers began organizing as a profession in the second half of the nineteenth century. They formed separate societies specific to areas of practice (e.g. civil engineering) and they continued the process of forming professional societies and formulating standards as their numbers surged, in spite of their intimate ties with business organizations. Over this same period, the education of engineers in institutions of higher education assumed increasing importance. The engineering curriculum traces its origins to the late eighteenth century in the École Polytechnique in France. With its emphasis on analytical methods, science, and mathematics, the French plan was the model for the first engineering school in the United States, West Point, established in 1802. The eighteenth-century French model remains discernible in the technical core of engineering education in the US. Vestiges of engineering's military past also survive, perhaps in part because military organizations provided the model for early large business organizations, especially the railroads, and thereby for industrial organizations of the late nineteenth century.

By the second decade of the twentieth century, engineering already showed most of the features that mark occupations as professions. Engineers depended on knowledge that was difficult to acquire and had theoretical coherence. They had formed professional societies and announced that they served the public. Apparently rejecting the notion that they were ordinary players in the rough and tumble of the marketplace, they had adopted standards of education and performance, including codes of ethics, to help them serve the public welfare. In subsequent decades, engineers revised their codes of ethics in response to developments in the wider society and to internal pressures. A legal ruling in 1978 required elimination of provisions that barred consulting engineers from competing on the basis of price. The emphasis of 1912 on "gentlemanly" conduct and "due regard" for the public gave way, after the revisions of the mid-1970s, to a clear announcement in the First Canon of most codes that "Engineers shall hold paramount the safety, health, and welfare of the public in the performance of their professional duties."

Professions are distinctive among occupational groups in creating communities of peers with standards that reach across and apply in the organizations that employ their members. Collegiality, with its emphasis on reciprocity and mutual support, constitutes a distinctive relationship among professional peers. Publications such as the Institute of Electrical and Electronic Engineers' *Spectrum*, which circulates to a large international membership, help to create and maintain a sense of a peer community of engineers.

Other professionals (e.g. physicians, accountants, lawyers) are employed in business organizations, but engineers often constitute a much larger proportion of a company's workforce and are usually more integral to producing the end product. While engineers and other professionals in business organizations are bound by the special standards of their respective professions, business managers have not organized as a profession and do not claim the special standards and status of a profession. This difference between engineers and managers, as occupational groups, can be a source of misunderstanding and tension in decision-making, even occurring between engineers and managers who were originally trained as engineers (Weil, 2002). The codes of ethics of engineers are rarely, if ever, given visibility in business organizations. Yet the primacy for engineers of safety and reliability is widely acknowledged.

Engineers' overarching ethical task is to mesh the demands for cooperating in an employer's enterprise with meeting the special standards – both technical and ethical – of the profession (that encompass, of course, an appropriate standard of care). In general terms, the codes provide guidance on how to carry out this meshing: treat the public welfare as paramount but fulfill the obligations of a faithful employee. Engineers are left on their own to find or devise specific mechanisms for making appropriate accommodations and to discover the advantages of allying with colleagues in support of responsible conduct.

Employers depend upon engineers for the reliable, uncompromised judgment of trained professionals; they and their engineer employees must, therefore, be concerned with threats to the reliability of judgment that conflicts of interest pose (Davis, 1982). When employers protect information for meeting the requirements of patent applications or supporting claims of trade secrecy, they present distinctive problems of confidentiality for engineers. Engineers must separate legitimate from exaggerated demands for secrecy and generic from locally specific knowledge, and they may have to weigh the claims of former employers when responding to certain demands for information from current employers (Frederick and Snoeyenbos, 1983).

Engineers must identify their ethical responsibilities in settings that are regulated by laws, codes, and government agency rules, at federal, state, and local levels, and by threats or outcomes of law suits. This means they must become familiar with legal requirements and cooperate with government officials and others to meet standards. Engineers must recognize their own individual responsibility although they are generally not targets of lawsuits, for plaintiffs target companies and firms. Government licensing is required for only a small number of engineering roles. Engineers, therefore, have to be mindful that they perform as *bona fide* professional engineers even though manufacturing businesses have influenced most states to exempt most engineering employees from licensing. As professionals, they must meet special standards articulated in codes of ethics as well as an appropriate standard of care, based in our ordinary morality.

Business ethics should address the situation of professional employees of business organizations. Professionals are needed and valued for the kind of informed judgment they bring to decision processes. It should be an important concern in business organizations to maintain climates conducive to the exercise of reliable judgment by professionals and to devise and maintain mechanisms that assure incorporation of professional judgment, including "bad news," in decision processes.

Bibliography

Accreditation Board for Engineering and Technology (1977). *Code of Ethics of Engineers*. New York: ABET.

Baron, M. (1984). *The Moral Status of Loyalty*. Dubuque: Kendall/Hunt Publishing. (Illinois Institute of Technology: Center for the Study of Ethics in the Professions.)

Broome, T. H., Jr. (1987). Engineering responsibility for hazardous technology. *Journal of Professional Issues in Engineering*, 113, 139–49.

Davis, M. (1982). Conflict of interest. *Business and Professional Ethics Journal*, 1 (4), 17–27.

Davis, M., Weil, V., Hollander, R., and Gibson, K. (1994). Symposium on engineering and business ethics. *International Journal of Applied Philosophy*, 8 (2), 1–21.

De George, R. T. (1981). Ethical responsibilities of engineers in large organizations: The Pinto case. *Business and Professional Ethics Journal*, 1 (1), 1–14.

Frederick, R. E. and Snoeyenbos, M. (1983). Trade secrets, patents, and morality. In M. Snoeyenbos, R. Almeder, and J. Humber (eds.), *Business Ethics: Corporate Values and Society*. Buffalo, NY: Prometheus, 162–9.

Layton, E. T. (1986). *The Revolt of the Engineers: Social Responsibility and the American Engineering Profession*. Baltimore, MD: Johns Hopkins University Press.

Vincenti, W. G. (1990). *What Engineers Know and How They Know It: Analytical Studies from Aeronautical History*. Baltimore, MD: Johns Hopkins University Press.

Weil, V. (2002). Engineering ethics. In R. E. Spier (ed.), *Science and Technology Ethics*. New York: Routledge, 59–88.

entrepreneurship and ethics

S. Venkataraman

Entrepreneurship is concerned with understanding how, in the absence of current markets for future goods and services, these goods and services are brought into existence by individuals and groups (Venkataraman, 1997). To the extent value is embodied in products and services, entrepreneurship is concerned with how the opportunity to create "value" in society is discovered or imagined and acted upon by some people. Often new products and services are brought to market by new firms. Therefore, entrepreneurship is also concerned with how people create new firms, nurture them, and renew older firms over time.

The field of business ethics, on the other hand, is concerned with the fairness of methods used to create this "value," and the ensuing distribution of the value among various stakeholders to the enterprise. Thus, if we understand entrepreneurship and ethics as the fields that together seek to describe, explain, predict, and prescribe how value is discovered, created, distributed, and perhaps destroyed, then together they represent two sides of the same coin: the coin of value creation and sharing.

Entrepreneurs, through their imagination, energy, talent, knowledge, contacts, and activities, attempt to create new wealth in societies. They do this in two ways: by reducing or eliminating existing inefficiencies in markets and firms or by bringing new products and problem solutions to people. When people create new businesses or firms to exploit inefficiencies or create and sell new and innovative products, we call them entrepreneurs and their activities entrepreneurial.

Inefficiencies arise (1) when it is difficult to remove poorly used resources from where they are currently employed and reapply them in ways that are more useful and (2) when different people have different information, conjectures, or ideas about the future. These inefficiencies offer enterprising people a rich pool of opportunities for the creation of successful new businesses. Practically every industry has pockets of such inefficiencies, although the scale and scope of such inefficiencies are different in different industries.

Opportunities to create new products arise because of limits to our current knowledge and also because we humans are creative and are constantly looking at the world around us in new ways. An example of limits to our knowledge would be the limitations in technology needed to satisfy certain known but unfulfilled market needs. For example, we know that the disease of cancer exists and that the market for a cure is both huge and worthwhile, but we have limited knowledge and means with which to develop a cure that would solve the problem. This known limitation is obviously a target for aspiring entrepreneurs in universities, in bio-

technology firms, and in large pharmaceutical companies. Every industry faces such technological frontiers – in design, manufacturing, distribution, sales, marketing, logistics, quality, etc. – and is therefore a source of both known and sometimes unanticipated opportunities.

It is from these major sources – stickiness of resources, information asymmetries, limited knowledge, and creativity – that new wealth is often created for the enterprising entrepreneur and for society.

Both Schumpeter (1976) and Adam Smith (much earlier) drew a profound connection between the personal profit motive and social wealth. Entrepreneurship is particularly productive from a social welfare perspective when, even in the process of pursuing selfish ends (where we interpret the word "selfish" to mean all things intended by Adam Smith, including greed, other regarding, and prudence (Werhane, 1991)), entrepreneurs also enhance social wealth by creating new jobs, higher standards of living, and net increases in real productivity. Arguably, were it not for the social surplus generated by private wealth seeking, the privilege and freedom to pursue selfish ends may not be accorded by societies to individuals at all.

Entrepreneurship involves joint production where several different stakeholders have to be brought together to create the new product or service (Shane and Venkataraman, 2000). The creative task of the entrepreneur is to identify, assemble, and institutionalize the joint production function in a way that meaningful surplus is created.

Typically, the entrepreneur does not own or control all the resources required to develop the market, establish the value-creating infrastructure, and eventually profit from his or her particular knowledge and aspirations. Most of these resources have to come from other people or institutions. Thus, the entrepreneur has to assemble, organize, and execute the value-creating infrastructure before potential profits can be realized.

The process of creating products and markets implies that much of the information required by potential stakeholders – for example, technology, price, quantity, tastes, supplier networks, distributor networks, and strategy – are not reliably available. Relevant information will only exist once the market has been successfully created (Arrow, 1974). Potential stakeholders thus have to rely on the entrepreneur for information, but without the benefit of the entrepreneur's "insight." Thus, decisions about all aspects of the new firm, its future and stakeholders' participation have to be made behind the classic "veil of ignorance" (Rawls, 1971).

Because of such information asymmetry the seeds of potential conflicts between stakeholders can be sown right at the inception of the firm, at the very forging of the joint production function. Indeed, scholars such as Knight (1957) and Kirzner (1985) have argued that without fundamentally different expectations and interpretations about the future, there is no entrepreneurial opportunity in the first place. The entrepreneurial opportunity owes its very existence to the differing information bases and expectations of the stakeholders.

When the process of creation occurs in an environment of differing information, interpretation, and expectations, ethics plays an important role in informing individuals of the appropriate behavior. Ethics provides the entrepreneurs and their stakeholders with guidance on the properties of fair and efficient exchange processes, contracts, and alternative mechanisms available to effectively reconcile competing claims during the creation process.

Entrepreneurial opportunities present people with possibilities for both a gain and a loss. By definition, entrepreneurship requires making investments (time, effort, and money) today without knowing what the returns will be tomorrow. Economist Frank Knight pointed out an important quality about entrepreneurial opportunities: there is a fundamental uncertainty about them. He observed that one cannot collect more information or perform more analysis to reduce uncertainty. Rather, only the collective actions of competing entrepreneurs, resource suppliers, and customers can reduce uncertainties. There is no meaningful way in which to predict the future prospects of an entrepreneurial opportunity and then act on it. Knight pointed out this important distinction between uncertainty (outcomes that cannot be imagined and are unknowable) and risk (both outcomes and their probabilities can be subjectively assigned). You

can insure against or diversify away risk, but you cannot insure against or diversify away uncertainty.

Because of uncertainty there is the possibility of unintended consequences during the creation process. While some of these consequences are positive, there are others that are perverse or harmful to others. The entrepreneurial process, by its very nature, is driven by people who are liable to make errors, are sometimes ignorant, sometimes ignorant about their ignorance, sometimes brilliant, mostly prosaic, sometimes knowingly deceitful, but mostly well intentioned, and most important of all, boundedly rational (Simon, 1947). Thus, value inequities and externalities are an essential byproduct of the creation process. Very often, such inequities and externalities arise due to unintended consequences, but sometimes they may be a product of willful deceit on the part of the entrepreneurs or their stakeholders. Inequities arise when some stakeholders enjoy more than their "fair" share of the benefits of entrepreneurial creation compared to others, which may not have been anticipated when commitments were made. At other times these stakeholders may actually have benefited at the *expense* of others. Such *externalities*, where one person's actions affect another, are sometimes willful, but often unanticipated. Pragmatically, one has to deal with such externalities as and when they arise. Ethics, again, plays a major role in guiding the entrepreneurs and their stakeholders on how to resolve the externalities created by the entrepreneurial process. From an ethics perspective, we may summarize three alternative mechanisms that address issues of inequities and externalities during the entrepreneurial process. One is embodied in a person (the moral person), one is embodied in a process (the bargaining process), and one is embodied in an external (to the firm) institution (the visible hand of law and government).

Moral persons employ and adhere to ethical norms that reflect high standards of right behavior. Moral persons not only conform to accepted high levels of professional conduct, they also frequently exhibit ethical leadership. Moral persons strive to operate well above and beyond what the law mandates. Sound moral principles such as justice, rights, utilitarianism, and the

Golden Rule are employed for decision-making and conduct (Carroll, 1995), and guide individuals in resolving inequities.

Central to the process view is the conception of the "value-creation activity as a contractual process among those parties affected" (Freeman, 1994: 67). Thus, an entrepreneurial enterprise is a nexus of multilateral contracts where value equilibration occurs over time through a process of bargaining among the various resource owners and stakeholders in the enterprise. The bargaining process is a dynamic one of give and take over time, all occurring within a mutually accepted framework of reconciliation rules, guided by legal notions of "fair contract" (Freeman and Evan, 1990).

Conflicts, especially about ex-post distributions, are an integral part of the value-creation process. Thus, emphasis is placed on the procedural aspects of multiple stakeholder co-ordination rather than upon the results of value-creating activity itself or upon the specific outcomes of the bargaining process (Donaldson and Preston, 1995).

In the event that the moral manager and/or the bargaining process do not satisfactorily perform the job of dealing with inequities and externalities, there is need for a countervailing force, in the form of an external visible hand. The visible hand augments moral persons and fair processes with an external creator and enforcer of laws to overcome problems of inequities and negative externalities, even if actions were taken in good faith (Hill and Jones, 1992). Thus, we have reporting requirements, monitoring agencies, enforcement agencies, etc., overseeing the activities of the entrepreneurs and their stakeholders.

People often forget that a competitive entrepreneurial process itself is another powerful way of dealing with inequities and externalities. The very process of entrepreneurial discovery serves as a fair and efficient mechanism to reconcile conflicting stakeholder claims. In this regard, the entrepreneurial process works in two ways: dealing with a value anomaly or externality stakeholder by stakeholder and by bringing about a fundamental change in a complete system of stakeholders. We may call these, respectively, the weak equilibrating process and the strong equilibrating process (Venkataraman,

1997, 2002). The strong equilibrating process overcomes some of the limitations of the weak process. The weak equilibrating process holds that whenever a stakeholder justifiably believes that the value supplied by him or her to an enterprise is more than the value received, the entrepreneurial process has an opportunity to redeploy the resources of the "victimized" stakeholder to a use where value supplied and received will be equilibrated. The strong equilibrating process holds that if the redeployment of individual stakeholders does not work freely and efficiently (for whatever reasons), and serious value anomalies and externalities accumulate within firms and societies, the entrepreneurial process will destroy the value anomalies by fundamental rearrangements in how resources and stakeholders are combined, a process commonly referred to as *innovation*. Such recombination may occur through invention of new products, new organizational forms, new processes of production, transportation, and communication, new markets, and new ways of organizing life in societies.

WEAK EQUILIBRATING PROCESS

Hayek (1945: 519) pointed out that in any collective, equilibration has to be brought about under circumstances where the knowledge required to bring about such equilibration exists neither concentrated in some integrated form nor is "given" to a single mind. Rather, such knowledge exists as "dispersed bits of incomplete and frequently contradictory knowledge which all the separate individuals possess."

The dispersion of information among different people has two implications. First, it is physically impossible for the value of all resources during the creative process to be in balance at any given time, that is, exist in a state of equilibrium. Thus, in most creative tasks most of the time, some resource owners will not get their due. Second, the existence of these inefficiencies is a reliable source of profit for those alert individuals who can discover and eliminate value inequities and externalities.

Value inequities and externalities represent entrepreneurial opportunities for individuals. By definition whenever there is an asymmetry in beliefs about the value of a resource (say between the value supplier and those who receive it) there exists inefficiency. Inefficiencies are a major incentive for alert individuals seeking to profit from them, and the central feature of a free market system is the abundant supply of such alert profit-seeking entrepreneurs (Kirzner, 1985).

An entrepreneur is one who realizes or conjectures (either through genuine insight and knowledge, or through mere luck) that some resources are underutilized in their current occupation and recombines them into potentially a more useful and fruitful combination. Such redeployment goes on all the time in a market economy and plays three important roles from an ethics perspective. First, it provides important information about the competitive value of alternative resources. Value inequities or anomalies can often be discovered only in reference to some external benchmark, and the entrepreneurial process provides this important information to the stakeholders, from which they can recognize the presence of inequities. Second, the competition for resources from opportunity-seeking entrepreneurs potentially forces current entrepreneurs to act as if each stakeholder is an end unto himself or herself and not a means to others' ends. Third, the entrepreneurial process can provide a viable exit route for victimized stakeholders.

Strong Equilibrating Force

The weak equilibrating force is a necessary but not sufficient condition for solving stakeholder anomalies. Historically, people in many societies have accepted significant disparities in fortunes and wealth, especially in free and democratic societies where people are confident that the disparities are outcomes of a fair process, in the sense of Rawls (1971). Often, however, there are systematic local problems, both in outcomes and in the working of the weak equilibrating force. Stakeholder inequities in some sections of the economy (for example, the giant widely held corporation or in some specific industries) may accumulate and may be spread over a wide spectrum of stakeholders. Moreover, such inequities may persist for non-trivial periods. The sources of such accumulation and persistence may be several. First, because the weak force harbors errors and ignorance, stakeholder inequities may never be discovered in the first place.

Second, even if these inequities are discovered, the affected group may be fragmented, or cannot coalesce into a concentrated power capable of changing the current order. Third, even if the victimized stakeholder groups are concentrated, there may be significant asymmetry in relative power and so they are powerless to alter the status quo. Fourth, even if power is not an issue, the stakeholders are so dispersed that their problems are economically unattractive for the entrepreneurial process to solve. Fifth, there may be conflicts of interests, lack of fairness, and a lack of ethics in those that are aware of and can correct the inequities. Finally, there may be willful desire to do harm on the part of some.

The persistence of accumulated inequities calls not for incremental change through the weak force, but for a fundamental qualitative change of the kind Schumpeter envisioned – a revolutionary change in economic order through a process of creative destruction. The entrepreneur is one such agent of change. As Schumpeter (1976) pointed out, the "fundamental impulse that sets and keeps" in motion such systemic change "comes from the new consumer goods, the new methods of production or transportation, the new markets, and the new forms of industrial organization." The history of business is littered with such entrepreneurially introduced innovations. Each succeeding innovation has altered the economic, political, and social landscape and, for our purposes, has brought about a fundamental qualitative change in relative stakeholder power. Entrepreneurs and entrepreneurship have the power to do immense good, but can also harm. However, the entrepreneurial process contains within itself the power to address the harm.

Bibliography

Arrow, K. J. (1974). Limited knowledge and economic analysis. *American Economic Review*, **64** (1), 1–10.
Carroll, A. B. (1995). Stakeholder thinking in three models of management morality: A perspective with strategic implications. In J. Nasi (ed.), *Understanding Stakeholder Thinking*. Helsinki: LSR Publications, 47–74.
Donaldson, T. and Preston, L. (1995). The stakeholder theory of the corporation: Concepts, evidence, implications. *Academy of Management Review*, **20**, 65–91.

Freeman, R. E. (1994). A stakeholder theory of the modern corporation. In T. L. Beauchamp and N. E. Bowie (eds.), *Ethical Theory and Business*. Engelwood Cliffs, NJ: Prentice-Hall, 66–76.

Freeman, R. E. and Evan, W. M. (1990). Corporate governance: A stakeholder interpretation. *Journal of Behavioral Economics*, **19** (4), 337–59.

Hayek, F. A. (1945). The use of knowledge in society. *American Economic Review*, **35** (4), 519–30.

Hill, C. W. L. and Jones, T. M. (1992). Stakeholder-agency theory. *Journal of Management Studies*, **29**, 131–54.

Kirzner, I. (1985). *Discovery and the Capitalist Process*. Chicago: University of Chicago Press.

Knight, F. H. (1957) [1921]. *Risk, Uncertainty, and Profit*, 8th edn. New York: Kelley and Millman.

Rawls, J. (1971). *A Theory of Justice*. Cambridge, MA: Harvard University Press.

Schumpeter, J. A. (1976). *Capitalism, Socialism and Democracy*. New York: Harper and Row.

Shane, S. and Venkataraman, S. (2000). The promise of entrepreneurship as a field of research. *Academy of Management Review*, **25** (1), 217–26.

Simon, H. A. (1947). Administrative behavior. New York: Free Press.

Smith, A. (1937). *The Wealth of Nations*. New York: Modern Library/Random House.

Venkataraman, S. (1997). The distinctive domain of entrepreneurship research. In J. Katz (ed.), *Advances in Entrepreneurship, Firm Emergence and Growth*. Place? JAI Press, vol. 3, 119–38.

Venkataraman, S. (2002). Stakeholder value equilibration and the entrepreneurial process. In R. E. Freeman and S. Venkataraman (eds.), *Ethics and Entrepreneurship*. Ruffin Series 3. Charlottesville, VA: Philosophy Documentation Center.

Werhane, P. (1991). *Adam Smith and His Legacy for Modern Capitalism*. New York: Oxford University Press.

environment and environmental ethics

Laura Westra

In the sense intended by Environmental Ethics (EE), "environment" refers specifically to the natural world of which humans are a part. It includes landscapes which function according to evolutionary natural processes. However, since humankind has substantially altered many natural systems, the "environment" also includes areas manipulated for human use, including landscapes where agriculture, agroforestry, and cities are located.

EE appears at first to be a species of applied ethics, like business ethics or bioethics, applying ethics to the problems of human interaction with the environment. Unlike those disciplines, however, EE goes beyond the appropriate application of familiar doctrines to a certain species of practical problems: it requires that we extend or transcend our accepted moral doctrines because it forces us to rethink the boundaries of the morally considerable. Whatever our moral persuasion, we must go beyond the "anthropocentric" paradigm (that is, the position that only humans are morally considerable and that they are at the "center" of our moral reasoning), to establish who or what might possess moral standing (Van DeVeer, 1986). EE is broader, more inclusive than other practical ethics; hence it is, in some sense, a *new* ethic, addressing as it does totally new problems in many areas (Callicott, 1984; Scherer, 1990; Westra, 1994a).

EE requires us to confront problems that cannot be easily resolved if we cling to pure anthropocentrism; they may remain intractable even if ours is a "weak" anthropocentrism, that is, one which admits environmental values beyond those of economic exploitation of nature (Norton, 1991). Thus the first question raised by EE is where do we draw the boundaries of the moral community? Is sentience necessary for the inclusion of non-human animals (Singer, 1993)? Or should we consider all individual organisms equally, because of their individual teleology, their unique desire to realize themselves, which supports their intrinsic worth (Taylor, 1986)? And what of natural "wholes" such as ecosystems (Rolston, 1988; Leopold, 1949; Westra, 1994a)? Many philosophers argue that *all* these entities are valuable, hence merit inclusion in the moral community, whereas others draw the line at sentience only, or limit themselves to individual rights (Regan, 1983).

The approach we choose will dictate how we respond to the many environmental problems we encounter: problems of pollution, resource depletion, animal exploitation, waste disposal, population explosion, and erosion and depletion of soils; problems involving the air we breathe, the sun that warms the earth, the water and land we need to survive, and biotic impoverishment of habitats, loss of species, climate changes – all of which affect our life-support systems. Aside from the moral considerability question, other novel aspects of environmental problems predicate the need for a new ethic. All actions in regard to the environment can now be defined as "upstream/downstream," as all our activities have unprecedented effects through the future (in time) and globally (in space). Nothing we do, given our increasing technological powers, can be viewed as yielding limited, spatially circumscribed consequences. Thus our actions now require new social constraints, as "traditionally broad concepts of liberty" are no longer appropriate (Scherer, 1990).

Further, our environmental moral conflicts are no longer limited to disagreements about external constraints, or conflicts about group preferences. Internal conflicts are also unavoidable: we *know* that not all our preferences and choices are acceptable, as our very lifestyle has been called into question. Each one of us must thus resolve the internal conflicts between "consumer" and "citizen," learning to modify and restrain the former, while emphasizing the latter and our commitment to our community and to life on earth (Sagoff, 1989). A new understanding of what it means to be moral, and an ecological ethics which is "deep" rather than "shallow" (Seed et al., 1988), is required, and a changed lifestyle, based on reproductive and consumerist restraint, a changed diet, and new intellectual or spiritual goals.

EE is a relatively new field, but several conflicting approaches are already discussed in the literature. I alluded earlier to the anthropocentric/non-anthropocentric dichotomy. Some argue that to view purely human concerns as central is nothing but "speciesism" (that is, a position that is based inappropriately on the "superior" value of our species over others), whereas others respond that only humans can be moral or even appreciate or discuss questions of value, hence the moral view must be human. Another conflict is that between individualists and holists. Some ask whether individual animals or plants have value or even rights. Others argue that wholes such as species, ecosystems, the land, or the biosphere might represent the most appropriate locus of value instead (Rolston, 1988; Leopold, 1949; Westra, 1994a). Yet another debate centers on the role of sciences

such as biology or ecology in environmental ethics.

Those who accept a holistic ethics tend to allow the scientific "is," uncertain and incomplete though it is, to provide the limits appropriate to the moral "ought" which dictates environmentally good actions (Rolston, 1988). Others prefer not to tie EE to the methodological difficulties and the predictive uncertainties of a young, science-like ecology, with its many approaches and varied scalar perspectives (Shrader-Frechette and McCoy, 1993).

In essence, EE is basic to social, political, and economic policy-making, and represents one of the major considerations required of business operations. Nowhere can the power and the reach of business have a deadlier impact on human and non-human life than through its interaction with the environment. By the same token, it is in the environmental realm that large corporate bodies, particularly multinationals, can make the greatest contribution to the public good, if their operation is seriously guided by an ecologically sound environmental ethics.

Examples of destructive business behavior are unfortunately more frequent and better known than their opposite actions. Bhopal and *Exxon Valdez* are names everyone has heard, whereas efforts like the funding of buffer zones sustainability next to Amisconde's Man-in-the-Biosphere project in Costa Rica, by McDonald's Corporation, has never made front-page news (Lacher and Cesca, 1995). Another environmental problem connected with some business operations is only now being clearly recognized in all its implications, although it has a long and nefarious history: that of "environmental racism." Both "risky business" operations and hazardous waste disposal facilities tend to permit economic considerations *only* to guide their siting policies, and thus most often choose poor areas where house and land values are lower. Hence, they tend to choose existing "brownfields," already present in and around areas inhabited primarily by persons of color (Bullard, 1994; Westra and Wenz, 1995).

When business practices are hazardous to human beings, through their environmental impact, corporations may simply respond by appealing to traditional moral theories to evaluate their activities. For instance, utilitarian doctrines will dictate that the "good" of the many should represent the proper goal of moral agents; and, provided that the "good" is defined and understood in communitarian terms, rather than as aggregate preferences or purely as economic benefits, this approach may work, at least in a limited manner. Deontological emphasis on respect for human rights, if it is based on Kant's doctrine of the absolute value of life, would not permit that human health and life be risked, no matter what other benefits might accrue to any of the parties involved. Finally, Rawlsian "fairness" might serve (a) to limit unjust burdens imposed on some stakeholders in the interest of business development or profit; and (b) to curtail the exploitation of the weakest and most powerless, and thus perhaps to attack "environmental racism" from another direction (see KANTIAN ETHICS).

In fact, many of the consequences of their operations can be made environmentally sound, simply through a consideration of their possible effect on human beings (thus remaining within the ambit of traditional moral theory, for instance the harm principle). Business should monitor closely their products, their processes, and their practices, in regard to both their internal and their external stakeholders, in order not to impose unacceptable risks, often unknown by those exposed to such risks and uncompensated (Westra, 1994b).

But there are other, more far-reaching problems (e.g., questions of siting location or waste disposal), where guidelines reaching beyond present, existing human stakeholders, to the non-human environment, may provide a more inclusive perspective. In general, it is hard to quantify, specify, or defend in a court of law, hazards to human health which may take years to develop. But both non-human animals and the ecosystem habitat we share with other creatures may already be affected, in a demonstrable, non-controversial way. It is in these cases that ethics that demand respect for the environment as such might be more effective from the moral standpoint and that of public policy. The same attitude may be found increasingly in new regulations and laws. For instance, land-use cases which might have been treated as a "taking" in earlier times, now may be dealt with under the heading of "police powers," to prevent owners' business choices and to protect some endangered and fragile ecosystems, such as wetland, for future generations, when all may depend on these ecosystems' "services."

At the international level, biodiversity treaties, or the ozone protocol, also indicate a trend to universal regulation, and away from the need to demonstrate harm to a specific individual before restraints may be instituted.

After all, even the Endangered Species Act demands the protection of *habitats*, in order to ensure their goals in regard to some species. Finally, even major economic players such as the World Bank have also changed their practices to emphasize the importance of environmental impact, which is now the major consideration in their lending policies (Goodland and Daly, 1995).

Bibliography

Bullard, R. (1994). *Dumping in Dixie*. Boulder, CO: Westview Press.

Callicott, J. F. (1984). Non-anthropocentric value theory and environmental ethics. *American Philosophy Quarterly*, 21, 299–309.

Goodland, R., and Daly, H. (1995). Environmental sustainability: Universal and non-negotiable. In L. Westra and J. Lemons (eds.), *Perspectives on Implementing Ecological Integrity*. Dordrecht: Kluwer Academic Publishers.

Lacher, T. and Cesca, R. (1995). Ethical obligations of multinational corporations to the global environment: McDonald's and conservation. In L. Westra and J. Lemons (eds.), *Perspectives on Implementing Ecological Integrity*. Dordrecht: Kluwer Academic Publishers.

Leopold, A. (1949). *A Sand County Almanac and Sketches Here and There*. New York: Oxford University Press.

Norton, B. (1991). *Toward Unity Among Environmentalists*. New York: Oxford University Press.

Regan, T. (1983). *The Case for Animal Rights*. Berkeley: University of California Press.

Rolston, H. (1988). *Environmental Ethics*. Philadelphia, PA: Temple University Press.

Sagoff, M. (1989). *The Economy of the Earth*. Cambridge, MA: Cambridge University Press.

Scherer, D. (ed.) (1990). *Upstream/Downstream: Issues in Environmental Ethics*. Philadelphia, PA: Temple University Press.

Seed, J., Macy, J., Fleming, P., and Naess, A. (1988). *Thinking Like a Mountain: Towards a Council of All Beings*. Philadelphia, PA: New Society Publishers.

Shrader-Frechette, K. and McCoy, E. (1993). *Method in Ecology*. Cambridge: Cambridge University Press.

Singer, P. (1993). *Practical Ethics*, 2nd edn. New York: Cambridge University Press.

Taylor, P. (1986). *Respect for Nature*. Princeton, NJ: Princeton University Press.

Van DeVeer, D. (1986). *Paternalistic Intervention*. Princeton, NJ: Princeton University Press.

Van DeVeer, D. and Pierce, C. (1995). *People, Penguins and Plastic Trees: Basic Issues in Environmental Ethics*. Belmont, CA: Wadsworth.

Westra, L. (1994a). *An Environmental Proposal for Ethics: The Principle of Integrity*. Lanham, MD: Rowman and Littlefield.

Westra, L. (1994b). Corporate responsibility and hazardous products. *Business Ethics Quarterly*, 4 (1), 97–110.

Westra, L. and Wenz, P. (eds.) (1995). *The Faces of Environmental Racism: Confronting the Global Equity Issue*. Lanham, MD: Rowman and Littlefield.

environmental risk

Rachelle D. Hollander

The first meaning of risk in *Webster's Ninth New Collegiate Dictionary* (1986) is "possibility of loss or injury." To risk is "to expose to hazard or danger." The meaning of environment is, most generally, "the circumstances, objects, or conditions by which one is surrounded," including biophysical factors determining the form and survival of organisms or ecosystems, and sociocultural factors influencing individuals and communities.

Environmental risk, then, as relevant to business ethics, encompasses those actions or inactions by which businesses give rise to and are affected by the possibility of biophysical or social loss or injury to entities of all kinds. This definition is more inclusive than that used in most discussion – where the environment and environmental risk are taken to be limited to biophysical, not social or cultural, factors.

This entry examines several components of this definition, focusing primarily on loss to biophysical systems. It concentrates on questions concerning probability and uncertainty, the notion of what counts as loss or injury and the relationship of this to other desired or desirable phenomena, and the normative nature and policy dimensions of the construct of risk.

RISK AS PROBABILITY

The likelihood of injury or harm may be well known or a subject of much dispute. In all but the most remote parts of the world, people know that the likelihood of serious harm from stepping immediately in front of a speeding car is very high. People understand and can estimate familiar, frequent risks. Although their very familiarity can lead to underestimation, individuals need not pursue elaborate exercises in quantification to make most of their decisions; nor need organizations do so in similar circumstances.

Away from this simple model, entire industries are built on such exercises. Consider mortality rates. An example of well-established probabilities are actuarial tables of human life expectancies in different parts of the world. Establishing such probabilities for particular categories of human lives or other elements of the environment is more complex. Whether we do it depends on the value we place on those elements and whether we have other acceptable ways of arriving at decisions.

Even well-established risks are subject to change that can come more or less rapidly, depending on social and environmental conditions. Many risks are subject to human influence or control. But the likelihood that individual, group, or organizational actions or inactions will result in increasing or decreasing risks to human lives or those of other species and ecosystems may not be well established. There may be greater or lesser degrees of uncertainty. Other forms of harm than those resulting in premature mortality need consideration and may be subject to even more uncertainty. If this is so, many risks to humans, other species, and ecosystems cannot be accurately measured. Many species on the planet have not been identified, so risks cannot be assigned at all. Here, rather than uncertainty, there is ignorance.

Inability to assign well-founded estimates of life expectancies or rates of environmental succession or decay, however, cannot be used to justify the position that there are no risks. The risks are unknown. When risks are unknown, the question arises of where the burden of proof should lie. If this question can be answered, it will be through a process of social negotiation, not quantification, although the negotiation may include the question of further research, and its risks, costs, and benefits.

This last point is true of finding answers to all questions of environmental risk. Consider the possibility of injury or harm from the release of lead into the environment. Lead is a metallic chemical element. All lead compounds are poisonous. Lead has had and continues to have many important commercial uses. Human beings of different ages and ethnicities exhibit different sensitivities. Many kinds of injury or harm that can be attributed to lead are well established; some are subject to some dispute. Actions can be taken to change commercial and waste disposal practices to get rid of, control, or minimize the use of lead so that the risk to the environment, in the plant, at home, or at large, is alleviated. Even with such a long-standing risk, about which a great deal is known, decisions will arise through an ongoing process of social negotiation.

Part of this negotiation process involves procedures called risk assessments. Scientists and engineers often undertake these assessments, under the auspices of businesses and industries that may perform them in deciding whether or not to develop or market a new product or continue an old one. They also undertake these assessments, as employees, under the auspices of governmental agencies charged to protect human or ecological health and safety; or, with grants and contracts from these agencies, in colleges and universities. Federal agencies support research to improve processes of risk assessment as well. These assessments are an important – albeit controversial – tool in the process by which organizations, groups, and individuals decide whether or not something poses risk and what to do about it.

RISK AS NORMATIVE CONSTRUCT

Although some risks are worth taking, people wish to avoid injury or harm. But care must be taken not to view this idea too simplistically. What exposures, actions, or inactions, at what levels, must be avoided? To whom? When? Whose responsibility is it to avoid exposing themselves or others to environmental risks, to alleviate results from such exposure, or to compensate? What evidence, of what kinds, suffices to establish risk? What kinds of regulation are appropriate? What about the international implications of risk exposures?

Business interests, among others, may accuse environmental or neighborhood groups or regulators of overreaction to environmental risks, pointing out that to some degree such risks are unavoidable, and the price of much that people hold dear. They may contrast environmental risks to economic risks. This particular normative construct of risk – the trade-offs view – is described further below, as are other normative approaches.

When risks are being debated, such as in considering the question of lead in the environment, it is useful to ask the following questions: Have persons' legitimate expectations for feasible control and due care been met or violated? Are there ways to improve the situation? According to what standards? (Hollander, 1994). The use of the shorthand term "risk" here goes beyond counting how many organisms, in what environments, at what ages, are injured or harmed, and how. It goes to questions about what kind of world we wish to see: what kinds of outcomes, institutions, procedures, and behaviors we value.

RISK PRIORITIES

Many people have strong views about the importance of environmental risk. In expressing these views, they often use arguments and develop positions that fall into categories identified by Aiken (1986): the top-priority, trade-offs, constraints, and interconnectedness views.

The top-priority view places an environmental risk at the top of a list of all kinds of risks – environmental and other – and insists that the proper way to proceed is to lower or overcome it. In this view, the top risk has priority even if another risk is increased by doing so.

The trade-offs view might agree to the list, but its proponents proceed by trying to compare what they take to be relevant risks in order to reduce the overall level of risk. This form of comparative risk assessment tends to be the approach of federal regulators in the US Environmental Protection Agency (EPA). Risk assessments often presuppose this normative view. The trade-offs view has to find a way to measure different kinds of risk for these comparisons to be made. It is not always easy to do this. Economists tend to use this normative view, but they have difficulty setting a monetary value on ecologists' views about ecological risks or environmentalists' views about the value of wilderness, for instance. And microbiologists may disagree with ecologists, even about what the relevant risks are.

Persons with the constraints view identify such issues as human rights and informed consent; whatever the ranking scheme, they indicate concern about human exposures to chemical toxins without their knowledge and/or beyond their control. Regulators in the EPA and in the Food and Drug Administration often take this view, along with the trade-offs view. The concept of environmental justice, beginning to play an important role in social deliberations about environmental risks, often presupposes the constraints view, asking whether it is fair for poor or minority communities to be faced with more environmental hazards than richer communities, which tend to have fewer residents of color.

The interconnectedness view points out that the natural world does not operate like a balance sheet, which can only be completed after the fact. Rather, it operates more like business decision-making environments in which risk is unavoidable and positive as well as negative. Life requires evolution, predation, and death. Interconnectedness means a negative can't be simply traded off against a positive; it may be necessary to the maintenance of a desirable whole. The desire to return wolves to the American Northwest may be an example of this view.

RISK POLICY

There is growing recognition that adequate answers to questions of acceptable risk and acceptable evidence of risk require acknowledging different positions groups take and behaviors they exhibit about what is risky and what to do about it. Adequate answers require attention to issues of process and conduct, as well as outcomes (Thompson, 1993).

The positions that different groups take about risk have consequences that themselves affect the risk. The groups include scientific and non-scientific institutions, business among them, in roles ranging from undertaking risk assessments; to attempting to bring different dimensions of risk to the attention of relevant scientists and policy-makers, in order to make them part of

formal processes; to disputing the results of risk assessments or risk management processes; to adopting or ignoring their results in policy or practice. Adequate risk assessment and management, and risk policy, will need to take these consequences into account.

Additionally, risk policy will need to be concerned with outcomes, structures, and procedures, and conduct or behavioral norms in order to understand the responses of individuals and organizations. In its initial forms exclusively and to a great extent now, quantitative risk assessment examines outcomes and distributions of outcomes. Assessments look for answers to questions of morbidity or mortality. As noted above, these are difficult questions to answer when limited to human beings, and questions concerning other species and ecosystems are even more complicated. Furthermore, environmental values go beyond concerns for morbidity and mortality, to those perhaps better viewed as bio- or enviro-aesthetic, and to feelings of awe or wonder. It is not clear that these values can be assimilated in a trade-offs analysis.

In addition to outcomes, issues of risk concern the structures and procedures by which risk decisions are made. These are not concerns about outcomes to humans or environments of exposures to putative hazardous substances or other factors influencing environmental degradation. They are concerns for the norms and procedures by which, and institutions in which, decisions get made. As in the constraints view, these are concerns for process and fairness in process and protection of human rights. They are concerns for integrity and public confidence in social systems, for feasible control and due care. The perception of risks from and to procedures and processes often lies behind people's reluctance to allow business, government, and other institutions to proceed as they would like and think they should be able.

A concern about conduct is a final element that should be considered in risk policy. This is a concern for how risk assessments get made and what their implications are for human behavior. It is a concern for the implications for humans and their impacts, that decisions are made in certain ways and not others. If decisions are made by one or another group of elites, or by democratic processes, what does that mean for how these individuals and groups will behave in the future? For how institutions will evolve, or how others will behave? To what habits of character will these procedures lead? Will they result in more care, or more carelessness? Will they lead to efforts to improve in the future, or to complacency?

For instance, should procedures be used that try to quantify the value of an individual human life as a basis for making social decisions? The concern about this procedure may not be just for its influence on outcomes or structures, but about its influence on human beings' regard for each other. The refusal to place monetary values on individual human lives need not mean that decisions about scarce resources lack justification. It would mean that the grounds could not rely on a consequentialist procedure that assigns monetary values to individual lives. Such a refusal takes the position that questions about norms, structures, human character, and conduct need to be incorporated into decision procedures.

See also *biodiversity; consequentialism; environment and environmental ethics; future generations; global warming; hazardous waste; marketing, ethics of; property, rights to; risk; technology, ethical issues in; transnational corporations*

Bibliography

Aiken, W. H. (1986). On evaluating agricultural research. In K. A. Dahlberg (ed.), *New Directions for Agriculture and Agricultural Research: Neglected Dimensions and Emerging Alternatives*. Totowa, NJ: Rowman and Allanheld, 31–41. (Presents four normative views in the context of setting agricultural research priorities.)

Brown, H. S. et al. (1993). *Corporate Environmentalism in a Global Economy: Societal Values in International Technology Transfer*. Westport CT: Quorum Books.

Cranor, C. F. (1993). *Regulating Toxic Substances: A Philosophy of Science and the Law*. New York: Oxford University Press.

Hollander, R. D. (1994). Is engineering safety just business safety? *International Journal of Applied Philosophy*, 8 (2), 15–19.

Krimsky, S. and Golding, D. (eds.) (1992). *Social Theories of Risk*. Westport, CT: Praeger. (Good introduction to different theories, approaches, models of risk assessment.)

MacLean, D. (ed.) (1986). *Values at Risk*. Totowa, NJ: Rowman and Allanheld.

MacLean, D. and Brown, P. (eds.) (1983). *Energy and the Future*. Totowa, NJ: Rowman and Allanheld.

Mayo, D. G. and Hollander, R. D. (eds.) (1992). *Acceptable Evidence: Science and Values in Risk Management*. New York: Oxford University Press. (Examines value dimensions in risk assessment processes and policies.)

Thompson, P. (1993). Food labels and biotechnology: The ethics of safety and consent. Discussion Paper, Center for Biotechnology Policy and Ethics, Texas A&M University. (Differentiates the outcomes, procedures, and character concerns over policies.)

equal opportunity

Paul de Vries

A standard of decision-making, stipulating that all people be treated the same, except when distinctions can be explicitly justified. This standard has been used to define fairness in lending, housing, hiring, wage and salary levels, job promotion, voting rights, and other concerns. Artificial barriers, prejudices, and personal preferences should neither restrict nor enhance the opportunities for anyone. Affirmative action programs set goals and quotas for hiring, promotion, and suchlike, but equal opportunity focuses on breaking down the artificial barriers and stereotypes.

The standard of equal opportunity is a frequent theme in American culture and tradition. Perhaps the most basic notion of the American free enterprise economy is the value of equal opportunity. Thomas Jefferson used equal opportunity as the foundational theme of the Declaration of Independence: Jefferson's argument is that God made us equal, and that equality is protected for basic opportunities: life, liberty, and the pursuit of happiness. It is also at the core of Martin Luther King Jr.'s famous "I Have a Dream" speech. He dreamt that his four little children would someday "not be judged by the color of their skin but by the content of their character."

Major thinkers in intellectual history have championed equal opportunity as well. Adam Smith made it a necessary part of an efficient and fair economy. For John Rawls, it is one of the three most elementary principles to which all rational beings should agree. Hilary Putnam, while acknowledging that the belief and practice of equality were first taught in the Bible, defends it as his model for "pragmatic realism."

The phrase "equal opportunity" contains two value-charged, ambiguous words. It seems "nice" to say that we are "equal," but there is no factual measure on which any two people are truly equal. "Equality" in this case is a standard for decisions and policies, not a description. Moreover, it is difficult to be against any "opportunity," for example; nevertheless, how much personal responsibility should be required is a matter of debate.

Some distinctions between people are pertinent, and decisions based upon these distinctions can be justified in ways that are consistent with equal opportunity. For example, when evaluating applicants for a women's professional basketball team, the management may justifiably exclude all men as well as those women who are not skilled in basketball. Similarly, many jobs require special training or even licensing, and equal opportunity is not violated when these criteria are recognized. People without accounting training need not be considered on an equal basis with those who are trained, when accounting is an important part of a job opening. Also, banks and mortgage companies do not violate equal opportunity when loan applicants are evaluated by relevant criteria: credit records, income, job stability, and the like.

The critical question is: "What distinctions between people are pertinent without equal opportunity being compromised?" Overt and subtle standards need to be evaluated; both conscious and subconscious patterns ought to be scrutinized. Even the most self-conscious egalitarians will likely have some unjustified implicit assumptions that color or twist their perceptions and decisions.

Statistical analyses of personal and corporate decisions help to reveal patterns that are otherwise difficult to recognize. For example, even a very conscientious bank may discover that it demands a higher credit rating for Latinos and blacks than it does for Asians and whites for the same kinds of loans. This pattern might be an unconscious aspect of a partially subjective process, even when the loan officer is black or Latino. Similarly, a statistical analysis of various corporate offices and levels may reveal a kind of "glass ceiling" for women and minorities. If, with few exceptions, there are no minorities or women in leadership and white men are exclusively promoted above a certain organizational level, equal opportunity is probably violated. Similarly, one can ask, is the ethnic diversity of the organization similar to the geographic region around it? If not, there may be artificial barriers that restrain equal opportunity.

Why is equal opportunity an important value standard? There are at least five reasons. First, an egoistic reason: people owe it to themselves to have broad contacts and objective evaluations of others, in order to expand their own horizons and increase the quality of those whom they then select as special friends, employees, advisors, etc. Second, a utilitarian reason: an organization or a group of people is better off when everyone is given a full equal opportunity to thrive. Third, a rights-based reason: merely by virtue of being human, everyone deserves the right to equal opportunity, regardless of any benefit or cost. To restrict equal opportunity is to dehumanize people and institutions. Fourth, as a direct application of the golden rule, equal opportunity is supported by justice reasoning. Any opportunity we enjoy we should want to be available to others, too, without prejudice. Fifth, there is a transcendent reason: every human being is an image of God, and is thereby an heir to certain privileges and opportunities that should not be arbitrarily restricted. Equal opportunity is every person's divine endowment which should be honored and protected with impartiality.

See also *discrimination in employment; racism*

Bibliography

de Vries, P. (1989). Adam Smith's "theory" of justice: Business ethics themes in *The Wealth of Nations. Business and Professional Ethics Journal*, 8 (1), 37.

King, M. L., Jr. (1986). *A Testament of Hope.* San Francisco: Harper Collins.

Putnam, H. (1987). *The Many Faces of Realism.* Chicago: Open Court.

Rawls, J. (1971). *A Theory of Justice.* Cambridge, MA: Harvard University Press.

Smith, A. (1976). *An Inquiry into the Nature and Causes of the Wealth of Nations.* Indianapolis, IN: Liberty Classics.

Sowell, T. (1990). *Preferential Policies*. New York: William Morrow.
Stasz, C. (1981). *The American Nightmare: Why Inequality Persists*. New York: Schocken Books.

ethics

Jan Narveson

Broadly speaking, ethics has always been the study of What We Should Do.

First, "we": ethics has never been entirely self-addressed, but rather is a general inquiry: the question is, what should *one* do, where "one" is anyone. It may also, however, be any one belonging to some identified group.

Second, "should": ethics is a "normative" inquiry. It is about what to do, what it would be good or bad, right or wrong, wise or unwise, to do. It is not merely an inquiry into what we actually do, into what makes us tick, the subject-matter of (human) psychology, rather than ethics. Nevertheless, ethical theories always say something about "human nature," in some way or other, as will be further noted below.

And third, the word "do": many ethical theories have concentrated on character, on what we should be like, rather than on the question of which actions we should perform. However, character is always presumed to have a bearing on action, to be borne out or exemplified in action. If it is separated from that practical interest, the study of character for its own sake would perhaps be found more nearly in aesthetics than ethics.

However, there is a narrower use of the term "ethics," one which applies to most of the moral philosophy of the past few centuries, though it is also applicable to much of the moral philosophy of earlier times as well. In this narrower use, ethics is concerned especially with norms for the conduct of people insofar as they are members of social groupings – of people *qua* members of society. In this more specialized use of the term, ethics is better referred to as "morals" or "morality." The philosophical study of morality has concerned itself especially with the project of finding, or at least determining, whether it is in principle possible to find, a set of moral principles or rules that would hold

good for all people, or (what is thought to be essentially equivalent) for all rational people. It is debatable whether there is or can be any such set of principles, and a historically prominent view called "relativism" holds that there cannot be, but that instead such sets of rules have to be fairly specific to individual societies or even individuals (*see* RELATIVISM, CULTURAL AND MORAL).

Morality is a set of rules for a group, but which groups, then? There are two answers. First, and primarily, there are what we may call "natural" groups, that is, groups which are together not by virtue of deliberate choice but by birth or happenstance: societies, cultures, and of course the group of all humans generally, which we may treat as a limiting case. The other sort of group, however, is the association, that is, groups whose members are such by virtue of having intentionally chosen to do what makes them members, or even intentionally chosen to become members as such. Thus, doctors are a group in the first sense, while the American Medical Association is one in the second. So we may speak of "medical ethics," "business ethics," and so on (*see* BUSINESS ETHICS).

There is a large question about specific ethical codes of these latter types. Business ethics is the ethics pertaining to people in their roles as transactors of business: that is the definition of the term. But are the principles of business ethics to be conceived as subordinate principles to more general principles of ethics that apply to everyone in their general relations of life? Or does the business connection actually generate special new principles? Are business people exempt from ordinary ethics and subject only to the special rules of their own calling? That is no longer a question of definition but of substantive theory (*see* CODES OF ETHICS).

Philosophical ethics is reflection about ethics in the above senses: attempts to think out the foundations of ethics, or its logical status, its basic ideas, or its basic principles. However, ever since the Middle Ages and perhaps before, philosophers have sometimes also attempted to apply these general principles to fairly specific real-life questions. That project was called "casuistry," a term widely used with some contempt. But it in fact designates a perfectly real and legitimate task, that of applying principles of ethics to the complexities of real life.

Having noted various distinctions about domains and types of ethical theories and studies, let us, finally, consider the question of what morality is. This is a question about which there has been considerable dispute, and the explanation offered here must be understood in that light – that is, as a discussable idea about which people still differ. To understand the idea of morals, we need the idea of a social rule. Two elements go into this notion. First, it is "social" if it applies to the whole of society, or of the society whose morality it is. And it is a "rule" if it rules out certain kinds of behavior, and calls for other kinds. Moreover, these must be kinds of behavior that the people subject to them might well not do otherwise. Moral rules call upon us to refrain from doing merely whatever we want. Second, a moral rule for a society is social in the sense that its enforcement is social. What is meant by this is that it need not be enforced nor legislated by a specific body of people designated or appointed for the purpose – that is law, not morals. Morality, however, is informal: there may be no authoritative setting down of these rules, and there is no designated, official enforcement. Rather, everyone participates in "enforcing" morality, by praising, blaming, rewarding, and punishing. The "morality" of a society, then, is that set of rules or principles or ideals such that people in that society generally accept that they apply to their own and others' behavior, and tend to reinforce the called-for behavior in others.

We can now make one more distinction, extremely important for philosophical purposes. The definition just supplied defines what we might call the "social sciences sense" of the term: the ethics of Society X is the set of rules which the members of X do actually attempt to get each other to conform to. However, one might suppose that the prevailing rules of some society, or even of humans in general, are defective in some way; and one might suppose they could be improved upon. A set of rules that is proposed as being what a society should have, whether or not it actually does, would be what we might call an exercise in "ideal" ethical theory. And the very deep question this raises

is whether it is really possible to do ideal theory in ethics. Can we actually conceive of rules that are still recognizably moral rules, and yet are only ideal rules that a society ought to have even though it does not (at least, as yet) actually have them, or not fully? Again, that large question is one philosophers must consider. But not only philosophers. Especially in societies with extensive cultural diversity, there is substantial disagreement among its members about just what exactly to praise and blame, reward and punish, and emulate in one's own behavior. Inevitably, many people will be in the position ascribed to philosophers: that is, of at least contemplating and very likely of promoting what is seen to be "reforms" of society's morality.

In the case of business ethics and similar more specific areas of ethical inquiry, the scope for reformative approaches is extensive. Business ethics is bound not to be well-defined. This is so for two reasons. First, it is a protean field encompassing very diverse activities, many of which are changing rapidly with the growth of technology. And secondly, business relations know no boundaries: people of the most diverse cultures engage in business interactions. These are bound to be affected by the differing ethical practices and expectations of the parties concerned. So there remains plenty of work for the philosopher concerned with business ethics, of both the analytical and the reformative type.

Europe, business ethics in

Henk van Luijk

In Europe, business ethics appeared on the scene from the mid-1980s onward, both as an academic discipline, taught at universities and business schools, and as a phenomenon within business circles. Signs of an academic maturation can be found in the number of professorships, in publications of books and journals, in courses at academic institutions, and in professional and scholarly associations. In 1984 the first European chair in Business Ethics was founded at Nijenrode University at the Netherlands Business School. Ten years later the number of chairs amounted to 15, including the prestigious Dixons Chair for Business Ethics and Corporate

Responsibility at the London Business School. Courses in business ethics are taught in many universities and business schools all over Europe. Numerous books and articles in the field have been published in various European languages. In 1992 a quarterly, *Business Ethics: A European Review*, was started; in 1995 a bilingual journal in French and English was launched; and in 1994 a collection of essays appeared under the telling title: *Business Ethics: A European Approach*. All this indicates that business ethics in Europe is not only taking shape, but is also taking a specific European shape, compared to its counterpart in the United States.

Worth mentioning also in this respect is EBEN, the European Business Ethics Network. Founded in 1987 as the outcome of the First European Conference on Business Ethics, EBEN in its first seven years has grown to over 500 members from both academia and the business world. The aim of the network is to foster the moral quality of decision-making processes in business, and to serve as a clearing house for exchange of experiences and for joint initiatives. What makes it specifically European is the emphasis on discussion and cooperation, involving academics, business representatives, governmental agencies, and the professions alike. It is not accidental that in the first major European volume on business ethics, Steinmann and Löhr's *Unternehmensethik*, a central place is given to *Diskursethik*, or "communicative ethics."

There are clear similarities between business ethics in the United States and in Europe. Both branches pay due attention to the description and analysis of single cases. In fact, this is the field in which commonly most of the available moral energy is invested. Cases in environmental management, personnel management, product quality, marketing practices, financial constructions, accounting techniques, proprietary knowledge, and business transactions abroad get the attention they deserve on both sides of the Atlantic. The same applies to corporate culture, the moral climate in the company, and the development of ethics codes. During the 1980s, corporate Europe lagged behind the US in elaborating ethics codes, but in the 1990s this was gradually being eliminated. Codes are more and more accepted in

Europe as a means to straighten the moral backbone of an organization and to keep fraudulent and criminal or semi-criminal influences outside its precincts.

There are also striking dissimilarities between Europe and the US in the topics studied and in the ways moral problems in business are handled. With regard to the topics studied it is revealing to compare the content of White's comprehensive anthology *Business Ethics: A Philosophical Reader* with the German *Lexikon der Wirtschaftsethik* (Lexicon of Business Ethics). The American *Reader* presents valuable studies on specific moral dilemmas that can arise between various interest groups and individuals in business, such as insider trading, sexual harassment, environmental responsibility, and privacy protection in the workplace. Some of these topics are treated in the German lexicon as well, but by far not all. Ample attention is given instead to topics like the ethical aspects of privatization, the moral foundation of co-determination rights of employees, the ethics of investment policies, and the moral proprieties of a market economy. In short, the German lexicon of business ethics encompasses many items that could also be covered under the heading of social and political philosophy and economic ethics. And in this respect the lexicon represents business ethics in Europe as a whole. This is not just a question of definition, European scholars obviously being more willing to use a broad definition of the field. Behind the difference in definition lies a deeper difference with regard to the prevalent conception of ethics. In the European context, ethics is not confined to the responsibility of the individual in distinct situations of conflict, but comprises as well a collective responsibility for the shaping of what is called, in German political terms, the *Soziale Marktwirtschaft*, a social market economy, in which the opportunities given in a free-market system are combined with the acceptance of a share in the fostering of the common good by corporations, governmental agencies, trade unions, and professional and other interest groups alike.

There are legal as well as political and cultural reasons why European business ethics is partly developing along its own lines. The legal reasons have to do with a fundamental difference in the legal systems. Citizens in the US, as in the United Kingdom, are accustomed to the *common law* system of British descent, with its extensive reliance on judge-made laws, whereas social arrangements in European countries are mainly based upon the *civil law* system stemming from the Roman and the Napoleonic empires, which places great trust in governmental officials and government-made provisions. These different legal systems pervade the way in which ethical conflicts are tackled. A moral culture based on common law generates winners and losers, whereas a culture based on civil law aims at balanced agreements. Ethical conflicts in business in Europe are less spectacular than on the other side of the Atlantic, not because European business people are less passionate or more ethical, but because they invest their ethical energy in settlements rather than in moral victories. Political and cultural reasons corroborate this picture. European political history is marked by a system of proportional representation and the accompanying necessity of frequent governmental coalitions. A give-and-take on the basis of a predefined common interest that is normal in political life has found its way also into corporate relations. European employers and employees meet each other at the negotiation table more often than in court or in the street on the barricades. Many issues that, in the US, are the subject of vehement ethical discussions and subsequent lawsuits, in Europe find their way to negotiated agreements between employers and trade unions, often with governmental agencies as supporting third parties, and eventually as law-giving institution.

The insight is that, in the domain of business relations, ethics cannot be confined to personal values and individual attitudes, nor to the analysis of single cases, or to the designing of codes and guidelines, important as all this undoubtedly is. Ethics in business, in its European variety, is as much about the moral solidity of the economic system we are able to establish. It is about the freedom of action we create for all market participants, not just for a few. And it is about the collective attention given to the unfortunate, an attention that is sedimented in welfare arrangements as the outcome of a long process of political as well as moral agreements. All these features taken together entitle us to

speak of a plainly *European* version of ethics in business.

Bibliography

Enderle, G., Homann, K., Honecker, M., Kerber, W., and Steinmann, H. (eds.) (1993). *Lexikon der Wirtschaftsethik*. Freiburg: Herder.

Harvey, B. (ed.) (1994). *Business Ethics: A European Approach*. Englewood Cliffs, NJ: Prentice-Hall.

Harvey, B., van Luijk H., and Steinmann, H. (1994). *European Casebook on Business Ethics*. New York: Prentice-Hall.

Steinmann, H. and Löhr, A. (eds.) (1989). *Unternehmensethik*. Stuttgart: Verlag Poeschel.

White, T. I. (ed.) (1993). *Business Ethics: A Philosophical Reader*. New York: Macmillan.

executive compensation

Paul G. Wilhelm

Executive compensation based on agency theory argues that equity holders (principles) delegate the responsibility of managing firms to top executives or agents, who are charged with using their specialized knowledge and the company's resources to generate the highest possible return to principals. Control problems often exist because the interests of agents and principals differ. Executives may exploit their privileged positions to gain excessive compensation or perks independent of the company's performance, at the expense of principals who may thereupon develop monitoring systems to counter the agent's avarice. The use of pay practices to align the interests of agents and principals is complicated by the difficulty of directly observing an executive's effort or behavior.

The executive compensation controversy can be addressed by trying to ensure that distributive justice, or the proper distribution of economic benefits and burdens, occurs. Following the principle of "to each according to merit," companies should hire, promote, and distribute bonuses to executives strictly on the basis of individual merit. Fair sales for most people are based on market competitiveness, meaning that salaries should be sufficient to attract and retain the number and quality of people needed to sustain the business in the long term.

In practice these ethical theories break down because there isn't any real competitive salary market for large company executive talent. A phantom market exists primarily in the minds of the CEO's hand-picked compensation committee. Hence the balancing of risk and rewards achieved in most occupations is nullified. The risk–reward profile of the American CEO is now heavily biased toward reward, such that elements of risk have been virtually eliminated through stock options and golden parachutes.

In a truly free market those executives with a proven track record at one or more companies would be in demand, offering their services to the highest bidder. However, there is little evidence of such movement among CEOs. In fact, most executive jobs at top firms are filled from within, where there is a high level of competition among the senior ranks of the corporation. Most competitors would probably take the CEO position, with its prestige and perks, for a reasonable pay raise of about 30 percent. However, the pay gap between the CEO and other senior-level executives is now much wider, with CEOs typically earning 60 percent more than the second highest paid executive.

Executives should be rewarded for decisions and judgments affecting the long-term future of the company. But, in fact, up to 90 percent of the pay of executives is geared to the current year's business results, and this leads to short-range rather than strategic decisions. Bonus schemes are not anchored to tough performance standards, which should be at least as difficult as those for division managers, plant managers, and other employees who are on incentive pay. CEOs and boards of directors should be evaluated regularly just like rank and file employees.

Responsibility can be restored to compensation committees of boards of directors by allowing shareholders to use the proxy system to nominate and elect independent directors who are more responsive and accountable to the long-term interest of shareholders. Investors could then get the information needed to better analyze performance pay plans and long-term income plans that executives now recommend for themselves. Executive salaries and their justifications should be unambiguously disclosed to stockholders and the general public. Performance control systems could then be better imple- mented to link pay with performance. No bonuses should be paid until earnings cover the cost of capital and surpass the rate of inflation. Revising methods of determining executive pay will help restore compensation levels that are fair and competitive.

exploitation

Jesse Taylor

Under the broadest interpretation, exploitation occurs whenever specific means are determined for accomplishing a task set by interest. The means then become instruments to be used in achieving interest-determined goals. Thus, human life itself is exploitative. However, given that exploitation is an inevitable consequence of human existence, it does not follow that all manifestations of it are necessary or morally acceptable.

To "exploit" is not merely to use, but to use to one's advantage. Although the origin of the word "exploit" goes back only to about the 1430s, the idea has its antecedents in Aristotle's *Nicomachean Ethics*. Roughly, Aristotle maintained that the good of a being is attainable only from actions that accord with its nature as a unique natural kind. This fostered the view that virtue of a species is acquired from its participation in species-specific activities. In the case of persons, if such activities include choosing one's own ends, appropriating materials for producing ends, and participating in activities to assure success, then persons are wrongfully exploited when denied the possibility of attaining their happiness as decision-making entities. Moreover, since Aristotle esteemed human existence as the highest form of organic life, exploitation may involve a reduction in status of equals by those holding a monopoly on the materials of human flourishing.

PSYCHOLOGICAL COMPONENTS

The concept of exploitation presupposes the existence of an ego, autonomy, freedom, interest, and a field of contingencies as modalities of interest. The ego establishes an interest in a subjectivity. The idea of human freedom is the condition that enables autonomy to manifest itself as a contingency. By virtue of the contingency displayed and expressed in individual autonomy, we may infer that interest as such, is not biologically given. Autonomy asserts itself as an appropriating transcendence that transforms interest into an objectivity of some kind.

METAPHYSICS OF EXPLOITATION

As a metaphysical phenomenon, exploitation is a necessary condition for human agency. As Sartre argued, human consciousness is best understood as a desire for being, rather than as being as such. Consciousness is constituted only from its interests and desires. Hence, from the onset of human existence, consciousness is parasitic, and, therefore, necessarily exploitative (Sartre, 1973).

As "exploitative" beings, we are fully responsible for the character of a human existence fashioned from contingencies admitting indefinite possibilities. This is to say, the manner of human existence is at bottom choice-determined. Persons do not determine their status as exploitative creatures; they do choose, however, to orient their interest one way or another, and to contemplate whether to adopt principles to constrain the scope and categories of human choices.

ASPECTS OF THE MORAL CONCEPTION OF EXPLOITATION

Considerations relating to "constraining principles" on exploitative propensities have traditionally fallen in the realm of political theory and ethics. It is only within the frameworks of such theories that a distinction between good and bad exploitative behaviors can be drawn. Most instances of "exploitation" are not morally objectionable. An even greater number of cases are borderline with respect to their moral permissibility. Among clear cases in which exploitation involves immorality are those that violate the Kantian dictum: "we must always treat persons as ends in themselves, and never as means merely," with special emphasis on the phrase, "as means merely" (see KANTIAN ETHICS). Kant believed that the supreme good of persons is their autonomy. Relations that subordinate autonomy can never be of benefit to persons as such, since a trade-off will necessarily involve

giving up an absolute value for a conditional value. Kant was, of course, mindful that there may be "circumstances" when allowing oneself to be exploited or even to exploit oneself may be advantageous for some purpose. However, since contingent objectives never change the "category" of human value, circumstances can never be used to justify exploitation considered immoral in the Kantian sense.

From a political perspective, it is frequently argued that where actions comply with sovereign laws, exploitative activities within legal constraints are acceptable. This method of interpreting exploitation is founded on the view that human value is defined by sovereigns. Where sovereign states manifest different conceptions of value, ideas of immoral exploitation are subject to relativity (see RELATIVISM, CULTURAL AND MORAL).

EXPLOITATION UNDER THE PYRAMID MODEL OF ORGANIZATIONAL STRUCTURE

The Pyramid Model of organizational structure is frequently cited as a mechanism with systemic exploitative properties. Put simply, it is believed that only upper-level organizational interests can be realized under the Pyramid Model. The problem associated with this form of exploitation is that most people (since they will exist at the bottom of the organizational chart) are denied the opportunity to develop as interest-bearing subjects. This implies that subjects of equal value are regarded as if they are not. The elite are given primacy of expression solely because of their economic advantages and rank. Thus, their domination of the lower ranks of the pyramid is one of power, not of intrinsic worth.

AN EGALITARIAN CONCEPTION OF EXPLOITATION

In contrast to the Pyramid Model, Marx and Engels argued that workers are necessarily disadvantaged, since their only commodity is their labor. The means of production belong to the ruling class. Workers must, for the sake of their survival, accept conditions of employment established by the ruling class, conditions often reducing the worker to the level of a product. To remedy this form of exploitation, Marx and Engels advocated a conception of property that would virtually obliterate the Pyramid Model by making "property" a communal phenomenon.

IDENTIFYING INSTANCES OF EXPLOITATION

The identification of unacceptable instances of exploitation is, at best, difficult. Since the roles of "ability," "interest," and "circumstances" in limiting human success cannot be fully determined, we can never be certain that social/political role assignments are not unduly restrictive. Our conception of "acceptable exploitation," therefore, could be derived from theory about "equality of opportunity" (see EQUAL OPPORTUNITY). If the theory permits frequent judgments of unjust exploitation, this would tend to give rise to theory modification or abandonment.

Bibliography

Becker, L. C. and Kipnis, K. (eds.) (1984). *Property: Cases, Concepts, Critiques*. Englewood Cliffs, NJ: Prentice-Hall.

Carnoy, M. (1984). *The State and Political Theory*. Princeton, NJ: Princeton University Press.

Cohen, G. A. (1988). *History, Labour, and Freedom*. Oxford: Oxford University Press.

Edwards, R. C. et al. (eds.) (1986). *The Capitalist System*. Englewood Cliffs, NJ: Prentice-Hall.

Machan, T. R. (ed.) (1986). *The Main Debate: Communism versus Capitalism*. New York: Random House.

Marx, K. and Engels, F. (1959). *Basic Writings on Politics and Philosophy*, ed. L. S. Feuer. Garden City, NY: Doubleday.

Sartre, J.-P. (1973). *Being and Nothingness*. New York: Washington Square Press.

Schweickart, D. (1993). *Against Capitalism*. Cambridge: Cambridge University Press.

Terkel, S. (1974). Here I am a worker. In L. Silk (ed.), *Capitalism: The Morning Target*. New York: Quadrangle, 68–9.

F

fairness

George Klosko

Exactly what constitutes fairness will depend on the specific nature of the decision process or institution in question. Consider, for example, a fair trial, a fair contest, a fair grade, a fair price, a fair agreement, a fair election. This variety of contexts entails a corresponding range of criteria of fairness. All of these, however, generally center on equal treatment of people, with departures from equality requiring justification.

The concept of fairness is closely related to a number of other moral concepts, such as equality, impartiality, and justice. Like these other notions, it centers on how people are treated by others, especially the requirement that they be treated alike, in the absence of significant differences between them. The distinctive focus of fairness is decision-making processes or institutions that apply rules. For instance, in regard to the application of rules, a fair procedure is one that applies them similarly to all cases, unless there are strong reasons for making exceptions in particular cases. Accordingly, an examination is graded fairly when all papers are judged by the same standards. "Fairness" is generally appealed to in assessing both the means through which decisions are made or rules applied, and the outcomes that are brought about. The former is generally described as "procedural" fairness, the latter as "distributive" fairness. Though these two concerns frequently coincide (i.e., fair procedures give rise to fair outcomes and unfair to unfair outcomes), this is not always the case, and so procedural and distributive fairness should be distinguished. However, though the notion of fairness pertains to both concerns, it is more closely associated with procedures, while the notion of justice bears more particularly on outcomes (*see* DISTRIBUTIVE JUSTICE).

According to the *Oxford English Dictionary*, "fairness" and cognate words have been used in English, with their present sense, at least as far back as 1460. But in other languages, closely related concepts are encountered many centuries earlier. For example, in Book V of Thucydides' *History of the Peloponnesian War* (late fifth century BC), the besieged people of Melos ask their besiegers to consider "that in the case of all who fall into danger there should be such a thing as fair play and just dealing (*ta eikota kai dikaia*)" between people (Thucydides, 1972: V, 90). Their request is that strong and weak peoples be treated similarly, regardless of differences in power. In his *Politics* (late fourth century BC), Aristotle makes the important observation that standards of justice or fairness are different in different regimes. In oligarchical regimes, ruled over by the rich, it is thought fair to treat people differently according to their merits, with amount of property constituting degree of merit. In democratic regimes, in contrast, it is considered fair to treat people alike – and so to distribute political offices through a lottery system – with free birth and citizenship constituting being alike (Aristotle, 1981: V, ch. 1). An important lesson of Aristotle's discussion is that there is no universally recognized standard of fair treatment, in terms of either procedures or distribution. Different ways of dealing with people can plausibly be represented as fair, as long as they treat people who are similar in important respects similarly.

Much of the attention "fairness" has received in recent years is because of the work of John Rawls and his theory of "justice as fairness." In his main work, *A Theory of Justice* (1971), Rawls argues that specific principles of justice can be justified by showing that they would be chosen by representative individuals placed in a carefully constructed, artificial choice situation. To ensure that the choice of principles is not influenced by people's particular interests, Rawls employs a hypothetical "veil of ignorance." Individuals are to make their decision without knowledge of their specific identities or attributes (e.g., economic or social position, religion, sex, age, etc.). Because of the representative individuals' concern that, once the veil of ignorance is lifted, they might turn out to be disadvantaged members of society, Rawls argues that they will choose principles that protect the weaker or "least advantaged" members. Rawls calls his theory "justice as fairness," because this name "conveys the idea that the principles of justice are agreed to in an initial situation that is fair" (1971: 12).

The need to promote fair distribution in cooperative enterprises has been appealed to by recent scholars – including Rawls – to establish obligations to support such associations. The "principle of fairness" (or fair play) was developed by H. L. A. Hart in 1955: "When a number of persons conduct any joint enterprise according to rules and thus restrict their liberty, those who have submitted to these restrictions when required have a right to a similar submission from those who have benefited by their submission" (Hart, 1955: 185).

The moral thrust of the principle of fairness is the fair – or just – distribution of benefits and burdens. When a number of people engage in cooperative activity to produce and consume benefits, other people who enjoy the benefits but do not share the costs of providing them (i.e., free-riders) treat the cooperators unfairly. In order to correct this situation, they too should cooperate, in spite of their desire not to (when a number of further conditions are also met). As Hart and other theorists have argued, the principle of fairness can establish people's obligations to bear the burdens of citizenship – most notably obeying the laws of their countries – even if they have not consented to do so.

In recent years, the concept of fairness has also figured prominently in social psychology. Researchers have studied decision processes in judicial, political, business, and other settings, in order to ascertain people's views about procedural fairness – or procedural justice, in this context interchangeable terms. Procedural considerations have been found to have strong effects on research subjects, which are not only distinct from considerations of outcome but frequently also more influential, even when outcomes are highly unfavorable. For instance, in assessing a variety of institutions – political, judicial, business – subjects have repeatedly been shown to place greater weight on their views of how decisions are made than on how the outcomes of the decisions affect them (see Lind and Tyler, 1988). Results of empirical tests have also complicated theorists' views concerning the nature of fairness. Subjects have been found to view a decision-making process as fair if it gives them the opportunity to be heard and treats them with respect, rather than focusing on the formal assurances of consistent treatment across cases on which philosophers have traditionally concentrated.

Bibliography

Aristotle (1981). *The Politics*, revd. edn., ed. T. A. Sinclair and T. Saunders. Harmondsworth: Penguin Books.

Bayles, M. (1990). *Procedural Justice: Allocating to Individuals.* Dordrecht: Kluwer.

Hart, H. L. A. (1955). Are There Any Natural Rights? *Philosophical Review*, **64**, 175–91.

Hochschild, J. (1981). *What's Fair: American Beliefs About Distributive Justice.* Cambridge, MA: Harvard University Press.

Klosko, G. (1992). *The Principle of Fairness and Political Obligation.* Savage, MD: Rowman and Littlefield.

Lind, E. A. and Tyler, T. R. (1988). *The Social Psychology of Procedural Justice.* New York: Praeger.

Rawls, J. (1971). *A Theory of Justice.* Cambridge, MA: Harvard University Press.

Thucydides (1972). *History of the Peloponnesian War*, trans. R. Warner. Baltimore, MD: Penguin Books.

Tyler, T. R. (1988). What is procedural justice?: Criteria used by citizens to assess the fairness of legal procedures. *Law and Society Review*, **22**, 103–35.

feminist ethics

Rosemarie Tong

A diverse range of women-centered *approaches* to moral theory and practice which aim to reinterpret, supplement, and reconceive traditional ethics so that it (1) includes women's as well as men's moral experiences and perspectives and (2) values women as men's moral equals. *Feminine* approaches to ethics favor an ethics of care that emphasizes the importance of nurturant human relationships. Not surprisingly, *maternal* approaches to ethics identify a good mother–child (parent–child) relationship as the most promising paradigm for what counts as a nourishing human relationship. In contrast, *feminist* approaches to ethics emphasize issues of male domination and female subordination, and argue "against patriarchal domination, for equal rights, a just and fair distribution of scarce resources, etc." (Sichel, 1991). Finally, *lesbian* approaches to ethics show how traditional ethics disciplines those who deviate from its norms, especially its norm of compulsory heterosexuality.

Although it is tempting to think that women-centered approaches to ethics are late twentieth-century developments, most of them have a long history. Mary Wollstonecraft, John Stuart Mill, Harriet Taylor, Catherine Beecher, Charlotte Perkins Gilman, and Elizabeth Cady Stanton all debated whether morality is or is not gendered. In large measure these eighteenth- and nineteenth-century thinkers set the stage for current discussions about whether "women's ethics" is indeed one of *care* and "men's ethics" one of *justice*, and whether women's traditional role as childbearers and childrearers has caused women, but not men, to think maternally.

FEMININE APPROACHES

Rather than denigrating typically "feminine" characteristics (e.g., nurturing, caring, compassion, benevolence, and kindness) as "soft" virtues for "weak" people, *feminine* ethicists such as Carol Gilligan have presented them as just as morally demanding as typically "masculine" characteristics (e.g., justice, independence, and rationality). In her book *In a Different Voice* (1982), Gilligan included a study of women making decisions concerning abortion. As she listened to these women's narratives, she heard a language of care that stressed intimate relationships and particular responsibilities instead of a language of justice that emphasized communal well-being and/or individual rights (*see* UTILITARIANISM; KANTIAN ETHICS). Although

Gilligan has repeatedly denied that she regards an ethics of care as uniquely "female" and an ethics of justice as uniquely "male," most of her interpreters nonetheless insist that for Gilligan morality is thoroughly gendered. As they see it, Gilligan's work reflects her disagreements with educational psychologist Lawrence Kohlberg about men's and women's relative abilities to develop as full moral agents.

Supposedly, men routinely ascend to Stage Five on Kohlberg's six-stage scale of moral development ("the social contract legalistic orientation"), while women rarely climb past Stage Three ("the interpersonal concordance or 'good boy–nice girl' orientation") (Kohlberg, 1971). Instead of viewing this gender difference as evidence of women's moral inferiority, Gilligan interpreted it as a sign that Kohlberg's methodology provided an account not of *human* but of *male* moral development. According to Gilligan, women typically achieve full moral personhood in a way that men typically do not. Whereas men are inclined to measure their moral progress in terms of how autonomous they are becoming, women tend to assess their moral progress in terms of how strongly they are connected to others (Gilligan, 1982: 76–92).

Another thinker who has developed a so-called feminine approach to ethics is Nell Noddings. She argues that ethics is about the overall goodness or badness of actual relationships between individuals. There are, she says, two parties in any relation: the "one-caring" and the "cared-for." When all goes well, the one-caring is motivationally engrossed in the cared-for, and the cared-for welcomes the one-caring's attention, spontaneously sharing his/her aspirations, appraisals, and accomplishments with him/her (Noddings, 1984: 9). For Noddings, caring is not a matter of being favorably disposed toward humankind in general. Instead, caring involves both continual communication with particular individuals and active engagement in their lives. Deeds count more than thoughts.

Noddings insists that caregiving is a fundamental *human* activity, something that men as well as women can and should do. She also claims that the one-caring can and should also be a cared-for. Nevertheless, most of the carers Noddings describes are women, some of whom seem to care too much – to the point of imperiling their own identity, integrity, and even survival. As a result, a number of critics have faulted Noddings (and Gilligan) for their apparent overemphasis on *women's* capacities for caring. According to critic Sheila Mullet, for example, genuine caring between men and women cannot occur in a patriarchal society. Unless women become men's full political, economic, social, and psychological equals, women cannot care for men in a truly voluntary manner (Mullet, 1988: 199).

MATERNAL APPROACHES

Clearly related to feminine approaches to ethics are so-called maternal approaches to ethics. Virginia Held, Sara Ruddick, and Caroline Whitbeck stress that the paradigm of contractual transactions between equally informed and equally powerful autonomous men does not serve to illuminate our typical moral transactions. Most of our relationships are between unequals: the young and the old, the client and the professional, the student and the teacher, and so on. As maternal thinkers see it, a good mother–child (or, better, mothering person–child) relationship is the best paradigm to use in assessing the moral quality of these inevitably imbalanced relationships. In the course of striving to preserve, help grow, and make socially acceptable their children, mothers/ mothering persons teach themselves as well as their children how to be responsible persons sensitive to the needs and interests of others (Ruddick, 1983: 215).

Two sets of critics have challenged maternal approaches to ethics. *Non-feminist* critics object that it is doubtful whether any one human relationship, however good, either can or should serve as the paradigm for all human relationships. *Feminist* critics express similar reservations, underscoring the point that the mother–child relationship is a particularly problematic choice for a moral paradigm, freighted as it is with enough patriarchal baggage to weigh down even the strongest of women. They reason that a better model for good human relationships is a successful friendship relationship. Created and maintained by a set of interlocking and reinforcing loves, trusts, and emotional commitments, the friendship relationship, like the mother–child relationship, strikes a wider range of moral chords than a legalistic rational-contractor relationship. It has the added advantage, however, of being more equal than a mother–child relationship.

FEMINIST APPROACHES

Given that feminine and maternal approaches to ethics have much in common with feminist approaches to ethics, it is challenging to specify what makes an approach to ethics "feminist" as opposed to "feminine" or "maternal." Ultimately, it might be the fact that feminist as opposed to feminine or maternal approaches to ethics tend to ask questions about women's *power*, even more than women's *goodness*, relative to men's. In other words, feminist approaches to ethics stress how traditional ethics mirrors and maintains systems, structures, and patterns of behavior that repress, suppress, and oppress women.

Among others, Alison Jaggar has claimed that traditional ethics contributes to women's subordination in at least five ways. First, traditional ethics shows little concern for women's as opposed to men's interests and rights. Second, it neglects women's issues on the grounds that few morally interesting questions arise in "women's world" – the realm of dishes and diapers. Third, traditional ethics frequently operates on the assumption that women's moral capacities are deficient compared to men's moral capacities. Fourth, it tends to overvalue allegedly masculine traits like "independence, autonomy, intellect, will, wariness, hierarchy, domination, culture, transcendence, product, asceticism, war, death" on the one hand, and to undervalue allegedly feminine traits like "interdependence, community, connection, sharing, emotion, body, trust, absence of hierarchy, nature, immanence, process, joy, peace and life" (Jaggar, 1992: 364) on the other. Fifth, traditionally ethics devalues women's moral experience by favoring "masculine" ways of thinking that focus on rules, universality, and impartiality over "feminine" ways of thinking that focus on relationships, particularity, and partiality.

Aware of the ways in which traditional ethics has disadvantaged women, Jaggar has concluded that, minimally, any feminist approach to ethics must proceed on the assumption that women and men do not share precisely the same situation in life; offer action guides "that will tend to subvert rather than reinforce the present systematic subordination of women"; provide strategies for dealing with issues that arise in private or domestic life; and "take the moral experience of all women seriously, though not, of course, uncritically" (Jaggar, 1991: 366). Women should not focus first and foremost on becoming more perfect carers. Rather, their primary aim should be to resist and overcome gender inequity.

Lesbian Approaches

That feminist approaches to ethics should be so bold as to focus on *women's* concerns is part of what makes them unique and controversial. In a similar vein, lesbian approaches to ethics dare to focus on lesbian concerns, thereby taking "particularity" to what even some heterosexual feminists regard as a fault. Although it is difficult to make generalizations about lesbian approaches to ethics, they usually entail a transvaluation of traditional moral values. Mary Daly, for example, insists that she whom the patriarch calls "evil" is in fact good, whereas she whom the patriarch calls "good" is in fact bad. If a woman is to escape the traps men have laid for her – if she is to assert her power, to be all that she can be – then she must realize that it is not good for her to sacrifice herself for the sake of the men and children in her life. What *is* actually good for women is precisely what patriarchy identifies as evil for women – becoming their own persons (Daly, 1984: 275).

Additionally, lesbian approaches to ethics usually urge women to replace the question "Am I good?" with the question "Does this contribute to my self-creation, freedom, and liberation?" Just because lesbian ethicists emphasize the role of choice as opposed to duty in ethics does not mean that lesbian ethics is relativistic. On the contrary, Sarah Lucia Hoagland observes that in choosing for herself, a lesbian chooses for other lesbians who in turn choose for her. Lesbians do not weave value in isolation from each other; they weave value together. Ethics is not an individualistic quest. Moral value does not emerge from somewhere inside of one's self or from far outside of one's self, but from the space between one's self and others. A lesbian approach to ethics is about lesbians becoming persons "who are not accustomed to participating in relationships of domination and subordination" (Hoagland, 1988: 241). Such persons have "the ability to travel in and out of each other's world" (Lugones, 1987). In Hoagland's estimation, an emphasis on "adventure, curiosity, desire seems to take the power out of (traditional) ethics, of being able to make each other behave; ethics ceases to be a tool of control" (Hoagland, 1988: 246). Ethics becomes instead a series of open questions, the partial and provisional answers to which emerge as playful souls weave tapestries of meaning together.

Woman-Centered Approaches and Business Ethics

As described here, women-centered approaches to ethics have much to offer the field of business ethics. From *feminine* approaches to ethics, business persons can learn about the value of care and consider ways to restructure the business world so that it becomes more responsive to the concrete needs of particular persons. Similarly, from *maternal* approaches to ethics, business persons can gain the courage to imagine a business world ruled not by the dynamics of a competitive relationship between two rational adult contractors, but instead by the dynamics of a cooperative relationship between a mothering person and a child. Were the business world to adopt feminine and maternal values, it might learn how to pursue maximum profit at minimum human cost – that is, in ways that do not permit the intentional, reckless, or negligent infliction of harm on vulnerable persons such as overworked employees, uninformed consumers, or struggling rivals.

Business persons can also learn much from feminist approaches to ethics. Minimally, they can come to see the gender disparities that characterize the business world. Women and minority men are not paid as much or promoted as quickly and noticeably as men (particularly white men). The "old boys" coexist with the equal-opportunity employers; glass ceilings and "tokenism" are just as much the order of the day as effective affirmative action programs. Moreover, the business world is still organized in ways that make it much more difficult for women than for men to combine family and career. Without supportive maternal (or parental) leave policies and without adequate childcare facilities, businesswomen cannot hope to achieve what businessmen can. Finally, women are far more likely to be sexually harassed by their employers and co-workers than are men.

Ideally speaking, business persons can also learn much from *lesbian* approaches to ethics, since structures and systems of male domination and female subordination undoubtedly impede the ability of business to produce quality goods, to provide excellent services, and to make substantial profits. Perhaps the best way for business to achieve its goals is for it to enable each and every person in its network of relationships to develop his/her talents fully. By encouraging all of their employees to be adventuresome, curious, and desirous and to welcome human difference as much as human similarity, employers might find themselves blessed with a fully productive workforce.

CRITIQUES OF WOMAN-CENTERED APPROACHES

Whether traditional ethics ultimately acknowledges feminist ethics as a *bona fide* moral enterprise partially depends on the ability of those developing women-centered approaches to ethics to persuade their non-feminist colleagues that ethics can legitimately focus on the concerns of a particular group of people: *women*. What distinguishes a feminist from a non-feminist moral perspective is a so-called feminist standpoint. Although feminists have not fully developed the concept of a feminist standpoint, most of them agree that it identifies women as oppressed persons whose status as victims gives them "access to understanding about oppression that others cannot have" (Bartlett, 1991: 385). Moreover, most feminists ground this privileged perspective in the contention that oppressed persons' pain, humiliation, and subordination motivate them to criticize "accepted interpretations of reality" and to develop "new and less disturbed ways of understanding the world" (Jaggar, 1983: 370).

As defined above, a feminist standpoint is vulnerable to at least two lines of criticism. One set of critics objects that it is based on the essentialistic notion "Woman" – the view that all women are the same (Tong, 1993: 10). In replying to this objection, feminist standpoint theor-

ists emphasize that just because they believe that women are like each other by virtue of their sex does not mean that they deny the many differences among women (class, race, ethnicity, sexual identity, and age). Feminist standpoint theorists do not wish to promote the idea of women understood as a collectivity (who all think the same thought), but the idea of women understood as a plurality (who think different thoughts) (*see* DIVERSITY; MULTICULTURALISM).

Another set of critics objects that feminist theory is "female-biased." Whereas traditional ethicists supposedly offered *everyone* objective truth, feminist standpoint theorists offer *women* subjective beliefs. To this criticism, feminist standpoint theorists respond that what traditional ethics identified as *the* truth was nothing of the sort. Like all knowledge, its knowledge was the product of a specific set of experiences – in its case, mostly the experiences of privileged white men. Largely missing from traditional ethics were the experiences of women as well as those of men of color and unprivileged white men. Therefore, far from being truly representative of human moral experience, traditional ethics was very selective.

CONCLUSION

What women-centered approaches to ethics share is a conviction that denial of perspective does not achieve neutrality; denial of plurality does not bring unity; denial of relationship does not achieve self-identity for the rational, autonomous self. Women-centered ethicists do not offer traditional ethics just another set of approaches, a set of pretty frames through which to view old moral sights. Rather, they offer traditional ethics a new set of spectacles to superimpose upon its old lenses, thus bringing into focus the full range of human moral experience in all its "gendered," "raced," and "classed" diversity.

Bibliography

Bartlett, K. T. (1991). Feminist legal methods. In K. T. Bartlett and R. Kennedy (eds.), *Feminist Legal Theory: Readings in Law and Gender*. Boulder, CO: Westview Press, 370–403.

Beecher, C. E. and Stowe, H. B. (1987). *The New Housekeeper's Manual*. New York: J. B. Ford.

Daly, M. (1984). *Pure Lust: Elemental Feminist Philosophy*. Boston, MA: Beacon Press.

Gilligan, C. (1982). *In a Different Voice: Psychological Theory and Women's Development*. Cambridge, MA: Harvard University Press.

Gilman, C. P. (1979). *Herland: A Lost Feminist Utopian Novel*. New York: Pantheon.

Held, V. (1993). *Feminist Morality: Transforming Culture, Society, and Politics*. Chicago: University of Chicago Press.

Hoagland, S. L. (1988). *Lesbian Ethics*. Palo Alto, CA: Institute of Lesbian Studies.

Jaggar, A. M. (1983). *Feminist Politics and Human Nature*. Totowa, NJ: Allanheld.

Jaggar, A. M. (1991). Feminist ethics: Projects, problems, prospects. In C. Card (ed.), *Feminist Ethics*. Lawrence: University of Kansas Press.

Jaggar, A. M. (1992). Feminist ethics. In L. Becker and C. Becker (eds.), *Encyclopedia of Ethics*. New York: Garland, 363–4.

Kohlberg, L. (1971). From is to ought: How to commit the naturalistic fallacy and get away with it in the study of moral development. In T. Mischel (ed.), *Cognitive Development and Epistemology*. New York: Academic Press, 164–5.

Kourany, J., Sterba, P., and Tong, R. (eds.), *Feminist Philosophies: Problems, Theories, and Applications*. Englewood Cliffs, NJ: Prentice-Hall.

Lugones, M. (1987). Playfulness, "world"-traveling, and loving perception. *Hypatia*, 2, 13.

Lugones, M. and Spelman, M. (1992). Have we got a theory for you!: Feminist theory, cultural imperialism and the demand for "the woman's voice." In M. Pearsall (ed.), Women and Values: Readings in Recent Feminist Philosophy. Belmont, CA: Wadsworth, 19–31.

Mill, J. S. (1970). The subjection of women. In A. S. Rossi (ed.), *Essays on Sex Equality*. Chicago: University of Chicago Press, 125–56.

Mullet, S. (1988). Shifting perspectives: A new approach to ethics. In L. Code, S. Mullet, and C. Overall (eds.), *Feminist Perspectives: Philosophical Essays on Method and Morals*. Toronto: University of Toronto Press.

Noddings, N. (1984). *Caring: A Feminine Approach to Ethics and Moral Education*. Berkeley: University of California Press.

Ruddick, S. (1983). Maternal thinking. In J. Trebilcott (ed.), *Mothering: Essays in Feminist Theory*. Totowa, NJ: Rowman and Allanheld, 213–30.

Sichel, B. A. (1991). Different strains and strands: Feminist contributions to ethical theory. *Newsletter on Feminism*, 90, 90.

Taylor Mill, H. (1970). Enfranchisement of women. In A. S. Rossi (ed.), *Essays on Sex Equality*. Chicago: University of Chicago Press.

Tong, R. (1993). *Feminine and Feminist Ethics*. Belmont, CA: Wadsworth.

Whitbeck, C. (1983). The maternal instinct. In J. Trebilcott (ed.), *Mothering: Essays in Feminist Theory*. Totowa, NJ: Rowman and Allanheld, 185–98.

Wollstonecraft, M. (1988). *A Vindication of the Rights of Women*, ed. M. Brody. London: Penguin Books.

fiduciary duty

John R. Boatright

is a duty of a person in a position of trust to act in the interest of another person without gaining any material benefit, except with the knowledge and consent of that other person.

The term describes the legal duty of trustees, guardians, executors, agents, and others who are in an explicit fiduciary relation, but a fiduciary relation may exist in law whenever one person has superior power or influence over another person and the other person places confidence in or relies on that person. Although it is primarily a legal term, fiduciary duty is also used to describe the purely ethical duty of a person in a position of trust. Thus, some breaches of fiduciary duty by lawyers (who are in a fiduciary relation with clients) constitute ethical but not legal misconduct.

In business, officers and directors of corporations are fiduciaries with a duty to act in the interest of the corporation and, to some extent, the stockholders (*see* STOCKHOLDER). Members of partnerships and joint enterprises are fiduciaries with respect to each other's interest; majority stockholders are considered in law to have a fiduciary duty similar to that of officers and directors; and minority stockholders in closely held corporations are fiduciaries under certain conditions. Corporations and their members may have a fiduciary duty toward employees, customers, and other constituencies in such matters as employee pension plans and client investment accounts, and the duty of loyalty that employees have to a firm is sometimes regarded as fiduciary in character.

The concept of fiduciary duty originated in common law for cases in which one person entrusts property to the care of another, and it remains a central concept in the law of trusts.

Use of the concept has been extended over time to other trust-like situations in order to prevent abuse when one person has superior power over another. Historically, fiduciary duty belongs to the law of equity, in which courts decide cases on the basis of justice or fairness instead of strictly formulated rules, and the concept developed as a means for imposing duties where precise rules cannot be easily formulated. Fiduciary duties are further unlike the specific duties created by contracts in that they are imposed on all persons in fiduciary relations and cannot be easily altered by the affected parties.

Among the features of fiduciary duty, the most prominent are:

1 *An open-ended duty to act in the interest of another.* The acts that a person in a fiduciary relation are required to perform are generally not specified in advance, so that a fiduciary has wide latitude in the means used to advance the interests of another. The standards for evaluating the performance of a fiduciary are commonly those of due care, good faith, and, in business, the business judgment rule, all of which can be satisfied by many different acts.
2 *A closed-in duty to avoid acting in self-interest.* Generally, the acts in a fiduciary's self-interest that violate a fiduciary duty are clearly stated in the law. Among such specific legal prohibitions are self-dealing, acceptance of bribes, direct competition, and use of confidential information.
3 *Strongly mandatory, moralistic character.* Whereas much of corporate law can be altered by agreement or contract between the affected parties, fiduciary duties are relatively unalterable. An agent can engage in self-dealing, for example, with the knowledge and consent of the principal, but courts hold such departures from fiduciary duty to very stringent standards. However, the fiduciary duty of corporate officers and directors cannot generally be waived, even with stockholder approval. Courts have also used highly moralistic words, such as *loyalty*, *trust*, and *honor*, to describe fiduciary duty, thereby giving their rulings moral as well as legal force.

The importance of fiduciary duty for business ethics lies principally in the question, to whom do officers and directors owe a fiduciary duty? The standard answer is that management has a fiduciary duty to stockholders and to stockholders alone, so that corporations ought to be run solely in their interest, which is to say that managers should seek to maximize stockholder wealth. This stockholder view of the corporation has been challenged on two different grounds. Some critics argue that the ethical basis of a fiduciary duty to serve the interests of stockholders has been undermined by the changed nature of corporate property, caused in part by the separation of ownership and control noted by Berle and Means. Stockholders, according to these critics, do not entrust their property to the managers of corporations but are merely investors who can be said to own only their stock, not the corporation. Thus, Dodd (1932) argued that corporate managers no longer had a strict fiduciary duty to serve the interests of stockholders but were free to operate the corporation for the benefit of diverse constituencies. In the famous Berle–Dodd debate, Berle (1932) agreed that the traditional ethical basis of management's fiduciary duty to stockholders had been undermined, but argued against freeing managers to serve other interests because of the danger of unbridled management discretion.

Other critics of the stockholder view of the corporation contend that the same conditions which create a fiduciary duty to serve the interests of stockholders also apply to other constituencies, with the result that a fiduciary duty is owed to these other constituencies as well. Thus, officers and directors may have a fiduciary duty to other investors, such as bondholders, to protect their investments; to employees to maintain remunerative employment; to consumers to meet their needs and to protect them against harm from defective products; and so on. Such arguments lend support to stakeholder theory as an alternative to the stockholder view.

Recent developments in corporate law reflect both of these grounds of criticism, and shifting understandings of the fiduciary duty of management remain central to the ongoing debate over the purpose of corporations and the interests that they ought to serve.

Bibliography

Bayne, D. C. (1958). The fiduciary duty of management: The concept in the courts. *University of Detroit Law Review*, **25**, 561–94.

Berle, A. A. (1932). For whom corporate managers are trustees: A note. *Harvard Law Review*, **45**, 1365–72.

Bratton, W. W. (1992). Public values and corporate fiduciary law. *Rutgers Law Review*, **44**, 675–98.

Clark, R. C. (1985). Agency costs versus fiduciary duties. In J. W. Pratt and R. J. Zeckhauser (eds.), *Principals and Agents: The Structure of Business*. Boston, MA: Harvard Business School Press, 55–79.

Dodd, E. M. (1932). For whom are corporate managers trustees? *Harvard Law Review*, **45**, 1145–63.

Frankel, T. (1983). Fiduciary law. *California Law Review*, **71**, 795–836.

Scott, A. W. (1949). The fiduciary principle. *California Law Review*, **37**, 539–55.

Sealy, L. S. (1962). Fiduciary relationships. *Cambridge Law Journal*, 69–81.

finance, ethical issues in

Raj Aggarwal

arise especially in transactions between parties characterized by unequal market powers and differential access to relevant information, particularly in areas where legal or regulatory rules are of uncertain effectiveness. Most financial transactions depend on implicit contracts and expectations of ethical behavior, and financial decisions are often made on behalf of principals by agents, agents that may have preferential access to information and who may face conflicts of interest in making such decisions. Ethical issues in finance are particularly important as they often involve conflicts between fiduciary responsibilities, self-interest, and responsibilities to other stakeholders.

NATURE AND IMPORTANCE OF ETHICAL ISSUES IN FINANCE

While many social values are reflected in laws, many others are reflected only in ethical guidelines restraining self-interest and balancing the often conflicting interests of various stakeholders. Many actions that favor certain stakeholders or are self-serving may be legal, but are often considered unethical. Ethical guidelines are a reflection of values and mores that are considered important by society. Unfortunately, there is often considerable disagreement in a society about what is considered unethical in finance. A case in point relates to disagreements, since at least biblical times, about appropriate interest rates on loans.

In recent years there have been continuing instances of unethical behavior related to financial activities (often leading to significant losses for the firms involved). Highly publicized cases in the late 1980s where unethical behavior in finance resulted in illegal activity include those that led to government actions against Michael Milken, Ivan Boesky, Salomon Brothers, Bank of Credit and Commerce International, futures traders, mutual fund managers, a number of defense suppliers, and other firms. Some of these actions led to the liquidation and loss of independence of major investment banking firms such as Drexel Burnham and Kidder Peabody. Serious ethical and legal questions are being raised about the suitability of the sales of many derivative products, even to managers of major corporations who are presumably sophisticated investors. American companies operating overseas have to conform to the Foreign Corrupt Practices Act that outlaws bribery overseas; and US companies continue to be prosecuted for violating its requirements. However, unethical behavior in finance is not limited to US companies. In the early 1990s, banks and other financial firms in Europe, Asia, and Latin America have been implicated in widespread corruption and unethical behavior. Clearly, ethical issues in finance are important and not limited to any one country.

THE MODERN SETTING OF ETHICS IN FINANCE

Business organizations are replete with opportunities for behavior that is self-serving or that favors certain stakeholders at somebody else's expense. For example, employees control the use and disposition of business assets and, more generally, managers and directors act as agents for principals such as owners and other suppliers of capital. Further, principals and agents have differential access to relevant information, and agents often face ethical dilemmas relating to the disclosure of adverse information. As another example, many business relationships depend on implicit contracts between the company and its various stakeholders. In these cases, the expectation of ethical behavior is critical to the efficient operation of a business. Similarly, ethical and moral values also influence the relationship between employees, managers, and their firms and, thus, the relative efficiency of alternative approaches to the organization of a firm (this is contended to be one of the main reasons for the differences in how work is organized between, say, US and Japanese firms). Consequently, modern financial economics, and finance theory and practice, are intimately concerned with ethical issues and behavior as indicated by the importance of topics such as agency theory, financial contracting under information asymmetry, moral hazard and adverse selection, and reputation acquisition in finance.

Ethical behavior in the financial industry is particularly important since financial decisions may involve other people's money, accumulated wealth, and other savings. It is impossible to develop and impractical to implement, for every possible contingency in the financial industry, rules of behavior constraining self-serving behavior or behavior favoring certain stakeholders. Laws, regulations, and corporate rules of conduct consequently often have to leave many details undefined, and the players have to look for guidance to commonly accepted values and mores as reflected in social expectations of ethical behavior.

Continuing unethical behavior in finance generally has a contagion effect. Even for firms that do not face failure and are not directly associated with unethical behavior, unethical behavior in an industry can lead to higher operating costs for all businesses in that industry due to the increased regulatory and legal actions designed to curb such behavior. Each major epoch of unethical financial behavior in the past has been followed by new government regulations and laws designed to reduce or at least minimize such unethical behavior. Some have even argued that most government regulations related to the financial industry originated as reactions against episodes of significant unethical behavior among some financial market participants. Unfortunately, persistence of scandals and unethical behavior in financial markets can erode confidence in such markets, and lead to a reduction in the number of market participants and, thus, to reduced efficiency of such markets. Ethical behavior in finance is often a tug of war between self-interest, market efficiency, and various concepts of fairness.

FORCES IMPACTING ETHICAL BEHAVIOR IN FINANCE

Ethical behavior reflects the constraining role of social conventions, and ethical behavior in finance often presents many dilemmas and choices between personal, organizational, and societal goals. In a market-based economy, social conventions as guides to ethical behavior can be of uncertain value as they are often in conflict with the notion, associated with Adam Smith and others, that the pursuit of self-interest by individuals leads to the maximum social good. These uncertainties and conflicts become particularly evident and even critical in economies that are in transition from centrally planned socialist economies to market-driven economies.

However, the pursuit of self-interest associated with Adam Smith's "invisible hand" is somewhat mitigated by the need to allow for market failures. Such failures can arise due to externalities, costly and asymmetric information, high transactions costs, unequal bargaining powers, barriers to entry and exit, and other factors limiting market participation. Regardless of the reason(s) for market failure, it is contended that the pursuit of self-interest and corporate shareholder wealth maximization must be restrained by appropriate laws, regulations, and social expectations for ethical behavior that reflect society's shared values and beliefs (Adam Smith, in fact, also recognized society's dependence on virtue).

Ethical behavior in finance can also be promoted by detecting and punishing unethical behavior. Such efforts to prevent or minimize unethical behavior in finance are generally based on regulation and disclosure of such activities. Of course, to be effective, such regulations and disclosure rules must be enforced and violators punished. However, as discussed above, such regulations and laws are likely to impose higher dead-weight costs on all participants in financial transactions and may lead to less efficient markets. Thus, the need for ethical behavior in finance also arises from the recognition that its absence is likely to encourage new laws and higher levels of government regulations against such behavior.

In some cases, it may be possible to discourage unethical behavior by redefining property rights, internalization of previous externalities, or by the explicit recognition of implicit contracts between the various stakeholders in a firm. For example, many new regulations and class action lawsuits against unethical business practices are based on demonstrating that such a business is appropriating or damaging property belonging to others. As another example, public pressure may be used to make explicit the implicit contracts between a company and the community in which it operates. However, redefinition of such property rights is often difficult, involves lengthy processes, or may be impossible in many cases in modern democratic societies. Of course, it is much more effective and economically efficient when ethical behavior is promoted (and unethical behavior constrained) by shared values and beliefs.

In addition, a reputation for ethical behavior can have many advantages. For example, firms build and maintain good reputations in order to convince clients that the risks of transactions are reduced. In doing so, they increase the value of implicit claims sold by the firm to its various stakeholders, and the firm's ability to attract and engage in profitable transactions. This is particularly important in finance as such transactions generally involve decisions about somebody else's assets. Trust and a good reputation are not only essential in such cases, but are also very efficient mechanisms for reducing and eliminating agency costs and costs of contractual enforcement. Finally, good reputations enhance the available opportunity set by reducing the risks faced by the parties in a transaction. Thus, firms with good ethical reputations gain access to wealth-enhancing opportunities not available otherwise.

Most finance professionals are taught that the overriding goal of the firm is to maximize shareholder wealth. Some contend that maximizing shareholder wealth in the long term is possible only with ethical behavior. Unethical behavior is costly as it damages a firm's reputation and, conversely, ethical behavior can be wealth

enhancing. However, shareholder wealth maximization alone will prevent unethical behavior only if the firm's stock price reflects the extent to which the benefits of such unethical behavior are less than the expected present value of the future costs of unethical behavior (in the form of penalties or lost reputation that impact a firm's risk or return). This implies that unethical behavior is disclosed publicly in a timely manner and that capital markets are able to assess its impact on share value accurately. Consequently, the goal of shareholder wealth maximization by itself is unlikely to lead to ethical behavior other than in some special cases. Thus, most finance professionals accept that the pursuit of the shareholder wealth maximization goal has to be constrained by behavior that certainly must be legal and preferably also ethical.

ETHICAL ISSUES IN FINANCIAL MANAGEMENT

Managers are agents for principals (owners and other stakeholders in a firm). Managers also have preferential access to information about the firm and its assets and liabilities. Members of a firm's board of directors share similar advantages relative to other owners. While managers and directors are restrained from taking advantage of their positions as agents by many laws and regulations, generally there is considerable room for unethical behavior. For example, accounting rules generally allow some flexibility and important information can be withheld. Similarly, the release of other material non-accounting information can also be withheld. Empirical evidence shows that the announcement of an issue of equity depresses the stock price as equity is sold to the public only when it is overpriced. Similarly, compensation of senior management is sometimes set by directors with insufficient attention to their fiduciary duties to stockholders allowing for overly generous stock options, golden parachutes, and other forms of managerial compensation.

ETHICAL ISSUES IN FINANCIAL TRANSACTIONS WITH STAKEHOLDERS

Managers can also take advantage of their preferential access to information in their dealings with other stakeholders such as suppliers, customers, the communities in which the firm operates, labor unions, and others. Problems arise when different parties in transactions between a firm and its stakeholders have different expectations regarding what is considered ethical. Suppliers and customers may behave opportunistically. A firm may ignore its implicit commitments to a community. A new owner may not accept many or all of the implicit contracts between a firm and its stakeholders. It has been suggested that the renegotiation of costly implicit contracts can be a major source of synergistic savings in a merger or acquisition. In these and other financial transactions between a firm and its stakeholders, implicit contracts are impacted and ethical issues become very important and even critical in many cases.

ETHICAL ISSUES IN THE FINANCIAL SERVICES INDUSTRY

Mandatory disclosure regulations as reflected in the 1933 and 1934 Securities Acts in the United States and in the 1900 British Companies Act are an attempt to reduce information asymmetry by requiring disclosure of certain minimum amounts of information and apply penalties for misrepresentation in all disclosures by issuers of securities. While it is possible that they may have reduced investor choice by increasing costs of security issuance and by reducing the choice set of available risky securities, these requirements have clearly increased the informational efficiency of financial markets.

Laws against insider trading in securities are another example of attempts to reduce information asymmetry among financial market participants. While there is some controversy regarding these laws and regulations, many of them are based on the notion that insider information does not belong to the person using it and, thus, its use is fraud or theft and is contrary to fiduciary responsibilities of insiders.

In recognition of the need to address the problems arising out of unequal market powers and asymmetric information, most professional associations in the financial services industry in the US have developed ethical guidelines for their members (e.g., the Chartered Financial Analysts Federation). In addition, many regulations and guidelines, such as the suitability rules regarding sales of securities, are an attempt to protect investors with low market power and

knowledge from firms with greater market power and knowledge. Suitability rules require that brokers determine if potential buyers of certain risky securities are suitable owners of such securities. For similar reasons, issuers of securities are required to issue securities at prices that are "fair and equitable." Both the New York and the Tokyo Stock Exchanges have in recent years appointed study groups and panels to recommend ways to improve the fairness and efficiency of financial markets for individual investors.

Another ethical issue in finance relates to the desire of many investors to invest only in firms that engage in ethical businesses. These investors are willing to limit their universe of investments, thus forgoing a possible better risk–return combination. A number of "socially responsible" mutual funds are available for the portfolio investment needs of such investors.

CONCLUSIONS

Ethical issues are ubiquitous and important in finance. Ethics act as important and cost-effective constraints on self-serving and other undesirable behavior by agents (such as managers) who have preferential information and who are responsible for the management of assets that belong to others (principals). Ethics in finance are especially important as it is impractical for laws, regulations, and corporate rules of behavior to cover every contingency in financial transactions between employees, managers, firms, and their various stakeholders. Financial transactions depend critically on implicit contracts, and the pursuit of shareholder wealth maximization must be constrained by expectations of ethical behavior. Further, unethical behavior in finance can lead to business failure and/or increased regulatory and legal costs for the industry, while a reputation for ethical behavior leads to an expanded opportunity set and can be wealth enhancing.

See also *accounting ethics; agency theory; corporate finance, ethical issues in; efficient markets; financial reporting; Foreign Corrupt Practices Act; insider trading; market for corporate control; mergers and acquisitions; risk; stakeholder theory*

Bibliography

Aggarwal, R. and Chandra, G. (1990). Stakeholder management: Opportunities and challenges. *Business*, **40** (4), 48–51.

Anand, P. and Cowton, C. J. (1993). The ethical investor: Exploring dimensions of investment behavior. *Journal of Economic Psychology*, **14** (2), 377–85.

Baumol, W. (1991). *Perfect Markets and Easy Virtue: Business Ethics and the Invisible Hand*. Cambridge, MA: Blackwell.

Bear, L. A. and Maldano-Bear, R. (1994). *Free Markets, Finance, Ethics, and Law*. Englewood Cliffs, NJ: Prentice-Hall.

Dobson, J. (1993). The role of ethics in finance. *Financial Analysts Journal*, November/December, 57–61.

Markowitz, H. (1992). Markets and morality. *Journal of Portfolio Management*, winter, 84–93.

Noe, T. H. and Robello, M. J. (1994). The dynamics of business ethics and economic activity. *American Economic Review*, **84** (3), 531–47.

Shefrin, H. and Statman, M. (1993). Ethics, fairness and efficiency in financial markets. *Financial Analysts Journal*, November/December, 21–9.

Williams, O., Reilly, F. K., and Houck, J. W. (eds.) (1989). *Ethics and the Investment Industry*. Savage, MD: Rowman and Littlefield.

financial reporting

Lawrence A. Ponemon

can be defined as the process of collecting, processing, and disclosing an organization's economic activity. Data collected in the financial reporting process are typically measured on a transactional basis (e.g., buying inventory or selling merchandise) in one functional currency (e.g., such as dollars, yen, or pounds sterling) using a set of standardized accounting rules known as generally accepted accounting principles (GAAP).

Three primary financial statements serve as the basic outputs of a financial reporting system. These include: the balance sheet, which measures the assets, liabilities, and equity of an organization at a point in time; the income statement, measuring revenues and expenses of an organization over a time period lasting no longer than one year; and the statement of cash flows, measuring the sources and uses of funds over the same time period as the income statement. Other outputs of

the financial reporting process are a plethora of special reports used for specific decision-making activities, such as capital expenditures, cash projections, and what-if analysis.

The three primary objectives of financial reporting are:

1   *Control* – helping to ensure that assets of an organization are secure and under management supervision.
2   *Accuracy* – creating a fiscal picture or snapshot of the company at given points in time that presents the economic reality of the company in a timely and unbiased manner.
3   *Accountability* – providing corporate directors, shareholders, and other key stakeholders of a company with information to evaluate the performance of the company and its management.

The stakeholders of financial reports include the organization's management, employees, stockholders, creditors, customers, vendors, governmental authorities, and labor unions. The ethical foundation of financial reporting is derived from the need to hold managers accountable for achieving the goals of investors. The physical separation of investors and managers during the early days of capitalism resulted in accounting rules or principles that specify what, when, and how economic transactions *ought* to be recorded in a company's financial books and disclosed to stakeholders.

The ethical imperative of financial reporting stems from the public's reliance on financial statements as a trusted summary of a company's economic reality for a given period of time. Financial reports that provide all relevant users with accurate and timely reports about the fiscal health of an organization are what the public expects. Financial reports that do not meet any one of the three fundamental objectives of control, accuracy, or accountability are believed to be unreliable or possibly even fraudulent.

Unreliable financial reports come about because of mistakes in the accounting process, technology glitches, or intentional manipulation. An example of unintentional error in financial reporting would be an underestimate of a liability due to duplicate payments to vendors because of a new application being implemented in the accounting department. The recording of inflated revenues by an accounting manager to show better earnings, however, is a clear intentional manipulation of the financial reporting process.

While many stakeholders can be influenced by intentional manipulation of financial statements, the consequences of nefarious activities usually involve two primary groups: the organization's senior management and investors. In most cases the organization's management is typically represented by the company's top executive management whose performance is inextricably linked to financial results such as profit or earnings per share (EPS). Investors are individuals and institutions who provide economic resources to the organization, and this group is typically represented by the corporate board members (especially those directors who are independent of management and do not have a significant economic stake in the company).

Competing economic interests of different stakeholder groups, such as management and investors, can cause actual or perceived ethical conflict within the organization. This conflict may motivate some managers in control over the financial reporting process (such as the CFO or CEO of the company) to make income, expense, or asset recognition decisions that ultimately compromise the reliability and integrity of financial reports. As a result of the potential for these kinds of conflict, the financial accounting process includes independent auditors who are independent of all key stakeholder groups. The auditor's primary role is to ensure that financial reports are prepared in accordance with proper accounting rules and, hence, can be relied upon to determine the fiscal health of a company.

Recent negative events in the marketplace – including unethical financial reporting practices of senior executives in very large companies – have resulted in greater control and public oversight of the financial reporting process. Such controls include more stringent rules that aim to enhance the transparency of a company's senior executive team and its board of directors. New requirements have also been imposed on auditors to better serve the public as a corporate watchdog.

See also *stakeholder theory; Sarbanes-Oxley Act; Securities and Exchange Commission.*

Foreign Corrupt Practices Act (FCPA)

Kenneth D. Alpern

A United States law passed in 1977 that prohibits publicly traded US corporations from making illicit payments to officials of foreign governments, to political parties and their officials, or to intermediaries for such purposes. The FCPA is an outcome of a series of investigations of the mid-1970s which revealed that some major US corporations maintained slush funds used for bribery and other dubious payments to officials of a number of foreign governments. Over 300 corporations admitted to hundreds of millions of dollars in such payments, one of which led directly to the fall of a Japanese government and imprisonment of its prime minister.

From the outset, the FCPA was criticized on a number of grounds, most prominently: vagueness, economic loss, and moral unsoundness.

Vagueness. Even after the 1988 amendments, still vague are: (1) what counts as acceptable payments to low-level officials for routine services such as clearance of customs, police protection, and utility service; (2) the extent of allowances for "reasonable and *bona fide* expenditure" – such as for travel and lodging – directly related to promotion of a product or execution of a contract; (3) the level of knowledge of intermediaries' activities that creates liability. It is generally agreed that the FCPA remains vague, perhaps as all laws must be, but the effect is disputed: Does the vagueness chill honest business dealings, or does it open the door to wider abuses?

Economic loss. Perhaps the strongest objection is that since businesses from other countries are not similarly restricted, the FCPA merely puts US corporations at a competitive disadvantage, resulting in lost profits to shareholders, fewer US jobs, and reduced US tax revenues. Among responses to this objection are that bribery and extortion payments are not often really necessary and that as a matter of fact, US businesses have not lost much in sales; and that a reputation for honest business dealings will pay off in improved long-term economic and political relations with foreign governments and citizens.

Moral unsoundness. Among moral objections, it has been argued that the FCPA imposes our moral standards on others, that morally valid concern for economic well-being outweighs prohibitions on bribery, and that the most common practice at issue is not bribery corruptly initiated by the US business, but rather extortion in which the business is the victim. Responses include that both bribery and extortion are illegal and judged immoral in virtually every country in the world, as confirmed by the secrecy of such dealings. And against any loss in short-term profit, it must be recognized that complicity in such illicit dealings corrupts the free market and moves international business closer to the state of nature.

The government has only infrequently laid charges under the FCPA and claims have been made that the 1988 amendments have emasculated the law. Large illicit transfers of funds may have become less frequent – or more cleverly disguised – but a law cannot have much impact without the general will that it be followed.

Bibliography

Alpern, K. D. (1993). Moral dimensions of the Foreign Corrupt Practices Act. In T. Donaldson and P. Werhane (eds.), *Ethical Issues in Business*, 4th edn. Englewood Cliffs, NJ: Prentice-Hall. (Defends the morality of the FCPA.)

Gillespie, K. (1987). The Middle East response to the US Foreign Corrupt Practices Act. *California Management Review*, summer, 9 30. (Economic impact of the FCPA.)

Pastin, M. and Hooker, M. (1980). Ethics and the Foreign Corrupt Practices Act. *Business Horizons*, December, 43–7. Reprinted in T. Donaldson and P. Werhane (eds.), *Ethical Issues in Business*, 4th edn., 1993. Englewood Cliffs, NJ: Prentice-Hall. (Argues that the FCPA is morally unsound.)

Pines, D. (1994). Amending the Foreign Corrupt Practices Act to include a private right of action. *California Law Review*, **82**, 185–229. (Contains a good general overview.)

US Government (1988). 15 USC §§ 78m(b), 78dd-1, 78dd-2, 78ff. (originally enacted as Pub. L. No. 95–213, 91 Stat. 1494 (1977), and amended by Foreign Corrupt Practices Act Amendments of 1988, Pub. L. No. 100-418, 5001-3, 102 Stat. 1107, 1415–25). (Codification of the FCPA.)

free speech in the workplace

John J. McCall

Free speech is the ability to express oneself without seeking prior clearance and without fear of subsequent reprisal.

Free speech is one of the first rights enumerated in the United States Constitution. Its position in that document reveals the moral importance that its framers accorded to the free expression of ideas. In the US context, however the right to free speech is a limited right possessed by citizens against their *government*. The constitutional protection of speech is a constraint only against government actions; it provides no bar even against a private employer's discharge of an employee for speaking, outside the workplace, on behalf of political causes opposed by the employer. (We should note, though, that such a discharge, while not unconstitutional, may be illegal according to statute in specific states.)

If the Constitution provides no protection for employee speech in the private sector, traditional US labor law provided scarcely much more. The doctrine of employment at will allowed employers to dismiss for any reason or for no reason (*see* JUST CAUSE).

An employer's almost total discretion to discharge has been limited in the last few decades. For example, courts have held that firing for speech disclosing serious product safety hazards violates public policy. Courts have also limited the traditional duty of loyalty the employee owes as an agent by excepting actions (including speech) that are illegal or unethical (*see* AGENCY THEORY). Perhaps the major legal protection for employee speech can be found in legislation. For instance, the Wagner Act (1935) makes it illegal to discharge employees for promoting unionization; the Occupational Safety and Health Act (1970) makes it illegal to discipline workers who request safety inspections of the workplace.

These protections notwithstanding, most commentators would accept that legal protection for employees' speech remains quite limited when compared to the more extensive constitutional protection from government interferences that citizens enjoy. The moral question is whether a more extensive right to free speech *ought* to apply to the workplace. The answer to that question will depend on the moral foundations that can be offered for a right to free speech.

Traditionally, rights to free speech have been justified as both instrumentally and intrinsically valuable. One instrumental defense of free speech holds that citizens' freedom of expression is required for the health of democratic government. If government can effectively control the speech of its citizens, it could prevent citizens from debating and criticizing government policy, effectively limiting democratic self-determination. If democracy has moral importance, so would a right to freedom of expression.

A second instrumental defense claims that the best hope for arriving at truth, if only in the long run, is through allowing competing opinions to be tested in a free marketplace of ideas.

A non-instrumental defense of free speech argues that it is a necessary condition for treating persons with due respect. Morality holds that human persons have a special moral status that requires they be treated with dignity. The source of that dignity is often explained by the fact that persons are unique in their autonomy, their ability to make reasoned choices about their lives. Respect for persons demands that they be able to engage in open discussion about important aspects of their lives.

Do these moral arguments justify an extension of free speech rights to the workplace? Some argue they do not. They would claim that (1) in a free competitive economy, employees can find alternative employment and avoid a specific corporation's restrictions on their speech; (2) rights against the government are necessary because the threat to the well-being of citizens from a totalitarian government is much greater and the avoidance costs much higher than for any specific authoritarian corporate policy (especially given (1), above); (3) strict control over the workforce is required for efficient production, and employee rights to free speech would undermine the necessary discipline.

Others find these reasons unconvincing in that (1) they overstate the difference, both in potential harm and avoidance costs, between governmental and corporate exercises of power; (2) alternative employment (a) requires forgoing time and firm-specific skills invested in one's job, (b) may not be readily available and, (c) in any case, may not be any different with regard to free speech; and (3) the need for efficiency has not been proven to preclude the possibility of carefully circumscribed employee rights (e.g., open communication may increase work satisfaction and productivity while threats of reprisal may dampen them). Most importantly, however, the proponents of employee rights to free speech will point out that the arguments critical of that right fail to address the crucial connection between respect and free speech.

Even those willing to defend employees' speech rights must admit that some limits on speech are necessary. For example, when, if ever, would outside political activities be grounds for corporate disciplinary action? Most proponents of employee rights would not accept an answer to that question that stated "whenever the political activities are in conflict with the economic interests of the firm," since that would threaten, say, an insurance company nurse from urging legislative passage of a single-payer health insurance system. Would support of racist policies by an employee of a firm with a large black client base be any different?

Similarly, proponents of employee rights to free speech still need to answer, with justifications, questions such as whether, and under what conditions, an act of whistleblowing ought to be protected, and how far should a right to express grievances about corporate policy to co-workers and supervisors go.

Recently adopted corporate racial and sexual harassment policies raise questions about the range of employee speech rights as well. Some have argued that these policies are vague in their definition of harassment and insufficient in their guarantees of due process for accused employees, with the effect that even acceptable speech is "chilled." So, even if one agrees that rights to free speech ought to extend to the workplace, much analysis remains before the specific content of that right can be identified.

Bibliography

Bingham, L. (1994). Employee free speech in the workplace: Using the First Amendment as public policy for wrongful discharge actions. *Ohio State Law Journal*, 55, 341.

Blades, L. (1967). Employment at will vs. individual freedom: On limiting the abusive exercise of employer power. *Columbia Law Review*, 67, 1405.

Ewing, D. (1977). *Freedom Inside the Organization*. New York: McGraw-Hill.

Martin, D. (1978). Is an employee bill of rights needed? In M. B. Johnson (ed.), *The Attack on Corporate America*. New York: McGraw-Hill.

Novosel vs. Nationwide Insurance Company. 721 F. 2d 894 (3d Cir 1983).

Summer, C. (1976). Individual protection against unjust dismissal: Time for a statute. *Virginia Law Review*, 62, 481.

Werhane, P. (1985). *Persons, Rights and Corporations*. Englewood Cliffs, NJ: Prentice-Hall.

Westin, A. and Salisbury, S. (eds.) (1980). *Individual Rights in the Corporation*. New York: Pantheon.

freedom of contract

J. Gregory Dees

is the view that competent individuals should be at liberty to enter into private, consensual exchange agreements of their choosing, without interference from third parties, including governments. To the extent that government has an active role in economic life, it is to protect this freedom and to help enforce the contracts made under it. Belief in freedom of contract is generally accompanied by an endorsement of extensive individual property rights.

This belief in individual liberty grew out of the major Western political and social transformations of the seventeenth and eighteenth centuries. The transformations were driven by doubts about external moral authority, increasing faith in individual rationality, and a new appreciation of the potential of freely functioning markets. Consent became the preferred ground for obligation in political and private life.

Freedom of contract is supported by two distinct, but often intertwined traditions: classical liberalism and free-market economics. Classical liberalism has its intellectual roots in John

Locke's writing on civil government and John Stuart Mill's work on liberty. It has received recent expression in the libertarianism of Robert Nozick. Classical liberalism emphasizes the inherent moral value of individual autonomy and private property rights. The core idea is that people should be free to govern their lives and their property, so long as they do not obstruct the rights of others to do the same. Free-market economics, on the other hand, derives the value of contractual freedom from a theory of social welfare (*see* WELFARE ECONOMICS). Often associated with Adam Smith, this line of reasoning has found more recent champions in Friedrich Hayek and Milton Friedman. They argue that prosperity (or, more precisely, economic efficiency) is a social good of overriding importance, and that it is best achieved when people are free to seek their own gain. Just as liberals are skeptical about external moral authority, these economists are skeptical about centrally controlled social engineering.

Though few would deny that contractual freedom has some value, critics have raised a number of questions about its legitimate extent. Even the proponents of freedom of contract recognize a need for limits. All but the most radical add two qualifications. The first is that private contractual agreements should not unjustly harm third parties. The second is that neither party to an agreement should use force or fraud. Breach of either condition could provide a rationale for societal intervention. For most proponents, these are the only conditions that justify interference with private contracts and they are to be interpreted very narrowly. Critics, however, support more extensive grounds for intervention. These may be simplified into three areas: remedying defects in voluntariness, protecting community interests, and preventing self-destructive behavior.

Defects in Voluntariness

Both the liberal and economic defenses of freedom of contract seem to rest on the idea that individuals make informed, rational, and free choices. The value of freedom is questionable when people make uninformed, irrational, or impaired choices. Critics argue that the prohibition against force and fraud does not go far enough. Even mentally competent adults who are not subject to force or fraud may lack crucial information and may not know they lack it; the costs of personally gathering missing information (search costs) may be very high; even if provided with the information, they may not have the education or capacity to understand it, especially with complex products; they may be pressed to make a decision without enough time to think it through; they may be in a state of mind that temporarily impairs their reasoning; they may be acting under some form of duress; they may be subtly manipulated in some way; or they may have very little relative bargaining power. Some critics go so far as to suggest that the very idea of a free choice that is not corrupted by social conditioning and constrained by external circumstances is a chimera.

More moderate critics use common defects in voluntariness to assert that societies have an obligation to create favorable decision-making conditions and to protect people when these conditions do not obtain. They argue for a wide array of regulations and legal protections, from information disclosure requirements to "cooling off" periods in which parties have a right to rescind a contract. Proponents respond that individuals can and should learn to protect themselves from unfavorable conditions. *Caveat emptor* is a common corollary to freedom of contract.

COMMUNITY INTERESTS

Some critics go further to argue that communities have a legitimate interest in many private contracts. Proponents open the door to community interests by acknowledging that unjust harm to third parties may justify social intervention. Though it is not what proponents had in mind, interpreted broadly, harm to third parties could include intangible harms to the community, its social fabric, and its shared values. In this regard, communities often attempt to limit the kinds of things subject to market exchange (or "commodified"). Economic exchanges that have been outlawed include the sale, for example, of sexual services (prostitution and surrogacy), votes in an election, public offices, human organs, oneself into slavery, and babies. In many early societies even land was not treated as a commodity to be owned or traded. Beyond blocking exchanges, communities might want to

regulate them to preserve shared values and objectives. Examples of social values potentially threatened by private contracts include distributive justice, preservation of human dignity, community aesthetics, and the absence of discrimination against religious, ethnic, or gender groups. Social values of this sort have been used to argue for rent control, minimum wage laws, health and safety regulations, zoning restrictions, affirmative action, and limits on the production and sale of pornography.

Communitarian critics of freedom of contract argue that harm to community values can justify social interference with private contracts. Proponents of contractual freedom counter this argument by pointing out the potentially oppressive results of allowing this type of restraint. Community values about the appropriate role and worth of women and minority groups have been used to justify discrimination. Proponents also point out the costs of these constraints. They argue, for instance, that minimum wage laws increase unemployment, and the absence of a market in human kidneys for transplants limits the supply and results in more deaths from kidney disease.

SELF-DESTRUCTIVE BEHAVIOR

A few critics of freedom of contract go further. Even when conditions of informed voluntary choice are met, people may choose to engage in economic exchanges that are not judged to be in their own long-term interest. This judgment may be made by the individuals themselves in more reflective moments, by elders who have more life experience, or by some collective social assessment. Even if such contracts are isolated and do not negatively impact others in the community, some would argue that society should play the role of protecting people from themselves. Examples in this area are difficult to identify because they often raise issues of voluntariness and community values as well. Common candidates, however, are drug laws, laws against assisted suicide, and laws against gambling. Liberal proponents tend to respond to paternalistic criticisms by arguing that it is none of society's business if individuals choose self-destructive paths that do not directly harm others. This is an objectionable form of *paternalism*. Economic proponents stress the fact that mentally competent adults are in a better position than anyone else to determine what is in their own best interest, even if their judgment is not perfect and even if it changes over time.

Courts and legislatures have been sympathetic to many of these criticisms, leading some observers to claim that freedom of contract is dead. However, others see this freedom expanding, as societies experiment with new commodities (such as sexual surrogacy and organ sales) and as former communist countries embrace free markets. What is certain is that the extent and limits of freedom of contract will continue to be a contentious and rich issue of debate for the foreseeable future.

See also *coercion; economic efficiency; economics and ethics; efficient markets; liberty; rational choice theory*

Bibliography

Andre, J. (1992). Blocked exchanges: A taxonomy. *Ethics*, 103, 29–47. (An extensive survey with references to the literature.)

Atiyah, P. S. (1985). *The Rise and Fall of Freedom of Contract*. Oxford: Oxford University Press.

Friedman, M. (1962). *Capitalism and Freedom*. Chicago: University of Chicago Press.

Hayek, F. (1960). *The Constitution of Liberty*. Chicago: University of Chicago Press.

Nozick, R. (1974). *Anarchy, State, and Utopia*. New York: Basic Books.

Paul, E. F., Miller F. D., Jr., and Paul, J. (eds.) (1985). *Ethics and Economics*. Oxford: Blackwell. (Particularly the essays by Amartya Sen and Allan Gibbard.)

Trebilcock, M. J. (1993). *The Limits of Freedom of Contract*. Boston, MA: Harvard University Press. (A comprehensive treatment.)

future generations

LaRue Tone Hosmer

The moral issue involved is the proper treatment of the people who will come after us as inhabitants of the earth.

This basic moral question can be expressed very simply: "What sort of world do we want to leave for our children?" Should we take what we need now in the way of the natural resources (scarce oil, ore, and timber), the public goods (clean air, water, and land) and the financial, social, and political capital that has been bequeathed to us, and leave the members of future generations to fend for themselves? Or should we restrict our usage of those resources, goods, and forms of capital out of a sense of duty to those not yet born?

The ethical analysis of this basic moral question is not simple. It is a form of inquiry frequently termed *transgenerational justice* (though certainly concepts of rights, benefits, and duties are also relevant), and it is made complex by empirical uncertainties, finite limits, value disagreements, and symmetrical inconsistencies. This entry will take up each of these complicating factors first, and then briefly discuss the various forms of ethical inquiry that have been attempted.

COMPLICATING FACTORS IN TRANSGENERATIONAL MORAL ISSUES

Most modern ethical theories assume a timeless world. It is a world limited to the interests of the persons living at a single period who make tradeoffs between those interests. Once we add the dimension of time – and this is time extending beyond the immediately adjacent generations – we add a number of very severe complications.

Empirical uncertainties. Forecasting economic, social, and technological change over a period of three to four generations is an exceedingly imprecise art. We do not know what future conditions will be like, and therefore it is frequently unclear what actions might be taken now in the hope of improving those conditions. For example, should we conserve our supplies of carbon-based energy (coal, oil, and natural gas), or should we rely on the hoped-for means of converting sunlight to electricity in quantities adequate to meet utility loads?

Finite limits. Regardless of technological advancements, most of the natural resources and public goods of this world are severely limited. Locke recognized this limitation when he made the proviso to the right of property ownership that "enough and as good be left for others" (*see* LOCKE, JOHN). Unless this proviso is accepted as a base for transgenerational issues, we are rapidly into the situation described by Hardin (1968), where the rational self-interests of many individuals are shown to destroy the limited resources and goods held in common.

Value disagreements. Population control is frequently prescribed as the cure for finite resources. Fewer total people will obviously have lower total demands, but we are left to decide how many people are too many, and that depends upon the style of life that is desired. You may want beautiful vistas and abundant wildlife. I may prefer large extended families. Both are doubtless "good" in any rational sense of that word, yet how are we to decide between them?

Symmetrical inconsistencies. Trade-offs between contemporaries can be considered as contracts based upon mutual advantage or mutual agreement, and it is hard to fault either as being morally "wrong" in some way. This simplifying view is not valid for future generations. Here we encounter a one-way street, where no mutual advantage or mutual agreement is possible. We can determine the basic quality of life of those living in the future; they cannot help or harm us in any way.

ETHICAL APPROACHES TO TRANSGENERATIONAL MORAL PROBLEMS

It is generally recognized that we hold certain moral obligations to future generations. It is the extent of those obligations that is in question, because each increase in the natural resources and public goods reserved for those not yet born results in a decrease in the living standards of some of those here now. Conversely, policies that will improve the welfare of less well-off contemporaries automatically entail some environmental risks or economic burdens for posterity. There have been three basic approaches to this problem, all of them generally unsatisfactory due to the special complications described previously.

Individual rights. It is easy to say that the members of future generations have rights (*see* RIGHTS). They obviously do. This approach, however, does not seem to help in the trade-offs between generations because there is no way of determining whose rights should predominate or whose values should hold sway.

Even the most basic right to life, when applied to future generations, becomes merely a right to survival, which most would agree is not enough.

Economic benefits. It has often been suggested that future benefits and harms be discounted back to present value to make them more readily comparable to contemporary benefits and harms (*see* SOCIAL COST-BENEFITS; ECONOMIC EFFICIENCY). The problem is that while the present cost of future benefits may legitimately be expressed in this way, it is morally awkward, at best, to attempt to think of a present value equivalent to such future harms as genetic ill-health or environmental destruction.

Distributive justice. Rawls attempted to overcome the symmetrical inconsistencies associated with future generations by proposing that each individual, choosing behind the veil of ignorance, was actually the head of a family with some degree of affection and concern for succeeding generations. This is an ingenious approach, but it presents difficulties, for we are not certain whether those succeeding generations – extended far enough to encounter both empirical uncertainties and value disagreements – will be better off or worse off than the present generation. If they are to be better off, then the "difference principle" would seem to preclude any sacrifice being made on their behalf. If they are to be worse off, then the amount of that sacrifice is still not clear (*see* DISTRIBUTIVE JUSTICE).

What ends are worth pursuing? This is the major issue confronted by consideration of individual rights, economic benefits/harms, and just agreements in the trade-offs between the welfare of present versus future generations. It is an area of inquiry that will receive continually increasing attention as we appear to approach the finite limits of our natural resources and public goods.

Bibliography

De-Shalit, A. (1992). Community and the rights of future generations: A reply to Robert Elliot. *Journal of Applied Philosophy*, 9, 105–15.

English, J. (1977). Justice between generations. *Philosophical Studies*, 31, 91–104.

Hardin, G. (1968). Tragedy of the commons. *Science*, **162**, 1243–8.

Hauerwas, S. (1974). The moral limits of population control. *Thought*, **49**, 236–49.

Jecker, N. (1992). Intergenerational justice and the family. *Journal of Value Inquiry*, **26**, 495–509.

Laslett, P. and Fishkin, J. S. (eds.) (1992). *Justice Between Age Groups and Generations*. New Haven, CT: Yale University Press.

Mueller, D. C. (1974). Intergenerational justice and the social discount rate. *Theory and Decisions*, **5**, 263–73.

Sikora, R. L. and Barry, B. (eds.) (1978). *Obligations to Future Generations*. Philadelphia, PA: Temple University Press.

G

game theory

Christopher W. Morris

the systematic study of *interdependent* rational choice. It may be used to explain, predict, and/or evaluate human behavior in contexts where the choices of individuals depend on what others choose to do. The seminal works were *The Theory of Games and Economic Behavior* (1944) by von Neumann and Morgenstern and a couple of papers by John Nash in the early 1950s. Four decades later, game theory is used widely in all of the social and policy sciences, moral and political philosophy, linguistics, and biology. In 1994 the Nobel Prize for Economics was awarded to John Nash, John Harsanyi, and Reinhard Selten for their defining contributions to the field (*see* RATIONAL CHOICE THEORY).

The theory of *independent* individual choice studies the decisions of a single individual choosing from a number of options or alternatives. The outcome of the individual's choice is understood to be the result of his or her choices and of the relevant intervening states of the environment or world (e.g., the weather). In contexts of decision-making *under certainty*, it is known exactly what outcome will be produced by each available choice or act. In these situations a rational choice will be one that maximizes the satisfaction of the agent's goals (or *utility*, a measure of the agent's values, goals, interests, or preferences). In contexts of *risk*, where only a probability can be assigned to any act bringing about a particular outcome, the most widely accepted view is that rational choice requires maximizing one's *expected* utility. (If no probabilities can be assigned, the decision problem may be thought of as one *under complete uncertainty* or *complete ignorance*. There is considerable disagreement about rational choice under uncertainty.) (*See* RISK.) In the basic neoclassical model of a competitive market, it is assumed that there are so many producers and consumers that none can influence the behavior of any other. This assumption, in effect, makes the decision problem facing any particular individual one of independent individual choice; if it is also assumed that every agent possesses full information, then the problem becomes one of individual choice under certainty.

Interdependent choice is more complex as the outcome is a result not only of the choices of the agent in question and the state of the world, but also the choices of other individuals. The problem is how to choose when the outcome is dependent on the choice of others? One cannot, as in individual choice under risk, assign a probability to the choices of others and maximize expected utility: one's choice depends on what the others choose, but their choice depends on what we choose. How then to form expectations regarding what others will do? A new element of *strategic* choice is introduced by interdependence. We may, then, think of game theory as the systematic study of strategic choice.

A problem of interdependent choice or a "game" consists of two or more agents (or "players"), each facing a choice of two or more acts or strategies ("moves"). An outcome results from the set of strategies chosen. Different sorts of games present different sorts of problems, and different conditions can facilitate the choice process. A particular set of "ideal" conditions simplifies game theory and made most of the early results possible: equal rationality (each agent is fully rational), complete information (each agent knows the rules of the game, the preferences of the other players), common knowledge (each knows that each knows the rules of the game, etc., and so on). Under these conditions there are, for certain types of games, sets of strategies that result in outcomes with attractive properties. One such property, which plays a crucial role in game theory, is that of an *equilibrium* outcome (or "Nash equilibrium"): a set of strategies (or outcome) is in equilibrium when no one can improve their position by unilaterally changing their strategy. Equilibria of this sort possess a type of stability: no one will rationally choose, by themselves, to upset it. If one is interested in *predicting* or *explaining* outcomes, the concept of an equilibrium outcome will be important, and, for normative purposes, it also proves significant.

It is important to distinguish games with two players from those with more ("*n*-person games"). The complexities introduced by having more than two players make *n*-person game theory more complicated and controversial. The second distinction that needs to be made is that between games where there is perfect conflict of interest and all others. The first are called "zero-sum" or "constant-sum" games, as the "sum" of the possible gains from interaction is zero or constant (e.g., two-person parlor games where one player wins, the other loses). With two-person zero-sum games, if we enrich the choice of strategies in certain ways, there is always at least one equilibrium outcome (and a convenient decision rule, the "minimax" rule).

Two-person zero-sum games are theoretically important but of less practical interest. Few choice problems facing humans, in spite of what is sometimes said about love and war, are genuine zero-sum or strictly competitive games. The class of "positive-sum" games is of greater interest for understanding human interaction. Here we must distinguish between situations where the interests or aims of individuals do not conflict at all, and situations of "mixed conflict" where there is some (but not complete) conflict. Situations with no conflict are games of "pure coordination" (e.g., the choice to drive on the right or the left of the road). With such problems it is thought to be desirable that outcomes not only be in equilibrium but also that they be "optimal" or "efficient" in a particular sense attributed to Pareto, the second important possible property of outcomes. An outcome is *Pareto efficient* if and only if there is no change that would improve one person's situation with-

out at the same time making another worse off. In other words, if an outcome is efficient in this sense, any change will make another worse off. In coordination games equilibria will often be efficient or "optimal" in this sense.

More troubling and perplexing are a variety of "mixed" games, with some conflict of interests. The well-known Prisoner's Dilemma (PD) is an example of such a game. A two-person PD is any situation facing two individuals, each with a choice of two acts or strategies, with four possible outcomes valued in a certain way. If we label the strategies "cooperate" and "defect," or "C" and "D," then the outcomes are such that each individual prefers joint cooperation (C, C) to joint defection (D, D). But each most prefers the outcome where he or she defects and the other cooperates (D, C) and least prefers the outcome where he or she cooperates and the other defects (C, D). In PDs played once, on the received conception of rationality (as well as many others), it is rational to defect whatever the other does. The result, then, is (D, D), an outcome which is an equilibrium but which is not Pareto efficient: (C, C) is mutually preferred to (D, D). Some find this result (and others like it) troubling – rational individuals do less well than they might. Others blame the situation or context and recommend that we focus our attention on the setting of choice (e.g., institutions). Yet others point to the fact that some PDs may have outcomes that are desirable to others (e.g., economic competition). It is games like these that may prove to be of most interest to students of economics and business. For instance, recently the idea of "corporate culture" has been fruitfully explored using game-theoretic models of "reputation" and related notions.

Bibliography

Axelrod, R. (1984). *The Evolution of Cooperation*. New York: Basic Books.
Eatwell, J., Milgate, M., and Newman, P. (1989). *Game Theory, The New Palgrave*. New York: W. W. Norton. (A useful set of articles from the new edition of the famous encyclopedia of economics.)
Fudenberg, D. and Tirole, J. (1992). *Game Theory*. Cambridge, MA: MIT Press. (Advanced text.)
Kreps, D. M. (1990). *Game Theory and Economic Modelling*. Oxford: Clarendon Press. (An accessible introduction, relatively non-mathematical.)

Schelling, T. C. (1967). What is Game Theory? In *Choice and Consequence*. Cambridge, MA: Harvard University Press, 213–42. (Introductory article, by a great writer.)

glass ceiling

Patricia G. Smith

A metaphor that refers to the invisible barrier that blocks the advancement of women and minorities to upper-level leadership positions, especially in the world of business. This phenomenon can be reported objectively as a statistical fact. It was noted in the early 1970s that although women and minorities had been entering the workforce in record numbers for over a decade, very few were able to progress to middle- or upper-level management. The EEOC (Equal Employment Opportunity Commission) reported in 1966 that while over 40 percent of white-collar jobs were held by women, their representation in upper-level management was so small as to be statistically insignificant. *Harvard Business Review*'s 1964 study concluded: "the barriers [for women in upper management] are so great there is scarcely anything to study." Not surprisingly, at that time many experts urged patience. Without denying that discrimination was a factor of concern, it does take time, they suggested, for any group to work its way up through the ranks.

Twenty years later little progress is apparent. In 1987 the US Department of Labor published a report – *Workforce 2000* – that brought attention to dramatic changes in the workforce, including almost 50 percent participation by women overall, the fastest-growing segment being married women of childbearing age, and especially mothers of preschool children. Yet the level of participation in upper management has remained virtually unchanged. A 1990 survey of the country's 1,000 largest corporations (*see* KORN/FERRY, 1990) reported that women and minorities now hold less than 5 percent of executive positions, representing a growth rate of less than 2 percent since 1979. This statistic has not changed in the most recent 1994 survey. The existence of the glass ceiling is clear, but its nature is nebulous and its causes controversial.

Insofar as it is the product of overt discrimination it is prohibited by law and actionable, if it can be proven. But much of the problem today seems to be a manifestation of subtle forces and pervasive presumptions that are very difficult to pinpoint in particular circumstances. Prejudices abound. For example, it is widely held that single women are bad investments for leadership training because they are more interested in marriage than a career (despite the fact that few women today stop working when they marry); and that women of childbearing age are similarly bad risks because they are likely to get pregnant (despite the fact that professional women take no more time off for pregnancy than men take for sick leave). Many executives claim that women and minorities do not make it to the upper ranks because they lack the characteristics needed for leadership positions. A number of studies have corroborated this attitude. One, for example (Basil, 1972), asked for a ranking of personal characteristics necessary for effective upper management and received the following top five: Decisiveness, Consistency and Objectivity, Emotional Stability, Analytical Ability, Perceptiveness and Empathy. All five of these characteristics were perceived by the executives and students surveyed as more common in men than in women. Thus, women as a class were perceived as lacking in leadership qualities, in drive and motivation, in strength and decisiveness. Similar studies have reviewed attitudes about minorities with similar results (e.g., Dickens and Dickens, 1982). The lack of scientific evidence for such attitudes in no way reduces their effects. And the perceptions are self-verifying. If women and minorities are preconceived as lacking leadership qualities, then they will quite naturally be passed over for the highest positions and channeled into support services. They will not be leaders, so they will not be perceived as leaders. Recent reports of the Department of Labor (Martin, 1991; and in 1994) noted that typical selection and grooming procedures for upper-level management, conducted by personal recommendation, informal meetings, and networking, tends to disadvantage women and minorities who remain outside the network. Yet no discrimination is verifiable in such circumstances. It is likely to be unconscious. Business leaders tend to select and groom successors who are more or less like themselves, and they perceive women and minorities as importantly different. For those being judged before they have a chance to perform, this creates and maintains an invisible barrier: the glass ceiling.

Bibliography

Basil, D. C. (1972). *Women in Management*. New York: Dunleen.
Catalyst (1983). *Barriers to Women's Upward Mobility: Corporate Managers Speak Out*. New York: Catalyst.
Catalyst (1990). *Catalyst's Study of Women in Corporate Management*. New York: Catalyst.
Dickens, F. and Dickens, J. (1982). *The Black Manager*. New York: American Management Association.
Korn/Ferry International and UCLA's Anderson Graduate School of Management (1990). *Korn/Ferry International's Executive Profile 1990: A Survey of Corporate Leaders*. New York: Korn Ferry International.
Martin, L. (Secretary of Labor) (1991). *Report on the Glass Ceiling Initiative*. Washington, DC: US Department of Labor.

global warming

Joseph R. DesJardins

The consequences of a build-up in a variety of "greenhouse gases" in the earth's upper atmosphere. These gases, primarily water vapor and carbon dioxide, along with trace amounts of ozone, methane, nitrous oxide, and chlorofluorocarbons (CFCs), trap heat within the atmosphere, much as the glass in a greenhouse functions to allow warming sunlight in while preventing the warmer air from escaping.

The issue of global warming generated extensive political and ethical debates beginning in the 1980s. Some observers claimed that human activities, primarily associated with burning fossil fuels in automobiles and industry, were significantly adding to the amount of carbon dioxide in the atmosphere. According to these observers, an increase in greenhouse gases would lead to global warming which, in turn, would cause considerable environmental damage and human suffering. As a result, these observers recommended policy changes to minimize the use of fossil fuels and otherwise limit the discharge of greenhouse gases. Critics replied by challenging the existence of the greenhouse effect, the fact of global warming, and the catastrophic predictions based on the alleged fact of global warming.

To understand these issues, it is therefore important to distinguish between the greenhouse effect, global warming, and the environmental and social consequences of such warming. The "greenhouse effect" is well-confirmed through observation and experiments over the past century and is now the prevailing scientific explanation of the atmosphere's role in regulating the earth's temperature. There is no serious scientific dispute about the reality of the greenhouse effect and the critical role of water vapor and carbon dioxide in causing this effect.

While some controversy lingered concerning the increase in atmospheric levels of greenhouse gases, there is little scientific dispute any longer on this issue. Measurements have demonstrated that the concentration of atmospheric carbon dioxide has increased significantly since the industrial revolution and now exists at levels unsurpassed in hundreds of thousands, if not millions, of years. Fossil fuel use in automobiles, electric utilities, industry, and home heating is primarily responsible for the increase in carbon dioxide. At the same time, worldwide deforestation has decreased nature's ability to remove atmospheric carbon dioxide through photosynthesis.

Controversy also continued around the allegation that *global warming* was resulting from the build-up of greenhouse gases. The evidence now seems to demonstrate that global warming is indeed occurring. In 2001 the United States National Climate Data Center, a body of the National Oceanic and Atmospheric Administration, confirmed that global surface temperatures have in fact increased by 0.6°C since the late nineteenth century and 0.4°C over the past 25 years. While global warming has not been uniform across the globe, worldwide the two warmest years on record are 1998 and 2001, and nine of the ten warmest years since record-keeping began in the mid-nineteenth century have occurred since 1990. This increase of global temperature closely parallels the increase in atmospheric greenhouse gases.

The ecological, climatic, and human effects of global warming remain unknown. Many variables could affect the future consequences of global warming. The climatic role played by oceans, the polar ice caps, and clouds, as well as human decisions concerning pollution, deforestation, fossil-fuel use, and agriculture, all have the potential for either increasing or decreasing global warming. A worst-case scenario predicts a rise in ocean levels due to melting of snow and ice in the earth's polar regions, climatic shifts, worldwide droughts and famine, and massive extinctions of plant and animal life. A best-case scenario would include a gradual adaptation to higher temperatures through shifts in population and agricultural centers.

Ethical issues raised by global warming include responsibility to future generations, justice questions concerning the allocation and distribution of resources and risks, responsibility to non-human life, and respect for the natural world. More generally, the question of how one ought to act and what public policies are appropriate in the face of scientific uncertainty about great risk, or what is sometimes called the precautionary principle, is particularly pertinent when considering global warming.

Bibliography

Brown, D. (2002). *American Heat: Ethical Problems With the United States' Response to Global Warming*. Lanham, MD: Rowman and Littlefield.

Houghton, J. T., et. al. (eds.) (2001). *The Scientific Basis of Climate Change: Third Assessment Report of the Intergovernmental Panel on Climate Change*. Cambridge: Cambridge University Press.

Drake, F. (2000). *Global Warming: The Science of Climate Change*. New York: Oxford University Press.

National Climatic Data Center (2003). *Global Warming*. Washington, DC: National Oceanic and Atmospheric Administration.

globalization

Georges Enderle

In recent years the debate on globalization has become widespread and highly controversial as it explores what globalization is, how it impacts the world, and what it should be (e.g., Stiglitz, 2002). Given all these controversies, the often-evoked image of the world as a "global village" seems rather innocent, harmless, and misleading, although it correctly points to the increasing interconnectedness of the world, due to an immense reduction in the cost of transportation and communication.

Globalization can be understood as a kind of international system in the making. It is "not simply a trend or a fad but is, rather, an international system . . . that has now replaced the old Cold War system, and . . . has its own rules and logic that today directly or indirectly influence the politics, environment, geopolitics and economics of virtually every country in the world" (Friedman, 2000: ix). Although economic globalization is of paramount importance and the main focus of this article, it would be shortsighted to conceive globalization in exclusively economic terms. This system in the making is about "global transformations" in the plural (Held et al. 1999; Held and McGrew, 2000, 2002), including political, cultural, and environmental globalization, migration, and the expanding reach of organized violence.

There are two different approaches to globalization: the first describes and analyses its actual objectives, its rules and logic, its activities and outcomes; the second evaluates these objectives, rules, logic, activities, and outcomes in normative-ethical terms. Therefore, disagreements about globalization can arise on many fronts. Among them are included the following: how these transformations are perceived; how they actually work; how they impact on the world; whether this international system in the making is a fate beyond the realm of human responsibility; if, however, globalization is a human construct, then who and what institutions should be held accountable; according to what ethical standards ought they to be evaluated; and what are the results of such evaluation. The following discusses basic features of economic globalization and reflects on its ethical implications.

The goal of economic globalization can be understood as the widest geographic extension possible of international economic integration, either as a process or a state of affairs, that moves beyond provincial, sectoral, national, and regional (i.e., transnational but less than global) integration. What is often called globalization relates, in fact, only to the triad of the United States, European Union, and Japan, at the factual exclusion of the rest of the world.

Taking the world as a single place, globalization's essential criterion is commonly seen in the equality of prices of equal goods and equal services (Machlup, 1977) and includes three necessary conditions: (1) division of labor, (2) mobility of goods and factors of production or both, and (3) non-discrimination in the treatment of goods and factors (with regard to origin, destination, etc.). Since all economic activities are conceived to be (virtually or actually) interrelated and interdependent, all economic actors in charge of planning and allocation must make their calculations on the basis of opportunity costs (i.e., the costs associated with not choosing the alternative option). As long as prices of equal items in any market (of goods, services, labor, capital, currencies) are different, the pursuit of economic efficiency and competition tends to equalize those prices.

In view of this overarching goal, the role of markets and competition has gained paramount importance in the international arena, entailing multiple and far-reaching processes of deregulation, liberalization, and privatization. At the same time, powerful multinational corporations have vigorously pushed forward these processes, thus justifying the qualification of globalization as "corporate driven."

While this general picture of economic globalization needs several qualifications, it has a strong empirical basis. Since the 1950s, an array of internationalization processes have integrated in a more systematic fashion, covering a large set of parameters including inter-country investment, production, marketing, and trade, and increased interfirm alliances and collaboration, often due to the importance of research and development and its interconnection with globalization (UN, 1991–). These recent developments are paralleled by international agreements on trade and investment (GATT, etc.), the creation of the World Trade Organization (WTO) in 1995, reform discussions about the International Monetary Fund (IMF) and World Bank (WB), and a host of other initiatives.

If one looks at the empirical evidence of the economic impact of globalization (which, overall, is not easy to establish), one finds a mixed picture that falsifies each of the two familiar slogans, namely that "with globalization, the world is a better place" and that "because of globalization, the rich get richer and the poor get poorer." It seems fair to state that, by and large, the impact of globalization has been beneficial in East Asia and China while detrimental to the Islamic world, Sub-Saharan Africa, and the environment. The poverty statistics of the World Bank show, from 1987 to 1999, an increase of the poor worldwide from 2.549 billion to 2.777 billion (when "poor" is defined as living on $2 or less per person per day), but a decrease of the poor worldwide from 1.183 to 1.151 billion (when "poor" is defined as living on $1 or less per person per day). Rich sources of information are the *World Development Reports* by the World Bank (WB, 1978–) and the *Human Development Reports* by the United Nations Development Program (UNDP, 1990–).

In order to understand and evaluate economic globalization, one has to investigate and account for not only economic activities and their impact, but also the institutions and the rules (or "the system") that govern and should govern these activities and consequences. (Similarly, in sports such as football or baseball, it goes without saying that the game consists of both the institutional setting with the rules and the playing of the players.) Hence the institution and the rules of the market are at stake.

It is useful to recall the strengths and weaknesses of the market in the domestic context of industrialized countries in order to investigate the question of what markets can and cannot provide in the international arena. Free and competitive markets, properly regulated, provide freedom to economic actors (individuals, organizations, and countries). They have an equalizing impact insofar as they are based on economic performance, expressed by the price system, as distinct from non-economic characteristics such as race, gender, religion, and nationality. They improve efficiency, promote innovation, and advance economic growth. At the same time, from economic theory and practical experience we know that economic growth is not necessarily sustainable in environmental terms. Markets by themselves cannot ensure an acceptable distribution of economic opportunities or results. Even if they are perfect, they fail in providing public goods. Moreover, some markets, particularly in the areas of labor, basic healthcare, and education, are inherently unreliable at maximizing aggregate output in these areas (Turner, 2001).

Given these strengths and weaknesses of the markets in the domestic realm, these same factors must be taken seriously in the shaping of economic globalization as well. Global markets need global institutions which should not only enhance freedom, efficiency, and economic growth. They should also promote sustainability and distributive justice, provide international public goods that are essential for living and collaborating in the "global village," strengthen fairness in labor markets, and ensure basic healthcare and education. The lessons learned in the domestic realm should be applied to "the international system in the making" in general and to economic globalization in particular. Global institutions and rules, supported and adapted at the local, regional, and national levels, are necessary in order to make economic globalization acceptable to the world population. The standards have to be fair, effective, democratic, and sustainable. However, by and large, these standards are not met by the present global institutional setting, including the IMF, WB, WTO, International Labor Organization (ILO), World Health Organization (WHO) and UNESCO.

While these four standards are essential to the creation of effective global institutions, they do not suffice single-handedly to make economic globalization succeed because the successful "game" depends not only on the quality of the rules but also on how "the players play." First and foremost, it is the moral responsibility of the "big players," that is, powerful nation-states, unions of states, and multinational corporations, to shape globalization, as indicated earlier. This enormous task includes two simultaneous tracks:

1   The big players have to direct their own conduct toward the goal of globalization "with a human face." Hence, on the part of business, initiatives such as UN Global Compact, Global Reporting Initiative, and Caux Principles for Business should be vigorously supported and advanced.
2   The big players must be determined to fairly participate in the establishment of the necessary global institutions, as outlined earlier, complementing this valuable kind of self-regulation.

Global institutions cannot be built and major actors in globalization cannot fulfill their responsibilities without universal ethical standards and a common ethical ground. Fortunately, in recent years, we have witnessed many important initiatives (CPWR, 1993; ID, 1994; CRT, 1994; Williams, 2002) and numerous publications (Donaldson, 1989; De George, 1993; Enderle, 1999; Singer, 2002) which struggle with the ethics of globalization. Of particular interest is Amartya Sen's work *Development as Freedom* (1999), in which the author offers universal ethical standards which are based on a sound philosophical foundation and can be measured and applied to assess policies of governments, international institutions, and multinational corporations. The standards are "real freedoms that people enjoy," substantiated in five interrelated types of freedoms: political freedoms, economic facilities, social opportunities, transparency guarantees, and protective security. Despite the tremendous complexities of the world, this perspective of "real freedoms" appears to indicate the direction for globalization "with a human face."

Bibliography

An Interfaith Declaration (ID): A Code of Ethics on International Business for Christians, Muslims and Jews (1994). Reproduced in *Business Ethics – A European Review*, 5, 1 (January 1996).

Caux Round Table (CRT) (1994). *Principles for Business*. www.cauxroundtable.org.

Council for a Parliament of World's Religions (CPWR) (1993). *Towards a Global Ethic (An Initial Declaration)*. Chicago.

De George, R. T. (1993). *Competing with Integrity in International Business*. New York: Oxford University Press.

Donaldson, T. (1989). *The Ethics of International Business*. New York: Oxford University Press.

Enderle, G. (ed.) (1999). *International Business Ethics: Challenges and Approaches*. Notre Dame, IN: University of Notre Dame Press.

Friedman, T. L. (2000). *The Lexus and the Olive Tree*. New York: Anchor Books.

Global Reporting Initiative (GRI). www.globalreporting.org.

Held, D. and McGrew, A. (eds.) (2000). *The Global Transformations Reader*. Cambridge: Polity Press.

Held, D. and McGrew, A. (eds.) (2002). *Governing Globalization: Power, Authority and Global Governance*. Cambridge: Polity Press.

Held, D., McGrew, A., Goldblatt, D., and Perraton, J. (1999). *Global Transformations: Politics, Economics and Culture*. Stanford, CA: Stanford University Press.

Kaul, I., Grunberg, I., and Stern, M. A. (eds.) (1999). *Global Public Goods: International Cooperation in the 21st Century*. New York: United Nations Development Program.

Machlup, F. (1977). *A History of Thought on Economic Integration*. New York: Columbia University Press.

Sen, A. (1999). *Development as Freedom*. New York: Knopf.

Singer, P. (2002). *One World: The Ethics of Globalization*. New Haven, CT: Yale University Press.

Stiglitz, J. E. (2002). *Globalization and Its Discontents*. New York: Norton.

Turner, A. (2001). *Just Capital: The Liberal Economy*. London: Macmillan.

United Nations (UN) (1991–). *World Investment Report*. Annually. New York: United Nations.

UN Global Compact. www.unglobalcompact.org.

United Nations Development Program (UNDP) (1990–). *Human Development Report*. Annually. New York: Oxford University Press.

Williams, O. F. (ed.) (2000). *Global Codes of Conduct: An Idea Whose Time Has Come*. Notre Dame, IN: University of Notre Dame Press.

World Bank (WB) (1978–). *World Development Report*. Annually. Washington, DC: World Bank and Oxford University Press.

World Bank (WB) (2002). *Globalization, Growth, and Poverty: Building an Inclusive World Economy*. New York: Oxford University Press.

H

hazardous waste

Laura Westra

is waste (solids, sludges, liquids, and container-ized gases) other than radioactive (and infectious) waste, which, by reason of its chemical activity or toxic, explosive, corrosive, or other characteristics, causes danger or likely will cause danger to health or the environment, either alone or when coming in contact with other wastes. "Waste" here refers to a movable object that has no direct use and is discarded permanently (Lagrega, Buckingham, and Evans, 1994). Wastes are an unintended byproduct of production processes. With the increasing use of toxic substances in production (both goods and services), many wastes are hazardous to human health and the natural environment. The definition of what exactly constitutes "hazardous" waste is highly debated and varies widely, depending on the country's laws. Most industrialized nations have laws (developed in the past 20 years) defining hazardous wastes, and specifying mechanisms for their containment, transportation, and disposal (Shrivastava, 1995; UNCLOS, 1982; Basel Convention and Related Legal Rules, 1995; UN Commission on Human Rights, 2001).

However, even the existence of numerous covenants and agreements among states has not slowed, let alone eliminated, this global problem, the results of which continue to inflict harm on human health and "physical integrity" (European Court of Human Rights, 1998). The harm is both direct and indirect, the latter affecting human beings through significant and often irreversible alterations to our habitat (Karr, 2000; Noss, 2000; Loucks, 2000: 177–90). This dual assault represents a significant assault on basic human rights (Shue, 1996) and it also carries within it a strong component of injustice for both the present populations of developing countries (Rees and Westra, 2003: 99–124) and for future generations (Westra, 2004). It also represents an attack on democratic values (1998 Arhus Convention on Public Participation; Postiglione, 2001).

Basic human rights to both security and subsistence (Shue, 1996) are under attack because of the health consequences of (a) transporting and (b) disposing of hazardous wastes when the ultimate disposal site is in a developing country. The transport itself is a hazard, but ultimately, both result in substantive harms, especially to impoverished vulnerable populations in North America (Westra, 2001) and in developing countries (Gbadegesin, 2001). As Barlow and Clarke suggest, we should be drawing a clear "line around the commons," as there are "certain goods and services that should not be traded, commodified, patented and privatized in the global economy," particularly "toxic waste and nuclear arms waste" (2002: 182).

In addition, turning ecosystems into brownfields to continue previous hazardous industrial practices, and to house hazardous wastes, also destroys the capacity of these natural systems to sustain life (Daily, 1997) and provide food for the overwhelming numbers of impoverished, famine-stricken populations (Pogge, 2001). Thus, the production of hazardous wastes is one of the clearest examples of the fact that "market transactions have consequences that are not limited to those who choose to engage in them" (Daly and Cobb, 1989: 52).

The existence of these threats has emphasized the need for environmental rights, such as claims to a "decent, healthy or viable environment," codified by Principle I of the 1972 Stockholm Declaration (see also 1994 UN Sub-Commission on the Prevention of Discrimination and Protection of Minorities' Declaration of Principles of Human Rights and the Environment; and Article 24 of the African Charter on Human and People's Rights). All these documents stress the interdependence of environmental rights and the fulfillment of all other human rights (Birnie and Boyle, 2002: 255).

The threats arising from hazardous waste are not clearly explained and publicized, thus the right of people to know, and hence to participate in decision-making, is also under threat (1998 Arhus Convention).

Given the common occurrence of hazardous waste being transported across borders, yet finding no country ready to accept it, we need to give serious consideration to the reduction of various forms of consumption from which the waste originates (Rees and Westra, 2003: 99–124). The emerging movement to consider and codify "ecological rights" (Taylor, 1998) demands such a step, as does the awareness of the injustice inherent in the "ecofootprint" of most Northern states, in relation to that of the South (Rees and Wackernagel, 1996). The reduction of hazardous wastes represents an immediate priority, as does the application of cleaner industrial technologies and practices, as well as regulations to eliminate completely those practices and products that depend on substances that present major health threats.

Finally, it is imperative to ensure that legal instruments are not only designed, but also enforced, to end the international trade in hazardous waste (Vallette, 1989). As corporate activities, together with military institutions, generate the greatest quantities of hazardous wastes, it is these activities we should scrutinize first, to protect the commons upon which we and future generations depend.

Bibliography

Arhus Convention on Access to Information, Public Participation in Decision-making and Access to Justice in Environmental Matters (1998). 4th UNECE Ministerial Conference.

Barile, G. (1985). Obligationes Erga Omnes e individui nel diritt internazionale umanitario. *Rivista di Diritto Internazionale*, **68** (5), 17–27.

Barlow, M. and Clarke, T. (2002). *Global Showdown*. Toronto: Stoddard Publishing.

Battin, M. P. (1996). The way we do it, the way they do it. In T. Mappes and D. De Grazia (eds.), *Biomedical Ethics*, 4th edn. New York: McGraw Hill, 393–400.

Birnie, P. W. and Boyle, A. (2002). *International Law and the Environment*, 2nd edn. Oxford: Oxford University Press.

Boyd, D. R. (2003). *Unnatural Law: Rethinking Canadian Environmental Law and Policy*. Vancouver: University of British Columbia Press.

Bridgeford, T. A. (2003). Imputing human rights obligations on multinational corporations: The ninth circuit strikes again in judicial activism. *American University International Law Review*, 18, 1009.

Callicott, J. B. (1989). *In Defense of the Land Ethic*. New York: State University of New York Press.

Christensen, R. L. (2002). Canada's drinking problem, Walkerton, water contamination and public policy. In S. C. Boyd, D. E. Chunn and R. Menzies (eds.), *Toxic Criminology*. Halifax: Fernwood Publishing, 97–111.

Daily, G. (1997). *Nature's Services*. Washington, DC: Island Press, 3–4.

Daly H. and Cobb, J. B., Jr. (1989). *For the Common Good*. Boston, MA: Beacon Press.

Gbadegesin, S. (2001). Multinational corporations, developed nations and environmental racism: Toxic waste, oil explorations and ecocatastrophes. In L. Westra and B. Lawson (eds.), *Faces of Environmental Racism*, 2nd edn. Lanham, MD: Rowman and Littlefield, 187–202.

European Court of Human Rights (1998). *Guerra vs. Italy*. Judgment of February 19. *Reports of Judgments and Decisions* 1998-I, § 57.

Hannikainen, L. (1988). *Peremptory Norms (Jus Cogens) in International Law – Historical Development, Criteria, Present Status*. Helsinki: Coronet Books.

Harrington, C. (2002). *Doe vs. Unocal Corp.*, 2002 WL 31063976 (9th Cir.2002). *Tulane Environmental Law Journal*, 16, 247–9.

Herman, E. S. and Chomsky, N. (2002). *Manufacturing Consent*. New York: Pantheon Books, Random House.

Hurrell, A. and Kingsbury, B. (1992). *The International Politics of the Environment*. Oxford: Oxford University Press.

Karr, J. R. (2000). Health, integrity and biological assessment: The importance of measuring whole things. In D. Pimente, L. Westra, and R. F. Noss (eds.), *Ecological Integrity: Integrating Environment, Conservation and Health*. Washington, DC: Island Press, 209–26.

Kummer, K. (1992). The international regulation of transboundary traffic in hazardous wastes: The 1989 Basel Convention, 41 ICLQ 530.

Lagrega, M. D., Buckingham, P. L., and Evans, J. C. (1994). *Hazardous Waste Management*. New York: McGraw-Hill.

Loucks, O. L. (2000). Pattern of forest integrity in the Eastern United States and Canada: Measuring loss and recovery. In D. Pimentel, L. Westra, and R. F. Noss (eds.), *Ecological Integrity: Integrating Environment, Conservation and Health*. Washington, DC: Island Press, 177–90.

Meron, T. (1986). *Human Rights Law-Making in the United Nations*. Oxford: Clarendon Press.

Meron, T. (1989). *Human Rights and Humanitarian Norms as Customary Law*. Oxford: Clarendon Press.

Noss, R. (2000). Maintaining the ecological integrity of landscapes and ecoregions. In *Ecological Integrity* 191–208.

Pogge, T. W. (2001). *Global Justice*. Oxford: Blackwell.

Postiglione, A. (2001). *Giustizia e Ambiente Globale*. Milan: Giuffrè Editore.

Provost, R. (2002). *International Human Rights and Humanitarian Law*. Cambridge: Cambridge University Press.

Rees, W. and Westra, L. (2003). When consumption does violence: Can there be sustainability and environmental justice in a resource limited world? In J. Agyeman, R. Bullard and B. Evans (eds.), *Just Sustainabilities*. London: Earthscan, 99–124.

Ridenour, A. (2001). Doe vs. Unocal Corporation, Apples and Oranges: Why courts should use international standards to determine liability for violations of the law of nations under the Alien Tort Claims Act. *Tulane Journal of International and Comparative Law*, 9, 581.

Scott, J. (2000). On kith and kine (and crustaceans):Trade and environment in the EU and the WTO. In J. Weiler (ed.), *The EU, the WTO and the NAFTA*. Oxford: Oxford University Press, 129–68.

Shrivastava, P. (1995). *Greening Business: Profiting Corporations and the Environment*. Cincinnati, OH: Thompson Executive Press.

Shue, H. (1996). *Basic Rights: Subsistence, Affluence and American Public Policy*. Princeton, NJ: Princeton University Press.

UN Commission on Human Rights (2001). 57th Session, Report on the adverse effect of the illicit movement and dumping of toxic and dangerous products and wastes on the enjoyment of human rights, UN Doc. E/CN.4/2001/55.

UNCLOS (1982). United Nations Conference on the Law of the Sea, Article 87 (2), 194 (2); 194 (1).

Vallette, J. (1989). *The International Trade in Waste: A Greenpeace Inventory*. Washington, DC: Greenpeace.

Westra, L. (2001). The faces of environmental racism: Titusville, Alabama, and BFI. In L. Westra and B. Lawson (eds.), *Faces of Environmental Racism*, 2nd edn. Place? Publisher? 113–40.

Westra, L. (2004). *Ecoviolence and the Law: Supranational, Normative Foundations of Ecocrime*. Ardsley, NY: Transnational Publishers.

healthcare ethics and business ethics

Ann E. Mills and Andrew C. Wicks

Healthcare ethics, which is a more specialized branch of the field widely known as bioethics, deals with ethical issues that arise in the healthcare setting. Some of the more significant subjects in healthcare ethics are the moral traditions and directives of healthcare workers, the healthcare worker–patient relationship, the rights and responsibilities of patients, access to healthcare, and the allocation of resources (Beauchamp and Childress, 1994).

One of the most interesting similarities between the fields of healthcare ethics and business ethics is their relatively recent emergence. A wide array of writings dating from ancient times can be found on ethics in both business and medicine. The writings and traditions of medicine, in particular, have a rich and extensive grounding in ethics. However, it is only within the past 40 years that both business ethics and bioethics have become distinct academic disciplines, which also correspond to wider social movements designed to reshape their respective practices.

Although it is difficult to determine precisely when they came into being, the "birth of bioethics" has been traced by historians and bioethicists to 1962, when a Seattle hospital faced the problem of allocating a scarce life-saving medical treatment (kidney dialysis) (Jonsen, 1993). Business ethics is a newer field and has no such defining moment. In the US it has origins in the movement for corporate social responsibility in the 1970s, and Watergate, and developed critical mass during the 1980s amid the popular reaction to the perceived excesses of that period – what some commentators called the decade of greed.

Numerous theories have been put forward as to why these movements have taken root. The factor that seems to be most commonly cited by researchers as the impetus for their emergence is the pluralistic character of modern American culture. However, there is considerable disagreement as to whether the diversity of values that allegedly gives rise to the need for business ethics and bioethics represents a healthy culture or a society in a state of moral decay (MacIntyre, 1988; Stout, 1988; Walzer, 1983). Other factors that have been cited include the increasing complexity of society (as well as healthcare and business), broader social changes, the rapid expansion of technology, the increased effectiveness and importance of medical treatment, and the growing influence of business on medicine. Finally, as these movements have grown, there is an ongoing ambiguity about the appropriate role for ethicists, particularly as they are being drawn into more practice-related roles as consultants and policy advisors. The question of what "expertise" ethicists have has been raised, but the status and function of ethicists is far from resolved in either field.

Another connection between business ethics and healthcare ethics is the alleged influence of business on the practice of medicine. This has become particularly evident in the past several decades. A number of studies have indicated a powerful interaction between medicine and business, especially as healthcare becomes more dependent on high technology, pharmaceuticals, private medical insurance, and other resources which are both directly and indirectly connected to business (Starr, 1982).

While there is disagreement regarding the extent to which business has reshaped medicine, there is widespread agreement that business has become an increasingly powerful influence in how medicine is practiced. E. Haavi Morreim (1992) has argued that the traditional model of the healthcare encounter found in the Hippocratic tradition, that of a doctor and patient, has been under pressure to change for some time and must include a wider array of interested parties or stakeholders in healthcare related decision-making. Private businesses, which provide the technology and resources that enable healthcare workers to provide care, are among the array of groups she believes deserve a legitimate role in how healthcare resources are allocated and delivered. Some authors have argued that the increasing influence of business is an alarming recent trend. Implicit in their argument is a belief that medicine has retained much of its distinctiveness and independence from business (Relman, 1992; Dougherty, 1990). However, as healthcare costs rise and the use of technology increases it appears that this interaction will be

expanding for the foreseeable future. As a result, it will be increasingly difficult to sharply distinguish healthcare from business; both at the institutional level and in terms of practitioners. Evidence for this can be found in the mission statements and practices of a number of health-related businesses, particularly the pharmaceutical industry.

There are also alleged connections between the central moral norms of both fields. Although little has been done to compare the moral traditions and concepts which structure the inquiry of ethicists in both fields, recent research makes a case that there are fundamental similarities between the two (Wicks, 1995a). Furthermore, if one can make a case that the line between healthcare and health-related businesses is becoming blurred, then it strengthens the basis for connecting the normative core of each field. Some authors are deeply suspicious of business and fear the traditions of medicine will be eroded or destroyed by any wholesale interaction between these institutions and their respective ethics (Relman, 1992; Dougherty, 1990). Others argue that a comprehensive meshing of (the ethics of) medicine and business (ethics) is necessary to serve the needs of society (Morreim, 1992; Agich, 1990; Wicks, 1995b).

Evidence that the latter view is becoming more widely accepted is provided by the Joint Commission for Accreditation of Healthcare Organizations (JCAHO). The JCAHO evaluates and accredits more than 15,000 healthcare organizations in the US. JCAHO accreditation, or equivalent accreditation from another accrediting agency, is a requirement for Medicaid and Medicare reimbursement. Thus, healthcare organizations, particularly hospitals, have strong financial incentives to incorporate JCAHO standards in their decision-making and practices.

Until 1995 the healthcare ethics standards promulgated by JCAHO focused on individual patient rights and responsibilities. In 1995 a new section was added: "Standards for Organization Ethics." These standards focused on a set of issues that had not been fully addressed by the usual healthcare regulatory mechanisms. These included "business" issues, like billing, patient transfers, and marketing, as well as contractual issues, and professional relationships both within and beyond the healthcare organization. JCAHO directed all healthcare organizations it accredits to pay attention to the likely effect of these issues on patient care and to align their practices in ways that reflected their commitment to their core values (Joint Commission, 1995).

A broader more process-oriented definition of healthcare organization ethics has since been advanced: "Organization ethics consists of [a set of] processes to address ethical issues associated with the business, financial, and management areas of healthcare organizations, as well as with professional, educational, and contractual relationships affecting the operation of the healthcare organization" (Spencer et al., 2000: 212). This definition encompasses all aspects of the operation of the healthcare organization and includes the articulation, application, and evaluation of the organization's mission and values statements. However, both approaches to "organization ethics" for healthcare acknowledge that the line between healthcare and health-related businesses has become blurred. Both approaches insist that healthcare organizations pay attention to these relationships by creating a positive ethical climate throughout the healthcare organization.

A positive ethical climate has at least two important characteristics. First, it is an organizational culture in which the mission and vision of the organization inform the expectations for professional and managerial performance and are implemented in the actual practices of the organization. Second, a positive ethical climate embodies a set of values that reflect societal norms for what the organization should value, how they should prioritize their mission, vision, and goals, and how the organization and the individuals associated with it should behave (Spencer et al., 2000). Since a positive ethical climate directs attention to the values and ideals associated with the intersection of the management, clinical, and professional roles of the healthcare organization, encompassing healthcare activities as well as healthcare business activities, a positive ethical climate may provide the basis for connecting the normative core of each field.

Finally, both fields are influenced by other disciplines. Philosophy and religious studies have proven to be particularly important resources to develop vibrant accounts of applied ethics. More specifically, business ethicists and bioethicists draw on these broader resources to develop a more systematic base from which to generate moral insights or theories that can be related to specific human activities.

Bibliography

Agich, G. (1990). Medicine as a business and profession. *Theoretical Medicine*, 11, 311–24.

Beauchamp, T. L. and Childress, J. F. (1994). *Principles of Biomedical Ethics*, 3rd edn. New York: Oxford University Press.

Dougherty, C. (1990). The cost of commercial medicine. *Theoretical Medicine*, 11, 275.

Joint Commission for Accreditation of Healthcare Organizations (1995). *Patient Rights and Organization Ethics: Comprehensive Manual for Hospitals.* Joint Commission for Accreditation of Healthcare Organizations.

Jonsen, A. R. (1993). The birth of bioethics. Special supplement of the *Hastings Center Report*, November/December, S1–15.

MacIntyre, A. (1988). *After Virtue*, 2nd edn. Notre Dame, IN: University of Notre Dame Press.

Morreim, E. H. (1992). *The New Medical Ethics of Medicine's New Economics.* New York: Klewter.

Reich, W. T. (ed.) (1978). *Encyclopedia of Bioethics.* New York: Free Press.

Relman, A. (1992). What market values are doing to medicine. *Atlantic Monthly*, March, 106.

Spencer, E., Mills, A., Rorty. M., and Werhane, P. (2000). *Organization Ethics for Healthcare Organizations.* New York: Oxford University Press.

Starr, P. (1982). *The Social Transformation of American Medicine.* New York: Basic Books.

Stout, J. (1988). *Ethics After Babel.* Boston, MA: Beacon Press.

Walzer, M. (1983). *Spheres of Justice.* New York: Basic Books.

Wicks, A. C. (1995a). Albert Schweitzer or Ivan Boesky? Why should we reject the dichotomy between medicine and business? *Journal of Business Ethics*, 14 (5), 6339–51.

Wicks, A. C. (1995b). The business ethics movement: Where are we headed and what can we learn from our colleagues in bioethics? *Business Ethics Quarterly*, 5 (3), 603–20.

Hinduism and business ethics

S. Prakash Sethi and Paul Steidlmeier

India and Hinduism – the dominant religion of a majority of its people – meet both the criteria of a strong culture and a history of highly developed civilization, and a deeply felt sense of morality based on religious tenets. Therefore, while on the surface India's people in general, and its business people in particular, may appear to be highly rational in their business and economic activities, and may even seem to make similar decisions to those made by business people in industrially advanced and Judeo-Christian societies of the West, it would be extremely misleading to conclude that they are similar, at least to the extent of decision-making in the economic arena, either at the macro or micro levels. The thought processes and the underlying sets of moral values in the two systems are quite dissimilar. For the same reason, two apparently inconsistent decisions, from the Western point of view, would appear quite consistent in the Indian framework because they conform to a common underlying moral rationale.

Basic Tenets of Hinduism

Hinduism, as it is practiced today, has evolved over a period of 3,000 years. In the process, it has assimilated a variety of religions and moral beliefs, as successive waves of invaders from the North, East, and West occupied the land and eventually became part of the landscape. This is why Hinduism can accommodate a wide variety of behaviors and moral rationales which, on the surface, may appear to be internally inconsistent.

Notwithstanding the bewildering varieties of religious rituals, multitudes of gods, sects, cults, and holy persons of all ilks and persuasions, most scholars of Hindu religion recognize that the doctrines of *samsara*, *karma*, and *moksha* lie at the core of Hindu philosophy (Milner, 1993). The description of the basic tenets of Hindu philosophy, in the present instance, is of necessity selectively confined to those concepts that are of particular relevance to the economic arena. *Samsara* pertains to the rebirth or the transmigration of self and has a great impact on the mode of thinking and way of life of people of the Hindu faith. *Karma* denotes fate or manifest

destiny in common parlance. It literally means "actions" or "deeds." The *law of karma* operates like a chain of causation, whereby the life of the individual self is determined by actions – the present life is the result of actions in the past life, and actions in the present life will determine the pattern for future lives. *Moksha* (*Nirvana*) refers to the liberation from the constant cycle of birth and death to become part of the ultimate infinite universe (i.e., union with God) (Uppal, 1977: 122–35).

Other concepts of Hindu religion are important in terms of their impact on the economic life and business conduct of the Indian people. These are: (a) *Dharma* – the notion of one's duty and obligation to others and to oneself, and the practice of virtue, in the discharge of life's day-to-day functions; (b) *Artha* – the acquisition of wealth for use; and (c) *Kama* – the enjoyments of the pleasures of life (Anand, 1963: 18–24).

The Hindu notions of heaven and hell are quite different to those prevailing in other religions, notably Christianity and Islam. There is no rainbow or pleasure dome at the end of the current life's journey. All actions – good and bad – are rewarded and punished in one incarnation or another; it is the soul that is everlasting, and it is the soul that seeks liberation from being trapped in the constant cycle of earthly forms. One's station in life is largely predetermined by one's actions in previous lives. *Karma* operates like an iron law of inescapable retribution. This notion acts as a coping mechanism where life's injustices and miseries, as well as possession and enjoyment of worldly goods, are accepted as part of one's fate. It provides a rational justification, propels people toward good deeds because they determine one's fate in the next life, and puts brakes on one's unbridled self-interest, for fear of retribution for bad deeds. The concept of *dharma* adds another dimension to *karma*, in that it defines one's duties and obligations to others (i.e., social hierarchy of kinship) and also suggests means for choosing among different moral values and alternative courses of action. *Dharma* is a set of moral guidelines for an individual to follow in everyday life in various spiritual aspects. Some important virtues that are stressed are truth, non-violence, sacrifice, purity, and renunciation or detachment. Great emphasis is placed on detachment from all associations with the material world (Uppal, 1977: 126–9).

Artha (wealth) and *kama* (enjoyment of life) are treated as important values that must be actively sought. They provide the vigor of the Indian entrepreneur, and the relative absence of guilt that accompanies enjoyment of life's munificence. Wealth and enjoyment of life, however, have to have a purpose, reaching toward liberation of soul or *nirvana*. *Artha* guides all acquisition and use of material means for sustaining life. The two holy books, Mahabharata and Panchatantra, illustrate Hindu philosophy toward material means and their enjoyment.

> What is here regarded as *Dharma* depends entirely upon wealth (*Artha*). One who robs another of wealth robs him of his *Dharma* as well. Poverty is a state of sinfulness. All kinds of meritorious acts flow from the possession of great wealth, as from wealth spring all religious acts, all pleasures and heaven itself... He that has no wealth has neither this world nor the next... Poverty is a curse worse than death. Virtue without wealth is of no consequence. The lack of money is the root of all evil. But material wealth is to be sought in ways consistent with the requirements of detachment or renunciation required under *Dharma* as explained above. *Kama* is the enjoyment of the appropriate objects of the five senses of hearing, feeling, seeing, tasting, and smelling, assisted by mind together with the soul. (Uppal, 1977: 129; see also Koller, 1970: 42–3)

The significance of actions raises some important questions for the sake of achieving "real-self" or *atman*: (1) Should we cease to perform actions, or in other words, is renunciation from all worldly activities the answer? (2) Is there any ordering of good actions versus bad actions? (3) Can an individual be guided to perform good actions? The answer to the first question is found in the sacred book, the Bhagavad Gita. It is maintained that action is necessary, "for no one can remain even for a moment without doing work; every one is made to act helplessly by the impulses born of nature." The crucial thing is to engage in worldly activities without becoming attached to them. "To action alone hast thou a right and never at all to its fruits; let not the fruits of action be thy motive; neither let there be any attachment to inaction. Therefore, without attachment, perform always the work that has to be done, for man attains to the highest by doing work without attachment" (Radhakrishnan, 1948: 119–38; see also Uppal, 1977: 128; Weber, 1958: 4).

HINDUISM AND CONTEMPORARY (WESTERN) BUSINESS PRACTICES AND ETHICAL NORMS

In a perfect world, Hindu religion and its followers would provide an ideal combination of attributes conducive to business development in general and ethical business conduct in particular. *Dharma* would indicate a heightened sense of duty and self-responsibility which could be counted upon as a basic value promoting people to meet their obligations, operate in a highly principled manner, and pursue the acquisition of wealth in a virtuous (fair) manner. *Karma* would suggest an acceptance of one's position in life, encourage one to regard work as a moral duty, and suggest that excellence be pursued for its own sake and not necessarily as a means to bigger financial rewards or higher status.

Wealth creation and enjoyment of means of life (*artha* and *kama*) are seen as having divine approval and should be enjoyed without any guilt or fear of opprobrium. In business conduct, especially dealing with Western types of businesses, the two concepts would imply a greater scope of cooperation and trust under conditions where the local partners visualize their gains in terms of *wealth accumulation* and *control of productive assets*, rather than being doled out as mere rewards, no matter how munificent.

While there may be common agreement as to the principles of *dharma* and *karma*, *artha* and *kama*, their interpretation takes place with a far wider latitude than is prevalent in Western work. Even more important, the degree to which different individuals would emphasize one value over the other under the Hindu philosophy is based to a greater extent on intuitive, or spiritually felt, emotions. Thus, one might find an Indian less compromising on a vaguely defined "principle" than otherwise reasonable people would consider plausible. It is not uncommon for Indians to take offense, and act almost irrationally, when they believe that a principle is at stake, or that a person has not acted in a morally responsible manner consistent with his status in life and in accordance with his stature in the social and transactional context of a given situation. Similarly, a devotion to work and separation of work from reward would make many an Indian work and excel to the extent that they might be perceived, from the point of view of a "non-Indian" socioeconomic framework, to be undermining a common level of expectations and skewing the relationship between supply and demand for services. Thus, contracts are likely to be honored; a full day's wage buys more than a full day's work; and business is conducted in a highly ethical manner. Consequently, norms of business conduct and behavior appear – at least to the uninitiated – to be inconsistent and illogical because they seem to be applied in different situations in such a manner that their rationale is not easily explained.

The other negative side-effects of Hindu philosophy are inherent in their very nature. *Karma* creates a sense of fatalism and pessimism and thus contributes to risk avoidance. It also rationalizes the inequities of a caste system which allows for exploitation of the less fortunate as a matter of divine right and the sufferers' inherent misfortune. While in times past the caste system was somewhat akin to a craft guild, with flexibility created for expertise, work specialization, and productivity gains, it also created a social order which was acceptable to the feudal system of political governance. Over time, it has become rigid and ossified, and inimical to individual growth. At the state level, it has created an ever-increasing class of "suffering minorities" seeking to codify social entitlement for an indefinite period (Dehejia and Dehejia, 1993; Milner, 1993; Mishra, 1962; Uppal, 1977).

In a business context it is not unusual for high-caste Hindus to exploit those of lower caste status with relatively little guilt or remorse. The classification also extends to social relationships. Thus, while modern businesses may easily integrate the workplace, the real integration is sometimes not easily achieved. At the social levels, groups do not seek integration or even intermingling. Where economic stakes are high, each caste is likely to create all types of subterfuges to favor its own group to the detriment of others. This phenomenon is all too apparent in any sociopolitical and economic arrangement involving power sharing or allocation of economic entitlement – jobs, for example. Only the truly uninitiated are oblivious to the subtle machinations of individuals and groups as they vie for power and influence.

Detachment of work from its reward has a number of implications for business behavior. Since work is revered for its own sake, there is often a tendency to disregard its adverse effects. Thus, poor work conditions, low pay, and other inequities may be condoned by the social system as the lot of the poor, the nature of work itself, and not the responsibility of the owner. Where responsibility is assumed, it is deemed to be a matter of conscience or good business practice rather than a moral imperative. The poor are poor because it is their fate. The rich have been chosen by the gods to accumulate wealth and do good deeds for their ultimate salvation – as it is their wont to do. One should not be surprised to find echoes of robber barons and the era of exploitative capitalism in America, where workers were ruthlessly suppressed so that capitalists could maximize surplus value and build bigger monuments to the glory of God and supremacy of Western civilization. The Taj Mahal and other monuments may inspire awe for their grand design and superb execution, but they also tell a story of untold suffering on the part of millions of craftsmen who worked and died in literal bondage to their feudal lords to glorify the latter's conquests and appeasement of gods.

Another stark example of differences between Western and Hindu notions of good works and the bearing of *karma* shows up in the domain of charitable activities. Wealthy Hindu business people would more likely spend a far bigger portion of their fortunes in building temples for their favorite gods to seek favors for the next life, rather than devote resources to helping the poor and building social institutions to help them. Socially responsible corporate behavior on the part of indigenous Indian businesses is primarily in the form of acts of charity on holy days, rather than treating the poor and disadvantaged as stakeholders deserving of help and entitled to dignity. Indian businesses, except for the Parsees (members of the Zoroastrian religious sect in India descended from Persians), are less prone to acts of civic philanthropy unless they have a religious tint.

The sense of duty or *dharma* manifests itself in a variety of ways in business conduct. At one level, it is the concept of devotion to principle, defined as one's primary obligation to one's values and social (i.e., group or kinship) responsibilities. A principle, for its own sake, is important and has propelled many a Hindu to make extreme sacrifices because to do otherwise would be a violation of *dharma*, a divine sin, and, therefore, morally repugnant. From the Western perspective, a person acting under the belief of his *dharma* is more likely to act irrationally, and is likely to make compromises to achieve a "win–win" solution. Thus an understanding of *dharma* and its situational and personal context is very important in determining the applicable norms of social behavior in a particular situation and given the particular set of people involved.

Dharma is also a fluid concept, specific to situation and person. In one case it may justify fighting and even killing one's own kin, while in another case it may justify fighting and even killing another person to protect one's own kin. The Western mind, not attuned to Indian thought processes and often applying a Western sense of cost-benefit rational analysis, could easily violate an Indian's concept of *dharma* and principle and thereby provoke a major confrontation. By the same token, *dharma* may force a person to act in ways which might violate the Western sense of social or commercial contact, although the Indian mind would feel absolved of responsibility because it was his duty to do so.

Hinduism also manifests itself in contradictory behavior of tolerance/intolerance when dealing with people of other cultures and religions. Although the Hindu religion is extremely tolerant of other religions and people's right to worship their own gods, this tolerance does not extend to according them the same privileges and rights as one accords to one's own in social or commercial dealings. One has a lesser duty or *dharma* to treat a business transaction or a person from another religion/community fairly when this treatment is likely to impair benefits or advantages to one's own self or one's kin. While such behavior may manifest itself just as easily in Western societies in terms of race or color bias, the system in India is likely to be more egregiously tolerant of discriminating behavior.

Artha and *kama* (i.e., acquisition of wealth and the means of its enjoyment) have a positive influence on business behavior in that they favor savings and consumption, thus contributing to economic growth. They also manifest themselves often in conspicuous consumption and wealth hoarding in non-productive assets. In part, these actions also arise out of a desire to avoid paying confiscatory taxes to a national government – a concept that is not central to the Hindu culture. Historically, the state has been seen primarily as the king's domain, known for its extortion of other people's labor rather than protection of its subjects. Thus, while India has all the trappings of a modern democracy, its foundations are still based on bribery and corruption, the coin of the realm of a feudal mindset. The corruption and buying of elections are endemic to India's democratic system. The bureaucracy's indifference to the plight of the masses is pervasive. Like most other developing countries of Asia and Latin America, nothing moves without paying a bribe, and this includes virtually all levels of government.

SUMMARY AND CONCLUSIONS

Hinduism as a religion exerts a strong influence on its followers. It accommodates a wide variety of behaviors and is quite flexible in applying various religious tenets to real-life situations. At the same time, it is highly spiritualistic, and seeks virtuous behavior and adherence to principle and social obligation. It creates conditions that rationalize the sanctity of work even when work is unpalatable and unrewarding. The accumulation of wealth and enjoyment of the means of life are stripped of their guilt connotations and Hindus are encouraged to pursue such activities provided they are undertaken within the framework of one's *dharma*. The system provides a built-in mode for coping with adversity. However, when carried to extremes, it engenders pessimism, risk avoidance, and a rationale for exploitation by the haves of the have-nots.

Bibliography

Anand, M. R. (1963). *Is There A Contemporary Indian Civilization?* Bombay: Asia Publishing House.

Dehejia, R. H. and Dehejia, V. H. (1993). Religion and economic activity in India: An historical perspective. *American Journal of Economics and Sociology*, 52, 145–54.

Kapp, W. P. (1963). *Hindu Culture, Economic Development and Economic Planning in India*. New York: Asia Publishing House.

Koller, J. (1970). *Oriental Philosophies*. New York: Scribner.

Radhakrishnan, S. (1948). *The Bhagavad Gita*. London: Allen and Unwin.

Milner, M., Jr.. (1993). Hindu eschatology and the Indian caste system: An example of structural reversal. *Journal of Asian Studies*, 52 (2), 298–319.

Mishra, V. (1962). *Hinduism and Economic Growth*. Bombay: Oxford University Press.

Uppal, J. S. (1977). *Economic Development in South Asia*. New York: St. Martin's Press.

Weber, M. (1946). The social psychology of the world religions. In H. Gerth and C. Wright Mills (eds.), *From Max Weber*. New York: Oxford University Press.

Weber, M. (1958). *The Protestant Ethic and the Spirit of Capitalism*. New York: Free Press.

Welty, P. T. (1973). *The Asians: Their Heritage and Their Destiny*. Philadelphia, PA: Lippincott.

history of business ethics

Thomas F. McMahon

Concern about ethical issues in business goes back as far as history itself; there has always been some form of mandate for people in commerce. The Egyptians were not to take money for passage across the river until after the passenger was safely there. In the Old Testament, interest was not to be taken on loans. For Aristotle, interest was also not to be levied on loans because money was "consumed" in its first use (like fruit) and therefore had no other use for which interest could be extracted. Cicero asked about price justice for goods in a starving city. Dionesian Roman Law prescribed that justice requires granting to each person what is his or her due.

Arguments against the position of the Roman Catholic Church toward business can be traced to scholastic theologians, especially to Thomas Aquinas. Some claim that, for Aquinas, a just price was determined by the inherent nature of the product and not by the market forces of supply and demand, although subsequent studies have shown that the medieval scholars acknowledged market forces in determining business ethics. In the medieval period the guilds furnished protection and standards for their respective groups. The Reformation and trade in the new world opened new horizons for business and its practices, including slavery, an upcoming middle class of merchants, and a rising sense of nationalism. Much later, Adam Smith's *Wealth of Nations* fits well into the overall surge into developing an industrial society and setting minimum standards for business behavior. Ethical principles such as Kant's categorical imperative and Bentham's utilitarianism also served the industrial revolution and its new ethical choices (*see* KANTIAN ETHICS; UTILITARIANISM). However, no set of ethical principles or practices emerged to guide the business practices of employers and employees. In the late nineteenth century the underpinning concepts of business ethics – power and rights – were exercised in such interacting arenas as courts of law, unions, trade associations, and professional societies (*see* RIGHTS). Social Darwinism, with its new evolutionary social ideology of progress in an industrial society, became prominent. In 1881 Pope Leo XIII reacted by writing his famous social encyclical (letter) on capital and labor. He used natural law principles and the theories of Thomas Aquinas to fortify his arguments for the rights of labor. The 1886 Haymarket riots in Chicago, however, exemplify conflict between employer and employees during this period of industrial growth.

In the early twentieth century, most of the books on business ethics were general in approach and provided an overview on an issue or a specific aspect or problem. For example, they did not deal with an overall problem of business ethics. The exception was Sharp and Fox (1937), who covered pricing, lying, and other topics relating to the economics of business. Issues dealing with employee rights, the environment, and international ethics would come at a much later date.

The first breakthrough for a general interest in business ethics came in Baumhart's revealing study, "How ethical are businessmen?", published in 1961 when the electrical industry price-fixing scandal shook the United States

(Baumhart and Raymond, 1961). It was the first empirical study which showed that ethical issues and problems were found in every industry, in most companies, and on all levels of the managerial pyramid. This revelation came at a time when business enjoyed an outstanding reputation for providing goods and services, where it was assumed that executives and managers acted in an ethical manner.

Following Baumhart's study, the principle-to-solution approach to ethical problems in business was frequently, but not exclusively, pursued through natural law concepts in conferences, textbooks, and general interest books. Furthermore, the manager was himself (*sic*) responsible and accountable: business ethics was personal and individual – it was not corporate. Issues and problems were generally perceived from an individualistic viewpoint. For example, the highest executives of the General Electric Corporation believed that the company did not have any responsibility for the managers who fixed prices. Padded expense accounts, bribery, "call girls," cheating, lying, pricing, and wages were some of the popular topics which were discussed and written about. Most of the concerns were personal, not corporate: how was this executive or manager responsible for his ethical problem? Courses in institutions of higher learning were generally called Business Ethics and were frequently taught in philosophy departments, although some were given by business law or management departments (*see* BUSINESS ETHICS).

The 1964 US Civil Rights Act and subsequent social legislation triggered an awareness of concerns which affected employees, the environment, and the community, both local and national. The term "business ethics" was frequently replaced with the phrase "the social responsibilities of business," thus incorporating prevailing social norms and expectations. The change of name reflected the shift in emphasis from the personal ethics of the manager to the overall position of the company on such issues as racial and sexual discrimination, air and water pollution, plant closing, and employee rights, the companies becoming legally and ethically responsible for implementing these changes. "Responsibility" as such implies having assumed an obligation and is thus accountable

and prescriptive in nature. Responsibility also refers to rights as well as to obligations. Furthermore, the philosophical approach to business ethics shifted from natural law to utilitarianism and Kant's categorical imperative. Rawls's theory of distributive justice became a necessary tool in the teaching of business ethics. By 1975, US colleges and universities offered over 550 undergraduate and graduate courses on business ethics, although most institutions used titles such as Business and Society. Textbooks and case books on business ethics proliferated, written primarily by philosophers who specialized in applied ethics. Bowie, Cavanagh, Davis, Donaldson, De George, Frederick, Garrett, Goodpastor, Sethi, Steiner, Velasquez, Walton, and Werhane are just a few of the authors who published anthologies and textbooks on business ethics. Centers for research and programs on business ethics as well as endowed chairs multiplied; business ethics became recognized as a distinct discipline in academia. Indeed, in 1976 the prestigious Academy of Management added a Social Issues in Management division.

The Watergate affair and payoffs to foreign government officials in the 1970s shifted emphasis once again in business ethics. Media attention on questions about who told subordinates to act illegally and/or unethically pierced the corporate veil of secrecy; personal accountability within institutional structures became the arena of concern. The question was: Who told whom to do what as it affected society? At the same time, payoffs to foreign government officials precipitated the 1977 Foreign Corrupt Practices Act. It also set the stage for discussing not only the issue of personal accountability, but also the question of cross-cultural differences and incompatible legal systems: Whose ethics does a business person follow when she/he is in a foreign country? Finally, business ethicians became concerned with political and social structures that permitted humans to be treated in an inhumane manner, such as apartheid, child labor, and land division. These changes led to a newer view of business decision-making in the form of what authors refer to as "social responsiveness," which requires a reaction of social pressures but also the "long-run role in a dynamic social system" (Sethi, 1974), which in turn should be anticipatory and preventative. Frederick (1978) calls corporate social responsibility CSR$_1$, which has a philosophic underpinning. He names corporate social responsiveness CSR$_2$, which refers to the capacity of the corporation to respond to social pressures; it is a more pragmatic effort in reacting to the corporate environment. While social responsibility relates more clearly to rights and obligations, social responsiveness reacts to pressures which are in effect various forms of power exercised by different groups affecting the corporation. Davis and Blomstrom, Post, Sethi, Wilson, and others have developed various categories to illustrate social responsiveness. Carroll has combined social responsibility, social responsiveness, and social issues to produce the "corporate social performance model."

Two sets of events in the 1980s encouraged business ethicians to consider insider trading and an unprecedented number of acquisitions and mergers. The former challenged the ethical as well as the legal practices of the financial community. First of all, using insider information unbalanced the competitive environment, but discussion on what constituted insider information left much gray area, while the law challenged violators like Boesky (see INSIDER TRADING).

Freeman (1984) and others developed the notion of stakeholders: "an individual or group who can affect or is affected by the actions, decisions, policies or goals of the organization." The notion of stakeholder broadened the relationship of the firm to different, and perhaps previously disregarded, elements in society, such as special-interest groups, social activists, environmentalists, and institutional social investing (see STAKEHOLDER THEORY). The proliferation of mergers and acquisitions occasioned "downsizing," "rightsizing," and "reorganization," which resulted at times in massive terminations of employees, including executives and managers. Middle management positions were frequently eliminated, employees felt a loss of job security, and they redirected their loyalty in the firm. Furthermore, the term "business ethics" now included the broader view of social issues. Authors included the social responsibilities of business, business and society, and perhaps even public policy under the now

more generic "business ethics." Indeed, the founding of the Society for Business Ethics resolved the concern of individual and social issues of business once and forever. Business ethics included both.

In the late 1980s and 1990s business ethics assumed an international flavor. European philosophers and business school professors in particular began to develop their own approaches. Up to this time, the Europeans and others depended primarily on material produced by American scholars. The political and economic changes in the Eastern European countries and the forming of the European Community raised specific issues in business ethics that had not been adequately treated previously by Americans, such as language and cultural changes when working in foreign countries. The European approach has strong philosophical tenets as well as interests in dealing with the ethics of economics. It also questions the moral individualism of American decision-making, which is closely linked to individual persons. Indeed, these new problem-type approaches should have a greater interdisciplinary analysis. The European approach is more collegial and investigates long-term interests of all concerned. Business ethics is thus conceived as a consensual ethic, possibly a result of the different variations of European social democracy. The European Business Ethics Network (EBEN) is the institutionalized network for European ethicians. Enderle, Mahoney, Ryan, and van Luijk are familiar names in the European setting.

Political events such as the North American Free Trade Agreement (NAFTA) and the General Agreement on Tariffs and Trade (GATT) raise business ethics issues. These agreements have international implications for business ethics in terms of jobs, relocation, investing, environment, and discrimination, both racial and sexual. It is too early to determine the precise ethical application of these issues, which standards will apply, and how they will be implemented. Furthermore, the legal disintegration of apartheid raises new problems in business ethics, such as ownership of property, foreign investing, and equal job opportunity (see EQUAL OPPORTUNITY).

International business ethics is different from national business ethics inasmuch as there is no sovereign power to settle claims; there are different derivative values from different cultures; there are problems of communication; and there are differences in interpretation and application.

The one constant in the history of business ethics has been change: in emphasis, in philosophy, in topics, in cases. Change is also noticeable in accountability: from the individual to the corporation and then returning to the individual within the corporation. Changing economic, financial, and marketing functions shifted production and distribution, which in turn brought new and sometimes different ethical problems. Business ethics has also broadened its scope from national and regional issues to international and global concerns. All this change has produced a complexity in business ethics that requires thorough inquiry and innovative solutions.

Bibliography

Baumhart, S. J. and Raymond C. (1961). How ethical are businessmen? *Harvard Business Review*, **39** (4).

Beauchamp, T. L. and Bowie, N. E. (eds.) (1993). *Ethical Theory and Business*, 4th edn. Englewood Cliffs, NJ: Prentice-Hall.

Buchholtz, R. A. (1992). *Business Environment and Public Policy*, 4th edn. Englewood Cliffs, NJ: Prentice-Hall.

Carroll, A. B. (1993). *Business and Society: Ethics and Stakeholder Management*, 2nd edn. Cincinnati, OH: South-Western.

Cavanagh, G. F. (1976). *American Business Values in Transition*. Englewood Cliffs, NJ: Prentice-Hall.

Davis, K. and Blomstrom, R. L. (1971). *Business, Society and Environment: Social Power and Social Response*, 2nd edn. New York: McGraw-Hill.

De George, R. T. and Pichler, J. A. (eds.) (1978). *Ethics, Free Enterprise and Public Policy*. New York: Oxford University Press.

Donaldson, T. and Werhane, P. H. (eds.) (1993). *Ethical Issues in Business: A Philosophical Approach*, 4th edn. Englewood Cliffs, NJ: Prentice-Hall.

Frederick, W. C. (1978). From CSR$_1$ to CSR$_2$: The maturing of business-and-society thought. Working paper No. 279, Graduate School of Business, University of Pittsburgh.

Frederick, W. C., Post, J., and Davis, K. (1992). *Business and Society: Corporate Strategy, Public Policy, Ethics*, 7th edn. New York: McGraw-Hill.

Freeman, R. E. (1984). *Strategic Management: A Stakeholder Approach*. Boston, MA: Pitman.

McMahon, T. F. (1975). *Report on the Teaching of Socio-Ethical Issues in Collegiate Schools of Business/Public Administration*. Charlottesville: University of Virginia Press.

Sethi, S. P. (ed.) (1974). *The Unstable Ground: Corporate Social Policy in a Dynamic Society*. Los Angeles: Melville Publishing.

Sharp, F. C. and Fox, P. G. (1937). *Business Ethics: Studies in Fair Competition*. New York: Appleton-Century.

van Luijk, H. J. L. (1990). Recent developments in European business ethics. *Journal of Business Ethics*, **9**, 537–44.

Velasquez, M. G. (1982). *Business Ethics: Concepts and Cases*. Englewood Cliffs, NJ: Prentice-Hall.

human resource management, ethical issues in

Martin N. Davidson

Human resource management (HRM) is the science of managing people systematically in organizations. The unique individual actor in the organization – a given executive, manager, line worker – is not the focus of HRM, *per se*. Rather, human resources practices and policies concerning recurring cycles of staffing, reward and compensation, and performance management inform how any person or group of people is introduced into the organization, managed while there, and exited from the organization. When these three overarching aspects of human resource management are designed effectively, the organization benefits from a management system that enhances the sustained competitive advantage of the organization. A critical part of designing these aspects effectively requires consideration of ethical concerns at each stage.

Staffing is comprised of systems designed to recruit and select employees to undertake required roles in the organization. The purpose of *recruiting* is to provide the organization with a group of candidates large enough for the organization to select the qualified employees that it needs. Needs are formalized by (1) job or position descriptions, which are written statements of content and organizational level of the job; and (2) hiring specification, which details background, experience, and skills requirements.

Selection is the mutual process in which the organization decides whether to make an offer of employment and, if offered, the candidate decides whether or not to accept. Typically, selection procedures follow several steps. The applicant completes a formal job application, participates in a screening interview, takes tests, submits to a background check, participates in a more in-depth interview, and receives a job offer. Of course, different employers may only use a subset of these steps.

Ethical dilemmas emerge at a number of junctures within the staffing process. Within recruiting, organizations distribute descriptions and specifications to labor pools – the sites within the population in which the organization believes it is likely to find qualified candidates. However, the determination of what pools are tapped is often subjective and systematically biased. For example, when an organization finds a rich pool that yields a number of successful hires, the organization will tend to return to that pool, to the exclusion of other options. The result of this seemingly rational pattern has been that other rich pools are overlooked (Williams, Labig, and Stone, 1993). This is bad practice from a human resource perspective: organizations do not want to miss opportunities to find highly qualified employees, especially when there are labor market shortages. But the problem is compounded when underutilized pools correlate with race, ethnicity, gender, or other demographic characteristics of individuals that are unrelated to job performance (Hardin, Reding, and Stocks, 2002).

This dilemma reaches even greater proportions as more global commerce leads many organizations to staff in other countries. For example, when executive recruiting choices are made among whether employees will be from the parent country (e.g., a US company operating in India), the home country (e.g., India), or a third country (e.g., Canada), there is a danger that parent country employees will be preferred because the organization knows how to recruit them. In addition to being a potentially suboptimal business decision, such a choice also neglects the possibility that host country talent could be infused in the organization. Moreover, it creates a scenario in which important social, cultural, and political nuances in leading a workforce in the host country may be misunderstood, ignored, or abused.

Parallel dilemmas emerge in the selection process. A great deal of research focuses on selection bias, including bias in screening applications, interview methods, and test development (Bertrand and Mullainathan, 2002). The objective of the multiple methods in the selection process is to predict who will be effective in the job. However, at virtually every step in the process, the capacity to make sound judgment is potentially undermined by human and systemic factors that introduce uncertainty into the assessment. In the midst of this bias-induced uncertainty, organizations are challenged to maintain rigorously commitments to fairness in the selection process.

Reward and compensation systems in organizations can be thought of as tools to attract, motivate, and retain employees. Choices managers make about reward systems can affect an organization's ability to hire and keep desirable employees in a competitive labor market, and of course, rewards can affect people's attitudes, feelings, and behaviors at work. There is a range of rewards that are distributed in organizations, both tangible and intangible. Tangible rewards include pay and its variants (e.g., base salaries, hourly wages, commissions, bonuses, profit sharing, deferred compensation, stock options), as well as non-monetary rewards such as promotions, private offices, company cars, benefits, and other perquisites. Examples of intangible rewards include recognition, personal satisfaction, pride, camaraderie, team spirit, and self-actualization (Harder, 1999).

Among the many challenges raised in reward and compensation, none is more prevalent than equity – the extent to which employees are compensated fairly. The simplest expression of the equilibrium that needs to be established to constitute fairness is equity theory (Adams, 1965). Equity theory says that people evaluate the ratio of what they are getting from a particular situation (*outcomes*) with what they are contributing to a situation (*inputs*), and compare this ratio to the outcome/input ratio for a *comparative referent*. If the ratio of someone's outcomes to inputs is equal to that of his or her comparative referent, equity exists. But if not, inequity exists, and the theory suggests that people are motivated to reduce this in some way. Put another way,

Person A's Outcomes/Person A's Inputs should equal Person B's Outcomes/Person B's Inputs in the eyes of both A and B. If A believes she is working as hard as B (inputs are equal), but that she is receiving fewer outcomes than B, A will seek to equalize the equation by (1) trying to increase A's outcomes (e.g., pushing for a raise for herself); (2) trying to reduce B's outcomes (e.g., getting B's perquisites revoked); (3) reducing A's inputs (working less vigorously); or (4) increasing B's inputs (e.g., offloading more work to B).

Each of these four situations includes an ethical challenge in how A affects her view of the equation. She can increase her outcomes by seeking a raise, but she can also increase her outcomes by taking office supplies home. People who feel underpaid or underappreciated commonly justify unethical acts by appealing to a larger sense of equity: "If I can't get my due through the company's bureaucratic procedures, then it's OK for me to get what I deserve my own way." It behooves an organization to tend to its equity issues, both because it is wrong to knowingly compensate people inequitably when standards of equity should apply, and because the consequences of maintaining an inequitable system of compensation can be very costly in other ways.

Interestingly, the basic process of assessing fairness becomes even more complicated when personal and social factors are introduced. For example, research demonstrates that the race or ethnicity of A can influence what is viewed as fair. When a white employee sees any colleague denied a raise (regardless of the race of the colleague), the employee is angered, but once a reasonable explanation for the treatment is offered, the employee is appeased. When a black employee sees a white colleague denied a raise, the employee is likewise appeased by a plausible explanation. But when the mistreated colleague is also black, the black employee is not so easily appeased. Even though he or she may understand and acknowledge the validity of the explanation, the black employee remains outraged by the injustice and motivated to prevent similar perceived mistreatment in the future (Davidson and Friedman, 1998). This example demonstrates the power that group identity and capacity to empathize with a mistreated other

can have on one's assessment of fairness and on one's reaction to that assessment.

Performance management includes the policies, processes, and behaviors the organization utilizes as a means of creating a work development relationship between the employee and the organization. Performance management includes socialization, training and development, performance appraisal, and positional movement such as promotion, demotion, transfer, and firings. *Socialization* is commonly thought of as the early experiences an employee has once she or he enters the organization. Here, the employee is "shown the ropes" using formal presentations about organizational history, daily work routine, and general organizational policies. In addition, the employee is introduced to colleagues who can educate the employee on the informal norms that operate in the workplace. For example, the formal orientation may explain that personal phone calls are not to be made from office phones, but the informal norm may be that everyone, including management, makes personal calls as long as they are local calls.

There are always potential ethical dilemmas as new employees seek to discern the difference between the formal and the informal conventions of work behavior. There often is no easy rule to help determine which formalities must be followed and which are flexible. As a result, new employees, who are already eager and anxious to understand their new environment, tend to be conservative and follow the formal guidelines. In addition, new employees are challenged to determine who is able and willing to serve the role as the "informant" who will orient the employee. The employee must determine who is trustworthy and, at a basic level, will behave in the employee's best interest. Unfortunately, it is sometimes difficult to select a helpful informant. The basic relational challenges (e.g., is the informant knowledgeable, likeable, etc.) are often exacerbated by group identity or cultural differences of individuals. If a new employee is from a different country, more experienced employees may shy from serving as an informant because they feel less comfortable dealing with the new employee. As a result, that employee fails to receive competent guidance and enters at a disadvantage, relative to a native newcomer.

Training and development are terms that capture two aspects of the professional learning process. Training programs are designed to maintain and improve current job performance. If an employee is a telemarketer, he may train to speak more clearly or to learn to operate the telephony. In contrast, developmental programs are designed to hone skills for future job assignments in the organization. Training can occur through on-the-job training methods such as job rotation, internship, or apprenticeships. Off-job training takes place in technologically equipped simulation spaces, in the classroom, or offsite. Employees may learn through a variety of pedagogies, including computer assisted learning or behavioral training including role playing.

In contrast, management development programs take a broader perspective on the individual employee. Training programs are often "cookie-cutter" in design – they are developed for a person holding a particular job and whoever cycles through that job can take the identical training. Developmental programs are increasingly shaped to take into account the unique competencies and weaknesses of an employee and help that employee improve through a more personalized educational approach. These programs tend to incur greater investments per person and tend to be focused on employees at the managerial and executive level. They may be structured as on-the-job or off-job learning experiences.

Developmental programs often include developmental relationships as core elements of the learning process. Whereas training may tend to be more short-term and may not even heavily use human instructors, developmental programs are often framed as longer-term learning opportunities requiring the input of more senior individuals who can mentor the employee. These mentors educate their protégés on the intricacies of the kinds of positions they may attain in the future. Since such information is often unique to the organization and more difficult to obtain, these developmental relationships are invaluable. No executive succeeds without a robust set of developmental relationships.

Performance appraisal is the process of feeding back information to employees on how well they are doing their work. This feedback can occur in two ways: informally on a more regular basis, and formally on a semi-annual or annual basis. Informal appraisal occurs on a daily basis ideally and is a regular process of offering feedback to alter undesirable behavior, or to reinforce desirable behavior. Informal appraisal relies on interpersonal skill in giving and receiving feedback and focuses on behaviors that are observable and that can be changed.

Formal performance appraisal has two purposes: evaluation and development. Formal appraisals include detailed performance data such as numerical ratings and written qualitative data. Based on those data, raises or other rewards, as well as pay cuts and other punishments, are prescribed. This constitutes the evaluative aspect of formal appraisal. The appraisal also includes suggestions for additional training to compensate for shortcomings or to bolster strengths. This constitutes the developmental aspect of appraisal.

Appraisal is typically one of the more difficult tasks in a manager's duties because it involves giving others information that often disconfirms their positive images of themselves and of their performance. Such disconfirming information breeds emotional upset for most employees and makes the task even more aversive for most managers. However, honest and accurate feedback is extremely valuable to employees and is the basis for advancement and professional success. Interestingly, managers who were reluctant to offer effective feedback were derailed from success in their own professional aspirations because they were perceived to lack integrity (Van Velsor and Leslie, 1995). In essence, these managers were not truthful in giving performance information, and even though the managers may not have been malicious in intent, the impact of their behavior hindered the ability of their subordinates to perform effectively. In turn, those subordinates felt betrayed.

These examples of interpersonal challenges in effectively appraising individuals take on greater importance when viewing appraisal accuracy from a more systemic perspective. A good deal of research demonstrates systematic bias in feedback frequency and accuracy based on individual characteristics such as gender and race. Sometimes the bias leads to unrealistically negative feedback based on a given characteristic (Chinander and Schweitzer, 2003), and sometimes to unrealistically positive feedback (Harber, 1998). In either case, the lack of true feedback is harmful.

The last step of the performance management stage is positional movement – promotion, transfer, and firing. If recruiting and selection represents input into the organization, positional movement represents output. *Promotion* is clearly a reward for effective performance and provides most employees with a sense of accomplishment and a tangible positive outcome. This movement creates higher levels of motivation for the employee promoted, but can serve as either an impetus for greater effort or a disincentive to try for colleagues who are passed over for promotion. *Transfers* can serve multiple purposes, from development to avoidance. High-potential employees may be transferred to give them a greater breadth of experience. Poor-performing employees may be transferred because her or his manager wishes to avoid the difficulty of disciplining or firing the individual. *Firing* results when an employee simply does not perform to required standards, or when the employee violates critical rules or regulations.

Though there are certainly ethical challenges in managing the decisions that lead to, and the practices that execute, these movements, another dilemma emerges for those left behind in these movements. As mentioned above, those not promoted may have encouraged or discouraged reactions to a colleague's promotion. In the case of transfers, the employee's former colleagues may have a range of reactions, from sadness to relief that the individual has moved on. In the developmental transfer, those left behind may respond as they would if the employee had been promoted – it would be seen as reward for effective performance. In the avoidance transfer, though, colleagues could question the integrity of the manager who made the transfer or of the organization for tolerating the practice of holding on to a poor performer. Finally, firing or layoffs can leave survivors frightened and demoralized because they experience the harshest possibility of the conclusion of a relationship with the organization.

At every aspect of the human resources cycle – staffing, reward and compensation, and performance management – a wide range of ethical issues and dilemmas may surface. This entry introduces a few important ones.

Bibliography

Adams, J. S. (1965). Inequity in social exchange. In L. Berkowitz (ed.), *Advances in Experimental Social Psychology*, Vol. 2. New York: Academic Press, 267–99.

Bertrand, M., and Mullainathan, S. (2002). Are Emily and Brendan more employable than Lakisha and Jamal?: A field experiment on labor market discrimination. Unpublished manuscript.

Chinander, K. R. and Schweitzer, M. E. (2003). The input bias: The misuse of input information in judgments of outcomes. *Organizational Behavior and Human Decision Processes*, **91** (2), 243–53.

Davidson, M. N. and Friedman, R. A. (1998). When excuses don't work: The persistent injustice effect among Black managers. *Administrative Science Quarterly*, **43** (1), 154–83.

Harber, K. D. (1998). Feedback to minorities: Evidence of a positive bias. *Journal of Personality and Social Psychology*, **74** (3), 622–8.

Harder, J. W. (1999). *Organizational Reward Systems*. Charlottesville, VA: Darden Graduate School of Business.

Hardin, J. R., Reding, K. F., and Stocks, M. H. (2002). The effect of gender on the recruitment of entry-level accountants. *Journal of Managerial Issues*, **14** (2), 251–66.

Van Velsor, E. and Leslie, J. B. (1995). Why executives derail: Perspectives across time and cultures. *Academy of Management Executive*, **9** (4), 62–72.

Williams, C. R., Labig, C. E., and Stone, T. H. (1993). Recruitment sources and posthire outcomes for job applicants and new hires: A test of two hypotheses. *Journal of Applied Psychology*, **78** (2), 163–72.

I

imperfect markets

S. Prakash Sethi

BUSINESS ETHICS IN THEIR HISTORICAL CONTEXT

Concern about business ethics, or the lack thereof, seems to be a historical phenomenon that recurs with remarkable regularity through periods of prosperity and hard times. Yet the conventional wisdom has it that with some exceptions, most businesses are honest and law abiding. The challenge for us, however, is to find some explanatory and predictive variables that would help us understand why, and under what circumstances, corporations and their executives are prompted to engage in unethical and even illegal conduct. Equally important, this approach would provide a direction that we might take to contain these circumstances and thus curb unethical conduct.

The extensive prevailing literature in business ethics primarily views the issue in individual-personal terms (i.e. corporate executive and the employee) and suggests that making corporations more ethical involves changes in executive behavior. While this approach has strong intellectual roots in moral philosophy and religion, it fails to explain the persistence of unethical and illegal behavior among corporations of all sizes, financial health, competitive market conditions, and level of individual executive compensation. As economic activity increases in complexity and technological orientation, it slips from its mooring in individual actions. Large-scale economic activity invariably requires collective action, where each individual contribution is connected, only remotely and indirectly, to the institution's purpose as a whole. Thus, individual acts are rewarded and punished, not so much

for their ethical content, but according to the notion of one's loyalty and commitment to the institution's success.

BUSINESS ETHICS, COMPETITIVE MARKETS, AND INDUSTRY STRUCTURE

To better understand the prevalence or lack of ethical conduct in business, we must look to prevailing industry structure and competitive dynamics in particular markets. Contrary to common beliefs, we assert that while highly competitive markets may promote efficiency, they do not guarantee ethical behavior and may indeed provide greater opportunities and incentives for unethical business behavior. Instead, it is the imperfect markets, with their above-market profits, that provide the conditions that induce corporations to act both ethically and unethically, depending on the unique characteristics of those markets, and the corporation's orientation in exploiting those characteristics for both good and evil.

Perfect competition and business ethics. "Competition keeps businesses honest." If this were true, it would follow that firms would act more ethically, even in the economic sense of maximizing social welfare, as markets approximate the ideal conditions of perfect competition. Unfortunately, this is not the case when applied to business morality. While efficient markets may prompt firms to act smart, they do not induce them to act ethically, and, " 'perfect' markets are highly imperfect in their enforcement of business morality" (Baumol, 1991: 24). The absolute discipline of ideal markets leaves little room for the individual firm to undertake voluntary activities that go beyond what is legally required. To do so would incur additional costs that a firm could not absorb, since buyers (being perfectly informed) would refuse to pay higher prices for products that could be bought more cheaply elsewhere.

Corporate structure and decision-making processes. Large corporations and their decision-making processes also militate against ethical standards. Group norms, and pressure to conform, exert strong influence on individuals to yield to demands for lower ethical standards when they are seen to be protecting the group at the cost of potential harm to "outsiders." Corporate decisions, from conception to implementation, involve hundreds and often thousands of individuals, each contributing an infinitesimal amount, and often with little or no understanding of its potential impact on the overall decision. The group orientation of corporate unethical behavior depersonalizes business leadership. The corporate personality diffuses the individual burden of guilt.

IMPERFECT MARKETS: OPPORTUNITIES FOR BEING VIRTUOUS

There are two conditions – given the competitive nature of markets – that must exist in order to create a potentially conducive environment for business to behave ethically: (1) there must be some imperfections in the marketplace that the firm can exploit to generate "above normal" profits (i.e., strategic slack); (2) the firm must be assured of garnering both economic and noneconomic benefits from such ethical conduct in terms of greater customer loyalty, public goodwill and trust, employee satisfaction, and reduced government regulation and oversight, to name a few.

The existence of strategic slack is a necessary but not a sufficient condition for companies to act more ethically than their competitors. Although it provides the resources to enhance managerial discretion, it does not direct it. A company's management may use its "slack" resources to enhance its ethical posture. It could just as easily use them to defy societal expectations and resist external pressures (Falbe and Sethi, 1989). Strategic slack affords management the arrogance of power to respond negatively to external forces of change. The ideological orientation of management may also influence its behavior by disregarding the needs of the general

community and those stakeholders who cannot directly impact its operations (Baumol, 1991; Sethi, 1994; Sethi and Steidemeier, 1991).

The second necessary condition – market reward for a firm's enhanced ethical and socially desirable behavior – is also rooted in market imperfections, especially as they relate to market concentration. A reputable firm inspires trust and confidence. Contrary to the conditions of ideal markets, the long-term prosperity and growth of a company depends on its ability to engender customer loyalty and also propels it to deal with its stockholders, employees, and suppliers in a fair and equitable manner. A similar approach toward the community-at-large augurs well for maintaining a high level of sociopolitical trust and puts high value on ethical and socially responsible behavior as an integral part of doing business and corporate ethos (Baumol, 1991; Heal, 1976; Sethi, 1994). It behooves the firm to sacrifice at least some of its short-term profits arising out of market imperfections and use them to build greater entry barriers against competitors and ensure long-term, above-normal profitability.

IMPERFECT MARKETS AND IMPEDIMENTS TO BEING VIRTUOUS

Imperfect markets have become a dominant condition and are likely to remain so for the foreseeable future. This raises an important question: How can the large corporation be induced to act ethically and socially proactively, without the burden of onerous governmental regulation and oversight, and minimize the cost of regulatory failure?

In one sense, society's moral and ethical values are public goods. All members of a society stand to benefit from their enhancement, regardless of their individual contribution. This may partially explain the inherent discrepancy in public trust and goodwill enjoyed by non-governmental organizations (NGOs) against that of the business community.

Profits are one measure of a corporation's reward for doing its job well. In this sense, the most profitable corporation is also the most socially responsible corporation and doesn't need to do anything else (Friedman, 1970). The problem of the free-rider does not exist (Sethi, 1994), since private firms must always try to maximize private gains by internalizing all possible profits and externalizing all possible costs.

Under conditions of imperfect markets, dominant firms cannot always control – for legal and other reasons – the behavior of rogue firms wishing to exploit an industry's stock of public trust for their own gain (i.e., become a free-rider). This condition is likely to be exacerbated where public trust in an industry or a firm's integrity is high. Industry members, therefore, must assume that other companies would follow suit and behave equally aggressively as free-riders, since they have more to lose from contributing to general public trust and moral and ethical values and everything to gain from being a free-rider. On the other hand, where industry standards of ethical norms are low, and so perceived by the public-at-large, deviance by an industry member to raise ethical standards and undermine industry's public stance would be severely resisted by the rest of the industry, with the deviant member subjected to intense public and private pressure to fall in line.

The one exception to this rule would take place where a firm's market position and resultant non-market rent are so strong that it must protect them at all costs by courting the goodwill of its customers, government regulators, and the public-at-large (Hirsch, 1976; Schelling, 1978). The incentive to do so, however, is not altruism, but a desire to preserve profits. This condition tends to undermine the value of a firm's contributions to enhancing society's stock of ethical and moral values because the company is viewed to be primarily acting in self-interest. By linking their good corporate citizenship activities to specific constituencies that enhance the business goals of the corporations, called "strategic giving," companies dilute their social import and the altruistic character of their "public or collective goods."

A third problem pertaining to companies' reluctance to pursue higher ethical standards is related to the authority and power of top managers within the organization structure; the nature of their rewards – financial and non-financial, private and social; the reference group to which these managers aspire to belong; and how these managers view themselves and are in turn viewed by society. Received legal theory and corporate hyperbole suggest that a company's managers work primarily to enhance the best interests of the firm's owners (i.e., stockholders), commensurate with some measure of acceptable risk. However, in practice this is far from true, as recent incidents of corporate fraud (e.g., Enron, WorldCom, Tyco) amply demonstrate. It is in the interest of corporate managers to perpetuate such a myth to protect their authority and power. Top managers hold most of the cards in controlling the destiny of the corporation and, except in dire circumstances, are hard to replace by discontented stockholders (Bolton, 1993; Loomis, 1993). The gap between the rhetoric of CEO accountability to shareholders and the reality of CEO and top management has caused a crisis in corporate governance, leading to the enactment of the Sarbanes-Oxley Act of 2002.

ALTRUISM AS A DESIRABLE INSTITUTIONAL AND PERSONAL GOAL

It would seem counter-intuitive to suggest that economic institutions could ever be made to seek altruistic goals as an integral part of their overall objectives. Yet this is precisely what needs to be done. An important characteristic of the American sociopolitical system is that most corporate leaders do not come from established social elites. Nor do they have recognized symbols of social class, such as titles. The public-at-large has little familiarity with their individual personalities and character, and colors them with the same brush as the corporation they manage. Devoid of mutual trust, people use political processes to impose rigid conditions on corporate behavior. Managers respond in kind by satisfying the form of the law and legal requirements without concerning themselves with the substance or objectives for which those requirements were imposed.

For corporate managers to act beyond the minimally prescribed and legally enforced norms of social conduct, it would be important to foster mechanisms for generating a higher threshold level of trust. This necessitates a redefinition of the successful corporation and the character of its leadership. Through social consensus, akin to that of other societal institutions (e.g., universities and churches), the highly admired and trusted corporation would display the dual characteristics of the financially successful enterprise with equally good corporate citizenship, defined in terms of corporate behavior that uses its economic power with self-restraint and strives toward distributive justice for other factors of production in relation to their contribution to the success of the enterprise.

Bibliography

Baumol, W. J. (1991). *Perfect Markets and Easy Virtue: Business Ethics and the Invisible Hand*. Cambridge, MA: Blackwell.

Bolton, J. R. (1993). A second look at boardroom reform. *Wall Street Journal*, June 2, A14.

Falbe, C. M. and Sethi, S. P. (1989). The concept of strategic slack: Implications for the choice of public policy strategies by corporations. Paper presented at the Ninth Annual Strategic Management Conference, "Strategies for Innovation," San Francisco, October 11–14.

Friedman, M. (1970). The social responsibility of business is to increase its profits. *New York Times Magazine*, September.

Heal, G. (1976). Do bad products drive out good? *Quarterly Journal of Economics*, **90**, 499–503.

Hirsch, F. (1976). *Social Limits to Growth*. Cambridge, MA: Harvard University Press.

Loomis, C. J. (1993). King John wears an uneasy crown. *Fortune*, January 11, 44–8.

Schelling, T. C. (1978). *Micromotives and Macrobehavior*. New York: W. W. Norton.

Sethi, S. P. (1994). Imperfect markets: Business ethics as an easy virtue. *Journal of Business Ethics*, **13** (10), 803–15.

Sethi, S. P. and Steidemeier, P. (1991). *Up Against the Corporate Wall: Modern Corporations and Social Issues of the Nineties*, 5th edn. Englewood Cliffs, NJ: Prentice-Hall.

information and international insider trading

Robert Conroy

While there are many issues that arise in international finance, the most persuasive has to do with the use of information. Information is a valuable commodity. Generally, information in a financial context is of two types. The first is public information. This is information that is in the public domain. This does not mean that it is known to everyone, but that it is available to anyone. There may be a fee to obtain the information but the key is its availability. Broadly, in an international context there is no issue about using this information to formulate and execute financial transactions.

The more important distinction has to do with non-public or insider information. This is information that is not available to everyone. The issue in this context is whether this information can be used to formulate and execute financial transactions. There is a great deal of evidence both in the United States and internationally that this type of information can be used to generate profits in financial transactions. This profit comes at the expense of those individuals or institutions that do not have access to the information. A key question is whether this is fair, and whether trading on such information should be barred either legally or ethically. Regrettably, this is viewed differently in different cultures.

The international view is the central issue which financial managers face when operating in different countries. In general, standards which apply to the use of non-public information come in three forms. The first is legal restrictions or prohibition. The second are rules governing the standards of practice of professional societies. Thirdly, there are individuals' own ethical standards that are the result of the individuals' cultural identity. In those cases where any or all of these conflict, the actions of the individual should be governed by the highest standard. This is true both domestically and in an international context.

The United States has taken the position that insider trading is inappropriate and has established legal prohibitions against using insider information. Moreover, prohibitions against using material non-public information are included in many professional societies' standards of practice. As such, in the United States there is a clear prohibition against such trading.

In an international context, the laws and customs in different countries can be quite varied. An individual can find that the local laws and customs are at variance with the established norms that had governed their actions in the past. Usually the dilemma is that the laws and customs allow practices that would be prohibited in their normal operating environment. The logical question is, what norms should the individual follow? In the case where the individual subscribes to a set of standards of practice that specifically prohibits insider trading, this prohibition should supersede the local law and customs.

In the absence of such guidelines the individual must make his or her own determination. If an individual believes that insider trading is wrong, then the local law and customs cannot relieve that individual of the responsibility to act in a way that is consistent with his or her own internal value system. On the other hand, if an individual does not hold the opinion that activities such as insider trading are wrong, then to the extent that the individual operates within the guidelines of local law and customs, such activities would be reasonable.

See *insider trading*

information, right to

Kevin W. Mossholder

The right to information involves access to information that is necessary for the effective discharge of stakeholders' duties. Stakeholders are entitled to information that permits them to function in roles defined by society or by agreement with others who have a mutual interest in outcomes affected by stakeholder actions. Information is power; it may be used in controlling others or empowering them. To the degree that the free flow of information is restricted by certain stakeholders, the potential for ethical violations of other stakeholders' rights will tend to increase (*see* STAKEHOLDER THEORY).

Information has become a "currency" for exchange between the organization and its stakeholders. As such, a central issue concerning the right to information is ensuring that an equitable balance is struck among parties in the information exchange process. Though moral and legal principles can be used to help in such determinations, the subjectivity involved in various stakeholders' perspectives precludes finding clear *a priori* boundaries between the right to know and the right to privacy. The following is an overview of the information rights of key organization stakeholders. It is based on the idea that stakeholder rights are important if organizations are to function effectively.

EMPLOYEE AS STAKEHOLDER

Employees should have access to information that is needed to function effectively in their organizational roles. Because of salary- and career-related factors, employees have an interest in performing at a satisfactory or greater level. Insufficient access to job-relevant information may unfairly inhibit job performance.

Performance, personnel, and other career-relevant data that are maintained as part of employees' permanent records (excluding some information involving other parties' confidentiality) should be open to inspection. When personnel decisions are made about employees, they should have adequate access to information that helped shape the decision. Employees who are demoted, transferred, or terminated have a right to know why such action was taken.

Maintaining privacy safeguards requires that employees be informed of monitoring efforts by the organization. Employees should also be informed of how personal information that may be collected by the organization will be kept confidential.

Employers also have certain information rights in the context of the employee–employer relationship. In general, employers are entitled to information pertinent to gainful organizational interests. Information employees possess that could affect organizational competitiveness should be communicated. Assuming it has been acquired ethically, information about competitors or unsolicited ideas from outsiders should also be communicated to the employer.

Organizations have the right to information concerning employees' acquisition of conflicting or competing interests. This right may also apply in cases where employees' immediate family members are involved in addition to or instead of the employees themselves. If employees have or have been asked to engage in behavior that violates organizational ethics codes, organizations are entitled to information bearing on the behavior. Given proper respect of employees' privacy rights, organizations have the right to information about unsafe employee behavior (e.g., drug use) in safety-sensitive jobs. They also may monitor workplace behavior where employees are informed and monitoring protects the organization's property and trade (see ORGANIZATION ETHICS).

CONSUMER AS STAKEHOLDER

Consumers have the right to be truthfully and accurately informed of a product's or service's content and purpose. This allows consumers to make rational choices among products. Advertising is a principal means of providing consumers with product information. Though advertisements may be designed to influence and persuade, the information communicated by them to consumers should accomplish this end in a manner that does not deceive, conceal, or withhold the truth.

Any information about potential safety defects or health hazards should be disclosed in such a way that it is readily understood by the consumer. Organizations should inform consumers about means of registering valid complaints, and about procedures to be followed for obtaining compensation for faulty products.

SHAREHOLDERS AND OTHER STAKEHOLDERS

Organization shareholders have a right to information about financial and other related information (e.g., pending lawsuits). They should expect the organization to provide them with reports of how well it has followed the law and protected shareholder investments. Other stakeholders having various information rights with respect to the organization may be identified through stakeholder analysis. Unions, suppliers, trade associations, political and advocate groups, the media, and the general public among other entities comprise the potential stakeholder pool. The legitimate information rights of various stakeholder groups should be determined when such groups are identified.

INFORMATION RIGHTS AND THE LAW

There are many laws governing information access in organizations. For example, a partial listing of the US laws pertinent to employee stakeholders could consist of the following: Freedom of Information Act, Fair Credit Reporting Act of 1971, Worker Adjustment and Retraining Notification Act of 1988, Polygraph Protection Act of 1988, and ERISA. When identifying stakeholder groups, an organization should be attentive to legal responsibilities they have regarding information availability. Not all rights will be addressed by law; however, applicable laws can help define where organizations can begin the process of meeting the information rights of their stakeholders.

Organizations must continually adapt to the environments in which they operate. In the "information age" an important part of this process necessarily includes addressing stakeholder rights to information. Interconnections through various electronic media will likely increase the scope of information demands on organizations. Given this circumstance, information rights and access will likely expand as an area of focus within the field of business ethics.

Bibliography

Weiss, J. W. (1994). *Business Ethics.* Belmont, CA: Wadsworth.

insider trading

Steven R. Salbu

is buying or selling securities with reliance on information that is not available to the public. Insider trading is also defined as trading by true corporate insiders, such as directors or officers of a firm, or by outsiders who are privy to non-public information and who trade in contravention of a FIDUCIARY DUTY.

Always a controversial issue, insider trading has entered center stage of the larger corporate governance question in the early years of the twenty-first century. As gross miscarriages of leadership led to mounting corporate scandals during this period, insider trading has been among the infractions of high-level executives who placed their own interests above those of other stakeholders, such as shareholders, employees, and the marketplace of investors in general.

Trading securities based on inside information was prohibited in the United States under common law early in the twentieth century. This prohibition was codified under the Securities and Exchange Act of 1934, under a broad proscription of fraud in the purchase or sale of securities (*see* SECURITIES AND EXCHANGE COMMISION). Under present judicial interpretation of the Act, insiders or outsiders who have a fiduciary duty to another must either disclose their inside information to the public or abstain from trading on the information. A second section of the Securities and Exchange Act of 1934 purports to mitigate insider trading practices more indirectly, by requiring disgorgement of short-swing profits by certain classes of insiders, regardless of whether trades have been made with the advantage of any inside information. Specifically, beneficial owners, directors, and officers must return any profits gained by a sale of stocks within six months of sale. Through the 1970s the United States was the only nation that both prohibited insider trading and vigorously prosecuted violators. More recently, industrialized nations in Asia and Europe have strengthened their insider trading laws and have begun to prosecute violators with some consistency.

Whether trading is unethical, and whether it is appropriate to outlaw insiders' trading behavior, are highly controversial questions. Those who support insider trading as ethically defensible tend to posit arguments of economic efficiency. Some contend that trades made on accurate inside information support an efficient market by contribution to the most rapid market assimilation of information, which drives stock prices closer to an equilibrium that accurately represents true asset values. Commentators supporting the practice have also argued that insider trading by directors and officers can benefit a company by providing an incentive for the most highly qualified candidates to fill high-level management positions. Finally, critics of the climate which presently disfavors insider trading have suggested that no one is harmed by the practice, and therefore it is morally supportable.

Those who condemn insider trading as unethical rely on arguments of both economic function and fairness. Some suggest that insider trading does in fact harm buyers or sellers who deal with the insider. They reason that innocent buyers or sellers who trade with insiders purchase stocks at higher prices or sell them at lower prices than they would agree to under parity of information, and are harmed to the extent of the difference between actual price and the price they would be

willing to set under informational parity. Other critics of insider trading focus on potential negative effects on the market at large rather than the potential harm to individual transactors. They reason that proliferation of selective insider advantage will tend to erode faith in the marketplace as a level playing field, causing anything from market sluggishness to market crash as disadvantaged investors withdraw their support. Some suggest that ethical consideration of insider trading must either supplant or supplement economic concerns with consideration of fairness issues. They contend that insider trading is wrong because transactions under disparate conditions of informational access are inherently unfair transactions.

These challenging ethical questions are exacerbated by both legal and pragmatic complications. Under present federal law in the United States, the statutory prohibition neither uses nor defines the term "insider trading," relying instead upon a more general ban on "fraud." Accordingly, cases arise in which a trader is uncertain whether particular practices at the margin are legal or illegal. The present lack of clarity under federal law presents several kinds of ethical problems. First, many consider laws unfair when they hold persons civilly and criminally accountable for behaviors that have not been clearly defined. The issue of due process under law is also an issue of the fundamental fairness of the legal system. Second, from a utilitarian standpoint, systematic discouragement of economic investment by enacting vague legal prohibitions that may tend to have a chilling effect on transactions, detracts from the greater social good. Among both supporters and critics of the practice of insider trading, many commentators agree that the present imprecision of the state of the law is unethical.

The problems of inadequate definition of insider trading are compounded by conceptual ambiguities, which suggest that precise circumscription of an unethical sphere of activity is pragmatically troublesome. For example, if we define insider trading as trading on information to which the public does not have access, we must then define the boundaries of public access. Yet information can exist in practice on a continuum, from "accessible to one person" to "accessible to all persons." The difficulties associated with trying to fix insider trading some-where along the access continuum quickly become evident. Likewise, difficulties exist in regard to defining precisely what is inside "information," as opposed to opinion or specu-lation. While some believe that information must be factual and verified to yield an unfair edge in trading, others contend that inside opinions con-fer advantage to the extent that they are expert or well informed. What comprises "inside infor-mation" is therefore a complicated question, which to date remains largely unresolved by both legal and ethical scholars.

Bibliography

Ayres, I. and Choi, S. (2002). Internalizing outsider trading. *Michigan Law Review*, **101**, 313–408.

Bagby, J. (1987). The evolving controversy over insider trading. *American Business Law Journal*, **24**, 571–620.

Levmore, S. (1988). In defense of the regulation of insider trading. *Harvard Journal of Law and Public Policy*, **11**, 101–9.

Macey, J. (1984). From fairness to contract: The new direction of the rules against insider trading. *Hofstra Law Review*, **13**, 9–64.

Moore, J. (1990). What is really unethical about insider trading? *Journal of Business Ethics*, **9**, 171–82.

Salbu, S. (1992). The misappropriation of theory of insider trading: A legal, economic, and ethical analysis. *Harvard Journal of Law and Public Policy*, **15**, 223–53.

Shaw, B. (1990). Shareholder authorized insider trading: A legal and moral analysis. *Journal of Business Ethics*, **9**, 913–28.

Werhane, P. (1989). The ethics of insider trading. *Journal of Business Ethics*, **8**, 841–5.

integrative social contracts theory

Thomas W. Dunfee and Thomas J. Donaldson

Integrative Social Contracts Theory (ISCT) is a normative theory of business ethics. ISCT is intended to provide a framework capable of guiding managers confronting ethical decisions. The theory weds the normative perspective of traditional philosophical social contract method-ology with the specificity of moral understand-ings among participants in economic, social, and political organizations. In this manner ISCT bridges empirical and normative research in business ethics.

THE HYPOTHETICAL MACROSOCIAL CONTRACT

ISCT is founded upon two kinds of contract, macrosocial and microsocial. The former, *macro-social contract*, is a hypothetical agreement about a broad normative framework designed to guide all economic arrangements. Unlike Rawls's approach, hypothetical contractors in the ISCT state of nature are not presumed to operate under a robust veil of ignorance. ISCT's con-tractors know at least their basic preferences and values, and thus confront only a partial veil of ignorance, namely one that hides information about their personal economic endowments and roles in society.

The initial contractors are assumed to be influenced by two critical factors. First, they recognize the constraints of bounded moral ra-tionality. Economic actors have limited ability to comprehend, interpret, and apply moral con-cepts. They understand that they lack a fool-proof moral calculus for sorting out economic conundrums. Second, the macro contractors recognize the need for some community-based morality that will aid their group endeavors, including economic ones. They understand that such a community-based morality can help optimize their own economic and social prefer-ences even as it avoids the economic analogue of a Hobbesian state of nature.

In response to these assumptions, the global-level contractors are presumed to design a uni-versal or macrosocial contract with the following terms:

1 Local communities may specify ethical norms for their members through *microsocial contracts* (called "moral free space").

2 Norm-generating microsocial contracts must be grounded in informed consent buttressed by a right of community members to exit and to exercise voice within their communities.

3 In order to be obligatory (legitimate), a microsocial contract must be compatible with hypernorms.

4 In case of conflicts among norms satisfying principles 1–3, priority must be established through the application of rules consistent with the spirit and letter of the macrosocial contract.

MICROSOCIAL CONTRACTS: ECONOMIC COMMUNITIES AND MORAL FREE SPACE

Economic communities, defined as self-determined, self-circumscribed groups who carry on economic activity and who are capable of establishing norms of ethical behavior for themselves, generate *microsocial* contracts that establish rules for their members in moral free space. *Authentic norms* are those that reflect agreement attitudes and behaviors of most members of a community. They constitute the ethical rules. Microsocial-generated authentic norms thus represent a general consensus among community members about economic rules and propriety.

In order to create binding obligations on community members, norms must be sufficiently authentic to represent consent by the community. This is only possible when a community recognizes appropriate rights to exit and to voice. Exit opportunities should be reasonably available, although they need not be costless. The opportunity to exercise voice needs to be evaluated within the context of organizational environment and decision-making processes.

HYPERNORMS: FROM AGREEMENT TO LEGITIMACY

Although a norm may be authentic to a community, it will not create a binding obligation on community members if it violates manifest, universal ethical principles called *hypernorms* in ISCT. Hypernorms are principles so fundamental that they constitute norms by which all other norms are to be judged. They are discernible in a convergence of religious, political, and philosophical thought. Authentic norms that are compatible with hypernorms are fully legitimate, creating morally binding obligations. Thus, in ISCT, *legitimate norms* are the only microsocial norms binding for the membership of the norm-generating community. Hypernorms are not merely constraints on illegitimate authentic norms, but may also affirmatively create binding moral obligations.

ISCT defines three types of hypernorms. *Procedural hypernorms* recognize rights essential to support the consent requirements of the macrosocial and microsocial contracts. They are specified in the macrosocial contract and include the rights of exit and voice vis-à-vis norm-gen-

erating microsocial communities. *Substantive hypernorms* specify fundamental conceptions of the right and the good and are exogenous to the macrosocial and microsocial contracts. Examples of substantive hypernorms include promise keeping, respect for human dignity, and the right to be informed concerning physical dangers in the workplace environment. *Structural hypernorms* are specified in the macrosocial contract. They recognize rights and principles essential for the establishment and successful operation of just institutions in society. Examples include the right to own property and the hypernorm of necessary social efficiency. This hypernorm identifies duties to maintain the efficiency of societal systems, including economic institutions designed to promote economic welfare and social justice. A norm, policy, or institution satisfies the efficiency hypernorm when it contributes to the efficiency of the provision of necessary social goods, that is, aggregate economic welfare or social justice. The hypernorm entails, among other things, that *economic* actors have duties to support efficient policies and institutions that promote liberty and due process, as well as minimal possibilities for health, food, housing, and education.

PRIORITY RULES FOR CONFLICTING LEGITIMATE NORMS

Individuals making ethical judgments may be confronted with conflicting legitimate norms as the result of multitudinous communities generating an array of norms. Individuals simultaneously belong to different communities, which may have directly contradictory norms. Many transactions cross communities (e.g., a Chinese firm doing business in the US) where there are directly conflicting norms. ISCT recognizes a set of six priority rules for sorting among mutually exclusive legitimate microsocial norms.

1   Transactions solely within a single community, which do not have significant adverse effects on other humans or communities, should be governed by host community norms.

2   Community norms indicating a preference for how conflict of norms situations should

be resolved should be applied, so long as they do not have significant adverse effects on other humans or communities.

3 The more extensive the community which is the source of the norm, the greater the priority which should be given to the norm.

4 Norms essential to the maintenance of the economic environment in which the transaction occurs should have priority over norms potentially damaging to that environment.

5 Where multiple conflicting norms are involved, patterns of consistency among the alternative norms provide a basis for prioritization.

6 Well-defined norms should ordinarily have priority over more general, less precise norms.

These rules are intended to be applied in a manner consistent with the letter and the spirit of the macrosocial contract and are not intended as a precise calculus. The six rules are to be weighed and applied in combination. Similar to the process of statutory interpretation, there is no precise hierarchy for the six rules, and instead, emphasis should be on the fit of the particular ethical principle with one or two of the principles, or with a convergence of the six priority rules toward a particular result.

THE MEANING OF ISCT

The term "integrative" is used to illustrate that ISCT is based upon a hypothetical social contract whose terms allow for the generation of binding ethical obligations through the recognition of actual norms created in real social and economic communities. A hypothetical social contract is thereby integrated with real or extant social contracts. The plural "contracts" is used to emphasize the fact that ISCT envisions multitudinous local community-based social contracts establishing binding ethical norms.

APPLYING ISCT

The application of ISCT to specific decision contexts requires that certain key determinations be made: (1) a relevant microsocial community must be identified; (2) relevant microsocial authentic norms must be determined; and (3) relevant hypernorms must be identified or specified. ISCT has been primarily developed and advo-

cated in the joint writings of Thomas Donaldson and Thomas Dunfee (1999, 1995, 1994). In their later writings (1999) they identify proxies and presumptions that may be employed to ease these critical determinations.

Identifying relevant communities requires identification of one or more communities holding an authentic norm relevant to the decision required. Although often similar to the process of stakeholder identification that looks for individuals affected by or holding a relevant interest in a decision, the ISCT process differs in that the search is for a sufficiently significant interest among the set of communities affected by or asserting an interest in a decision.

Once a relevant community is determined, the following proxies and presumptions are suggested for determining relevant authentic norms. An authentic norm is presumed to exist when supported by the following sources. The more sources that support a particular candidate for an authentic norm, the stronger the presumption in its favor.

An authentic norm may be presumed to exist on the basis of the following:

• Many people in the community believe it exists and are able to express it in words.
• Inclusion in a formal professional code.
• Inclusion in a corporate code.
• Commonly listed in the media as an ethical standard for the relevant community.
• Commonly referred to as an ethical standard by business leaders.
• Identified as a standard in competent opinion surveys.

The presumption in favor of authentic norm status may be overcome on the basis of:

• Evidence of substantial deviance from the putative norm.
• Evidence of an inconsistent or contrary norm in the same community.
• Evidence of coercion relating to the norm within the relevant community.
• Evidence of deception influencing the emergence or evolution of the norm.

The more proxies supporting the existence of an authentic norm, the stronger the contrary evidence required to conclude that the authentic norm is, in fact, ersatz.

Finally, the following is suggested as a means for identifying substantive hypernorms. If two or more of the following types of evidence confirm widespread recognition of an ethical principle, the decision-maker should operate on the basis of a rebuttable presumption that it constitutes a hypernorm. The more types of evidence in support of a hypernorm, the stronger the presumption.

Evidence in support of a principle having hypernorm status includes:

- Widespread consensus that the principle is universal.
- Inclusion in well-known global industry standards.
- Support by prominent non-governmental organizations such as the International Labor Organization, the UN, or Transparency International.
- Support by regional government organizations such as the European Community, the OECD, or the Organization of American States.
- Consistently referred to as a global ethical standard by international media.
- Consistency with precepts of major religions.
- Support by global business organizations such as the International Chamber of Commerce or the Caux Roundtable.
- Consistency with precepts of major philosophies.
- Support by a relevant international community of professionals, e.g., accountants or environmental engineers.
- Consistency with empirical findings concerning universal human values.
- Support within the laws of many different countries.

CRITICISMS OF ISCT

Hypernorms have been a lightning rod in ISCT. The lack of a specified set of hypernorms is disconcerting to some. Soule (2002: 199) has expressed concern about the ability of managers to identify hypernorms and argues: "the chances for carelessly or opportunistically locating wrong, rogue, or conveniently self-serving hypernorms are significant." Shaw (2000) concurs, arguing that it is too easy to read personal preferences into hypernorms. Others have expressed concern that hypernorms, as defined in ISCT, are not sufficiently extensive to protect important rights such as freedom from gender-based discrimination (Mayer and Cava, 1995). Husted (1999) critiques the theory as inherently conservative, relying excessively on the status quo and requiring a stronger test of compatibility between hypernorms and authentic norms. He also expresses concerns that the definition of community is too amorphous, making it problematic to identify authentic norms. Boatright (2000) believes ISCT is excessively majoritarian while lacking adequate theoretical underpinnings. Hartman, Shaw, and Stevenson (2003) conclude that ISCT, standing alone, is not capable of providing adequate guidance to managers confronting issues pertaining to global labor standards.

CONCLUSION

To date, commentators have applied ISCT to a variety of practical issues, including credit card marketing to college students (Lucas, 2001), ethical norms in Russia (Puffer and McCarthy, 1997), bribery (Dunfee, Smith, and Ross, 1999), global labor standards (Hartman, Shaw, and Stevenson, 2003), the role of corporations in contributing to sustainable peace (Dunfee and Fort, 2003), and the distribution of life-saving pharmaceuticals (Reisel and Sama, 2003). It has served as a basis for empirical research testing the impact of national context on ethical decision-making (Spicer, Dunfee, and Bailey, forthcoming). Douglas (2000), Husted (1999), Shaw (2000), and others have proposed modifications in the theory.

ISCT contributes to the impact of the growing portfolio of specialized theories through its use as legitimization for the relevance of community and professional ethical norms. It encourages decision-makers to consider the norms of all relevant communities and thus ensures a broad consideration of stakeholder interests. Even as it does so, ISCT acknowledges the role of manifest universal standards, and thus allows its adherents to embrace pluralism without falling into relativism. Perhaps most important to those who have utilized it, ISCT attempts to provide a pragmatic framework for dealing with cross-cultural conflicts.

Bibliography

Boatright, J. R. (2000). Contract theory and business ethics: A review of *Ties that Bind*. *Business and Society Review*, **105** (4), 452–66.

Donaldson, T. and Dunfee, T. W. (1994). Towards a unified conception of business ethics: Integrative social contracts theory. *Academy of Management Review*, **19** (2), 252–84.

Donaldson, T. and Dunfee, T. W. (1995). Integrative social contracts theory: A communitarian conception of economic ethics. *Economics and Philosophy*, **11** (1), 85–112.

Donaldson, T. and Dunfee, T. W. (1999). *Ties that Bind: A Social Contracts Approach to Business Ethics*. Cambridge, MA: Harvard Business School Press.

Douglas, M. (2000). Integrative social contracts theory: Hype over hypernorms. *Journal of Business Ethics*, **26** (2), 101–10.

Dunfee, T. W. and Fort T. L. (2003). Corporate hypergoals, sustainable peace, and the adapted firm. *Vanderbilt Journal of Transnational Law*, **36** (2), 563–617.

Dunfee, T. W., Smith, N. C., and Ross, W. T. (1999). Social contracts and marketing ethics. *Journal of Marketing*, **63**, 14–32.

Hartman, L. P., Shaw, B., and Stevenson R. (2003). Exploring the ethics and economics of global labor standards: A challenge to integrative social contracts theory. *Business Ethics Quarterly*, **13** (2), 193–220.

Husted, B. W. (1999). A critique of the empirical methods of integrative social contracts theory. *Journal of Business Ethics*, **20** (3), 227–35.

Lucas, L. A. (2001). Integrative social contracts theory: Ethical implications of marketing credit cards to US college students. *American Business Law Journal*, **38** (2), 413–40.

Mayer, D. and Cava, A. (1995). Social contract theory and gender discrimination. *Business Ethics Quarterly*, **5** (2), 257–70.

Puffer, S. M. and McCarthy, D. J. (1997). Business ethics in a transforming economy: Applying the integrative social contracts theory to Russia. *University of Pennsylvania Journal of International Economic Law*, **18** (4), 1281–1304.

Reisel, W. D. and Sâma, L. M. (2003). The distribution of life-saving pharmaceuticals: Viewing the conflict between social efficiency and economic efficiency through a social contract lens. *Business and Society Review*, **108** (3), 365–87.

Shaw, B. (2000). Review essay: *Ties that Bind*. *American Business Law Journal*, **37** (3), 563–78.

Soule, E. (2002). Managerial moral strategies: In search of a few good principles. *Academy of Management Review*, **27** (1), 114–24.

Spicer, A., Dunfee, T. W., and Bailey, W. J. (forthcoming). Does national context matter in ethical decision-making?: an empirical test of integrative social contracts theory. *Academy of Management Journal*.

integrity

Lynn Sharp Paine

Integrity, in the sense relevant for business ethics, is the quality of moral self-governance. Derived from the Latin word *integritas*, meaning wholeness, completeness, or purity, integrity has been widely praised both as a virtue and as a quality essential for personal well-being and social effectiveness. Psychologists have found integrity to be essential to an individual's sense of identity and self-worth, enabling the successful navigation of change and challenge. Links between integrity and the ability to gain and maintain the trust of others have often been noted. Many purveyors of practical advice, including Cicero and Benjamin Franklin, have counseled that integrity is the cornerstone of worldly success. According to Franklin, "no Qualities [are] so likely to make a poor Man's Fortune as those of Probity and Integrity" (quoted in Beebe, 1992: 8).

Although integrity has been defined in a variety of ways, it is generally identified with one or more of the following related characteristics.

Moral conscientiousness. Integrity involves moral conscientiousness and a desire to do what is right. Persons of integrity are trustworthy and resistant to corruption. They can be relied on to be truthful, to be fair, to stand by their promises, to follow the rules – or, at least, to challenge them openly and fairly. Such persons are faithful to the moral requirements of the roles in which they serve. When acting as a fiduciary for others, for example, they can be counted on to exercise independent judgment unbiased by personal advantage (*see* FIDUCIARY DUTY). They are scrupulous in dealing with conflict of interest or improper influences which might taint their judgment.

Moral accountability. Integrity involves personal accountability. Persons of integrity accept responsibility for themselves and what they do. They rarely appeal to external forces to explain or justify their behavior. They do not pass the buck or seek exculpation in excuses such as "He made me do it," "I was just following orders," "I had no choice." Nor do they see themselves as slaves of their own desires. Integrity is associated with a high degree of self-control and self-awareness.

Moral commitment. Integrity is often identified with having a set of distinctive and strongly held commitments. Persons of integrity have a set of anchoring beliefs or principles that define who they are and what they believe in. They stand for something and remain steadfast when confronted with adversity or temptation. In some instances – for example, Gandhi's commitment to non-violent resistance or Martin Luther King's commitment to civil rights – their anchoring beliefs become the driving force of their lives. Individuals who have no defining commitments, who are too easily swayed by the crowd, who tailor their beliefs to their audience, or who capriciously change their fundamental values are generally thought to be lacking in integrity. While integrity is incompatible with dogmatic adherence to unexamined belief, it does imply constancy of purpose and willingness to take a principled stand.

Moral coherence. Integrity connotes coherence or consistency in a variety of senses: among commitments, among moral judgments, between belief and expression, and between word and deed. Hypocrisy, dishonesty, and self-deception, perhaps the most common failures of integrity, all involve forms of incoherence. Although perfect coherence in all the above senses is unattainable – and perhaps undesirable – persons of integrity generally strive for harmony between principle and practice and for coherence among who they are, who they perceive themselves to be, and how they present themselves to the world. Authenticity and sincerity are often regarded as hallmarks of integrity.

These different aspects of integrity, though related, can sometimes conflict, creating difficult moral dilemmas for decision-makers. For example, managers' role-related obligations may conflict with their personal commitments. Conscientious persons may be torn between blowing the whistle on misconduct they observe and adhering to the conventional bounds of their assigned responsibilities. Despite its associations with harmony and personal well-being, integrity requires that individuals deal with such conflicts and overcome the tensions inherent in them.

While philosophers and psychologists have approached integrity from different perspectives, it is tempting to speculate that the moral expressions of integrity may rest on the psychological foundation of a well-integrated personality. If true, this connection would lend credence to Aristotle's view that virtue and personal well-being are closely linked and rooted in human nature. In this regard, it is interesting to note that Erik Erikson (1950), the well-known psychoanalyst and developmental psychologist, regarded integrity as encompassing ethical and psychological wholeness and as the final and highest stage of personal development.

Though integrity has been widely admired, some philosophers have questioned its usefulness as a moral standard. The philosopher John Rawls, for example, has called integrity a secondary moral concept, one of form rather than content, with no moral purchase until informed by a theory of right and wrong. According to Rawls (1971: 519), integrity is compatible with almost any guiding principles or commitments; even a tyrant, he says, could exhibit a high degree of integrity.

Others have argued that while integrity allows for some latitude in content, it is not entirely open-ended. Integrity-conferring commitments must be important, and they must be morally sound (McFall, 1987). There is a note of irony in attributing integrity to the mafioso who only "takes out" those who deserve it. Similarly, a "tyrant with integrity" would appear to be a contradiction in terms insofar as a tyrant is someone who exercises absolute power brutally and in flagrant violation of law and morality. According to this line of thought, integrity is a powerful moral concept precisely because it focuses on form as well as content and because it is compatible with a range of personal commitments.

Whether moral integrity can be properly ascribed to entities other than individual persons has been a matter of debate. In recent years, however, executives and management theorists have become concerned with corporate or organizational integrity. New US standards for sentencing corporations convicted of wrongdoing have reinforced this concern. Under the 1991 Federal Sentencing Guidelines, organizational culpability was made a critical factor in determining corporate fines, thus giving managers added incentives to promote moral self-governance in their companies.

While organizational integrity is sometimes thought to require nothing more than the personal integrity of the organization's members, research suggests that organizational strategies, structures, and systems are important factors in supporting organizational integrity. Research also suggests that individual integrity is best thought of not as a stable personality trait established once and for all in early life, but as a process of interacting with the world which can be supported or inhibited by the context in which the individual acts. These findings imply that executives concerned about organizational integrity should focus both on developing the personal capabilities of individuals in their companies and on establishing the organizational conditions required for moral self-governance.

Bibliography

Badaracco, J. L., Jr. and Ellsworth, R. R. (1989). *Leadership and the Quest for Integrity*. Boston, MA: Harvard Business School Press. (Executive perspectives.)

Beebe, J. (1992). *Integrity in Depth*. College Station: Texas A&M University Press. (A psychological perspective.)

De George, R. T. (1993). *Competing with Integrity in International Business*. New York: Oxford University Press. (A philosophical perspective.)

Erikson, E. H. (1950). *Childhood and Society*. New York: W. W. Norton. (A developmental perspective.)

Halfon, M. S. (1989). *Integrity: A Philosophical Inquiry*. Philadelphia, PA: Temple University Press. (A philosophical perspective.)

McFall, L. (1987). Integrity. *Ethics*, 98, 5–20. (A philosophical perspective.)

Paine, L. S. (1994). Managing for organizational integrity. *Harvard Business Review*, March/April, 106–17. (An organizational perspective.)

Rawls, J. (1971). *A Theory of Justice*. Cambridge, MA: Harvard University Press. (A philosophical perspective.)

Srivastva, S. and Associates (1988). *Executive Integrity: The Search for High Human Values in Organizational Life*. San Francisco: Jossey-Bass. (Organizational and executive perspectives.)

Taylor, G. (1985). *Integrity: Pride, Shame, and Guilt*. Oxford: Clarendon Press, 108–41. (A philosophical perspective.)

intellectual property

Paul Steidlmeier

The World Intellectual Property Organization (WIPO) characterizes intellectual property as "creations of the mind," which are treated as property. This article first clarifies the different principal forms of intellectual property, and then examines its ethical basis in light of four considerations: (1) what "creations of the mind" should count as private property; (2) the means to acquire and protect it; (3) monopoly power in terms of both the exclusion of others over time and pricing; (4) the rights of third parties. The article concludes with an overview of global policies and processes of managing intellectual property.

THE NOTION OF INTELLECTUAL PROPERTY

Intellectual property refers to patents, copyrights, trademarks, and trade secrets and is distinct from tangible property, such as land, buildings, or commodities.

Patents generally protect inventions of new processes and products over a specified number of years (17 years in the US). Since patents are published with the description of the underlying research, they eventually spread new discoveries around the globe as well as spur further innovation. The fact that critical information is published, however, makes it extremely easy for people to pirate the innovations straight away.

In distinction to patents, copyright protects the expression or concrete representation of ideas and artistic creations (over periods ranging from 50 to 100 years) (*see* COPYRIGHT). Copyright covers many forms of expression, notably literary and artistic works and, more recently, computer programs. Copyright has been particularly threatened by piracy in the areas of the media and software.

A trademark is a symbol, word, or figure used by a company to designate its goods and distinguish them from others. It has recently been expanded (by the EU) to include geographic origins (especially of wine and cheese). A trademark is usually registered with a government agency to ensure its use exclusively by the owner without limitations of time. Cashing in on another's valuable trademark hits all sorts of markets, from the fashion and medical industries to agriculture and computers.

Trade secrets represent a company's product or process innovations, but they do not represent a legal grant of rights from a national government as patents, copyrights, and trademarks do (*see* TRADE SECRETS). They tend to be governed (in the US) by state law and cases and are tried in state rather than federal courts. Requirements of novelty and innovation to qualify as a trade secret are less strict than with patents and copyrights. Trade secrets are generally not limited by time and can be maintained indefinitely. Increasingly, trade secrets are targets of industrial espionage unless actively protected by the firm that holds them.

ETHICAL ISSUES

There is a lively debate over the ethical foundations of intellectual property, ranging from whether these "creations of the mind" should be considered as private property rights at all, to legitimate means of acquiring and protecting it, to setting boundaries for monopoly powers associated with it, and to protecting the rights of third parties (*see* RIGHTS).

What should count as property? To patent scientific ideas and information as property is a very new development in human history, indeed. It stems primarily from the West in the late eighteenth and nineteenth centuries. One of the principal disputes concerns what should count as property in the first place. Traditionally, intellectual ideas have been treated as part of the public domain – much like the alphabet, nuclear physics, the "green revolution," or a cure for a disease such as polio. While applications such as a particular keyboard, a nuclear plant design, a

specific seed strain, or a medicinal formula developed from the ideas might be patented or copyrighted, the idea itself could not be. The medical technology to overcome polio, for example, was not patented, while specific company products developed to wipe out polio were protected.

Ownership of property in general represents (1) a *right* that people have regarding (2) a (commercial) *resource* (3) over *time*. Four general sets of philosophical arguments emerge to legiti̇nate a set of intellectual property rights: (1) the inventor's rights to the fruit of one's labor and effort; (2) the inventor's rights to livelihood; (3) the inventor's rights to liberty and self-realization; and (4) social benefits derived therefrom in terms of efficient production of beneficial social outcomes as part of the common good.

Western private business interests generally view technology itself – not just a specific product – as a private good and a commercial commodity. The EU, however, differs from the US in several important respects; for example, in the EU the patenting of algorithms as well as some genetic discoveries are outlawed and the limits on software eligibility are more restricted.

The intellectual property rights advocated by North American and European companies are primarily based upon modern Western values and culture, which are more individualistic in tone. In other cultural settings such arguments do not find the same legitimacy. Non-Western developing countries, for example, increasingly link property rights to broader foundations of human rights, particularly to what are articulated as rights to economic development. People in many developing areas view the knowledge base of technology as a common good and, because it represents non-applied ideas, as non-commercial. If ideas, not simply applications, can be transformed into commodities and traded in the market, then the very foundations of further technological innovation become entangled in the perpetuation of monopoly interests (*see* MONOPOLY).

If creations of the mind do not ethically count as property, the debate is over. If, however, it is determined that intellectual property rights are, indeed, ethical rights (rather than merely social or legal conventions), three related items are particularly disputed: (1) the means to acquire and protect intellectual property; (2) monopoly power in terms of the exclusion of others over time and pricing; (3) the rights of third parties.

Means to acquire and protect intellectual property. Following from the above, approaches to the acquisition of intellectual property differ according to whether one defines ideas, information or technology as either a private or a common good (*see* INFORMATION, RIGHT TO; TECHNOLOGY, ETHICAL ISSUES IN).

If an idea or technology is viewed as a common good, the information it embodies is open to all. It is not a commodity to be bought and sold. Only specific applications of a technology in terms of products and processes can be considered a commercial commodity or private property.

If an idea or technology is viewed as a privately owned commodity, however, the approach to its acquisition is a contractual agreement between the owner and acquirer. This may take the form of direct sales, licensing, or agreements to provide technical, engineering, or managerial assistance. Even if it is granted that intellectual innovations can be treated as private property, the dispute is not over with respect to how property is to be acquired. Namely, who should hold the rights? In the United States, the person "first to invent" enjoys the property rights, whereas in Europe and most other countries it is the person "first to file." At issue is who is entitled to enjoy the fruits of scientific labor. The problem is further complicated by the fact that many inventors work in corporate and government organizations, which demand that researchers sign away any such rights as a condition of employment.

Protection of intellectual property goes hand in hand with legitimate means to acquire it. Advocates of strong intellectual property rights argue that protection stimulates economic progress in several ways: by providing an incentive for people to spend money on research and innovation, by improving the quality of competition, by enhancing an economy's prospects for growth and development, by providing the consumer with better products over time, and by providing new jobs through the continual dynamic transformation of the economic structure. It is recognized that all these benefits may

cause disruptions, requiring, for example, continual process improvements, retraining of the workforce and so forth; but, overall, there is progress.

The means to protect intellectual property are straightforward enough and encompass market contracts, economic sanctions against violators, legal action, ideological struggles over legitimation, and a variety of political measures including lobbying and political action committees, domestically, and diplomacy, internationally.

The acquisition and protection of intellectual property is rendered more complex by the issues of whether the owner should enjoy exclusive monopoly powers in excluding others and, if so, for how long and under what conditions.

Monopoly power, the exclusion of others over time, and pricing. The owner's interests are usually protected by the grant of unconditional monopoly power over a number of years (ranging from around 17 years for patents to 70 years or more for copyrights, and unlimited for trademarks and trade secrets, depending on the jurisdiction). The arguments for such grants of monopoly power are put forward in essentially utilitarian terms: the allure of monopoly profits provides strong incentives for researchers to produce a rich stream of social benefits (*see* UTILITARIANISM).

This argument is countered by many developing countries that insist monopoly power should be mitigated by social objectives of justice, welfare, and efficiency, which are required to secure minimum levels of social well-being. The *exclusion of others* over *time* from intellectual property innovations becomes particularly important for developing countries, because it threatens their very prospects for development and more fundamental human rights to life. When the factor of time is applied to intellectual property rights, it not only raises the issues of inheritance but also of limits of monopoly power associated with patents and copyrights. One point put forward by developing countries in the intellectual property debate calls for restricting the period of patent monopoly, rather than granting patent holders generous monopolies of 17 years or more. In fact, they argue this point in a utilitarian fashion; namely, that if technology were more widely distributed to developing countries, greater social benefits would accrue both in terms of overall growth as well as in terms of the marginal productivity of technical applications at different stages of development.

Exclusion of others is especially called into question when the property owner does little or nothing with the property for the public good. Some multinationals are known to acquire young companies and their promising technologies to eliminate them as competition rather than develop their potential. The alleged failure to productively exploit patents has led Brazil and India, among others, to adopt policies such as compulsory licensing, shortened times of monopoly grants, and even the loss of patent rights, especially in areas of health sciences and agriculture that are critical to human well-being. These new views on intellectual property rights link them to expanded notions of human rights and to distributive justice, not just to the dynamics of self-interest and a utilitarian calculus of overall social benefits.

Even within Western thought, however, a more communitarian view of property rights has persisted. Taking the idea of public domain applied to tangible property, it could be argued, for example, that the public interest is so compelling that a country's law may stipulate that a patent be "worked" or that it face "compulsory licensing"; that is, a patent must be fully exploited so as to speed the rapid and wide diffusion of new technologies, which is a legitimate and compelling public interest. In the aftermath of the "9/11" disaster in the United States, just such an approach was advocated by the US government with respect to drugs needed to treat anthrax.

Monopoly powers not only raise the issue of accountability but also the corollary issue of a fair price and a just rate of return. The issue of access and price highlights the question of whether there is a moral obligation to aid the disadvantaged, reminiscent of Rawls, and whether, indeed, it is the obligation of the property owner rather than society at large to do so. Traditionally, the monopoly pricing of intellectual property is legitimated in terms of providing incentives to expend the energy to innovate and, in so doing, produce a wide array of social benefits, as well as in terms of covering the costs of wide-ranging research efforts over the long term, especially given the fact that many such efforts end in failure. Yet, even when monopoly is allowed, opponents argue, those ends could be served without giving free reign to exploitative pricing.

In the end, monopoly control and pricing are generally disputed on the grounds of social benefits and costs and distributive justice (*see* DISTRIBUTIVE JUSTICE). Debate has been especially heated in the healthcare industries if for no other reasons than that they touch basic human needs so directly. The need for regulation of monopoly pricing is increasingly being felt in the health industries in the context of government sponsored health plans. In the debate, the strong property rights group emphasizes values of individualism, utilitarianism, and procedural justice (liberty, opportunity, incentives, fruits of one's labor), while the latter emphasizes communitarian bonds, broader patterns of distributive justice, and an approach to human rights that entails specific economic rights and rights to development (*see* COMMUNITARIANISM).

The rights of third parties. Another major moral problem arises from the above and focuses on the legitimate rights of third parties. The modern Western notion of property (derived principally from John Locke and Adam Smith) recognizes the property owner as the one having the *greatest possible interest* in a thing (consistent with a fair legal system). That is, from the start, the property owner is recognized as the *principal stakeholder* but not the only stakeholder in the product or process. The rights of the other stakeholders are defined by conditions of access and the consequences, which they bear from the property owner's actions. The moral question with respect to a particular resource is this: What constitutes a fair set of reciprocal rights and duties between all stakeholders, defined as those with a legitimate interest in the resource?

There is not much of a conceptual problem of fairness, when the innovation in question or the pricing which governs access to it causes harm to a third party, and the owner is then held morally and legally liable for damages. The main moral problem pits the moral principle that the inventors have the right to the fruits of their labor versus the principle that those in society have a right to be able to meet their basic needs or rights to livelihood. When such people do not have access to a needed product, the question is whether the property owner has the responsibility to provide such access or whether society at large bears the responsibility to resolve the issue through social policy such as an income supplement.

MANAGEMENT AND SOCIAL POLICY

When all is said and done, intellectual property is far easier to acquire but more difficult to protect than tangible property. In distinction from land, intellectual property is divisible and easily acquired without expropriating the owner's access to and use of the resource. With intellectual property violations, the owner does not lose property but, rather, the exclusive rights to its imputed stream of economic benefits. Owners do not lose the property itself but their monopoly control over it. In effectively losing their exclusive rights to intellectual property, owners forgo a stream of profits as well as the decision-making power over possible uses of the property in question. All this suggests that the social management of intellectual property evokes a different set of social rules than physical property.

In practice, there are two general types of solutions to intellectual property problems that are usually employed in tandem: (1) legal–political policies and (2) economic and commercial strategies. Each has a mixed record in terms of efficacy and portends different ethical and socio-economic consequences.

Legal–political paths. International copyright protection is afforded by the Berne Convention, which originated in 1886 and has been expanded through five subsequent Berne Acts (the latest being Paris 1971). The Paris Convention of 1883 covers patents as well as trademarks. The area of trade secrets is the least protected of all and is usually covered by state and local law. Business enterprises usually meet threats in this area by taking measures to tighten internal security and by placing restrictive clauses in contracts of those who deal with sensitive proprietary information. The Paris, Berne, and other conventions are vague to the extent that their interpretation in a particular case depends upon local case law.

Interesting developments are taking place in global negotiations over what should be protected as property and how. The US government looks kindly upon patent and copyright extensions, while other parts of the world would shorten the time of protection and demand compulsory licensing. In addition, developing countries seek to have their unique plant genetics, traditional knowledge, and folklore protected from "mining" by the developed countries' multinationals. Increasingly, both sides link their positions to global negotiations regarding trade and development. Trade related intellectual property issues (TRIPS) are on everyone's agenda as they are articulated as "linkages," which affect the valid participation in the agreements under negotiation.

All this being the case, companies increasingly realize that they cannot rely on global politics, agreements, and regulations to manage their intellectual property, for it leaves their intellectual property rights very vulnerable. Increasingly, they turn to strategies to exploit their property as a commercial asset rather than merely protect it as a right.

Economic and commercial path. The economic and commercial path has been growing in popularity mainly because the legal–political path leaves companies in a risky position. Besides that, it is slow and costly, maintains jurisdictional ambiguities, and fails to keep pace with technological innovations and life-cycles. Over the past decade the mass media and pharmaceutical industries have been especially hard hit and have been forced to redesign their business plans and to begin to treat their intellectual property more as an asset or commodity to be strategically exploited in market terms than just as a right to be protected in political and legal terms.

Technology itself makes the protection of intellectual property rights problematic. Anything digitized is difficult to police, so copyright is vulnerable; patents are published information and easily appropriated; innovations and trade secrets can be engineered around; trademarks can be easily falsified.

Many industries face a strategic crisis as they find their traditional business plans, which are based upon strict legal and political protection of their property rights, in shambles. In the context of AIDS drugs, for example, the pharmaceutical industry has faced a demand for compulsory licensing, which is remarkable in that the licensing crosses national borders in an agreement negotiated through the WTO in 2003. In setting up dual pricing systems the agreement invites the strategic threat of reverse imports. The software industry has seen a strong and sustained push toward open systems and architecture (Linux). Companies such as Hewlett-Packard, Sun, IBM, and Intel try to hasten the pace of innovation as well as derive benefits from complementary assets as they try to craft viable business models, which are capable of withstanding competitive dynamics and the sophisticated technologies of pirating, as well as weak legal protection.

Companies have embarked on strategies to change the cost structure of intellectual property. When allowed by antitrust, companies increasingly collaborate on basic research. Cross-licensing between companies is also growing rapidly. Technology development itself is increasingly rooted in ties to universities and tied to venture capital sources and takes shape as spin-offs of innovative companies. All of these strategic innovations change the cost structure of innovation and also accelerate the "pay-back period" of return on investment. Increasingly, companies treat intellectual property as a commodity or asset to be managed profitably in the here and now, not just as a right to be protected over an anticipated monopoly period.

In the end, the management of intellectual property remains very dynamic. The debate will continue over (1) what creations of the mind should count as property rights, (2) what boundaries should be set for how it is to be acquired and protected, (3) the limits on monopoly powers, and (4) the rights of third parties. Holders of property rights will increasingly employ both legal–political strategies to protect their property rights and commercial strategies to exploit them in market terms.

Bibliography

Besen S. M. and Raskind, L. J. (1991). An introduction to the law and economics of intellectual property. *Journal of Economic Perspectives*, **5** (1), 3–27.

Chapman, A. R. (2002). The human rights implications of intellectual property protection. *Journal of International Economic Law*, **5** (4), 861–82.

Correa, C. M. (2003). *Intellectual Property Rights, the WTO and Developing Countries*. Penang: Third World Network.

Drahos, P. and Mayne, R. (eds.) (2002). *Global Intellectual Property Rights: Knowledge, Access and Development*. New York: Palgrave, Macmillan.

Gadbaw, R. M. and Richards, T. J. (1988). *Intellectual Property Rights – Global Consensus, Global Conflict?*, Boulder, CO: Westview Press.

Hope, J. (2002). Traditional economic justification for intellectual property laws. Open Source Biotechnology Project, Research School of Social Sciences, Australian National University, Canberra, ACT0200.

Sell, S. K. (2003). *Private Power, Public Law: The Globalization of Intellectual Property Rights*. New York: Cambridge University Press.

Siebeck, W., Evenson, R. E., Lesser, W., and Primo Braga, C. A. (eds.) (1990). *Strengthening Protection of Intellectual Property in Developing Countries: A Survey of the Literature*. Washington, DC: World Bank.

Spector, H. M. (1989). An outline of a theory justifying intellectual and industrial property rights. *European Intellectual Property Review*, 11, 270–3.

Teece, D. J. (2001). *Managing Intellectual Capital: Organizational, Strategic and Policy Dimensions*. New York: Oxford University Press.

United Nations High Commissioner for Human Rights (2002). Intellectual property and human rights. Sub-commission on Human Rights Resolution 2000/7.

World Intellectual Property Organization (2003a). *WIPO Guide to Intellectual Property Worldwide*. Geneva: World Intellectual Property Organization.

World Intellectual Property Organization (2003b). *WIPO Intellectual Property Handbook: Policy, Law and Use*. Geneva: World Intellectual Property Organization.

international business ethics

Thomas J. Donaldson

Ethical issues surrounding transnational corporations are numerous and fall into at least eight major categories: bribery and sensitive payments, employment issues, marketing practices, impact on the economy and development of host countries, effects on the natural environment, cultural impacts of transnational operations, relations with host governments, and relations with the home countries.

While discussions of the responsibilities of transnationals has occurred for decades, few analyses cast explicitly in terms of ethics occurred until the late 1970s. It was then that moral philosophers and business academics began exploring specific issues in international business ethics. Since then, two distinct schools of thought have arisen concerning transnational responsibilities: they may be called the "minimalist" and the "maximalist" schools. The minimalist school argues that a transnational's moral responsibilities are tied directly to its economic purposes: to make profits for its investors and products or services for the public. Minimalists deny that it is the responsibility of the corporation to help the poor, encourage the arts, or contribute to social causes – except insofar as doing such things is consistent with its more fundamental mission of making profits. Minimalists assert transnationals have moral responsibilities, but these are largely subsumable under the heading of "not harming" and not directly violating the rights of others. In contrast, the maximalist believes that corporations are unique in their level of organization and ability to control wealth, and that, in turn, they have the duty to reach out and help others. If housing and water supplies are substandard in the local area, then the company should work toward their improvement. And if malnutrition is a serious problem, the transnational should both develop nutrition programs and facilitate their implementation. Both minimalists and maximalists agree that transnationals should meet certain minimum ethical standards in conducting their business, but they disagree about whether transnationals should exceed this minimum.

The most-used means of expressing minimum standards is through the moral language of rights. Many international documents which articulate rights, including the United Nations' *Universal Declaration of Human Rights*, have gained broad acceptance among nations. A list of rights to which most nations and individuals would agree is the following:

1   The right to freedom of physical movement.
2   The right to ownership of property.
3   The right to freedom from torture.
4   The right to a fair trial.

5   The right to non-discriminatory treatment (i.e., freedom from discrimination on the basis of such characteristics as race or sex).
6   The right to physical security.
7   The right to freedom of speech and association.
8   The right to minimal education.
9   The right to political participation.
10   The right to subsistence.

All individuals, nations, and corporations are understood to have correlative duties in connection with these rights. Moreover, most experts agree that these duties include not only refraining from depriving people of the objects of their rights directly, but also, at least in some instances, helping protect people from being deprived of their rights. For example, a transnational operating in a developing country has correlative duties regarding the right to minimal education. In turn, the transnational would violate the right to minimal education if it hired 8-year-old children for full-time, ongoing labor and thus deprived them of the opportunity to learn to read and write. Here the violation would be passive rather than active; it would happen not through the company's actively removing the means for minimal education, but by passively failing to protect the right from deprivation.

Another example of failing to honor a right by failing to protect it from deprivation involves the prospective purchase of land in a third world nation by a transnational corporation, where the intent is to convert the land to the production of a cash, export crop. Suppose the land in question is owned by absentee landlords but worked by tenant farmers. Suppose further that the tenant farmers each year have been able to take a portion of the crop barely sufficient for their own nutritional needs, but that the conversion of the land to a cash crop (forced by the transnational's purchase) will have the effect of driving the farmers to the slums of a nearby city, where they will suffer malnutrition as a result. If this were true, then the transnational may violate the farmers' right to subsistence by its actions, even though it would not have taken food from anyone's mouth. The violation of the right would be passive; it would occur as a result of not honoring the duty to protect the right to subsistence from deprivation.

An approach that is satisfied with merely honoring rights, such as the above, is a minimalist approach to international business ethics. In contrast, De George's book, *Competing with Integrity in International Business* (1993), is a good example of the maximalist approach. De George advances ten guidelines that he believes apply to American multinationals operating in less-developed countries. According to him, such multinationals should:

1 Do no intentional direct harm.
2 Produce more good than harm for the host country.
3 Contribute by their activity to the host country's development.
4 Respect the human rights of their employees.
5 Respect the local culture and work with and not against it.
6 Pay their fair share of taxes.
7 Cooperate with the local government in developing and enforcing just background institutions.
8 Recognize that majority control of a firm carries with it the ethical responsibility for the actions and failures of the firm.
9 Make sure that hazardous plants are safe and run safely.
10 When transferring hazardous technology to less-developed countries, be responsible for redesigning such technology so that it can be safely administered in the host country.

As De George's rules imply, one of the most difficult contexts for transnational ethics involves clashes between home- and host-country norms or laws. The problem is especially acute when the norm or law appears substandard from the perspective of the transnational's home country. When wage scales, pollution standards, norms prohibiting bribery, and treatment of minorities appear substandard in a foreign country, should the transnational take the high road of adhering to the home-country standards, or should it take the expedient route of embracing the host-country standards?

Embracing either extreme would be morally problematic. Always to adopt the home-country standard would sometimes disadvantage the host country. For example, a transnational that always paid workers in host countries the same wage rates as paid in the home country could damage foreign development in the host country, since attractive wage rates are often the principal incentive for transnational investment overseas. Furthermore, the trade-offs among competing economic and social goods may be different in the host than in the home country. A third world country barely able to feed its malnourished population may prefer somewhat higher levels of pollution and more productivity (say, of food and fertilizer) than would a developed nation.

On the other hand, always to adopt the host-country standard would be pernicious. Laws and regulations in many developing countries are frequently unsophisticated, and a lack of technological knowledge coupled with inefficient bureaucratic mechanisms may preclude effective government control of industry. Blindly to adopt a developing country's standards for asbestos or for the dumping of hazardous waste could have tragic human consequences. While no simple answers exist, Donaldson, De George, and others have argued that certain principles can be articulated for the purpose of addressing such problems of norms in conflict.

In a directly practical vein, coalitions of governments and transnational corporations are increasingly articulating shared responsibilities in formal documents. Sometimes the responsibilities are formalized as the result of voluntary efforts by companies who are members of the same industry, as in the instance of the World Health Organization's Code on Pharmaceuticals and Tobacco, and the World Intellectual Property Organization's Revision of the Paris Convention for the Protection of Industrial Patents and Trademarks. Sometimes they are formalized as the result of international economic arrangements, as in the instance of the principles of intellectual property circumscribed by the General Agreement on Tariffs and Trade (GATT). And sometimes they are formalized as a result of decisions by truly global institutions, as in the instance of the OECD's *Declaration on International Investment and Multinational Enterprise.*

Bibliography

De George, R. T. (1993). *Competing with Integrity in International Business.* New York: Oxford University Press.

Donaldson, T. (1989). *The Ethics of International Business.* New York: Oxford University Press.

Donaldson, T. (1991). The ethics of conditionality in international debt. *Millennium: Journal of International Studies,* **20** (2), 155–69.

Enderle, G. (1989). The indebtedness of low-income countries as an ethical challenge for industrialized market economies. *International Journal of Applied Philosophy,* **4** (3), 31–8.

Guidelines for Multinational Enterprises (1984). Added to the 1976 *OECD Declaration.* In *International Investment and Multinational Enterprises: Revised Edition 1984.* Paris: Organization for Economic Cooperation and Development, 11–22.

Kline, J. (1985). *International Codes and Multinational Business: Setting Guidelines for International Operations.* Westport, CT: Quorum Books.

Moran, T. H. (1977). *Multinational Corporations and the Politics of Dependence: Copper in Chile.* Princeton, NJ: Princeton University Press.

O'Neill, O. (1986). *Faces of Hunger: An Essay on Poverty, Justice, and Development.* London: Allen and Unwin.

Preston, L. E. and Windsor, D. (1991). *The Rules of the Game in the Global Economy: Policy Regimes for International Business.* Dordrecht: Kluwer.

Shue, H. (1980). *Basic Rights.* Princeton, NJ: Princeton University Press.

Waldman, R. J. (1980). *Regulating International Business Through Codes of Conduct.* Washington, DC: American Enterprise Institute.

International Society of Business, Economics, and Ethics

Georges Enderle

ISBEE, formed in 1989, is the first worldwide professional association to focus exclusively on the study of business, economics, and ethics. Its professional orientation involves people not only with academic competencies but also with practical competencies in responsible management positions (such as vice-presidents and issue managers) and entrepreneurs of medium-sized and small companies. Individual membership consists of academicians, managers of business firms and of not-for-profit organizations, and others who have an interest in business ethics. Organizational membership includes companies and other organizations. ISBEE is strongly international in character with members from around the world.

ISBEE developed in response to a felt need to bring together individuals in traditionally distinctive fields – economics, business, law, and philosophy – and different practical areas – human resources, marketing, finance, social and environmental concerns. What characterizes these individuals is their common interest in the ethical dimension of economic, social, and environmental issues that affect domestic and global firms and hence individuals and broader structures as well. The organization offers a global network of persons and organizations and a wide range of professional activities, including quadrennial congresses, proceedings, a newsletter, and a webpage.

The mission of ISBEE is to provide a forum for the exchange of experiences and ideas; to enhance cooperation in cross-functional and cross-cultural projects; and to discuss the ethical dimension of economic, social, and environmental issues which affect companies nationally and internationally. ISBEE supports a cross-disciplinary approach with the participation of both academicians and practitioners. It schedules its conferences and programs to encourage both formal and informal sharing of ideas and projects.

ISBEE cooperates with regional and national networks of business ethics around the globe: the Society for Business Ethics (North America), the European Business Ethics Network (EBEN), the Japan Society for Business Ethics Studies (JABES), the Latin American Business Ethics Network (ALENE), and the African Business Ethics Network (BEN–Africa). It actively supports the creation of business ethics networks, particularly in developing countries. In 2002, ISBEE entered an institutional affiliation with the Caux Round Table (CRT).

A culminating event of ISBEE's activities is the World Congress of Business, Economics, and Ethics, held every four years. Past congresses have taken place in Tokyo (1996) with keynote speakers such as Amartya Sen (Nobel Prize winner in Economics) and Hans Küng (initiator of *Global Ethic*), in São Paulo (2000) with Mark Moody-Stuart (Shell) and Muhammad Yunus (Grameen Bank), and in Melbourne (2004) with Ewald Kist (ING Group) and Narayana Murthy (Infosys, India). In addition, ISBEE has been supporting regional conferences in São Paulo (1998, 2003), Shanghai, (2002), Oslo (2003), and Zambia (2003).

Membership in ISBEE is open to persons and organizations in all countries who are interested in business and economic ethics, from either a practitioner or academic perspective. Email: isbee@nd.edu; webpage: http://www.isbee.org.

Internet and business ethics

Richard T. De George

The Internet is a global communication network of networks, all using a standard TCP/IP protocol. The Internet includes and makes possible email, chat rooms, online conferencing, the worldwide web, Telnet, newsgroups, and a host of other means of transferring information and communicating with people around the globe. It has made possible the globalization of businesses, which are able to coordinate their many activities wherever they take place around the world. It has also made possible telework for employees, sales via the worldwide web, and one-on-one marketing on a scale previously unimagined. It is changing the way business is done, and in the process is raising new ethical issues, on which no general consensus has yet emerged. Nonetheless, in many ways the Internet is simply another tool used by business, and from that point of view, lying, misrepresentation, deceptive advertising, fraud, theft, and so on are clearly as unethical when done on the Internet as when done through any other medium.

A few ethical issues arise with respect to the Internet itself as a business. One example is the practice of cyber-squatting. This consists of registering a domain name of a well-known company, such as IBM (e.g., IBM.com), or the names of celebrities or politicians, before they do and selling the domain name in question to that company or individual for a large profit. Although registering a domain name might cost as little as $30.00, the company in question might be willing to pay many thousands of dollars for it – and one company paid over $7 million. The practice, if done deliberately for the purpose of reselling it, is arguably unethical. Although it is now illegal in the United States, it remains legal in a large number of countries.

A second set of issues concern Internet Service Providers (ISPs), which provide the connection between an individual's computer and the Internet, usually for a fee. One question is the responsibility that an ISP has for the content of the sites provided. The ethical issue is usually argued by analogy. Is the ISP's role similar to that of a newspaper, and so responsible for what appears on it; or is it similar to that of a telephone company, which simply makes possible a connection and cannot be held responsible for what people say using the phone lines; or is it something other? If notified that a user is perpetrating fraud, does the ISP have the responsibility to terminate that user? A second issue has to do with the privacy that subscribers to an ISP deserve. Should an ISP turn over the names of subscribers without a court order to do so for cause? A third issue is whether ISPs (or governments) have any obligation to help guarantee universal accessibility to the Internet by all people, and whether they have the right to censor what they allow access to, making it impossible to access what the ISP (e.g., if it is state owned) does not wish its users to see.

The majority of ethical issues, however, have to do not with the Internet as a business, but with business over the Internet or business uses of the Internet. Business done over the Internet is often called e-business or e-commerce, which can be either business-to-business (B2B) or business-to-customer (B2C).

Although B2B raises some ethical issues, for the most part they are comparable to issues in brick and mortar business transactions, namely, those dealing with monopoly practices, price fixing, collusion, and the like. Although B2B tends to dominate the e-business market, more attention has been focused on issues in B2C, perhaps because individual customers are more vulnerable than businesses, which are frequently better able to protect their interests in ways that individual consumers cannot. Even here, however, some practices such as fraud, misrepresentation, deceptive advertising, and the like are clearly unethical and raise no new ethical problems. Issues that have drawn the most attention are privacy, security, spam, pornography, employees' use of the Internet, legal jurisdictions, and intellectual property.

The issue of privacy arises in many ways, one of which is the possibility of tracking customers beyond their activities on a business's own site. This might be done by following the user from one's site to other sites, or by the use of "third party cookies" (which consists of placing "cookies" or a string of information about a customer's visits to sites that carry banner ads for any of the products advertising with a given advertising agency). The aim of such tracking is frequently to determine the interests of the shopper so that the customer can be targeted with one-on-one advertising, or be sent ads about products in which he or she is likely to be interested. Many users object to the fact that information is gathered on them without their knowledge and so without their consent. Whether consent is tacitly given by web-browsing because the practice of tracking is now fairly well known is debated, with many privacy advocates arguing that informed consent (using opt-out as the default) and explicit consent for tracking are ethically required.

Security issues also arise in a variety of ways. One question is the extent of the moral responsibility of Internet businesses to protect their customers' records, credit cards, and personal information against theft by hackers. Second, since surfing the web, entering into chat rooms, and engaging in other interactive activities on the Internet puts one in contact with unknown parties, issues of safety arise. As a result, it is not uncommon for email providers, such as Hotmail, and chat rooms to suggest that users use pseudonyms to disguise their identities. This in turn makes it even more difficult to be sure with whom one is dealing – which leads to electronic attempts to make up for the lack of security, via encryption, various techniques to verify that one is communicating with the person intended, and

proxy servers which help hide one's computer address. Although generally accepted, some see the need for such electronic techniques as a response to the lack of trust that generally pervades Internet use.

Spam is the equivalent of junk mail, and consists of messages or ads that are sent in bulk to thousands or even millions of recipients at one time. If sent in great enough numbers, they can overload the capacity of ISPs, and if received in large enough numbers from different sources, they can fill a recipient's mailbox, making it impossible to receive other email, or they pose the chore of sorting through hundreds of emails in which one has no interest, wasting valuable time and causing great annoyance. The practice is therefore seen by many as unethical. There are filters that some ISPs supply to their users to block spam, but much still gets through. Those who use spam often defend the practice as simply a legitimate form of advertising and no more unethical than junk mail. Nonetheless, the activity is so inexpensive that it is used much more than junk mail, and the cost is borne more by the receiver in terms of annoyance and time than by the sender. There have been some attempts to make at least certain types of spam illegal.

Many complain that pornography is rampant on the Internet, and it is certainly readily available. One issue that the United States has tried, so far unsuccessfully, to legislate against, is the availability of pornography by children or minors. Whether or not supplying pornography to (and viewing it by) consenting adults is unethical is debated, but in most jurisdictions it is legal. Yet supplying such material to children is illegal, and arguably unethical. Unlike movie theaters and video stores, which can allow entry only to adults, and unlike TV, which is regulated if available free, pornography on the Internet can be readily accessed by anyone, despite some attempts at age verification. Many sites are also often found inadvertently through search engines, for instance under "games," which contain links to many pornographic sites.

Corporations often claim that they are being robbed by employees who spend unreasonable amounts of time on the Internet or using personal email. What is ethical or unethical for employees with respect to Internet and email use is not a matter of simple right and wrong. The reason is that legally an employee's computer belongs to the employer who supplies it, and who has legal access to everything on the computer. Since the computers belong to the employer, the employer can determine how much access to the Internet by way of email and web browsing it will allow employees. While some people argue that respect for one's employees demands that companies not track employee use and not prohibit all personal use, there is general agreement that at a minimum, from an ethical point of view, employees should be informed of the company's policy and should be told what is and what is not permitted.

The Internet crosses borders between states and countries with impunity. Although this is convenient for users, it raises innumerable problems for legal jurisdictions. Which laws apply, those of the state or country in which the sender or website is located or those in which the receiver is located? One email virus, the "I Love You" bug, which did billions of dollars damage worldwide, was launched by a student in the Philippines, which at the time had no law against such activity. The student could not be prosecuted. Child pornography, illegal in most jurisdictions, is not illegal in some, and so the receiver but not the sender might be subject to prosecution. The issue of taxes and who has the authority to levy and collect taxes on Internet sales is still unresolved. In this instance what is fair with respect to e-businesses in the United States that compete with brick and mortar or with mail order businesses is also not yet resolved. The privacy laws in the European Union are different from the laws in the United States. If each were limited to its own jurisdiction, there would be no problem. But individuals transact business across borders on the Internet. The obvious but difficult solution is to harmonize the rules and laws in all jurisdictions. But there are so many areas to be covered and so many differences that harmonization is very difficult.

The issue of ownership of intellectual property is exacerbated by the Internet, in part because of the question of jurisdiction and the difference in views of ownership of intellectual property in different parts of the world, but also because of the ease with which digital information – whether in the form of text or music or visuals or movies – can be downloaded. The case of Napster raised the question of the legitimacy of peer-to-peer exchanges in which users made their records available to anyone who wished to download them through the intermediary of Napster. Although the US courts found against Napster, it has been replaced by programs which enable copying from individual to individual without any intermediary. Such practices are being fought vigorously by record, video, and motion picture companies for copyright infringement, and this has led to various forms of legislation, which critics claim go too far in protecting material that is in the public domain. Thus the ethics of copying, trading, copyright, and appropriate legislation are all hotly debated issues. Similarly, the patenting of business methods using the Internet, which is beginning in the United States, is contested as unethical by some.

The issues of ethics and business on the Internet will remain thorny and disputed for the foreseeable future, despite certain broad areas of agreement.

Bibliography

De George, R. T. (2003). *The Ethics of Information Technology and Business.* Oxford: Blackwell.

Johnson, D. (2001). *Computer Ethics,* 3rd edn. Upper Saddle River, NJ: Prentice-Hall.

Spinello, R. A. and Tavani, H. (eds.) (2001). *Readings in CyberEthics.* Boston, MA: Jones and Bartlett Publishers.

invisible hand, the

David Kirkwood Hart

The assumption that society benefits most when individuals are allowed to define and pursue their own self-interests, with minimal interference from governments or other authorities. However, this assumption also presumes there is some guiding natural force – seldom mentioned and almost never defined – that ensures a just equilibrium will result from such self-interested behaviors.

The concept of the invisible hand first emerges in the work of Adam Smith, who mentions it in two brief passages in his two major books. Nowadays the term has been captured by the economists, but, originally, it had more to do with Smith's moral philosophy than it did with merely his economic ideas. It is this larger, moral conception that is of greatest interest for business ethics.

Smith, profoundly influenced by Stoicism, believes the invisible hand is a beneficent force of nature, operating without human intention and within a system of natural liberty, which allocates social goods in a rough and ready, but generally fair, distribution. This eventually results in the greatest happiness for the greatest number, a concept he borrows from his mentor, Francis Hutcheson.

Some argue that Smith's ideas about the invisible hand come from the rather unsavory philosophy of unmitigated self-interest advocated by his contemporary, Bernard Mandeville, who argued that the pursuit of "private vices" resulted in "publick benefits." But Smith devoted a hefty chapter in his first book, *The Theory of Moral Sentiments* (1759), to discrediting Mandeville's ideas. Indeed, it can be argued that Smith's conception of the invisible hand was his answer to Mandeville.

Turning to Smith's writings, aside from a casual and contradictory reference in an early essay, "The history of astronomy," the two major references to the invisible hand are in his two major books. The most famous and frequently quoted passage, in his second book, *The Wealth of Nations* (1776), is actually the least explanatory of the two. In a section discussing the "natural balance of industry," Smith notes that investors like to keep their capital close to home, which works to the advantage of the local community. Further, the main reason they invest is to increase their profits. Thus:

> As every individual, therefore, endeavours as much as he can both to employ his capital in the support of domestick industry, and so to direct that industry that its produce may be of the greatest value; every individual necessarily labours to render the annual revenue of the society as great as he can. He generally, indeed, neither intends to promote the publick interest, nor knows how much he is promoting it. (Smith, 1776: 456)

The important point here is that intelligent individuals, who possess capital, direct the full force of their intelligence to improving domestic industry so as to make a profit. Even though their motive is profit, the entire society benefits from that collective application of intelligence. As a result:

> By preferring the support of domestick to that of foreign industry, he intends only his own security; and by directing that industry in such a manner as its produce may be of the greatest value, he intends only his own gain, and he is in this, as in many other cases, led by an invisible hand to promote an end which was no part of his intention. (Smith, 1776: 456)

This passage might seem to support the popular, but erroneous, argument that Adam Smith was the precursor of economic Social Darwinism. But that is far off the mark, as can be seen in his earlier and longer explication of the term in *The Theory of Moral Sentiments*. There Smith presents his moral philosophy, intending that all of his later works would be interpreted in terms of it. The foundation of that system rests upon the primacy of sympathy, which is the ability of all individuals to understand one another. Moreover, Smith knows that society is a mixed bag: some people are unabashedly self-interested, but others are both virtuous and caring. It is upon the latter that he constructs his ideal society.

The main issue that leads Smith to the notion of the invisible hand is the incomprehensible complexity of society. It is impossible for any individuals or groups, including the government, to comprehend society well enough to allow them to systematically plan and guide the society toward good ends. Indeed, he notes that he had "never known much good done by those who affected to trade for the publick good. It is an affectation" (Smith, 1776: 456).

Smith wants to free humankind from the paternalism of those individuals and groups who believe they can direct and control society for its own best good. The villain is "the man of system": the individual who believes that he or she can devise and execute plans which will guarantee desired social benefits.

Smith recognizes the impossibility of any human plan being able to encompass the fullness and complexity of society. Thus, organizational systems, externally imposed, are bound to fail, and people will suffer as a result. Smith advises us to let the human chess pieces move of their own volition, guided primarily by their individual virtue, and an invisible hand will lead them all toward a just outcome.

It is significant that the concept of the invisible hand is introduced in a passage attacking the "splenetic philosophy" of Mandeville. Smith begins by condemning the silly ostentation of the wealthy: "If we consider the real satisfaction which all these things are capable of affording, by itself and separated from the beauty of that arrangement which is fitted to promote it, it will always appear in the highest degree contemptible and trifling" (Smith, 1759: 183). He knew, however, that the rich would continue to spend lavishly, out of "their natural selfishness and rapacity." But since the stomachs of the wealthy can contain no more than the stomachs of the poor, what do the wealthy hope to obtain? The answer is clear: most of them serve only their vanity.

However, out of such self-indulgence will often come social good. The wealthy are led by an invisible hand to make nearly the same distribution of the necessaries of life, which would have been made, had the earth been divided into equal portions among all its inhabitants, and thus without intending it, without knowing it, advance the interest of the society, and afford means to the multiplication of the species (Smith, 1759: 184).

Thus, without intending it, and in an economic system of natural liberty, such spending provides indirectly for the working men and women. As H. B. Acton writes: "An unintended result of action is thus something that is not specifically aimed at by any member of a group of agents but that arises as a result of each agent's successful pursuit of his particular aim" (Acton, 1993: 174).

So ordinary people are employed in building the mansions of the rich; they tend their fields, flocks, and gardens; they run their industries; they manufacture and repair their goods; and so on. For these services, they are compensated, and this brings about a relatively just distribution of material benefits. Smith clearly understands the savage inequities of tyrannies and

monopolies, but he attacks them at other places in his books.

The most important thing for Adam Smith is the happiness of all individuals, which is not necessarily related to their comparative shares in economic goods. Thus, he continues his description of the invisible hand by pointing to its moral significance:

> When Providence divided the earth among a few lordly masters, it neither forgot nor abandoned those who seemed to have been left out in the partition. These last too enjoy their share of all that it produces. *In what constitutes the real happiness of human life, they are in no respect inferior to those who would seem so much above them.* In ease of body and peace of mind, all the different ranks of life are nearly upon a level, and the beggar, who suns himself by the side of the highway, possesses that security which kings are fighting for. (Smith, 1759: 184–5; emphasis added)

In the ideal, then, the invisible hand concerns much more than economics: it concerns the moral happiness of all individuals encompassed within a larger society.

Such happiness comes through virtuous character. Throughout *The Theory of Moral Sentiments* Smith repeats the admonition that for the ideal to exist, all individuals must act virtuously. What is not clearly understood by too many contemporary readers is how much Smith's ideal rests upon individual virtue, and that is certainly the case with the invisible hand: it only works as it should when all participants play fair. For Adam Smith, the optimal functioning of the invisible hand is predicated upon widespread virtue (Smith, 1759: 82–91).

However, that ethical conception has been lost to modernity, and the invisible hand has been reduced down to an unintentional (and largely inexplicable) ordering factor among rational utility maximizers competing in free markets, which results in a reasonable distribution of economic goods within that society. This view of the invisible hand relies more upon the utilitarianism of Jeremy Bentham and his followers than it does upon Adam Smith. For them, the primal motivation for each individual is the minimization of pain and the maximization of pleasure. Since such pleasures and pains come mostly from the physical needs of individuals, it follows that citizens serve society best by following their material instincts. Adam Smith conceives of the invisible hand quite differently. For him, it operates best as the result of intentional and voluntary virtue. The greatest contribution individuals can make to the collective good is the development and actualization of their own virtue.

Bibliography

Acton, H. B. (1993). *The Morals of Markets and Related Essays*, ed. D. Gordon and J. Shearmur. Indianapolis, IN: Liberty Classics.

Morrow, G. R. (1923). *The Ethical and Economic Theories of Adam Smith*. Clifton, NJ: Augustus M. Kelley.

Muller, J. Z. (1993). *Adam Smith in His Time and Ours*. New York: Free Press.

Smith, A. (1759; 1790). *The Theory of Moral Sentiments*, ed. D. D. Raphael and A. L. Macfie. Indianapolis, IN: Liberty Classics.

Smith, A. (1776). *An Inquiry into the Nature and Causes of the Wealth of Nations*, ed. R. H. Campbell and A. S. Skinner. Indianapolis, IN: Liberty Classics.

Werhane, P. H. (1991). *Adam Smith and His Legacy for Modern Capitalism*. New York: Oxford University Press.

Islam, business ethics and

Abdulaziz A. Sachedina

Islam, the third and last of the Abrahamic religions to emerge, literally means "submission to God's will." It was proclaimed by Muhammad (born 570 CE), the Prophet of Islam and the founder of Islamic public order in the seventh century CE in Mecca, Arabia. Mecca was the most important trading center of western and central Arabia. Meccans played a dominant role in the creation of a culture that developed and nurtured a socioeconomic system based on Islamic justice. Islam required a good public order in which spiritual interests were organically related to individual material well-being. Hence, the law of the marketplace was given almost equal weight with the regulations connected with acts of worship in the mosque.

The market mechanism is an integral part of the Islamic economic system because the institution of private property depends on it for its operation. It also provides for consumers to express their desires for the production of goods of their liking by their willingness to pay the price. But the profit motive that is essential for the operation of free enterprise, if not controlled, could also become a tool of greed and violate Islamic goals of social and economic justice and equitable distribution of income and wealth. The strictures against usury in the Qur'an can be seen as the clear distinction Islam makes between legitimate trade with profit and unchecked individual greed to increase one's possessions without engaging in trade in a market economy. According to Muslim jurists:

> The law in order for the people to benefit mutually permits buying and selling. There is no doubt that this can also be a cause of injustice, because both buyer and seller desire more profit and the Lawgiver has neither prohibited profit nor has He set limits to it. He has, however, prohibited fraud and cheating and ascribing to a commodity attributes that it does not possess. (al-Jaziri, *Kitab al-fiqh 'ala al-madhahib al-arbaa*)

MARKET ECONOMY AND CONTRACTUAL RELATIONS

Islam, as it developed in the regions inhabited by other monotheistic faiths like Judaism, Christianity, and Zoroastrianism, shared an ethos of public order founded upon justice. It required the practice of a minimum of moral virtues intended to be a kind of "rule of life." Along with certain rules, which were practical and material, temporary and external, Muslim ethicists explicitly decreed various permanent restrictions designed to discipline both the body (rules about lawful foods and earning, about dress and public behavior) and the mind (prohibited subjects of thought and conversation that led to the corruption of conscience). In addition, Islam required certain expiatory works of charity to compensate for the sins of omission and commission, primarily to inculcate sociability. Whereas the ritual acts, whether performed publicly in a group or privately, were the homage humankind paid to God and were intended to affect the conscience of the practicing believer, commercial engagements were closely tied to the notions of interpersonal justice and were intended to affect public behavior. In this latter sense, the rites are instruments provided by God for attaining a higher level of conscientious development needed for assuming greater social responsibilities.

The main concern of Islamic public order was not so much collective interest as individual justice in transactions that had to be protected outside of close friendships and family ties. It was expected that, contrary to the claims of tribal kinship and noble family lineage that determined social relations in pre-Islamic Arabia, most human relations under Islam would take the form of contract relations rather than be determined in advance by social status. Many provisions in the law attempted to back those who were weak in one way or another against the strong who might take advantage of them. On the whole, faith in Islam constituted ten parts, of which only one part was related to the God–human relationship and claimed the status of a common universal obligation. The remaining nine parts were related to human relationships determined by contractual responsibilities and specific social and cultural experience.

Muslim juridical writings give detailed rulings related to the acquisition and disposal of private and business property and the purchase and sale of merchandise. The underlying principle operative in market law is twofold: the autonomy of the individual to own productive resources to further her/his economic interest and the protection of the consumer from harm. The pursuit of individual economic interest has to be regulated within a communitarian ethic requiring the individual to take the competing interests of the community at large as morally binding. Therefore, any individual business undertaking seen to cause harm to the moral and spiritual fabric of society is to be condemned and prohibited. The protection of the consumer was regulated through the principle of non-maleficence (*al-darar al-muhtamal*). This principle requires that resource-owners would not seek to cause harm to buyers by false evaluation and other means to increase sales. Hence, deceptive advertising is regarded as morally wrong and legally punishable. The principle of public interest (*maslaha*) requires that free mutual consent of the buyer and the seller be regarded as a necessary condition for any business transaction. The Qur'an provides the grounds for the ruling: "O believers, consume not your goods between you in vanity, except there be trading, by your agreeing together" (K. 4:29). Individual freedom in negotiating business transactions is recognized in the directive given by the Prophet: "Leave people alone, for God provides them sustenance through each other" (*Sahih al-Muslim, Kitab al-Buyú, Hadith* 1522). Thus, freedom of enterprise leaves the conduct of a large part of the production and distribution of goods and services to individuals or voluntarily constituted groups. However, even this otherwise absolute freedom is regulated by the legal principle of public interest that requires that the good of its commission – when compared to the harm – should be predominant.

SHARIA AND THE EMERGENCE OF PRINCIPLES FROM CASES

Islamic ethics, mediated through God's will, is an integral part of Islamic law – the Sharia. The Sharia determines the specifics of a system in which judgments of public interest and equity are causally related to the overall prosperity of the community in this and the next life. The end of humanity is happiness, and this is attained fully through the rewards of God on the Day of Judgment for everything that humans do to improve the quality of the spiritual/moral and material life of humanity.

Islamic jurisprudence (*fiqh*) was developed to determine normative Islamic conduct as detailed in the Sharia, the Sacred Law. The Sharia is the divinely ordained blueprint for human conduct, which was inherently and essentially religious. The juridical inquiry in discovering the Sharia code was comprehensive because it necessarily dealt with every case of conscience covering God–human relations, as well as the ethical content of interpersonal relations in every possible sphere of human activity. Most of the legal activity, however, went into settling more formal interpersonal activities that affected the morals of the community. These activities dealt with the obligation of doing good to Muslims and guarding the interests of the community. Hence, in the area of economics, the Sharia dealt with negative and positive limits governing economic activities of consumption, production, distribution, and exchange.

Human conduct is to be determined in terms of how much legal weight is borne by a particular rule that rendered a given practice obligatory or merely recommended. For instance, if it is deemed that bribery, which is ethically and legally forbidden, becomes necessary under an unjust system in order to influence a decision leading to the betterment of the community, then the law excuses it after a careful risk-benefit analysis. Cases involving blatant moral–spiritual corruption are excluded in this ruling. Likewise, it had to be decided whether an obligatory act, because of its social relevance and the degree of applicability of a given rule or precedent, was to be enforced by penalties in the courts or left to God's judgment in the hereafter. Thus, for instance, transactions involving selling or buying of alcohol were regarded as illicit and punishable by the Sharia courts because of its social relevance. However, a Muslim businessman living in the West where he sometimes has to entertain his non-Muslim clients with alcohol while abstaining himself, although a sinful act in itself, is regarded as being beyond the jurisdiction of the Sharia court.

As developed in classical Islamic legal theory, justifications in religious–moral action consist of a dialectic between judgments in specific cases and the generalizations derived from rationale in cases in the light of which generalizations themselves are modified. Hence, to derive a specific ethical judgment – for example, that an act of distribution of surplus wealth among the needy is obligatory – is to confirm that it satisfies a certain description of the religious–moral concept of justice according to one's belief in social responsibility. Social responsibility, as part of the generalizable command to be just, could then be applied to other acts. Taking the specific case of interest, interpreted as covering any money payment for money, the koranic position was interpreted as a social responsibility not to make a loan to someone in need the occasion of profiting from their distress. At the same time, the ethical requirement that human beings must treat each other fairly, made interest in Muslim societies a major resource for investment in cases where – if two businessmen were agreed – then it might be legitimate for the one who was to profit by the consequences of the present deal with the other to be bound to share his profit in a complementary future deal. The convergence between the divine command that human beings must

treat each other justly and the rational cognition of justice being good underscores the importance of formulating specific moral–legal judgments first and then searching for principles that can be generalized and applied to new cases.

There is a correlation between known moral convictions and God's purposes as mentioned in the revelation. Hence, when the Qur'an banned transactions involving interest, the purpose was clearly to protect the financially weak against the wealthy taking advantage of them. General moral beliefs like the protection of the weak in society are guided by the revelation that views interest as a form of disregard for the downtrodden in society, and seek their application in specific situations (like engaging in contracts that call for taking interest), thereby furthering the authenticity and relevance of religiously and morally governed economic activity. Although the system allowed the latitude to cope with changing conditions of the community, the predominant concern among lawyers was the fear of arbitrariness in the decisions of those who held financial and political power.

MARKET ETHICS AND THE CHARGING OF INTEREST (*RIBA*)

Perhaps one of the most difficult issues in Islamic concern for fairness in business dealings was its prohibition of business transactions that called for charging interest in its koranic meaning, that is, covering money payment for money. Muslims have struggled with the problem of interest ever since the Qur'an categorically denounced it. Jurists have interpreted the koranic prohibition as permitting exceptions as cases required in different contexts. There have been a number of rulings issued at different times in the history of Islamic jurisprudence when a distinction was made between usury (*riba*) and interest to circumvent the categorical prohibition. Other scholars believed there was a difference between Muslim and non-Muslim financial institutions, allowing Muslims to receive interest from the latter institutions while prohibiting it from the former.

From early times, transactions with a fixed time limit and payment of interest (*riba*), as well as speculations of all kinds, formed an essential element in the highly developed Meccan system of trade at the time when the Prophet emerged. A debtor who could not repay the capital (money or goods) with the accumulated interest at the time it became due, was given an extension of time in which to pay, but at the same time the sum due was doubled. The practice was prevalent during the early part of the Prophet's mission in Mecca before he migrated to Medina in the year 622 CE, and he denounced it. Like other social reforms introduced by the Prophet in a developing community, a prohibition against interest was introduced in stages in the Qur'an, beginning with the verse: "O believers, devour not usury [*riba*] doubled and redoubled, and fear you God" (K. 3:130).

Clearly, the Qur'an regards usury as a practice of unbelievers and demands as a test of belief that it should be abandoned. The Prophetic traditions elaborate the koranic passages in the matter of interest on loans only, declaring interest-taking as one of the gravest sins. All who take part in transactions involving interest are cursed, the guilty are threatened with hell, and various kinds of punishment are described. In spite of all this, there exist reports which foresee that transactions involving interest will prevail (*Al-Muwatta'*, Imam Malik).

The koranic denunciations of usury were occasioned by the needs of a developing community faced with socioeconomic imbalances. Consequently, as it appears in the Qur'an, in some instances related to interpersonal justice it softens its position on a matter against which it has fulminated elsewhere, recognizing the human conditions that prompt such behavior. At other times, the Prophet, as its interpreter, moderated the koranic stance by providing exceptions to the overall prohibition. The case of usury evidently points to this revelation–history confrontation in the early community. A number of traditions show that the severe prohibition of usury was moderated by reference to the changed circumstances of a transaction involving specific items and the way they exchanged hands in active trade. In general, Muslim jurists developed cases to permit exceptions to the categorical prohibition in the Qur'an. The cases were reported in the traditions that were open to various interpretations. There were monetary transactions that led to principles that now govern when and where interest may be accepted. For instance, some Muslims practiced money exchange during the Prophet's lifetime. They asked the Prophet if this was all right. The Prophet said: "If it is from hand to hand [*yadan bi-yadin*, that is, immediately], there is no harm in it; but if it is delayed [*nasa'an*] it is not right" (*Sahih al-Bukhari, Kitab al-Buyù, Hadith* 14). Some jurists extrapolated these traditions to maintain the view that *riba* consists only in the increase of the original amount of a loan in a business agreement with a fixed period (*dayn*); others opined that there is no *riba* if the transfer of ownership takes place immediately. In other words, interest was to be permitted if transfer of ownership took place at once.

CONTEMPORARY ATTITUDES TOWARDS INTEREST (*RIBA*)

Based on the rulings inferred by the earlier jurists, there now exists a view among some Muslim jurists that interest is permitted if transfer of ownership of goods capable of *riba* takes place immediately (Schacht, 1995). The more strict Muslims, in their limitation of *riba*, exchange goods of the same kind in equal quantities as laid down in some traditions. In the case of loans, which is generally understood to be the koranic reason for prohibition of interest, it is forbidden to make a condition that a larger quantity shall be returned without regard to the kind of article. In premodern judicial decisions gold and silver are generally regarded as items capable of *riba*. Outside of precious metals there are differences of opinion about the items that are liable to usury ordinances. Thus, for instance, should all business dealings in things of the same kind be considered capable of *riba*? Opinions vary according to the documentation used to deduce juridical decisions.

The structure of the greater part of the law of contract is explained by the endeavor to enforce prohibition of usury and risk (*maysir*). Muslims are prohibited either from taking or paying interest. *Riba* in a loan exists not only when one insists upon the repayment of a larger quantity, but also if any advantage at all is demanded. Therefore, even a bill of exchange (*suftaja*) is sometimes actually forbidden, because the vendor, who is regarded as the creditor, reaps the advantage of avoiding the cost of transport.

This did not prevent the extensive spread of this arrangement in the Muslim middle ages. However, Muslim merchants were always conscious that a direct breach of the prohibition of usury was a grave sin. To this day, therefore, conscientious Muslims not infrequently refuse to accept bank interest.

The importance of *riba*-based commerce and its requirement to charge interest have given rise to a number of methods to evade the prohibition. Some Sunni schools and the Shiites have recognized such methods of evasion in their discussion about the purpose of divinely ordained restrictions. These methods are not seen as contrary to the strict enforcement of the prohibition in applied jurisprudence. Application of two juristic principles: (1) "Necessity overrides prohibition," and (2) "No harm and harassment in Islam," has made it possible for jurists to rule that the rationale and inner significance of the koranic ordinance reveal the need to take into consideration the situational aspects of the original prohibition. Hence, one can conjecture about the philosophy of laws leading to the categorical prohibition of interest because of its adverse impact upon those who are manipulated in society; or one can regard it as distasteful but maneuver carefully to make interest fall within the acceptable limits required by the rule "No harm and no harassment" of otherwise lawful transactions. Moreover, in the case of deferred sales (*buy-uàl-àjal*), in which either the delivery of the item or the payment of its price is deferred to a later date, where all would tend to fall under a sale which is used as a means of procuring *riba*, there is no certainty, nor even a strong probability, that such a sale leads to evil. Hence, if *A* sells his car to *B* for $10,000, with the price being payable in six months' time, and *A* buys the same car for $8,000 from *B* with the price being payable immediately, this transaction in fact amounts to a loan of $8,000 to *B* on which he pays an interest of $2,000 after six months. There is a strong probability that this sale would lead to *riba*, although there is an element of uncertainty. It is for this reason that some jurists have regarded this type of transaction as valid and the basic legality of sale must be held to prevail (Kamali, 1991: 315–16).

Nevertheless, more strict jurists have regarded any loan contract specifying a fixed return to the lender as immoral and illegal, regardless of the purpose for which a loan is sought, its amount, or the prevailing institutional framework. Accordingly, they have condemned an array of common business practices as un-Islamic and unethical. But most business people simply consent to the Western model, as long as the financial institution happens to be non-Muslim. In this decision they have been guided by a majority of jurists who justify their rulings by regarding modern bank interest as something different than the *riba* (usury) mentioned in the Qur'an. Their supporting argument discusses the lexical meaning of the word *riba*, which literally means "increase." Since not every increase or profit is unlawful, the text remains ambiguous as to what type of increase it intends to forbid. Moreover, some of these jurists regard banking with interest as permissible, as long as a person does not negotiate the interest and the bank is non-Muslim. However, there is a powerful minority juridical opinion that takes the koranic prohibition as explicit and categorical.

Bibliography

None of the works listed below directly deal with issues in business ethics in Islam; nor do they address contemporary issues that form part of the ongoing debate in the areas of corporate social responsibility, advertising, conflict of interest and conflict of obligation, and environmental responsibility. With the technicalization of the Muslim world, international trade regulations have replaced or ignored the classical juristic rulings of the premodern Islamic law of transactions.

Ahmad, K. (ed.). (1980). *Studies in Islamic Economics*. Leicester: Islamic Foundation.

Kamali, M. H. (1991). *Principles of Islamic Jurisprudence*. Cambridge: Cambridge University Press.

Sadr, Ayatollah Baqir al- (1982). *Islam and Schools of Economics*. Karachi: Islamic Seminary.

Schacht, J. (1995). *Riba*. In the *Encyclopaedia of Islam*, 2nd edn., Vol. 8, 1491–3. Leiden: Brill.

Siddiqi, M. N. (1981). *Muslim Economic Thinking: A Survey of Contemporary Literature*. Leicester: Islamic Foundation.

Taleqani, S. M. (1983). *Islam and Ownership*, Trans. A. Jabbari and F. Rajaee. Lexington: Mazda Publishers.

Israel, business ethics in

Dove Izraeli

In Israel's business world and academia there is little awareness of Business Ethics as a specific field of inquiry and activity. Few businesses have either a formalized code of ethics or a specialized organizational function to deal with issues of social responsibility. Furthermore, the need for such measures to promote business ethics is not an issue with any priority on the public agenda. This is not to say that Israeli business practice is unethical. On the contrary, studies of ethical attitudes and behaviors among business professionals reveal that Israelis have relatively high ethical standards (Izraeli, 1988; Izraeli and Glass, 1994). These are infused with the ideals and standards of over 3,000 years of the Jewish tradition of law and ethics, reenforced with turn-of-the-century socialist ideals of a free and just society that imbued the founders of modern Israel (Eisenstadt, 1985) (*see* JUDAISM, BUSINESS ETHICS AND).

Compared to other Western democracies, Israel has a more centralized, state-regulated economy, with a high level of government control and intervention in many aspects of economic life. Most of Israel's capital comes from abroad and is funneled through government bodies. Centralized control of resources was functional for massive immigrant absorption and military defense. However, the widespread dependence of business on government and the close ties that developed among the economic, political, and administrative elites became a major source of corruption. The dominant political parties used their control over access to economic opportunity and jobs as a political resource to secure their own power and political patronage in the government, while trade-union controlled economic enterprises were common, if not the norm (Aharoni, 1991). In response to competitive pressures from a global economy, Israel's economy is moving toward greater liberalization and privatization. At the same time an increasing number of private firms have gone public. However, the new consciousness prevalent in the West concerning business's responsibility toward stakeholders and the environment is still in an embryonic stage.

STAKEHOLDERS

Israeli business people have a narrow and limited conception of who the stakeholders are in their companies. An illustrative example is an advertisement by an Israeli business daily of a publication listing the approximately 500 corporations trading on the Tel Aviv stock exchange and "the stakeholders" – referring to those who own 5 percent or more of the corporate shares. The implication is that other people – workers, suppliers, consumers, the public at large – have no stake in the firms. This failure to recognize all people affected by the actions of business firms as stakeholders is quite remarkable, considering that only a few months prior to the advertisement a sizable portion of the population lost a large amount of their investments following a major stock market crash precipitated by insider information and manipulation of the market. The business community's incognizance of the existence of wider circles of stakeholders and its indifference to them is detrimental to Israel's standing in the global business market.

ECOLOGY

Environmental protection is another issue that to date has failed to involve the business community, which continues to be a major offender. There is growing awareness among the Israeli public of the protracted reduction in environmental quality, reflected, for example, in the increase in pollution and noise levels (Gabai, 1994). The contribution of business to environmental pollution, however, has not been given sufficient public attention.

Most of the initiative in this respect has come from government, which in 1973 established the Environmental Protection Service. Subsequent governments set up specialist units for the study, protection, and fostering of ecology which, in 1988, were transferred to the newly established ministry of the environment. Numerous citizen groups have organized around ecology issues. Within the domain of social responsibility the ecology lobby is probably the strongest.

COMBATING CORRUPTION

The Knesset (Israeli parliament) has been the prime mover in passing legislation and creating institutions and specialized agencies for coping with corruption and regulating the ethical behavior of the business community. These include the State Comptroller's Office, the Ombudsman's Office, special police units for "white-collar crime," and the requirement of internal auditors for all government offices and public companies. The courts and especially the Supreme Court have played a very significant role in defining the boundaries and reaffirming the norms of ethical behavior.

The media, with its strong tradition of investigative reporting, plays a central role in exposing business scandals and supporting individual citizens harmed by business or establishment corruption. In addition, there are dozens of citizen groups active on a wide variety of issues. In many cases, however, their dependence on government funds has undermined their effectiveness as watchdogs on government and business.

EMERGING TRENDS

Recent developments include an emerging awareness of the need to pay special attention to Business Ethics. Israeli academics, influenced by developments in American academia, have introduced social responsibility in business and management as a field of teaching and research in all business schools in Israel's universities, and the first generation of graduates is beginning to have an impact on the field of practice. A number of pioneering business firms have sought consultation for introducing socially responsible policies that reflect a new understanding of the stakeholder concept. Some, especially subsidiaries of American multinationals and headquarters of Israeli multinationals, have adopted official codes of ethics. Progress toward peace and Israel's growing integration into the global economy are factors encouraging the continued liberalization of Israel's economy and the awareness of the need to promote business ethics.

Bibliography

Aharoni, Y. (1991). *The Israeli Economy: Dreams and Reality.* New York: Routledge.

Eisenstadt, S. N. (1985). *The Transformation of Israeli Society.* Boulder, CO: Westview Press.

Gabai, S. (1994). *The Environment in Israel.* State of Israel, Ministry of the Environment.

Izraeli, D. (1988). Ethical beliefs and behavior among managers: A cross-cultural perspective. *Journal of Business Ethics,* 7, 263–71.

Izraeli, D. and Glass, D. (1994). The changing ethical beliefs and behavior of Israeli managers. In U. Berlinski, A. Friedberg, and S. B. Werner (eds.), *Corruption in a Changing World: Comparisons, Theories and Controlling Strategies.* Jerusalem: Chen Press, 448–58.

J

Japan, business ethics in

Iwao Taka

In Japan, ethics is bound up with a religious dimension (two normative environments) and a social dimension (a framework of concentric circles). The normative environments, influenced by Confucianism, Buddhism, and other traditional and modern Japanese religions, emphasize that not only individuals but also groups have their own spirit (*numen*) which is connected to the ultimate reality. The framework of concentric circles lets moral agents apply different ethical rules to the circles. The dynamics of these religious and social dimensions lead to a different view of both individuals and corporations from that dominant in the West.

THE RELIGIOUS DIMENSION – TWO NORMATIVE ENVIRONMENTS

The religious dimension supplies a variety of concrete norms of behavior to the Japanese in relation to the ultimate reality that may be called the normative environment. There are mainly *two* influential normative environments in Japan: the transcendental normative environment and the group normative environment.

Transcendental normative environment. In the transcendental environment, everyone has an equal personal *numen* (soul, spirit). This idea has been philosophically strengthened by Confucianism and Buddhism. In the case of neo-Confucianism, people are assumed to have a microcosm within themselves, and are considered condensed expressions of the universe (macrocosm). Their inner universe is expected to be able to connect with the outer universe.

In the case of Buddhism, every living creature has an equal Buddhahood, a Buddhahood which is similar to the ideas of *numen* and microcosm. Buddhism has long taught: "Although there are differences among living creatures, there is no difference among human beings. What makes human beings different is only their name."

In addition, however, under the transcendental normative environment, not only individuals but also jobs, positions, organizations, rituals, and other events and things incorporate their own *numina*. These *numina* are also expected to be associated with the *numen* of the universe.

Deities of Shintoism, Buddhism, and the Japanese new religions, which have long been considered objects of worship, are often called the "great life force of the universe." In this respect, the life force can be sacred and religious. On the other hand, many Japanese people have unconsciously accepted this way of thinking without belonging to any specific religious sect. In this case, it is rather secular, non-religious, and atheistic. Whether holy or secular, however, the significant feature of Japan is that this transcendental normative environment has been shared by Japanese people.

Inasmuch as Japanese people live in such a normative environment, the meaning of work for them becomes unique. Work is understood to be a self-expression of the great life force. Work is believed to have its own *numen*, so that work is one of the ways to reach something beyond the secular world. Accordingly, Japanese people unconsciously and sometimes consciously try to unify themselves with the great life force by concentrating on their own work.

Whereas Western managers place priority on innovation, Japanese managers and workers put emphasis on *Kaizen* (continuous improvement of products, of ways to work, and of decision-making processes). While innovation can be done intermittently, *Kaizen* can be carried on continuously by almost every person.

In this way, the transcendental environment has supplied many hard workers to the Japanese labor market, providing an ethical basis for "diligence." However, it has not created extremely individualistic people who pursue only their own short-term interests. Because they have hoped for job security and life security in the secular world, they have subjectively tried to coordinate their behavior so as to keep harmonious relations with others in their group. Within this subjective coordination, and with a long-term perspective in mind, they pursue their own purposes.

Group normative environment. The second or group normative environment necessarily derives from the transcendental normative environment, insofar as the latter gives a special raison d'être not only to individuals and their work, but also to their groups. As a result of the transcendental environment, every group holds its own *numen*. The group acquires this raison d'être, as long as it guarantees the life of its members and helps them fulfill their potentials.

But once a group acquires its raison d'être, it insists upon its survival. An environment in which norms regarding the existence and prosperity of the group appear and affect its members is called the "group normative environment," and the set of the norms in this environment is called "group logic." Groupism and a group-oriented propensity, which have often been pointed out as Japanese characteristics, stem from this group normative environment.

The Japanese often face an ethical dilemma arising from the fact that they live simultaneously in these two different influential normative environments. In the transcendental environment, groups and individuals are regarded as equal *numina* and equal expressions of the great life force. In the group environment, however, a group (and its representatives) is considered to be superior to its ordinary members, mainly because the members are not related to the force in the same way. The only way for members to connect with the life force is through the activities of their group.

SOCIAL DIMENSION – ETHICS OF CONCENTRIC CIRCLES

Due to human-bounded cognitive rationality or cultural heritage, Japanese moral agents, whether individuals or corporations, tend to conceptualize the social environment in a centrifugal order similar to water ripples. Although there are many individuals, groups, and organizations which, taken together, constitute the overall social environment, the Japanese are likely to categorize them into four concentric circles: family, fellows, Japan, and the world. On the basis of this way of thinking, Japanese people and organizations are likely to attribute different ethics or moral practices to each circle.

The concentric circles of corporations. First, corporations have a *quasi-family circle*. Of course, though corporations do not have any blood relationships, they might have closely related business partners (e.g., parent, sister, or affiliated companies). Vertical *keiretsu* (vertically integrated industrial groups like Toyota, Hitachi, or Matsushita) might be a typical example of the quasi-family circle. In this circle we find something similar to the parent–child relationship.

The main corporate members (about 20–30 companies in each group) of horizontal *keiretsu* (industrial groups such as Mitsubishi, Mitsui, Sumitomo, Dai Ichi Kangyo, Fuyo, and Sanwa) might be viewed as quasi-family members. Nonetheless, most of the cross-shareholding corporations in the horizontal *keiretsu* should be placed in the second circle, because their relations are less intimate than commonly understood.

Second, in the *fellow circle*, each corporation has its own main bank, fellow traders, distant affiliated firms, employees, steady customers, and the like. If the corporation or its executives belong to some outside associations like *Nihon Jidousha Kogyo Kai* (Japanese Auto Manufacturers Association), *Doyukai* (Japan Association of Corporate Executives), or *Keidanren* (Japan Federation of Economic Organizations), the other members of such outside associations might constitute part of its fellow circle. And if the corporation is influential enough to affect Japanese politics or administration, the Japanese governmental agencies or ministries and political parties might constitute part of its fellow circle.

Recognition within the fellow circle requires that there must be a balance between benefits and debts in the long run. On account of this, if a corporation does not offer enough benefits to counterbalance its debts to others in this circle, the corporation will be expelled from the circle, being criticized for neither understanding nor appreciating the benefits given it by others. On the other hand, if the corporation can successfully balance benefits and debts or keep in the black, it will preferentially receive many favorable opportunities from other companies or interest groups. For these reasons, every corporation worries about the balance sheet of benefits and debts in the fellow circle.

Third, in the *Japan circle*, fellow-circle ethics are substantially replaced by the principle of free competition. Competitors, unrelated corporations, ordinary stockholders, consumers (for ordinary corporations, the Japanese government constitutes part of this circle), and so forth, all fall within this circle. Yet almost all corporations in this circle know well that long-term reciprocal ethics are extremely important in constructing and maintaining their business relations because of their similar cultural background. This point makes the Japan circle different from the world circle.

Fourth, in the *world circle*, corporations follow the principle of free competition, subject to the judicial system, with less worry about their traditional reputations. The behavioral imperatives for corporations turn out to be producing or supplying high-quality and low-price products, taking much more market share, and using the law to resolve serious contractual problems.

Dynamics of the concentric circles. What are the dynamic relations among these circles and how are they interrelated? Generally speaking, the relations are similar to those of "operation base and battlefield." For example, when the second circle of an individual is recognized as a battlefield, the first circle takes on the role of operation base. When there is severe competition among the members of the second circle, individuals look for peace of mind from their first circle. I cannot show the same picture in relations between the first and second circles of corporations as clearly as for those of individuals, due to the fact that a corporation does not have similar feelings toward its quasi-family members as does an individual. But when it comes to Japan as a whole, I can draw almost the same picture between the first, second, and third circles of corporations as for those of individuals. At this level, while Japan is viewed as a battlefield, an individual person or an individual corporation expects that both the first and second circles of each of them will serve as an operation base. These multi-layered inner circles can be called "multiple operation bases." When the fourth is understood as a battlefield, however, this third circle also turns into one of the multiple operation bases (conversely, I can postulate the existence of multiple battlefields).

JAPANESE PERSPECTIVE ON AMERICAN BUSINESS ETHICS ISSUES

Job discrimination and the transcendental logic. In the transcendental normative environment, whatever job people take, they are believed to reach the same goal or the same level of human development. Because of this logic, the Japanese are unlikely to evaluate others in terms of their job (specialty). They would rather evaluate one another in terms of their attitudes toward work. It is not important for the Japanese to maintain the principle of the division of labor. Of importance is the process and the result of work. If people cannot attain goals in the existing framework of the division of labor, they are likely to try other alternatives which have not been clearly defined in the existing framework. This kind of positive attitude toward work is highly appreciated in Japan.

Employees' interest and the group logic. In the group normative environment, the group is believed to hold its own *numen* and is expected to guarantee the members' life. A corporation is thought to exist for its employees rather than for its shareholders.

Even in Japan, shareholders are legal owners of a company, so that the shareholders might use their legal power to change the company in a favorable way for themselves. Therefore, many Japanese corporations have invented a legitimate way to exclude the legal rights of shareholders (i.e., "cross-shareholding"). This is the practice in which a corporation allows trusted companies to hold its own shares, and in return the corporation holds their shares. By holding shares of one another and refraining from appealing to shareholders' rights, they make it possible to manage the companies for the sake of employees. Because this cross-shareholding is based on mutual acceptance, any attempts to break this corporate consortium from the outside, whether Japanese or foreign, are often stymied by the consortium of the member corporations.

In Japan, when executives face serious difficulties, they first reduce their own benefits, then dividends and other costs and, after that, employees' salaries or wages. If the situation is extremely hard to overcome with these measures, they sell assets and only as a last resort do they lay off workers. Even in this case the executives often find and offer new job opportunities for those who are laid off, taking care of their family's life.

Claims against the Japanese market and the ethics of concentric circles. Because of the framework of concentric circles – especially the ethics of the fellow circle – foreign corporations often face difficulties entering the Japanese market. Although the Japanese admit that the market is very hard to enter, a majority of them believe it is still possible to accomplish entry.

Even if the Japanese market has many business-related practices such as semi-annual gifts, entertainment, cross-shareholding, a "triangular relationship" among businesses, bureaucracy, and the Liberal Democratic Party, a long-term relationship is formed mainly through a series of business transactions. That is to say, the most important factor in doing business is whether suppliers can respond to the assemblers' requests for quality, cost, and the date of delivery, and the like, or how producers can respond to the retailer's or wholesaler's expectations.

Foreign corporations might claim that because they are located outside Japan, they cannot even enter the Japan circle. In return, the Japanese business community is likely to insist that if they understand the "long-term reciprocal ethics" they can enter the Japan circle; and what is more, might be fellows of influential Japanese corporations. As I have described,

what makes the Japan circle different from the world circle is that people in the Japan circle know well the importance of this ethics. In fact, foreign corporations successfully enjoying the Japanese market include IBM, Johnson and Johnson, McDonald's, Apple, and General Mills, which have well understood this ethics.

In this respect, realistically, the Japanese community interprets criticism by the American counterpart of the Japanese market as unfair and unethical. To put it differently, the Japanese believe that if foreign corporations understand the long-term ethics, they can easily be real members of the Japanese business community.

ETHICAL ISSUES OF THE JAPANESE BUSINESS COMMUNITY

I have shown how Japanese corporations conceive the American business society and its business-related practices from the viewpoint of the two normative environments and the concentric circles. Yet the Japanese business community is not without its own ethical problems. On the contrary, there are many problems it has to solve.

In order to reveal some of the issues, this article will confine itself to the concept of fairness, hypothetically interpreted as "openness," since fairness generally implies treating every agent equally according to the same rule, or opening the market or organizations for every agent who is willing to follow the same rule. On the basis of this simplified definition, I will cover two levels of ethical issues: opening Japanese organizations and opening the Japanese market (see FAIRNESS). Moreover, I will identify three ethical prime values in order to discuss problems and possible solutions. By "prime values" I mean the core concepts of transcendental logic, group logic, and the fellow circle's ethics.

Discrimination and the transcendental logic. The prime value here is that "everybody has an equal microcosm." Whether men or women, Japanese or foreigners, hard workers or non-hard workers, everybody has to be treated equally as a person. When we observe organizational phenomena from the viewpoint of this value, two issues of discrimination emerge.

First, the transcendental logic has worked favorably only for male society. That is, in this normative environment, Japanese women have been expected to actualize their potentials through their household tasks. Those tasks have been regarded as their path toward their goal. Of course, insofar as women voluntarily agree with this thinking, there seems to be no ethical problem. And, in fact, a majority of women have accepted this way of living to date. Nonetheless, now that an increasing number of women work at companies and hope to get beyond such chores as making tea to more challenging jobs, Japanese corporations have no longer been allowed to treat women unequally.

Second, the transcendental normative logic itself has often been used to accuse certain workers of laziness. As far as a worker voluntarily strives to fulfill his or her own potential according to the transcendental logic, this presents no ethical problems. Nevertheless, once a person begins to apply the logic to others and evaluate them in terms of their performance, the transcendental logic easily becomes the basis for severe accusations against certain workers. If a person does not follow this teaching, refusing overtime or transfers, he will jeopardize his promotion and be alienated from his colleagues and bosses, since he is not regarded as a praiseworthy diligent worker. Even if he is making efforts to fulfill his potential in fields unrelated to work, he is not highly appreciated, simply because what he is doing is not related to the company's work.

Employees' dependency and the group logic.   In the group normative environment, groups are regarded as having a higher status than their individual members. Because members are inclined to take this hierarchical order for granted, they come to be dependent on the groups. This dependency of the agents, whether of individuals or groups, brings the following two problems into the Japanese business community: (1) the individual members of the group refrain from expressing their opinions about ethical issues, and (2) they tend to obey organizational orders, even if they disagree with them. The first tendency is related to decision-making, while the second affects policy implementation.

When we look at these two tendencies from the viewpoint of this prime value, they will be translated into the following two ethical issues: (1) Japanese corporations are likely to exclude

employee participation in ethical decision-making; (2) in some cases, they might not guarantee employees' right to life.

The dependency trait ends up excluding different opinions or ideas. *A fortiori*, in exchange for job security, the rank and file rarely raise questions about the decisions made by management, even if those decisions are against their own sense of what is right. In this respect, the rank and file are likely to take no ethical responsibility for decisions. Because the authority and responsibility of individuals are not clearly defined in Japanese organizations, individual employees do not regard involvement in wrongdoing as their own responsibility, but rather as the responsibility of middle management. Even in middle management, however, it is not clear who will take responsibility for wrongdoing. And top management quite often does not know exactly what employees or middle management are doing in daily business.

The dependency trait is inclined to force individual members to devote their time and energy to work. Such dependency might encourage individual employees to behave ethically if higher groups such as *Doyukai*, *Keidanren*, or the board of directors seriously proclaimed the necessity of business ethics. If a member pursues his own interest in a company, this behavior often harms the interests of other members. In this case, other members exert social pressure to comply with the group's aggregate interest. For this reason, in the group normative environment, a member is likely to give up on his own interest and obey group orders.

A typical example which shows this tendency of members to waive their basic rights is *karoshi* (death caused by overwork). In 1991 the Japanese labor ministry awarded 33 claims for *karoshi*. Since it is very hard to prove a direct and quantifiable link between overwork and death, this number is not large enough to clarify actual working conditions, but is certainly large enough to show that there is a possibility for turning group logic into unconditional obedience.

This corporate climate not only jeopardizes an employee's right to life, but also hampers the healthy human development of individual members. Because of this, the Japanese business community has to alter its group-centered approach and create a democratic approach within which individuals can express their opinions more frankly than before.

Exclusiveness of the concentric circles. The Japanese conceptualization of the social environment in a centrifugal framework is closely connected with Confucianism (the differential principle): it allows people to treat others in proportion to the intimacy of their relationships.

In looking at the opening of the Japanese market from the viewpoint of this prime value, there appear to be at least two issues: (1) The Japanese business community has to make an effort to help foreigners understand the concept of long-term reciprocal ethics. This effort will bring moral agents of the world circle into the Japan circle. (2) The Japanese community has to give business opportunities to as many newcomers as possible. This effort will bring newcomers into the fellow circles.

The first issue is how to transfer foreign corporations from the world circle to the Japan circle. Takashi Ishihara (1989) recommends that Japanese corporations follow the spirit of fairness. This fairness implies that they treat foreign companies the same as they treat other Japanese firms. To put it differently, the concept of fairness encourages Japanese corporations to apply the same ethical standard to all companies.

Although this is a very important point of fairness, there is a more serious problem involved in opening the market, which is how to let newcomers know what the rules are and how the Japanese business community applies those rules. As mentioned before, for the purpose of constructing and maintaining business relationships with a Japanese company (a core company), a foreign firm has to be a fellow of the company. In this fellow circle, every fellow makes efforts to balance benefits and debts with the core company in material and spiritual terms in the long run, since maintaining a long-term balance is the most important ethic. Yet such a balance is too complicated for the foreign corporation to attain as long as benefits and debts are rather subjective concepts.

Even if they can enter the Japan circle successfully, there still remains another problem: how those foreigners already within the Japan circle can enter fellow circles of influential Japanese corporations. This is related to the second issue of opening the Japanese market.

Even when foreign companies understand and adopt long-term reciprocal ethics, they might not be able to enter those fellow circles if they rarely have the chance to show their competitive products or services to influential corporations. On account of this, as an ethical responsibility, Japanese corporations should have access channels through which every newcomer can approach equally.

I conclude:

1   From the transcendental prime value, the Japanese business community has to change its discriminatory organizational climate.
2   From the group prime value, it has to alter the group-centered climate into a democratic ground.
3   From the prime value of the concentric circles' ethics, it has to have access channels open to every newcomer.

These ethical suggestions might hurt the efficiency or competitiveness of Japanese corporations, so they need to be discussed in relation to economic factors. What is more, in order to proceed in the direction of these suggestions, each corporation will have to establish its own specific code of business ethics.

Bibliography

Benedict, R. (1946). *The Chrysanthemum and the Sword: Patterns of Japanese Culture.* New York: Meridian.
Egami, N. (1989). *Nihon Minzoku to Nihon Bunka* (Japanese People and Culture). Tokyo: Yamakawa Shuppansha.
Imai, K. and Komiya, R. (1989). *Nihon no Kigyo* (Japanese Corporations). Tokyo: Tokyo University Press, 131–58.
Ishihara, T. (1989). *Keizai Doyukai* (Annual Report of Japan Association of Corporate Executives).
Japanese Fair Trade Commission (1991). *Annual Report of the Japanese Fair Trade Commission: White Paper of Antimonopoly.* Tokyo: JFTC, 88–92.
Kyogoku, J. and Kyogoku, J. (1983). *Nihon no Seiji* (Politics of Japan). Tokyo: Tokyo University Press.
Upham, F. K. (1987). *Law and Social Change in Postwar Japan.* Boston, MA: Harvard University Press, 14–16.
Yamamoto, S. (1979). *Nihon Shihonshugi no Seishin* (The Spirit of Japanese Capitalism). Tokyo: Kobunsha, 118–41.

journals of business ethics

James R. Glenn, Jr.

The topic of business ethics is available to readers in print and increasingly online in a variety of forms: books (authored and edited), general readership newspapers, and a vast array of periodicals and professional publications that can be categorized in many different ways. What follows is one attempt to organize this last group of publications in a way that might be useful.

ACADEMIC JOURNALS WITH BUSINESS ETHICS AS A PRIMARY FOCUS

Journals addressed primarily to scholars and utilizing peer reviewing (**P** = print version; **O** = online version; **C** = CD-ROM):

Business Ethics: A European Review, 1992–, quarterly. **P, O.**
Business Ethics Quarterly, 1991–, quarterly (Society for Business Ethics). **P, C.**
Business and Professional Ethics Journal, 1981–, occasionally. **P, O.**
Business and Society, 1960–1991 (Roosevelt University); 1992–, quarterly (International Association for Business and Society). **P.**
Employee Responsibility and Rights Journal, 1988–, quarterly (Council on Employee Responsibilities and Rights). **P, O.**
Ethics and Information Technology, 1999–, quarterly. **P, O.**
Journal of Academic Ethics, 2003–, quarterly. **P, O.**
Journal of Business Ethics, 1980–, monthly. As of 2004 incorporating *International Journal of Value-Based Management*, 1988–2003, as well as *Teaching Business Ethics*, 1997–. **P, O.**

PERIODICALS WITH BUSINESS ETHICS AS A MAJOR FOCUS

Magazines and journals that advocate good business and professional ethics, address business and professional ethics, address the business and professional community, and do not utilize academic peer reviewing:

Business Ethics, 1986–, bimonthly. **P, O.**
Business and Society Review, created by Milton Moskowitz in 1972, quarterly (now published by the Center for Business Ethics at Bentley College). **P, O.**
Electronic Journal of Business Ethics and Organization Studies, 1996–, annual. **O.**
Ethical Performance, 1999–, 11 issues/year. **O.**
Issues In Ethics, 1987–, quarterly (Markkula Center for Applied Ethics). **P.**
Ethikos, 1987, and *Corporate Conduct Quarterly*, 1991–8, bimonthly. **P, C.**
International Business Ethics Review, 1997–, annual (International Business Ethics Institute). **P, O.**
Journal of American Academy of Business, 2002–. **P, O.**
Online Journal of Business Ethics, 1995–2000 (Center for Business Ethics, University of St. Thomas). **O.**

PROFESSIONAL PUBLICATIONS THAT INCLUDE ARTICLES ON BUSINESS ETHICS

Many utilize academic or professional peer review, but not all. Most are addressed to identifiable academic, professional, or business constituencies. All have published three or more articles on business ethics in the last 16 years, and the last few years have seen a notable increase in attention to this topic.

Academy of Management Executive
Academy of Management Journal
Academy of Management Review
Accounting, Auditing and Accountability Journal
Across the Board
American Bankers Association: ABA Banking Journal
American Business Law Journal
Australian Accountant
Business
Business and Economic Review
Business Forum
Business Horizons
Business Insights
California Magazine
California Management Review
Canadian Business Review
Chartered Accountants Journal of New Zealand
CPA Journal
Common Boundary
Co-op American Quarterly
Executive
Executive Excellence

Harvard Business Review
Humanomics
Information Management Journal
Internal Auditor
International Management
International Journal of Management
International Journal of Management and Decision-making
International Journal of Public Administration
Journal of Accountancy
Journal of American Academy of Business
Journal of Banking and Finance
Journal of Blacks in Higher Education
Journal of Business Strategy
Journal of Corporate Accounting and Finance
Journal of Education for Business
Journal of International Business Studies
Journal of Management Development
Journal of Management Education
Journal of Management Inquiry
Journal of Management Studies
Journal of Property Management
Journal of Public Affairs
Journal of Socioeconomics
Leadership and Organization Development Journal
Management Accounting
Management Decisions
Management Review
Marketing
Public Affairs Quarterly
SAM Advanced Management Journal
Security Management
Sloan Management Review
Social Justice Research
Utne Reader
Vital Speeches
Working Women

A computer search on ABI/Inform for articles on business ethics between January 1987 and July 1994 produced 978 citations. Using the same key words from the previous collection date to August 31, 2003 produced 6,400 citations. A search for business ethics journals from the previous date until August 31, 2003 produced 3,422 citations. The addition journals added to the list had at least five articles. While ABI/Inform is generally regarded as the most extensive business journal database, for whatever reasons, there are journals that regularly address business ethics that are not included in

this database; for example, premier journals such as *Business Ethics Quarterly* and *Business and Society*. A Yahoo search for business ethics journals produced 254,000 citations and a Google search produced 410,000.

BUSINESS PUBLICATIONS THAT REGULARLY INCLUDE COVERAGE OF BUSINESS ETHICS

A sampler of publications addressing a broad business readership (stories may appear with or without attribution of authorship):

Business Week
Computerworld
The Economist
Fortune
Inc.
Industry Week
Wall Street Journal

NEWSLETTERS FOCUSING ON BUSINESS ETHICS

Newsletters produced by individuals, ethics centers and institutes, professional associations, special interest groups, government agencies, and consulting firms:

At The Center, 2002–, quarterly (Markkula Center for Applied Ethics). **P.**
Benchmarks, 1994–?, monthly (Minnesota Association for Applied Corporate Ethics).
BizEthicsBuzz, 2002, monthly (Business Ethics). **O.**
Business Ethics Resource, 1987–?, quarterly.
Business and Society, 1968–74, biweekly. **P.**
Business and Society Briefings, 1992–? (Conference Board).
CBE News, 1992–, biannual (Center for Business Ethics).
CasePlace.org (Aspen Institute's Business and Society Program). **O.**
Center For Ethics Studies Newsletter (Center for Business Ethics).
Conference Board Newsletter, 2001– (Conference Board). **P, O.**
Corporate Examiner (Interfaith Center on Corporate Responsibility).
Ethical Management, monthly.
Ethics Matters, 2003– (Center for Business Ethics). **O.**
Ethical Performance, 11 issues/year. **P, O.**

Ethically Speaking, semiannual (Association for
Practical and Professional Ethics).
Ethics and Policy, 1974– (Center for Ethics and
Social Policy).
Ethics in Action, bimonthly (Josephson Institute
of Ethics).
Ethics Journal, 1991–2000 (Ethics Resource
Center). **P**.
Ethics Today, 2000–2 **P**. Now *Ethics Today
Online*, monthly, 2002 (Ethics Resource
Center). **O**.
Executive Citizen, 1992–, quarterly.
Executives Alert (National Center for Ethics).
Management Ethics (Canadian Centre for Ethics
and Corporate Policy). **P**.
New Leader.
On Achieving Excellence.
*Research Report of the Council on Economic Prior-
ities*

NEWSLETTERS FOCUSING ON THE BUSINESS
OF ETHICAL INVESTING

Published by individuals and organizations ad-
vising or evaluating the ethical performance of
businesses for potential or current investors:

Clean Yield
Franklin Research's Insights
Good Money
Green Money Journal
Investing for a Better World

Judaism, business ethics and

Moses Pava

Jewish ethics, since its biblical origins, has recognized and celebrated the dignity, value, and
meaning of humanly productive activities, including economic activities. Jewish business
ethics educates and harnesses individual human
desire and initiative and directs them toward
legitimate social ends. In Judaism there is no
notion of original sin, but rather humans are
thought to possess both evil *and* good inclinations (the *yetzer tov* and the *yetzer ra*). As the
biblical prophet Moses summarized his law
more than three thousand years ago, humans
have both an opportunity and a responsibility

to choose intelligently between them (see Deuteronomy 30:19).

THE BIBLICAL FOUNDATION OF JEWISH
BUSINESS ETHICS

The Torah (or the Pentateuch) contains numerous legal norms and models of aspiration relevant to economic and agricultural matters. For
example, Leviticus 19 reads: "When you reap
the harvest of your land, you shall not reap
wholly the corner of your field nor gather the
gleaning of the harvest, but you shall leave them
for the poor and the stranger." Deuteronomy 25
states: "You shall not have in your house diverse
measures, a great and a small. A perfect and just
weight shall you have."

These laws and many others convey both
specific legal obligations and important ethical
principles, especially as interpreted by the
rabbis. For example, the Torah's prohibition
on "putting a stumbling block before the
blind" has served for centuries as a summary
statement of Jewish attitudes toward conflicts
of interest and a warning against selling defective
merchandise.

Judaism's prophetic writings continue this
insistence on the centrality of ethics in the economic sphere. For example, Isaiah chastises the
Israelites for fasting and sitting in sackcloth and
ashes when their fellow countrymen are
suffering from poverty and lack of food. The
prophet rhetorically asks: "Is that what you call
a day acceptable to the Lord?" He continues:
"This is the fast day that I esteem precious:
Loosen the chains of wickedness . . . Share your
food with the hungry, take the poor to your
home, clothe the naked and never turn from
your fellow" (ch. 58).

The prophet Amos, echoing the verse com-
manding just weights from Deuteronomy, cited
above, underscores a similar message to the
upper classes who were oppressing the poor of
his generation: "Hear this, you that would swallow the needy and destroy the poor of the land,
saying, when will the new moon be gone, that we
may sell grain? . . . Making the ephah small and
the shekel great, and falsifying the balances of
deceit? That we may buy the poor for silver, and
the needy for a pair of shoes" (ch. 8).

Tellingly, in underscoring the importance of
ethics and empathy for the poor, both of these

biblical prophets contrast ethics with ritual observance by noting the emptiness of the latter without the former.

RABBINIC INTERPRETATIONS AND EXTENSIONS

The rabbis of the ancient world accepted the Jewish Bible as their binding constitution. They too viewed human initiative as inherently valuable, a perspective they inherited from their close reading of the Torah. In every instance the rabbis felt an obligation to interpret the biblical text in light of contemporary social and economic conditions. Economic justice was so important to the rabbis that they believed the first question asked in the world-to-come is, "Have you been honorable in business?" (Shabbat 31a).

Economic justice and Hillel's prosbol.   An important example of the rabbinic attitude in the area of business ethics is Hillel's innovation of the *prosbol.* According to a literal reading of the biblical text in Deuteronomy, all debts must be released in the sabbatical year. Hillel, one of the most famous interpreters of rabbinic law, recognized that the inability to collect loans at the end of the seventh year had now, in his time, become a hindrance to economic development and communal welfare. The required cancellation of loans after the seventh year created a tremendous barrier to making funds available for legitimate economic purposes. Hillel's solution is recorded in the talmudic tractate of Gittin.

According to the talmud, the *prosbol* is a legal document that allows the lender and borrower to circumvent the cancellation of the debt. The concept underlying the document is that while an individual is prohibited from collecting a loan at the end of the seventh year, the rabbinical court is not. Therefore, the court can legally collect the funds from the borrower and turn them over to the lender. The effect was to nullify the law without violating it, in order to meet the reasonable commercial needs of the community.

Changing the law for the sake of God.   In another important illustration of the rabbinic emphasis on economic justice, the rabbis altered the requirements of the sacrificial service in order to prevent merchants from exploiting worshipers by charging exorbitant prices for the needed sacrificial birds. Rashi, the preeminent Jewish commentator of the middle ages, stated that this case provides an example of changing the law "for the sake of God."

Beyond the letter of the law.   The Jewish tradition is keenly aware of the need for unambiguous signals about the contours of proper legal behavior. On the other hand, the inherent limitations of any rule-based legal code present the possibility for unethical and antisocial activities with the law's approval. Jewish law is consciously aware of this tension inherent in all legal codes. The concept of *lifnim mishurat hadin* (usually translated as beyond the letter of the law) is offered as a possible solution. A famous talmudic case illustrates the central importance of *lifnim mishurat hadin* for Jewish business ethics.

It once happened that Rabbah hired porters to transport a barrel of wine. As the porters were carrying the wine, the barrel broke and all of the wine it contained was lost. Rabbah seized the porters' garments and refused to pay them their agreed upon wages. The porters took Rabbah to court and "sued" him for the return of their garments and for payment of their wages. "We are poor men, have worked all day, and are in need; are we to get nothing?" The rabbi who was serving as judge on this case ordered Rabbah, "Go and pay them." Rabbah, himself an expert on Jewish law, turned to the rabbi and judge and rhetorically asked, "Is that really the law?" The rabbi, knowing that there was no specific legal requirement for Rabbah to pay the porters, responded: "Even so you must pay the porters," citing the general biblical obligation "to keep the path of the righteous."

The common theme in each of the above examples is the rabbinic emphasis on the creative interpretation of biblical law. In order to promote the continuation of the Jewish community through radically changing circumstances, the rabbis neither invented nor discovered wholly new ethical laws. Rather, they applied existing law and tradition in an expansive attempt to solve practical problems in a spiritually meaningful way. In every case, the rabbis looked back in order to construct a better and more equitable future for the Jewish community.

The Contemporary Relevance of Jewish Business Ethics

In today's pluralistic and highly competitive business environment, there is an increasing demand for a heightened awareness of business ethics. An understanding of the rich heritage of Jewish texts related to business issues is an important and invaluable resource to help promote and understand higher standards for business ethics.

Judaism is particularly well suited to participate in today's business ethics debates. Increasingly, business ethicists, like Pat Werhane, Joseph Badaracco, and many others, have noted that business ethics requires moral imagination. This implies that business ethics is about creativity, identity stories, uncertainty, and an enhanced appreciation for other people's perspectives, more than universal rules, certainty, and specific codes of conduct.

Beyond doubt, one of the most cited examples of an authentic Jewish business ethics is the story of Shimon ben Shetach.

His students once purchased a donkey from a heathen neighbor. Just before they delivered the donkey to their teacher, the students noticed an expensive pearl hidden in the saddle bag. "Rabbi," they said, "if you sell this expensive pearl, you can now devote yourself full-time to the study of Torah." Shimon ben Shetach said, "Return the pearl to its rightful owner." The students were confused. "Doesn't everyone agree that if you find something belonging to a heathen you make keep it for yourself?" The teacher responded, "Do you think that Shimon ben Shetach is a barbarian? I would rather hear the heathen bless God than have all riches of the world."

The students in this story believe that business ethics is about following a set of predetermined rules – everyone agrees if you find something belonging to a heathen you may keep it for yourself. The teacher, Shimon ben Shetach, however, recognizes a deeper truth. Business ethics is also about who we are becoming – "Do you think that Shimon ben Shetach is a barbarian?" Some ethical choices are so important that they determine our identity.

Shimon ben Shetach believes that he has found a better understanding of their shared biblical inheritance, an interpretation which fits with the biblical material, but one that promotes the inherent interests of the community in a more profound and fundamentally ethical way than his students' interpretation. Before Shimon ben Shetach, there is no tradition that requires him to return the pearl to its original owner. The binding norm derives from a creative and novel interpretation on Shimon ben Shetach's part. He recognizes that ethics is not only about following well-trodden rules, but also depends on how one frames a question. History remembers Shimon ben Shetach as a paradigm of the covenantal leader in business precisely because of the moral imagination his decision exemplifies.

In summary, Judaism, unlike many other traditions, has never denigrated business and wealth, but rather has always recognized an appropriate place for business in society. Judaism's ancient and unbroken chain of tradition and interpretation encapsulates a deep and profound practical wisdom

In a revealing comment, the Talmud imagines God criticizing the Roman Empire. "In times to come, the Holy One Blessed be He will proclaim, 'You foolish ones among the peoples, all that you have done, you have done only to satisfy your own desires. You have established marketplaces to place courtesans therein, and baths to revel in them'" (Avodah Zarah 2b). As this hypothetical conversation illustrates, the satisfaction of desires alone is not a sufficient justification for engaging in economic activities. The author of this rabbinic parable understood the importance of and necessity for marketplaces. He does not suggest that engaging in secular activities is inappropriate. Rather, the point of a religiously informed business ethics is that economic activities are never to be viewed only as ends in themselves. Economic activities at the individual, organizational, and national level are a means toward building a just and caring society in which the best of human spiritual values may flourish.

Perhaps no one captured the essence of Jewish ethics better than Rabbi Abraham Joshua Heschel, one of the outstanding Jewish leaders of the twentieth century. He wrote:

> The dichotomy of faith and works which presented such an important problem in Christian

theology was never a problem in Judaism. To us, the basic problem is neither what is the right action nor what is the right intention. The basic problem is: what is right living? . . . Right living is like a work of art, the product of a vision and of a wrestling with concrete situations. (Heschel, 1955: 296)

One of the best examples of Heschel's insight can be found specifically in the area of Jewish business ethics.

Bibliography

Heschel, A. J. (1955). *God in Search of Man*. New York: Harper and Row.

Levine, A. (1980). *Free Enterprise and Jewish Law*. New York: Ktav.

Pava, M. L. (1997). *Business Ethics: A Jewish Perspective*. New York: Ktav.

Tamari, M. (1987). *With All Your Possessions*. New York: Free Press.

just cause

John J. McCall

is a policy requiring that dismissal of employees be for a just or good reason.

A just cause dismissal policy is best understood in contrast to a strict employment at will (EAW) rule which allows employers absolute discretion to fire an employee. The essence of just cause policies, on the other hand, is to limit the employer's authority to discharge. While there may be many different instantiations of just cause policies, all will address the following: reasons, procedures, and remedies.

What constitutes a good or just reason for dismissal is impossible to define exactly in a brief policy or statute. Typically, "just cause" is defined loosely (e.g., as reasonable and job-related grounds for dismissal) and left to arbitrators or labor courts to define more precisely through their decisions. It is, however, clearly understood that union membership, race, sex, personal bias, political opinions, religion, or ethnicity are invalid reasons; theft, fighting on the job, drug use on the job, excessive absenteeism, or substandard performance are acceptable reasons.

There are interesting corollaries of requiring good reasons: (1) If inadequate performance is a

valid reason for discharge, then employers must specify what counts as adequate performance. (2) More broadly, a just cause policy must understand "valid reason" as requiring more than an employer's subjective belief, say, that an employee stole or used drugs at work. Some substantial evidence must be available to make such a belief reasonable. Failure to require these things of employers will obviously make a demand for just cause ineffectual in protecting employees from unfair dismissals.

Just cause policies will also require that some procedures be available to review discharge actions. At the very least, some mechanism for external and independent assessment of the merits of the employer's reasons must be made available to the employee. Arbitrators or labor courts usually fill this role. While not essential, less formal internal pre-termination hearings or appeals mechanisms are consistent with the spirit of just cause in that these will help prevent unfair discharges. Once the employee completes the probationary period required for coverage, most just cause policies also require prior notice of intent to dismiss and written provision of the reasons.

Finally, all just cause policies must include some remedy for those cases where a firing is found to be unjust. Possible remedies include reinstatement and/or monetary damages. In jurisdictions governed by just cause, monetary damages are usually limited by statute to some small multiple of wages.

While most Western industrialized nations have adopted some form of just cause policy, US state laws almost universally represent a modified EAW rule. In the US, employer discretion to discharge is no longer absolute, having been limited incrementally by judicial precedents or statutes that identify impermissible grounds for dismissal. However, aside from those enumerated exceptions, US employers may still fire for any or no reason. Exceptions to this are public employees and union workers, both of whom enjoy protections similar to "just cause," and those who work for corporations that have voluntarily adopted a just cause policy.

Interestingly, some employer groups in the US are urging the adoption of a just cause standard because they find state law so uncertain and because firings found to violate the law can bring damage awards far greater than those allowed by just cause statutes. For these reasons, the Billings Chamber of Commerce supported Montana's 1987 just cause law.

Since 1980, just cause statutes have been introduced in ten states. The debate over these proposals is in part a moral debate involving issues of fairness, justice, and collective welfare (*see* JUSTICE; UTILITARIANISM). Proponents of such statutes are moved by the substantial harms that can accompany job loss. In addition to lost income, workers and their families suffer insecurity, depression, and loss of self-respect. They argue that it is unfair to impose these costs on the estimated 150,000+ workers a year discharged without just cause and due process.

Opponents of just cause claim that broad employer authority to dismiss is necessary for workplace discipline and motivation. (Implicit in this argument is the belief that job security and work output are inversely related.) They also point to the need for employer flexibility in the competitive global economy. They argue that just cause is not required by fairness, since workers and employers have equal ability to terminate the relationship. Finally, they claim that just cause must be inefficient, since if it were efficient, the labor market would force employers to provide it.

Defenders of just cause respond to these challenges by arguing:

1 The motivator under EAW is fear of job loss and psychological literature is unanimous on fear being a poor motivator. At most, fear will assure that workers conform to minimum external standards. It will probably also assure workers who lack innovation and who are dispirited.
2 Those who point to drones as the paradigm of workers with job security need to show that is typical under job security, and if it is, that security and not some other variable (e.g., lack of autonomy) is the cause of low productivity.
3 The appeal to needed flexibility in a competitive economy is a red herring, since all just cause policies accept layoffs due to economic conditions.
4 While formally equal, individual employees and employers are not often in positions of equal bargaining strength. As a result, it is not surprising that the private labor market does not typically provide job security. It is also not surprising that grievance procedures are one of the first demands of organized workers.

It remains to be seen which set of arguments carries the day in the continuing US debate. It also remains to be seen whether European labor rules experience any great change as a result of increased global competition and local unemployment. (So far, changes have been small and limited mainly to increased allowance for temporary workers.)

See also *due process; free speech in the workplace; freedom of contract; work, right to*

Bibliography

Beerman, J. and Singer, W. J. (1989). Baseline questions in legal reasoning: The example of property in jobs. *Georgia Law Review*, 23, 911.

Edwards, R. (1993). *Rights at Work: Employment Relations in the Post-Union Era*. New York: Twentieth Century Fund.

Epstein, R. (1984). In defense of the contract at will. *University of Chicago Law Review*, 51, 947.

Krueger, A. (1991). The evolution of unjust dismissal legislation in the United States. *Industrial and Labor Relations Review*, 44, 644.

Paull, K. (1991). Employment termination reform: What should a statute require before termination – some lessons from the French, German, and British experiences. *Hastings International and Comparative Law Review*, 14, 619.

Singer, W. J. (1988). The reliance interest in property. *Stanford Law Review*, 40, 614.

Summer, C. (1976). Individual protection against unjust dismissal: Time for a statute. *Virginia Law Review*, 62, 481.

Werhane, P. (1985). *Persons, Rights and Corporations*. Englewood Cliffs, NJ: Prentice-Hall.

justice

Thomas J. Donaldson

Any inquiry about "the circumstances of justice" is ultimately one about the scope of justice. It is, in other words, a part of the broader search for the conditions which must obtain for questions of justice to have meaning. Clearly, some such conditions must obtain. To ask whether last year's weather treated my house justly is nonsense, but to ask whether the rich citizens of second-century Rome treated their poorer fellow citizens justly makes sense. But what, precisely, gives sense to the latter question while denying it to the former? The practical implications of this question may be significant, for it appears that one must determine the conditions of justices in order to confront a host of vexing issues: Can one nation treat another unjustly? Can one generation treat a future generation unjustly? Can people treat animals unjustly?

While discussion about the "circumstances of justice" are cut from the larger cloth of the inquiry into the scope of justice, they encompass a narrower range of issues. The phrase "circumstances of justice" refers implicitly to a key set of disputed issues about the conditions of justice, and to specific "circumstances" asserted by the British philosopher David Hume (1711–76). Indeed, it was Hume who coined the phrase "circumstances of justice." Hume argued that people usually find themselves in circumstances manifesting four general characteristics which limit the possibility of justice: dependence, moderate scarcity, restrained benevolence, and individual vulnerability.

1   *Dependence.* According to Hume, individual human beings are not entirely self-sufficient. In addition to requiring nature's cooperation in the form of, for example, air and water, they rely upon the cooperation of their fellows to achieve certain critical goods.
2   *Moderate scarcity.* Most people find themselves confronted neither by a dramatic material abundance, which would make a conflict of material interests impossible, nor by a dramatic scarcity, which would make decent life impossible.
3   *Restrained benevolence.* Humans tend neither to be saints nor devils; they manifest generosity, but only to a point. While they frequently sacrifice on behalf of family, friends, nation, and humankind, they tend over the long term to reveal a deep-seated and resilient self-interest.

4   *Individual vulnerability.* Humans are vulnerable to one another. No matter how powerful or intelligent, an individual may succumb to attacks by weaker fellows.

The twentieth-century American philosopher John Rawls made use of Hume's interpretation of the circumstances of justice in his well-known account of distributive justice, *A Theory of Justice* (1971). He explicitly states that his own account adds "nothing essential" to Hume's "much fuller" discussion, and proceeds to employ Hume's insights in establishing limits on the scope of distributive justice. He refers to the circumstances of justice as "the normal conditions under which human cooperation is both possible and necessary," and gives special attention to the condition of modern scarcity, which he defines as the existence of natural resources "not so abundant that schemes of cooperation become superfluous," nor "conditions so harsh that fruitful ventures must inevitably break down."

But even if Rawls's account is identical to Hume's – a claim questioned by many observers – one may wonder whether the so-called circumstances of justice are, in truth, necessary either for the meaningful application of such terms as "just" and "unjust" or for the existence of just institutions.

For example, it seems at first glance that if people have either an extravagant abundance of material goods, or an extreme scarcity, then issues of justice will not arise. But first impressions may be misleading. Suppose that an extravagant abundance of material goods exists. Might not questions of justice nonetheless arise over, say, the bestowing of awards in public contests, or in structuring systems of seniority and status? Or, alternatively, suppose that a dramatic scarcity of goods exists. Might not questions of justice arise in determining, say, who should be utterly deprived in order for others to survive?

Much turns on the sense of "necessary" intended. If the circumstances of justice are said to be necessary for the term "justice" even to have meaningful application to states of affairs, then obvious counter-examples must be considered. For example, imagine a society populated by utterly selfish people – rational brutes preying on one another. Might such a society not still be labeled "unjust" from the perspective of an external observer? Hence, some critics argue that while the condition of restrained benevolence may be practically necessary for the emergence of just institutions, it is unnecessary for the meaningful application of concepts of justice even to societies that lack such institutions.

Even the presumably less stringent test of being "necessary for the emergence of just institutions" is subject to controversy. Extending the example mentioned above, some argue that even conditions of dramatic scarcity are compatible with the existence of cooperative schemes used to effect damage control and maximize human survival.

It should be added that controversy sometimes also surrounds the meaning of key terms specifying the circumstances of justice. Rawls, for example, believes that distributive justice is inappropriate in international contexts owing to the low level of international dependence. While asserting that distributive justice concerns the distribution of the fruits of cooperation, he proceeds to note that nations are more or less self-sufficient schemes of social cooperation. "The boundaries" of the cooperative schemes to which the principles of distributive justice apply, Rawls argues, "are given by the notion of a self-contained national community." But how much dependence is necessary? Might it be enough simply that the wealth of developed industrial nations owes itself, at least in part, to dealings with industrially underdeveloped nations? Or is it perhaps enough that the financial destinies of most nations are currently intertwined by mutual systems of money, commerce, and regulation? That distributive justice has international application in this sense is precisely the claim made by many contemporary philosophers.

Hence, while the discussion of the "circumstances of justice" belongs to the historical stream of discussion about the conditions of justice generally, it reflects the special focus given to it by Hume in the eighteenth century. For this reason, even appealing to the "circumstances of justice" may imply adopting a particular approach to the broader issue of the scope of justice.

See also *distributive justice*

Bibliography

This entry is reprinted from pp. 653–5 of Lawrence C. Becker and Charlotte B. Becker (eds.), *Encyclopedia of Ethics*, New York: Garland Publishing, 1992, where it appeared under the title "Justice, circumstances of."

Beitz, C. (1979). *Political Theory and International Relations*. Princeton, NJ: Princeton University Press.

Hubin, D. C. (1979). The Scope of Justice. *Philosophy and Public Affairs*, 9, 3–24.

Hume, D. A. (1957) [1751]. *An Inquiry Concerning the Principles of Morals; with a supplement: A dialogue*, ed. C. W. Hendel. New York: Liberal Arts Press.

Hume, D. A. (1988) [1737]. *Treatise of Human Nature*, ed. L. A. Selby-Bigge. Oxford: Oxford University Press.

Rawls, J. (1971). *A Theory of Justice*. Cambridge, MA: Harvard University Press.

K

Kantian capitalism

Norman E. Bowie

Kant's moral philosophy, especially the three formulations of the categorical imperative, can provide a compelling vision of what a business corporation ought to look like if it were organized as a moral firm. The first formulation of the categorical imperative, "Act only on that maxim by which you can will at the same time that it become a universal law," provides a kind of moral minimum for a capitalist system and the businesses within it. Certain activities, if they were to be universalized in business, would make business impossible. Kant's own example to illustrate his point was the following. Suppose you desperately needed money. Is it morally permissible to ask a friend to lend you some money but with no intention of paying it back? To find out, Kant would require us to universalize the maxim of the action, "Is it morally permissible for anyone in desperate financial circumstances to promise to repay borrowed money with no intention of doing so?" Kant answers with a resounding "no"!

Immediately I see that I could will the lie but not a universal law to lie. For with such a law there would be no promises at all, inasmuch as it would be futile to make a pretense of my intention in regard to future actions to those who would not believe this pretense or – if they hastily did so – would pay me back in my own coin. Thus, my maxim would necessarily destroy itself as soon as it was made a universal law (Kant, 1990: 19).

Notice that Kant is not saying that a lying promise will lead to bad consequences in business, although it will. Rather, he is saying that a universalized maxim of lying promises undermines the very notion of promise keeping itself.

Such a maxim is logically self-defeating. This argument applies with equal force to theft, the passing of bad checks, and the breaking of contracts. Occasionally, the real world provides illustrations of Kant's point. A seafood company in Ocean City, Maryland had the following notice posted on the wall: "We will not accept checks and here is why." Below the note was a row of checks stamped "Returned: Insufficient Funds." That seafood shop would no longer do business with those who wanted to pay by check. In that micro world, a certain practice had become impossible because too many people passed bad checks. Passing bad checks became sufficiently universal so that paying by check in this seafood store became impossible.

When Russia instituted capitalism in the early 1990s, it faced several great difficulties. Since few Russian companies would tell the truth about their financial situation, it had great difficulty in establishing a stock market. Only when there was greater transparency about financial affairs was something like a modern stock market possible. Russian companies also had great difficulties getting parts and other supplies. Suppliers had not been paid or had been paid much too late. The result was predictable. Suppliers were reluctant to provide parts or would insist on payment before shipping.

Kant's insistence that we only act on principles that can be universally acted on is a good corrective to these types of situations and provides a kind of market morality for capitalism.

The second formulation of the categorical imperative stipulates that we treat the humanity in a person as an end and never as a means merely. This formulation is often called "the respect for persons principle." Kant believed that persons had a dignity that was beyond all price. What distinguishes persons from everything else on earth is that they are free beings (autonomous.) Persons are free in two senses. First, their actions are not solely causally determined by the laws of nature. Second, persons are capable of acting under laws that they make themselves. Persons can be self-governed. As such, persons are responsible creatures and are capable of living under the moral law. This is what gives people dignity and entitles them to respect.

This principle requires that a manager treat employees differently from the other factors of production. Machinery and capital are mere things, but employees are persons; they ought not to be interchangeable with machinery and capital. Deception and coercion should be ruled out of business relationships because they treat a person as merely a means to the ends of the deceiver or coercer.

Whether the standard employer–employee relationship is coercive is highly contested. Consider layoffs. Employers tend to argue that employees are well aware of layoffs when they take the position and furthermore, employees have the right (which they frequently exercise) to take positions elsewhere. There is no coercion involved in this idea of the standard labor contract. On the other hand, many employees argue that in times of relatively high employment and job insecurity, employees must really accept offers on employers' terms. You take what you can so you can eat and have a roof over your head, but you certainly do not freely accept the threat of a layoff merely to enhance stockholder wealth. Resolving this debate requires a mutually agreed upon definition of coercion.

Respecting people also requires a concern about their autonomous development. Managers need to adopt management practices that enhance employee autonomy rather than stifle it. One such practice is open book management. Open book management was developed by Jack Stack at the Springfield Remanufacturing Company. Under open book management, all employees are given all the financial information about the company on a regular basis. In a sense every employee becomes a chief financial officer. Open book management goes far in correcting the existence of informational asymmetry that is so typical in most businesses. It also enhance employee self-respect. Under open book management, employees would know if cost cutting is really needed and might agree to a collective pay cut or collectively reduced hours rather than a layoff. Other practices that support the autonomy of employees are participative management, teamwork, and quality circles.

Kantian leaders are different as well. On the traditional view, CEOs are decision-makers. However, a Kantian CEO pushes decision-making down the organization. They give others the tools and skills they need to make decisions themselves. They do not make decisions for others. In this way the Kantian CEO respects and enhances the autonomy of other stakeholders in the organization.

Kant's third formulation of the categorical imperative roughly says that you should act as if you were a member of an ideal kingdom of ends in which you were both subject and sovereign at the same time. This formulation requires that business organizations are governed by rules that all can endorse. Since all endorse them, everyone is sovereign with respect to the rules. And since all agree to live under the rules, all are at the same time subject to the rules.

Kantian capitalism does not require that there be unanimous consent regarding every decision in a business. However, it could be argued that a Kantian firm would accept the following principles. Let us call them the principles of a moral firm.

1 The business firm should consider the interests of all the affected stakeholders in any decision it makes.
2 The firm should have those affected by the firm's rules and policies participate in the determination of those rules before they are implemented.
3 The interests of one stakeholder (e.g., the stockholder) should not automatically be given priority in all cases of conflict.
4 When a situation arises where it appears that the interest of one set of stakeholders must be subordinated to the interests of another set of stakeholders, that decision should not be made solely on the grounds that there is a greater number of stakeholders in one group than in another.

5   No business rule or practice can be adopted which is inconsistent with the first two formulations of the categorical imperative.
6   Every profit-making firm has a limited, but genuine, duty to be a sustainable organization. That means that profitability must be consistent with sound environmental practice and with recognition that a firm has various social responsibilities.
7   Every business firm must establish procedures designed to ensure that relations among stakeholders are governed by principles of justice.

The first principle is a straightforward principle for any moral theory that takes respect for persons seriously. Since autonomy is what makes humans worthy of respect, a commitment to principle 2 is required. Principle 3 provides a principle of organizational legitimacy; it ensures that those involved in the firm receive some minimum benefits from being a part of it. Principle 4 rules out utilitarianism as a criterion for decision-making in the moral firm. Principle 6 is an extension of Kant's principle of beneficence to the corporate level. Principle 7 is a procedural principle designed to ensure that whatever rules the organization adopts conform to the basic principles of justice.

Adherents to Kantian capitalism face a special challenge with respect to the purity of motive. For Kant, the only thing which is good without qualification is the good will. If something is done out of prudence or even sympathy, it may be a good thing to do but it is not a moral act. Many of the good things that a business does contribute to the bottom line. Thus, J. W. Marriott, Jr. of the Marriott Corporation described Marriott's decision to hire those on welfare as follows: "We're getting good employees for the long term but we're also helping these communities. If we don't step up in these inner cities and provide work, they'll never pull out of it. But it makes bottom line sense. If it didn't we wouldn't do it" (Milbank, 1996: A1).

Doesn't the appeal to the bottom line disqualify Marriott's act as a moral act? It might be a good thing to do, but how can Marriott deserve any moral credit for it? The problem only arises if one separates making a profit from behaving ethically. However, a manager of a business has a contractual obligation to serve as an agent for the stockholders. Contracts are a kind of promise and an obligation to keep one's promises is one of the strongest obligations a Kantian can have. Thus, Marriott is behaving morally when it helps the inner-city communities and makes a profit in doing so. There is a moral win–win for all the participants. Indeed, finding such win–wins is what a Kantian capitalist is morally obligated to do.

Kant was a figure of the Enlightenment and one of the key features of the Enlightenment was its cosmopolitan perspective. Despite the fact that Kant never traveled more than 26 kilometers from Konisberg, his philosophy is completely cosmopolitan in outlook. His great concern was with the progress of the human community and with the ways that the human community could live in peace. For Kant, national boundaries had at most derivative significance. Contemporary capitalism is also cosmopolitan and no respecter of national boundaries. Many have argued that capitalism contributes to peace. You do not have wars with your trading partners.

Kant's moral philosophy certainly cannot address every issue in business ethics or the morality of capitalism. For example, the obligations of business to a sustainable environment are perhaps handled better by another ethical perspective. However, if the adoption of Kantian capitalism could provide a moral minimum for business, ensure that employees are treated with respect, structure firms as moral communities, and help establish a more cosmopolitan and peaceful world, Kant's moral philosophy would make a large contribution to business ethics.

Bibliography

Bowie, N. E. (1999). *Business Ethics: A Kantian Perspective.* Oxford: Blackwell.
Bowie, N. E. (2000). A Kantian theory of leadership. *Leadership and Organization Development,* **21** (4), 185–93.
Kant I. (1957). *Perpetual Peace,* trans. L. White Beck. Indianapolis, IN: Bobbs-Merrill.
Kant, I. (1990). *Foundations of the Metaphysics of Morals,* trans. L. White Beck. New York: Macmillan.
Kant, I. (1996). *The Metaphysics of Morals,* trans. M. J. Gregor. New York: Cambridge University Press.

Milbank, D. (1996). Hiring welfare people, hotel chain finds, is tough but rewarding. *Wall Street Journal*, October 31, A1.

Kantian ethics

John Marshall

The moral theory of Immanuel Kant (1724–1804) or any theory that incorporates some of Kant's central claims, or claims similar to Kant's.

KANT'S MORAL THEORY

Kant's most basic claim is that nothing can be conceived to be good unconditionally and without qualification except a good will. This he explicates and defends in the *Foundations of the Metaphysics of Morals* (1785) and in the *Critique of Practical Reason* (1788). He argues along the following lines.

THE HYPOTHETICAL IMPERATIVE

We (human beings) have needs, desires, reason, and a will. Our will is our capacity to act in accordance with rational principles (that is, to act for reasons). When we will any action we act on more or less general principles (maxims); these contain a description of our action, a description of our purpose, and a (putatively) justifying rationale. If, for example, the maxim of my action is to return library books in order to accommodate other users, then although there are indefinitely many true descriptions of what I am doing as I return a book, this is the description under which and the purpose with which I act. My rationale might in turn refer to a more general maxim, for example, my maxim to do my part in mutually advantageous cooperative schemes – my maxim of fairness. As it happens, our maxims often fail to contain fully justifying rationales, even when they appear to us to do so. They often fail, that is, to conform to relevant principles of rationality. In this respect our maxims are unlike those of a perfectly rational will. For us, then, the principles of rationality are imperatives and expressed with an "ought."

One valid principle of rationality is *the* hypothetical imperative – that we ought to do what is necessary to achieve our goals. If my goal is health and a long life, for example, then this imperative declares invalid maxims of taking no exercise and eating rich foods. All maxims this imperative declares as valid, on the other hand, are themselves hypothetical imperatives. Should we agree there were no principle of rationality other than *the* hypothetical imperative, then all valid imperatives would be based on our desires and inclinations and a perfectly rational will would be good only conditionally – good only as a means.

THE GOOD WILL AND THE CATEGORICAL IMPERATIVE

If a perfectly rational will is to be good unconditionally, therefore, there must be some principle of practical rationality other than *the* hypothetical imperative. That there is such a principle (or that we believe there is) is contained in the concept of duty. For to act from duty is not to act from inclination or desire; indeed, to act from duty may require acting contrary to all inclination. To illustrate: consider the difference between the merely warm-hearted Good Samaritan and the Good Samaritan who acts from duty. Both make the well-being of others their end. The maxim of the former, however, is a hypothetical imperative. For him, the needs of the stranger in distress are reasons to act only conditionally on his warm-hearted nature. For the Samaritan who acts from duty, by contrast, the stranger's needs are unconditional reasons for acting; his maxim is therefore a categorical imperative, chosen simply because it is a law. One who chooses maxims on this basis acts from respect for law as such. The basic principle of all action from duty, therefore, is one that sets out the conditions under which a maxim could be a categorical imperative. This formal principle of all categorical imperatives is called *the* categorical imperative: "I ought never act in such a way that I could not will that my maxim should be a univeral law." This is the supreme regulative principle of the good will.

AUTONOMY, DIGNITY, AND THE REALM OF ENDS

If all imperatives were hypothetical then the condition of the human will would be (as many moral theorists assume) heteronomy, a will always bound to serve inclination. But if the condition of our will were heteronomy, then one with effective power could always coerce us to do his will by making the price of non-compliance higher than we can pay. If, for example, self-preservation is my strongest inclination and heteronomy the condition of my will, then death is a price I cannot pay. I could not, for example, resist the threat of my sovereign to kill me should I refuse to bear false witness against an innocent man whom he wishes, on some plausible pretext, to execute. On the other hand, if I know that I ought to resist him – that resistance is duty – then I know that I can resist him and know that the condition of my will is autonomy. If, therefore, the categorical imperative is valid then autonomy is the condition of our will.

What is more, as the example illustrates, if I take the categorical imperative to be valid, I also take myself to have dignity, a value beyond any price (or exchange value); furthermore, I must grant that what holds for me holds for moral agents generally. The validity of the categorical imperative entails that moral agents are ends in themselves, each having a value that limits the value of anything that can be produced through action. That moral agents have dignity implies, negatively, that we are never to act on maxims to which others could not freely and rationally consent and, positively, that we are to make the morally permissible ends of others our own ends. Thus, beginning with the idea that the supreme principle of morality is a categorical imperative, we arrive at the formula of humanity: "Act so that you treat humanity, whether in your own person or in that of another, always as an end and never as a means only."

The idea that we are all ends in ourselves leads to the conception of a realm of ends, an ideal of moral community in which we are united under common moral laws to which we freely consent (each having a veto), laws which define equal rights to freedom from interference by others (external freedom) and which establish social and political conditions favorable to individual development and happiness. This conception of a realm of ends interprets the concept of a categorical imperative: our maxim is a categorical imperative if and only if it could serve as a law in a realm of ends. (This interpretation of the idea of a categorical imperative

has inspired recent work in contractarian moral theory.)

DEFENSE OF THE CATEGORICAL IMPERATIVE

Up to this point it has been shown only that if the concept of duty is not a vain delusion, then (a) the categorical imperative is a valid rational principle for us, (b) we are agents with autonomy, (c) we are ends in ourselves. It remains to defend the categorical imperative. The key is autonomy of the will. In the final analysis, Kant's defense comes to this: the autonomy of the will is the inescapable fact of our own reason; we reject it on pain of rational incoherence.

THE SYSTEM OF DUTIES

In the *Foundations* Kant sketches a decision procedure – the law-of-nature test – for determining what our specific duties are. The test itself is not the categorical imperative, but an adaptation of it. It requires first that we form a universalized counterpart of our personal maxim; for example, the maxim of the liar would become the law of nature: all lie when it suits their purposes. Then we are to ask whether this could be conceived or willed as a law of nature. If not, then action on that maxim is morally impermissible. The test seems (satisfactorily) to rule out lying promises and ignoring the needy. We cannot conceive the maxim of the lying promiser as a universal law, for a lying promise is a possible means to one's ends only if it is the *exception* and not the universal rule. Similarly, we cannot rationally will not to be helped when we cannot achieve our ends without aid (this would contradict the hypothetical imperative), so we cannot consistently will the universal law of no help. Thus, to help the needy is a law we must, on pain of contradiction, legislate for ourselves. Unhappily, as critics have noted, the test can seem also to have counter-intuitive results. The fact of the matter, however, is that there is no consensus in the critical literature about what precisely the test is, how it is supposed to work, or what it is designed to accomplish. Since, in *The Metaphysics of Morals* (1797), where Kant sets out his system of duties, he does not use the law-of-nature procedure, this late work sheds no light on it.

The Metaphysics of Morals divides duties into two sets: duties of justice (*Recht*) (also called juridical duties), concerned with enforceable external freedom, and duties of virtue, concerned with unenforceable internal freedom. Each set has a fundamental principle derivable from the categorical imperative. The universal law of justice enjoins us not to interfere with the morally permissible activity of others (VI 231). An act is wrong if it violates this law (or its derivatives); yet since coercive prevention of wrongdoing is not wrong, these duties can be enforced. It follows that such duties are duties to perform or not to perform certain acts. If I refrain from assaulting you or if I honor my contract, I perform my duty, even if I act solely from self-interest. Indeed, it is because we are naturally inclined to act from self-interest that these duties can be enforced. (In connection with the juridical duty not to steal, Kant develops a theory of original entitlement to land different from Locke's labor theory.)

The fundamental principle of duties of virtue is to act in accordance with a maxim of ends that we can will as a universal law. Like the universal law of justice, this is directly implied by the humanity formula (VI 395). Since duties of virtue are duties to adopt ends, they leave us some latitude in deciding how they are to be achieved. (They are duties of wide requirement.) For example, in fulfilling the duty of benevolence I may permissibly be guided by personal attachment in my choice of beneficiary. They divide further into duties to ourselves – to make our own natural and moral development our end; and duties to others – to make their well-being and happiness our end. Some duties of virtue, however, are of narrow requirement (e.g., duties not to lie or willingly to end our lives). (Kant's view that lying is a violation of a duty to oneself and is never permitted is controversial.) *The Metaphysics of Morals* is not a tidy book; yet only in it do we find the substantive morality Kant believes follows from his claim that the good will is the single unqualified good.

KANTIAN THEORIES

A theory may be labeled Kantian if it displays some of the distinguishing marks of Kant's theory: that moral rules or moral reasons are categorical, that persons are ends in themselves, that moral agents are self-governing (i.e., have autonomy), that the value of consequences of action is conditional on the value and integrity of moral agents, that moral principles are universalizable, that the fundamental principle of morality is formal, absolute, and grounded in our rationality, and that substantive morality is a rational construction. Theories described as Kantian for one or other of these reasons may nonetheless diverge from Kant's theory in other ways. Some contemporary accounts of moral reasons agree with Kant's that these are not conditional or agent-desire dependent, but reject Kant's doctrines of the categorical imperative and of autonomy. Others stress the value of agent integrity as a bulwark against consequentialism, but they reject Kant's interpretation of agent integrity. Many contemporary theorists follow Kant in saying that moral rules must be universalizable and impartial, while at the same time they reject Kant's view that moral rules command categorically. In the theory of R. M. Hare, a theory frequently described as Kantian, the universalizability thesis is defended on narrowly linguistic grounds – an appeal to ordinary meaning – and the moral use of "ought" is subordinated to prudential rationality (the only principle of rationality Hare accepts), with the un-Kantian result that moral imperatives which are categorical in form, command hypothetically.

Kant's own theory is often described as rigorist, absolutist, formalist, and deontological. Kant is rigorist in insisting on the purity of the moral motive (respect for law) unmixed with inclination; still he believes that we have a duty to cultivate, for example, "the compassionate natural feelings in us," and to rid ourselves of feelings of envy, ingratitude, and malice (VI 456–62). Kant is absolutist in that he holds the moral law, which is a strictly formal (contentless) principle, to be absolutely valid for all moral agents, but only on some interpretations of Kant's substantive system of duties does he endorse absolute duties (e.g., never to lie, never to torture, never to kill an innocent human being, whatever the consequences). Kant is a deontologist in this sense, that the categorical imperative sets formal conditions that outcomes of possible actions must meet in order to have value and to be worth promoting. Yet, unlike standard deontological theorists, he does not share with consequentialists the view that there is a way to rank outcomes from best to worst independently of how they might be achieved or by whom. He also rejects the standard deontologist's view that there is a set of moral rules (absolute or prima facie) presented to us directly by our reason (or moral intuition) and demanding our obedience. In Kant's view, such rules could command only hypothetically and the rationality of obedience would presuppose some inclination (e.g., an implanted or acquired desire to follow rules of this kind). The substantive morality of *The Metaphysics of Morals* is, to be sure, anti-consequentialist, but only in its theory of justice do we find even an approximation of a deontological ethics and even this part of the theory derives from the theory of the good will. Finally, a theory is rightly labeled Kantian if it builds on the idea that we are all free and equal moral persons with autonomy (in something like Kant's sense of autonomy). This conception of persons goes hand-in-hand with the (constructivist) idea, the organizing idea of Kant's realm of ends, that the system of duties, rights, and virtues is the legislative product of mutually harmonious willing of free and equal moral persons.

Bibliography

Beck, L. White (1960). *A Commentary on Kant's Critique of Practical Reason*. Chicago: University of Chicago Press. (A classic work by one of America's most distinguished Kant scholars.)

Herman, B. (1991). *The Practice of Moral Judgment*. Cambridge, MA: Harvard University Press. (Excellent discussion of the role of the categorical imperative in moral judgment.)

Hill, T., Jr. (1991). *Dignity and Practical Reason*. Ithaca, NY: Cornell University Press. (Collection of essays, especially clear and readable, on a range of topics in Kant's ethics.)

Kant, I. (1785). *Grundlegung zur Metaphysik der Sitten*, in volume 4 of the Prussian Academy Edition. Several translations are available. Trans. by L. White Beck as *Foundations of the Metaphysics of Morals* (Library of Liberal Arts, 1959); by H. J. Paton as *Groundwork of the Metaphysics of Morals* (Harper, 1964); and by J. Ellington as *Grounding for the Metaphysics of Morals* (Hackett, 1983).

Kant, I. (1788). *Kritik der praktischen Vernunft*, in volume 5 of the Prussian Academy Edition. Trans. L. White Beck as *Critique of Practical Reason* (Library of Liberal Arts, 1956).

Kant, I. (1797). *Metaphysik der Sitten*, in volume 6 of the Prussian Academy Edition. Trans. M. Gregor as *The Metaphysics of Morals* (Cambridge, 1991).

Kant, I. (1902–). *Gesammelte Schriften*, Prussian Academy Edition. 28 vols. Berlin: Walter de Gruyter. (In most translations of Kant's works one can find page numbers referring to this edition. Under the editorship of P. Guyer and A. Wood, Cambridge University Press is currently preparing new translations of Kant's works.)

Nell (O'Neill), O. (1975). *Acting on Principle: An Essay on Kantian Ethics*. New York: Columbia University Press. (Excellent study of the law-of-nature procedure for testing maxims.)

O'Neill, O. (1989). *Constructions of Reason: Exploration of Kant's Practical Philosophy*. Cambridge: Cambridge University Press. (Collection of illuminating, interpretive essays, some dealing specifically with practical problems.)

Paton, H. J. (1971). *The Categorical Imperative: A Study in Kant's Moral Philosophy*. Philadelphia: University of Pennsylvania Press. (Commentary on the *Groundwork*.)

Sullivan, R. J. (1989). *Immanuel Kant's Moral Theory*. Cambridge: Cambridge University Press. (Comprehensive.)

L

labor unions

Barry Castro

Labor unions generally are able to negotiate with employers by threatening to withhold, and occasionally withholding, the labor of their membership. That is their primary power in the bargaining process. That power is significantly enhanced if their members *qua* employees have specialized skills or are for some other reason difficult to replace. Union negotiators must balance their interest in maximizing employee pay and securing favorable working conditions against their interest in uninterrupted employment. They cannot be either entirely unwilling to recommend that their members withhold their labor or too anxious to have them use that weapon. The management representatives with whom they bargain are analogously in the process of balancing their interest in lower levels of compensation for their workforce with an interest in uninterrupted production. Additionally, there is a societal interest in ongoing production and all sorts of procedures for public conflict resolution may be required by law – especially in contexts where the goods or services involved are defined as critical to the society as a whole. There is also a societal interest in distributive justice and both unions and employers are likely to play an active role in influencing the way the public defines that interest. Finally, those negotiating on both the labor union and the management sides, and potentially governmental facilitators as well, will all be subject to varying degrees of intra-organizational political pressure, which may stimulate or inhibit quick settlement. That is the basic context. Most often there is labor peace and the threat of strike or lockout is muted. Labor unions can then serve to constrain the more militant elements in the labor force and,

particularly in owner-managed firms, employers can more easily define their employees as stakeholders to whom they are genuinely committed.

When unions are effective in increasing wages, they will, other things being equal, also increase the costs of the goods or services that their members produce. These cost increases are likely to be reflected in increasing prices and decreasing profits. Price increases are likely to reduce the use of the relevant goods or services. Declining profits are likely to increase the speed at which labor is displaced by capital. Either may stimulate the flight of capital to low labor cost sectors. Whether cost increases are associated with price increases or decreasing profit margins, they may occasion a movement of people and capital that cannot but subvert pre-existing social networks between both business people and people in general. Unions are likely to oppose the movement of capital, but not primarily for this reason. Union strategists, like business strategists, will ordinarily place an almost exclusive priority on the interests, particularly the short-term interests, of the organizations to which they are affiliated.

Individual employees are clearly at a disadvantage in negotiating wages with large employers. Collective bargaining through labor unions is one very basic way that imbalance may be redressed. Unions also may be able to redress a power imbalance through their efforts to organize hitherto unorganized workers, through lobbying efforts, through their abilities to bring matters to the attention of the press, and through their support for or opposition to particular political candidates. Additionally, unions may act to strengthen the civil liberties of their membership. They can provide members with a variety of safeguards against arbitrary dismissal or reassignment. They generally make available a grievance procedure that guarantees members access to due process and offers redress for harassment. Unions are often an important force in attaining (and sustaining) measures that enhance the safety of employees. They are also likely to be active in constraining the length of the normal working week. In all of these ways, unions can move society in general toward a broader engagement with ethical questions that come out of the workplace, an engagement that begins in the workplace but is not confined to it.

Unions can provide benefits that have a subjective dimension as well as a substantive one. Members who feel very little control over their work can find a sense of personal power in union activities that restore a perhaps battered sense of dignity. Unions can provide many members with access to positions of local leadership that help them to develop their abilities and strengthen their senses of their own power. Unions can certainly increase their members' consciousness of a collective strength that may provide an important counterweight to their awareness of very limited personal power. In political unions, they can provide members with all the enthusiasms and self-affirmation that movement politics generally can provide those who embrace them.

While labor unions generally tend to reduce overall wage inequality among their members, they can also increase the power of one group of employees relative to another (skilled relative to unskilled labor, older union members relative to those newly employed or yet to be employed, people of one gender, ethnicity, or race relative to others). While unions generally have an equalizing effect on wages, they have also instituted two-tier systems that privilege one group of workers as opposed to a second, and in so doing add to the stratification of the workforce. Unions can reinforce adversarial views of the workplace and constrain easy collaboration. They can substitute contractual stipulations for freely evolved normative relations. They can make commitment to the work itself more difficult, and in so doing, subordinate a craft or professional orientation to class solidarity. They are countervailing organizations and their means of countervailence are inevitably contractual and bureaucratic – with all of the limitations associated with those means. To the extent employer–employee relations can be interpersonally mediated, especially in smaller owner-managed firms, these contractual and bureaucratic modalities can constitute frustrating interferences with more flexible human relations.

Unions can be organized around particular skills, around particular employers, around particular industries, and around particular political positions or affiliations. Their focus can range from something close to the provision of services for a fee to their role as an instrument of class solidarity. Each of these organizational forms is likely to raise ethical questions. An emphasis on the well-being of a narrowly defined membership excludes concerns with other workers and with the larger polity. Thus, for example, an emphasis on the skilled crafts workers who are relatively few in number and difficult to replace, may powerfully reduce the leverage of those with fewer skills. It may also marshal organized resistance to technological innovation. Class-based political unionism is more likely to be focused on the attainment of distributive justice in general. It is, however, vulnerable to all of the liabilities of populist politics.

Unions, much more than business corporations, are apt to at least nominally embrace democratic and egalitarian norms. They will often present themselves in the language of shared values. They are, nonetheless, likely to develop oligarchic hierarchies that maintain a long-term privileged tenure. A local leadership may well be truly representative of the local membership. That is less likely to be the case on state and national levels, where the union can become a lot like a business that sells services. The dissonance between the norms of a service organization and the personal commitment associated with a democratic movement for distributional justice may be considerable.

Union leaders, like business leaders, may have a wide variety of orientations to their role. They may be idealists with strong commitments to the union as an instrument through which social justice can be achieved. They may see themselves as agents of a narrowly defined membership. They may see their role in the context of a historic tradition of working-class struggle. They may act on that vision independently or in affiliation with a political party or political movement. Alternatively, union leaders may see their primary political role as securing their own re-election. Much like corporate managers, they may simply be committed to doing their job, advancing their careers, and seeing to the interests of their organizations. Many union leaders will be complicated mixes of all of these orientations. That is important to emphasize because decisions that make ethical sense in one orientation may well make a good deal less sense in another.

It will in any case not be easy for anyone who has functioned as a union leader to let go of that role and go back to his or her ordinary work. That is especially likely to be the case in blue-collar situations – less likely to apply when membership work is itself prestigious and well paid (e.g., in Actor's Equity or the American Association of University Professors). A leadership's interest in maintaining the way of life made possible by its incumbency can be a strong motivation for that leadership to find ways to insulate itself from political challenges inside the union. On the other hand, democratic process may genuinely be regarded as less important than other union values – values that it may be argued would be compromised by too rigorous a commitment to that process. Differentiating between rationalization for vested interest and a genuine prioritization of values is likely to be ethically difficult.

Another difficulty may be based on the powerful leverage of the union leader's position. That power is based on control of the relevant supply of labor, something likely to have considerable value to employers, who may seek in one way or another to buy the cooperation of the leadership. The processes involved can be subtle – merely a matter of union leaders being invited into prestigious associations that they had previously been denied access to or the prospect of desirable managerial jobs being offered to them down the road. Union leaders' defenses against such cooptation will be difficult – very difficult if they see their position as largely a career step rather than an expression of some deeper commitment.

Bibliography

Commons, J. R. (1966). *History of Labor in the United States*. New York: A. M. Kelly. (The first significant history of unions up to the 1920s.)

Dickman, H. (1987). *Industrial Democracy in America: Ideological Origins of National Labor Relations Policy*. LaSalle, IL: Open Court.

Dunlop, J. T. (1990). *The Management of Labor Unions: Decision-making With Historical Constraints*. Lexington, MA: Lexington Books.

Freeman, R. B. (1989). *Labor Markets in Action: Essay in Empirical Economics*. Cambridge, MA: Harvard University Press.

Industrial and Labor Research Association (1993). *Employee Representation: Alternatives and Future Directions*. Madison, WI: Industrial Relations Research Association.

Montgomery, D. (1988). *Workers' Control in America: Studies in the History of Work, Technology, and Labor Struggles*. New York: Cambridge University Press.

Perlman, S. (1979) [1928]. *Theory of the Labor Movement*. Philadelphia, PA: Porcupine Press.

leadership

Jack Weber

Leadership has often been contrasted with management. Indeed, Warren Bennis and Burt Nanus (1985) claimed "organizations are over-managed and under-led." While endorsing the validity of the distinction, John Kotter (1990a) claims effective management and inspired leadership are both necessary in an increasingly complex and volatile business environment. In this view, good management provides the degree of order and consistency necessary in large, complex organizations through planning, structuring jobs and relationships, staffing, directing and delegating, comparing behavior with plan, and problem solving and taking corrective action. By contrast, inspired leadership is about envisioning alternative futures, enrolling and aligning people in a common direction, and "satisfying basic needs for achievement, a sense of belonging, recognition, self-esteem, a feeling of control over one's life, and the ability to live up to one's ideals" (Kotter, 1990b).

However, this view of leadership is a relatively recent one. Historically, there have been three main schools in the study of leadership: the trait, behavioral, and situational/contingency approaches. These and related perspectives have spawned thousands of definitions of leadership, most of them implying that leadership is about influencing an individual or group to do what "the leader" wants done in a superior–subordinate relationship. After examining briefly the methodologies and tenets of the main schools, we will explore more recent work, and the forces calling for a new paradigm of thinking about leadership.

An early approach to the study of leadership at the beginning of the twentieth century is the "great person" theory, which attempted to identify the traits or qualities which separated leaders from non-leaders by studying "great people" in history (Bass, 1990). This approach spawned interest in examining the lives of exemplary individuals, as if the unique accomplishments of those leaders were expressions of some underlying traits or extraordinary personal "gifts," not to be found in the general public. As this research failed to identify a generalizable set of traits that could be used to identify leaders, it confirmed a belief by others that leaders were born and not made. Or, as one researcher put it, leaders have a "natural unlearned power" with an instinct for the "propitious moment" (Hillman, 1995). But however inspiring the lives of people like Lincoln, Gandhi, Churchill, and others were to study, for the average person, there seemed to be little chance to enhance one's own effectiveness as a leader by exposure to their lofty example.

A more practical approach was the notion that leadership was perhaps learnable. Behavioral theorists at the University of Michigan in the late 1940s (e.g., Rensis Likert (1961) and fellow researchers at the Institute for Social Research) attempted to identify patterns of leadership behavior associated with high- and low-performing groups in various organizations. In general, they asserted that "employee-centered" managers who emphasized the well-being of their subordinates had more productive work groups than "production-centered" managers who focused on getting work done. Much related research in the 1950s was predicated on similar notions of sharply contrasting styles of leadership (e.g., autocratic vs. democratic, task-oriented vs. relationship-oriented, etc.).

However, subsequent research by Ralph Stogdill and his associates at Ohio State University (Stogdill, 1974) suggested that a leader's style wasn't a discrete point on a continuum, but rather two independent dimensions: "initiating structure" and "consideration." Those high on the first dimension tended to be primarily concerned about influencing subordinates to set goals and produce results, while those high on the latter dimension were primarily concerned with establishing supportive relationships with people they led.

While initially the Ohio State researchers believed that a leader high on consideration would have more highly satisfied and/or more highly performing subordinates than a leader high on initiating structure, later research suggested that both were important. This led Robert Blake and Jane Mouton (1978) to suggest that "concern for people" and "concern for production" were two independent dimensions of leadership behavior and could be measured by a 9-by-9 "managerial grid." They also implied that there was one best leadership style, the so-called "9, 9" team-manager style, who was high on both dimensions.

The premise of "one best style" was challenged by Fred Fiedler and his associates (Fiedler and Chemers, 1984), who argued that the effectiveness of a leader was based upon "situational contingency," that is to say, a match between the leader's style and the requirements of the situation. In their classic popular article on "How to choose a leadership pattern," Tannenbaum and Schmidt (1973) argue that the degree to which a leader invites others to participate in making decisions depends upon the leader's assumptions about his/her own and others' abilities, the skill and education of the subordinates, and other elements of the circumstances.

A variation on this theory included Paul Hersey and Ken Blanchard's (1988) "situational leadership" theory, in which the authors argue that a leader needs to adjust his/her relative emphasis on "task behaviors" (e.g., providing guidance and direction) and "relationship" behaviors (e.g., providing emotional support) according to the "readiness" of the followers, viz., their willingness and ability to perform a particular task.

A significant shift away from the trait, behavioral, and situational contingency approaches to the study of leadership was pioneered by Kouzes and Posner (1987), who analyzed the patterns and themes in the "personal best" leadership experiences of some 550 managers. Rather than focusing on "style," they identify five common behavioral practices that managers are engaging in when they are leading vs. managing: (1) challenging the process, (2) inspiring a shared vision, (3) enabling others to act, (4) modeling the way, and (5) encouraging the heart.

At the threshhold of the twenty-first century, as leadership is increasingly about responding to and creating often discontinuous change, leading inevitably requires relentlessly questioning the status quo or "business as usual." At the simplest level, leadership is a challenge to how people have behaved in the past. For example, a "quality revolution" may require people to spend more time in "quality improvement teams" and learn new skills in group problem solving or statistical process control. More fundamentally, however, leadership often represents a challenge to deeply held assumptions or beliefs (e.g., that "individuals are more effective than groups"). And finally, when organizational transformations are required, leadership must challenge people at the level of their worldview – and the organization at the level of its shared worldview or "paradigm" (e.g., that "low cost and high quality" are not necessarily mutually exclusive).

As Einstein said, "the world that we have made by the level of thinking we have done thus far creates problems that we can't solve at the level of thinking we were at when we created them." Thus, leadership will increasingly require leaders to challenge people to think and act in new ways, to reflect on and question their own deeply rooted assumptions, and ultimately confront the unexamined premises which have shaped the history of their enterprise.

Increasingly, leadership is mostly closely associated with the notion of vision. By contrast to managerial goals, which are often an extension of what has been done in the past and/or a prediction of what is to come, vision is value based, engages people emotionally, and presumably inspires people to extraordinary accomplishment. Leaders devote a significant amount of time in conversations (Shaw and Weber, 1990) with key stakeholders in developing a shared image of a future state that their team and/or organization could and should become (see STAKEHOLDER THEORY). When this is crystallized, leaders see it as their responsibility to engage the energies and enthusiasm of all stakeholders in this view of

the future through speaking passionately for their vision, listening openly to what others say and for what is in the "unsaid," so as to facilitate the reshaping of the vision in ways that broadly capture the imagination and spirit of everyone.

Developing and communicating a shared vision not only provides opportunities for leaders to challenge others to think and act in new ways, but also to find ways to empower individuals, groups, and organizational units to translate the vision into action. In doing so, they must confront their own managerial assumptions and practices concerning others' capacity to assume responsibility.

However, the flattening of organizations and the creation of self-managed work groups means that not only do managers need to be willing to give up control and empower others, but also fundamentally rethink the nature of leadership (Ghoshal and Bartlett, 1995). Similarly, re-engineering and redesigning organizations around horizontal processes such as "order fulfillment" and so-called business transformation, have promoted the notion that leadership, rather than being rooted in hierarchical authority, is increasingly shifting to one's capacity to influence peers and others over whom one lacks formal authority. Similarly, changing demographics and diversity in the workplace, globalization of business, deregulation of markets, telecommuting, accelerating technological change, and the impact of information technology on emerging network models of organization call for paradigm shifts in how we think about leadership (see WOMEN IN LEADERSHIP).

The world is changing so rapidly, the stakes are so high, and issues are so complex, that one person can no longer lead an organization. Rather, leadership and the freedom to exercise initiative needs to be exercised throughout the organization to serve customers better, to dramatically increase productivity, decrease cycle times, spur innovation, and to help people find meaning in their work. And as organizations increasingly require the exercise of discretion, it can only happen when leaders work to align members on a set of guiding principles.

Several years ago a friend gave me a beautiful quotation from George Bernard Shaw's *Man and Superman* that included the following line: "This is the true joy in life, the being used for a purpose recognized by yourself as a mighty one." While it clearly speaks to man's universal search for meaning, it speaks to the opportunity that leadership provides to inspire people to go beyond ordinary limits of service and accomplishment, to enable people at all levels of the enterprise to transcend the frustrations of organizational life and achieve a sense of purpose through their work, and to align people throughout the enterprise on a set of shared values.

In their classic study of America's best-run companies, Peters and Waterman (1982) note that "the excellent companies are the way they are because they are organized to obtain extraordinary effort from ordinary human beings" (*see* TOM PETERS ON EXCELLENCE). In attempting to explain this phenomenon, the authors point to what Burns (1978) called "transforming leadership": leadership that builds on our need for meaning, and creates an engaging and widely shared sense of institutional purpose. Under this view, leadership is an opportunity to personally exemplify and call forth the commitment and urge for transcendence that we all seek. Since we dream about but rarely find this kind of leadership, the task is ours.

Bibliography

Bass, B. M. (1990). *Bass and Stogdill's Handbook of Leadership*, 3rd edn. New York: Free Press.

Bennis, W. and Nanus, B. (1985). *Leaders: The Strategies for Taking Charge*. New York: Harper and Row.

Blake, R. R. and Mouton, J. S. (1978). *The New Managerial Grid*. Houston: Gulf.

Burns, J. M. (1978). *Leadership*. New York: Harper and Row.

Fiedler, F. E. and Chemers, M. (1984). *The Leader Match Concept*, 2nd edn. New York: John Wiley.

Ghoshal, S. and Bartlett, C. A. (1995). Changing the role of top management: Beyond structure to processes. *Harvard Business Review*, January/February, 86–96.

Hersey, P. and Blanchard, K. (1988). *Management of Organizational Behavior*. Englewood Cliffs, NJ: Prentice-Hall.

Hillman, J. (1995). *Kinds of Power: A Guide to Its Intelligent Uses*. New York: Currency/Doubleday.

Kotter, J. P. (1990a). *A Force for Change: How Leadership Differs from Management*. New York: Free Press.

Kotter, J. P. (1990b). What leaders really do. *Harvard Business Review*, May/June, 103–11.

Kouzes, J. M. and Posner, B. (1987). *The Leadership Challenge: How to Get Extraordinary Things Done in Organizations*. San Francisco: Jossey-Bass.

Likert, R. (1961). *New Patterns of Management*. New York: McGraw-Hill.

Peters, T. J. and Waterman, R. H., Jr. (1982). *In Search of Excellence: Lessons from America's Best Run Companies*. New York: Harper and Row.

Shaw, G. and Weber, J. (1990). *Managerial Literacy: What Today's Managers Must Know to Succeed*. Homewood, IL: Dow Jones-Irwin.

Stogdill, R. (1974). *Handbook of Leadership*. New York: Free Press.

Tannenbaum, R. and Schmidt, W. (1973). How to choose a leadership pattern. *Harvard Business Review*, May/June, 3, 3–11.

learning organizations

Lynn A. Isabella

Every so often the work of an organizational scholar creates significant interest and shapes an entire new direction for managerial thought. The concept of the learning organization, popularized by Peter Senge, is such a concept. Through his seminal book, *The Fifth Discipline: The Art and Practice of the Learning Organization*, Senge (1990) set forth a set of organizational characteristics which, taken together, create an internal capability for organizations to thrive in a world of increasing interdependence. His premise was simple. For organizations to cope with the continual change and uncertainty posed by today's – not to mention the future's – business environment, those companies and the individuals in them need to learn. People are the core, because an organization only learns if its people learn.

The premise seems simple enough: individuals learn so companies learn. However, Senge points out that we, in our organizations, are somewhat learning impaired. To learn first means to tackle our learning disabilities, which he summarized as follows (Senge, 1991):

1 *Our tendency to equate our job with our identity.* In other words, we are what we do. This focus keeps individuals from seeing the larger system in which their work unfolds. They become more concerned about self

than about the impact of themselves or their decisions on others or other parts of the organization.

2 *Our belief that the enemy is "out there."* In fact, to coin a familiar phrase, we have met the enemy and it is us, according to Senge. As long as we attribute blame to an outside agent, we miss exploring our own role and the consequences internally of our actions or inactions.

3 *The illusion of taking charge.* Our proactive stance encourages us always to find the problem and fix it. But do we really understand the problem we are fixing and do we really understand how our own actions in past solutions might have contributed to these problems today?

4 *We have a fixation on events.* Concentrating on discrete events, such as quarterly results or percent budget cuts, keeps us from seeing the systemic declines that might result from any of these events. We see the trees, but never the forest.

5 *We delude ourselves that we learn from experience.* However, the full effect of our actions may not be apparent for years, thus we are not really learning from "experience." The experience on which we base our learning may be short-term results rather than longer-term consequences.

6 *We hold to a myth of teams.* What we call a team, according to Senge, is not that at all. We ascribe team attributes and team-centered actions to groups who are less team oriented and more individually oriented.

Working on our disabilities takes discipline – precisely five distinct disciplines. While the goal is learning and striving toward a learning organization, achieving that status is a process, not an end point. The five disciplines and a brief description of each follows.

Discipline 1: Systems Thinking

Systems thinking involves seeing interrelationships and patterns, how seemingly disconnected pieces actually fit together. Too often, individuals see only their business unit, their product, or their slice of the working world, yet their actions or decisions may have ramifications for other areas. For example, a decision made to change a product's design characteristics may satisfy customer demand, but might cause havoc with that product's manufacturing process and associated costs. Without considering how the system is affected by a change in one part, all parts ultimately suffer. By engaging in systems thinking, we are encouraged to think of implications and consequences ahead of time and to see the relationships between seemingly unrelated business aspects. It is our desire for systems thinking that has encouraged a cross-functional focus in our organizations, as well as discussions of crossing lines of business.

Discipline 2: Personal Mastery

This discipline, according to Senge, consists of several important elements. Personal vision is the first cornerstone. Without a sense of a future state or ultimate desires, actions have no context or meaningful purpose. Learning individuals need a sense of where they are headed. This vision may not be highly specific or completely defined, but it is a sense of direction and value. Years ago, the Japanese heavy equipment manufacturer Komatsu articulated its future state of "Surround Caterpillar." This became the personal vision for Komatsu managers as they strove to maneuver their company competitively against Caterpillar.

Personal vision is not enough. With vision, there needs to be a sense of creative tension that addresses the gap between the current reality and the future state – both where a company is now and where it might go in the future represent pulls. The creative tension comes to play in how the company balances its priorities and masters its movement toward the future with consideration for its past.

Finally, part of personal mastery involves a commitment to the truth. Sometimes a search for the real truth means discussing what have been termed the "undiscussables." Other terms might be "sacred cows," or most recently, "confronting the brutal facts" (Collins, 2001). There can be little personal mastery without an honest and accurate evaluation of present conditions.

Discipline 3: Mental Models

Individuals enact their realities and predicate their actions on their interpretations (Weick,

1979). All too often, however, our mental models, the frameworks we use to interpret our work, are not explicit to us. For example, we might view a boss as being ineffective when she does not invite us to a meeting. Behind this evaluation might be our own mental model that says "A boss should include all subordinates" or perhaps "I like to be included in all activities." Recognizing our mental models, testing them for their validity and appropriateness, is key to managing our mental models.

Discipline 4: Shared Vision

Organizations that become great have a sense of purpose and direction that is shared. Vital for a learning organization is a sense of focus and energy that guides the actions and decisions of those who work within it. What do we want to become or create as a company? Creating this vision and ensuring that it is shared by organizational members becomes the job of the leader.

Discipline 5: Team Learning

While the differences between teams and groups have since been explicated (Katzenbach and Smith, 1993), Senge's inclusion of this discipline brought attention to the internal dynamics with a team setting that accounted for extraordinary performance. His contention was that the process of dialogue, not discussion, was instrumental to a team's learning and therefore ultimately to its performance. Too often, teams engage in discussion or debate, arguing positions or looking for weaknesses in logic. While discussion has its place, teams need to engage more in dialogue, a free flow of ideas and conversation between individuals without judgment or evaluation. Senge contended that we are skilled debaters in our organizations, but need to master the skills of dialogue. Doing this can unleash creativity and innovation.

Since the introduction of the concept of the learning organization, there have been countless books and articles targeting the general concept or the individual disciplines. Yet there is no doubt that a fundamental shift is occurring in how we view companies. The concept of the learning organization put into words what many have believed and felt. Learning is the only sustainable competitive advantage. But learning is a lifetime process. Whenever we learn, there is still more to learn.

Bibliography

Collins, J. (2001). *Good to Great: Why Some Companies Make the Leap . . . And Others Don't*. New York: Harper Business.

Katzenbach, J. and Smith, D. (1993). *The Wisdom of Teams: Creating the High Performance Workplace*. Boston, MA: Harvard Business School Press.

Senge, P. (1990). *The Fifth Discipline: The Art and Practice of the Learning Organization*. New York: Doubleday/Currency.

Senge, P. (1991). Learning organizations. *Executive Excellence*, 8 (9), 7–9.

Weick, K. (1979). *The Social Psychology of Organizing*, 2nd edn. Reading, MA: Addison Wesley.

legal ethics and business ethics

William S. Laufer

The history of legal ethics is often traced to a retired Presbyterian Sunday School teacher, George Sharswood, who went on to become the Chief Justice of Pennsylvania and founder of the law school at the University of Pennsylvania. In the midst of the tumultuous 1850s, Sharswood observed that the moral temptations and perils were great, perhaps too much for lawyers to resist: "There is no class . . . among whom moral delinquency is more marked and disgraceful" (Sharswood, 1854: 170). In prescribing a set of professional ethics for members of the bar, he reasoned: "the responsibilities, legal and moral, of the lawyer, arise from his relations to the court, his professional brethren, and to his client" (Sharswood, 1854: 174). "It is the duty of counsel," Sharswood wrote, "to be the keeper of the conscience of the client; not to suffer him, through the influence of his feelings or interest to do or say anything wrong in itself, of which he would afterward repent" (Sharswood, 1854: 175). The ethical principles found in the writing of Sharswood, as well as the scholarship of David Hoffman and Thomas Goode Jones, laid a foundation for the development of early state codes of ethics for lawyers (Alabama adopted one of the first codes in 1887), and the passage of the American Bar Association's

Table 1

Core issues in legal ethics	Coverage of ABA Model Code (1992)	Coverage of ABA Model Rules (1992)
Ethics in the profession of law	Integrity of profession	Competence
Ethics and the adversary system	Making counsel available	Scope of representation
Conflicts of interest	Unauthorized practice of law	Diligence
Perjury and confidentiality	Confidences and secrets	Communication
Ethics in the provision of legal services	Independent judgment	Confidentiality of information
	Competence	Prohibited transactions
	Zeal within the law	Imputed disqualification
	Improving the legal system	Successive government and private employment
	Appearance of impropriety	Former justice or arbitrator
		Organizations as client
		Disabled client
		Safekeeping property
		Declining or terminating representation
		Adviser
		Intermediary
		Meritorious claims and contentions
		Expediting litigation
		Candor toward tribunal
		Fairness to opposing party counsel
		Advocate in non-adjudicative proceedings
		Truthfullness in others
		Communication with represented persons
		Dealing with unrepresented persons
		Respect for rights of third person
		Responsibilities of a partner or supervisory lawyer
		Responsibilities of a subordinate lawyer
		Responsibilities regarding non-lawyer associates
		Professional independence of lawyer
		Unauthorized practice of law
		Restrictions on right to practice
		Pro bono public service
		Accepting appointments
		Membership in legal services organization
		Law reform activities affecting client interests
		Communicating concerning lawyer's services
		Advertising
		Direct contact with prospective clients
		Communication of fields of practice

(ABA) Canons of Professional Ethics (1908) (Papke, 1986).

For nearly a century, the pioneering work of Sharswood, Hoffman, Jones, and the Canons of Professional Ethics served as a guide and reference for the ethical challenges and controversies. By the mid-twentieth century, however, there was a need for an elaborate set of ethical principles reflecting the bar's collective interest in self-regulation. Without a modern recodification of ethical principles, there was a fear that wayward lawyers would be increasingly vulnerable to external regulation and sanction (Wilkins, 1992). This need was addressed with the passage of the ABA's Model Code of Responsibility (1969/1992) ("Model Code"), the first comprehensive model codification of legal ethics. The Model Code was adopted in nearly every state with only a few changes. Following criticism by scholars, jurists, and members of the bar, the ABA issued a new codification in 1983, called the Model Rules of Professional Conduct (1983/ 1992) ("Model Rules"). Unfortunately, the Model Rules were not well received by all jurisdictions. Some states rejected the Model Rules and others modified them. Some retained the Model Code, and a few adopted sections of both (Hazard and Hodes, 1994). All states await the completion of the Restatement Third of the Law Governing Lawyers drafted by the American Law Institute. At present, the professional regulation of lawyers is a matter of idiosyncratic state law. Not surprisingly, commentators have called for the creation of national ethical standards for lawyers, uniform standards codified in federal law that would apply across all states.

With all of the differences in ethics laws, there are five core ethical issues that capture much of the variance in state ethics codes and reflect a common set of problems facing the business and practice of law: (1) ethics in the profession of law, (2) ethics in our adversary system, (3) conflicts of interest, (4) perjury and confidentiality, and (5) ethics in the provision of legal services (Davis and Elliston, 1986). In table 1 the substance of these five issues is compared with the coverage of the Model Code and Model Rules.

Ethics in the Profession of Law

Legal ethics and business ethics differ in scope and specificity. Legal ethics is underwritten by a very limited set of professional requirements and norms, such as requirements relating to competence and integrity. The legal profession is given significant responsibility for enforcement of ethical requirements and norms through a special system of adjudication that disciplines those who violate ethics rules (cf. Hazard, 1991). Business ethics, in contrast, reflects a host of diverse professional, industry, and corporate norms that are both internally and externally regulated. The distinction is made clear by the fact that there are only two formal mechanisms for the ethical regulation of attorney conduct: (1) a fitness test as an entry requirement, and (2) state code disciplinary proceedings for the sanctioning of unprofessional behavior. The former (1) requires that all candidates for admission to the bar of a particular jurisdiction be of "good moral character." Fitness boards evaluate fitness in light of community standards (Elliston, 1986).

The latter (2) appears in the authority given to the state bar associations to self-regulate, discipline, and sanction, through private reprimand, censure, probation, suspension from practice, and disbarment. Professional self-regulation, for example, often requires inquiries into attorney integrity and competence. It is no coincidence that the first canon of the Model Code mandates: "A lawyer should assist in maintaining the integrity and competence of the legal profession" (Model Code, 1992). This canon not only makes attorney competence and integrity an individual responsibility (the breach of which is subject to disciplinary actions), but also requires the disclosure of any member of the bar who falls short of its strictures (see also Model Code, Canon 6). The Model Rules specify explicit standards relating to legal knowledge and skill; thoroughness and preparation; and the need to maintain competence over time (Model Rules, Rule 1.1). Legal ethics in both the Model Rules and Model Code are reflected in a self-regulating set of professional norms (aspirational "ethical considerations") with explicit disciplinary rules governing misconduct.

Ethics and the Adversary System

Lawyers representing different or opposing clients generally have adverse interests. They approach the law and the legal system as adversaries. The active participation of attorneys in shaping, reshaping, and framing facts and arguments in the courtroom stands in sharp contrast to the inquisitorial system of justice (Laufer, 1995). Notably, to some moral philosophers, the adversary system promotes an amoral view of life (see Wasserstrom, 1975; Bayles, 1983; Luban, 1983). To many lawyers and legal ethicists, the adversary system is fundamental to our system of justice, reflecting certain core values and rights, such as the right to personal autonomy and equal protection of the laws (Freedman, 1992).

Central to the adversary system are lawyers in the role of the advocate. As Fuller and Randall (1958) noted some years ago: "In a very real sense it may be said that the integrity of the adjudicative process itself depends upon the participation of the advocate. This becomes apparent when we contemplate the nature of the task assumed by the arbiter who attempts to decide a dispute without the aid of partisan advocacy." Partisan advocacy is required under both the Model Rules and Model Code. The former requires that an attorney, as an advocate, "zealously asserts the clients under the rules of the adversary system" (Model Rules, 1992, Preamble). Even though lawyers must act with "zeal in advocacy," the Model Rules do not require the taking of every advantage or opportunity on the client's behalf. Professional discretion allows for limits to be placed on efforts to vindicate a client. The Model Code, however, is less forgiving. Canon 7 requires that "A lawyer should represent a client zealously within the bounds of the law." Short of pursuing frivolous litigation, this may be accomplished through any permissible means to seek any lawful objective (Model Code EC-7–1). Disciplinary rules allow for sanction of those who fail to zealously represent a client's interests (Model Code, DR 7–101 and DR 7–102).

Conflicts of Interest

Conflicts of interest are unavoidable in a profession that promotes multiple and often conflicting roles. As the preamble of the Model Rules states, "A Lawyer is a representative of clients, and officer of the legal system and a public system having special responsibilities for the quality of justice" (Model Rules, Preamble). Multiple responsibilities and multiple obligations (to client, the court, and the system of justice) can create significant conflicts. These conflicts may be confounded by situations that require the simultaneous representation of divergent interests; problems arising from successive representations; and problems that arise from personal conflicts (Hejmanowski, 1993).

The Model Rules prescribe a fundamental loyalty to the client underwritten by an independence of professional judgment (see also Canon 5, Model Code). Model Rule 1.7, for example, requires the declination of withdrawal of representation where an impermissible conflict of interest arises before or during representation. Adverse interests, whether personal or professional, are not permitted. To gauge the existence or extent of a conflict in situations that are not explicitly covered by Model Rules, lawyers must consider the "duration and intimacy of the lawyer's relationship with the client or clients involved, the functions being performed by the lawyer, the likelihood that the actual conflict will arise and the likely prejudice to the client from the conflict if it does arise" (Rule 1.7, Comment, Other Conflict Situations).

Conflict of interest provisions apply to individuals and institutions alike. Some critically important conflicts occur at the institutional level between and among large, often decentralized, law firms (Epstein, 1992). Firm structure and firm practices may create additional conflicts. Problems related to specialization in law are particularly troublesome (Schneyer, 1991; Rhode, 1985).

Perjury and Confidentiality

In a classic paper, Professor Monroe H. Freedman (1966) raised three of the hardest questions facing the criminal defense lawyer: (1) Is it proper to cross-examine for the purpose of discrediting the reliability or credibility of an adverse witness whom you know is telling the truth? (2) Is it proper to put a witness on the stand when you know he will commit perjury? (3) Is it proper to give your client legal advice when you have reason to believe that the knowledge you give him will tempt him to commit perjury?

The controversy over confidentiality, perjury, and disclosure is made far more complex by the conflicting provisions found in the Model Code and Model Rules. The former *allows* for only certain disclosures and breaches of lawyer–client confidentiality. The latter *permits* or *requires* a far greater disclosure (Landesman, 1980). According to the Model Rules, the central task of the advocate – to zealously and persuasively present the client's case – is qualified by the primacy of the advocate's duty of candor to the court. Thus, according to the Model Rules,

A lawyer shall not knowingly: (1) make a false statement of material fact or law to a tribunal; (2) fail to disclose a material fact to a tribunal when disclosure is necessary to avoid assisting a criminal or fraudulent act by the client; (3) fail to disclose to the tribunal legal authority in the control jurisdiction known to the lawyer to be directly adverse to the position of the client and not disclosed by opposing counsel; or (4) offer evidence that the lawyer knows to be false. If a lawyer has offered material evidence and comes to know of the falsity, the lawyer shall take reasonable remedial measures.

ETHICS IN THE PROVISION OF LEGAL SERVICES

Legal commentators have engaged in an interesting but largely academic debate on the merits and limitations of mandatory *pro bono* service, i.e., requiring lawyers to donate services for free to represent those in need of legal services who cannot afford to retain counsel. Mandatory *pro bono* service is more than a personal duty, it is a duty owed to the courts; it is a duty arising from the privilege of licensure; it is a duty of an officer of the court (Strossen, 1993; Coombs, 1993; Macey, 1992). Mandatory *pro bono* representation amounts to involuntary servitude; it is taking of property without just compensation, and it violates the equal-protection rights of those required to give service. The parallels to debates over corporate social responsibility are nothing short of remarkable.

THE FUTURE OF LEGAL ETHICS

In reflecting on the core ethical issues and the future of legal ethics, Hazard (1991) observes that the historical or traditional function of the legal profession has undergone significant change in recent years. The narrative that once defined the legal profession (i.e., an attorney is an advocate who defends a client threatened with

the loss of life and liberty by government oppression) is tired and dated. Courts, legislators, and administrative agencies have interposed themselves in matters that were once the exclusive province of the profession.

The result for legal ethics? Legalized regulation of ethics will increasingly replace professional self-regulation; case law and statutory law will become increasingly intrusive; and the "bar" will lose its time-honored normative status to the normative power of courts and regulatory agencies. According to Hazard, it is simply a matter that leadership goes where the action is. Law practice is increasingly specialized. It is found in large firms, law departments, government agencies, and corporations. The professional relationships of the "bench and the bar" are a thing of the past. The client is now the business organization, not the indigent; the transaction is regulatory in nature, not criminal; the outcome will have as its remedy money or property, not freedom; and justice will be all but incidental. If Hazard is right, and much evidence supports his view, business and legal ethics may soon face many of the same challenges as the regulation and narrative of law and business converge.

Bibliography

Bayles, M. (1983). Professionals, clients and others. In W. L. Robinson et al. (eds.), *Profits and Professions*. Clifton, NJ: Humana Press, 65–73.

Coombs, M. (1993). Your money and your life: A modest proposal for mandatory pro bono services. *Boston University Public Interest Law Journal*, 3, 215–38.

Davis, M. and Elliston, F. A. (eds.) (1986). *Ethics and the Legal Profession*. Buffalo, NY: Prometheus.

Elliston, F. A. (1986). The ethics test for lawyers. In M. Davis and F. A. Elliston (eds.), *Ethics and the Legal Profession*. Buffalo, NY: Prometheus.

Epstein, R. A. (1992). The legal regulation of lawyers' conflicts of interest. *Fordham Law Review*, 60, 579.

Freedman, M. H. (1966). Professional responsibility of the criminal defense lawyer: The three hardest questions. *Michigan Law Review*, 64, 1469.

Freedman, M. H. (1992). Professionalism in the American adversary system. *Emory Law Review*, 41, 467.

Fuller, L. L. and Randall, J. D. (1958). Professional responsibility: Report on the joint conferences. *American Bar Association Journal*, 44, 1159–1218.

Hazard, G. C., Jr. (1991). The future of legal ethics. *Yale Law Journal*, 100, 1239.

Hazard, G. C., Jr. and Hodes, W. (1994). *The Law of Lawyering: A Handbook on the Model Rules of Professional Conduct*, 2nd edn. Englewood Cliffs, NJ: Prentice-Hall.

Hejmanowski, L. E. (1993). An ethical treatment of attorney's personal conflicts of interest. *Southern California Law Review*, **66**, 881.

Landesman, B. M. (1980). Confidentiality and the lawyer–client relationship. *Utah Law Review*, **54**, 765–86.

Laufer, W. S. (1995). The rhetoric of innocence. *Washington Law Review*, **70**, 329–421.

Luban, D. (1983). The adversary system excuse. In D. Luban (ed.), *The Good Lawyer: Lawyers' Roles and Lawyers' Ethics*. Totowa, NJ: Rowman and Allanheld, 83–122.

Macey, J. R. (1992). Collective discharge of duty or compelled free service? *Cornell Law Review*, **77**, 1115–23.

Marks, F. R. and Cathcart, D. (1974). Discipline within the legal profession. *University of Illinois Law Forum*, **34**, 193–236.

Papke, D. R. (1986). The legal profession and its ethical responsibilities: A history. In M. Davis and F. A. Elliston (eds.), *Ethics and the Legal Profession*. Buffalo, NY: Prometheus.

Rhode, D. L. (1985). Symposium on the law firm as a social institution: Ethical perspectives on legal practice. *Stanford Law Review*, **37**, 589.

Schneyer, T. (1991). Professional discipline for law firms? *Cornell Law Review*, **77**, 1–46.

Sharswood, G. (1854). *An Essay on Professional Ethics*. Philadelphia, PA: T. and W. Johnson.

Strossen, N. (1993). Pro bono legal work: For the good of not only the public, but also the lawyer and the legal profession. *Michigan Law Review*, **91**, 2122.

Wasserstrom, R. (1975). Lawyers as professional: Some moral issues. *Human Rights*, **5**, 1.

Wilkins, D. B. (1992). Who should regulate lawyers? *Harvard Law Review*, **105**, 801–87.

legal issues for business and business ethics

Timothy L. Fort

One can make an argument that most legal issues that affect business have some kind of ethical component. Anglo-American law does distinguish between acts that are *malum in se* (wrong in their own right) and *malum prohibitum* (wrong because the sovereign says they are wrong). Even a *malum prohibitum* law, however, tends to have some ethical dimension. There may be nothing morally shocking in going 35 miles per hour in a 30 mile per hour zone. But the reason for the 30 mph speed limit is not simply arbitrary; there are reasons for why that speed limit makes sense for the safety of the relevant road. Moreover, because compliance with the law is one standard for determining ethical business behavior, nearly *any* law can be considered relevant for the proper conduct of corporate affairs. This is not to argue that all laws are just, but that society frequently makes judgments about ethical propriety on the basis of legal compliance.

As a result, the universe of relevant, potential legal issues for business and business ethics is daunting. Rather than attempting (and inevitably failing) to list all the relevant issues, one can break the legal issues affecting business and business ethics into three categories: constitutional, regulatory, and private.

Generally speaking (and referring primarily to US legal issues) the Constitution is a restriction of the power of governments rather than business. It is not unconstitutional, for instance, for a business to discriminate on the basis of race or religion. It is unconstitutional for the federal government to do so via the Constitution and the Bill of Rights and it is unconstitutional for states and their subsidiaries (i.e., local governments) to do so. It *is* constitutional for the US Congress to pass laws that outlaw discrimination pursuant to, for instance, the Commerce Clause, which gives Congress the right to regulate interstate commerce. Thus, the 1964 Civil Rights Act was a constitutional enactment by Congress that outlawed racial discrimination that might otherwise be done by private business. Many similar examples exist. Obviously, the Constitution is not irrelevant to business, but typically it reaches business through the constitutional acts of a government that regulates business. This means that most of the interaction between the law and business exists through the passage of legislation or through judicial actions.

Regulatory principles represent a major attempt for societal regulation of business affairs. Securities regulation, which controls many issues of insider trading and corporate governance, environmental regulation, and employment law are perhaps the three most immediately obvious kinds of laws that directly attempt to require businesses to follow certain standards of proper behavior. Many other direct and indirect models exist as well. Criminal Law,

Antitrust Law, and the Uniform Commercial Code represent additional direct regulatory efforts. Reflexive approaches, such as embodied in the Federal Sentencing Guidelines, attempt to create the incentives for corporations to construct self-governing institutional frameworks to mitigate potential wrongdoing. Thus, the Federal Sentencing Guidelines offer "carrots" in the form of reduced severity of sentencing options if corporations proactively develop codes of conduct, provide training sessions, and maintain other kinds of reporting incentives, while holding out a "stick" of more severe sentences if the carrots are ignored and wrongdoing continues. This reflexive approach also characterizes sexual harassment law and securities law in the form of the Sarbanes-Oxley Act of 2002.

Private law is a third kind of legal issue with which businesses must be concerned. Private law in the common law system has deep roots in judicial development of doctrines that protect people from things such as fraud, personal injury, and property infringement. Private law has also been amplified in many legislative reforms. Regulatory law frequently takes the form of a suit filed by a government agency, although private rights of action are also granted. In private law, however, the typical plaintiff is a private, non-governmental party. Even if the plaintiff is a governmental body, the source of the law is generally that of a private law doctrine, the most prominent of them being contracts, torts, and property. In each of these bodies of law, rules have been established to punish wrongdoing. Thus, a person who has been defrauded by another person could sue for breach of contract; a person who has taken advantage of another person's incapacity (such as being under the age of contractual consent) can have the transaction voided; a sloppy manufacturer can be held liable in tort for the damages occurred by their malfeasance; and a person whose property has been trespassed can sue for damages.

less developed countries, business ethics in

Sita C. Amba-Rao

Business ethics in less developed countries (LDCs) includes study of values and standards of moral behavior with regard to economically developing and emerging countries, involving a range of global ethical issues: business relationships in society, business–government roles, ethical challenges in a free market, universal standards versus country norms, intercultural ethics comparisons and views from LDCs, corporate and transnational codes of ethics, stakeholder interests, and ethics study, education, and dissemination.

SIGNIFICANCE

Until the 1970s there were few studies or discussions about ethics in business affairs in the West, and until the 1980s, ethics was not an issue of concern in the developing or newly emerging countries of Eastern Europe, Asia, Africa, or Latin America. However, major societal forces since the mid-1980s, particularly the political and economic upheavals of the 1990s, spurred interest in business and academic worlds (*see* INTERNATIONAL BUSINESS ETHICS and country-specific topics.) These forces, for example, are: violent struggle for regime change and the peace process in the Middle East and for democracy in Central and Eastern Europe; the transformation of economic systems to capitalism in most of the LDCs; the huge potential for consumerism and economic growth in China and India; the East Asian economic surge, influencing the whole world; financial scandals in Western countries. These factors and continuing economic problems such as unemployment, discrimination, sustainable development, and fair trade demand attention to ethical guidelines beyond law and market forces.

ROLE OF MULTINATIONAL CORPORATIONS

Through the 1970s and 1980s, as multinational corporations (MNCs) from many countries developed and influenced social and economic outcomes, they found contrasts between their home-country laws and practices and those of host countries. Further, the economic gap between industrialized Western countries and LDCs widened. The LDCs include countries at various stages of development, along with the newly emerging economies of Central Europe and the former Soviet bloc. Intending to soften perceived weaknesses in local practices, Western-based MNCs adopted their home-country practices with regard to human and environmental factors such as the use of child labor and environmental pollution. In the process, however, the MNCs confronted cultural differences in acceptable ethical norms and behavior and, therefore, tended to follow host country norms. These conflicting views created dilemmas between following country-specific norms (cultural relativism) and universal principles of human rights and dignity. In the last two decades many scholars have developed ethical theories and models that could aid in understanding and reconciling intercultural differences in ethical norms and expectations in business operations (DeGeorge, 1993; Donaldson, 1989).

Two other dominant issues concern MNC's role in LDCs: MNC's power compared with LDC host governments, and lack of enforceable international laws following economic globalization. First, because of power differences influencing outcomes in LDCs, MNCs are vulnerable to charges of undermining host government interests and resources. Consequently, MNCs need to pay special attention to their operations in LDCs.

Under the idea of Corporate Social Responsibility, the MNC would make a commitment to the host country's societal goals in addition to the firm's economic goals (see also STAKE-HOLDER THEORY; CORPORATE SOCIAL PERFORMANCE). This approach takes a systemic view of mutual obligations. In the global context, the major stakeholder is the host government where the relationship is governed by mutually acceptable rules regarding fair distribution of costs and benefits. The argument is that the responsibility of the corporations is to satisfy the socioeconomic needs of the host country while making profits.

The second issue is about the need to adopt internal controls in the absence of enforceable international regulations. Many firms with integrity developed codes at company level. Similarly, some scholars justify "transcultural corporate ethics" (Frederick, 1991: 165). A number of international initiatives in regulating multinational corporate activities and governments exist at different levels, including the levels of firms/industries, countries, business and government, and world organizations.

While international codes are not legally enforceable, social, moral, and political influences have significant impact on corporate behavior in some aspects, such as technical clarification, information sharing, and safety. Other areas are subject to controversy and conflicting interests and viewpoints, hence fail to obtain consensus or enforcement; for instance, the longstanding proposal "UN Code of Conduct for Transnational Corporations," with its comprehensive and diverse provisions. Nevertheless, continuing discussions and information sharing promote understanding and compromise, reflecting an evolutionary process.

ALTERNATE APPROACHES

Other approaches evolved by scholars in search of solutions to ethical dilemmas in LDCs include the "extant social contract" (Dunfee, 1991; Donaldson and Dunfee, 1994) and "adoptive stakeholders" (Tavis, 1988). The extant social contract calls for respect for the existing understanding of moral behavior in a business culture, considering the local ethical context; for instance, behavior based on personal relationships in business. Yet this does not nullify the universally applicable norms. On the contrary, this approach calls for a reconciliation between a universal code of conduct and cultural tradition avoiding either of the extremes – an optimizing rather than a maximizing goal.

According to the principle of "adoptive stakeholders," corporations have a special responsibility in the developing host countries, because of stakeholder disadvantages. For example, there may be a lack of consensus on social expectations, inability of consumers to make informed choices, and regulatory inadequacies. Consequently, stakeholder interests are represented by external interest groups, as in the case of the Nestlé boycott against indiscriminate sale of infant formula in many developing countries. Thus, these activists became surrogates or adoptive stakeholders. Extending this approach to MNCs, Tavis (1988) argues that the local subsidiary represents the multinational corporation in adopting stakeholders. Due to its central position, the subsidiary could ensure that its constituents' needs are represented to corporate headquarters, and inform government policy in the host country. Similarly, surveys of developing countries will aid in identifying relevant social needs.

However, others oppose social activism on the part of MNCs, beyond business necessity or enlightened (long-term) self-interest (Werhane, 1994; Sternberg, 1994). A similar advocacy role, that of a trustee, for corporations, reflecting communal interests, is posited by religious activism, for example liberation theology (Sethi and Steidlmeier, 1990).

RECENT DEVELOPMENTS

More recently the challenges for international business ethics with reference to LDCs have been addressed by several scholars, including those from LDCs. The dominant theme of these recent writings is that business ethics is based on a diversity of factors of time and place. While there is agreement regarding issues, consensus is elusive on solutions because of cultural value conflicts.

There is also agreement that while some issues need to be dealt with in a country context – historical, social, political, economic – other challenges are clearly in the domain of basic rights and the dignity of human beings. In this respect, certain things need to change, including institutionalized systems and practices such as gender discrimination in the Middle East and caste discrimination in India (despite existing legislation). Where necessary, MNCs or other "outside" institutions such as NGOs should act as intermediaries or change agents.

In addition to recognizing ethical dilemmas, related concepts concerning moral behavior attained dominance and are frequently discussed: INTEGRITY, accountability, sustainability, and transparency. Due to some explosive financial scandals and fraud in the Western world, and the widening power gap between developing and developed countries, transparency of activities and information was promoted by institutions such as International Transparency at Berlin.

The most comprehensive of the recent studies are two sources edited by Enderle (1997, 1999). He identified several issues and described approaches to them. These were expanded in a worldwide survey and analyses of several issues concerning business ethics by scholars from specific countries or regions, half of whom were

from LDCs. Individual scholarly views, as well as the analyses of the survey, were presented in the First World Congress of Business, Economics and Ethics at Berlin in July 1996, and further refined and published.

In the volume of worldwide views (Enderle, 1999), several LDCs from Eastern Europe, the former Russian bloc, Africa, Latin America, and Asia are represented. After reviewing the analyses and identifying current ethical challenges involving problems such as poverty, development, the environment, and population, Enderle presents five approaches to address such problems:

1 Economic as well as non-economic analyses of problems are in order, to create trust through integrity and, in turn, to solve many organizational problems.
2 Cultural differences are relevant; for example, views on intellectual ownership and management.
3 Religious traditions provide a common ground for ethical dilemmas. Spiritual resources can be utilized for reciprocal learning; for example, Western analytical ethics and India's intuitive or conscious ethics;
4 Action is needed at three levels: individual (leaders), organizational, and systemic (country or region). Global firms can create or change values by means of "sensitivity" or "ecology" conscious management. For example, the Caux Roundtable Principles for Business are developed by European, Japanese, and US executives based on the Japanese *Kyosei* philosophy of living and working for the common good.
5 The role of individual leaders is important in providing information and creating trust among followers as part of integrity management.

These scholars recognize that law and market forces are inadequate guidelines for businesses in a complex global economy and, therefore, affirm that a multiple approach with concerted action at all levels should be directed toward common ethical guidelines. In a similar vein, Enderle (1997) summarized the reports of country surveys, arriving at the same conclusion, and gleaned certain issues of specific significance for the LDCs: the relevance of semantics, corruption, leadership, corporate responsibilities, and the importance of international issues to the LDCs. These are abstracted below:

1   Semantic differences brought into focus the diversity of meanings and applications of ethical terms. Further, ethical challenges differed among countries. It is necessary to strengthen the moral climate from within a country's culture, rather than follow Western culture.
2   Corruption is stressed by many LDCs as a major problem to be eliminated.
3   Leadership is required to implement "organizational integrity." The call for professional ethics among managers is clear.
4   Corporate responsibility: a diversity of stakeholders is recognized; corporate governance and the mutual accountability of companies and stakeholders are important; businesses are expected go beyond law and act with self-enlightened interest, for the common good.
5   International importance: the LDCs are engrossed in domestic issues, yet have made international connections with neighboring countries, noting that the internationalization of business ethics should be by mutual learning and communication.

These and additional ethical issues relevant to LDCs are analyzed by other authors, as well. The first four views listed below are presented in Hoffman et al. (1994) and the last two by Stewart and Donleavy (1995).

1   Limitations of the market economy call for a new role for business, governments, and non-government organizations (NGOs), as intermediaries for resources and representation of LDC interests.
2   Value systems can be modified with internal initiatives or external interventions. For example, the Hong Kong government set up an independent commission against corruption. Thus, Hong Kong became a neighboring model to learn from, instead of the West.
3   Intellectual property rights are viewed by some LDCs as a monopoly of the West, while others assert it is a fundamental principle of property rights everywhere.
4   Sustained development involves concern for feeding the poor while maintaining the long-term sustainability of land.
5   Finding a common ground in religious values should lead to practical rules of behavior and not simply a theology orientation; thus, "business with conscience," based on values such as fair trade or money lending without greed, should be encouraged.
6   LDCs must be part of the global dialogue on ethics in order to contribute to the world economy.

The significance of these recent developments is that much of their substance reflects LDC views and realities. Regarding cultural context and inherent human rights, questions arise such as what does "cultural context" mean in practical terms, and who determines this? Is the process free of coercion? Cultural autonomy with individual responsibility should be encouraged, but not opportunism or an "anything goes" attitude. Issues such as fair trade, the sustainability of the environment, patents, child labor, and discrimination based on gender or caste can cause ambiguities. Further, an attempt at culture change requires reciprocity and symmetry for the groups involved; that is, a mutual understanding and two-way communication and influence. As global business ethics develops, there is a need to examine, clarify, and resolve cultural relativism. Such studies directly involving LDCs enhance ethical decision-making.

INSTITUTIONAL AND PROFESSIONAL ROLES

Governments of LDCs will need to undertake legal and administrative reforms with changes in the political–economic system, and corporations will have to consider internal systemic change (Amba-Rao, 1993) (*see* STRATEGY AND ETHICS). The role of professionals, such as those in marketing and the environment, is crucial in recognizing ethical contexts in economies that are undergoing major changes. Initiatives of government, education, and business in meeting these challenges will be the subjects of further scrutiny and study (*see* ORGANIZATIONAL CULTURE).

Bibliography

Amba-Rao, S. C. (1993). Multinational corporate social responsibility, ethics, interactions and third world governments: An agenda for the 1990s. *Journal of Business Ethics*, **12**, 75–94.

DeGeorge, R. T. (1993). *Competing with Integrity in International Business*. New York: Oxford University Press.

Donaldson, T. (1989). *The Ethics of International Business*. New York: Oxford University Press.

Donaldson, T. and Dunfee, T. W. (1994). Toward a unified conception of business ethics: Integrative social contracts theory. *Academy of Management Review*, **19** (2), 252–84.

Dunfee, T. W. (1991). Business ethics and extant social contracts. *Business Ethics Quarterly*, **1** (1), 23–51.

Enderle, G. (1997). A worldwide survey of business ethics in the 1990s. *Journal of Business Ethics*, **16**, 1475–83. (The entire issue is devoted to the survey report and papers.)

Enderle, G. (1999). *International Business Ethics: Challenges and Approaches*. Notre Dame, IN: University of Notre Dame Press.

Frederick, W. C. (1991). The moral authority of transnational corporate codes. *Journal of Business Ethics*, **10**, 165–78.

Freeman, R. E. and Gilbert, D. R., Jr. (1988). *Corporate Strategy and the Search for Ethics*. Englewood Cliffs, NJ: Prentice-Hall.

Hoffman, W. M., Kamm, J. B., Frederick, R. E., and Petry, E. S., Jr. (eds.) (1994). *Emerging Global Business Ethics*. Westport, CT: Quorum Books.

Sethi, S. P. and Steidlmeier, P. (1990). A new paradigm of the business/society relationship in the third world: The challenge of liberation theology. In W. C. Frederick and L. E. Preston (eds.), *Research Issues and Empirical Studies*. Greenwich, CT: Jai Press, 279–93.

Sternberg, E. (1994). Relativism rejected: The possibility of transnational business ethics. In W. M. Hoffman et al. (eds.), *Emerging Global Business Ethics*. Westport, CT: Quorum Books, 143–50.

Stewart, S. and Donleavy, G. (1995). *Whose Business Values?: Some Asian and Cross-Cultural Perspectives*. Hong Kong: Hong Kong University Press.

Tavis, L. A. (1988). *Multinational Managers and Host Government Interactions*. Notre Dame, IN: University of Notre Dame Press.

Tavis, L. A. (1994). Bifurcated development and multinational corporate responsibility. In W. M. Hoffman et al. (eds.), *Emerging Global Business Ethics*. Westport, CT: Quorum Books, 255–74.

Werhane, P. H. (1994). The moral responsibility of multinational corporations to be socially responsible. In W. M. Hoffman et al. (eds.), *Emerging Global Business Ethics*. Westport, CT: Quorum Books, 136–42.

leveraged buyouts

Thomas M. Jones

A leveraged buyout (LBO) is a transaction which transforms a publicly traded corporation into a privately owned firm through the use of newly issued debt. A typical LBO begins when an investor or group of investors determines that a firm's assets are undervalued; that is, when market value drops below asset book value. Investors can then reap rewards by buying the firm's stock at a premium from shareholders and redeploying its assets. Funds for the buyout are often obtained through the issuance of high-risk, high-interest bonds, called "junk bonds" when they do not meet the standards of investment-grade bonds. LBOs can be big business; in 1988, $64 billion worth of LBOs were undertaken (Sherrid, 1989).

In order to realize the profit potential of LBOs, investors must either sell off assets (i.e., divisions of the firm) to reduce the debt burden taken on by the "leveraging" of the buyout, or employ them more efficiently through various cost-cutting measures. The pressure to make interest payments on large amounts of newly acquired, high-interest debt magnifies the importance of efficient operation.

ETHICAL ISSUES

Attempts to cut operating costs introduce some thorny ethical issues. Employees often lose their jobs as firms tighten their economic belts; employees who are retained often become demoralized and suffer psychological stress. When plants are consolidated, entire communities may suffer significant losses. Buyers of sold-off divisions may repudiate pension obligations, warranty claims, and/or supply contracts, thus harming retired employees, customers, and/or suppliers.

"Junk bonds" add another ethical issue. Bond rating services, noting that the firm has taken on large amounts of high-risk debt, reduce the rating on the firm's previously existing investment-grade bonds, resulting in losses for the firm's pre-LBO bondholders. For conservative investors, who bargained for high-grade (low-risk, low-interest) corporate bonds, such losses may be particularly painful.

LBOs also play a role in the economy as a whole. The increased debt load taken on by leveraged firms increases the risk of defaults and bankruptcies. In an economic downturn, the failure of highly leveraged firms could exacerbate, or even precipitate, a major recession. Further, LBOs represent a major factor in what has become a highly volatile and speculative stock market, itself a major contributor to what has been called a "casino" society.

MANAGEMENT-LED LBOs

A significant proportion of LBOs are initiated not by investors outside the firm, but by managers of the firm itself. This phenomenon is not surprising, since insiders are well positioned to determine that the firm's assets are undervalued. Managers, with the financial backing of junk bonds underwritten by investment bankers, offer to buy company stock at a premium over the market price. To some authors (Houston and Howe, 1987), the existence of this premium fulfills the ethical duties of participating managers because social wealth is increased. To others (Bruner and Paine, 1988), the premium must be *fair*, which means that it is based on a "synthetic" buyout price.

Other authors (Stein, 1985, 1987; Jones and Hunt, 1991) identify additional ethical issues raised by *management-led* LBOs. First, since the brokerage firm which attests to the virtues of the planned buyout and the fairness of the offer is hired by the firm's managers, an "unfair" judgment is highly improbable. Second, managers may manipulate the firm's earnings downward in order to reduce the cost of the buyout (Stein, 1987). While some financial manipulation is routinely done for corporate purposes, thus benefiting stockholders (Briloff, 1981), manipulation for the benefit of managers at the expense of stockholders is ethically unsound.

A third ethical problem arises with respect to the valuation of the firm. Unlike outside investors, managers can gauge the value of the firm after "restructuring" with considerable precision. Stein (1985) argues that managers are thus (1) trading on inside information; and (2) violating disclosure rules when they buy "their" firm without disclosing its true value. The conflict of interest in management-led LBOs is also readily apparent. As fiduciaries of shareholders, managers should seek the highest possible price for company shares; as bidders, they may seek the lowest possible price (*see* FIDUCIARY DUTY).

The principal problem many observers have with management-led leveraged buyouts is that participating managers often reap enormous returns on relatively small investments. Large returns are often justified in terms of high risk. Since highly leveraged investments are often quite risky, high potential returns may be deserved. When managers, who know the financial capabilities of the firm with substantially more certainty than do outside investors, bid for the firm, their "deserved" return would seem to be substantially smaller.

THE ETHICS OF LEVERAGED BUYOUTS

A short list of key considerations for judging the ethics of individual LBOs is in order. First, in any utilitarian analysis, costs to non-stockholder constituents of the firm – especially bondholders, employees, customers, suppliers, and neighboring communities – must be included. Second, the fairness of enriching investors (especially managers) and shareholders at the expense of these groups must also be considered. Further, the fairness of the bid to stockholders must be judged in view of the fact that most actions which managers could undertake to enhance their wealth after an LBO could also be undertaken to enhance shareholder wealth before (or instead of) an LBO. Managerial motives are also at issue; using corporate constituents merely as means to managerial ends violates Kantian principles. A libertarian perspective (Nozick, 1974) would call into question the potentially coercive nature of LBOs from the perspective of employees or bondholders. In short, LBOs, like many complex transactions, are morally complex. Recourse to simple formulae such as "creating shareholder wealth" is rarely appropriate.

Bibliography

This entry is based on Jones and Hunt (1991) below.

Briloff, A. (1981). *The Truth About Corporate Accounting*. New York: Harper and Row.

Bruner, R. F. and Paine, L. S. (1988). Management buyouts and managerial ethics. *California Management Review*, **30** (2), 89–106.

Houston, D. A. and Howe, J. S. (1987). The ethics of going private. *Journal of Business Ethics*, 6 (7), 519–25.

Jones, T. M. and Hunt, R. O. (1991). The ethics of leveraged management buyouts revisited. *Journal of Business Ethics*, 10, 833–40.

Nozick, R. (1974). *Anarchy, State, and Utopia*. New York: Basic Books.

Sherrid, P. (1989). Debt on trial. *US News and World Report*, February 13.

Stein, B. J. (1985). Going private is unethical. *Fortune*, November 11, 169–70.

Stein, B. J. (1987). Shooting fish in a barrel. *Barron's*, January 12, 6–7, 20, 22, 24.

liberal–communitarian debate

Thomas E. Wren

The liberal–communitarian debate, which took its present form in the early 1980s, can be traced back to the beginning of the modern age, when liberalism emerged as a political and philosophical movement. John Locke in seventeenth-century England and Immanuel Kant in eighteenth-century Prussia developed theoretical views of society and human nature that stressed equality, personal autonomy, individual rights, and universalizable (and supposedly universal) moral principles. Considering the standard predilection within liberalism for autonomous reasoning rather than unquestioning acceptance of received opinions, it is not surprising that the views of these thinkers were at odds with the pre-Enlightenment political philosophies then prevailing, all of which assumed the legitimacy and necessity of traditional political authority and hierarchical social structures. Thus Locke, Kant, and other early liberals can be thought of as reacting against what might be called the proto-communitarianism of their day, which culminated in William Blackstone's outrageously complacent belief that in English law and society "All is as it should be," and echoed Aristotle's ancient notion that the *polis* is the natural normative base of all human activity. However, proto-communitarian theory grew out of then-current theological conceptions of society (Christendom, the divine right of kings, etc.), whereas today's communitarian views (including those most friendly to religion) begin with the relatively secular psychological insight that social affiliation is not only a profoundly urgent human need but also the ground for all thinking, valuing, and self-awareness (*see* LIBERALISM; COMMUNITARIANISM; KANTIAN ETHICS; UNIVERSALIZABILITY).

Contributors to today's liberal–communitarian debate generally take the publication of John Rawls's *Theory of Justice* in 1971 as the starting point of the contemporary discussion, since in that work Rawls attempted to replace then-current utilitarian rationales for liberal democratic systems with more recognizably Kantian principles such as impartiality, universalizability, and respect for persons (*see* UTILITARIANISM). Using his heuristic device of an "original position" in which perfectly rational individuals deliberate and choose the most adequate (i.e., most just) institutions for distributing burdens and benefits, Rawls effectively projected his vision of the American political system onto a timeless, transcultural intellectual screen.

The most important early reactions to Rawls's book were Michael Sandel's *Liberalism and the Limits of Justice* (1981) and Alasdair MacIntyre's *After Virtue* (1984), each of which argued against Rawls's model of an individual moral agent as a solitary, autonomous, utterly rational holder of desires and beliefs, and replaced this model with that of a self which is culturally embedded and socially engaged from its first moments of self-awareness to its most sophisticated achievements of selfhood or personal identity. Over the next several years other important contributors to the communitarian literature emerged, most notably Charles Taylor (1989a, 1989b) and Michael Walzer (1983, 1987). Predictably, this literature has evoked counter-replies from Rawls (1993) and other partisans of liberalism, such as Ronald Dworkin (1985) and Will Kymlicka (1989), as well as from Jürgen Habermas (1994). As the debate continued in the 1990s, some convergence took place, which was reflected in a softening of the rhetoric. Thus, Daniel Bell (1993) and others began to use such phrases as "the communalization of liberalism" and "liberal communitarianism."

By the end of the 1990s much of the fire had gone out of the debate, at least the part that consisted in technical philosophical analysis.

Few if any communitarian thinkers now doubt that notwithstanding the wide variety of cultural differences there are important philosophical and political reasons to speak of universal human rights. Exactly what those rights are, as well as such questions as how they are to be identified or ordered, are issues that remain unresolved, but the earlier hard conceptual opposition between universal human rights and culture-specific values no longer exists.

In spite of this qualification, however, it remains true that the contemporary liberal–communitarian debate operates at several levels. At the level of political theory, it is still primarily a debate over the relationship between legal or governmental structures and cultural structures such as religious institutions or ethnic groups and their traditions. At the level of moral theory, it is a debate over the relationship of values and obligations, or more specifically, over whether conceptions of what is good can logically ground principles about what is right, or vice versa. Finally, at the level of what is sometimes called philosophical psychology, it is a debate over the nature of the self.

POLITICAL THEORY

At the first level, liberals continue to argue that laws and other social institutions are – or should be – neutral with respect to individual persons' conceptions of the good or even those shared conceptions of the good that are specific to a cultural group. The liberal position is that these institutions, as well as the political system as a whole, exist to secure and distribute fairly the economic resources needed by each person to pursue his or her conception of the good life, and to preserve for each the maximum liberty to do so that does not interfere with the liberty of other persons. Within this tradition there are a variety of views concerning the question of group rights, some arguing that only rational individuals are rights-bearing subjects and others arguing that among the basic rights that individuals have is the right to a cultural identity. This right claim leads to what is usually called "identity politics," in which communitarian values are supported on the essentially liberal grounds that since people have a right to a cultural identity the state has an obligation to provide cultural groups with the necessary protections of their traditions and values. In multicultural societies, consequently, politics consists in a series of compromises between groups with conflicting conceptions of the good (see Ingram, 2000, 2004; Bell, 2000).

Communitarians, on the other hand, argue that political structures are inevitably shaped by conceptions of the good, even though these conceptions are culture-specific. In other words, not only is there nothing wrong with the state giving special support to particular traditions and values (e.g., stamping "In God we trust" on coins), but in some cases doing so is vital to the well-being of the state itself (e.g., preserving a sense of national identity that can hold the nation together in times of crisis). Much of the political unrest over the last several decades has involved what might be called "national communitarianism," in which the very fact that one lives in a political system is understood to create the moral imperatives and values traditionally associated with patriotism. Few communitarians, if any, would go so far as to deny that one has no moral obligations at all to persons outside one's community (including one's national community), but many accept without hesitation the claim by David Miller (1997) and others that one's fellow nationals may and in many cases *should* receive preferential treatment.

Between these two positions are at least two intermediate ones. The first one was introduced by Taylor and Walzer and became increasingly prominent during the 1990s, to the effect that democratic liberalism is itself "a fighting creed." That is, the liberalism found in Western democracies expresses a particular conception of the good as well as a principle of impartial justice. This view was further refined at the end of the decade in Rawls's final work, *The Law of Peoples* (1999), which suggested that people would normally choose to live in liberal democracies but made no attempt to argue *a priori* for the moral superiority of liberal democracies over "decent peoples" (societies with a reasonable consultation hierarchy, basic human rights, and a shared conception of a common good). As international relations become increasingly globalized in the present decade, thanks to the rapid flow of information, goods, and labor across national borders, it seems inevitable communitarian political systems, including even the most resolutely monocultural nation-states, will have to open their borders to other cultures and, in consequence, adopt policies and attitudes that correspond in fact if not in theory to the model of an overlapping consensus that was introduced by Rawls (1993).

The second intermediate position was also introduced at the beginning of the 1990s, when Elizabeth Frazer and Nicola Lacy (1993; see also Frazer, 1999) proposed what they call "dialogic communitarianism," an approach that includes features from both sides of the debate. It is liberal in its demand for universal access to political institutions and open political dialogue, and communitarian in its emphasis on relational processes of mutual recognition and identity formation. Their basic idea of an effective political discourse that is at once open to all and protective of cultural diversity is carried to a new level of sophistication and comprehensiveness in the more recent work of Iris Marion Young (2002).

MORAL THEORY

At the second level, that of ethics or moral philosophy, liberals hold that morality is primarily a matter of procedural rightness, such that it would be wrong to use unfair or otherwise unacceptable procedures in order to attain substantive goods or ends, no matter how worthy these goals are in themselves. This is an essentially deontological (duty oriented) conception of morality, in contrast to the teleological (goal oriented) conceptions of communitarianism and, in a quite different sense, classical utilitarianism. As with most if not all deontological conceptions, the central principle of rightness is that of impartiality, or in Kantian terms, the universalizability criterion of the Categorical Imperative. Moral judgments about the rightness of an action are made from a perspective that transcends the perspective of the individual agent, such that their validity can be recognized by any competent reasoner, regardless of his or her historical circumstances and regardless of how he or she would be affected by the action in question. So construed, personal morality is seen as a set of universalizable moral rules, corresponding to the Rights of Man celebrated in the moral and political rhetoric of the Enlightenment.

Communitarianism, on the other hand, refuses to adopt the detached perspective of the impartial reasoner, insisting instead that all perspectives, including moral perspectives, are inherently historical and hence relative to one's socialization history. For communitarians, moral principles express the community's sense of its own history and its own conception of the good, which can be thought of either as the common good, as individual flourishing, or as some combination thereof. Communitarians today generally distance themselves from the rather simplistic cultural relativism that was popular in the 1960s, though there are obvious similarities between the two views. Unlike most relativists, many communitarians adopt a hermeneutical theory of moral knowledge, according to which it is possible for someone outside a moral tradition to "fuse horizons" (Gadamer, 1976) and thereby come to a significant, albeit partial, understanding not only of what it is like to have another moral perspective but also of how one's own moral perspective appears to outsiders. Whether this is a genuinely middle position between universalism and moral relativism is itself a matter of debate, but since the early 1990s communitarians have tended – somewhat paradoxically – to incorporate the rhetoric of universal human rights into their own discourse. The liberals of the 1980s, they claim, were not universal enough, since their substantive conceptions of morality were ethnocentric, in that they were consciously modeled on the practices of modern Western democracies. Thus, at the end of the decade, Taylor (1999) argued that to be fruitful, discussions of human rights should recognize that the same moral norms can have different philosophical foundations in different cultural contexts. Setting aside questions of justification in favor of questions of application can, he claimed, bring different cultural traditions together without subordinating any of them. Taylor's vision of a *de facto* moral universality, which is reminiscent of the "overlapping consensus" that Rawls outlined much earlier in his *Political Liberalism* (1993), does not resolve the liberal–communitarian debate but rather dissolves it, in the sense that it renders it uninteresting in light of the larger and more urgent discussions of ethics in a globalized society.

PHILOSOPHICAL PSYCHOLOGY

At the third level, that concerned with the moral self, the liberal–communitarian debate has turned on the question of whether human personality is best thought of individualistically, which is to say in terms of autonomy and its correlates (freedom, critical thinking, self-realization), or collectively, which is to say in terms of historical embeddedness and its correlates (relationships, cultural identity, loyalty, shared sense of a common good). Each side was able to mount telling objections against the other's position in terms of abuses all too common in our own century. For instance, liberals pointed to the conformism characteristic of "authoritarian personalities" whose tendencies toward fascism are now well documented (Adorno et al., 1950), and communitarians decried the rootlessness and anomie of decontextualized individuals as "the malaise of modernity" (Taylor, 1991).

Here, as in the two other levels discussed above, the contrast between liberals and communitarians has softened over the last decade. Contributors to the discussion of moral selfhood now tend to combine elements of both positions, understanding socialization both as a necessary condition for the possibility of any experience whatever and also as an intrinsically historical process riddled with ethnocentricity and other sorts of contingency. In this middle view, attachments to other persons and groups are seen as prior to choice (I simply find myself as a member of a family, nation, etc.), but those groups and attachments are not thereby immune to criticism. True, such criticism can be launched from without as well as from within: from without, as when one criticizes one's legal system in terms of a "higher law," or from within, as when one criticizes one's legal system in terms of other statutes and judicial decisions that are part of the system itself. But however it is launched, it *is* criticism, and for that reason these contributors believe the old liberal objection to communitarianism as mindless conformism and personal stultification fails.

In short, the fact that we are historical beings who come to maturity in specific historical and geographical locations, cultural traditions, etc., does not constitute an argument against the liberal ideal of moral autonomy. Liberals do not deny the fact that our moral choices are made within contexts that are themselves unchosen, any more than communitarians deny that moral maturity consists largely in a conscious recognition and affirmation of the values we call "ours."

Bibliography

Adorno, T. W., Frenkel-Brunswik, E., Levinson, D. J., and Sanford, R. N. (1950). *The Authoritarian Personality*. New York: Harper and Row.

Aristotle (1985). *Nicomachean Ethics*, ed. and trans. T. Irwin. Indianapolis, IN: Hackett.

Bell, D. (1993). *Communitarianism and Its Critics*. Oxford: Clarendon Press. (A good non-technical introduction to the whole liberal–communitarian debate, with special sympathy for the communitarian position.)

Bell, D. (2000). *East Meets West: Human Rights and Democracy in East Asia*. Princeton, NJ: Princeton University Press.

Blackstone, Sir W. (1979). *Commentaries on the Laws of England*, 4 vols. Chicago: University of Chicago Press. (Facsimile of first edition of 1765–9.)

Dworkin, R. (1985). *A Matter of Principle*. Cambridge, MA: Harvard University Press.

Frazer, E. (1999). *The Problems of Communitarian Politics*. Oxford: Oxford University Press.

Frazer, E. and Lacey, N. (1993). *The Politics of Community: A Feminist Critique of the Liberal-Communitarian Debate*. Toronto: University of Toronto Press.

Gadamer, H.-G. (1976). *Philosophical Hermeneutics*. Berkeley: University of California Press.

Habermas, J. (1994). The new conservativism: Cultural criticism and the historians' debate. In A. Gutmann (ed.), *Multiculturalism and the Politics of Recognition*, 2nd edn. Princeton, NJ: Princeton University Press.

Ingram, D. (2000). *Group Rights: Reconciling Equality and Difference*. Lawrence: University of Kansas Press.

Ingram, D. (2004). *Rights, Democracy, and Fulfillment in the Era of Identity Politics: Principled Compromises in a Compromised World*. Lawrence: University of Kansas Press.

Kant, I. (1959) [1785]. *Foundations for the Metaphysics of Morals*, ed. and trans. L. W. Beck. Indianapolis, IN: Bobbs-Merrill.

Kymlicka, W. (1989). *Liberalism, Community and Culture*. Oxford: Clarendon Press.

Locke, J. (1924) [1690]. *An Essay Concerning the True and Original Extent and End of Civil Government*, Book Two of *Two Treatises of Government*. London: Guernsey Press.

MacIntyre, A. (1984). *After Virtue*. South Bend, IN: University of Notre Dame Press.

Macedo, S. (2000). *Diversity and Distrust*. Cambridge, MA: Harvard University Press.

Mason, A. (2000). *Community, Solidarity and Belonging: Levels of Community and Their Normative Significance.* Cambridge: Cambridge University Press.

Miller, D. (1997). *On Nationality.* Oxford: Oxford University Press.

Rawls, J. (1971). *A Theory of Justice.* Cambridge, MA: Harvard University Press.

Rawls, J. (1993). *Political Liberalism.* New York: Columbia University Press.

Rawls, J. (1999). *The Law of Peoples, with The Idea of Public Reason Revisited.* Cambridge, MA: Harvard University Press.

Sandel, M. (1981). *Liberalism and the Limits of Justice.* Cambridge: Cambridge University Press.

Taylor, C. (1989a) Cross purposes: The liberal–communitarian debate. In N. Rosenblum (ed.), *Liberalism and the Moral Life.* Cambridge, MA: Harvard University Press.

Taylor, C. (1989b). *Sources of the Self: The Making of the Modern Identity.* Cambridge, MA: Harvard University Press.

Taylor, C. (1991). *The Ethics of Authenticity.* Cambridge, MA: Harvard University Press. (Originally published in Canada in 1991 under the title *The Malaise of Modernity.*)

Taylor, C. (1999). Conditions of an unforced consensus on human rights. In J. R. Bauer and D. Bell (eds.), *The East Asian Challenge for Human Rights.* New York: Cambridge University Press.

Walzer, M. (1983). *Spheres of Justice.* Oxford: Blackwell.

Walzer, M. (1987). *Interpretation and Social Criticism.* Cambridge, MA: Harvard University Press.

Young, I. (2002). *Inclusion and Democracy.* Oxford: Oxford University Press.

liberalism

Richard E. Flathman

can be understood in two separable but related ways. On the one hand, it is a porous and fluctuating political or ideological tendency and force. As such it has promoted freedom, rights, privacy, pluralism, and – at its best – a robust individuality. On the other hand, it is a fractious family of theories, whose authors share the values just mentioned, while disagreeing as how best to construe and implement them.

In the first perspective, liberalism is a disposition of belief and thought that, from the seventeenth century forward in Western Europe and North America, challenged religious intolerance, authoritarianism, mercantilism, and *diri-*

gisme, and – if less insistently – entrenched social inequalities. Having achieved wide – albeit contested – acceptance throughout much of the Western world, liberalism is now a political and moral outlook located uneasily between left and right oppositional forces.

Leftist critics of liberalism object to its acceptance of the structural inequalities that disfigure contemporary liberal democracies. In their turn, traditional conservatives complain of its voluntarism and suspicion of hierarchy and authority, a criticism that communitarians and classical republicans extend to what they regard as liberalism's overly abstract but nevertheless community-dissolving individualism. By contrast, those self-styled recent "conservatives" who associate themselves with Adam Smith and free-market economics deride the statist and "tax and spend" proclivities of welfare-state liberalism. In much of the rest of the world, liberalism continues as a source of dissent against tendencies similar to those that animated early liberal thinking.

In the second, more resolutely theoretical perspective, liberal thinkers can be differentiated in various partly complementary, partly competing ways. A schema given prominence by John Rawls features a distinction between justice- and rights-oriented liberalisms as distinct from utilitarian or otherwise teleological formulations that give pride of place to conceptions of the human good. Rawls claims that the former type of theory, which he traces to John Locke and Immanuel Kant, best secures the liberal value of respect for individual persons. If liberalisms of this kind have difficulty accommodating ambitious conceptions of the common good – hence perhaps also active participatory democracy – they support procedural considerations such as the rule of law and constitutionalism. By contrast, utilitarian liberalisms, associated with John Stuart Mill and recent welfare economics, privilege substantive conceptions of the general welfare. If the latter jeopardize justice and individual rights, they may encourage a vigorous democratic process (*see* KANTIAN ETHICS; WELFARE ECONOMICS).

The distinctions on which this account depends, valuable in signaling tensions internal to both liberal theory and practice, invite amendment along various lines. Mill struggled to provide a well-protected place for justice and rights, an effort continued by his "rule-" and "indir-ect-" utilitarian successors. Numerous welfare-state liberals are strongly committed to rights such as those enshrined in the United States Constitution, including rights to privacy as regards familial, vocational, sexual, and other matters of "lifestyle." Conversely, rights- and justice-oriented liberal theorists accept the de-sirability of a domain of end-directed public policy and tacitly acknowledge that conceptions of ends or goods are necessary to delineating and construing justice and rights. Notions of justice and rights are given priority in the "basic structure" (Rawls) of society, but utilitarian considerations operate freely within the con-straints of the latter.

An alternative account, which seeks to encom-pass liberal thinkers and tendencies that are dif-ficult to classify in the terms just discussed, features a distinction between agency- and virtue-oriented liberalisms. Theories of the first of these two types foreground individuals as actors, initiators, and creators. Agency liberals do not deny that reasoning should play a role in action, but they stress that acting involves de-sires and intentions, imagination and will. As Hobbes famously put it, reason is a "scout" for the passions, not their master. In tolerably favor-able circumstances human beings form and sat-isfy a diversity of incommensurable desires and interests, thereby distinguishing themselves one from the other.

Agency liberals manifest a non-dogmatic skepticism concerning the power of reason to arrive at uncontestable truths about morals and politics. Accordingly, they fear misbegotten but often determined attempts to subject thought and action to the rule of reason. Diversity and dissonance invigorate activity and heighten the prospects for individual and collected gratifica-tion. Because interests and desires frequently conflict, restrictions on conduct are necessary. But for this purpose agency liberals look first and foremost to "adverbial" *virtus* rather than end-directed principles or rules. The primary political *virtu* is civility, and agency liberals emphasize qualities of character such as magnanimity and fastidiousness, courage and free-spiritedness.

Classically formulated by Hobbes, the elem-ents of agency liberalism are evident in thinkers such as Benjamin Constant, Wilhelm von Hum-boldt, in the individuality-affirming aspects of the thinking of Mill, and in recent writers such as Isaiah Berlin and Stuart Hampshire.

For virtue liberals, human affairs can be just and humane only if they are disciplined by virtues firmly grounded in deliberative rational-ity. Ends that are shareable because based on reason are superior to those that divide, and some ends are categorically inadmissible. There is a realm of activity that is properly private, but its scope should be determined by public reason; the distinction between public and private cir-cumscribes the authority of the state but not of reason and morality. Of persons who "find that acting justly is not a good," "their nature is their misfortune" (Rawls, 1971: 576). Political society, acting coercively as it judges necessary, is entitled to discipline and punish such unfortunates.

The classic proponents of this version of lib-eralism are Kant and T. H. Green. Among con-temporary thinkers, John Rawls and Jürgen Habermas are the most influential representa-tives of this orientation. The large body of writing affirmatively influenced by these thinkers gives virtue liberalism great promin-ence in the current literatures of political and moral philosophy.

These important differences noted, and rec-ognizing that liberalism as both force and idea is currently on the defensive, Jose Ortega y Gasset was correct to say that liberalism is "the noblest cry that has ever resounded in this planet" (1932: 84).

See also *communitarianism; liberalism–communi-tarian debate; utilitarianism*

Bibliography

Arblaster, A. (1984). *The Rise and Decline of Western Liberalism*. Oxford: Blackwell.
Berlin, I. (1969). *Four Essays on Liberty*. Oxford: Oxford University Press.
Constant, B. (1988). *Political Writings*. Cambridge: Cambridge University Press.
Flathman, R. E. (1992a). Liberalism. In L. Becker (ed.), *Encyclopedia of Ethics*. New York: Garland. (The above entry borrows from this publication.)
Flathman, R. E. (1992b). *Willful Liberalism*. Ithaca, NY: Cornell University Press.

Freeden, M. (1978). *The New Liberalism*. Oxford: Clarendon Press.

Gasset, Jose Ortega y (1932). *The Revolt of the Masses*. New York: W. W. Norton.

Green, T. H. (1986). *Lectures on the Principles of Political Obligation and Other Writings*. Cambridge: Cambridge University Press.

Hampshire, S. (1989). *Innocence and Experience*. Cambridge, MA: Harvard University Press.

Hayek, F. A. (1960). *The Constitution of Liberty*. Chicago: University of Chicago Press.

Hobbes, T. (1955). *Leviathan*. Oxford: Blackwell.

Humboldt, W. von (1969). *On the Sphere and Duties of Government*. Cambridge: Cambridge University Press.

Kant, I. (1948). *Groundwork of the Metaphysics of Morals*, trans. H. J. Paton as *The Moral Law*. London: Hutchinson.

Kant, I. (1964/5). *Metaphysics of Morals*. Most of the first part trans. J. Ladd as *The Metaphysical Elements of Justice*. Indianapolis, IN: Library of Liberal Arts. The second part trans. M. Gregor as *The Doctrine of Virtue*. New York: Harper and Row.

Locke, J. (1948). *A Letter Concerning Toleration*. Oxford: Blackwell.

Locke, J. (1960). *Two Treatises on Government*. Cambridge: Cambridge University Press.

Mill, J. S. (1951). *On Liberty, Utilitarianism, and Representative Government*. New York: E. P. Dutton.

Rawls, J. (1971). *A Theory of Justice*. Cambridge, MA: Harvard University Press.

Rawls, J. (1993). *Political Liberalism*. New York: Columbia University Press.

Ruggerio, G. de (1927). *The History of European Liberalism*. Oxford: Oxford University Press.

Smith, A. (1937). *The Wealth of Nations*. New York: Modern Library.

libertarianism

Tibor R. Machan

PEDIGREE AND ESSENTIALS

Libertarianism emerged from the classical liberal tradition, as a purified or more consistent version of its pedigree. The focus is on the political priority of individual (negative) liberty. Libertarianism views the basic rights of every (adult) individual to life, liberty, and property as the central normative claim underlying the political, legal, economic, and social system most suitable for human community life.

Although there are several strains of libertarianism, the differences concern mainly the philosophical argument from which the conclusion emerges that each individual possesses the basic rights to life, liberty, and property. Some of these strains use somewhat different terms, some eschewing talk of rights, some stressing the utility of efficiency or practical value, or, again, the progressive prospects to be obtained from regarding individual liberty as the highest public good.

Still, the conclusions of these different lines of argumentation issue in the affirmation of the political value of a system of laws that focus on establishing and protecting the sovereignty of the individual citizen in all spheres of his or her life – religious, artistic, economic, scientific, and so forth.

Libertarianism stresses, perhaps somewhat misleadingly, the fundamentality of the right to private property. Here, too, different strains of arguments for this kind of polity will advance somewhat different grounds for why this right is to be recognized and legally protected. Two major views appear to have emerged as prominent: a more or less descriptive or positivist line of argument, and one that involves normative or prescriptive considerations.

POSITIVIST (ECONOMIC) LIBERTARIANISM

The positivist line of argumentation focuses on the common human objective of prosperity or wealth, something preeminently likely in a society wherein private property rights are respected and protected. Prosperity, along these lines, is determined subjectively – that is, by reference to how citizens perceive themselves to be satisfied, enriched, fulfilled, successful, etc.

As in the tradition of most non-cognitivist approaches to values, this (neo-Hobbesian, *homo economicus*) version of libertarianism regards only a value-free approach to understanding society as intellectually defensible. Value judgments are non-cognitive, except in the limited sense that one can identify, by reference to what people do (i.e., their revealed preferences), what is good for them. From within this framework, negative individual liberty – identified as the absence of physical intrusion by others upon the person and property of any individual – would most effectively secure mutual, widespread progress toward what is taken to be the common objective of everyone, namely satisfaction of preferences.

NORMATIVE (MORAL) LIBERTARIANISM

The normative libertarian takes value judgments to be objectively determinable, albeit most often agent relative (i.e., depending upon many individual, social, and other aspects of the individuals involved). Among the few universalizable objective values is the central condition – to be secured by everyone within a community – of individual self-determination, personal sovereignty, or autonomy. This value, as others, is established by reference to what and who the individual is, namely, essentially self-directed, in possession of the unique capacity of free will.

Because the morally successful individual must, first and foremost, take the initiative to do the right thing, to act ethically, the condition of liberty (spelled out by the set of basic individual rights) is an indispensable precondition for everyone's moral development. Private property, in turn, is viewed here as the concrete implementation of the condition of moral autonomy and political sovereignty – it is supposed to constitute the precondition for a life guided by one's own moral choices, for better or worse. Private property pertains to one's life and what one acquires or obtains in it without force or fraud. This is taken to enable one to make free determination of the course one's life will take while others are no less enabled, so far as human choices make a difference for this purpose.

INDIVIDUALISM

Individualism – also referred to as psychological or ethical egoism – is often taken to be a crucial component of libertarianism, although strictly it would play a role at the foundations underlying this political outlook (see EGOISM, PSYCHOLOGICAL EGOISM, AND ETHICAL EGOISM). Some version of individualism, but not necessarily the type referred to (mostly by critics) as atomistic, is closely linked to libertarianism.

The crucial individualist element is personal determination of or responsibility for one's conduct, so that the individual person is taken to be decisively (though not exclusively) involved in initiating judgment and shaping conduct. Sociability is compatible with the position, even as an essential component, provided it is not coercively imposed. Because of the nature of human beings as basically self-directed, the social or communitarian dimension of life is introduced by libertarianism as requiring freedom of choice (e.g., in the selection of social ties among adult human beings).

JUSTICE, EQUALITY, ETC., VIA LIBERTARIANISM

Whether one approaches the libertarian framework from a positive or normative framework, the concrete socioeconomic result would be a constitutional system that stresses the supreme significance of individual liberty. Such notions as "justice," "equality," "order," "welfare," etc., have a significant role in the development of the libertarian's basic legal framework or constitution, albeit never superseding the right to individual liberty.

Thus, libertarian justice consists in a system's focus upon the standards of due process that disallow any policy involving involuntary servitude, regardless of how worthy the objective might be (e.g., fighting crime, defending the country, fostering the arts, sciences, healthcare, education, recreation, etc.). It is not that such objectives necessarily lack widespread acceptance or even objective value. Yet the precondition of having to reach them without the violation of individual rights (for example, by means of taxation, universal conscription, transfer or redistribution of wealth) is the central prerequisite of justice. Equality, too, is understood by reference to the mutual condition of liberty that every citizen must enjoy – that is, everyone is equal in respect of having the right to life, liberty, and property, regardless of whether equality prevails in natural assets, good fortune, health, well-being, sexual appeal, etc. Thus, libertarianism tolerates various types of social injustice, such as personal betrayal, economic exploitation, and racial discrimination, so long as no force and fraud are involved. Furthermore, while it is egalitarian at the political and legal levels of community life, there is no insistence upon the political priority of equality in economic, educational, athletic, or similar opportunities, let alone equality of conditions or results, level playing fields, etc. The main reason is, briefly, that to establish such equality is a pipe dream – clearly those attempting to establish the equality in question would always fail to be equal to others in the central respect of being authorized to violate individual rights.

Libertarianism is concerned with political – not social or economic or racial or ethnic – justice and equality. While the latter are not, by at least some libertarian lights, incapable of being identified and sought out, they must be pursued without recourse to the violation of individual rights to life, liberty, and property. Order, progress, cultural diversity, ethnic, racial, and gender harmony are similarly regarded as possibly valid but never primary values for a good political community.

COMPARATIVE (NON-UTOPIAN OR IDEALISTIC) ASSESSMENT

There is no room here to consider the innumerable theoretical objections, let alone aversions, expressed against libertarianism. Put simply, libertarians take most of them to stem from utopian or idealistic thinking.

Indeed, at the level of comparative political thinking, the libertarian may be distinguished by a lack of utopianism. (This is especially true of the normative libertarian, who does not see human nature as conducive to perfectibility or any institutional guarantee against immoral conduct – imprudence, dishonesty, stinginess, greed, sloth.)

Accordingly, when it comes to assessing the merits of libertarianism, it is argued that it should be done comparatively: which polity is most likely or highly probable to do justice to the most rational assessment of human good. Utopian or idealistic thinking judges political theories by impossible standards and, thus, encourages misguided public policy and legal measures. Because individuals are fallible and cannot be engineered to be morally good, the utopian aspirations of many competing political, social, and economic frameworks need to be set aside. When this is done, so the libertarian holds, the polity of individual liberty comes off as superior to all live options and contenders.

When it comes to the libertarian approach to business ethics, what stands out is the principled insistence on the public policy of *laissez-faire*, not embarking on any type of prior restraint (analogously with the public policy of respecting and protecting the right to freedom of the press or religion). Yet this does not tell the whole story because libertarians are people who do not confine their interest to politics alone. As far as libertarianism is concerned, business ethics – albeit not strictly speaking concerned with politics and public policy but with answering the specialized question "How ought a person embarking on commerce, as an amateur or professional, conduct themselves?" – draws on ethical not political theory. Whatever sound ethical theory human beings ought to live by will have implications for the various roles human beings take on in their lives, including the role they have as commercial or business agents. Libertarianism is not directly concerned with what ethical theory is sound, although in the defense of libertarianism it is usually stressed that commercial and business activities are morally at least unobjectionable if not outright morally proper (as per the exercise of the virtue of prudence in a social context).

Bibliography

Friedman, M. (1962). *Capitalism and Freedom*. Chicago: University of Chicago Press.

Hayek, F. A. (1954). *Capitalism and the Historians*. Chicago: University of Chicago Press.

Hospers, J. (1971). *Libertarianism*. Los Angeles, Nash.

McGee, Robert W. (1992). *Business Ethics and Common Sense*. Westport, CT: Quorum Books.

Machan, T. R. (1988). *Commerce and Morality*. Lanham, MD: Rowman and Littlefield.

Machan, T. R. (1995). *Private Rights and Public Illusions*. New Brunswick, NJ: Transaction Books.

Narveson, J. (1991). *The Libertarian Idea*. Philadelphia, PA: Temple University Press.

Nozick, R. (1974). *Anarchy, State, and Utopia*. New York: Basic Books.

Rand, A. (1967). *Capitalism: The Unknown Ideal*. New York: New American Library.

Rasmussen, D. and Machan, T. R. (eds.) (1996). *Liberty for the 21st Century*. Lanham, MD: Rowman and Littlefield.

Rothbard, M. N. (1973). *Power and Market*. New York: Macmillan.

von Mises, L. (1951). *Human Action*. New Haven, CT: Yale University Press.

liberty

George G. Brenkert

is commonly regarded as one of the fundamental values or principles of modern Western society. Ideally, it characterizes individuals within both political and economic systems. Though there is widespread agreement that liberty is highly desirable, there is much less agreement as to what it is.

The word "liberty" has a Latin origin and captures the same ideas as "freedom," which has a Germanic derivation. Liberty is usually taken, most simply, to be the situation of individuals who are not constrained by others (or the state) in their choice of goals or course of action. This liberty of non-constraint, or negative liberty, is one of two standard views of liberty. The term "negative liberty" is not pejorative. It simply refers to the lack of constraint.

However, a complete view of negative liberty requires definition of both the nature and extent of such constraint. First, does constraint refer simply to physical impositions placed upon a person by the intentional actions of others? There have been various objections to this external and intentional interpretation of constraint. Some have argued that the constraint which limits one's freedom may be unintentionally imposed. If a night custodian locks a door, unintentionally leaving a manager inside the building, the custodian has reduced the manager's liberty. Similarly, a person's freedom, it is argued, may also be reduced by psychological pressures and threats, as when a supervisor demands that a subordinate act in certain ways subject to possible dismissal. Finally, others have maintained that even the internal, psychological states of individuals, for example great fears or anxieties created in a working situation, may also limit their liberty.

Thus, interpretations of negative freedom as simply the lack of intentional, physical constraint are of disputable adequacy. Suppose, however, that the preceding disputes can be resolved. Another crucial issue remains. Since people must live together and by their actions may constrain each other, what is the extent of the lack of constraints required for freedom? At what point may a person's actions be restricted so as to secure freedom for others (or themselves)?

There are several prominent responses. Some claim that a person's actions may be limited when they harm another person, though "harm" has itself received various interpretations: (1) violating a person's important human interests; (2) violating individual rights (to religion, opinion, expression, property); and (3) impairing practices and systems in the public interest. Others maintain that grave offense to other persons (e.g., pornography), or even the immorality of one's actions (e.g., prostitution), are grounds for limiting a person's behavior so as to secure freedom. Each of these responses has its own advantages and disadvantages. However, the appeal to harm has been thought by many to be the least controversial response.

Accordingly, negative freedom exists when people are relieved of a broad range of constraints and those that are imposed on them derive from one of the liberty-limiting principles just noted. Since people may choose under such conditions to act in a variety of ways, such freedom is sometimes linked with equality of opportunity (see Friedman and Friedman, 1980; Berlin, 1969). In any case, the enjoyment of negative liberty requires a social and legal system in which some actions are restrained. Absolute freedom, in the sense of a total lack of constraints, would destroy itself.

It should be noted that liberty, as so far described, characterizes a passive condition of an individual. Certain constraints do not exist; various opportunities or alternatives are present. It is an individualistic view, not necessarily connected with democracy or self-government. An enlightened despot, for example, might allow a greater extent of negative freedom than a democratically run fundamentalist society.

Some have argued that negative freedom is an incomplete or inadequate account of liberty. They contend that liberty is not simply a lack of certain forms of constraint ("freedom from"), but that it is the self-determination (or self-realization) by individuals of their affairs ("freedom to"). Liberty, on this view, is a positive and active condition of a person. This is the second standard view of liberty, commonly referred to as "positive freedom." It is closely related to the notion of autonomy. Berlin claims that this form of freedom answers the question, who or what controls one's actions? For Berlin, this is a different question from the one negative freedom asks, namely, what is constrained? Others, however, claim that liberty requires both negative and positive aspects. Those who defend positive freedom admit that one's self-determination is fostered by the lack of constraints, but they place their emphasis on the self-determination, not the lack of constraints.

This positive view of liberty also requires additional clarification and qualification. It would appear that even those individuals who set their course based on irrational emotions or desires and inadequate knowledge have engaged in a form of self-determination. Nevertheless, many defenders of positive freedom are reluctant to characterize such acts as free. Accordingly, they specify that only certain kinds of self-determination (e.g., those embodying particular forms or degrees of rationality) are instances of freedom.

However, some have argued that this opens the door for others (including the state) to determine when people's self-determinations fulfill these additional conditions for freedom and to impose those conditions on them. In short, they undertake to force people to be free. There is, however, no necessity to this. It is one thing to claim that people do not fulfill certain conditions of positive freedom. It is another to force them to fulfill those conditions and, hence, to be free.

Finally, defenders of positive freedom must also specify the relation of an individual's own self-determinations to those of other members of one's society. Frequently this has been done by means of theories of participation in a democratic order in which each individual is to have a say in those issues which significantly affect him or her. The manner in which this is possible within large, urban societies is a crucial issue for positive freedom.

Traditionally, both views of liberty have been applied to political states and their relations to their citizens. Within such views, negative liberty requires exemption from various forms of interference or constraint. Positive liberty requires some form of participation in the determination of the affairs of state. Within economic organizations, both forms of liberty have traditionally been realized more fully by entrepreneurs, owners, and (perhaps) upper management. In recent years, however, there has been an attempt to extend both forms of

liberty more broadly to employees (see Ewing, 1977). Demands for negative liberty have taken the form of demands for employee rights such as freedom of expression and privacy. Positive liberty has been linked with due process and various forms of participation within the firm.

Positive and negative freedom carry different implications for the relation between freedom and economic (and political) resources. If one adheres to negative freedom, the absence (or presence) of resources which enable one to engage in various activities may be desirable, but does not detract from, or add to, one's freedom. Various resources may make one's freedom more valuable, but do not alter the extent of one's freedom. However, resources play a necessary role in positive freedom. One cannot be self-determining, for example, if one does not have the wherewithal to do so.

When freedom is linked with economic resources, questions of the relation of freedom and equality arise. Freedom is sometimes said to be opposed to equality. This view assumes that equality requires that limits or constraints be placed on some to promote the resources of others (hence, greater equality). Defenders of this view tend to assume that liberty is defined by the lack of restraints and that equality requires the elimination of differences (see Friedman and Friedman, 1980). Neither assumption must be made. Defenders of equality may allow for various justified differences. Proponents of liberty may opt for positive liberty as a form of self-determination which recognizes the interdependence of individuals in a society. When liberty and equality are so viewed, liberty may itself require that resources be apportioned equally rather than enjoyed disproportionately by various parts of society. In these circumstances, freedom and equality need not be opposed (see Norman, 1987).

Liberty is frequently connected to rights. For example, individuals are often said to have a right to liberty. This is a global claim regarding liberty. It implies that a person's (positive or negative) liberty is entitled to certain protections. On the other hand, and more specifically, liberty is also often said to consist of a number of rights, whose protection is often supposedly guaranteed by constitutions. The nature of these rights, whether positive or negative, reveals the nature of liberty being defended.

In modern times, a common distinction has been drawn between political and civil liberties. Political liberties consist of rights that individuals have to participate in the political realm: for example, the rights to vote and to run for office. Civil liberties, then, consist of rights one might have outside a political realm, such as rights to religion, to free speech, and not to be tortured.

The liberties guaranteed by the constitutions of nations and states extend to the citizens and individuals within the authority of those political entities. Such guarantees do not necessarily hold between private individuals, or employers and employees. Thus, though a government may be prohibited by its constitution from interfering with a citizen's freedom of speech, privacy, and due process, these protections do not thereby extend to the workplace. The attempt to extend the protection of individual liberties to the workplace is a movement which has gained considerable momentum in recent decades (see Ewing, 1977).

Finally, though liberty is often viewed as an unambiguous good, this is too simple. The constraints or limits of a social, political, or economic system may also serve to give individuals a sense of security and identity. Lack of such limits, it has been argued, creates people who may feel isolated and anxious (see Fromm, 1965). In this situation, they may be willing to surrender their freedom to others. Accordingly, liberty is one value, albeit a very important one, among others such as justice, equality, community, fraternity, and security. A healthy society and workplace will accord liberty a significant place. However, they must also weigh it against other important values.

Bibliography

Berlin, I. (1969). Two concepts of liberty. In I. Berlin (ed.), *Four Essays on Liberty*. Oxford: Oxford University Press, 118–72.

Ewing, D. W. (1977). *Freedom Inside the Organization*. New York: McGraw-Hill.

Friedman, F. and Friedman, R. (1980). *Free to Choose*. New York: Avon Books.

Fromm, E. (1965). *Escape from Freedom*. New York: Avon Books.

Gray, T. (1991). *Freedom*. Atlantic Highlands, NJ: Humanities Press International.

Hayek, F. (1960). *The Constitution of Liberty*. Chicago: University of Chicago Press.

Mill, J. S. (1956). *On Liberty*. Indianapolis, IN: Bobbs-Merrill.

Norman, R. (1987). *Free and Equal*. Oxford: Oxford University Press.

lobbyists

Alan R. Beckenstein

are persons whose primary function is to influence the outcome of the public policy process. The origin of the term derives from the room outside of a legislative chamber in which the "lobbyists" waited for an opportunity to speak to legislators.

Historically, to some citizens, the label "lobbyist" has carried a negative connotation. Public opinion has typically been suspicious about the combination of politics and money. Some lobbyists have been assumed to supply money – in the form of bribes, gifts, or campaign funds – to politicians who serve the interest group's favored agenda.

Political theorists and constitutional scholars emphasize the free-speech aspects of lobbying activity. In a democratic society, political activity is a legitimate function of individuals and groups, including business organizations. Active participation by all segments of society contributes to a strong system of checks and balances. Most importantly, lobbyists exercise their basic right to free speech.

Efforts to control lobbying activities have been proposed for at least a hundred years. The free-speech arguments have prevailed in moderating zealous reform attempts. The US Foreign Agents Registration Act of 1938 and the Federal Registration of Lobbyists Act of 1946 have been the notable reforms. These Acts basically require lobbyists to register themselves as such with Congress and to report significant lobbying expenditures. In 1995 Congress passed the Lobbying Disclosure Act, which established standards for disclosure of contacts between lobbyists and Members of Congress where such contact is intended to "influence" the Members. The primary emphasis of this legislation was to limit severely the amount of gifts and campaign donations that could be given to legislators and to close loopholes in the rules requiring disclosure of a lobbying activity.

The scope of lobbying activity increased greatly during the post-World War II period. The number of lobbyists registered with Congress in 1961 was 365 and had risen to 23, 011 in mid-1987 (Smith, 1988: 29). This was an adaptation to new media and technology. The ability to communicate at grassroots levels and to conduct mass marketing campaigns altered the possible influence channels for interest groups. Information about supporters of members of Congress became available through information technology. This allowed lobbyists an opportunity to use indirect influence to affect the positions of legislators. These channels supplemented the traditional direct lobbying efforts of face-to-face contact. Even these direct efforts became more complicated as the size of Congressional staffs grew rapidly during the same time period.

A sensitive issue for lobbyists is the so-called "revolving door" of public service. Former government officials often land positions in which access to those who succeeded them in office is a valuable commodity. Restrictions exist that limit former officials from doing business in their area of public responsibility for a period of one year. These restrictions are often difficult to define; access created for colleagues can frequently substitute for direct contact.

The term "lobbyist" once referred only to those who sought to influence Congress. It now is applied to broader public policy activities, including the activities of the executive branch in influencing Congress, foreign governments influencing one another, and state and local governments influencing the federal government. It also applies to actions taken to influence regulatory agencies.

Bibliography

Congressional Quarterly (1994). Stiff limits on gifts to members will ride on final lobby bill. September 24, 2656–7.

Congressional Quarterly Almanac (1993). Senate passes lobbying disclosure bill. 50–2.

Mack, C. S. (1989). *Lobbying and Government Relations.* New York: Quorum Books.

Smith, H. (1988). *The Power Game.* New York: Ballantine Books.

M

managerial ethics and the ethical role of the manager

Christopher McMahon

The ethical dimension of management is determined by the social role that managers are understood as playing. Three possibilities are especially worthy of consideration. They are that managers are agents acting on behalf of a principal or client, that managers are trustees for various corporate constituencies, and that managers are partners with governmental officials in an integrated system of political authority.

If managers are agents acting on behalf of a principal/client, the moral dimension of management is the same as in any agency relationship (*see* AGENCY THEORY). In such a relationship, the agent consents to act on behalf of and under the direction of the principal, who in turn consents to have the agent's actions count as the principal's for moral or legal purposes. The duties of an agent are performance (to do what he or she has undertaken to do), obedience (to accept the reasonable directions of the principal, which may involve performing the undertaken task in what seems to be a mistaken way), and loyalty (not to act contrary to the interests of the principal).

The moral strength of these duties is influenced by the intrinsic moral importance of the task the agent has undertaken to perform, but is not exhausted by it. The duties of an agent can have considerable moral force even when the task undertaken has no intrinsic moral importance if the interests of the principal would be seriously damaged by failure to perform the task, or to perform it well. Of special significance here is the case where the principal is not knowledgeable enough to determine whether the agent is performing well or to instruct the agent on how to proceed. The problem of the control of an expert agent by a relatively inexpert principal is sometimes called an "agency problem."

The model of agency is applicable to the provision of many professional services, and it is characteristic of paradigmatic professions such as the law that the agent is much more knowledgeable than the principal/client. Thus the moral problems that arise when an agent has expertise that the principal lacks are central to professional ethics. In addition to prohibitions against exploiting the vulnerability of the principal/client, professional ethics may call for the abridgment of the duty of obedience. If employing the means suggested by an inexpert client would, in the judgment of the agent, be extremely foolish, the agent may have no duty to comply.

Managers of corporations are often thought to be agents of the shareholders, but this claim is not supported by the law. The law of corporations does not regard the directors (or the other managers) as having the same duties to the shareholders that agents have to principals. For example, one of the duties of agents is obedience to the reasonable directions of the principal or principals, but although shareholders sometimes make corporate decisions directly by voting their shares, corporate constitutions usually provide no way that the shareholders as a group can routinely give instructions to managers. And while legal relations do not necessarily determine moral relations, the lack of an institutional mechanism that would enable shareholders to give instructions to managers also argues against the view that managers function morally as the agents of the shareholders. The difficulties encountered in regarding the managers of corporations as agents of the shareholders leads to the second way of characterizing the moral dimension of management. This approach can be introduced by noticing that the idea that the primary moral task of managers is to serve the shareholders can be accommodated without regarding managers as agents of the shareholders. They can be regarded instead as trustees. A trustee has a fiduciary duty to advance the interests of the beneficiary of the trust, but has no duty to obey the beneficiary. Even if legally managers are not trustees for the shareholders, the model of trusteeship may provide a more accurate representation of the moral relation between managers and shareholders than the model of agency.

The primary importance of the model of trusteeship, however, is that it provides an alternative way of accommodating the fact that the interests of the shareholders are not the only interests that managers must take into account. The model of agency accommodates this fact by saying that an agent may not do on behalf of a principal anything that would violate the rights of other people. A similar point can be made in connection with the model of trusteeship. A trustee may not advance the interests of a beneficiary in any way that would violate the rights of other people. But the model of trusteeship also seems to allow another possibility. We can say that, morally, managers have the status of trustees not only for the shareholders but also for some other groups.

This is the core of the "stakeholder" model of managerial ethics (see STAKEHOLDER THEORY). The fact that the interests of certain groups other than the shareholders – most importantly, employees, customers, suppliers, and neighbors of corporate facilities – are routinely affected by managerial decisions is registered by regarding them as having, like the shareholders, a "stake" in managerial decisions. And the idea of trusteeship is used to explain how these interests are to be reflected in managerial decision-making. Morally, managers are trustees for all routinely affected groups, with the same duty to protect or advance their interests (without violating the rights of people who fall outside them) that they have to protect or advance the interests of the shareholders.

This way of representing the moral significance of the interests of non-shareholders for managerial decision-making is not free of difficulty, however. There is no transaction that establishes a relation of trusteeship between non-shareholder groups and managers. Apparently, then, the possession by managers of this role must be derived from some general moral principle according to which each moral agent is a trustee for all others – or all others whose interests he or she routinely affects. But this drains from the role of trustee any distinctive content capable of distinguishing it from other relations in which individuals might stand to each other, and reveals the stakeholder view as a variant of the moral theory of utilitarianism, according to which each is required to maximize the total aggregate satisfaction of all affected interests.

Whether or not the stakeholder view is best regarded as a variant of utilitarianism, it shares an important defect with utilitarianism. It provides no way of regarding some, but not all, interests routinely affected by managerial decisions as creating legitimate moral claims. If we wish to characterize routinely affected interests in a way that reflects such distinctions, the conceptual apparatus of rights or fairness with which we started is preferable. Some interests are such that frustrating them violates stringent rights or constitutes serious unfairness, while others, equally strongly felt by those whose interests they are, lack this feature. So a right-based way of representing the moral claims of non-shareholders, whether routinely affected or not, actually yields a subtler view than the stakeholder theory. The members of routinely affected groups sometimes have rights that constrain what managers may do to promote narrower organizational goals.

There is a third way of understanding the social role of managers. Managers can be regarded as serving not the shareholders, or all the stakeholders, but rather as serving the employees. On this view, the shareholders join consumers, suppliers, and neighbors as an affected group that has a right to fair treatment in the course of managerial efforts to promote narrower organizational goals. To be more precise, they become investors, understood as suppliers of a certain kind – suppliers of capital – who have a right to a fair price for what they provide, which in this case means an adequate return on investment. But they have no right that managers derive organizational goals from their interests. These goals are rather determined by the concerns, especially the moral concerns, of the employees.

The justification for this way of looking at the social role of managers arises from an important difference between employees and other groups affected by managerial decisions. Managers have authority over employees. But where there is authority, consideration must be given to what makes it legitimate. In the governmental sphere, legitimate authority is authority that serves the interests of those over whom it is exercised. Legitimate rulers rule in the interests of the governed. That is, they have the job of facilitating mutually beneficial cooperation among the governed. If managerial authority is relevantly similar to governmental authority, then managers should be regarded not as servants of the shareholders or all the stakeholders, but as servants of the employees with the task of facilitating mutually beneficial cooperation among them.

If managers have this social role, their primary moral duty is to exercise authority in a way that enables the employees more successfully to achieve their moral aims in their work (while appropriately respecting the rights of other groups). To the extent that managers are understood as exercising the legal property rights of non-employee owners, these must be defined so that the directive power they confer on managers does not exceed legitimate authority.

This approach can be challenged by questioning whether managerial authority is relevantly similar to the authority of governments. Earlier we saw that the law of corporations does not regard managers as agents of the shareholders. But legally, employees often have the status of agents of their employers. In corporate contexts, this means that employees are agents of the corporation that employs them. Managers are supervising agents to whom the corporation's authority as principal has been delegated. Viewed in this way, managerial authority is different from the authority of governments. On standard contractarian political theories, for example, the people are not the agents of the state; rather, the government is an agent or trustee of the people. Defenders of this third view of the social role of managers must, then,

do more than simply point out that managerial authority has to be legitimate. They must vindicate the claim that what makes managerial authority legitimate is the same thing that makes the authority of governments legitimate. One way of doing this is explored in McMahon (1994).

In the political sphere, it is generally accepted that cooperation-facilitating authority should be democratically exercised, at least in the sense that those exercising it should be elected by those over whom it is exercised. So this third approach points to the conclusion that managers should be elected by the employees. But legitimate social purposes may be served by corporate constitutions that also give investors some role in choosing managers – as in the system of co-determination – and strong unions may provide a way of satisfying the demand for democracy without instituting the election of managers by employees.

On all of these ways of understanding the social role of managers, the moral structure of managerial decision-making is the same. There is some goal that managers are understood as being responsible for promoting, and there are constraints, deriving from rights, on what managers may do to promote these goals. The three views differ only on what the goal of managers is: either to advance the interests of the shareholders, to advance the aggregate interests of all the stakeholders, or to facilitate mutually beneficial cooperation among the employees. Ordinarily, constraints deriving from rights limit absolutely what can be done to promote non-moral goals, but it may be possible to regard some managerial goals as underwritten by deeper moral considerations. In cases of this sort, the constraints on managerial action provided by rights may have to be balanced against the moral benefits associated with the goals. Many moral problems have this structure.

A further question can be raised about the moral dimension of management. Are the moral considerations that managers face the same as those faced by ordinary citizens, or are the requirements of morality strengthened or weakened in the domain of management? Two possibilities must be distinguished here.

The first is that although the moral considerations that managers face in their capacity as managers are the same as those faced in ordinary life, the factual situation of managers combines with these considerations in such a way that actions that would be impermissible for ordinary citizens become permissible for managers. For example, the closing of a plant may devastate a whole town, and an ordinary citizen would not normally be justified in doing something that had this effect. But managers may be faced with a situation in which the failure to take this step would result in greater losses to the employees and others down the road, and thus the balance of ordinary moral considerations may justify it.

The second way that managerial morality could depart from ordinary morality is that managers could face a different set of moral considerations than ordinary citizens. Of particular interest here is the idea that in the world of business, some ways of treating people that would ordinarily be prohibited are permissible. This point must be distinguished from the previous one. The claim is not that moral considerations applicable to all sometimes justify managers in performing actions that ordinary citizens would not be justified in performing, but rather that certain moral considerations applicable to ordinary life are inapplicable to the business world.

This claim is dubious, however. Managerial ethics depends on the social role of management, and it is hard to think of any legitimate social purposes that would be served by regarding the world of business as one in which some ordinary moral considerations do not apply. The closest we can come is to make the converse point. There is a class of moral considerations that identify social states of affairs the promotion or maintenance of which is important from the moral point of view. These morally important social values include the preservation of the environment, the advancement of knowledge, the development of culture, the fostering of community, the promotion of social prosperity, and the protection of public health. Considerations of this kind have little significance outside organizational contexts since nothing much can be done to affect them. Thus they are not a part of the morality of ordinary life. But like governmental officials, the managers of large nongovernmental organizations must take these

values into account, and the moral desirability of promoting them may sometimes outweigh – and thus justify departing from – more familiar moral considerations. To say this, however, is to say that managers must be sensitive to more, rather than fewer, moral considerations than other people.

Bibliography

Dahl, R. (1985). *A Preface to Economic Democracy*. Berkeley: University of California Press.

Frascona, J. (1964). *Agency*. Englewood Cliffs, NJ: Prentice-Hall.

Goldman, A. (1980). *The Moral Foundations of Professional Ethics*. Totowa, NJ: Rowman and Littlefield.

McMahon, C. (1994). *Authority and Democracy: A General Theory of Government and Management*. Princeton, NJ: Princeton University Press.

Mason, E. (1959). *The Corporation in Modern Society*. Cambridge, MA: Harvard University Press.

Nagel, T. (1978). Ruthlessness in public life. In S. Hampshire (ed.), *Public and Private Morality*. Cambridge: Cambridge University Press, 75–91.

market for corporate control

Susan Chaplinsky

refers to the role that capital markets play in disciplining the management of firms to take actions to improve shareholder value. Free and well-functioning capital markets provide an ongoing assessment of a firm's performance through the value that investors are willing to pay for a firm's securities. The security of most relevance in this context is equity or common stock because control of a firm usually requires that a party obtain a majority of the outstanding equity shares. Theoretically, the firm's common stock represents the fair value of the net benefits that investors foresee accruing on the stock over all future years. The returns or benefits received by shareholders arise from dividends or other cash payments and from the price appreciation of the shares (capital gains). Because investors can compare how a particular firm fares in relation to peer firms, they are able to use capital market information to identify "underperforming" and "over-performing" firms. Depending on the reason for and the extent of under-performance, a firm may find itself subject to takeover pressure. Takeover pressure is often prompted by a bidder's belief that the current market value of a target firm is less (i.e., its current stock price is low) than what it would be worth if the assets were deployed differently. For example, a bidder might believe that the target's share price would increase if it sold off some unrelated lines of business and instead concentrated on its core business. However, since this strategy may be at odds with the one pursued by the existing management, implementing these changes may require that a bidder gain control of the firm and oust management. Regardless of whether a bidder is ultimately successful in gaining control, the actions of the bidder and even the threat of takeover often are sufficient to prompt management to reassess its own performance and make changes to improve shareholder value. In this way, the market for corporate control provides an "external review" of management's actions which works to enhance the incentives to increase shareholder value.

An important related issue is why managers appear to require an external force – such as the discipline of the capital markets – to maximize shareholder value. Berle and Means (1932) first noted that the ownership and the control of assets is separated in many publicly held US corporations. This separation results because managers who have decision-making authority over the day-to-day operations of the firm typically did not have large ownership or equity stakes in the firms they managed. Jensen and Meckling (1976), following on this observation, argue that costs arise because managers and shareholders have different incentives. For example, when managers are paid a fixed salary their decisions have different consequences for them than for shareholders who are residual claimants. Thus, a manager may overspend on certain items that enhance his or her welfare (e.g., fancy carpeting for the office, a corporate jet) which reduce the available earnings that could be paid to shareholders. In general, the differing incentives can lead managers to pursue their own self-interest at the expense of maximizing shareholder value. The principal–agent literature puts forth a number of suggestions to improve the firm's internal control process to reduce the potential

for agency costs. These include (1) giving managers a larger ownership stake in the firm, (2) tying executive compensation to stock market performance, and (3) increasing the oversight provided by boards of directors. For a variety of reasons, the firm's internal control process may still fail to offer sufficiently strong incentives to maximize shareholder value (Jensen, 1993). When this happens the capital markets remain a powerful, disinterested check on the management's actions – a court of last resort. Some argue, therefore, that the greatest protector of shareholder interests is a free and unfettered market for corporate control.

Bibliography

Berle, A. and Means, G. (1932). *The Modern Corporation and Private Property.* New York: Macmillan.
Jensen, M. (1993). The modern industrial revolution, exit, and the failure of internal control systems. *Journal of Finance*, **48** (3), 831–81.
Jensen, M. and Meckling, W. (1976). Theory of the firm: Managerial behavior, agency costs and ownership structure. *Journal of Financial Economics*, 3, 305–60.

marketing and the consumer

Donald P. Robin

Marketing is defined, in part, as an open and non-coerced exchange of values between the marketer and the consumer. The consumer is the final user of the utility he or she derives from the exchange and is the focus of marketing efforts developed to create enough perceived consumer value to precipitate the exchange.

OVERVIEW

Society has set very broad limits on the freedom of choice in these exchanges in an effort to maximize consumer satisfactions and the utility created by them. During his term as US president, John F. Kennedy announced a consumer bill of rights, and one of the four rights he created focused on the consumer's opportunity to choose from among several available goods and services. Legal constraints were developed throughout the twentieth century to prevent business combinations that would reduce the available choices.

Marketers have responded with a large and widely varied array of goods and services, offered at differing prices, available in many locations, and with a range of available consumer information. Generally, marketers have developed this mix in order to maximize the value that they receive from the exchange process. However, because consumers have options, they must also focus on the wants and needs of the consumer.

Fortunately for society, the marketing exchange is not a "zero sum game" and in most (but certainly not all) exchanges, positive value or utility is created when the exchange occurs. Specifically, both parties are usually better off after the exchange than before it occurred. This outcome can exist because the marketer and the consumer differently value that which is exchanged. Typically, the marketer gains economic utility, while the consumer gains a functional and/or psychological utility.

OPPORTUNITIES FOR ETHICAL PROBLEMS

Perhaps the most fundamental opportunity for ethical problems to develop occurs because of consumers' inability to evaluate the market basket available to them on dimensions that they would consider important. The plethora of exchange opportunities available to the consumer creates options that cannot reasonably be evaluated in all important dimensions because (1) the consumer lacks the technical skill, or (2) the consumer is overwhelmed by the task and chooses not to evaluate opportunities beyond a very basic list of characteristics. Consumers often overcome this sometimes massive ignorance about important factors in an exchange by placing trust in the producer or retailer.

Marketers seldom have perfect information about the important characteristics of the products and services they sell. Nevertheless, their information is usually far superior to their customers' level of knowledge. For convenience in this discussion, this difference in level of information between the marketer and the consumer is called the "knowledge gap." The abuse of the knowledge gap is the basis for a variety of unethical behaviors by marketers.

To some degree, the remaining three "rights" in President Kennedy's consumer bill of rights are concerned with abuses of this knowledge gap. One of these rights is for the consumer "to

be informed and protected against fraudulent, deceitful, and misleading statements, advertisements, labels, etc.; and to be educated as to how to use financial resources wisely." A second right is for the consumer "to be protected against dangerous and unsafe products." And a third right is for the consumer "to be heard by government and business regarding unsatisfactory or disappointing practices." With perfect knowledge and understanding of all important characteristics of the marketing exchange, the consumer shouldn't need any of these "rights." However, consumers are often closer to total ignorance than perfect knowledge even in the case of regularly purchased items, and when the trust is broken, the marketer has acted unethically and the consumer must be protected. Note that marketers may not understand that they have broken consumers' trust.

While abuses will undoubtedly continue to exist, many marketers seem to understand that long-term profitability can be achieved and maintained by not abusing the knowledge gap and honoring the consumers' trust. Consumers tend to look for marketers they can trust, and they can become extremely loyal to those who attempt to act in accordance with that trust. Alternatively, should consumers find out that their trust has been violated, it becomes very difficult for a marketer to win them back. The outcome of most marketing exposés supports that contention. However, opportunities to take advantage of the knowledge gap can frequently produce at least short-term profits, and vigilance is necessary. Perhaps the most important role of government and consumer advocates in preventing unethical behavior is to fill the knowledge gap with relevant information.

Most good basic marketing textbooks will have a section or chapter on marketing's ethical interface with the consumer.

Bibliography

Evans, J. R. and Berman, B. (1994). *Marketing*, 6th edn. New York: Macmillan, esp. ch. 5.

Laczniak, G. R. and Murphy, P. E. (1993). *Ethical Marketing Decisions: The Higher Road*. Boston, MA: Allyn and Bacon.

Pride, W. M. and Ferrell, O. C. (1989). *Marketing: Concepts and Strategies*, 6th edn. Boston, MA: Houghton Mifflin, ch. 2.

Smith, N. C. and Quelch, J. A. (1993). *Ethics in Marketing*. Homewood, IL: Richard D. Irwin.

marketing, ethics of

Patrick E. Murphy

Marketing ethics is the systematic study of how moral standards are applied to marketing decisions, behaviors, and institutions. The moral standards aspect of this definition has to do with the application of ethical theories (e.g., utilitarianism, duty-based, virtue ethics) to marketing issues. Furthermore, implicit in this definition is the understanding that ethics contains a normative aspect; that is, what is right or correct. Ethical questions arise in many marketing decisions, including whether to introduce a new product, the price to offer, and choice of advertising strategy. The behavior of marketers like salespeople, who are often judged only on the amount of product sold without investigating the methods used to acquire those sales, comes under scrutiny. As marketing has become more commonplace at non-profit institutions such as hospitals and museums, ethical questions now have surfaced which are rather similar to those faced by business firms.

Ethical issues in marketing have existed since the first things of value were traded. However, serious study of marketing ethics has only begun in the last 25 years. Marketing ethics sometimes is labeled as an oxymoron because certain marketing practitioners, like used car dealers, advertising copywriters, and telemarketers, commonly violate ethical precepts. This stereotypical judgment of marketing has been replaced with the understanding that most marketers not only hold to a higher standard of ethics but also recognize that the short-term financial payoff gained by ethical transgressions is often supplanted by long-term damage to both balance sheet and reputation.

MARKETING THEORY

Substantial effort has been expended by scholars to develop theoretical models that stipulate the factors leading to an ethical marketing decision. Most of this work employs one or more accepted ethical theories like utilitarianism, duty and rights, and virtue ethics. The thrust of these models has concentrated on individual moral development (Kohlberg's stages), organizational moral development (from amoral to highly ethical companies), contingency theory (opportunity to engage in unethical activity and relative importance of peers and top management), and the theory of reasoned action (rational persons must recognize the ethical dimension of a decision and determine the potential consequences of it) (Laczniak and Murphy, 1993; Smith and Quelch, 1993). Robin and Reidenbach (1993) propose a "workable ethical philosophy" for marketing with three distinct characteristics: moral relativism, bounded/constrained relativism, and descriptive ethics.

Another thrust of the research in theoretical work within marketing ethics is theory testing. Recent empirical studies have investigated the application of Kohlberg's theory in a study of marketing practitioners and testing the importance of commitment and trust in relationship marketing (emphasizing ongoing relationships with customers rather than short-term transactions). (See articles in *Journal of Marketing*, 1992–5.)

MARKETING PRACTICE

Although a myriad of marketing decisions contain ethical ramifications, several topics that are widely accepted as major areas of marketing practice are examined here. They are: market segmentation/targeting, marketing research, product development, pricing, distribution, personal selling, advertising, and international marketing.

Segmenting the market to appeal to smaller groups with more homogeneous needs is one of the major premises of marketing management. The needs of some segments like children and the elderly have long been protected by public policy-makers. Growth in the new immigrant population in the US and increases in school dropout rates indicate that the segment of "market illiterates" likely will grow in the future. Furthermore, the segmentation strategy employed by R. J. Reynolds in marketing Dakota cigarettes to women (historically an acceptable segment) drew such criticism that the product was withdrawn from the market. Ethical questions can arise from both inclusion and exclusion of certain market segments (Smith and Quelch, 1993: 188–95).

Marketing research techniques are used by all marketers. Research practitioners usually operate in an ethical manner because of their commitment to the scientific method and professionalism. The marketing researcher has several duties to respondents in any type of research (i.e., not to deceive, to protect privacy and anonymity). Many marketing research firms operate as consultants to companies and a set of duties exists to be forthright with one another in financial dealings and research requirements. Researchers also have duties to the general public when the research results are disseminated in the media. One emerging ethical issue is corporate intelligence-gathering, where companies attempt to gain information about their competitors (Laczniak and Murphy, 1993: ch. 3).

Product development and management is a cornerstone of marketing because the marketing process must begin with a product (defined as goods, services, or ideas). Ethical questions are continually being asked about product safety and product counterfeiting. Laws do protect both consumers and marketers from abuse, but ethical issues sometimes arise when the law is being followed. Socially controversial products, like the "sin" categories of tobacco and alcoholic beverages and firearms, consistently are questioned from an ethical standpoint. The environmental compatibility or incompatibility of many products, including all packaged goods, chemicals, plastics, and many others, are being scrutinized by consumers and policy-makers. The whole "green-marketing" movement of the last several years, where companies have promoted the environmental benefits of their products, has raised suspicion on the part of consumers and led to some state and federal regulatory restrictions. This issue is one likely to raise even more attention in the future.

Pricing of products within marketing is a central marketing decision. In an era of increasing competition in the retail sector, traditional guidelines on markups and pricing strategies are growing obsolete. Although price gouging of specific segments like the elderly and market illiterates does still occur, price sensitivity is the watchword for many consumers and most indus-

trial buyers. Thus, ethical concerns seem to be arising more frequently since some marketers fail to disclose pertinent data about product quality or features in pricing their products to promote low prices. For example, a current strategy practiced by discount retailers is to offer very low prices on computer hardware and software without divulging they are last year's model or not expandable. Other pricing-related issues pertain to non-price price increases (reducing product quality or quantity while keeping the price the same) and pricing in the service sector where airlines, rental car firms, and some financial institutions have been criticized for not giving relevant information about prices being offered.

The distribution element of marketing contains a number of different firms, starting with suppliers to manufacturers, then to wholesalers and retailers, and finally to end consumers. At each point of interface in this "channel" of distribution, potential ethical issues arise. One of the most prevalent is the power and control within the channel, meaning that large members of the channel may coerce smaller ones into price concessions and unreasonable delivery demands. Another ethical issue pertains to gift giving or bribery, because most of these organizations employ buyers and purchasing agents who may be influenced by these techniques. Competition between firms within the same level (retailer vs. retailer) and different levels (manufacturer vs. retailer) of the channel cause some managers to rationalize unethical conduct when competition becomes intense (Laczniak and Murphy, 1993: 110–13).

More people are employed in the personal-selling function than any other marketing area. Consequently, the issue of ethics in selling touches many marketing practitioners. Salespeople seem to be most prone to act unethically when one or more of the following situations exist: when competition is intense; economic times are difficult; compensation is based exclusively (or primarily) on commission; questionable dealings are common industry practice; sales training is non-existent or abbreviated; the individual has limited selling experience. Sales managers operate in a position above the sales rep and are charged with administering the territories of salespersons, setting quotas, and evaluating competition. Ethical sales managers strive for fair treatment of salespersons and competitors as well as regular communication with their salespeople about company policies and personal ethical concerns.

Advertising is the most visible area of marketing and often charged with ethical abuse. Some observers argue that advertising often reaches unintended audiences who may view the ad as being misleading when the targeted segment understands the message. Advertising is inherently intrusive and causes irritation or suspicion even when conducted ethically. Some of the most pertinent ethical questions deal with the persuasiveness of advertising messages, the advocacy role played by advertising agencies, the responsibility to audiences, and the media's stance with respect to advertising. One of the curious features of ethics in advertising is that the involvement of several separate groups (advertiser, agency, and media) has led to generally lower standards for the field than one would expect. These issues and others are explored in more depth in advertising ethics.

The complexities of marketing in the international sphere have meant even greater ethical scrutiny of business. Different cultures, traditions, and values have added a new set of challenges to marketing managers interested in satisfying marketplace needs. Two of the factors associated with ethical problems in international marketing are cultural relativism and economic development. Historical activities like massive bribery of foreign government officials is not only unethical but also illegal under the Foreign Corrupt Practices Act, and "dumping" of products in third world countries where many industries have codes making such practices unacceptable seems to be an exception now. As multinational corporations have expanded their operations to even more far-flung countries, they have weighed the importance of consistent policies with sensitivity to local needs and customs. This situation requires an even higher level of ethical concern, and this observer believes that multinationals must operate at the highest rather than lowest common denominator (see Laczniak and Murphy, 1993: ch. 8) (*see* GLOBALIZATION).

MARKETING ETHICS IN THE FUTURE

Several challenges facing marketing practitioners need to be tackled. First, ethical questions in small and medium-sized firms are equally important as those confronted by global marketers. Since most of the growth in the future is projected to be in these smaller operations, the founders and owners of these firms need to specify clearly their ethical position. For example, product development criteria, selling tactics, and pricing philosophy should be discussed with regularity from an ethical viewpoint. Barriers to communication are much lower than in large corporations, but a willingness to grapple with and discuss ethical issues must exist for meaningful interaction to occur in these businesses.

Second, codes of ethics must be tailored to the marketing function and be made more specific. The good news about codes is that 90 percent of large US companies have such a code, and an increasing number of multinationals headquartered in other countries have some written ethical policies. However, few codes offer meaningful guidance for salespeople and marketing executives. Such guidance should ideally go beyond policy manuals, and these marketing codes should be made available to all stakeholders. Less than 50 percent of current codes are public documents (Murphy, 1995). Another strategy that companies might use is a series of ethical audit questions pertinent to marketing (Laczniak and Murphy, 1993: 292–7).

Third, most major ethical questions facing companies in the future will require both a philosophical and a technical analysis. Some companies use trained ethicists that assist them with these issues. In addition, technical experts with strong scientific backgrounds are also needed to properly evaluate many of these questions. For example, environmental problems resulting from product use and disposal should probably be confronted in this manner.

Fourth, the dynamic tension between ethics and competition must be kept in balance. Getting ahead and winning are part of the competitive nature of the marketplace. This tension will likely only be heightened in the increasingly competitive world of the twenty-first century.

Companies must compete in an uncertain global market where the playing field is not always level. The top managers of large and small businesses need to assert their role as "leaders" to ensure that ethics has an important role to play in all companies (Murphy and Enderle, 1995).

Laczniak (1993) identified four challenges to academic researchers studying marketing ethics. The first one is to develop alternative paradigms to the past work which has applied normative ethical theories or proposed positive models of marketing ethics. A second challenge requires more cross-cultural evaluation. Increasingly, researchers are comparing consumer attitudes and/or marketing practices from several countries. Third, both societal and professional "performance gaps" exist between accepted behavior of marketers and the aspiration levels of society or the profession. Fourth, researchers should become informed advocates for improved ethical practice by marketing managers.

Bibliography

Laczniak, G. R. (1993). Marketing ethics: Onward toward greater expectations. *Journal of Public Policy and Marketing*, 12, 91–6.

Laczniak, G. R. and Murphy, P. E. (1993). *Ethical Marketing Decisions: The Higher Road*. Boston, MA: Allyn and Bacon.

Murphy, P. E. (1995). Corporate ethics statements: Current status and future prospects. *Journal of Business Ethics*, 13, 1–14.

Murphy, P. E. and Enderle, G. (1995). Managerial ethical leadership: Examples do matter. *Business Ethics Quarterly*, 5, 115–26.

Murphy, P. E. and Laczniak, G. R. (1981). Marketing ethics: A review with implications for managers, educators and researchers. In B. M. Enis and K. J. Roering (eds.), *Review of Marketing, 1981*. Chicago: American Marketing Association, 251–66.

Murphy, P. E. and Pridgen, M. D. (1991). Ethical and legal issues in marketing. *Advances in Marketing and Public Policy*, 2, 185–244.

Robin, D. P. and Reidenbach, R. E. (1993). Searching for a place to stand: Toward a workable ethical philosophy. *Journal of Public Policy and Marketing*, 12, 97–105.

Smith, N. C. and Quelch, J. A. (1993). *Ethics in Marketing*. Homewood, Il.: Irwin.

Tsalikis, J. and Fritzsche, D. J. (1989). Business ethics: A literature review with a focus on marketing ethics. *Journal of Business Ethics*, 8, 695–744.

Marxist ethics

Carol C. Gould

The concept of a Marxist ethics may seem like a contradiction in terms. Marx's focus was the critique of capitalism from the standpoint of political economy. He was skeptical of the abstract ideas implicit in much of normative ethics, such as "human beings" or "rights." In his work *The German Ideology*, he refers to morality itself as a form of ideology, expressing the interests of the dominant class in society (Tucker, 1978: 154). Instead, Marx believed that our focus should be on the concrete social and historical situation and particularly on the often oppressive relations within which people have historically worked to meet their material needs. Thus, along with criticizing his predecessor G. W. F. Hegel's idealism for the undue power it bestowed on rationality at the expense of these material conditions, Marx roundly rejected the liberal individualist tradition in philosophy from Locke through Kant to Bentham, with its project of ethics as a rights-driven or value-driven endeavor.

Along similar lines, in his early work *On the Jewish Question*, Marx criticizes the abstraction contained in the French Declaration of the Rights of Man and of the Citizen, and regarded rights of liberty and property as expressing the prerogatives of bourgeois individuals seeking to accumulate property and pursue their narrow self-interests, within a bourgeois state that functions to uphold a capitalist economic system. In the *Critique of the Gotha Program* he further states that all rights are by their nature rights of inequality, inasmuch as they necessarily disregard the significant differences among people's needs. By contrast, Marx's own focus is resolutely on a person's practical situation, and especially the social class within which they work, and he offers a critique of the relations of exploitation and domination that have structured these class relations throughout history. Further, in terms of conceptions of justice and new models of society and economy, Marx tended to say little. He regarded speculative utopian theorizing as lacking a ground in social reality, and seems to suggest that the character of alternative societies should be left to future participants to determine and create.

Nonetheless, it is clear that Marx's condemnation of capitalism is infused with ethical values and norms, and in particular, that he sees it as a profoundly unjust system, especially in regard to its modes of alienating and exploiting the working class. The critique he offers, along with certain positive conceptions presented at various points in his work, in fact implies an understanding and deep appreciation of the values of freedom, justice (especially in relation to equality and reciprocity), and social cooperation. Indeed, some theorists have argued that what we might call Marx's ethical humanism and his criticism of liberal individualism are key contributions to the philosophical tradition and among his most enduring legacies.

The paradox entailed here – of Marx's justice-infused perspective coupled with his rejection of the project of individual ethics – can be resolved. To do so requires understanding his approach as one that conceives the equal freedom of all individuals as emerging through a historical and social process of overcoming the forms of oppression characteristic of class societies of the past and the present. Further, this full freedom of individuals presupposes the development of a form of communal society in which alone it can flourish. This society, Marx and Engels write in *The Communist Manifesto*, is to be "an association, in which the free development of each is a condition for the free development of all" (Tucker, 1978: 491). Thus, for Marx, our ethics must be a social ethics, and one sensitive to the historical conditions for its realization, and conversely, the critique of society is one that is necessarily imbued with implicit normative conceptions.

Marx tended to present his most direct reflections on values and norms in his philosophical manuscripts and other writings that remained unpublished for much of his life or that were published posthumously. Indeed, a perusal of his reflective *Economic and Philosophic Manuscripts of 1844* or his masterpiece, the *Grundrisse*, provides important clues to finding and interpreting the various ethical references in his published works as well. These latter include many works of a more political nature, several co-authored with Friedrich Engels, as well as his

magnum opus *Capital*. Some of these published writings reflect the effort to achieve a value-free social science popular during the period of his work, and even perhaps show a certain economic reductionism.

In his *1844 Manuscripts* Marx analyzes human beings as characterized by free, creative activity, manifested primarily in their transformative activity of working on nature, as well as in contexts of social interaction. It is precisely this freedom that he suggests the laborer loses as a result of the "free labor contract" of capitalism, which in fact, he proposes, proves to be an illusion: in giving the capitalist control over his labor power for a period of time, the worker becomes alienated from his own activity and thus from his humanity. Freedom requires, by contrast, that the worker be in control of his own work, and inasmuch as this is social labor, jointly in control of it with others.

Further, the worker is alienated from the product of his work by giving it up to the capitalist who sells it for a profit. The exploitation of the worker originates in this transfer, which the worker is forced to make due to lack of property (i.e., access to the means of production), which are instead under the control of capital. Yet workers are, for Marx, the very source of the surplus value that is the basis of the profits, and thus the growth and eventual concentration, of capital. The worker, by contrast, does not in fact gain in proportion to his work (contrary to the claims made for capitalism) but is only paid a fixed sum, the wage or salary.

It can be seen, then, how Marx's early moral critique of alienation and exploitation maps onto, and perhaps even forms the core of, his economic critique of capitalism. The apparent equality of capital and workers in the "free" labor contract masks the deep inequality between them in the process of production. As Marx puts it, the more the worker works, the greater becomes the power over and against him and the more he loses control of his own creative life activity (Tucker, 1978: 72). This lack of equality and reciprocity, which Marx sees as built into the capitalist system itself and thus as systemic to it, reveals its deeply unjust nature. Finally, in this system, workers are not only alienated from their own work and from the capitalists, they are also alienated from each other, and stand in competitive rather than co-operative relations with others. Moreover, they, like the objects they produce, are transformed into products to be bought and sold; in being treated as exchange values, they lose their intrinsic worth, in a phenomenon Marx referred to in *Capital* as "the fetishism of commodities" (Tucker, 1978: 319).

In insisting that the free development of each is a condition for the free development of all, Marx places emphasis on the full elaboration of the human powers of individuals, a position worked out in his *Grundrisse* and other writings. In contrast to capitalism, in which individuals develop one-sidedly, with an emphasis on consumption and acquisition of goods, Marx presents a vision of many-sided individuals, who have developed a wide range of talents and capacities (Marx, 1993: 488). This echoes the formulation in the *German Ideology*, where the image of the free individual in a society of the future is presented as one where "it is possible for me to do one thing today and another tomorrow, to hunt in the morning, fish in the afternoon, rear cattle in the evening, criticize after dinner, just as I have a mind, without becoming hunter, fisherman, shepherd, or critic" (Tucker, 1978: 160).

In the sustained analysis in Marx's *Grundrisse*, the possibility of the emergence of such free, many-sided individuals is seen as premised on capitalism's development of a world market, which disregards borders, and in which individuals relate to others in increasingly multiple, universalistic, and cosmopolitan ways (Marx, 1993: 409–10). Further, it presupposes a highly developed technological society that produces a level of material abundance, thus reducing necessary labor to a minimum. Much of this labor would be done by machines, or more precisely, automatic systems of machinery (Marx, 1993: 692). Science and technology thus come increasingly to drive the production process, allowing considerable free time for people to develop their talents (Marx, 1993: 611–12). Finally, in the communal society envisioned for the future, co-operative arrangements among workers would come to replace the exploitative and oppressive relations characteristic of capitalism.

Marx presents certain explicit principles of distributive justice for a socialist society and for the subsequent communist form of society that would emerge from it in his work *The Critique of the Gotha Program*. He argues that the first step, in socialism, is to realize the distributive principle that is supposedly, but not really, inherent in capitalism, namely, that workers be rewarded for their work. Where capitalism actually lacks any proportionality between work and reward, inasmuch as workers are limited to a salary or wage no matter how much or how well they produce, under socialism as the system emerging from capitalism, workers will contribute according to their abilities and be remunerated according to their work. In the subsequent emergence of a fully communal society of the future, a different principle comes to be operative. In a society of abundance, which has overcome the relative scarcities of capitalism and socialism, it will be possible to distribute economic and social goods and benefits according to the principle "from each according to their ability, to each according to their needs" (Tucker, 1978: 531). Individuals would be required to contribute what they can, up to their fully developed abilities, and could expect to have their needs met from the results of the social production process. It is also worth noting that Marx and Engels envisioned this society as one that recognizes women's equality, in contrast to forms of class society in which women were inevitably treated as "instruments of production."

Immanent in Marx's critique of capitalism and explicit in his projection of future forms of society are therefore the ethical values and norms of the free development of individuals, the fundamental equality of all human beings, and a conception of strongly cooperative relations of people socially organized to meet their material needs. His ethics is thus essentially a social ethics, rather than simply a moral or individualistic one concerning the treatment that each individual owes others, as in the Kantian or utilitarian traditions in ethics. Methodologically, Marx's view implies that to understand a situation ethically, we need to look at the particular relations of domination and exploitation in which people stand and take note of the role played in their lives by structural oppression (e.g., social systems of class or gender domination), and not only to consider the particular intentions or interests of the individual person. He insisted, too, that full and equal respect for human dignity and freedom requires for its realization profound changes in the form of society.

It remains to consider the import of Marx's views for some of the themes that have played a role in business ethics, several of which came to prominence in response to his critique of capitalism. One obvious impact derives from Marx and Engels's emphasis on the power of, and necessity for, trade unions. They argued that it is only through this means that the collective power of the workers can be harnessed to negotiate benefits in the face of increasingly powerful capitalist corporations. In a different and later context, a right to form unions came to be recognized as one of the human rights in the Universal Declaration of Human Rights (1948). A somewhat less obvious, but perhaps equally important, idea stemming from Marx's theory is that of worker or employee self-management and the related notion of employee stock ownership plans. Thus, several interpreters of Marx have felt that his emphasis on cooperation in economic life requires not only democratic input into macroscopic economic planning, but also more crucially perhaps, democratic management in firms. This does indeed appear to be entailed in Marx's early and consistent critique of workers' alienation from their own work under capitalism, and the correlative demand that they come to exercise joint control over their own work. Likewise, the importance that Marx placed on work rather than leisure as the main expression of an individual's free creative activity gives rise to the desideratum of developing an economy that provides meaningful work for everyone. To the degree that there is still drudgery to be done in an advanced economy of the future, Marx would say that it needs to be shared in a fair way by everyone.

Finally, the centrality that Marx gave to economic life, coupled with the idea that it should be under the workers' control, suggests the need for not only political, but also economic, democracy, and not only in the workplace but also beyond it. Regrettably, despite Marx's acute analysis of existing economic formations and his sensitivity to this range of ethical issues, he did not say much about what such economic democracy should look like. His preoccupation with the critique of capitalism, infused as I have indicated with moral outrage at its injustice, seems to have pushed to the side the delineation of a more adequate alternative. The project of creating such an alternative was left to his Marxist successors, where the results range from clearly undemocratic and ineffective proposals of centralized state planning, at odds with Marx's own emphasis on the free development of individuals and his own internationalism; to more contemporary market socialist theories; to plans for self-managing economic and political regions like Mondragon in Spain; and on a smaller scale to employee-owned firms. As to which political economic arrangements are best able to provide for the equal freedom and development of individuals and more democratic forms of their participation in economic and social life, that remains a question for future research in this tradition.

Bibliography

Bowles, S. and Gintis, H. M. (1999). *Recasting Egalitarianism: New Rules for Communities, States, and Markets*, vol. 3. London: Verso.

Braverman, H. (1999). *Labor and Monopoly Capital: The Degradation of Work in the Twentieth Century*. New York: Monthly Review Press.

Brenkert, G. (1983). *Marx's Ethics of Freedom*. London: Routledge.

Cohen, G. A. (2000). *Karl Marx's Theory of History: A Defence*. Princeton, NJ: Princeton University Press.

Cunningham, F. (1990). *Democratic Theory and Socialism*. Cambridge: Cambridge University Press.

Gould, C. C. (1978). *Marx's Social Ontology*. Cambridge, MA: MIT Press.

Gould, C. C. (1990). *Rethinking Democracy*. Cambridge: Cambridge University Press.

Lukes, S. (1990). *Marxism and Morality*. Oxford: Oxford University Press.

Macpherson, C. B. (1990). *Democratic Theory: Essays in Retrieval*. Oxford: Oxford University Press.

Marx, K. (1992–3). *Capital: A Critique of Political Economy*, vol. 1, trans. B. Fowkes; vols. 2 and 3, trans. D. Fernbach. Harmondsworth: Penguin Books.

Marx, K. (1993). *Grundrisse: Foundations of the Critique of Political Economy*, trans. M. Nickolaus. Harmondsworth: Penguin Books.

Marx, K. and Engels, F. (1975–). *Collected Works*. New York: International Publishers.

Ollman, B. (1990). *Alienation*, 2nd edn. Cambridge: Cambridge University Press.

Peffer, R. G. (1990). *Marxism, Morality and Social Justice*. Princeton, NJ: Princeton University Press.

Roemer, J. E. (1994). *A Future for Socialism*. Cambridge, MA: Harvard University Press.

Schweickart, D. (2002). *After Capitalism?* Lanham, MD: Rowman and Littlefield.

Tucker, R. C. (ed.) (1978). *The Marx–Engels Reader*, 2nd edn. New York: Norton.

meaningful work

Joanne B. Ciulla

is work that is worthwhile, significant, satisfying, and conducive to personal growth, worth, and well-being. As a social construction, the idea of meaningful work reflects the value that a culture places on the activity of work and the value and status of various kinds of work. As a personal construction, meaningful work reflects the aspirations, ideals, and values that comprise a person's view of him or herself and a satisfying life. The British social commentator and craftsman William Morris offers this characterization of meaningful work: "Worthy work carries with it the hope of pleasure in rest and the hope of pleasure in our daily creative skill" (Morris, 1885: 21).

History of the Meaning of Work

People have not always thought that work should play the central role in a person's life (de Grazia, 1962). For the ancient Greeks, work itself had little value and the good life was a life of leisure. In *The Politics*, Book II, Aristotle says that work is best done by slaves, because it ties them to necessity. He says that slaves are not human because they lack the freedom to decide, deliberate, and plan the future. Greek myths depict boring repetitive work as the worst punishment – Sisyphus is doomed to push a rock up a hill and the Dianides spend eternity filling leaking water jars.

The craft guilds of the middle ages endowed craft work with new meanings. Guilds tied the identity of a person to his craft, hence came the proliferation of occupational last names such as Baker, Carpenter, and Goldsmith. Guilds gave craftsmen and women affiliation to a specific community, privileged technical knowledge, standards of workmanship, and ethical norms of behavior.

The Renaissance gave us the Promethean view of work that exalted human ingenuity and the image of humans as inventors and creators of their own destiny; whereas the Reformation promoted the idea that all of work was inherently meaningful in that it was a calling that demonstrated one's worthiness to God.

Meaningful Work and Industrialization

The intrinsic value of work as a calling stands in sharp contrast to the instrumental view of work that came with industrialization (Clayre, 1974). One way to understand meaningful work is by understanding alienation. For Karl Marx, work is the central human activity. Marx believed that wage labor under capitalism led to alienation because it did not pay people for what they produced, but rather compensated them for the freedom that they lost at work. In the *1844 Manuscripts* Marx argues that capitalism alienates people from themselves, each other, their product, and their creativity.

The scientific approach to management focused on increased productivity. Scientific management stripped work of many elements that give it meaning. It broke down the social relationships of workers and systematized work so that it required little skill or knowledge. Managers did the thinking and workers performed the physical motions. The goal of scientific management was to replace expensive labor with cheap labor and gain absolute control over production. The sole meaning of work under scientific management was manifested in the pay that a worker received for producing the most goods in the least amount of time.

Models of Meaningful Work

One major assumption about meaningful work is that mental labor is more meaningful than physical labor. Technology rids us of difficult physical labor and repetitive work, but it also deskills some kinds of work (Braverman, 1980). One way that management mediates the effects of deskilled labor is by redesigning jobs. Implicit in job redesign are assumptions about meaningful work, such as the need for variety, creativity, and empowerment.

Today's ideal of meaningful work is often based on the professions. That is why more work groups call themselves professionals. The professional has autonomy, respected identity with other professionals, and pride in the notion of using specialized knowledge to help others. Norman Bowie (1990) argues that companies should focus on providing meaningful work and treating employees as professionals. He suggests that by treating employees as the primary stakeholder, companies might be more profitable than if they only focused on profits (see STAKE-HOLDER THEORY).

MEANINGFUL WORK AND BUSINESS ETHICS

The concept of meaningful work raises these questions about the ethics of business: Do people have a right to meaningful work? Do employers have an ethical obligation to provide meaningful work to their employees? To answer these questions, we have to ask: Is it possible for a company to create meaningful work for all employees?

A job may be meaningful to one person and a form of daily humiliation to another (Terkel, 1974). In the popular management book *In Search of Excellence* (1982), Peters and Waterman assert that the role of managers is to "make meaning." However, their approach raises questions as to whether this kind of management is a form of psychological manipulation. Meaning can be found in the aesthetic qualities of a job, its end product, or its usefulness. It can also be derived from the relationship of the worker to others in the organization.

The right to meaningful work is difficult to establish, because it cannot be clearly defined for everyone. However, we can use ethical principles like negative harm and respect for persons to argue that employees have a right to work that does not degrade them physically and mentally and respects their dignity and autonomy as a person. Similarly, an employer's obligation to supply meaningful work is difficult to support. However, one may argue that an employer has an obligation to provide conditions conducive for finding meaning in work (Ciulla, 1990). These conditions include a healthy moral environment where all employees are treated fairly and with respect and appreciation, open communication between management and employees, ongoing training and job enrichment, employee involvement in the structure and organization of their job, and a safe workplace.

In liberal societies people also have the right to seek meaning outside of the workplace. This means that employers have an obligation to provide working hours and conditions that do not impair a person's ability to seek a meaningful life (Ciulla, 1990) (see WORK AND FAMILY). Despite its abstract nature, meaningful work is central to ethical management. It focuses attention on how people's experience in the workplace contributes or detracts from their non-economic ideal of the good life.

Bibliography

Bowie, N. E. (1990). Empowering people as an end for business. In G. Enderle, B. Almond, and A. Argandoña (eds.), *People in Corporations: Ethical Responsibilities and Corporate Effectiveness*. Dordrecht: Kluwer Academic Publishers, 105–12.

Braverman, H. (1980). *Labor and Monopoly Capital: The Degradation of Work in the Twentieth Century*. New York: Monthly Review Press.

Ciulla, J. B. (1990). On the demand for meaningful work. In G. Enderle, B. Almond, and A. Argandoña (eds.), *People in Corporations: Ethical Responsibilities and Corporate Effectiveness*. Dordrecht: Kluwer Academic Publishers, 113–18.

Clayre, A. (1974). *Work and Play: Ideas and Experience of Work and Leisure*. London: Weidenfeld and Nicolson. (Good discussion of nineteenth-century ideas of work and life.)

Gini, A. R. and Sullivan, T. J. (eds.) (1989). *It Comes with the Territory: An Inquiry Concerning Work and the Person*. New York: Random House. (Excellent collection of classic and contemporary readings on work.)

Grazia, S. de. (1962). *Of Time, Work and Leisure*. New York: Twentieth Century Fund. (One of the best books on this topic.)

Morris, W. (1885). *Useful Work and Useless Toil*. London: Socialist League Office, Socialist Platform Number 2.

Schwartz, A. (1982). Meaningful work. *Ethics*, 92, 634–46.

Terkel, S. (1974). *Working*. New York: Pantheon Books. (Wonderful interviews on work.)

Werhane, P. (1985). *Persons, Rights and Corporations*. Englewood Cliffs, NJ: Prentice-Hall, ch. 7.

media, ethics of

Deni Elliott

may seem to be an oxymoron, particularly to anyone who has felt misused by media. But "media," even when the discussion is confined to the United States, refers to a diffuse collection of corporations. The media include profit and not-for-profit companies and companies that take as their primary description one of three basic thrusts: news/information, persuasion in the form of public relations or advertising, and entertainment. Each kind of company has its own social function and resulting moral responsibilities.

"Media" also include two major divisions in medium – print and electronic – that impact on their capabilities and methodologies, though not necessarily on their responsibilities. Broadcasting live events, for example, raises questions of appropriateness of material for the audience as well as questions of privacy for the individuals involved in the event. Privacy and appropriateness of material are ethical issues for news coverage by print media as well, but they rarely require the split-second decision-making required in "live" broadcast coverage.

Sometimes charges of unethical behavior are based on a misunderstanding of the specific media role rather than on actual malfeasance, as when a local auto dealer condemns a newspaper for running an article that tells consumers how to be savvy car buyers. Other times, lowered expectations of a particular medium – "what can you expect from television?" – derail needed analysis of media behavior.

As different kinds of media have different social functions, understanding those functions is vital to making judgments concerning the ethics of practitioners' actions. In any profession, acting in a morally acceptable way means meeting one's moral obligations and not causing unnecessary harm in the process.

ENTERTAINMENT MEDIA

The social function of entertainment media is self-explanatory. Those media practitioners exist to produce written, audio, or visual programming and materials that will appeal to designated audiences. This social function is accompanied by an economic function that all other for-profit companies share, namely to make money for the stockholders or owners. But neither the social nor the economic function alone provides justification for action that could be predicted to cause harm to individuals or identifiable groups.

The element of harm becomes important in determining the morality of entertainment media when one considers the effect of violence on children, the effect of pornography on women, and the effect of promoting unattainable lifestyles to vulnerable audiences. Whether groups or individuals are depicted in ways that continue a history of discrimination is also a matter of ethical concern. The question of whether violence, pornography, unattainable lifestyles, or stereotypical depiction cause harm is a matter of debate in the scholarly literature. Whether harm caused is "unnecessary," and thus unjustified, and in need of regulation is a matter of debate among advocacy groups, media representatives, and policy-makers.

PERSUASIVE MEDIA

Persuasive media, which include public relations and advertising, exist to sell their clients' ideas or images to designated publics. The editorial or opinion pages of a newspaper are also examples of persuasive media, but the intent is slightly different in that here the rationale is to create a public forum or a showcase of informed opinion on important issues of the day. The newspaper *showcases* ideas; public relations and advertising practitioners *sell* them. The persuasive message is necessarily one-sided and distorted by its lack of completeness. That is not, in itself, an ethical concern, but the line between withholding information in the name of advocacy and the withholding of information in what counts as deception is not clear.

The designated public for advertising is consumers targeted for product use. More directly than entertainment media, advertisers sell status and fantasy. One doesn't merely buy a particular brand of toothpaste or running shoe, one also buys an image, that will inspire love, acceptance, or envy. If the product is out of the price range of the targeted consumer (such as designer footwear targeted to inner-city youth), or if the consumer is unable to separate fantasy from product (such as children and advertised toys), then the advertiser may be causing unnecessary harm in marketing the product.

When the product itself has questionable merit, such as tobacco, then any marketing becomes an ethical issue. In this debate, the legality of tobacco use and of free speech in promoting legal, albeit dangerous, products, is set against the ethical precept of "do not cause unnecessary harm."

Public relations practitioners who work as "information agents" or "public information officers" for corporations or governmental agencies also target consumer audiences, but many public relations practitioners target news media as a way of achieving a larger audience and as a way of adding credibility to their message. If news media report the message developed by public relations in a way that does not expose the bias of the information, it is more likely to be accepted as accurate and complete than information that the public understands originates with a biased, self-interested source.

NEWS MEDIA

News media in the US have the social function of telling citizens what they need to know for self-governance. The information that we need to know for self-governance is a varied lot and includes information about our governmental processes, the bureaucrats who facilitate the process, and the leaders we elect; it includes information about our economic structure and pragmatic information about how our tax dollars are spent. It includes information about our community and our fellow citizens.

But, as with the other media, news media are restrained in meeting this social function by the moral dictate that they ought not to cause unnecessary harm. Harms caused to sources, story subjects, and consumers in the process of reporting the news include the causing of pain through undesired attention or intrusion, depriving people of freedom or pleasure by turning the spotlight of public scrutiny their way. The harms include the breaking of promises to sources who have been promised anonymity. The harms include the deception of story sub-jects by use of undercover reporting and the deception of consumers when information is illegitimately or incorrectly left out of a story. Whether the news organization is meeting its social function of telling people what they need to know for self-governance serves as a basis for determining when the harm caused is "necessary" and when it is not.

THE SPECIAL PROBLEM OF ENFORCEMENT IN MEDIA ETHICS

Media organizations and professional societies, particularly those related to news presentation, have shown increasing interest in ethics issues over the past two decades. Attention to ethical transgressions by individual organizations and professional societies is particularly important, because media constitute the only industry with US First Amendment protections. The law limitations provide after-the-fact sanctions for the publication of libelous material or material that fits the very narrow definition of legal invasion of privacy. Codes of ethics articulated by professional societies can only be accepted by their members, not enforced. The First Amendment precludes the regulation of the press by anything other than voluntary means. Codes of ethics developed within news organizations may be enforced in the respect that an individual's unwillingness to subscribe to an organizational policy may result in discharge. But no journalist can be barred from the profession; no news organization can be prevented from printing or broadcasting what it terms news (see CODES OF ETHICS).

BLURRED DISTINCTIONS CREATE HYBRID MORAL PROBLEMS

The distinctions between the three types of media become blurred, creating new ethical concerns. Different media have different jobs to do. If one cannot identify a media product as informative, persuasive, or entertaining in primary intent, there is no basis upon which one can argue that the medium is failing to meet its moral responsibility.

The blurring between entertainment and opinion writing becomes an issue in the publication of cartoons that have a strong political message. Some newspapers call these comics, forms of entertainment; some put politically charged cartoons on the editorial page, considering them to be persuasive products; others refuse to run such hybrids, charging that the creation of such cartoons is a misuse of the cartoonist's fame and influence.

The blurring between news and entertainment becomes a factor in trying to decide if television magazines such as *Hard Copy* and *Untold Story* are news or if they are entertainment. Producers for these segments certainly don't hold themselves to the journalistic standards of "news" programs, yet their saleability is their believability. And their interviews look and sound enough like news interviews that all but the most sophisticated viewer may be tricked into believing that the shows are "news."

The blurring between entertainment and persuasion becomes a factor when children's television programming is created as a marketing tool for merchandise. Watchdog groups have convinced federal agencies of the special vulnerability of children to advertising and have succeeded in curtailing advertising that wraps around children's programming. However, when the product *is* the show, few limitations apply. Creators of such merchandise-propelled programming counter that there is no important difference between the selling of dolls or toys that spin-off from a popular program and creating a program to stimulate children's interest in particular dolls or toys.

Finally, the lines between news and persuasion blur when news media provide press releases or video news releases without appropriate warning to the reader or viewer. Without identification of the author or producer of the piece as an advocate, the audience is likely to accept the piece as information produced by a disinterested party.

Bibliography

Baker, L. (1993). *The Credibility Factor: Putting Ethics to Work in Public Relations*. Homewood, IL: Irwin.

Black, J. and Barney, R. (1993). *Doing Ethics in Journalism*. Greencastle, ID: Society of Professional Journalists.

Blyskal, J. and Blyskal, M. (1985). *PR: How the Public Relations Industry Writes the News*. New York: William Morrow.

Christians, C., Rotzoll, K., and Fackler, M. (1991). *Media Ethics: Cases and Moral Reasoning*, 3rd edn. New York: Longman.

Cooper, T. (1988). *Television and Ethics: A Bibliography*. Boston, MA: G. K. Hall.

Ellul, J. (1973). *Propaganda*. New York: Vintage.

Goodwin, G. (1994). *Groping for Ethics in Journalism*, 3rd edn. Ames: Iowa State University Press.

Gross, L., Katz, J., and Ruby, J. (eds.) (1988). *Image Ethics: The Moral Rights of Subjects in Photographs, Film, and Television*. New York: Oxford University Press.

Jaksa, J. and Pritchard, M. (1994). *Communication Ethics: Methods of Analysis*, 2nd edn. Belmont, CA: Wadsworth.

Johannesen, R. (1990). *Ethics in Human Communication*, 3rd edn. Prospect Heights, IL: Waveland Press.

Limburg, V. (1994). *Electronic Media Ethics*. Boston, MA: Focal Press.

Montgomery, K. (1989). *Target Prime Time: Advocacy Groups and the Struggle over Entertainment Television*. New York: Oxford University Press.

Patterson, P. and Wilkins, L. (1994). *Media Ethics: Issues and Cases*, 2nd edn. Madison, WI: Brown and Benchmark.

Schudson, M. (1984). *Advertising: The Uneasy Persuasion*. New York: Basic Books.

mergers and acquisitions

Robert S. Harris

Corporate mergers have played a prominent role in shaping the structure of business. Technically speaking, there are many different ways in which two (or more) firms can combine. For example, in a statutory merger, when two or more firms combine, one company survives under its own name, and the others cease to exist as legal entities. In a statutory consolidation, on the other hand, all the combining companies cease to exist as legal entities, and an entirely new, consolidated corporation is created. Some mergers are consummated after amicable negotiation between managers of acquiring and acquired firms. Other business combinations occur despite bitter disagreement between two sets of managers. In such hostile takeovers, the acquiring firm often goes over the heads of the acquired firm's management to the shareholders by means of a tender offer. A tender offer is an offer to pay existing shareholders some specified amount of cash or securities if these shareholders will sell (tender) their shares of stock to the acquiring firm. For present purposes, we will use the broader term *merger* to refer to combinations of firms without making these detailed distinctions.

Mergers have motivated intense public debate about their effects and desirability. Much of this debate is ultimately grounded in fundamental ethical and value judgments. Almost inevitably, mergers raise issues about the rights of a wide spectrum of stakeholders in the modern corporation (*see* STAKEHOLDER THEORY). Does the merger create value to owners, or does it simply serve managerial interests? Are there detrimental consequences to employees, communities, or consumers? Are decision-makers who craft mergers compromised with conflicts of interest?

Many of the issues raised by mergers and acquisitions stem from the complex set of interrelationships in a corporation. In the simplest sense an acquisition involves a buyer purchasing an asset (or assets) from the existing owner for some agreed-upon compensation. If an individual purchases a used car from another person, there are issues about truthful representation of the quality and legal ownership of the car; however, a single individual buyer typically negotiates directly with a single individual seller with relatively little effect on others not directly party to the negotiation. Like a car sale, a corporate acquisition involves basic issues of truthtelling, but the rights to property and the effects on many parties (who are not empowered legally to participate in the acquisition negotiation) are much more complicated (*see* PROPERTY, RIGHTS TO).

Insights as to why corporate mergers take place and the ethical issues they raise can be sharpened by realizing that a merger results in a new set of legal and other contracts among economic interests (*see* CONTRACTS AND CONTRACTING). These contracts (and their predecessors), however, involve only a subset of the stakeholders affected by the corporate combination. The legal, regulatory, and political context will shape the powers and responsibilities of specific stakeholders in the recontracting process involved in a merger and, as a result, influence the effects a merger may have on a particular group. A society's structure of corporate governance cedes certain decision-making powers to

management and the board of directors, who in turn have certain responsibilities. This command system (the shape of which may vary dramatically across political and cultural boundaries) replaces direct market transactions for a wide array of important economic decisions. In effect, the governance structures set down the rules of the market for corporate control.

This perspective highlights a number of points:

1 The interests of people with decision authority determine incentives for merger (*see* AGENCY THEORY).
2 These interests are shaped by provisions of contracts.
3 Such contracts are incomplete and do not cover all contingencies.
4 Mergers may lead both to changes in total value and redistribution of such value.

As a result, mutual understandings (implicit contracts and "goodwill") play a crucial role inside and between firms – even though such understandings are often not written, legally enforceable contracts. The legal system sets the context for trade-offs among particular stakeholder interests in a merger. At a more fundamental level, however, the society and its political process will ultimately shape legal and other standards. Generally, market-based, capitalistic views favor the rights of owners, but the fabric of corporate governance is a complicated balance of rights and interests of different groups. These interests work their way through the business, legal, and political system.

Some of the principal ethical concerns raised in mergers surround the rights, duties, and obligations of the following stakeholders:

● *Consumers.* When two firms combine to increase market power, the result may be higher prices and profits as competition is lessened. While such profits are beneficial to owners, consumers may be worse off. In part, to protect consumer interests, governments often pursue regulatory and antitrust policies designed to foster competition.

- *Employees.* Mergers may lead to job reductions and revamping (or elimination) of contracts with employees. Particularly troubling are the status of promises about future compensation (e.g., through pension plans) and the status of implicit contracts between the firm and employees. For instance, the workers and prior management may have had unwritten agreements (implicit contracts) about job advancement and security.
- *Managers.* As prime decision-makers in mergers, managers may have conflicts of interest arising from concerns about their own job security and compensation. These pressures may lead them to pursue acquisitions of other firms and perhaps resist takeovers of their own company. On the other hand, managers may receive large payments (golden parachutes) upon completion of a takeover while their employees lose jobs. Furthermore, managers (and the board of directors) must deal with the disparate effects a merger may have on different stakeholders.
- *Communities.* Sometimes a merger may result in the postmerger company planning to lay off workers and close facilities. A specific closure may be inevitable for a firm to remain competitive, or it may be only one of many management options. What are the rights and responsibilities of communities in such a context?
- *Boards of directors.* Boards are often the final arbiter of the merger and must conclude whether the merger agreement is in the best interests of the corporation and what constitutes such best interests. The legal context of corporate structure and governance shapes specific board responsibilities to consider different stakeholder views.
- *Advisors and financial intermediaries.* With their compensation often contingent on an agreement being struck, such parties may not have incentives consistent with sound advice and performance.
- *Classes of security owners.* A great number of conflicts may arise among classes of security holders. For instance, equity holders may see a benefit from increasing debt in part to siphon off value from existing debt claimants

who have inadequate legal protection from value downgrades due to the increased risk of default. Different generations of security holders may also have disparate interests. For instance, insider trading laws are written expressly to prevent someone with privileged information from profiting from such information by exploiting the ignorance of existing owners. The structure and desirability of such laws raises a host of issues about rights and privileges of different groups.

A more detailed list of issues is beyond the scope of this entry. What is clear is that through the conduct of many decision-makers, society will develop a governance context for mergers to accommodate its view of the claims of different parties. Once such a context is set, pressures will exist for debate among different claimants, and that debate will likely engender a reassessment of the context over time.

Bibliography

Coase, R. H. (1937). The nature of the firm. *Economics*, **4**. (A classic treatment of the firm as an organizational structure.)

Copeland, T. E. and Weston, J. F. (1988). *Financial Theory and Corporate Policy*. Reading, MA: Addison-Wesley. (A survey of corporate finance with chapters detailing the financial theory of and empirical evidence about mergers.)

Freeman, R. E. (1984). *Strategic Management: A Stakeholder Approach*. Boston, MA: Pitman. (An explication of the stakeholder perspective.)

Hanly, K. (1992). Hostile takeovers and methods of defense: A stakeholder analysis. *Journal of Business Ethics*, **11**, 895–913. (An example of a stakeholder analysis.)

Jensen, M. C. (1993). The modern industrial revolution, exit, and the failure of internal control systems. *Journal of Finance*, **48**, 831–80. (A view of a transformation in organizational form.)

Jensen, M. C. and Meckling, W. H. (1976). Theory of the firm: Managerial behavior, agency costs, and ownership structure. *Journal of Financial Economics*, **2**, 305–60. (An influential article on ownership structure.)

Kester, Carl W. (1991). *Japanese Takeovers*. Boston, MA: Harvard Business School Press. (An interesting look at the Japanese context.)

Williamson, O. E. (1985). *The Economic Institutions of Capitalism*. New York: Free Press. (A view of economic organizational forms.)

meritocracy

Maureen A. Scully

is a social system in which merit or talent is the basis for sorting people into positions and distributing rewards, such that the positions of highest authority are occupied by those of greatest merit. The term "meritocracy" is a satirical invention of Young (1958), who wrote a fable about a future society that could not abide the perfect meritocracy it created. The term is now applied, without the irony, to advanced capitalist systems of status attainment and reward allocation, usually to distinguish them favorably from aristocratic or class-based systems, where birth or family privileges determine an individual's status (Bell, 1972). A meritocracy relies on three principles (Daniels, 1978): (1) merit is a well-defined and measurable basis for selecting individuals for positions; (2) individuals have equal opportunity to develop and display their merits and to advance; (3) the positions into which individuals are sorted are mapped to stratified levels of rewards (such as income or status). An organization or an entire society might espouse and try to operate on meritocratic principles.

Proponents of meritocracy highlight several advantages. A meritocracy is fair in that everyone has an opportunity to advance and rewards are proportional to meritorious contributions; merit is distinguished from equality or need, other fair bases of reward. Meritocracy motivates people. Functional sociologists argue that meritocracy directs the most talented people into the most functionally important positions and thereby enhances a society's survival and efficiency.

The idea of meritocracy enters into ethical discussion about social systems – whether societies or organizations – in two ways, which are addressed in the following sections. First, a social system can be evaluated for the extent to which it lives up to meritocratic promises. Second, the moral basis of meritocracy as a distributive system can be assessed. This critical stance is less common, because meritocracy is accepted as a fair and legitimate principle and deeply woven into the culture and political rhetoric in many advanced capitalist societies and organizations.

THE PURSUIT OF MERITOCRACY AS FAIRNESS

In societies, debate rages over whether equal opportunity and meritocracy have been achieved. One position is that class and privilege, not talent, determine who gets ahead, so the society is not a true meritocracy. It follows that programs should be created to improve opportunities for the disadvantaged, redistribute wealth, and assist the undeservingly poor. An opposing position is that talent and hard work drive advancement and that the society is a meritocracy or a close enough approximation. It follows that no redress is needed and people in the lowest positions should work harder. At stake in this debate is the question of whether a society is just.

In organizations, reward systems that are variations on meritocracy, such as pay-for-skills or pay-for-performance, are assessed from the standpoint of the three principles of meritocracy. There are discussions about whether chosen measures of merit are appropriate and measurable, whether biases compromise equality of opportunity, and how steeply and how high the reward curve should rise (*see* AFFIRMATIVE ACTION PROGRAMS). At the societal and organizational levels, the focus is often on fine-tuning a meritocracy.

THE MORAL TENOR OF LIFE IN A MERITOCRACY

A second ethical approach to meritocracy probes whether a perfectly fine-tuned meritocracy has undesirable implications, three of which are considered here: privileging a dominant class while denigrating the poor, amplifying unearned differences in merit, and potentially compromising cooperation.

First, meritocratic ideology legitimates inequality, by painting a picture where "success comes to those whose energies and abilities deserve it, failures have only themselves to blame" (Mann, 1970: 427). Meritocracy is a "ruling ideology" (Marx and Engels, 1978: 64) that may serve the privileged by justifying their status and curbing resistance. Weber (1978: 953) writes: "every highly privileged group develops the myth of its natural superiority." The concomitant feelings of inferiority among those in lower positions have been called "the hidden injuries of class" (Sennett and Cobb, 1972). However, empirical evidence suggests that people in the lowest positions are not necessarily overcome by belief in meritocracy and have ways of making sense of their position other than blaming themselves (Scully, 1993). While meritocratic ideology may not fully legitimate inequality, it may raise enough uncertainties about distributive justice that resistance is not mobilized.

Second, the links between merit and reward may be difficult to justify on the grounds of moral desert inasmuch as merit may be unearned or a weak basis for special treatment. Historically, the Protestant ethic justified the link between hard work (as an indicator of moral rectitude) and wealth (as a possible indicator of salvation). However, merit, whether ability (such as IQ) or the capacity to exert effort and achieve goals, may be inherited or beyond an individual's control (Sher, 1979). If so, it becomes difficult to argue that a person's very "life chances" (income, housing, education) should be linked to their merits. For example, a society where people with mental handicaps routinely receive fewer resources seems cruel. Moreover, a meritocracy seems to assume that performance must be coaxed from the talented, which suggests they are more petulant than morally deserving. An alternative system, which may be more idealistic than practical, might be designed around the talented sharing their gifts without extra rewards. Meaningful work can be its own reward.

Third, merit-based differences are divisive. They can create a climate where cooperation and concern for others are mitigated and where smug success and embarrassing failure charge the tenor of social life. For example, organizations are discovering that the individualistic and competitive spirit of merit-based rewards can undermine teamwork. Because meritocracy is such a taken-for-granted ideal, the search for alternative reward systems for societies and organizations has been difficult (Donnellon and Scully, 1994). A less competitively individualistic society, perhaps based on communitarianism, might distribute occupations and tasks by merit but not skew rewards in other domains by merit (Walzer, 1983). The inclusion of meritocracy in the lexicon of business ethics is a reminder to evaluate the very assumptions about fairness and the social contract that guide the everyday operations of individuals and organizations.

Bibliography

Bell, D. (1972). On meritocracy and equality. *Public Interest*, **29**, 29–68.

Daniels, N. (1978). Merit and meritocracy. *Philosophy and Public Affairs*, **3**, 206–23.

Donnellon, A. and Scully, M. (1994). Teams, merit, and rewards: Will the post-bureaucratic organization be a post-meritocratic organization? In A. Donnellon and C. Hecksher (eds.), *The Post-Bureaucratic Organization*. Thousand Oaks, CA: Sage.

Mann, M. (1970). The social cohesion of liberal democracy. *American Sociological Review*, **35**, 423–39.

Marx, K. and Engels, F. (1978). *The German Ideology*, trans. C. J. Arthur. New York: International Publishers.

Scully, M. (1993). *The Imperfect Legitimation of Inequality in Internal Labor Markets*. Working Paper 3520-93. Cambridge, MA: Sloan School of Management.

Sennett, R. and Cobb, J. (1972). *The Hidden Injuries of Class*. New York: Vintage Books.

Sher, G. (1979). Effort, ability and personal desert. *Philosophy and Public Affairs*, **8**, 361–76.

Walzer, M. (1983). *Spheres of Justice: A Defense of Pluralism and Equality*. New York: Basic Books.

Weber, M. (1978). *Economy and Society: An Outline of Interpretive Sociology*, vol. 2, ed. G. Roth and C. Wittich. Berkeley: University of California Press.

Young, M. (1958). *The Rise of the Meritocracy*. New York: Penguin Books.

methodologies of business ethics research

Gary R. Weaver and Linda Klebe Treviño

comprise the variety and justification of methods by which business ethics research is undertaken. Business ethics research conventionally is divided into two approaches: normative and descriptive. Normative research is concerned with evaluating or prescribing the behavior of business persons and organizations. Descriptive research, by contrast, focuses on describing individual and organizational behavior so that it can be explained and possibly predicted. This conventional division of business ethics into two fairly distinct fields can be criticized as theoretically untenable and ethically undesirable (see below). But the distinction between normative and descriptive business ethics research *at least* captures a variety of important *surface* differences of current practice in the field, even if those differences fade at a deeper level of scrutiny.

Normative research focuses on what ought to be, and typically is the province of persons trained in philosophy, religious studies, or related liberal arts subjects. Such persons may see themselves filling the role of external critic of established business practices. By contrast, descriptive business ethics research usually is performed by applied social scientists, and often takes place within business organizations and business schools. It displays a more pragmatic approach to issues, and arguably is less prone to take a critical stance toward the established norms and goals of business. More importantly, mainstream social science theory (at least in the US) generally forgoes questions of what ought to be in favor of queries into what is. The goal is to explain the behavior of business organizations and their members. Business policies and practices are studied to discover what influences them and what they in turn influence. Although questions of their ethical propriety may be important, those are questions which range beyond the scope of conventional social science inquiry.

Language and Style

These different institutional homes and academic outlooks incorporate significant differences of style and language. Mainstream empiricists utilize the consensually agreed upon methods of their social scientific training, whether it be laboratory experimentation, business database studies, or surveys. Research is guided by relatively formal design criteria which, if judiciously followed, are thought capable of supporting explanatory models of business behavior. Data typically are analyzed utilizing a variety of quantitative statistical methods (e.g., regression analysis).

By contrast, philosophically driven research includes nothing like the highly specified research methods of social science. Although there is methodological self-reflection in normative ethics generally, it tends to be individualized to the task and author at hand. Any generally applicable normative method is best described

informally in terms of intellectual virtues such as consistency, clarity, avoidance of emotional manipulation, etc. Thus, whereas descriptive work has relatively standardized forms of method and presentation, normative work is much more eclectic and idiosyncratic.

Differences of language and presentation, plus different attitudes toward methodological uniformity, can contribute to misunderstanding. For example, normative theorists usually use the phrase "ethical behavior" to refer to behavior which in fact is ethically proper. Descriptive researchers, however, use the term "ethical" in a non-normative sense. For them, "ethical behavior" denotes the behavior of a person or organization confronted with ethical issues or choices, regardless of whether or not the behavior in question is normatively proper.

Assumptions about Human Agency

The normative and descriptive domains invoke explanatory models that rest upon distinct and sometimes unstated assumptions about human agency. The normative approach typically assumes that actions are performed with some degree of autonomy and responsibility. For some (metaphysical – as distinct from political – libertarians), this assumption entails a denial that ethical action easily can be placed in the kind of causal or nomological nexus empiricists usually seek. For other normative theorists (sometimes called "soft" determinists), the assumption of autonomy and responsibility attendant to ethical deeds suggests that not all causal factors are on an equal footing. Autonomous and responsible actions involve the agent's choices, *even if* those choices are causally determined. Thus, only causal factors that work through a person's choices preserve autonomy and moral responsibility.

Searches for the causal antecedents of behavior, then, can be problematic to normative theorists, as the goal of such a search conflicts with a normative assumption about human agency. To some normative theorists, success on the part of the empiricist in finding the sources of behavior risks compromising one's ability to impute normative significance to the behavior. Moreover, to some normative theorists, ethically proper action is self-explanatory, needing no additional explanation in social scientific terms.

In contrast, management researchers – even if they admit that in some sense individuals should be considered ethically responsible for their actions – nevertheless are more interested in finding causal determinants of ethical behavior (e.g., reward systems, codes of conduct, individual characteristics). External determinants of behavior are more interesting and useful for study because they are factors a manager can control. For example, a manager can manipulate reward systems in order to influence subordinates' behavior. In the descriptive approach, both ethically proper and improper actions are viewed as complex phenomena that should be explained by a combination of causal factors. Even whistleblowing, often presumed to be an example of autonomous, ethically proper action, is understood by social scientists to be the product of multiple internal and external causal factors.

Role of Abstraction vs. Empirical Detail

Modern normative ethical theory typically (though not universally) pursues a standard of moral reasoning or action which holds for persons in general. Consequently, normative theory often is framed at an abstract level, and is distanced from the specifics of any particular social setting. Even though normative inquiries often rely on the detailed study of real-life cases in business ethics, that kind of empirical detail often merely provides a venue for applying normative theories or unearthing implicit counterintuitive implications of such theories. It is only at the level of dealing with particular issues that normative theory is context sensitive; its general principles typically are framed in context-neutral fashion.

While normative business ethics thus displays a bias toward abstraction, descriptive business ethics leans in the opposite direction. Even though the abstract concepts of empirical psychology and sociology may play key roles in empirical business ethics research, those concepts are expected at some point to be empirically or observationally defined so that they can be concretely measured. Thus, the social scientist may devalue the philosopher's moral judgments because they cannot be evaluated by standardized empirical tests, nor be used to predict or explain behavior. But the social scientist's statements about "ethical" behavior may seem of secondary value to a normative theorist, because they do not address the evaluative questions of right and wrong.

Basis for Evaluating Theoretical Claims

The "method" of normative ethical theory – insofar as there is a common one – involves achieving what Rawls (1971) calls a reflective equilibrium between theoretical constructions (i.e., general normative principles) and persons' considered moral judgments. Everything from the formal sciences to common norms and intuitions is relevant in this process. Importantly, actual moral practice functions among the criteria for evaluating moral theories; were a normative theory to prescribe gratuitous punishment, we would have at least prima facie grounds for rejecting the theory. But these grounds are only prima facie; inconsistency with current moral practice in no way *necessitates* the rejection of a normative principle. After all, the point of such principles is to guide and possibly correct current practice. Normative claims and principles, in short, are to be evaluated according to an open-ended array of evidence, concerns, and insights, all tied together by generalized standards of good argument (e.g., no unseemly emotional appeals, no efforts to intimidate, etc.) rather than by some precisely defined methodology.

In descriptive business ethics, the initial stages of theory development may proceed in somewhat intuitive fashion. However, on the conventional account, an acceptable theory ultimately must contribute to one's ability to explain and predict. Thus, theory justification is accomplished via a putatively natural scientific model of empirical confirmation or disconfirmation, or through the theory's pragmatic ability to predict behavior and solve problems. Although critics of this conventional view of science argue that (a) the ideas of empirical confirmation and disconfirmation are beset with conceptual problems, and (b) that a variety of non-rational factors enter into the acceptance or rejection of a theory, the bulk of descriptive research on business ethics maintains this traditional empiricist (or neo-positivist) view of the goals and methods of inquiry.

CONVENTIONAL EMPIRICAL APPROACHES

The prominent research methods within conventional descriptive business ethics fall within two broad categories: experimental and correlational research. Within both categories, researchers are expected to begin with hypotheses rooted in social science theory. They then are to design a study that will test the hypothesized relationships.

Experimental approaches are used when the researcher wants to investigate a causal relationship between two variables, essentially investigating whether some phenomenon, X, "causes" another, Y. Experiments can be conducted in laboratory or field settings. The experimenter manipulates one or more independent variables (X, above), and then measures variations in the dependent variable (Y, above). The two major criteria for evaluating experimental research are *internal* and *external* validity. If an experiment is internally valid, the researcher can be confident that the independent variable "caused" the dependent variable. Laboratory experiments are generally thought to be higher in internal validity because the investigator has maximum control over the independent variables. For example, a laboratory experimenter might hypothesize that individuals would be more likely to steal under certain circumstances, and then randomly assign subjects to conditions that represent either the presence or absence of those circumstances. External validity has to do with the generalizability of the research results. Laboratory experiments are lower in external validity because they are conducted in artificial settings that strip away much of the complexity of real-life settings. Field experiments are higher in external validity because they are conducted in actual organizational settings, but they are lower in internal validity because the antecedent conditions (the Xs) are more difficult to control.

Correlational approaches are used when the research has hypothesized relationships among variables which cannot be manipulated by the researcher. Data to test the hypotheses may come from archival sources, or from surveys the researcher administers. For example, the researcher might hypothesize that individuals' cynicism toward business ethics will be higher for business school students and lower for older,

more experienced members of the business community. A survey could be conducted of members of both groups, and their responses could be compared. Or the research might hypothesize that corporate crime is higher in firms that are in financial difficulty. In this case, archival data about convictions and financial performance could be collected and subjected to correlational analysis.

ALTERNATIVE EMPIRICAL APPROACHES

There is, however, descriptive business ethics research which departs from the standard, quantitatively oriented methods. These approaches involve a variety of qualitative techniques which eschew numerical analysis for some form of in-depth verbal description or textual and verbal analysis. This research does not claim to provide generalizable claims in the fashion of quantitatively oriented research, but often is presented as a basis for building theories which can then be tested by more conventional quantitative techniques. Constructing a robust theoretical model of some category of phenomena may require intimate familiarity with it, familiarity best obtained by extensively talking to, observing, or living among the people involved. Qualitative research, in the fashion of interviews and ethnographic research such as participant observation, provides the basis for that kind of in-depth understanding.

The theoretical account resulting from qualitative research *may* be shaped into a formal model and then subjected to quantitative empirical test. But more radical non-quantitative research questions this possibility, and argues for the unavoidably malleable, interpretive character of all social or behavioral phenomena. In this view, any efforts to quantitatively assess phenomena by "objective" means (such as survey research) disguise the fact that the resulting portrait is *artificially* static. Quantitative methods, according to this alternative view, treat essentially interpretive phenomena as considerably more fixed and objective than we are entitled to claim.

More importantly, radically interpretive empirical research rejects the assumption of a normative/empirical distinction which underlies the conventional approaches to business ethics research. Rather, it argues that even the mainstream empiricist methodology imposes a normative standard on its subjects. Conventional empiricists may go so far as to admit that normative concerns lead them to study some phenomena rather than others (e.g., ethical concerns may prompt one to study the effects of certain forms of organizational discipline). But conventional empiricists would argue that standardized empirical methods guarantee that any conclusions will be value neutral, favoring no particular ethical position. To the critic of conventional methodology, however, such "objective" methods inherently favor a particular set of ethical claims (usually held to be those of the status quo or dominant power structure). For example, conventional empirical research on the effects of punishment on employees focuses on whether or not punishment is effective in changing behavior. But in doing so, this ostensibly neutral research assumes a consequentialist view of punishment (i.e., behavioral consequences are all that matters), and defines the relevant consequences from a managerial standpoint (rather than from the standpoint of, for example, a labor union organizer). To the critic, then, empirical business ethics research – despite its methodological and stylistic differences from normative research – does not avoid normative issues so much as hide them.

INTEGRATIVE APPROACHES

The more radically interpretive approach to empirical methodology, then, suggests the possibility of more integrative approaches to business ethics inquiry, in which normative and empirical considerations are not so readily isolated. Various types of integrative methods are well known in other fields. Kohlberg's work on moral development, to take just one example, uses normative principles or categories not only to label levels of moral development, but also to carry out some of the explanatory work in accounting for an individual's transition from one type of moral reasoning to another. (In Kohlberg's view, people move toward higher levels of moral reasoning in part *just because* they are higher, i.e., morally preferable.)

Within business ethics research, however, integrative methodologies are rare. Most typically, they occur when the empirical methods used are of the more interpretive, qualitative sort. (Jackall's *Moral Mazes* (1988) exemplifies this ap-

proach, simultaneously describing the ethical assumptions and standards of managerial work *and* the normative ethical problems attendant to those standards.) Integrative empirical work in the conventional quantitative tradition is rarer, however, as the underlying assumptions of that approach usually work against integrative tendencies. Extant work which attempts such integration generally uses normatively articulated categories to initially frame issues and phenomena, which then are analyzed according to conventional empirical methods (e.g., Victor and Cullen, 1988).

See also *business ethics; journals of business ethics; research centers for business ethics*

Bibliography

Donaldson, T. (1994). When integration fails. *Business Ethics Quarterly*, **4** (2), 157–71.
Jackall, R. (1988). *Moral Mazes: The World of Corporate Managers*. New York: Oxford University Press.
Rawls, J. (1971). *A Theory of Justice*. Cambridge, MA: Harvard University Press.
Trevino, L. K. (1992). Experimental approaches to studying ethical/unethical behavior in organizations. *Business Ethics Quarterly*, **2** (2), 121–36.
Trevino, L. K. and Weaver, G. R. (1994). Business ethics/business ethics: One field or two? *Business Ethics Quarterly*, **4** (2), 113–28.
Victor, B. and Cullen, J. (1988). The organizational bases of ethical work climates. *Administrative Science Quarterly*, 33, 101–25.
Victor, B. and Stephens, C. U. (1994). Business ethics: A synthesis of normative philosophy and empirical social science. *Business Ethics Quarterly*, **4** (2), 145–57.
Weaver, G. R. and Trevino, L. K. (1994). Normative and empirical business ethics: Separation, marriage of convenience, or marriage of necessity? *Business Ethics Quarterly*, **4** (2), 129–33.

monopoly

*Samuel M. Natale, William G. O'Neill,
Sebastian A. Sora*

is exclusive control over producing or selling a commodity or service. By definition, when a monopoly exists there are not numerous sellers in a market, each having a share, but only one seller having 100 percent of the market. Also, by definition, a monopoly is a market in which new sellers are, by one means or another, barred from entering. A monopoly may be held by the state or by a private interest. It may be due to the nature of the commodity itself or it may be established by some form of legislation. Additionally, such factors as original patents and sizable initial investment in start-up costs may effectively bar or discourage other sellers from entering a market – at least for a time.

Service monopolies are inherently different than goods monopolies. Such monopolies are generally local but dominant and can be national, as in the US Postal Service. Such monopolies can be less efficient but still remain economically viable (Geddes, 2000). Monopoly may also be created in effect by mergers (Gonsalves, 1989; Velasquez, 1988).

Monopolies raise at least three closely related moral issues: (1) a basic issue of justice in price (commutative justice); (2) the issue of efficiency of the economic system amid concentration of power (distributive justice); (3) the issue of corruption and other negative effects on economic society.

COMMUTATIVE JUSTICE

In the nineteenth and early twentieth centuries giant corporations began to have great control over the economy of a country. The United States was certainly an example.

The Interstate Commerce Act (1897) and the Sherman Antitrust Act (1890) were introduced to combat these effects. These measures, together with the Clayton Act and the Federal Trade Commission Act (both 1914), eventually succeeded in gaining control over these problems. After 1930, extensive regulation of business on all governmental levels developed, as well as an ongoing debate over the usefulness and appropriateness of government regulation as opposed to self-regulation of business (Beauchamp and Bowie, 1988).

The classic focus of concern on justice and pricing distinguishes the possibility of a just monopoly, when the control by monopoly is for the common welfare, from an unjust monopoly, which damages the common good. Competitive pricing to undercut competitors is not seen as wrong, but pricing below or above the level of a just price through monopolistic power is seen as

wrong (Gonsalves, 1989). The determinants of just price and the factors that ought to be considered in this judgment are highly disputed, but the standard of "whatever the buyer is willing to pay" is manifestly insufficient. Monopoly sellers can, for example, limit supply sufficiently to secure an artificially high price. The seller violates a principle of commutative justice by selling the commodity at more than it is actually worth to him and by forcing the buyer to pay more than it is worth to him (Velasquez, 1988).

Additional producers and sellers are interested in there being additional supply. Otherwise the economic system is forcibly restricted to limiting the agency of those involved in the system to mere utility in producing profits (see Sen, 1987, on utility and agency). Such a restriction is morally questionable in view of larger considerations. Increased competition has been the cumulative effect of antitrust actions through the decades. Antitrust action has also restrained mergers among competitors (Shepherd, 1986).

DISTRIBUTIVE JUSTICE

On the level of larger questions of distributive justice, monopolistic practices damage the efficiency of an economic system and undercut the moral arguments arising for the distribution of resources under that system. The general justification of profit maximization cannot be widened to include monopoly (Arrow, 1973). Monopoly, or even oligopoly, increases the difficulty to the level of impossibility for survival of small businesses in an economy. Control over a series of products in one industry – the food industry, for example – can effectively squeeze the consumer through the total costs of the market basket cumulatively by small increases over numerous items (Shaw and Barry, 1992). Monopolies can influence the efficiency of the distribution of goods in an economy through controlled shortages to produce higher prices, through a disinclination to efficient consumption of resources to produce a commodity, through disinclination of efficiency to reduce costs of production, through the maneuvering of some products unnecessarily to the level of high-priced luxuries, through requiring purchasers to purchase other items in order to be able to purchase some desired commodity, etc. (Velasquez, 1988).

One of the largest antitrust cases involved AT&T. AT&T agreed to divest itself of all its regional Bell operating companies. AT&T has increasingly been competing aggressively and successfully in a host of new endeavors (Stewart, 1993).

The victim or beneficiary in such situations is the system itself, as an instrument of not only economic efficiency but also of social justice. The choice of a social system is important to economic justice, but in both private-property and socialist systems, markets exist and true competition militates against price wars and other abuses of market power (Rawls, 1971) (see DISTRIBUTIVE JUSTICE). It should be noted that there is the concept of a "natural monopoly." In such a case, with the correct government oversight, the monopoly improves the efficiency of the economic system. It is not necessary that such monopolies be coercive (Foldvary, 1999).

CORRUPTION AND NEGATIVE EFFECTS

Monopolies are open to the kinds of concerns that characterize a general corruption of the system and a wounding of society. Monopolistic practices deviate from justice by producing a gravely exaggerated inequality of power over the consumer, allowing sellers to dictate terms to the consumer instead of responding to the market (Velasquez, 1988).

Monopolistic practices are among the factors contributing to the overweening power of corporations in dangerous areas of concern, nationally and internationally. Giant corporations can effectively negotiate by themselves with governments and influence legislation to serve their interests in franchising, tariffs, and other matters (Shaw and Barry, 1992).

At base, what is at stake is an inequality of knowledge poisoning the moral foundation of bargaining in an economy (Fried, 1979). Knowledge is important to genuine determination of preference by a consumer. Neither the supplying of this knowledge, nor the responsible shepherding of it in the interests of the economic society and the consumer, is likely to occur in the case of monopoly or in the similar effects of oligopoly.

Bibliography

Andrews, E. L. (1994). ATM case on monopoly settled. New York Times, April 22, D1.

Arrow, K. J. (1973). Social responsibility and economic efficiency. Public Policy, 21. Reprinted in Shaw and Barry (1992).

Beauchamp, T. L. and Bowie, N. E. (1988). Ethical Theory and Business, 3rd edn. Englewood Cliffs, NJ: Prentice-Hall.

Foldvary, F. (1999). Natural Monopolies, The Progress Report. Benjamin Banneker Center for Economic Justice and Progress, Baltimore, MD.

Fried, C. (1979). Right and Wrong. Cambridge, MA: Harvard University Press.

Fuhrman, P. (1987). Do it big Sammy. Forbes, 140, 278–80.

Geddes, R. (2000). Hoover Digest 2000. Stanford, CA: Stanford University Press.

Gonsalves, M. A. (1989). Right and Reason: Ethics in Theory and Practice. Columbus, OH: Merrill.

Rawls, J. (1971). A Theory of Justice. Cambridge, MA: Harvard University Press.

Sen, A. (1987). On Ethics and Economics. Oxford: Blackwell.

Shaw, W. H. and Barry, V. (1992). Moral Issues in Business, 5th edn. Belmont, CA: Wadsworth.

Shepherd, W. G. (1986). Bust the Reagan trustbusters. Fortune, 114, 225–7.

Stewart, J. B. (1993). Whales and sharks. The New Yorker, 68, 37–43.

Velasquez, M. G. (1988). Business Ethics, Concepts and Cases, 2nd edn. Englewood Cliffs, NJ: Prentice-Hall.

moral climate

Ann E. Mills

One component of the organizational culture is what some organizational theorists call the "moral climate" of an organization. The moral climate of an organization can be perceived as the functional analogue of the character of an individual. A person's character is a group of relatively stable traits connected with practical choice and action. Similarly, an organization's moral climate is defined by the shared perceptions of how moral issues should be addressed and what is morally correct behavior for the organization (Victor and Cullen, 1988). Just as personal ethics often affects what an individual will do when faced with moral dilemmas, corporate moral climate guides what an organization and its constituents will do when faced with issues of conflicting values. Moral climate includes both content – the shared perceptions of what constitutes ethical behavior – and process: how ethical or moral issues will be dealt with.

Organizational moral climate consists of the shared perceptions of the "general and pervasive characteristics of [an] organization [of a system] affecting a broad range of decisions" (Victor and Cullen, 1988: 101). Since most organizations can be thought of as "open systems," affected by and affecting the external environment, moral climate defines the organization in both its internal and external relationships.

The moral climate of organizations is often articulated via value statements, mission statements, organization codes of ethics, policies addressing specific ethical issues, and most importantly, through its effect on the attitudes and activities of everyone associated with the organization. For a code of ethics does not necessarily mean that persons associated with a particular organization will be guided by it. Nevertheless, these self-proclaimed standards are a means by which stakeholders can judge the organization, and hold it accountable.

Obviously, one could create or perpetuate a negative as well as a positive moral climate in any organization. A positive moral climate has at least two important characteristics. First, it is an organizational culture where the mission and vision of the organization are consistent with its expectations for professional and managerial performance and consistent with the goals of the organization as they are actually practiced. Second, a positive ethical climate is one that embodies a set of values that reflect societal norms for what organizations should value, how they should prioritize their mission, vision, and goals, and how they, and their professionals and managers, should behave (Spencer et al., 2000).

As described here, moral climate refers to the character of the organization. There is another use for this expression as well. It can also refer to the social/political/economic/religious environment in which the organization is embedded. In this usage it is obvious that the external moral climate can affect the organization and its internal climate and so affect the organization's decision-making, possibly preventing the organization from doing what it considers the moral thing to do (see ORGANIZATIONAL MORAL DISTRESS).

Interest in the practical effects of an organizational moral climate has engaged both scholars and managers. Thomas Peters and Robert Waterman, in their ground-breaking book *In Search of Excellence* (1982), identified the inculcation of "shared values" among employees in organizations as one of the foremost reasons for the success of America's "best run" or "excellent" companies. They argued that the commitment to high performance was the result of intrinsic motivation, a belief that the task at hand was inherently worthwhile, and that excellent companies tap the inherent worth of a task by putting it in the context of their core values. Peters and Waterman crystallized their ideas in the famous McKinsey 7-S Framework in which shared values are linked to the organization's structures, systems, style, staff, skills, strategy, and structure (Peters and Waterman, 1982: 10).

More recently, in a six-year project, James Collins and Jerry Porras set out to identify and systematically research the historical development of a set of what they called "visionary companies," to examine how these companies differed from a carefully selected control set of comparison companies (Collins and Porras, 1994: 2). Their interest lay in explaining the enduring quality and prosperity of these visionary companies. They found that visionary companies (those that could be identified at the premier organization in its industry, as being widely admired by its peers, as having a long track record of making a significant impact on the world around it, as well as generating a remarkable long-run performance as measured by the stock market) displayed an organization-wide commitment to their stated core values and a sense of purpose in realizing their missions. Collins and Porras concluded:

> Contrary to business school doctrine, "maximizing shareholder wealth" or "profit maximization" has not been the dominant driving force or primary objective through the history of visionary companies. Visionary companies pursue a cluster of objectives, of which making money is only one – and not necessarily the primary one. Yes, they

seek profits, but they are equally guided by a core ideology – core values and a sense of purpose beyond just making money. Yet, paradoxically, the visionary companies make more money than the more purely profit-driven comparison companies. (Collins and Porras, 1994: 8)

Insofar as a positive moral climate must include attention to the legal parameters within which it operates, it can be argued that the government has an interest in the moral climate of organizations. In 1991 the US Department of Justice (DOJ) extended the Federal Sentencing Guidelines to include organizations. According to the Guidelines, even though individual agents are responsible for their own criminal conduct, organizations are additionally vicariously liable for offenses committed by their agents, and as such can be held culpable for the individual's actions (An Overview, 2003: 2). Organizations may therefore be responsible for any financial restitution or punishment associated with an individual's criminal behavior while acting as an agent or employee of the organization. The range of fines or other punishments for the organization is based on the seriousness of the offense and the culpability of the organization.

The DOJ recognizes that an organization cannot control every action taken by every individual associated with the organization. But it also realizes that organizations can try to promote a climate or a culture in which it is unacceptable to break the law. According to the Federal Sentencing Guidelines, organizations can do this through effective programs to prevent and detect violations of the law (An Overview, 2003: 2). Evidence that efforts in this direction have been made reduces the level of culpability and thus the fines to the organization. Since the fines associated with organizational wrongdoing are large, since there is no guaranteed protection against individual wrongdoing in any organization, and since fines associated with wrongdoing can be reduced by as much as 95 percent, organizations have a powerful motive to establish programs designed to prevent and detect violations of the law. The Federal Sentencing Guidelines offer explicit and detailed instructions on what they consider to be the characteristics of such programs. These characteristics include documented standards and policies, high-level oversight of the program, effective communication, and disciplinary mechanisms (An Overview, 2003: 3). Today, these programs, often called corporate compliance programs, though some are called ethics programs, are found in nearly every medium to large organization.

Researchers have theorized that corporate compliance programs or ethics programs can have one or more aims. A compliance program can have the sole goal of detecting or preventing legal violations, or its goals can be broader. For instance, it can aim to develop and evaluate the organizational mission, to create a positive ethical climate within the organization that perpetuates the mission, to develop decision models for ensuring this perpetuation is reflected in organizational activities, and to serve as a cheerleader, evaluator, and critic of organizational, professional, and managerial behavior. Or it can incorporate both goals, since disobeying the law or circumventing regulations is ordinarily not considered appropriate moral or legal behavior.

There is interest in evaluating the effects of the two types of programs on corporate behavior. Gary Weaver and Linda Treviño call the first type of ethics program "compliance" oriented and the second type of ethics program "values" oriented. Compliance oriented ethics programs emphasize rules, monitor employee behavior, and discipline misconduct. The second type, values oriented programs, emphasizes support for employees' ethical aspirations and the development of shared values (Weaver and Treviño, 1999: 317).

Weaver and Treviño argue that both types of programs seek to "bring some degree of order and predictability to employee behavior" (Weaver and Treviño, 1999: 316) and that the two orientations are not mutually exclusive. For example, a values oriented ethics program could exist with rules, accountability, and disciplinary mechanisms. But according to Weaver and Treviño their studies of both types of programs indicate that, all things being equal, "a focus on monitoring and discipline in an ethics program is more likely to engender a contractual employee attitude toward the organization, rather than a perception of organizational support and trust, or increased salience for one ethical obligation as an organizational member" (Weaver and Treviño, 1999: 317).

A contractual employee attitude can be understood as an attitude where shared values between the organization and employee are irrelevant – the employee is to perform some function for which that employee is paid and that employee is monitored to ensure that function is performed. But Weaver and Treviño indicate that according to their data, a focus on monitoring implies distrust of employees, and this may encourage a response to the ethics program which is calculated and self-interested. This response is unlikely to encourage organizational commitment or communication. Nor, in the words of Peters and Waterman, is it likely to lead to a commitment to high performance.

Communication is, of course, at the heart of an effective compliance or ethics program, for without it, values cannot be shared or wrongdoing reported. Thus, it seems, there is a contradiction: communication is needed for an effective compliance program, but Weaver and Treviño supply data suggesting that a compliance program without a value orientation encourages non-communication. They state: "A values orientation, in particular, appears to add distinctive and desirable outcomes that cannot be achieved by a perceived focus on behavioral compliance. Moreover, a values orientation appears important to fully realizing the potential benefits of compliance activities such as reporting misconduct" (Weaver and Treviño, 1999: 317).

Thus, a compliance approach to creating programs aimed at influencing the moral climate of the organization may not realize the benefits described by Peters and Waterman and Collins and Porras. Moreover, a compliance approach to generating a moral climate is not helpful when the organization is faced with difficult moral or ethical choices. For this, a values orientation is necessary.

Bibliography

An Overview of the Federal Sentencing Guidelines (2003) Available http://www.ussc.gov/orgguide.HTM.

Collins, J. and Porras, J. (1994). *Built to Last: Successful Habits of Visionary Companies*. New York: Harper Collins.

Peters, J. T. and Waterman, R. H., Jr. (1982). *In Search of Excellence*. Thorndike, ME : G. K. Hall.

Spencer, E., Mills, A., Rorty. M., and Werhane, P. (2000). *Organization Ethics for Healthcare Organizations*. New York: Oxford University Press.

Victor, B. and Cullen, J. (1988). The organizational bases of ethical work climates. *Administrative Science Quarterly*, **33**, 101–25.

Weaver, G. and Treviño, L. (1999). Compliance and values oriented ethics programs: influences on employees' attitudes and behavior. *Business Ethics Quarterly*, **9** (2), 315–17.

moral development

John W. Dienhart

is a rational process of acquiring moral values. According to moral development theory, we do not adopt moral values uncritically; rather, we adopt moral values only if we have the conceptual and emotional resources to understand them, and only if they help us resolve interpersonal problems. Moral autonomy is possible because we have some choice over which values to adopt and how to interpret them.

Moral development theory is associated with three names: Jean Piaget, Lawrence Kohlberg, and Carol Gilligan.

PIAGET: MORALITY AND RATIONALITY

Piaget published *Le Jugement moral chez l'enfant* in 1932, the heyday of psychoanalysis and the beginning of behaviorism. Psychoanalysis and behaviorism, though different in many ways, both view morality as a set of *external rules* imposed on individuals.

Piaget rejected the external-rule interpretation of morality. Studying the behavior of young males, Piaget argued that morality develops as a result of *internal rational processes* (see KANTIAN ETHICS). We develop morally as we become involved in increasingly complex social arrangements. We adopt moral rules and principles because they help us cope with these complex social environments. While embraced by those in education, Piaget was largely ignored by research psychologists until Kohlberg devised more precise ways to measure moral development.

KOHLBERG: AN ETHIC OF RIGHTS

In the late 1950s Lawrence Kohlberg began an 18-year study of 50 men and boys to evaluate and refine Piaget's theory. On the basis of that and many subsequent studies, Kohlberg argued that there are three levels of moral development, each of which has two stages.

Level I: Pre-Conventional Level. Individuals have a limited understanding of, but not loyalty to, social or moral rules, which are valuable only if they promote self-interest. Individuals make moral judgments in terms of concrete consequences to themselves (*see* CONSEQUENTIALISM).
Stage 1: Punishment and Obedience Orientation. Right acts are those that are not punished. Punishment consists of either corporal punishment or the loss of a privilege. Authorities are obeyed because of their power to punish.
Stage 2: Instrumental-Relativist Orientation. Right acts promote self-interest now or in the future. Individuals understand how reciprocity can justify current loss to secure greater rewards later.
Level II: Conventional Level. Individuals understand how moral rules bind groups together. They make moral judgments in terms of rule-following and the concrete consequences to their group, and so can justify self-sacrifice. One's group is viewed as morally superior to others.
Stage 3: Interpersonal Concordance of "Good Boy/Nice Girl" Orientation. Right acts promote the good of a small group, such as a family. Reciprocity is valuable because it holds a group together. There is loyalty to the group, its rules, and authorities.
Stage 4: Law and Order Orientation. Right acts follow group rules or promote the good of a large group, like a nation. There is loyalty to the large group, its laws, and leaders.
Level III: Post-Conventional Level. Individuals use universal ethical standards. The partiality of Levels I and II is rejected in favor of impartiality, which views all human beings, groups, and societies as equally valuable.
Stage 5: Social-Contract Legalistic Orientation. Right acts and policies are those that are fair or promote the good of the group. Laws can be unjust. Principles of social contract theory and utilitarianism are not clearly distinguished. There is loyalty to laws or groups that respect human beings.
Stage 6: Universal Ethical Principle Orientation. Right acts and policies respect human dignity. Utilitarianism is rejected. There is loyalty to universal principles, not to laws or groups.

People move through these stages serially. Each stage provides the foundation for the next, integrating the values of previous stages. Stage 5, for example, reinterprets the values of self, family, and nation in terms of fairness and the good of all. Value adoption is rational: people move to later stages because they are better for resolving problems.

GILLIGAN: AN ETHIC OF CARE

Carol Gilligan argues that Piaget and Kohlberg ignore the moral importance of interpersonal relationships. She argues that up to one-third of women, but virtually no men, define moral responsibility in terms of caring relationships.

Care reasoning has three levels. Women move to later levels because later levels are better for resolving problems. In the *first level* of care reasoning, right actions promote one's own interests, but self-interest is understood in terms of successful interpersonal relationships. As women become more empathetic and dependent on how others view them, they move to the *second level* of care reasoning, in which right actions promote the good of others, as dictated by conventional expectations. These expectations can lead women to neglect themselves, making them unable to serve the interests of others. If women perceive this conflict, they move to the *third level* of moral reasoning, in which right actions nurture all people and relationships as much as possible. Level three balances caring for oneself with caring for others.

Although the view that only women use care reasoning is widely disputed, many now accept that these two kinds of reasoning exist. The nature of these two types of reasoning and their relationships to each other and to gender is far from settled.

IMPLICATIONS FOR BUSINESS

Since we use moral reasoning to evaluate and understand relationships and conflicts, it occurs in all aspects of life, including business. The issue, then, is not whether ethics has a role in business decision-making, but what that role is.

Descriptively, we can ask: "What kind(s) of moral reasoning do people use in business?" *Normatively*, we can ask: "What kind(s) of moral reasoning should people use in business?" Moral development theory can help us answer the first question by giving us research categories and procedures; it is less helpful in answering the normative question, except insofar as it can help us design effective reasoning strategies (*see* PRACTICAL REASONING).

Bibliography

Dienhart, J. (1992). *A Cognitive Approach to the Ethics of Counseling Psychology*. Lanham, MD: University Press of America. (An assessment of rational and non-rational theories of moral acquisition.)

Duska, R. and Whelan, M. (1975). *Moral Development: A Guide to Piaget and Kohlberg*. New York: Paulist Press. (An excellent introduction to moral development.)

Friedman, M. (1987). Beyond caring: The demoralization of gender. In M. Hanen and K. Nielsen (eds.), *Science, Morality and Feminist Theory*. Calgary: University of Calgary Press, 87–110. (An insightful discussion of how care and rights reasoning fit together.)

Gilligan, C. (1977). Conception of the self and of morality. *Harvard Educational Review*, **47** (4), 481–517.

Gilligan, C. (1992). *In a Different Voice*. Cambridge, MA: Harvard University Press. (Gilligan's major work.)

Gilligan, C., Ward, J. V., and Taylor, J. M. (eds.) (1988). *Mapping the Moral Domain*. Cambridge, MA: Harvard University Press.

Kohlberg, L. (1981). *Essays on Moral Development, Vol. 1: The Philosophy of Moral Development*. San Francisco: Harper and Row.

Kohlberg, L. (1984). *Essays on Moral Development, Vol. 2: The Psychology of Moral Development*. San Francisco: Harper and Row.

Piaget, J. (1965) [1932]. *The Moral Judgment of the Child*. New York: Free Press.

moral dilemmas

Walter Sinnott-Armstrong

are situations where moral requirements conflict, and *neither* requirement is *overridden*. Different people have very different kinds of situations in mind when they talk about moral dilemmas. If a contractor could gain a large profit by deceiving a customer, some might call this a moral dilemma, even if the moral factors all fall on one side and conflict only with self-interest. Similarly, conflicts between morality and law or religion are sometimes called moral dilemmas.

People even talk about moral dilemmas when it is not clear whether morality is relevant at all. A manufacturer, for example, might be said to be in a moral dilemma if she suspects but does not know that a certain customer is using her products in harmful and illegal ways. What makes this a moral dilemma is that it is hard to tell whether there are moral reasons against selling to this customer.

Moral philosophers have recently discussed a narrower set of situations as moral dilemmas. They usually define moral dilemmas as situations where an agent morally *ought* to do each of two (or more) acts but cannot do both (or all). However, it often seems that one ought to do something (such as give to a certain charity) that one is not morally required to do. The most common examples of moral dilemmas include moral obligations or requirements, so it is natural to limit moral dilemmas to situations where an agent cannot fulfill all applicable moral *requirements*.

Some philosophers refuse to call a situation a moral dilemma when one of the conflicting requirements is clearly stronger, such as when one must break a trivial promise to avoid a serious harm. To exclude such resolvable conflicts, "moral dilemmas" can be defined, as in the original, formal definition, to include all and only situations where an agent cannot fulfill all applicable *non-overridden* moral requirements.

It is also common to define moral dilemmas as situations where every alternative is morally wrong. This is equivalent to the two previous definitions if an act is morally wrong exactly when it violates a moral requirement or a non-overridden moral requirement. However, we usually do not call an act "wrong" unless it violates an overriding moral requirement. Then the definition in terms of "wrong" makes moral dilemmas impossible, since overriding moral requirements cannot conflict. So it is preferable to define moral dilemmas in terms of non-overridden moral requirements.

Some would object that this definition includes trivial requirements and conflicts, so one might require that the conflicting moral requirements be *strong*. One also might want to add that the agent must be aware of the moral requirements and must be able to satisfy each by itself. But such additions will not affect the basic logical issues about whether it is possible for moral requirements to conflict without resolution.

Bibliography

Gowans, C. W. (1987). *Moral Dilemmas*. New York: Oxford University Press.

Gowans, C. W. (1994). *Innocence Lost: An Examination of Inescapable Wrongdoing*. New York: Oxford University Press.

Morton, A. (1991). *Disasters and Dilemmas: Strategies for Real-Life Decision-making*. Cambridge, MA: Blackwell.

Sinnott-Armstrong, W. (1988). *Moral Dilemmas*. Cambridge, MA: Blackwell.

moral imagination

Patricia H. Werhane

The idea of moral imagination derives historically from the work of Adam Smith and Immanuel Kant. According to Smith, imagination plays a key role in "fellow understanding," our ability to place ourselves in the situation of another (the function of sympathy) and thus make moral judgments about others. Imagination is also important as each of us steps back in order to evaluate ourselves and others from a more impartial perspective on the basis of societal moral rules and sometimes to critique and revise those rules (Smith, 1976: I.i) For Kant, imagination is a key component of experience, understanding, and reasoning. Kant argues that imagination

works on three levels. The reproductive imagination synthesizes our sensations, the productive imagination creates the data of experience, memory, and knowledge, and the creative imagination enables us to formulate new ideas and think "out of the box" (Makkreel, 1990).

However, neither Smith nor Kant uses the term *moral* imagination. More recently, the notion of moral imagination has been explicated in detail by Mark Johnson. In an important book, Johnson defines moral imagination as "an ability to imaginatively discern various possibilities for acting within a given situation and to envision the potential help and harm that are likely to result from a given action" (Johnson, 1993: 202).

In business ethics, moral imagination is defined as

> the ability in particular circumstances to discover and evaluate possibilities not merely determined by that circumstance, or limited by its operative mental models, or merely framed by a set of rules or rule-governed concerns. In management decision-making, moral imagination entails perceiving norms, social roles, and relationships entwined in any situation. Developing moral imagination involves heightened awareness of contextual moral dilemmas and their mental models, the ability to envision and evaluate new mental models that create new possibilities, and the capability to reframe the dilemma and create new solutions in ways that are novel, economically viable, and morally justifiable. (Werhane, 1999: 93)

Being morally imaginative includes:

- Self-reflection about oneself and one's situation.
- Disengaging from and becoming aware of one's situation, understanding the mental model or script dominating that situation, and envisioning possible moral conflicts or dilemmas that might arise in that context or as outcomes of the dominating scheme.
- The ability to imagine new possibilities. These possibilities include those that are not context-dependent and that might involve another mental model.
- Moral imagination requires that one evaluate from a moral point of view both the original

context and its dominating mental models, and the new possibilities one has envisioned (Werhane, 1999).

Moberg and Seabright have expanded on this notion of moral imagination and developed more fully the ways in which it can enrich the managerial decision-making process. They define moral imagination as "a reasoning process thought to counter the organizational factors that corrupt ethical judgment" (Moberg and Seabright, 2000: 845) and they integrate moral imagination into Rest's four-stage model of ethical decision-making, clarifying its role in the identification of moral issues, the formation of moral judgment, the development of moral intent, and the guidance of moral behavior.

All these thinkers focus on moral imagination at the individual or managerial level. However, moral imagination is not merely a function of the individual imagination. Rather, moral imagination operates on organizational and systemic levels as well, again as a facilitative mechanism that may encourage sounder moral thinking and moral judgment. It is these latter phases that have been neglected. In an organizational context, managers are often trapped within an institutional culture that creates mental habits that function as boundary conditions, precluding creative thinking. To change or break out of a particular mindset requires a well-functioning moral imagination. Similarly, a political economy can be trapped in its vision of itself and the world in ways that preclude change on this more systemic level. Thus moral imagination, the ability to get out of these models and traps, is critical at all levels.

How does moral imagination work on the organizational and systemic levels?

A truly systemic view thus considers how... [a phenomenon]...operates in a system with certain characteristics. The system involves interactions extending over time, a complex set of interrelated decision points, an array of actors with conflicting interests...and a number of feedback loops...Progress in analyzing [ethical issues]...can only be made with a full understanding of the systemic issues. (Wolf, 1998–9: 1675)

Moral imagination involves engaging in a systemic multiple perspectives approach. This includes the following:

- Concentration on the network of relationships and patterns of interaction, rather than on individual components of particular relationships, spelling out the networks of relationships from different perspectives.
- A multi-perspective analysis that is both descriptive and normative, taking into account various perspectives of the manager, the citizen, the firm, community, state, law, tradition, background institutions, history, and other networks of relationships.
- Then taking an evaluative perspective, asking: What values are at stake? Which take priority, or should take priority?
- Becoming proactive, both within the system and in initiating structural change.

In this process one describes the system and its networks of interrelationships in order to grasp the interconnectedness of the system. One investigates what is not included in the system (its boundaries and boundary-creating activities) and what mindsets are predominant, asking who are the stakeholders (individuals, associations, organizations, networks, agencies), what are the core values of each set of stakeholders, and what sort of consensus can be concluded from what is often a disagreement about core values of each stakeholder. Additionally, one outlines the core values of the system and speculates as to what these *should* be. Finally, one should think about whether and which organizations or individuals within the system might be capable and willing to risk challenging bits of the system and carry out change. The result: "moral imagination and systems thinking encourage networked systems analysis that is engaged and critical, creative and evaluative, and values grounded. This process encourages constructive change within a network of relationships" (Werhane, 2002).

Bibliography

Cohen, D. V. (1998). Moral imagination in organizational problem solving: An institutional perspective. *Business Ethics Quarterly*, Ruffin Series 1, 123–47.

Johnson, M. (1993). *Moral Imagination*. Chicago: University of Chicago Press.

Larmore, C. (1981). Moral judgment. *Review of Metaphysics*, 35, 275–96.

Makkreel, R. (1990). *Imagination and Interpretation in Kant*. Chicago: University of Chicago Press.

Moberg, D. and Seabright, M. (2000). The development of moral imagination. *Business Ethics Quarterly*, 4, 845–84.

Smith, A. (1976) [1759]. *A Theory of Moral Sentiments*, ed. A. L. Macfie and D. D. Raphael. Oxford: Oxford University Press.

Werhane, P. H. (1999). *Moral Imagination and Management Decision Making*. New York: Oxford University Press.

Werhane, P. H. (2002). Moral imagination and systems thinking. *Journal of Business Ethics*, 38, 33–42.

Wolf, S. (1998–9). Toward a systemic theory of informed consent in managed care. *Houston Law Review*, 35, 1631–81.

moral mazes

Robert Jackall

The metaphor "moral mazes" refers simultaneously to the labyrinthine structure of large bureaucratic organizations and to the ethical quandaries that such organizations regularly create for men and women who work in them.

Bureaucracies not only rationalize work, but also behavior and attitudes. Though each organization has its own constructed "institutional logic" and its own ethical standards, bureaucracies, whether public or private, share certain structural features that shape the moral ethos of big organizations. Typically, bureaucracies require and create patterns of predictable routine, impersonal rules and procedures, and patterns of delimited authority in order to maximize organizational efficiency. In the process, bureaucracies bring together people who have little in common with each other except the impersonal rules that govern their behavior. Since these rules are not given but made, they vary widely not only between different organizations, but even within the same organization, depending on who has the authority and power to make the rules. Moreover, authority and power shift in organizations, depending on changes in the markets or external exigencies that determine organizational frameworks and fates.

Bureaucracies place powerful premiums on certain behavior, and reward those able to discern those premiums and behave accordingly. Both the premiums themselves and conformity to them are ambiguous because they are constantly subject to peers' and superiors' interpretations, making compulsive sociability in an attempt to discern and shape those interpretations an occupational virtue. Though specific premiums and requisite conformity to them vary considerably depending on the nature and purpose of particular bureaucracies and on organizational leadership, all bureaucracies require varying degrees of self-rationalization of their members. Voluntary self-rationalization produces the deepest internalization of organizational goals, creating relatively enclosed social worlds that cause people to bracket moralities to which they might adhere in their homes, churches, or other social settings. Occupational rules-in-use gain ascendancy over more general ethical standards. Moral choices become inextricably tied to organizational fates.

Within such a context, bureaucracies typically separate men and women from the human consequences of their actions. For instance, top managers rarely meet workers fired because of their decisions; they rarely visit communities devastated economically because of their reallocation of resources; they rarely encounter consumers inadvertently injured by their companies' products; they rarely meet specific men or women who have become "cases" under procedures they have authorized. Such insulation heightens rational decision-making according to the impersonal criteria at the core of every modern bureaucracy, even as it makes notions such as the "ethics of brotherhood" irrelevant. Further, despite claims to the contrary, bureaucracies also separate people from internal accountability for their actions. Bureaucratic hierarchies generally encourage superiors' usurpation of credit for the work of subordinates. Moreover, few bureaucracies have formal tracking systems to allot blame for mistakes; men and women who are upwardly mobile can outrun their mistakes, leaving others to bear blame for them. At the upper levels of organizations, among men and women of proven and relatively equal abilities, the allocation of credit and blame, and corresponding success and failure, is thus very often experienced as arbitrary, indeed capricious. In short, big organizations often seem to be vast systems of organized irresponsibility – even, perhaps especially, to those within them.

Organizational leaders can attempt to impose standards of moral evaluation and practical moral reasoning to guide their charges' actions. But since there is no necessary connection between the good of a particular individual, the good of an organization, and the common good, every set of standards that leaders might assert is arbitrary to some extent and subject to constant negotiation and reinterpretation by competing organizational interests. Leaders can impose certain standards by dint of effort and authority and sometimes those standards become deeply institutionalized in a particular organization. Typically, however, standards last only as long as leaders themselves do. When looking up provides little direction, men and women in large organizations look around. They turn to each other for moral cues for behavior and come to fashion specific situational moralities for specific significant others in their world. As it happens, the guidance that they receive from each other is as profoundly ambiguous as the social structure of big organizations. Moral rules-in-use for all issues become indistinguishable from the rules for achieving success or avoiding failure. Ethical issues often get translated into problems of public relations. Men and women in large organizations thus often find themselves caught in an intricate set of moral mazes, unable even to discern the terms of their quandaries, let alone a way out of the thicket.

Bibliography

Bensman, J. (1983). *Dollars and Sense: Ideology, Ethics, and the Meaning of Work in Profit and Nonprofit Organizations*, revd. edn. New York: Schocken Books.

Jackall, R. (1988). *Moral Mazes: The World of Corporate Managers*. New York: Oxford University Press.

Weber, M. (1946). Religious rejections of the world and their directions. In H. H. Gerth and C. Wright Mills (eds.), *From Max Weber*. New York: Oxford University Press.

moral muteness

Frederick Bird

What is moral muteness? People are morally mute if they fail forthrightly to voice moral concern regarding issues about which they possess moral convictions. Hypocrites act deceptively, claiming moral convictions that they do not in fact hold. People who are morally mute are deceptive as well, but in a quite different way, because they fail to disclose and communicate overtly moral convictions that they in fact hold.

Moral muteness assumes at least four different forms. First, many people in business are morally mute because they fail to speak out about activities they judge to be harmful or wrong. They witness discrimination against minorities, they know colleagues are padding expense accounts, they observe managers misusing executive perks, or they see the cavalier disregard for the legitimate complaints of particular customers – and they say nothing. They learn that agents retained by their firms in developing countries are offering bribes to government officials – but they remain quiet. They hear stories that a purchasing agent is paying a certain long-time supplier much higher prices for goods that could be obtained much more inexpensively from alternative sources – and they do nothing in response. As happened for a large number of people working in the thrift industry in the 1980s, they witness their colleagues making a large number of questionable loan decisions – and they remain silent (Mayer 1990). In all these examples business people are morally mute because they have failed to speak up about practices which they privately consider as either blatantly harmful, decidedly wrong, or at least potentially so.

Second, people are morally mute as well by not representing their own moral views as forthrightly as they might. They mute their moral concerns by remaining silent about moral ideals they would like to put into place. They might hope, for example, that their organizations would create more opportunities for minorities, adopt more environmentally sustainable practices, or provide more skill training opportunities, but they say nothing directly. They mute their moral concerns as well by not bargaining hard for positions about which they hold moral convictions. In order to avoid overt conflicts, they too easily or too quickly compromise.

Third, one of the most prevalent expressions of moral muteness is exhibited in the way supervisors or colleagues provide muted feedback and appraisals on the work of others. One manager commented: "I inherited a manager who had sloppy dress, bad teeth, and poor personal hygiene; previous managers couldn't bring themselves to give him feedback." Another confessed: "Our managers are chicken to confront in the performance appraisal interview. All our employees have satisfactory or better ratings, and everybody has potential. It's just not true" (Bird, 1996: 45, 48). Like assigning inflated grades in school, the failure to provide forthright and honest feedback leaves others without clear understanding of their shortfalls and available opportunities for learning.

Fourth, we are morally mute as well when we disguise genuine moral concerns as if they were simply matters of economic calculation or organizational politics. This tendency to mask ethical issues predominantly in other terms as matters of finance, strategy, or pragmatics is widespread. Our concerns for just treatment, honest communications, and socially responsible practices are rephrased as matters of competitive advantage or self-interest. We can appropriately argue that people experience something like moral amnesia when they use decidedly non-moral terms to raise what on closer examination are clearly ethical concerns. One of the best-known examples of this kind of moral amnesia is the essay by Milton Friedman entitled "The social responsibility of business is to increase its profit" (1971). The title and a quick read of this essay make it seem that Friedman is arguing that the ethical responsibility of businesses does not extend beyond profit making so long as this is done legally. On closer examination, the essay is filled with moral arguments about the responsibilities of executives to employees and customers as well as shareholders, the importance of operating without deception and in keeping with standards of fair competition, and the responsibility of using organizational resources effectively without waste. The failure overtly to acknowledge these ethical concerns makes it much more difficult to encourage and invite open discussions of everyday moral issues that business organizations face.

In many cases, moral muteness is a matter of degree. Few business people totally mute their moral concerns. In many cases what business people do is to whisper their moral concerns or state them indirectly. They raise objections with a few colleagues about what they regard as their firms' misleading advertising, unfair promotion policies, or loosely interpreted adherence to air quality standards. They hesitantly and in passing note their concern with the way their firms use agents to skirt legal requirements. They bury their criticism of the way their firms manage security problems, sourcing, or consumer complaints within larger reports, where they can be easily overlooked. In an often-cited case that involved the manufacturing of a braking system for US Air Force planes, several engineers quietly cautioned the superiors in their company that the four-disk brake under construction would not provide sufficient braking strength and, therefore, constituted a safety hazard. In spite of these warnings, their superiors decided to proceed with initial flight tests, in part in order to keep to their agreed-upon manufacturing schedule. In the company's test flights the new brakes did not allow the planes to come to a stop within the expected distance. The engineers who raised the safety concerns altered the report to allow the planes to coast longer distances. They submitted the report but did not sign their names to it. They knew the brakes as constructed constituted a safety hazard. They had quietly voiced their concern. Even though they believed firmly that weakness of the brakes would become publicly evident as soon as they were utilized by the Air Force, they made no further efforts to communicate their concerns. Yet it was clearly in their firm's interest to learn of this braking problem. Later, at much greater expense, the firm had to redesign and rebuild the brakes they were working on because their malfunctioning became clear as soon as the Air Force tested them (Vandiver, 1972).

Why do business people so often muffle their expression of moral concern? Why do they so frequently respond inattentively to moral concerns expressed by others? What are the primary underlying causes of moral muteness and deafness?

Several individual factors seem especially important. To begin with, many people mute their moral convictions either because they believe they cannot make a difference and/or because they believe that moral considerations call for heroic actions they feel ill-prepared to follow. For example, if they learn that their firm is probably making payoffs to secure contracts, they are likely to assume their alternatives are either to speak out publicly and put their jobs at risk or to remain silent and keep their positions. They view their alternatives almost exclusively in relation to exit or loyalty. When they conclude that they cannot act morally unless they act like saints, what they frequently suffer from is a lack of moral imagination that would lead them to explore varied ways they might voice their concern without having to put themselves at extraordinary risk (Hirschman, 1970). For example, in a case like the one just cited, they might voice concern by raising questions, by proposing to experiment with alternative strategies to develop business contacts, by voicing concern anonymously either within or beyond the organization, and/or by seeking assistance from colleagues or relevant community groups. Moral resignation in many cases follows from excessively inflated notions of what moral convictions require from us, combined with an inability to think creatively about quite different possible ways of responding. Moral imagination, in contrast, invites us to consider varied alternatives, to begin in small ways where we can, and to seek out allies (Nielsen 1987, 1989).

Additionally, as individuals, we often fail to speak out about moral concerns because we fear being implicated. We fear that we will be adversely affected because now others will begin to expose ways we may at times have cut corners. We fear that as we speak out, we will be dragged along by unfolding events, which will in turn take increasing amounts of our time and energy. Finally, we fear reprisals from those whose misconduct is being exposed. All these fears call for realistic assessments. Still, often by effectively preparing our cases, by remaining clear about the issues at stake, by using our imagination, and by seeking the support of colleagues, we can protect ourselves both from being further implicated and from becoming over-committed.

Nonetheless, the extent to which individuals feel free to voice their moral concerns is often greatly affected by the milieu and structures of organizations of which they are a part. In several decisive ways business organizations promote and reinforce moral silence and its corollary, moral deafness. For example, many organizations effectively discourage or block overt expressions of dissent, questioning, and criticizing. They do so in the first place by not establishing accessible means for employees, managers, and other stakeholders to raise concerns, air complaints, and make inquiries. Few firms have established effective due process or employee voicing systems that might allow and encourage constituents of organizations regularly to express their moral concerns (Ewing, 1989; Saunders and Leck, 1993). Moreover, many firms that establish some kind of mechanism for employees to speak out about moral issues tend to invite primarily the most accusatory expressions. They establish anonymous hotlines or especially welcome statements providing evidence of violations of organizational standards. These mechanisms do not invite two-way discussions. Rather than risk possibly irretrievably damaging someone else's reputation or career, and rather than risk reprisals for actions that seem only a little out of line, many business people have chosen to remain silent. Accusatory forms for raising moral concerns do not invite discussions, inquiries, or tentative explorations. Other firms further stifle open communication by penalizing people when their concern about some particular violations turn out to be unfounded. In the process they suppress efforts to question and seek clarification about moral issues.

Certain top-down patterns of organizational direction and accountability also foster moral muteness. Directions and policies are expected to begin at the top and subordinates are then checked for their compliance. The difficulty with this pattern is not that it is hierarchical. Most patterns of authority are, after all, hierarchical. Rather, problems arise because the communications between superiors and subordinates are not two-way, reciprocating, and interactive. Subordinates are given little room to set agendas, initiate concerns, or bargain about priorities (Westley, 1990). Because subordinates work within parameters set by superiors, they are unlikely to raise moral issues not overtly contained within these limits (Ackerman, 1975).

In an ironic way, certain forms of self-serving moral talk seem to give rise to moral muteness and moral deafness. Minimally, they seem to discourage give and take conversations about moral issues. Occasionally, business people use moral talk to call attention to their high ideals, to point to praiseworthy performance for which they or their firms claim credit, and to expose the blatant moral abuses of others. These are indeed legitimate uses of moral discourse so long as they do not become too prevalent and they are balanced with uses of moral discourse for self-criticism and learning, for problem solving, for mobilizing support, and the like (Bird, Westley, and Waters, 1990; Waters, 1980). The problem with praising, blaming, and idealizing is that, when they become the dominant expression of moral concern, they make it seem as if ethics is almost entirely concerned with the acts of saints and sinners (Waters, 1980). As a result, the everyday uses of moral discourse – to think about and address problems, to share common values, to exercise judgment, and to set forth and undertake responsibilities – are ignored or marginalized. Instead, ethics is associated in a very limited way with exceptionally good or deplorably bad conduct. Correspondingly, the excessive use of moral talk to praise, idealize, and blame tends to discourage rather than invite moral discussion and deliberation. Furthermore, people often praise, blame, or idealize to reinforce their own positions. As a result, many others do not voice their genuine moral concerns, in part because talking overtly about moral issues often seems to be associated with the morally questionable practices of cutting off debate, diverting attention from other genuine moral concerns, and singing one's own praises.

Bibliography

Ackerman, R. (1975). *The Social Challenge to Business.* Cambridge, MA: Harvard University Press.

Bird, F. (1996). *The Muted Conscience: Moral Silence and the Practice of Ethics in Business.* Westport, CT: Quorum Books.

Bird, F. (2001). Good governance: A philosophical discussion of the responsibilities and practices of organizational governors. *Canadian Journal of Administrative Studies*, 18 (4), 298–312.

Bird, F., Westley, F., and Waters, J. A. (1990). The uses of moral talk: Why do managers talk ethics? *Journal of Business Ethics*, 8, 75–89.

Ewing, D. W. (1989). *Justice on the Job: Resolving Grievances in the Non-Union Workplace.* Boston, MA: Harvard Business School Press.

Friedman, M. (1971). The social responsibility of business is to increase its profit. *New York Times Magazine*, September 13, 32–3.

Hirschman, A. (1970). *Exit, Voice, and Loyalty.* Cambridge, MA: Harvard University Press.

Mayer, M. (1990). *The Greatest Bank Robbery Ever: The Collapse of the Savings and Loan Industry.* New York: Charles Scribner's Sons.

Nielsen, R. (1987). What can managers do about unethical management? *Journal of Business Ethics*, 6, 309–20.

Nielsen, R. (1989). Changing unethical behavior. *Academy of Management Executive*, 3 (2), 123–30.

Saunders, D. and Leck, J. D. (1993). Formal upward communication procedures: Organizational and employee perspectives. *Canadian Journal of Administrative Studies*, 10 (3), 255–68.

Vandiver, K. (1972). Why should my conscience bother me? In R. Heilbroner et al. (eds.), *In the Name of Profit.* Garden City, NY: Doubleday.

Waters, J. A. (1980). Of saints, sinners, and socially responsible executives. *Business and Society*, winter, 66–73.

Westley, F. (1990). The microdynamics of inclusion: Middle managers and strategy. *Strategic Management Journal*, 11, 337–52.

moral projection, principle of

Kenneth E. Goodpaster

is formulated as follows: "It is appropriate not only to describe organizations (and their characteristics) by analogy with individuals, it is also appropriate normatively to look for and to foster moral attributes in organizations by analogy with those we look for and foster in individuals" (Goodpaster, 1983). The intuitive idea is straightforward: to explore the analogy between persons and organizations in order to determine whether and how it might guide descriptive and normative ethical thinking about either.

Critics of the principle of moral projection (Ranken, 1987) have argued that the analogy between persons and organizations is not only imperfect in certain respects, but also dangerous, in that it could have the effect of reducing needed attention to individual responsibility in corporate settings. Defenders reply that affirming corporate responsibility is not inconsistent with affirming individual responsibility as well in situations where both apply.

Put in its simplest terms, the principle of moral projection states that we can and should expect no more and no less of our institutions (taken as moral units) than we expect of ourselves (as individuals). In particular, moral responsibility is an attribute that we should look for and try to foster in individuals. The principle of moral projection, therefore, invites us to explore the analogues of moral responsibility for organizations. "Corporate responsibility" could then be seen as the moral projection of the idea of responsibility in its ordinary (individual) meaning, viz. perception, reasoning, and action rooted in a basic concern for stakeholders (Stone, 1976: 114).

See also *moral status of corporations*

Bibliography

Goodpaster, K. E. (1983). The concept of corporate responsibility. *Journal of Business Ethics*, 2 (1), 1–22. (An earlier formulation appears in Goodpaster and Matthews (1982) Can a corporation have a conscience? *Harvard Business Review*, January–February.)

Ranken, N. (1987). Corporations as persons: Objections to Goodpaster's "principle of moral projection." *Journal of Business Ethics*, 6 (8), 633–7. (Also see Goodpaster (1987), The principle of moral projection: A reply to Professor Ranken. *Journal of Business Ethics*, 6 (4), 329–32.)

Stone, C. (1976). *Where the Law Ends: The Social Control of Corporate Behavior*. New York: Harper and Row.

moral status of corporations

Larry M. May

The moral status of the corporation is dependent on the moral features of the corporation and on the moral status of the members of the corporation. At the heart of the philosophical subfield called business ethics are central questions of metaphysics, ethical theory, and social philosophy related to the status of the business corporation. Of chief concern are these questions: Is the corporation ontologically distinct from the individual persons who compose it? Does the corporation have responsibilities, and to whom? Does the corporation have moral rights and are they equivalent to those of individual humans? Does the regulation of corporations pose special moral problems? Questions of ontology, responsibility, and rights have always been the proper purview of philosophy and so it is easy to understand why philosophers have gravitated recently to these questions in business ethics.

The moral status of the corporation is intimately linked with its metaphysical status, for only if the corporation is a distinct moral entity, specifically a moral agent, does the corporation have a distinct moral standing, separate from the entities (individual human persons) who make it up. Of course, the corporation could have an auxiliary or dependent moral status even if the corporation was not a moral agent. While this is in itself an important point, most of what follows will ignore this alternative. Instead, the focus will be on questions of agency, responsibility, and rights of a corporation *per se*.

The corporation exists, but what kind of existence is this? There are at least three ways to answer this question. First, the corporation may exist in the way that a "heap" exists, as merely the category which stands for the collection of entities which happen to compose it. Second, the corporation may exist as a "unity," where the form of the corporation (its organizational structure) is what renders it unique, but where the substance of the corporation is entirely made up of other things. Third, the corporation may exist somehow in its own right, as a formally and substantially "unique thing."

The question of whether the corporation is an agent can be addressed in a similar way to the question of whether the corporation exists. First, a corporation may be an agent in the sense that "corporate action" is merely a shorthand way to refer to how discrete individual human persons act. Second, a corporation may be an agent vicariously through the various actors who make up the corporation and who are facilitated in their actions by the corporation's organizational structure. Third, a corporation may be an agent in its own right, perhaps as much an actor as is the collection of body parts that make up a human actor. The law treats corporations as full-fledged legal persons that can act in their own right. This is commonly known as "the legal fiction of the corporate person," and hence it is not necessarily useful in determining whether the corporation is a moral person.

One way to approach the question of corporate agency is to ask whether the commonsense understanding of corporate actions can be reduced to individual human actions. In this context the corporation cannot really act on its own; only individual human persons can act. But it is very difficult to make sense completely of corporate actions, such as "Gulf Oil Company acquired XYZ Company," without referring to corporations, or to features of individual human persons. Of course, merely because it is hard to make these complete reductions does not yet tell us that corporate agents should be admitted into our moral universe. But until complete reductions are made, it is intelligible to think of corporations as moral agents.

If corporations are moral agents, what kind of agents are they? Corporations may be full-fledged moral agents or they may be partial or vicarious agents. In order to be full-fledged moral agents there must be some sense in which they can act in a morally significant way on their own. Following the model of individual human action, a locus of choice or intention must be found from which moral actions could issue. The corporate boardroom is the most obvious place to look for such choice or intention. Here the individual choices or intentions of the board members are transformed so that what emerges is a collective choice or intention. For the choices to be the choices of a full-fledged moral agent they must at least resemble the choices that a single human individual would make. But there is a wide diversity of viewpoints about what constitutes choice for a single human individual, and it is not clear what criteria must be satisfied for a collective choice to be ascribable to a corporation. Nonetheless, the more these choices and intentions resemble those cases of individual human choice or intention, the

stronger the case for thinking that a corporation is a full-fledged moral agent.

Vicarious or secondary agency is a weaker form of corporate agency than full-fledged agency. One way to understand vicarious agency is in terms of individual humans who have been authorized to represent the corporation, thereby providing the corporation with a way in which it can act *through* the actions of these individuals. It is common to speak of an employee "acting within the scope of his or her authority." Such expressions belie a moral fact: that for certain previously established purposes, a given act can be given two descriptions. The act always remains primarily an act of a discrete individual human; and the act is secondarily (or vicariously) also an act of a corporation. Whenever authority has been so conveyed, then it is relatively easy to establish this weaker sense of moral agency on the part of a corporation.

Corporations may be morally responsible for harms in several different ways. Most obviously, if a person is harmed directly as a result of a corporate intentional decision, then the corporation is morally responsible for this harm. Responsibility may also apply to corporations for harms that result from negligence, recklessness, or simple omission. Such cases are more or less problematic, depending on the difficulty of telling whether the corporation's contribution to a harm was in some sense morally faulty. In Anglo-American law there are three main types of fault: intentional wrongdoing, negligence, and recklessness.

Corporations can engage in intentional wrongdoing and hence be morally responsible and blameworthy on this basis. It is rare that a corporation sets out to do wrong to a person in the same way that an individual agent might intend to do harm to another out of revenge or anger. The most obvious explanation for the rarity here is that corporations do not have any recognized way of displaying or feeling anger or revenge. The corporation can make decisions, and those decisions may be based on the emotional reactions of the members of the board of directors. Nonetheless, corporations could decide to harm a person, especially if it would advance the interests of the corporations to do so. But normally the threat of adverse publicity will make this very unlikely. Far more common is that corporations decide to do things which will risk harm to persons so as to more expeditiously advance their interests.

Corporate negligence is the most common basis upon which corporate moral responsibility can be based. Negligence is the failure to display due care, that is, care which a reasonable person would take. Decision-making in the corporate domain is so focused on serving the goals of the charter, or the interests of investors, etc., that it is relatively common for corporations to fail to take into account the possible harms of their decisions. But for these failures to constitute moral negligence, it must also be the case that reasonable people would have taken those possible harms into account. An interesting example concerned a decision by the Boeing Company to build their 727 line of aircraft so that all of the backup electrical systems were in the same part of the plane. In the event of an accident it was possible that all of the backup systems could be disabled at once, leaving the plane unmaneuverable and the passengers on the plane in great peril. Of course, no one at Boeing intended to harm anyone by making this decision. But it did seem unreasonable for them to have done this, given the risks of harm to their passengers. This is a fairly straightforward case of corporate moral negligence.

An example of corporate moral recklessness concerned a decision by the Ford Motor Company to place the gas tank on the Ford Pinto in a position so close to the back of the car that it could explode upon fairly low-speed collisions. What made this case one of recklessness was that key members of Ford's management knew of the problem and knew that it would cost very little to fix it, but decided to take the risk. Here, a rare internal memorandum surfaced which indicated that Ford had actually calculated how many people were likely to die and how much Ford would be likely to lose in wrongful-death lawsuits, compared to how much it would cost to fix the Pintos so that it was far less likely the gas tanks would explode. This was judged in a court of law in Indiana to be reckless because of the decision to go ahead with a known risk that no reasonable person would inflict on the populace. The moral assessment would be similar.

In addition to the responsibilities to individual persons, corporations also have more broadly based social responsibilities. While it is controversial how extensive these responsibilities are, nearly everyone recognizes the responsibility that corporations have not to harm or risk harm to the larger society, by such acts as discriminatory hiring or polluting the water sources in a particular locale. Milton Friedman, a well-known critic of most social responsibilities for corporations, has said that the chief social responsibility of business corporations is to make a profit. But even this view supports the general idea that there are various customs in each locale, concerning what are appropriate and inappropriate actions which affect the overall well-being of a society.

On the other side of the balance sheet from corporate moral responsibilities, are corporate moral rights. Corporate moral rights can be divided into commercial and non-commercial rights. Commercial rights generally concern rights to property, rights to profit, and generally rights to determine how the corporation is run. Non-commercial corporate rights concern such things as rights to free speech, and generally rights to exert influence in the public domain. The basis of rights can come from the moral agency of the corporation, or from the moral interests of the corporation. In either case, the ascription of moral rights to corporations is based on an analogy to the ascription of moral rights to persons.

Commercial rights of corporations are moral if they affect moral duties, liberties, privileges, or immunities. The property rights of corporations are moral rights if, for instance, they restrict the range of moral options that individuals or groups have in behaving toward that corporation. Property rights generally are rights to the exclusive (or nearly exclusive) ownership and use of a given thing. In most modern corporations, ownership and control are divided to the extent that, while the shareholders own the corporation, it is normally management (in a sense employed by the shareholders) which controls the activities of the corporation. The property rights of a modern corporation create moral options related to control for managers and moral options related to ownership for shareholders, but the divided nature of corporate property makes it often hard to tell who should be afforded what moral privilege or immunity.

Corporate rights to profit are even harder to ascertain morally. While it seems reasonable that corporations are morally entitled to keep whatever surplus value is generated from their production processes, things get cloudier when these profits are generated by windfalls or exploitative conditions. Indeed, the moral right to profit seems to virtually everyone to be limited based on how that profit was generated. The same could be said of all commercial corporate rights. Since commercial rights themselves are justified by their social productiveness, when the overall social effect is negative, rights may be restricted as well. The corporation generally has the right to decide how it is run as long as its being run this way is not likely to be harmful to the overall social welfare.

Non-commercial rights of corporations derive their moral force from analogy with similar rights for individual humans. The Anglo-American legal tradition recognizes corporations as legal persons with very similar rights to other persons. Morally, to the extent that corporate agents resemble human agents, corporations will have a basis for rights to free speech similar to that which human persons have. But the problem with this strategy is that corporations are not the kind of agents whose voices necessarily add to the political process when they participate. Indeed, corporations have a history of drowning out the rest of the voices in a political debate. And these corporations are rarely the kind of agents who are vulnerable and hence in need of the kind of protection which free-speech rights afford. For these reasons, most corporations will not have the same, or as weighty, non-commercial rights as will individual humans.

Finally, corporations may be considered morally virtuous or morally evil, but from a more roundabout route. While a plausible case can be made for seeing corporations as limited agents, it is far harder to see them as having characters that can be morally assessed except in a very derivative form. But the leading members of a corporation may convey a character to a corporation by the way these members conduct themselves while acting on the behalf of the corporation. It is also possible for a succession of virtuous leading members of a corporation to convey good character to a corporation over many years. But should the moral characters of the leading members change, then so will the "character" of the corporation. The regulation of corporations does not pose the same sort of moral problems as it does for individual humans, except in limited cases of rights violation, since the lack of distinct moral character of the corporation means that there is no prima facie basis for respecting corporate autonomy.

Bibliography

Berle, A. A. and Means, G. C. (1933). *The Modern Corporation and Private Property*. New York: Macmillan.

Copp, D. (1979). Collective actions and secondary actions. *American Philosophical Quarterly*, 16, 177–86.

De George, R. (1990). *Business Ethics*, 3rd edn. New York: Macmillan.

Donaldson, T. (1982). *Corporations and Morality*. Englewood Cliffs, NJ: Prentice-Hall.

French, P. A. (1984). *Collective and Corporate Responsibility*. New York: Columbia University Press.

Fuller, L. L. (1967). *Legal Fictions*. Stanford, CA: Stanford University Press.

May, L. (1987). *The Morality of Groups*. Notre Dame, IN: University of Notre Dame Press.

Soloman, R. C. (1992). *Ethics and Excellence: Cooperation and Integrity in Business*. New York: Oxford University Press.

Velasquez, M. (1983). Why corporations are not morally responsible for anything they do. *Business and Professional Ethics Journal*, 2, 1–18.

Werhane, P. (1985). *Persons, Rights, and Corporations*. Englewood Cliffs, NJ: Prentice-Hall.

motives

Edwin M. Hartman

You have a motive for performing an act if and only if there is something to be said for it from your point of view. You have a motive for doing anything that is in your interest, though in some cases you may have a stronger motive for not doing something of that kind. Motives can be causes of behavior even though we sometimes identify them through the behavior they cause, and usually cannot identify the law-like regularities that link cause and effect.

Philosophers have long argued over whether one has any motivation to be moral. "Why should I be moral?" is a standard question in moral philosophy. Some philosophers who have posed it have thought moral behavior to be costly in itself – for example, to involve sacrifices and missed opportunities – and so to need some compensating justification. Religions have promised post-mortem rewards: some people have held that honesty and other virtues, for organizations as well as individuals, constitute the best policy. Game theorists have demonstrated that universally selfish behavior may make everyone in a community worse off than all would be if all were unselfish (see GAME THEORY).

One assumption common to nearly all the philosophers of the Western tradition, with Aristotle as the most notable exception, is that narrow self-interest is the motive behind all or most intentional actions, and the most comprehensible reason for acting. Psychological egoism, the doctrine that all intentional actions are that way, can defend itself finally only by retreating into tautology. There is no good reason to deny that many acts are motivated by charity, concern for one's family and friends, patriotic sentiment, or compassion: in some instances it would be extraordinary for an agent to put personal convenience ahead of the chance to avert disaster for someone else.

Kant, much influenced by Christian pietism, suggests that moral action is a matter of goodness winning out over the agent's natural selfishness. Some of Kant's successors in business ethics have been read as arguing that moral action is necessarily unselfish, even if it must be opposed to one's own best interests – to put it crudely, that being moral must hurt (see KANTIAN ETHICS).

One's interests are in fact primary motivators; in the sense that they may encompass the prosperity of one's friends, the happiness of one's children, the success of one's organization or even one's favorite charity. For some people, these are components of happiness. Aristotle states that the surest sign of character is what gives one pleasure: good people find pleasure in good deeds, bad ones in bad. The one who manages to resist temptations to be immoral is less praiseworthy and less reliable; the one who does the right thing in hope of some reward is worse yet. Worst is the agent for whom morality is no motivating consideration at all.

Among the philosophers who believe that morality can be a motive for acting are so-called internalists, who argue that an agent has no moral obligation to do anything that he or she has no motive for doing. One assumption that supports internalism is that moral obligation is something one may accept or not. Internalism suggests a contract theory of morality, but not all contract theorists are internalists. The more common view is externalism, according to which whether an act is morally good is a matter of whether it meets moral standards that are separate from (external to) the agent. Moral realism, the view that there are actual moral facts that our moral theories seek to state or explain, implies externalism, but not the other way around.

One of the abiding questions of ethics is whether a good act is necessarily done out of good motives, as opposed to selfish ones, for example. Consequentialists like Mill answer negatively, deontologists like Kant affirmatively. Kant goes so far as to claim that only the good will really counts in morality, and that one is not in the fullest sense responsible for the consequences of one's good intentions. Few moral philosophers and fewer managers would agree that it is enough to be well-meaning (see CONSEQUENTIALISM).

I may have a motive for an action and yet not do it. For example, I may find there is reason to fire an employee because of bad performance, but may refrain out of personal loyalty. Or I may fire the employee on account of both incompetence and dishonesty. A corporate decision to support a local charity may have multiple motives in a similar way. The two motives are then jointly sufficient conditions of the behavior, whether or not either by itself would suffice.

A manager who wants a moral organization might prefer that the employees do the right thing for the best possible reason, but would likely settle for one in which morally good behavior is the result of incentives carefully designed to motivate the selfish. To a manager who wants employees to be motivated by moral considerations a strong corporate culture is an attractive vehicle, for it can to some degree socialize employees to want to be honest, loyal, and so on – that is, to be people of good character in Aristotle's sense.

It is a largely empirical question whether and when an appropriate corporate culture is a more effective device for ensuring moral behavior than are the incentives of money and status. The former may well be more effective and the latter less so for large, diversified organizations in turbulent environments: for in these, position descriptions and performance criteria will not form a valid or reliable basis for incentives, especially where teamwork is essential to production. There it is more effective to get employees to identify with the organization's success, which will then be itself a motivator. In any case, if employees are as selfish as Kant suggests all people are, managers will have great difficulty in creating a moral organization, no matter what they do.

Bibliography

Aristotle (1985). *Nichomachean Ethics*, trans. T. Irwin. Indianapolis, IN: Hackett.

Davidson, D. (1980). *Essays on Actions and Events*. New York: Oxford. (Contains an influential defense of the view that reasons are causes of actions.)

Kant, I. (1959). *Foundations of the Metaphysics of Morals*, trans. L. W. Beck. New York: Liberal Arts Press.

Mill, J. S. (1957). *Utilitarianism*. Indianapolis, IN: Bobbs-Merrill.

Sen, A. K. (1987). *On Ethics and Economics*. Cambridge, MA: Blackwell. (Includes a critical analysis of psychological egoism.)

motives and self-interest

Robert H. Frank

A *New Yorker* cartoon once depicted a distinguished looking gentleman taking his grandson for a walk in a wood. "It's good to know about trees," he tells the boy, adding: "Just remember, nobody ever made big money knowing about trees." This advice nicely captures the modern economist's view of human nature. Unselfish motives may exist, the economist reluctantly concedes, but in our bitterly competitive world, people indulge them at their peril.

Cynical though it is, the self-interest model has yielded important insights. It tells us, for example, why car pools form in the wake of rising fuel prices; why divorce rates are higher in countries that have liberal welfare benefits; why energy use is lower in apartments that have separately metered utilities; and so on.

Yet many other behaviors do not fit the me-first caricature. When traveling, we leave tips in restaurants we never expect to visit again. We donate anonymously to private charities. We often incur costs to dispose of unwanted pesticides properly rather than simply pour them down the drain. Soldiers dive atop hand grenades to save the lives of their comrades. Seen through the lens of modern self-interest theory, these behaviors might seem the human equivalent of planets traveling in square orbits.

Recent research, however, suggests how noble human behaviors might not only survive the ruthless pressures of the material world, but might actually be nurtured by them as well. This research builds on the observation that people often confront problems in which the conscious, direct pursuit of self-interest is self-defeating.

An example is the case of the owner of a profitable business who is currently weighing an opportunity to open a branch in a distant city. He knows that if he hires an honest manager the branch will return high profits, but that otherwise it will lose money. One of his employees wants the job and is fully qualified for it. The owner would be willing to double her current salary if he could be sure that she would manage honestly. He knows, however, that if she manages dishonestly, she will be able to make three times her current salary.

In standard economic models, this option spells doom for the branch operation. Reasoning from the self-interest model, the owner concludes that since the employee could earn more by managing dishonestly, she will do so. And since this means the branch will be a loser, the owner does not open it. The irony, of course, is that this choice leaves both the owner and his employee worse off than if the owner were to open the branch and the employee were to manage it honestly.

In this scenario we have what economists call a "commitment problem." This problem could be solved if the employee could credibly commit herself to manage honestly. In situations like these the pursuit of material self-interest proves self-defeating.

Traditional economic models try to solve commitment problems by changing the material incentives people face. For example, the owner might try to hire an investigator to monitor the branch manager's performance. But in many cases, the relevant behavior simply cannot be monitored. In such cases, traditional models suggest that solutions do not exist.

Yet commitment problems can often be solved even when behavior cannot be monitored. Solutions require that we relax the assumption that people are motivated only by narrow self-interest. Suppose, for example, that the owner had some means of discovering that his employee was a trustworthy person, and would manage his branch operation honestly even though she could earn much more if she cheated. He could then open the branch with confidence, even though he could not monitor his manager directly. Both the owner and the manager would gain.

This solution relies on two premises: first, that there are people who behave honestly even when they could earn more by cheating; and second, that reliable means exist for identifying these people. The first premise is uncontroversial, but the second invites scrutiny. After all, all managerial candidates have strong incentives to portray themselves as trustworthy, so personal declarations of honesty cannot carry much weight. Investigating a candidate's past record will be illuminating only in those cases where someone has actually been caught doing wrong. It will reveal little about the many cheaters who were shrewd enough to avoid detection. If these methods fail, how can trustworthy persons be identified?

The key is to recognize that honest behavior is motivated not by rational calculations but by emotions – by moral sentiments, to use Adam Smith's term. The employee who walks away from a golden opportunity to cheat is motivated by her sympathy for the owner's interests, and by her feelings of self-esteem, which depend strongly on right conduct. The problem for the would-be cheater is that the emotions that motivate honest behavior are difficult to fake. Once we get to know a person well, we are able to make reliable judgments about her character. The cheater's goal is to appear trustworthy, but given our ability to detect the presence of the emotions that motivate trustworthiness, the easiest way to *appear* trustworthy is actually to *be* trustworthy.

The irony is that the *homo economicus* caricature that populates conventional economic models often does worse, even in purely material terms, than his genuinely trustworthy counterpart. In his single-minded quest to further his own material interests, he becomes unattractive as a partner in situations that require trust. By contrast, the trustworthy person values honest behavior for its own sake, and therefore is much in demand in these situations. The material rewards he reaps are no less valuable for having come unbidden.

Bibliography

Akerlof, G. (1983). Loyalty filters. *American Economic Review*, 73, 54–63.

Frank, R. H. (1988). *Passions Within Reason*. New York: W. W. Norton.

Frank, R. H., Gilovich, T. D., and Regan, D. T. (1993). The evolution of one-shot cooperation: An experiment. *Ethology and Sociobiology*, 14, 247–56.

Gauthier, D. (1985). *Morals by Agreement*. Oxford: Clarendon Press.

Hirshleifer, J. (1987). On the emotions as guarantors of threats and promises. In J. Dupre (ed.), *The Latest on the Best: Essays in Evolution and Optimality*. Cambridge, MA: MIT Press, 307–26.

Schelling, T. (1978). Altruism, meanness, and other potentially strategic behaviors. *American Economic Review*, 68, 229–30.

Sen, A. K. (1985). Goals, commitment, and identity. *Journal of Law, Economics, and Organization*, 1, 341–55.

Skyrms, B. (forthcoming). Darwin meets *The Logic of Decision*: Correlation in evolutionary game theory. *Philosophy of Science*.

multiculturalism

Michael H. Prosser

is an appreciation of diversity, which may range beyond ethnic or racial identities to diverse lifestyles or health-challenged individuals; openness and acceptance of alternative lifestyles; people of different backgrounds living constructively together, cooperating, and getting things done together; and cultures sharing power. Cultural power sharing promotes ideal multiculturalism as the opposite of such negative "isms" like racism, ethnocentrism, sexism, and xenophobism, which stress the fragmented relationship of negative prejudice and power, and racial, cultural, sexual, and domestic/foreign imbalances.

Within larger groupings of society, ideal multiculturalists consist of people in multicultural organizations genuinely committed to a diverse representation of their membership; sensitive to maintaining open, supportive, and responsive environments; working toward and purposefully including elements of diverse cultures in their ongoing operations; and authentic in their responses to issues confronting them with equal power sharing as a primary goal. Gudykunst and Kim identify a model for multicultural human development: "If strangers successfully overcome the multitude of challenges and frustrations that invariably accompany the process of cultural adaptation, they develop a mental and behavioral capacity more adaptable, flexible, and resilient than that of people who have limited exposure to the challenges of continuous intercultural encounters" (Gudykunst and Kim, 1992: 253).

Multiculturalists are uniquely a heritage of the late twentieth century, shaped as much by intercultural and international travel and exchange, computers, Internets, and satellites as by their own personality traits. Peter Adler notes that these new people cannot be defined by the languages they speak, though they are more and more likely to be bilingual or multilingual, nor by their professions, places of residence, or cognitive sophistication. Instead, they are recognized by their developing inclusive outlooks and worldviews, by how they see the universe as a dynamically moving process, by their reflection on the interconnectedness of life and their cultural ecology in their own thoughts and actions, and by how they remain open to new experiences. Adler suggests that the universal character of multicultural persons is an abiding commitment to essential similarities between people everywhere, while paradoxically maintaining an equally strong commitment to their differences. He stresses their psychocultural adaptiveness, always undergoing personal transitions; maintaining indefinite self-boundaries; and continuously living in a state of creative tension (cited in Prosser, 1989: 70–3). Thus, the ideal multicultural society serves as a symbol of acceptance and protection for all, including those who least have power.

Multicultural persons often find themselves working in multinational organizations with a dominant home country or cultural base where the major organizational decisions are made, or in international organizations where power is shared more evenly among cultural groups. Geert Hofstede suggests that since power sharing is an important ingredient of effective multicultural relationships, there are common challenges in managing multicultural, multinational, or international organizations. These include the necessity to create their own strong and unique subcultures, especially with considerable cultural diversity in the organizations themselves; choosing partner cultures very carefully, while deciding how much power and decision-making is to be shared; organizing international headquarters sensitively with organizational rewards facing outwards rather than inwards to the center; forming well constructed international teams, for example, with members who themselves have the potential of exemplifying ideal multicultural characteristics; and deciding whether to accept or try to change local cultural habits in host countries and cultures which affect the constructive aspects of the organizations (Hofstede, 1984: 273–6).

Contemporary ethical issues for multicultural persons and multinational and international organizations are significant. Among the strongest cross-cultural sets of ethics developed since World War II has been the 1948 Universal Declaration of Human Rights, with officially accepted principles by all nations joining the United Nations, but honored often only in the breach. Because ethical principles typically are culture specific, multiculturalists tend to form their ethical perspectives either from the viewpoint of their own cultures, or seek to accommodate the opposite culture's ethical precepts. Dean Barnlund states that current ethical questions which influence intercultural/multicultural encounters are entirely new, and call for a metaethic to be used by people from different cultures when ethical dilemmas arise (cited in Gudykunst and Kim, 1992: 264–5). Such a metaethic remains still only an outline.

Gudykunst and Kim stress that the final goal of all multicultural persons is to build community, for the good of the whole, with a full recognition of cultural diversity, and initiated both by societies and individuals, whether at a domestic or international level. To this end, these authors recommend those seeking truly multicultural lives to attempt to live their own lives by following seven community-building principles: *be committed, be mindful, be unconditionally accepting, be concerned for themselves and others, be understanding, be ethical, and be peaceful* (Gudykunst and Kim, 1992: 267–8). The end goal of the ideal multicultural person would seem to aspire toward becoming a "citizen of the world," acknowledging with Socrates that "I am neither a citizen of Athens, nor of Greece, but of the world."

Bibliography

Gudykunst, W. B. and Kim, Y. Y. (1992). *Communicating with Strangers: An Approach to Intercultural Communication*, 2nd edn. New York: McGraw Hill.

Hofstede, G. (1984). *Culture's Consequences: International Differences in Work-Related Values*, abridged edn. Beverly Hills, CA: Sage.

Prosser, M. H. (1989). *The Cultural Dialogue: An Introduction to Intercultural Communication*. Washington, DC: SIETAR International.

multinational corporations

Richard T. De George

are corporations that have operations in more than one country (host countries) but are controlled by a headquarters in a home country. Multinationals have been the focus of three groups of ethical disputes.

1   By which rules are multinationals bound: those of the home country or those of the host country? One view defends the position that "when in Rome, do as the Romans do." This is rejected by those who equate this view with ethical relativism and argue that although a company should obey local laws and customs whenever possible, a multinational may not, for example, employ forced labor or discriminate on the basis of race or gender, even if these practices are locally accepted.

2   The differential in power between large, powerful multinationals and less developed countries has led to such charges as exploiting labor and resources; undermining local cultures; raising expectations that cannot be fulfilled; ignoring the safety and health of host countries; and causing malnutrition and starvation by buying up the most productive land for cash crops. Multinationals have an obligation to take special care when operating in less developed countries.

3   Because of the lack of adequate international institutions and laws, some charge that multinational companies can fix prices in transfer payments, avoid taxes, and circumvent national legal restrictions. The problems and temptations of multinationals have led to international and industry codes and other attempts at international control. Many companies of integrity, conscious of the ethical pitfalls facing multinationals, have adopted their own codes or guidelines to ensure ethical activity.

Bibliography

Barnet, R. J. and Ronald, E. M. (1974). *Global Reach: The Power of the Multinational Corporations*. New York: Simon and Schuster.

De George, R. T. (1993). *Competing With Integrity in International Business*. New York: Oxford University Press.

Donaldson, T. (1989). *The Ethics of International Business*. New York: Oxford University Press.

Hoffman, W. M., Lange, A., and Fedo, D. A. (eds.), (1986). *Ethics and the Multinational Enterprise*. Lanham, MD: University Press of America.

multinational marketing

Brian Harvey

is marketing across national boundaries, often by companies whose manufacturing operations are also multinational. Multinational marketing has generated some specific ethical issues that are represented by well-known cases. These cases relate to particular products, such as pesticides, pharmaceuticals, armaments, and infant formula. They also concern the methods used to promote them, ranging from the sales and advertising techniques employed to the extent of the existence of bribery and corruption. The concerns focus especially on the impact of Western multinational corporations on less developed countries and, as a consequence, embrace the role of corporate, industry, home-government, and international codes in regulating the process of multinational marketing.

A Western multinational's marketing and promotion practices in less developed countries were at the heart of the Nestlé infant formula case. An exhaustive account of the controversy has been given by Prakash Sethi (1994). Critics argued that Nestlé irresponsibly persuaded poor mothers to buy an artificial food that they could not afford, and that they could not use safely in conditions of low water quality and hygiene. By encouraging a move away from breast feeding, and the use of an infant formula product that was likely to be diluted and contaminated, the critics claimed that the company was adding to the incidence of infant disease and death. The marketing and promotion methods used included direct promotion to mothers, consumer advertising, free samples in hospitals, inducive packaging and labeling, promotion to doctors and other healthcare workers, saleswomen dressed as nurses to "promote" or "educate" mothers of newborn babies in hospitals, and commission-based compensation systems (Sethi, 1994: 120)

Nestlé's position was that the company was a legitimate and accepted participant in the multinational market for a product that was safe and useful, and that they used marketing practices that were both legal and ethical.

The multinational marketing of pharmaceuticals and pesticides presents industrial corporations with some fundamental ethical challenges. A pharmaceutical product may be banned in the home country (for example, the United States), but less developed countries may not have the means to regulate or effectively monitor the pharmaceuticals market. A multinational marketer has the opportunity to exploit the situation by deceptive changes in the product's formulation, name, or country of origin. But it might be argued that conformity to home-country regulations is not an ethical requirement for a corporation in its multinational marketing. For example, the potential net social benefits of a product's use may be different in the different circumstances of a less developed country; the effectiveness of the pesticide DDT in combatting malaria could well be regarded as outweighing the increased risk of human cancer in a DDT-contaminated environment – a consideration that caused it to be banned in some countries. But in what forum can such a decision legitimately be made? The absence of an institutional framework for making such decisions in the host country, or internationally, means that corporations and industries cannot escape the necessity to confront issues of business ethics and regulate themselves. Richard De George argues "not to cause direct harm and to produce more good than harm to the host country remain the operating ethical norms, together with the general prohibition against deception and lying" (De George, 1993: 62).

De George's principles might also be applied to the multinational marketing of banking and financial services. Snoy (1989) illustrates the ethical issues in international lending to less developed countries: to what extent should banks accept responsibility, or a share of it, for the social impact of the selection of projects to be funded, or of the efficiency and honesty with which the funds are applied to those projects; and where development projects fail, what represents a fair sharing of the burden of financial adjustment? De George quotes the example of the Bank of Commerce and Credit International to epitomize the harm a bank can do: "Beyond facilitating fraud and embezzlement, it provided a financial conduit for illegal drug and arms traffic, laundered illegally acquired moneys

[and] supplied secret accounts for illegal flight capital" (De George, 1993: 68).

Bibliography

De George, R. (1993). *Competing with Integrity in International Business.* New York: Oxford University Press.

Sethi, S. P. (1994). *Multinational Corporations and the Impact of Public Advocacy on Corporate Strategy: Nestlé and the Infant Formula Controversy.* Boston, MA: Kluwer.

Snoy, B. (1989). Ethical issues in international lending. *Journal of Business Ethics*, August, 635–9.

nanotechnology

Rosalyn W. Berne

Nanoscience and nanotechnology involve the study, control, manipulation, and assembly of multifarious nanoscale components into materials, systems, and devices to serve human interests and needs. Since a nanometer measurement is equivalent to one billionth of a meter, scientific research and technological development at this scale is fantastically small. Documents from the US National Nanotechnology Initiative describe nanotechnology as "the ability to work at the molecular level, atom by atom, to create large structures with fundamentally new properties and functions" (Roco and Bainbridge, 2001). Nanoscience and nanotechnology seek to understand and then mimic nature, by imitating nature's own mastery of the atoms. The Nano Business Alliance, a US trade group, estimates nanotechnology's annual global revenues to be $45.5 billion, including microelectronic devices, while the National Science Foundation has projected that number to be $1 trillion by the year 2015.

Early inspiration and vision for the pursuit of nanoscience and nanotechnology is widely credited to physicist Richard P. Feynman and his December 1959 speech at the annual meeting of the American Physical Society at the California Institute of Technology entitled, "There's plenty of room at the bottom." He concluded that speech with a financial challenge, offering $1,000 to the "first guy who can take the information on the page of a book and put it on an area 1/25,000 smaller in linear scale in such a manner that it can be read by an electron telescope." In 1982 Gerd Binnig and Heinrich Rohrer invented the scanning tunneling microscope (STM), which made Feynman's challenge technically feasible and essentially marked the technological beginning of nanoscience and nanotechnology research. IBM patented the invention and demonstrated the microscope's incredible power by writing the initials "IBM" with thirty-five individual xenon atoms.

Thirty years after Feynman's speech, also at the California Institute of Technology, US President Bill Clinton gave an address on science and technology to students and faculty, in which he announced "a major new national nanotechnology initiative worth $500 million." The US National Nanotechnology Initiative followed. Many other initiatives have been launched worldwide in Japan, Taiwan, Singapore, South Africa, South Korea, Brazil, Germany, France, Australia, Switzerland, and the European Union. The significant annual increases in their financial appropriations points to significant political and economic motivations of governments to fuel the pursuit of this new area of scientific knowledge and to accelerate and advance technical understanding and control of the material world. Together with private, major corporations, venture capital groups, start up businesses, and other private and national laboratories, the enormity of the financial investments in nanoscience and nanotechnology initiatives is unparalleled.

The National Science Foundation touts nanoscience as leading to "dramatic changes in the ways materials, devices, and systems are understood and created," and lists among the envisioned breakthroughs "orders-of-magnitude increases in computer efficiency, human organ restoration using engineered tissue, 'designer' materials created from direct assembly of atoms and molecules, and the emergence of entirely new phenomena in chemistry and physics." One industry leader testified before the House

Science Congressional Subcommittee: "Nanotechnology is becoming nanobusiness faster than anyone imagined...With a plethora of products on the market and more on the way, it is no longer prudent to view nanotechnology as just a science" (Marty, 2003). US Senator Barbara Mikulski stated, "We are poised to take the next major leap into the future where the possibilities are endless" (cited in Roco and Bainbridge, 2001: appendix B).

Business has taken an active and aggressive leadership role in nanotechnology policy, information dissemination, and economic development. The industry association Nano Business Alliance, for example, was founded to "advance the emerging business of nanotechnology and Microsystems." Its stated mission is "to create a collective voice for the emerging small tech industry and develop a range of initiatives to support and strengthen the nanotechnology business community." The statement does not include any mention of ethics. The alliance's founding leaders were House Speaker Newt Gingrich and venture capitalist Steve Jurvetson, as well as leaders from HP, IBM, GE, AGFA, Deloitte and Touche, the NNI, and others. Although US based, the alliance also has affiliates in the EU, Canada, and Israel.

Nanotechnology pioneer K. Eric Drexler envisions that molecular assemblers could make possible low cost solar power; cures for cancer and the common cold; cleanup of the environment; inexpensive pocket supercomputers; accessible space flight; and limitless acquisition and exchange of information through hypertext (Drexler et al., 1991). Some dismiss such claims as "hype," not representative of scientifically grounded reality. Nobel Laureate Richard Smalley, Harvard University chemist George Whitesides, and others, dispute Drexler's claims of what will actually be the likely result of our abilities to build devices and enact various technological processes at such miniscule scales. For example, Smalley (2001) disagrees with Drexler that we will one day be able to create self-replicating, self-assembling devices. Whitesides (2001) concurs, saying that we have no sense of how to design a self-sustaining, self-replicating system of machines. There is a great deal of speculation and debate over future outcomes and applications, and no one knows if the machines we create will be able to do the things hoped for, such as "scavenge molecules from their environment to reproduce themselves, creating an unlimited number of molecular robots that can perform feats of engineering that defy our imagination" (Michio, 1997).

The Canadian-based ETC group, a nanotechnology watchdog organization, is concerned that nanotechnology development is moving quickly, without any real oversight regarding environmental safety, public health, and other societal concerns. ETC identifies three phases of nanotechnology development. The first (which is already well underway) involves bulk production of nano-scale particles for use in sprays, powders, coatings, fabrics, etc. In these applications, nanoparticles contribute to lighter, cleaner, stronger, more durable surfaces and systems. In the second phase, the goal is to manipulate and assemble nanoscale particles into supra-molecular constructions for practical uses. Third would be the phase of mass production (possibly self-replicating nanoscale robots) to manufacture any material, on any scale. Finally, according to the ETC, nanomaterials will be used to affect biochemical and cellular processes, such as for engineering joints, performing cellular functions, or combining biological with non-biological materials for self-assembly or repair (Genomes to Atoms, 2003).

Early development has already produced nanoscaled devices such as nanoscale storage and nanotube transistors, molecular transistors and switches, atomic force microscopes, focused ion and electron beam microscopes, novel materials, nanowires and nanostructure-enabled devices, non-volatile RAM, nano-optics, nanoparticle solubilization for drug delivery, and nano-encapsulation for drug delivery (Forbes/Wolfe, 2003). Private investors and major companies worldwide continue to commit large and increasing amounts of funding to the potentially revolutionary breakthroughs and spin-offs of nanotechnology in intellectual property, instrumentation, novel materials, modeling, platform techniques, and nano-biotechnology (Forbes/Wolfe, 2003).

Ethics-concerned critics point to the rapid emergence of nanoscience and nanotechnology as a social–cultural undertaking, fueled by scientific ingenuity, political pressures, venture capital motivations, and dominant conceptions of public good. They assert nanoscience is going forward too quickly, before adequate moral meaning and evaluation can be created. They express concern that moral meaning and evaluation should not wait until after nanoscience discovery and nanotechnology developments emerge from the laboratory. They suggest that we take nanoscience and nanotechnology seriously now, while it is still developing (e.g., Mnyusiwalla, Daar, and Singer, n.d.). Further, because of such potential dangers as freely migrating carbon nanotubes penetrating plant, animal, and human cells, or uncontrollable self-assemblers, if we do not take heed now, it may soon be too late for society to respond effectively and proactively, and to avert any consequential and irreversible harms. Conversely, there are those who defend the pursuit of nanoscience and nanotechnology on moral grounds as relatively benign enterprises, representing a good and natural evolution in scientific inquiry. They suggest that as with any new technology, responsibility for the development of nanotechnology lies principally with the larger society and in the making of public policy. Further, they tend to reject suggestions of a precautionary hold on the development of nanotechnology as keeping humanity from its rightful self-improvement.

In his essay "Why the future doesn't need us," Bill Joy (n.d.) reflected on the potential dangers of genetics, nanotechnology, and robotics, and made just such a suggestion – arguing that it is better to relinquish research and development in this field than to proceed without knowing its possible harmful consequences: "These possibilities are all thus either undesirable or unachievable or both. The only realistic alternative I see is relinquishment: to limit development of the technologies that are too dangerous by limiting our pursuit of certain kinds of knowledge." His writing unleashed vigorous and emotional debate from various sectors of public discourse, and especially from nanotechnology proponents such as Christine Peterson of the Foresight Institute. Foresight has put forward self-regulation guidelines for the development of nanotechnology which, if adopted by research scientists and industries involved, it believes should suffice in addressing ethical concerns over the safe development of nanotechnology. However, there is still lack of agreement and consensus over distinctions of fact and fiction in the future outcomes of nanoscience and nanotechnology development, and few clearly articulated nodes of ethical concern.

Extreme reactions, expressed in such writings as Michael Crichton's novel *Prey*, reflect fear over the lack of control we may have with some nanotechnology mechanisms and devices. Such expressions call for moral reflection over assumptions about the inevitability of nanotechnology's development, the risks and harms imbedded in precise, atomic manipulation by humans, and our potential inability to undo our technological ingenuities. Short of the more dramatic and explicit nodes of ethical concern expressed in science fiction (such as nanobot swarms seeking to eat human flesh), there are questions pertaining to equity and access, environmental safety, irreparable and mysterious changes to food, water, and air, privacy and security, and the philosophical considerations of introducing mechanical systems into biological organisms such as the human body. One key ethics consideration is what society should expect from corporations involved in nanotechnology developments. To protect society from possible harm, external controls may have to be put in place to regulate and govern the types of nanotechnology that companies produce. Or will corporations exercise genuine moral responsibility in the development of nanotechnology? Such responsibility might include agreeing to self-regulation, or abiding by more widely adopted rules, principles, and codes, such as those proposed by the Foresight Institute, and/or becoming involved in public policy, citizen review groups, and the like. Provision for access to new fields of educational and technical training is also a socio-ethical node of concern for business, as is the ethical responsibility over risk taking with novel and unpredictable, relatively untested new materials and devices, with public and environmental safety, and the more philosophical questions of how to identify what role industry should play in the "precise human control and manipulation of matter." The release of nanoscaled devices into waterways and into the atmosphere spurs ethical concerns over environmental accidents and abuses. The tremendous potential capability of nanotechnology to improve surveillance systems brings into question the privacy rights of citizens. Its potential to produce powerful and precise new weapons brings into question the purposes and meanings of military combat and intervention. Miniaturization and hybridization of commonly used electronic devices calls into question the assumption that faster and cheaper is equal to better, and raises issues about how market imperatives may be overly influential in leading the rapid development of nanotechnology.

Given the especially subtle but fundamental changes nanotechnology may represent to the way we live our lives, and of the functions of our planet, notions of technological determinism seem to be at stake as well. Given the enormity of potential good to human health, there are also questions to be considered as to who will receive the benefits of nanotechnology developments, at what cost, and to whom. Ownership, power, and control issues regarding devices and processes that are fundamentally invisible to the human eye stimulate interesting ethical challenges to the writing of property law, as much as to the fundamental beliefs and values of human communities. Some political rhetoric uses the language of competition in describing the national nanoscience initiative as a race for the acquisition of nanotechnology. This raises the ethical questions of which countries or world powers will have primary control over the applications of nanotechnology, and what will be their relationships with corporations. If private citizens or companies will have access to the raw materials of nanotechnology, such as carbon nanotubes, or eventually, assemblers, then who will oversee or control the use they make of those materials, such as the building of experimental devices or weapons of mass destruction? Other, perhaps surprising, nodes of ethical concern are likely to emerge, as nanoscience progresses into palpable, more fully appropriated new technologies.

Through the tools now at our disposal, extensions of human hands and eyes (such as the atomic force and atomic probe microscopes) allow us to observe and manipulate atoms directly, move them, rearrange them, and reconfigure them at will. Claims are being made that the material ability of humans to manipulate the atoms, and, from the bottom up, to create atomically built hybrids of synthetic, mechanical, and biological components into novel devices, suggests that we are now embarking on an incredibly powerful, tremendously exciting, but possibly dangerous undertaking. At the very least, the emergence of nanotechnology could mean fundamental and beneficial changes to our relationships with our bodily and material worlds, as we gain greater power to manipulate our environment to the perceived enhancement and welfare of human life.

Where might such awesome abilities lead us? Where does business aim to go with them? What will it mean when nanoscience and nanotechnology enable us to achieve our stated and desired goals? What we do with the knowledge we gain and how we take advantage of this next phase in our technological capacity may determine the changing substance of our material, social, cultural, economic, moral, and perhaps even spiritual lives. Are we prepared to accept and adapt to those changes with full awareness? Are businesses pursuing new product nanotechnology development with conscientious commitment to public and consumer well-being? The ethical challenges are as daunting as the material ones.

Bibliography

Major portions of this entry also appear in M. M. Hubbard (snr. ed.) (2004). *Encyclopedia of Science, Technology and Ethics*. Farmington Hills, MI: Macmillan Library Reference.

Drexler, K. E. et al. (1991). *Unbounding the Future: The Nanotechnology Revolution*. New York: William Monroe.

Forbes/Wolfe (2003). Nanotech Report, 2 (3), March. Subscription electronic newsletter. New York: Forbes and Angstrom Publishing.

Genomes to Atoms, The Big Down, Atomtech: Technologies Converging at the Nano-Scale (2003). January. Available on line at www.etc.org/publications.

Joy, B. (n.d.). Why the future doesn't need us. http://www.wired.com/wired/archive/8.04/joy.html.

Michio, K. (1997). *Visions: How Science Will Revolutionize the 21st Century*. New York: Anchor Books.

Marty, A. (2003). Statement to the Committee on House Science, March 19. Document available at http://web.lexis-nexis.com/.

Mnyusiwalla, A., Daar, A., and Singer, P. (n.d.). Mind the gap: Science and ethics in nanotechnology. Available at http://www.utoronto.ca/jcb/pdf/nanotechnology_paper.pdf

Roco, M. C. and Bainbridge, W. S. (2001). *Societal Impli-cations of Nanoscience and Nanotechnology*. Dordrecht: Kluwer Academic Publishers.

Smalley, R. E. (2001). Of chemistry, love and nanobots. *Scientific American*, September, 77.

Whitesides, G. (2001). The once and future nanoma-chine. *Scientific American*, September, 81.

New Zealand, business ethics in

Alan E. Singer and Alan J. Robb

Since the environment and conduct of New Zea-land business has become increasingly inter-nationalized, business ethics "in" this island nation of 4 million people is now only partially defined by national geography and identity. Accordingly, the main focus of this entry will be upon the more distinctive features of the local culture, institutions, and *zeitgeist*.

In New Zealand there is a national culture that strongly values practicality, while it respects individuality. This is reflected in commerce in general, but especially in the high regard for engineering, construction, and agriculture. In almost all fields, there is a keen monitoring of overseas developments, coupled with a real will-ingness to experiment. Yet, at the same time, there remains some ambivalence toward overseas competition, a tendency to look inwards for solutions to local problems, with an orienta-tion toward cooperative problem solving in groups.

Many people in New Zealand derive a special sense of enlightenment and spiritual replenish-ment from the land itself, and the surrounding oceans. Concern for the environment is now manifest in the Resource Management Act, which creates individual and collective liabilities for pollution, while requiring decisions about resource use to be framed as problems of con-strained optimization. This sense of the land is, in turn, related to the continuing vitality of an indigenous Maori culture. Maori business has some separate institutional arrangements that successfully coexist with and operate alongside the mainstream. Moreover, a number of syner-gies appear to exist between the ethos of Maori business and the more economically rational practices of the mainstream. These synergies may be found in areas such as consensual deci-sion-making, commitments to shared ideals, and the guardianship of natural resources. The latter, in particular, now sees a happy coinci-dence of imperatives flowing from ecological and strategic concerns. Both the tourism indus-try and the cooperative management of exports demand maintenance of the clean and green national image that yields positive country-of-origin effects for a great many Kiwi products and services.

Cooperatives contribute significantly to the New Zealand economy. Some 20 of the top 200 businesses are cooperatives. All share the international cooperative alliance principles expressed thus: "In the tradition of their found-ers, cooperative members believe in the ethical values of honesty, openness, social responsibil-ity, and caring for others." In other areas of business ethics there has been much less conver-gence between cultural ideals and practical real-ity. The concept of a "fair go" is important for the people of New Zealand, yet it has increas-ingly become subordinated to an ideology of the market in all spheres of life. This ideology has itself been heavily marketed by powerful coali-tions, ostensibly and arguably for collective benefit. For example, Equal Employment Op-portunity (EEO) legislation, aimed at directly improving the lot of women, Maori, and Pacific Islanders, quickly became a political football, with the right wing insisting that the market provides equitable outcomes. Thus, concepts of fairness from the center left, such as that con-ceived by Rawls or Kant, are not currently in vogue.

Together with the ethos of the "fair go" comes a corresponding dislike of privilege; yet, paradoxically, the families and associates of the early (ca. 1850) European settlers continue even now to play a disproportionate role in the man-agement, ownership, and control of larger New Zealand businesses (still small by world stand-ards). Moreover, in Maori business, there is some similar tension between positions based upon lineage versus levels of management expertise. Of course, New Zealand is by no means unique among former UK colonies in this regard, nor in its time-honored tendency to indulge in a "fair" share of restrictive and collusive business practices.

There is another characteristic of the Kiwi ethos of relevance to business ethics, that of "she'll be right" (i.e., all will be well). This folksy sentiment may well have been one factor (among others) in some of the more blatant recent lapses of business and professional ethics. Examples include the disappearance of all of a client's funds in the course of a routine domestic property transaction, as well as notable incidences of audited accounts showing profit for important companies about to enter receivership. Nonetheless, there has been considerable willingness to experiment with institutional arrangements. Recently, there have been strong moves to clarify directors' responsibilities, strengthen supervisory agencies, and create a heightened sense of collegiality among various industry bodies. In addition, the serious fraud office in New Zealand is now valiantly and quite successfully striving to prosecute various forms of corporate crime. Despite this, there remains some unease about general standards of business and professional integrity.

A further distinctive element concerns ethics in sports. As in the UK, the links between business and sports have been greatly strengthened, in recent times, with a rapid transition towards professionalism. All the generally accepted limitations of market-based societies have become writ large in this arena, including (1) the distinction between entertainment and actual sporting achievement, (2) sponsorship funds directed at sports that have more TV appeal, (3) limitation of access for those who cannot pay, and (4) controversies about promotions involving liquor and tobacco. Legal battles continue, particularly in the latter arena. Conflicts have also arisen between institutionalized sports practices and commercial principles. For example, a bylaw of the NZRL (rugby league) was recently found to be an "unreasonable restraint of *trade*."

There are many features of business ethics "in" New Zealand that reflect similar developments elsewhere. Most notably, the *zeitgeist* has been influenced by Thatcherism, with a marked transition away from welfare statism. Income tax and national debt have been reduced, with commensurate reductions in public and welfare expenditure. Many former government departments have been restructured as State Owned Enterprises (SOEs), charged with being as

profitable as the private sector but also with "endeavoring to accommodate or encourage community interests" – yet many of the new SOE managers were then recruited from the private sector.

The resulting rise of a hoped-for "enterprise culture" has not been uniformly pretty to observe. For example, when the 1980s wave of corporate acquisitions crashed on these particular shores, the debris revealed a quite astonishing level of criminal activity. Quite a number of "enterprising" corporate high flyers of that decade have since been convicted. There have also been changes to the takeover code, aimed at protecting minority (ownership) interests. In the push to improve business ethics, many have settled upon a mission of customer service (TQM, or "total quality management") coupled with "satisfactory" rates of return.

There is a growing responsiveness to social issues, as required by law (e.g., EEO) or to accommodate pressure groups. For example, triple bottom line reporting has begun to be practiced by some companies, while sustainability reporting is now entering the language of the commercial sector. The New Zealand Business Council for Sustainable Development provides resources for companies seeking guidance on these matters. The accounting profession has extended its annual report awards to include categories for Environmental reporting, Human Resources reporting, and Corporate Governance reporting.

In 1999 a national management magazine commenced an award for Business Ethics and Sustainability. Companies identified as making outstanding contributions to ethical management practices in New Zealand have been 3M New Zealand for its ethical approach to environmental management (1999), NZ Post for its employee relations policies (2000), Methanex NZ for leadership in stakeholder dialogue (2001), and Norske Skog Tasman for learning and development opportunities provided to employees (2002).

Despite these developments, New Zealand remains at the point where it must face the central question of business ethics: direct involvement by business in meeting needs, particularly for those who lack the ability to pay (for reasons related to poor health, limited capability, matters of conscience, or bad luck). Several New Zealand companies have set recent precedents here, by establishing charitable trusts, by funding local school science labs, or by recruiting from the long-term unemployed. It remains an irony that members of the accounting and legal professions, both advocates for promoting socially concerned ethical behavior, should themselves remain active in promoting tax-avoidance schemes that probably undermine the tax base, but certainly promote guileful behavior more generally, with consequent damage to the social fabric.

Bibliography

Alam, K. F. (1993). Ethics in New Zealand organizations. *Journal of Business Ethics*, **12** (6), 433–40.

Brennan, M., Ennis, M., and Esslemont, D. (1992). The ethical standards of New Zealand business managers. *New Zealand Journal of Business*, **14**, 100–24.

Chartered Accountants Journal of New Zealand (2003). Feature: Ethics, sustainability, governance. **82** (8), 8–25, 34–6.

Deeks, J. and Enderwick, P. (1994). *Business and New Zealand Society*. Auckland: Longman Paul.

The Press (1994). Editorial on New Zealand culture. September 10, Christchurch.

Reid, B. (1994). New Zealand seeks the middle ground. *Time International*, March 14, 40–5.

Singer, A. E. (1994). Doing strategy as doing good: The new pragmatism. *New Zealand Strategic Management*, **1**, 44–51.

normative/descriptive

Carroll U. Stephens and Jon M. Shepard

The field of business ethics explores the antecedents and consequences of moral behavior in the economic sphere. To do so, the field draws upon two distinct theoretical bases: philosophy and the social sciences – most often social psychology and organization theory. The former base is normative, prescriptive, and held to represent values. The latter is descriptive, empirical, and held to represent "value-free" facts. Within business ethics, a distinct division of labor appears to exist between scholars who were trained in the normative, philosophical tradition and those in the descriptive, social science tradition.

The normative/descriptive distinction in business ethics has its roots in the fact/value split articulated in ancient Greek philosophy and nineteenth-century European logical positivism. This schism is problematic for two reasons. First, it is philosophically questionable. Second, even if it were predicated upon sound theory, it would be inappropriate in a field that definitionally comprises both prescriptive and descriptive elements.

For the pre-Socratic Greek philosophers (sixth century BC), there was no fact/value distinction, because the two categories corresponded: the normative and the descriptive were assimilated through the assumption that value (e.g., justice) was founded on nature. Knowledge of fact and value was based upon reason, and observation of the natural world. The fact/value dichotomy began to arise with the Sophists (fifth and fourth centuries BC), but they too developed a correspondence theory of truth for statements about values: since value of any kind is determined by human convention, it is factual for those who agree on the truth of a value. In other words, truth is determined by logic and argumentation. The Socratic tradition (fifth and fourth centuries BC) was a reaction to the ethical relativism of the Sophists. By taking an absolutist stance, Socrates, Plato, and Aristotle resolved the fact/value problem. According to their theory, value is determined by nature and can be ascertained through the use of reason. Plato found value (e.g., justice, courage, wisdom, temperance) in the other-worldly forms that exist beyond empirical observation. Although Aristotle rejected Plato's other-worldly theory of the forms, he believed that value existed in nature and could be discovered, albeit imperfectly, through deliberation based on the use and refinement of practical wisdom.

Values and empirical forms became further distinguished in the nineteenth century, with the advent of Comtean positivism, which later developed into logical positivism. A very strong paradigm in the contemporary social sciences, logical positivism assumes that (a) facts are entirely distinct from values, and (b) social scientists discern truth that is independent of any value judgments and has no normative implications (Comte, 1854; Ayer, 1946).

Yet despite Comte and the logical positivists, a number of thinkers argue that there is no absolute demarcation between fact and value. All science entails value-laden decisions about what to study and how to study it, and – as the social constructionists (e.g., Berger and Luckmann, 1967) have argued – social reality is inarguably open to multiple, value-based interpretations. Pirsig (1991: 66) draws upon Socratic philosophy and William James's radical empiricism to argue:

> Values are not outside of the experience logical positivism limits itself to. They are the *essence* of this experience. Values are *more* empirical, in fact, than subjects or objects. Any person of any philosophic persuasion who sits on a hot stove will verify without any intellectual argument whatsoever... that the *value* of his predicament is negative. This... is not just a vague, woolly-headed, crypto-religious, metaphysical abstraction. It is an *experience*. It is not a description of experience. As such it is completely predictable. It is verifiable by anyone who cares to do so. It is reproducible, of all experience it is the least ambiguous, least mistakable there is.

The evasion of normative content is untenable in the field of business ethics, since ethics, by definition, advances moral claims. Hence the field cannot be purely non-normative, studying the causes and impacts of organizations' moral behavior without specifying, in philosophical terms, what constitutes morality. Neither can the field be strictly normative. Although the objective of moral philosophy is finding and defending normative positions, philosophers nonetheless have always utilized implicit models of human behavior. Throughout history, much of what we have come to understand about ourselves has had its bases in philosophical inquiry. In recent times, these models of human behavior have been explicitly enhanced by the empirical social sciences. For instance, John Rawls's *A Theory of Justice* (1971) – widely deemed to be one of the great works of twentieth-century philosophy – drew heavily upon the empirical findings of developmental psychologist Lawrence Kohlberg (1969). Rawls's extensive theory of the principles undergirding the construct of justice includes psychologically descriptive discussion of which system of distribution an individual would choose if he or she did not know what his or her natural endowments and position in the social structure would be. The theory's compelling power derives, in part, from Rawls's use of a psychologically tenable decision model: he notes empirical evidence that the principles embedded in his model of justice do indeed serve as decision heuristics for people at high stages of moral development.

However, social science research on topics related to ethics must elucidate constructs as defined by *philosophers* if such research is to have any claim to studying what it purports to. For instance, psychological research on moral development would be invalid and logically impossible in the absence of a specification of morality – a definition of what ought to be rather than what is.

When the normative/descriptive distinction in business ethics is dissolved, single works of scholarship may draw upon both bases. Under such a method, the specification of ethicality is a philosophical one – for example, Kantian deontology (*see* KANTIAN ETHICS). Social science theories and techniques then are used to determine how this condition of ethicality may be brought about, and/or what its consequences are. Questions such as how organizations may be designed to foster goals of corporate social performance, and what occurs when businesses behave unethically, are at the heart of business ethics research. Such questions cannot be fully addressed without both normative and empirical components. To ignore the normative aspects is to risk amoral social science, and to ignore the descriptive aspects is to risk unreal philosophy.

Bibliography

Ayer, A. J. (1946). *Language, Truth, and Logic*, London: Victor Gollancz.

Berger, P. and Luckmann, T. (1967). *The Social Construction of Reality*. New York: Doubleday.

Comte, A. (1854). *The Positive Philosophy*, trans. H. Martineau. New York: D. Appleton.

Donaldson, T. (1994). When integration fails. *Business Ethics Quarterly*, 4 (2), 157–70.

Frederick, W. (1994). The virtual reality of fact vs. value. *Business Ethics Quarterly*, 4 (2), 171–4.

Kohlberg, L. (1969). Stage and sequence: The cognitive-developmental approach to socialization. In D. Goslin (ed.), *Handbook of Socialization Theory and Research*. Chicago: Rand McNally.

Pirsig, R. (1991). *Lila: An Inquiry into Morals*. New York: McGraw-Hill.

Rawls, J. (1971). *A Theory of Justice*. Cambridge, MA: Belknap Press.

Trevino, L. and Weaver, G. (1994). Business *ethics/Business* ethics: One field or two? *Business Ethics Quarterly*, **4** (2), 113–28.

Weaver, G. and Trevino, L. (1994). Normative and empirical business ethics. *Business Ethics Quarterly*, **4** (2), 129–44.

Werhane, P. (1994). The normative/descriptive distinction in methodologies of business ethics. *Business Ethics Quarterly*, **4** (2), 175–80.

Victor, B. and Stephens, C. (1994). Business ethics: A synthesis of normative philosophy and empirical social science. *Business Ethics Quarterly*, **4** (2), 145–56.

O

obedience, to authority and to the law

Dawn R. Elm

Obedience: behavioral compliance with a set of standards or rules formulated by an individual or by a group. In either case, an individual is being obedient to authority when he or she behaves in a manner prescribed by these standards or rules.

Authority refers to the right or power of the individual or group who formulated the standards to ensure compliance. Such authority is generally conveyed by the capability to enforce the standards. Authority is a function of the perceived legitimate power of the group or individual who formulated the standards. Legitimate power is power derived from the position or role of the group or individual. For example, typical sources of legitimate power and authority can be found in the roles of parent, supervisor, teacher, and various law enforcement and judicial positions. The law can be considered a formal set of rules and standards that is associated with significant legitimate power and authority in society.

The psychological and moral implications of obedience to authority have been investigated by various researchers. Milgram (1974), for example, examined why individuals abandon their responsibility when obeying their supervisor inside a hierarchy. He suggested that the hierarchical structure of organizations causes individuals to deny responsibility for their actions because they are following orders (obeying authority). Carroll (1978) and Jackall (1988) both described how difficult it can be for managers to behave morally inside a hierarchical business organization when obeying a supervisor may be a condition of continued employment or advancement (*see* MORAL MAZES).

The moral implications of obedience to the law have also been discussed by numerous scholars. A useful distinction between *moral legalism* and *pure legalism* can be found in Beauchamp and Bowie (1993), as well as a variety of other business ethics texts. Moral legalism refers to using the law as a moral standard or rule; that is, the moral thing to do is to obey the law. Pure legalism refers to obeying the law as a means to help coordinate social activities, but does not always constitute moral behavior. The morality of an individual's action is determined by a moral rule or standard which supersedes the law. Therefore, although morality and law are closely connected, they are distinct. Obeying the law does not necessarily result in moral behavior.

See also *justice; legal ethics and business ethics; organization ethics; organizational theory, ethical issues in*

Bibliography

Beauchamp, T. L. and Bowie, N. E. (1993). *Ethical Theory and Business*, 4th edn. New York: Simon and Schuster.

Carroll, A. (1978). Linking business ethics to behavior in organizations. *SAM Advanced Management Journal*, 43, 4–11.

Jackall, R. (1988). *Moral Mazes: The World of Corporate Managers*. New York: Oxford University Press.

Milgram, S. (1974). *Obedience to Authority*. New York: Harper and Row.

opportunity cost

James R. Freeland

Opportunity cost exists whenever choosing one alternative precludes the choice of another alternative in a world of scarcity. It is an important principle of rational decision theory. It arises when some alternatives are not formally considered in a rational analysis.

For example, suppose a person is faced with the choice of whether or not to play a colleague in handball for an hour. In making a rational choice, if this person made the choice by considering only the value (utility) received from playing handball, the analysis would be incomplete because the opportunity cost of the next best alternative (perhaps working on a revision of a book) was not considered. In making the choice of whether to play handball, one must consider the cost of the lost opportunity (working on the book revision).

Samuelson and Nordhaus define opportunity cost in the following way: "The value of the next best use for an economic good, or the value of the sacrificed alternative. Thus, say that the best alternative use of the inputs employed to mine a ton of coal was to grow 10 bushels of wheat. The opportunity cost of a ton of coal is thus the 10 bushels of wheat that *could* have been produced but were not" (Samuelson and Nordhaus, 1992: 743). The idea of "best alternative" recognizes there may be many alternative uses of a resource, but that the opportunity cost is determined by the most valuable benefits sacrificed. This implies that the correct opportunity cost can only be determined by considering the specific details of a specific problem situation.

The concept of opportunity cost serves to remind us that the out-of-pocket dollar outlays are not a complete measure of the cost. The concept is sometimes misapplied and misunderstood in practice because of the practical difficulty of determining the value of the next best alternative. As an example, consider the cost of getting an MBA degree. The out-of-pocket costs for tuition, fees, books, and room and board might total $60,000. However, the true cost of getting the MBA degree must also consider the cost of the next best alternative (e.g., working as a financial analyst). Suppose one could earn $40,000 by working as a financial analyst during the same amount of time it takes to get the MBA degree. Then the true cost of getting the MBA is actually $100,000. One way to avoid having to consider the opportunity cost in this way is to formally consider the choice between two alter-

natives: (1) get an MBA degree, or (2) work as a financial analyst. The cost of (1) is $60,000. This should be compared to the cost of (2), which is the most valuable benefit sacrificed.

Bibliography

Heymann, H. G. and Bloom, R. (1992). *Opportunity Cost in Finance and Accounting.* New York: Quorum Books.
Samuelson, P. A. and Nordhaus, W. D. (1992). *Economics*, 14th edn. New York: McGraw-Hill.

organization ethics

Richard P. Nielsen

is the study of ethical issues in organizations. From a behavioral perspective, ethical issues in business, government, and non-profit organizations are much more similar than they are different. Equally, the bureaucratic and organizational causes of unethical behavior in business, government, and non-profit organizations are more similar than they are different. This is why organizational scholars study organizational ethics phenomena and not solely business ethics, government ethics, or non-profit organization ethics issues.

For example, problems of fair treatment of employees, occupational health and safety, product/service safety, abuse of power, responsibility to external constituencies, pollution, bribery, privacy, conflict of interest, equal opportunity, preferential treatment, unjust discharge, etc., exist across business, government, and non-profit organizations. Similarly, causes of unethical behavior such as greed for money and/or power, fear of upper-level powerful managers, organizational requirements to obey orders, organizational isolation, routinized "in the box" job behavior, and thinking that does not include the ethical as part of "my job," lack of organization civil liberties that might protect employees from retaliation for raising ethical issues, etc., exist in business, non-profit, and government organizations.

Organization ethics may be following a developmental path similar to that of organization behavior. Organization behavior is taught in schools of management, business, public administration, education, engineering, nursing, public health, and medicine. This was not always the case. The behavioral sciences were introduced into business schools in the 1920s and it took almost 50 years for organization behavior to be taught in professional schools across economic sectors. Organization ethics may be following a similar pattern. In the 1980s organization ethics was introduced into schools of management and business. Since then a few schools of government and public administration have begun to teach it, and it is spreading to other professional schools. The day may come when most ethics courses in management schools are called organization ethics instead of business ethics.

Bibliography

Ewing, D. W. (1977). *Freedom Inside the Organization: Bringing Civil Liberties to the Workplace*. New York: McGraw-Hill.

Hirschmann, A. O. (1970). *Exit, Voice, and Loyalty: Responses to Decline in Firms, Organizations, and States*. Cambridge, MA: Harvard University Press.

Nielsen, R. P. (1993). Organizational ethics from a perspective of action (praxis). *Business Ethics Quarterly*, 3 (2), 131–51.

Nielsen, R. P. (1996). *The Politics of Ethics: Methods for Acting, Learning, and Sometimes Fighting Others in Addressing Ethics Problems in Organizational Life*. New York: Oxford University Press.

organizational culture

Clarence C. Walton

A distinctive characteristic of a community having a significant history, organizational culture consists of shared assumptions and fundamental beliefs validated over time as essential to the group's successful handling of problems relevant to its internal cohesiveness and external adaptations. Taken for granted as the most realistic way to view the organization and its environment, such beliefs and assumptions are automatically transmitted to new employees as guides for their acting, thinking, and feeling toward the entity's operation.

Situated at the intersection where many disciplines (anthropology, sociology, psychology, philosophy, history, and organizational theory) meet to offer diverse definitions of organizational culture, it is not surprising that the term seems surrounded by ambiguities.

Previously ignored – even considered as irrelevant – organizational culture had clearly come of age when the *New York Times* (January 7, 1983) described it as the catchphrase "management consultants are breathing into the ears of American executives." An even surer sign of the term's acceptance came when companies followed the lead of Ford, Polaroid, TRW, Proctor and Gamble, and Pacific Telesis in investing millions in efforts to define more precisely their respective cultures. Since culture is the organization's foundation, architects of change had to understand how much restructuring the foundation could support.

Organizational cultures are developed in various ways: World War II gave a Rosie-the-Riveter culture to war-production facilities; IBM's outstanding past performances made the Big Blue a model for other cultures; charismatic founders in the mold of Thomas Watson of IBM, General Johnson of Johnson and Johnson, and Harley Proctor of Proctor and Gamble who, convinced that the lives and productivity of their employees were shaped by the workplace, sought to build an environment in which both could thrive. An intriguing historical footnote is the question whether Sears-Roebuck surpassed arch-rival Montgomery-Ward because Sears's General Robert Wood had more humanistic values than MW's Sewell Avery. There are, of course, other heroes: Thomas Edison, Charles Steinmetz, and Gerald Swope at General Electric, Knute Rockne at Notre Dame, Theodore Vail and Walter Gifford at American Telephone and Telegraph, and hundreds of others.

On the other hand, hard-driving and successful executives like Harold Geneen of International Telephone and Telegraph, and Richard Snyder of the Simon and Schuster publishing house, left their respective companies with badly battered cultures. The hero-hellion tale suggests that a culture's making may be more than the company's maker. Job security, high wages, aesthetically pleasing workplaces, and onsite health and recreational facilities are among the ways new leaders and employees enrich and redefine the culture.

Within organizations are subcultures. The sales division, for example, may have a "gung-ho" ideology; research and development, a visionary "can do" outlook; and engineering, a careful, meticulous approach. But all subcultures partake of the essential qualities of the entity's larger culture that serve as both an integrative and control agent over the various parts.

Distinctions are now in order. *Organizational culture* is not the same as *corporate structure*, which may reflect (a) Weberian bureaucratic models that provide impartial treatment of people and standardized procedures, or (b) patrimonial structures that emphasize personalities, an emphasis that often results in politicking, Machiavellian intrigues, and discreet maneuvering to win the boss's favor.

A more important distinction exists between *culture* and *climate*. The *organizational climate*, often determined by taking the pulse of employees, seeks to answer such questions as these: What are the workers' expectations of the enterprise? Do they find their expectations being met? Are they proud of being an Organization X's employee? The climate is more like public opinion – transitory, subject to sudden change, and an uncertain base for judging the company's underlying character.

CULTURE'S IMPORTANCE

That culture plays a significant role in business is illustrated by the way company breakups and corporate mergers are handled. The most dramatic example of breakup came in 1984 in the court-ordered division of AT&T. To dismantle efficiently, the company established headquarters in Basking Ridge, New Jersey. On the center's walls were posted every conceivable item: schedules, charts, alternatives and options, and the like. Missing was the word *culture* – an omission that added confusion to the dismantling process.

A second example of culture's importance occurs during mergers or takeovers. Postmortems of failures have tended to focus on such factors as over-inflated purchase prices, unrealistic projections for earnings, or potential economies of scale. Ignored was the possibility of a mismatch of corporate cultures. One example occurred in 1984 when General Motors purchased Electronic Data Systems from H. Ross Perot. At the time it was thought that EDS's hard-driving entrepreneurial spirit would be crushed by the bureaucracy of the giant purchaser. In reality, the reverse occurred: loyalty to the boss became the prime requisite for employees.

ETHICAL QUESTIONS

By its very nature, organizational culture raises important moral questions: Are individuals trustworthy or not? More prone to good or to evil? Capable of increasing their understandings of right and wrong? On another level is the question of truth: Is it what most people say truth is? Is it what the boss declares? Is everyone's opinion as good as everyone else's?

On the institutional plane the question centers around the meaning of the corporate person – a definition used in the American legal system. What does *person* mean? While many terms have been coined to describe the perspective of the disputants on this issue, one useful distinction is that between (1) the moral person's view and (2) the structural restraint paradigm. Under the first, all agents are moral agents because they behave *intentionally* – and organizations act with intent, an intent that may differ from the intention of even certain directors and officers. Corporations are, therefore, full-fledged members of the moral community on equal standing with humans. The organization is not simply an agency among agencies; it is the stage on which actors perform. As role-holders their actions might be quite different from their personal behavior and beliefs.

Firmly opposed to this position is the structural restraint camp, which insists that individuals, not entities, act. Simply establishing goals implies that other moral considerations are either automatically excluded or considered irrelevant. Persons alone have intellects and free wills and only they can bear moral responsibility for their actions. Hiding under a collective cloak is no excuse for evading individual responsibility.

While scholars debate, managers act. Perhaps leadership's most important function is to know when and how to create, recreate, and, when necessary, destroy the organization's culture.

Bibliography

Deal, T. W. and Kennedy, A. A. (1982). *Corporate Cultures*. Reading, MA: Addison-Wesley.

Frost, P. J. et al. (1985). *Organizational Culture*. Beverly Hills, CA: Sage.

Hofsteder, G. (1980). *Culture's Consequences*. Beverly Hills, CA: Sage.

Ott, J. S. (1989). *The Organizational Culture Perspective*. Chicago: Dorsey.

Schein, E. H. (1985). *Organizational Culture and Leadership*. San Francisco: Jossey-Bass.

Walton, C. (1992). *Corporate Encounters*. New York: Dryden.

organizational decay

Howard S. Schwartz

is a process in which an organization shifts its focus from coping with the real world to dramatizing a fantasy about itself. It is a progressive condition that builds upon itself, enlisting more and more of the organization's energies and resources, until the capability of the organization to deal with the real world becomes problematic.

PSYCHOLOGY OF ORGANIZATIONAL DECAY

In the beginning of psychological life, the fusion of infant and mother creates for the infant a sense of being the center of a loving world. Freud (1955, 1957; Chasseguet-Smirgel, 1985) refers to this experience as *primary narcissism*. Inevitably, the fact of the world's indifference presents itself to us, resulting in anxiety. To defend against anxiety, we develop a fantasy of the return to the state of narcissistic fusion. Freud called this fantasy the *ego ideal*. It represents for us a life free of anxiety.

Our projection of the ego ideal into organizations is what lies behind their attraction for us. In doing this, we picture ourselves in our organizational roles as being the center of a loving world – perfectly good, free of tension, able to do what we want and be loved for it. When we do this, we have taken the organization as our ego ideal. An image of the organization functioning as an ego ideal is called the *organization ideal*. Unfortunately, we are not the center of a loving world. The ego ideal, whether in the form of the organization ideal or any other form, is never realized.

Organizations attempt, in various ways, to preserve the fantasy of the ego ideal, while registering that it has not been attained. In corporate life, the most common means for this is through the idea of hierarchy. Hierarchy explains how the organization can be the ego ideal, while our lives as organization participants are not perfect. It is because those who really represent the organization, its high officials, have attained the organization ideal, even if we have not. In this way, the organization enlists our anxiety as a powerful motivational force, which it can direct by specifying criteria for promotion.

To maintain the fantasy of the organization ideal as a motivational force, the corporation must dramatize its own perfection and the perfection of its high officials. But the organization and its officials are not perfect. Hence, the organization that operates this way must shift its focus toward the creation and embellishment of a fantasy of perfection, and deny the reality that stands at variance with it. This is the root of organizational decay.

SOME ASPECTS OF ORGANIZATIONAL DECAY

1   *Commitment to bad decisions.* The organization ideal, being perfect, makes only perfect decisions. An organization in a state of decay compels the belief that its decisions have been perfect, no matter how imperfect they may have been. The subsequent policies of the organization amplify this error, degrading the organization's capacity to make good decisions in the future and leaving the original problems unresolved.

2   *Advancement of participants who detach themselves from reality, and discouragement of reality-oriented participants who are committed to their work.* As the organization's capacity to make good decisions erodes, successful idealization of the organization becomes increasingly difficult. At the same time it becomes increasingly urgent as an organizational priority. Promotion criteria shift toward those who are best at advancing and maintaining this fiction, in the face of increasing variance with reality. These people can either be cynics, whose elevation degrades the moral character of the organization, or individuals with a high capacity for self-delusion, who simply do not have much

engagement with reality at all. Reality-oriented participants tend to become discouraged and alienated.

3   *The narcissistic loss of reality among management.* When the organization becomes the dramatization of its own perfection and that of its high officials, individuals are subjected to organizational pressure to maintain this performance. Those in positions of power, who are central in exerting this pressure, often having been assisted in their rise to power by the lack of a firm connection with reality, can easily take this performance as an authentic reflection of their real perfection. In this way, they may lose touch with reality altogether (*Business Week*, 1991).

4   *Transposition of work and ritual.* In the decaying organization, productive work loses its meaning; work becomes a ritualized performance. At the same time, rituals associated with the process of promotion, increasingly divorced as they are from the organization's function, come to be supercharged with meaning. Employees' energy is redirected accordingly.

5   *Creation of the organizational jungle.* Progress through the hierarchy, which is supposed to mean increasing freedom from anxiety, may make it worse. The cause of the anxiety cannot be acknowledged, and the necessity of maintaining the fantasy of the organization ideal means that one has to deal with it in isolation. Often, individuals attribute its cause to others, who are experienced as threats to their security, threats that may be dealt with by gaining hierarchical advantage over those seen as posing them.

6   *Creation of the enemy without.* Another way of dealing with anxiety is by attributing it to forces outside the organization, seen as bad, who make demands on the organization, seen as all good. This may be the source of some of the antisocial activity of otherwise perfectly decent organizational citizens.

Morality is not a matter that affects organizational life only occasionally. It is always present in the obligation to do good work. Organizational decay, by construing the organization as its own moral universe, interferes with the mor-

ality of the work process. This places many organizational participants in a condition of sustained moral dilemma, torn between what they need to do to get their work done, and what they need to do to advance within the organization. Resolution of this continuing dilemma requires a realistic sense of what life has to offer and a deep appreciation of the meaning of our relationships to others.

Bibliography

Business Week (1991). Cover story: CEO Disease: Egotism can breed corporate disaster – and the malady is spreading. April 1, 52–60.

Chasseguet-Smirgel, J. (1985). *The Ego Ideal: A Psychoanalytic Essay on the Malady of the Ideal.* New York: Norton.

Freud, S. (1955). *Group Psychology and the Analysis of the Ego.* Standard edition, ed. L. Strachey, Vol. 18. London: Hogarth Press.

Freud, S. (1957). *On Narcissism: An Introduction.* Standard edition, ed. L. Strachey, Vol. 14. London: Hogarth Press.

Jackall, R. (1988). *Moral Mazes: The World of Corporate Managers.* New York: Oxford University Press. (Organizational decay processes from a sociological perspective.)

Schwartz, H. S. (1990). *Narcissistic Process and Corporate Decay: The Theory of the Organization Ideal.* New York: New York University Press.

Trento, J. J. (1987). *Prescription for Disaster: From the Glory of Apollo to the Betrayal of the Shuttle.* New York: Crown. (Organizational decay processes at NASA.)

Wright, J. P. (1979). *On a Clear Day You Can See General Motors: John Z. De Lorean's Look Inside the Automotive Giant.* New York: Avon. (Organizational decay processes at General Motors.)

organizational dilemmas

John M. Darley

A dilemma is a choice between two conflicting alternatives where both cannot be realized. In an ethical context of a business setting, "organizational dilemmas" may be choices faced by business decision-makers in which to choose to behave ethically is also to choose to behave in ways that may harm a corporation's profit margins or even threaten its continued existence. These are the sorts of decisions faced when, for instance, asbestos manufacturers received medical reports that asbestos inhalation caused lung cancer in workers, tobacco manufacturers received scientific reports on the cancer-causing properties of cigarette smoking, or the Robbins corporation received reports that its contraceptive device, the Dalkon Shield, drew dangerous bacteria into the bodies of its users.

THE CAUSES OF UNETHICAL RESOLUTIONS TO ORGANIZATIONAL DILEMMAS

When episodes of corporate malfeasance are discovered, and large numbers of persons are involved, a great deal of public anger is generated. While the public condemnation is appropriate, it is also worth carrying out a close examination of the organizational dynamics that led to these results; an examination that might allow for the reduction of these incidents. The first result of such an examination suggests that organizations that engage in harm-doing to their workers, the consumers of their products, or the general public fall into two categories: in the first category the corporate leaders intend to commit the practice, in the second they do not, but, as we will see, complex organizational processes often cause it to happen.

Organizations that seek to do harm. In the first category, it becomes obvious that the organizational principals plan to commit the unethical or illegal actions in order that they personally or the organization gains what profits can be made. The assumption is that the nature of the actions can be concealed, or the consequences of its detection minimized. Examples of this abound: "boiler room" stock-brokerage houses that push dreadful stock on customers, siding contractors who disappear with customers' deposits. Some large and apparently respectable companies have also engaged in these practices: for example, newspaper reports on the settlements that the Prudential Corporation is making with investors lured into "safe investments" that tumbled in value. Nor is it always customers that are the target of such behaviors; the Film Recovery System Corporation hired illegal immigrant workers who could not read English in order that they would not know their health was being endangered by the toxic chemicals they were required to handle without safety precautions.

If the corporate management intends that unethical or illegal solutions to organizational dilemmas be chosen, then how is it that they make certain that the corporate subordinates resolve dilemmas in the direction of acting unethically or illegally when they face concrete choices to do so? Broadly, this is accomplished in two ways. First, they recruit workers who will act questionably. Investigators of businesses running swindles by telephone reveal that the average telephone swindler has worked for a number of such operations before, moving to new ones as legal prosecution closes down the old ones. Second, the corporation uses techniques for the "socialization" of ordinary individuals into acting unscrupulously. These methods of socialization can be specified by organizational social scientists; here we simply mark that they change the individuals involved, generally making them active participants in unethical actions, thus adding to the pool of those who are recruitable for similar actions in the future, and who will independently engage in those actions without organizational pressures to do so.

The social control of organizations in which the top management is complicit in harm-doing actions can take three general forms: voluntary change in the corporate structure to eliminate inappropriate pressures, government monitoring to detect wrongdoing, followed by fines, criminal prosecutions, or interventions to force changes in corporate structure, or consumer boycott actions. Many scholars (e.g., Clinard and Yeager, 1980: 229–325) who have examined the actual workings of these social controls on corporate behavior do not find them altogether effective, although some think that they could be strengthened and made effective.

Organizations that get entrapped in wrongdoing. In other cases, the wrongdoing in a corporation is not condoned by the management; instead, it begins at some lower level within the organization. These cases deserve considerable analytic interest because, unlike the cases in which the top of the organization intends unethical actions, it seems that corporate practices could be effective in detecting and stopping these actions. While no definitive surveys identify frequencies, it is clear that in a number of cases in which unethical actions begin in some unit of a corporation, those practices capture the acquiescence of those higher in the hierarchy, and moves are made to cover up the practices. A number of factors bring this about: loyalties to subordinates, superiors' feelings of negligence and mismanagement for not detecting the practices earlier, corporate commitments to the quality of the product now discovered flawed or to the industrial practice now discovered dangerous, and/or costs incurred to date that would be wasted if the wrong were to be corrected; perhaps most importantly, the humiliation of being a part, although an unwitting part, of an unethical action. For these reasons, corporations sometimes attempt to cover up the unethical actions. In doing so, they often encourage behaviors that are as unethical as the actions that they cover up, and as a second consequence, continue the initial unethical actions, such as when defective and dangerous products have been marketed by corporations long past the point when they discovered that they were dangerous.

How this can be avoided is a question that calls for a good deal of attention. Corporate codes of ethics are helpful if the corporation has a history of taking them seriously. Protected mechanisms for reporting violations to corporate authorities that will take them seriously also have been recommended; outside directors may be used in this fashion. Other mechanisms for supporting those within the organization who "blow the whistle" are important because traditionally whistleblowing is frequently a punished activity.

Bibliography

Clinard, M. and Yeager, P. (1980). *Corporate Crime*. New York: Free Press.
Schlegel, K. and Weisburd, D. (eds.) (1992). *White Collar Crime Reconsidered*. Boston, MA: Northeastern University Press.

organizational moral distress

Ann E. Mills and Patricia H. Werhane

Moral distress has been identified at the individual level and defined as the anguish a person may experience faced with a situation in which the individual knows the right thing to do but is prevented from doing it by institutional constraints (Jameton, 1984: 81). In this article, we take a broader approach and apply the idea of moral distress to the organizational level. We call this concept "organizational moral distress."

Most organizations suffer some form of distress at some time in their lives as they make decisions pursuant to their goals. We distinguish organizational moral distress from organizational distress by noting that organizational moral distress arises because of a situation characterized by a "values misalignment" as opposed to the distress that organizations commonly face as they negotiate competitive markets.

Organizational moral distress is the distress one or more organization stakeholders or stakeholder groups experience because of a misalignment of values between the operationalized values of the organization and the values the organization says it endorses, or between the organization's values and its internal or external stakeholders, or because its stakeholders perceive the organization's mission and values differently. Thus, organizational moral distress can occur in at least four ways – and they can overlap in specific cases. We look more closely at these four situations and present a case to illustrate each form of organizational moral distress.

Organizational moral distress will occur when the mission of the organization is not operationalized in practice. In this case, there is a gap between what the organization does and what the organization says it does.

Organizations generally have mission statements that include the values they deem important for the success of their enterprise – and it is this self-proclaimed standard that is intended to guide the organization and its stakeholders through difficult or complex decision-making. In addition, it is a standard for accountability and judgment about the organization as well as the systems and structures it creates to perform its mission. These systems and structures can reinforce the organization's mission and support its values or they may not, but in both cases they represent the operationalized values of the organization.

Perhaps the most famous case of an organization employing systems and structures to support values different than its stated values is that of Enron. Enron's mission statement prided itself on four key values: respect, integrity, communication, and excellence. However, the values that actually guided decision-making seemed to rest on greed and arrogance. Not only were greed and arrogance apparent in Enron's business and accounting practices, they were also apparent in the systems and structures Enron created to fulfill its mission. For example, the usual checks and balances designed to handle corporate conflicts of interest were ignored. For instance, those that stood to gain from a proposed project conducted the evaluations to determine their worth to the company. Another example is the notorious "rank and yank" performance reviews, in which bonuses could only be distributed if reviewers were unanimous in their decisions concerning themselves and others. Reviewers, however, reported to those that were being evaluated. The result was incentives that created "a mercenary, cut-throat culture" that treated its workers like "dog meat" (Hassell, 2001).

Organizational moral distress will occur when the values of the organization and the values of its internal stakeholders are misaligned.

All individual stakeholders and stakeholder groups bring to the organization their own values. Often, the values of the individual or group will conflict with the organization values and it is generally up to the organization to accommodate (or not) these values. For instance, outside legally prescribed limits, it is up to the organization to decide whether or not it can accommodate an individual's family values. In these cases, organizational moral distress can often be avoided by the organization being clear about its values in the hiring process. Processes of self-selection or mediation can also resolve potential or actual conflict. In extreme cases, conflict between values of the individual or group and the organization can be resolved through strikes or termination of the individual or group, or even through organization demise.

Another potential source of this sort of organizational moral distress occurs when the organization employs or contracts with professionals. An organization may employ lawyers, or engineers, or accountants. Other organizations may employ physicians, or chemists, or nurses.

Professional individuals or groups are often associated with professional bodies, such as the American Institute of Certified Public Accountants, that subscribe to specific values deemed important to the profession. Generally, the employing organization will incorporate, at least in part, those values with its own. For instance, the mission and values statements of legal, medical, and accounting organizations reflect similar values as those associated with their specific professional associations. Yet the employing organization will often also endorse other values and these may potentially conflict with professional values. For instance, the mission statement of Deloitte and Touche reads: "To help our clients and our people excel" (http://careers.deloitte.com/crs/missionstatement.asp.). Yet the American Institute of Certified Public Accountants proclaims that the highest duty of certified public accountants is to the public (http://www.aicpa.org/about/vision.htm.). Thus, organizational moral distress can occur as a result of conflict between the individual's and/or group's professional values and the organization's values.

The more easily identifiable cases of this sort of organizational moral distress are often associated with whistleblowers. Consider the role of Sherron Wadkins in the Enron case, in which she tried to warn her bosses that the company would implode in accounting scandals and was ignored. But the AOL Time Warner case also belongs in this category, in that it can be regarded as a failure of leadership to align internal stakeholder values to organization values.

On January 10, 2000 Gerald Levin, CEO of Time Warner, and Steve Case, chairman of America Online, announced a $350 billion merger. The merger was envisioned as a partnership of equals. AOL Time Warner's mission statement is "To become the world's most respected and valued company by connecting, informing, and entertaining people everywhere in innovative ways that will enrich their lives." Its values include creativity, agility, teamwork, integrity, and responsibility. AOL Time Warner proclaims, "We treat one another with respect – creating value by working together within and across our businesses" (http://www.aoltimewarner.com/corporate_information/mission_and_values.adp). Yet less then two years later

Levin had abruptly retired and three years later Steve Case, having survived an attempt to oust him, had floated the idea of AOL spinning off from the Time Warner group. Stock prices for the combined company peaked at $56.60 in May of 2001 and hit bottom in July 2002 at $8.70. Currently, it is trading at around $14.00.

Newsweek analyst Johnnie Roberts suggests that easy answers – the end of the dot-com boom and the events of September 11, 2001 – aren't sufficient to explain why the company went into such a tailspin. He suggests that the real answer lies in the incompatibility of the two men involved. The results were power struggles, ill-defined duties, and lack of collaboration and communication between the two men and their subordinates. AOL executives behaved as if they and no one else had a stake in the marriage. For instance, AOL's Michael Kelly, who became AOL Time Warner's financial chief, in an address to senior executives of both companies, recalled that when AOL purchased Netscape, AOL fired everyone. Another example was the propensity of AOL executives to aggressively forecast earnings and profits. Time Warner's Joan Nicolais preferred to offer Wall Street what she considered to be more accurate numbers and furiously opposed this aggressiveness. She was eventually replaced as the head of AOL Time Warner Investment Communications Officer (Roberts, 2002).

Organizational moral distress will also occur when stakeholder individuals or groups perceive the organization's mission and values differently.

All organizations balance competing goals, for instance quarterly returns and future investment. Equally, many organizations balance competing values, for instance community welfare and employee welfare. Individual stakeholders or groups may agree upon the values of the organization, but they may prioritize them differently or they may misunderstand their application. This kind of organizational moral distress can occur as a result of the differing functions of individuals or groups, which will influence their perceptions and priorities.

For instance, consider the recent American Airlines controversy. The corporate vision of AMR, the parent group of American Airlines, is to be the world's leading airline by focusing on industry leadership in the areas of safety, service, product, network, technology, and culture. Its mission statement reads in part: "AMR fosters an inclusive environment that allows all employees to contribute to the overall success of the company by: balancing the needs of the company with the needs of employees" (http://www.amrcorp.com/corpinfo.htm). No distinction in the mission statement is made between different groups of employees.

AMR, facing bankruptcy, after a continual slowdown of air traffic after the September 11 attack, won concessions from its unions totaling $1.8 billion. Concessions included pay cuts, benefits and contract changes, as well as allowing the airline to lay off 7,000 employees. Almost simultaneously with the announcement of an agreed package of concessions, came the news that AMR had arranged for special accounts to ensure funding of executive retirement benefits and protect these funds in the event of a bankruptcy. In the face of a furious reaction from its unions, as well as an impending public relations disaster, Donald Carty, CEO, resigned.

Organizational moral distress will also occur when the organization is prevented from doing what it perceives as the right thing to do by external stakeholders. In this example, the organization knows or believes it knows the right action to take in a particular circumstance, but is prevented from doing so by one or more external stakeholders.

Perhaps no other industry has generated more controversy in the last few years than the biotech industry, with its discovery and exploration of new technologies like stem cell research. The mostly small companies that make up this industry believe passionately in the potential of stem cell research to develop regenerative technologies that can eventually be used against diseases like Parkinson's, Alzheimer's, and cancers. Yet their research depends on the use of cells obtained from days-old embryos, which has raised profound ethical and moral questions. The result of the controversy is a ban on any research that "harms or destroys" embryos and a complete ban on the use of any stem cell line developed after August 9, 2001 for any organization that receives federal funding for such research. These injunctions have had consequences for those organizations that believe in the potential of such research – and that rely on public funding to conduct their research. An example is the University of California.

The biology department at the University of California, San Francisco (UCSF), formerly headed by Roger Pedersen, is a leader, along with John Hopkins and the University of Wisconsin, in stem cell research. Although biotechnology company Genron has always funded stem cell research at UCSF, Pedersen and his colleagues worried that the ban might also affect indirect costs.

The university, determined to make sure that its researchers stayed at the top of the field, and aware that of the 78 cell lines identified before the August ban only 7 were possibly viable, decided to set up a privately funded laboratory off-campus where its researchers can work on new cell lines. The program was moved off-campus and Pedersen himself resigned to relocate to Cambridge University in England, where the government actively supports stem cell research. He retains a faculty position at the UCSF and is actively recruiting other United States' scientists to work in England (Perez-Pena, 2003).

Bibliography

Hassell, G. (2001). The fall of Enron: Pressure cooker finally exploded. *Houston Chronicle*, December 9.

Jameton A. (1984). *Nursing Practice: The Ethical Issues.* Englewood Cliffs, NJ: Prentice-Hall.

Perez-Pena, R. (2003). Broad movement is backing embryo stem cell research. *New York Times*, March 16, 20.

Roberts J. (2002). How it all fell apart: Steve Case and Jerry Levin created AOL Time Warner in a marriage of convenience. The inside story of what went wrong. *Newsweek*, December 9, 52.

---

organizational theory, ethical issues in: Part 1

Robert A. Phillips

It has been said that no one deserves more credit for victory in World War II than Henry Ford. His development of the assembly line made available the tools of victory without which the most brilliant strategy and staunchest determination are insufficient. It was the *organization* of

productive capacity that is credited. Similar credit has been attributed to the organization of the Manhattan Project, the moon landing and, of course, General Motors and the other behemoths of twentieth-century commerce. When so considered, it is not surprising that organization theory would be rife with ethical content. Indeed, Shafritz and Ott trace organization theory back to Exodus chapter 18, in which Moses's father-in-law Jethro instructs Moses on how to delegate his responsibilities for rendering judicial decisions. Verses 25–6 say:

> And Moses chose able men out of all Israel, and made them head over the people, rulers of thousands, rulers of hundreds, rulers of fifties, and rulers of tens. And they judged the people at all seasons: the hard cases they brought unto Moses, but every small matter they judged themselves.

The first two excerpts in Shafritz and Ott's (2001) compendium of organization theory are from Socrates and Adam Smith – two people as well (or better) known for their moral philosophy as for their contributions to organization theory.

An overview of the history of organizational theory as an academic discipline presents a sense of oscillation between the technical and humanist approaches. In what follows, I will briefly describe the work of some of the seminal scholars in the field of organization theory and the perspective advanced by each. This will be followed by an equally brief suggestion of some of the ethical issues that surround each perspective. This discussion will be far from exhaustive. Rather, it is intended to give the reader the broadest sense of the domain of the field and the moral questions that may arise in this domain.

CLASSICAL ORGANIZATION THEORY

Socrates and Moses notwithstanding, it is reasonable to begin discussion of organization theory where we might also begin a discussion of economic theory: Scotland in 1776, in the person of Adam Smith. Though widely recognized as the father of modern economics, at least for his analysis of the division of labor, Smith may also be considered the father of organization theory. Smith argues that the great benefit to the productive capacity of society arises due to the division of labor. By undertaking only one small part of overall production each individual is able to increase her dexterity, minimize time switching between jobs, and improve that part of the process through innovation.

The question then becomes one of just how many such divisions are optimal. No one is more famous for his thoughts on this aspect of the division of labor than Frederick Taylor – originator of "scientific management." Taylor's time and motion studies determined the optimal number of smaller activities for any given productive task, the proper tool for the job (e.g., what size shovel moves the maximum amount of coal), how long each activity should take a typical worker, etc. For classical organization theorists, organizations are like machines, so organization theory is akin to an engineering problem (consider another classical work by Henry Towne, "The engineer as economist"). Efficiency was the goal and people were typically considered interchangeable parts of the organizational machine. The search was for the "one right way" to organize production. Notably, both Smith and Taylor considered – to varying extents – the moral dimensions of their models. Though believing that the division of labor was in many ways good for society and the workers, Smith recognized, for example, that the division of labor tends to dull the mind. He writes:

The man whose whole life is spent in performing a few simple operations, of which the effects, too, are always the same, or very nearly the same, has no occasion to exert his understanding . . . He naturally loses, therefore, the habit of such exertion, and generally becomes as stupid and ignorant as it is possible for a human creature to become. (Cited in Heilbroner, 1986: 155)

Taylor (1911) was less circumspect about the effects of his program on the workers. He believed that, "Without any question, the large good which so far has come from scientific management has come to the worker." To Taylor's credit, his system was seen by many as a progressive force in its day (he counted Justice Louis Brandeis among the early defenders of Taylorism), but questions nevertheless emerge. What are the moral implications of treating people like machine parts? Are they to be thrown out when worn down? Are people so easily interchangeable for one another? What are the effects on one's self-perception of being treated this way? Taylor was profoundly concerned with fairness (e.g., "a fair day's work for a fair day's wage"), but his measure of fair was determined by the best workers working their hardest, often to their very limit. Is this a just metric? Should any provision be made for human weakness and disparities of strength and talent? If not this, then what is the proper expectation of a fair day's work?

THE ORGANIZATIONAL BEHAVIOR PERSPECTIVE

At least in part as a response to the mechanistic perspective of classical organization theory, there emerged a more humanistic stream of research around questions concerning how *individuals* acted and reacted within organizations and groups. Research on issues such as motivation, group dynamics, leadership, teamwork, and the effect of organizational environment on individual behavior came to the fore. Beginning with the famous Hawthorne Experiments of Roethlisberger and Mayo, researchers began to consider the effects of group norms, workplace socializing, treatment of and attention paid to employees by management, and the interaction effects among these and other factors on workplace performance. Mary Parker Follett wrote important treatises on the giving and taking of orders and the psychological influences in play in organizations. Douglas McGregor (1960) contrasts Theory X (essentially the assumptions of Taylorism) with Theory Y. The latter provides a more optimistic picture of human nature that assumes that, rather than lazy and opportunistic, people take pride and fulfillment from work. Often the assumption that workers see work as a necessary evil can be self-fulfilling because of the way managers treat them using this assumption. Chester Barnard (1968) argued money is of limited value as a motivator and that other incentives (e.g., prestige, pride, association with desirable others, etc.) play an equal or overriding role in motivating people.

But ethical questions emerge from this more humanistic perspective as well. When does altering the environment to produce desired individual behaviors cross into illegitimate psychological manipulation? Can social psychological *perceptions* of justice be used to replace *actual* workplace justice? Can the other incentives Barnard describes be used opportunistically by companies, perhaps even cheating employees out of their material due? What if the majority of employees of a given company or industry are irredeemably lazy and shiftless? Is it morally permissible to treat these people more instrumentally rather than risk being taken advantage of? In short, do the moral rules change when the chary assumptions of the organizational behavior perspective do not hold? Finally, if managers and organizations are able to exert this sort of influence over the actions and perhaps the personality of others, what sort of people are they obliged to mold? While more subtle, such questions are nevertheless vital to the project of organization theory.

ORGANIZATIONAL ECONOMICS

As the pendulum between humanist and technical approaches swung back toward the latter, the field of organizational economics emerged. Preeminent in this area are Williamson's transaction cost economics and Jensen and Meckling's "agency theory." Like Chester Barnard, agency theory is concerned with incentives and motivations of individuals in organizations. However, agency theorists and organizational economists have a far less charitable view of human nature. The fundamental premise of organizational economics is that the separation of risk-taking (often simplistically referred to as "ownership") and decision-making (a.k.a., control) creates an agency problem. Given that people are opportunistic (self-interest-seeking with guile), what can be done to prevent managers from shirking their duties and/or using a firm's resources for their own benefit rather than that of the principal?

The moral issues attendant to the organizational economics perspective are enormous. Are people truly opportunistic? Does the assumption of opportunism tend toward self-fulfillment? As with Taylorism, what constitutes shirking? Who is the principal? Who, if anyone, "owns" the firm? What moral baggage comes with such ownership? What is the nature of the "property rights" assumed of principals? What responsibilities are concomitant to these property rights? What role do concepts such as trust and reputation play in minimizing agency and transaction costs?

POWER AND POLITICS ORGANIZATION THEORY

Whereas the organizational economics literature perceives the organization as an institution primarily characterized by rationality, the power and politics perspective sees the organization as a place where relationships of power – and often conflict – play out. Whereas the "structuralist" school focuses on the authority of the formal hierarchy (e.g., relationships as viewed on an organization chart), the power and politics perspective examines power derived from a variety of relations (e.g., expertise, charisma, connections, etc.). The power and politics lens is perhaps the most obviously morally laden of the frameworks examined so far. The ends to which power is applied are often taken as given. The obvious moral question for such studies is the legitimacy of these ends. What means are justified to achieve what ends? Equally obvious is the fact that any time there is conflict, there will be issues of distributive and procedural justice. What duties are owed to the powerless?

Obviously, much is omitted from this limited introduction. Among the areas not covered are the vital topics of systems theory, organizational culture, organizational development and change, the social psychology of justice, the effects of boundaryless and virtual organizations, critical theory and postmodernist approaches, and many other topics. As non-state organizations increase in power and influence around the globe, one may reasonably expect the field of organization theory to examine all the more closely the moral issues attendant to the various perspectives.

Bibliography

Barnard, C. I. (1968) [1938]. *The Functions of the Executive*. Cambridge, MA: Harvard University Press.

Barney, J. B. and Ouchi, W. G. (1986). *Organizational Economics*. San Francisco: Jossey-Bass.

Coase, R. H. (1937). The nature of the firm. *Economica*, **4**, 386–405.

Cyert, R. M. and March, J. G. (1963). *A Behavioral Theory of the Firm*. Englewood Cliffs, NJ: Prentice-Hall.

Follett, M. P. (1995). *Mary Parker Follett: Prophet of Management*, ed. P. Graham. Boston, MA: Harvard Business School Press.

Gabor, A. (2000). *The Capitalist Philosophers*. New York: Times Business.

Heilbroner, R. L. (ed.) (1986). *The Essential Adam Smith*. New York: W.W. Norton.

Jensen, M. C. and Meckling, W. H. (1976). Theory of the firm: Managerial behavior, agency costs, and ownership structure. *Journal of Financial Economics*, 3, 305–60.

McGregor, D. M. (1960). *The Human Side of Enterprise*. New York: McGraw-Hill.

March, J. G. and Simon, H. A. (1958). *Organizations*, 2nd edn. Cambridge, MA: Blackwell.

Pfeffer, J. and Salancik, G. (1978). *The External Control of Organizations*. New York: Harper and Row.

Phillips, R. A. (2003). *Stakeholder Theory and Organizational Ethics*. San Francisco: Berrett-Koehler.

Roethlisberger, F. J. and Dickson, W. J. (1939). *Management and the Worker*. Cambridge, MA: Harvard University Press.

Shafritz, J. and Ott, J. S. (2001). *Classics of Organization Theory*. Fort Worth, TX: Harcourt.

Smith, A. (1982a) [1790]. *The Theory of Moral Sentiments*, ed. D. D. Raphael and A. L. Macfie. Indianapolis, IN: Liberty Classics.

Smith, A. (1982b) [1776]. *The Wealth of Nations*, ed. D. D. Raphael and A. L. Macfie. Indianapolis, IN: Liberty Classics.

Taylor, F. W. (1911). *The Principles of Scientific Management*. New York: Norton.

Thompson, J. D. (1967). *Organizations in Action*. New York: McGraw Hill.

Towne, H. R. (1886). The engineer as economist. *Transactions of the American Society of Mechanical Engineers*, 7, 428–32. Reprinted in Shafritz and Ott (2001).

Williamson, O. (1985). *The Economic Institutions of Capitalism*. New York: Free Press.

organizational theory, ethical issues in: Part 2

Shaker A. Zahra and Peggy A. Cloninger

Organizational theory (OT) focuses on the behavior of companies or units, and their leaders and members. It examines those factors that determine the behavior of these groups and their consequences for organizational effectiveness. OT theorists have offered many insights into human motives and behaviors. They have also devoted considerable intellectual energy to the study of formal and informal organizations, and examining rational and political processes. Consequently, OT can enrich our understanding of the roots and consequences of business ethics.

Although OT scholars and business ethicists focus on many common issues, they espouse different views of organizational and human behaviors. While these views may occasionally conflict, they often complement one another. This article explores areas of convergence and divergence between OT and business ethics by focusing on three levels of analysis. The first is the concept of the firm and its implications for human behavior. The second is inter-organizational relations. The third is the relationship between the company and society.

THE CONCEPT OF ORGANIZATION AND ITS IMPLICATIONS FOR HUMAN BEHAVIOR

The concept of the firm represents an important starting point for scholars of both business ethics and OT. Whereas economics and finance theorists view the firm as a web of contracts, OT and business ethics scholars espouse a broader and more complex definition. Both groups believe that formal contracts among organizational members, and ensuing rights and obligations, are only a part of the concept of the organization. A deeper appreciation of human behavior can be achieved by delving into the values of different organizational members, because these values undergird the choices made by individuals and groups. Differences in, and clashes of, values often induce differences in orientations, interests, and behaviors. Thus, by exploring the causes and manifestations of value differences, the stage is set to understand and explain the behavior of groups and individuals within the organization.

OT researchers further suggest that organizations are political entities, where individuals attempt to pursue their interests. To achieve organizational goals, formal and informal controls are needed. These controls help promote cohesion and unity of direction, thus reducing conflicts. Still, conflicts persist because of the divergence of interests and differences in power among members of the organization.

Nowhere is conflict more recognized in OT research than in the relationship between principals (owners) and agents (managers). A large body of research suggests that the rise of public corporations has resulted in the dispersion of ownership which, in turn, has resulted in loss of control by owners over their companies. Professional managers have become centers of power in the large contemporary organization. These managers own very little or no stock in the companies they run. Lacking connection to the company and its owners, managers may pursue goals that do not maximize shareholders' value or that undermine their property rights. Conflicts of interests are represented in a multitude of managerial actions such as over-diversification (Hoskisson and Hitt, 1994), excessive compensation, and mis-directing corporate resources.

Conflicts between principals and agents are at the very core of scholarly conversation in OT and business ethics. Much attention has centered on governance systems that align the interests of the two groups, an interest that has generated a large number of studies (Zahra and Pearce, 1989). The company's board of directors is widely viewed as the ultimate means of corporate control. Yet in reality boards have often failed to align the interests of shareholders and managers. Instead, many boards have become subservient to managers. Moreover, attempts to empower boards have not been very successful (Pearce and Zahra, 1991).

Researchers in OT and business ethics have explored different ways to empower boards and make them true instruments of corporate governance. OT scholars have focused on restructuring the board composition, information flows, and decision-making processes. They have also explored ways to provide incentives to senior managers to place shareholders' interests ahead of other groups. Conversely, business ethicists have attempted to understand when and why conflicts of interests between principals and agents arise, outline guidelines to ensure alignment of their goals, and explore the effect of corporate and professional codes of ethics on this alignment. Clearly, contributions by business ethicists complement those offered by OT researchers (*see* CONFLICT OF INTEREST; CODES OF ETHICS).

The relationship between individual employees and the organization is another key area of interest to both OT and business ethics. In OT, both the structuralist and Marxist schools have given this issue special attention. The Marxist view states that the separation of ownership of the tools of production from labor creates conflicts between owners and workers (employees). This happens because owners have an incentive to exploit their workers to maximize their profits. Structuralists view the organization somewhat differently. They assert that the formal structure perpetuates the domination of owners over labor. They also claim that work organizations often dehumanize employees, stifle their initiative and creativity, emphasize compliance and conformity, and foster feelings of anomie and alienation. The individual is thus exploited for the good of the owners.

Not all OT researchers accept the Marxist or structuralist views. Some have advocated several more enlightened views of the organization, conceiving more humanistic organizations that foster creativity, enhance individuality, and provide an environment conducive to human growth. Promoting these more humanistic organizations has become a central theme in the current research in OT. Managers have been admonished to build a wholesome quality of working life (QWL) in order to better integrate organizational and individual goals and needs.

One outcome of the debate on the nature of the relationship between the individual and the organization is a growing recognition of the rights and obligations of employees. Here, business ethicists have much to offer OT researchers. There is an obvious fundamental difference between OT theorists and business ethicists. Whereas ethicists appear interested in balancing different interests and promoting moral conduct, OT scholars are more interested in cultivating human capabilities and talents to improve performance and increase productivity. This subtle difference seems to permeate the current theoretical and empirical discussions of employee rights and responsibilities.

Some business ethicists build their arguments within philosophical discussions of human nature and values. They focus on stages of moral development and, accordingly, prescribe appropriate behaviors. Conceptual models of ethical behavior abound. According to Reidenbach and Robin (1990), these models converge empirically on three major dimensions. The first relates to moral equity, which in turn embodies beliefs about the fairness, justice, morality, and acceptability of behavior. The second dimension is relativistic in nature and refers to whether or not a behavior is culturally acceptable. The third dimension is contractual in nature, insofar as it indicates commitment to and consistency with formal and informal work contracts.

This three-dimensional classification shows the potential contribution of business ethicists to the study of behavior in the organization. Yet, like other classifications, it also highlights the difficulty awaiting managers in attempting to ensure ethical behaviors: employees often have very different frames of reference, vary in their cognitive development, and may have different goals and expectations. Accommodating individual differences can sometimes create perceptions and feelings of inequity. Moreover, a group's agreement on a definition of acceptable behavior does not guarantee it is ethical.

The difficulty of prescribing ethical behavior in work organizations becomes apparent in discussions of employee rights and responsibilities. There is no universal agreement on these rights, the approaches the company should take to support and protect them, the limits to be placed on these rights, or the conditions under which these rights can be changed. Further, balancing the rights and responsibilities of different employees may induce conflicts that paralyze the firm, lower productivity, and threaten the very existence of the organization (Werhane, 1985).

Doing what is ethically right can sometimes have unintended negative effects. Consider, for example, companies that have attempted to address past discriminatory hiring practices. These efforts have produced charges of reverse discrimination by groups traditionally favored in corporate hiring (see AFFIRMATIVE ACTION PROGRAMS). Likewise, corporate efforts aimed at helping women break through the glass ceiling have been criticized by male employees. Similarly, granting women maternity leave has sparked controversy, leading to charges of favoritism. Some male employees have sued their employers to establish their right to paternity leave. Doing the ethically right thing can sometimes fuel conflicts that divide the labor force. Of course, this does not mean that companies should not do the right

thing; it merely suggests that sometimes business ethics are as hard to implement as they are hard to define. Therefore, occasionally, OT theorists have avoided discussions of the ethical implications of their strategies for organizational change.

The issues are as complex for the individual as they are for the company. Should an employee blow the whistle on her/his managers if they are engaged in unethical or illegal activities? (see WHISTLE BLOWING). Should they accept as a fact of life the special programs enacted to redress past corporate hiring practices? Should they comply with poorly designed work routines, rather than question their managers' authority? Answering these and similar questions requires considerable soul searching because there are no absolutely correct answers.

INTER-ORGANIZATIONAL RELATIONSHIPS AND BUSINESS ETHICS

OT researchers also focus on inter-organizational relationships that affect the company's ability to secure resources and accomplish its goals. Companies develop joint ventures, join trade associations, and support lobbying on behalf of the industry. Companies also signal their moves to competitors to promote goodwill in the industry. OT theorists acknowledge the fact that some inter-organizational activities can stifle competition and reduce consumer welfare. This happens through interlocking directors, either directly or indirectly, to coordinate the activities of two or more companies. Inter-organizational links, while useful in many cases, can harm the competition in an industry.

Another area of interest is the growing use of competitive analysis, where companies collect and analyze data about their rivals' operations and strategies. Competitive analysis is now widely viewed as a requirement for success. However, some companies use questionable techniques for this purpose. For example, they may spy on their competitors or bribe their employees to gain access to data on a rival's operations. A recent study concluded that managers believe that rising competition, concern over their company's survival, and careerism promote ethical violations in competitive analysis. Surprisingly, managers also indicated these actions can harm the competition in an industry, reduce trust, and inhibit the flow of information in the market (Zahra, 1994).

A third area that has received some attention in the literature is the mutual interdependence of companies. Increasingly, companies are dependent on each other for survival; one company's products are inputs into another company's operations. With the ongoing massive restructuring of the US economy, for example, companies have divested and farmed out some of their operations. Will this interdependence stifle long-term competition and reduce consumer welfare? When are these actions ethical? Whose values should OT researchers use in evaluating the ethical nature of these transactions? Greater attention to these questions can enhance the contribution of business ethics to the study of OT.

OT researchers tend to view inter-organizational relationships as essential to competing in today's global economy. However, the ethical implications of these transactions are not clear. At a first glance, some transactions funnel information to competitors and may lead to tacit collusion. Others may strengthen the bargaining power of existing companies and can stifle the entry of new companies. Still other transactions may prolong the existence of marginally efficient companies, and may undermine the long-term interests of shareholders and society.

Clearly, the ethics of inter-organizational relations deserve greater attention in the literature. Guidelines on ethical versus unethical inter-organizational relations are needed. Business ethicists need to consider three questions that may determine whether an action is ethical or not: Will the action reduce competition in the market? Will the action reduce consumer satisfaction and welfare? Will the action inhibit industry evolution?

The Organization and its Society

OT and business ethics researchers have shown considerable interest in a company's relationship with its society. Both groups appear to accept the multiplicity of, and conflicts among, the company's goals. They disagree, however, on the importance of different organizational goals and how best to reconcile any trade-offs among them. The stakeholder approach (Freeman and Gilbert, 1988) has become the focal point in discussing these disparate views, including recent discussions of the environment in which the earth is recognized as the "ultimate" stakeholder (see STAKEHOLDER THEORY).

Business ethicists have contributed greatly to research into the relationship of the company and society. For instance, they have highlighted the important role of the firm in enhancing social welfare, improving living conditions, nurturing human growth, and protecting the environment and natural resources. This discussion has influenced companies' efforts to promote ethical behavior among managers and employees. Many of these recommendations have become an integral part of corporate codes of ethics. OT scholars have accepted this view and incorporated it into their discussions of the organizational mission and goals.

The debate on the corporate social role has entered a new phase. In today's global economy, managers must deal with a complex array of stakeholders, with different goals, interests, and values. Business ethicists are therefore confronted by a number of challenging questions. Whose values should dominate the mission and goals of the global corporations? Whose work ethics should guide employee behavior? If societies differ in their definition of ethical behaviors, can these different views be reconciled? What are the implications of cultural and ethnic diversity for corporate codes of ethics? These basic questions are now receiving some attention in the literature. However, as the globalization of the world economies continues, these issues are likely to become more complex. Transnational clashes of values will become a centerpiece in discussions of business ethics and OT (see GLOBALIZATION; INTERNATIONAL BUSINESS ETHICS; MULTINATIONAL CORPORATIONS).

Conclusion

This article has focused on the role of business ethics in OT. It has suggested that business ethicists and OT theorists share many common interests, but still differ in their conclusions. Business ethics research has enriched OT discussions of the nature of the firm and its impact on employee behavior, inter-organizational relationships, and the role of the organization in society. While researchers have focused on the nature of the firm's relationship with society or individuals, many gaps remain in the literature on inter-organizational relationships. The growing use of these transactions suggests a need for greater attention to their ethical implications. Moreover, there is need for understanding the ethical issues associated with transnational organizations. By giving greater attention to the changing dynamics and nature of competition in the global marketplace, business ethics can further enrich future OT research. Clearly, business ethicists and OT scholars have much to learn from each other.

Bibliography

Freeman, R. E. and Gilbert, D. R., Jr. (1988). *Corporate Strategy and the Search for Ethics*. Englewood Cliffs, NJ: Prentice-Hall.

Hoskisson, R. E. and Hitt, M. A. (1994). *Downscoping: How to Tame the Diversified Firm*. New York: Oxford University Press.

Pearce, J. and Zahra, S. (1991). Relative powers of CEOs and boards of directors: Associations with corporate performance. *Strategic Management Journal*, 12, 135–53.

Reidenbach, R. and Robin, D. (1990). Toward the development of a multidimensional scale for improving evaluations of business ethics. *Journal of Business Ethics*, 9, 639–53.

Werhane, P. (1985). *Persons, Rights and Corporations*. Englewood Cliffs, NJ: Prentice-Hall.

Zahra, S. (1994). Unethical practices in competitive analysis: Patterns, causes and effects. *Journal of Business Ethics*, 13, 53–62.

Zahra, S. and Pearce, J. (1989). Boards of directors and corporate financial performance: A review and integrative model. *Journal of Management*, 15, 291–334.

P

Pareto optimality

Dana R. Clyman and Thomas M. Tripp

A Pareto optimal allocation is one from which it is impossible to improve any party's share without diminishing the share of another party.

When allocating resources, whether through a negotiation process, political process, or simply by edict, the question arises: How do you know whether the final allocation is a "good" one? Regardless of one's philosophy, a necessary condition for "goodness" with which few people would argue is Pareto optimality. One would never want to accept a non-Pareto optimal allocation, because such an allocation could always be improved upon for at least one party – if not for all parties – without requiring any sacrifice from any other party.

This idea is presented graphically in figure 1, which depicts the collection of possible resolutions of a two-party allocation decision, as measured by the value each party derives from each possible resolution. The points on and within the curve represent the values to the parties of the possible allocations. Because no allocations are mapped to points outside the curved boundary, that boundary represents the

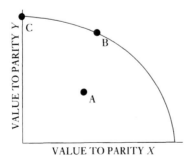

VALUE TO PARITY *X*

Figure 1

collection of Pareto optimal allocations. No allocation represented by a point within the curved space is Pareto optimal because there is always another allocation on the curved boundary that is preferred by both parties.

For instance, compare the allocations whose values to the parties are depicted by points A and B. No matter what the value systems are to which the individuals subscribe, as long as the individual's values are measured accurately, then both parties must prefer allocation B to allocation A. It follows immediately, therefore, that all "good" allocations are Pareto optimal.

But are all Pareto optimal allocations good? Consider allocation C. This allocation could be described as "*Y* gets everything; *X* gets nothing." In a multiparty allocation decision, equivalent allocations are those where one party or a few parties get everything, and everyone else gets nothing. Few would welcome such outcomes. The reason is clear: *Pareto optimality says nothing about fairness.* In other words, while few would disagree with the idea that Pareto optimality is a *necessary* condition for assessing the "goodness" of allocations, few would argue that it is *sufficient* (*see* FAIRNESS).

There is also an additional problem with Pareto optimality. When one moves from few parties to many, the concept itself becomes less useful. The reason is that, as the number of parties increases, the probability increases dramatically that at least one party would be made worse off whenever one allocation is replaced by another. In other words, in multiparty allocation decisions, a far greater percentage of the collection of possible allocations are Pareto optimal. And, in the extreme, when all allocations are Pareto optimal, Pareto optimality cannot discriminate among allocations. Hence, as the number of parties increases, the Pareto optimality condition loses its power.

Nevertheless, the condition is still necessary. One should never accept an allocation – no matter how many parties – that is not Pareto optimal. Furthermore, in two-party allocation decisions, like one-on-one negotiations, Pareto optimality is a powerful tool for discriminating among alternatives.

Bibliography

Clyman, D. R. (1995). Measures of joint performance in dyadic mixed-motive negotiations. *Organizational Behavior and Human Decision Processes*, **64**, 38–48.

Clyman, D. R. (1996). Measuring cooperation in negotiations: The impossible dream. In R. J. Zeckhauser et al. (eds.), *Wise Choices: Decisions, Games and Negotiations*. Boston, MA: Harvard Business School Press, 388–99.

Deutsch, M. (1975). *Distributive Justice*. New Haven, CT: Yale University Press.

Lax, D. A. and Sebenius, J. K. (1987). Measuring the degree of joint gains achieved by negotiators. Unpublished manuscript, Harvard University.

Lind, E. A. and Tyler, T. R. (1988). *The Social Psychology of Procedural Justice*. New York: Plenum Press.

Raiffa, H. (1982). *The Art and Science of Negotiation*. Cambridge, MA: Harvard University Press.

Tripp, T. M. and Sondak, H. (1992). An evaluation of dependent variables in experimental negotiation studies: Impasse rates and Pareto efficiency. *Organizational Behavior and Human Decision Processes*, **51**, 273–95.

participatory management

Michael Maccoby

The concept of participatory or participative management has been used in the context of traditional hierarchical industrial organizations or bureaucracies. It means that, to a greater or lesser extent, managers share their power with employees, managers, or non-managers who are lower in the structure. The opposite of participative management is autocratic or dictatorial management.

This overview first describes the experience of participative management in traditional industrial organizations and then reports recent organizational initiatives that have redefined participative management in terms of empowerment and interactive management.

Within the traditional organizational framework, there are three degrees of participative management: consultation, value-based influence, and formal power sharing. Consultation is the form of participation wherein a manager seeks the viewpoints of subordinates before making a decision. There is no commitment by the manager to act according to the wishes or suggestions of subordinates (Weber, 1964). Value-based influence implies a commitment by management to take account of subordinates' viewpoints before making decisions. Typically, there is agreement that managers will honor explicitly stated values. In some of the most effective companies, these values try to balance the interests of a number of stakeholders, in particular, owners, customers, and employees (Kotter and Heskett, 1992) (*see* ORGANIZATIONAL CULTURE). Formal power sharing entails a more democratic form of governance in which some, but not necessarily all, so-called managerial decisions are made by consensus or vote. This type of participation or co-determination is not usually adopted freely, but is typically forced on management by the political system or stakeholder power (e.g., unions, environmental groups). It is then up to management to make good use of co-determination by adopting a participatory style of leadership.

An example of co-determination is the German Works Council, where members elected by the employees can make some decisions concerning changes in work rules and also influence top management's strategic decisions. Another example is the General Motors Saturn factory in Spring Hill, Tennessee, where union officials, elected by workers, formally share power with plant management.

Participatory management often implies that while managers may listen to or even share power with those lower in the hierarchy, they reserve the right to make the final decisions. Exceptions to this rule are those cases where through collective bargaining there is a contractual agreement with a union to share power – for example, in setting wages and evaluating working conditions. In some organizations there is a mixture of consultation, influence, and power sharing, depending on the type of decisions involved.

WHY DOES MANAGEMENT INVITE PARTICIPATION?

The purposes of practicing participatory management are to arrive at better decisions, to achieve employee buy-in for implementing management decisions, and to increase employee motivation. By listening to frontline employees, managers gain information and ideas. Workers may find processes ineffective, inefficient, or cumbersome. They may offer suggestions for improvement. Especially in the age of service, frontline employees are in the best position to hear customer complaints and ideas for improvement. Experience demonstrates that at all organizational levels, when people feel they have been heard and their views given serious consideration, they are more likely to support management decisions and implement management plans.

Beginning with the pioneering research on worker morale at the Western Electric Hawthorne plant in Chicago in the 1930s, there has been evidence that by giving employees a say in how work is performed, satisfaction with work usually improves (Rothilsberger and Dickson, 1939) (see the discussion of resistances to participation, below, for exceptions). Surveys indicate that a majority of employees believe that participation in these areas will improve organizational effectiveness and quality. Employees in the US want to have a say in deciding how to do their jobs and organize the work; deciding what training is needed for their jobs; setting work schedules, including breaks, overtime, and time off; setting goals for their work group; deciding how to work with new equipment or software; and setting safety standards and practices.

Japanese industries took the lead in the 1960s and 1970s by integrating participative management into a total quality management system, including the idea that all workers have internal and external customers they must satisfy. Workers are encouraged to participate in continuous improvement and are rewarded for ideas adopted by management. At Toyota Motors, in the early 1990s, there were about 50 ideas per worker per year proposed and of these 80 percent were adopted, with workers rewarded with bonuses for those adopted. Japanese management also allows workers to experiment with changing work methods. In most large Japanese companies, worker representatives are consulted on strategic decisions.

The participation of unions as institutions in management decisions is required by law in Germany and Sweden, where union representatives sit on supervisory boards. This participation can range from a more perfunctory information sharing, with minimal consultation, to significant involvement in shaping and implementing policies. In the US, in some companies, the United Autoworkers (UAW), United Steelworkers (USW), United Needletraders Industrial and Textile Employees (UNITE), and Communication Workers of America (CWA) have reached contractual agreement to participate with management in decisions ranging from market strategy to process changes. In these cases, the unions also encourage management to involve frontline employees in decision-making.

LIMITS TO PARTICIPATORY MANAGEMENT

The ability to participate in a meaningful way depends on such factors as size of group, participants' knowledge of the situation, and speed of decision-making required. There are occasions when management wants to limit the number of people involved in sensitive negotiations because of possible negative consequences if the information becomes known publicly.

There are also cases where employees reject invitations to participate. For example, union representatives have refused to participate in decisions which might adversely affect their members. Although generally union members want their leaders to participate with management, there are instances in which participation could erode their political support. Crozier (1964) showed that many French bureaucrats rejected opportunities to participate in order to protect autonomy and the right to object, or in the case of union members, grieve a management decision.

An issue is the fear by employees that by volunteering ideas to improve productivity, they may no longer be needed and lose their jobs. In the large Japanese companies, participation has been reinforced by promises of employment security. In the US, some unions have bargained for employment security, while others in industries undergoing continual restructuring and rationalization have negotiated programs for retraining and continual learning to enhance employability.

Effective participatory management requires a high level of mutual trust, otherwise managers will not share information and their subordinates will not want to open themselves to possible manipulation or exploitation. The most effective participative management is based on practicing values such as respect, honesty, and an attempt to obtain mutual benefit from decisions. (Participatory management also requires that employees are educated sufficiently about management goals so they can contribute meaningfully to decisions. Equally, it requires facilitative skills and the willingess to listen to employees on the part of managers. Maccoby (1988) has found that managers with an "expert orientation" have a hard time learning from subordinates.)

In 1994 the Communication Workers of America studied examples in which they had participated with the management of telecommunication companies. They found that when participation was value based and information was shared sufficiently, there were significant benefits to both management and employees. However, they also found cases of pseudo-participation and promises for participation made by a manager who then left his or her position and was replaced by someone who took advantage of the trust previously developed.

Beyond Participative Management

A new organizational model is emerging. It is flatter than the traditional industrial bureaucracy, with fewer middle managers. The ideal is that top management determines strategy and the frontline is empowered to implement and adapt it (*see* EMPOWERMENT). To some degree, these elements have been part of good management in the past. What is most different is the movement from autonomous functions to interactivity and heterarchical cross-functional teams.

The new organizational model has resulted from four factors: the shift in the mode of production in manufacturing as well as in service industries, the lessons of total quality management, the competitive demand for speed in bringing new products to market, and the significant development in the 1980s and 1990s of information and telecommunications technology (IT). IT allows manufacturing processes to be automated and information to be shared rapidly to and from the front lines. Furthermore, the new IT has allowed management to "re-engineer" processes to cut out layers of control and communication.

Under this model, instead of following directions, the frontline employees must be "empowered" to use judgment and make decisions that will both satisfy customers and implement management strategy. In the case of continuous process technology, quick decisions must be made for purposes of safety and to avoid product losses.

In the heterarchical, cross-functional team or network, leadership shifts according to who has the appropriate knowledge. An example is a concurrent design process which replaced a linear design process that moves from design to engineering to production. Instead, designers, engineers, marketing experts, and frontline production employees (and in some cases, customers) work together, share different types of knowledge, and make decisions by consensus. The results are better products, produced more rapidly.

The management model proposed by Ackoff (1994) redefines participatory management as interactive management, based on the concept of the organization as a social system with the goal of satisfying the main stakeholders: customers, employees, and owners. The interactive planning process requires that management design an "ideal future" which is interpreted and implemented by people in different parts of the system. A continual dialogue is led by management concerning how to close the gaps between the present state and the organization's ideal design.

This interactive approach to continual transformation and employee empowerment was the basis for AT&T's Workplace of the Future and was agreed to by its unions – CWA and IBEW – in their 1992 and 1995 contracts (Heckscher et al., 2003). Each business unit and division had a planning council which included union representatives who were there not because of their demand for power, but because they facilitated communication, and by emphasizing employee needs and protecting their contractual rights, they increased trust in the process. The planning council was led by management with the value-based participatory approach. The council designed the ideal future, developed an education program with the aid of professors from Rutgers University, and interactively supported attempts by the various workplaces to interpret and implement it. However, this participation ended in 2000 when new leadership at AT&T became adversarial to union organizing in newly acquired units and the unions withdrew from participation.

In the new interactive model, with or without union cooperation, participatory management no longer depends on a few innovative managers. It engages everyone in the organization in learning what is needed for success by all stakeholders. Interactive management becomes the most effective way of developing a customer-responsive, efficient, and highly motivated organization.

Bibliography

Ackoff, R. (1994). *The Democratic Corporation: A Radical Prescription for Recreating Corporate America and Rediscovering Success*. New York: Oxford University Press.

Crozier, M. (1964). *The Bureaucratic Phenomenon*. Chicago: University of Chicago Press.

Heckscher, H., Maccoby, M., Ramirez, R., and Tixier, P. (2003). *Agents of Change: Crossing the Post-Industrial Divide*. Oxford: Oxford University Press.

Kotter, J. and Heskett, J. (1992). *Corporate Culture and Performance*. New York: Free Press.

Maccoby, M. (1988). *Why Work: Leading the New Generation*. New York: Simon and Schuster.

Rothlisberger, F. J. and Dickson, W. J. (1939). *Management and the Worker*. Cambridge, MA: Harvard University Press.

Weber, M. (1964). *The Theory of Social and Economic Organization*. New York: Free Press.

political philosophy and business ethics

Allen Buchanan

The definition of *political philosophy* is itself a matter of controversy, especially among those who identify themselves as political philoso-phers. There is perhaps even less agreement on proper methodology than on what constitutes the subject matter of political philosophy. However, most if not all of the following questions are widely recognized to be the proper concern of political philosophy.

- Under what conditions, if any, is political authority and, in particular, the authority of the state, legitimate? What are the scope and limits of state authority – what are the legitimate functions of the state? What is the proper division between the public and private sectors in a society – which functions are best performed by government, which by the private sector (including the market and non-profit organizations)?

- Assuming that the state is to be the ultimate guarantor of justice, through the threat of coercive enforcement of principles of justice, which principles of justice are appropriate (under which sorts of circumstances, for which types of societies)?

- What is the nature of political obligation? When can persons rightly be said to have an obligation to obey the law or the commands of those in positions of political authority? What are the scope and limits of political obligation – when is resistance to political authority justifiable?

- What are the moral justifications for various forms of government, including democracy and federalism?

- What sorts of conduct are ethically permissible or obligatory for government officials? (To what extent, if any, can appeals to the higher good of the country or "national security" justify behavior on the part of officials that would otherwise be immoral?)

- More generally, how, if at all, does the ethics of governmental organizations differ from the ethics of individuals or of private sector organizations? Under what conditions can members of political units (citizens) or officials (in government bureaucracies) be said to be collectively, as distinct from individually, responsible for outcomes resulting from their actions or omissions?

- What are the rights and duties of membership in political units (especially states)? What are the moral justifications for various proposals for determining criteria for membership (e.g., ethnicity, religion)? What is the moral case for a rights of immigration and emigration, rights of political sanctuary, etc.?

- What are the moral constraints that bear on war, considered primarily as an activity of states? (Traditional political philosophy distinguishes between the moral justification for going to war and the morality of what is permissible in the conduct of war.)
- To what extent are the legitimate goals of political association (the establishment of justice, security, etc.) best served by a state-centered system as opposed to one in which other political units (regional associations such as the European Union, confederations, etc.) have a more prominent role?

This list of questions, which is not intended to be exhaustive, should make it clear that political philosophy is primarily concerned with normative issues, even though the exploration of normative questions invariably requires conceptual analysis and rests on empirical assumptions about institutions and human nature as well. If there is a theme that unifies these questions, it is the investigation of the *morality of the institutionalized uses of power, and ultimately of coercive power.*

The proper definition of *business ethics* is, if anything, even more contested than that of political philosophy. As with political philosophy, there are contrasting views on both methodology and subject matter. The following alternative conceptions of business ethics are among those currently most prominent in the field, although a number of them have come under strong criticism. As we shall see, each has important (though usually unstated) implications for what the relationship between business ethics and political philosophy is.

RULE-EGOISM

According to this conception, business ethics is concerned exclusively with the ethical conduct of business people as they go about their business activities. In other words, like most of the other conceptions listed below, the rule-egoist model limits business ethics primarily if not entirely to the consideration of ethical questions *within* the sphere of business, without explicitly investigating ethical issues concerning the *institution* of business as a whole. More specifically, according to the rule-egoist model, it is the task of political philosophy, not of business ethics, to investigate the justifications for using markets as the basic institution for producing and distributing the material requirements of human welfare. Instead, it takes the existence of the market, and hence of a distinct sphere of business activity, for granted and asks: Why should people engaged in business act ethically? The answer this view gives is disarmingly simple: Business people should act ethically because it is in their long-term interest to do so. The assumption is that business activity is purely self-interested and that by following moral rules business people can, at least in the long run, best serve their self-interest.

One prominent variant of rule-egoism is the "social responsibility" view of business ethics. The defining thesis of the social responsibility view is that business people can best serve their interests (and the common interest of the business community as a whole) by acting ethically so as to preempt regulation imposed by government upon business. The idea is that by acting ethically (and making the public aware that they are doing so) business people can convince the public and their legislative representatives that such external controls are not necessary because business people can be counted on to do what is right without the threat of government coercion.

The rule-egoist conception is flawed on a number of counts. First, it provides no guidance whatsoever in cases in which there is not a close congruence between self-interest and what is ethical – and is quite implausible if it claims that the two never diverge.

Second, the rule-egoist position simply assumes that there is an independent and adequate list of moral principles available in society at large which business people can simply follow in order to maximize their own interests. In this sense it adopts an uncritical attitude toward received moral principles. Indeed, rule-egoism is not properly described as an ethical theory at all. Instead, it is only a theory of why business people should be ethical – taking it for granted that there is no problem of determining what being ethical requires.

Third, rule-egoism tends to overlook entirely (or at least to minimize) the fact that corporate interests (for example, the interest in maximizing profit or growth or market share) and the interests of a given individual within the corporation can and do diverge. Indeed, some of the most vexing ethical dilemmas in business have to do with the conflict between loyalty to organizational interests and a proper regard for one's own interests as an individual, including one's interests in the well-being of one's family. Political philosophy takes this general type of conflict as one of its central problems, especially in its investigation of the scope and limits of the individual's obligation to obey the law and the duties of government officials to comply with institutional policies. Saying that business people ought to act ethically because it is in "their interest" sheds no light on these issues.

Fourth, rule-egoism, at least in its "social responsibility" version, begs important questions by assuming that existing conceptions of self-interest (or corporate interests, or the interests of the business community as a whole) are legitimate and beyond ethical criticism.

Questions about the moral character of business institutions as a whole, or of the market system, are never broached within this model. Because of this exclusion, the rule-egoist model divorces questions of political philosophy entirely from the domain of business ethics. In particular, the justice of market systems is never an object of inquiry. Yet whether behavior within a given institution is ethically permissible generally depends at least in part upon whether the institution itself is compatible with the requirements of justice. By offering a conception of business ethics that is entirely independent of political philosophy's concern about the justice of institutions, the rule-egoist model presents an unduly foreshortened picture of the domain of ethical issues concerning business (*see* EGOISM, PSYCHOLOGICAL EGOISM, AND ETHICAL EGOISM).

THE SIMPLE LEGALIST/LOYAL AGENT MODEL

This conception of business ethics is suggested by a widely cited article by Milton Friedman entitled "The social responsibility of business is to increase its profits" (1970). The central claim is that the only ethical obligation of business people, who are viewed as agents of the corporation's shareholders, is to maximize profits, subject only to conformity to legal requirements (contract law, antitrust law, etc.). Legal requirements are seen as "rules of the game" necessary for preventing fraud and theft and avoiding anti-competitive practices that interfere with the functioning of the market in the production of human welfare. Clearly, this view, like rule-egoism, fails to consider either the possibility that a market institution within which corporations operate is subject to ethical criticism (for example, on grounds of justice), or the problem of determining exactly what moral constraints ought to be observed, in what circumstances, in the pursuit of profit. In addition, the simple legalist/loyal agent conception of business ethics assumes without argument that (a) all shareholders are concerned exclusively with maximizing profit (rather than with the pursuit of ethical values) and (b) managers have no ethical responsibilities to try to educate or convince shareholders that certain ways of pursuing profit are inappropriate. Here again, an unduly restricted conception of business ethics overlooks important ethical issues that are the stock-in-trade of political philosophy, in particular the moral obligations of persons in positions of authority within institutions to dissent from policies they regard as unethical and to be a voice for reform within the organization.

Friedman suggests that the pursuit of profit maximization is subject to the constraint of "ethical custom" as well as the law. However, his view here is subject to the same criticism advanced above against rule-egoism, namely, that it adopts a wholly uncritical attitude toward what are commonly taken to be valid ethical principles, assuming that there is no problem of determining what ethics requires. In effect, Friedman is able to conclude that the only moral obligation of business people is to maximize profits only by assuming that there are no cases in which there are serious questions about whether the means by which profit maximization is pursued are ethical. Most importantly, Friedman's conception of business ethics lacks any plausibility unless it is assumed that the institution of the market is itself beyond any serious ethical criticism. In that sense, the simple legalist/loyal agent view is able to exclude issues of political philosophy from the domain of business ethics only by assuming that political philosophy has already provided an adequate justification for the "rules of the game" of the market, including the overriding commitment to profit maximization.

THE CASUISTRY MODEL

According to this conception of business ethics, the proper subject matter of ethical inquiry is the concrete case in which an ethical problem arises; and the proper method of inquiry is to argue by analogy from cases in which we have a confident consensus on what the right thing to do is, to those cases in which we are unsure about what is ethical. The casuistry model does not deny the role of general principles in business ethics (or in ethics generally). However, it does include a substantial degree of skepticism about the possibility of systematic ethical theory, and insists that whatever general principles we eventually endorse should emerge from reflection on the concrete realities of particular cases.

The casuistical approach suffers from two main limitations. First, by its own admission, it is not helpful for exploring ethical issues about large-scale institutions, whose characteristics are necessarily more abstract than the features of particular cases, and about whose legitimacy we may have no clear moral intuitions. Second, and more importantly, the casuistry model assumes, quite implausibly, that the nature of our ethical responses to particular cases that arise within a framework of institutions are not themselves influenced – and possibly distorted by – morally questionable features of the framework itself. For this reason, there are serious doubts about the reliability of the results casuistry yields even in its attempt to cope with particular ethical problems, quite apart from its apparent inability to engage larger issues of the justice of the institutional framework within which these particular problems arise.

MANAGERIAL PROFESSIONALISM

A fourth conception tacitly restricts the domain of business ethics to the ethical problems encountered by managers. Indeed, the fact that much, perhaps the greater part, of the contemporary business ethics literature is addressed exclusively to managers shows the pervasiveness of this conception. In effect this constitutes a reduction of business ethics to a particular kind of role morality or a species of professional ethics.

One obvious flaw of this approach is that it either denies the fact that employees who are not managers face serious ethical problems in business or facilely assumes that the solution to all such problems lies primarily in the hands of managers. Quite apart from this indefensible elitism, the managerial professionalism view has another grave defect, one which it shares with each of the preceding conceptions of business ethics: it precludes inquiry into the ethical status of the institutions within which the role of manager exists. Once again, an impoverished conception of business ethics results from the exclusion of the sorts of larger institutional issues that are the subject of inquiry in political philosophy.

AN ALTERNATIVE CONCEPTION OF BUSINESS ETHICS – BLURRING THE BOUNDARY BETWEEN BUSINESS ETHICS AND POLITICAL PHILOSOPHY

A more fruitful conception of business ethics recognizes that for a number of reasons it is implausible to make such a sharp separation between business ethics and political philosophy. Instead, we should think of these as being fields which are in part complementary and in part overlapping.

The preceding critical analysis of several influential conceptions of business ethics reveals that what political philosophy and business ethics have in common is this: both are concerned with the *morality of the uses of collective power in organizations operating in the public sphere*. There are differences, of course, the most important being that the power of political institutions, at least of the most inclusive of these, includes the explicit and legally sanctioned use of coercion. In spite of this difference, however, there are many important similarities. In both business and government, there are complex issues concerning the ethics of whistleblowing and, more generally, of the permissibility and obligatoriness of dissent, conscientious refusal, and of obligations to work for reform within the organization. In both business and government, ethical codes and principles are often invoked to cope with conflicts of interest that are inherent in principal–agent relationships, due to the asymmetry of knowledge between principal and agent and in recognition of the fact that assuring a perfect congruence of interests between principal and agent through material incentives (or through monitoring and the threat of penalty) is often impractical or too costly. Furthermore, a growing body of social science research indicates that moral commitments and values (including honesty and fairness) play a crucial role in achieving stable cooperation within organizations, regardless of whether they are in the private or the public sector. Finally, business competition and war are similar in that they are both zero sum interactions (in which one party's gain is another's loss). To that extent both business ethics and political philosophy are concerned with the ethical constraints on competition in which the stakes, in terms of welfare and power, are high.

Given that both political philosophy and business ethics are concerned with the ethics of institutions and with the moral uses of institutionalized power in the public sphere, researchers in both should be willing and able to borrow from one another. In addition, recent developments in the evolution of the global economy make the case for cooperation even stronger and may even call into question our ability to distinguish the two fields. Increasingly, we are witnessing the emergence of extremely powerful transnational institutions that are partly economic and partly governmental in nature. Examples include the European Union and the World Bank (whose leaderships include both officers of banks and representatives of national governments). For this reason as well, business ethics and political philosophy are becoming even more closely linked.

Bibliography

Clegg, S. (1989). *Organization Theory and Class Analysis: New Approaches and New Issues*. New York: Walter de Gruyter.

De George, R. T. (1993). *Competing with Integrity in International Business*. New York: Oxford University Press.

Donaldson, T. and Werhane, P. (1988). *Ethical Issues in Business: A Philosophical Approach*, 3rd edn. Englewood Cliffs, NJ: Prentice-Hall.

Freeman, R. E. (1991). *Business Ethics: The State of the Art*. New York: Oxford University Press.

Friedman, M. (1970). The social responsibility of business is to increase its profits. *New York Times Magazine*, September 13.

Goodin, R. and Pettit, P. (1993). *A Companion to Political Philosophy*. Oxford: Blackwell.

Kymlicka, W. (1990). *Contemporary Political Philosophy: An Introduction*. Oxford: Clarendon Press.

Pateman, C. (1970). *Participation and Democratic Theory*. Cambridge: Cambridge University Press.

Velasquez, M. G. (1992). *Business Ethics: Concepts and Cases*, 3rd edn. Englewood Cliffs, NJ: Prentice-Hall.

positive organizational scholarship

Scott Sonenshein

Positive Organizational Scholarship (POS) pursues the scientific study of positive outcomes, attributes, and processes within organizations. The field does not favor a single theory, but rather positions itself as an umbrella term that encapsulates how, when, and why individuals achieve the good life in work contexts. Given that business ethics scholars study relationships between work contexts and the pursuit of the good life, there are obvious bridges linking business ethics and POS. By articulating these connections, I will start an important conversation between the two fields that will strengthen both of them.

In order to elucidate the connections between business ethics and POS, I first offer a definition of POS. Afterwards, I describe POS's intellectual heritage in positive psychology. While positive psychology is certainly not the only intellectual discipline to have influenced POS, I specifically highlight positive psychology because of its direct role in helping establish POS. Finally, I conclude with a discussion of two important connections between POS and business ethics, suggesting how the two fields of inquiry can build off each other's strengths and accomplishments.

WHAT IS POSITIVE ORGANIZATIONAL SCHOLARSHIP?

A useful approach for defining POS is to understand the meaning of "Positive," "Organizational," and "Scholarship" (Cameron, Dutton, and Quinn, 2003b). By "Positive," researchers refer to positive states and positive dynamics associated with those states. Most organizational scholarship focuses on negative states such as inefficient performance, production errors, or unethical behaviors, as well as negative dynamics that lead to those states (Cameron, 2003). POS does not deny the importance or legitimacy of researching these organizational phenomena. Rather, the field calls for the expansion of organizational research to include a more purposeful focus on positive phenomena. POS researchers focus on constructs such as resilience – making improvements even under adverse circumstance (Sutcliffe and Vogus, 2003); positive deviance – significant departures from norms in honorable ways (Spreitzer and Sonenshein, 2003, 2004); and high-quality relationships – life-giving relationships that create meaning (Dutton, 2003; Dutton and Heaphy, 2003). These constructs focus on when, how, or why individuals pursue and/or how organizations enable excellence, well-being, and virtue.

POS's emphasis on "Organizational" refers to the importance of situating the study of positive phenomena within work contexts. For POS researchers, context plays a central role in enabling individuals to achieve the good life. Instead of serving as a medium to dehumanize individuals, POS claims that organizations actually have the potential to help their members fulfill the good life.

Finally, POS researchers stress the importance of "Scholarship." Careful theoretical development and empirical research help separate POS research from the recommendations given by pop psychologists and the prescriptions of management gurus. No doubt, POS scholars openly embrace a set of value assumptions. These value assumptions play a prominent role in guiding the questions that researchers pose. For example, POS clearly favors questions that address how individuals achieve the good life, and how organizations enable individual, group, and organizational excellence. Moreover, POS starts from the universal premise that all individuals want to achieve the good life. However, unlike pop psychologists and management gurus, POS leaves describing and explaining the exact means and mechanisms for achieving the good life to empirical exploration. POS

researchers emphasize the importance of using objective research methods, even if their research questions inevitably reflect normative biases. The prominence of the scientific method in POS reflects the field's conscious desire to integrate the study of positive phenomena within mainstream organizational research by using longstanding empirical methodologies.

INTELLECTUAL ROOTS OF POSITIVE ORGANIZATIONAL SCHOLARSHIP

Many intellectual disciplines have influenced the development of POS, such as appreciative inquiry in organizational development (Cooperrider et al., 1999) and community psychology (Jahoda, 1958). However, for the sake of brevity, I will focus on the discipline with the most direct, and perhaps most widespread, influence on the development of POS: positive psychology. POS arose, in part, from the cross-pollination of psychology and organizational behavior departments (Bernstein, in press).

Positive psychology (for an extensive overview of the field, see Snyder and Lopez, 2002) was formally introduced in 1998 by Martin Seligman during his tenure as president of the American Psychological Association (APA) (Seligman, 1999). Seligman observed that the overwhelming majority of psychology research focused on curing disease and dysfunction. Clinical diagnostic materials such as the *Diagnostic and Statistical Manual of Mental Disorders* (DSM) (American Psychiatric Association, 2000) embrace a "disease model of human nature" (Peterson and Seligman, 2003b: 15). Psychologists have concentrated on how to cure diseases – that is, how to take individuals from a negative state of dysfunction to a neutral state called normal. While curing disease is obviously a worthwhile endeavor, psychology has surprisingly paid little attention to how individuals can achieve a positive state of well-being, flourishing, and excellence. Positive psychologists, in the words of Seligman (2002: xii), wonder more about "how to go from plus two to plus seven" and "not just how to go from minus five to minus three and feel a little less miserable." The objective of both positive psychology and POS is not how to make improvements so as to take individuals or organizations from negative states to slightly less negative or neutral states. Rather, both intellectual viewpoints focus on the majority of the population – those already at a normal level of functioning – and seek to elevate these individuals into a state of enhanced well-being, excellence, and virtue.

Far from calling for a ban on traditional psychology – referred to as "business-as-usual-science" (Peterson and Seligman, 2003b) – POS scholars and positive psychologists think that the study of both negative and positive states demands legitimate intellectual attention. That is, the goal is not to denigrate the tremendous progress made by organizational behavior and psychology over the past century. Instead, POS and positive psychology attempt to rectify the significant imbalance of negative to positive research projects scholars undertake by widening the research agendas in their respective fields. At the heart of this plea is a call for recognizing that studying the good life is as legitimate a scientific endeavor as studying disease or organizational dysfunction.

Connections between Business Ethics and Positive Organizational Scholarship

Since its inception in 2001, POS has made remarkable progress. For example, POS has published the first scholastic reader on positive organizing (Cameron, Dutton, and Quinn, 2003a) and the first special issue of a journal dedicated to POS research (Cameron and Caza, 2003). Moreover, over 50 scholars now openly align themselves with POS, and scores of others conduct research consistent with POS's main tenets (University of Michigan Business School, 2003). Yet, in order for POS to expand from a developing field into a fully established intellectual paradigm, researchers need to make progress on two important fronts, both of which require tighter integration with business ethics scholarship. First, POS researchers need to invest in additional theoretical development about the good life. Second, POS researchers need to recognize and build off prior work in business ethics that poses similar questions. By making progress on both of these fronts, POS can craft a deeper contribution to the organizational studies literature. POS can use its empirical tools to garner a better understanding of how

to reach the good life, an important question for business ethics scholars as well.

Further Theoretical Development of the Good Life

One of the most important contributions that business ethics can make to POS is to help with defining what constitutes the good life. POS scholars and positive psychologists both claim to help individuals reach the good life, but are remarkably vague about what exactly constitutes the good life. For some researchers, the good life focuses on subjective well-being (SWB) (Diener, 2000), and for others, the good life emphasizes virtues (Cameron, 2003; Peterson and Seligman, 2003a). But while POS scholars often refer to the good life in general, and SWB and virtues in particular, POS scholars, trained as social scientists, are not well suited for expanding these concepts or articulating their philosophical bases. When, how, and why individuals achieve the good life may require empirical investigation. But what constitutes the good life inevitably necessitates philosophical discussion, something with which business ethics scholars can aptly help. Take, for example, Robert Solomon's work on virtues, which emphasizes the importance of character in business. Solomon grounds his theory using an Aristotelian approach that recasts the way we conceptualize organizations in a manner consistent with POS. In Solomon's words, his work is a "battle in a war against those myths and metaphors and other forms of conceptual isolationism that lead us to think about business as a game – or worse, as a jungle or a war for survival" (Solomon, 1992: 19). Solomon's work not only describes the way we live, but it also describes the way we *ought* to live. It provides a set of aspirational ideals for which we ought to strive. Questions about *ought* – and discussions about how we *ought* to live – are not understandable merely through empirical descriptions but rather require philosophical articulation as well.

While business ethicists can provide POS researchers with the content of the good life, I think POS can offer business ethics a set of important empirical findings that help scholars understand more about how to achieve – and the social and psychological consequences of achieving – the good life. The description and explanation of organizational processes and psychological enablers that help individuals reach the good life can disseminate important information to scholars and practitioners interested in bringing the good life to organizational contexts.

OVERLAP OF INTELLECTUAL INTERESTS

At their very cores, business ethics and POS share important value assumptions often overlooked by other management disciplines. Both disciplines seek to influence mainstream management and organizational research to adopt positive and affirmative assumptions about human behavior, including that individuals have moral agency and can exist as moral creatures. The two disciplines can affirm the similarities of their intellectual interests and build off each other's strengths in order to influence the larger management literature. For example, one of the more recent influential developments in business ethics addresses the importance of conceptualizing organizations as being capable of fostering the good life (e.g., Hartman, 1996). Business organizations are not the only type of ethically impoverished institutions described most prominently by Robert Jackall (1988). As early as 1994, R. Edward Freeman (1994) called for an end to the separation between "business" and "ethics," suggesting that theoretical work often treats business and ethics as conceptually distinct. Too much attention, Freeman (1995) argued, is placed on describing business organizations as radically self-interested or exploitative. The separation of business and ethics is manifested in many well-engrained dichotomies, such as the purpose of the firm, the moral norms used to describe business, and the conceptualization of human behaviors within organizations (Wicks, 1996). This "negative" view of business leads to a focus on compliance ethics, as opposed to more aspirational understandings of business ethics (Paine, 1994). While business ethicists have lamented the implicit theoretical separation of business and ethics, they have offered little empirical support that business and ethics can converge in the empirical world. Positive organizational scholars can help document how individuals achieve the good life within work contexts – and how work contexts are at least equally capable of fostering the good life as they are at taking it away. POS's concentration on

empirical testing can demonstrate that Freeman's intuition about the separation of business and ethics is correct: namely, that despite the preponderance of research that separates business from ethics, there are many positive, and integrative, stories we can tell about business and ethics.

CONCLUSION

POS and business ethics ultimately center their energies on improving the human condition. Whereas business ethics instructs us about our endpoint – legitimate views of the good life – POS helps us reach that endpoint by describing and explaining the underlying processes and dynamics that lead to the good life. An understanding of both destination and journey can help individuals achieve the excellence and well-being valued by both positive organizational scholars and business ethicists. The common world descriptions implicit in most management theories consider organizations ethically impoverished institutions that deny individuals their moral agency and strip away their humanity. Greed, radical self-interest, corruption, and the exclusive pursuit of shareholder returns overshadow the compassion, loyalty, relationships, and extraordinary performance within organizations. While both views may exist in the empirical world, we unfortunately know very little about the latter view. POS's call for expanding research agendas to encompass understanding of the good life should receive a warm welcome from business ethicists who think that the good life serves as the very foundation on which we build and understand business organizations.

Bibliography

American Psychiatric Association (2000). *Diagnostic and Statistical Manual of Mental Disorders DSM-IV-TR (text revision)*, 4th edn. Washington, DC: American Psychiatric Association.

Bernstein, S. (in press). Positive organizational scholarship: Meet the movement: An interview with Kim Cameron, Jane Dutton and Robert Quinn. *Journal of Management Inquiry*.

Cameron, K. (2003). Organizational virtuousness and performance. In K. Cameron, J. Dutton, and R. Quinn (eds.), *Positive Organizational Scholarship*. San Francisco: Berrett-Koehler.

Cameron, K. and Caza, A. (2003). Special issue on contributions to positive organizational scholarship. *American Behavioral Scientist.*

Cameron, K., Dutton, J., and Quinn, R. (eds.) (2003a). *Positive Organizational Scholarship.* San Francisco: Berrett-Koehler.

Cameron, K., Dutton, J., and Quinn, R. (2003b). Foundations of positive organizational scholarship. In K. Cameron, J. Dutton, and R. Quinn (eds.), *Positive Organizational Scholarship.* San Francisco: Berrett-Koehler.

Cooperrider, D. L., Sorensen, P. F., Whitney, D., and Yaeger, T. F. (eds.) (1999). *Appreciative Inquiry: Rethinking Human Organization Toward a Positive Theory of Change.* Champaign, IL: Stipes Publishing.

Diener, E. (2000). Subjective well-being: The science of happiness and a proposal for a national index. *American Psychologist*, 55 (1), 34–43.

Dutton, J. E. (2003). *Energize Your Workplace: How to Create and Sustain High-Quality Relationships at Work.* Ann Arbor: University of Michigan Business School Press.

Dutton, J. E. and Heaphy, E. (2003). The power of high quality connections. In K. Cameron, J. Dutton, and R. Quinn (eds.), *Positive Organizational Scholarship.* San Francisco: Berrett-Koehler.

Freeman, R. E. (1994). The politics of stakeholder theory: Some future directions. *Business Ethics Quarterly*, 4 (4), 409.

Freeman, R. E. (1995). *The Business Sucks Story.* Paper presented at the Society for Business Ethics, Vancouver.

Hartman, E. M. (1996). *Organizational Ethics and the Good Life.* New York: Oxford University Press.

Jackall, R. (1988). *Moral Mazes.* New York: Oxford University Press.

Jahoda, M. (1958). *Current Concepts of Positive Mental Health.* New York: Basic Books.

Paine, L. S. (1994). Managing for organizational integrity. *Harvard Business Review*, 72 (2), 106–18.

Peterson, C. and Seligman, M. E. P. (2003a). *The VIA Classification of Strengths and Virtues.* Washington, DC: American Psychological Association.

Peterson, C. and Seligman, M. E. P. (2003b). Positive organizational studies: Lesson from positive psychology. In K. Cameron, J. Dutton, and R. Quinn (eds.), *Positive Organizational Scholarship.* San Francisco: Berrett-Koehler.

Seligman, M. E. P. (1999). The president's address. *American Psychologist*, 54, 559–62.

Seligman, M. E. P. (2002). *Authentic Happiness.* New York: Free Press.

Snyder, C. R. and Lopez, S. J. (eds.) (2002). *Handbook of Positive Psychology.* New York: Oxford University Press.

Solomon, R. C. (1992). *Ethics and Excellence.* New York: Oxford University Press.

Spreitzer, G. and Sonenshein, S. (2003). Positive deviance and extraordinary organizing. In K. Cameron, J. Dutton, and R. Quinn (eds.), *Positive Organizational Scholarship.* San Francisco: Berrett-Koehler.

Spreitzer, G. M. and Sonenshein, S. (2004). Toward the construct definition of positive deviance. *American Behavioral Scientist*, 47 (6), 828–47.

Sutcliffe, K. M. and Vogus, T. J. (2003). Organizing for resilience. In K. Cameron, J. Dutton, and R. Quinn (eds.), *Positive Organizational Scholarship.* San Francisco: Berrett-Koehler.

University of Michigan Business School (2003). Positive organizational scholarship website: http://www.bus.umich.edu/Positive/.

Wicks, A. C. (1996). Overcoming the separation thesis: The need for a reconsideration of business and society research. *Business and Society*, 35 (1), 89–118.

practical reasoning

Douglas N. Walton

is a goal-driven, knowledge-based, action-guiding species of reasoning that meshes together goals with possible alternative actions that are means to carry out those goals, in relation to an agent's given situation as he or she sees it, and concludes in a proposition that recommends a prudent course of action. Practical reasoning is a defeasible kind of argumentation, in that it is tentative in nature – subject to revision as new information concerning the agent's changing circumstances comes to be known. Practical reasoning is crucial to the underlying framework of virtue ethics, where it defines the right personal characteristics needed to undertake a prudent course of action in relation to an agent's ethical goals as applied to a given situation (*see* VIRTUE ETHICS).

An example would be the case of a manufacturer who wants to market a drug, but knows that satisfying the regulatory safety requirements will involve costly testing of the drug. To arrive at a prudent line of action, the manufacturer might take a close look at how the drug would be tested, including such factors as who would carry out the tests, how much this would cost, what options are available, how long it would take, and so forth. They would then put this information together with their goals in manufacturing, making a judgment of how much of a priority manufacturing this particular drug should be for them. Their deliberations on the question should take the form of practical reasoning that meshes their general goals as a company with specific information about this drug, and the means necessary to manufacture it under current, or reasonably predictable, circumstances.

Practical reasoning, in its simplest form (Walton, 1990), is an inference with a goal premise and a means premise: "G is my goal ; carrying out action A is the means, in this situation, to realize G; therefore, I should carry out A." Although this simple structure gives the reader a basic idea of how practical reasoning works, other factors need to be taken into account. In Walton (1991: 109), these other factors are expressed in the form of critical questions that should be asked in a given case. One factor is that there may be more than one means available, so that the various possible alternative lines of action may need to be compared. Another factor is that the agent may have multiple goals, so that it may be necessary to decide which goals have priority over others. There may even be practical conflicts (i.e. conflicts between carrying out one goal and carrying out another), where the line of action required to carry out one goal would interfere with, or cancel out, the line of action required to carry out the other. Another factor is that of side-effects. The practical reasoner needs to ask critical questions about the likely consequences, both positive and negative from the point of view of her goals, of carrying out a contemplated action. A final factor is that the contemplated action may require prior actions to carry it out. Often, a number of preparatory actions are needed. Thus, in complex practical reasoning, it is not just a single action in isolation that needs to be considered. Typically, it is a connected sequence of actions that leads toward the goal.

Bibliography

Walton, D. N. (1990). *Practical Reasoning: Goal-Driven, Knowledge-Based, Action-Guiding Argumentation.* Savage, MD: Rowman and Littlefield.

Walton, D. N. (1991). *Begging the Question: Circular Reasoning as a Tactic of Argumentation.* New York: Greenwood Press.

pragmatism and business ethics

Sandra B. Rosenthal

The application of ethics to the business context often takes one of two approaches, one emphasizing the study of cases without any extensive theoretical background, the other emphasizing the application of abstract ethical theories embodying universal principles to specific cases. The former tends toward a "my opinion versus your opinion" analysis without a conceptual backdrop for sound reasons, while the latter is frequently a very sterile and abstract approach to ethics that does not connect with the dynamics and problems of the business world.

Moreover, the litany of conflicting theories and principles gives rise to a kind of ethical smorgasbord with no guidelines for choice among varying theories, some of which may give conflicting signals concerning the right decision and result in totally different courses of action. The basis for choice, which now becomes the heart of moral reasoning and the very foundation for moral decision-making, remains mysterious, outside the realm of theoretical illumination, and ultimately ignored. Adding to the problem, the application of a moral rule to a specific case can be used by ill-intentioned individuals to justify all kinds of behavior which common sense judges to be immoral. Moreover, actions done with the best of intentions by virtuous people may nonetheless be misguided and can only be so judged by something other than intentions. Rules seem to judge intentions, yet bad intentions can misuse rules. Part of the problem of making ethical decision-making relevant for the business community may be an implicit, unexpressed, but nonetheless pervasive and "commonsense" perception by practitioners that the above problems are in fact the case.

Classical American pragmatism offers a unique philosophical framework that provides a unifying ground for how and why we evaluate rules and traditions and choose among various principles in an ongoing process of dealing with change and novelty. At the same time, this pragmatic theory cannot be set over against the case approach to business ethics, for it is a theory that demands the return to situations in their concrete fullness and richness as the very foundation for the development of moral decision-making as inherently contextual and situational, and for the emergence of moral "rules" as tentative working hypotheses abstracted from the fullness of concrete decision-making. In so doing pragmatism focuses on a relational understanding of humans, communities, and corporations alike, thereby moving beyond the long tradition of atomic individualism which ultimately places the individual and the group in an irreconcilable conflict, with all the moral pitfalls this involves. Rather, there is an ongoing process of adjustment between the unique creativity of the individual entity of whatever sort, and the conforming dimension of the "common other" within which it is embedded and with which it is inextricably intertwined as an organic whole. Value emerges within these relational contexts, and the adjustment between the two dimensions of the shared and the unique gives rise to the novel and creative dimensions of moral decision-making.

Value situations, like all situations as understood within the pragmatic context, are open to inquiry and require the general method of experimentalism by which a progressive movement from a problematic situation to a meaningfully resolved or secure situation takes place. This method involves creatively organizing experience, directing one's activity in light of that creative organization, and testing for truth in terms of consequences: does the organization work in bringing about the intended result? In the case of value inquiry as the embodiment of experimental method, this involves moving from a situation filled with problematic or conflicting valuings to a resolved or meaningfully organized experience of the valuable through an expansive reconstruction or reintegration of the situation.

Morality is to be discovered in concrete human experience where conflicting interests and desires need to be adjudicated, rather than in conflicting moral principles or rights that are debated in the abstract. Our concrete decision-making is influenced by all sorts of conflicting guidelines, and such decision-making cannot be simplified to accord with any single one of them. Added together, traditional theories are contradictory because they are each attempting to substitute for a concrete, rich moral sense operative in decision-making some one consideration which is found operating there in various degrees at various times and in various situations, turning it into a moral absolute to determine what is the moral course to follow at all times and in all situations. Any rule, any principle, any scheme, is an attempt to make precise and abstract some consideration which seems to be operative in concrete moral experience, but this experience is ultimately too rich and creative to be adequately captured in that manner.

Traditional moral theories can be useful in shedding light on moral situations and providing additional guidelines for evaluating the moral aspects of different courses of action. It is not that traditional moral theories do not get hold of something operative in our concrete moral decisions, but that in lifting out one aspect, they ignore others, reducing moral action to some fixed scheme. Utilitarian theories, deontological theories, virtue theories, individualisms, and communitarianisms all get at something important, but they each leave out the important considerations highlighted by the other theories. And the relative weight given to any of these, as well as to a host of other considerations in coming to a decision as to what ought to be done, will depend on the novel and complexly rich features of the situation in which the need for the decision arises. In this process, we are often reconstructing moral rules. Principles are not directives to action, but are suggestive of actions. Just as hypotheses in the technical experimental sciences are modified through ongoing testing, moral principles are hypotheses which require ongoing testing and allow for qualification and reconstruction. The most important habits we can develop are habits of intelligence and sensitivity, for neither following rules nor meaning well can suffice. But bringing about good consequences in the contextual richness of different situations through moral decision-making helps develop, as byproducts, both good character traits as habits of acting and good rules as working hypotheses needing ongoing testing and revision.

Moral reasoning as concrete, then, is not working downward from rules to their application, but working upward from the full richness of moral experience and decision-making toward guiding moral hypotheses. The resolution of conflicting moral perceptions, which provide the context for new ideals, cannot be resolved by a turn to abstractions, but through a deepening sensitivity to the demands of human valuings in their commonness and diversity. Such a deepening does not negate the use of intelligent inquiry, but rather opens it up, freeing it from the products of its past in terms of rigidities and abstractions. In the area of ethics, this deepening focuses intelligent inquiry on the experience of value as it emerges within human existence, allowing us to grasp different contexts, to take the perspective of "the other," to participate in dialogue with "the other" to determine what is valuable.

Moral reasoning as concrete rather than abstract and discursive incorporates in its very dynamics moral sensitivity and moral imagination. The operation of reason cannot be isolated from the human being in its entirety. Moral reasoning involves sensitivity to the rich, complex value-ladenness of a situation and to its interwoven and conflicting dimensions, the ability to utilize creative intelligence or moral imagination geared to the concrete situation, and an ongoing evaluation of the resolution. The goal is not to make the most unequivocal decision, but to provide the richest existence for those involved. This requires an enrichment of the capacity to perceive the complex moral aspects of situations rather than a way of simplifying how to deal with what one does perceive. Moral maturity in fact thus increases rather than decreases moral problems to be mediated, for it brings to awareness the pervasiveness of the moral dimension involved in concrete decision-making. When we slide over the complexities of a problem, we can easily be convinced that absolute moral principles are at stake. And the complexities of a problem are always context dependent and must be dealt with in the context of a concrete situation.

This position, of course, rules out absolutism in ethics, but it equally rules out subjectivism and relativism, for it is rooted in the conditions and demands of human living and the desire for meaningful, enriching lives. We create and utilize norms or ideals in the moral situation, but which ones work is dependent upon their ability to integrate, harmonize, and expand the real relational value-laden contexts within which humans are embedded. While the experience of value arises from specific, situational contexts shaped by a particular tradition, this is not mere inculcation, for the deepening process in getting beneath rules or principles offers the openness for breaking through inculcated tradition and evaluating one's own stance. In this way we are operating not in closed perspectives, but rather in perspectives that open onto broad human community.

The pragmatic view attempts to combine the commonness of humans *qua* human with the uniqueness of each human *qua* human in a way which allows for a value situation of intelligently grounded diversity accompanied by an ongoing process of evaluation and continual testing, thereby avoiding both dogmatic imposition or irresponsible tolerence. Though moral diversity, just as diversity in general, can flourish within a community, when such diversity becomes irreconcilable conflict, intelligence must offer growing, reconstructed contexts which can provide a workable solution. These ingredients of concrete moral decision-making discussed above have implications for understanding the pragmatic concepts of both workability and growth.

Workability cannot be taken in the sense of workable for oneself only, for individuals are inextricably tied to the community of which they are a part. Nor can workability be taken in terms of the short-range expedient, for actions and their consequences extend into a indefinite future and determine the possibilities available in that future. Finally, workability in the moral situation cannot be taken in terms of some abstract aspect of life such as economic workability, etc., for moral situations are concrete, and workability in the moral situation must concern the ongoing development of the concrete richness of human experience in its entirety. Workability and growth go hand in hand. Workability involves resolution of conflict through reconstructed expanded contexts, and the expanding understanding of varied and diverse interests through a widening of perspective is precisely concrete growth. Workability and growth, properly understood, are inherently moral, and the ethical dimension of business decisions involves consideration of both in their concrete fullness. In this way, pragmatism can hold that the ultimate goal in the nurturing of moral maturity is the development of the ability for ongoing self-directed growth.

What particular skills, then, must be cultivated if ethics is to thrive in the business context? What is needed is the development of the re-organizing and ordering capabilities of creative intelligence, the imaginative grasp of authentic possibilities, the vitality of motivation, and a deepened sensitivity to the sense of concrete human existence in its richness, diversity, and complexity. The importance of this latter cannot be over-stressed. It is this deepened, "felt" dimension that regulates the way one selects, weighs, and conceptually orders what one observes. The vital, growing sense of moral rightness comes not from the indoctrination of abstract principles but from attunement to the way in which moral beliefs and practices must be rooted naturally in the very conditions of human existence. It is this attunement which gives vitality to diverse and changing principles as working hypotheses embodied in concrete moral activity. And it provides the ongoing direction for well intentioned individuals to continually evaluate and at times reconstruct ingrained habits and traditions. Humans cannot assign priority to any one basic value, nor can their values be arranged in any rigid hierarchy, but they must live with the consequences of their actions within concrete situations in a process of change.

The cultivation of the ethical skills highlighted by the pragmatic position will allow those engaged in business activity to utilize ongoing change in the concrete contexts of corporate life, with the increasing complexity, pluralism, and diversity these contexts manifest, to bring about ongoing enriching growth of the firm in its multiple relations. In this process, theory is not sacrificed for practice but, rather, theory embodies practice. The balancing of and choice among moral rules as working hypotheses and their ongoing reconstruction when needed lends itself to, indeed demands, the use of cases in all their situational richness and the bottom up approach to moral decision-making which this incorporates.

Bibliography

Aristotle (1985). *Nicomachean Ethics*, trans. T. Irwin. Indianapolis, IN: Hackett.

Dewey, J. (1983). *Human Nature and Conduct*. In J. A Boydston (ed.), *The Middle Works*, Vol. 14. Carbondale: Southern Illinois University Press.

Dewey, J. (1990). *Logic: The Theory of Inquiry*. In J. A Boydston (ed.), *The Latter Works*, Vol. 12. Carbondale: Southern Illinois University Press.

Kant, I. (1959). *Foundations of the Metaphysics of Morals*, trans. W. W. Beck. New York: Library of Liberal Arts.

Rawls, J. (1971). *A Theory of Justice*. Cambridge, MA: Harvard University Press.

Rosenthal, S. (1986). *Speculative Pragmatism*. Amherst: University of Massachusetts Press.

Ryan, A. (1974). *John Stuart Mill*. London: Routledge and Kegan Paul.

Schneewind, J. B. (ed.) (1965). *Ethical Writings*. New York: Collier.

praxis

Richard P. Nielsen

is the theory and method of appropriate action for addressing ethics issues and developing ethical organizations.

The difference between theoria and praxis in organizational ethics is not the same as the difference between theory and application. Organizational ethics praxis focuses on ways of acting in addressing concrete ethics situations. Its units of analysis are not the ethical issues themselves, but rather the action methods for addressing and influencing concrete ethics issues and developing ethical organizations.

The perspective of praxis (theory and method of action) is important and different from the perspectives of theoria (theory of understanding), epistemology (ways of knowing/learning), and ontology (ways of being/existing). Praxis is the least developed area within the field of organization ethics.

Within the area of organizational ethics praxis theory, the approaches that have received the most attention include forcing; for example, top-down punishment-based ethics codes and different types of bottom-up forcing methods, such as various forms of secret and public whistleblowing, obstruction, and adversarial processes. Types of organizational ethics action approaches that have received considerably less, but nonetheless significant, attention are organization due process systems, such as grievance and arbitration procedures that include ethics cases in the due process systems; integrating, for example, win-win problem solving negotiating methods and integrative ethics organizational change and development methods; and dialogue methods. The distinction between integrating and dialogue may seem a bit ambiguous here, but it will be considered in more detail later. A key to the difference is that dialogue has a priority concern for the ethical, while integrating has a more or less equal concern for ethical and other organizational effectiveness criteria.

In classical philosophy, a contrast is made between two dimensions of life within the whole person: understanding (theoria) and action (praxis). There can be some confusion in the Greek-to-English translation from praxis to practice. Praxis/practice does not refer to the mundane, or to an anti-intellectual person, or to a person who is not concerned with ideas or theory. The end of the praxis dimension of life is living well or living appropriately within the *polis*, within the community, within the organization. According to Bernstein (1971: x), " 'Praxis' in this ... sense signifies the disciplines and activities predominant in man's ethical and political life" within the *polis*, within the community, within the organization. In contrast, the end of the theoria dimension of life is knowing or wisdom for its own sake. Within the whole person, both dimensions and perspectives are important; they can and should inform one another.

While classical, scholastic, modernist, postmodernist, and hermeneutic discourse ethics philosophers all consider the concept of praxis somewhat differently, the basic contrast between a perspective of understanding more or less for its own sake (theoria) with a perspective of acting and living appropriately (praxis) is maintained. In an organizational ethics context, for example, theoria focuses on whether or not it is ethical to expose workers to certain levels of a particular chemical. Praxis focuses on how to act in addressing the worker–chemical exposure issue, for example (1) through such forcing methods as punishment-enforced safety codes, whistle-

blowing, etc.; (2) through internal due process, grievance, and arbitration systems; (3) through integrative, win-win negotiating or participative organizational development efforts, for example, with and between those more concerned with safety and those more concerned with reducing costs; (4) through dialogue among managers, or dialogue among managers, workers, and health experts, about what the ethical thing to do is; (5) through some sequence or combination of the above praxis methods.

As referred to above, both perspectives can inform one another. For example, interpretation and explanation theories can precede action and theories of action; and conversely, experiences and theories of action can precede and inform interpretation and explanation theories. That is, one can first theorize about the content of an ethics issue and as a result of such theorizing then theorize about how to act well in addressing the issue in the concrete case, and then act appropriately. Conversely, one can act well in addressing an ethics issue in the concrete case and later theorize about how one acted in addressing the ethics issue, as well as theorize about the content of the ethics issue based on the experience. However, there can also be discontinuities. For example, one can, through theoria, understand that a particular, concrete organizational behavior that one sees and even is part of is unethical. Nonetheless, one can choose not to theorize about how to act in addressing the issue and also not act at all because of lack of interest, concern, courage, and/or constraints, etc. Similarly, one can act well or poorly in addressing an important ethical situation and nonetheless not theorize much or at all about the issue or how to act.

Why should we be concerned about differences in perspectives of theoria and praxis? The more we understand that there are different and multiple action/praxis methods, the more our degrees of freedom and choices increase, so that we can potentially live and act better and more appropriately with respect to the ethical. If we know we have action choices with their relative and contingent strengths and weaknesses, potentially, we can live and act better, more appropriately, more fully.

Confusion or inattention to differences between the theoria and praxis perspectives can lead to needless cognitive either/or controversies with respect to ideas with implicitly different emphases on the learning and action dimensions, when those ideas might be complementary rather than antagonistic. In addition, such either/or interactions in the praxis dimension can needlessly alienate and render ineffective on the praxis dimension potentially fruitful and cooperative interpersonal relationships and interactions that could help advance theoria concerns. Understanding these differences can facilitate potential integration, at least to some extent, of apparently mutually exclusive models when differences between theoria and praxis are attended to.

A serious problem that is often overlooked and that sometimes occurs is that what is effective as an ethics learning method is not always effective as an ethics action method. For example, whether we approach dialogue from perspectives of learning, action, or combined learning–action can be important. While Socratic dialogue can be used from both learning and action perspectives, its strength can be more as learning than action. For example, in the case of Roger Boisjoly and the Challenger Launch, at the time the events of this case were unfolding Boisjoly, in effect, was not able to distinguish and separate dialogue as learning from dialogue as action. He incorrectly assumed that since dialogue was effective as a way of learning and knowing what was ethical, it would be equally effective as interpersonal and inter-organizational praxis method. At the time, the correspondence between dialogue as learning and action appeared so obvious and direct that he was unable to consider alternative praxis methods such as negotiating, and secretly or publicly blowing the whistle. With an understanding of the praxis limitations of Socratic dialogue, Robert Greenleaf, in the case of gender discrimination within AT&T, successfully used Woolman dialogue to build upon and correct this potential praxis weakness in Socratic dialogue by intentionally and specifically including and combining praxis-focused elements with epistemological elements. This is not to suggest that Socratic dialogue is always more effective than Woolman dialogue from a learning perspective, or that Woolman dialogue is necessarily more effective than Socratic dialogue from an

action perspective. While this may be the case and a potential area for empirical research, the point is that it can be very important to recognize and attend to differences in the perspectives of epistemology and praxis in organizational ethics contexts.

There are great opportunities for research and theory-building in this area. First, as referred to above, organizational ethics praxis has not been studied nearly as much as organizational ethics theoria and epistemology. It is an area in relative need of development. Second, from an epistemological perspective, we can study how different praxis methods can combine epistemological and praxis elements that can then be more and less effective relative to learning and knowing about the ethical. This can help us make appropriate choices of learning/knowing methods. Third, from a praxis perspective, we can try to learn more about how there are different and multiple action methods that can increase our degrees of freedom and choices so that we can potentially live and act better and more appropriately with respect to the ethical. If we know how we have action choices with their relative and contingent strengths and limitations in organizational ethics contexts, potentially we can live and act better, more appropriately, more fully. Fourth, we can try to learn more about how epistemology and theoria can inform praxis and praxis can inform epistemology and theoria in organizational ethics contexts. Potentially, these are three dimensions of the whole person that may be able to mutually strengthen each other and the whole person. There are opportunities for considering how these distinctions among dimensions within the whole person can be inseparable parts of the same whole, both with respect to a whole and healthy person, and the whole and healthy organization and organizational community.

Bibliography

Bernstein, R. J. (1971). *Praxis and Action*. Philadelphia: University of Pennsylvania Press.

Ewing, D. (1989). *Justice on the Job: Resolving Grievances in the Nonunion Workplace*. Boston, MA: Harvard Business School Press.

Nielsen, R. P. (1990). Dialogic leadership as ethics action (praxis) method. *Journal of Business Ethics*, **9**, 765–83.

Nielsen, R. P. (1993a). Organizational ethics from a perspective of action (praxis). *Business Ethics Quarterly*, 3 (2), 131–51.

Nielsen, R. P. (1993b). Woolman's I am we triple-loop, action-learning: Origin and application in organization ethics. *Journal of Applied Behavioral Science*, 29 (1), 117–38.

preferential treatment

Ming S. Singer

typically refers to selecting or promoting a less "qualified" minority candidate over a more "qualified" non-minority applicant. Qualification is defined in terms of job-relevant merits. Job-relevant merits can include objective performance indices or test scores that have been proven to be valid predictors of job performance. In the academic literature, preferential treatment is alternatively termed preferential selection, preferential hiring, reverse discrimination, or diversity-based hiring.

Preferential treatment should be clearly distinguished from the practices of either "equal opportunity" or "affirmative action" in personnel functions. Equal opportunity ensures that all potential candidates are given equal chance and treatment in the competition for limited job vacancies. Equal opportunity is not a race- or gender-conscious practice and the final allocation decision is based solely on proven job-relevant merits. In theory, preferential treatment is then the opposite to equal opportunity, in that not all candidates are treated equally and that certain groups of job candidates are given preferences over the others.

Affirmative action, as defined by Seligman (1973), can take on any of these four meanings: (a) pure or passive non-discrimination, (b) pure affirmative action, (c) affirmative action by preferential treatment, or (d) quota hiring. With reference to this definition, preferential treatment involves both (c) and (d). Preferential treatment therefore can be considered as a subset of affirmative action.

The main characteristics of preferential treatment are: (1) it is race- or gender-conscious; (2) it is redistributive in nature as a means of resources allocation; (3) it is intended for specified target groups; and (4) it is intended as a temporary measure.

The justifications for and against preferential treatment are well documented in the philosophical literature. The most frequently cited justification is that preferential treatment obeys the compensatory justice principle in providing compensations to minorities for past discriminations they suffered. Other justifications have been put forward by proponents of preferential treatment: the practice helps to equalize life chances so that minorities can compete with non-minorities on equal terms; it helps to broaden the talent pool of organizations; it ensures having minority role models in the workforce; and it ultimately helps to reduce inequality and to achieve justice in society.

Opponents of preferential treatment argue that proponents of the practice misinterpret the principle of compensatory justice. Compensation for past discrimination should not be required of all members of non-minority groups, nor should reparation go to all minority group members. Further, opponents argue that preferential treatment itself violates the principle of justice by discriminating against non-minority candidates; and that allocation of employment resources should be based on job-relevant merits rather than personal characteristics.

Philosophical debate aside, there has been ample empirical research pertaining to the practical consequences of preferential treatment in employment practices. Using utility analysis, researchers have addressed the question of the economic consequences of preferential treatment in employee selection. Findings suggest that, relative to the net gains of hiring based on merits, preferential hiring would result in less gain or a loss in overall workforce efficiency in the economy. However, this effect could be reduced by adopting the "top-down within-group" method of selection, which appears to result in the least amount of productivity loss and at the same time, significantly increases the minority hiring rate (e.g., Hartigan and Wigdor, 1989).

Social-psychological research (e.g., Heilman and Alcott, 2001; Kravitz et al., 1997; Kravitz and Klineberg, 2000) has shown that preferential treatment may have adverse consequences for individual beneficiaries whom the practice intends to benefit (e.g., negative self-perception and self-evaluation of own abilities or performance). Preferential treatment may also have a negative influence on relations between minority and non-minority groups. However, other authors have noted positive social-psychological consequences of preferential treatment (e.g., feelings of being more respected by others, or raising minorities' expectations of being able to "make it").

The perceived fairness of preferential treatment in employment practices has been studied from the perspective of organizational justice theories. This perspective enables researchers to examine the very core of the issue: concern for social justice in any multicultural society. Although people in general perceive the practice as unfair, researchers have delineated various conditions under which preferential treatment may be seen as less unfair or even fair (e.g., framing the practice in different terms, the discrepancy in merits between candidates, or personal experience with unfair employment-related treatments) (e.g., Singer, 1993).

In the United States the legal status of preferential treatment is not always clear. The Civil Rights Act of 1964 and Title VII of the Act prohibited the use of either preset hiring quotas or any non-job-relevant factors as criteria for employment practices. The Supreme Court has ruled, on several occasions, that a numerical hiring or promotion quota is a lawful remedial action aiming at rectifying employers' past discriminations against minorities. However, between 1964 and 1991, the Supreme Court was not consistent in its interpretations of the Act, and consequently inconsistent in its rulings over alleged cases of preferential treatment in employment practices. These inconsistencies were partly due to, and closely tied to, the then inconclusive and often conflicting findings in psychometric research on differential validity, test fairness, subgroup differences in job-related abilities, and subgroup norming, as well as validity and accuracy in performance predictions.

By the beginning of the 1990s it had become clear that psychometrically sound tests do not discriminate against minority job candidates. The reason for the persistently lower minority hiring rate was found to be due primarily to subgroup ability differences (e.g., Gottfredson,

1994; Gottfredson and Sharf, 1988; Schmidt, Ones, and Hunter, 1992). Consequently, merit-based selection that uses valid tests would inevitably result in a lower minority hiring rate. Under the Civil Rights Act of 1991, employment discrimination is defined in terms of "disparate hiring outcome" rather than "disparate treatment of individual candidates." The Act also stipulates that subgroup norming based on minority status is unlawful.

The United States Supreme Court, in a recent landmark ruling (June 23, 2003), rejected a rigid university admission system that automatically grants additional points to minority candidates (case no. 02–0516), but nonetheless upheld a preferential treatment policy that gives race a significantly less prominent role in admission decisions (case no. 02–0241). The Court's ruling thus allows for a "narrowly tailored use of race" in selection decisions in order to increase the potential benefits of student diversification in educational institutions. This ruling of the Supreme Court will without doubt have a far-reaching impact on preferential treatment in other hiring practices in government agencies and the wider business world. With this ruling in place, the key question surrounding preferential treatment is likely to shift from one of legality to one of how to reach the goal of social justice expediently so that preferential treatment will no longer be required.

See also *affirmative action programs; equal opportunity; multiculturalism; organization ethics; organizational theory, ethical issues in*

Bibliography

Gottfredson, L. S. (1994). The science and politics of race norming. *American Psychologist*, **49**, 955–63.

Gottfredson, L. S. and Sharf, J. C. (eds.) (1988). Fairness in employment testing. Special issue of *Journal of Vocational Behavior*, 33 (3).

Hartigan, J. A. and Wigdor, A. K. (1989). *Fairness in Employment Testing*. Washington, DC: National Academy Press.

Heilman, M. E. and Alcott, V. B. (2001). What I think of you think of me: Women's reactions to being viewed as beneficiaries of preferential selection. *Journal of Applied Psychology*, **86**, 574–82.

Kravitz, D. A. and Klineberg, S. L. (2000). Reactions to two versions of affirmative action among whites, blacks, and Hispanics. *Journal of Applied Psychology*, 85, 597–611.

Kravitz, D. A., Harrison, D. A., Turner, M. E., Levine, E. L., Chaves, W., Brannick, M. T., Denning, D. L., Russell, C. J., and Conard, M. A. (1997). *Affirmative Action: A Review of Psychological and Behavioral Research*. Bowling Green, OH: Society for Industrial and Organizational Psychology.

Schmidt, F. L., Ones, D. S., and Hunter, J. E. (1992). Personnel selection. *Annual Review of Psychology*, 43, 627–70.

Seligman, D. (1973). How "equal opportunity" turned into employment quotas. *Fortune*, March, 160–8.

Singer, M. (1993). *Diversity-Based Hiring: An Introduction from Legal, Ethical and Psychological Perspectives*. London: Avebury.

pricing, ethics of

Daniel T. Ostas

A central tenet of the capitalist creed exhorts the wise business person to buy cheap and sell dear. But can it be unethical to sell a good or service at too high a price? In answering this question, it is helpful to distinguish between *legal* norms of conduct and alternative *ethical* concerns. As a general rule, the American common law permits the seller to seek his or her highest price. The common law focuses on consent. So long as the buyer consents to the price, it is presumptively fair and enforceable. The law seeks to assure that the buyer's consent is meaningful through the doctrines of fraud, duress, undue influence, and unconscionability. It is illegal to lie, to coerce, or to abuse the trust of one's trading partner. However, if the buyer fails to prove fraud or the like, the courts will enforce the contract price, no matter how outrageous that price may appear to an outside observer (Ostas, 1992: 580).

Ethical analysis suggests alternative concerns. First, a "fair" price in an ethical sense may simply mean the market price. Under this view, a price that far exceeds the market would be unfair and unethical even if the buyer consented to it. Historically, the common law embraced such an ethic. Employing the doctrine of *laesio enormis*, American courts in the eighteenth and early nineteenth centuries routinely inquired into the substantive fairness of contractual prices (Horwitz, 1977: 173–80). Prices that significantly exceeded the market rate were not enforced. The market provided an objective benchmark by which to judge the fairness of pricing. By the mid-nineteenth century, the belief in an external notion of value had been discredited in favor of respect for individual autonomy, and the parties alone could determine the value of the commodity or service traded.

Discrimination in pricing raises a second ethical concern. Perhaps it is unethical to discriminate between buyers, demanding a higher price from one class of buyers than another. For example, it is clearly unethical to discriminate between buyers on the basis of race, religion, or ethnicity. "Red-lining" in inner-city lending provides an example. Price discrimination can appear in other contexts as well. Consider the effects of a natural disaster such as a flood. Electricity is out and there is a sudden demand for gasoline-driven electric generators. Can a seller demand its highest price in such a setting? Traditionally, the common law answer is "yes"; so long as buyer and seller consent to the price, the price is fair. State legislatures, by contrast, typically answer "no." Responding to public outcries of "price gouging," state legislatures typically impose a more generous ethic, demanding that the seller not take undue advantage of the necessitous condition of its trading partners. Price discrimination also can be used as a competitive weapon. A large chain-store may charge an unusually low price in hopes of driving its smaller competitors out of business. Again, the common law permits such practices; both ethical analysis and antitrust legislation impose an alternative moral vision of "fair" competition.

The presence of monopoly power also affects the ethics of pricing. Perhaps if a seller has exclusive control over a needed product, fairness would demand that that product be offered at a price that reflects the monopolist's costs. For example, regulated monopolies, such as utilities, must justify price increases before regulatory commissions, where consumer groups have a right to air their concerns. Since the buyer and seller do not have equal bargaining power, the market is not trusted to generate an ethically acceptable price. Yet in other arenas the law permits the monopolist to seek its highest price. For example, a pharmaceutical company has no legal duty to offer its patented life-saving drug at an affordable price. Legally, the company can set its price so as to maximize its profits, even if this means that people in need will not get the drug. Again, ethical analysis suggests an alternative ethic.

Before condemning the common law too harshly, it is important to note that the law itself embodies an ethic. In fact, the common-law approach to pricing can be defended on either libertarian or utilitarian grounds (Epstein, 1975: 293). Libertarianism elevates the principles of individual autonomy and individual liberty to positions of the highest order. Positive laws that interfere with the liberty and autonomy rights of individuals are impermissible and immoral. From a libertarian perspective, only the parties to a contract can determine whether a price is fair, and individuals have no duty to share their property rights with others. Utilitarianism will argue that a regime of freedom of contract generates the greatest good for the greatest number. To a utilitarian, personal autonomy and liberty are not ends in themselves, but rather, are means to generating prosperity for the greatest number. Borrowing from Adam Smith, a utilitarian may argue that attempts to regulate prices will interfere with the invisible hand of the market and lead to unintended negative consequences (*see* INVISIBLE HAND). Given a competitive free market, the best public policy is one that firmly embraces the right of an individual or company to set its own price.

The common law rests on a presumption that individuals should be empowered to set the terms of their own bargains. Ethical analysis suggests some pragmatic limitations to this presumption. First, a price that exceeds the market price gives evidence that some sort of misrepresentation, duress, or abuse of trust may have occurred during the contract negotiations. Ethical reasoning demands that parties treat one another with respect, providing full disclosure of relevant information, and not taking undue advantage (Shell, 1991: 93). Second, although private autonomy and respect for private property are important ethical concerns, they are not the only ethical concerns raised by pricing. Price discrimination on the basis of prejudice (red-lining), to take advantage of a necessitous condition (flood), or to destroy a competitor (chain-store) all violate ethical standards of fair

play. And finally, the presence of monopoly power generates an affirmative ethical duty to offer one's product at a price reasonably tied to one's costs. Such ethical concerns provide a useful supplement to traditional common-law principles.

Bibliography

Chamberlin, E. (1985). *The Theory of Monopolistic Competition.* Cambridge, MA: Harvard University Press.

Darr, F. (1994). Unconscionability and price fairness. *Houston Law Review*, **30**, 1819–91. (Explores the factors that lead common-law courts to find a price to be unfair and unenforceable.)

Epstein, E. (1975). Unconscionability: A critical reappraisal. *Journal of Law and Economics*, **18**, 293–315. (Defends a general regime of freedom of contract on both utilitarian and libertarian grounds.)

Fried, C. (1981). *Contract as Promise.* Cambridge, MA: Harvard University Press. (Links the legal duties of contracting with the ethical duties generated by promising.)

Horwitz, M. (1977). *The Transformation of American Law: 1780–1860.* Cambridge, MA: Harvard University Press. (A seminal work on the history of the common law of contracts.)

Macneil, I. (1980). *The New Social Contract: An Inquiry into Modern Contractual Relations.* New Haven, CT: Yale University Press. (Identifies a communitarian ethic at the core of contractual endeavors.)

Ostas, D. (1992). Predicting unconscionability decisions: An economic model and an empirical test. *American Business Law Journal*, **29**, 535–84. (Concludes that modern courts require evidence of some sort of negotiating impropriety to hold a price unenforceable.)

Shell, G. (1991). When is it legal to lie in negotiations? *Sloan Management Review*, **32**, 93–101. (Explores the interface between law and ethics in contract negotiations.)

Prisoner's Dilemma

Daniel R. Gilbert, Jr.

The Prisoner's Dilemma is an analytical device designed to demonstrate difficulties inherent in voluntary human cooperation.

William Poundstone (1992) locates the origins of the Prisoner's Dilemma in the cold-war era. The Prisoner's Dilemma quickly became popular, he argues, among game theorists who doubted that American and Soviet leaders could practice nuclear self-restraint (*see* GAME THEORY). The Prisoner's Dilemma is customarily defended as a fact of human societies. Robert Frank (1988: 257) claims that prisoner's dilemmas abound. A species of game theory, the Prisoner's Dilemma frequently has been applied to problems of business competition (Oster, 1990; McMillan, 1992; Murnighan, 1991; Dixit and Nalebuff, 1991; Frank, 1988).

The Prisoner's Dilemma storyline involves two prisoners who are suspected of committing a single crime. The prisoners sit in separate prison cells awaiting interrogation. The prisoners are pure egoists who rationally prefer less jail time to more jail time. The story also includes, in the background, a district attorney who lacks sufficient evidence to obtain any conviction without a confession from at least one of the prisoners.

The key ingredients in the Prisoner's Dilemma framework are the payoffs that the district attorney offers the prisoners. Each prisoner is enticed with an offer of little or no jail time *if* she/he confesses *and* the other does not confess (Murnighan, 1991). If both confess, they both can expect lengthy prison terms. If both remain silent, they receive shorter prison terms than if both had confessed. The longstanding moral of the Prisoner's Dilemma is that it is better for the prisoners to cooperate with each other by each keeping silent. Yet, this moral continues, each prisoner's egoism undermines the likelihood of such a solution. Each, as an egoist, goes for the "sucker offer": cooperate with the district attorney by confessing in anticipation of a reward.

Numerous commentators use the Prisoner's Dilemma to make a point about the prospects for human cooperation (Murnighan, 1991; Axelrod, 1984; Frank, 1988). In so doing, they venture into the territory of ethics and, in particular, the territory of any ethics that deals with human communities (*see* COMMUNITARIANISM). In this regard, the Prisoner's Dilemma is ripe for four kinds of ethical scrutiny. Each deals with the suitability of the Prisoner's Dilemma as a way of talking about human community (*see* PRAGMATISM AND BUSINESS ETHICS).

First, there is reason to question whether the Prisoner's Dilemma supports any ethical conception of the "good life." The nameless prisoners have no known pasts, no known ties to one another, no known ties to others (such as family members), and no known life aspirations (Gilbert, 1996; Solomon, 1992). These are characters who simply prefer more to less. At issue is whether this austere view of humanity can serve as a useful guide for living in association with other human beings (Taylor, 1991; Poundstone, 1992). Frank (1988: xi) tries to add "more noble motives" to such a conception of human beings.

Second, there is reason to question whether cooperation is taken seriously in the Prisoner's Dilemma account. Robert Axelrod (1984: vii) introduces his application of the Prisoner's Dilemma with this question: When should a person cooperate and when should a person be selfish in an ongoing interaction with another person? Cooperation, on this view, is *one* among several optional actions that an *individual* could take in relation to another party. On this view, defection from cooperation is also a feasible alternative for the parties to the Prisoner's Dilemma. This conception of cooperation differs from the customary ethical premise that human cooperation is a jointly created result.

Third, there is reason to question whether human community, as something more than reciprocity, is taken seriously in the Prisoner's Dilemma account (*see* FEMINIST ETHICS). Axelrod (1984) takes the Prisoner's Dilemma to the doorstep of human community. He argues that if each prisoner takes a so-called *tit for tat* approach in an iterated Prisoner's Dilemma, then a self-sustaining process of reciprocity will result. Still, there is no common good, no shared sense of "us," in the Prisoner's Dilemma framework, no matter how long and how frequently the two parties interact.

Fourth, there is reason to question whether voluntary human cooperation is taken seriously in the Prisoner's Dilemma account. The payoffs are controlled by the district attorney. Neither prisoner has any way of knowing what the other is saying or what payoffs were offered to the other. The critical question then is whether the Prisoner's Dilemma contains room for anything other than a solution that is imposed by someone acting outside the two prisoners' cells (Gilbert, 1996; Poundstone, 1992). All of Axelrod's (1984) proposals for promoting cooperation involve third party interventions in the prisoners' lives.

The Prisoner's Dilemma is increasingly vulnerable to challenge from a group of business ethics scholars who work in a social contract tradition. Among these contractarian projects are the works of Donaldson and Dunfee (1994) regarding integrative social contracts theory; Freeman (1984, 1994) regarding a stakeholder theory of the firm; Evan and Freeman (1987) regarding "Kantian capitalism"; and Gilbert (1992) regarding strategy, ethics, and conventions.

As contractarians, these writers each start from the premise that human beings are inevitably connected in the patterns of human relationships called communities. They then move to consider what humans should do to protect and to enhance their associations, toward the elusive goal of human solidarity (Rorty, 1989). In so doing, these writers challenge a premise that is central to the Prisoner's Dilemma: persons can live meaningfully by behaving uncooperatively. These contractarians, in short, are working to replace "prisoner" with new metaphors for human beings (Rorty, 1989).

Bibliography

Axelrod, R. (1984). *The Evolution of Cooperation*. New York: Basic Books.

Dixit, A. and Nalebuff, B. (1991). *Thinking Strategically: The Competitive Edge in Business, Politics, and Everyday Life*. New York: W. W. Norton.

Donaldson, T. and Dunfee, T. (1994). Towards a unified conception of business ethics: Integrative social contracts theory. *Academy of Management Review*, 19, 252–84.

Evan, W. and Freeman, R. E. (1987). A stakeholder theory of the modern corporation: Kantian capitalism. In T. Beauchamp and N. Bowie (eds.), *Ethical Theory and Business*, 3rd edn. Englewood Cliffs, NJ: Prentice-Hall, 97–106.

Frank, R. (1988). *Passions Within Reason: The Strategic Role of the Emotions*. New York: W. W. Norton.

Freeman, R. E. (1984). *Strategic Management: A Stakeholder Approach*. Boston, MA: Pitman.

Freeman, R. E. (1994). The politics of stakeholder theory: Some future directions. *Business Ethics Quarterly*, 4 (4), 409–21.

Gilbert, D., Jr. (1992). *The Twilight of Corporate Strategy: A Comparative Ethical Critique*. New York: Oxford University Press.

Gilbert, D., Jr. (1996). The prisoner's dilemma and the prisoners of the prisoner's dilemma. *Business Ethics Quarterly*, 6 (2), 165–78.

McMillan, J. (1992). *Games, Strategies, and Managers*. New York: Oxford University Press.

Murnighan, J. K. (1991). *The Dynamics of Bargaining Games*. Englewood Cliffs, NJ: Prentice-Hall.

Oster, S. (1990). *Modern Competitive Analysis*. New York: Oxford University Press.

Poundstone, W. (1992). *Prisoner's Dilemma: John von Neumann, Game Theory and the Puzzle of the Bomb*. New York: Doubleday.

Rorty, R. (1989). *Contingency, Irony, and Solidarity*. Cambridge: Cambridge University Press.

Solomon, R. (1992). *Ethics and Excellence: Cooperation and Integrity in Business*. New York: Oxford University Press.

Taylor, C. (1991). *The Ethics of Authenticity*. Cambridge, MA: Harvard University Press.

privacy

Rogene Buchholz

is the state of being free from intrusion or disturbance in one's private life or affairs (Flexner, 1987). One's private life is considered to be that which is not of an official or public character, that solitary or secluded part of life that does not include the presence of others. The private part of life is the most intimate and personal part of life that is not exposed to the public or available to outsiders for whatever reason. Privacy refers to that sphere of life where one's behavior, thoughts, feelings, etc., are unknown to others and are not available for their scrutiny.

The self requires a space of its own to be what it is, and this space is the private world. While people play many social roles in the context of a society, the underlying self, the so-called real person, is seen as the ultimate moral unit, deserving of protection and respect in its own right, and not just because of the functional role it occupies. Its sources of dignity are detachable from the specific social fields it occupies. Because the self is not dependent on any particular context for its value, it implicitly imposes a limit on what can be done to beings to achieve any particular social objective. It is capable of standing in opposition to society or taking a critical attitude toward things going on in society, even if this critical attitude is unwelcome.

Yet the self is not an atomic unit independent of other selves. Our dependence on others accounts for most of our moral qualities and accounts for most of what we are and can hope to become. This susceptibility to others is a prime and salutary feature of being human, but it also threatens us in ways that need to be limited. In different historical settings, and in different contexts, different levels of susceptibility to others are appropriate. The concept of privacy limits the amount and effectiveness of social control over an individual. In various settings, different levels of self-direction are appropriate. Privacy protects the individual by limiting scrutiny by others and the control some of them have over our lives (Schoeman, 1992).

On the narrow end of the spectrum, privacy relates exclusively to personal information and describes the extent to which others have access to this information. A broader conception extends beyond the informational domain and encompasses anonymity and restricted physical access. The most embracing characterizations of privacy include aspects of autonomy, particularly those associated with control over the intimacies of personal identity. For advocates of this interpretation, privacy is the measure of the extent an individual is afforded the social and legal space to develop the emotional, cognitive, spiritual, and moral powers of an autonomous agent (Schoeman, 1992).

As social beings, we may be more vulnerable to social than to legal coercion, and the strategies that we construct to combat social coercion will be different from those that insulate us from legal coercion. The strategies that protect individuals from the overreaching power of government are mostly dependent on legal remedies. In the social realm, the defenses will have to be of a more nuanced and informal character as represented in social norms. Given the awareness of the danger of social control, it is curious that so little mainstream philosophical attention is placed on the rights and wrongs of social control mechanisms (Schoeman, 1992).

With respect to privacy, it is interesting to note that the US Constitution does not explicitly mention a right to privacy, although the Bill of Rights does protect what could be called zones of privacy, including the free exercise of religion and security from unreasonable searches and seizures. Not until 1966, however, did the Supreme Court affirm that a right to privacy exists

in a case involving a Connecticut law restricting contraception. While this case pertained to marriage and the family, it wasn't long before this right to privacy was transformed into an individual right that has had many permutations. In *Roe vs. Wade* Justice Blackmun had the following to say about the constitutional right to privacy:

> The Constitution does not explicitly mention any right of privacy. In a line of decisions, however . . . the Court has recognized that a right of personal privacy, or a guarantee of certain areas or zones of privacy, does exist under the Constitution. In varying contexts, the Court of individual Justices have, indeed, found at least the roots of that right in the First Amendment . . . in the Fourth and Fifth Amendments . . . in the penumbras of the Bill of Rights . . . in the Ninth Amendment . . . or in the concept of liberty guaranteed by the first section of the Fourteenth Amendment . . . These decisions make it clear that only personal rights deemed "fundamental" or "implicit in the concept of ordered liberty" . . . are included in this guarantee of personal privacy. (*Roe vs. Wade*, 410 US 113, 1973)

The Fourth Amendment to the Constitution guarantees the right to be secure in one's person, houses, papers, and effects against unreasonable search or seizure. The First Amendment affords people free exercise of religion and freedom of speech, the press, and assembly – freedoms we associate with freedom of conscience. The Fifth Amendment ensures that people cannot be required to testify against themselves, and the Fourteenth Amendment provides that they cannot be deprived of life, liberty, or property without due process of law. In tort law there are four categories of individual protection: (1) intrusion upon a person's seclusion, solitude, or private affairs; (2) disclosure of private, embarrassing facts; (3) public disclosure of a person in a false light; and (4) appropriation of another's name, image, or other aspect of identity, for one's advantage or profit, without that person's consent (Schoeman, 1992: 12).

Privacy has been held to be the most comprehensive of all rights and the right that is most cherished by civilized individuals. It has also been described as the kernel of freedom and as the most basic right from which all other freedoms stem (Rotenberg, 1993). Whether privacy is this basic is subject to debate, but there seems no doubt that privacy serves some basic human need, that there is some kernel to the self that needs to be protected from intrusion and from scrutiny by other people. There apparently are some things that must be kept inviolate and unknown in order for humans to have some space that is entirely their own and is unavailable to others.

The question in an advanced society with all kinds of interconnections between people, and where people are dependent on one another for the performance of certain jobs, is: Where does the sphere of privacy end and the public's need to know begin? Many of the issues that involve privacy in our society can be stated in terms of the individual's right to privacy versus the society's need to know. Other issues, particularly with regard to private property, can be stated in terms of the right to use things in one's own interests versus the public's right to regulate that usage in the public interest. These questions are complex and have no easy answers.

The rapid advances in computer and telecommunications technology have taken individual records and individual papers from the home and private safes and out of the control of the individual. The record-keeping explosion of the computer age has prompted both government and the private sector to keep previously unimagined records and papers relating to the individual (Freeman, 1987). The right to privacy is not absolute in an organized society, for society's need to know must always be balanced against the individual's right of privacy in most democratic societies.

With regard to business organizations, privacy is an issue relating to drug testing, testing for AIDS, computer privacy, and other issues. Drug abuse constitutes a significant problem in the workplace, contributing to impaired productivity and job performance, increased accidents and injuries, violations of security, theft of company property, and diminished employee morale. Highly focused programs such as drug testing can be a valuable deterrent in discouraging nonusers from beginning to use drugs, deterring experimental users from graduating to more serious abuse, motivating non-addicted users to discontinue using drugs for fear of getting caught, and challenging addicted users to seek medical help.

Drug testing is especially appropriate in safety-related work, particularly where public safety is involved. In 1994, new US federal regulations doubled the number of workers that needed to be tested for drug and alcohol use at work. Government required both random alcohol and drug testing each year for 25 percent of transportation workers in such safety-sensitive areas as trucking, aviation, railroads, and pipelines. Only random drug testing was required before. The rules also covered mass-transit workers, and expanded drug testing to intrastate truckers and bus drivers (Newman, 1994).

These new rules were expected to cover 7.5 million workers as compared with 3.5 million before. In addition to the new coverage required by these rules, testing for drugs was on the rise generally, as more companies were testing job applicants and employees. An American Management Association survey reported that in 1993, 85 percent of the 630 companies surveyed had drug-testing programs, including 73 percent of manufacturers and 66 percent of financial service companies. Since 1987 the number of companies with drug-testing programs has tripled (Newman, 1994).

Drug tests can be applied to many different kinds of samples and materials, but most often urine is tested because of the ease of getting a sample, the speed of conducting the analysis, and the low cost involved. But urine tests can be considered an invasion of privacy because the tests can disclose numerous other details about one's private life, such as whether or not an employee or applicant is pregnant or is being treated for various medical conditions in addition to evidence of illegal drug usage. Drug testing is less intrusive if the actual giving of the sample is not observed, since most people using the toilet or urinal usually have an expectation of privacy. However, the absence of supervision means that an employee who does use drugs is able to substitute someone else's "clean" urine or otherwise tamper with the sample.

Testing for AIDS has many of the same problems with regard to privacy, but is different in many important respects. For one thing, there is as yet no cure for AIDS, so identifying people who have the disease will not help them to get on some rehabilitation program. AIDS sufferers also run a greater risk of discrimination than do people on drugs, because the same elements of fear are not present. Once identified as a carrier of the AIDS virus, an individual runs the risk of losing friends, employment, housing, and insurance, despite laws protecting them from discrimination. Another problem is that the results of testing can be misleading as well as inaccurate and lead to unjust treatment of individuals. In spite of these problems, however, much of the general public believe mandatory testing is necessary, particularly in those instances where there is a risk of exposure, where they are willing to set the right to privacy aside in the interests of protecting public health.

Problems in the computer field traditionally had to do with security breaks into the computer network, the accuracy of credit information, and other such problems. Technological changes have brought other issues on the agenda of concern, such as the monitoring of electronic mail (email) and employee performance. Do employers have the right to read employees' electronic mail correspondence, or do employees who work on the equipment own the data even though the employer owns the infrastructure or pays for the service? Is it an invasion of privacy to monitor employees' performance using computer technology without their knowledge? Companies have been encouraged to develop policies on these issues and legislation has been introduced into Congress to require companies to alert workers in advance if they regularly monitor email messages and place limits on how many times a worker could be monitored for performance.

These examples are only a few of the many areas in the workplace where privacy is a concern. The issue, as mentioned before, is generally stated as the employer's or public's need to know versus the individual's right to privacy. This way of stating the issue looks on the surface to be some collective body such as the public pitted against the individual who wants privacy to be respected. However, in the final analysis, the issue really concerns one individual or set of individuals against another individual or set of individuals. People who fly in airplanes are at risk under normal circumstances, and they want to know if they are faced with an additional risk involving pilots who may be on drugs and not able to function properly. Individual managers may want to know what kind of conversations are taking place between employees over electronic mail, but employees want to keep these conversations private, as they do other conversations with fellow employees.

In all of these cases, decisions have to be made about where the zone of privacy ends and where other members of the public have a legitimate right to know in order to protect their own interests. What protections are needed to preserve that core of the individual and protect that space that is necessary for human beings to function, and what intrusions on this space are valid to promote other people's legitimate interests in knowing something about that individual and what he or she is doing? These are difficult questions that any society and its institutions have to continually grapple with as technology and society change, bringing up new issues that were not previously of concern.

Bibliography

Coombs, R. H. and West, L. J. (1991). *Drug Testing: Issues and Options*. New York: Oxford University Press.

DeCew, J. W. (1994). Drug testing: Balancing privacy and public safety. *Hastings Center Report*, 24 (2), 17–23.

Fay, J. (1991). *Drug Testing*. Boston, MA: Butterworth-Heinemann.

Flexner, S. B. (1987). *The Random House Dictionary of the English Language*, 2nd edn. New York: Random House.

Freeman, W. (1987). *The Right of Privacy in the Computer Age*. New York: Quorum.

Furchgott, R. (1992). Invasion of privacy. *Self*, 14 (12), 128–31.

Handlin, O. (1993). The Bill of Rights in its context. *American Scholar*, 62 (2), 177–86.

Newman, A. (1994). Drug testing firms face pluses, minuses in new rules. *Wall Street Journal*, March 15, B4.

Peterman, L. (1993). Privacy's background. *Review of Politics*, 55 (2), 217–46.

Pillar, C. (1993). Privacy in peril: How computers are making private life a thing of the past. *Macworld*, July, 124.

Rotenberg, M. (1993). Communications privacy: Implications for network design. *Communications of the ACM*, August, 61.

Schoeman, F. D. (1992). *Privacy and Social Freedom*. New York: Cambridge University Press.

Viles, P. (1994). Privacy a murky area in First Amendment law. *Broadcasting and Cable*, **124** (3), 70–4.
Worsnop, R. L. (1993). Privacy in the workplace. *CQ Researcher*, **3** (43), 1011–24.

procedural justice

Dierdre N. McCloskey

is the doctrine that justice is not fairness of outcome but fairness of procedure in arriving at the outcome. A procedural definition of the just goes back to John Locke (b. 1632), and behind him to ancient Roman law. "Procedural" justice stands against "substantive" justice, Roman law against Greek philosophy. In the vocabulary of the philosopher Robert Nozick, who in 1974 revived procedural justice, substantive justice is an "end-state" principle. According to end-state or substantive definitions of justice, if someone is now a millionaire, and you regard great wealth as obscene in a world of poverty, you will regard the outcome as unjust. By contrast, Locke and Nozick start and end with private property, to which someone is entitled. "A distribution is just," writes Nozick (1974: 151), "if it arises from another just distribution by legitimate means," such as a market or a court in a republic. The theory is historical, looking back to the origins of wealth.

Thus, Andrew Carnegie the steelmaker was entitled to his wealth if he acquired it by legitimate means from people who had in turn acquired it by legitimate means, back to the Flood. Procedural justice would not, for example, acknowledge the justice of a gospel of wealth, commonly defended on the grounds that the millionaire should "give back to the community some of what he has taken" (the gospel of wealth could be defended perhaps on other grounds, such as magnanimity). The free exchanges in which Carnegie partook to acquire his wealth were legitimate, not takings. Nozick makes the point in his famous Wilt Chamberlain example. Four million people each voluntarily pay a quarter to see exhibitions of Chamberlain's prowess as a basketball player. Chamberlain therefore becomes a millionaire. According to an end-state theory such as that of Nozick's colleague at Harvard, John Rawls, Chamberlain's wealth is

just only if allowing it to accumulate will improve the welfare of the least-advantaged person in the community. On the contrary, Nozick replies, Chamberlain has a natural right to the fruits of his labor. He is entitled to his wealth if he acquired it without force or fraud. Procedural justice therefore fits smoothly with libertarianism, anarchism, and classical liberalism. It is hostile to utilitarianism (and other theories of the just that urge the government to adjust end states). "Commutative justice" (the term is from Aquinas) is justice in market exchanges, with the proviso that the exchanges take place at the just price. For modern economics and for libertarian philosophers like Nozick, the just price is any price voluntarily contracted. In the words of H. B. Acton, "Commutative justice is found when freely made agreements are kept, and it is maintained when there are laws for punishing fraud and for enforcing the fulfillment of contracts" (1993: 125). In English legal terms, procedural justice is that of common-law courts, as against equity. In economic terms, it is that of markets as against governments.

See also *communitarianism; justice; libertarianism; utilitarianism*

Bibliography

Acton, H. B. (1993). *The Morals of Markets and Related Essays*, ed. D. Gordon and J. Shearmur. Indianapolis, IN: Liberty Fund.
Nozick, R. (1974). *Anarchy, State, and Utopia*. New York: Basic Books.

products liability

John J. McCall

is an area of law determining the conditions under which a manufacturer/seller is required to provide financial compensation for injuries caused by defective products.

Prior to the industrial revolution, products liability law was effectively governed by a principle of *caveat emptor* ("buyer beware"). That principle precluded injured consumers from ever recovering damages in court. At the beginning of this century, the ruling legal doctrines were a conjunction of privity of contract and negligence. The privity doctrine allowed consumer suits only against parties with whom they had direct contractual relations; this requirement effectively insulated manufacturers from suits, since manufacturers were removed in the chain of distribution from the end purchaser. The negligence standard required that successful consumer suits had to prove the defendant seller was negligent for letting a defective product into the marketplace. (A defective product is one that is judged to be "unreasonably dangerous.")

In 1916 a New York court case, *McPherson vs. Buick Motors*, eliminated the privity requirement and thus exposed manufacturers to increasing numbers of product liability suits. Other state jurisdictions gradually followed New York's lead in establishing simple negligence as a standard for manufacturer liability. However, by the 1960s, that standard was challenged as a number of states began to recognize a consumer's cause of action even in cases where negligence was not established. In California, a 1963 ruling in *Greenman vs. Yuba Power Products* established a doctrine of strict liability. Under this standard, manufacturers would be held strictly liable for injuries caused by defective products. The plaintiff is under no burden to establish negligence. Strict liability has become the norm for product liability in most states and for most product categories.

The shift to strict liability and away from a negligence standard signifies an important change in the function of product liability law. Prior to the adoption of strict liability, the decision to compensate an injured consumer was, at least arguably, based on a finding that the defendant was at fault and liability could be seen as a penalty for negligent behavior. Once strict liability was adopted, however, the conception of product liability law shifted from a fault-finding exercise to an attempt to provide a mechanism of compensation for consumers injured by defective products. The law became a scheme of no-fault insurance where the premiums for that insurance are paid by the manufacturer.

An obvious result of the loosened requirements on consumer suits is an increased frequency of consumers bringing suits and recovering damages. This is not to suggest that business is without available legal defenses, however. A corporation may block or diminish monetary judgments by showing that consumers voluntarily assumed risk, misused, or were contributorily negligent; or by establishing that the risk of the product is outweighed by its social benefits.

Given the increased financial exposure of corporations under strict liability, it is not surprising that they, and their insurance carriers, lobbied for state and federal legislation to change the law and return to the negligence standard. The arguments used in this lobbying effort raise issues of morality and public policy. Some of the arguments assert that strict liability is harmful to society. Others claim that strict liability is unfair to business because it imposes liability in cases where the business is not at fault. The first line of argument concentrates on the social costs of strict liability. Opponents claim that it has led to an explosion of liability suits and damage awards, with drastically increased insurance premiums. This in turn leads, they claim, to increased product prices, products being withdrawn from the market, decreased investment in research and development of new products, and depressed employment.

Those favoring strict liability argue (1) the general decrease in accidents because manufacturers have greater safety incentives under strict liability outweighs the other harmful economic effects; and (2) the law can make exceptions for product categories if strict liability leads to the unavailability of socially essential products (as California courts have done for prescription pharmaceuticals).

Defenders of strict liability also respond to the charge that it unfairly imposes liability on faultless manufacturers. Since even opponents of strict liability will accept manufacturer liability where there is negligence, the issue at hand is essentially a question about how to assign the costs for injuries from defective products when no one is at fault. If we abandon strict liability, its proponents argue, and return to negligence, then the full cost of the accident falls on the injured party, who of course bears no responsibility for the defect. They contend that it would be fairer to allocate the cost to a corporation, which is also faultless, because the corporation can spread the cost of the accident broadly among the consumers of its product.

More recently, critics of current products liability law have abandoned a frontal assault on strict liability and have instead lobbied for more limited policy changes. These efforts have met with some success, as the majority of states have enacted reform legislation since 1995. Recent state legislative actions include a limit on punitive damage awards (usually to a small multiple of compensatory damages); a requirement that a substantial portion of punitive awards be paid to the state instead of the plaintiff; a limit on non-economic (i.e., pain and suffering) damages to $250,000; and financial penalties for filing what the court determines is a frivolous suit. These reforms aim to reduce the incentive to bring suits by reducing the potential return to both plaintiffs and their lawyers. A central ethical question concerning these reforms is whether they reduce the financial pressure on business at the cost of denying fair recompense to some worthy plaintiffs.

The current debates over the increased use of class action suits in liability cases, the appearance of suits against gun manufacturers (for negligent marketing leading to injuries caused in crime), and McDonald's (for obesity-related health damage), and the explosion in medical malpractice insurance premiums are just a few of the contemporary developments that assure continued controversy over products liability.

See also *compensatory justice; fairness; risk*

Bibliography

American Tort Reform Association (n.d.). http://www.atra.org.

Brenkert, G. (1984). Strict products liability and compensatory justice. In W. M. Hoffman and J. M. Moore (eds.), *Business Ethics: Readings and Cases in Corporate Morality*. New York: McGraw Hill.

Calabresi, G. (1970). *The Costs of Accidents: A Legal and Economic Analysis*. New Haven, CT: Yale University Press.

Coleman, J. (1976). The morality of strict tort liability. *William and Mary Law Review*, 18, 259.

Coleman, J. (1992). *Risks and Wrongs*. Cambridge: Cambridge University Press.

McCall, J. (2000). Fairness and strict liability. In J. DesJardins and J. McCall (eds.), *Contemporary Issues in Business Ethics*, Belmont, CA: Wadsworth.

Miller, A. (1982). *Miller's Court*. New York: Houghton Mifflin.

Posner, R. (1973). Strict liability: A comment. *Journal of Legal Studies*, 2, 205.

Sunstein, C. et al. (2002). *Can Tort Juries Punish Competently?* Chicago: University of Chicago Press.

Thomson, J. J. (1986). *Rights, Restitution and Risk*. Cambridge, MA: Harvard University Press.

professional codes

Michael Davis

is generally shorthand for "code of professional ethics," a set of standards governing the conduct of members of a certain occupation. Whether or not a business has its own code of ethics, many of its employees or contractors may. There are, for example, codes of ethics for lawyers, accountants, and actuaries, for engineers, chemists, and computer scientists, for professionals in purchasing, marketing, and personnel. A professional code is neither a (purely) personal code, ordinary morality, nor (mere) law. What, then, is it?

A professional code states ("codifies") *standards of practice*, whether by describing preexisting practice (as a dictionary definition does) or by creating the practice (as a definition in a statute does). A code that does not state an actual practice (more or less) is a possible code, not an actual one.

A professional code need not be *written*. An oral formulation will do. However, in any society where writing is common, most professional codes are in writing for the same reason most technical standards are: writing makes them easier to recall, easier to transmit to newcomers, and so on.

A code of ethics – any code of ethics – states standards of practice for a *group*. For example, a corporate code states how employees of a certain business should conduct themselves. It does not apply to everyone. In this respect, codes of ethics resemble laws rather than morality. They are relative. Codes of ethics are nonetheless part of morality in at least two ways. First, their standards must be *morally permissible*. (A "torturer's code of ethics" could only be ethics in scare quotes, an ethic or ethos much as counterfeit "money" is money only in a degenerate sense.) Second, the standards in question must *morally oblige members of the relevant group.* A code of ethics cannot, however, oblige because it restates common moral standards or applies them to new circumstances. A code of ethics must require something ordinary morality merely permits. A code of ethics, by definition, always sets a standard of conduct "higher" (that is, more demanding) than ordinary morality. How can a code of ethics be both a morally obliging standard and a standard higher than ordinary morality?

The answer is simple: a code of ethics must be part of morality because of some (morally obliging) convention, for example, an oath or contract. The convention must, in conjunction with some ordinary moral standard (e.g., "Keep your promises"), add a new moral standard.

Here then, is a crucial difference between codes of ethics and law. Law as such achieves order by threatening liability, legal restraint, or punishment; a code of ethics achieves order by getting novel moral commitments from people who take such commitments seriously. A code of ethics is, therefore, always a personal code; its claim results from a person's commitment, not from external force. A code of ethics is nonetheless never merely a personal code; the commitment in question must be shared with others, the rest of the group.

A *professional* code is the code of ethics of a certain kind of group, a *profession*. What is a profession? For our purposes, a profession is a group of people organized to earn a living by providing a service at a standard higher than law, market, and (ordinary) morality demand. A profession must be a group. There can no more be a profession of one than a club of one. A profession must be organized. Without organization, there is only a particular occupation. But not just any organization will do. The organization must be designed to help its members earn a living. An organization concerned only to help others would be a charity or other service group, not a profession.

The service a profession provides may be of any (morally permissible) sort from which its practitioners can earn a living (though in fact professions tend to be organized by relatively well-educated occupations). The professional need not be an independent consultant (for example, the traditional lawyer). The profes-sional may be an employee, whether of government or private business. Indeed, even such occupations as plumber, secretary, or peddler could organize as a profession. All they need to do is adopt (and generally follow) standards for earning a living higher than law, market, and morality impose. (Without such higher standards, the resulting organization would be a trade association, labor union, or similar organization of self-interest.)

Why would any occupation want to be a profession? Why, in other words, would rational people voluntarily burden their livelihood with demands neither law, market, nor morality make? The answer, of course, must be that the people in question believe that they benefit overall from taking on those burdens. One profession may organize to protect its members from market pressure to do what law and morality forbid. The code of such a profession would emphasize the aid each member owes those who do what law and morality require when client, employer, or government try to get them to do something else. Another profession may organize to protect the reputation of its members. Its code would emphasize practices designed to prevent the appearance of wrong-doing. And so on. Most professional codes reveal a mix of such purposes.

A professional code cannot achieve its purpose unless members of the profession in fact generally do as the profession's code requires. Professional codes thus create a cooperative practice: each participant benefits (primarily) from what the others do and would not do did they not believe the rest were generally doing the same. Since the standards of a cooperative practice are morally obliging if participation in the practice is voluntary and the standards themselves are morally permissible, each person who voluntarily maintains membership in a profession, is morally obliged, even without oath or contract, to practice it as its code says.

Bibliography

Bayles, M. (1989). *Professional Ethics.* Belmont, CA: Wadsworth.

Davis, M. (1987). The moral authority of a professional code. *Authority Revisited: NOMOS XXIX.* New York: New York University Press.

Kultgen, J. (1988). *Ethics and Professions*. Philadelphia: University of Pennsylvania Press.

profit, profits, and profit motive

F. Neil Brady

In popular usage, profit is loosely associated with a "markup" of merchandise or a rate of return on capital. The average person typically thinks of profit as what is left over from revenues after all the bills have been paid. A normal profit is often defined as the implicit cost of the resources contributed by the owners. A more technical definition of profit becomes quite elusive, and probably no concept in economics is used with such a wide range of meanings.

Profit in Economic Theory

The history of economic thought regarding the word "profit" is important to the field of business ethics. What generally makes the issue of profit an ethical issue are distributional questions such as "Who gets to profit?" and "How much do they deserve?" Answers to these questions depend on being able to determine the source of profits. Many factors enter into the profitable business venture: available capital, competent management, entrepreneurial ideas, skilled labor, market advantage, and sheer luck. Ethically speaking, profit should be distributed to the most deserving source, and economists have argued for 200 years over the nature of profit.

Adam Smith was one of the first to articulate a theory of profit. He argued that social classes were partly defined by their source of income: landlords collected rent, laborers received wages, and businessmen earned profits. Smith was one of the first to see that profit was a major motivating force in economies. Indeed, he saw that it was often potential for profit that attracted resources into those activities that produced goods and services most desired by buyers. But why should profit exist at all? Why would anyone want to pay more for a product than what it cost to produce it? There are several answers. Smith mentions two. One is that profit represents the surplus value created by labor returning to the capitalist as profit after wages are deducted. Both Ricardo and Marx articulated this view more fully, referring to profit as a form of exploitation of one social class over another. The other view mentioned by Smith is the idea that profits are related directly to the cost of production and are, therefore, a fixed component of price.

There are more factors in profitable business activity than either labor or the costs of production. Alfred Marshall lists money capital, physical capital, management, land, and labor as the productive factors in economies. His view of the factor most deserving of profit was management: management provides business ability, energy, and organization; and management takes the risks associated with business ventures. Therefore, since management takes the risks, it should earn the profit (and take the losses).

Of course, any risk that can be estimated or measured can also be insured. Therefore, if profit arises from risk-bearing, profit should disappear as the cost of insurance against loss. Frank Knight pointed out, however, that there is a difference between risk and uncertainty. Risk is insurable; uncertainty is unmeasurable and is, therefore, uninsurable. Therefore, according to Knight, profit arises from the bearing of uncertainty, not just risk. He was less clear about who, exactly, bears uncertainty. To say that entrepreneurs, creditors, or managers bear uncertainty is to view the matter too narrowly. Indeed, entrepreneurship and innovation are diffused throughout organizations, as all levels of personnel assume uncertainty in various forms. For example, good ideas often are generated by labor, yet they may be least likely to realize a profit from their contribution. Also bearing the burden of innovation are the suppliers of previously needed inputs to production who have lost their market, and the suppliers of new equipment who need to redesign. Paradoxically, those most likely to profit from innovation are often those with the weakest claim to such an improvement – shareholders and management.

So profit can be attributed to a variety of sources, and deciding the equitable distribution of profits has been one major theme in business ethics. Various profit-sharing programs are popular among organizations that assume employees contribute strongly to profit.

PROFIT IN SOCIAL THEORY

Social theory has also contributed to this discussion. Foremost among the contributors in recent decades are Robert Nozick and John Rawls. In his *A Theory of Justice* Rawls argues that economic and social inequalities are justified only when they ultimately result in benefits to those most in need. Because markets frequently fail to accomplish this, government functions to provide for the redistribution of profits. Like health and education, wealth is the product of a social context, without which it could not occur, and upon which all citizens begin with an equal claim. But society can do better for all its citizens by encouraging the use of skills and talents on behalf of society. Thus, corporations are chartered, managers are given executive compensation, and entrepreneurs are made wealthy *so long as those least advantaged in society are made better off in the process*. Thus, for Rawls, profit (or wealth accumulation) is directly linked to the production of social good at all social levels.

Robert Nozick countered with a more individualistic view of profit-making. His "Wilt Chamberlain example" (1974: 161–4) is famous for attempting to demonstrate that great wealth is just, so long as it derives from a history of just transactions. His view is that the moral status of wealth accumulation should be judged, not by some ideal distributive pattern of social justice, but at the micro level by the moral status of the individual economic transactions that gave rise to the wealth. His *Anarchy, State, and Utopia* (1974) has come to be regarded as a major modern statement of libertarian philosophy.

Not only might profit-making be socially allowed, but to some it is also the prime moral imperative for business activity. Milton Friedman has argued that the sole social responsibility of business is to increase its profits without deception or fraud, implying that other "socially conscious" motives are improper for business. Such "extra-profit" motivations might include responding to the interests of people who are affected by corporate activity but who are not actual shareholders, such as employees, consumers, and the local community on which the firm depends for good will and cooperation. Like Friedman, some would see the firm as simply an economic entity legally bound to pursue exclusively the will of the shareholders who, it is assumed, are motivated simply by return on investment. This "libertarian" outlook underlies the popular creed "Greed is Good," since the pursuit of self-interest is thought to contribute to efficient markets and the general health of an economy.

In contrast, others see businesses as embedded in a social context which encourages interests beyond those of sheer profitability, to include the pursuit of a variety of goods that businesses, because of their economic and political power, are often in a unique position to bring about. Hence, successful businesses commonly contribute to worthy societal causes. Of course, it is possible that such seeming social consciousness may ultimately be motivated by the utilitarian realization that the success of a corporation relies partly on its public perception as a "good citizen" rather than as a "Mr. Scrooge." So, regardless of theory, the nature of actual business motivations remains elusive from case to case. Additionally, estimates of the importance of the profit motive must be tempered by the realization that the chief motivating factor for some business persons is the pride they take in providing a product or service of superior quality or that directly contributes to the well-being of society. In their minds, profitability might be a secondary motivating factor. So the pursuit of profit may or may not be the prime motivating factor in business activity, but it is likely not the only one.

Bibliography

Arnold, N. S. (1987). Why profits are deserved. *Ethics*, 97, 387–402.

Friedman, M. (1970). The social responsibility of business is to increase its profits. *New York Times Magazine*, September 13, 32–3, 122–6.

Knight, F. (1971). *Risk, Uncertainty, and Profit*. Chicago: University of Chicago Press.

Marshall, A. (1948). *Principles of Economics*. New York: Macmillan.

Nell, E. (1987). On deserving profits. *Ethics*, 97, 403–10.

Nozick, R. (1974). *Anarchy, State, and Utopia*. New York: Basic Books.

Obrinsky, M. (1983). *Profit Theory and Capitalism*. Philadelphia: University of Pennsylvania Press.

Rawls, J. (1971). *A Theory of Justice*. Cambridge, MA: Harvard University Press.

property

Eric Mack

refers both to (a) a normative relationship between agents and things and (b) the things that stand in that normative relationship to agents. In the paradigm case of property, an individual is related to some physical object (e.g., a sheep or a knife) by having an exclusive right to use, control, transform, consume, and exchange or donate that object as he chooses. In virtue of that property relationship, that object is the property of that agent. It is his to do with as he sees fit. In the paradigm case, the property holder's right of disposition is only subject to the constraint that he not dispose of his property in ways that violate others' rights. The owner of the knife may not thrust it into anyone else's chest or sheep. However, many instances of property diverge in one or more respects from this basic paradigm. An agent's property need not be a physical object, but can instead be a more abstract thing such as a flow of water, a segment of the electromagnetic spectrum, an industrial process, or a number of shares in corporation X. Distinct agents may have property in different aspects of the same thing; for example, one may have the usual land ownership rights while another may hold the subsurface mineral rights. And distinct agents may jointly own particular things (e.g., the "community" property of married couples).

The paradigm presented and its variants are all cases of *private* property. Yet it is often claimed that property can be communal, state (i.e., public), or private and that no one of these is the privileged form of property. What is classified as communal property exists when numerous individuals are each free to use and consume some common resource. For example, each hunter in the tribe is free to reconnoiter the tribal territory and take what game she finds – as long as that game is not already being taken by another hunter. What is classified as state property exists when the use, control, transformation, and consumption of certain things is governed by explicit political decisions about public schemes of use, control, etc., or about who shall be charged with formulating such schemes. While communal "property" and state "property" do share with private property

the feature that non-owners (e.g., members of other tribes or other states) are excluded, it is plausible to view all these relations as property relations only if one insists on classifying every set of norms which govern the use, control, etc., of things in a given society as property rules. Such an insistence tends to obscure the special character of property rules and of societies in which property rules largely govern the disposition of things.

The distinctive character of genuine (i.e. private) property regimes can be illustrated by means of a case discussed by Harold Demsetz (1967). Demsetz describes the emergence of property rights in beaver-hunting areas among a number of Indian tribes in Eastern Canada during the eighteenth century. Prior to the advent of the beaver-pelt trade, the hunting territory of each tribe and the beaver it contained was communal "property." Each hunter had the right to hunt anywhere within that territory and to take any beaver he first found. However, when European demand for beaver pelts caused a vast increase in the value of these pelts, a continuation of this communal system would have led to the destruction of the beaver population. For each hunter then had a strong incentive to take as much as possible from the commons and had very little incentive to bear costs to conserve or enhance the beaver population. Any hunter's efforts to conserve or enhance the population would immediately be exploited by some other hunter.

One solution which might have been attempted to avert a tragedy of the commons would have been the conversion of the beaver and their habitat to public "property" to which a politically determined scheme of conservation and exploitation would be applied. This would have required widely shared and articulated knowledge of the whole habitat, of the best methods and schedules for harvesting beaver furs throughout it, and of the human and non-human resources available for effective use in the public scheme of beaver exploitation. It would also have required effective mechanisms to enforce the rulings of the Beaver Production Council. However, the actual solution which emerged was a system of family-owned, private rights to beaver-producing subregions. This allowed particular hunters to reap the rewards of their own conservation and enhancement of the beaver populations within their own protected domains and to attune their hunting of the beavers to the special conditions they individually faced. No collective decision had to be reached about any comprehensive scheme, and enforcement costs were limited to ensuring that neighboring property holders did not trespass on one another's domains.

Unlike the public "property" solution to communal "property" problems, this private rights solution displays the essential features of a property scheme. Decision-making is radically decentralized because distinct agents enjoy secure discretionary control over particular things. This allows them to reap the benefits of their own investments in attention, effort, and resources and requires them to suffer the costs of their own failures of investment. Economic coordination among agents arises not from any collectively adopted or imposed plan, but rather through multiple, interconnecting, bilateral, market and contractual accommodations.

Is private property morally justified? The tale of the beavers and like narratives suggest a consequentialist vindication, namely that private property facilitates rational economic decisions (*see* CONSEQUENTIALISM). But many have opposed private property regimes precisely because they undercut communal or public life. Many others charge that such regimes, unless augmented by redistributive programs, yield grave distributive injustices. On the other hand, defenders of private property argue that property is a fundamental right, that private holdings which emerge from peaceful acquisition, production, and trade are, for that very reason, just, and often even deserved.

See also *economic liberty*

Bibliography

Demsetz, H. (1967). Toward a theory of property rights. *American Economic Review*, 57, 347–59.

Epstein, R. (1985). *Takings: Private Property and the Power of Eminent Domain*. Cambridge, MA: Harvard University Press.

Honor, A. M. (1961). Ownership. In A. G. Guest (ed.), *Oxford Essays in Jurisprudence*. Oxford: Oxford University Press, 107–47.

Munzer, S. (1990). *A Theory of Property*. Cambridge: Cambridge University Press.

Paul, E. (ed.) (1990). *The Monist*, Issue on Property Rights, 73 (4).

Pennock, J. R. and Chapman, J. W. (1980). *NOMOS XXII: Property*. New York: New York University Press.

Waldron, J. (1988). *The Right of Private Property*. Oxford: Clarendon Press.

property, rights to

Kenneth Kipnis

POSSESSION AND PROPERTY

Property rights are a complex, socially constituted bundle of obligations and permissions. It is a common mistake to think of property as one thing and the rights that attach to it as another. We can think of a baseball as part of a system of rules and practices within which it is used. If we found such an object in an ancient tomb, we could say it was *just like* a baseball. But if we knew the game wasn't played when the object was buried, we couldn't say that is what it was.

Similarly, there is a critical difference between the way the squirrel is in possession of its acorns and the way the corporation owns the forest. Unlike the mere possession of things, the ownership of property presupposes an elaborate system of rules governing the social allocation of things to persons. Just as our ancient artifact does not become a baseball until it is fitted into the practices of the game, so the things it is possible to possess – songs, lands, genetically engineered species, inventions, crops, manufactured items, mineral deposits, airplane tickets, stock certificates, trademarks, taxicab licenses, secret recipes, dolphins, human cell lines, news reports, athletic teams, and so on – do not become property until they are fitted into a complex system of legal arrangements.

In 1919 Wesley Newcomb Hohfeld tried to show how complex legal arrangements could be built out of four fundamental relationships: what are now called claim-rights, liberties, powers, and immunities. Each of these "Hohfeldian rights" specifies a unique reciprocal relationship involving at least two parties. When you owe me a dollar, I have a *claim-right* against you that you pay me and, reciprocally, you have the duty to pay. The claim-right and the duty are part of a single relationship: the one entails the other. Likewise, if I am at *liberty* to eat in the cafeteria, then, reciprocally, everyone else lacks the right that I not eat there. If I have the *power* to permit people to take the short cut through my backyard, then, reciprocally, whether another person is at liberty to take the short cut or not is subject to my decision-making authority. Everyone else is liable to me in that way (i.e., is subject to my power to give or withhold permission). And lastly, if I have *immunity* as an official representative of a foreign government, then I am not subject to arrest in the way everyone else is. Reciprocally, the police lack that legal power in my case: nothing they do to me can count as a valid arrest. A claim-right correlates with a duty. A liberty to do something correlates with the absence of a right that one not do that thing. A legal power correlates with a liability. And an immunity correlates with the absence of a power. Much as atoms make up molecules, so Hohfeld thought that complex social practices could be constructed out of these elements.

In its original sense, property connoted all that was proper to some person. John Locke (1967), for example, included as property one's life and one's liberties in addition to one's estates. C. B. Macpherson (1977) has noted that since Aristotle, the concept of property has traditionally included the right not to be excluded from those things society had designated as common: for example, access to and right to use public parks and waterways. It was not until the seventeenth century – not until the rise of capitalism and those market systems that have come to dominate social life in the West – that conceptions of property have more narrowly focused on goods that can be exchanged in market transactions. What makes market systems (i.e., the practices of business) possible are, in part, socially backed understandings of exchangeable entitlements.

THE ANALYSIS OF OWNERSHIP

In a 1961 article, A. M. Honoré analyzed the familiar concept of ownership into its "incidents." Much of what he says about ownership can be understood in terms of Hohfeldian rights. At the foundation is the right to possess: a claim-

right to be in exclusive control coupled with the liberty to exercise "such control as the nature of the thing admits." Stories, lands, and groceries admit to different sorts of control. If one owns a story, a movie producer may not adapt it without permission. Hikers may not trespass across one's land. It is a crime to steal another's groceries. This liberty to exercise control over one's property is exclusive: all others are prohibited from interfering unless the owner exercises a power of permission. Honoré notes that the practices of ownership entail the existence of remedies available to the owner in the event that the right to exclusive control is violated. If the groceries are stolen, the owner/victim has the power to summon the police and, if it is provably known who did it, to have the thief charged with a crime.

Three additional rights are closely related: the right to use, the right to manage, and the right to the income. One is at liberty personally to enjoy one's property at one's sole discretion: this is the right to use. One has the liberty and unique power to decide how and by whom one's property shall be used: this is the right to manage. And one comes to own whatever fruits, rents, or profits one's property generates: this is the right to the income. The right to the capital includes the power to give away one's property and the liberty to consume, waste, or destroy it. The right to security involves an immunity from expropriation: generally, property is transferred only with the consent of the owner. Honoré adds what he calls the "incident of transmissibility": at the death of the owner, what has been owned as property can pass to the owner's successors.

The foregoing discussion should make it clear that there is no singular "right" to property. Rather, ownership is best understood as a package of claim-rights, liberties, powers, and immunities. It is commonplace that these elements can be divided and reassembled in a myriad of ways. A trust, for example, can be set up so one party – the beneficiary – has the right to the income while a second party – the trustee – has the right to manage. When one rents an apartment, one has the right to use it for a fixed period during which many of the owner's rights are suspended. Corporations, as fictional persons, own property themselves, but corporate officers manage the business as agents of the corporation (*see* AGENCY THEORY). The stockholder, as owner of the corporation, has rights to the income. This separation of management rights from the other rights of ownership is a striking feature of many contemporary business organizations.

Honoré discusses duties and liabilities associated with ownership. Chief among these is the prohibition against harmful use: owners have a duty not to use their property in ways that harm others. Likewise, the general immunity against expropriation will not protect owners against having their property taken from them following non-payment of debts, bankruptcy, or as a consequence of state expropriation (as, for example, when lands are condemned to build a highway). Those who lose property in this last way may have a claim-right to just compensation. Rights are often shaped by regulations and exceptions conceived in the public interest. Zoning laws may restrict what I can construct on my land. And although owners ordinarily have exclusive control, under exigent circumstances government officials (police and firefighters, for example) and even ordinary citizens may be at liberty, without consent, to enter private premises or take into their possession the property of others.

THE JUSTIFICATION OF PROPERTY RIGHTS

Conceived in this way, a system of property rights is a complex social artifact empowering owners to make socially enforceable claims. It is not much of an exaggeration to think of ownership as a kind of sovereignty. Morris Raphael Cohen (1927) has written: "In a régime where land is the principal source of obtaining a livelihood, he who has the legal right over the land receives homage and service from those who wish to live on it." Much as the justification of political authority has long been a central concern of philosophy, so philosophers have worried about the legitimacy of property rights. Lawrence Becker (1977) distinguishes between general and specific justifications of property. The former explains why there ought to be any property rights at all. The latter explains why there ought to be some specific sort of property right: Should beaches be private property down to the water? While it is not possible to provide a comprehensive overview of this literature, two important strands of the debate are worth sketching.

John Locke in chapter 5 of the *Second Treatise of Government* (1967) sets out the classic exposition of what has become known as the labor theory of property. Even prior to the establishment of law, Locke argues, there is a natural right to property. When, for example, a fisherman catches a fish in the ocean, it seems plain enough that the fish properly belongs to him. Locke would point out that the value of the fish in the boat is far greater than its value while it was in the ocean. The fisherman's labor makes the difference, for the fish in the boat is the original fish "mixed" with that labor. For this reason it would be wrong for a bystander to seize the fish in the boat, unjust to take for oneself "the benefit of another's pains, which he had no right to." Locke adds that the argument justifying appropriation applies only when the fisherman takes no more than he can make use of and only provided there is "enough and as good left in common for others." This latter condition – the "Lockean proviso" – grows in importance as the world's resources are depleted. Many critics have pointed out that Locke's general justification cannot specifically justify the ownership of land. Robert Nozick (1974) wonders why mixing one's labor with an unowned thing isn't simply a way of losing one's labor.

While, in justifying property, Locke tends to look backward at the laborer's initial appropriation, utilitarian and economic theorists see regimes of property rights as engineered mechanisms that, if well designed, can promote the general happiness or the broadest satisfaction of preferences (*see* UTILITARIANISM). Jeremy Bentham (1931), for example, builds his general justification of property upon the precariousness of mere possession. "Without law there is no security," and where there is no security, disorder and impoverished misery are, according to Bentham, inevitable consequences. Law creates "a fixed and durable possession" and so encourages people to labor now for that which they may reasonably expect to enjoy in the future. Property, in at least some of its implementations, can promote human well-being by securing a more efficient – and, therefore, a more affluent – social order.

It may be useful to take note of the social perspectives underlying these two approaches to justification. While Locke appeals to justice, utilitarians and economic theorists appeal to a concern for the general well-being. There is more than a kernel of truth in each perspective. For our choices in configuring the claim-rights, liberties, powers, and immunities that are associated with property will affect the justice of our economic institutions and the general well-being of those in our community. Although, in our individual pursuits of property and the good life, we may fixate upon what we want for ourselves, we might also do well to reflect on how our historically contingent, evolving regime of property rights could be improved and how accommodations to emerging circumstances might further shared aspirations for a more perfect community.

See also *economic efficiency; justice; rights*

Bibliography

Becker, L. C. (1977). *Property Rights: Philosophic Foundations*. London: Routledge and Kegan Paul. (An important overview and analysis of the major arguments for and against property rights.)

Becker, L. C. (1979). Property theory and the corporation. In M. Hoffman (ed.), *Proceedings of the Second National Conference on Business Ethics*. Washington, DC: University Press of America.

Bentham, J. (1931) [1830]. *Principles of the Civil Code*, ed. C. K. Ogden. London: Kegan Paul. (Chapters 7–12 set out Bentham's account. The text is available in Bentham's *Theory of Legislation*.)

Cohen, M. R. (1927). Property and sovereignty. *Cornell Law Quarterly*, 13, 8–29.

Hohfeld, W. N. (1919). *Fundamental Legal Conceptions*. New Haven, CT: Yale University Press.

Honoré, A. M. (1961). Ownership. In A. G. Guest (ed.), *Oxford Essays in Jurisprudence*. Oxford: Clarendon Press, 107–47. (The standard analysis of ownership.)

Locke, J. (1967) [1689]. *Two Treatises of Government*, 2nd edn., ed. P. Laslett. New York: Cambridge University Press. (Chapter 5 of the second treatise sets out Locke's account.)

Macpherson, C. B. (1962). *The Political Theory of Possessive Individualism*. Oxford: Clarendon Press. (An important study of the Lockean account of property.)

Macpherson, C. B. (1977). Human rights as property rights. *Dissent*, 24, 72–7.

Nozick, R. (1974). *Anarchy, State, and Utopia*. New York: Basic Books.

psychology and business ethics

David M. Messick

Psychology is the scientific study of human thought and action. An informal survey of several texts on business ethics suggests that Lawrence Kohlberg (1981) stands out from all other psychologists in his impact on this field. Kohlberg's influence is also great in the study of moral psychology. But in business ethics, as in moral psychology, to focus on Kohlberg to the exclusion of others would seriously confine the ways in which psychological research illuminates the moral nature of humans generally and in business contexts specifically. We note, for instance, that Kohlberg's theory is developmental, internal, normative, and rule based. Following Piaget, Kohlberg proposes that humans undergo a fixed developmental sequence in the way they reason about moral issues. The sequence of stages is presumed to be invariant; people differ in the rate at which they progress through the stages; and people stop at different stages. Higher stages in the sequences are "better" than lower stages in that they represent more mature concepts of morality and justice. Morality, in Kohlberg's theory, is a quality of mind, and it is a cognitive quality that characterizes one's reasoning about moral dilemmas.

Kohlberg's theory is, at best, an incomplete account of the psychology of human morality. For instance, it ignores the chasm that separates the way people reason about ethical dilemmas from the way they actually behave therein. It downplays the role of the environment in determining behavior and tends to portray judgments as rule based rather than context based. It privileges some ethical principles to the exclusion of others (e.g., justice as opposed to caring). It has little room for the emotional side of morality, for moral outrage directed at violators, for instance, or for sympathy, pity, shame, or guilt. Finally, Kohlberg's theory tells us little about how people perceive the causal texture of behavior that underlies judgments of praise and blame.

There is a voluminous research literature on a number of psychological issues that are relevant to business ethics. These include empathy and sympathy, altruism, cooperation, social influence, social conflict and its management, behavioral decision-making, lying, aggression, social

comparison, prejudice, discrimination and intergroup relations, illusions and self-deception, distributive justice, procedural justice, and risk
perception and communication, to mention
only a few. In this article, I will describe three
of these areas. I have chosen the three areas for
their pertinence to problems in business ethics.
They are intergroup relations, social influence,
and cooperation.

INTERGROUP RELATIONS

As business becomes more global and the demographics of the labor force change, it becomes
critical to understand the dynamics of intergroup processes, especially those that occur in
the minds of individuals. Recent social psychological research has made progress understanding the interrelated phenomena of prejudice,
discrimination, ethnocentrism, and stereotyping
(Fiske and Taylor, 1991). All of these phenomena involve reacting to persons on the basis of
their group membership rather than on information about them as individuals. Stereotyping
consists of responding to a person in terms of
presumed qualities of the group to which the
person belongs – women, African Americans,
Italians, Jews, or men, for instance. The content
of stereotypes for all of those groups will generally be different, but the ways in which stereotypical information seeps into judgments and
decisions about people will be the same. Ethnocentrism, on the other hand, refers to the distinction that we draw between "us" and "them."
Recent work on the cognitive underpinnings of
ethnocentrism suggests that we see and react to
"outgroups" differently from ingroups even
though the classification into ingroups and outgroups is not stable. At this moment an ingroup
can be your gender and the next it can be your
country or your firm.

The ways in which stereotypes and ethnocentric views of outgroups work are subtle, especially in a time in which discrimination and bias
are viewed as unacceptable and indeed illegal in
many contexts. Managers know that it is illegal
to deny a promotion to an employee because the
person is a woman or a Catholic. However, that
does not mean the effects of stereotypes are non-
existent. The use of stereotypical information is
especially likely in a couple of circumstances.
First, when the person is the only or one of just

a few of the type, he or she is especially likely
to be responded to stereotypically. A black
employee who is the only black in the office
will have her "blackness" highlighted more
than if there were many other black employees.
Thus the first person of "their" type to move
into a position in a firm can expect to be labeled
with "their" stereotype. Second, stereotyping is
likely to occur when the criteria for evaluation
are vague, ambiguous, or subjective. Being "able
to get along with people" is more vague and
subjective than "generating $100,000 of business
a month." Stereotypes are more likely to influence the former than the latter judgment.

Like stereotypes, ethnocentric decisions or
judgments are often subtle. A promotion is
given to someone who is like "us" because one
feels uncomfortable with "them." There is good
evidence (Brewer, 1979) that discrimination
often works through a process of ingroup favorability rather than through outgroup derogation.
We make little exceptions to aid ingroupers that
we fail to make for outgroupers. This is a plausible hypothesis to explain why blacks and Hispanics are denied home loans proportionally
more often than white applicants. Even when
"equated" for credit worthiness, minority applicants are refused more often than whites. The
ingroup favorability idea suggests that the difference may be less a matter of qualified minorities being refused than of unqualified whites
being granted loans. Racial, gender, or ethnic
discrimination in business settings may well
work through the subtle ways of favoring the
ingroup (otherwise known as white males) rather
than by derogating or harming the outgroup.

SOCIAL INFLUENCE

Most experimental psychologists place great
weight on the environment as a cause of human
behavior and this is nowhere more important
than with the social environment. A line of
research that was begun more than 50 years ago
has demonstrated the importance of the social
surround. Milgram's (1974) disturbing experiments on obedience to authority demonstrated
how incorrect people's beliefs were (and probably still are) about how difficult it would be to
induce one person to harm another merely
through the urging of a legitimate authority.
Milgram coaxed his subjects to deliver what

they believed to be exceedingly painful and possibly fatal electric shocks to another participant. He noted that the single most important consequence of submitting one's self to the legitimate authority is the loss of the sense of responsibility. The subordinate becomes a pawn with no sense of moral responsibility for the harm that he is inflicting.

Latane and Darley (1970) and others found a somewhat paradoxical effect of the social environment that they called the *bystander effect*. This phenomenon refers to the finding that people are less likely to intervene in an emergency to help another person if they witness the emergency with other bystanders than if they witness it alone. In other words, the bystanders inhibit people's natural tendencies to come to the aid of a person in need. (It does not follow because each person in a group is less likely to help than they would be alone, that the victim is less likely to receive help when witnessed by a group. All it takes to get help is one volunteer.) This bystander effect has several causes. One is that we learn about the world by observing how other people respond to it. If we witness an emergency and see that no one else is doing anything, we may interpret the situation as one that does not merit intervention. A second cause may be that we (self-servingly) diffuse our responsibility and assume that someone else will take care of the problem. If there are multiple witnesses then we cannot be personally blamed (either by ourselves or others) for doing nothing.

Social circumstances that foster poor decision-making are profoundly unethical in that poor decision-making will squander resources and put people in harm's way. One syndrome of this sort has been described as *groupthink* (Janis, 1982). Groupthink is a pattern of group decision-making that results when a group places undue emphasis on conforming to the culture of the group and spends too little of its resources on getting the decision right. Groupthink represents the disastrous implosion of conformity pressures whose features include illusions of invulnerability, illusions of the group's morality (and the immorality of outgroups), and a powerful tendency to censor group members who appear to disagree with the group. Such suffocating social climates interfere with the accurate processing of infor-

mation, with the exploration of alternative courses of action, and with the thorough appraisal of the risks and benefits of the options. Janis has attributed some of the worst political decisions of this century to groupthink, decisions including the disastrous Bay of Pigs invasion and the failure to prepare for the Pearl Harbor attack.

Finally, Cialdini (1988) has written about the psychological processes that subtend the strategies and tactics that are used to influence people's behavior. He identifies six principles of social influence that are manifested in business applications ranging from selling cars to soliciting contributions to charitable organizations. Cialdini discusses the ways in which these six principles (they are reciprocation, commitment, authority, social validation, scarcity, and liking) can be and are used to attain compliance with the influencer's goals. One interesting aspect of these ideas is that they all stem from basic social psychological processes. Reciprocation, for instance, appears to be a universal feature of human social interaction. People tend to return favors and to reciprocate harm. Such a principle is one of the cornerstones of our social nature. This principle is exploited, however, when a charitable organization sends addressed mailing labels to prospective contributors. Sending an inexpensive gift like mailing labels evokes the reciprocal favor of returning a cash contribution. The tactic is used with the intention of generating money, not with the intention of maintaining the fabric of a social community. The question is raised: When are such tactics manipulative and improper and when are they acceptable?

Most psychologists would look to the social environment to explain unethical behavior in business and other organizations. Darley (1992) offers an extreme position that most evil is organizationally grounded.

COOPERATION IN SOCIAL DILEMMAS

Social dilemmas are situations in which there is a conflict between what is good for a group and what is good for the individual. More precisely, they are situations in which each individual in a group has a clear incentive to behave in a way which, if engaged in by all, produces less desirable outcomes than would have been achieved if all members did what was *not* in their individual interest. To illustrate a social dilemma, the world's fisheries are critically depleted, partly because each nation's interests are best served by harvesting as much as possible from the sea. The collective consequence is overharvesting that is the fault of no single nation. Corruption exists in some organizations because it is in no individual's interest to report it. However, the corruption will eventually stain everyone in the organization, including those who declined to report it, and the damage may be far worse than the cost of blowing the whistle. Inducing people to cooperate in such situations, to act against their individual short-term interest to achieve individual and collective long-term benefits, is at the heart of the problem of cooperation (Messick and Brewer, 1983; Komorita and Parks, 1994).

Psychological research on cooperation has focused on two interrelated strategies: changing the people or changing the structure. The first of these strategies attempts to promote cooperation by altering individuals' values, motives, expectations, or trust in the others in the group. It has been shown that in some circumstances people are willing to act on behalf of their group when there are no possible individual interests to be served. One factor that is essential to developing that level of cohesion and trust is the ability of the members to communicate about the task. Communication allows promises to be made, intentions to be expressed, and a sense of community to develop. Communication also promotes empathy and friendship among group members.

Communication among members is not feasible in many contexts. In cases where the group is too large, dispersed, or diffuse, structural solutions can be sought. Structural solutions may involve changing the payoffs to individuals to enhance the incentive to cooperate, for instance. Appointing a single individual or agency to make decisions on behalf of the group, or changing the nature of the alternatives that the people have, are other types of structural changes. Regulation of one sort or another may be called for. Some states, for instance, require teachers to pay a "fee" even if they are not members of the public teachers union, to eliminate the incentive for teachers to free-ride on the union dues of those teachers who are union members. Proposals for California citizens to install catalytic converters voluntarily were dismal failures because citizens could not justify the cost of more than $100 when the impact of their single acts on the quality of the air in California would be negligible. California state law now mandates that all cars have these pollution control devices. This is a good structural solution to a behavioral problem of cooperation.

Bibliography

Brewer, M. B. (1979). In-group bias in the minimal intergroup situation: A cognitive motivational analysis. *Psychological Bulletin*, **86**, 307–24.

Cialdini, R. B. (1988). *Influence: Science and Practice*. Glenview, IL: Scott Foresman.

Darley, J. M. (1992). Social organization for the production of evil. *Psychological Inquiry*, **3**, 199–218.

Fiske, S. T. and Taylor, S. E. (1991). *Social Cognition*. Reading, MA: Addison-Wesley.

Janis, I. L. (1982). *Groupthink*. Boston, MA: Houghton Mifflin.

Kohlberg, L. (1981). *The Philosophy of Moral Development*. New York: Harper and Row.

Komorita, S. S. and Parks, C. D. (1994). *Social Dilemmas*. Madison, WI: Brown and Benchmark.

Latane, B. and Darley, J. M. (1970). *The Unresponsive Bystander: Why Doesn't He Help*. New York: Appleton-Century-Crofts.

Messick, D. M. and Brewer, M. B. (1983). Solving social dilemmas: A review. *Review of Personality and Social Psychology*, **4**, 11–44.

Milgram, S. (1974). *Obedience to Authority*. New York: Harper and Row.

public/private distinction

Leslie P. Francis

The view that there is a line to be drawn between areas of human life open to social inspection or regulation, and areas of human life immune to such scrutiny.

Since the publication of J. S. Mill's *On Liberty* in 1859, the distinction between public and private spheres has been a mainstay of liberal political theory. The distinction has figured prominently in arguments such as Mill's that special kinds of information or choices ought to be protected from government interference. In business ethics, for example, the distinction plays a central role in controversy over whether aspects of an employee's life outside the job are proper subjects of employer intervention. The public/private distinction has also been crucial to the view that a range of social institutions – markets, families, or churches, for example – can and should operate without government interference.

The line between public and private has been drawn descriptively, legally, and normatively, and there have been frequent confusions among these levels of delineation. Mill drew the line descriptively in terms of the effects of actions: actions which affect only oneself are self-regarding, but actions which have consequences for others are other-regarding. Noting that there are few actions utterly without ripple effects, others have drawn descriptive lines between what is seeable by others and what is hidden or unseen, or between what has been traditionally regarded as intimate and what has not.

In law, the public/private distinction has served to identify actors of different types. In the United States, for example, state employees' managers have special constitutional obligations to respect rights and may be sued for damages if they do not. The public/private line has also been used to characterize places. Again in the US, if a shopping center is a public forum, then it is subject to constitutional claims, such as the right of free speech on the premises. The public/private distinction also has been drawn between types of law: contract law, property law, and tort law are generally characterized as "private law," governing arrangements among individual actors; criminal law, administrative law, and environmental law are matters of "public law," structuring affairs between individuals and the government.

There are many different normative accounts of what ought to be protected as private. One view of privacy centers on information about the individual that ought to be immune from scrutiny by others: health records, financial information, information about group affiliations and friendships, juvenile offense records, and the like (see INFORMATION, RIGHT TO). Another account focuses on spaces –

homes, bodily cavities, cars, purses, or desk drawers – that ought to be protected from intrusions without consent. Still another account looks to liberties, such as choices about marriage, reproduction, education, art and literature, or religion, for insulation from interference.

The public/private distinction, in all of its permutations, has come under fire from both the left and the right as a problematic manifestation of liberal individualism. Some critics argue that the distinction is meaningless; others, that it marks out many different continua on which we might locate social relationships. Other critics contend that insistence on a line between public and private results from and protects certain entrenched interests against others. Communitarian critics argue that decisions often defended as private, such as what movies to see or whether to have an abortion, threaten the fabric of community and contribute to modern alienation. Economic leftists argue that the market is not a private affair; legal choices such as whether to treat employer–employee relationships as matters of private law have important consequences for the structure of public labor relations. Feminists argue that institutions such as the family have oppressed women, and that insulating these institutions from public scrutiny deepens that oppression. Liberals reply that recognition of a private sphere in some form is crucial to the protection of liberty and self-respect. Perhaps the most difficult question for liberals, and the one on which they most disagree, is how to view social but non-governmental institutions such as markets or churches in terms of a public/private dichotomy.

See also *communitarianism; feminist ethics; liberalism*

Bibliography

Benn, S. I. and Gaus, G. F. (eds.) (1983). *Public and Private in Social Life.* New York: St. Martin's Press.
Crittenden, J. (1992). *Beyond Individualism: Reconstituting the Liberal Self.* New York: Oxford University Press.
Daly, M. (ed.) (1994). *Communitarianism: A New Public Ethics.* Belmont, CA: Wadsworth.

Fox-Genovese, E. (1991). *Feminism Without Illusions: A Critique of Individualism.* Chapel Hill: University of North Carolina Press.

Gavison, R. (1992). Feminism and the public/private distinction. *Stanford Law Review*, 3, 1–45.

Kymlicka, W. (1989). *Liberalism, Community, and Culture.* Oxford: Clarendon Press.

Mill, J. S. (1859). *On Liberty.* Numerous editions are available.

Moore, M. (1993). *Foundations of Liberalism.* Oxford: Clarendon Press.

Singer, B. J. (1993). *Operative Rights.* Albany: State University of New York Press.

Symposium on the Public/Private Distinction (1982). *University of Pennsylvania Law Review*, 130, 1289–1608.

R

racism

Jesse Taylor

A belief that one's ethnic stock is superior. The term "racism" is an evaluative offspring of the concept "race." In spite of the parental relationship, however, racism is an independent phenomenon that has flourished in the midst of controversy surrounding "objectivity" with respect to the concept of "race" itself (Zack, 1993). Conceptually, the idea of "race" is concerned merely with metaphysical or biological classifications of people in accordance with attributes or characteristics considered usually ascribable as group-identifying properties. By contrast, racism assigns values and stereotypes to those race categories in order to fix race relations along a continuum of "superior-race-to-inferior-race." From this perspective, we understand racism primarily from what it seeks to accomplish as a value thrust, rather than as an action with independently definable properties. In this context, racism is viewed as an "occasional phenomenon" (Gadamer, 1993: 144–59) of actions that are not intrinsically racist. However, the lack of tangible characteristics does not obscure the fact that the display of racism in many practices and attitudes is frequently undeniable (Gault, 1992).

Racist. A member of a racial group considered elite as determined by political, social, economic, etc., powers, and who willfully participates in practices designed to maintain the elite status of the racial group of which one is a member. There is an element of controversy associated with this conception of a racist. It eliminates blacks, for instance, as possible racists. However, since one could not claim social, political, or economic benefits from their black racism, it seems pointless to suppose that such racism exists. It is conceivable that what is considered "black racism" is merely a conditioned response to "white racism," thus not racism at all.

Epistemology of racism. Our judgments that some actions are racist are open to debate for the same reasons as "held to be a work of art" may be subject to debate over whether or not something is actually art. As in art, disputes concerning racism will be settled with a heavier emphasis on value rather than factual considerations. That is, since racism is not definable as an independent act (Austin, 1956), its being is understood as the outgrowth of judgments about purposes and consequences of actions that are in fact fully definable. There are clear cases of racism that tend to reinforce a "pecking order" among racial groups so as to give privilege to the so-called elites. At bottom, we understand racism as a commitment to that pecking order, or to one's involvement in practices that help to maintain privileges of those considered racial elites.

Science and racism. It is unlikely that science will ever settle disputes concerning racial superiority. Debates on this issue involve judgments that are immune to sensory input by virtue of their roles in constituting frameworks for judgments. In this respect, racism is viewed as a phenomenon of reflective consciousness. As such, it belongs to the Kantian realm of "art" as opposed to that of "science." On the other hand, even if racial superiority could be established scientifically, it may yet be morally wrong to oppress human beings, since inferiority would not change nature's requirement to function in accordance with the full gamut of their humanity (Williams, 1991).

Equality and racism. Racism is antithetical to prevailing conceptions of equality. Thriving on the idea of race as a "great-making quality," racism views the worth of a person as constrained within the scope of their racial identity. The interest of a race considered superior (generally as defined by those holding political and economic power) will supersede the interests of all others without regard to questions of justice or to impact upon the victims. Such subordination of interests persists in spite of its incompatibility with conceptions of equality advanced by Locke, Kant, Rawls, and other prominent social/political scholars (*see* KANTIAN ETHICS). For them, human equality is not to be defined in terms of abilities as such, since they vary from person to person and even with respect to a particular person at different times or circumstances. Equality is concerned with dispositional aspects of humanity that are universal, not with relative manifestations of those dispositions in individuals or in groups. This conception of equality evokes a kind of "form over function" standard for personhood. This standard forbids applying restraints to one's natural or metaphysical identity based on a notion that some should not be allowed to exist as fully human, since others are considered "better fit" to achieve the same metaphysical task. On this issue, Locke, Kant, and Rawls have clearly taken the position that it is morally impermissible to restrain the natural dispositions of persons to exist as such.

Universality of racism. Slavery and its consciousness have made it impossible to live in America without the residual effect of racism having some influence on how our judgments of others and ourselves are determined. Racism has also become institutionalized to the degree that many of us participate in racist practices without our knowledge (Appiah, 1990). Persons actually viewed as racist, however, are among those privileged to the advantages of the racial elite, and who support the stereotypes that establish a hierarchy among racial groups.

Color and racism. Color alone is not a race problem for persons of color. Blind persons would perhaps choose to be sighted if the means were available to them, but one's color is not an impediment to one's human potential. Under Rawls's "veil of ignorance," for example, it is perfectly conceivable that as many persons would choose black as a color of preference as those disposed to choose white (among those wishing to express a color preference at all). The idea of color as a cause of racial problems gives rise to the view that color is a qualitative aspect of humanity. Once it is clear that color problems stem from a socially created color criterion, rather than from color itself, it is clear that racism has nothing to do with color as such.

Racism as vice. Although racist sentiments tend to vary with political and economic climates, most people reject racism as an admirable human quality. Just as persons who find themselves "selfish" in undesirable respects can foster a better sense of altruism from practice, persons who are discontented with their racism can participate in practices that can help to reduce their racism considerably. In this sense, we can think of racism as a vice and the absence of it a virtue. So conceived, it is possible to cultivate non-racist potential that exists in actual racists, provided that they are unhappy with their racism. There are no assurances that racism will ever be fully eliminated. However, with general agreement that racism and selfishness are not good human qualities, the elimination of both can be espoused as worthy goals.

Bibliography

Appiah, K. A. (1990). Racisms. In D. T. Goldberg (ed.), *Anatomy of Racism*. Minneapolis: University of Minnesota Press.

Austin, J. L. (1956). A plea for excuses. In W. T. Jones, F. Sontag, et al. (eds.), *Approaches to Ethics*. New York: McGraw-Hill.

Cashmore, E., Banton, M., et al. (1994). *Dictionary of Race and Ethnic Relations*, 3rd edn. New York: Routledge and Kegan Paul.

Feagin, J. R. (1992). The continuing significance of racism: Discrimination of black students in white colleges. *Journal of Black Studies*, 22, 546–78.

Fredrickson, G. M. (1988). *The Arrogance of Race: Historical Perspectives on Slavery, Racism, and Social Inequality*. Middletown, CT: Wesleyan University Press.

Gadamer, H.-G. (1993). *Truth and Method*, 2nd edn. New York: Continuum.

Gault, C. H. (1992). *In My Place*. New York: Harper Collins.

Giovanni, N. (1994). *Racism 101*. New York: William Morrow.

Williams, P. (1991). *The Alchemy of Race and Rights*. Cambridge, MA: Harvard University Press.

Zack, N. (1993). *Mixed-Race and Anti-Race*. Philadelphia, PA: Temple University Press.

rational choice theory

R. Edward Freeman

is a body of literature that explores the idea that humans can and sometimes do make choices that are based on principles of rationality. Rational Choice Theory encompasses a large body of work, including much of modern economics. This article is confined to the use of rational choice theory in ethics (*see* GAME THEORY).

Sometime during the 1950s, moral philosophers became concerned with a question that is as old as Plato and Aristotle: Why should one be moral? Plato believed that if a person knew the right thing to do she would automatically do the right thing. Aristotle held out the possibility of weakness of will or *akrasia*, that a person could know the right but fail to do it because of some defect of character. Marked by Kurt Baier's *The Moral Point of View*, published in 1958, philosophers began to ground an answer to "Why be moral?" in theories of reason and rationality.

At the same time, John Rawls (1971) and later David Gauthier (1986) picked up the social contract tradition begun by Hobbes and began to develop theories of social institutions that grounded the morality and justice of institutions in theories of rationality. Thus, ethics and political philosophy merged around the notion that humans could rationally choose the ethical point of view and design political and social institutions that were based on principles of rational choice.

The publication of Rawls's magisterial *A Theory of Justice* is the landmark event in the application of rational choice theory to ethics. Rawls asked us to imagine an original position of hypothetical contractors behind a "veil of ignorance" trying to decide which principles of justice were rational to accept. Suppose that no one knew the position that she was likely to occupy

once the veil was lifted, and hence no rational chooser would make an exception for herself. The principles chosen, according to this argument, would be in line with the rational choice principle called "minimax." Under conditions of total uncertainty, where the consequences of choice are important, rationality dictates choosing the alternative which has the least worst outcome.

The important point here is not whether or not minimax is the correct principle; rather, it is that Rawls connected ethical and political philosophy with an entire stream of research in economics in a manner that was novel. A whole body of scholarship on Rawls began to appear in economics journals. Psychologists who studied how people actually make decisions began to become relevant to ethicists. In short, ethics based on rational choice theory became more interdisciplinary, and Rawls became required reading in many graduate seminars in a number of academic disciplines.

Rational choice theory consists of a number of different decision or choice problems. The first could be called "decision-making under uncertainty," and consists of the principles or axioms or theories that a decision-maker should or does use when she has several alternatives each of which is probabilistically determined by states of nature. Sometimes the decision-maker has no control over the state of nature, and sometimes she can act as if she can influence which state actually occurs. In a famous example, Leonard Savage supposes that a chef has already cracked five eggs into a bowl that will contain the eggs for a six-egg omelet, and wants to proceed rationally with the sixth egg. If she cracks the sixth egg into the bowl with the others and it is rotten, then all eggs will have to be discarded. Alternatively, if it is a good egg, the omelet will proceed quickly. Or, she can crack the sixth egg into a separate bowl, sparing the five good eggs, but incurring a cost of washing the bowl. One theory, Bayesian Decision Theory, asks the chef to put a probability judgment on the state of nature that is defined by whether or not the egg is rotten, and to maximize her utility taking into account the costs of washing the bowl, etc. Now there are certain problems for which probability assignments make little or no sense. Rawls argued that the basic problem of choosing principles of justice was just such a problem. These special cases of uncertainty have been called "decision problems under ignorance."

A second kind of rational choice problem is one of interdependent choice, whereby two or more decision-makers determine the final outcome of a situation. This is the province of game theory. A third kind of rational choice problem is called the "social choice problem." Suppose that individuals in a society must decide on a voting rule by which to make social decisions. Which voting rules are rational to choose? Kenneth Arrow (1963) showed that there is no voting rule that obeys a few very simple conditions of rationality. In addition, the subsequent research on social choice theory for the past 45 years has led to a new understanding of the conditions of rationality.

The so-called Arrow Paradox illustrates a strategy in much of rational choice theory. Axioms or conditions are proposed, and general possibility theorems are proved which show that certain decision rules can be derived or not from the axioms. If one can prove an impossibility result, then new conditions or modified axioms are proposed and the process begins anew. Daniel Ellsberg, Maurice Allais, and Robert Nozick have each proposed paradoxes that occur with regard to one foundational principle of rational choice theory, the "sure thing principle." The PRISONER'S DILEMMA illustrates a paradox about the interdependence of certain choices in game theory.

Rational choice theory continues to be a wealth of insight for moral philosophers, but among some philosophers, questions have been raised about its foundations. Why, for instance, must morality be grounded in individual choice, in general and rational individual choice in particular? What normative work is the term "rational" doing in such a theory? The attempt to ground ethics in rationality is just one more attempt to reduce all of human behavior to mere reason, negating or minimizing other kinds of behavior. This critique of rational choice theory argues that the primacy of the individual ignores the view that the very best of human activity may well be a function of human communities and the capacity to care for others, rather than a function of individual self-interested choices.

Bibliography

Arrow, K. (1963). *Social Choice and Individual Values*, 2nd edn. New Haven, CT: Yale University Press.

Baier, K. (1958). *The Moral Point of View*. Ithaca, NY: Cornell University Press.

Campbell, R. and Snowden, L. (eds.) (1985). *Paradoxes of Rationality and Cooperation*. Vancouver: University of British Columbia Press.

Gauthier, D. (1986). *Morals By Agreement*. Oxford: Oxford University Press.

Luce, D. and Raiffa, H. (1957). *Games and Decisions*. New York: John Wiley and Sons.

Rawls, J. (1971). *A Theory of Justice*. Boston, MA: Harvard University Press.

reflective equilibrium

Kai Nielsen

is a coherentist method of explanation and justification used in ethical theory, social and political philosophy, philosophy of science, philosophy of mind, and epistemology. Its initial articulation was made by Nelson Goodman, but its more familiar and extensive utilization is in moral and social philosophy, where it was initiated by John Rawls and Stuart Hampshire and was later amplified by Norman Daniels and Kai Nielsen. Its most forceful critics are Richard Brandt, David Copp, Joseph Raz, Jean Hampton, and Simon Blackburn.

As a method of justification in ethics it starts with a society's, or cluster of societies', most firmly held considered judgments (principally their moral judgments) and seeks to forge them into a consistent and coherent whole that squares with the other things that are reasonably believed and generally and uncontroversially accepted in the society or cluster of societies in question. The considered judgments appealed to can be at all levels of generality, though the point of departure will usually be from particular considered judgments which in turn will be placed in a coherent pattern with more general moral principles, middle-level moral rules and with, as well, moral practices (more strictly, with the verbal articulations of the practices). Suppose a particular moral belief fails to be compatible with a general moral principle in turn supported by many other firmly held particular considered judgments, other general moral principles, and middle-level moral rules. Then that particular considered judgment should either be modified until it is so consistent or be excised from the corpus of considered moral judgments and the moral repertoire of that society. If, by contrast, a general moral principle (say the principle of utility) is incompatible with a considerable number of firmly held considered judgments, then it should also be either similarly modified or rejected. The idea is to shuttle back and forth between particular moral judgments, general principles, medium-level moral rules, and moral practices, modifying, where there is an incompatibility, one or the other, until we have gained what we have good reason to believe is the most consistent and coherent pattern achievable at the time. When this is attained a reflective equilibrium has been reached.

The idea is to seek to maximize the coherence of our moral beliefs and practices. But there is no assumption that any reflective equilibrium that has been attained will be *final* and will not subsequently be upset. It will be upset (and this is something we should expect to happen, historically speaking, repeatedly) if either we come to have a still more coherent pattern, or because, as the situation changes, new moral judgments enter the scene which conflict with some of the beliefs in the reflective equilibrium which has been established. When that is so we need to get a new consistent cluster of beliefs and moral practices. So, in such situations, the extant reflective equilibrium is upset. In that case, a new, more adequate one has to be brought into existence which will contain either a larger circle of coherently related beliefs and practices or will instead, while not enlarging the web of belief, articulate a more coherent package of beliefs and practices. The expectation is that this pattern of reasoning will continue indefinitely, and, in doing so, yield, if it is pursued intelligently, ever more coherent conceptions of moral belief and practice, while never attaining final closure.

Fallibilism is the name of the game. No ultimate critical standards are sought and no principles or beliefs, not even the most firmly held, are, in principle, free from the possibility of being modified or even abandoned, though some moral truisms may always *in fact* be unquestioningly accepted. But this non-absolutism is not skepticism, for, if a reflective equilibrium is achieved, we will have found a rationale for our moral beliefs and practices by seeing how they are in a consistent and coherent pattern. Justification, on this conception, is attained in this way.

The coherentist pattern of explanation and justification described above is still a narrow (partial) reflective equilibrium. It collects together moral and like-considered judgments, moral practices, medium-level moral rules and, as well, moral principles, including very general ones. But this would simply be coherentism that does not take into consideration facts about the functioning of economies and other parts of the social structure, conceptions of human nature, social facts, political realities, and scientific developments. Rawls, Daniels, and Nielsen seek a wider reflective equilibrium which takes these matters into consideration as well. It is called wide (broad) reflective equilibrium. Besides seeking to forge a coherent pattern of the moral matters mentioned above, it seeks – continuing to seek to maximize coherence – an equilibrium which takes into account our best corroborated social scientific theories and theories of human nature, firmly established social and psychological facts, and political realities, such as the extent and intractability of pluralism in the society or cluster of societies where the reflective equilibrium is sought. It also should take into consideration what it is reasonable to believe in the society or societies in question and whether the *de facto* pluralism in question is a reasonable pluralism. The thing is to achieve a consistent cluster of moral, factual, and theoretical beliefs that would yield the best available account of what the social situation is, what possibilities obtain in the society, and of what it is reasonable and desirable to do. Such an account is through and through coherentist and holistic, justifying our beliefs and practices by showing the coherency of their fit with each other.

In taking one account of such beliefs and practices to be superior to another, we do so by ascertaining which account yields the superior fit of our beliefs and practices. But wide reflective equilibrium accounts do not suffer from the defects of pure coherentist theories where any consistent set of beliefs, no matter how unrealistic, is justified simply in virtue of the fact of being a consistent system. In reflective equilibrium, we seek a cluster of *considered judgments* in wide reflective equilibrium. We do not seek just any consistent cluster of beliefs, for we start with considered judgments and return to them as well.

Some critics of reflective equilibrium have argued that there is no coherent system of moral beliefs and practices *to be discovered* by careful reflection and analysis. Instead, we have inherited from history a mass of conflicting views, unreflectively gained, held, and persisted in. These views are views which are not infrequently ideological. They often are the non-principled result of brute compromises between contending parties, of religious biases and class, ethnic, racial, and gender prejudices. This unrationalized mélange is not supportive of (the objection goes) the idea of there being an underlying coherent whole, whose deep underlying structure is to be unearthed by careful investigation. What we have instead is simply a clutter of conflicting beliefs and practices revealing a jumble rather than a coherent pattern. To this it has been, in turn, responded that philosophers who are defenders of reflective equilibrium are also *constructivists*. The pattern of consistent beliefs, including very centrally moral beliefs, is *not* a structure to be discovered or unearthed, as if it were analogous to a deep underlying "depth grammar" of language, but something to be *forged* – constructed – by a careful and resolute use of the method of reflective equilibrium. We start from our considered judgments, which involves the seeing of things by our own lights. Where else could we start? We can hardly jump out of our cultural and historical skins. But that is no justification or excuse for remaining there. If we use the method of reflective equilibrium, we will, after careful examination, reflection, and a taking of the relevant moral considerations to heart, modify or excise some considered judgments, persistently seeking a wider and more coherent web of beliefs and practices. We will so proceed until we have constructed a consistent and relevantly inclusive cluster of beliefs and practices. But it is not a question of discovering some underlying moral structure that has always been there. Such "moral realism" is mythical.

Other critics of reflective equilibrium have argued that reflective equilibrium, both narrow and wide, is ethnocentric, relativist, and conservative. Similar responses to those made to the previous criticism can be relevantly made here. There is no escaping starting with our considered judgments. However, the very fact of such a starting point is not a manifestation of ethnocentrism. In seeking to maximize coherence and to get the full range of relevant considerations into as coherent and inclusive a pattern as we can, the moral and empirical beliefs and conceptions of others – sometimes, culturally speaking, very different "others" – need to be taken into consideration. If our particular considered judgments are in conflict with either well-established factual claims, well-grounded and established social theories, or carefully articulated moral theories, they must be up for critical inspection and (at least) possible rejection. If they conflict with the considered judgments of other peoples whose considered judgments square better with a careful appraisal of the facts or the most carefully articulated social, biological, and natural-scientific theories, as well as with reflectively articulated general moral principles, then we have good reasons to accept these considered judgments rather than our own. This is true even of our more general considered judgments where they conflict with such massively supported considered judgments. The method of reflective equilibrium is a *self-correcting* method which gives us, as we repair or rebuild the ship at sea, a *critical* morality. So, though we start inescapably with our considered judgments, if we apply reflective equilibrium resolutely, our account will not be, or at least need not be, ethnocentric. Similar considerations obtain for the claim that reflective equilibrium is relativistic or inherently conservative.

A somewhat different criticism of reflective equilibrium claims that it does not push questions of justification far enough. It does not come to grips with the foundational, or at least fundamental, epistemological issues that would show us what moral knowledge really is or what warranted moral beliefs really are, so that we could defeat a determined global ethical skepticism. An underlying *assumption* of reflective equilibrium is that our considered judgments have an *initial credibility*. But unless we can show how we could establish these considered judgments to be true or warranted, that assumption will not be justified and we will not really have faced the epistemological questions that need to be faced if we are to come to have a genuinely objective ethical theory philosophically defended. Defenders of reflective equilibrium will in turn respond that such a foundationalist quest is both impossible and unnecessary. There is no just knowing moral propositions to be true or warranted. There is no just noting that they rest on some direct correspondence of moral propositions to the facts (moral or otherwise). There are no such fact-like entities for moral propositions to correspond to. But the recognition of this should not, they argue, lead to the abandonment of all notions of objectivity in morality. Cross-culturally agreed-on considered judgments set in a wide reflective equilibrium give us an inter-subjectivity, reflectively sustainable, that is all the moral objectivity we can get and all that we need.

This brief account cannot do justice to the complex issues that divide defenders of wide reflective equilibrium and their critics. These issues are now at the forefront of discussions concerning justification and explanation in ethics and social philosophy. Rawls and Hampshire provide the classical articulations of reflective equilibrium and Brandt and Hare the classical statements of its critique. Daniels, Nielsen, and Rorty provide cutting-edge defenses of wide reflective equilibrium and Raz, Copp, and Hampton cutting-edge statements of its critique. It is to these writings that the reader should turn for a more thorough analysis of these issues.

Bibliography

Blackburn, R. (1993). Can philosophy exist? In J. Couture and K. Nielsen (eds.), *Méta-Philosophie: Reconstructing Philosophy?* Calgary: University of Calgary Press, 83–106.

Brandt, R. (1979). *A Theory of the Good and Right.* Oxford: Clarendon Press.

Copp, D. (1985). Considered judgments and moral justification. In D. Copp and D. Zimmerman (eds.), *Morality, Reason and Truth: New Essays on the Foundations of Ethics.* Totowa, NJ: Rowan and Allanheld, 141–68.

Daniels, N. (1996). *Justice and Justification.* Cambridge: Cambridge University Press.

Hampshire, S. (1983). *Morality and Conflict.* Cambridge, MA: Harvard University Press.

Hampton, J. (1989). Should political philosophy be done without metaphysics? *Ethics*, 99, 791–814.

Hampton, J. (1993). The moral commitments of liberalism. In D. Copp, J. Hampton, and J. E. Roemer (eds.), *The Idea of Democracy.* Cambridge: Cambridge University Press.

Nielsen, K. (1982). On needing a moral theory: Rationality, considered judgments and the grounding of morality. *Metaphilosophy*, 13, 97–116.

Nielsen, K. (1991). *After the Demise of the Tradition: Rorty, Critical Theory and the Fate of Philosophy*, Boulder, CO: Westview Press.

Nielsen, K. (1994). How to proceed in social philosophy: Contextualist justice and wide reflective equilibrium. *Queen's Law Journal*, 20, 89–138.

Rawls, J. (1971). *A Theory of Justice.* Cambridge, MA: Harvard University Press.

Rawls, J. (1974). The independence of moral theory. *Proceedings and Addresses of the American Philosophical Association*, 48, 5–22.

Rawls, J. (1993). *Political Liberalism.* New York: Columbia University Press.

Raz, J. (1982). The claims of reflective equilibrium. *Inquiry*, 25, 307–30.

Rorty, R. (1988). The priority of democracy to philosophy. In M. D. Peterson and R. C. Vaughan (eds.), *The Virginia Statute For Religious Freedom.* Cambridge: Cambridge University Press, 257–82.

regulation

Wesley A. Magat

As defined in the classic treatise of Alfred Kahn (1970: 3), "regulation is the explicit replacement of competition with governmental orders as the principal institutional device for assuring good performance" from an industry.

Several aspects of this definition are important. First, systems of regulation are imposed by law through the political-choice process because some segments of the population prefer the outcomes that emerge from an administrative process to those resulting from the operation of unfettered markets. These groups may also prefer some aspects of the regulatory process itself, such as their sense of its fairness, to the market process of resource allocation.

Second, industries, and the businesses and consumers who comprise those industries, are

regulated in order to improve upon the performance of the industries, at least as measured or
perceived by some segments of the population.
Welfare economics focuses on policies for maximizing social efficiency, defined as the sum of
the benefits to consumers and companies from
markets, whereas political economists tend to
stress the distributional gains and losses
resulting from regulation.

Third, regulation operates through agencies
who act as the agents of the administrative and
legislative branches of the government in carrying out laws. Regulatory agencies are constrained by their enabling statutes, by
procedural restrictions such as the US Administrative Procedure Act (in the US context), and
by the political forces which act upon the agencies. They carry out their missions through setting rules, or regulations, and by adjudicating
requests from affected parties such as an electric
utility company.

One of the most famous results in economics
is Adam Smith's (1776) observation that economic welfare can be maximized by organizing
the distribution of goods and services through
perfectly competitive markets. Much regulation
can be justified as responses to so-called "market
failures," that is, social inefficiencies arising
from the operation of imperfectly competitive
markets. From a political point of view, the
logic is straightforward. If a market fails due to
a market imperfection, then society can improve
aggregate economic welfare by imposing regulations that force the market to operate as if it were
perfectly competitive. Political forces can
impose regulations on an economy even if those
regulations only benefit the groups in political
power at the expense of other groups, sometimes
with an overall decrease in the aggregate level of
economic welfare in the economy. In the latter
case, the regulations stay in place until the political coalition behind them disintegrates or is
beaten by another coalition, at which time the
regulations are dismantled or the industry is
deregulated (e.g., the American airlines industry
was deregulated in 1978 after 40 years of regulation).

Based on the theory of market failure or the
pursuit of political aims other than economic
efficiency, several justifications for regulation
can be identified (see Breyer, 1982).

Natural monopoly. If the number of companies
in a market is small and if barriers to entry into
the industry limit the competition from potential
rivals, then the producers in the industry can
raise their prices above the competitive levels
without fear of a large loss of sales and profits.
One of the entry barriers that limits the number
of firms in an industry is due to increasing
returns to scale. If the average cost of production
falls dramatically at high volumes and industry
demand is only strong enough to support one
firm, or at most a few firms, at this high rate of
production, then small companies are unable to
enter and compete in the market because of their
marked cost disadvantage. Local telephone companies, electric utilities, and natural-gas distribution companies provide good examples of this
kind of "natural monopoly" for which rate regulation limits the price charged to consumers of
their products.

Spillover costs. When the costs of producing
some product, such as paper, spill over to other
producers (e.g., in the form of polluted water
that must be cleaned before use) or to consumers
(e.g., in the form of air pollution which causes
respiratory problems), then markets fail to maximize economic welfare. Without facing sufficient incentives to bear the costs of the
spillovers, companies tend to produce too
much of the products or they devote too few
resources to reducing the spillover effects.
Hence the potential justification for government
regulation, such as standards on the levels of
hydrocarbon emissions from automobiles, emis-
sion taxes on hydrocarbons emitted by electric
utilities, and allocations of radio broadcast frequencies to avoid the spillover costs (namely, the
interference) that would be imposed upon
existing stations from new stations broadcasting
on the same frequencies.

Inadequate information. For markets to function
smoothly, consumers and producers must possess accurate information about the availability
of goods, their prices, and their quality. However, it is difficult to exclude others from the use
of product information once it is produced or
discovered, making information itself a good
which is under-supplied in markets and thus
a candidate for government programs that

encourage further supply. The US National Weather Service provides information directly, while EPA's gas mileage labeling requirements ensure that this information is available to new car buyers (see Viscusi and Magat, 1987; Magat and Viscusi, 1992).

Paternalism.   Regulation is sometimes justified on the basis that consumers sometimes make decisions which are not in their own best interests. This argument can easily become a slippery slope, quickly overriding freedom of choice in many economic decisions, but for certain classes of decisions government paternalism is at least arguable. State regulation of alcohol sales to minors and inebriated adults is one commonly accepted example of a paternalistic regulation. There is strong evidence that even well-educated adults have difficulty in accurately assessing health and safety risks, and in making self-protection decisions concerning these low-probability risks. Both of these risks provide a potential justification for banning the direct sale to consumers of certain chemical and pharmaceutical products.

Moral hazard.   Markets cannot function well without contracts written over private exchanges, and efficient contracts cannot be written unless the actions of parties involved in the contract are observable. Otherwise, the problem of moral hazard arises. Employers may underinvest in the safety levels of their work environments if these safety levels are not observable by employees; consumers may use products carelessly if the products are covered by warranties and other forms of insurance; and doctors and their patients may agree to excessive levels of medical care if a third-party insurer pays without the ability to observe levels of care. In all of these cases government regulation has been suggested as a way of correcting the market failure.

Redistribution.   Regulation is a political response by groups of citizens to override the outcomes of the market process. Given the ability of every level of government to create winners and losers from regulatory action, it is not surprising that much government regulation is motivated at least in part by efforts to redistribute resources, whether it be set-aside provisions for women and minority firms in government contracts and

spectrum sales, grandfathering or relaxed pollution standards for existing versus new sources of pollution, or regulatory barriers to entry into long-distance telephone markets. (For further discussion, see Schmalensee and Willig, 1989: ch. 22; Magat, Krupnick, and Harrington, 1986; Cohen and Stigler, 1971.)

While the examples in this entry are based on American regulatory institutions, the general principles behind the political causes and economic justifications for regulation are shared by all market-based economies.

See also *corporate social performance; efficient markets; environment and environmental ethics; global warming; hazardous waste; Securities and Exchange Commission*

Bibliography

Baumol, W. J. (1977). On the proper cost test for natural monopoly in a multiproduct industry. *American Economic Review*, 67, 809–22.

Breyer, S. (1982). *Regulation and its Reform.* Cambridge, MA: Harvard University Press.

Cohen, M. and Stigler, G. (1971). *Can Regulatory Agencies Protect Customers?* Washington, DC: American Enterprise Institute for Policy Research.

Derthick, M. and Quuirk, P. J. (1985). *The Politics of Deregulation.* Washington, DC: Brookings Institution.

Kahn, A. E. (1970). *The Economics of Regulations: Principles and Institutions.* New York: John Wiley.

Magat, W. A., Krupnick, A. J., and Harrington, W. (1986). *Rules in the Making.* Washington, DC: Resources for the Future.

Magat, W. A. and Viscusi, W. K. (1992). *Informational Approaches to Regulation.* Cambridge, MA: MIT Press.

Noll, R. G. and Owen, B. M. (1983). *The Political Economy of Deregulation.* Washington, DC: American Enterprise Institute.

Schmalensee, R. and Willig, R. D. (eds.) (1989). *Handbook of Industrial Organization.* Amsterdam: North-Holland.

Smith, A. (1776). *An Inquiry into the Nature and Causes of the Wealth of Nations.* London: W. Strahan, T. Cadell.

Spulber, D. F. (1989). *Regulation and Markets.* Cambridge, MA: MIT Press.

Viscusi, W. K. and Magat, W. A. (1987). *Learning About Risk: Consumer and Worker Responses to Hazard Information.* Cambridge, MA: Harvard University Press.

Viscusi, W. K., Vernon, J. M., and Harrington, J., Jr. (1992). *Economics of Regulations and Antitrust.* Lexington, MA: D. C. Heath.

relativism, cultural and moral

Norman E. Bowie

Cultural relativism is a descriptive claim that ethical practices differ among cultures; that, as a matter of fact, what is considered right in one culture may be considered wrong in another. Thus, the truth or falsity of cultural relativism can be determined by examining the world. The work of anthropologists and sociologists is most relevant in determining the truth or falsity of cultural relativism, and there is widespread consensus among social scientists that cultural relativism is true.

Moral relativism is the claim that what is really right or wrong is what the culture says is right or wrong. Moral relativists accept cultural relativism as true, but they claim much more. If a culture sincerely and reflectively adopts a basic moral principle, then it is morally obligatory for members of that culture to act in accordance with that principle.

The implication of moral relativism for conduct is that one ought to abide by the ethical norms of the culture where one is located. This position is captured by the popular phrase: "When in Rome, do as the Romans do." Relativists in ethics would say: "One ought to follow the moral norms of the culture." In terms of business practice, consider this question: "Is it morally right to pay a bribe to gain business?" The moral relativist would answer the question by consulting the moral norms of the country where one is doing business. If those norms permit bribery in that country, then the practice of bribery is not wrong in that country. However, if the moral norms of the country do not permit bribery, then offering a bribe to gain business in that country is morally wrong. The justification for that position is the moral relativist's contention that what is really right or wrong is determined by the culture.

Is cultural relativism true? Is moral relativism correct? As noted, many social scientists believe that cultural relativism is true as a matter of fact. But is it?

First, many philosophers claim that the "facts" aren't really what they seem. Early twentieth-century anthropologists cited the fact that in some cultures, after a certain age, parents are put to death. In most cultures such behavior

would be murder. Does this difference in behavior prove that the two cultures disagree about fundamental matters of ethics? No, it does not. Suppose the other culture believes that people exist in the afterlife in the same condition that they leave their present life. It would be very cruel to have one's parents exist eternally in an unhealthy state. By killing them when they are relatively active and vigorous, you ensure their happiness for all eternity. The *underlying* ethical principle of this culture is that children have duties to their parents, including the duty to be concerned with their parents' happiness as they approach old age. This ethical principle is identical with our own. What looked like a difference in ethics between our culture and another turned out, upon close examination, to be a difference based on what each culture takes to be the facts of the matter. This example does, of course, support the claim that as a matter of fact ethical principles vary according to culture. However, it does not support the stronger conclusion that *underlying* ethical principles vary according to culture.

Cultures differ in physical setting, in economic development, in the state of their science and technology, in their literacy rate, and in many other ways. Even if there were universal moral principles, they would have to be applied in these different cultural contexts. Given the different situations in which cultures exist, it would come as no surprise to find universal principles applied in different ways. Hence, we expect to find surface differences in ethical behavior among cultures even though the cultures agree on fundamental universal moral principles. For example, one commonly held universal principle appeals to the public good; it says that social institutions and individual behavior should be ordered so that they lead to the greatest good for the greatest number. Many different forms of social organization and individual behavior are consistent with this principle. The point of these two arguments is to show that differences among cultures on ethical behavior may not reflect genuine disagreement about underlying principles of ethics. Thus, it is not so obvious that any strong form of cultural relativism is true.

But are there universal principles that are accepted by all cultures? It seems so; there does seem to be a whole range of behavior, such as torture and murder of the innocent, that every culture agrees is wrong. A nation-state accused of torture does not respond by saying that a condemnation of torture is just a matter of cultural choice. The state's leaders do not respond by saying, "We think torture is right, but you do not." Rather, the standard response is to deny that any torture took place. If the evidence of torture is too strong, a finger will be pointed either at the victim or at the morally outraged country: "They do it too." In this case the guilt is spread to all. Even the Nazis denied that genocide took place. What is important is that *no* state replies that there is nothing wrong with genocide or torture.

In addition, there are attempts to codify some universal moral principles. The United Nations Universal Declaration of Human Rights has been endorsed by the member states of the UN, and the vast majority of countries in the world are members of the UN. Even in business, there is a growing effort to adopt universal principles of business practice. In a recent study of international codes of ethics, Catherine Langlois and Bodo B. Schlegelmilch (1990) found that although there certainly were differences among codes, there was a considerable area of agreement. William Frederick has documented the details of six international compacts on matters of international business ethics. These include the aforementioned UN Universal Declaration of Human Rights, the European Convention on Human Rights, the Helsinki Final Act, the OECD Guidelines for Multinational Enterprises and Social Policy, and the United Nations Conduct on Transnational Corporations (in progress) (Frederick, 1991). The Caux Roundtable, a group of corporate executives from the United States, Europe, and Japan, are seeking worldwide endorsement of a set of principles of business ethics. Thus, there are a number of reasons to think that cultural relativism, at least with respect to basic moral principles, is not true, that is, that it does not accurately describe the state of moral agreement that exists. This is consistent with maintaining that cultural relativism is true in the weak form, that is, when applied only to surface ethical principles.

But what if differences in fundamental moral practices among cultures are discovered and

seem unreconcilable? That would lead to a discussion about the adequacy of moral relativism. The fact that moral practices do vary widely among countries is cited as evidence for the correctness of moral relativism. Discoveries early in the century by anthropologists, sociologists, and psychologists documented the diversity of moral beliefs. Philosophers, by and large, welcomed corrections of moral imperialist thinking, but recognized that the moral relativist's appeal to the alleged truth of cultural relativism was not enough to establish moral relativism. The mere fact that a culture considers a practice moral does not mean that it is moral. Cultures have sincerely practiced slavery, discrimination, and the torture of animals. Yet each of these practices can be independently criticized on ethical grounds. Thinking something is morally permissible does not make it so.

Another common strategy for criticizing moral relativism is to show that the consequences of taking the perspective of moral relativism are inconsistent with our use of moral language. It is often contended by moral relativists that if two cultures disagree regarding universal moral principles, there is no way for that disagreement to be resolved. Since moral relativism is the view that what is right or wrong is determined by culture, there is no higher appeal beyond the fact that culture endorses the moral principle. But we certainly do not talk that way. When China and the United States argue about the moral rights of human beings, the disputants use language that seems to appeal to universal moral principles. Moreover, the atrocities of the Nazis and the slaughter in Rwanda have met with universal condemnation that seemed based on universal moral principles. So moral relativism is not consistent with our use of moral language.

Relativism is also inconsistent with how we use the term "moral reformer." Suppose, for instance, that a person from one culture moves to another and tries to persuade the other culture to change its view. Suppose someone moves from a culture where slavery is immoral to one where slavery is morally permitted. Normally, if a person were to try to convince the culture where slavery was permitted that slavery was morally wrong, we would call such a person a moral reformer. Moreover, a moral reformer would almost certainly appeal to universal moral principles to make her argument; she almost certainly would not appeal to a competing cultural standard. But if moral relativism were true, there would be no place for the concept of a moral reformer. Slavery is really right in those cultures that say it is right and really wrong in those cultures that say it is wrong. If the reformer fails to persuade a slaveholding country to change its mind, the reformer's antislavery position was never right. If the reformer is successful in persuading a country to change its mind, the reformer's antislavery views would be wrong – until the country did in fact change its view. Then the reformer's antislavery view would be right. But that is not how we talk about moral reform.

The moral relativist might argue that our language should be reformed. We should talk differently. At one time people used to talk and act as if the world were flat. Now they don't. The relativist could suggest that we can change our ethical language in the same way. But consider how radical the relativists' response is. Since most, if not all, cultures speak and act as if there were universal moral principles, the relativist can be right only if almost everyone else is wrong. How plausible is that?

Although these arguments are powerful ones, they do not deliver a knockout blow to moral relativism. If there are no universal moral principles, moral relativists could argue that moral relativism is the only theory available to help make sense of moral phenomena.

An appropriate response to this relativist argument is to present the case for a set of universal moral principles, principles that are correct for all cultures independent of what a culture thinks about them. This is what adherents of the various ethical traditions try to do. The reader will have to examine these various traditions and determine how persuasive she finds them. In addition, there are several final independent considerations against moral relativism that can be mentioned here.

First, what constitutes a culture? There is a tendency to equate cultures with national boundaries, but that is naive, especially today. With respect to moral issues, what do US cultural norms say regarding right and wrong? That question may be impossible to answer, because

in a highly pluralistic country like the United States, there are many cultures. Furthermore, even if one can identify a culture's moral norms, it will have dissidents who do not subscribe to those moral norms. How many dissidents can a culture put up with and still maintain that some basic moral principle is the cultural norm? Moral relativists have had little to say regarding criteria for constituting a culture or how to account for dissidents. Unless moral relativists offer answers to questions like these, their theory is in danger of becoming inapplicable to the real world.

Second, any form of moral relativism must admit that there are some universal moral principles. Suppose a culture does not accept moral relativism, that is, it denies that if an entire culture sincerely and reflectively adopts a basic moral principle, it is obligatory for members of that culture to act in accord with that principle. Fundamentalist Muslim countries would reject moral relativism because it would require them to accept as morally permissible blasphemy in those countries where blasphemy was permitted. If the moral relativist insists that the truth of every moral principle depends on the culture, then she must admit that the truth of moral relativism depends on the culture. Therefore the moral relativist must admit that at least the principle of moral relativism is not relative.

Third, it seems that there is a set of basic moral principles that every culture must adopt. You would not have a culture unless the members of the group adopted these moral principles. Consider an anthropologist who arrives on a populated island: How many tribes are on the island? To answer that question, the anthropologist tries to determine if some people on some parts of the island are permitted to kill, commit acts of violence against, or steal from persons on other parts of the island. If such behavior is not permitted, that counts as a reason for saying that there is only one tribe. The underlying assumption here is that there is a set of moral principles that must be followed if there is to be a culture at all. With respect to those moral principles, adhering to them determines whether there is a culture or not.

But what justifies these principles? A moral relativist would say that a culture justifies them. But you cannot have a culture unless the members of the culture follow the principles. Thus it is reasonable to think that justification lies elsewhere. Many believe that the purpose of morality is to help make social cooperation possible. Moral principles are universally necessary for that endeavor.

Bibliography

Benedict, R. (1934). *Patterns of Culture*. New York: Penguin Books.
Bowie, N. (1988). The moral obligations of multinational corporations. In S. Luper-Foy (ed.), *Problems of International Justice*, Boulder, CO: Westview Press.
Frederick, W. C. (1991). The moral authority of transnational corporate codes. *Journal of Business Ethics*, **10** (3), 165–77.
Harman, G. (1975). Moral relativism defended. *Philosophical Review*, **84**, 3–22.
Hatch, E. (1983). *Culture and Morality*. New York: Columbia University Press.
Krausz, M. and Meiland, J. (1982). *Relativism: Cognitive and Moral*. Notre Dame, IN: University of Notre Dame Press.
Ladd, J. (1973). *Ethical Relativism*. Belmont, CA: Wadsworth.
Langlois, C. and Schlegelmilch, B. B. (1990). Do corporate codes of ethics reflect national character? Evidence from Europe and the United States. *Journal of International Studies*, **21**, (9), 519–39.
Mackie, J. (1977). *Ethics: Inventing Right and Wrong*. Harmondsworth: Penguin Books.
Rachels, J. (1993). *The Elements of Moral Philosophy*, 2nd edn. New York: McGraw-Hill.
Sayre-McCord, G. (1991). Being a realist about relativism (in ethics). *Philosophical Studies*, **61**, 155–76.
Wong, D. (1984). *Moral Relativity*. Berkeley: University of California Press.

religion and business ethics

Martin Calkins

Today's business ethics is, in part, the product of religious leaders' steadfast interest in business's relationship to certain social issues. In the West, these leaders represent Judaism, Roman Catholicism, and Protestantism.

Judaism, the root of Christianity, provided business ethics with an operative set of norms. These norms, the most prominent being the Ten Commandments (Exodus 20:1–17), are an admixture of judgment (*mishpat*) and loving kindness (*hesed*) and are reflective of God's covenant with the Israelites. They continue to influence and regulate the behavior of contemporary businesses as the basis of the "blue laws" that regulate business hours ("Remember the sabbath day, and keep it holy"), as the source of the idea that transactions should involve proper entitlement ("You shall not steal"), and as the basis for the expectation of truth-telling in negotiations ("You shall not bear false witness against your neighbor").

Coming out of this tradition, Christians believe that Jesus Christ fulfilled ("I have come not to abolish but to fulfill," Matthew 5:17) and reinterpreted ("the sabbath was made for humankind, and not humankind for the sabbath," Mark 2:27) Jewish law. The New Testament is replete with examples of how Jesus interpreted the law to pertain to business transactions and the economy. In it, Jesus addresses business's relationship to worship (the story involving the money changers in the Temple, Matthew 21:12–13 and John 2:14–16), he calls into question the relationship of work to wages (the story of the vineyard laborers, Matthew 20:1–16), he considers the worthiness of risk-taking and enterprise (the parable of the talents, Matthew 25:14–30), and he recognizes the propriety of tax payment (in encouraging Jews to pay the taxes due Caesar, Matthew 22:20–1). Scripture also relates how, prior to his arrest and conviction, Jesus himself was an object of barter in being sold by a traitorous disciple (see the story of Judas's blood money, Matthew 27:3–8).

Early Christian leaders tried to emulate Jesus by carrying on his concern for the justice of economic transactions, especially as they applied to the needy. St. Paul, for one, emphasized the idea of labor as a form of worship; that is, a way by which we might participate in creation and the building up of God's Kingdom. Paul referred to early Christian disciples as ones who "work with me in Christ Jesus" (Romans 16:3) and repeatedly encouraged his audiences to excel in "the work of the Lord" (1 Corinthians 15:58).

Later, St. Ambrose and St. Augustine considered different aspects of labor; in particular, the link between work and entitlements. St. Ambrose's (333–97) theistic property ethic, for example, held that certain entitlements are part of our birthright. He argued that since we share a common natural poverty at birth and death, we have a justified claim to nature's wealth-producing resources. The wealthy, he claimed, because they have resources in abundance, have a duty to make restitution to the needy among us who have been deprived of this birthright.

Following Ambrose, St. Augustine (354–430) asserted that the poor are the result of Adam's Fall and original sin (Genesis 3). The poor are poor, he argued, because the propertied few have denied them access to the wealth that belongs to all. In paradise, Augustine reasoned, Adam was gifted with the wisdom to fulfill God's created order and was able to recognize that society should hold resources in common. After the Fall, however, attempts to live according to a system of common ownership were undermined as significant numbers of people insisted on remaining attached to an "earthly city" and a life regulated by personal and selfish desires.

Centuries after Augustine, St. Thomas Aquinas (1225–74) considered the theological and philosophical implications associated with commutative justice (the justice between two equals in regard to private transactions) and distributive justice (the rendering of rewards according to proportion). Thomas's Aristotelian and Augustinian based virtue theory, for example, held that justice to be a personal characteristic of habitual action that enables people to flourish in accord with God's plan. This Thomistic theory became the cornerstone of most Christian teaching for the following three hundred years.

With the Protestant Reformation, however, Christian ethics bifurcated into two branches: (1) a Protestant branch that sought to be prophetic and capable of discerning the moral status of current practices and (2) a Roman Catholic branch that sought to prescribe and proscribe specific acts. The difference between the two approaches is evident in Max Weber's and Pope Leo XIII's writings on the economy.

Max Weber (1864–1920) is known for his commentary on the link between Protestantism and capitalism. His larger body of work, however, described the evolution of the modern institutional and organizational order of "rational bourgeois capitalism" and the psychological conditions that made possible the development of large-scale business enterprises. As part of his inquiry, he investigated the connections between religious affiliation and social stratification and posited that something integral to Protestantism must have had something to do with the success of German business leaders. He then looked to the four principal forms of ascetic Protestantism (Calvinism, Pietism, Methodism, and the sects growing out of the Baptist movement) and argued that the development of an economic spirit (an *ethos* attaching to an economic system) is likely sourced in (1) Luther's notions of "the call" and the moral justification of worldly activity and (2) Calvin's spirit of Christian asceticism and notion of a relationship between prosperity and salvation.

Although the accuracy of his work is being questioned at present, Weber's provocative thesis impelled subsequent Protestant educators (Reinhold Niebuhr, John Howard Yoder, and others) to offer different sorts of important and influential commentaries on capitalism. Yoder's notion of "servant strength," for example, called into question the ethics of power that underlies the connections that Weber observed.

During and after the Reformation, the Roman Catholic Church remained immersed in casuistry and scholasticism. In the nineteenth century it began to apply these methodologies to issues associated with capitalist economies. Due to the work of German-speaking Catholics such as Adam Müller (1779–1829), Franz Von Baader (1765–1841), Adolph Kolping (1813–65), and Wilhelm von Ketteler (1811–77), the church began to consider the issue of worker alienation and the social suffering that attended to the transition from a feudal crafts system to a modern industrial order. Ketteler, in particular, was influential in an ability to move Pope Leo XIII (papacy: 1878–1903) to promulgate *Rerum Novarum* (*The Condition of Labor*, 1891), the Catholic Church's first major social encyclical on the economy. *Rerum Novarum*, which considered the dignity of labor, the rights and just wages of workers, and workmen's associations, has been celebrated subsequently in a number of anniversary encyclicals, the most recent being Pope John Paul II's *Centesimus Annus* (*On the Hundredth Anniversary of Rerum Novarum*, 1991).

In the US, prominent Catholic lay and clerical leaders who addressed economic and business concerns in the recent past include Orestes

Brownson (1803–76), Dorothy Day (1897–1980), Peter Dietz (1878–1947), and John A. Ryan (1869–1945). In addition, in the twentieth century, the US Catholic Bishops produced two major pieces on the economy: *The Pastoral Letter of 1919* and *Economic Justice for All* (1986), the latter being a collaborative and inclusive venture that addressed a broad sweep of economic issues with particular attention paid to the economically needy.

Bibliography

Avila, C. (1983). *Ownership, Early Christian Teaching.* New York: Orbis Books.

Clifford, R. J., SJ (1990). Exodus. In Raymond E. Brown, Joseph A. Fitzmyer, and Roland E. Murphy (eds.), *The New Jerome Biblical Commentary.* Englewood Cliffs, NJ: Prentice-Hall, 44–60.

De George, R. T. (1987). The status of business ethics: Past and future. *Journal of Business Ethics,* 6, 201–11.

Delacroix, J. and Nielsen, F. (2001). The beloved myth: Protestantism and the rise of industrial capitalism in nineteenth-century Europe. *Social Forces,* 80 (2), 509–53.

Gordon, B. (1994). Theological positions and economic perspectives in ancient literature. In H. G. Brennan and A. M. C. Waterman (eds.), *Economics and Religion: Are They Distinct?* Boston, MA: Kluwer Academic Publishers, 19–40.

Gustafson, J. M. (1981). *Ethics from a Theocentric Perspective.* Chicago: University of Chicago Press.

Marshall, G. (1982). *In Search of the Spirit of Capitalism.* London: Hutchinson.

Naughton, M. (1992). *The Good Stewards: Practical Applications of the Papal Social Vision of Work.* Lanham, MD: University Press of America.

O'Brien, D. J. and Shannon, T. A. (eds.) (1992). *Catholic Social Thought – The Documentary Heritage.* New York: Orbis Books.

Weber, M. (1958). *The Protestant Ethic and the Spirit of Capitalism,* student's edn. New York: Charles Scribner's Sons.

Yoder, J. H. (1984). *The Priestly Kingdom.* Notre Dame, IN: University of Notre Dame Press.

Zweig, M. (ed.) (1991). *Religion and Economic Justice.* Philadelphia, PA: Temple University Press.

research centers for business ethics

Mark Rowe

are dedicated to the study of what is good or right for individuals and groups of individuals engaged in business activity. More particularly, these organizations investigate and analyze the application of moral concepts and principles to business decision-making and action, usually with the aims of developing greater awareness and understanding of ethical issues in the business environment, and promoting best practices to address them. Business ethics centers are most effective when they bridge theoretical inquiry and practical application, and guide organizations in the development of ethical business cultures.

Business ethics centers are generally not-for-profit organizations, and although most have been established within business schools and universities, some exist independently. Funding and support for institution-based centers are usually provided by the host institution or by corporate and individual donors, government grants, revenue-generating activities (such as executive education programs, conferences, and publishing), and sometimes by all of these sources in combination. Independent centers may derive funding from donors, grants, and programs and also from consulting revenues.

Significant active research in business ethics began in the mid-1970s, as the field became more widely recognized as a legitimate subject for study and teaching. Demand for such research was driven by the heightened social and ethical consciousness that emerged in the wake of a decade of civil unrest, environmental concern, and consumer enfranchisement – and especially after a series of high-profile scandals such as Watergate and the aerospace industry bribes. Among the oldest business ethics centers are the Center for Business Ethics, founded in 1976 at Bentley College in Waltham, Massachusetts, and the Olsson Center for Applied Ethics, which became active at the Darden Graduate School of Business, University of Virginia, at around the same time.

There are now close to 200 centers worldwide, over 120 of which are in the United States alone. Regions newly significant for interest in business ethics which have seen the creation of centers include Latin America, South Korea, Japan, and South Africa. Typically, centers are small, with a full-time director, one or more research and consulting staff members or associates, and several full- and part-time support staff. In the university setting it is common for faculty members to be affiliated with such centers. They are often charged with teaching business ethics within a broader discipline-based curriculum and, especially now in business schools, integrating the subject into students' general education.

The particular focus of individual centers varies widely but, in general terms, all of them work to stimulate, support, conduct, and disseminate research related to business ethics and corporate social responsibility. Very few centers now concern themselves solely with conducting or collecting research. Even when the majority of a center's time and resources are used in this way, it is likely that there will be subsidiary activities such as organizing occasional conferences or publishing reports. Most centers have multiple functions, often a combination of research with teaching and the preparation of teaching materials, organizing conferences and seminars, and the provision of speakers and scholars for media interviews. A growing number of centers offer advisory and networking services to corporations and other organizations. Some centers are repositories for books, journals, videos, and corporate ethics materials. Among centers that publish business ethics newsletters or magazines, the trend is toward online publications to enable more timely and cost-effective dissemination of ideas and information. The Ethics Resource Center in Washington, DC and the Institute of Global Ethics in Camden, Maine are notable trendsetters in this regard.

Centers differ in the degree of specialization within the field of business ethics, ranging from an interest in business generally to a specialist focus on particular industries or professions. Prominent centers in the former category include the Zicklin Center for Business Ethics Research at Wharton, University of Pennsylvania, the Center for Business Ethics at Bentley College (above), and the Institute of Business Ethics in London, UK. At the other end of the spectrum is the Isbell Center for Hospitality Ethics at Northern Arizona University and the Silha Center for the Study of Media Ethics and Law at the University of Minnesota.

Research methodologies employed at centers also differ widely, depending on the nature of the subject matter, the research objectives, and the resources available. Some centers conduct empirical research to investigate, evaluate, and explain companies' practices, using qualitative methods such as case studies and interviews, as well as quantitative analysis of large-sample survey data that might have been gathered with the assistance of a specialist survey firm. Research is also carried out using secondary sources such as corporate public publications, public filings, media coverage, and directories. The work of some centers requires a greater degree of theoretical abstraction, grounded in the discipline of philosophy.

revolving door

Lynn A. Isabella

is a commonly used metaphor that represents the fluid and continuous movement of individuals in and out of organizations. Imagine a steady stream of people from two directions passing through a spinning door. Their entrance as well as their exit is easy, quick, and relatively unencumbered; individuals are constantly in motion passing through. However, because hiring, training, and retraining individuals is costly, a constant revolving door of personnel has serious financial implications.

Revolving doors can exist in different ways for different reasons. Specific jobs or positions can become known as places where individuals quickly come and go; alternatively, the culture of an organization can come to be known as one where the tenure of people within the company is short. For example, a number of companies have jobs that become known as "stepping stones" within an organization. These are positions through which people rotate on their way somewhere else. One is never expected to remain long; one rarely sees the consequences of actions initiated. At the organizational level, companies can become known as "revolving door" cultures. These are companies who expect (consciously or unconsciously) that employees will remain for short periods of time and then move on. These companies are extremely demanding of people's time and energies, workloads are heavy, and the atmosphere intense. Such a company may have an unintended (or intended) philosophy of people as expendable resources: use them as long and as hard as one can, then hire another to begin the cycle again.

The revolving door phenomenon can have ethical implications for companies and for the individuals who work in them. For companies, as individuals pass through their doors quickly, so can company secrets, client data, and other proprietary information. Companies as a result often go to great lengths to protect that data. It is not uncommon for employees, especially high-level executives, when leaving or being asked to leave, to do so immediately and under guard or to be asked to sign an agreement limiting industry access. At the individual level, the revolving door may represent a constant supply of fresh talent for a company, but at the expense of perhaps unwitting but eager employees, who believe they are being hired into a position of promise.

Bibliography

Arthur, M., Hall, D., and Lawrence, B. (eds.) (1989). *Handbook of Career Theory*. New York: Cambridge University Press.

Feldman, D. (1989). Careers in organizations: Recent trends and future directions. *Journal of Management*, 15, 135–56.

Hall, D. T. (1976). *Careers in Organizations*. Pacific Palisades, CA: Goodyear.

Schien, E. (1978). *Career Dynamics: Matching Individuals and Organizational Needs*. Reading, MA: Addison-Wesley.

rights

Alan Gewirth

The claiming of rights is one of the strongest ways of demanding protection of persons' interests. At the same time, many aspects of the appeal to rights are intensely controversial. The controversies bear not only on the normative and substantive issues of who has rights to what, but also on basic conceptual issues.

Hohfeld's Distinctions

The standard starting point for dealing with the conceptual issues is Wesley N. Hohfeld (1879–1918), who saw that the phrase "a right" was used with different meanings in the legal literature. To avoid the resulting confusion, he distinguished four meanings of this phrase. First, if *A* has a *claim-right* to *X* against *B*, then *B* has a correlative *duty* to *A* to refrain from interfering with *A*'s having or doing *X*, or, in some situations, a duty to give *X* to *A* or to help *A* to have or do *X*. Thus, *A* has a claim-right to life against *B* and all other persons in that they have a correlative duty to refrain from taking *A*'s life; and if *B* promised to meet *A* at the bookstore at noon, then *A* has a claim-right against *B* that *B* meet him there and then, and *B* has a correlative duty to meet *A* as promised.

Second, if *A* has a *liberty-right* (or *privilege*) to *X* against *B*, then *B* has a correlative *no-right* (i.e., no claim-right) that *A* not do *X*. Hence, *A* has no duty to refrain from doing *X*; but also, in contrast to the case of claim-rights, *B* has no duty to refrain from interfering with *A*'s doing *X*. Thus, if *A* and *B* simultaneously engage in a footrace, each has a liberty-right to win the race if he can – neither has a duty to refrain from winning it – and each has no right that the other not win. The liberty-right is hence the opposite of a duty, just as the no-right is the opposite of a claim-right.

Third, if *A* has a *power* (or *power-right*) to *X* with regard to *B*, then *A* is in a legal or other justified position to effect a change in some relevant status of *B*, and *B* has a correlative *liability* to undergo this change. Thus a religious official has a power-right to perform a marriage ceremony between a man and a woman, so that their legal status is changed from being unmarried to being married to each other.

Fourth, if *A* has an *immunity* (or *immunity-right*) to *X* against *B*, then *A* is free or exempt from *B*'s legal or other justified power or control with regard to *X*, and *B* is under a correlative *disability* to affect the legal or other relevant status of *A*. Thus, *A* has an immunity to being forced to testify against himself in a criminal case, and the state has a correlative disability to force him to testify. The immunity is the opposite of a liability, and the disability is the opposite of a power (power-right).

These distinctions clarify many of the diverse usages of the phrase "a right," but they also leave many conceptual problems unresolved. For example, what do all these types of "rights" have in common? Hohfeld said they are all "legal advantages," but this is vague.

THE ELEMENTS OF CLAIM-RIGHTS

Despite the possible interconnections between Hohfeld's types, it is generally agreed that claim-rights are the most important kind of rights, especially because of their stringency as entailing strict duties to forbear or assist. The general structure of a claim-right is given by the following formula: *A* has a right to *X* against *B* by virtue of *Y*.

There are five main elements here: first, the *subject (A)*, of the right, the right-holder; second, the *nature* of the right, what being a right consists in or what it means for someone to have a right; third, the *object (X)* of the right, what it is a right to; fourth, the *respondent (B)* of the right, the duty-bearer, the person or group that has the correlative duty; and fifth, the *justifying ground (Y)* of the right.

THE PROBLEM OF REDUNDANCY

This formula with its elements helps to elucidate some of the chief conceptual problems that have been raised about rights. One is the problem of redundancy, which takes two forms. The first form concerns the relation between the subject's rights and the respondent's duties. Since rights and duties are correlative, this is taken to mean that the right of *A* against *B* is the "same relation" as (or, as Hohfeld said, is "equivalent" to) the duty of *B* to *A*. But if they are the "same relation," then isn't one of them redundant?

A main answer is that claim-rights and strict duties have objects that differ in valuational content. Rights are justified claims to certain benefits, the support or protection of certain interests of the subject or right-holder. Duties, on the other hand, are justified burdens on the part of the respondent or duty-bearer: they restrict his freedom by requiring that he conduct himself in ways that directly benefit not himself but rather the right-holder. But burdens are for the sake of benefits, and not conversely. Hence duties, which are burdens, are for the sake of rights, whose objects are benefits, so that rights are the justifying reasons for duties. Thus, rights and duties are distinct, and neither is redundant.

In opposition to this answer, it is sometimes contended that the objects of rights are not always benefits to the right-holder. Examples are the right to smoke excessively and the right to have a promise to oneself kept that will benefit not oneself but only some third party. There are at least three replies:

1 The right to smoke and to engage in other self-harming actions may be taken as species of the right to freedom, which is in general a good to the right-holder. Thus the objects of rights are general goods for the right-holder, even if all their specific varieties may not be good for her.

2 Rights would not be *claimed* unless the claimant *thought* there was some value in her having the object of the right.

3 In the case of third-party beneficiaries, the person to whom a promise is made also has an interest in the promise being kept, so that to this extent she too derives benefit from it.

These considerations lead to a second form of the problem of redundancy. In the formula given above, the object (*X*) of the right – the object consisting in certain benefits or interests – seems to do most or all of the work for which the right is invoked, so that the concept of rights is again declared to be redundant. For if what is so important about rights is the support or protection of certain benefits or interests, then why isn't such protection sufficient; why do we also need rights to these interests?

There are several more answers. All involve that rights, especially when they are moral, provide certain indispensable normative additions to simply having or being protected in certain interests or benefits. To begin with, *A*'s having a moral right to *X* adds to his having *X* or his being protected in having *X* the important qualification that there is strong justification both for his having *X* and for his being protected in having *X*. This justification, moreover, is of a special sort, in that, when *A* has a right to *X*, this means that he is personally entitled to have *X* as his due, as what belongs personally to him, so that it is normatively necessary that *A* be protected in having or doing *X*.

Rights as Normatively Necessary Personal Entitlements

These aspects of personal entitlement and normative necessity bear on three specific relations among the elements of rights distinguished above. First, rights are normatively necessary in the relation between the subject and the object, in that the subject has personal property in, and thus justified personal control over, the object, so that it is personally owed to him as his due and for his own sake, not because it adds to overall utility. Second, rights are also normatively necessary in the relation between the subject and the respondent, in that the former is in a position to make a justified personal claim or demand, not merely a request or a plea, against the latter for the support or protection of his having the object of his right. In this way the respondent has duties that are personally owed to the subject. Third, rights are normatively necessary in the relation between the subject and the object, on the one hand, and the justifying ground, on the other, in that this ground supplies the warrant or title, and thus the necessitating premise, for the object's being personally owed to the subject and hence for the requirement that the subject have, and be protected in having, the object to which he has a right. In view of these stringent aspects of normative necessity, the question arises whether rights can ever be overridden. This will be discussed below.

The Nature of Rights

These three diverse relations between the subject, on the one hand, and the respondent, the object, and the justifying ground, on the other, also have a direct bearing on the conceptual question of the nature of a right. Two different theories focus on different elements in the structure of a right given above. The "benefit theory" emphasizes the relation between the subject and the object of rights. Since the object consists in certain benefits or interests of the subject, the benefit theory holds that for a person to have a right is for him to be the directly intended beneficiary of someone else's performance of a duty, or, in a further version, that some projected benefit or interest of his is a sufficient ground for other persons having duties. The "choice

theory," on the other hand, emphasizes the relation between the subject and the respondent of rights. The theory holds that to have a right is to be in a justified position to determine by one's choice how other persons (the respondents) shall act.

Each theory is plausible, but each also incurs difficulties. It has been held that the choice theory does not explain how children and mentally deficient persons may have rights; but this could be taken care of by the consideration that such persons can be represented by other persons who make claims for them. Another, perhaps more serious difficulty for the choice theory is that it implies that subjects may waive their rights; but some rights, such as those provided by the criminal law or by welfare legislation, cannot be waived. On the other hand, it seems to follow from the benefit theory, unlike the choice theory, that animals have rights, since they have certain interests and thus are capable of being benefited. Some thinkers have endorsed this conclusion, and have used it to reject the choice theory. At the same time, however, the choice theory has the distinct advantage that it views the right-holder as an active claimant on her own behalf, and thus as having an indispensable element of autonomy and dignity, in contrast to the passive recipience that the benefit theory seems to attribute to right-holders. This defect of the benefit theory can, however, be substantially remedied if it can be shown that a full justification of the theory involves that all morally justified rights have, as their most general objects, the fulfillment and support for each right-holder of the necessary conditions of action and of generally successful action. This will be further discussed below. It seems, then, that despite the possible divergences of the benefit and choice theories, the most acceptable account of the nature of rights must involve some combination of the two theories that incorporates the strong points of each while omitting its negative features.

The Nature of Moral Rights

The justifying ground of legal rights consists in the statutes and other provisions of positive municipal law. But it is also often said that persons have certain rights even if these are not recognized or enforced by positive laws, such as when it is asserted that slaves have a right to be free. In such cases the having in question, like the rights themselves, is moral, not legal.

There are two different views on the nature or existence of moral rights. On one view, for such rights to exist means that, while they fulfill certain moral criteria, they are embodied in positive laws or other social rules. On another view, moral rights exist or are had even when they are not so embodied; it is sufficient that they fulfill or derive from justified moral principles or other morally relevant considerations. Against this latter view it is objected that because of the diversity and conflicts of moral principles, there would be no way of definitively determining whether anyone has moral rights, in contrast to the determinate answers provided by positive laws. This point is often adduced in criticism of the undisciplined proliferation of rights-claims that are invoked by various protagonists in political and legal controversies. But against the former, positivist view it is objected not only that it incurs the same difficulty of ascertainment when it seeks to evaluate positive laws by moral criteria, but also that it makes unintelligible the recognized practice of appealing to rights even when they are not embodied in positive laws or ongoing social rules, and even in opposition to such laws and rules. Against the specifically legal positivist view it is further objected that it does not provide for those moral rights which, by general agreement, are not and should not be embodied in positive laws, such as the rights, in ordinary interpersonal relations, not to be lied to and not to be subjected to broken promises, as well as the rights of children to receive loving care from their parents.

The Justifying Ground of Moral Rights

To ask who has what moral rights to what is to ask a normative and substantive question, not only a conceptual one, although conceptual considerations also figure in the answers one gives. If for moral rights to exist, they must be justified by sound moral principles or other morally relevant grounds, where do we look for such principles or grounds? An important emphasis has been that human beings have interests. But not all interests generate rights. In view of the nor-

mative necessity involved in rights, it would seem that the interests that ground them must also involve necessity. Such necessity could be obtained if the interests consisted not in contingent, dispensable desires or goods, but rather in the goods that are necessary for human action or for having general chances of success in achieving one's purposes by action.

For such a general grounding of general moral rights to be successful, the necessary conditions of actions and of generally successful action would have to be carefully specified. The two main such conditions are freedom and well-being. Freedom is the procedural necessary condition of action; it consists in controlling one's behavior by one's own unforced choice while having knowledge of relevant circumstances. Well-being is the substantive necessary condition of action; it consists in having the general abilities and conditions needed for achieving one's purposes. Since the agency-needs that are here called "necessary" pertain not only to bare action but also to generally successful action, the necessity in question can accommodate the varying degrees in which practical abilities and conditions are needed for action. Thus, well-being falls into a hierarchy of goods ranging from life and physical integrity to education and opportunities for acquiring wealth and income. According to the general substantive theory here sketched, all actual or prospective agents have equal moral rights to freedom and well-being, and their having these rights is grounded in their enduring needs for the necessary conditions of their action and generally successful action. An argument can be given for the moral principle that grounds this thesis.

Moral Rights as Solely Negative

According to one libertarian view, all moral rights are negative: they set absolute "side constraints" on actions in that their correlative duties require refraining from actions that interfere with persons' freedom. A difficulty with this view is that it cannot handle conflicts of rights. Suppose A is going to murder B, and the only way to prevent this is for C to steal the car of D, who is entirely innocent in relation to A's murder project. Here the absolute rights not to be murdered and not to be stolen from come into unresolvable conflict.

To deal with such cases, it has been suggested that rights construed as side constraints should be supplemented by "consequential analysis" that trades off the lesser badness of infringing one right by the greater badness of infringing another. A related suggestion is the general idea presented above that rights fall into a hierarchy according to the degree of their objects' needfulness for action, so that the right not to be stolen from is overridden by the right not to be murdered when these rights are in conflict.

Such a procedure has been called a "utilitarianism of rights." But this phrase is misleading if it implies a constant readiness to interfere with rights for the sake of regularly achieving some sort of weighted minimization of rights violations. A "utilitarian" approach of this sort is different from considerations that are restricted to wide disparities in degrees of importance between the interests that are the objects of the respective rights, as in the above example.

What, however, of situations where the rights that are in conflict have objects that are of the same degree of importance? A recurrently adduced example is the one in which a casual bystander can save ten innocent persons from being murdered only if he murders one of the persons himself. It has been suggested that, since the function of rights is to protect justified personal interests, and since the interests in this example are on a par, the rights theorist must seriously consider participating in this abominable project.

The rejections of such participation can, however, be justified on grounds of rights. For the rights to life of the nine other innocent persons do not extend to the right to life of the tenth person. In general, if a person has a right to X, then he has a right to anything else Y that may be necessary for his having X, *unless* someone else already has a right to Y and Y is as important for action as is X. For example, if Jones is starving and cannot obtain food by his own efforts, while Smith has abundant food, then Jones's right to life overrides Smith's property right in the food, so that Jones has a right to as much of Smith's food as he needs in order to prevent starvation. But if Smith has only enough food to prevent his own starvation, then Jones does not have a right to it because Smith's not starving is as important for his action as Jones's not starving is for his. It

is for such a reason that the nine other innocent persons do not have a right that the tenth person be murdered in order to prevent their being murdered. Hence, if the casual bystander were to murder the tenth person, he would be violating that person's right to life, while if he were to refrain from the murder, he would not be violating the others' rights to life, since they do not have a right that the tenth person be murdered in order to prevent their murder.

POSITIVE RIGHTS

A second view of the contents of moral rights is that they are positive as well as negative. If the ultimate justifying ground of rights is the needs of agency, including well-being, then positive welfare rights are justified when persons cannot fulfill their needs of well-being by their own efforts so that positive assistance by other persons is required, in cases ranging from relief of starvation to provision of educational resources. As in the case of negative rights, the application of the positive rights model requires consideration of degrees of needfulness for action, so that, for example, taxation that removes a relatively small part of affluent persons' wealth is justified, and is not a violation of the taxed persons' rights, if this is needed in order to prevent other persons' starvation or to provide opportunities for education. More than in the exclusively negative theory of rights, the positive theory requires recourse to institutional, especially state, provision for various rights, as against leaving such provision solely to individual initiative. Thus, on this view, moral rights are social and economic as well as political and civil.

UTILITARIANISM AND RIGHTS

Utilitarianism raises two kinds of questions for theories of rights. One is whether it can "accommodate" rights (i.e., whether the requirements of rights can be justified by the utilitarian principle that the rightness of actions is to be determined by consequentialist considerations about the maximizing of total or average utility). It has been contended that utilitarianism can require that special protection be provided for the special interests and needs that are the objects of rights. A chief reply to this thesis is that, since the aim of utilitarianism is ultimately aggregative, to maximize utility, the distributive protections provided by even the most important rights would be at best only contingently maintained, since the rights could be overridden whenever the maximization of utility required this.

A second question about the relation of utility to rights goes in the reverse direction. Even if utilitarianism cannot adequately accommodate rights, is this always a fault? Isn't it also true that rights cannot accommodate utilitarianism, in that the insistence on individual rights may block the fulfillment of important communal goals? This question underlies the charge, which goes back at least to Jeremy Bentham (1748–1831) and Karl Marx (1818–83), that rights are egoistic because they involve claims for the fulfillment of individual interests, so that they may operate to submerge the values of community or society.

Two replies can be given to this charge. The first relies on the thesis sketched above about the varying degrees of importance or needfulness of the objects of rights. Thus, the theory of rights may allow for the exercise of eminent domain where an important community project like the building of a new public school requires that some persons be forced to give up their property rights in their houses at a certain location (with due compensation). But the theory cannot allow, for the reasons indicated above, that an innocent person be killed in order to prevent certain even severe harms from befalling the community as a whole.

A second reply is that human rights, which are universally distributed moral rights, require of each person that he act with due regard for other persons' interests as well as his own. For since, in principle, each person has human rights against all other persons, every other person also has these rights against him, so that he has correlative duties toward them. The concept of human rights thus entails a reciprocal universality: each person must respect the rights of all the others while having his rights respected by all the others, so that there must be a mutual sharing of the benefits of rights and the burdens of duties. The human rights thus involve mutuality of consideration and, thus, a kind of altruism rather than egoism. By requiring mutual aid where needed and practicable, the human rights make for social solidarity and a community of rights.

Bibliography

An earlier version of this entry appeared in L. C. Becker and C. B. Becker (eds.) (1992), *Encyclopedia of Ethics.* New York: Garland.

Dworkin, R. (1977). *Taking Rights Seriously.* Cambridge, MA: Harvard University Press. (Rights as "trumps.")

Feinberg, J. (1973). *Social Philosophy.* Englewood Cliffs, NJ: Prentice-Hall. (Analysis and conflict of rights.)

Feinberg, J. (1980). *Rights, Justice, and the Bounds of Liberty.* Princeton, NJ: Princeton University Press. (Importance of rights; their relation to claims.)

Finnis, J. (1980). *Natural Law and Natural Rights.* Oxford: Clarendon Press. (Rights account for the requirements of practical reasonableness.)

Flathman, R. E. (1976). *The Practice of Rights.* Cambridge: Cambridge University Press. (Rights are adversarial; communitarian objections.)

Gewirth, A. (1978). *Reason and Morality.* Chicago: University of Chicago Press. (Rights based on necessary conditions of action.)

Gewirth, A. (1986). Why rights are indispensable. *Mind,* 95, 329–44. (Answers conceptual and moral objections against rights.)

Hohfeld, W. N. (1964) [1919]. *Fundamental Legal Conceptions as Applied in Judicial Reasoning.* New Haven, CT: Yale University Press. (Classic fourfold typology.)

Lyons, D. (ed.) (1979). *Rights.* Belmont, CA: Wadsworth. (Good collection, including Lyons's "Rights, claimants, and beneficiaries" (58–77), which argues for the benefit theory.)

Martin, R. and Nickel, J. W. (1980). Recent work on the concept of rights. *American Philosophical Quarterly,* 17, 165–80. (Extensive bibliography.)

Melden, A. I. (1977). *Rights and Persons.* Berkeley: University of California Press. (Rights based on personhood.)

Sen, A. (1982). Rights and agency. *Philosophy and Public Affairs,* 11, 3–29. (Discusses a "goal rights system" wherein the fulfillment or non-fulfillment of rights is included in the consequential evaluation of states of affairs.)

Shue, H. (1980). *Basic Rights: Subsistence, Affluence, and US Foreign Policy.* Princeton, NJ: Princeton University Press. (Basic rights include subsistence as well as security and liberty.)

Sumner, L. (1987). *The Moral Foundation of Rights.* Oxford: Clarendon Press. (Argues against natural law and contractualist theories of rights and for consequentialist theory.)

Thomson, J. (1990). *The Realm of Rights.* Cambridge, MA: Harvard University Press. (Examines what rights are and which rights there are.)

Tuck, R. (1979). *Natural Rights Theories: Their Origin and Development*. Cambridge: Cambridge University Press. (Histories of rights theories from twelfth to seventeenth centuries.)

Waldron, J. (ed.) (1984). *Theories of Rights*. Oxford: Oxford University Press. (Good introduction and bibliography.)

Wellman, C. (1985). *A Theory of Rights*. Totowa, NJ: Rowman and Allanheld. (A right is a complex structure of legal positions having a central core.)

Wolgast, E. H. (1980). *Equality and the Rights of Women*. Ithaca, NY: Cornell University Press. (Women's rights based not on egalitarian reasoning but on distinctiveness and interdependence.)

risk

W. Michael Hoffman

To be at risk: To be subject to harm from some process or activity. The degree of risk is a function of the probability and severity of that harm. Given the multitude of ways in which people can be harmed, most people are at risk to some degree most of the time. In addition, since things other than people can be harmed – for example, property, animals, the natural environment – these things can also be described as being at risk from certain processes or activities.

Safety is defined in terms of risk. It is sometimes said that something is safe if it is free from risk, but nothing can be absolutely risk free. Both risk and safety, therefore, come in degrees and involve decision problems as to whether something is too risky or safe enough. So a thing is thought to be safe only if its risks are judged to be acceptable, quite often by a person or group empowered to make that decision for a larger society.

In making a decision about safety, two necessary and distinct activities come into play: measuring risk and judging the acceptability of that risk. The measurement of risk involves an objective scientific assessment of the probabilities and consequences of events. A risk estimate can predict the likelihood that some event will happen, but is unable to pinpoint the occurrence of any specific harmful event.

Unlike the empirical activity of measuring risk, judging safety or the acceptability of risk is a normative activity. This brings up the question: Who makes the judgment that a certain risk is acceptable, and by what criteria? And since risk implies the probability of harm to persons, to say that a risk is acceptable implies that the justification for undertaking the risk, or not avoiding it, overrides the moral rule "do no harm." Thus, judgments about acceptable risk for persons are necessarily moral judgments, at least in part.

The remainder of this entry will concentrate on acceptable-risk decision criteria, and will sometimes use environmental risk for the purposes of illustration, although in the field of business ethics, product and workplace safety are equally important areas of risk assessment.

Two essential components of any plan to deal with risk problems are clarity about the goals the decision is intended to achieve and the means proposed to achieve them. But before this can be done by a corporation, for example, risk problems, such as those about pollution or hazardous waste, are other difficulties that need to be addressed.

The first difficulty is problem definition. If there is uncertainty about how to define the problem, there will be uncertainty about the goals and what would constitute solving the problem. It has been claimed that plant species are diminishing because of business activities such as logging and large-scale farming. Is this a risk problem, and if so, what kind of risk? What would count as a solution to the problem?

The second difficulty is disagreement about which facts are relevant to the problem. Is the loss of plant species a problem because of their possible use in healing, because such loss affects the ozone layer, or because the loss of plant variety is a bad thing in itself? How the risk problem is defined will have a major influence on which facts are taken to be relevant, and vice versa.

Finally, there often is a conflict of values, or even confusion about what values we hold or ought to hold. Many claim that the environment is intrinsically valuable. Others argue that it has value only because it serves human ends. Difficulty over values affects how we define the risk problem and how we identify relevant facts.

There are certain characteristics that any acceptable solution to a risk problem must possess – characteristics that are also helpful with problem definition, identification of facts, clarification of values, determination of goals and the means to those goals. The following criteria have been suggested for any acceptable judgment about a risk problem. Unacceptable decisions fail to meet one or more of the criteria. A proposed solution to an environmental risk problem is acceptable only if it is:

1 *Politically implementable*: proposed solutions that do not take account of the political situation are not realistic.
2 *Economically feasible*: if the plan places unreasonable burdens on corporate productivity and profitability, it will destroy the base from which successful action is possible.
3 *Legally defensible*: there is a fundamental obligation to obey the law, except in extreme situations; law is necessary for social order and constructive action.
4 *Technically plausible*: if the technical means to accomplish the solution are not available or if they are excessively problematic, then any proposed solution becomes pure speculation.
5 *Environmentally manageable*: the proposed solution should be one that does not result in catastrophic or irreversible harm to the environment.
6 *Ethically responsible*: a decision to a risk problem is ethically responsible only if:

(a) It poses no unreasonable threat to human life or health. People should not be exposed to foolish risks – those with goals that are unworthy of the potential harm. To act negligently is to act so as to cause harm by taking unreasonable risk.
(b) It fairly distributes benefits and burdens. No solution is ethically acceptable, for example, if it allocates all benefits to some, and all burdens to others, or if it treats people unequally.
(c) It neither unjustifiably violates moral rights nor unjustifiably forces a dereliction of moral duties. A moral right can justifiably be set aside only by other, more stringent moral rights.
(d) It gives due consideration to the values and interests of all those affected. It will often be necessary to act against the values and interests of some, but only after serious consideration is given to every possible way to accommodate them.

(e) It provides compensation in the event of unexpected or excessive harm. Victims must not be expected to bear such harm with no prospect of reparation.
(f) It is voluntarily accepted, to the extent possible, by those affected, or, at least, those affected are given a fair opportunity to participate in the decision-making process. The only exceptions are where people voluntarily give up the opportunity to participate.
(g) It treats persons not merely as means to some goal, but as ends in themselves. All human beings must be treated with dignity and respect and not as simply tools for others to use.

Bibliography

Fischhoff, B., Lichtenstein, S., Slovic, P., Derby, S. L., and Keeney, R. L. (1981). *Acceptable Risk*. New York: Cambridge University Press.

Frederick, R. E. and Hoffman, W. M. (1990). The individual investor in securities markets: An ethical analysis. *Journal of Business Ethics*, 9, 579–89.

Frederick, R. E. and Hoffman, W. M. (1994). Environmental risk problems and the language of ethics. *Business Ethics Quarterly*, 5, 699–711.

Fried, C. (1987). Imposing risks upon others. In G. Sher (ed.), *Moral Philosophy: Selected Readings*. San Diego, CA: Harcourt, 699–710.

Hoffman, W. M. (1984). The Ford Pinto. In W. M. Hoffman and J. M. Moore (eds.), *Business Ethics: Readings and Cases in Corporate Morality*. New York: McGraw-Hill, 585–92.

Hoffman, W. M. and Fisher, J. V. (1984). Corporate responsibility: Property and liability. In W. M. Hoffman and J. M. Moore (eds.), *Business Ethics: Readings and Cases in Corporate Morality*. New York: McGraw-Hill, 176–82.

Lowrance, W. W. (1976). *Of Acceptable Risk*. Los Altos, CA: William Kauffman.

Mayo, D. G. and Hollander, R. D. (eds.) (1991). *Acceptable Evidence: Science and Values in Risk Management*. New York: Oxford University Press.

Shrader-Frechette, K. S. (1991). *Risk and Rationality*. Berkeley: University of California Press.

roles and role morality

Alan H. Goldman

Roles are positions in business or the professions to which different social functions attach; role morality is the assumption of different normative ethical systems for different roles. The central issue here is whether different social roles require distinct norms or moral frameworks to guide their behavior. For there to be truly distinct role moralities, it is not sufficient that those in different social roles or professions enter into unique relations with others. All social roles involve relations that uniquely define them to be the roles they are. Instead, moral considerations that arise elsewhere must be weighed differently, must be systematically augmented or diminished in their weight, against opposing considerations in proper moral deliberations in these social contexts. An occupant of the role (for example, a lawyer or business manager) must be called upon to ignore certain moral rights, or certain utilities or disutilities, that would otherwise be morally decisive.

Often such special norms reflect some value central to the definition of the social role in question, and the norm gives that value extra weight for the occupant of the role. Lawyers are called upon to ignore the interests of third parties in zealously pursuing the legal objectives of their clients within the bounds of law. Journalists routinely ignore what others might properly perceive as rights to privacy in developing news stories for their reading publics. In business, the central values lie in efficient use of resources in providing desired goods to the consuming public and in providing stockholders a good return on their investments. Thus, some have argued (e.g., Friedman, 1979) that business managers ought not to forgo profit (which measures efficiency and provides returns) on perceived moral grounds.

From the point of view of moral theory, however, the basic question is how such special norms can be morally acceptable, how the concept of distinct role moralities is even coherent. From the point of view of a rights-based or individualist moral theory, it seems that we can override moral rights only for the sake of protecting more central or important rights in the context in question. Otherwise, rights must be voluntarily waived or previously forfeited by wrongdoing in order to be safely ignored. This fundamental demand of the moral framework seems to hold in all social contexts. From the point of view of a utilitarian or collectivist moral theory, it seems that we can impose costs or

forgo benefits only to prevent greater harm or realize greater collective good, and once more this constraint appears to govern all contexts to which the theory applies. Thus, if business managers perceive that pursuit of maximal profit imposes serious harm on the public (say in decisions regarding product safety, waste disposal, or relocation), how can it be morally coherent to suggest that such pursuit is their proper role?

The answer is that such norms are at least possible, or coherent, given sufficient complexity in a moral framework. In a multi-leveled framework there can be a distinction between an agent's perception of a morally required course of action and her authority to act on that perception. This distinction exists in several moral theories, including Mill's (1955), and it rests on the fact of fallibility in moral perception and moral reasoning. A major argument by defenders of adversarial legal systems to the conclusion that lawyers ought not to restrain their clients on extra-legal moral grounds is that their moral perceptions may be eccentric or incapable of objective justification. Similarly, if a business manager seeks to sacrifice style or raise prices in order to impose safer products on the public, despite market research that indicates contrary preferences, the result may be not what she predicts, but loss of market share to the competition.

In other cases the justification of special norms does not appeal to fallibility in gauging the consequences of actions considered one at a time, but instead to the results of every occupant of the social role reasoning directly from those consequences. Waste disposal provides a good example here. Each small business may reason correctly that the effect of its disposing of wastes in the cheapest way possible is negligible. But if all reason in the same way, the result can be disastrous to the health of the entire community. Here it seems that a special norm restricting the pursuit of maximum profit is in order. Norms governing other roles may be justified in the same way. A teacher should grade based only on quality of work submitted, even though the effect of taking other considerations into account in individual cases might be known to be utility maximizing. A journalist's passing up a single story because of qualms about privacy might not harm the public, but the cumulative effect of all journalists forgoing stories because of such qualms might be significant deprivation of information to the public. Such norms result in a consistency or uniformity in the behavior of role occupants beyond that achievable without them.

It can be argued that norms of the type just considered are either not special or not necessary. A Kantian will hold that moral reasoners must always think of everyone's acting in the way proposed (*see* KANTIAN ETHICS). But this test is not always relevant. Telling a lie in order to avoid a greater evil can be justified, even though if everyone lied in similar circumstances, the strategy might be useless and hence unjustified. It is permissible not to vote in a local election even though the result of no one voting would be disastrous. The universalizing test is relevant only when many individuals would act in a cumulatively harmful way on the basis of (individually) correct consequentialist reasoning in the absence of special constraint. This criterion does apply to various social roles, as indicated above, generating special norms and hence role moralities.

It can be argued, as in the pollution example, that a business manager ought not to impose higher costs on his corporation unless these are required by law. The appeal here would be to a moral division of labor (between managers and legislators), and it would reinstate the profit principle as the sole fundamental norm for business. Those who defend special role moralities often make such appeals, but they must be closely scrutinized. Any justification of special role moralities, even if coherent, must be carefully criticized, given the sacrifice of normally important moral factors involved.

Bibliography

Bayles, M. (1989). *Professional Ethics*. Belmont, CA: Wadsworth, ch. 2.

Fried, C. (1978). *Right and Wrong*. Cambridge, MA: Harvard University Press, ch. 7.

Friedman, M. (1979). The social responsibility of business is to increase its profits. In T. Donaldson and P. H. Werhane (eds.), *Ethical Issues in Business*. Englewood Cliffs, NJ: Prentice-Hall, 191–7.

Goldman, A. H. (1980). *The Moral Foundations of Professional Ethics*. Totowa, NJ: Rowman and Littlefield.

Kadish, M. R. and Kadish, S. H. (1973). *Discretion to Disobey*. Stanford, CA: Stanford University Press, chs. 1, 2.

Mill, J. S. (1955). *On Liberty*. Chicago: Gateway.

Wasserstrom, R. (1975). Lawyers as professionals: Some moral issues. *Human Rights*, 5, 1–24.

Russia, business ethics in

Deryl W. Martin and Jeffrey H. Peterson

Business ethics in Russia most accurately could be described by the ancient maxim, *caveat emptor* (buyer beware). Virtually all domestic business transactions are legally unregulated and self-policing. To appreciate the origin of the Russian ethos, one must understand that the simplest economic concepts we often take for granted are relatively new to the Russian people. For example, though perhaps initially inconceivable, the notions of property rights, ownership, freedom of contract, profit – and even the idea of a market itself – are ideas only now evolving in modern Russian society (*see* PROPERTY, RIGHTS TO; FREEDOM OF CONTRACT; PROFIT, PROFITS, AND PROFIT MOTIVE). With the collapse of the principle of centralized planning, the Russian people are, as a matter of necessity, embracing capitalism to provide for their daily needs. Absent a legal basis to enforce sanctions and lacking a history of contract law, Russians continue to grapple with the ethics of unbridled commerce. The variety of ethical misdeeds arising from this legal void are well documented (see, for example, Meirovich and Reichel, 2000).

It became legal in 1991 for private Russian concerns to broker the buying and selling of virtually any commodity (see Kolosov, Martin, and Peterson, 1993). With the attendant and requisite expansion of that which constitutes private property, several businesses developed for the purpose of making a market in which the buying, selling, and trading of such property is accommodated. Due primarily to the lack of accurate and reliable information concerning supply, demand, and ownership encumbrances, performance on the agreements to trade goods on these "exchanges" is not guaranteed by market owners – unlike more developed markets in

Western and other cultures. Without a legal structure to enforce contract compliance, all Russian business transactions occur in a legal vacuum where self-interest and personal (microeconomic) decisions aggregate to societal (macroeconomic) outcomes (see Martin and Peterson, 1991; Werhane, 1989; Appressyan, 1997). Thus, the nature of these markets is consistent with the notion of *caveat emptor* in its strictest sense.

The state of business ethics in Russia continues to evolve. Despite the potential repercussions of an unregulated environment, new Russian businesses are being created exponentially and existing companies are thriving. Gradually, these new enterprises are becoming the provider of the bulk of life's basic goods for the Russian people as they grapple with the ethics of their unfamiliar economic freedom, and begin to examine the implications of the development of civil society in Russia (Taylor and Kazakov, 1997). It is perhaps most important to note that although the notion of private property is again new to their culture, Russian businessmen and women apparently realize that behaving in an ethical fashion – fulfilling contractual obliga-

tions – is in their long-run self-interest. The continued existence of markets indicates that economic agents in Russia have overwhelmingly chosen to eschew the short-term gain associated with contract default in favor of building the reputational capital necessary for successful operation in self-regulating markets.

Bibliography

Appressyan, R. G. (1997). Business ethics in Russia. *Journal of Business Ethics*, 16, 1561–70.

Kolosov, M. A., Martin, D. W., and Peterson, J. H. (1993). Ethics and behavior on the Russian Commodity Exchange. *Journal of Business Ethics*, 12, 741–4.

Martin, D. W. and Peterson, J. H. (1991). Insider trading revisited. *Journal of Business Ethics*, 10, 57–61.

Meirovich, G. and Reichel, A. (2000). Illegal but ethical: An inquiry into the roots of illegal corporate behavior in Russia. *Business Ethics: A European Review*, 9 (3), 126–35.

Taylor, T. C. and Kazakov, A. Y. (1997). Business ethics and civil society in Russia. *International Studies of Management and Organization*, 27 (1), 5–18.

Werhane, P. H. (1989). The ethics of insider trading. *Journal of Business Ethics*, 8, 841–5.

S

safety, worker

Joseph Grcic

The development of the industrial revolution radically transformed the nature of human work and human relations. Every year in the US over 10,000 workers are killed on the job and about 2.8 million are injured. There are over 100,000 deaths from diseases due to exposure to physical and chemical hazards in the workplace. The medical and other costs of work-related deaths and injuries are estimated at over $8 billion yearly. Work safety issues include reducing workplace hazards and implementing safety standards without significant reductions in efficiency. It concerns such matters as the hazardous nature of some work, its organization (hours, speed), and the quality of the work environment. Although the safety of work continues to improve in the West due to labor unions, legislation, and enlightened entrepreneurs, attention is still focused on industries where exposure to such substances as textiles (brown lung disease), paint odors (emphysema), benzene (leukemia), lead (sterility), microwaves (cataracts, lower sperm count), petrochemicals (tumors, sterility), coal dust (black lung), asbestos (cancer, asbestosis), and excessive noise (hearing loss) still occurs.

Initially, concern for worker safety came in the form of compensation for injuries, as it did in Germany in the late nineteenth century. In the US, legislation to compensate workers started as early as 1920, but it did not cover the reduction of workplace hazards. Conservative free-market defenders objected to government interference in the marketplace, which they claimed raised prices and weakened the freedom of contract, a cornerstone of capitalism. Defenders of increased regulation argued that workers were often in a weak bargaining position and usually had to take any job available.

An important case involving worker safety concerned the Johns Manville (now Manville) corporation, a manufacturer of asbestos. Corporate documents show that the company knew as early as the 1930s that its workers were in danger of developing cancer from exposure to asbestos but did nothing to protect them. When this information became public in the 1980s, thousands of employees sued the company, leading Johns Manville to establish a fund to pay employees and to declare bankruptcy.

In 1970, Congress passed the Occupational Safety and Health Act (OSHA) requiring employers to maintain certain minimum conditions to protect their workers. The law mandated that a safe work environment be provided through appropriate supervision and training of workers. Penalties for violation range from monetary judgments to criminal prosecution of specific individuals responsible within the firm.

Today, worker safety continues to be important for employees and employers. Concern about secondhand cigarette smoke has led employers either to ban smoking in the workplace or to provide special smoking areas. Injury due to repetitive hand motions by keyboard operators is another focus of regulators. Many employee-rights advocates believe that OSHA is understaffed and too influenced by the private sector it seeks to regulate, while others debate the nature of acceptable risk. The global nature of the marketplace that allows firms to move to areas with minimal or no provision for safety of workers is also a concern. Some ethicists argue that the best way to reduce dangerous and unhealthy working conditions is to restructure the modern corporation toward greater democracy and to empower employees, for example, by giving workers a voice in plant safety, and/or by installing them on the boards of directors, thus enabling them to influence relevant safety policies directly.

Bibliography

De George, R. T. (1990). *Business Ethics.* New York: Macmillan.

Grcic, J. (1985). Democratic capitalism: Developing a conscience for the corporation. *Journal of Business Ethics,* 5, (2), 145–50.

Shaw, W. H. and Barry, V. (eds.) (1995). *Moral Issues in Business,* 6th edn. Belmont, CA: Wadsworth.

Velasquez, M. G. (1982). *Business Ethics: Concepts and Cases.* Englewood Cliffs, NJ: Prentice-Hall.

Werhane, P. H. (1985). *Persons, Rights and Corporations.* Englewood Cliffs, NJ: Prentice-Hall.

Sarbanes-Oxley Act

Jenny Mead and Robert J. Sack

On July 30, 2002, in response to a series of financial scandals that had rocked the corporate world in the United States, the Sarbanes-Oxley Act (SOX), HR 2673, or "Corporate and Criminal Fraud Accountability Act," was signed into law. After the Enron collapse in the fall of 2001, Senator Paul S. Sarbanes (D, Maryland) proposed a set of dramatic new laws. However, Representative Michael G. Oxley (R, Ohio) proposed a set of milder laws. While those two proposals were working their way through the legislative process, the huge fraud at telecommunications giant WorldCom became apparent, and any political support for a milder set of reforms disappeared. In fact, some have suggested that the new Act be called the "WorldCom Act." The law was intended to bolster public confidence in the United States' capital markets and impose new duties and significant penalties for non-compliance on public companies and their executives, directors, auditors, attorneys, and securities analysts. The provisions of the new law primarily apply only to public companies filing form 10-K with the Securities and Exchange Commission, their auditors, and securities analysts.

The Act deals with a wide variety of corporate governance issues, as outlined in the following text, and it is sure to have an impact on many people who work in the finance side of publicly held companies. But there appear to be two areas where the Act will have its most dramatic effect:

1   The Act requires the chief executive officer and the chief accounting officer of every company of publicly held companies to sign a report that is to be included with every filing the company makes with the Securities and Exchange Commission, stating that they have reviewed the filing and that, to the best of their knowledge and belief, the filing – including the financial statements for the period – contains no material misstatement. They are also required to attest to their belief that the company has an adequate system of internal control, and that the system was effective, as of the date of the report. In the Congressional hearings into the collapse of Enron and WorldCom, a number of the key executives from those firms testified that they did not know about the underlying frauds, that these frauds were the work of their accounting staff people.

2   These attestation provisions have had a number of interesting effects. Most importantly, many companies have adopted a build-up approach to these new responsibilities. The companies have asked the heads of the operating units and the key functional units to sign a similar attestation, forcing those people to think carefully about their own role in their companies' reports to their stockholders. Following on that new perspective, we have seen at least one chief financial officer resign his post, and send a letter to the company's audit committee, outlining his concerns about the company's financial accounting. It is also important to note that the Act contains new protections for whistleblowers.

3   The Act virtually eviscerates the accounting profession. Under the Act a new quasi-governmental body (independent, but under the jurisdiction of the SEC) took over the setting of audit standards, the determination of rules of independence for auditors, the investigation of apparent failed audits, and the enforcement of professional standards and rules. The new board (the Public Company

Accounting Oversight Board, or PCAOB) has been staffed with some dedicated people, and it will be interesting to see how the accounting profession evolves under their leadership.

The major provisions of the Sarbanes-Oxley Act are as follows.

TITLE I: PUBLIC COMPANY ACCOUNTING OVERSIGHT BOARD

- The five-member PCAOB oversees the audit of public companies, establishes audit report standards and rules, and inspects, investigates, and enforces compliance on the part of registered public accounting firms and those associated with these firms. The board, a corporate entity funded by fees imposed on public companies, operates as a non-profit corporation that will exist indefinitely until dissolved by Congress, and its decisions are subject to oversight and review by the SEC. To restrict ties to the accounting industry, only two members may be certified public accountants; member terms are five years.
- Requires auditing standards to include a seven year retention period for audit work papers; a second partner review and approval; evaluation of whether internal control structures and procedures include records that accurately reflect transactions and disposition of assets; only senior managers and directors may authorize receipts and expenditures; and description of both material weaknesses in internal controls and of material non-compliance.
- Mandates continuing inspections of public accounting firms for compliance, annually for firms providing audit reports for more than 100 issuers and three years for those providing audit reports for less than 100 issuers.
- The PCAOB is empowered to impose disciplinary or remedial sanctions on registered firms and their associates for intentional conduct or repeated instances of negligent conduct.
- Directs the SEC to report to Congress on adoption of a principles-based accounting system by the US financial reporting system.

TITLE II: AUDITOR INDEPENDENCE

- Prohibits auditors from simultaneously performing specified non-audit services for a client such as bookkeeping, investment banking, or actuarial services.
- Requires five year auditor rotation of lead partner.
- Auditors must report to the audit committees on critical accounting policies and practices used in the audit, alternative treatments and their ramifications within GAAP, and material written communications between the auditor and senior management of the issuer.
- Places a one year prohibition on an auditor performing audit services if the issuer's senior executives had been employed by that auditor and had participated in the audit of the issuer during the one year period preceding the audit initiation date.

TITLE III: CORPORATE RESPONSIBILITY

- Company CEOs and CFOs must certify that financial reports and conditions are accurate and fairly presented. These officers are responsible for effective internal controls ensuring that reported information is correct.
- In the event of accounting restatement of financial material because of non-compliance, the CEO and CFO forfeit certain bonuses and compensation from the company.
- Although required to be on the board, audit committee members must otherwise be independent, with no affiliation with or compensation from the issuer.
- Company directors and executive officers are banned from trading their company's stock during pension fund blackouts.

TITLE IV: ENHANCED FINANCIAL DISCLOSURES

- Financial reports filed with SEC must reflect all material correcting adjustments and disclose all material off-balance sheet transactions and relationships that might have affected the financial status of an issue.
- With some exceptions, a corporation is prohibited from giving personal loans to its executives and directors.

- Senior management, directors, and principal stockholders must disclose changes in securities ownership of swap agreements within two business days (formerly ten business days) after the close of the calendar month.
- Annual reports must contain internal control reports stating management responsibility for these controls and assessing their effectiveness.
- Requires disclosure of whether a company had adopted an ethics code for its senior financial management.
- Regular and systematic SEC reviews of periodic disclosures by issuers required.

TITLE V: ANALYST CONFLICTS OF INTEREST

- Restricts investment bankers' ability to pre-approve research reports.
- Protects analysts from employer retaliation after writing negative analyses of publicly traded companies.
- Strengthens structural division in registered brokers or dealers between analysts and investment bankers.
- Prohibits supervision of research analysts by people involved in investment banking activity.
- Establishes blackout periods for broker or dealer participants in a public offering from distributing reports related to the offering.
- Strengthens full disclosure requirements for research analysts making public appearances and for brokers and dealers in their research reports.

TITLE VI: COMMISSION RESOURCES AND AUTHORITY

- Authorizes additional funds for the commission to carry out its functions, powers, and duties.
- Expands SEC's disciplinary authority by allowing it to consider orders of state securities commissions when deciding whether to limit brokers and dealers' activities, functions, or operations.
- Authorizes federal courts to prohibit people alleged to have violated securities laws from participating in an offering of penny stock.
- Authorizes the SEC to censure any individual appearing before the commission who has engaged in unethical or improper professional conduct.

TITLE VII: STUDIES AND REPORTS

- Authorizes the commission to conduct studies on securities professionals who have participated in, but not been penalized for, securities violations; factors leading to consolidation of public accounting firms and the impact of this reduction on the securities market; SEC enforcement actions taken against companies which violate reporting requirements and restatement of financial statements; the role and function of credit rating agencies in the operations of the securities market; and a GAO study of whether investment banks and financial advisors assisted public companies in manipulating their earnings and obfuscating their true financial conditions.

TITLE VIII: CORPORATE AND CRIMINAL FRAUD ACCOUNTABILITY

- Imposes criminal penalties for obstructing or influencing either a federal investigation or a matter in bankruptcy by concealing, falsifying, destroying, or altering information. Auditor failure to retain review work papers for five year period results in ten year prison sentence.
- Provides whistleblower protection for employees of a publicly traded company who participate or assist in an investigation of fraud or other misconduct by federal regulators, Congress, or supervisors.
- Any person who knowingly defrauds shareholders of a publicly traded company is subject to a fine or imprisonment of up to 25 years.
- Certain debts incurred in violation of securities fraud laws are non-dischargeable in bankruptcy.
- Extends the statute of limitations to permit a private right of action for a securities fraud violation to not later than two years after its discovery or five years after the date of the violation.

TITLE IX: WHITE COLLAR CRIME PENALTY ENHANCEMENTS

New penalties imposed for violations:

- Mail fraud: 20 years, $250,000.
- Wire fraud: 20 years, $250,000.

- Violations of the Employee Retirement Income Security Act of 1974 (or pension fund fraud): 10 years, $500,000.
- Certification of false financial report: 20 years, $5 million.
- Securities fraud (new provision): 25 years and $250,000.

TITLE X: CORPORATE TAX RETURNS

- A corporation's federal income tax return should be signed by its CEO.

TITLE XI: CORPORATE FRAUD ACCOUNTABILITY

- Amends federal criminal law to establish a maximum 20 year prison term for tampering with a record or otherwise impeding an official proceeding.
- Violating the 1934 Security Exchange Act: 20 years, $5 million.
- Authorizes SEC to prohibit a violator of rules governing manipulative, deceptive devices, and fraudulent interstate transactions from serving as officer or director of a publicly traded company.
- SEC may seek injunction to freeze extraordinary payments earmarked for designated persons or corporate staff under investigation for possible violations of federal securities law.

Bibliography

Bloomenthal, H. S. (2002). *Sarbanes-Oxley Act in Perspective*. St. Paul, MN: West Group.
Hamilton, J. and Trautmann, T. (2002). *Sarbanes-Oxley Act of 2002: Law and Explanation*. Chicago: CCH.

Securities and Exchange Commission

Robert J. Sack

The SEC was established as part of the Roosevelt administration's response to the crises of the 1929 depression. The commission is primarily responsible for administration of the laws governing the purchase and sale of securities in interstate commerce and the operation of securities exchanges in the United States.

When the securities laws were originally debated, some argued that the SEC should evaluate each security offered for sale and express an opinion as to its safety. However, Congress was evidently concerned that the power implied in that judgment might be abused, and so the federal securities laws – and the activities of the SEC – require only that investee companies provide full disclosure of relevant facts. *Caveat emptor* was retained as a bulwark of the market, but with the understanding that the buyer was entitled to full and fair information (Loss and Seligman, 1989: 171–80).

Even with that conceptual limitation, the SEC has considerable power. It exercises its authority in two primary ways (Phillips and Zecher, 1981: 9):

1 Establishing standards for the disclosure documents which companies are required to file when they want their securities sold to the public.
2 Initiating civil enforcement actions against companies and their officers, alleging either fraud or failure to comply with the laws and filing standards.

The SEC does not have authority to bring criminal charges, but may ask a civil court to bar individuals from acting as an officer of a publicly held company, and to assess fines and recover damages. More commonly, an enforcement action results in an injunction, which orders the defendant to comply with the law in the future, or an order to cease and desist from certain practices. The theory behind those apparently innocuous sanctions is that the financial community will be reluctant to do business with those who have been stigmatized by such a court order, and so the activities of those people will be circumscribed. That theory may work for those who stumble into trouble, but it appears to be less effective for those who intend to abuse the markets for their own benefit (see, for example, the front page article in the May 12, 1995 issue of the *Wall Street Journal*).

The SEC was established in part to correct abuses in the securities markets and in part to restore confidence in the market and thereby get the economy moving again. The dichotomy of that dual role – police chief/confidence builder – has plagued the SEC since its founding. It is apparent in the current controversy over the disclosures that should be required of foreign companies. Some foreign companies, especially from Germany, argue that because they comply with the disclosure requirements established by their own financial communities, the SEC ought to accept those disclosure documents as a basis for selling securities in the United States. The SEC is under considerable pressure to agree, because those international securities transactions would promote world trade, would enhance the United States as a world leader in capital formation, and would provide opportunities for US investors to diversify their portfolios. The SEC has so far insisted that foreign firms comply fully with the requirements imposed on domestic companies, arguing that the current disclosure system in the United States is the best in the world, and that protection of the US investor is the SEC's first priority. However, in an increasingly global economy that is an increasingly difficult argument (AAA/SEC Liaison Committee, 1995: 82).

Some argue that the SEC is unnecessary because market forces will do a more efficient job of enforcing disclosure by companies who wish to sell securities (Kitch, 1994, explores this idea thoroughly). The theory behind that argument is that – in the long term – a company that provides above-average disclosures will have below-average costs of capital, because its shareholders will enjoy less information risk. That relationship has not been proven, however, at least in part because there are few companies who provide more than the required disclosures. In any event, those arguments have been largely academic: there seems to be an understanding in the securities industry (and in Congress) that the pressures of the marketplace will tempt some companies and managers beyond their ethics, and that a legitimized restraining authority serves the interests of all (Seligman, 1982, 563–8; Beatty and Hand, 1992).

Bibliography

AAA/SEC Liaison Committee (1995). Mountaintop issues from the SEC. *Accounting Horizons*, 9 (1), 79–86.

Beatty, R. P. and Hand, J. R. M. (1992). The causes and effects of mandated accounting standards: SFAS No. 94 as a test of the level playing field theory. *Journal of Accounting, Auditing and Finance*, 7 (4), 509–30.

Kitch, E. W. (1994). *The Theory and Practice of Securities Disclosure*. Working Paper, University of Virginia School of Law, Charlottesville.

Loss, L. and Seligman, J. (1989). *Securities Regulation*. Boston, MA: Little, Brown.

Phillips, S. M. and Zecher, J. R. (1981). *The SEC and the Public Interest*. Cambridge, MA: MIT Press.

Seligman, J. (1982). *The Transformation of Wall Street: A History of the Securities and Exchange Commission and Modern Corporate Finance*. Boston, MA: Houghton Mifflin.

Skousen, K. F. (1983). *An Introduction to the SEC*. Cincinnati, OH: Southwestern Publishing.

self-interest

James B. Wilbur

is the motivational element in human action that relates any interest to the self to whom the interest belongs. With regard to the object of a self's interest, however, the phrase is ambiguous. It may refer to whatever any self may be interested in or it may mean that people are interested only in themselves. The former is nicely expressed in the couplet "the world is so full of a number of things, I am sure we should all be as happy as kings," and the latter expresses the doctrine of egoism, commonly known as selfishness (*see* EGOISM, PSYCHOLOGICAL EGOISM, AND ETHICAL EGOISM).

Historically, actions arising from desire or passion as sources of interest were well understood in both the ancient (Plato, *Republic*, 434–40; *Phaedrus*, 248–57) and medieval (Dante, *Inferno*) worlds. But it was not until the seventeenth and eighteenth centuries, with their this-worldliness and their emphasis upon the individual, coupled with the attempt to develop a science of man suggested by and modeled upon Newtonian mechanics, that self-interest and egoism became the measure of human motion. The specification of such self-interest varied widely: self-preservation in Hobbes; raising the power of one's being in Spinoza; acquiring pleasure and avoiding pain in Locke and early Utilitarians, such as Bentham; the aesthetic feeling in free, creative activity in Shaftsbury; the greatest happiness for the greatest number in J. S. Mill; and competitive success in the free-market system of Adam Smith. This emphasis upon "interest-in-the-self" has tended to make the narrow understanding of the phrase dominant in our tradition almost to the exclusion of any "social interests" a self may have. At the same time, such a selfish ethic was considered to be no ethic at all because of its lack of any "other-regarding" interests. Attempts have been made to modify the "selfish" aspect through the use of an "enlightened self-interest" that counselled consideration for others, but this merely uses others as instruments for the ends of self and is morally objectionable. It won't do unless the others are treated as ends in themselves and then the object of interest is no longer the self. Thus, the narrow meaning has come to express basic human concern coupled with a sense of moral disapproval to such a degree that the mere presence of self-interest in any activity tends to poison whatever other-regarding interests may be involved in that activity. On these grounds, since every interest belongs to a self, it would be next to impossible for purely altruistic activity to occur (Broad, 1949) (see ALTRUISM AND BENEVOLENCE). An adequate conception of "self-interest" must be found in order to protect the moral value of individualism.

Considered in itself, "self-interest," whether of the self-regarding or other-regarding variety, is a type of activity founded upon the capacity of our consciousness to be aware that we are aware, to have ends and purposes as objects for ourselves, be they of ourselves or of something else. Within the context of management and considering the vast power corporations exercise in communities, the question becomes: How can we be reasonably sure that such power will be exercised in the public interest? (Silk and Vogel, 1976: 128–9). As long as the distinction between ownership and management was not recognized (Berle and Means, 1934: 348) the problem was not difficult: owners could be held directly responsible. But when corporations went public and shareholders were seen as owners, then the problem became more difficult, for, while management must satisfy many interests, including those of the shareholders, there is often very

little to guard the interests of the public, and even those of the corporation itself, from the self-interest of the managers. In the last century, to protect the public we have increasingly used government to make laws and public agencies to apply them, only to discover that the people we elect to do the job are just as subject to considerations of self-interest in the narrow sense as are managers. It has become a very difficult problem.

A large portion of the difficulty arises from our failure to consider any other aspect of our activity of self-interest than its consequences; all decisions are to be made in terms of the bottom line, the end result. But self-interested activity involves more than just results and consequences (see CONSEQUENTIALISM). It requires freedom of choice and continuous concern. It requires structured alternatives and it requires consistency (Wilbur, 1992: 16–19, 29, 44–5). And the degree to which these enabling conditions are present and maintained is the degree to which self-interest as an activity is possible. So, no matter what object your self-interest may have, there are some interests you ought to have, the conditions that enable self-interested activity. And the conditions that enable your self-interested activity are the same for everyone's self-interested activity. When you maintain them for yourself, you maintain them for everyone. For example, these considerations are what make freedom of choice such a terribly important human condition, and they help to constitute an adequate and morally acceptable conception of self-interest. In a famous passage, often held to be obviously false, Adam Smith held that if everyone pursues their own self-interest, then "as if led by an invisible hand" they will promote the good of society. The conception of an adequate self-interest suggested here casts a different light upon what Adam Smith said (Smith, 1930: 421). In another famous passage, Kant said "act so that you treat humanity, whether in your own person or that of another, always as an end and never as a means only" (Kant, 1959: 75–6), and the only way to treat someone as an end is to maintain the enabling conditions of self-interested activity (see KANTIAN ETHICS). They constitute the limitations within which self-interested activity for anyone can be maintained without destroying it for everyone.

Bibliography

Berle, A. A. and Means, G. C. (1934). *The Modern Corporation and Private Property*. New York: Macmillan.

Broad, C. D. (1949). Egoism as a theory of human motives. *Hibbert Journal*, **48**, October, 105–14.

Dante Alighieri (1977). *Divine Comedy, Part I: The Inferno*, trans. J. Ciardi. New York: W. W. Norton.

Kant, I. (1959). *Foundations of the Metaphysics of Morals*, trans. L. W. Beck. New York: Liberal Arts Press.

Plato (1961). *Collected Dialogues*, ed. E. Hamilton and H. Cairns. New York: Bollingen Foundation, Princeton University Press.

Silk, L. and Vogel, D. (1976). *Ethics and Profits: The Crisis in Confidence in American Business*. New York: Simon and Schuster.

Smith, A. (1930). *Wealth of Nations*. London: Cannon.

Wilbur, J. B. (1992). *The Moral Foundations of Business Practice*. Lanham, MD: University Press of America.

sexual harassment

John Hasnas

is the abuse of one's position of authority over an employee in order to exact sexual favors from the employee or to discomfort or humiliate the employee because of his or her sex. "Sexual harassment" is a term with both a legal and a moral meaning, which, although related, are not identical. The tendency to conflate these meanings has been the source of much confusion and indicates the need to clearly distinguish between the term's legal and moral applications.

Legally speaking, sexual harassment is a form of sex discrimination. This is because, although the federal government is empowered by the Civil Rights Act of 1964 to prohibit employment discrimination on the basis of an individual's race, color, religion, sex, or national origin, it possesses no statutory authority to directly regulate interpersonal relationships in the workplace. Therefore, the only forms of sexual harassment that are legally actionable are those that discriminate against an employee because of his or her sex.

There are two distinct types of legally prohibited sexual harassment: quid pro quo harassment and hostile environment harassment. Quid pro quo harassment occurs when an individual's employment opportunities are conditioned upon his or her entering into a sexual or social relationship with an employer (i.e., when the opportunities are given or withheld as the quid pro quo for the relationship). Quid pro quo harassment may consist in either threats of adverse employment consequences if one does not enter the relationship, or offers of advancement if one does. It should be noted that such threats or offers must be directed toward the employee *because of the employee's sex*. If they are equally directed toward individuals of both sexes, as they might be by a bisexual supervisor, they would not constitute legally actionable sexual harassment because they would not be discriminatory in nature.

Hostile environment harassment occurs when an employer engages in conduct that has the purpose or effect of creating a working environment that is intimidating, hostile, or offensive to the members of one sex. Hostile environment harassment consists in unwelcome behavior of a sexual nature that is sufficiently distressing to interfere with an individual's ability to perform his or her job, even when the behavior is not designed to elicit sexual favors. Such behavior must be severe and pervasive enough to alter the conditions of the victim's employment and may not consist in merely a few isolated incidents. Once again, the behavior must have a sexually discriminatory effect. General intimidating or offensive behavior (i.e., behavior that would be intimidating or offensive to all employees regardless of their sex) does not constitute legally actionable sexual harassment. It should be noted that unlike quid pro quo harassment which requires intentional conduct, hostile environment harassment may consist in any course of action, intentional or not, that has the effect of creating a hostile working environment.

Morally speaking, sexual harassment consists in intimidating conduct directed toward individuals in subordinate employment positions by those with power over them for the purpose of exacting sexual favors that would not otherwise be granted (May and Hughes, 1987). This definition could reasonably be extended to include intimidating conduct that is designed to belittle or denigrate an employee because of his or her sex. From the moral perspective, sexual harassment is an abuse of power in the employment relationship, and as such, is objectionable primarily because of its oppressive, rather than discriminatory, nature. Thus, the actions of a bisexual harasser would constitute morally objectionable sexual harassment, even though they would not be legally actionable. Further, isolated instances of oppressive, sexually degrading conduct that would be inadequate to make out a legal case of hostile environment harassment could still constitute morally objectionable sexual harassment. However, because the evil of sexual harassment is its oppressive nature, and because oppression requires intention, there can be no negligent or inadvertent sexual harassment in the moral sense. Unlike legal sexual harassment, conduct that unintentionally creates an offensive working environment for the members of one sex would not lie within the moral significance of the term.

Bibliography

Dodds, S. M., Frost, L., Pargetter, R., and Prior, E. W. (1988). Sexual harassment. *Social Theory and Practice*, 14, 111–30.

Epstein, D. (1996) Can a "Dumb ass woman" achieve equality in the workplace? Running the gauntlet of hostile environment harassing speech. *Georgetown Law Journal*, **84**, 399–451.

Estrich, S. (1991). Sex at work. *Stanford Law Review*, **43**, 813–61.

MacKinnon, C. (1979). *Sexual Harassment of Working Women*. New Haven, CT: Yale University Press.

May, L. and Hughes, J. C. (1987). Is sexual harassment coercive? In G. Ezorsky (ed.), *Moral Rights in the Workplace*. Albany: State University of New York Press, 115–22.

US Supreme Court (1986). *Meritor Savings Bank vs. Vinson*, 477 US 84.

US Supreme Court (1998). *Oncale vs. Sundowner Offshore Services*, 523 US 75.

Volokh, E. (1997). What speech does "hostile work environment" law restrict? *Georgetown Law Journal*, **85**, 627–48.

social cost-benefits

Mark Sagoff

Economists in the 1940s and 1950s, who developed cost-benefit analysis, analogized the government to a firm. They thought that public works projects, such as dams, should return a profit to society on its investment. The Flood Control Act of 1938 required a weighing of economic pluses and minuses; for example, the value of irrigation and electricity against the amortized capital cost of building a dam. It permitted the government to finance water projects only when "the benefits to whomsoever they accrue [are] in excess of the costs."

A cost-benefit approach is uncontroversial in relation to governmental projects – including "pork barrel" projects – that provide goods and services, such as electricity and irrigation, for which ordinary markets set prices. It becomes controversial, however, insofar as it replaces public deliberation and legislative intent in the administration of laws that express public values and morality. When Congress outlawed child labor, for example, it regulated markets for moral not economic reasons.

Similarly, Congress has passed environmental laws largely because of ethical concerns, for example, about the extinction of species and the protection of public safety and health. Can the cost-benefit approach apply to public policy in the area of the environment, civil rights, education, the support of the arts, and so on? These policies at present follow from political deliberation through which we form and express our values as a nation. Should they be based instead on the preferences of individuals determined and aggregated by the techniques of cost-benefit analysis?

Cost-benefit aggregation presupposes that all values are subjective. It assimilates ideals and moral commitments to wants and preferences of the sort individuals satisfy in markets. The cost-benefit approach enters these preferences into a social welfare calculus on which policy is then based. Moral deliberation, in contrast, is supposed to be educative. Rather than depend on the "given" or "exogenous" consumer preferences of individuals, it seeks to inform, educate, and constitute public opinion within legitimate democratic political institutions and processes. According to this approach, the public consists not of consumers seeking to promote their own welfare, but of citizens deliberating over shared values, objectively grounded moral beliefs, or conceptions of the common good.

The cost-benefit approach begins with an answer to the moral question: What is the goal of public policy? The goal of public policy, it assumes, is the same as that of the market, namely, to elicit and satisfy consumer wants and preferences. The theory of welfare economics on which cost-benefit analysis rests equates the public good with the maximum satisfaction of preferences that individuals are willing to pay to satisfy. The theory defines "welfare" or "well-being" in terms of the satisfaction of those preferences.

Critics of the cost-benefit approach, including many environmentalists, believe, on the contrary, that democracy is seized with ethical questions, not just economic ones. Environmentalists argue, for example, that persons and property should be protected by right from pollution, as from any form of invasion or coercion. Accordingly, legislation seeks to minimize pollution rather than to maximize welfare. What is more, environmentalists do not believe that smoking, pollution, and other assaults on health improve welfare even if people voluntarily smoke, accept risky jobs, and so on. The role of government may be to create new options and to educate and improve preferences, rather than simply to take them as they come.

Those who defend cost-benefit analysis reply that if people are assumed to be the best judges of their own well-being, the economically efficient outcome – that is, the one that maximizes the satisfaction of preferences weighted by willingness-to-pay – will (tautologously) maximize the well-being or welfare of those individuals. A perfectly competitive market – that is, a market in which all goods are fully owned and people can trade costlessly – would allocate resources to those willing to pay the most for them, and it would therefore reach the welfare-maximizing, efficient outcome. If the role of the government is the same as that of a perfectly competitive market, that is, to allocate resources to those willing to pay the most for them, then cost-benefit analysis is a legitimate basis for public policy. Since markets often fail to capture all willingness to pay, especially in relation to the environment, managers trained in cost-benefit analysis should determine these "unpriced" preferences and allocate resources accordingly.

Many economists are developing techniques to "price" ethical values and political convictions as if they were subjective or personal "consumer" preferences. The primary technique, contingent valuation methodology, involves asking people how much they are willing to pay for outcomes to which they are morally committed (for example, the existence of an endangered species or a wilderness area they do not expect to visit). Even if citizens would pay only a few dollars each for these "existence" values, the aggregate sum might be substantial.

Cost-benefit analysis, insofar as it treats principled beliefs, moral commitments, and reasoned positions as "externalities" consumer markets have failed to "price," raises several difficulties. First, preferences, being mental states, are unobservable. Analysts must infer them from what a person says or does. However, anything a person says or does – including the answers he or she gives on surveys – can be interpreted in any number of ways. Accordingly, cost-benefit analysis greatly extends the power of governmental officials who, by asking questions and interpreting answers in one way rather than another, obtain the results they want. Since market "failures," "existence" values, and other "unpriced" preferences are pervasive and ubiquitous, moreover, the cost-benefit approach, for all its insistence on free markets, opens the door to centralized planning.

Second, the worth of an ideal or a principle cannot be determined by asking what people are willing to pay for it. Nobody asks economists how much they are willing to pay for their view that social welfare, as they define it, should be a basis of regulatory policy. Why should willingness-to-pay measure the importance of opposing principled positions and moral theories? People who believe that it is wrong to accelerate the extinction of species, for example, do not express a subjective preference. They affirm a policy position opposed to the assumptions of a cost-benefit approach.

Third, having a preference, however ill-informed or poorly considered, may give the individual a reason to try to satisfy it, but what reason has the government to seek to satisfy that preference? The reply that the satisfaction of preference maximizes well-being is trivially tautological if "well-being" or "welfare" is defined in terms of preference satisfaction. Otherwise, it is false. For example, people as a rule do not report they become happier when their incomes rise, and they can satisfy more of their preferences.

Plainly, cost-benefit analyses have an important role to play in reviewing "pork barrel" public works projects and subsidies to industry. One may question the applicability of cost-benefit analysis to regulatory policies, however, in which a nation attempts to do what is right but not necessarily what cost-benefit analysts say is efficient.

Bibliography

Hart, H. L. A. (1979). Between utility and rights. *Columbia Law Review*, 79, 828–31.

Kelman, S. (1981). *Cost-Benefit Analysis: An Ethical Critique*. Washington, DC: American Enterprise Institute for Public Policy Research.

Posner, R. (1979). Utilitarianism, economics, and legal theory. *Journal of Legal Studies*, 8, 103–19.

Sagoff, M. (1981). At the shrine of Our Lady of Fatima *or* why political questions are not all economic. *Arizona Law Review*, 23, 1283–96.

Sagoff, M. (1984). On preserving the natural environment. *Yale Law Journal*, 297, 205–67.

social sciences and business ethics

Alex C. Michalos

It is convenient to think of the social sciences as the organized pursuit of law-like regularities and theories regarding human action, and to think of business ethics as the theory and practice of human action aimed at securing a good life in a market, a mixed market, or an exchange economy. Perhaps the most important word in this brief definition is "convenient," because it emphasizes the fact that what is being offered is merely a stipulative definition or conventional understanding about the key words designating this subject-matter.

Although there is no general agreement about the proper way to define the social sciences and its diverse disciplines, there are different identifiable, self-defined, specialized research communities (i.e., professional or learned societies), academic departments, and scholarly journals.

So one way to proceed to an exhaustive analysis of our subject would be to list the appropriate social science societies and types of academic departments and journals, and then examine their particular relations to business ethics. One would still have borderline cases, one of the oldest being history and one of the newest being evaluation science (Michalos, 1992). Among the social sciences, one would include family studies, geography (especially economic and social geography), political science, policy science, planning (urban, rural, and regional), sociology (especially criminology, quality of work life, sociology of work or labor studies, industrial relations and social indicators, psychology, economics, organizational behavior) and anthropology.

Unfortunately, the suggested strategy of approaching our subject is oversimplified because it assumes that we are confronted with a many–one relation (many disciplines to one business ethics), when in fact we are faced with a many-to-many relationship, because different people construe ethics and business ethics in different ways. One theoretical approach in the study of ethics is consequentialism (including utilitarianism as a particular species). However, it too comes in many forms, which increases the variety of subheadings on the business ethics side of the relationship to be correlated with the social sciences side.

A few examples will suffice to illustrate the great importance of social scientific research to consequentialism. Ruut Veenhoven maintains an excellent website called World Database of Happiness that includes a Bibliography of Happiness with over 3,400 titles of scientific studies, a Catalog of Happiness Queries with over 500 standardized measures, a list of Happiness in Nations with results from over 1,800 surveys in 112 nations, and a detailed file of Correlational Findings on Happiness with over 7,400 findings from 705 studies in 140 nations. In Michalos (1991) it was reported that biennial computer searches of the research literature carried out over a dozen years on the key words "happiness" and "satisfaction" had revealed an average annual publication rate of over 1,100 titles for nearly 20 years.

Although few philosophers have ventured into this empirical work in the consequentialist moral tradition, social scientists have been very active and social scientists working on business ethics are increasingly drawing on this tradition. Collins (2000) wrote a very thorough review of the first 1,500 articles published in the *Journal of Business Ethics*, covering the period from its first issue in 1982 through 1999. Among other things, he showed that (1) survey research accounted for 14 percent of the articles published in 1982, increased to 51 percent in 1996, and decreased to 33 percent in 1999; (2) "researchers consistently report that survey respondents perceive their own ethical standards to be higher than those of their peers"; (3) ethical sensitivity is "by far the most researched topic among" the first 1,500 articles, with, for example, most studies showing that "women are more ethically sensitive than men"and that "upper level managers are less tolerant of unethical behavior than those of lower organizational rank"; (4) most large firms in the United States have codes of ethics but there are a variety of "social control mechanisms" such as moral/social audits, stakeholder analysis, and ethics programs; (5) "people perceive corporate social performance and reputation as a multidimensional concept beyond economic performance and obeying the law"; and (6) the three most frequently studied professions are accounting, marketing, and finance.

Georges Enderle edited a special issue of the *Journal of Business Ethics* (Volume 16, Number 14, October 1997) that included a fine set of reviews of business ethics in the 1990s in Australia and New Zealand, Japan, China, the Philippines, India, South Africa, Russia, the Czech Republic, Eastern and Southern Africa, the Middle East, Central and Eastern Europe, Latin America, and North America. As one might have expected, the reviews revealed a wide variety of views about the meaning of "business ethics," a variety of cultural settings, and a variety of approaches to identifying and addressing central issues.

Loe, Ferrell, and Mansfield (2000) wrote a review of 188 empirical studies of ethical decision-making in business, and found that the most frequently studied issues involved the role of gender and moral philosophy. The *Journal of Business Ethics* accounted for the greatest

number of such studies (61), with the *Journal of Business Research* (8) and the *Journal of Marketing Science* (7) a distant second and third.

Sabrin (2002) examined 13 journals focusing on business ethics in the five-year period 1995–99 in order to measure "the most productive business ethics scholars." Over half of the 2,371 business ethics scholars included in the study "published less than a single article during the entire five-year period." What is perhaps most interesting about this investigation is that "the 'top' MBA schools were not the ones whose faculties were doing business ethics research. Most of the top producing schools had MBA programs that were either unranked or were ranked relatively low." Speculating on why that might be the case, Sabrin said: "perhaps ethics, like religion, is left to the individual to decide for himself or herself."

Another way to measure the impact of social science on business ethics is by means of the most recent issue of the *Journal Citation Reports* of the *Social Sciences Citation Index*. Examining the "Cited Journal Listing" for 1992 (Grid: M5), one finds that only one (8 percent) of the 12 journals that are listed as citing *JOBE* in 1992, 1991, and 1990 was not a social science journal. Going in the other direction, one finds that every one of the 48 journals cited by authors in *JOBE* was a social science journal (Grid: H9, 19). In 2001, *JOBE* was cited 73 times, all by articles in social science journals. Every one of the 296 journals cited by *JOBE* articles in 2001 was a social science journal.

Finally, then, it is worthwhile to mention that although the focus of the present entry is on different ways of measuring the impact of social science on business ethics, the causal arrows of influence obviously run in both directions. Business ethics has had and will likely continue to have a profound impact on social science. Indeed, it does not seem to be an exaggeration to say that we have not witnessed such a morally provocative influence on the social sciences since the turn of the twentieth century, when virtually all of these sciences were driven by reform-minded researchers committed to improving the human condition with the help of their new tools of social analysis.

Bibliography

Collins, D. (2000). The quest to improve the human condition: The first 1,500 articles published in *Journal of Business Ethics*. *Journal of Business Ethics*, 26, 1–73.

Loe, T. W., Ferrell, L., and Mansfield, P. (2000). A review of empirical studies assessing ethical decision-making in business. *Journal of Business Ethics*, 25, 185–204.

Michalos, A. C. (1991). *Global Report on Student Well-Being, Vol. 1: Life Satisfaction and Happiness.* New York: Springer-Verlag.

Michalos, A. C. (1992). Ethical considerations in evaluation. *Canadian Journal of Program Evaluation*, 7, 61–75.

Robertson, D. C. (1993). Empiricism in business ethics: Suggested research directions. *Journal of Business Ethics*, 8, 585–600.

Sabrin, M. (2002). A ranking of the most productive business ethics scholars: A five-year study. *Journal of Business Ethics*, 36, 355–79.

socially responsible investing

Andrea Larson

refers to activities that direct capital to companies that take action to promote equity, support a healthy environment, and build communities. SRI is typically focused on corporations with "sustainable" practices and strategies that maximize economic, social, and environmental performance while sustaining, and preferably renewing, communities and ecosystems. SRI investors avoid companies that manufacture products or employ practices they believe are harmful to society. Typically, investments flow to companies with a proactive environmental record, positive employee relations, and strong community involvement. The aim is to promote good business across economic, environmental, and social performance indicators – and to get high returns while so doing.

SRI has been practiced for hundreds of years. Beginning as early as the seventeenth century, Quakers refused to invest in and profit from companies associated with the slave trade or war-related activities. This was the start of what is today called negative screening. By the early twentieth century religious groups refused

to invest in companies involved in the production of alcohol or tobacco products. In the 1980s avoidance investing resulted from the public outcry associated with companies investing and profiting from South Africa. The anti-apartheid campaign in South Africa was the first widespread recognition of the power of social investing.

From the 1960s onwards there were a number of events that bolstered the SRI movement in the United States. Vietnam War protests, civil rights battles, and the assassination of Dr. King were followed by federal legislation, including the National Environmental Policy Act, the Consumer Bill of Rights, the Food and Drug legislation spurred on by the thalidomide case, and the Highway Safety Act. The results offered proof that people could bring about significant changes by demanding that corporations take greater responsibility commensurate with their influence in society. In the 1980s and early 1990s SRI portfolio management firms such as Franklin Research and Development and US Trust of Boston were born. Social investment funds like Calvert and Working Assets were created and a number of associations, like the Social Investment Forum, were founded. The creation of these institutions marked the beginning of positive screening. Investors understood that corporations had the capacity to impact society and the environment in both positive and negative ways through their business practices. SRI investors began to analyze the practices of corporations and take positive practices into account when making investment decisions.

Three SRI strategies have evolved over time: screening, shareholder advocacy, and community investment. Positive and negative screens were used: positive to reinforce desired behavior as it improved (e.g., sound labor practices or responsible environmental actions) and negative to exclude firms from lists (e.g., tobacco and alcohol distribution or sale, animal testing). Shareholder advocacy engaged stockholders with companies to change firm practices through negotiation, formal resolutions (petitions to corporate boards), and block voting at annual meetings. Investments by firms in neighborhoods through corporate support of community banks, credit unions, loan funds, or microenterprise lending constituted community investments. Results were measured in terms of jobs, affordable housing, and other vital signs of community renewal.

Between 1993 and 2003 there was a rapid rise in funds invested in socially responsible portfolios. The growth and success of SRI in the United States since the mid-1990s signaled a fundamental shift in the business environment, characterized by a public desire to see and support a convergence of business issues and larger social concerns. SRI reflected investors' growing desire to screen out investments in firms perceived to have adverse effects on society and to favor those companies whose actions appear to enhance public health, environmental well-being, and improved quality of life.

The fundamental principle behind SRI is the alignment of financial goals and social/environmental responsibility. Investors are not asked to give up returns in order to invest responsibly. In fact, investors demand that socially responsible funds perform as well as – if not better than – non-screened funds. To the surprise of many, the performance of socially responsible funds exceeded the performance of the overall stock market between 1997 and 2003. The investment bank and brokerage firm Smith Barney stated in 2001:

> Socially responsible investing has moved into the mainstream of the United States as a result of demographic and business trends that are present in our economy today. There are two current trends, which imply that socially responsible investing is not simply a fad, or short investing strategy. On the business side, there is evidence of convergence between social and business interests. Socially aware investors are looking closely at the practices of businesses specific to environment, labor policies, and overall ethical track record. Businesses are not only recognizing the trend in socially aware investing but they are also recognizing that investments in sustainable practices yield long-term financial results. (www.smithbarney.com)

The pool of invested capital in the SRI category grew substantially in a short period of time.

By 2003 approximately $1 out of every $9 under professional management in the United States was invested using SRI screens. Of the nearly 12 percent of all investment assets under professional management in the United States, $2.32 trillion out of $19.9 trillion resided in a professionally managed portfolio utilizing one or more screening strategies.

Trends in SRI are a signal of changing investor preferences and values that reflect the shifting social and political conditions in which businesses now operate globally. Together with engaging customer demands, new scientific data, legislative and regulatory requirements, and more active non-governmental criticism of business practices, SRI can be seen as an important indicator of emerging definitions of "good business" in the twenty-first century. Today, companies ignore these indicators and trends at their peril. Firms that can find opportunity for innovation and competitive differentiation will benefit.

Financial markets have become more attuned to responsible behavior and its implications for future economic performance. SRI indexes (e.g., Domini, Citizens Index) have outperformed the general market indexes. This success in financial markets is based upon the market's ability to uncover value, assess risk, and judge expected future performance. The market expects these companies to outperform the general market, due to their leadership in adopting low risk and sustainable practices and innovations. The belief is that, over the long run, all companies will implement.

Growth in socially responsible investing

1984	1995	1997	1999	2001
$40 billion	$639 billion	$1.18 trillion	$2.16 trillion	$2.32 trillion

Source: 2001 report on socially responsible investing trends in the United States, Socially Responsible Investing Forum, http://www.socialinvest.org/areas/research/trends/2001-Trends/htm (March 2003 updated version)

All corporations fall on a spectrum between being simply reactive and integrating sustainable business methodology as a core value. The current convergence of business issues and social issues, as recognized by the financial markets, is forcing companies to examine their practices and policies. As the factors driving this convergence gather momentum and strength, companies may no longer have the option to change. Regulatory demands, consumer preferences, financial markets, and international requirements may demand that companies change. Current data support the conclusion that SRI does not have to come with financial sacrifices and that, in some instances, it may even outperform unscreened portfolios. Consequently, those that perceive the inefficiencies and take advantage of the slow-to-react corporations will create and capture significant value. The key to this new business model is the creation of economic value in collaboration with the creation of social value.

societies for business ethics

Archie B. Carroll

Societies for business ethics are organizations created for and sustained by individuals interested in the subject of business ethics. Such societies are typically based in academia and are composed primarily of academic members, but are also open to practitioner members. Such organizations periodically meet to discuss their common interests, and they frequently hold annual meetings for discourse among members. Societies for business ethics typically publish periodic newsletters and sponsor working groups, and some sponsor journals or periodicals for thought and research on the topic of business ethics.

Prominent societies for business ethics include the Society for Business Ethics (SBE), the International Association for Business and Society (IABS), the International Society of Business, Economics, and Ethics (ISBEE), the European Business Ethics Network (EBEN), the Social Issues in Management (SIM) Division of the Academy of Management, and the Associ-

ation for Practical and Professional Ethics (APPE).

SOCIETY FOR BUSINESS ETHICS

SBE is an international organization of scholars engaged in the academic study of business ethics. Founded in 1980, SBE has a number of important objectives, among which are the following: to promote the study of business ethics; to provide a forum in which moral, legal, empirical, and philosophical issues of business ethics may be openly discussed and analyzed; to provide a means by which those interested in and concerned with business ethics may exchange ideas; to promote research and scholarship; to promote the improvement of business ethics teaching in universities and organizations; to develop and maintain a friendly and cooperative relationship among teachers, researchers, and practitioners in the field of business and organizational ethics.

SBE conducts an annual meeting for the presentation of research, and issues a newsletter with information of interest to members. SBE publishes a journal, *Business Ethics Quarterly*, for the dissemination of the most important scholarship in the field, along with other publications, including the Ruffin Lecture Series. For more information about SBE, consult http://www.societyforbusinessethics.org/.

INTERNATIONAL ASSOCIATION FOR BUSINESS AND SOCIETY

IABS is a learned society devoted to research and teaching about the relationships between business, government, and society. Business ethics is one of its most important subjects. IABS was founded in 1990 and now has over 300 members worldwide from over 100 universities in more than 20 countries, as well as members from various corporations and non-profit organizations. IABS is a multidisciplinary association which attracts scholars and executives from all the disciplines of business and management.

Key objectives of IABS are to advance research, teaching, and professional standards in the field of Business and Society by facilitating exchange of information and ideas, and encouraging and assisting activities which advance knowledge of the business and society relationship. The research domain of IABS covers the various aspects of the interface between management and the social–political dynamics of the surrounding society. This domain includes, among others, research on business ethics, corporate social responsibility, performance and citizenship, and emerging social issues in business.

IABS organizes annual conferences, which generally meet two years in North America and one year outside North America. International locations have included Belgium, Austria, France, and the Netherlands. IABS publishes a quarterly newsletter, which is posted on its webpage, and sponsors a journal, *Business and Society*, a peer-reviewed scholarly journal devoted to research, discussion, and analysis of the relationship between business and society. The web page for IABS may be found at http://www.iabs.net/.

International Society of Business, Economics, and Ethics

ISBEE is a worldwide professional association that focuses exclusively on the study of business, economics, and ethics. ISBEE's professional orientation involves people not only in academe, but also those with practical competencies in responsible management positions. Membership also includes entrepreneurs of medium-size and small companies. ISBEE is strongly international in character, with members from around the world.

ISBEE developed in response to a sensed need to bring together individuals in traditionally distinct fields – economics, business, law, and philosophy – and from different practical areas – human resources, finance, social and environmental concerns, and marketing. The mission of ISBEE is to provide a forum for the exchange of experiences and ideas; to enhance cooperation in cross-functional and cross-cultural projects; and to discuss the ethical dimension of economic, social, and environmental issues which affect companies nationally and internationally. The organization supports a cross-disciplinary approach with the participation of both academicians and practitioners. It schedules its conferences and programs to encourage both formal and informal sharing of ideas and projects.

A culminating event of ISBEE's activities is the World Congress of Business, Economics, and Ethics, held every four years. Past congresses have taken place in Japan and Brazil. ISBEE's web page is http://www.isbee.org/.

European Business Ethics Network

EBEN is the only international network dedicated wholly to the promotion of business ethics in European private industry, public sectors, voluntary organizations, and academia. EBEN is a not-for-profit association, registered in the Netherlands. EBEN members include business people, consultants, public managers, academics, and students. EBEN's role is to promote values-based management, ethical leadership, and increased awareness about companies' responsibility in society.

The members of EBEN are concerned with promoting business ethics education and training as well as improving practices. EBEN is recognized on the world stage as representing European views on business ethics. Members from all over the world have joined together to advance business ethics by becoming active in the network. The diversity of membership of EBEN (from 33 countries in the year 2000) means that there are many varied views within the group about business ethics. EBEN is an inclusive network that accepts this plurality of perspectives.

EBEN supports initiatives at cross-European, national, and regional levels. National networks of EBEN are established or developing in Germany, Spain, the UK, the Netherlands, the Czech Republic, and Poland. There are active groups in a number of other countries, and always the possibility of forming more established National EBEN networks. The web page for EBEN is http://www.eben.org.

Social Issues in Management Division, Academy of Management

The Academy of Management, founded in 1936, is the oldest and largest organization of management scholars in the world. In 2003 it had 13,732 members from 90 nations. SIM is one of the academy's original divisions, created in 1971. The domain of SIM encompasses the exploration and analysis of various environmental and stakeholder influences upon the organization and the organization's effect upon these groups. The SIM domain includes:

- The social environment: topics such as corporate social responsibility, corporate philanthropy, stakeholder management, and corporate social performance.
- The ethical environment: topics such as corporate codes of ethics, corporate crime, individual ethical behavior, the influence of the organization on ethical conduct, ethical implications of technology, and the assessment of personal values and corporate culture.
- The public policy environment.
- The stakeholder environment.
- The international environment.

Each year, SIM holds its annual meeting in conjunction with the Academy of Management. Each meeting provides the opportunity for the presentation and discussion of scholarly papers addressing business ethics and other domain-related topics. Research on business ethics is published in the Academy of Management's major journals: *Academy of Management Journal*, *Academy of Management Review*, *Academy of Management Executive*, and *Academy of Management Learning and Education*. The academy also publishes a Best Papers Proceedings for each annual meeting.

ASSOCIATION FOR PRACTICAL AND PROFESSIONAL ETHICS

APPE was founded in 1991 to encourage interdisciplinary scholarship and teaching of high quality in practical and professional ethics by educators and practitioners who appreciate the practical–theoretical aspects of their subjects. The association facilitates communication and joint ventures among centers, schools, colleges, business and non-profit organizations, and individuals concerned with the interdisciplinary study and teaching of practical and professional ethics.

Ethics centers have proliferated over the past two decades, as have media stories reflecting heightened concern over the ethical behavior of organizations, politicians, and professionals. Colleges and universities are rethinking their curricula to address concerns about educating for civic and professional responsibility. These

phenomena underscore a growing conviction that the need has never been more urgent for practical ethical discourse in civic and professional life.

APPE sponsors a newsletter, *Ethically Speaking*. It holds an annual meeting and it also provides its members with access to resources of institutional members. APPE's website is http://www.indiana.edu/~appe/.

Societies for business ethics serve an important need in promoting research and studious inquiry into the nature and application of business ethics knowledge. Doubtless, there are other such societies, but the six major societies discussed above provide a solid foundation for further exploration into the topic.

socioeconomics

Amitai Etzioni

The neoclassical paradigm assumes that people have one overarching goal: satisfying their wants. Historically, these wants were depicted as materialistic; more recently, satisfaction derived from other sources has been added, such as the pleasure gained from helping the poor, but the core concept remains self-centered and hedonistic and Me-istic: people are propelled by *their* wants, *their* self-interest, *their* profits. Research in this tradition further assumes that a person's various "tastes" can be neatly ordered into one unitary pattern of desire, with a common denominator to "trade-off" various items (apples for oranges, etc.), a notion at the heart of economics. In contrast, my finding is that people have several wants, including the commitment to live up to their moral values, and that these wants cannot be neatly ordered or regulated by prices. This finding provides a starting point that is fundamentally different from that of the neoclassical paradigm.

SOCIOECONOMICS BASED ON THE I–WE PARADIGM

This paradigm assumes a divided self, which *does* have the hedonistic urges assumed by the neoclassical paradigm (albeit those too are affected by the values of the society in which the person lives). However, far from mindlessly pursuing these desires, the person is viewed as a judging self which examines its urges and evaluates them by various criteria, the most important of which are moral/social values. A struggle ensues: under some conditions, urges win out; in others, morals triumph.

There are many ways of classifying ethical positions. Socioeconomics is moderately deontological, where a deontological position is the notion that actions are morally right when they conform to a relevant principle or duty. Deontology stresses that the moral status of an act should not be judged by its consequences, the way utilitarians do, but by the intention. Moderate deontologists take consequences into account but as a secondary consideration (*see* UTILITARIANISM).

The significance of incorporating this moral dimension into the concept of human nature is that it is perhaps the most important feature that separates us from animals. Our moral commitments and our urges do not often pull us in the same direction. Much of human life is explainable as a struggle between the two forces, and a study of the conditions under which one or the other prevails. Even a modicum of introspection provides first-hand evidence of this significant, perpetual inner conflict. Those who have never experienced such conflict are either born saints or utterly debased (Etzioni, 1988).

Having resolved the conflict and decided upon a goal, how does a person go about selecting a course, the means to the goal? Neoclassicists say, *rationally*; that is, by using empirical evidence and logical inference. Much of this approach is contradicted by the observation that most choices are influenced heavily by normative/affective (N/A) factors; that is, by people's values and emotions. These factors shape to a significant extent the information that is gathered, the ways in which it is processed, the inferences that are drawn, the options that are considered, and the options that are finally chosen.

Entire categories of means, whether "efficient" or not, are judged to be unacceptable and *automatically* ruled out of consideration. Thus, most reasonably competent daughters and sons of the American middle class consider it unthinkable not to attend college. About a third of those entitled to collect welfare refuse

to apply, because it's "not right." Furthermore, emotions (e.g., impulse) cut short deliberation (when it does occur). While emotions and values have often been depicted as "distorting rationality," which they can do, they also agitate against using means that may be efficient in the narrow sense but are indecent or hurtful to others or the community. Furthermore, N/A factors can often play a positive role in decision-making, especially by mobilizing or inhibiting action or generating or communicating information. In short, the moral order deeply affects not merely what we seek to accomplish but also the way we proceed.

THE INDIVIDUAL IN COMMUNITY

The neoclassical paradigm draws on and contributes to the Whiggish tradition of investing all moral rights in the individual; the legitimate decision-maker is assumed to be the individual. All attempts to modify a person's tastes are viewed as inappropriate interventions (hence the term "consumer sovereignty"). Moreover, the government is usually blamed for attempts to redirect individuals, and such redirections are treated as intrinsically coercive. In contemporary terms, the neoclassical paradigm is essentially libertarian (*see* LIBERTARIANISM).

A recent philosophical trend, the communitarian movement, attempts to correct this radical individualism. Communitarianism builds on the observation that individuals and communities are mutually dependent, and that certain "public goods," not just the individual, are fundamentally of merit – for example, defense, basic research, public education. Some extreme communitarians entirely neglect individual rights in the name of societal virtues, the motherland, or some other such cause. A much more defensible position may be found in recognizing that both individual rights *and* duties to the community have the same basic moral standing, hence the I–We paradigm. It follows, for example, that we need to both recognize the individual *right* to a trial by jury of peers, and the individual's *obligation* to serve on a jury; to be defended, and to pay for defense; to benefit from the savings of past generations, and to save for future ones.

The voice of the community is typically moral, educational, and persuasive. If coercion is relied upon, this indicates that the community has been weakened, with too many members engaged in activities previously considered unthinkable. The more effective policy is not to enhance the government but to rebuild the social and moral community. This shift starts with a change of paradigms, from the neoclassical to a new approach that encompasses rather than ignores the concept of community, one that balances (*not* replaces) individualistic tendencies with concern for community, and one that reaches beyond the realm of material incentives and sanctions to the role of values, particularly shared values, as long as they are *freely endorsed and not imposed*.

Empirical work on the role of community has shown unequivocally that social collectivities are major decision-making units, often providing the context within which individual decisions are made. Moreover, in many areas collectivities, if properly structured, can both render more rational decisions than their individual members (though not necessarily highly rational ones) and account for more of the variance in individual decision-making than do individual attributes (see Etzioni, 1988).

Another crucial function of community is to contain the conflict and limit the scope of market competition. This social context is not merely a source of constraints on the market but also a precondition for its ability to function. Three types of elements sustain market competition in this way:

- Normative factors, such as a commitment to fairness in competition and to trust that this commitment will be shared by others.
- Social bonds, reflecting the fact that competition thrives, not in impersonal systems of independent actors unbound by social relations, as implied by the neoclassical paradigm, not in the socially tight world of communal societies, but in the middle range where social bonds are strong enough to sustain natural trust and low transaction costs, but not so strong as to suppress exchange orientations.
- Governmental mechanisms as the arbiter of conflicts, where normative factors and social bonds have proved insufficient constraints, and the enforcer of judgments. These crucial

roles illustrate the need to move beyond the conceptual opposition between "free competition" and "governmental intervention," which implies that all interventions are injurious and that unshackled competition can be sustainable.

The essential capsule of competition is thus best considered as an intertwined set of normative, social, and governmental mechanisms, which have a distinct role but also can, within limits, substitute for one another.

Bibliography

Etzioni, A. (1988). *The Moral Dimension: Toward a New Economics*. New York: Free Press.

South Africa, business ethics in

Gedeon J. Rossouw

BACKGROUND

Business ethics both as a practice and academic field suffered under the apartheid regime in South Africa. During the final years of the apartheid era, South African corporations were barred by sanctions from participating in the world market. Consequently, they felt themselves compelled to find alternative access to world markets. Ingenious, but often illegitimate and immoral, ways were found to circumvent the sanction barriers. Such attempts at sanction busting were praised rather than repudiated by the government and the business community. This led to a business culture that endorsed immoral means of doing business as good business practice.

In the context of the liberation struggle against apartheid, immoral business practices were sometimes endorsed as legitimate means to achieve a moral end. Fraudulent actions and deliberate deceit were legitimized as necessary means to overthrow an illegitimate government. In was within this situation that the term "struggle bookkeeping" was coined.

TEACHING

The emergence of business ethics as an academic field coincided with the demise of the apartheid regime. By the late 1980s the first courses in business ethics were introduced at a few business schools. Over the next decade there was a steady growth in the number of business schools that introduced courses in business ethics. By the turn of the twenty-first century it had become commonplace to have at least an elective module in business ethics at business schools. There is no dominant model for teaching business ethics at business schools in South Africa. At some schools business ethics is part of the mandatory core curriculum, others offer it only as an elective, while others claim that it is integrated into all subjects offered.

Besides the courses at business schools, business ethics modules are also offered in a variety of other university disciplines, including philosophy, human resource management, business management, and accounting and auditing. The introduction of business ethics at undergraduate level – especially in commerce faculties – was triggered by business scandals that cast business and specifically the accounting and auditing professions in a negative light. In response to these negative perceptions, external pressure by professional bodies was exerted upon institutions of higher learning to include business ethics in the undergraduate curriculum.

A Technikons module on business ethics is included in the generic business management program. All Technikons in South Africa share a common generic curriculum. This generic curriculum is supposed to form 70 percent of the curriculum offered at each of the Technikons. The remaining 30 percent is complied on the initiative of the department or lecturer presenting the course. The generic business management program includes the theme of business ethics, but does not prescribe the content of business ethics. A recent survey on the teaching of business ethics at Technikons revealed that the business ethics module is in need of extensive development (see Alberts, 2002).

RESEARCH

The research agenda of business ethics is driven by the realities of post-apartheid South Africa and the African context. The need to rebuild the moral fiber of the business community dominates that agenda. The bulk of research is focused on how ethics can be institutionalized in corporations. The two Corporate Governance Reports for South Africa published in 1994 and 2002 gave further impetus to this research by recommending that corporations should actively manage their ethics. In addition, corporate social responsibility, affirmative action, and HIV/AIDS in the workplace have also attracted a fair amount of research. More recently, IT-related ethical issues have also become part of the research focus.

BUSINESS ETHICS INSTITUTES

The proliferation of business ethics modules at institutions of higher learning also resulted in the emergence of centers and institutes with a business and professional ethics focus. Several such centers and institutes currently exist in South Africa. These institutes typically focus on being research and resource centers, while simultaneously providing consultancy services. The initiative for the formation of an African network of business ethics also originated in South Africa and eventually resulted in the formation of the Business Ethics Network of Africa (BEN-Africa) in 2000. In 2003 BEN-Africa had members in 25 African countries. BEN-Africa publishes regular newsletters, presents an annual conference, and has its own website (www.benafrica.org).

ETHICS IN BUSINESS

In 1994, the year of South Africa's first democratic elections, the first corporate governance report for South Africa was published. It soon became known as the King Report on Corporate Governance, named after Mervin King (SC) who chaired the committee that drafted the report. Commissioned by the main players in the private sector, the report adopted an inclusive corporate governance model, which advocated that boards of directors should not only pursue the interests of shareholders, but also be responsible to all their stakeholders. It also encouraged corporations to commit themselves to the highest standards of ethical behavior.

Although the recommendations of the King Report were not legally enforced, they were nevertheless embraced by corporate South Africa and became very influential. After the publication of the King Report the number of companies with codes of ethics increased sharply. In 2000 a second committee on corporate governance was convened which drafted the Second King Report on Corporate Governance, published in 2002. The King 2 report once more embraced the inclusive approach to corporate governance and extended it further. It went beyond the recommendation of King 1 in recommending a culture of triple bottom line reporting. Specifically with regard to ethics, it advised companies to engage with their stakeholders in determining their ethical standards. It also advised companies to actively manage and institutionalize ethics. There is also an expectation that companies should account their ethics performance, submit it to independent verification, and ultimately disclose it to shareholders.

The King 2 report once more advocated a self-regulatory regime where corporations are encouraged to adopt good governance as best business practice. Despite the lack of legal enforcement of the standards of governance recommended by King 2, they are widely endorsed by the South African business community. The recommendations of King 2 have since been reflected in the revised listing requirements of the JSE Securities Exchange, as well as in law reform that is still in the making. The public sector is also included in the scope of King 2.

King 2 distinguishes three areas of ethical obligation for business. First, there is organizational integrity, which refers to the standards of behavior adopted by the organization as well as the institutionalization thereof. Second, there are the internal social obligations of organizations that refer specifically to safety and health issues, employment equity, and the development of human capital. Special emphasis is placed on the responsibility of business with regard to HIV/AIDS and gender equity. Third, there are the external social obligations of organizations that focus mainly on corporate social responsibility, black economic empowerment, and societal transformation.

Bibliography

Alberts, E. (2002). Integration of business ethics in the curriculum of human resource management at Technikons in South Africa. Unpublished doctoral dissertation in Afrikaans. Johannesburg: Rand Afrikaans University.

Barkhuysen, B. (1999). A survey of the current status of business ethics as academic field in Africa. Unpublished masters' dissertation. Johannesburg: Rand Afrikaans University.

Rossouw, G. J. (1997). Business ethics in South Africa. *Journal of Business Ethics*, 16, 1539–47.

South America, business ethics in

Maria Cecilia Coutinho de Arruda

Business ethics in South America, as in many other countries, combine the positive (values, honesty, transparency, respect) and negative (corruption, fraud, bribery, inside information, human rights violations, lack of punishment). Because business ethics has been in the news all over the world for several years, business leaders from all South American countries (SACs) often ask for a specific definition of the term. There are clear rules and laws about correct and ethically sound business behavior, but few regions in these countries enforce compliance. Complicity and connivance in business are so common that in general the South American public profoundly distrusts business and government. Citizens, politicians, and business leaders seem to be confused by the concept of ethics and even more skeptical when this concept is related to business. Too often, public speeches and discussions of business ethics are more oratorical and superficial than they are serious and indicative of a strong commitment to moral values. Following the lead of many political and business leaders, and in the knowledge that many individuals from higher social classes go unpunished, many ordinary citizens of SACs justify unethical and even criminal behavior.

In order to raise the ethical level of business policies and performance, the Center of Studies for Ethics in Organizations – Fundacao Getulio Vargas, São Paulo (CENE-FGV-EAESP) – was founded in 1992. Through workshops, conferences, consulting, teaching, and training, CENE-FGV-EAESP has significantly supported companies, professionals, and academics interested in developing ethical parameters and principles to face the modern requirements of the business world in Brazil and Latin America. Thanks to its efforts, the Asociacion

Latinoamericana de Etica, Negocios y Economia (ALENE), or Latin American Business Ethics Network, was created in 1998. ALENE's annual meetings in different SACs allow a deep and productive discussion of the serious problems that exist in the region. These conferences generate many publications that enable the integration of academics and business leaders from several SACs. ALENE members have played an important role in the International Society of Business, Economics, and Ethics (ISBEE), bringing cases and experiences that can help further ethics in developing countries.

In the 1990s, South American corporations began emphasizing business ethics practices. Codes of ethics or value statements have been articulated in over 80 percent of Brazilian companies, around 50 percent of Argentine firms, and a significant percentage in other SACs. By offering better wages, benefits, and work conditions, these companies and corporations try to drive their internal policies toward social justice (*see* JUSTICE).

By improving manufacturing processes and quality control, the society produced new, better, healthier, and more sustainable products for the marketplace. By paying their taxes honestly, these companies contributed significant income to the government. The process of globalization led multinational companies in SACs to review their ethical statements. They began to deal more carefully with such issues as diversity, sustainability, and prejudice concerning sex, age, and social status.

In order to guarantee high levels of ethical performance, it was necessary to create laws, agreements, business and professional associations, and voluntary technical norms. As an example, the Brazilian Association of Toy Makers – Associacao Brasileira de Fabricantes de Brinquedos (ABRINQ) – a strong association of over 300 toy manufacturers in Brazil, prepared a voluntary technical norm to avoid the production of all dangerous features in any toy. The government supported the initiative, making this norm mandatory in all toy manufacturing companies. ABRINQ member companies now have an active foundation organized to avoid child labor in Brazil.

Rich in natural resources, SACs have been attractive to international investors, particularly large corporations. Nevertheless, economic growth in SACs has been very unequal. The new flow of wealth has protected elite members of society, who prospered by working for the government and became even wealthier after acquiring auctioned assets. The newly created jobs have tended to be temporary, low paid, and concentrated in specific economic sectors. Although managing privatization changes became a highly profitable activity, the drive toward making companies more competitive resulted in many middle- and lower-class workers losing their jobs.

With these trends, another ethical problem arose in SACs: the concentration of investments in large cities, while distant and rural regions struggle to survive, with little chance of receiving short-term investments. Even in urban areas, many South American citizens live in slums, with little or no access to running water, electricity, drainage systems, adequate housing, education, and health. Chile, Argentina, Bolivia, Peru, and Brazil have established governmental programs to reduce the social price of economic development of the 1990s, but poverty is still an important issue in the business ethics arena: over 30 percent of SAC populations live in real poverty, according to the Economic Commission for Latin America (CEPAL), a regional sector of the United Nations located in Santiago, Chile.

The unfair income distribution in most SACs is a consequence of inflation-generated materialism and corruption in governmental agencies, which do not distribute resources in a manner established by law. The culture of the Brazilian *jeitinho* (finding an unethical and easier way to solve any problem) persists among all social classes in most SACs (Appy, 1992: 50). The inflationary culture led to a devaluation of professional work, an impulse to seek easy ways of earning money, and a general irresponsibility and lack of concern about productivity (*see* PROFIT, PROFITS, AND PROFIT MOTIVE).

Often, it is difficult for businesses to adopt ethical practices in their relationships with government agents, clients, suppliers, and stakeholders. Bribery, percentages, gifts, and other "payments" have become usual or mandatory in many sectors, and real moral dilemmas concerning managerial ethics and the ethical role of the manager have appeared. Illiteracy and low levels of education in SACs also promote unethical practices. Even though religion (primarily Roman Catholicism) is extremely important in SACs, many people seem to have lost their ability to distinguish between right and wrong. A complete revolution in habits seems necessary to change people's attitudes toward moral values. Some business executives already play an important role in this effort by avoiding any kind of corruption, paying their bills on time, protecting the environment and environmental ethics, and having the courage to be honest.

Recognized as less-developed countries, SACs have faced increasing competition in world markets, which induced industrialized nations to cluster together in regional economic blocs: the European Union (EU), the North American Free Trade Agreement (NAFTA), and some alliances among Japan and its East Asian neighbors. SACs felt the need to face both fair and unfair competition. Argentina, Brazil, Paraguay, and Uruguay created the Common Market of South America (MERCOSUR) in March 1991 in an attempt to integrate their economies and defend themselves from discriminatory tariffs from other countries. After many difficulties, the MERCOSUR countries are facing new developments, as AFTA – the American Free Trade Area – has gained strength.

Most SACs have gone through deep political and economic changes in the last few decades. The influences of different ideologies and the lack of governmental action in significant areas such as education, health, housing, and social welfare made private and non-governmental organizations more aware of their social responsibility. The Instituto Ethos – Business and Social Responsibility – was founded in 1998 in São Paulo, Brazil to supplement the Brazilian government's social action. Its mission is to generate awareness and to mobilize and help companies manage their businesses in a socially responsible way. The institute brings together hundreds of companies in various sectors, formally committed to the construction of a fair and environmentally sustainable society. A large number of initiatives throughout the country has encouraged the creation of similar organizations in Argentina and Chile.

In Brazil, the FIDES Foundation – Fundacao Instituto de Desenvolvimento Empresarial e Social – and IBASE – Instituto Brasileiro de Analises Sociais e Economicas – have worked on the Social Balance Sheet (SBS) as a tool to report on the status of business social actions. Although not mandatory, many companies have filled out FIDES-IBASE forms to prepare and publish their SBS in order to inform society, clients, and stockholders about their social responsibility activities developed during a specific period. Other SACs have begun implementing this practice.

After dealing with socially responsible activities related to society as a whole, companies now seem more interested in internally reinforcing compliance with their codes of ethics. CENE-FGV-EAESP has helped many Brazilian companies to create their own business ethics statements and to implement solid business ethics programs. Nevertheless, the most recent concern of business ethics in several SACs has been with ethics in corporate governance. Because of a number of scandals that came to light, the executives, boards, and stockholders of the largest organizations have discussed and revised their best practices with more attention on their ethical perspective.

South American business schools have introduced business ethics to their curricula so to better prepare undergraduate and graduate students to make ethical business decisions in present or future positions. The Fundacao Getulio Vargas – São Paulo is the first business school in Latin America to offer business ethics as a specific concentration area in MS and PhD programs.

At both the micro and macro levels, business ethics has come to the forefront in South America. Companies, universities, and governmental agencies have begun to implement successfully ethical systems based on solid moral values.

See also *Foreign Corrupt Practices Act; organization ethics; religion and business ethics; social cost-benefits; socioeconomics; work and family*

Bibliography

Appy, R. E. (1992). Etica empresarial e inflacao. In N. G. Teixeira (ed.), *A Etica no Mundo da Empresa*. São Paulo: Pioneira, 47–55.

Arruda, M. C. C. (2002). *Codigo de Etica: Um Instrumento Que Adiciona Valor*. São Paulo: Atlas.

Arruda, M. C. C., Whitaker, M. C., and Ramos, J. M. R. (2003). *Fundamentos de Etica Empresarial e Economica*, 2nd edn. São Paulo: Atlas.

Ashley, P. A. (2003). *Etica e Responsabilidade Social nos Negocios*. São Paulo: Saraiva.

Debeljuh, P. (2003). *El Desafio de la Etica*. Buenos Aires: Temas Grupo Editorial.

Humberg. M. E. (2002). *Etica na Política e na Empresa*. São Paulo: Editora CLA.

Monett, L. (1994). The political economy of MERCO-SUR. *Journal of Anti-American Studies and World Affairs*, 3 (4), 101–41.

Newton, L. and Ford, M. M. (1992). *Taking Sides: Clashing Views on Controversial Issues in Business Ethics and Society*, 2nd edn. Guilford, CT: Dusking Publishing.

Schmidt, E. (2000). *Etica y Negocios para America Latina*, 3rd edn. Lima: Universidad del Pacifico; OXY.

Steinberg, H. (2003). *A Dimensao Humana da Governanca Corporativa: Pessoas Criam as Melhores e as Piores Praticas*. São Paulo: Editora Gente.

stakeholder theory

R. Edward Freeman

A *stakeholder*: any group or individual which can affect or is affected by an organization. This wide sense of the term includes suppliers, customers, stockholders, employees, communities, political groups, governments, media, etc. A narrower definition is that the stakeholders in a firm are designated as suppliers, customers, employees, financiers, and communities.

Stakeholder theory: a set of propositions that suggest that managers of firms have obligations to some group of stakeholders. Stakeholder theory is usually juxtaposed with stockholder theory: the view that managers have a fiduciary duty to act in the interests of stockholders. "Stakeholder" is an ironic twist of "stockholder" to signal that firms may well have broader obligations than the traditional economic theory has assumed.

The recent history of stakeholder theory has been well documented by Donaldson and Preston (1995). One can find vestiges of the concept in many areas of business, from finance, strategic management (cf. Mason and Mitroff, 1982), organization theory (cf. Thompson, 1967; Dill, 1958), and ethics (cf. Freeman, 1994). The actual word "stakeholder" first appeared in the management literature in an internal memorandum at the Stanford Research Institute (now SRI International, Inc.) in 1963. It was meant to generalize the notion of stockholder as the only group to whom management need be responsive. Thus, the stakeholder concept was originally defined as "those groups without whose support the organization would cease to exist." Stemming from the work of Igor Ansoff and Robert Stewart in the planning department at Lockheed, and later Marion Doscher and Stewart at SRI, the original approach served an important information function in the SRI corporate planning process. The Swedish management theorist Eric Rhenman, who is perhaps the originator of the term, was instrumental in the development of stakeholder thinking in Scandinavia, where the concept became one of the cornerstones of industrial democracy. (See Nasi, 1995, for the history of the concept in Scandinavia.)

Donaldson and Preston (1995) suggest the research on stakeholders has proceeded along three often confused lines. First, there is instrumental stakeholder theory, which assumes that if managers want to maximize the objective function of their firms, then they must take stakeholder interests into account. Second, there is the descriptive research about how managers, firms, and stakeholders in fact interact. Third, there is a normative sense of stakeholder theory that prescribes what managers ought to do vis-à-vis the stakeholder. To this framework we can add a fourth dimension, the metaphorical use of "stakeholder," which depicts the idea as a figure in a broader narrative about corporate life. We shall combine the first two senses of stakeholders and call that the *analytical* approach to stakeholder theory, while the second two senses can be called the *narrative* approach to stakeholder theory.

THE ANALYTICAL APPROACH TO STAKEHOLDER THEORY

Any business needs to be understood at three levels of analysis. The first concerns how the business as a whole fits into its larger environment, or the *rational* level. The second concerns how the business relates to its environment as a matter of standard operating procedures and routine management processes, or the *process* level. The third concerns how the business executes actual *transactions*, or deals or contracts with those individuals who have a stake.

An example of the rational level is to think of business strategy as a game played, for example, between IBM and AT&T. IBM does action X and AT&T responds with action Y. An example of what we mean by the process level would be to look internally and see how the performance and reward procedures work at both AT&T and IBM. An example of the transactions level would be to closely examine the behavior of IBM and AT&T salespersons to see how each treats customers, and to examine the terms of various contracts, deals, promises, and individual motivations of each player. Obviously, these three levels of analysis are connected. In fact, we argue that in successful businesses they fit together in a coherent pattern.

The rational level. The rational level of the stakeholder framework must give an accurate picture of the place of a business in its larger environment. It must identify those groups who

have a stake, and it must depict the nature of the relationship between stakeholder and firm.

Who are those groups and individuals who can affect and are affected by the achievement of an organization's purpose? How can we construct a stakeholder map of an organization? What are the problems in constructing such a map? Ideally, the starting point for constructing a map for a particular business is a historical analysis of the environment of that particular firm. In the absence of such a historical document, figure 1 can serve as a checkpoint for an initial generic stakeholder map.

Figure 1 depicts a stakeholder map around one major strategic issue for one very large organization, the XYZ Company, based primarily in the United States. Unfortunately, most attempts at stakeholder analysis end with the construction of figure 1. The primary use of the stakeholder concept has been as a tool for gathering information about generic stakeholders. Table 1 is a chart of specific stakeholders to accompany figure 1 for the XYZ Company. Even in table 1 some groups are aggregated, in

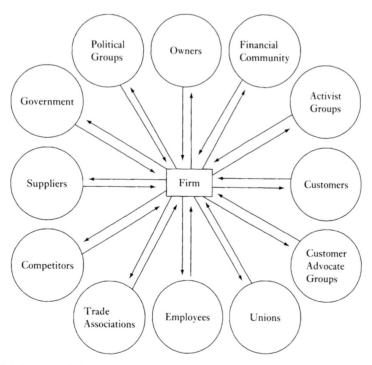

Figure 1 Stakeholder map of a large organization

order to disguise the identity of the company. Thus, "Investment Banks" would be replaced by the names of those investment banks actually used by XYZ. Table 2 is an analysis of the stakes of some of those specific stakeholder groups listed in table 1. Thus, the stake of Political Parties no. 1 and no. 2 is as a heavy user of XYZ's operations, and as being able to elevate XYZ to national attention via the political process. Customer Segment no. 1 used a lot of XYZ's product, and was interested in how the producer could be improved over time for a small incremental cost. Customer Segment no. 2 used only a small amount of XYZ's product, but that small amount was a critical ingredient for Customer Segment no. 2, and there were no readily available substitutes. As shown in figure 1 and tables 1 and 2, the construction of a rational stakeholder map is not an easy task in terms of identifying specific groups and the stakes of each. The figure and tables are enormously oversimplified, for they depict the stakeholders of XYZ as static, whereas in reality, they change over time, and their stakes change depending on the strategic issue under consideration.

The process level.   Large, complex organizations have many processes for accomplishing tasks. From routine applications of procedures and policies to the use of more sophisticated analytical tools, managers invent processes to accomplish routine tasks and to make complex tasks routine. To understand organizations and how they manage stakeholder relationships, it is necessary to look at the standard operating procedures – the organizational processes that are used to achieve some kind of fit with the external environment.

Organizational processes serve multiple purposes. One purpose is as a vehicle for communication and as symbols for what the corporation represents. Standard operating procedures depict what activities are necessary for success in the organization. And the activities necessary for success inside the organization must bear some relationship to the tasks that the external environment requires of the organization if it is to be a successful and ongoing concern. Therefore, if the external environment is a rich multi-stakeholder, the strategic processes of the

Table 1   Specific stakeholders in a large operation

General	Specific
Owners	Shareowners
	Bondholders
	Employees
Financial community	Analysts
	Investment banks
	Commercial banks
	Federal Reserve
Activist groups	Safety and health groups
	Environmental groups
	"Big business" groups
	Single-issue groups
Suppliers	Firm no. 1
	Firm no. 2
	Firm no. 3
	etc.
Government	Congress
	Courts
	Cabinet departments
	Agency no. 1
	Agency no. 2
Political groups	Political party no. 1
	Political party no. 2
	National League of Cities
	National Council of Mayors
	etc.
Customers	Customer no. 1
	Customer no. 2
	etc.
Customer advocate groups	Consumer Federation of America
	Consumers' Union
	Council of Consumers
	etc.
Unions	Union of Workers no. 1
	Union of Workers no. 2
	etc.
	Political action committees of unions
Employees	Employee segment no. 1
	Employment segment no. 2
	etc.
Trade associations	Business Roundtable
	NAM
	Customer trade organization no. 1
	Customer trade organization no. 2
	etc.

Competitors	Domestic competitor no. 1
	Domestic competitor no. 2
	Foreign competitor no. 1
	etc.

Table 2 Stakes of some special stakeholders

Stakeholder	Stake
Customer segment no. 1	High users of produce
	Improvement of product
Political parties nos. 1 and 2	High users of product
	Able to influence regulatory process
	Able to get media attention on a national scale
Customer segment no. 2	Low users of product
	No available substitute
Consumer advocate no. 1	Effects of XYZ on the elderly
Employees	Jobs and job security
	Pension benefits
Consumer advocate no. 2	Safety of XYZ's products
Owners	Growth and income
	Stability of stock price and dividend

organization must reflect this complexity. These processes need not be rigid analytical devices, but rather existing strategic processes that work reasonably well with a concern for multiple stakeholders.

The transactional level. The bottom line for stakeholder management has to be the set of transactions that managers in an organization have with stakeholders. How do the organization and its managers interact with stakeholders? What resources are allocated to interact with which groups? There has been a lot of research in social psychology about the so-called transactional environment of individuals and organizations, and we shall not attempt to recapitulate that research here. Suffice it to say that the nature of the behavior of organizational

members and the nature of the goods and services being exchanged are key ingredients in successful organizational transactions with stakeholders.

Corporations have many daily transactions with stakeholder groups, such as selling things to customers and buying things from suppliers. Other transactions are also fairly ordinary and unexciting, such as paying dividends to stockholders and negotiating a new contract with the union. Yet when we move from this relatively comfortable zone of transactions to dealing with some of the changes that have occurred in traditional marketplace stakeholders and the emergence of new stakeholder groups, there is little wonder that transactions with the corporation's stakeholder map become a real source of discontent.

If corporate managers ignore certain stakeholder groups at the rational and process level, then there is little to be done at the transactional level. Encounters between corporation and stakeholder will be, on the one hand, brief, episodic, and hostile, and on the other hand, non-existent if another firm can supply stakeholders' needs. Successful transactions with stakeholders are built on understanding the legitimacy of the stakeholder and having processes to routinely surface their concerns. However, the transactions themselves must be executed by managers who understand the currencies in which the stakeholders are paid. There is simply no substitute for thinking through how a particular individual can win and how the organization can win at the same time.

The Narrative Approach to Stakeholder Theory

"The stakeholder theory" can be unpacked into a number of stakeholder theories, each of which has a "normative core," inextricably linked to the way that corporations should be governed and the way that managers should act. On the narrative approach, "stakeholder theory" is thus a genre of stories about how we could live. A "normative core" of a theory is a set of sentences that includes, among others:

1 Corporations ought to be governed . . .
2 Managers ought to act to . . .

where we need arguments or further narratives which include business and moral terms to fill in the blanks. This normative core is not always reducible to a fundamental ground like the theory of property, but certain normative cores are consistent with modern understandings of property. Certain elaborations of the theory of private property, plus the other institutions of political liberalism, give rise to particular normative cores. But there are other institutions and other political conceptions of how society ought to be structured, so that there are different possible normative cores. Such a "reasonable pluralism" is what is meant by the idea of "enterprise strategy," but even that concept is too much in the instrumental/descriptive mode.

One normative core of a stakeholder theory might be the doctrine of Fair Contracts. Another might be Feminist Standpoint Theory, rethinking how we would restructure "value-creating activity" along principles of caring and connection. A third would be an Ecological (or several ecological) Normative Principles. Figure 2 is suggestive of how these theories could be developed.

Any normative core must address the questions in columns A or B, or explain why these questions may be irrelevant, as in the ecological view. In addition, each narrative must place the normative core within a more full-fledged account of how we could understand value-creating activity differently (column C).

Research is proceeding along both the analytical and narrative lines. The rich panoply of concepts that is stakeholder theory threatens to replace, once and for all, the old way of thinking about the publicly held business as the sole property of stockholders, and offers the opportunity to build a wider shared vision of business into the twenty-first century.

Bibliography

Dill, W. (1958). Environment as an influence on managerial autonomy. *Administrative Science Quarterly*, 2 (4), 409–43.

Donaldson, T. J. and Preston, L. E. (1995). The stakeholder theory of the corporation: Concepts, evidence, and implications. *Academy of Management Review*, 20 (1), 65–91.

Freeman, R. E. (1984). *Strategic Management: A Stakeholder Approach*. Boston, MA: Pitman.

Freeman, R. E. (1994). The politics of stakeholder theory: Some future directions. *Business Ethics Quarterly*, 4 (4), 409–21.

Mason, R. and Mitroff, I. (1982). *Challenging Strategic Planning Assumptions*. New York: John Wiley and Sons.

Nasi, J. (1995). *Understanding Stakeholder Thinking*. Helsinki: LSR-Julkaisut Oy.

Thompson, J. (1967). *Organizations in Action*. New York: McGraw-Hill.

	A. *Corporations ought to be governed . . .*	B. *Managers ought to act . . .*	C. *The background disciplines of "value creation" are . . .*
Doctrine of Fair Contracts	. . . in accordance with the six principles. (Freeman, 1994)	. . . in the interests of stakeholders	– business theories – theories that explain stakeholder behavior
Feminist Standpoint Theory	. . . in accordance with the principles of caring/connection and relationships (Freeman, 1994)	. . . to maintain and care for relationships and networks of stakeholders	– business theories – feminist theory – social science understanding of networks
Ecological Principles	. . . in accordance with the principle of caring for the earth. (Freeman, 1994)	. . . to care for the earth.	– business theories – ecology – other

Figure 2   Stakeholder theory

stockholder

Max B. E. Clarkson and Michael Deck

is the owner of one or more shares of the authorized common stock issued by a corporation; also called shareholder. Share certificates specify the number of shares owned, which entitles the holder to a proportionate share of any distribution of the corporation's residual equity, after the payment of the claims of creditors, employees, and governments. The shares are not assessable and the stockholder has no liability for claims against the company. The stockholder's return on investment may be realized through dividends or an increase in the value of the shares. But there may also be no dividends and the company's shares may decline in value or become worthless.

Stockholders have rights, such as voting for directors and auditors, attending annual or special meetings, and voting on changes in the capital structure of the company. However, the stockholders do not "own the company." The corporation is not a piece of property. The board of directors, elected by the stockholders, is legally responsible for the management of the corporation. The fiduciary duty of the board is to the corporation itself and not solely to the stockholders in order to maximize their wealth. "Constituency statutes," now enacted in over forty states, recognize explicitly that the board may consider the best interests not only of stockholders, but also of the corporation's other stakeholders, such as the employees, customers, suppliers, and communities.

The corporation is a legal construct of society for accomplishing economic and social ends through the attraction and employment of private capital. Economic theory as commonly taught asserts that the relationship between the stockholder and the management of a publicly held corporation is a simple extension of the relationship between an entrepreneur (as principal) and a hired manager (as agent). This leads to the erroneous notion that "managers are agents of the stockholders." Managers are in fact and in law agents of the corporation.

strategy and ethics

Daniel R. Gilbert, Jr.

is a genre of management thought that deals with the question: Whose voices should be taken seriously, and on what terms, with regard to the future course of an organization? (*see* CORPORATE GOVERNANCE). Strategy and ethics is a liberal challenge to long-standing beliefs about the legitimacy of business and organizations. Strategy and ethics occupies a position on an educational margin between business policy and strategic management, on one hand, and business ethics and business and society, on the other.

A GENEALOGY OF STRATEGY AND ETHICS

A genealogy of thinking about strategy and ethics can be traced across four "generations," each of which is distinguished by a particular meaning of "good" management policy.

First, strategy and ethics emerged as an expression of the premise that it is "good" policy for executives to know themselves. "Know and admit to your own voice" is the imperative. Kenneth Andrews (1980: 85) argued that executives should pay close attention to the values by which they can live: "Strategy is a human construction; it must in the long run be responsive to human needs. It must ultimately inspire commitment. It must stir an organization to successful striving against competition. Some people have to have their hearts in it" (*see* VIRTUE ETHICS).

Second, strategy and ethics evolved as an expression of the premise that it is "good" policy for executives to pay attention to other voices raised outside their organizations. "Listen to the rhetorics of other general views of the world" is the imperative here. This imperative is manifest in the competitive strategy approach to strategic management, where Michael Porter (1985) has identified the "five forces" of buyers, suppliers, rivals, new entrants, and purveyors of substitute products. These are generic voices in the vicinity of an organization. This imperative is also manifest in the study of business and society, where Lee Preston and James Post (1975) argued that business organizations are one part of a pattern of "interpenetrating systems."

Third, strategy and ethics has taken a new turn on the premise that it is "good" policy for executives to listen carefully, and to be prepared to respond, to specific persons expressing their own voices. "Listen to what specific persons are saying about their specific stakes" is the imperative here. These persons are called stakeholders. R. Edward Freeman (1984: 46) defined a stakeholder as "any group or individual who can affect or is affected by the achievement of the organization's objectives." Freeman argued that a stakeholder approach to strategy should involve considerations of "distributive justice" (*see* STAKEHOLDER THEORY; DISTRIBUTIVE JUSTICE).

Fourth, strategy and ethics has evolved more recently on the premise that it is "good" policy for executives to justify corporate strategies in accordance with certain common ethical principles. "Think carefully about the specific terms of your relationships with others and find ways to agree on those terms" is the imperative here. Freeman and Gilbert (1988) give the name "Personal Projects Enterprise Strategy" to one version of this imperative. They propose that strategies should honor, among others, a principle of personal autonomy and a principle of voluntary agreement.

Gilbert has gone further to argue that strategy is inseparable from a person's ethical responsibility to contribute to human solidarity. He calls this account "Strategy Through Convention" (Gilbert, 1992). Edward Stead and Jean Stead (1992) have extended this particular generation of strategy and ethics by linking strategic management to an environmental ethics.

An Opposing View to Strategy and Ethics

Strategy and ethics should not be confused with strategic ethics. Strategic ethics is an argument that institutions can be structured to safeguard the rights of a strategist against the encroachment of other people. Strategic ethics is based on the assumption that trust is fleeting in human relationships, because people are prone to opportunism unless they are given incentives to act

otherwise. Oliver Williamson (1985) proposed one set of safeguards based on minimizing transactions costs. Robert Axelrod (1984) proposed a "tit for tat" strategy as a workable safeguard.

Strategic ethics is an antithesis of the strategy and ethics genre of management thought. On the strategic ethics view, the praiseworthy strategist is adept at rationally maximizing the gains from relationships with others (*see* EGOISM, PSYCHOLOGICAL EGOISM, AND ETHICAL EGOISM). On the strategy and ethics view, the praiseworthy strategist is adept at bringing different voices into strategic deliberations and actions.

Strategy and Ethics, and Feminist Ethics

Three feminist ethics themes are prominent in the strategy and ethics genre. First, strategy and ethics educators create a prominent place for new and distinct voices in their accounts about business and organizations. This emphasis parallels a feminist concern with giving voice to those who have previously been silenced in modern institutions. This facet of strategy and ethics challenges a traditional view that the history of an organization can be explained in terms of the exploits of one more-or-less-omniscient mastermind, usually the chief executive.

Second, strategy and ethics educators create an account in which new and different voices participate in debates about the legitimacy of modern business institutions. This emphasis parallels a feminist concern with empowering those who were previously powerless. This facet of strategy and ethics challenges the traditional view – for example, articulated by Andrew Carnegie (1920) – that ordinary citizens should trust business leaders to practice as wise stewards who have the good of society foremost in their minds.

Third, strategy and ethics educators spread a belief that some liberal conception of a common good can be advanced as a direct consequence of management practice. This emphasis parallels a feminist concern with empathy and human connection. This facet of strategy and ethics challenges a traditional view from neoclassical economics – sustained in strategic management

– that the greatest social good will come as a byproduct of the market mechanism.

Bibliography

Andrews, K. (1980). *The Concept of Corporate Strategy*, revd. edn. Homewood, IL: Richard D. Irwin.

Axelrod, R. (1984). *The Evolution of Cooperation*. New York: Basic Books.

Carnegie, A. (1920). *The Autobiography of Andrew Carnegie*. Boston, MA: Houghton Mifflin.

Freeman, R. E. (1984). *Strategic Management: A Stakeholder Approach*. Boston, MA: Pitman.

Freeman, R. E. and Gilbert, D. R., Jr. (1988). *Corporate Strategy and the Search for Ethics*. Englewood Cliffs, NJ: Prentice-Hall.

Gilbert, D. R., Jr. (1992). *The Twilight of Corporate Strategy: A Comparative Ethical Critique*. New York: Oxford University Press.

Porter, M. (1985). *Competitive Strategy: Techniques for Analyzing Industries and Competitors*. New York: Free Press.

Preston, L. and Post, J. (1975). *Private Management and Public Policy: The Principle of Public Responsibility*. Englewood Cliffs, NJ: Prentice-Hall.

Stead, W. E. and Stead, J. (1992). *Management for a Small Planet*. Thousand Oaks, CA: Sage.

Williamson, O. (1985). *The Economic Institutions of Capitalism: Firms, Markets, Relational Contracting*. New York: Free Press.

sweatshops

Denis G. Arnold

The term "sweatshop" is typically used to denote a factory where workers are subjected to working conditions that harm their well-being. These might include dangerous health and safety conditions, extremely low wages, extremely long work hours, physical or psychological abuse by supervisors, and disregard for local labor laws.

The resurgence of illegal sweatshops in North America and Europe has received considerable attention. However, it is the offshore labor practices of North American and European based multinational enterprises (MNEs) and their contractors that have been most controversial. This is partly due to the fact that many of the labor practices in question are legal outside North America and Europe, or are tolerated by corrupt or repressive political regimes. Unlike the recent immigrants who toil in the illegal sweatshops of North America and Europe, workers in developing nations typically have no recourse to the law or social service agencies.

Disagreements regarding sweatshops are at the core of contemporary debates regarding globalization. Many economists argue that what is needed are more, not fewer, sweatshops. This position is grounded in the idea that the exploitation of a natural resource such as labor will allow developing nations to attract foreign direct investment. This, in turn, will stimulate economic growth and increase employment levels. Providing workers with wages and working conditions above what the market demands will, it is argued, raise unemployment levels. Furthermore, because sweatshop workers often earn more than they otherwise would, it is argued that they are fortunate to have such jobs. For these reasons, such economists reject calls for new regulations governing the treatment of workers in factories in developing nations.

In reply, anti-sweatshop activists and numerous non-governmental organizations argue that the necessary preconditions for a free market in labor often do not exist in developing nations because of the desperate circumstances of workers and the coercive influence of governmental, or quasi-governmental, organizations. These critics accuse MNEs such as Disney and Nike of the ruthless exploitation of workers in their contract factories in developing nations. This position is grounded in the idea that core labor standards should be respected. Furthermore, because sweatshops produce many negative externalities, such as social disruption caused by urban migration and the growth of slums around free trade zones, it is argued that their benefits are overstated. For these reasons, such critics urge the imposition of new regulations governing the treatment of workers in factories in developing nations.

A third position calls upon MNEs to voluntarily improve the health and safety conditions in their offshore factories and to increase wages and benefits. This view is grounded in the idea that MNEs must, at a minimum, respect the basic human rights of workers. Furthermore, this view holds that it is strategically valuable for MNEs to respect workers' rights because doing so may result in strategic advantages like improved relationships with key stakeholders such as customers and investors. This view is supported by the fact that some MNEs such as Motorola have long placed a high priority on respect for the basic human rights of workers. If some MNEs are capable of treating workers with dignity and respect while remaining profitable, then *mutatis mutandis* it should be possible for others to do the same.

In response to the public uproar over the use of sweatshop labor, several MNEs have recently implemented innovative new programs aimed at improving the well-being of their workers. Nike, Mattel, and Adidas–Salomon have each put in place a series of morally imaginative programs concerning such important issues as child labor, worker health and safety, and worker education. These programs have been studied by academics and now serve as models for other companies that wish to improve their global labor practices.

Bibliography

Arnold, D. G. and Bowie, N. E. (2003). Sweatshops and respect for persons. *Business Ethics Quarterly*, **13** (2), 221–42.

Arnold, D. G. and Hartman, L. P. (2003). Moral imagination and the future of sweatshops. *Business and Society Review*, 108 (4), 425–61.

Hartman, L. P., Arnold, D. G., and Wokutch, R. E. (2004). *Rising Above Sweatshops: Innovative Management Responses to Global Labor Challenges*. Westport, CT: Praeger.

Maitland, I. (2004). The great non-debate over international sweatshops. In T. Beauchamp and N. E. Bowie (eds.), *Ethical Theory and Business*, 7th edn. Englewood Cliffs, NJ: Prentice-Hall.

Rosen, E. I. (2002). *Making Sweatshops: The Globalization of the US Apparel Industry*. Berkeley: University of California Press.

Sethi, S. P. (2003). *Setting Global Standards: Guidelines for Creating Codes in Multinational Corporations*. Hoboken, NJ: Wiley.

taxation, ethics of

Julie A. Roin

Any one may so arrange his affairs that his taxes shall be as low as possible; he is not bound to choose that pattern which will best pay the Treasury; there is not even a patriotic duty to increase one's taxes. (Judge Learned Hand, *Helvering vs. Gregory*, 69 F.2d 809, 810 (2d Cir. 1934))

The code of conduct that passes for tax ethics in the United States has been described by one commentator as an "uneasy truce between notions of personal avarice and good citizenship" (Holden, 1991). Perhaps because of the additional difficulties of arranging such a truce in the context of complex yet ambiguous tax rules, the parameters of acceptable taxpayer behavior have been more fully explored in the context of the federal income tax than any other. This entry focuses on the standards developed in the income tax context and allows readers to extrapolate from them to other situations.

STANDARDS FOR TAX RETURN REPORTING

Although the Internal Revenue Service has extensive audit powers, it has never had the resources necessary to investigate more than a small fraction of the returns filed. The vast majority of taxpayers must therefore self-assess their tax obligations. It is plainly illegal, and not simply unethical, to lie to the Internal Revenue Service by filing a tax return containing false statements. Fraud on, and making false statements to, the Internal Revenue Service are felonies which can lead to the imposition of substantial monetary penalties as well as incarceration. Similarly, taxpayers may on their returns take only positions that they believe in

good faith to be correct. Though incorrectly reporting the tax consequences of transactions (as opposed to misreporting factual issues, such as the existence of transactions) rarely leads to criminal charges, substantial civil penalties can be invoked for "negligence" (which includes the failure to make a reasonable attempt to comply with the tax law) and the disregard of rules and regulations (including careless, reckless, and intentional disregard of the same). The traditional baseline for acceptable (and perhaps "ethical") tax behavior has been that necessary to avoid the imposition of this civil penalty.

Good faith does not require resolving all ambiguous questions in favor of the government. Taxpayers may take any position for which they believe in good faith a "reasonable basis" exists under the law. Because taxpayers often lack detailed knowledge of the tax laws, they may rely on a professional tax preparer's conclusion as to the merits of a particular tax position. The professional organizations that regulate lawyers and accountants allow their members to advise tax-reporting positions where there exists "some realistic possibility of success if the matter is litigated." The professional need not believe that the position will prevail if the matter is actually litigated. A lawyer, for example, may advise the statement of positions most favorable to the client if the lawyer has a good faith belief that those positions are warranted in existing law or can be supported by a good faith argument for an extension, modification, or reversal of existing law. A lawyer can have a good faith belief in this context even if the lawyer believes the client's position probably will not prevail (ABA, 1985).

In drafting its standards for enrolling and disciplining agents practicing before it, the Treasury Department concluded the realistic possibility standard would be satisfied if "a reasonable and well-informed analysis by a person knowledgeable in the tax law would lead such a person to conclude that the position has approximately a one in three, or greater, likelihood of being sustained on its merits" (Circular 230, 10.34). A professional return preparer, according to these same standards, may sign returns incorporating such positions, as well as positions which, though not "frivolous," fail the realistic possibility standard but are adequately disclosed to the Internal Revenue Service on the return. Preparers should not sign returns incorporating weaker positions in the absence of disclosure, nor should they advise taking such positions without first explaining to their clients the penalties they risk incurring, as well as any opportunities of avoiding such penalties through disclosure. Taxpayers seeking to avoid the negligence penalty are held to a slightly different standard than tax preparers. No penalty attaches to reporting positions supported by "substantial authority." Treasury's definition of "substantial authority" closely resembles that of the "realistic possibility of success" standard applicable to tax preparers (Treas. Reg. §1.6662–4(d)(2)). But taxpayers have less leeway than preparers with respect to weaker claims. Whereas preparers can avoid penalties by disclosing all non-frivolous claims, disclosure protects taxpayers only with respect to positions for which "a reasonable basis" exists. This "reasonable basis" standard is "significantly higher than not frivolous or not patently improper" (Treas. Reg. §1.6662–3(b)(3)). Taxpayers, unlike tax preparers, thus run the risk of incurring a penalty when taking non-frivolous positions that lack "a reasonable basis." This statutory scheme may encourage taxpayers to take such positions without disclosing them to the Internal Revenue Service, creating a conflict of interest between them and their tax advisor or preparer – and raising ethical questions about the preparer's duty of representation.

Post-Return Behavior

Concerns about acceptable behavior do not end with the filing of tax returns. One perennial issue is whether taxpayers who discover errors on previously filed returns are obligated to file correct, amended returns. There is no statutory or regulatory authority requiring taxpayers to file amended returns; nonetheless, lawyers believe that they have an ethical obligation to advise their clients to file such returns and that they may be required to withdraw from further representation with regard to the matter should the client decide not to file such a return. The precise extent of such a required withdrawal can be uncertain due to the multi-year effect of some tax decisions.

Once unlucky enough to be the targets of audits, taxpayers and their agents should cooperate with the tax authorities. Both taxpayers and their advisors should provide records and other information requested by the Internal Revenue Service unless they have reasonable cause to believe that such material is covered by a legal privilege. The criminal penalty against fraud and perjury continues in effect; furthermore, if a taxpayer is represented by an attorney, the attorney is prohibited by legal canons (as well as by the Treasury Department's disciplinary rules which apply to all taxpayer agents, not just attorneys) from "mislead[ing] the Internal Revenue Service deliberately, either by misstatements or by silence or by permitting the client to mislead" (ABA, 1985). As attorneys are also forbidden from revealing client confidences, when confronted with a client intent on misleading or lying to the Internal Revenue Service, an attorney must withdraw from representing the client. Whether a given course of conduct (or silence) rises to the level of "misleading" can be the subject of dispute.

It again bears repeating that the above discussion summarizes a minimalist definition of acceptable tax behavior. Those who ascribe to Justice Holmes's aphorism that "taxes are what we pay for civilized society" believe that far more candor and cooperation is required before taxpayers can call their actions with regard to the tax system "ethical." On the other hand, because tax laws are designed in part to influence behavior, even the most conscientious taxpayer will have trouble deciding when legal strategies to minimize taxes are appropriate responses to economic legislation and when they merely exploit tax "loopholes."

Bibliography

American Bar Association (1985). Comm. on.Ethics and Professional Responsibility, Formal Op. 85–352. Available from ABA, 750 N. Lake Shore Drive. Chicago, IL.

American Institute of Certified Public Accountants (1985). Statements on Responsibilities in Tax Practice No. 1. Available from AICPA, 1211 Avenue of the Americas. New York.

Cooper, G. (1980). The avoidance dynamic: A tale of tax planning, tax ethics, and tax reform. *Columbia Law Review*, **80**, 1553–1622.

Holden, J. P. (1991). Practitioners' standard of practice and the taxpayer's reporting position. *Capital University Law Review*, **20**, 327–44.

Holden, J. P. and Friedman, R. E. (1992). Income tax return accuracy: Taxpayer responsibility and practitioner responsibility. *USC Law Center Tax Institute series on Major Tax Planning*, **44** (1), 10-1–10-22. (Slightly expanded version of first article.)

Schenk, D. H. (1991). Conflicts between the tax lawyer and the client: Vignettes in the law office. *Capital University Law Review*, **20**, 387–420.

US Treasury Department Circular No. 230. Available from the Treasury Dept., Main Treasury Building, Washington, DC.

teaching business ethics

Gerald F. Cavanagh

provides education in the cognitive and habitual skills needed to make ethical judgments on business matters. Ethics is a system of moral principles for distinguishing right from wrong, and the methods of applying them. Ethics enables one to make better decisions and ultimately to develop virtue and character. Business ethics equips one to systematically look beyond one's own interests to the interests of others. The terms "ethical" and "moral" are often used interchangeably.

Business ethics provides the language, concepts, and models that aid one in making moral judgments. Teaching business ethics provides practical guidance through three steps: (1) gathering relevant factual information; (2) analysis using the ethical norms(s) that are most applicable; (3) making the judgment as to whether the act or policy is ethical or not. The facts gathered must be appropriate and sufficient for judging (*see* METHODOLOGIES OF BUSINESS ETHICS RESEARCH). The moral norms most often used are rights and duties, justice, utilitarianism and caring. The flow chart in figure 1 presents one approach to teaching business ethics.

The ethical norm of personal rights and duties indicates a person's entitlement to something and parallel duties to others. Rights stem from the human dignity of the person, and enable individuals to pursue their own interests. Rights also impose the duties of correlative prohibitions or requirements on others.

Justice requires all parties to be guided by fairness, equity, and impartiality. Justice calls for even-handed treatment of individuals and groups in the distribution of benefits and burdens of society, in the administration of laws and regulations, and in the imposition of sanctions. Justice considers how all stakeholders are impacted by the consequences of a business act, including workers, customers, the poor, and the community.

The norm of utilitarianism enables one to judge that an act is right if it produces the "greatest good for the greatest number," or the greatest net benefit when all the costs and benefits (financial and otherwise) are taken into account. The decision process is similar to a cost-benefit analysis applied to all stakeholders who are touched by the decision.

The norm of caring stems from our relationships to other people; it is an extension of family life. Personal relationships, trust, teamwork, and communication are built upon caring. Caring engages our emotions, as does any ethical reasoning. In making any ethical judgment, it is essential to consider the interests of others, and this requires one to empathize with those that are affected by one's decisions.

Ethics is the foundation for, but goes beyond, legal ethics. Law specifies the minimum requirement. To provide a level playing field in a healthy society, legislation is necessary. For example, if pollution were not regulated, unethical firms would benefit financially, at least in the short term. However, ethics often calls us to actions above what the law requires.

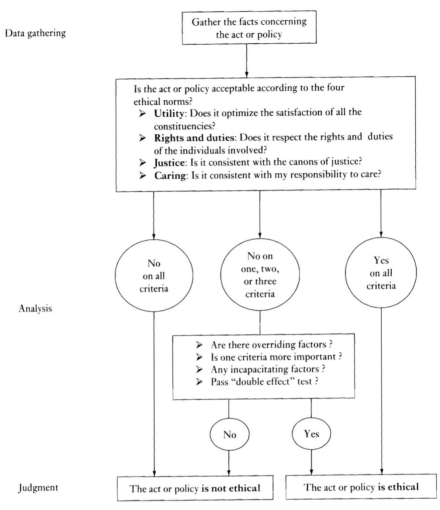

Data gathering

Gather the facts concerning
the act or policy

Is the act or policy acceptable according to the four
ethical norms?
  ➢ **Utility**: Does it optimize the satisfaction of all the
    constituencies?
  ➢ **Rights and duties**: Does it respect the rights and duties
    of the individuals involved?
  ➢ **Justice**: Is it consistent with the canons of justice?
  ➢ **Caring**: Is it consistent with my responsibility to care?

No
on all
criteria

No on
one, two,
or three
criteria

Yes
on all
criteria

Analysis

  ➢ Are there overriding factors ?
  ➢ Is one criteria more important ?
  ➢ Any incapacitating factors ?
  ➢ Pass "double effect" test ?

No   Yes

Judgment   The act or policy **is not ethical**   The act or policy **is ethical**

Figure 1   Flow diagram of ethical decision making
Source: Adapted from Gerald F. Cavanagh, Dennis J. Moberg and Manuel Velasquez, "Making Business Ethics
Practical," *Business Ethics Quarterly* (July 1995).

PEDAGOGY FOR BUSINESS ETHICS

Teaching business ethics requires one to consider substantive business issues with regard to
the ethics of the individual, the firm, and the
market system. First, issues internal to the
firm, such as work, employee rights, worker
satisfaction, worker safety, and discrimination
in employment are often treated. Second, the
environment external to the firm: customers,
advertising, media, energy use, pollution, the
environment, and sustainability (*see* ENVIRON-
MENT AND ENVIRONMENTAL ETHICS).
Third, the strengths and weaknesses of the busi-

ness system itself are examined. Citing the positive ethical outcomes of the market system, such
as quality products, services, and jobs, along
with freedom and innovation, we strive to lessen
the negative outcomes, such as suppression of
worker wages, environmental degradation, and
the fostering of selfishness, greed, and corruption.

Teaching business ethics today demands
that one understand other peoples and cultures and their ways of thinking and
acting (*see* MULTICULTURALISM, ISLAM, JU-
DAISM, HINDUISM, and specific country
profiles).

Good teaching demands active learning and interaction (see Piper et al., 1993). Standard methods of teaching business ethics include input (reading, lecture, film), business cases (*see* CASE METHOD), web information and communication, written assignments, discussion, and projects (often with teams to teach cooperation). There are excellent business ethics texts available, such as Velasquez (2002), De George (1999), Boatright (2002), and Cavanagh (1998). Good Internet sites are also available, as are films. A journal, *Teaching Business Ethics*, provides some useful material.

PERSONAL VALUES, CHARACTER, AND MORAL DEVELOPMENT

Ethics provides the skills to decide specific acts or policies. Ethical values also influence ethical behavior and moral development (*see* VALUES). Consistently making ethical decisions deepens a lasting belief that a certain goal or mode of conduct is morally better than the opposite goal or conduct and this supports more ethical behavior and ultimately virtue and good character. This can then develop better managerial values and support a more ethical climate within the organization.

Bibliography

Boatright, J. R. (2002). *Ethics and the Conduct of Business.* Upper Saddle River, NJ: Prentice-Hall. (Well organized, comprehensive overview of business ethics.)

Cavanagh, G. F. (1998). *American Business Values: With International Perspectives*, 4th edn. Upper Saddle River, NJ: Prentice-Hall. (Historical and behavioral overview of values, along with ethics and cases.)

De George, R. T. (1999). *Business Ethics*, 5th edn. Upper Saddle River, NJ: Prentice-Hall. (Clear, philosophical approach.)

Donaldson, T., Werhane, P. H., and Cording, M. (2002). *Ethical Issues in Business: A Philosophical Approach*, 7th edn. Upper Saddle River, NJ: Prentice-Hall. (Excellent collection of philosophical articles and cases.)

Hosmer, L. T. (2002). *The Ethics of Management*, 4th edn. Homewood, IL: Irwin. (Ethics cases by strategic management expert.)

Piper, T., Gentile, M., and Parks, S. D. (1993), *Can Ethics Be Taught? Perspectives, Challenges and Approaches at Harvard Business School.* Boston, MA: Harvard Business School. (Overview of Harvard Business School's experience with teaching business ethics.)

Teaching Business Ethics (1997–2003). Vols. 1–7. (A journal on the subject.)

Velasquez, M. G. (2002). *Business Ethics: Concepts and Cases*, 5th. edn. Upper Saddle River, NJ: Prentice-Hall. (Comprehensive, engaging text with cases interwoven.)

Selected Internet sites

Aspen Business Ethics Case Studies http://www.caseplace.org

Business Ethics (emphasis on Canada) http://www.businessethics.ca

Business and Sustainable Development http://www.busglobal.com

Caux Round Table Principles for Business http://www.cauxroundtable.org

Ethics Classroom http://www.ethicsclassroom.info/

Ethics Resource Center http://www.ethics.org

Santa Clara Markkula Center for Applied Ethics (excellent links to many other sites) http://www.scu.edu/ethics

Transparency International http://www.transparency.org

UN Global Compact http://www.unglobal.compact.org

teams

Robert A. Phillips

A team refers to a special subclass of cooperative scheme characterized by a particularly high degree of interdependence and close-knittedness and often focused on a single goal. While sports examples abound, a good, non-athletic example may be a project team within a manufacturing firm. Although the members may all be employees of the same corporation and thus have obligations to that organization and the economy at large as members of these respective cooperative schemes, they are also part of a team with the concomitant increase in ethical content. They spend many hours a day together, they share a common goal, they are more likely to go out of their way to assist teammates, and they depend upon one another more than the organization at large. The concept of a team, on this understanding, indicates a higher level of commitment than many other similar cooperative schemes and therefore will contain a higher level of ethical content.

The necessity of cooperation in value creation and exchange relationships (i.e., virtually all economic interactions) is readily apparent. This need to cooperate leads inexorably to the demand that individual economic entities work as parts of teams. There are many things that can only be done by teams and many others which can be done better by teams than by individuals. Further evidence of the importance of teams can be seen in the preeminent role of building "team skills" in most business schools. One's ability to work as part of a team is, more often than not, vital to success in the business world.

However, insofar as most issues with high ethical content occur in interpersonal contexts – indeed, some would argue that ethics for a hermit is an empty or meaningless concept – the benefits of cooperative behavior carry with them a great deal of ethical baggage. A good starting point is to ask this question: Does a person have greater obligations to a "teammate" than to society at large? If so, what is the source and nature of this increased obligation?

Philosophical justification for behavior within teams can be found (in addition to its utility for those of consequentialist leanings) in the concept of fairness or fair play (*see* CONSEQUENTIAL-ISM). Alluded to by John Locke (1690) and Adam Smith (1790), and later by H. L. A. Hart (1955), the principle of fairness finds its most sophisticated defense in the work of John Rawls. The "principle of fairness," combined with certain natural duties, represents the moral rules for individuals in Rawls's much-acclaimed *A Theory of Justice* (1971). As Rawls puts it in another work:

> The principle of fair play may be defined as follows. Suppose there is a mutually beneficial and just scheme of cooperation, and that the advantages it yields can only be obtained if everyone, or nearly everyone, cooperates. Suppose further that cooperation requires a certain sacrifice from each person, or at least involves a certain restriction of his liberty. Suppose finally that the benefits produced by cooperation are, up to a certain point, free: that is, the scheme of cooperation is unstable in the sense that if any one person knows that all (or nearly all) of the others will continue to do their part, he will still be able to share a gain from the scheme even if he does not do his part. Under these conditions a person who has accepted the benefits of the scheme is bound by a duty of fair play to do his part and not to take advantage of the free benefit by not cooperating. (Rawls, 1964: 9–10)

The principle takes as one of its major concerns the issue of free-riders within a cooperative scheme. One of the greatest problems with using teams is that there are often members of a team who fail to do their share. Free-riders hope to be carried along by the success and effort of others within the cooperative scheme while themselves contributing far less than their role and the benefits they receive would dictate. The principle of fairness provides a moral foundation for the obligations of individuals within a co-operative scheme as well as the obligations of the scheme to the individual in the form of provision of a fair share of the benefits of the scheme.

Although providing solutions to the myriad ethical issues would be rather difficult (if not impossible) in the abstract, it might nonetheless be useful to at least point out some of the possible areas of controversy inasmuch as the recognition of ethical content in a situation may help properly frame the issues. Can the majority (ethically) force their will on the minority or an individual for the sake of the team goal or purpose? Should the individual *voluntarily* yield to the team for the sake of the goal? Should such a goal or purpose come from within or from outside the team and will the source make a difference in the level of commitment required? What about the assigning of responsibility and accountability both within teams and for the effect of the team as a whole on the rest of the world? Where is the line between team leadership and coercion? What are the obligations of being a follower? These are just a few of the possible ethical pitfalls to be aware of when thinking about teams, especially in a business context.

Bibliography

Hart, H. L. A. (1955). Are there any natural rights? *Philosophical Review*, **64**, 175–91.

Katzenbach, J. R. and Smith, D. K. (1993). *The Wisdom of Teams*. Boston, MA: Harvard University Press.

Locke, J. (1690). *Second Treatise of Government*, para. 130. Numerous editions are available.

Rawls, J. (1964). Legal obligation and the duty of fair play. In S. Hook (ed.), *Law and Philosophy*. New York: New York University Press, 3–18.

Rawls, J. (1971). *A Theory of Justice*. Cambridge, MA: Harvard University Press.
Smith, A. (1790). *Theory of Moral Sentiments*, Part II, Section II, ch. II. Numerous editions are available.

technology, ethical issues in

Kristin Shrader-Frechette

The US government projects cost increases for drugs of between 10 and 14 percent, per year, through at least 2011. US consumers claim the pharmaceutical technologies are too expensive, given that Canadians pay $34 for the same dose of the cancer drug Tamoxifen that costs US citizens $240. They also say that because the US National Institutes of Health, using citizens' tax dollars, funded most research on Tamoxifen and other drugs, citizens typically "pay twice" for pharmaceuticals. Yet the drug industry makes greater profits than any other contemporary enterprise. In response, the pharmaceutical companies claim it cost nearly four times as much to bring a new drug to market, in 2003, as in 1990. But the US Food and Drug Administration says that, since 1989, only 15 percent of new drugs provided remedies that were superior to those already on the market. It says most of the costs of new drugs is for advertising, for less desirable products, and not for research (Greider, 2003; see Huffington, 2003).

Who is right in the pharmaceutical technology battle? Ethicists have a variety of answers, not only to this problem but also to other technological problems, such as World Trade Organization agreements that override national environmental and safety standards (see Wallach and Sforza, 1999). In part as a result of such trade agreements, the World Health Organization says, for example, that the application of chemical technologies annually kills at least 40,000 persons worldwide. Most of these deaths are from use of pesticides in developing nations that are banned in the developed world. As the drug and pesticide cases illustrate, the design and employment of technologies often raise troubling ethical issues, questions about right and wrong.

Most of the ethical issues concerning technology focus on questions of risk. Some of these questions include whether persons have been informed adequately about technological dangers, whether they have consented to them, whether the risks are equitably distributed, and whether risk imposers have been compensated for the threats they generate.

Technological risks can be divided into two main types, societal and individual. Societal risks (such as those from underground gasoline storage tanks) are largely involuntarily imposed. Individual risks (such as those from using a regulator to engage in scuba diving) are largely voluntarily chosen. Societal risks often raise greater ethical questions than individual risks because their potential victims typically have less choice regarding whether or not to accept them. For example, people choose whether to become scuba divers and what kind of breathing equipment to use. Usually, however, they have less choice over whether to allow a gas station to be built near them.

Much ethical debate focuses on whether technological risks ought to be evaluated by members of the technical community (Cooke, 1992; see Sunstein, 2002) or by laypersons who are most likely to be their victims (Freudenburg, 1988). Scientists and engineers often treat the assessment of technological risks as the paternalistic prerogative of experts, in part because they claim that the definitions of irrational, ignorant, or risk-averse laypersons could impede social and technological progress (Douglas and Wildavsky, 1982; Sunstein, 2002). Many moral philosophers argue, in response, that evaluations of technology are not only matters of scientifically defensible outcomes but also matters of just procedures, because they affect public welfare (Cranor, 1992; Shrader-Frechette, 1991, 2002). Also, because even scientists and engineers have well-known prejudices in defining and estimating technological risks – such as the over-confidence biases in giving overly positive estimates of risk (Cooke, 1992; Kahneman, Slovic, and Tversky, 1982) – ethicists claim that we need democratic, as well as technical, evaluations of technology.

Other ethical controversies concern what level of technological safety is safe enough. Utilitarian philosophers, who emphasize maximizing overall welfare, typically argue that we can serve the greater good by accepting low levels of risk and by not forcing industry to spend money to avoid unlikely hazards, such as nuclear core melts or chemical explosions. Harsanyi (1975), for example, argues that "worst cases" of technological risk rarely occur. He claims that forcing industry to avoid worst cases is too conservative, impedes social progress, and over-emphasizes small probabilities of harm. Egalitarian philosophers, who emphasize the equal rights of all persons to protection from harm, maintain that the people deserve protection, even from unlikely technological threats. Shrader-Frechette (1991, 1993), for example, argues that because the probabilities associated with technological risks are often uncertain, the public deserves protection from them, even if they are small. Their size is dwarfed by potentially catastrophic consequences such as global warming or toxic leaks (see Rawls, 1971). Some egalitarian philosophers also claim that fairness and equal treatment require technology assessors and decisionmakers to reverse the burden of proof and place it on those who impose technological risks rather than on those likely to be their victims. They say that because causal chains of harm are difficult to prove – and because risk victims are less able than risk imposers to bear the costs of faulty technological evaluations – those who design, implement, apply, or benefit from a technology should bear its greatest risks (Cranor, 1992).

Still other ethical issues regarding technology address the criteria under which it is acceptable to impose some hazard (for example, chemical effluents) on workers or on the public. One important criterion for risk imposition is the equity of distribution of the risks and benefits associated with an activity. For example, Parfit (1983) argues that temporal differences among people/generations are not a relevant basis for discriminating against them with respect to risk. He and others maintain that a technological risk is less acceptable to the degree that it imposes costs on the future but awards benefits in the present. Commercial nuclear fission, for example, benefits mainly present generations, whereas its risks and costs – because of radioactive waste – will be borne primarily by members of future generations.

On the one hand, many economists evaluating technology follow the utilitarian philosophy. They question notions of distributive equity and argue that a bloody loaf of bread – earned through dirty or risky technologies – is better than none at all, because such technologies bring tax and employment benefits. On the other hand, egalitarian philosophers evaluating technology argue for "geographical equity" (Shrader-Frechette, 1993, 1995) and "environmental justice" (Bullard, 1993). They maintain that technological risks should be distributed equally across generations, regions, and nations. Otherwise, they claim, economically and socially disenfranchised persons will bear disproportionate burdens of technological risks. Economically, educationally, or socially disenfranchised persons also are less likely than others to be able to give genuine free informed consent to technological and workplace risks (MacLean, 1986; Rescher, 1983; Bullard, 1993; Shrader-Frechette, 2002). Chemical facilities and hazardous waste dumps, for example, tend to be located in areas where income, education, and political power are the lowest.

To such equity and consent arguments, some utilitarian ethicists have responded that no instances of distribution or consent are perfect. They claim that the greater good is achieved by risk-for-money trade-offs when workers accept jobs in dangerous technologies or when citizens accept the tax benefits of a hazardous technology in their community. Egalitarians like MacLean (1986) claim, however, that some values (like bodily health and environmental security) ought not to be traded for financial compensation. Gewirth (1982) also argues, for example, that persons have a moral and legal right not to be caused to have cancer. Such ethical debates over risk imposition and trade-offs generally focus on opposed views about rights, paternalism, human dignity, equal treatment, and adequate compensation for technological risk (Thomson, 1986).

Another aspect of the consent and compensation debate over technological risk concerns liability. Current US laws, for example, excuse nuclear power plant licensees from 99 percent of their liability for accidents, even when they intentionally violate safety laws. Technologists justify this liability limit on grounds of economic efficiency and the necessity to promote essential, but dangerous, technologies. A number of ethicists argue that these exclusions violate citizens' rights to due process and to equal protection (Shrader-Frechette, 1993, 1991).

As this discussion of equity, consent, and compensation reveals, the ethical issues associated with technology may be just as important as the scientific and safety issues. Once we understand the magnitude of these ethical issues, we are forced to ask about a technology, not only "how safe is safe enough?" but also "how safe is equitable enough?" or "how safe is voluntary enough?" or "how safe is compensated enough?"

Bibliography

Bullard, R. D. (1993). *Confronting Environmental Racism.* Boston, MA: South End Press.

Cooke, R. (1992). *Experts in Uncertainty: Opinion and Subjective Probability in Science.* New York: Oxford University Press.

Cranor, C. (1992). *Regulating Toxic Substances: A Philosophy of Science and the Law.* New York: Oxford University Press.

Douglas, M. and Wildavsky, A. (1982). *Risk and Culture.* Berkeley: University of California Press.

Freudenburg, W. (1988). Perceived risk, real risk: Social science and the art of probabilistic risk assessment. *Science*, 242, 44–9.

Gewirth, A. (1982). *Human Rights.* Chicago: University of Chicago Press.

Greider, K. (2003). *The Big Fix.* New York: Public Affairs.

Harsanyi, J. (1975). Can the maximin principle serve as a basis for morality? *American Political Science Review*, 69, 594–605.

Huffington, A. (2003). *Pigs at the Trough.* New York: Crown.

Kahneman, D., Slovic, P., and Tversky, A. (eds.) (1982). *Judgment under Uncertainty: Heuristics and Biases.* Cambridge: Cambridge University Press.

Kates, R. and National Academy of Engineering (eds.) (1986). *Hazards: Technology and Fairness.* Washington, DC: National Academy Press.

Kneese, A. V., Ben-David, S., and Schulze, W. D. (1982). The ethical foundations of benefit-cost analysis. In D. MacLean and P. Brown (eds.), *Energy and the Future.* Totowa, NJ: Rowman and Littlefield, 59–74.

MacLean, D. (ed.) (1986). *Values at Risk.* Totowa, NJ: Rowman and Allanheld.

National Research Council (1983). *Risk Assessment in the Federal Government: Managing the Process.* Washington, DC: National Academy Press.

National Research Council (1993). *Issues in Risk Assessment.* Washington, DC: National Academy Press.

Parfit, D. (1983). The further future: The discount rate. In D. MacLean and P. Brown (eds.), *Energy and the Future.* Totowa, NJ: Rowman and Littlefield, 31–7.

Porter, A. L., Rossini, F. A., Carpenter, S. R., and Roper, A. T. (1980). *A Guidebook for Technology Assessment and Impact Analysis.* New York: Holland.

Rawls, J. (1971). *A Theory of Justice.* Cambridge, MA: Harvard University Press.

Rescher, N. (1983). *Risk: A Philosophical Introduction.* Washington, DC: University Press of America.

Sagoff, M. (1988). *The Economy of the Earth.* Cambridge: Cambridge University Press.

Shrader-Frechette, K. (1991). *Risk and Rationality: Philosophical Foundations for Populist Reforms.* Berkeley: University of California Press.

Shrader-Frechette, K. (1993). *Burying Uncertainty: Risk and the Case Against Geological Disposal of Nuclear Waste.* Berkeley: University of California Press.

Shrader-Frechette, K. (1995). Technology assessment. In W. T. Reich (ed.), *Encyclopedia of Bioethics.* New York: Macmillan.

Shrader-Frechette, K. (2002). *Environmental Justice: Creating Equality, Reclaiming Democracy.* New York: Oxford University Press.

Srinivasan, M. (ed.) (1982). *Technology Assessment and Development.* New York: Praeger.

Sunstein, C. (2002). *Risk and Reason.* Cambridge: Cambridge University Press.

Thomson, J. J. (1986). *Rights, Restitution, and Risk.* Cambridge, MA: Harvard University Press.

Unger, S. H. (1994). *Controlling Technology: Ethics and the Responsible Engineer.* New York: John Wiley.

Wallach, L. and Sforza, M. (1999). *Whose Trade Organization?* Washington, DC: Public Citizen.

Winner, L. (1977). *Autonomous Technology: Technics Out of Control as a Theme in Political Thought.* Cambridge, MA: MIT Press.

Tom Peters on excellence

Tom Peters

Ethics is a hot business topic, and that is a potential boon to us all. Unfortunately, the heightened awareness has spawned an industry of mindless, "do good, be good" writings. But dealing with ethics is not so easy.

1. Ethics is not principally about headline issues – responding to the Tylenol poisoning or handling insider information. Ethical concerns surround us all the time, on parade whenever we deal with people in the course of the average day. How we work out the "little stuff" will

determine our response, if called upon, to a Tylenol-sized crisis. When disaster strikes, it's far too late to seek out ethical touchstones.

2. High ethical standards – business or otherwise – are, above all, about treating people decently. To me (as a person, business person, and business owner) that means respect for a person's privacy, dignity, opinions, and natural desire to grow; and people's respect for (and by) co-workers.

3. Diversity must be honored. To be sure, it is important to be clear about your own compass heading; but don't ever forget that other people have profoundly different – and equally decent – ethical guidance mechanisms.

4. People, even the saints, are egocentric and selfish; we were designed "wrong" in part from the start. Any ethical framework in action had best take into account the troublesome but immutable fact of man's inherently flawed character.

5. Corporations are created and exist to serve people – insiders and outsiders – period.

6. By their very nature, organizations run roughshod over people. Organizations produce powerlessness and humiliation for most participants, with more skill than they produce widgets.

7. Though all men and women are created equal, some surely have more power than others. Thus, a central ethical issue in the workplace (and beyond) is the protection of and support for the unempowered – especially the frontline worker and the customer.

8. For employees and managers alike, fighting the impersonal "they"/"them" (the/every bureaucratic institution) is almost always justified on ethical grounds.

9. While one can point to ethically superior (and profitable) firms, such as Herman Miller, most of us will spend most of our working life in compromised – i.e., politicized – organizations. Dealing with "office politics," "brown-nosing," etc., is a perpetual ethical morass. A "pure" ethical stance in the face of most firms' political behavior will lead you out the door in short order, with only the convent, monastery, or ashram as alternatives. The line between ethical purity and arrogant egocentricism (i.e., a holier-than-thou stance toward the tumult of everyday life) is a fine one.

10. Though I sing the praises of an "action bias," ethical behavior demands that we tread somewhat softly in all of our affairs. Unintended consequences and the secondary and tertiary effects of most actions and policies far outnumber intended and first-order effects. As a manager, and a "change agent," dropping out may be the only decent/ethical path; our best-intended plans so often cause more harm than good. (Think about it: leaving the world no worse off than when you arrived is no mean feat.)

11. The pursuit of high ethical standards in business might well be served by the elimination of many business schools. The implicit thrust of most MBA programs is that great systems and great techniques win out over great people.

12. Can we live up to the spirit of the US Bill of Rights in our workplaces? Can "good business ethics" and "good real-life ethics" – and profit – coincide on a routine basis? One would hope that the answer is yes, although respect for the individual has hardly been the cornerstone of American industry's traditional approach to its workforce.

13. Capitalism and democracy in society are messy. But capitalism has far fewer downsides and far more upsides than any alternative so far concocted. The same can be said for the firm – where "democracy" and "capitalism" are served by wholesale worker participation and widespread ownership.

14. Great novels, not management books, might help. There are no easy answers, but there are fertile fields for gathering ideas. If you wish to be appropriately humbled about life and relationships and the possibility of ethical behavior, read Dostoyevsky, Forster, or Garcia Marquez instead of Drucker, Blanchard, or Peters. Then reconsider your latest magisterial proclamation.

15. Each of us is ultimately lonely. In the end, it's up to each of us and each of us alone to figure out who we are, who we are not, and to act more or less consistently on those conclusions.

Anyone who is not very confused all the time about ethical issues is out of touch with the frightful (and joyous) richness of the world. But at least being actively confused means that we are actively considering our ethical stance and that of the institutions we associate with.

That is a good start. (1989 TPG Communications. All rights reserved.)

trade agreements, ethics of

John Dobson

Almost all trade agreements today are administered by the World Trade Organization (WTO). The WTO is based in Geneva, Switzerland, and is recognized by practically every country that undertakes international trade. The WTO has also garnered much attention because of its ability to act as a lightning rod for various antiglobalization protest groups. This controversial aspect was demonstrated perhaps most dramatically during the WTO meetings in Seattle, Washington, in November of 1999. This four day meeting saw some of the worst urban rioting that the US had ever experienced. There appears to be no single reason for this widespread hostility to the WTO: John Dobson (2001: 1) describes it as "a manifestation of the groundswell of anxiety concerning questions of externalities and sustainability in the face of global capitalism's advance."

In order to understand the moral controversy surrounding the WTO it is necessary to understand its history. Although officially formed in 1992, the WTO had a long prior history as the General Agreement on Tariffs and Trade (GATT). As was also the case with the International Monetary Fund (IMF) and the United Nations (UN), GATT was formed as a result of the Bretton Woods agreement of 1946. GATT's stated aim was to dismantle the cobweb of tariff barriers and achieve free trade.

Thus GATT essentially arose from a desire to escape the mercantilist protectionism that had characterized international trade in the years between the two world wars. International trade was recognized as a non-cooperative "Prisoner's Dilemma type" game in which the optimum solution could be reached only through some form of cooperation between players, the primary players being governments of developed nations (*see* PRISONER'S DILEMMA).

In order to achieve this objective, GATT was founded on three basic principles: (1) nondiscrimination: a country is prohibited from

levying different tariffs on the same good imported from different countries; (2) reciprocity: reductions in tariffs should be balanced between countries; (3) impartial adjudication of trade disputes, through processes developed and controlled by GATT.

For the first three decades of its existence GATT appeared to serve the international community of developed nations well. Trade barriers worldwide were reduced, and membership in GATT grew from 23 countries at its inception to over 100 countries by the time of its transformation into the WTO. The membership of GATT, therefore, expanded from essentially a club for developed nations into an organization spanning all stages of the development life-cycle.

From an ethical perspective, as GATT grew larger it became increasingly criticized on the grounds that its espoused ideology of free trade was merely a facade to conceal an underlying mandate of profit maximization for the world's large multinational corporations (MNCs). This criticism became even more widespread and vociferous when GATT became the WTO, probably because of the apparent power held by the latter to influence trade flows to and from developing countries. Indeed, the moral criticism of the WTO generally concerns the dealings of MNCs in developing countries. The moral question surrounding the WTO is thus in essence one of free trade versus fair trade: does the WTO's avowed promotion of free trade and the eradication of trade protection actually benefit all parties, including the less powerful, or does it merely benefit the MNCs based in the developed world?

Bibliography

Business Ethics Quarterly (2001). The battle in Seattle: Two conflicting views of corporate culture. *Business Ethics Quarterly*, 11 (3) (July).

trade secrets

Robert E. Frederick

Information a firm reserves for its exclusive use, or for use by other firms to which it grants a license. In this respect trade secrets and patents are similar. But trade secrets differ from patents in four important ways.

First, while a patent is an official grant of certain rights from the US government to the patent holder, and patent cases are tried in federal courts, trade secrets are governed by state law and cases are usually tried in state courts. Second, patents expire after 17 years. The information can then be used by anyone. But trade secrets can be maintained indefinitely. The Zildjian family, for example, has kept its trade secret for manufacturing cymbals since 1623. Third, patented information must meet strict standards of novelty and unobviousness, and must represent a genuine advance in a particular field. The requirements for something to qualify as a trade secret are much less strict. In most states as long as information has some degree of novelty, cannot be readily discovered by public inspection, has genuine commercial utility, and, most importantly, is actively protected from disclosure by the firm that holds it, then it can qualify as a trade secret. Fourth, although the information in a patent is public, patent law protects it from any use not authorized by the patent holder. But trade secret law is quite different. A trade secret cannot be used if it is acquired by improper means (e.g., industrial espionage or unauthorized disclosure by an employee). However, if a firm *X* independently discovers *Y*'s trade secret, then *X* can legally use the information. *Y* cannot sue to prevent *X* from using it, nor can *Y* require that *X* pay a licensing fee.

Unpatentable proprietary information, such as customer lists and marketing plans, can be held as trade secrets. But so can patentable information. Whether to hold such information as a trade secret or apply for a patent is a matter for the firm to decide. In some cases keeping information secret, whether patentable or unpatentable, seems clearly justified. But is it always justified? Suppose, for instance, that a utility firm discovers a pollution-free fusion process for making electricity cheaply, but decides to keep the process secret. Or suppose a pharmaceutical firm discovers and keeps secret an inexpensive and effective cure for AIDS. In both these cases it seems obvious that the information ought to be disclosed, even if unpatentable, because the public benefit of disclosure would greatly outweigh anything the firm gains by keeping the secret. If this is right, then on some occasions a decision about whether to keep information as a trade secret has a moral as well as a commercial dimension. If benefit to the public could be significantly increased by revealing the secret, or if harm to the public could be significantly decreased, then the firm may have a moral obligation to disclose the information that overrides considerations of profit or other business advantage.

Bibliography

Baram, M. (1968). Trade secrets: What price loyalty? *Harvard Business Review*, 6, 66–74.

Del Mar, D. (1974). *The Security of Industrial Information*. New Hope, PA: Chestnut Hill Press.

Frederick, R. and Snoeyenbos, M. (1983). Trade secrets, patents, and morality. In M. Snoeyenbos, R. Almeder, and J. Humber (eds.), *Business Ethics*. New York: Prometheus Books.

Rosenberg, P. D. (1982). *Patent Law Fundamentals*, 2nd edn. New York: Clark Boardman, ch. 3.

Unkovic, D. (1985). *The Trade Secrets Handbook: Strategies and Techniques for Protecting Corporate Information*. Englewood Cliffs, NJ: Prentice-Hall.

transforming justice

Thomas F. McMahon

may be defined as a theory on the interaction between rights and power that makes justice operative. Transforming justice is a conceptualization of justice which seeks to incorporate the vitality of power in the very definition of justice. Although transforming justice does have human rights for its basis, it does not subscribe to the strengths or weaknesses of other theories of justice (*see* RIGHTS).

How does transforming justice differ conceptually from the more traditional theories of justice and rights? The fundamental difference rests in the concept that justice cannot, and therefore will not, become an existential reality unless its theory also contains the notion of power. Power is what makes justice "transforming" – for example, moving away from inequality in fact toward equality in deed.

The "interaction" between rights and power in transforming justice challenges the traditional view that rights and power are to be treated as parallel factors in human behavior. It is in the practical order – not necessarily in abstract notions – where rights and power interact to produce transforming justice.

RIGHTS

Rights are claims by one entity for or against another entity, either human or corporate. A right is a relationship; it is not a thing. In a way, a right is a means to an end, such as the equality of justice (*see* JUSTICE). Rights are obtained through some source or title, such as contract. Rights are qualitative and thus "inform" the person, whether human or corporate. Rights are also dichotomous: either a person has them or not. There are no degrees. In this sense, they cannot be measured in terms of more or less.

Justice has rights for its object: by respecting the rights of others, a person gives another what is her/his due. Indeed, the ancient Roman definition of justice states that each person is to give the other what is his/her due. From another perspective, a person, by respecting the rights of another, empowers the other. However, different theories of rights frequently provide various, and sometimes conflicting, sources or titles of rights. In a pluralistic society where many value systems exist in the same geographical and social context, a particular claim of one person or group might not be recognized or acknowledged by others. Thus arises conflicts of rights.

POWER

The problem of conflict of rights creates one of the most perplexing problems in determining how transforming justice applies to concrete situations. Power is the capacity to bring about change in others according to the intent of the agent (powerholder). Like rights, power is relational; it always deals with another entity: human, corporate, or systemic. Power is quantitative: it can be measured, usually by its effect or impact. Furthermore, as quantitative, power can be added to or subtracted from, as every politician is aware on election day. Power can also be viewed as interacting. Political power can generate economic or social power; moral power can influence political power.

The source of power, unlike the title of rights, may be less certain. Depending upon the kind of power, it can be obtained through inheritance, contract, force, competition, manipulation, fraud, or a combination of these. However, of itself, power is ethically neutral. The manner of obtaining power and its subsequent use determine whether it is an ethical good or an ethical evil.

JUSTICE

Justice will be considered under the form of moral virtue. A moral virtue leads to action. Its value is in the behavior it elicits in the person who possesses it. Although a moral virtue, like every virtue, "perfects" the person who possesses it, it also leads the person to some form of controlled behavior. While the moral virtue of temperance perfects the person in moderation in food and drink, the moral virtue of justice leads to behavior which refers to the rights or claims of some other person apart from the agent. Unlike temperance, justice is not subjectively determined by the peculiar limitations of the agent, but is objectively determined by the established rights of the other person. Unlike power, which can be added to or subtracted from, the moral virtue of justice "qualifies" the person in the sense that "value added" is understood in the process of production (*see* VIRTUE ETHICS).

As a general rule in transforming justice, rights must precede power in transforming justice. Or, to put the rule in a negative frame, ethically evil power must not be used to obtain a right: "might does not make right."

In transforming justice, the "value added" is the capacity to move the agent to respect the claims of others or have others respect the agent's claims. Thus, power becomes a means to the end of justice, which is equality, among other things. Rights become the grist for the mill of transforming justice. Transforming justice, however, uses power to make certain that these rights are respected both by the agent and by the receiver.

Finally, the traditional theories of justice, although they are directed toward others, have no way of "moving" the agent or the other person to respect rights. For example, racial and sexual discrimination still exist in spite of the civil rights laws pertaining to women and minorities.

This kind of social justice needs to be made operative. With power as an integral part of its concept, transforming justice can only exist in an operating form. Transforming justice is a moral virtue in the fullest sense; it can be that "value added" which modifies by qualifying humans and, consequently, their behavior to recognize or to receive rights. As a practice it leads to new approaches to such issues as racial and sexual discrimination, employee rights, company re-organization, terminations, and many other dis-turbing ethical issues which executives and managers have to face.

Bibliography

Berle, A. A. (1969). *Power*. New York: Harcourt, Brace and World.

Boatright, J. R. (1993). *Ethics and the Conduct of Business*. Englewood Cliffs, NJ: Prentice-Hall.

Gewirth, A. (1984). The epistemology of human rights. *Social Philosophy and Policy*, 1, 1–2.

Gewirth, A. (1992). Rights. In L. J. Becked (ed.), *Encyclo-pedia of Ethics*. New York: Garland.

McMahon, T. (1973). The moral aspects of power: Power and the word of God. In F. Bockle and J.-M. Pohier (eds.), *Concilium: Religion in the Seventies*. New York: Herder and Herder.

Ozar, D. T. (1986). Rights: What they are and where they come from. In P. H. Werhane, A. R. Gini, and D. T. Ozar (eds.), *Philosophical Issues in Human Rights: Theories and Applications*. New York: Random House, 5–25.

Werhane, P. H. (1985). *Persons, Rights, and Corporations*. Englewood Cliffs, NJ: Prentice-Hall.

transnational corporations

Thomas J. Donaldson

A single company operating in two or more nations, with one part exerting at least partial control over the others. Yet while the trans-national is *trans*-national by virtue of operating in many countries, and while in theory a trans-national need not have a "home country" base (in contrast to a multinational corporation), it sometimes retains significant uni-nationality. Its upper management is usually dominated by nationals of a single country, its stock is usually owned largely by residents of a single country, and its charter emanates from a single country (*see* MULTINATIONAL COR-PORATIONS).

The meteoric rise of the transnational, which has occurred almost entirely since World War II, owes itself to a small set of key economic factors. These include a shortage of cheap labor in de-veloped countries, increasing relevance of econ-omies of scale, improved transportation, better communication, and increased worldwide con-sumer demand. These factors have proved espe-cially potent set against a backdrop of the production life-cycle. A new piece of technol-ogy, such as the portable compact disk player, is usually the product of research and development in a highly industrialized economy. Later, do-mestic rivals enter the market, competing with the original group of companies. At the same time, an export market develops in which com-peting producers are forced to seek other geo-graphic areas in which profit margins are higher. Still later, as profit margins shrink, costs are reduced by tapping cheaper labor markets.

Three strategic and structural stances charac-terize transnationals (Doz, 1980). The first is a *multi-domestic* stance that utilizes domestic plants servicing their respective home markets. Taking such a stance, the home-country head-quarters often serves as little more than a con-venient umbrella under which largely autonomous domestic operations operate. Host-country management typically retains con-siderable managerial prerogatives, and products are tailored neatly to host-country tastes.

The second generic stance is that of the *global* transnational. In contrast to the multi-domestic stance, the global stance unifies key elements of its global business, including manufacturing ac-tivities, managerial decision-making, and market strategy. Such a stance frequently employs standardization, economies of scale, and volume in order to enhance global competitiveness. Often, subsidiaries in host countries will special-ize in efficiently manufacturing a single com-ponent, with the result that a circle of subsidiaries cooperate to create the final prod-uct. Each subsidiary obtains from the others what it needs but does not produce. Corporate headquarters devotes considerable attention to arranging a minimizing of total expenses and a maximizing of revenues. In this way, centralized control is assumed.

The third and final stance allows a mixture of the first two. Called the *administratively controlled* stance, it operates without a formal integrative strategy, and permits economic variables to shape individual business decisions. While each major decision is either made by, or at least approved by, home-country corporate headquarters, individual decision contexts are evaluated on their own merits, without reference to a broader, integrative scheme.

All three types of stance operate against the backdrop of a global profit-maximizing imperative. That is to say, the transnational operates in a transnational context for the *purpose* of earning more money than it would if remaining a domestic activity, with the consequence that factor prices can be minimized in sophisticated ways. If labor costs or taxes are too high in country X, the transnational can either move entirely to country Y or shift key components of its production process to country Y. Whereas domestic firms must pay for capital at the going rate, transnationals are free to choose among competing rates. And, if government officials fail to cooperate in country X, the transnational – far more so than its domestic counterpart – can force concessions by threatening to move or restructure.

Bibliography

Barnet, B. and Muller, R. (1974). *Global Reach: The Power of Multinational Corporations*. New York: Simon and Schuster.

Buckley, P. J. and Casson, M. C. (1976). *The Future of the Multinational Enterprise*. London: Holmes and Meir.

Caves, R. E. (1982). *Multinational Enterprise and Economic Analysis*. Cambridge: Cambridge University Press.

Chandler, A. (1986). The evolution of modern global competition. In M. E. Porter (ed.), *Competition in Global Industries*. Boston, MA: Harvard Business Review Press.

Doz, Y. L. (1980). Strategic management in multinational companies. *Sloan Management Review*, winter, 27–46.

Dunning, J. H. (1981). *International Production and the Multinational Enterprise*. London: Allen and Unwin.

Johnson, H. G. (1985). The multinational corporation as a development agent. *Columbia Journal of World Business*, 4, 25–30.

Porter, M. E. (1990). *The Competitive Advantage of Nations*. New York: Free Press.

Vernon, R. (1966). International investment and international trade in the product cycle. *Quarterly Journal of Economics*, **80** (2), 190–207.

Zysman, J. and Tyson, L. (eds.) (1983). *American Industry in International Competition: Government Policies and Corporate Strategies*, Ithaca, NY: Cornell University Press.

trust

LaRue Tone Hosmer

is clearly essential in the conduct of human affairs. Most people would agree that neither stable social relationships nor efficient economic transactions are possible without a high level of trust on all sides. Indeed, Fukuyama (1995: 7) went even further in his classic work on this topic, and claimed "a nation's well-being, as well as its ability to compete, is conditioned by a single, pervasive cultural characteristic: the level of trust inherent in the society."

Scholars, however, have never been able to agree upon a precise definition of trust. Part of the problem is the number of applications. Trust can be viewed as reliance upon the outcome of an event, the behavior of a person, the competence of a professional, the reciprocity of a group, or the loyalty of an organization. Another part of the problem is the multiplicity of the disciplines. Trust has been included in the conceptual frameworks of psychology, social psychology, sociology, organizational behavior, and economic theory. But probably the main cause is the simple familiarity of the construct: "In both serious social thought and everyday discourse it is assumed that the meaning of trust, and its many apparent synonyms, is so well known that it can be left undefined or to contextual implications" (Barber, 1983: 7).

This entry will attempt to review, very briefly, the alternative definitions that have been proposed over time for the construct of trust, and then combine the essentials into a new definition. The new definition will be relevant to business ethics. One of the unusual aspects of the existing definitions from both the behavioral and economic sciences is the frequent inclusion of implied moral duties, assumed personal virtues, and inferred benevolent outcomes. By making these explicit, moral philosophy may be able to provide a more exact definition of trust. This, at all events, will be attempted.

Position of vulnerability. One of the earliest definitions (Deutsch, 1958) proposed that trust was a non-rational choice in which the possible loss if the trust was broken was much greater than the expected gain if the trust was fulfilled. Essentially, trust was viewed as an optimistic confidence in the outcome of an uncertain event.

Condition of dependence. Another early definition (Zand, 1972) accepted the vulnerability aspect, but felt that the decision to trust went beyond optimistic confidence in the outcome and necessarily involved giving up control and becoming dependent upon the actions of others. Trust was now viewed as an optimistic confidence in the behavior of another person.

Reliance on character. Barber (1983) added two necessary conditions to the decision by the trustor to give up control. The first was an assumption of technically competent role performance by the other person; the second was morally correct role performance by that person. Trust was now seen as reliance upon the competence and character of another person.

Dimensions of character. Butler and Cantrell (1984) emphasized character over competence, and attempted to define the character traits that were needed to develop trust. These were integrity (reputation for honesty and truthfulness), consistency (reliability and predictability), loyalty (benevolence and support), and openness (willingness to share ideas and information).

Probability of opportunism. Williamson (1985) proposed that it was impossible to determine the trustworthiness of others in economic transactions and therefore companies could not rely upon assumptions of competence or character. Instead, they had to negotiate detailed contracts and install explicit controls to ensure compliance. Trust was something to be imposed.

Control by tradition. Granovetter (1985) rejected the "trust has to be imposed" argument of the economists. He said that economic behavior was embedded in informal social relationships.

Zucker (1986) followed with the definition that trust was a set of social expectations based upon "fair" social rules and generally accepted "rights" shared by all participants.

Probability of cooperation. Gambetta (1988: 217) also rejected the "trust has to be imposed" argument and thought the goal was unforced cooperation. Trust, he wrote, "is the probability that the person with whom we are in contact will perform an action that is beneficial or at least not detrimental high enough for us to consider engaging in some form of cooperation."

Emphasis upon benevolence. Butler (1991) later placed much greater emphasis upon the loyalty dimension of trust, moving from a general reputation for benevolence by the trustor toward an implicit promise by that person or organization not to bring harm to the trustee. Trust was now defined as an implicit promise of "fair" treatment.

Importance of reputation. Hill (1990) proposed that it was possible to reduce the transaction costs of contracts and controls in principal–agent relationships, and achieve greater cooperation at lesser cost, by evaluating the past opportunistic actions of agents. Trust became, once again, an optimistic expectation for the "proper" behavior of others.

Importance of reciprocity. Friedland (1990: 317) reported that in games with an infinite number of plays, a persistent finding was that a matching or "tit-for-tat" reciprocal strategy was the most favorable because it elicited in adversaries more cooperative than competitive behavior. Trust was said to be a "genuine responsiveness by one player to the needs of the partner."

Importance of responsiveness. Bromily and Cummings (1992:4) proposed very explicitly that "trust is the expectation that an individual or group will (1) make a good faith effort to behave in accordance with commitments both explicit or implicit, (2) be honest in whatever negotiations preceded those commitments, and (3) not take excessive advantage of others."

Importance of good will. Ring and Van de Ven (1992: 488) also provided an explicit definition of trust as a mixture of two aspects: "predictability in expectations [of the behavior of others] and confidence in the good will of others." Good will was generally described as the benevolent duty to attend to the interests of others.

Clearly, under conditions of trust, the person who trusts (trustor) is vulnerable to the outcome of an uncertain event and dependent upon the actions of an uncontrolled person (trustee). Trustors place themselves in that awkward position because they rely on (1) the personal character of the trustee through a reputation for integrity, consistency, loyalty, and openness; (2) the social expectations of the group for "fair" rules and accepted "rights"; (3) an implied promise from the trustee for "beneficial" treatment and "proper" behavior; (4) a general assumption of "good faith" negotiations and "good will" treatments.

These are all terms that have a moral base, and perhaps that is the underlying reason for the lack of a widely accepted definition of the construct of trust. Moral concepts are an anomaly in most of the behavioral and economic sciences. Perhaps what is needed is to make the moral content explicit rather than implicit, and that can be done by reference to the ethical principles of moral analysis, with the following proposed definition: "Trust is the expectation by one person, group, or firm of ethically justifiable behavior – that is, morally correct decisions and actions based upon ethical principles of analysis – on the part of the other person, group, or firm in a joint endeavor or cooperative exchange."

Bibliography

Barber, B. (1983). *The Logic and Limits of Trust.* New Brunswick, NJ: Rutgers University Press.

Bromily, P. and Cummings, L. L. (1992). Transaction costs in organizations with trust. Working paper No. 28, Strategic Management Research Center, University of Minnesota.

Butler, J. K. (1991). Towards understanding and measuring conditions of trust: Evolution of a condition of trust inventory. *Journal of Management,* 17, 643–63.

Butler, J. K. and Cantrell, R. S. (1984). A behavioral decision theory approach to modeling dyadic trust in superiors and subordinates. *Psychological Reports,* 55: 190–28.

Deutsch, M. (1958). Trust and suspicion. *Journal of Conflict Resolution,* 2, 265–79.

Friedland, N. (1990). Attribution of control as a determinant of cooperation in exchange interactions. *Journal of Applied Social Psychology,* 20, 303–20.

Fukuyama, F. (1995). *Trust: The Social Virtues and the Creation of Prosperity.* New York: Free Press.

Gambetta, D. (1988). Can we trust trust? In D. Gambetta (ed.), *Trust: Making and Breaking Cooperative Relations.* Cambridge, MA: Blackwell, 213–38.

Golembiewski, R. T. and McConkie, M. (1975). The centrality of interpersonal trust in group processes. In C. L. Cooper (ed.), *Theories of Group Processes.* New York: John Wiley and Sons.

Granovetter, M. (1985). Economic action and social structure: The problem of embeddedness. *American Journal of Sociology,* 91: 481–510.

Hill, C. W. L. (1990). Cooperation, opportunism and the invisible hand: Implications for transaction cost theory. *Academy of Management Review,* 15, 500–13.

Ring, P. S. and Van de Ven, A. H. (1992). Structuring cooperative relationships between organizations. *Strategic Management Journal,* 13, 483–98.

Williamson, O. W. (1985). *The Economic Institutions of Capitalism.* New York: Free Press.

Zand, D. E. (1972). Trust and managerial problem solving. *Administrative Science Quarterly,* 17, 229–39.

Zucker, L. G. (1986). Production of trust: Institutional sources of economic structure, 1840 to 1920. In B. M. Star and L. L. Cummings (eds.), *Research in Organizational Behavior,* Vol. 8. Greenwich, CT: JAI Press, 53–111.

truthtelling

Mitchell S. Green

From the point of view of ethics, truthtelling is not a matter of speaking the truth but is rather a matter of speaking what one *believes* to be the truth. So, too, liars do not necessarily say what is false; they say what they believe to be false. Further, one can mislead without lying. An executive answering in the affirmative the question whether some employees are in excessive danger on the job will mislead if he knows that in fact most employees are but does not say so. Yet he does not lie. Similarly, there is no lie in an advertisement suggesting that those who use a certain product will garner wealth and power. This article deals with the ethical and practical dimensions of truthtelling and lying only.

Sincerity is a virtue and yet lies both great and trivial are sometimes in the best interest of the liar or even the party to whom they are addressed. While some, such as Augustine and Kant, have taken the view that lies are morally objectionable under any circumstances, others such as Grotius and Mill have thought there to be conditions under which lying is morally acceptable, and perhaps even obligatory. This latter position raises the question whether there are general principles in the light of which one may determine the moral status of a lie.

Our deeming sincerity a virtue may be due to the fact that each of us is better off in a society in which people are truthful most of the time than we would be in a society in which, say, people lie as often as they tell the truth. This fact may create a presumption against lying, so that even those who are not deeply moved by the claims of morality will require special grounds for lying rather than being veracious. If so, then the general principles mentioned above could help to shed light on this presumption and the conditions under which it is reasonably overturned.

The Rationality of Truthtelling

That each of us is better off living in a society in which people are truthful most of the time than we would be in a society in which, say, people lie as often as they tell the truth, may be brought out with the following example. You and another person, X, are both people who act in their own best interest, and you have been placed in separate rooms. In each room there are two buttons, one red and the other green. If you both push the same button (no matter the color) then you each receive a large reward, say $1 million each. If you push different buttons then you each receive a small reward, say $1 each. You receive a slip of paper from X with the words, "I have just pushed the green button." Each of you knows that the other is self-interested and each knows that the other is aware of the structure of the situation. Can you infer from these facts alone which button it would be rational to push?

It may seem obvious that the rational thing to do is to push the green button. But as Hodgson (1967) has pointed out, this inference presup-poses that X, as a rational agent, is inclined to tell the truth. You have no reason to accept X's message as veracious unless you have reason to believe that veracity is in X's best interest. Perhaps X believes that the rational thing to do is to assert the opposite of what he believes to be the case. Unless this possibility can be ruled out it is difficult to see what ground you could have for pushing the green rather than the red button.

There is nothing intrinsically more rational about driving on the right side of the road than driving on the left. However, *given* that in a certain society the regularity is to drive on the right side of the road, sane drivers in this society have no incentive to deviate from this regularity. The regularity of driving on the right side of the road thus seems to be an *equilibrium*: an outcome that is a function of the choices of multiple agents, and such that no such agent has an incentive to deviate from this outcome. It has been suggested by Lewis (1969, 1972) that the practice of asserting only what you believe is another such equilibrium, in that given that speakers generally do so there is typically no reason to deviate from this regularity. This may be what Samuel Johnson has in mind in suggesting that even in hell the devils tell one another the truth.

If we assume that X in the above scenario is from the same society as ours we may be able to infer that X's message is sincere. On this basis we may then infer that the rational choice is to push the green button. This allows us to see the importance of conventions such as truthtelling in societies like ours. Were there no such convention we would be at a loss to know what to make of one another's utterances even if we knew what their words meant.

Each of us benefits from the practice of truthtelling. This suggests that in an individual case even the self-interested, amoral agent will presume against lying. What sorts of considerations can overturn this presumption?

Conditions That May Excuse Lying

It has been said that it is easy to tell one lie but hard to tell only one, since the covering up of a lie can involve one in further untruths or dissimulation. What is more, the liar runs the risk of being found out, with the consequent tarnishing of the liar's credibility. Nevertheless, it seems to be in one's best interest to lie to an enemy who, were they to have the truth, would do you harm. Further, there seem to be cases in which not only is it in one's best interest to lie, one is right to do so. A farmer hiding Jews from Germans acts heroically in lying to Nazis who come to his door asking whether he is keeping any Jews in his house. Ethicists and theologians have dealt at length with the question of the conditions under which a lie is morally acceptable.

Augustine held all lies to be morally blameworthy, while conceding that some lies are more blameworthy than others. Following him, Thomas Aquinas held that only some lies constitute mortal sins. Kant held a more stern view, claiming that not only are lies wrong in all circumstances, but that the liar destroys his dignity as a person. Similarly, we find in Dante's *Inferno* that liars are tormented in the eighth circle of hell, and so are superior only to traitors.

Adopting a more temperate view, Grotius (1925) held that stating what one knows to be false is a lie only if it violates the right of liberty in judgment of the person to whom it is addressed. One with evil intentions gives up this right, and children have yet to acquire it, so lies to such people may be justified. However, an ailing person seems to have all his rights in place and yet a lie to such a person may well be justified.

Bok (1978) suggests four major conditions that can excuse lies: avoiding harm, producing benefits, fairness, and veracity itself. Concerning the first condition, some lies are done for the sake of preventing some evil greater than the evil of lying itself. The example of the farmer protecting the lives of the Jews he is harboring is a case in point. Similarly, a lobbyist for a large firm may believe that preventing the layoffs that would result from her company's losing a large government contract justifies lying to public officials. Other untruths are calculated to produce benefits, as in the case of a lie told to a person on her deathbed to lift her spirits, or in the giving of a placebo.

Third, fairness is sometimes invoked as exculpating a lie. One form that this appeal takes is in the thought that the other party would have no qualms about deceiving the liar. Also, some might take their lie to be fair on the ground that it rectifies some earlier wrong done to them. Fourth, one might try to justify a lie on the ground that it is required to preserve one's reputation for veracity. One who has told a justified lie may need to tell other lies in order to protect her reputation for veracity. Bok argues forcefully that although each of these four conditions can legitimate a lie, we are all too prone to invoke them opportunistically in an effort to justify our deceits. One way to resist this tendency may be to highlight the respect in which the norm of truthfulness is one of many public commodities.

LIARS AS FREE-RIDERS

Each of us benefits from an ability to presume that others are on the whole veracious. In light of this we see that the opportunistic liar is a "free rider": such a person exploits a public commodity for her own purposes, such that were many others to do the same this commodity would cease to exist. The commodity that the practice of veracity creates is the ability to rely upon the word of others as in all likelihood sincere. Those interested in the preservation of diverse commodities for the future will scrutinize carefully any claim to justify a departure from the norm of truthfulness.

Bibliography

Aquinas, T. (1922). *Summa Theologica*, trans. by the Fathers of the English Dominican Province. London: Burnes Oates and Washburn. (Distinguishes among the degrees of turpitude of various kinds of lie.)

Augustine, St. (1952). "Lying" and "Against lying." In *Treatises on Various Subjects*, ed. R. J. Deferrari. New York: Catholic University of America Press. (Early and highly influential prohibition against all forms of lying.)

Bok, S. (1978). *Lying: Moral Choice in Public and Private Life*. New York: Pantheon. (A philosophical account with attention paid to practical issues.)

Grotius, H. (1925). *On the Law of War and Peace*, trans. F. Kelsey. Indianapolis, IN: Bobbs-Merrill. (Defines lying in terms of the rights of those to which the lie is addressed.)

Hodgson, D. H. (1967). *Consequences of Utilitarianism*. Oxford: Oxford University Press. (Questions the source of the norm of truthtelling on purely instrumental grounds.)

Kant, I. (1949). On a supposed right to lie from benevolent motives. In *The Critique of Practical Reason and Other Writings in Moral Philosophy*. Chicago: University of Chicago Press. (Defends a view of lying as unjustified under all circumstances.)

Lewis, D. (1969). *Convention: A Philosophical Study*. Cambridge, MA: Harvard University Press.

Lewis, D. (1972). Utilitarianism and truthfulness. *Australasian Journal of Philosophy*, **50**, 17–19. (Each of these two works by Lewis defends a conception of a norm of truthfulness as an equilibrium.)

Williams, B. (2003). *Truth and Truthfulness: An Essay in Genealogy*. Princeton, NJ: Princeton University Press. (A philosophical and historical defense of the norm of truthtelling.)

United Kingdom, business ethics in

Jane Collier

INTRODUCTION

It may be overly optimistic to proclaim that business ethics in the UK has finally come of age, but during the last decade there have been some encouraging developments and significant "green shoots." The idea of ethics in business is no longer viewed as an oxymoron. Courses in business ethics proliferate in business schools, in executive education and professional training programs, and in staff development programs. Corporates commit to greater social responsibility, and consultancies devise ways to make that commitment credible. Research centers in universities as well as individual academics undertake leading-edge research that gets published either in-house or in academic journals, and papers on aspects of business ethics are published with increasing frequency in mainline management and professional journals. Conferences that bring together academics and practitioners proliferate, and international links are continually being forged and strengthened.

It is not difficult to identify the contextual factors that contributed to the increasing acceptance of the need for ethics in business. On the legal side, the 1985 Companies Act emphasized the rights of employees, and this was rapidly followed by developments in EU legislation culminating in the Social Charter of 1989. On the political side, the governments of the 1980s pushed back the boundaries of the state, but the consequent culture of greed and scandal led to pressure on companies, already vulnerable in a time of rapid technological and organizational change, to "clean up their act." And finally, on the business side, corporate difficulties emerging

as a consequence of that vulnerability led to the establishment of the Committee on the Financial Aspects of Corporate Governance and the publication of its report in 1992 (Cadbury, 2002). More recently, the Labour government instituted a number of measures designed to protect and reinforce the rights of stakeholders. For instance, the Public Interest Disclosure Act, which came into force in July 1999, lays down the rights of employees and the duties of employers in cases of whistleblowing, and is internationally recognized as a benchmark for whistleblowing legislation. The Pensions Act of 1995 outlines the rights of holders of pension plans to information on their future benefits, and the Late Payment of Commercial Debts (Interest) Act 1998 gave small firms with 50 or less employees a statutory right to interest for the late payment of commercial debts.

ISSUES

A central focus of UK business ethics theory and practice is the notion of corporate social responsibility to stakeholders. In the UK, businesses tend to express their commitment to CSR by listing their values in mission statements rather than by identifying specific social objectives and responsibilities. Internal aspects of CSR, such as employee rights and safety issues, are covered by comprehensive UK and EU legislation, but wider corporate social responsibility and related business behavior in a global context continues to give cause for concern, not least because it is difficult to translate "values" from one culture into another. This concern has been expressed not only by stakeholder groups such as consumers, anti-globalization campaigners, and NGOs, but also now by institutional investors. One of the most significant recent UK developments has been the rise of "socially responsible investment," partly as a consequence of an amendment in 2000 to the Pensions Act (1997) requiring trustees to declare their stance in relation to the social and environmental aspects of their investments, and partly due to investor fears of the effects on reputation of corporate irresponsibility in the global context. Socially responsible investment is a growing trend in the London market: it entails ongoing "engagement" on the part of institutional investors with companies in order to encourage best CSR practice (Collier, 2004). Engagement requires dialogue, but it also imposes an implicit duty on institutional investors to use their vote at AGMs. The Myners Report (2001) (whose provisions have not yet become statutory) makes this requirement explicit. It should be said here that the earlier UK ethical investment movement, although insignificant in market terms, served to raise the question of investor responsibility; however, the new factor in the situation is the pressure that institutional investors can now exert on companies and the "countervailing power" that they possess in consequence. Investors realize that long-term shareholder value depends on social and environmental best practice, and in particular on the efficient management of risk arising from normal company operations, which may threaten this.

Media exposure of issues affecting violation of worker rights, child labor, cruelty to animals, or environmental degradation tends to result in short-term consumer boycotts and longer-term loss of market share. Investor engagement aims to avoid such contingencies.

The other major focus of UK business ethics is corporate governance. The UK differs from the US in that societal responses to challenges tend to take the form of self-regulation rather than the introduction of regulatory measures. In order for self-regulation of corporate conduct to work, corporate governance structures and the institutions that support them must be sound. Good governance is seen not only as the basis of good business, but also as the springboard from which companies can articulate and put into practice the values which they see as underpinning their approach to CSR. There have been a number of reports since the Cadbury Report that have attempted to refine best practice in govern-

ance; the most recent of these have been the Higgs Report (2003) on governance and the Smith Report (2003) on audit committee reform. Both of these will now form the basis of a new Combined Code of Practice that will operate on the basis of "comply or explain (non-compliance)." There is some resistance on the part of companies to "being told" what good governance is, just as companies insist that their values rather than external strictures should drive their approach to CSR, but investor activism presents a united front in response to these arguments, and investor coalitions (particularly cross-border coalitions) wield a considerable amount of power.

INSTITUTIONS

There has been a significant growth in organizational and institutional frameworks supporting the development of corporate social responsibility. In terms of networks, the oldest "voice of responsible business" is Business in the Community, founded two decades ago, which is a network of 700 member companies operating in 200 countries worldwide committed to continually improving their positive impact on society and sharing best practice. A newer network with a more specific focus is the Ethical Trading Initiative, an alliance of companies, non-governmental organizations (NGOs), and trade union organizations committed to working together to identify and promote ethical trade. Members, including multinational companies and national companies sourcing abroad, are committed to the promotion of worker rights and the ending of child labor, forced labor, and sweatshops. Other alliances include Tomorrow's Company, a networking hub for businesses wishing to explore the future of sustainable success, and the Institute of Business Ethics, which works with companies seeking to build relationships of trust internally and to meet the challenges of external change and complexity. The IBE is perhaps best known for its expertise in developing corporate codes of ethics (Webley, 2003).

In terms of reputation effects, it is becoming important for major UK companies to report on their social, ethical, and environmental performance. Many companies do this on the web, and in order to present hard data they use indicators (usually) selected from the Global Reporting Initiative. These measurements are professionally verified, but in addition an increasing number of companies are using the AA1000 Assurance Standard developed by Account Ability. AA1000 is the world's first assurance standard developed to ensure the credibility and quality of reporting on social, environmental, and economic performance: it thus audits the quality of the whole report rather than specific indicators. The rise of socially responsible investment has also led to a need for indices that reflect CSR components, and in response FTSE has created the FTSE4Good Index Series. Indices have been designed to measure the performance of companies meeting globally recognized corporate responsibility standards and hence to facilitate investor knowledge of corporate behavior where companies are too far away to monitor.

RESEARCH

Business ethics research has expanded in line with these developments in the corporate sector. A number of research centers and chairs have been established in universities such as Bath, Cambridge, Brunel, Nottingham, Ashridge, and Warwick. These serve to develop and coordinate project and consultancy activities. Research clusters also exist in many other universities, and research findings are published in US and UK management and business ethics journals, as well as in the Blackwell journal *Business Ethics: A European Review*. This journal has now been in existence for 12 years, but it is noticeable that in recent years both the quantity and the quality of the papers has shown marked improvement (as has the number of subscriptions). There has also been an increase in the number of books published in the UK by teachers and researchers. Many of these explore specific areas such as governance or the environment; others are texts for use in the variety of courses now offered (Fisher and Lovell, 2003).

The most active and useful network for academics and practitioners working in the fields of business and corporate social responsibility is the European Business Ethics Network. Founded in 1987, it aims to support and encourage teaching and research throughout Europe,

including Central and Eastern Europe. Over time the national networks have become stronger, and the UK network holds a successful annual conference each year. However, collaboration with others in the wider European academic and practitioner forum is seen as essential if new best practice initiatives, such as those involving social partnerships, are to be facilitated.

TEACHING: THE CONTEXT

Business ethics teaching in the UK takes place primarily in management schools and departments. Whereas by the first decade of the twentieth century the major schools of management education had been established in both Europe and the US, in the UK the first business schools were only established in the 1960s. University academics saw management studies as lacking disciplinary coherence, and management education as merely vocational. To make matters worse, industry saw little value in creating an academic subject out of what was seen as a set of practical skills (Engwall and Zamagni, 1998). By the mid-1960s the London and Manchester Business Schools had begun to function and their example encouraged universities, polytechnics, and other colleges to develop management degrees and other management qualifications. The next 30 years saw the continual development and customization of MBA programs by colleges and universities, but in general management education in the UK touches a very small proportion of British managers. Reasons for this include the anti-intellectualism of management culture, the antipathy of employers, and a general lack of understanding and agreement as to what constitutes effective management education.

TEACHING BUSINESS ETHICS IN THE UK

During the 1980s there was significant growth in the number of business ethics courses offered by universities and business schools, particularly at the undergraduate level. In 1988 a questionnaire was sent to universities, polytechnics, and colleges of higher education in order to ascertain the nature and extent of UK business ethics teaching provision (Mahoney, 1990). The results indicated that the teaching of business ethics in the UK lagged a long way behind that in the US. Initiatives were disparate and uncoordinated, teaching was done in law and philosophy departments as well as in business departments, little supportive material was available, and two thirds of the respondents indicated that students had very little (if any) interest in the subject. In 2000 the Institute of Business Ethics sponsored another survey. The questionnaire was circulated to 105 institutions of higher education (five of these were purely postgraduate). The results indicated that while business ethics is taught at about half of the postgraduate and professional institutions, it is often a separate non-compulsory module, and is thus not integrated into the mainstream course of study. However, in contrast to the findings of the earlier study, students – particularly at postgraduate level – tend to respond positively in terms of receptivity and willingness to courses offered (Cowton and Cummins, 2003). A further difference is that the subject is now taught almost exclusively in business as opposed to philosophy departments, and teachers are not trained philosophers.

Bibliography

Cadbury, A. (2002). *Corporate Governance and Chairmanship: A Personal View*. Oxford: Oxford University Press.

Collier, J. (2004). Responsible shareholding and investor engagement in the UK. In G. Brenkert (ed.), *Corporate Integrity and Accountability*. Thousand Oaks, CA: Sage.

Cowton, C. J. and Cummins J. (2003). Teaching business ethics in UK higher education: Progress and prospects. *Teaching Business Ethics*, 7 (1), 37–54.

Engwall, L. and Zamagni, V. (1998). *Management Education in Historical Perspective*. Manchester: Manchester University Press.

Fisher, C. and Lovell, A. (2003). *Business Ethics and Values*. Harlow: Pearson Education.

Mahoney, J. (1990). *Teaching Business Ethics in the UK, Europe and the USA*. London: Athlone Press.

Myners, P. (2001). *Review of Institutional Investment: Final Report*. London: H.M. Treasury.

Nelson, J. and Zadek, S. (2001). *Partnership Alchemy: New Social Partnerships in Europe*. Copenhagen: Copenhagen Center.

Sorrell, T. and Hendry, J. (1994). *Business Ethics*. London: Butterworth Heinemann.

Webley, S. (2003). *Developing a Code of Business Ethics*. London: Institute of Business Ethics.

universalizability

Richard M. Hare

A thesis about moral statements, held by most, though not all, moral philosophers, namely that to make a moral judgment about one situation commits one to accepting a similar judgment about any situation having the same universal non-moral properties, no matter what individuals occupy what roles in the two situations. The thesis is associated above all with Kant, but is related to the views of earlier thinkers, and to the Christian (and pre-Christian) golden rule. "Individuals" is best taken (though Kant thought otherwise) to include all sentient beings, human or non-human (*see* KANTIAN ETHICS).

The thesis is crucial for moral reasoning. The following confusions about it are common.

1   Universalizability is not the same as generality or simplicity, although simple general rules do have a place at the intuitive level of moral thinking. The universal non-moral properties in question may be highly specific. Thus a believer in the universalizability of moral statements does not have to believe that they ought always to be made in accordance with very simple general rules. Specific (even very detailed) differences between situations may make a moral difference, provided that they can be expressed without reference to individual roles. Thus a lie told to someone in one situation could be wrong, but a lie told to someone in a subtly different situation not wrong, if the difference were morally relevant. Kant was unclear about this.

2   References to individuals are not the same as specifications of relations in which the individuals stand. Thus, if Jane is John's mother, it is not a breach of the thesis to say that John has a certain duty to Jane in virtue of being her son. The universal principle here is that all sons owe this duty to their mothers – for example, to care for them in old age, or to do so in certain minutely specified circumstances. It is not relevant that a son can have only one (genetic) mother.

3   It is likewise not relevant that no two actual people and no two actual situations are

exactly similar. Hypothetical people and situations can be imagined that *are* exactly similar in their non-moral universal properties, and we can ask what should be done in these exactly similar situations if *we* occupied different roles in them (for example, that of the victim of a dirty trick that we are thinking of playing in our present actual role).

4 The roles in the situations include the desires of the people in them; so I cannot argue, "I wouldn't mind it being done to *me*," if my victim very much minds it being done to *him*.

The argument from universalizability thus goes as follows: we say to someone planning a wrong act, "Are you prepared to say that the same ought to be done to you, if just the same situation were to recur, but with you in your victim's place?" Most people, if they understand what "ought" means, will say that they are not.

utilitarianism

David Lyons

A moral theory that regards welfare, or the good of individuals, as the ultimate value, and evaluates other things, such as acts, solely by their promotion of that value (*see* VALUES). Utilitarianism gives content to the idea that doing the right thing means doing good – making the world better than it otherwise would be. The theory has proved to be perennially attractive and resilient in the face of challenging objections.

Utilitarianism is a normative, not a descriptive theory (*see* NORMATIVE/DESCRIPTIVE). It does not assume that our actions or value judgments reflect an unqualified commitment to promoting welfare. Utilitarians assume a critical attitude toward conventional morality and existing institutions. The founders of modern utilitarianism, Jeremy Bentham (1748–1832) and John Stuart Mill (1806–73), were effective advocates of social reform.

Utilitarianism is regarded by many theorists as a species of consequentialism, which asserts that "intrinsic" value (the most basic kind of value) should be brought into existence, and

that acts, motives, and institutions should accordingly be judged by their "instrumental value" (their capacity to realize basic value). As a species of consequentialism, utilitarianism holds that the good of individuals is the only basic value and should accordingly be maximized. Non-utilitarian varieties of consequentialism regard some other things, such as beauty, knowledge, or justice, as intrinsically valuable.

Utilitarian theories incorporate various conceptions of welfare. Bentham embraced a "hedonistic" conception, in terms of "pleasure" and the absence of "pain." Mill believed that the pleasures which differentiate human beings from other animals are "higher" and more valuable than physical pleasures. He advanced a complex conception of human welfare, which emphasizes the exercise of distinctive human faculties.

Some objections to utilitarianism concern a particular conception of welfare, such as hedonism, and do not challenge the utilitarian idea that right conduct depends on the promotion of welfare. Other criticisms concern the theory's focus on welfare to the exclusion of other goods, and do not challenge the consequentialist idea that right conduct depends on the promotion of intrinsic value.

Utilitarianism (and more generally consequentialism) may be contrasted with theories claiming that some set of rights or duties (rather than a value such as welfare) is morally basic. John Locke (1632–1704) held, for example, that certain "natural" rights are morally basic. Immanuel Kant (1724–1804) developed a theory within which duties are morally basic (*see* RIGHTS; KANTIAN ETHICS).

More recently, W. D. Ross argued that morality imposes a diverse set of obligations, or "prima facie duties," including some that are essentially "backward looking," such as honoring one's moral commitments and compensating others for wrongful injuries one has done them. Utilitarianism, by contrast, is essentially "forward looking": moral requirements are held by it to be grounded on the difference conduct can make to the future history of the world. Commitments one has made, wrongs one has done to others, indeed past events generally, are morally relevant, according to utilitarianism, only insofar as they affect the future consequences of conduct. Utilitarians accordingly recognize particular moral rights or duties when, but only when, they believe the recognition of those rights or duties would promote welfare. Critics see this facet of utilitarianism as evidence of a fundamentally misguided approach to moral responsibility.

Some utilitarians have argued that utilitarianism satisfactorily accommodates moral rights and obligations. To succeed, their arguments must overcome what may be called the trumping problem. It means little to embrace moral rights and obligations if they are not accorded special weight in practice. If I have promised to help you with a particular task, I am not morally free to decide what to do when the time comes by determining whether my helping you would maximize welfare. My obligation can be outweighed by important conflicting considerations, but it outweighs the utilitarian consideration that I might do a trifle more good by breaking my promise. Precisely because of his commitment to maximizing welfare, it would seem that a utilitarian should be guided by that utilitarian consideration. If so, the obligation is accorded no weight at all in practice, and the utilitarian's recognition of it would seem empty. Similar difficulties attach to the utilitarian recognition of moral rights. It is unclear whether utilitarianism (or any form of consequentialism) can solve this problem.

Utilitarianism differs from ethical egoism, a normative theory which holds that an individual may properly serve her own interests, however her self-serving conduct might affect others (see EGOISM, PSYCHOLOGICAL EGOISM, AND ETHICAL EGOISM). Ethical egoism says that one should take others' welfare into account only insofar as helping, hurting, or ignoring others would have an impact on one's own welfare.

Utilitarianism regards the welfare of any single individual as no more or less important than the welfare of any other individual. At the level of principle, therefore, it rejects the conventional assumption that a political community may properly serve its own interests first and that its public officials are morally bound to give priority to those interests. Utilitarianism holds that a policy reflecting that conventional assumption might be justified, but only if and when such a division of labor would maximize welfare throughout the world. Utilitarianism requires that laws and public policy serve as far as possible the interests of all who may be affected. No individual's interests may be discounted or double-counted because of her location, citizenship, nationality, class, race, creed, or gender – indeed, for any reason whatsoever.

Although utilitarianism may be considered egalitarian because it requires that equal consideration be given to all, it does not assume that all individuals should be treated the same. It would endorse unequal treatment whenever the general welfare would be maximized by unequal treatment. Because different individuals have different needs, differential treatment is in some respects unproblematic. Medicine, for example, should be allocated only to those who require it.

But utilitarianism also implies that one may properly favor one's family or friends only if and when such a policy would best serve the general welfare. Critics have regarded this as an implausible consequence of the theory. They believe that a conscious commitment to utilitarianism would undermine meaningful relationships with other persons, because close relations with others involve according their interests special weight.

Critics argue further that a distinctively human life involves commitment not only to some other persons but also to some personal projects. Given the vast array of unmet needs around the world – indeed, within our own communities – it would seem that a conscientious commitment to promoting welfare would place unrelenting demands on one's time, resources, and efforts. Critics believe that utilitarianism demands more sacrifice than it is reasonable for a morality to require. We draw a distinction between acting as morality requires and acting above and beyond the call of duty. Critics believe that utilitarianism's demands on the individual obliterates this distinction.

Some utilitarians believe that welfare is best served when economic resources are distributed equally. This notion is based on the phenomenon of "diminishing marginal utilities." A hundred dollars is more useful to an impoverished person than to someone who is affluent. The quality of life for a poor man can be improved more than the quality of life for a rich man would be decreased if a hundred dollars were transferred from the rich man to the poor man. In practice, however, such transfers have considerable costs, which constitute utilitarian obstacles to economic equalization. If justice requires equal distribution of resources, then utilitarianism will have difficulty accommodating its dictates.

Bentham came to believe that the interests of those who occupy high public office tend to conflict with the interests of their subjects. Because those who are ruled far outnumber those who rule, he held that welfare is best served when public policies are dedicated to promoting the "greatest happiness of the greater number." That famous slogan thus reflects an application of the utilitarian principle, not the principle itself.

As the foregoing suggests, it often seems that the interests of different individuals can come into conflict in the real world. Whenever that happens, utilitarianism does not care whose interests are served, so long as welfare in the aggregate is promoted as much as it is possible to do. Critics of utilitarianism charge that, as a consequence, utilitarianism can have morally objectionable implications. It is imaginable, for example, that the aggregate welfare would best be served by exploiting some individuals for the benefit of others. Systems like that have existed in our world – serfdom and slavery are uncontroversial examples – which some have defended as beneficial on the whole. For such a system to be condoned by utilitarianism, however, the total benefits generated must not merely exceed the total costs; the system must promote welfare to a greater degree than any alternative system that is available. Critics hold that, even if utilitarian support for such a system is in fact unlikely, utilitarians wrongly reject such systems by calculating benefits and costs rather than recognizing that exploitative social systems violate inviolable rights.

In practice, exploitative systems attack not only the living standard of those who are exploited but also their dignity and self-respect. It is unclear whether utilitarianism can fully account for those terrible costs. The possibility that it can is suggested by the fact that one's

quality of life is devastated by conditions that undermine dignity and self-respect.

As many of these examples imply, utilitarianism assumes that "interpersonal comparisons of utility" are possible. Consider first commonplace estimates of self-interest. These require rankings of alternatives involving benefits and costs; they do not strictly require that we sum and therefore measure benefits and costs. Utilitarianism assumes that welfare gains and losses to a given person are measurable, and that the units of measurement for gains are equivalent to those for losses. It then adds a significant complication: it assumes, further, that units of measurement for gains and losses have interpersonal validity. It presupposes that there is some way of rigorously comparing the gains and losses of one person with the gains and losses for any other person. Utilitarianism makes no sense otherwise. But no one has ever adequately explained how such measurements can be made.

One should reject utilitarianism if one has good reason to believe that interpersonal comparisons of utility are not merely difficult but impossible. Believing this, some theorists have developed evaluative principles that do not require interpersonal comparisons, such as certain conceptions of economic efficiency. Consider the concepts of "Pareto superiority" and "Pareto optimality": allocation of resources B is Pareto superior to allocation of resources A if, and only if, the move from A to B would result in someone gaining without anyone losing. And A is a Pareto optimal allocation of resources if, and only if, it is impossible to reallocate resources from A so that some person gains without anyone losing. These concepts require that we determine whether anyone gains or loses, but they do not require that we compare one person's gain or loss with anyone else's gain or loss.

Although no one has yet proved that interpersonal comparisons of utility are in principle possible, commonplace reasoning frequently involves such comparisons. And the reasoning which has led theorists to reject interpersonal comparisons of utility may be questioned. It is based on the assumptions that welfare must be understood in terms of "pleasures" and "pains," and that these are "private," inaccessible to others, so that it makes no sense to think we might objectively measure the intensity of a pleasure or pain. But pleasure without pain is just one particular conception of welfare. It seems plausible to suppose that it is in a person's interest to have good health, ample resources, interesting opportunities, good companionship, and self-respect. In supposing this, one need not assume that such advantages can be analyzed exhaustively in terms of pleasure and the absence of pain. Whether welfare, properly understood, is susceptible to the necessary measurements remains to be seen.

Some utilitarians believe that right conduct is determined by actual consequences. Others believe it depends on the consequences that one can reasonably predict. Each alternative offers difficulties. On the first view, if all the available evidence is misleading, utilitarianism can condemn one's conduct even if one has acted most conscientiously. On the second view, utilitarianism can imply that it is wrong to do what actually has the best consequences. Utilitarians address these difficulties in part by distinguishing between judgments of acts and judgments of persons.

As a moral theory, utilitarianism applies the welfare criterion in order to determine which acts are morally right and which are morally wrong. The simplest and most important form of the theory applies the welfare criterion directly to conduct. The result is "act utilitarianism," which holds that each and every act should promote welfare as much as possible. Utilitarianism has recently been given different forms. One is "rule utilitarianism," which applies the welfare criterion indirectly to acts and directly to social rules. Rule utilitarianism says that conduct should conform to social rules which promote welfare as much as possible. Rule utilitarianism can itself be developed in various ways.

Critics have advanced many objections to utilitarianism beyond those already mentioned. For example, we usually assume that competent adults should be left free to find their own ways, which includes making their own mistakes (so long as they exercise due care for others' welfare). Invasions of that freedom are condemned as paternalistic. It would seem that utilitarianism must sometimes approve or even require such interventions. Utilitarians have, however, disagreed. Because his conception of welfare places a premium on the individual's free exercise of her own judgment, developing her own goals, and working toward them, Mill (for example) believed that utilitarianism, properly understood, would not condone objectionable paternalism.

See also *altruism and benevolence; privacy; welfare economics*

Bibliography

Bentham, J. (1789). *An Introduction to the Principles of Morals and Legislation*. (Many editions are currently available.)

Glover, J. (1990). *Utilitarianism and Its Critics*. New York: Macmillan. (A useful collection of studies, with an extensive bibliography.)

Mill, J. S. (1863). *Utilitarianism*. (Many editions are currently available.)

Moore, G. E. (1912). *Ethics*. Oxford: Oxford University Press. (A twentieth-century classic.)

Scheffler, S. (1988). *Consequentialism and Its Critics*. New York: Oxford University Press. (A useful collection, with an extensive bibliography.)

Sidgwick, H. (1874). *The Methods of Ethics*. London: Macmillan. (A highly esteemed classic of utilitarianism. A seventh edition was published in 1907.)

Smart, J. J. C. and Williams, B. (1973). *Utilitarianism: For and Against*. Cambridge: Cambridge University Press.

V

values

David T. Ozar

The verb "to value," like the nouns "value" and "values," and the adjective "valuable," have a wide range of meanings in ordinary speech because they are used in many different contexts. But all of these meanings and all uses of these words build on one central idea: to value something is to consider it a candidate for action aimed at achieving it. We speak and think most clearly, in other words, if we consider the verb "to value" as the primary guide to the meanings of these words. Then the adjective, "valuable," tells us that someone values the thing so described; and the nouns "value" and "values" pick out the characteristics that valuing focuses on, that is, the characteristics that make a thing a candidate for action aimed at achieving it. If we interpret these words in this way, then an uncommon but accurate synonym for "valuable" would be "choiceworthy" (a term borrowed here from Terrence Irwin's translation of Aristotle's *Nicomachean Ethics*). It is difficult to think of any exact synonym for the more abstract nouns, "value" and "values," although the word "goodness" sometimes means almost the same thing as "value."

The activity of valuing involves a valuer and something valued. The valuer must be the kind of being that acts and is drawn to action by characteristics in things. Thus, there is a link between talk of values and people's *motivations* for acting (*see* MOTIVES). But valuing is not simply reactive; it involves judgment, and this is why a person can provide a satisfactory answer to the question, "Why did you do that?" by citing the value/values that the action is aimed at achieving. That is, values refer to people's *reasons* for acting and their judgments about such reasons. This is why ethics, as the study of people's judgments about what they ought to do, always has an important place for values (i.e., for the characteristics that people value and so aim to achieve in their actions) (*see* ETHICS).

In addition to a valuer, the activity of valuing also involves something valued. It is an intentional activity; that is, it is not wholly self-contained in the valuer, but links the valuer to something else, to the thing valued, via the characteristics (values) in it which prompt or explain action aimed at achieving it. In this respect, statements about valuing are always, in part, descriptions of something, since they identify characteristics of things that the valuer takes to be real and worth acting for. But statements about valuing also serve as explanations of actions, as reasons offered to other persons to explain why a certain action was done in the past or is being done in the present or is being considered for the future. In this way statements about valuing always play a normative function as well, showing other persons who want to understand our actions why these actions are reasonable (*see* NORMATIVE/DESCRIPTIVE).

Things valued can be of many sorts. But the characteristics of things that valuing picks out are characteristics that make action worthwhile. So it is appropriate to ask if there is any class of characteristics that is fundamentally worthwhile to act for, or whether the valuableness of things – what is worth acting for – is completely variable. Answering this question requires a three-step sorting process.

First, some things are valued only "instrumentally," that is, as means to other things. For example, I value taking the subway in order to get to my destination. I value getting to my destination, let us say, in order to shop for something; and I value shopping in order, in one possible scenario, to give my friend a birthday gift; and so on. It seems obvious, however, that this chain of explanations cannot go on forever and still be an adequate explanation. Instead, we expect to find, at the end of such a chain, something that is not valued for the sake of something else; that is, something (or things) valued "for its own sake," as we commonly express it. In philosophers' terminology, things valued for the sake of something else are called "instrumentally" valuable; and a thing valued "for its own sake" is said to be "intrinsically valuable."

Second, is there any common characteristic among the things that people consider intrinsically valuable? This is a disputed point. But a good case can be made that, for humans, only *experiences* are intrinsically valuable, and that all the non-human things that humans value, and all other characteristics of humans besides experiences that humans value, are all valued instrumentally and for the sake of certain kinds of experiences that these things are means to in various ways.

The third question is whether there is any pattern in the experiences that humans value intrinsically. Is there some fairly definite set of experiences that are intrinsically valued by humans generally and that are the only ones that humans generally value intrinsically? This is a highly disputed question that has been written about, pro and con, by philosophers, psychologists, and other theorists about the human condition, as well as by novelists, playwrights, and many others for centuries. There are some very plausible candidates for experiences that all people, at least all people of mature years and sound mind, intrinsically value. Among these are: pleasure (or certain kinds of pleasure); self-determination or autonomy; certain kinds of human relationships (e.g., just exchanges; fulfilling one's social role; friendship; love); and a sense of integrity or of the unity of the self (*see* INTEGRITY; JUSTICE; ROLES AND ROLE MORALITY; TRUST).

Those who argue that there is no such pattern can point to the wide range of things that people value in daily life. But much of this diversity of human aims disappears once these aims are sorted out specifically in terms of the experiences that people intrinsically value. A more

serious objection for those who see a pattern in these intrinsic values concerns the qualifier: "at least all people of mature years and sound mind." Is this a legitimate qualifier or a way of avoiding evidence contrary to the proposed pattern?

The judgments people offer to explain their actions have been of interest to philosophers and other moral theorists for many centuries (*see* PRACTICAL REASONING). One tradition of theorizing about these judgments has paid particular attention to value statements and to the characteristics of things they identify as choiceworthy. This approach to moral theory is commonly called utilitarianism or consequentialism. But these theorists might very accurately be called "Value-Maximizers," because they hold that what a person morally ought to do in any situation in whichever course of action available to an actor will produce the maximum of intrinsic value (i.e., of experiences worth having for their own sake). These theorists describe human moral reflection at its best as a process of (1) evaluating alternative courses of action to determine what instrumental and then what intrinsic values they would yield (and what disvalues and hindrances to values as well), and for whom; and then (2) comparing these evaluations to determine which course of action yields the greatest value. On the value-maximizers' account of morality, this course of action is the one that the actor ought to do.

There have been many varieties of value-maximizing moral theories. Some have held that each human ought to maximize values for self alone; others have seen morality as maximizing values for everyone affected by a course of action; and others have offered other, more complex answers to the "for whom?" question. They have also differed in their views about what sorts of experiences are intrinsically valuable (*see* EGOISM, PSYCHOLOGICAL EGOISM, AND ETHICAL EGOISM).

The other traditions of moral theorizing, on the other hand, consider valuing to have, not a central, but at best a subordinate role within sound moral reflection. They have consequently paid much less attention to value statements and to the characteristics that humans value in things, and have explained moral reflection in a variety of other ways.

See *fairness; justice; Kantian ethics; liberalism; libertarianism; rights; virtue ethics*

virtue ethics

Daryl Koehn

OVERVIEW

A virtue ethic, like any ethic, describes human character and action in an evaluative manner. Virtue ethicists, such as Plato and Aristotle, believe that all human beings aim at being happy. In the language of virtue ethics, happiness is the "end" of human action. Agents are happy when they are doing well or thriving. More specifically, human beings are happy when they are fulfilling their peculiarly human potentialities. While a cat will be satisfied leading an animal's life of sensation and appetite, a human being needs something more. A human's life will not be a full one unless that person is, in addition to sensing and desiring, also maximally exercising the specifically human capacity to choose and to reason.

For the virtue ethicist, the process by which an organism realizes its particular potential and grows into its peculiar being or actuality is natural. Indeed, the Greek word for nature – *physis* – simply means a growing characterized by a successive and progressive realization of a certain end state. Since this fulfilling growth only occurs under specific conditions, it is the task of the virtue ethicist to specify these conditions. By doing so, the virtue ethicist hopes to make his or her audience more aware of the conditions to which they must pay attention if they, too, want to realize their nature or, equivalently, to be happy.

What are these conditions? First and foremost, human happiness depends upon participation in community, be that the community of a household, a clan, a business, or the larger political community. A community is "natural" if human growth (i.e., actualization) depends upon it. The human family is natural because no child becomes an adult without parents who nurture the child and teach her skills for survival. Similarly, human beings are "by nature" political beings because they cannot fully realize their peculiarly human rationality without participation in the larger political community. By providing and enforcing a rule of law, the political regime frees its citizens from having to constantly protect themselves from marauding thieves and murderers. In addition, the law makes for regular and predictable interactions among citizens. Such predictability, in turn, helps make deliberation possible. People can plan actions only when there is some stability in their environment (e.g., when banks do not arbitrarily choose not to open on some day; or when airlines do not willy-nilly refuse passengers because of their race or sex, etc.). Furthermore, by legislating public education, including the teaching of ethics, the political regime not only develops agents' ability to think and reason about the human condition and the surrounding world. It also aims at getting its citizens to see the necessary connections between their happiness and that of the community at large. Educated citizens will demonstrate the loyalty needed for the community to continue to be healthy and for subsequent generations to have a chance at actualizing their human potentiality.

Human happiness depends upon a second condition as well. To be happy, the agent must be virtuous. Virtue is not to be taken as some extraordinary or saintly goodness. Rather, a human virtue is a state or condition that serves to realize some dimension of human potential. Thus, while it would be better for soldiers to fight only in wars they know to be just, Aristotle treats even unthinking courage as virtuous. The soldier who acts to take a stand in the face of death thereby develops his or her ability to take risks and confront the consequences. Insofar as this ability is a critical life skill, this "false" courage is virtuous.

While "false" courage is a virtue, truly courageous persons do not fight to death simply because ordered to do so. Instead, they consider whether a given situation demands such a stance. Their thoughtfulness points to a third condition for human happiness. To fully (i.e., excellently) realize their human potentiality, persons must learn to deliberate well. Deliberation does not consist of merely identifying means to an end. Someone who deliberates rethinks the end at the same time as she analyzes means to the end. Thus, the deliberative daughter who is considering how best to care for her elderly mother will try to identify various options for care. Some means might include placing the mother in a nursing home, getting a residential nurse, or having the mother stay with the daughter. If the daughter is on the road to becoming virtuous, she uses her thinking about these various alternatives to further clarify what will count as "caring" for her mother. If she thinks the mother would like an in-house nurse because that will preserve the mother's independence, then the deliberative daughter refines her end of caring for her mother. "Caring" now means not merely physically tending to her mother but also meeting her mother's need for independence. Deliberation, unlike means–end cunning, examines the end along with the means in figuring out how best to achieve a desired end.

The person who fails to deliberate and who relies instead on simple cunning is little more than a crafty animal. Animals, too, can identify means to an end. To the extent an agent is little more than an animal, that agent is neither a virtuous nor a happy *human being*. The virtuous person's happiness inheres in the active life of deliberating. By consistently trying to deliberate about how best to act, agents develop their deliberative skill. They thereby realize their specifically human capacity to deliberate instead of merely engaging in cunning calculations. They also come to grasp important connections between the ends and means, linkages not apparent to vicious persons who fail to deliberate. Consequently, they are less frustrated because the end their action brings about tends to be the end they foresaw and wanted to achieve. The virtuous person's reward is happiness understood as an entire life of satisfying actions, while the vicious person's punishment is a life of actions that produce both unexpected and unintended consequences for himself and others.

Relevance of Virtue Ethics to Business

While virtue ethicists care about issues such as workers' rights and consumer protection, they are also concerned to raise the larger question of the meaning and goodness of business. Business is a practice, akin to the other professions and arts. Like all other professionals, business persons either realize or fail to realize their happiness through their activity at work. Persons who

view their jobs with "another day, another dollar" mentality are not likely to be happy. Such a mentality turns action into a means to make money. In terms of the above discussion, the agent with this mentality becomes little more than a cunning animal.

The virtuous business person, by contrast, always asks whether a proposed act will help to actualize his human being. If, for example, an act manifests contempt for his fellow citizens and for the law, the agent will refrain from it. For business, like the household, is a part of the larger political community. The virtuous person does not deliberately act in ways that destroy the laws that make his and others' happiness possible. Instead, the business person who desires to be happy will strive to make friends within the corporation, friends who can help the agent arrive at sound choices. The virtuous business person will also support his or her corporation's charity drives and other community projects. From the perspective of the virtuous agent, there can be no question as to whether business should be socially responsible. Insofar as business is a part of society, the acts of corporations and their employees will affect the society at large and, hence, the happiness of persons who are by nature political beings.

Distinctive Insights of the Virtue Ethics Approach

Virtue ethics has become increasingly popular among business ethicists who think this mode of analysis offers important and distinctive insights. According to virtue ethics, what makes an action good is not its conformity to some rule(s) but rather its tendency to fulfill human actuality. Virtue ethics resembles situation ethics inasmuch as both emphasize the need to evaluate particular, and possibly unique, features of a situation in arriving at a decision.

Unlike situation ethics, however, virtue ethics employs a non-relativistic standard for evaluating a course of action. Stated roughly, that principle is: What is humanly good and desirable is what actualizes human being. Not every decision made with respect to a situation is equally good. A sloppy, ill-considered decision or a choice that undermines the happiness of other members of the political community is not as fine and good as a carefully thought through choice consistent with (and preservative of) human virtue. Since what counts as being consistent with human virtue is itself often not immediately obvious in a particular situation, the agent who desires to be happy will investigate this question as well with her friends and colleagues.

One strength, then, of virtue ethics is its ability to provide non-relativistic, yet situation-sensitive, guidance to agents. Virtue ethics is also appealing because it brings to the fore features of action often overlooked by other modes of ethical analyses. Suppose, for example, that a businessman wonders whether he should bribe government officials in order to get a government contract. The Kantian ethicist will argue that the action will not be right if a description of the act's maxim involves the agent in a contradiction of will (*see* KANTIAN ETHICS). If we take the maxim in this case to be "Act to circumvent government rules and regulations in order to be able to do business with government," the maxim is clearly self-contradictory. Since all governments require rules in order to govern, the agent's envisioned act commits him to a practice that would destroy the very institution with whom he wants to do business. No rational agent therefore can will this act. Hence, it is immoral from the Kantian point of view.

While the virtue ethicist will acknowledge the force of the Kantian objection, it will not be decisive. She will urge the businessman to consider the consequences of this act for his character and long-term ability to lead a happy life. He should deliberate as to how the proposed means (bribing) may impact the end (doing business with the government). To successfully work with the government, the corporation's representatives will need to develop mutual trust. Doing so may be difficult if the relation begins in an underhanded fashion. Furthermore, if the businessman does win the business through a bribe, he cannot claim honestly that he succeeded because he had the superior product or because of his ability to help the customer see what service is best for the customer. The businessman is little more than a conduit for money in this case. He adds little to the transaction. Since his action does not develop any of his particularly human capacities, the virtue ethicist will suggest that the businessman who relies

upon bribery may wind up feeling dissatisfied and alienated from his work.

Virtue ethics may also be contrasted with utilitarianism. The utilitarian will consider whether the act of bribing maximizes the happiness of the society as a whole. One could argue that the act would benefit the bribed official. In the short run, bribery might benefit the company and the businessman as well, assuming the company gets the contract and is not simply tricked by the government official into paying ever more in bribes. If these and other benefits outweigh the various costs of bribery (e.g., the company has to pay bribery fees it would not have to pay if the bidding system were not corrupt), then the utilitarian will judge the action a good one and will recommend its performance.

The virtue ethicist will listen to the utilitarian's analysis. But once again it will not be decisive. Unlike the utilitarian, the virtue ethicist does not assign equal weight to all benefits and costs. Virtue ethics weighs those consequences impacting human growth most heavily. The businessman who pays the bribe initially may be overjoyed at winning the contract. How, though, will he win the next contract? He has not developed his selling skills, and not all contracts can be procured through bribes. By taking the easy route of offering a bribe and by failing to take a stand against corruption, the businessman is choosing a path not likely to serve him well in the future. The virtue ethicist is more inclined than the utilitarian to evaluate each choice from the perspective of the whole of life. As Aristotle puts it, "one swallow does not a summer make" nor does a single act make for a happy life.

WEAKNESSES OF VIRTUE ETHICS ANALYSIS

Critics of virtue ethics worry that the approach is too simplistic. The analysis posits a timeless, invariable human nature. Yet recent discoveries of anthropology show that humans have changed dramatically over time. If so, then it is questionable whether happiness can be said to be the human good. If human nature is indeed variable, happiness, too, must change over time.

In addition, since the virtue ethicist makes claims that are simultaneously descriptive and evaluative (e.g., "all men are by nature political"), some critics have alleged that this approach confuses descriptive with prescriptive claims. If "ought" cannot be derived from "is," then virtue ethics must be on shaky ground.

Of course, these criticisms are themselves controversial. Readers should consult materials listed below and judge the relative merits of virtue ethics for themselves.

Bibliography

Aristotle (1975). *Nicomachean Ethics*, trans. H. Rackham. Cambridge, MA: Harvard University Press.

Broadie, S. (1991). *Ethics with Aristotle*. New York: Oxford University Press.

Donaldson, T. (1992). The language of international corporate ethics. *Business Ethics Quarterly*, 2 (3), 271–82.

Hartman, E. M. (1996). *Organizational Ethics and the Good Life*. New York: Oxford University Press.

Plato (1968). *Republic*, trans. A. Bloom. New York: Basic Books.

Rorty, A. (1980). *Essays on Aristotle's Ethics*. Berkeley: University of California Press.

Salkever, S. (1990). *Finding the Mean: Theory and Practice in Aristotelian Political Philosophy*. Princeton, NJ: Princeton University Press.

Sherman, N. (1989). *The Fabric of Character*. Oxford: Clarendon Press.

Solomon, R. C. (1993). *Ethics and Excellence*. New York: Oxford University Press.

welfare economics

Kaushik Basu

is the study of decision-making with the aim of enhancing *social* welfare, in contrast to an *individual's* happiness or a *firm's* profit. It is therefore a subject which should be of value to government, since government is meant to be an agency for promoting social welfare. It should, however, also be of interest to an individual who is not committed solely to enhancing his or her own happiness, or even to the "enlightened" firm or business corporation that seeks not only to increase its profit but also has some commitment to the general well-being of society.

Suppose in choosing between two projects, *A* and *B*, all the relevant facts are known. It is known how much and who will gain from each project, how much damage each project will do to the environment, and so on. This is in itself of course not enough to choose between the projects. The choice depends on *what* it is that one is seeking to achieve. If a certain firm is evaluating these projects in order to maximize its profits, the facts may point to the choice of *A*. If the aim is to maximize social welfare, then the same facts point to *B*. However, the second decision-problem is in some fundamental ways more complicated than the first one because unlike "profits," what constitutes "social welfare" may itself be controversial.

It follows that welfare economics has two main concerns. The first is the abstract problem of deciding what constitutes social welfare, given that individuals in a society have widely divergent and often conflicting objectives. The second concern is the more mundane one of deciding how to choose between projects, taxation schemes, industrial regulation, environ-

mental policy and so on, given some agreed-upon notion of social welfare. The former concern relates welfare economics to moral philosophy and ethics, a boundary with considerable intellectual trespassing (Sen, 1987). The latter explains the overlap of welfare economics with issues of cost-benefit analysis and public policy (Atkinson, 1983; Ng, 1979).

Regarding the constitution of social welfare, one of the earliest and, in economics, arguably the most influential position has been a utilitarian one. With roots a respectable two centuries ago and in the works of Jeremy Bentham (1748–1832) and the two Mills (James, 1773–1836 and John Stuart, 1806–73), UTILITARIANISM is an ethical doctrine that requires us to maximize the sum total of everybody's utility or happiness. Hence, a welfare economics wedded to utilitarianism would simply sum the total benefit that results from each project or action, giving equal weight to all human beings, and then recommend the project that yields the larger aggregate welfare.

Though the utilitarian method has been and still is widely used in assessing the goodness of alternative government policies or projects, like tax schemes or new airports, it came under severe attack in the first half of this century. One set of criticisms pertained to the fact that utilitarianism requires us to *sum* everybody's utility. It is easier to agree that social welfare should *depend* on every individual's utility, but not necessarily be their sum. We may, for instance, argue that if a project impoverishes a rich man by two dollars (assuming for simplicity that dollars measure individual utility) and enriches a poor person by one dollar, this may be a desirable project even though the sum total of utility in society is lowered. The Bergson–Samuelson social welfare function (see Samuelson, 1947;

Graaff, 1957) allows for such flexibility which is not there in the utilitarian system.

The second criticism of utilitarianism, and one that also applies to the Bergson–Samuelson method, is that it entails interpersonal comparisons between different people's utility. But can we really compare one person's happiness with another's? (See Basu, 1995, for discussion.) How do we know whether a dollar would make Guildenstern or Rosencrantz happier? So if we have only one dollar to give away and we want to maximize social welfare, whom do we give it to?

A method that tries to circumvent this problem and has been immensely influential in modern welfare economics is the method of Vilfredo Pareto (1848–1923) (*see* PARETO OPTIMALITY). Welfare economics defines a *Pareto improvement* for a society as any change that leaves no one worse off and at least one person better off. A *Pareto optimal* state is then defined as a situation from where no further Pareto improvements are made.

One reason why the idea of Pareto optimality shot into prominence in economics was the discovery of a major theorem, the so-called Fundamental Theorem of Welfare Economics. The Fundamental Theorem is essentially a formalization of conjectures which date at least as far back as the writings of Adam Smith (1723–90). It states that, given some condition, perfect competition in an economy ensures that the economy will attain Pareto optimality. The importance of this theorem stems from the fact that it has been used – perhaps somewhat cavalierly – to justify a variety of government policies, for example, the enactment of antitrust legislation in order to encourage competition among firms, and, also, at times, to justify unbridled *laissez-faire*.

An advance which gave welfare economics a big boost was the discovery of a theorem of gigantic proportions – Kenneth Arrow's (1951) general impossibility theorem. An Arrovian social welfare function – "SWF" – is a rule by which individuals' rankings over a set of alternatives (e.g., candidates in an election) are converted into a social ranking. Instead of fixing a particular SWF, Arrow developed some reasonable axioms that we would want any SWF to satisfy. The impossibility theorem demonstrates that no SWF can satisfy these axioms. The theorem was remarkable because it was so unexpected; its proof relied on no standard mathematics but just careful chains of deduction. A large literature emerged to "solve" the problem (see Sen, 1970). The literature has grown so as to straddle the formal algebra of voting theory on the one hand and the conceptual world of moral philosophy on the other.

Instead of being a separate field of study, welfare economics is increasingly a method of analysis that underlies diverse branches of economics. With one foot in the groves of academe and the other in the practitioner's workplace, welfare economics is here to stay as an essential part of the economist's repertoire.

Bibliography

Arrow, K. J. (1951). *Social Choice and Individual Values.* New York: Wiley.

Atkinson, A. B. (1983). *Social Justice and Public Policy.* Brighton: Wheatsheaf; and Cambridge, MA: MIT Press.

Basu, K. (1995). On interpersonal comparison and the concept of equality. In W. Eichhorn (ed.), *Models and Measurement of Welfare and Inequality.* Berlin: Springer-Verlag, 491–510.

Graaff, J. de V. (1957). *Theoretical Welfare Economics.* Cambridge: Cambridge University Press.

Ng, Y.-K. (1979). *Welfare Economics.* London: Macmillan.

Samuelson, P. A. (1947). *Foundations of Economic Analysis.* Cambridge, MA: Harvard University Press.

Sen, A. K. (1970). *Collective Choice and Social Welfare.* San Francisco: Holden-Day.

Sen, A. K. (1987). *On Ethics and Economics.* Oxford: Blackwell.

welfare rights

Carl P. Wellman

are rights to or concerning well-being. Primarily, welfare consists in the state or condition of doing or being well; good fortune, happiness, or well-being of a person, community, or thing. Hence, primary welfare rights are often called rights to well-being. It is useful to classify the various conceptions of rights to welfare roughly on the basis of three distinct concepts of welfare. In the relevant senses, the word "welfare" is used to refer to (1) the happiness or well-being of a person, (2) a source of happiness or personal well-being, or (3) the organized provision for the basic well-being of the needy members of a community.

Gregory Vlastos is the most influential advocate of the first conception. He argues that there is a fundamental human right to well-being. The content of this right is best described as the well-being or welfare of each individual person, that is, the enjoyment of value in all the forms in which it can be experienced by human beings. One person's right to well-being is equal to that of every other person simply because one person's well-being is as valuable as that of any other's. From this generic human right to well-being Vlastos derives more specific welfare rights, such as the moral rights to education, medical care, or work under decent conditions. At this point his reasoning moves to the second conception of welfare rights best illustrated by the writings of Martin Golding. He contrasts option rights, that involve a limited sovereignty over persons or things, with welfare rights, claims to the goods of life which are conferred by the social ideal of a community. The content of each welfare right is some element in or means to the right-holder's personal good or well-being. Examples of the former might be health or freedom from pain; instances of the latter would be food or education. The clearest version of the third sort of conception is Carl Wellman's definition of a primary welfare right as a right to some welfare benefit or benefits. A welfare benefit is any form of assistance – monetary payment, good, or service – provided to an individual because of his or her need. Although the most obvious examples are public welfare benefits, such as (in the US context) social security payments or food stamps, there are also private welfare benefits, such as the disaster relief provided by the Red Cross or the food and shelter the Salvation Army offers to the homeless.

In order to understand fully the language of welfare rights, one must not only identify the relevant meaning of "welfare," but also the presupposed conception of a right. Most discussions of welfare rights interpret them according to Wesley Newcomb Hohfeld's conception of a claim. Thus, to assert that Jones has a right to adequate medical care is to say that Jones has a claim against some second party to be provided with medical care and that this second party has a duty to Jones to provide such medical care to him or her.

This interpretation poses a conceptual problem when resources are so scarce that adequate medical care is unavailable. Since no individual or government can have any duty to do the impossible, there could be no universal human right to medical care. Joel Feinberg, who adopts a claim theory of rights, suggests that in such cases one is using "a right" in a manifesto sense asserting a potential claim-right that ought to determine present aspirations and guide present policies. H. J. McCloskey avoids this predicament by adopting an entitlement theory of rights. Rights are entitlements *to* do, have, enjoy, or have done, not claims *against* others. Thus, although a welfare right involves an entitlement to the efforts of others or to make demands on others to aid and promote our seeking after or enjoying some good, the special circumstances will determine who, if anyone, has any implied duty.

Most libertarians conceive of rights negatively as claims that others *not* interfere with one's liberty of action or private property (*see* LIBERTARIANISM). Although most liberals accept such negative rights, they also assert various positive rights, claims against others to provide one with goods or services (*see* LIBERALISM). Because welfare rights seem to be positive rather than negative rights, welfare liberals can and usually do affirm their existence, while many libertarians conclude that there is a conceptual incoherence in any attempt to combine the negative concept of a right with the positive concept of an implied duty to provide welfare benefits. James Sterba suggests that there are negative as well as positive welfare rights. Those who lack the resources necessary to satisfy their basic needs have rights that others not interfere with their taking what they need from those who possess more than they basically need. Because welfare rights can be either negative liberty-rights or positive claim-rights, Sterba defines them as rights to acquire or to receive those goods and resources necessary for satisfying one's basic needs.

However one defines "welfare rights," it is essential to distinguish between the very different species of rights to which this expression can refer. The two most important genera are legal rights conferred by the rules or principles of some legal system and moral rights conferred by moral rules or reasons. Some legal welfare rights, such as the right to education, are in legal systems such as ours civil rights, rights possessed by every member of the society simply as a citizen. Others are special legal rights, rights one possesses by virtue of some more limited status, such as the right to Aid to Families of Dependent Children one possesses by virtue of one's status as an impoverished parent. The two most basic species of moral rights are human rights, rights one possesses simply as a human being, and civic rights, rights one possesses as a member of some society. Moral philosophers disagree about whether welfare rights, such as the right to social security or the right to an adequate standard of living, belong in the former or the latter category. The significance of this issue is in where the nature of implied duties lies. If these are civic rights, then it is one's society that has the obligation to provide for these rights; if they are human rights, then presumably other governments and even individual citizens of other nations also bear some responsibility for assisting those in need.

Another distinction that cuts across the previous classification is that between primary and secondary welfare rights. Carl Wellman distinguishes between primary welfare rights to welfare benefits and secondary welfare rights concerning, but not to, welfare benefits. This distinction can and should be generalized to cover all three conceptions of welfare. Examples of secondary welfare rights are the legal right of a recipient of some welfare benefit to a fair hearing before the termination of this benefit and the moral right of a worker that her employee provide equal pay for equal work.

Discussions of welfare rights are confusing, in part because the expression "a welfare right" is used with such diverse meanings. Those who wish to think clearly about the political, legal, and moral issues concerning welfare ought not to try to identify the correct, or even the best, conception of welfare rights. Different conceptions are appropriate for different purposes. What is important is to recognize their differences in order to understand more fully the meaning of any given assertion or denial of a welfare right and to think and debate the relevant issues more accurately and fruitfully.

See also *rights; welfare economics*

Bibliography

Feinberg, J. (1980). *Rights, Justice, and the Bounds of Liberty*. Princeton, NJ: Princeton University Press.

Golding, M. (1968). Towards a theory of human rights. *Monist*, **52**, 521–49.

Hohfeld, W. N. (1919). *Fundamental Legal Conceptions*. New Haven, CT: Yale University Press.

McCloskey, H. J. (1965). Rights. *Philosophical Quarterly*, **15**, 115–27.

Sterba, J. P. (1981). The welfare rights of distant peoples and future generations. *Social Theory and Practice*, **7**, 99–119.

Vlastos, G. (1962). Justice and equality. In R. Brandt (ed.), *Social Justice*. Englewood Cliffs, NJ: Prentice-Hall, 31–72.

Wellman, C. (1982). *Welfare Rights*. Totowa, NJ: Rowman and Allanheld.

Wellman, C. (1985). Welfare rights. In K. Kipnis and D. Meyers (eds.), *Economic Justice*. Totowa, NJ: Rowman and Allanheld, 229–45.

whistleblowing

Ronald F. Duska

is a practice in which employees who know that their company is engaged in activities that (a) cause unnecessary harm, (b) are in violation of human rights, (c) are illegal, (d) run counter to the defined purpose of the institution, or (e) are otherwise immoral, inform the public or some governmental agency of those activities. The ethical problem is whether and under what conditions whistleblowing is acceptable behavior and/or morally required behavior. Whistleblowing, if required, would involve a conflict between the obligation of loyalty the individual is presumed to have to the company and the obligation to prevent harm the individual is presumed to have to the public. But the exact nature and demands of these conflicting obligations to the company and the public are disputed.

Most business ethicists claim that employees have some obligation to the company or employer, which is usually characterized as an obligation of loyalty. Whistleblowing violates that obligation. In that context the company is viewed as analogous to a sports team. In sports, whistleblowing is the function of neutral, detached referees who are supposed to detect and penalize illicit behavior of opposing teams. It is neither acceptable nor a responsibility of a player to call a foul on one's teammates. If the analogy holds, what is unacceptable in sports is also unacceptable in business. From this perspective, whistleblowing is viewed as an act of disloyalty ("finking," "tattle tale") and there is a presumption against it. Consequently, a countervailing obligation to the public would be the only justification for overriding the obligation to the team or company. There is a wide range of views on the issue, ranging from the position that whistleblowing as an act of disloyalty is never justified, to the opposite position that employees owe no loyalty to a company and given their right to freedom of expression they can ethically disclose whatever they wish about a company, except where their work contract expressly or at least implicitly prohibits it.

Most business ethicists writing on whistleblowing maintain a fiduciary obligation of loyalty that whistleblowing violates, so the burden of proof or justification falls to the whistleblower. However, defenders of whistleblowing maintain that in conditions where companies violate ethical and/or legal constraints, whatever obligation of loyalty an employee has is abrogated, and whistleblowing is not only permissible but may also be morally required, on the grounds that individuals have a responsibility to the general public to prevent harm or illegal activity. Hence the conflict of obligations we mentioned. However, it is possible to argue that even if the illegal or immoral behavior of the company abrogates the responsibility of loyalty, there is no consequent good samaritan obligation to the general public to "blow the whistle."

So two arguments are needed: one to show whistleblowing is permissible, a second to show it is required. This latter argument is quite important, since blowing the whistle can lead to harm to the whistleblower. Under what conditions is one required to do what would likely harm oneself?

The argument for the permissibility of whistleblowing sets down a set of conditions to be met before a whistleblower can justifiably inform on her company.

1 The whistleblowing should be done for the purpose of exposing unnecessary harm, violation of human rights, illegal activity, or conduct counter to the defined purpose of the corporation, and should be done from the appropriate moral motive, that is, not from a desire to get ahead, or out of spite or some such motive. Nevertheless, whether the act of whistleblowing is called for is not determined by the motive of the whistleblower but by the company acting either immorally or illegally.

2 The whistleblower should make certain that his or her belief that inappropriate actions are ordered or have occurred is based on evidence that would persuade a reasonable person.

3 The whistleblower should have acted only after a careful analysis of the danger: (a) how serious is the moral violation? (minor moral matters need not be reported); (b) how immediate is the moral violation? (the greater time before the violation occurs the greater chances that internal mechanisms will prevent the anticipated violation); (c) is the moral violation one that can be specified? (general claims about a rapacious company, obscene profits, and actions contrary to public interest simply will not do).

4 Except in special circumstances, the whistleblower should have exhausted all internal channels for dissent before informing the public. The whistleblower's action should be commensurate with one's responsibility for avoiding and/or exposing moral violations. If there are personnel in the company whose obligation it is to monitor and respond to immoral and/or illegal activities, it would be their responsibility to address those issues. Thus, the first obligation of the would-be whistleblower would be to report the unethical activities to those persons, and only if they do not act, to inform the general public.

5 The whistleblower should have some chance of success. Ought implies can, so if there is no hope in arousing societal or government pressure, then one needlessly exposes oneself

and one's loved ones to hardship for no conceivable moral gain.

But these conditions speak mainly to the *permissibility* of blowing the whistle. A further, often overlooked question is under what conditions is it morally required (*obligatory*), if ever, for an employee to blow the whistle. The literature on this subject is sparse, except that there seems to be a good deal of tacit agreement that some sort of good samaritan principle is operative here. Hence, if there is an obligation to prevent harm, under conditions where there is a need and the person is capable of preventing the harm without sacrificing something of comparable moral worth, and if the person is the last resort, then that obligation would operate in the case of whistleblowing. Conditions 4 and 5 may be read as assuming that there is a responsibility to blow the whistle. But to show that obligation requires showing there is an obligation to the general public to prevent harm (Simon, Powers, and Gunneman, 1972).

In the corporate context, the company is seen as a team and expects loyalty. Forsaking the team to function as a detached referee to blow the whistle is seen as disloyal and cause for punitive action. In such a culture, to blow the whistle requires a certain moral heroism. Given the fact that society depends on whistleblowers to protect it from unscrupulous operators, justified whistleblowers need some protection. To assure the existence of necessary whistleblowers (somebody's got to do it), sound legislation is needed to protect the whistleblower.

Finally, whistleblowing is not restricted to the area of business. It occurs in all walks of life. Professionals may be held to the standards of their profession, that sometimes require blowing a whistle. For example, accountants and engineers have a dual obligation to their clients and to the public. Hence, they have a fiduciary responsibility to report certain illegal or potentially harmful activities if they encounter them in the course of their auditing or accounting or constructing. These obligations come from the professional status of the accountants and engineers, just as such obligations extend to all professionals, such as doctors and lawyers, who have obligations to their profession and the public to blow the whistle on colleagues who violate certain canons of appropriate behavior. But beyond the professions, whistleblowing is required in other walks of life: for example, the participants in an honor code have a responsibility to report violations. While such whistleblowing activity is viewed unfavorably, it is a necessary part of human activity.

Enlightened companies, aware that harmful, immoral, or illegal behavior that needs to be reported is likely to occur from time to time, have begun to make provisions for regularizing the monitoring of behavior, with ombudspersons or corporate responsibility officers. Such offices provide an outlet for those who feel obliged to report the unseemly behavior of their companies, without the need to go public. These provisions are desirable because they will alleviate the necessity of going public and blowing the whistle on harmful or illegal behavior.

Bibliography

Bok, S. (1980). Whistleblowing and professional responsibility. *New York University Professional Quarterly*, 11 (summer), 2–7.
De George, R. (1986). *Business Ethics*, 2nd edn. New York: Macmillan.
Duska, R. F. (1985). Whistleblowing and employee loyalty. In J. R. Desjardins and J. J. McCall (eds.), *Contemporary Issues in Business Ethics*. Belmont, CA: Wadsworth, 295–300.
Glazer, M. P. and Glazer, P. M. (1989). *The Whistleblowers: Exposing Corruption in Government and Industry*. New York: Basic Books.
Larmer, R. A. (1992). Whistleblowing and employee loyalty. *Journal of Business Ethics*, 11, 125–8.
Nader, R., Petkas, P., and Blackwell, K. (1972). *Whistleblowing*. New York: Bantam Books.
Simon, J. G., Powers, C., and Gunneman, J. P. (1972). *The Ethical Investor*. New Haven, CT: Yale University Press.
Westin, A. F. (1981). *Whistle Blowing: Loyalty and Dissent in the Corporation*, New York: McGraw-Hill.

women in leadership

Robin J. Ely

refers to the exercise of leadership by women. Equal Employment Opportunity legislation together with the press for equality in the workplace brought about by the Women's Movement have likely provided the impetus for this relatively new area of inquiry in the field of leadership. This work now constitutes one of the four main themes in contemporary leadership research (Calas and Smircich, 1988). It has centered primarily on questions about whether or not men's and women's leadership styles and, to a lesser extent, leadership effectiveness are different in ways that are consistent with cultural stereotypes.

LEADERSHIP STYLE

In their meta-analysis of the literature on gender and leadership style, Eagly and Johnson (1990) found evidence for both the presence and absence of leadership-style differences between the sexes. There was no support in organizational studies and minimal support in laboratory studies for the gender-stereotypic expectation that women lead in an interpersonally oriented style and men in a task-oriented style. Consistent with stereotypic expectations, however, this analysis revealed overall that women tended to adopt a more democratic or participative style than men did. Researchers have typically offered either person-centered explanations for sex-difference findings, such as socialized differences in female and male personality or skills (Hennig and Jardim, 1977), or situation-centered explanations, such as differences in the power and status of the organizational positions women and men hold (Kanter, 1977).

Although much of the sex-difference research in the leadership field has been motivated by feminist interests in promising gender equity, recent critics have argued that assumptions underlying this work have served to reinforce bias against women. For example, implicit in much of this research is the concern that sex differences reflect or have been used to legitimate the unequal treatment of men and women; therefore, an assumption underlying this work is that such differences should be repudiated and, in an ideal world, eradicated. Critics of this approach argue, however, that this assumption reinforces an asymmetric view of the role gender plays in leadership: it casts men's leadership as generic leadership uninfluenced by masculine gender and male experience; as such, men's leadership constitutes the presumed gender-neutral norm against which women's leadership

is measured and evaluated. To the extent that women deviate from this norm their leadership is viewed as less effective or absent altogether. Hence, comparative studies of leadership have tended not only to devalue women but also in so doing to narrow our understanding of what might constitute the full range of effective leader behavior.

This criticism has led some feminist scholars to reconceive the meaning of leadership to include the relational and emotional competencies women have developed as leaders in the domestic sphere of home and family, competencies, they argue, that men tend to lack (Helgesen, 1990). Hence, rather than seeking to overcome traditional feminine experience, these scholars exalt it, urging organizations to accommodate women in their feminized difference. In contrast to traditional research on women in leadership, much of this work rests on the assumption that neither organizations nor leadership are gender neutral; rather, gender bias permeates both organizations and organizational research in ways that devalue women and limit understanding. Evidence for the validity of this perspective has been largely descriptive, based on case studies of women's experiences in organizations and on reinterpretations of previous sex-difference findings (Helgesen, 1990; Rosener, 1990).

More recently, scholars whose work is grounded in poststructural feminism have offered yet another perspective on women and leadership style. This perspective represents a thoroughgoing break from the preoccupation with sex differences characteristic of previous research. Again, these scholars take issue with the unexamined assumptions underlying this work, arguing that the very focus on difference itself, regardless of whether and how it is recast and revalued, is both a source and a consequence of relations of domination. Juxtaposing the leadership literature with contemporaneous literature on sexuality and subjecting both to a cultural analysis called deconstruction, Calas and Smircich (1991) analyze leadership as a form of male homosocial seduction. As such, leadership promotes the values of masculinity in organizations, including masculine definitions of femininity. Hence, they argue, just as masculine identity and masculine experience have shaped the contours of discourse on leadership, so too have they shaped the contours of what we have come to believe are women's essential qualities of nurturance and caretaking. According to a poststructural feminist perspective, theories of women's leadership that attribute these (or any other) qualities, whether repudiated or exalted, to all women, are further oppressive because they elide racial, ethnic, class, and sexual identity differences among women and obfuscate forms of sexism to which different women are differentially subjected. They recommend abandoning general theories of either women or leadership in favor of partial and highly contextualized narratives to explore new meanings and new possibilities for the exercise of leadership by both women and men.

LEADERSHIP EFFECTIVENESS

Research on women's leadership effectiveness has centered largely on the role of sex bias in both real and perceived effectiveness. A meta-analysis of experimental research on sex bias in leader evaluations showed a small overall tendency for people to evaluate women leaders less favorably than men (Eagly, Makhijani, and Klonsky, 1992). Researchers have typically attributed such findings to the cultural stereotypes people hold about men and women which put women at a relative disadvantage.

Research in organizational settings has tended to be more qualitative and theoretical, focusing primarily on structural determinants of leader effectiveness (Kanter, 1977). This work has suggested that where women leaders are situated in the organization's power structure and the number of women who are in the organization's senior ranks are key to understanding both how they are perceived and how well they will do in leadership positions. Because women tend to be in low-power positions they are both less desirable and less effective as leaders; at the same time, their token status in many organizations heightens their visibility and creates increased performance pressures, isolation, and stereotyped roles for women leaders. Finally, there is some literature from a psychodynamic perspective that explores the unique difficulties women face in leadership roles, difficulties that stem from unconscious fantasies and fears of women's power and the strongly held stereotype that women possess legitimate authority only to nur-

ture (Bayes and Newton, 1978; Dumas, 1980). According to this perspective, these dynamics make it difficult for women leaders to mobilize resources in effective ways. Research in either laboratory or organizational settings that measures and compares men and women leaders' effectiveness along specific dimensions is scant and inconclusive.

Bibliography

Bayes, M. and Newton, R. M. (1978). Women in authority: A sociopsychological analysis. *Journal of Applied Behavioral Science*, 14, 7–20.
Calas, M. B. and Smircich, L. (1988). Reading leadership as a form of cultural analysis. In J. G. Hunt, R. Baliga, P. Dachler, and C. Schreisheim (eds.), *Emerging Leadership Vistas*. Lexington, MA: Lexington Books, 201–26.
Calas, M. B. and Smircich, L. (1991). Voicing seduction to silence leadership. *Organization Studies*, 12, 567–601.
Dumas, R. G. (1980). Dilemmas of Black females in leadership. *Journal of Personality and Social Systems*, 2, 3–14.
Eagly, A. H. and Johnson, B. T. (1990). Gender and leadership style: A meta-analysis. *Psychological Bulletin*, 108, 233–56.
Eagly, A. H., Makhijani, M. G., and Klonsky, B. G. (1992). Gender and the evaluation of leaders: A meta-analysis. *Psychological Bulletin*, 111, 3–22.
Helgesen, S. (1990). *The Female Advantage: Women's Ways of Leadership*. New York: Doubleday Currency.
Hennig, M. and Jardim, A. (1977). *The Managerial Woman*. Garden City, NY: Anchor Press/Doubleday.
Kanter, R. M. (1977). *Men and Women of the Corporation*. New York: Basic Books.
Rosener, J. (1990). Ways women lead. *Harvard Business Review*, November/December, 119–25.

women in the workplace

Barbara A. Gutek

Most women have always been "at work," but traditionally, fewer women than men have engaged in paid work. In 1890, for example, women made up only 17 percent of the US labor force; by 1980, women were 44 percent of the US labor force. In 1985, 54.5 percent of the US women 16 years of age and older were employed (*Statistical Abstract of the United States*, 1988: table 627). In 2000, over all, 63.9

percent of Americans age 16 and older were in the labor force, including 57.5 percent of all women 16 years or older. In the Scandinavian countries, typically, 75 percent or more of adult women are in the labor force. In general, during the 1970s and 1980s, women increased their share of the labor force in most countries of the world (United Nations, 1991), although the rate of increase has slowed in the past decade or so. Furthermore, in all areas of the world today, women in the prime childbearing years (25–44) are more likely to be employed than either younger or older women (United Nations, 1991: table 6.8). This represents a change in most of the industrialized countries where, in the past, women of prime childbearing years were less likely than either younger or older women to be employed.

The topic of "women at work" as a coherent subfield is less than 25 years old and it is interdisciplinary, involving researchers from management, psychology, sociology, economics, etc. It is worth noting that the research tends to focus disproportionately on women in non-traditional jobs (i.e., management and the male-dominated professions) and women at higher organizational ranks (managers and executives). Likewise, the research focuses disproportionately on women who are white and middle or upper class. These features characterize research on work in general, not just women at work.

In all of the research, gender figures prominently, and women and their experiences are either overtly or covertly compared with men. Sex difference is a common theme in the research and encompasses both differences between men and women and differences between the treatment of men and women. Women tend to work in "women's jobs," jobs defined in a particular time and place as appropriate for women. Although there are some consistencies across countries, cultures, and organizations (e.g., jobs involving children tend to be labeled women's jobs), examples of one job being a "man's job" in one country, culture, or organization, and a "woman's job" in another are common. This is true, for example, of medicine, sales, and clerical work.

Women's work is characterized by horizontal and vertical segregation. Horizontal segregation means that women and men work in different occupations. In 1970 in the US about 55 percent of women worked in the 20 most female-dominated occupations (Jacobs, 1989: table 2.4). Sex segregation is most often measured by the index of segregation (also known as the index of dissimilarity, D) which tells the percentage of one sex who would have to change jobs so that they would be distributed across jobs the same as the other sex. In the US, sex segregation has declined from about 76 in 1910 to 62 in 1981 (Jacobs, 1989), and it has done so, not because more men are working in jobs traditionally held by women (they are not), but because women have moved into traditionally male jobs such as law, medicine, management, and the professorate.

Vertical segregation means that men and women are located at different places in the hierarchy in their work. Women tend to be located in lower-level positions in their occupations and in their organizations, whereas men are found in jobs throughout the hierarchy. Women are said to face a glass ceiling, in that they are rarely found above certain hierarchical levels. Like horizontal segregation, vertical segregation is also decreasing, except at the top.

In general, the research on women at work fits into one of three categories: sex differences, problem focused, and changes initiated to alleviate problems.

One type of research focuses on differences and similarities between the sexes. Among the topics covered are the following: differences in masculinity and femininity and their implications; differences or similarities in management style or leadership style; sex differences in career choices and career interests; and differences and similarities in achieving style. Early research focused on traits or characteristics believed to be associated with women more than men, such as fear of success. A few areas are notable for the lack of expected sex differences. For example, while there is an active debate about whether men and women exhibit different leadership styles, the extant research suggests that men and women in leadership positions exhibit few differences. And despite the fact that women's and men's job experiences tend to differ, they tend to report similar levels of job satisfaction, and in recent years, job commitment.

A large body of research on women at work focuses on problems faced by women. These topics include the following, listed with some researchers and theorists in each field: biases in selection, placement, performance appraisal, and promotion (Nieva and Gutek; Swim et al.); sexual harassment (Fitzgerald; Gutek; Pryor; Terpstra and Baker); obstacles to achievement, advancement, and attainment of positions of leadership (Larwood; Morrison); lack of mentoring (Ragins; Fagensen); sex discrimination (Heilman; Crosby); the pay gap (England; Olson; Konrad); stereotyping (Fiske; Borgida); lack of job mobility (Brett); conflict between work and family responsibilities (Pleck; Brett; Davidson; Cooper). Research starting in the late 1970s on the problems faced by tokens (women who are numerically rare) (Kanter; Laws), including the problems faced by women when there are few women in top management positions in the organization (Ely), continue to be relevant.

A third type of research focuses on the success or failure of attempts to alleviate problems faced by working women (see, for example, Ely, Foldy, and Scully, 2003), including the impacts of laws and other programs aimed at providing equal opportunity, addressing affirmative action, establishing the comparable worth of jobs, and eliminating sexual harassment. But laws are not the only approach to alleviating problems faced by working women. In general, the type of solution sought depends on the way the problem is defined. Nieva and Gutek (1981) listed four models of problem definition and some problem-solving strategies that follow from them. They are: the individual-deficit model, wherein the problem is defined as problem people; the structural model, wherein organizational structures and policies hamper women (see Kanter, 1977); the sex-role model, wherein social roles and role expectations and role stereotypes hamper women; and the intergroup model, wherein men and women are viewed as opposing groups fighting over a limited amount of desirable jobs, power, and influence. They conclude that the most commonly proposed solutions fit the individual-deficit model. Women are given opportunities to overcome their "deficits" through training and self-help materials targeted at

them. Examples include dressing for success, assertiveness training, and how to write a business plan or obtain venture capital. Increasingly, men too are targets of training aimed at sensitizing them to issues like sexual harassment and sex discrimination.

Overall, the topic of women at work has attracted a lot of research attention over the past 20 years or so. Recent major reviews of the literature can be found in Ely, Foldy, and Scully (2003) and Cleveland, Stockdale, and Murphy (2000). While the field is not bereft of theory, much of the research continues to be descriptive, an approach well suited to a topic that is fraught with misperceptions and misinformation.

Bibliography

Cleveland, J., Stockdale, M., and Murphy, K. (2000). *Women and Men in Organizations: Sex and Gender Issues at Work*. Mahwah, NJ: Lawrence Erlbaum.

Ely, R. J., Foldy, E. G., and Scully, M. A. (2003). *Reader in Gender, Work, and Organization*. Oxford: Blackwell.

Gutek, B. A. (1993). Changing the status of women in management. *Applied Psychology*, 43(4), 301–11.

Gutek, B. A. and Larwood, L. (eds.) (1987). *Women's Career Development*. Newbury Park, CA: Sage.

Jacobs, J. (1989). *Revolving Doors: Sex Segregation and Women's Careers*. Stanford, CA: Stanford University Press.

Kanter, R. M. (1977). *Men and Women of the Corporation*. New York: Basic Books.

Nieva, V. F. and Gutek, B. A. (1981). *Women and Work: A Psychological Perspective*. New York: Praeger .

Statistical Abstract of the United States (1988). Washington, DC: US Government Printing Office.

Swim, J., Borgida, E., Maruyama, G., and Meyers, D. G. (1989). Joan McKay versus John McKay: Do gender stereotypes bias evaluations?*Psychological Bulletin*, 105(3), 409–29.

United Nations (1991). *The World's Women: Trends and Statistics, 1970–1990*. Social Statistics and Indicators, Series K, No. 8. New York: United Nations.

US Bureau of Census website: www.census.gov/Press-Release/www/2002/dp_comptables.html

work

A. R. Gini

As adults there is nothing that more preoccupies our lives than our work. We will not sleep as much, spend time with our families as much, eat as much, or recreate and rest as much as we work. Whether we love our work or hate it, succeed in it or fail, achieve fame or infamy through it, like Sisyphus we are all condemned to push and chase that thing we call our job, our career, our work, all of our days (Ciulla, 2000; Gini, 2000).

In its most benign sense, work can be defined as any activity we need or want to do in order to achieve the basic requirements of life and/or to maintain a certain lifestyle.(Sullivan, 1989: 115). The paradox of work is that while many of us wind up hating it, or are simply worn down and exhausted by it, most of us start off eagerly seeking it out. We want to work. Work in this society is seen both as a means and an end in itself. As a means, work is the vehicle by which we can achieve status, stuff, and success. As an end, work allows us to conform with one of our most cherished myths, the "Protestant Work Ethic." This ethic holds that work is good and that all work – any work – demonstrates integrity, responsibility, and fulfillment of duty.

In the long run work can prove to be a boon or a burden, creative or crippling, a means to personal happiness or a prescription for despair. But no matter where a person winds up on this spectrum one thing is clear: work is one of the primary means by which adults find their identity and form their character. Simply put: *where* we work, *how* we work, *what* we do at work, and the general ethos and culture of the workplace indelibly mark us for life.

Karl Marx has argued: "As individuals express their lives, so they are" (Marx, 1967: 409). It is in work that we become persons. Work is that which forms us, gives us a focus, gives us a vehicle for personal expression, and offers us a means for personal definition. "Work," argues John Paul II, "makes us human because we make something of ourselves through our work." Individuals need work in order to finish and define their natures. Just as work is not a simple given or fixed thing, said John Paul, so too human personalities. Both are facts continuously being produced by human labor (John Paul II, 1982: 112).

For good or ill, we are known and we know ourselves by the work we do. The meter and measure of work serves as our mapping device to explain and order the geography of life. Our work circumscribes what we know and how we select and categorize the things we choose to see. The lessons we learn in our work and at work become the metaphors we apply to life and others, and the means by which we digest the world. As Samuel Butler said: "Every man's work, whether it be literature or music or pictures or architecture or anything else, is always a portrait of himself."

Philosopher Adina Schwartz (1982) has argued that, at the level of mental health, work is a basic requirement of adult life. As adults, we need work in the same way that children need to play in order to fulfill themselves as persons. Unfortunately, this thesis applies even to those of us who spend our lives laboring at "bad jobs" – jobs that Studs Terkel refers to as "too small for our spirit" and "not big enough" for us as people. Jobs that are devoid of prestige. Jobs that are physically exhausting or mindlessly repetitive (Terkel, 1974: 521). Jobs that are demeaning, degrading, and trivial in nature. Even these kinds of jobs – though we are often loathe to admit it – provide us with a handle on reality, an access to services and goods, and a badge of identity.

Given the centrality of work in adult life and its impact on the development of personality and character, few students of business ethics and organizational development will be surprised by the contention that the ethos of workplace, corporate culture, and the mores of management influence the ethical norms and moral values of individual workers both on and off the job. Robert Jackall in his important book *Moral Mazes* argues that no matter what a person believes in off the job, on the job all of us, to a greater or lesser extent, are required to suspend, bracket, or only selectively manifest our personal convictions. What is right in the corporation is not what is right in man's home or his church. What is right in the corporation is what the guy above you wants from you (Jackall, 1988: 109).

Jackall contends that the logic of every organization (any place of business) and the collective personality of the workplace conspire to override the wants, desires, or aspirations of the individual worker. For Jackall, the primary imperative of every organization is to succeed. This logic of performance leads to the creation of a private moral universe – a moral universe that

by definition is totalitarian (self-ruled), solipsis-
tic (self-defined), and narcissistic (self-
centered). Within such a milieu truth is socially
defined and moral behavior is determined solely
by organizational needs. The key virtues, for all
alike, become goal preoccupation, problem solving, survival and success and, most importantly,
playing by the house rules. In time, says Jackall,
those initiated and invested in the system come
to believe that they live in a self-contained
worldview which is above and independent of
outside critique and evaluation.

Jackall argues that all corporations are like
fiefdoms of the middle ages, wherein the Lord
of the Manor (CEO, President) offers protection, prestige, and status to his vassals (managers) and serfs (workers) in return for homage
(commitment) and service (work). In such a
system, says Jackall, advancement and promotion are predicated on loyalty, trust, politics, and
personality much more than experience, education, ability, and actual accomplishments. The
central concern of the worker/minion is to be
known as a "can-do guy," a "team-player,"
being at the right place at the right time, and
master of all the social rules. That's why in the
corporate world, says Jackall, 1,000 "atta-boys"
is wiped away with one "Oh, shit"! (Jackall,
1988: 72).

As in the model of a feudal system, Jackall
maintains that employees of a corporation are
expected to become functionaries of the system
and supporters of the status quo. Their loyalty is
to the powers that be; their duty is to perpetuate
performance and profit; and their values can be
none other than those sanctioned by the organization.

Although Jackall's theory is a radical one and
deals primarily with large corporations, the logic
of his analysis can be applied to any place of
employment. We are a nation of workers, a society of employees. Statistics indicate that over 80
percent of the workforce are employed in organizations of twenty or more people. Every organization, corporation, or place of business has a
meter and measure of its own. In a very real
sense the workplace serves as a metronome for
human development and growth. The individual
workplace sets the agenda, establishes the values,
and dictates the desired outcome it expects from
its employees. Although it would be naive to

assert that employees simply unreflectively
absorb the manners and mores of the workplace,
it would be equally naive to suggest that they are
unaffected by the modeling and standards of
their respective places of employment. Work is
where we spend our lives, and the lessons we
learn there, good or ill, play a part in the development of our moral perspective and how we
formulate and adjudicate ethical choices.

In claiming that workers can become functionaries of the logic of performance and organizational ethics of the institutions they work for,
Jackall is in no way denying the value of a more
classic normative analysis of ethical decision-
making or the importance and responsibilities
of individual moral agency. He is not claiming
that individuals are ethically absolved when they
capitulate to the status of being an organizational
toady. Rather, he is trying to explain *how* the
imperatives of the workplace and the requirements of life facilitate and encourage the abdica-
tion of personal responsibility and autonomy.
After all, if work is the primary vehicle for the
achievement of personal success, status, prestige, and financial security, who of us is above
the temptation to cut corners, turn a blind eye,
or simply overlook the requirements and niceties
of ethics? But whatever way we choose, the
lesson to keep in mind is this: "As individuals
express their lives, so they are." The "portrait"
we paint of ourselves at work is how we are
known to ourselves and others.

CONCLUSION

Because work looms so large in our lives I believe
that most of us don't reflect on its importance
and significance. For most of us, work is – well –
work, something we have to do to maintain our
lives and pay the bills. However, work is not just
a part of our existence that can be easily separated from the rest of our lives. Work is not
simply about the trading of labor for dollars.
Perhaps because we live in a society that markets
and hawks the fruits of our labor and not the
labor itself, we have forgotten or never really
appreciated the fact that the business of work is
not simply to produce goods, but also to help
produce people.

Was Descartes wrong? Perhaps it isn't *Cogito
ergo sum* but, rather, *Laboro ergo sum.* We need
work, and as adults we find identity and are

identified by the work we do. If this is true then we must be very careful about what we choose to do for a living, for what we do is what we'll become. To paraphrase the words of Winston Churchill, first we choose and shape our work, then it shapes us.

Bibliography

Cuilla, J. (2000). *The Working Life.* New York: Times Books.

Gini, A. (2000). *My Job My Self.* New York. Routledge.

Jackall, R. (1988). *Moral Mazes.* New York: Oxford University Press.

Marx, K. (1967). The German Ideology. In L. Easton and K. Guddot (eds. and trans.), *Writings of the Young Marx on Philosophy and Society.* New York: Doubleday.

John Paul II (1982). *Laborem Exercens.* In G. Baum (ed.), *The Priority of Labor.* New York: Paulist Press.

Schwartz, A. (1982). Meaningful work. *Ethics,* **92,** 634–46.

Sullivan, T. J. (1989). What do we mean when we talk about work? In A. R. Gini and T. J. Sullivan (eds.), *It Comes With the Territory.* New York: Random House.

Terkel, S. (1974). *Working: People Talk About What They Do All Day and How They Feel About What They Do.* New York: Pantheon Books.

work and family

Robin D. Johnson

Work, family: Programs, policies, and practices designed to help people manage the boundary between work–professional life and family–personal life.

Work–family programs include parental leave, child and elder-dependent care support (onsite daycare, child–elder care referral services, financial subsidies for dependent care), flexible work systems (part-time work, compressed work week, flextime), job sharing, work–family sensitivity training, and work from home options (telecommuting, virtual office). Some companies have relabeled their existing general employee benefits "work–family programs" (e.g., employee assistance programs, disability insurance/income, tuition aid, etc.). What these programs share is an intent to help employees manage the boundary between their personal (family, private) lives and their professional (public, work) lives. Considerable difference of opinion remains about which programs to implement, how much influence companies, individuals, and government will have in determining programs, and who will or who should pay for these programs.

Early discussions about work and family focused attention on the *creation–establishment* of programs and policies designed to limit, if not eliminate, the intrusion of dependent concerns on employee work productivity. More recently the discourse regarding work–family programs has included issues of implementation of coherent, consistent, and fair work–family policies. Companies that have tried various work–family programs initially found their implementation challenging. Work–family policies were and are often misaligned with, or undermined by, other corporate policies, social norms, and gender-role expectations. Barriers include widespread belief in the existence of, and necessity for, a boundary between work and family lives; what some executives see as unrealistic expectations that companies take care of dependents resulting from individuals' personal decisions; a gap between policy and everyday managerial practice when employees attempt to use work–family programs; employer liability; invasion of privacy; and unfairness to or backlash from those who do not have dependents. Aligning programs, policies, and practice can grow into a major effort to change organizational culture.

RESEARCH, AREAS OF INQUIRY

Programs. In addition to widespread research on the specific types of programs needed, much of the program-oriented research is designed to assess the potential benefits to companies with enlightened work–family programs and policies implemented by sensitive managers. Research asserts that work–family programs can decrease absenteeism, tardiness, turnover, and product waste while increasing employee commitment, morale, and empowerment – for women and men, frontline workers and executives.

Policies and practices. Many companies attempt to mandate acceptance of work–family programs, adding them to a menu of other human-resource management programs for the increasingly diverse workforce. This strategy of trying to implement work–family programs while keeping existing systems and cultural values in place caused implementation difficulties. Managers frequently (re)interpret work–family in fairly narrow terms (flextime for women parents only, for example). In most cases the onus is on employees to present some plan for maintaining productivity while using the work–family program, or to accept some negative consequence (e.g., a "mommy track" or limited promotion opportunity). The negotiation between the manager and the employee often ends up with one (the manager) or both of them prioritizing work over family. If an employee has a risk-averse manager it is possible that the request to use some work–family program will be denied. In the US, work–family programs are still seen mostly as privileges from benevolent organizations implemented by sensitive managers. The practice varies considerably in other cultures. Whatever the culture, where work–family programs exist – either by corporate benevolence or social requirement – managerial responses to employee requests determine how these programs are used in practice.

THEORIZING

The work–family boundary.   It is argued that the boundary between work and family, if it exists, is permeable, asymmetrical (i.e., work interferes more with family than family interferes with work), or mythical. Moreover, insistence that work should be separate from family is dysfunctional for society, unrealistic given current workforce demography (working parents, more women as paid workers, greater number of dual career couples, more single male and female parents, an aging population, different family structures by sexual orientation and ethnicity, etc.), gendered (has a more negative impact on women than on men), and unfair.

The dichotomy: work vs. family.   Productivity and other business needs were often placed in contrast to or conflict with employee needs. This mirrors the public/private dichotomy. The boundary theories mentioned above challenge the assumed separateness of the two spheres. The dichotomy theories also challenge the unequal valuation of the two spheres, while exploring the possibilities for integrated, blended lives at home and at work.

Definition of family.   In the early stages of work–family programs, most companies defined family for employees – trying to limit their costs – and enforced their definition of family as a nuclear-tied (by birth or marriage) male–female relationship. In implementation, companies often find both their presumed right to define family and their narrow definition of family challenged by employees. Alternative definitions of family include extended family (by blood and marriage), friends, cohabitants, and emotional supporters. The process of defining family, and the actual definition of family in any organization, are an important aspect of work–family program implementation.

Rethinking work assumptions.   Many see work–family relationships as requiring changes in our assumptions about work. Work–family researchers have mentioned at least two assumptions that need rethinking: (1) face time = commitment, and (2) heroes who put out fires should be rewarded.

With changes in both technology and workforce demographics, it is easy to work from a number of locations. However, organizations frequently require "face time": time in front of a manager in order for that manager to see the employee as real and committed. For work–family to succeed it is argued that face time must be decoupled from attributions about employee commitment. The second assumption – firefighters are heroes to be rewarded – refers to a tendency to seek, recognize, and reward people who are able to handle organizational crises well (called firefighters). Often, little attention is paid to who started the fire or, more importantly, what could have been done to prevent it in the first place. Fire-crisis prevention in an organizational system that lauds firefighters as heroes is *invisible work*. Firefighters have tended to be male. Invisible work keeping fires from starting has tended to be done by females. Rethinking the firefighter as hero assumption, and shifting the reward focus to collective task performance (requiring relational skills correlated with women's managerial style) rather than individual heroics (requiring firm command-control leadership correlated with men's style) would mean a reassessment of the contribution to the organization from both men and women, and more gender equity in our organizations.

Connecting work–family to gender equity. Balancing work and family is a top priority for women and men that cuts across class, race, and national culture. Much of the earlier research and common discourse assumed work–family was a women's issue. This notion has (and continues to be) challenged by men who are becoming more outspoken about their changing roles. In one study, dual earners both restructured their work, although women restructured work more than men did. Researchers argue that the increase in women at work has expanded women's roles rather than caused a redefinition of gender roles for both men and women. Cross-culturally, it is argued that in the more "masculine" cultures these gender roles are more distinct (and presumably gender equity more difficult to attain), and in more "feminine" cultures gender roles are more blended, so that gender equity at work becomes less of an issue altogether. Mazrui and Mazrui (2001) describe how the separate-but-(un)equal doctrines/practices for gender in Islamic countries is being affected by technology and Internet access. Examining practices, assumptions, and policies that cause unequal opportunities and constraints (hence, gender inequity) is a continuing area for research and inquiry.

The ideas for this entry originated in my role as a researcher with the Ford Foundation Work–Family/Gender Equity Project. All collaborators from this project have published works on this subject. Collaborators include Lotte Bailyn, Susan Eaton, Joyce Fletcher, Dana Friedman, Ellen Galinsky, Maureen Harvey, Deborah Kolb, James Levine, Barbara Miller, Joyce Ortega, Leslie Perlow, and Rhona Rapoport. The Center for Gender in Organizations was established as a result of our work: www.simmons.edu/gsm/cgo/. The entry supplements those findings with research published in the articles listed in the bibliography.

Bibliography

Ely, R. J. and Myerson, D. E. (2000). Theories of gender in organizations: A new approach to organizational analysis and change. Center for Gender in Organizations CGO Paper, No. 8.

Fletcher, J. K. (2001). Invisible work: The disappearing of relational practice at work. Center for Gender in Organizations CGO Insights No. 8.

Frone, M. R., Russell, M., and Cooper, M. L. (1992). Prevalence of work–family conflict: Are work and family boundaries asymmetrically permeable? *Journal of Organizational Behavior*, 13, 723–9.

Hall, D. T. (1990). Promoting work, family balance: An organization-change approach. *Organizational Dynamics*, winter, 5–18.

Hochschild, A. (1997). *The Time Bind: When Work Becomes Home and Home Becomes Work*. New York: Metropolitan Books.

Hochschild, A. and Machung, A. (1989). *The Second Shift: Working Parents and the Revolution at Home*. New York: Viking.

Hofstede, G. et al. (1998). *Masculinity and Femininity: The Taboo Dimension of National Cultures*. Thousand Oaks, CA: Sage.

Karambaya, R. and Reilly, A. H. (1992). Dual earner couples: Attitudes and actions in restructuring work and family. *Journal of Organizational Behavior*, 13, 585–601.

Lewis, S. (2000). Work and family issues: Old and new. In R. Burke and D. Nelson (eds.), *Advancing Women's Careers*. Oxford: Blackwell, ch. 5.

Linehan, M. and Walsh, J. S. (2001). Key issues in the senior female international career move: A qualitative study in a European context. *British Journal of Management*, 12, 85–95.

Mazrui, A. and Mazrui, A. (2001). The digital revolution and the new reformation: Doctrine and gender in Islam. *Harvard International Review*, spring, 52–5.

National Research Council (1991). *Work and family: Policies for a Changing Workforce*. Panel report on Employer Policies and Working Families, Committee on Women's Employment and Related Social Issues and Commission on Behavioral and Social Sciences and Education, ed. M. A. Ferber and B. O'Farrell, with L. Allen. Washington, DC: National Academy Press.

Schor, J. B. (1992). *The Overworked American: The Unexpected Decline of Leisure*. New York: Basic Books.

work, right to

James W. Nickel

The United Nations' *Universal Declaration of Human Rights* (1948) declares a right to work: "Everyone has the right to work, to free choice of employment, to just and favorable conditions of work, and to protection against unemployment."

An effectively implemented right to work would guarantee the availability of remunerative productive activity.

Is it morally imperative to provide work to people who are unemployed? This is the question posed by the idea of a right to work. There are, however, two other ways in which the phrase "right to work" is used. Sometimes this phrase is used to refer to the freedom to choose and refuse employment, the freedom from forced labor. This freedom is an important human right, and is widely recognized as such. The phrase "right to work" is also sometimes used to refer to freedom from compulsory union membership.

There are proven measures available to ameliorate the problem of unemployment. Free public schools allow each person to prepare for participation in the economy. Work programs for young people that combine work experience and job training can be created. Tax and other incentives to hire more people can be given to industries. Economic policies designed to run the economy at a rapid rate can be adopted. Protection can be provided to the temporarily unemployed through universal unemployment insurance. And government can become the employer of last resort, guaranteeing a job to every person who is able to work, wants a job, and has been unable to find one. It is unlikely that a right to work can be fully implemented without government becoming the employer of last resort.

Why would anyone think that access to productive employment is something that is, or ought to be, a matter of right? The recognition of rights is often spurred by the recognition of serious problems, and unemployment has been an extremely serious problem for contemporary societies. Unemployment in the range of 5 to 15 percent is not uncommon, and unemployment among youths and minorities is often much higher. For most people, inescapable unemployment has very bad consequences. It deprives them of what is usually the most important source of income, it denies them the opportunities for self-development that employment provides, and it makes unavailable one of the main areas in which they can gain respect from self and others. Extended involuntary unemploy-

ment typically stigmatizes its victims. The longer unemployment lasts, the worse its consequences tend to be (Kelvin and Jarrett, 1985).

To put the case positively, access to employment is extremely important because remunerative work provides the most prevalent, reliable, and acceptable means of providing for one's survival, flourishing, and self-respect. Nonfinancial benefits include the satisfaction of self-sufficiency; the satisfaction of doing a task skillfully; friendly relations with one's co-workers; producing goods or services that benefit society; and escaping from unwanted freedom due to the fact that one's job schedule structures one's activities and time (Arneson, 1990).

An argument based on the claim that work is one of the most important areas for gaining self-respect and the respect of others is usually used by advocates of the right to work. Although abilities and dedication can be demonstrated in areas other than employment (for example, in games or volunteer work), it is in the performance of useful activities carrying monetary rewards that self-esteem and respect for others are most likely to be created and maintained.

Another argument for guaranteed access to employment suggests that a system of private property cannot pass tests of fairness if it consigns many people to inescapable unemployment. If unemployed people find that current economic arrangements allow them neither appropriate property that will support their lives and liberty (because all valuable property is already owned by individuals or the state) nor to find paid employment, these economic arrangements are unfair because they deny to some the means of survival, respect, and self-development, while providing access to those means to others who lack stronger claims.

One may be receptive to people's claim to assistance in meeting their vital needs while rejecting the right to work. It may be argued that guaranteeing people a minimum income will be less expensive and produce less inefficiency and corruption than guaranteeing them jobs. Economists generally prefer distributions of money or vouchers to in-kind provision because this allows for more efficient use of resources by the recipient (see Thurow, 1976, for a critical assessment of this preference). But a person with a minimum income who wants a job will find it very difficult to buy one, and voters may find public provision of employment more palatable than income grants. Arneson sees an advantage in providing minimum-wage jobs rather than income grants because doing this will benefit those members of the unemployed who are most needy while excluding "non-needy bohemians" (Arneson, 1990).

Jon Elster (1988) objects to a politically implemented right to work on the grounds that it is self-defeating to create a right to work for the purpose of promoting self-respect. To engender self-respect, work must result in the production of a good or service that is considered valuable. A right to government jobs that were visibly supported by heavy subsidies and that produced few social benefits would do little to promote self-respect. (See Arneson, 1990, for a criticism of this argument.)

Bibliography

Arneson, R. (1990). Is work special? Justice and the distribution of employment. *American Political Science Review*, **84**, 1127–47.

Elster, J. (1988). Is there (or should there be) a right to work? In A. Gutmann (ed.), *Democracy and the Welfare State*. Princeton, NJ: Princeton University Press.

Ginsburg, H. (1983). *Full Employment and Public Policy: The United States and Sweden*. Lexington, MA: Lexington Books.

Kelvin, P. and Jarrett, J. (1985). *Unemployment: Its Social Psychological Effects*. New York: Cambridge University Press.

Nickel, J. (1978). Is there a human right to employment? *Philosophical Forum*, **10**, 149–70.

Nickel, J. (1987). *Making Sense of Human Rights*. Berkeley: University of California Press.

Thurow, L. (1976). Government expenditures: Cash or in-kind aid? *Philosophy and Public Affairs*, **5**, 361–81.

Van Parijs, P. (1995). *Real Freedom for All*. Oxford: Oxford University Press.

Index

Printed in the USA/Agawam, MA
July 8, 2011

559497.028

DATE DUE

GAYLORD   PRINTED IN U.S.A.